Psychology
a dynamic science

Psychology

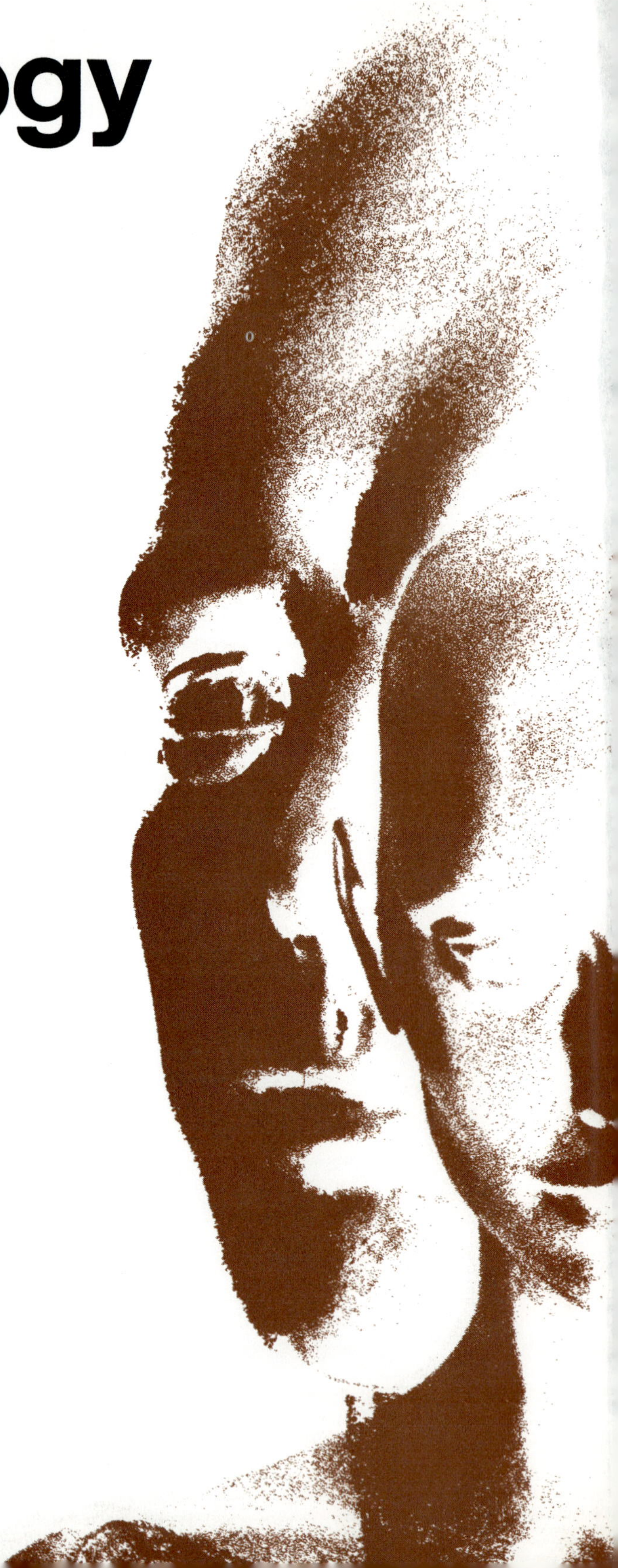

Eugenie Bertus

a dynamic science

Kurt Schlesinger
Philip M. Groves

Desmond S. Cartwright
John R. Forward
William F. Hodges
Steven F. Maier
Richard K. Olson
Victor L. Ryan
Barbara Sanders
Carol Schneider
James R. Wilson
Stephen Young

University of Colorado

wcb

Wm. C. Brown Company Publishers
Dubuque, Iowa

Perceptual dynamics are illustrated in one of M.C. Escher's impossible perspectives shown on the opposite page. (M.C. Escher, *Other World.* Escher Foundation—Haags Gemeentemuseum—The Hague.)

Library of Congress Catalog Card Number 75–18074

ISBN 0–697–06620–7

Printed in the United States of America

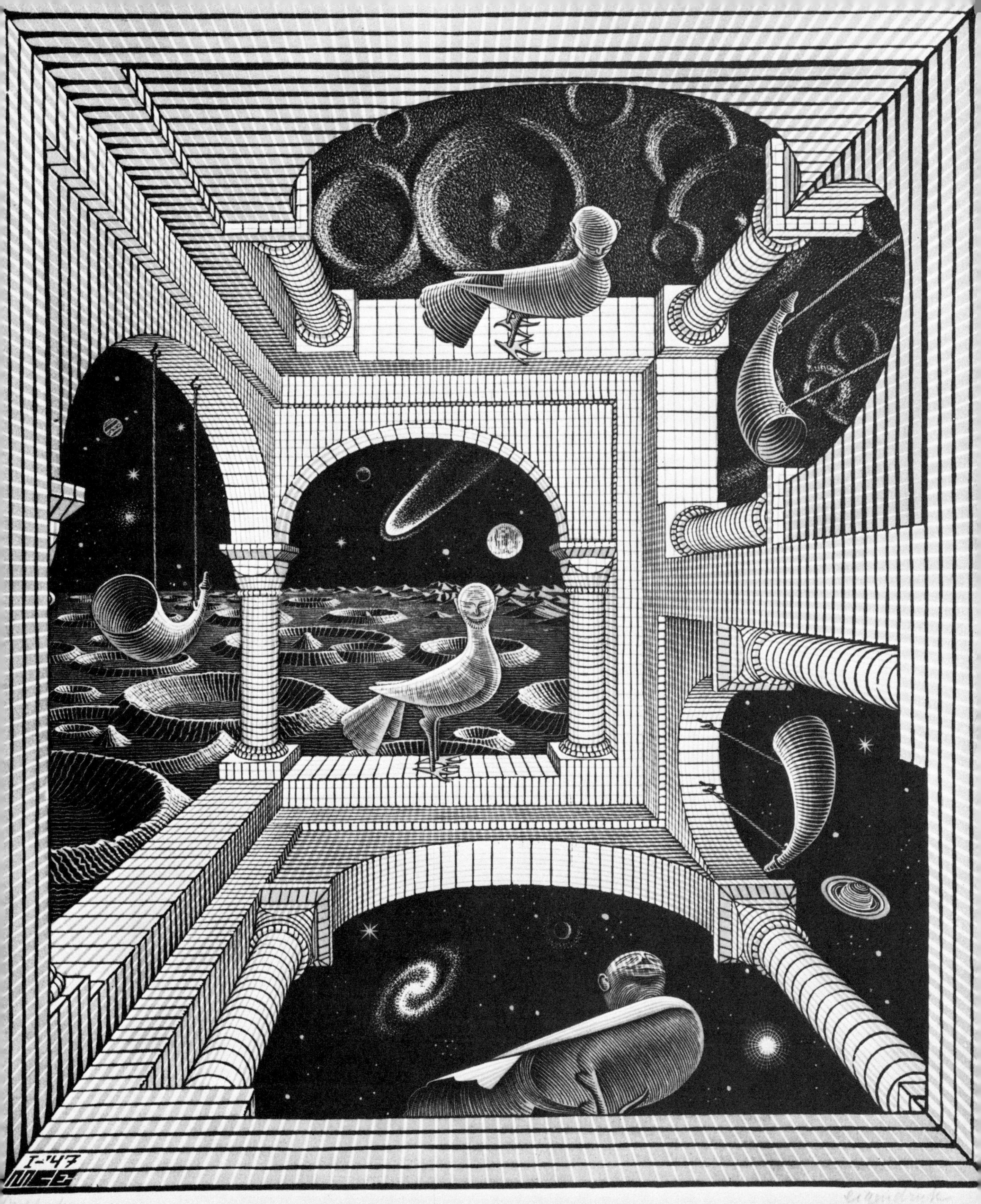
I-'47

Contents

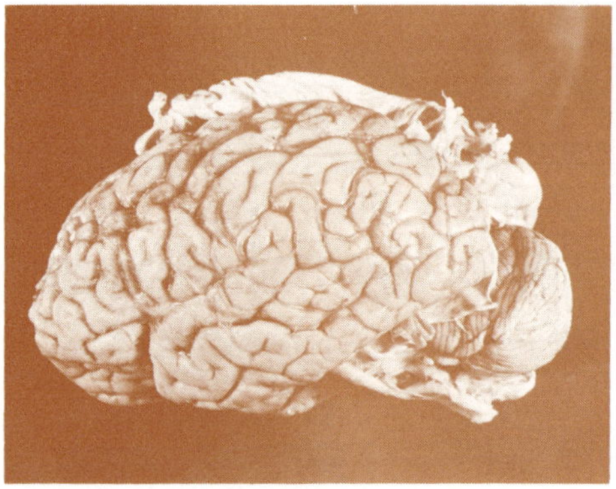

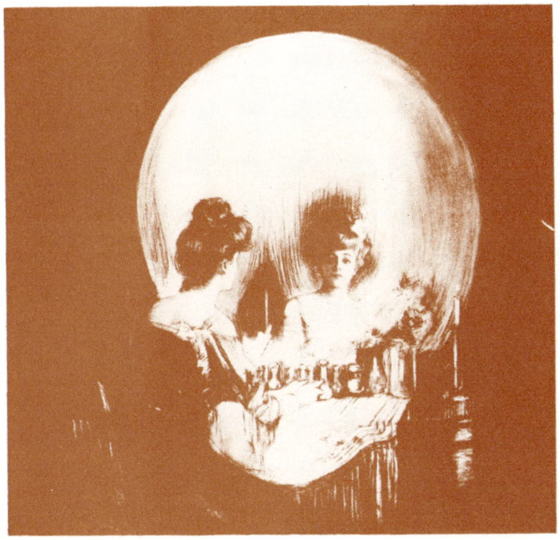

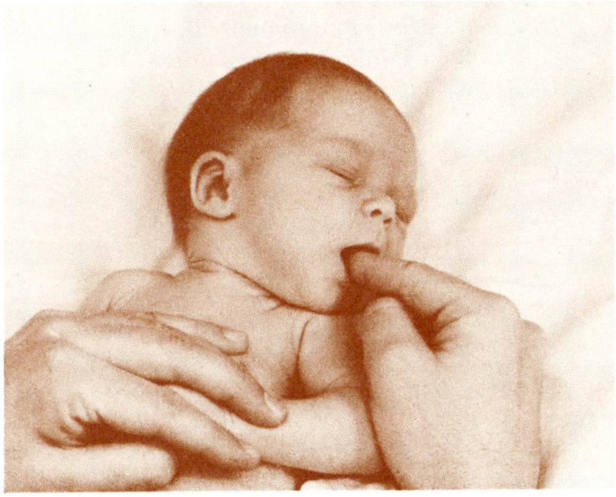

4

Developmental Processes and Behavior 229

5

Adaptive Behavior 315

7

Personality and Abnormal Behavior 491

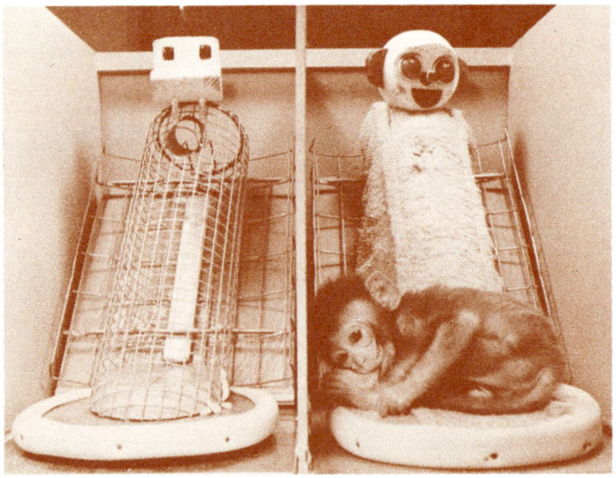

Preface

The goal of psychology, to understand human behavior, is of great interest to nearly everyone. Because of this, introductory psychology courses are among the most popular in college curricula today. However, understanding human behavior means many things to many people—students, laymen, and professional psychologists alike. If nothing else, attempting to write a comprehensive and up-to-date textbook of psychology illustrates this fact. As an academic discipline psychology is unified by its subject matter, the behavior of organisms; but, it is divided both by the myriad of approaches used to study behavior and by the fact that different psychologists are interested in special aspects of their field. This fact is reflected in the way introductory psychology courses are incorporated into the general college curriculum. In some instances, the first course in psychology carries social science credit, in other instances the student is given natural science credit for this course. In the majority of cases, the course may satisfy either or both of these requirements. For these reasons, introductory psychology textbooks must provide the student with a broad overview of the field. In this book we have attempted to give the student a scholarly framework from which to view psychology both as a social and as a biological discipline. In addition, we have tried to write a book that provides the student with a useful and contemporary survey of psychology, as well as one that will prepare those students who may wish to continue studying psychology with the background necessary for more specialized work.

We have organized our book around eight substantive areas of psychology. Chapter 1 describes psychology as a science and a profession and presents some of the methods which psychologists use in studying behavior. The second section deals with the biological bases of behavior. The facts and theories developed in this section are frequently integrated into other chapters in the text. Three of the chapters in this section (Behavioral Genetics, Hormones and Behavior, and Drugs, the Nervous System, and Behavior) are unique as they are not commonly found in other introductory psychology textbooks. In addition to being of interest to most college students, these topics continue to grow as important and integral aspects of modern psychological research and theory.

The third section of the text deals with the sensory systems and perception. Perhaps more than any other area of psychology, a treatment of perception must utilize many of the research findings and concepts derived from the wealth of information recently accumulated on the biological mechanisms which underlie our sensory and perceptual processes. We have presented this material in terms of the available information on sensory systems, information processing, and general models of perception.

Developmental psychology, the fourth section, represents an important area of research and theory. We have dealt with perceptual, intellectual, social, and psychosexual development. The chapter on psychosexual development is, perhaps, the most unique of all the chapters in this text. Its need is evident from the interest and questions which abound in our society today, as well as many others, concerning physiological and behavioral differences between the sexes and the many factors that influence their development.

The fifth section on adaptive behavior discusses both human and animal learning and memory research. We have also included a chapter which deals with some of the contemporary research and theories on the biological mechanisms of learning and memory, because of the widespread interest and importance of this topic in many modern psychology departments.

Section six focuses on consciousness, motives, and emotions. Biological as well as social concepts relevant to these topics have been included.

Personality and abnormal behavior are discussed in section seven. Included are chapters on personality theory, psychopathology, psychotherapy, and community mental health. This last chapter on community mental health reflects the view that developments in this area will soon change our concepts of dealing with mental health in modern Western society.

Section eight deals with social psychology. This section places the behavior of the individual within a modern social context and illustrates some of the basic subject matter of social psychology as it relates to contemporary social problems.

A discussion of statistics is included as the Appendix for instructors who wish to provide the student with material on basic statistical methods.

PSYCHOLOGY: A DYNAMIC SCIENCE represents the cooperative effort of twelve authors. Each chapter was written by an author or authors whose professional interests and research are directed toward that particular area. The experience has been a lesson in what close interaction and cooperation between individuals with diverse interests and different backgrounds can accomplish. We are indebted to our coauthors and friends and would like to acknowledge their scholarly contributions.

A special challenge is created when twelve individuals write one book, the most obvious being overlap of coverage, continuity of material, scholarship, and style. We have attempted to deal with these challenges in a number of ways. First, all authors participated in frequent meetings and discussions, which naturally centered around how best to complete this task. Secondly, we utilized a great many consultants as each phase of the book was being developed. All chapters were critically reviewed by a number of specialists in that particular area of psychology. Then each section was critiqued as a unit and, finally, the entire manuscript was thoroughly reviewed by individuals particularly concerned with introductory psychology courses and students. We heartily thank the following 37 reviewers for their careful analysis and extremely valuable suggestions and criticisms:

Merle Meyer (University of Florida), John Belknap (University of Texas—Austin), Paul Shinkman (University of North Carolina at Chapel Hill), Richard Maslow (San Joaquin Delta College), Robert Eason (University of North Carolina—Greensboro), Amado M. Padilla (University of California, Los Angeles), Michael Gabriel (University of Texas—Austin), Frank Landy (Penn State University), Stephen Reisman (University of Massachusetts), Irving J. Saltzman (Indiana University), Lyle Bourne (University of Colorado), Judith Rodin (Yale University), James Juola (University of Kansas), Carol Eckerman (Duke University), Howard Wolowitz (University of Michigan), Norman Adler (University of Pennsylvania), James P. Thomas (University of California—Los Angeles), Jim Hall (Northwestern University), John R. Newbrough (George Peabody College), Donna M. Gelgand (The University of Utah), David Goldfoot (University of Wisconsin), Gary Lynch (University of California—Irvine, Raymond Cattell (Pinebrook Hills), Alexander Pollatsek (University of Massachusetts), John A. Harvey (University of Iowa), Albert A. Harrison (University of California—Davis), Sandra Scarr-Salapatek (University of Minnesota), John L. Fuller (SUNY Binghamton), Richard Solomon (University of Pennsylvania), James McGaugh (University of California—Irvine), Wilse B. Webb (University of Florida), James M. Whitehouse (Drake University), David Perkins (California State University, Fullerton), Paul Levitt (University of Colorado).

A third technique which we utilized in insuring the continuity of style was to enlist the aid of a marvelously talented professional writer, Ms. Elizabeth Bowman. Her efforts were paramount in producing the final copy and we gratefully acknowledge her contribution.

We also wish to acknowledge the help of Mary Ann Gundel, Lynda Hart, Nancy Lucci, and Kathleen Wilson who helped us in preparing the manuscript, typing, proofreadings, etc. Without their patient help this book would never have been finished.

Edward Bowers, Jr., our editor at Wm. C. Brown Company Publishers, has encouraged us, helped us, and, on occasions, even cajoled us. He has been instrumental in the development of this text. In the process, he has become more than an editor, he has become our friend. Dave Corona, art director, and Mary Jones, our production editor, have also worked patiently with us and we owe them many thanks. Finally, we acknowledge the help of our friend Larry Brown, who has done everything possible to make our association with Wm. C. Brown Company Publishers a very pleasant experience.

KURT SCHLESINGER
PHILIP M. GROVES

Psychology
a dynamic science

William James (1842-1910) James pioneered the development of American psychology and was one of the leaders of the functionalist school. His monumental work "Principles of Psychology" published in 1890 was one of the most highly regarded and widely read expositions of theory and research at that time.

John Broadus Watson (1878-1958) The father of Behaviorism. His theory of behaviorism developed in opposition to structuralism, functionalism, and Gestalt psychology. The theory argues that the subject matter of psychology should be overt responses emitted by organisms because only these can be measured.

Section

1

An Introduction to the Study of Behavior

1

Psychology: Science and Profession

Psychology is the study of *behavior*. However, such a definition is neither meaningful nor satisfactory because it lacks refinement. According to the *American Psychological Association* (APA), the professional society to which most American psychologists belong, psychology is a scholarly discipline, a science, and a profession. The APA says:

> As a *scholarly discipline,* psychology represents a major field of study in academic settings, with emphasis on the communication and explanation of principles and theories of behavior.
>
> As a *science,* it is a focus of research through which investigators collect, quantify, analyze, and interpret data describing animal and human behavior, thus shedding light on the causes and dynamics of behavior patterns.
>
> As a *profession,* psychology involves the practical application of knowledge, skills, and techniques for the solution or prevention of individual or social problems; the professional role also provides an opportunity for the psychologist to develop further his understanding of human behavior and thus to contribute to the science of psychology.

Most students have some preconceptions concerning the nature of psychology. It involves, they think, the diagnosis and therapy of mental disorders, or the theories of Sigmund Freud, or parapsychology, or transcendental meditation, etc. These preconceptions are not entirely inaccurate; psychology does study all of these subjects. In looking over the contents of this book, you will notice that we intend to cover what appears to be an odd assortment of topics. Chapter 2, for example, is concerned with behavioral genetics. Chapter 3 introduces the anatomy and physiology of the nervous system. Chapter 12 is devoted to the topic of memory, while Chapter 21 deals with attitudes and attitude change. Thus you have reason to ask what these diverse subjects have in common. The answer is that they are all part of the subject matter of psychology. But there is more to psychology than these examples suggest.

It is no wonder, then, that it is difficult to define psychology and to determine its boundaries. One way to describe psychology is to indicate various areas of specialization (i.e., subfields) which constitute psychology. Specialization has occurred in nearly all academic fields, including the humanities and the social, biological, and natural sciences. As a discipline progresses, more and more knowledge is acquired; and thus it becomes increasingly difficult for a single individual to be knowledgeable in all aspects of a particular field.

During the fourteenth, or fifteenth, or sixteenth century, it was possible for one person to be proficient in several disciplines. Leonardo da Vinci is a remarkable example: Not only was he one of the greatest painters who ever lived, but he was also a sculptor, an architect, a biologist, a hydraulics engineer, an inventor, and the forerunner of modern aeronautics, among other things. Today, a da Vinci would be impossible, because it is unlikely that any individual could be completely knowledgeable in even one field. There is simply too much information for any one person to absorb. But despite the fact that a scholar must be a specialist, he shares with other specialists in his field certain basic interests. For example, regardless whether a biologist specializes in genetics, zoology, physiology, or cell biology, he shares with all other biologists a basic interest in living organisms and vital processes. Similarly, a physician may specialize in surgery, pediatrics, or orthopedics, but no matter which aspect of medicine he chooses, his basic interest is the prevention, treatment, and cure of disease.

Another reason for specialization is that each individual, because of differences in training and technical skills, brings to his studies a different perspective. The skills and interests characteristic of the clinical psychologist, for instance, are not the same as those of a psychologist who is interested in investigating the physiology of the nervous system. Specialization, then, is the result of increased knowledge, and psychology is no exception.

Some Areas of Specialization

The chapter titles in this book reflect many of the areas of specialization that exist in psychology. But to give you a better idea of the work that psychologists do, we have listed some of the major subfields of psychology and briefly described some of the issues that occupy professionals working in each. Figures 1.1 and 1.2 also illustrate the degree of specialization in psychology.

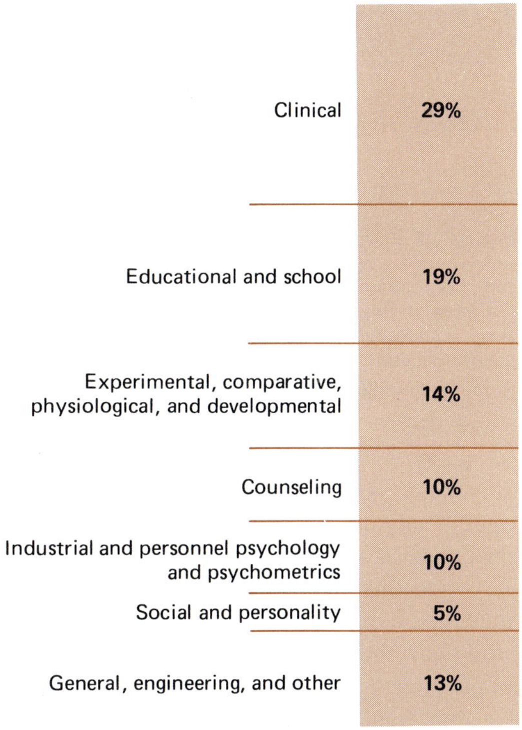

Figure 1.1 Some of the subfields of psychology and the percentage of psychologists who specialize in each of these fields. (From *A Career in Psychology*. Copyright 1970 by the American Psychological Association. Reprinted by permission. Taken from 1968 National Register of Scientific and Technical Personnel.)

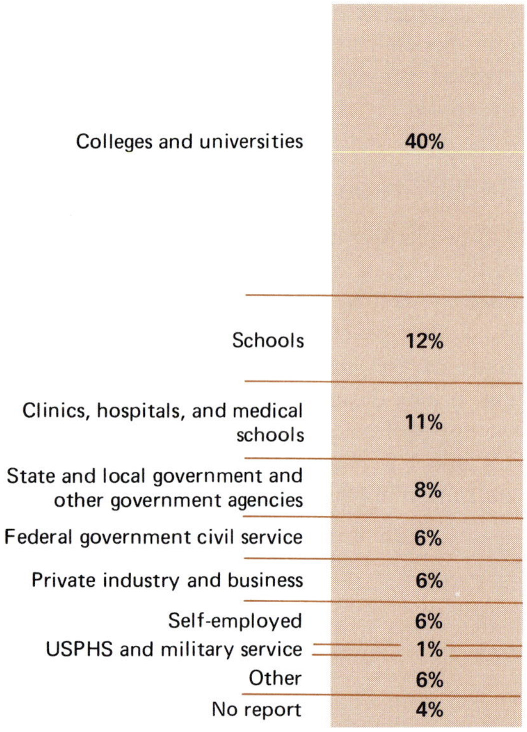

Figure 1.2 Psychologists work in many different settings. This figure lists the percentage of psychologists employed in various settings. (From *A Career in Psychology*. Copyright 1970 by the American Psychological Association. Reprinted by permission. Taken from 1968 National Register of Scientific and Technical Personnel.)

Biological Psychology Biological psychologists study the effects of biological processes on behavior, that is, the effects of biochemical, genetic, and physiological factors that influence behavior. For example, they might study how the removal of a certain area of the brain affects some behavior, such as eating. Or they might be interested in investigating the genetic basis for intelligence. These and many other related topics will be covered in Section 2: Biological Bases of Behavior.

Clinical Psychology Clinical psychologists are interested in abnormal behavior or, more accurately, maladaptive behavior: its causes, diagnosis, and treatment. An individual working in this field might study the interactions that occur in families when one member suffers from a particular kind of emotional problem. Other clinical psychologists might devise diagnostic tools, such as personality tests (discussed in Chapter 17), to identify individuals who suffer from a certain kind of maladjustment. Or he might use a therapeutic tool, such as psychotherapy, to treat individual patients. Many of the topics that are especially interesting to clinical psychologists will be discussed in Section 7: Personality and Abnormal Behavior.

Comparative Psychology This branch of psychology studies the similarities and differences in the behavior of organisms of different species. Comparative studies of many behaviors and the factors that influence them in animals of different species reveal to the comparative psychologist how certain behaviors might have evolved. In many cases, animals of a particular species are especially well suited for studying certain types of behavior patterns or the mechanisms underlying them. Such information often has general significance for understanding behavior that extends well beyond the specific knowledge gained about a single species of organism. Throughout this book you will find comparative studies of many different species.

Counseling Psychology In many ways, psychological counseling is similar to clinical psychology. However, the emphasis in clinical psychology is on maladaptive behavior and in psychological counseling more on normal behavior. Counseling psychologists use their knowledge about behavior to help individuals cope with everyday problems. In addition, they measure interest, aptitude, temperament, and the like to do academic, professional, and rehabilitation counseling.

Developmental Psychology This branch of psychology studies the development of an organism's behavior from its prenatal origins through maturity, to the end of life. The kind of research a developmental psychologist does might involve studying the development of a particular behavior in human infants and relating it to some aspects of biological growth. Or he might study social learning and relate it to other aspects of social development. These and similar topics will be discussed in Section 4: Developmental Processes and Behavior.

Educational Psychology Educational psychologists examine the interactions of students with their educational environment. Research in this field might focus on how different environments affect a child's desire to learn, for example, schools and churches; how different types of curricula affect students' mastery of different subjects; or how individual differences in learning ability among pupils affect the relations between pupils and teacher, or among pupils.

Industrial Psychology Industrial psychology is concerned with the behavior of individuals in relation to their work. A specialist in this field might analyze the way work is organized in the automotive industry and relate this information to the productivity of the workers. Or he might develop training programs that would maximize the potential of employees. Industrial psychologists are often called on to develop appropriate selection procedures to fit the right person to the right job.

Learning and Memory This branch of psychology is concerned with the learning and memory storage process. A researcher in this field might be interested in finding out whether there are different ways of remembering for different kinds of materials. A psychologist who is interested in the learning process might do research to test various theories that have been proposed to explain learning. Or he might investigate how rewards affect the rate at which different organisms will learn certain tasks. Learning, memory, and their biological relationships will be examined in Section 5.

Sensation and Perception This area of psychology treats all aspects of sensory and perceptual processes. For example, a psychologist working in this field might investigate how individuals see color or hear pitch. Or he might want to discover how the senses of smell and taste interact or whether they interact at all. Applied work in this field could involve the design of dials and gauges for airplane cockpits that pilots could read easily. A detailed account of how we obtain information from the world around us and integrate this information into meaningful patterns will be discussed in Section 3.

Social Psychology Social psychologists study behavior in terms of social interactions. For example, a social psychologist might study the qualities necessary for leadership in a particular group situation or how group pressure affects the behavior of individuals. He might study how attitudes develop in a particular social setting and devise techniques that will be useful in changing attitudes. Or he might examine the similarities and differences in the social structures of different cultural settings. Social psychology will be discussed in Section 8.

In this brief outline, you have seen that psychology has many faces. Most important, however, you have seen that psychologists are either actively engaged in experimental research or involved in the practical application of knowledge gained from research. In the following section 3, we will briefly consider the history of psychology as well as some of the methods used in experimental research in psychology.

History of Psychology

Psychology has been described as a discipline with a long past but a very short history. This popular aphorism is meant to convey two meanings. First, that concern with and thinking about psychological problems dates back to antiquity. Throughout history, philosophers have asked such questions as: What is the nature of knowledge, how is it acquired, and how are the mind and the body related. At least since the times of the early Greeks, medicine has wrestled with the problems of mental illness and epilepsy. And, finally, at least since the early nineteenth century, biologists have studied issues which today we would consider to be within the domain of psychology. Johannes Müller, for example, studied the relation between neural activity and sensation and perception; Charles Darwin asked questions about the relation of behavior to adaptation and survival.

The second meaning is that psychology, in the sense of being an independent academic discipline, is a very recent development. Although it is difficult to set an exact date, it is customary to say that psychology was born in 1879, the year that Wilhelm Wundt (1832–1920) established the first laboratory devoted exclusively to psychological research at the University of Leipzig.

It is historically accurate to say that for many centuries psychology was developing within other disciplines, and that it was born 100 years ago in Germany. It is also fair to say that during its infancy, psychology was greatly influenced by its founder, Wilhelm Wundt. One of his students, E. B. Titchener (1867–1927), was appointed to the chair of psychology at Cornell University and from there influenced the course of American psychology in the direction of structuralism, the "school of psychology" developed by Wundt and his students.

This "school" was so named because its goal was to describe the structure of the mind. More specifically, the ambitious task which structuralists set for themselves was to describe the "generalized human mind" in terms of the elements which made it up; to count the elements of consciousness in terms of the number of colors, tastes, smells, and so forth, of which it was thought to be constructed. To qualify as an element of mental life a sensation had to be irreducible. For this reason, structuralism is often referred to as a kind of mental chemistry. The structuralists soon discovered that sensations were not the only irreducible elements of consciousness, but also included certain types of images and several affects (emotions such as pleasantness and unpleasantness). Elements of consciousness were discovered by the method of *introspection,* a technique by which trained observers were taught to "look inward" and report their experiences. Synthesis, or the process by which the elements of the mind were put together to form more complex aspects of consciousness, was also studied.

To dissect the mind into its elements, the structuralists had available to them the *psychophysical methods* developed earlier by the physicist-philosopher G.T. Fechner (1801–1887). These methods are described in greater detail in Chapter 6; however, the task which Fechner had set himself was to measure sensations, and he had developed ideas and methods which allowed him to quantify certain aspects of mental life. To study synthesis, the work of Herman Ebbinghaus (1850–1909) was available; he had studied human verbal learning and memory quantitatively and had developed certain ideas which governed the association of stimuli and responses. These methods will be discussed in greater detail in

Chapter 12. The rules by which ideas become associated into ever more complex ideas had previously occupied the so-called *British Empiricsts,* philosophers such as John Locke and Bishop Berkeley.

The first serious challenge to structuralism was an American invention called *functionalism.* This school of thought was developed in the philosophy department at Harvard by William James (1842–1910), and in psychology departments at the University of Chicago by James R. Angel (1869–1949) and John Dewey (1859–1952), and at Columbia University by Edward L. Thorndike (1874–1949) and Robert S. Woodsworth (1869–1962). The functionalists argued that the elements of consciousness or mental chemistry should not be the major preoccupation of psychologists. Rather, psychologists should study what functions consciousness serves. In more modern terms, functionalists have focused their study on the adaptive value of behavior; in this they were greatly influenced by Charles Darwin's theory of evolution. They did not reject the emphasis which structuralists had placed on consciousness, nor their method of introspection. Instead, they argued that there exist obvious connections between the mind and *behavior,* and that the adaptive values of the mind (i.e., its functions) should be studied.

Functionalists were also interested in the question of how the nervous system controls the activity of other bodily organs and behavior. An interesting example of such "biological" interests is James' theory of emotional behavior described in Chapter 16. Finally, some of the functionalists, particularly William James, argued that psychologists should study "streams of consciousness" which characterize mental life more properly than the elements of consciousness into which the structuralists were trying to dissect the human mind.

By far, the greatest challenge to both structuralism and functionalism was another American development, a school of thought which came to be known as *behaviorism.* This school is largely identified with the ideas and work of the psychologist John B. Watson (1878–1958). He took exception with both the subject matter which up to then had formed the basis of psychology and with the methods used by psychologists. He argued most convincingly that the "private mental life" of human beings, into which introspection provided a window, could never be studied objectively. The only things which could be objectively analyzed and quantitatively measured, according to the behaviorists, were overt responses emitted by organisms—that is, behavior. Responses, according to this point of view, were elicited by stimuli; therefore, behaviorism also became known as $S \rightarrow R$ psychology. The task for psychology, then, was to study the relations between stimuli and responses and to discover the laws which govern their association. Two other points need to be made concerning early behaviorism: First, Watsonian behaviorism was also referred to as a kind of "black box" psychology because studying the central nervous system, where stimuli and responses presumably become associated, was ruled outside the domain of psychology. Second, early behaviorists were *empiricists,* the opposite of *nativist,* in that they argued that all behaviors result from experience, and none are determined by heredity.

Since according to the behaviorists the proper subject matters of psychology were stimuli, responses, their relations, and the laws which govern their association, methods had to be discovered which would allow one to study these phenomena objectively and quantitatively. It was indeed fortunate that at about this time the work of the Russian physiologists Ivan Pavlov (1848–1936) and

Vladimir Bechterev (1857–1927) became available to English-reading scholars. Pavlov had described his research at the now famous Charing Cross lecture in London in 1906, and Bechterev had been translated into French and German in 1913, languages with which American psychologists were familiar. In this lecture, Pavlov had described his famous work on classical conditioning, which will be discussed in some detail in Chapter 11. This phenomenon allowed researchers to study stimuli-response relations and to describe some of the laws which govern their association. Classical conditioning, a form of learning, became the method of behaviorism and, for this reason, this school of psychology became intimately associated with the study of learning and memory.

It was also at about this time, during the late nineteenth and early twentieth centuries, that two other schools of thought were developed that were to have a profound influence on psychology. One school, Gestalt psychology, was developed in Berlin by Max Wertheimer (1880–1943), Wolfgang Köhler (1887–1967), and Kurt Koffka (1886–1941). The other school of thought *psychoanalysis,* was developed in Vienna by Sigmund Freud (1858–1939).

According to the Gestalt psychologists, the analysis of the mind or behavior, practiced by the structuralists and behaviorists respectively, was in error because experience and behavior were "wholes" with properties unequal to the sum of their parts. The mind is not the sum of elements, sensations, ideas and emotions, but rather it is the interaction of these elements into complex wholes. The Gestalt psychologists made their points elegantly by analyzing certain types of perceptions and pointing out that figures, for example, are seen as wholes and not as elements.

Psychoanalysis, on the other hand, was not developed in academia but rather in the clinic and private consulting rooms of physicians who were concerned with treating neurotic patients. As such, psychoanalysis is a method of therapy that came to replace earlier forms of treatment such as hypnosis. But, it is much more than a form of treatment and the details of this theory will be covered in Chapter 17. Suffice it to say here that psychoanalysis is a theory of personality as well as a theory of personality development. Whereas previous schools of psychology had emphasized the conscious aspects of behavior, psychoanalysis placed great emphasis on its unconscious character.

Finally, one other development needs to be mentioned and that is the interest in individual differences in behavior which appear to be ubiquitous. Individual differences in behavior interested Francis Galton (1822–1911) and Alfred Binet (1857–1911). These individuals were fascinated by the differences in behavior from one individual to another, and they studied and measured these differences. In the hands of Galton, this fascination led to the development of a branch of psychology known as behavioral genetics (Chapter 2), whereas Binet's work laid the foundations for the so-called mental testing movement—that is, the development of intelligence tests, personality tests, and tests of all types.

This, in a nutshell, is the early history of psychology. Its true character cannot really be described in a few pages; fortunately, several excellent "histories" of psychology have been written; for example, E. Boring's *History of Experimental Psychology* (1950) and M. Wertheimer's *A Brief History of Psychology* (1970). We can confidently refer students to these textbooks for a far more adequate history of psychology.

Where do we stand today? Schools of psychology, in the sense used to describe the functionalists, the Gestalt psychologists, etc., are no longer important within psychology. What we see today are trends which emphasize certain subject matters, certain points of view, and certain methodologies. These are discussed throughout this textbook. Several important current trends are cognitive psychology, humanistic psychology, biological psychology, community mental health, and operant conditioning and its practical applications (e.g. behavior modification).

Psychology as a Science

To do behavioral research, psychologists have adopted the basic methodology of science and have invented techniques and methods that are especially suitable for studying behavior. Psychological research differs from experiment to experiment, depending in part on the problem being studied, the area of study (e.g., whether the research is biological or social), the investigator's theoretical orientation, the setting in which the work is being done, and so forth. But regardless of how experimental work in psychology is categorized—as field research, clinical research, or laboratory research—its overall purpose is the same. Therefore, before we describe the specific methods used in psychological research, a discussion is in order of the major goals of this research.

Goals of Psychological Research

In general, the goals of psychological research are threefold: (1) to describe, measure, and classify behavior, (2) to predict and control behavior, and (3) to understand and explain behavior.

Description, Measurement, and Classification of Behavior

If psychologists share with all other scientists the desire to describe a particular phenomenon accurately, it follows that the first goal of psychological research is to *describe* behavior. An example of descriptive research is given in box 1.1.

Once a behavior has been fairly well described, it is often necessary to *measure* it quantitatively. In certain instances, this task is relatively easy. For example, we would not find it difficult to count the number of errors a rat makes in running a maze or the number of times a bird will retrieve its eggs if they are scattered a certain distance from the nest. In other situations, however, it is extremely difficult to measure behavior. We can, by pointing out instances of anxious or depressed behavior, describe what we mean by anxiety or depression. But how do we measure these two states quantitatively? First, we would have to develop adequate measuring instruments. Thus one of psychology's goals is to develop such instruments.

Finally, after we have described behavior and developed appropriate techniques to measure it, we must *classify* behavior. At one level, classification of behavior presents no serious problems. For example, few would disagree that a rat nursing its pups or a bird retrieving its young to the nest is exhibiting a behavior that could be classified as maternal. At another level, however, attempts to classify behavior are extremely difficult. Scott's (1958) attempt to classify a variety of behaviors across species illustrates this problem vividly (see table 1.1).

Prediction and Control of Behavior

A major goal of science is to predict and control the occurrence of natural phenomena. Astronomers, for example, attempt to predict the behavior of comets, geologists try to predict the location of ores and oils, and psychologists attempt to predict behavior.

To *predict* behavior, the psychologist can rely on a variety of techniques. One method of predicting future behavior is on the basis of past performance. For example we could use a student's high school grades to predict what his college grades will be. However, because other factors such as motivation influence college grades, we should not be surprised if the student's grades do not perfectly predict his performance in college.

Often, psychologists use tests and *correlational techniques*—a mathematical expression for the fact that certain variables tend to change together systematically—to predict behaviors. (See discussion in the Appendix.) For instance, we would expect that an individual who expresses satisfaction with his job would also express strong interest in it. We could test this assumption by giving an interest test to all those recently hired into a certain profession and subsequently ask them to rate their job satisfaction. If, as expected, those who rate high on job satisfaction tend to have high scores on the interest test, we could say that the two factors are positively correlated. However, if their interest test scores were not related to job satisfaction, we would say that there was zero correlation between the two factors. And if high scores on the interest test were related to a low degree of job satisfaction, we would say that interest and job satisfaction are negatively correlated. In the appendix of this book, these statistical methods are discussed in greater detail and are illustrated diagrammatically.

Once the psychologist is able to predict, with some degree of accuracy, the occurrence of a particular behavior, it is natural for him to try to control it. In other words, control goes hand-in-hand with prediction. If, for example, psychologists could predict the occurrence of a mental disorder by using a psychological test, it would be logical for them to try to prevent the disorder from occurring. In general, if we can predict the occurrence of a phenomenon because certain conditions exist, then we can prevent (or control) its occurrence by changing the conditions. Conversely, if we can predict the occurrence of a behavior because certain conditions exist, then we can produce the behavior by creating the necessary conditions.

Box 1.1

Description in Psychology: Sexual Behavior in the Rat and Fish

Sexual behavior differs greatly among the different species, not only in terms of observable behavior, but also in terms of the underlying mechanisms that cause the behavior. To illustrate these differences, we will describe the characteristic sexual behavior of two very different organisms—the rat and a species of fish called the three-spined stickleback.

When a male rat is placed with a female rat in heat, sexual behavior may or may not occur. If it does, the usual sequence of events is as follows: First, the two rats explore each other by sniffing and licking. Then the male attempts to mount the female. If she is receptive, she arches her back, raises her head high, and moves her tail to one side. This behavior is called a *lordosis* response. The male then mounts, and penetrates her (achieves intromission) and makes a series of pelvic thrusts at regular intervals. After the male dismounts, he tends to groom himself for a time. He then mounts the female again, and the entire sequence is repeated over and over again until he ejaculates. He then clasps the female with

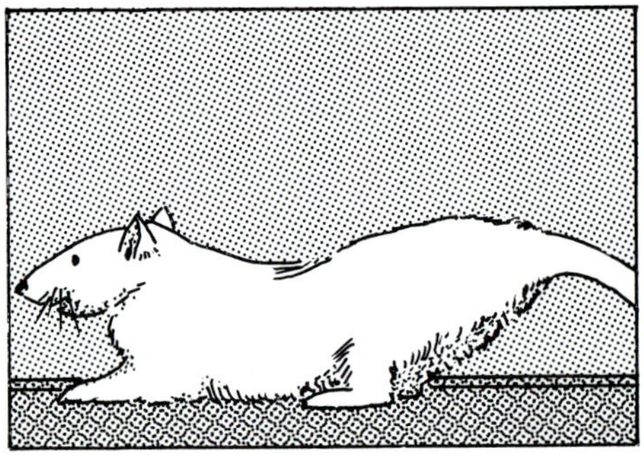

In principle, control over behavior is no different from the physicians' attempt to control disease. Smallpox and polio are controlled through immunization. And once it is possible to predict with accuracy that the incidence of lung cancer and heart disease is much greater in smokers than in nonsmokers, his forepaws; sometimes the male falls to his side carrying the female with him. In the rat multiple intromissions are necessary to prepare the female for pregnancy.

Male stickleback fish are territorial animals; that is, they chase other members of their species from their breeding groups. However, when a female stickleback enters the territory of a male, and he recognizes she is receptive, he attempts to mate by doing a characteristic mating dance. He swims over the nest he has built at the bottom of the river; the female follows him and deposits her eggs in the nest. The male then swims over the nest and fertilizes the eggs. These behaviors are illustrated in box figure 1.1.

As you can see, the mating behavior of these animals is vastly different. However, on the basis of observations and descriptions such as these, students of animal behavior have determined that sexual behavior in many species consists of a series of characteristic actions that always follow one another in a specific sequence.

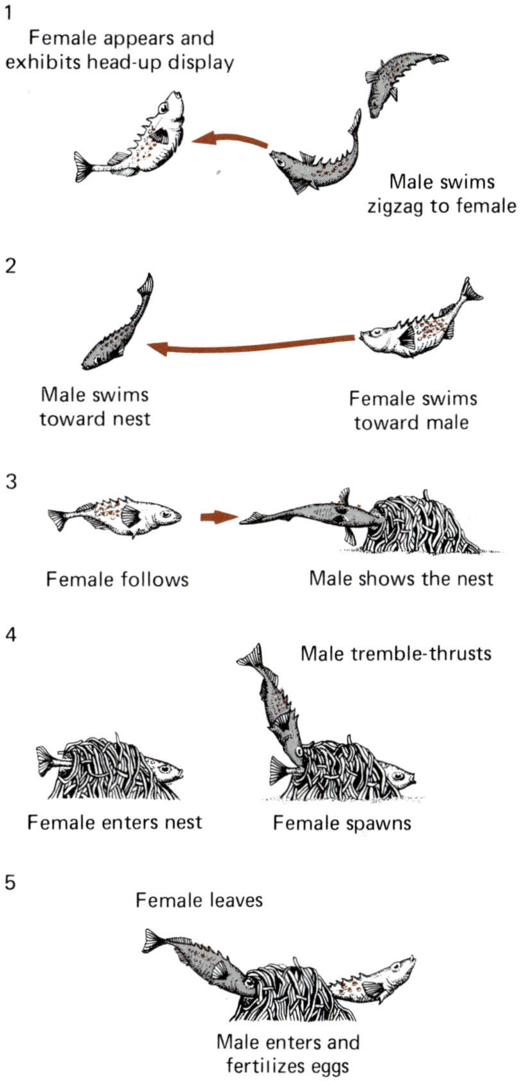

1
Female appears and exhibits head-up display
Male swims zigzag to female
2
Male swims toward nest
Female swims toward male
3
Female follows
Male shows the nest
4
Male tremble-thrusts
Female enters nest
Female spawns
5
Female leaves
Male enters and fertilizes eggs

Box Figure 1.1 a. Illustrates a female rat exhibiting lordosis response elicited by stroking the animal's side. Note that the response includes an arching of the back which elevates the genital region. The tail is pushed to one side. These behaviors facilitate intromission. During mating, the female in heat exhibits this behavior in response to the male's palpitation of her side. b. Illustrates the sequential courtship behaviors in stickleback fish. (a. from E. J. Farris and J. Q. Griffith, Jr. eds., 1949. *The Rat in Laboratory Investigation*. Philadelphia: J. P. Lippincott Company. b. from Schneider and Tarshis. *An Introduction to Physiological Psychology*. Copyright 1975 by Random House, Inc.)

then attempts will be made to control smoking behavior. If withdrawal from cigarettes causes irritability and aggressiveness, as some animal studies have indicated, then we can attempt to control such behavior with tranquilizers and the like. The important point to keep in mind is that control does not necessarily imply understanding. It is not necessary to understand why smoking causes lung cancer and heart disease before attempting to control smoking. It is also unnecessary to understand why withdrawal from cigarettes leads to irritability before one prescribes drugs to control behavior during withdrawal.

Table 1.1 J.P. Scott's Classification of Behavior.

Categories of Behavior (after Scott, 1958)	Description
1. Ingestive Behavior	Refers to all responses involving the acquisition of food. From relatively simple behaviors, such as nectar collection by bees, to predator-prey interactions, to elaborate ceremonies related to eating in humans.
2. Shelter-seeking	Refers to behaviors which optimize environmental conditions for the organisms, behaviors which avoid noxious or dangerous stimuli.
3. Agonistic Behavior	Refers to any behavior which involves "struggling," such as fighting, "bluffing," fleeing, "freezing," etc.
4. Sexual Behavior	Refers to all behaviors which have to do with courtship and copulation.
5. Epimeletic Behavior	Refers to care-giving behavior, such as feeding, cuddling, cleaning, etc.
6. Et-epimeletic	Refers to care-soliciting behaviors, such as the emitting of vocal signals and other behaviors which elicit epimeletic behavior from adults.
7. Eliminative Behavior	Refers to the compliment of ingestive behavior, but includes such behaviors as the cleaning of nests, the marking of territories, etc.
8. Allelomimetic Behavior	Refers to behaviors in which two or more animals do the same thing, i.e., a type of mimicry, such as flock formation in birds, herding in cattle, etc.
9. Investigative Behavior	Refers to all behaviors through which the animal explores its environment and other animals either of the same or of a different species.

Source: From J.P. Scott, *Animal Behavior.* Chicago: University of Chicago Press.

From the practical standpoint, however, control of behavior creates special problems. No one would argue that the attempt to control criminal behavior is a socially desirable undertaking. In fact, our prison systems are often criticized for failing to rehabilitate convicts. In other words, society applauds and sometimes demands control of certain kinds of behavior. In other cases, however, we are outraged when behavioral control is attempted. Remember how shocked we were when we learned that brainwashing techniques were being used on American prisoners of war in Korea? Our outrage was based on two factors: one, that attempts were being made to control people's thoughts, feelings, and behavior, and, two, that those attempts were frighteningly successful.

There is little doubt that as we learn more about behavior, we will be better able to control it. Thus the ethical and moral issues involve not only what behavior should be controlled and who should do the controlling, but also whether behavioral controls should be attempted at all, even if the ultimate goal is the betterment of the human condition.

Understanding and Explaining Behavior

Another major goal of science is to explain and understand natural phenomena. A major goal of psychology is to explain and understand behavior. Understanding involves assembling the known facts about behavior, gaining insights into the relationships among observable behavior, and deriving principles and models that will explain behavior. These principles can then be organized into more comprehensive frameworks called *theories.* In science, theories serve many functions. They are explanatory tools; they serve to integrate and systematize knowledge; and they make possible the formulation of new assumptions, or *hypotheses,* which can then be tested experimentally.

Finally, it is important to recognize that in science facts always remain facts, but our understanding of the facts changes continuously. In other words, theories are useful tools for understanding behavior, but theories are always subject to change. As new facts are discovered, a theory must either be modified to incorporate them or else be discarded altogether and replaced by a new theory.

Methods of Psychological Research

Now that we have outlined the overall goals of psychological research, we will describe the methods used in this research. First, we will discuss the experimental method, which is the foundation of all scientific research, and demonstrate its use in psychological research.

Experimental Method

When one thinks about scientific research, the first image that comes to mind is that of a scientist working in the laboratory. In the laboratory, the scientist can test the ideas, hypotheses, and predictions he has formulated on the basis of previous work. First, he outlines the problem or hypothesis as clearly as possible. Then he works out an appropriate *experimental design* that specifies the conditions under which measurements will be made, the instruments that will be used, and how the results will be analyzed. After completing his research and analyzing the results to his satisfaction, he will usually publish his findings in a scientific journal so that other scientists can repeat the experiment to ensure themselves of the accuracy of his findings. In other words, the experimental method makes it possible to replicate (repeat) research findings. Because work that can be repeated can be accepted as accurate with great confidence, *replication* is one of the cornerstones of science. Another reason for publishing the results of research is to inform other scientists of progress in their field. The publication of scientific research is especially important because it places science in the public domain, where it properly belongs.

Hypotheses As we have already seen, an experiment usually begins as an idea or hypothesis. There are two basic kinds of hypotheses that generate experimental research (Underwood, 1949): (1) "Let's see what will happen if . . ." kind of hypothesis and (2) "According to the work of ______, this should happen if . . ." kind of hypothesis.

Let's assume that a psychologist is interested in studying the effects of anxiety on test performance. How would he proceed, using the first kind of hypothesis? He might decide to give one group of subjects a set of instructions designed to make them extremely anxious before taking a certain test. He would then give neutral instructions to another group before they took the same test. The first group is commonly called an *experimental group;* the second group is termed the *control group.* The control group is similar in all respects to the experimental group, except that it is not exposed to the experimental variable—in this case, the anxiety-producing test instructions. Depending on the results of this experiment, the psychologist would conclude that anxiety improves, has no effect on, or adversely affects test performance.

Another psychologist, working with the second type of hypothesis, might reason as follows: A number of experiments I have read indicate that increasing the level of anxiety has detrimental effects on certain types of performance. I have also read that situations X and Y increase levels of anxiety in human subjects, whereas situation Z has no measurable effect on anxiety. According to what I have read, situations X and Y should decrease performance while situation Z should have no effect on performance. If the hypothesis is correct the control groups' performance should be superior to that of the experimental group. The experimenter would then expose an experimental group to either situation X or situation Y and the control group to situation Z. The performance of both groups would then be measured on the same task. Depending on the results of this experiment, the psychologist would conclude that anxiety as produced by situations X or Y increases, decreases, or has no effect on performance.

The second type of hypothesis is often more useful than the first because it is based on previous research findings. Hence, in the second experiment, the psychologist would be able to confirm or deny a prediction based upon research already conducted in this area.

Experimental Variables When using the experimental method to test a hypothesis, the scientist is simultaneously concerned with a number of factors called *variables.* These experimental variables are commonly classified as independent, dependent, and control variables.

The *independent,* or antecedent, variable is the factor that the experimenter manipulates in the experiment so that he can study its effects. In the experiments involving the effects of anxiety on test performance, the degree of anxiety was the independent variable.

The *dependent,* or consequent, variable is the variable that is being studied. It is that measure which is expected to change as a consequence of some experimental treatment. In the experiment just described, the test scores obtained by the subjects were the dependent variable.

Variables other than those which are being manipulated may affect the dependent variable. These are called *control* variables and the experimenter attempts to neutralize their effects so that he will be able, as accurately as possible, to assess the effects of the independent variable on the dependent variable. Two control variables that psychologists have learned to consider carefully in many experiments are the *placebo effect* and *experimenter bias.* These variables are discussed in box 1.2.

Experimental Design To use the experimental method most effectively, an investigator must manipulate the independent variable in a systematic way. In addition, he must use appropriate control procedures to interpret the results of his experiment. This is best accomplished by working out the experimental design carefully before beginning his experiment.

For example, suppose the investigator wants to know whether previous learning makes it easier for human subjects to learn something new. What experimental design would be appropriate? He could select a group of subjects and divide them at random into an experimental and a control group: the experimental group would learn task A; the control group would not. After a certain time interval, both groups would learn task B. This experimental design can be expressed as follows:

Box 1.2

The Placebo Effect and Experimenter Bias

Suppose a psychologist wants to study the effects of a psychedelic drug such as lysergic acid diethylamide (LSD) on motor skills required to drive a car safely. His first step is to divide a sample of human subjects randomly, or on the basis of some other sampling technique, into an experimental group and a control group. The experimental group receives LSD; the control group does not. All subjects are then tested on a driving simulator and are scored on their performance.

Let's assume that control subjects generally do better on the driving test than the experimental subjects. What can we conclude, based on these results? It would be natural for us to conclude that LSD adversely affects the motor skills necessary to drive a car. But isn't it possible that because the members of the experimental group were aware they had received LSD, their performance was affected by their expectations of how the drug was supposed to affect them?

To control this possibility, all the subjects in the experiment could be told that half of them will receive LSD and the other half will not. But no one should know whether he is a member of the experimental or control group. To accomplish this experiment, control subjects can be given a placebo, a pill that contains no active ingredients. If the performance of those subjects who received the placebo is affected, the psychologist can be more certain that expectations about what the drug might do are responsible for their behavior.

Although this technique is better than no controls at all, we still must contend with the possibility that the psychologist himself may, perhaps unconsciously, influence in subtle ways the subjects' performance on the driving test. To avoid this pitfall, the person conducting the driving test, like the subjects, should not know which subjects have received LSD. In other words, both the subject and the experimenter should be ignorant of who belongs in the experimental and control groups. This technique is often termed the "double-blind" procedure.

Experimental Group	Control Group
Learns task A	Does not learn task A
Learns task B	Learns task B

If the subjects in the experimental group learned task B more easily or quickly than those in the control group, the experimenter would conclude that learning task A facilitates the learning of task B. If the experimental group did not learn task B as easily or quickly as did the control group, he would conclude that learning task A interferes with learning task B.

A somewhat more complicated experimental design would be needed to investigate the following problem. Psychologists have known for some time that under certain circumstances humans as well as other animals recall information better if their memory is tested under the conditions that existed when the material to be remembered was learned. Evidence suggests that subjects will recall information better while intoxicated if they were intoxicated when they learned the material. This phenomenon, *state-dependent learning,* can be tested using the following design:

Group	Training Situation	Testing Situation
1	Intoxicated	Sober
2	Intoxicated	Intoxicated
3	Sober	Sober
4	Sober	Intoxicated

If an investigator discovers that groups 2 and 3 remember the information better than do groups 1 and 4, he would be entitled to conclude that, in this situation, recall is dependent on the similarity in the subject's physiological state at the time of original learning and of retesting.

Laboratories are not the only settings in which psychologists do research. Some conduct experiments in the field, others in clinical settings, etc. It is to some of these settings that we turn our attention.

Field Studies

Long before science moved into the laboratory, researchers used field studies to investigate interesting phenomena in nature. Today, scientists still frequently use field studies—either as a supplement to their laboratory work or as an alternative, when laboratory experimentation is inadequate or impossible.

In the field-study method, the scientist simply goes into the field and observes nature, but with a specific question in mind. Obviously, however, the control of many variables is more difficult in the field than in the laboratory. This technique has been used successfully, for example, to study the migratory behavior of fish and birds, social behavior among primates such as baboons and chimpanzees, and social interactions among children. In many field studies, the subjects are unaware of the investigator's presence.

The following examples will illustrate the field-study method of behavioral research. By tagging young salmon near or at their hatching sites, investigators have found that individual fish return, years later and after an ocean journey of many thousands of miles, to the same riverbed to lay their own eggs. The salmon find their way home, utilizing a variety of sensory cues, including the odor of the water in which they were born (Hasler, 1960). It is also known that if fertilized salmon eggs are moved to a new site before they hatch, the adult salmon will return years later to the place where they were hatched, not where their eggs were laid.

Another interesting example of the useful information obtained from field studies concerns the ability of primates to use tools. Although chimpanzees, for instance, are rarely observed using tools in the laboratory, we know, on the basis of extensive studies of chimpanzees and other primates in their natural environment (van Lawick-Goodall, 1970), that many primates continually use tools in the wild.

Clinical and Individual Case Studies

The *clinical method* is another technique used frequently in behavioral research, most often to study abnormal behavior. The work of Sigmund Freud is perhaps the most illustrious example of this type of research. Dissatisfied with the methods of treating neuroses that were available during the late 1800s, Freud developed his own technique, which primarily consisted of listening to patients talk about their feelings and problems. After repeatedly observing that his patients were unaware of the nature and origin of their emotional problems, he developed a comprehensive theory of neurosis and a rational treatment based on this theory.

The clinical method is still used extensively. The clinical psychologist explores an individual's life history in great depth, especially from the developmental point of view, and takes careful note of the individual's current situation. On the basis of these observations, he attempts to determine the origins of the patient's emotional problems and outlines a course of treatment.

Although the techniques used in *individual case studies* do not differ significantly from those used in clinical studies, the focus of the individual case study may or may not be abnormal behavior. The psychologist interviews the subject at length to obtain biographical and other information and may administer a variety of psychological tests. On the basis of these data, he is able to say something about the subject's personality traits, interests, habits, and so forth.

Data collected in this fashion can then be compiled for groups of individuals and used experimentally. For example, criminals can be compared with law-abiding citizens; psychologists can be contrasted with musicians; married persons can be compared with divorced persons. On the basis of comparisons such as these, psychologists attempt to gain insight into why certain individuals and not others become criminals, choose certain professions, get divorces, and so on.

Surveys

Suppose you are a college admissions officer faced with choosing a limited number of students for admission to a college. How would you decide which applicants will successfully complete a four-year course of study? Or imagine that you are the manager of a political campaign, and your candidate is about to take a public stand on an issue. How would you find out which statements will affect the voting behavior of his constituents?

Clearly, neither clinical nor individual case studies are appropriate for collecting information about the behavior of large populations. Survey methods, on the other hand, are ideally suited to such situations. There are several methods of studying the behavior of large numbers of people, including psychological tests, interviews, and questionnaires.

Psychological Tests

Psychologists have developed and standardized numerous tests to measure different aspects of behavior. One test you are familiar with is the intelligence or I.Q. test, which can be administered either to groups or to individuals. Thus our hypothetical college admissions officer might sift through the records of all incoming freshmen from previous years to collect their I.Q. scores and to determine whether they did well in college. After compiling such data, he might discover that students whose I.Q. scores were below a certain level were less likely to do well in college than were those who had higher scores. He could then decide to admit only those applicants who scored above a certain point on I.Q. tests. However, he is more likely to use several criteria, such as high school grades, in addition to the I.Q. scores, to set standards for admission. The reason may be that other researchers have found that students who do relatively well in high school, despite marginal I.Q. test scores, tend to be better risks than those who have high I.Q. scores but receive low high school grades.

Interviews

Earlier we said that the interview is one of the fundamental techniques used in clinical and individual case studies. But this technique can be adapted easily for use in surveys. In the *structured* interview, a number of respondents are asked a predetermined set of questions, and after the answers are tabulated, conclusions can be drawn concerning groups of individuals. In the *unstructured* interview, the questions depend on the responses of the subject and on the interviewer's hypotheses about the underlying reasons for these responses. For example, let's assume that a political candidate, during a period of economic recession, is running for office in Michigan and wants to make a public statement about solving the nation's economic problems. His campaign manager, faced with predicting what effects such a statement might have on the Michigan voters, conducts an unstructured interview with auto workers and farmers. In all likelihood the two groups feel differently about what action needs to be taken to correct the economic situation. Therefore the campaign manager will be careful to ask one group one kind of question and the other group another kind of question; moreover, he will tailor his questions not only to each group, but also to individuals.

Questionnaires

Figure 1.2 contains an example of the kind of questionnaire that a college instructor might distribute among his students to gauge the effectiveness of his course and method of presentation. On the basis of students' responses, he could decide whether to continue using a certain textbook, whether his examples and illustrations were appropriate, and

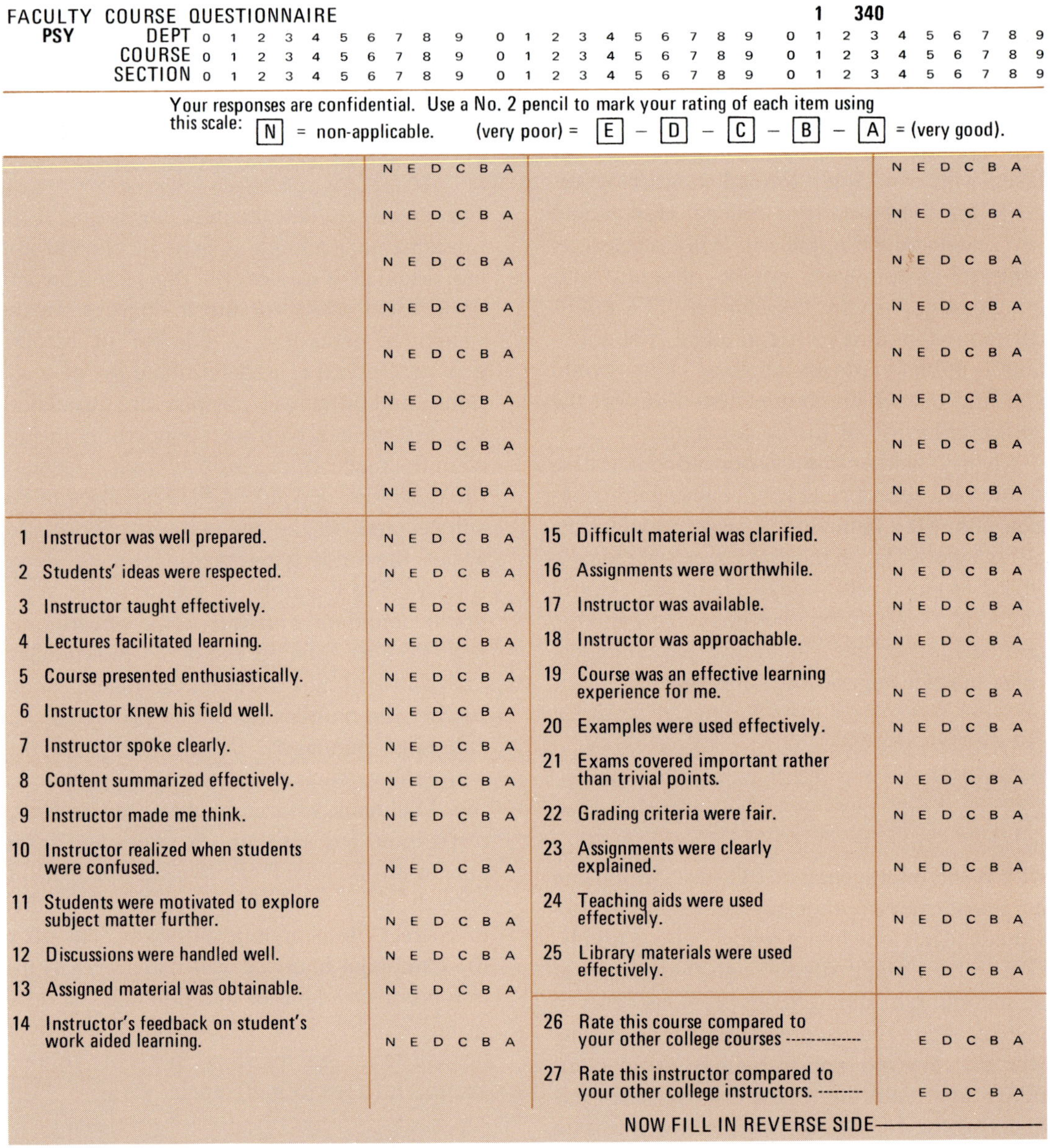
FACULTY COURSE QUESTIONNAIRE 1 340

PSY

DEPT	0	1	2	3	4	5	6	7	8	9	0	1	2	3	4	5	6	7	8	9	0	1	2	3	4	5	6	7	8	9
COURSE	0	1	2	3	4	5	6	7	8	9	0	1	2	3	4	5	6	7	8	9	0	1	2	3	4	5	6	7	8	9
SECTION	0	1	2	3	4	5	6	7	8	9	0	1	2	3	4	5	6	7	8	9	0	1	2	3	4	5	6	7	8	9

Your responses are confidential. Use a No. 2 pencil to mark your rating of each item using this scale: [N] = non-applicable. (very poor) = [E] – [D] – [C] – [B] – [A] = (very good).

	N E D C B A		N E D C B A
	N E D C B A		N E D C B A
	N E D C B A		N E D C B A
	N E D C B A		N E D C B A
	N E D C B A		N E D C B A
	N E D C B A		N E D C B A
	N E D C B A		N E D C B A
	N E D C B A		N E D C B A
1 Instructor was well prepared.	N E D C B A	15 Difficult material was clarified.	N E D C B A
2 Students' ideas were respected.	N E D C B A	16 Assignments were worthwhile.	N E D C B A
3 Instructor taught effectively.	N E D C B A	17 Instructor was available.	N E D C B A
4 Lectures facilitated learning.	N E D C B A	18 Instructor was approachable.	N E D C B A
5 Course presented enthusiastically.	N E D C B A	19 Course was an effective learning experience for me.	N E D C B A
6 Instructor knew his field well.	N E D C B A	20 Examples were used effectively.	N E D C B A
7 Instructor spoke clearly.	N E D C B A	21 Exams covered important rather than trivial points.	N E D C B A
8 Content summarized effectively.	N E D C B A	22 Grading criteria were fair.	N E D C B A
9 Instructor made me think.	N E D C B A	23 Assignments were clearly explained.	N E D C B A
10 Instructor realized when students were confused.	N E D C B A	24 Teaching aids were used effectively.	N E D C B A
11 Students were motivated to explore subject matter further.	N E D C B A	25 Library materials were used effectively.	N E D C B A
12 Discussions were handled well.	N E D C B A	26 Rate this course compared to your other college courses ---------------	E D C B A
13 Assigned material was obtainable.	N E D C B A	27 Rate this instructor compared to your other college instructors. ---------	E D C B A
14 Instructor's feedback on student's work aided learning.	N E D C B A		

NOW FILL IN REVERSE SIDE

Figure 1.3 A sample of a course evaluation questionnaire. Reverse side allows student to make additional comments about various aspects of the course. (University of Colorado, 1973. Used by permission of Ronald G. Taylor and Robert Whetstone.)

whether his lectures contained the proper mix of practical and theoretical material.

Another less structured questionnaire might require the students to recall three instances from class that led them to believe that the course was useful and three that indicated to them that it was not useful. By tabulating these results, the instructor could again reach decisions about the effectiveness of his course.

Information gathered during surveys is useful, not only because it provides answers to practical questions such as how voters will react, but also because it generates further research hypotheses. For example, let's suppose that our college admissions officer reads a book by McClelland et al. (1953), who surveyed a large number of college students and discovered that individuals differ in terms of their need for achievement. Those with a strong need to achieve view their parents as distant and themselves as independent of authority. Students with little need for achievement indicate that they are close to their parents and consider them friendly and helpful. Based on the results of McClelland's study and on his own survey that students with good high school grades but relatively low I.Q. scores tend to earn respectable grades in college, the admissions officer might predict that these students have a strong need to achieve. As an experimenter he might then decide to put this hypothesis to the experimental test using one or several of the experimental methods discussed above.

Use of Animals in Psychological Research

Although human behavior is the ultimate interest of most psychologists, you will find that much of the research described in this book uses lower animals as subjects. Some of the reasons for using animals are quite simple. For example, animals can be maintained in the laboratory under controlled conditions, and techniques and procedures can be used on them that cannot be used on humans. In other words, psychologists use animals in research primarily for both ethical and practical reasons.

But does what we learn about the behavior of pigeons, rats, or chimpanzees apply to human behavior? The answer is that sometimes it does and sometimes it does not. However, one of psychology's basic goals is to establish general laws of behavior which often apply across species. In other words, psychologists often find that what they learn about the rat's behavior will apply to some aspects of the behavior of human beings. There will be variations, of course, but many general principles hold across species. Hence, many principles that underlie animal behavior apply to human behavior. Modern biology also gives us faith in this belief. For example, much of what biologists have learned about the genetic material of viruses applies as well to the human genetic material. In addition, much of what is known about the nervous system of humans and its role in human behavior has been discovered or suggested by research on animals. This is because there are many fundamental similarities between animal and human nervous systems and biological processes.

Nevertheless, it is important to remember that what we learn in animal research may or may not apply to humans. Although many psychologists have faith in the generality of their finding, they always make generalizations cautiously and attempt, as best they can, to test such generalizations by observation and experimentation.

Finally, keep in mind that experiments in psychology are never undertaken lightly. They are governed by a code of ethics issued by the American Psychological Association, which stresses two general points: (1) psychological research must be conducted for the purpose of contributing to psychological science and human welfare and (2) each researcher is personally responsible for the ethical standards of his research as well as those of his assistants and students. Animal research is also governed by a code of ethics issued by the National Institutes of Health, which stresses that humane treatment of animal subjects is of paramount importance.

Summary

In this introductory chapter, we have tried to define what psychology is and how psychologists work. We said that although psychology has many faces, its underlying purpose is the study of all aspects of human and animal behavior. We also pointed out that psychologists use a variety of methods, depending on their goals, the problem they are studying, and the subjects they use.

Because psychology is a science, an academic discipline, and a profession, it follows that psychologists engage in both field studies and laboratory research, teach in academic and other settings, and function as professionals in private practice, hospitals and mental health centers, government, and industry.

Since psychology's goals are to describe, measure, and classify behavior, to predict and control behavior, and to understand and explain behavior, the psychologist uses all the methods of science, especially the experimental method, and, on the basis of research, attempts to construct theories which explain behavior.

The general statement that understanding man's behavior is of paramount importance is beyond dispute. Few would argue against the principle that understanding mental illness, learning and memory, motives, and emotions would be of great benefit to mankind. The fact that more than fifty percent of all hospital beds in the United States are occupied by mental patients would seem to suggest that the need to understand human behavior is critical.

James Olds (1922-) Together with Peter Milner, Olds discovered the phenomenon of self-stimulation. Today, Olds is one of the pioneers in investigating learning and memory from a physiological perspective.

Gregor Mendel (1822-1884) Augustinian monk who laid the foundation for the modern science of genetics. His classical experiments led to the development of the law of independent assortment and the law of segregation.

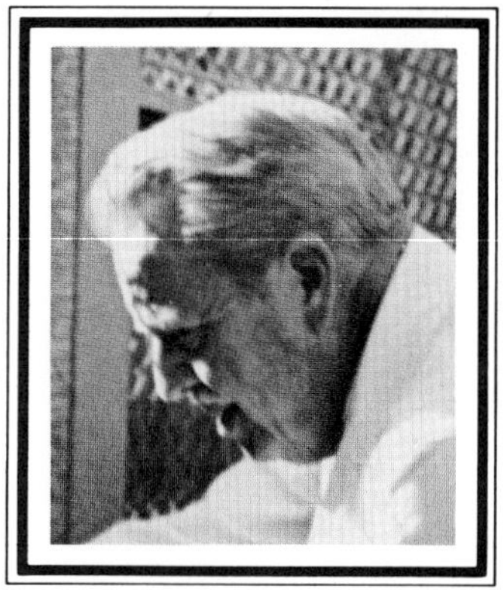

Frank Beach (1911-) For over three decades, Frank Beach has been one of the leading investigators on neural, experiential, and hormonal determinants of motivated behavior. His work on the biological mechanisms of sexual behavior form a cornerstone of this field. He has also made important empirical and theoretical contributions to comparative psychology.

Section

2

The Biological Bases of Behavior

2

Behavioral Genetics

Behavioral genetics is a relatively new area of research and specialization and is part of the broader and more traditional field of biological psychology. If one reads the research literature in psychology, he can find scattered articles on subjects that today would be classified as behavioral genetics. However, the first textbook that attempted to systematize the field was not published until 1960 (Fuller and Thompson), although interest in the questions which concern behavioral genetics dates back to antiquity.

The discipline of behavioral genetics can be defined as that field which asks questions about the *degree* and the *nature* of the heritable causes of behavior. This definition suggests that the work of the behavioral geneticist is of two types: First, he attempts to discover the degree to which the individual differences in behavior observed in populations are related to heredity. Second, he is concerned with the ways by which genes affect behavior. A behavioral genetic analysis of a trait attempts to answer the following questions, which are paraphrased from Thiessen (1972):

1. Is the trait influenced by differences in heredity?
2. What proportion of the individual differences in the behavior are caused by genetic and environmental factors?
3. How is the effect of heredity on behavior changed during the course of development, and how do environmental changes affect the expression of heredity?
4. What are the mechanisms that mediate between the gene and the behavior?
5. Does the behavior have adaptive significance; in other words, does it contribute to the reproductive fitness of the organism, and is it subject to natural selection?

This chapter will illustrate the kinds of research used in attempting to answer these questions. To understand behavioral genetics, you will need some knowledge of genetics itself. Accordingly, the first section will be devoted to a discussion of three basic areas of genetics: classical Mendelian genetics, quantitative genetics, and molecular genetics.

Introduction to Genetics

Mendelian Genetics

The birth of the science of genetics occurred with the publication of the classic experiments performed by Gregor Mendel, an Augustinian monk who was interested in the inheritance of certain traits in common, garden variety peas. Mendel had noticed that certain plants were *true breeding* for some traits: for example, some tall plants only produced tall progeny and certain dwarf plants only produced dwarf plants; some green plants produced only green offspring while some yellow plants produced only yellow progeny. In an attempt to explain this phenomenon, Mendel mated plants with different characteristics and counted the frequency with which the trait occurred in the progeny. In crosses involving true-breeding tall and true-breeding dwarf plants, for example, Mendel noted that all the progeny were tall. In another experiment, he noted that all the offspring from crosses of true-breeding plants with smooth seed skins and wrinkled seed skins were smooth-skinned. In other words, the F_1 *hybrid* plants (i.e., the first filial generation) were always like one of the parental types. The parental type which was recovered in the F_1 hybrid was termed the *dominant trait,* and the trait that failed to appear in the hybrid was termed the *recessive trait.* (Note that dominance and recessiveness refer to the trait, not to the underlying genetic material.) Mendel continued his experiments by crossing two F_1 hybrid plants with each other: for example, two hybrids derived from mating a tall with a dwarf plant. In this second filial generation, or F_2 cross, both parental types were recovered, and always in the same proportion: three tall plants and one dwarf plant. He also noted that the dwarf plants derived from the F_2 cross always bred true whereas the tall plants were of two types; one of the three tall plants bred true and two did not.

Mendel obtained similar results for each of the traits he studied. To explain these data, he proposed the following model: The expression of these traits depends on heritable "factors," and each plant possesses two factors for each trait. In true-breeding plants, the factors are identical. Thus true-breeding tall plants possess factors TT, whereas true-breeding dwarf plants possess factors tt. Each plant passes on one of these factors to its progeny in its sex cells or *gametes.* The offspring of a TT by tt cross will therefore contain factors Tt, and because T is dominant the plant will be tall. If two Tt plants are crossed, each can pass on factor T or t in its gametes, and thus it follows that one-fourth of the offspring will be TT (tall), one-half will be Tt (tall), and one-fourth will be tt (dwarf), giving a ratio of three tall for every one dwarf plant.

The results of this experiment and the explanatory model Mendel devised have been formalized into Mendel's first law, or the *law of segregation,* so called because the paired factors separate (segregate) when gametes are formed. Schematic representations of his results and the model that explains them are contained in figure 2.1.

Mendel also crossed plants that differed from one another in more than one trait: for example, true-breeding tall and yellow plants were crossed with true-breeding dwarf and green plants. Because tall is dominant over dwarf and yellow dominant over green, all F_1 hybrid plants were tall and yellow. In the F_2 generation, however, four types of progeny were produced: tall-yellow, tall-green, dwarf-yellow, and dwarf-green. The ratio of these

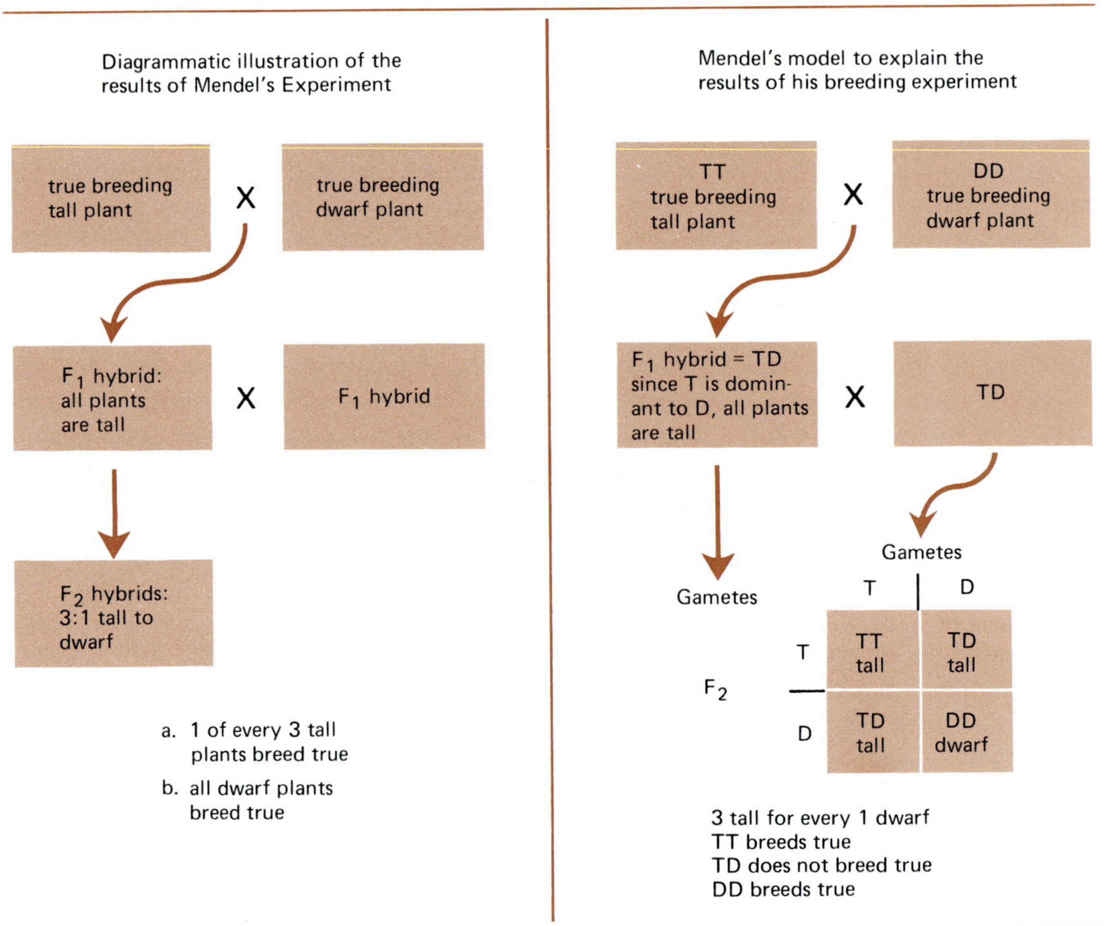

Figure 2.1 Illustration of Mendel's classic experiment and theory which led to the formulation of the law of segregation. The left side of the diagram illustrates the actual experimental procedure and the results, while the right side illustrates Mendel's explanatory model.

four types was 9:3:3:1. The model used to explain these results is illustrated in figure 2.2. This has been formalized as Mendel's second law, the *law of independent assortment,* which states that the factors underlying different traits such as size and color are transmitted independently of each other.

Although Mendel published his data in 1865, they were totally ignored for almost thirty years. One reason was that the biological mechanisms that would have explained his findings were not known at the time. These mechanisms began to be understood when biologists investigated the structure of cells, a field of study known as *cytology.*

Cytology can be thought of as having its origins in the late 1600s when several investigators, notably Hooke and Malpighi, discovered that all living matter had a common structural basis, that is, it was made up of cells. The culmination of this discovery was the so-called *cell theory* postulated by

Assume TT = true breeding tall GG = true breeding green

TTYY X DDGG DD = true breeding dwarf YY = true breeding yellow

Remember T dominant over D; Y dominant over G

F_1 = TDYG X TDYG

Gametes	TY	TG	DY	DG
TY	TTYY tall yellow	TTYG tall yellow	TTYG tall yellow	TDYY tall yellow
TG	TTYG tall yellow	TTGG tall green	TDGY tall yellow	TDGG tall green
DY	TDYY tall yellow	TDYG tall yellow	DDYY dwarf yellow	DDYG dwarf yellow
DG	TDGY tall yellow	TDGG tall green	DDGY dwarf yellow	DDGG dwarf green

Therefore: 9 tall yellow: 3 tall green: 3 dwarf yellow: 1 dwarf green

Figure 2.2 Mendel's classic experiment, which led to the formation of the law of independent assortment.

Schleiden and Schwann, circa 1839. The cell theory is perhaps the greatest unifying principle of biology.

Today we know a great deal about the structure and function of cells. Figure 2.3 represents an idealized and simplified diagram of a cell. In Chapter 3, the structure of a specialized type of cell, the nerve cell, will be discussed in detail.

Most cells share certain common features. They are enclosed by an envelope called the *cellular membrane*. In some types of cells, especially the nerve cell, this membrane is a highly complex structure, as you will see in Chapter 3. Most cells contain an inner body, or *nucleus,* which is separated from the remainder of the cell, or *cytoplasm,* by the *nuclear membrane*. Both the nucleus and the cytoplasm contain many intracellular organelles. Notice in figure 2.3 that within the nucleus are located several elongated structures called chromosomes. All cells multiply by dividing in one of two ways; in both cases, however, each daughter cell receives a nucleus and its own complement of chromosomes.

The kind of cell division that occurs in somatic cells—cells that form the *soma* or body of all plants and animals—is called *mitosis*. The other type of cell division occurs in sex cells, cells that form the germ plasm, and is called *meiosis*. Figures 2.4a and 2.4b are diagrammatic illustrations of the mitotic and meiotic processes. Note that prior to mitosis the cell contains pairs of chromosomes. During mitosis, however, the chromosome number doubles, the nuclei then divide, and each daughter cell receives a full complement of chromosomes. During meiosis, on the other hand, each daughter cell inherits only one-half the original number of chromosomes, or the *haploid* number of chromosomes; hence meiosis is referred to as reduction division. During fertilization, when sperm and egg combine to form the *zygote,* the full chromosome complement of the species, or the *diploid* number, is reestablished.

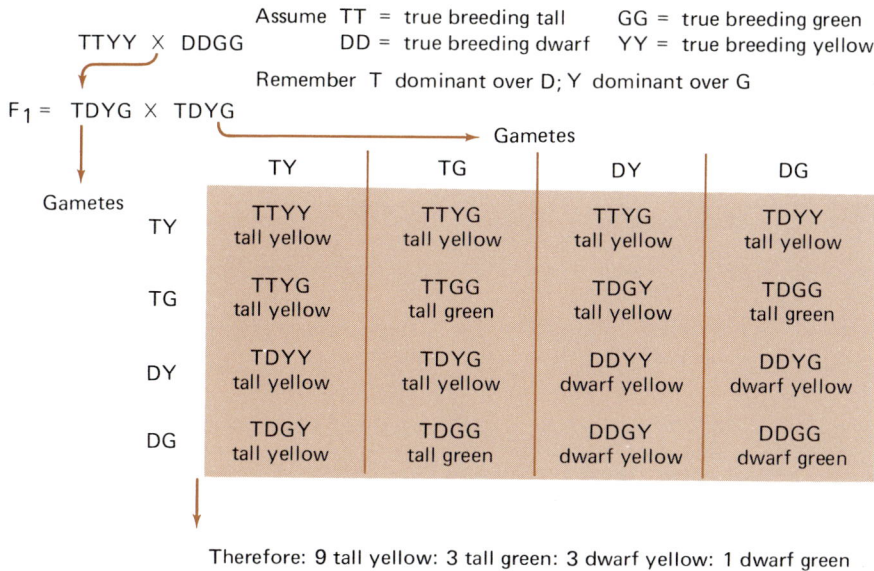

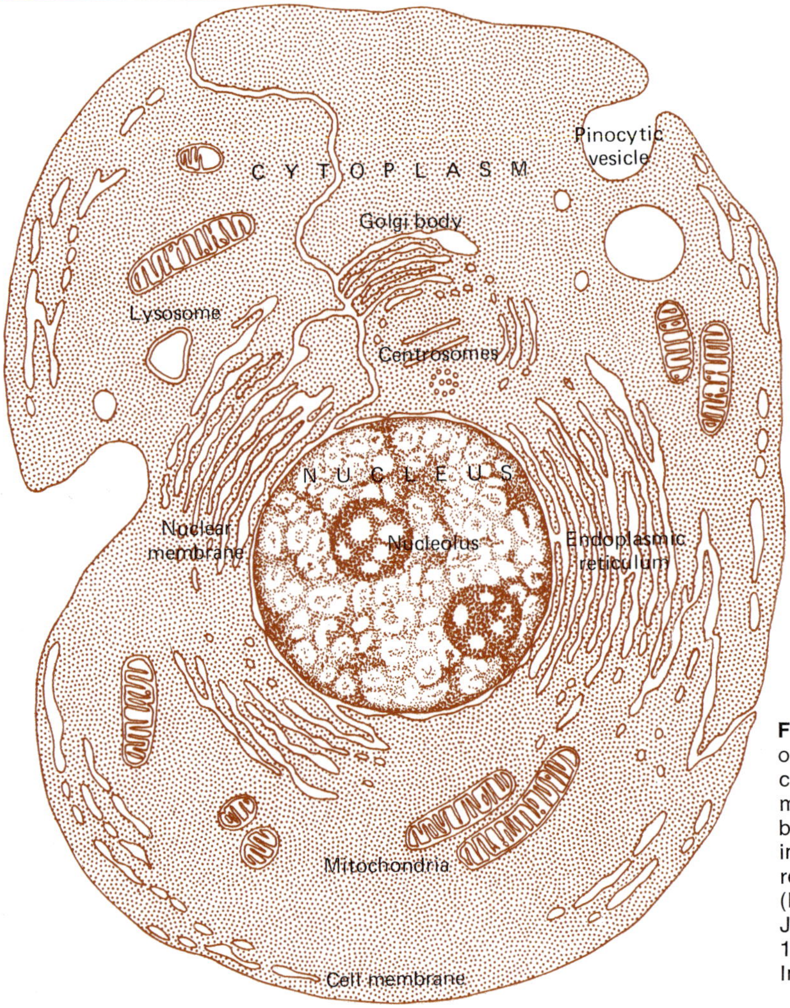

Figure 2.3 Simplified diagram of a cell. Note that the cell is contained within a cellular membrane and includes a number of subcellular organelles including the endoplasmic reticulum, mitochondria, etc. (From "The Living Cell" by Jean Brachet. Copyright © 1961 by Scientific American, Inc. All rights reserved.)

When Mendel's publication was rediscovered around the turn of the century, the cytological basis of cell reproduction was sufficiently well understood so that many geneticists began to see a relationship between the two types of research. In 1903 the great American geneticist Walter S. Sutton published a paper entitled *The Chromosomes in Heredity,* in which he postulated that the "factors" Mendel had proposed were located on chromosomes. And if his hypothesis was correct, then Mendel's results could be explained. Remember that during meiosis, the chromosome number is reduced by one-half; thus the 9:3:3:1 ratios that Mendel obtained can be explained if we assume that the two factors for size and number are located on separate chromosomes (i.e., that the two factors are inherited independently).

Mendel was extremely fortunate in choosing to study factors that were located on different chromosomes, and thus obeyed the law of independent assortment. It soon became obvious that not all cell factors obeyed this

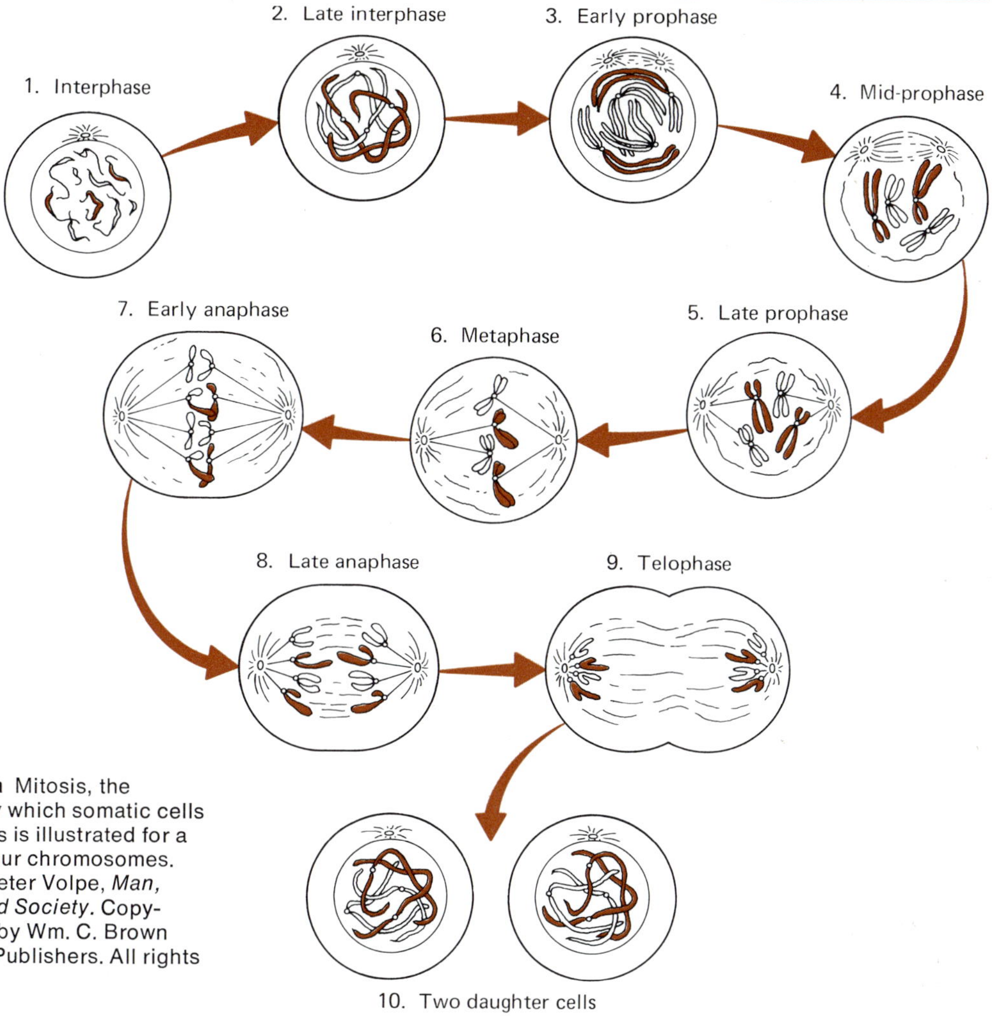

Figure 2.4a Mitosis, the process by which somatic cells divide. This is illustrated for a cell with four chromosomes. (From E. Peter Volpe, *Man, Nature, and Society*. Copyright 1975 by Wm. C. Brown Company Publishers. All rights reserved.)

law; the traits they regulated were associated more often than predicted by Mendel's second law. Thus the factors had to be located or *linked* on the same chromosome. It was then discovered that the degree of linkage between two factors—that is, the extent to which they are inherited jointly—varied from between approximately 50 and 100 percent. A physical basis for this linkage was found in the cytological observation that during meiosis, like or *homologous* chromosomes join together along their long axes and physically exchange genetic material—a process called *crossing over*. Another famous geneticist, Thomas H. Morgan, soon discovered that there was a quantitative relationship between the amount of crossing over and the physical distance that separates two factors on a chromosome. This discovery allowed geneticists to map individual factors on individual chromosomes, each factor occupying a particular position or *locus* on a chromosome.

By now, you have probably realized that what Mendel called factors are now called

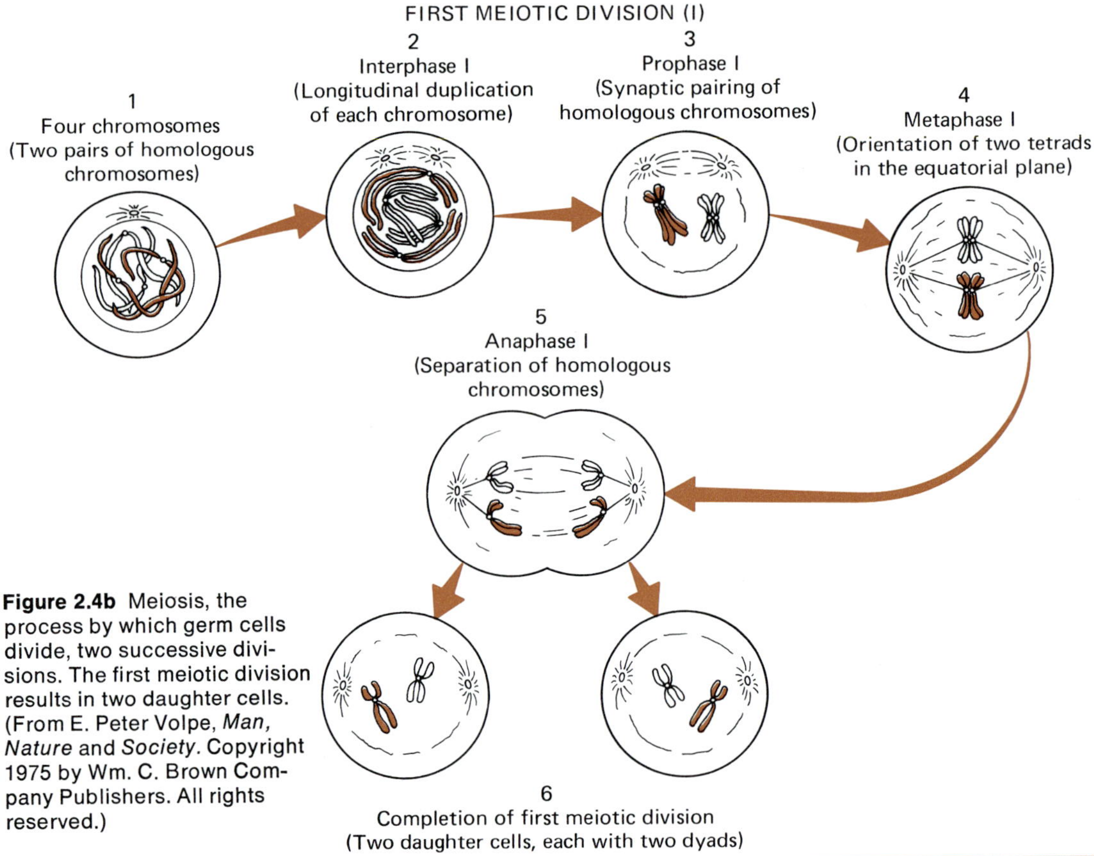

Figure 2.4b Meiosis, the process by which germ cells divide, two successive divisions. The first meiotic division results in two daughter cells. (From E. Peter Volpe, *Man, Nature* and *Society*. Copyright 1975 by Wm. C. Brown Company Publishers. All rights reserved.)

genes. All an organism's genes constitute its *genotype*. The *observed trait* (e.g., size or color) is termed the *phenotype*. You should also be aware that the cells of all animals of a given species contain the same number of pairs of chromosomes. Man, for example, characteristically has twenty-three pairs. One pair, called the sex chromosomes, determines the organism's sex. The human female has one pair of homologous sex chromosomes, XX. Males have one pair of XY. Genes located on these sex chromosomes are called *sex-linked* genes. The remaining chromosomes (twenty-two pairs in the case of humans) are called *autosomes*.

Today it is possible to photograph and separate the chromosome complement of an organism's cells—a process called *karyotyping*. Figure 2.5a illustrates a normal human karyotype. Figure 2.5b illustrates a karyotype obtained from an individual suffering from Down's syndrome (mongolism), which will be discussed more fully on page 45 of this chapter. Notice that the individual with Down's syndrome has three chromosomes 21, instead of the normal pair. This extra chromosome forms the cytological basis of Down's syndrome, which is often called *trisomy 21* (see fig. 2.5b).

Quantitative Genetics

The traits measured by Mendel were dichotomous: in other words, each plant could be

Figure 2.4c The end result of meiosis is the formation of four haploid (daughter) cells, each with only half the original number of chromosomes.

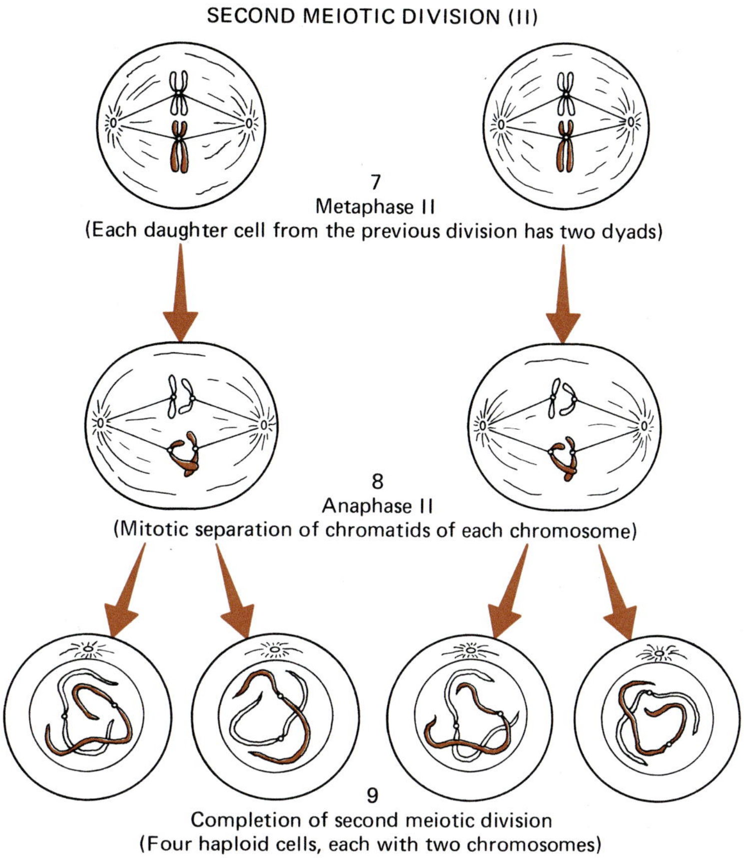

categorized as belonging to one of two mutually exclusive classes, for example, tall or dwarf, yellow or green, and so forth. In nature, however, most traits are not dichotomous but are continuously distributed. If we measure traits such as height or intelligence, we discover that people are not tall or short or low or high in intelligence, but rather that they vary in height and levels of intelligence continuously over some range. Assume that height and intelligence are both determined in part by genetic factors, as in fact they appear to be. At first glance, these traits do not seem to obey the laws of classical genetics. In fact they do, but the techniques used to study dichotomous variables are inadequate for the genetic study of continuously distributed variables. Why is this the case? Traits such as intelligence and height are controlled by many genes rather than single genes—that is, they are *polygenically* determined. Furthermore, many of the genes that determine such traits act additively, each gene adding a small increment to the expression of the trait. Finally, environmental factors contribute significantly to the expression of traits such as height and intelligence. These factors result in a continuous distribution of measurements for polygenically controlled traits, as illustrated in box 2.1. To study such traits, biometricians have devised a variety of quantitative techniques. Two of them—the coefficient of genetic determination and research with twins—will be discussed in the next section.

Box 2.1

Polygenetically Controlled Traits

1. Assume that a trait such as height is controlled by genes at two different loci, *A* and *B*. Assume that each of these genes can exist in two forms, *A* and *a*, *B* and *b*. For the moment, also assume that environmental factors do not contribute to the expression of the trait.

2. Next, assume that the genes act additively—each contributing an increment to the expression of the trait. Genes A and B each contribute one point; genes a and b contribute none.

3. Now, consider the mating of genotypes AABB by aabb. The phenotypic measurements will be 4 and 0, respectively, for these two parental types. Genotypically, however, all offspring in F_1 generation will be AaBb, and all will have a phenotypic score of 2. Thus each F_1 hybrid can produce four types of gametes: AB, Ab, aB, and ab. The results of an F_1 by F_1 mating are given in box figure 2.1a; the genotype of each offspring is shown, and the phenotypic score is given in parentheses. Therefore, the distribution of phenotypic scores will be one F_2 offspring with a score of 4, four F_2 offspring with scores of 3, six with scores of 2, four with scores of 1, and one with a score of 0. This represents a continuous distribution, as illustrated in box figure 2.1b.

4. Now assume that environmental factors contribute significantly to the expression of the trait and can affect the phenotypic scores by 0, ±1, ±2, ±3, and so on. Also assume that the environmental effects act randomly and that the trait is measured in eighty individuals. When this is done, data shown in the graph below are obtained. In theory, however, if the effects of the environment are random and if an infinitely large number of measurements are made, their net effect will be zero. The range of the distribution will be extended, but it will still be symmetrical.

5. Thus when more than one gene contribute to the expression of a trait and when each of these genes has only a small and additive effect, a continuous distribution of scores is obtained, as shown in the symmetrical distribution in box figure 2.1c.

Female gametes

Male gametes	AB	Ab	aB	ab
	AB	Ab	aB	ab
AB	AABB (4)	AABb (3)	AaBB (3)	AaBb (2)
Ab	AABb (3)	AAbb (2)	AaBb (2)	Aabb (1)
aB	AaBB (3)	AaBb (2)	aaBB (2)	aaBb (1)
ab	AaBb (2)	Aabb (1)	aaBb (1)	aabb (0)

Box Figure 2.1a

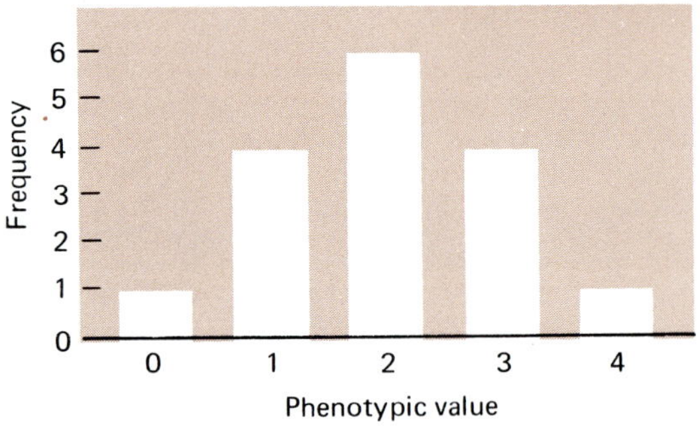

Box Figure 2.1b

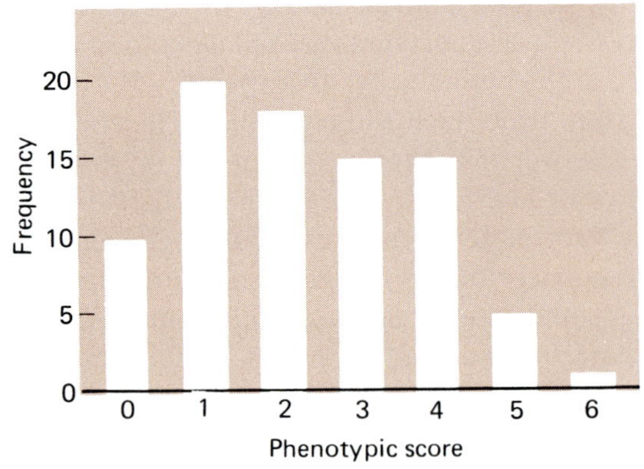

Box Figure 2.1c

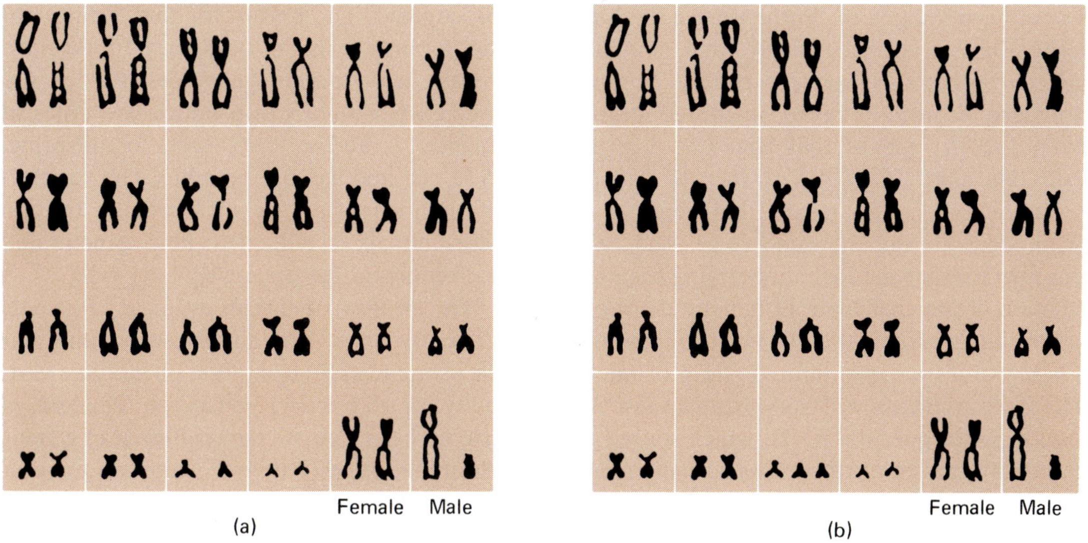

Figure 2.5 Karyotype of a normal male and female (a.) and of a male and female with Down's syndrome, mongolism (b.); note the atypical number of chromosomes number 21 in this case. (Reprinted by permission of Margery Shaw, M.D., Dept. of Biology, M.D. Anderson Hospital, Houston, TX and The Upjohn Company, Kalamazoo, MI.)

Coefficient of Genetic Determination

The *coefficient of genetic determination* is a statistical answer to the question: How much of the variability in a population, with respect to any trait, is attributable to genetic factors? Variability is defined as the dispersion of measurements around the average. (You will find it helpful at this point to turn to the Appendix, where the meaning of the term variance is discussed.) The underlying assumption is that total phenotypic variability (S_P^2) equals the variability attributable to genetic factors (S_G^2) plus the variability attributable to environmental factors (S_E^2). In this discussion, we will assume that genetic and environmental factors do not interact. Thus

$$S_P^2 = S_G^2 + S_E^2$$

The coefficient of genetic determination, or the proportion of total phenotypic variability attributable to genetic factors, can be expressed as follows:

$$S_G^2 / S_P^2 \quad \text{or}$$
$$S_G^2 / S_G^2 + S_E^2$$

Many techniques are available to determine the value of the coefficient of genetic determination. Here, we have chosen an example that involves *inbred* genetic material, not only because it is easy to present, but because inbred material is commonly used by behavioral geneticists. Inbreeding is defined as the mating of organisms that are related more closely than by chance. Many types of inbreeding are possible: brother and sister, offspring and parent, first cousins, and so forth. But regardless of which inbreeding scheme is used, the results are *isogenicity* and *homozygosity*. *Isogenicity* means that all organisms in an inbred population are genetically identical—as identical as two monozygotic (one-egg) twins.

Twenty generations of brother-sister matings results in virtual isogenicity, and animals mated brother by sister for twenty generations are technically called an inbred strain. *Homozygosity* means that genes at a given locus are alike (e.g., AA), whereas its opposite *heterozygosity* means that genes at a given locus are not the same (e.g., Aa). We can now present the logic underlying the calculation of the coefficient of genetic determination. Let's assume that we want to measure a behavioral trait in an inbred strain of mice. The measurements will vary from mouse to mouse, so the question is: To which source of variability can we attribute this variance? Because animals from an inbred strain are isogenic (i.e., they do not vary genetically), the only source to which we can attribute this variance is the environment. If we measure this same behavioral trait in another inbred strain, again the measurements will differ from mouse to mouse and, by analogous reasoning, we must attribute this variability to S^2_E.

What will happen if we mate mice of these two different inbred strains to each other? Members of the F_1 hybrid generation are now heterozygous but are still isogenic. The reason for this, considering only a single locus, is the following: Say that all mice in the first inbred strain were genetically AA at this locus, while mice in the second inbred strain were genetically aa at this locus; in other words, each group was isogenic and homozygous. All F_1 hybrids derived from this cross will be Aa, or heterozygous, *but* because the genetic material in all these animals is the same (Aa), they will be isogenic. Now let us measure the trait in the F_1 hybrid animals. The variability in these measurements must also be attributed to S^2_E. We now have three separate estimates of S^2_E and they differ. The arithmetic average of these three values is our most stable estimate of S^2_E.

If we now mate F_1 hybrid animals to each other, we will find that the F_2 generation is *not* isogenic. The reason for this, again considering only a single locus, is the following: We are now mating genotypes Aa by Aa. Since each animal can produce two types of gametes, A and a, three types of offspring, (AA, Aa, and aa) are possible. The variability obtained when we measure the trait in these animals is related to *both* genetic and environmental factors, or $S^2_G + S^2_E = S^2_P$.

We can now obtain an estimate of genetic variability, or S^2_G, by simply subtracting our best estimate of S^2_E from total phenotypic variability, or $(S^2_G + S^2_E) - (S^2_E) = S^G_2$. And, in turn, we can calculate the coefficient of genetic determination, $S^2_G/S^2_G + S^2_E$, which is the proportion of total phenotypic variability attributable to genetic factors. If we then multiply the result by 100 we obtain the percentage of variability of this trait in this population that is caused by genetic factors. Box 2.2 illustrates the way an actual coefficient of genetic determination is calculated.

Twin Research

Another technique that behavioral geneticists frequently use to study polygenetically controlled traits is the so-called twin method. There are two types of twins: identical or *monozygotic* (MZ) twins and fraternal or *dizygotic* (DZ) twins. MZ twins originate from the splitting of a single fertilized egg or ovum and are thus genetically identical. DZ twins originate from the fertilization of two different ova and are no more alike genetically than are ordinary siblings. Therefore, the variability in any given behavioral trait, averaged across pairs of MZ twins, must be attributed solely to environmental factors. But the variability in behavioral traits, averaged across pairs of DZ twins must be attributed to environmental *and* genetic factors. These variabilities from DZ and MZ twins can be used to estimate a parameter similar to the coefficient of genetic determination. Box 2.3

Box 2.2

Coefficient of Genetic Determination

1. The data used in this box to illustrate the calculation of the coefficient of genetic determination are taken from DeFries and Hegmann (1970), who measured the amount of locomotor activity in two inbred strains of mice and certain generations derived from them. In this illustration, the data have been averaged, and only the scores obtained in male animals will be considered.

2. You will recall that the coefficient of genetic determination is defined as the proportion of total phenotypic variability in a trait which is attributable to genetic factors in a given population. Here, we are interested in determining the contribution of genetic factors to locomotor activity in mice. In the data below, note that the average activity scores and the group variances are both given.

Inbred strain A	Average activity score	= 4.67
	Variance	= 6.33
Inbred strain B	Average activity score	= 15.73
	Variance	= 4.86
F_1 hybrids	Average activity score	= 14.54
	Variance	= 11.25
F_2 hybrids	Average activity score	= 11.97
	Variance	= 16.15

3. Before we consider these data, let's digress a moment by looking at the *average* locomotor activity scores. Notice, for example, that mice of inbred strain B are, on the average, three to four times more active than mice from inbred strain A. If we assume that mice from these two strains have been reared under identical or nearly identical environmental conditions, then these differences in locomotor activity must be related to genetic factors. In other words, strain differences are valid evidence that genetic factors contribute to the expression of locomotor activity in mice.

4. Now let us return to the business of calculating the coefficient of genetic determination: First, the two inbred strains and the F_1 hybrids are isogenic. Thus we can obtain an estimate of the influence of environmental factors on locomotor activity in mice by averaging the variations in locomotor activity for strain A, strain B, and the F_1 hybrid:

$$S_E^2 = \frac{(6.33 + 4.86 + 11.25)}{3} = 7.48$$

Our best estimate of total phenotypic variance, $S_G^2 + S_E^2$, is the variance in the F_2 generation:

$$S_P^2 = S_G^2 + S_E^2 = 16.15$$

By subtraction we obtain an estimate of the variance caused by genetic factors,

$$(S_G^2 + S_E^2) - (S_E^2) = S_G^2 = 16.15 - 7.48 = 8.67.$$

The coefficient of genetic determination is the proportion of total phenotypic variance related to genetic factors, or

$$\frac{S_G^2}{S_G^2 + S_E^2} = \frac{8.67}{16.15} = 0.54$$

Multiplying by 100 we obtain a value of 54 percent. Therefore, 54 percent of the variability in locomotor activity in this population is caused by genetic factors.

shows how one such parameter, Holzinger's H', can be calculated.

The twin method has been used extensively in research, particularly to estimate the contributions of genetic factors in mental illness and in the inheritance of I.Q. test scores. However, you should be aware that there are several shortcomings to this method. First, determinations about the zygosity of twins are not always accurate; this is particularly true in some of the early research in this area. Second, the twin method assumes that environmental factors are similar for DZ and MZ twin pairs, but there is some doubt about the validity of this assumption, Third, DZ and MZ twins do not have the same prenatal en-

Box 2.3

Holzinger's H'

1. H' = variance within DZ twins, (S^2_{DZ}) minus the variance within MZ twins (S^2_{MZ}) divided by the variance within DZ twins (S^2_{DZ}), or

$$H' = \frac{S^2_{DZ} - S^2_{MZ}}{S^2_{DZ}}$$

When this formula is used, the effects of heredity are *underestimated* because the average genetic correlation of DZ twins is 0.5.

2. However, the following assumptions are inherent in this method: (a) environmental and genetic factors are additive, (b) MZ and DZ twins have equivalent averages on measures of the trait, and between-pair variances are the same, and (c) environmental effects are equivalent in MZ and DZ twins.

3. The example discussed below is taken from data published by Vandenberg (1962), who estimated the heritable component of certain personality variables. To measure personality, he used the Thurstone Temperament Schedule, a pencil and paper test that is used to assess various aspects of personality. This particular example illustrates the so-called *stability* scale; if an individual scores high on the stability scale, he is probably the kind of person who remains calm in a crisis, refuses to be distracted while studying or working, and is not irritated when interrupted. The following example uses data obtained from 37 pairs of male twins: 24 MZ pairs and 13 DZ pairs. The obtained $S^2_{DZ} = 13.86$ and $S^2_{MZ} = 8.09$. Therefore, $\frac{13.86 - 8.09}{13.86} = \frac{5.77}{13.86} = 0.416$

Accordingly this would mean that approximately 41.6 percent of the variability in "stability," among the 37 pairs of twins as measured by Thurstone's test, is caused by genetic factors. But remember that Holzinger's H' underestimates the contributions of genetic factors to the total phenotypic variability.

vironments. For example, because MZ twins result from the splitting of a single egg, the amount of cytoplasmic material differs from that in other eggs. DZ twins, on the other hand, are sometimes affected by a common circulation when their placentas happen to fuse.

To control for some of these difficulties, several refinements have been made in the twin method. Two common ones are the *twins-reared-apart method* and the *co-twin control method*. In the first procedure, MZ twins reared together are compared with MZ twins reared apart. The rationale for this method is that the environments of MZ twins reared together are extremely similar, while the environments of twins raised apart are not, thus the differences between these populations can be attributed solely to environmental factors. In the co-twin control method, both twins are treated as nearly alike as possible, except on one variable. For example, one twin may receive extensive training on a motor performance skill; the other is not given such training. Later, the performance of both twins is measured, and any differences can be attributed to training because genetically the individuals are exactly alike.

Molecular Genetics

Molecular genetics and molecular biology are concerned with questions about the physical nature of genetic material, how the genetic material replicates itself, and how it codes for the production of proteins. Briefly, we will discuss what the genetic material is, as well as its role in controlling the production of proteins (enzymes) in cells.

Molecular biologists had known for years that either proteins or deoxyribonucleic acid (DNA) had to be the genetic material because chromosomes, on which the genetic material is found, consist of DNA and proteins. However, it was not until 1952 that DNA, rather than protein, was demonstrated to be the genetic material. Hershey and Chase (1952) used bacteriophages (or phages for short)—viruses that infect bacteria by attaching themselves to the bacterial cell wall. This process, termed infection, occurs and approximately twenty minutes later the bacterium bursts open, and about two hundred phages, identical to the infecting particle, emerge. Because bacteriophages are simple organisms composed of only two compounds—about fifty percent DNA and fifty percent proteins—they were ideally suited to answer the question of whether the genetic material was composed of DNA or proteins.

Although we are oversimplifying it somewhat, the classic Hershey-Chase experiment was conducted as follows: First, phages were radioactively labelled with an isotope of sulfur (S^{35}). Since proteins do contain sulfur and DNA does not, only the proteins in these phages were radioactively labelled. Another sample of phage was labelled with an isotope of phosphorus (P^{32}). Because phosphorus is a component of DNA but not of proteins, these viruses had only their DNA radioactively labelled. Next, both S^{35}- and P^{32}-labelled phages were allowed to infect a culture of bacteria. By special techniques, the infection was stopped at various intervals, and the material within the bacterium was identified. This material was P^{32}-labelled DNA; thus, only the DNA, not the protein, entered the bacterial cell. Since the DNA was the only physical link between the single infecting phage and the two hundred or so viruses that emerged, it followed that DNA was the genetic material.

The next problem facing molecular biologists was to identify the structure of DNA. This search culminated in the monumental discovery of Watson and Crick (1953), who found that DNA exists in nature as long molecules composed of two intimately associated pairs of DNA chains. Each chain is composed of four types of repeating *monomers,* or *nucleotides* composed of phosphoric acid and a form of sugar, deoxyribose. In addition, each nucleotide contains one of four bases containing nitrogen: thymidine, cytosine, adenine, and guanine. Figure 2.6a illustrates the structure of one such nucleotide with guanine as the base. A molecule of DNA is a long chain of such nucleotides attached to each other; something on the order of 200,000 nucleotides form a DNA chain. (One such linkage is illustrated in fig. 2.6b.) Finally, two such chains intertwine to form a spiral—the famous DNA double helix (see fig. 2.6c). The two chains are held together by hydrogen bonds between adjacent bases: thymidine pairing only with adenine, and cytosine only with guanine. These hydrogen bonding possibilities are illustrated in figure 2.6d.

After it was discovered that DNA contains the genetic information, the next problem was to determine the nature of the genetic code. The only difference in the DNA of a bacterium and a human being is the particular arrangement of the bases along the DNA chain. These arrangements of the bases along the DNA chain are the genetic information. The alphabet of the genetic code consists of three such bases or triplets. Thus "thymidine-thymidine-thymidine" is a code.

What does DNA do? It does two things: First, it makes or codes for a daughter DNA, a chemical process called *duplication* or *replication.* Second, it makes or codes for another large molecule, *ribonucleic acid (RNA),* which is similar in structure to DNA, except that the sugar is ribose and one of the bases is uracil rather than thymidine. RNA contains the genetic information from the DNA and controls the production of specific proteins in the cytoplasm of a cell. The process by which DNA codes for RNA is termed *transcription;*

Figure 2.6a Structure of the nucleotide.

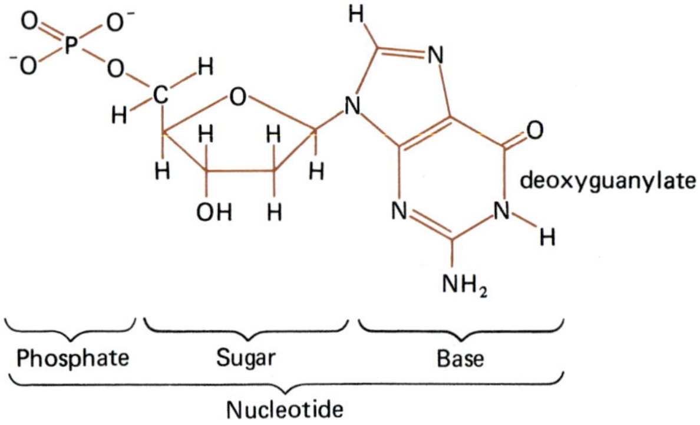

Figure 2.6b Ester linkages between nucleotides.

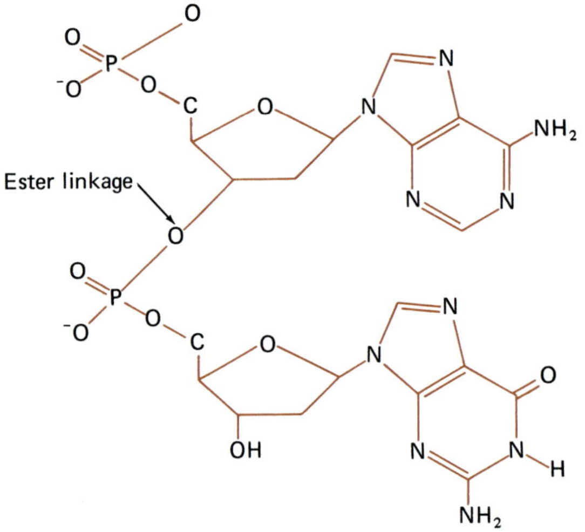

Figure 2.6c Hydrogen base pairing.

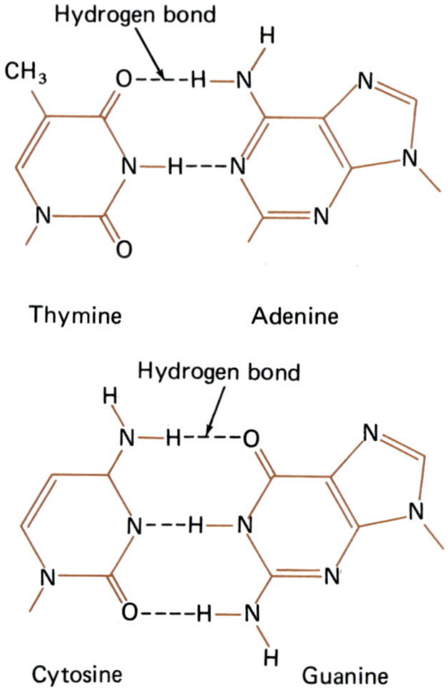

the process through which RNA controls the synthesis of proteins is termed *translation.*

$$\begin{array}{l} \text{DNA} \xrightarrow{\text{transcription}} \text{RNA} \xrightarrow{\text{translation}} \text{Proteins} \\ \downarrow \ \text{duplication (replication)} \\ \text{DNA} \end{array}$$

The control of protein synthesis is illustrated in figure 2.7. One kind of RNA that DNA produces is called messenger RNA (mRNA), which is similar to DNA. It contains the same information as does DNA because the ordering of bases in the RNA is similar to that on the DNA. This mRNA migrates to the cytoplasm, where it associates with one of the cytoplasmic particles, the *ribosomes.* Ribosomes are made of proteins and another class of RNA, *ribosomal RNA.* This unit—the mRNA associated with the ribosome—in turn forms a unit called a polyribosome, which is the cell's protein-synthesizing unit.

Also present in the cytoplasm of the cell is a third class of RNA, *amino*-acid-transfer RNA (tRNA). Compounds such as phenylalanine, tyrosine, leucine, and valine are among the twenty-odd amino acids found in cells. Through another chemical reaction, the

Figure 2.6d DNA helix.

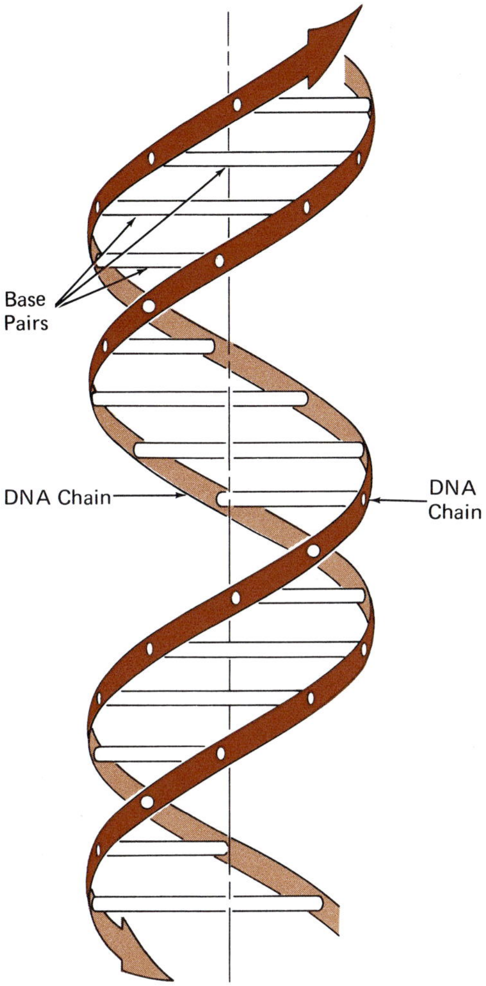

tRNAs attach to amino acids, and these units are brought to the polyribosome. Because of the code, however, only specific tRNA-amino-acid units can attach to the polyribosome at specific places.

Next, the amino acids attach to each other to form long chains called *polypeptides* which in turn combine with each other to form *proteins.* It is important to understand that what makes one protein different from another is the particular ordering of amino acids in a protein. This ordering is determined by the sequence of the bases on the mRNA, which in turn, depends on the sequence of the bases on the DNA. Thus the specificity of proteins resides in DNA; that is, it depends on the ordering of bases on the DNA molecule.

One important kind of protein produced by cells are *enzymes.* Enzymes are organic catalysts that make certain chemical reactions possible. Cells do not continuously produce all the enzymes that are coded in their DNA. Nor do all cells within a particular organism make the same proteins, although the genetic material is the same in all cells. (Even the most complex organism starts life as a single cell.) How is this possible? This is possible because certain portions of the DNA within a cell are inactive at certain times. For example, some enzymes are made only in the presence of the molecules they attack. These enzyme systems are called *inducible* enzymes. Certain parts of the DNA are inactive or *repressed,* and the process by which they become active is called *derepression.* Enzyme induction, repression, and derepression have been studied intensively in lower organisms, and much is known about these processes in bacteria. However, the mechanisms by which these processes work in the cells of higher animals are not fully understood, except that *hormones* (see Chapter 10) appear to be involved in the regulation of enzyme synthesis in higher forms.

In the next section, the basic information about genetics we have just described will be related to our main interest—how psychologists use genetics in the study of behavior.

Behavioral Genetics

This section is divided into two parts. The first part describes experiments in behavioral genetics within the classical, single-gene, Mendelian framework; the second part deals with experiments in behavioral genetics within the quantitative, polygenic framework.

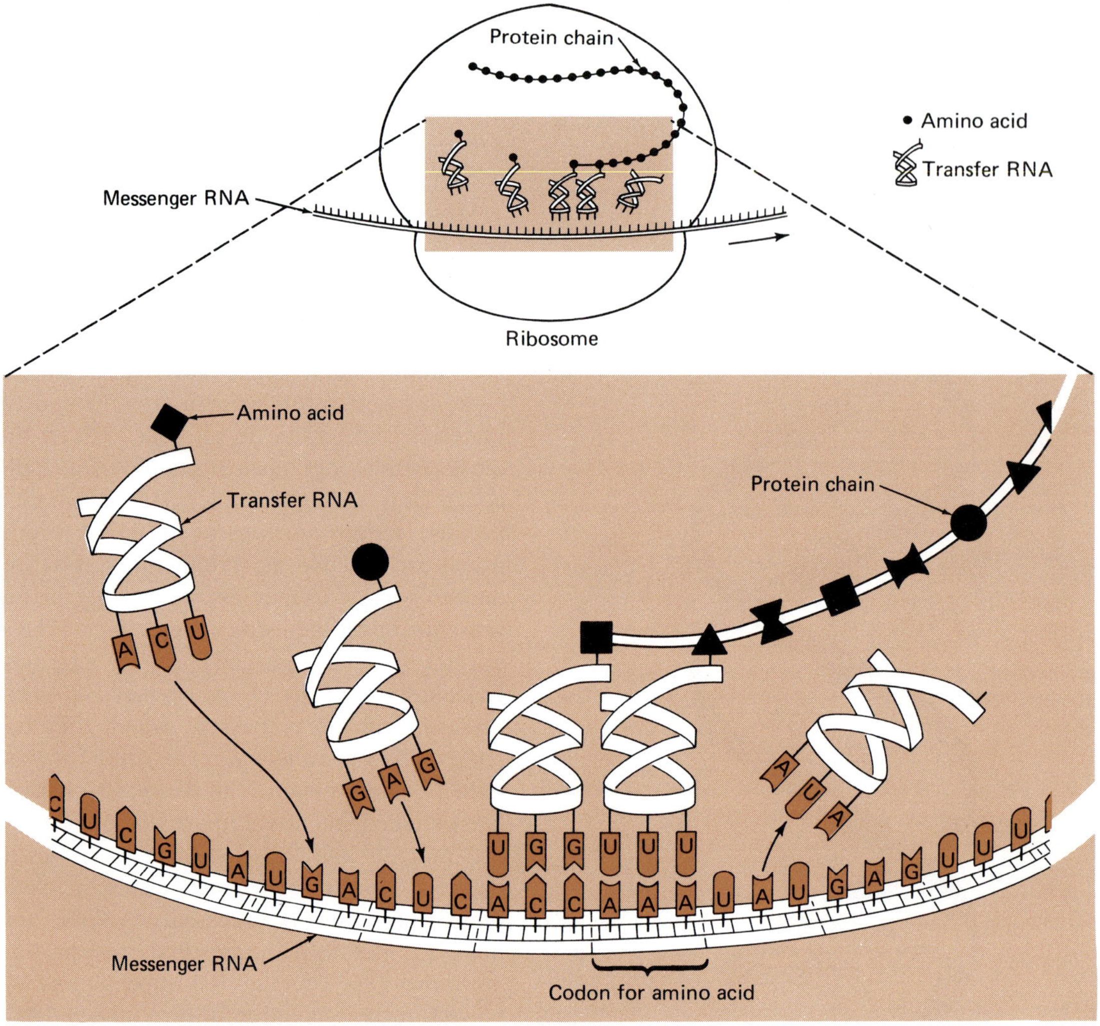

Figure 2.7 The polypeptide chain is synthesized as the ribosome moves along messenger RNA (mRNA). Amino acids are brought into proper position by specific transfer RNA's that couple briefly with complementary triplets on mRNA. This figure illustrates the model for control of protein synthesis by the genes. Messenger RNA is synthesized on the DNA of the gene. This mRNA then goes into the cytoplasm and becomes associated with ribosomes. The various types of transfer RNA (tRNA) in the cytoplasm pick up the amino acids they are coded for and bring them to the ribosomes as it moves along the mRNA. Each tRNA bonds to the mRNA at a point where a triplet of bases is complementary to an exposed triplet on the tRNA. This ordering of the tRNA molecules automatically orders the amino acids, which are then linked by peptide bonds. Synthesis of the polypeptide chain thus proceeds, one amino acid at a time, in an orderly sequence as the ribosomes move along the mRNA. As each tRNA donates its amino acid to the growing polypeptide chain, it uncouples from the mRNA and moves away into the cytoplasm, where it can be used again. (From E. Peter Volpe, *Man, Nature, and Society.* Copyright 1975 by Wm. C. Brown Company Publishers. All rights reserved.)

Single Genes and Behavior

One frequently studied type of mental retardation is called phenylketonuria (PKU). Although individuals suffering from PKU show a variety of symptoms, the most serious is mental retardation. The I.Q. test scores of untreated PKU individuals are very low; according to some estimates, fifty percent of the untreated cases have I.Q. test scores of less than twenty. Although these data must be accepted with caution because they were obtained from institutionalized cases, it is fair to say that PKU individuals usually suffer from severe mental retardation. Other symptoms commonly associated with PKU are accentuated superficial and deep reflexes and a high incidence of epileptic seizures.

PKU is transmitted by a single autosomal recessive gene. When two unaffected heterozygous carriers of the disease have progeny, their chances of having a PKU offspring are one in four, and, on the average, two of their three normal offspring will carry the trait. The disease does not afflict one sex more than the other, and occurs in six out of every 100,000 in the general population. An example of the inheritance of PKU in a family is shown in figure 2.8.

The cause of PKU is well understood: It is the result of an inborn error of metabolism. PKU individuals lack the genes that code for a particular enzyme found only in the liver; the enzyme's function is to convert the amino acid phenylalanine to another amino acid—tyrosine. Because PKU individuals lack this enzyme, an important metabolic step is blocked. In affected individuals, phenylalanine is converted through abnormal metabolic pathways into compounds such as phenylpyruvic acid, and the disease can be considered a liver pathology. However, many symptoms of PKU occur in the central nervous system. Precisely how this liver pathology results in abnormalities of the central nervous system remains unknown, but there are several pos-

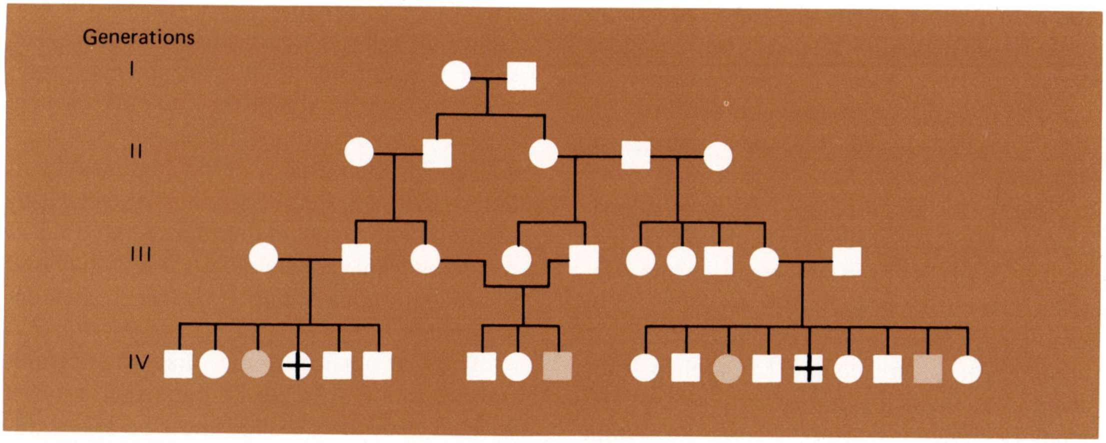

Figure 2.8 A pedigree collected over four generations of a family in which phenylketonuria, which results in mental retardation, was detected. In such a pedigree, females are represented by a circle, males by a square. Affected individuals are represented by filled in circles and squares. Individuals marked with a cross were probably affected with the disease, and all died before reaching maturity. (After Folling, A., Mohr, O. L., and Ruud, L., "Oligophrenia phenlprouvica, a recessive syndrome in man," *Norske Videnskaps/ Akademi I Oslo, Matematisk-Naturvidenskapelig Klasse,* 1945.)

sible explanations: For example, abnormally high levels of phenylalanine may be toxic to nerve cells. It is also possible that one or more of the abnormal phenylalanine metabolites that the PKU individuals produce are toxic to the nervous system.

It is possible to treat PKU individuals. Tests for PKU are now routinely performed in newborn infants, and if PKU is detected, the infant is placed on a dietary regimen low in phenylalanine. If started early enough, dietary management seems to alleviate many symptoms of the disease. This suggests that the brain is most vulnerable to damage during infancy, that is, during the period of most rapid differentiation and development.

Unaffected heterozygous carriers of the disease can also be detected. The carrier metabolizes normal dietary quantities of phenylalanine at approximately the same rate as do normal individuals, and excess amounts of this amino acid are not found in carriers. However, when carriers are given excess amounts of phenylalanine, they metabolize the excess more slowly than do normal individuals. The ability to detect heterozygous carriers of PKU makes it possible to use genetic counseling to great advantage. Two carriers can be advised that their chances of having a PKU child are one in four.

Finally, the production of PKU in experimental animals by dietary and pharmacological means has been an interesting and relatively recent research development. For example, if animals are injected with excess amounts of phenylalanine from birth, they show some deficits in learning ability and memory functions. But, several important questions about experimentally induced PKU remain unanswered: (1) Does the learning deficit outlast the treatment? (2) How early during development must the treatment be started to produce the maximal effects? (3) Are learning and memory deficits exhibited in all or only some learning situations?

Multiple Genes and Behavior

Because most behaviors are determined by many genes rather than by single genes, we will now turn our attention to behaviors that are polygenically determined. In this section we will consider the inheritance of intelligence and the use of selective breeding techniques in behavioral genetic research.

The Inheritance of I.Q. Scores

Psychologists have debated for years about the degree to which behavior is determined by genetic and environmental factors. But today the controversy about the question of *nature* versus *nurture* has intensified, especially with respect to the question of race and intelligence. One reason for the controversy is that the issues underlying the problem are improperly stated and poorly understood, especially by that mythical creature, "the intelligent layman." Phrasing the question in terms of heredity versus environment gives rise to a pseudo-issue because there is no answer. Genes do not act in a vacuum but always in some environment, and environments always affect biological organisms. In other words, heredity and environment continuously interact, and to state that a particular behavior is determined solely by heredity or solely by environment is patently nonsense. All traits—morphological, physiological, *and* behavioral—are determined jointly by genes and environment.

This is not to imply that the nature-nurture question is not an important issue; it is. However, the question must be asked differently. On the basis of previous sections in this chapter, you probably realize how it should be asked: *How much* of the variability associated with the measurement of a specific behavioral phenotype can be attributed to genetic factors and how much can be attributed to environmental factors. Remember that this question must be asked about populations, not individuals.

Before we begin our discussion of intelligence, a few preliminary remarks are necessary. One absolute requirement must be met before a behavioral genetic analysis of a trait is possible, and that is: Can the trait be measured reliably? (At this point, you will find it useful to review the section on reliability and validity in the Appendix.) The test-retest reliability of I.Q. test scores obtained by using the Wechsler Intelligence Test with adults is approximately 0.85, which makes the test a highly reliable measuring instrument. Whether the test is valid—that is, whether it measures anyone's preconceptions of what intelligence is—is unimportant in this context. It also does not matter whether I.Q. tests predict how well someone will do in school, for example. In other contexts, a test's validity is crucially important, but it is not an issue in the genetic analysis of a trait. (Intelligence tests are discussed in Chapter 13.)

Faced with analyzing a trait such as I.Q. scores, how does a behavioral geneticist proceed? The question can be broken into three parts. First, are there single genes that affect I.Q. scores, and do these genes express themselves as dominant or recessive? Second, are there any chromosomal abnormalities associated with the autosomes or sex chromosomes that affect I.Q. scores? And, third, are I.Q. scores that fall within the "normal" range determined in part by polygenic systems, and how much of the variability in intelligence test scores can be attributed to genetic factors?

Single Dominant Genes

There are a few single dominant genes that affect I.Q. test scores. The best-known example of this phenomenon is *Huntington's Chorea,* one of a class of defects that causes progressive degeneration of the central nervous system. Although we know that the basal ganglia (see Chapter 3) degenerate, we do not understand the genetic defect that causes this degeneration. The clinical symptoms associated with the disease are involuntary jerking of the body and limbs. As the disease progresses, intellectual functions also degenerate and ultimately the patient dies.

Huntington's Chorea is transmitted as a single, dominant autosomal gene that is usually transmitted by an affected carrier to half his children. The overt clinical symptoms generally appear at age forty. Because the carrier cannot be detected prior to the development of clinical symptoms and because his symptoms usually appear when he is past his reproductive prime, genetic counseling has, so far at least, not been especially useful.

Single Recessive Genes

There are many single recessive genes that affect measures of intelligence. PKU is only one of a large class of genetically caused diseases that affect amino acid metabolism.

Abnormalities Associated with Autosomes

In the late 1950s, Lejeune, Grautier, and Turpin (1959) studied the karyotypes of a number of patients with Down's syndrome (mongolism) and found an abnormal number of chromosomes in the nuclei of cells of these individuals. Patients with mongolism have forty-seven chromosomes instead of the normal forty-six; one of the smaller chromosomes (number 21) is present in triplicate. Thus Lejeune and his colleagues concluded that the underlying genetic defect in Down's syndrome resulted from the fusion of a normal haploid gamete with an abnormal gamete, which was haploid for all chromosomes except chromosome 21.

The clinical symptoms associated with trisomy 21 are quite varied: for example, fissuring of the tongue; flattening of the nasal bridge; short stature; short, broad neck; and mental retardation. Intelligence test scores indicate that the degree of mental retardation among victims of Down's syndrome varies from severe (scores of less than 20) to relatively mild (scores as high as 65). Although the early literature suggested that patients with trisomy 21 have low linguistic ability, recent work indicates that, generally speaking, the linguistic ability of these patients compares favorably with other mental retardates.

An important feature of trisomy 21 is the relationship between the mother's age and the frequency of the disease. Forty percent of all cases of Down's Syndrome are born to mothers who are forty years of age or older. Because older women have older husbands, it was thought that the father's age might be a factor. However, statistical analyses have proven this is not the case in most instances. The majority of cases are the result of a defect in the maternal gamete, which occurs during meiosis.

Abnormalities Associated with Sex Chromosomes

Many different aberrations of the sex chromosomes affect intelligence test scores. A few of these abnormalities are illustrated in figure 2.9. The intelligence test scores associated with them indicate that the lower the I.Q. score, the greater the amount of excess chromosomal material.

One of the more interesting diseases associated with abnormal sex chromosomes is called *Turner's syndrome*. Here, the basic genetic defect involves the absence or partial absence of the second X chromosome; the karyotype of Turner's syndrome shows twenty-two autosomes but only one X chromosome. Turner's syndrome has been estimated to occur in one out of every three thousand female births.

The degree of retardation associated with the disease is quite small; in fact, these patients may not be retarded at all. Interestingly, the disease appears to be characterized by a specific cognitive defect in the nonverbal area of behavior. Most standard intelligence tests can be divided into *verbal* and *nonverbal* items. Patients with Turner's syndrome have low scores on some of the nonverbal subtests, especially in relation to the scores they obtain on the verbal parts of the test. These patients suffer from a condition called space form blindness; for example, they perform poorly on right-left directional discrimination tests.

Polygenic Systems

As you have just seen, genetic factors can affect intelligence scores. However, you may wonder whether I.Q. scores that fall within the "normal" range are influenced by heredity. The answer to this question is yes, and, in the main, the evidence for this conclusion comes from three sources: twin comparison studies, family correlation studies, and studies of adopted children.

One of the early *twin comparison studies* in which the intelligence test scores of DZ and MZ twins were compared was done by Newman, Freeman, and Holzinger (1937). These investigators tested fifty identical twins and

Number of X chromosomes	Number of Y chromosomes: 0	Y	YY	YYY
0				
X	100 (60)	100	76 (6)	80 (1)
XX	100	84 (43)	58 (19)	n.r.[a]
XXX	51 (28)	52 (12)	48 (1)	n.r.
XXXX	40 (3)	35 (22)	n.r.[a]	n.r.
XXXXX	very low (2)	n.r.[a]	n.r.	n.r.

Source: Moor, 1967
[a]n.r. = not reported

Figure 2.9 Mean I.Q. test scores of individuals with abnormal numbers of sex chromosomes. Numbers in parentheses represent number of cases tested. (From "What do we know today about the inheritance of intelligence and how do we know it." In *Intelligence: Genetic and Environmental Influences.* Robert Cancro (ed.). Baltimore: Grune and Stratton, 1971. Reprinted by permission of Steven G. Vandenberg.)

fifty like-sexed fraternal twins, using the Stanford-Binet Intelligence Test. The correlation of the scores between DZ twin pairs was 0.62 and between MZ twin pairs was 0.90. (Recall that a correlation may range from −1.0 to +1.0. A correlation of 0 means that the two variables are unrelated while a correlation of +1.0 means that the variables are perfectly correlated.) Newman and his colleagues also tested seventeen DZ and MZ twin pairs who had been reared apart and found that the correlation in I.Q. test scores of these twins did not differ significantly from those obtained for twins reared together. More recently, Shields (1962) reported correlations of 0.77 in intelligence test scores of MZ twins reared apart and 0.76 in MZ twins reared together.

It is also possible to obtain correlations among DZ and MZ twins on subtests of standard I.Q. tests and to estimate the heritable components of these scores. Vandenberg (1968), for example, found that the following abilities, often measured on intelligence tests, have a genetic component: spatial visualization, word fluency, number ability, certain types of reasoning, and perceptual and clerical speed.

Because one can argue that the environment of identical twins is more alike than the environment of fraternal twins, the greater similarity in I.Q. test scores among MZ twins can be attributed to environmental factors. However, it is much more difficult to attribute the *similarities* in the correlations in intelligence test scores between MZ twins raised together and apart to environment. One argument which can be used to support the environmental viewpoint is that MZ twins reared apart do share a common environment at a crucial stage of development (early infancy), because they are seldom separated immediately after birth. Vandenberg and Johnson (1968) compared the correlations on I.Q. tests of MZ twins separated before nine months of age with those of twins separated after one or more years and found no significant differences in these correlations. Therefore, it is difficult to argue that the similarities in I.Q. test scores between twins raised apart and together are not related in part to genetic factors.

Erlenmeyer-Kimling and Jarvik (1963) reviewed the findings obtained in ninety-nine separate studies involving *family correlations:* that is, studies in which the I.Q. test scores of individuals of varying degrees of biological relationship were compared. These data are summarized in figure 2.10. Each point in the figure represents the results of one experiment, and the vertical bars represent the median correlation coefficients for all experiments on relatives of a particular degree of genetic relationship. In studying this figure, keep in mind that the expected correlation, based on a genetic model, would be 1.00 between MZ twins, 0.5 between DZ twins, 0.5 between siblings, and 0.0 between unrelated persons, regardless of whether they are raised together or apart. Notice that in many instances, the observed median correlations come close to those expected on theoretical grounds. However, because the correlation among MZ twins is not 1.0 but approximately 0.80, and because the correlation among unrelated persons reared together is not 0.0 but approximately 0.23, environmental factors must also be important in determining intelligence test scores. Erlenmeyer-Kimling's and Jarvik's summary is generally regarded as strong evidence that genetic factors are important determinants of I.Q. test scores because they reviewed almost one hundred separate experiments which spanned approximately fifty years, were performed in many different countries, and used many different kinds of intelligence tests.

In *studies of adopted children,* the intelligence test scores of adopted children are compared with those of both their biological and adoptive parents. The results of one experi-

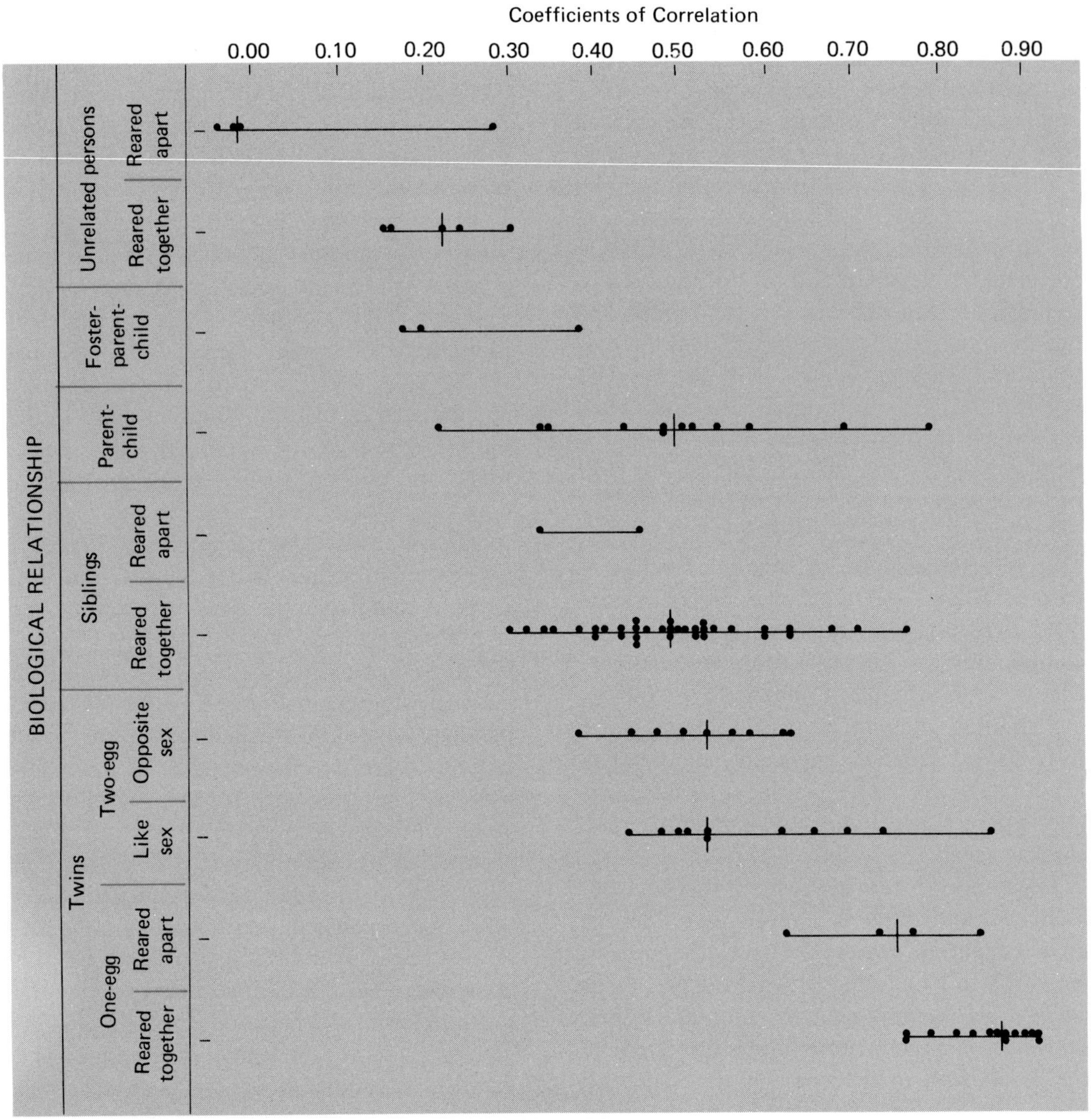

Figure 2.10 Correlations in I.Q. test scores in relatives of varying degrees of genetic resemblance. Each point represents an average correlation coefficient; there are data for 99 different studies, the vertical bars are the median correlation for each degree of biological relationship. (From Erlenmeyer-Kimling, L. and Jarvik, L. F., "Genetics and intelligence: A review," *Science,* Vol. 142, pp. 1477–1479, 13 December 1963. Copyright 1963 by the American Association for the Advancement of Science.)

ment of this type are summarized in figure 2.11.

Note that there is almost no correlation between the I.Q. test scores of the children of all ages and the educational level of their adoptive parents, while the correlation between the children six years or older and their biological parents is approximately 0.35.

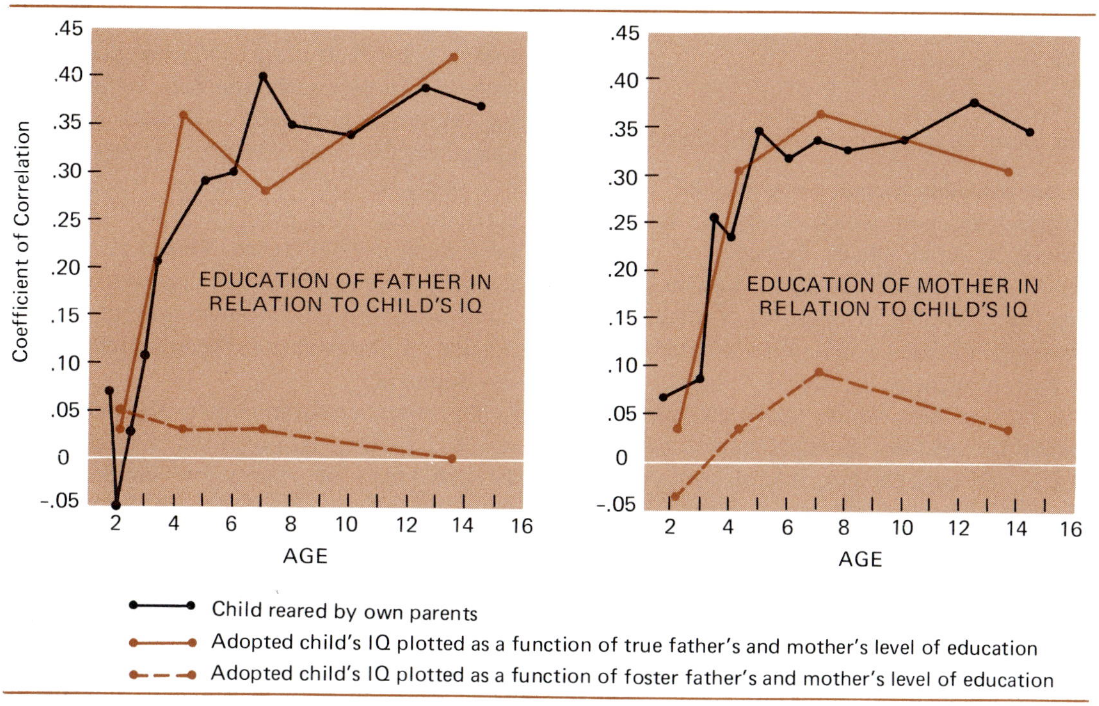

Figure 2.11 Resemblance of I.Q.'s between adopted children and foster and biological parents as a function of age. (After Marjorie Honzik, "Developmental studies of parent-child resemblance in intelligence." *Child Development* 28, 1957, pp. 215, 228. Reprinted by permission of Marjorie Honzik and the Society for Research in Child Development, Inc.)

Since it is difficult to explain the lack of a correlation between adoptive parents and adopted children on environmental grounds, these data are evidence for a genetic component in I.Q. scores. Notice, however, that the parents' educational level, not their I.Q. test scores, was used to obtain these correlations. However, because educational achievement is correlated with I.Q. test scores, the difference in variables does not invalidate the conclusion that heredity, in part, determines I.Q. scores.

All the studies described in this section on the inheritance of I.Q. scores suggest that intelligence, within the normal range, as measured by standardized intelligence tests, has a genetic component. Although each study presents certain difficulties, especially in terms of interpretation, together the experiments present an impressive body of evidence for several reasons: First, the same correlations between degree of genetic resemblance and I.Q. test scores have been obtained with a variety of methods and tests, such as the twin studies, family correlation studies, and studies of adopted children discussed here. Other research using other methods could have been cited; but the results and conclusions would have been the same. Second, the data have withstood the test of time: in this review, studies made fifty years apart have been considered and the results have always been the same. Third, the data have been collected in many countries on several continents and, again, the results have always been the same.

There can be little argument that I.Q. test scores have a genetic component. What is most impressive about these data is how large the contribution of heredity is in determining I.Q. test scores.

Environmental Determinants of Intelligence

In the previous section we presented experimental evidence which showed that the genetic material affects measures of intelligence. More specifically, the data indicated that the variability in measures of intelligence obtained in human populations is determined, in part, by genetic factors. In this section we will present data which show that environmental factors also affect measures of intelligence. Although the information contained in these two sections may seem contradictory, remember that all behaviors—including intelligence—are determined jointly by environmental and hereditary factors.

One environmental variable that affects measures of intelligence is *nutrition.* In this context it is important to distinguish between the diet eaten by the pregnant mother and the diet of her child after birth. There is fairly compelling evidence that the mother's diet influences the intelligence of her offspring; that is, if maternal nutrition is inadequate, the child's intelligence is affected. With respect to postnatal nutrition, we have only realized fairly recently that severe starvation can have devastating developmental effects on children. For example, severe protein starvation makes children listless, indifferent, and sluggish, and lowers their intelligence. Cabak and Najdanovic (1965) reported that children who were hospitalized for malnutrition before the age of two had lower I.Q. test scores than control subjects, and none of them had an I.Q. test score of more than 110. These studies strongly suggest that an adequate diet, particularly adequate in proteins, is necessary for normal brain development and that in the absence of an adequate diet, measures of intelligence are adversely affected. Adequate dietary management can also be shown to improve children's performance on intelligence tests. In one study, phenylketonuric children placed on diets low in phenylalanine before the age of six months, improved, whereas children placed on the same diet after six months did not improve. Of the children treated very early, seventy-four percent showed some improvement in intelligence. This study, as well as many others, points out that proper nutrition during early development is extremely important with respect to subsequent intellectual development.

The social environment, or the *conditions of child rearing,* can also affect intelligence. In one study of twenty-five children who were placed in an orphanage where they received little social stimulation, the average I.Q. score obtained in the sample was sixty-five. Thirteen of the children were transferred to an institution for the mentally retarded, and each child was assigned to a mentally retarded woman who acted as a "foster" mother. All these women lavished considerable attention on the children. On the average the I.Q. test scores of the children increased by twenty-eight points. The I.Q. scores of the twelve children who remained in the orphanage decreased over time.

Many other instances of the effects of manipulating social and sensory stimulation on the development of intellectual functioning have been reported. For example, Kagan (1972) found that certain cultural practices in Guatemala deprive children of these types of stimulation. When the methods of child rearing were modified, the children's intellectual development improved. Other studies in England and the United States indicate that cultural and economic deprivation can adversely affect intellectual development. For instance, the I.Q. scores of children reared on canal boats in England and in remote areas of Appalachia decrease as a function of time.

These studies of environment raise several important questions. First, is the lack of sensory stimulation or inadequate maternal care responsible for the results? Although no definitive answer to this question is available at the present time, it is likely that the lack of sensory stimulation and inadequate mothering has severe negative effects on children's intellectual development. Second, are the effects of early deprivation reversible? In the United States, the Head Start program was a large-scale attempt to overcome the effects of early deprivation by providing deprived children with medical, nutritional, and educational opportunities. Medical attention included the correction of sensory disabilities such as hearing loss, and provided warm, nutritious meals. Furthermore, since relatively few children were assigned to each teacher, they received large amounts of individual attention. Finally, parents were involved in the program on a volunteer basis. A program such as Head Start can be evaluated in a number of ways. For example, eighty percent of the parents felt that their children had improved. On the other hand, no long-term gains in I.Q. scores could be measured as a result of participation in Head Start. Therefore, the program has been called a failure. This may be the case, but children spent little time in the program, and perhaps it was overly optimistic to expect marked intellectual improvement in such a short period of time. In another study, called the Milwaukee Project (Strickland, 1971), different results were reported. In this program, children of mothers with I.Q.'s of less than seventy were given long-term, intensive compensatory training in the areas of education and social and sensory stimulation. And in this sample, long-term gains in intelligence test scores were observed.

Personality traits have also been shown to affect measures of intelligence. Individuals whose I.Q. scores improve with time are found to be aggressive, self-assertive, and self-initiating, while individuals whose I.Q. scores decrease over time apparently lack these personality traits. On the basis of the studies discussed here and in the previous section, what can we conclude about the relative influence of genetic and environmental factors on intelligence test scores? Jenck (1972) concluded that the variability in I.Q. test scores was related to the two factors in the following proportions: forty-five percent to heredity and thirty-five percent to environment. The remaining twenty percent was related to the interaction of genetic and environmental factors. Although we may disagree with Jenck's percentages, he has provided us with a starting point for future research on the relative contributions of genetic and environmental influences on intelligence as well as other types of behavior.

Genetic Determinants of Schizophrenia

The contribution of genetic factors to the expression of human behaviors other than intelligence has also been studied extensively. In the main, this research has used data obtained from twin studies and family correlation studies to demonstrate that genetic factors contribute significantly to important aspects of human behavior.

One behavioral trait that has frequently been examined from the genetic point of view is schizophrenia, a mental disorder that will be discussed at some length in Chapter 18. Much of the data have been reviewed critically by Shields, Gottesman, and Slater (1967). Despite the fact that this evidence is fairly convincing that schizophrenia depends in part on heritable factors, it has been plagued by one methodological difficulty that affects nearly all work in human behavioral genetics: it is extremely difficult to separate genetic and environmental contributions to the expression of the behavior in an unambiguous way.

In 1970 Heston published a paper that makes a most convincing case for the importance of genetic factors in schizophrenia. He used the adopted child method, and the details of the experiment were as follows: First, he selected forty-seven subjects who had been given up for adoption before the age of one month. These subjects were born to schizophrenic mothers, but were raised in foster or adoptive homes. The control group consisted of fifty individuals who had also been given up for adoption during the first month of life and had been raised in foster homes, but did not have biological mothers who were schizophrenic. Both groups were then evaluated on the basis of psychiatric interviews as well as school, police, medical, and Veterans Administration records. The results were evaluated by teams of clinicians who had no knowledge of the biological mothers' psychiatric status. Some of the results of this study are shown in table 2.1, and they provide convincing evidence that schizophrenia does indeed have a heritable component.

Selective Breeding

Selective breeding—a procedure used to produce animals and plants with desirable traits—dates back to the beginnings of civilization. Today, it is fair to say that selective breeding and inbred-strain comparison studies (which we discussed earlier) are the two most frequently used techniques in behavioral genetic experiments on animals. Basically, selective breeding involves the mating together of individuals with similar traits; after several generations, one obtains a population of organisms that differ, on the average, from the base population. For example, if we select from a herd of cows the animals that give the most milk and allow only these animals to reproduce, after many generations we would obtain a herd of dairy cows that in general, gives more milk than did the original herd. The numerous breeds of dogs that exist today were produced in this way.

Selective breeding for behavioral traits is no different from selective breeding for morphological or physiological traits, except that the traits selected for are behavioral. For example, breeds of dogs that are adept at herding sheep were originally selected and bred for this behavior. Similar processes that occur in nature, called *natural selection,* underlie Charles Darwin's theory of evolution.

To understand selective breeding, you need to appreciate two related facts. First, animals are chosen for selective breeding on the basis of some *phenotype* they manifest, not because they possess certain genes. If the phenotypic differences (the basis on which the animals are chosen) are determined, at least in part, by hereditary mechanisms, then selective breeding will be successful. To put it another way: a successful selective breeding experiment is *prima facie* evidence that the trait in question is determined, in part, by genetic factors. Second, genetic variability (S_G^2) with respect to the trait selected for must exist in the population from which the animals are selected if selective breeding is to be successful. In other words, selective breeding procedures will fail if the population from which we select happens to be an inbred strain. Remember that inbreeding exhausts genetic variability, and genetic variability is precisely what is needed in selective breeding. One way to test for isogenicity is to attempt selective breeding. If it fails, we know we are dealing with an isogenic line—at least with respect to the genes that underlie the trait in question.

Tryon Experiments

One classic selective breeding experiment for a behavioral trait was begun during the 1920s by R. C. Tryon, who selected rats on the basis of how they performed in a maze. Tolman, Tryon, and Jeffress (1929) constructed an automatic, self-recording, complex T-maze, which when tested proved to be a very reliable measuring instrument. Using this maze, a large-scale selective breeding program was begun. Tryon (1940) selectively bred for

Table 2.1 Foster-Rearing Studies of Schizophrenia

A comparison of individuals born to schizophrenic mothers and raised in a foster home and a control group born to normal parents and also raised in a foster home with regard to exhibiting the following types of behavior (Traits Exhibited). Note that individuals born to schizophrenic mothers are more likely to exhibit psychiatric symptoms than are control subjects.

Traits Exhibited	Number of Experimental Subjects (Number = 47)	Number of Control Subjects (Number = 50)
Schizophrenic symptoms	5	0
Mental deficiency	4	0
Antisocial personalities	9	2
Neurotic personality disorders	13	7
More than one year in penal or psychiatric institution	11	2
Discharged from armed forces for psychiatric or behavioral reasons	8	1

Source: "The Genetics of Schizophrenic and Schizoid Disease," Heston, L.L., *Science*, Vol. 167, pp. 249–256, 16 January 1970. Copyright 1970 by the American Association for the Advancement of Science.

what he called maze "bright" and maze "dull" rats. The original population of rats was relatively heterogeneous. In other words, some of the rats learned the maze quickly and made few errors while others learned the maze slowly and made many errors. The brightest female rats were then mated with the brightest male rats; the dullest female rats were mated with the dullest male rats. The two lines established with this procedure were then bred for twenty-one generations. The results of this experiment are illustrated in figure 2.12. Notice that the selective breeding was successful. After just seven generations of selective breeding, the two lines of rats differed so greatly that the distributions of their error scores no longer overlapped; that is, the brightest animal in the dull line was duller than the dullest animal in the bright line.

Why was this experiment so important? First, it demonstrated that the ability of rats to learn a maze has a genetic component. Today this news is not startling. At the time, however, most psychologists had an environmental bias, and this discovery was quite important. Second, lines of animals that differ

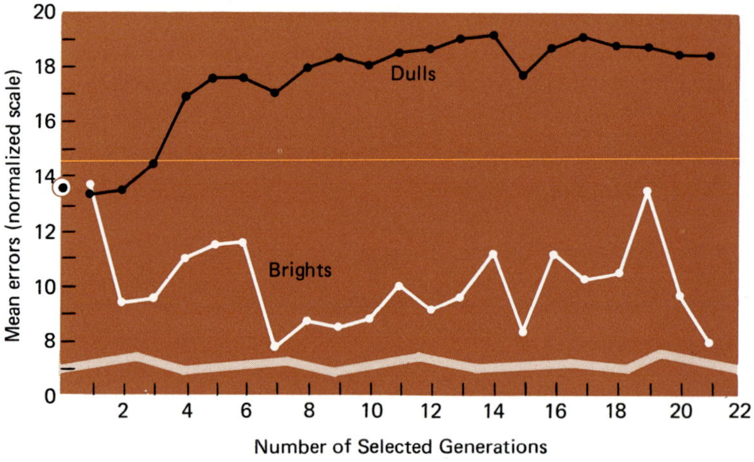

Figure 2.12 The results of Tryon's selective breeding in rats for maze brightness and maze dullness. (From McClearn, G. E., "The inheritance of behavior." In *Psychology in the Making*, L. J. Postman (ed.). New York: Alfred A. Knopf, Inc., 1963. Reprinted by permission.)

from one another in terms of a specific behavioral dimension are now available for other types of research concerning the genetic basis of behavioral variation.

This experiment was in fact performed. Maze-dull and maze-bright rats were placed into such a maze to determine whether they used visual or spatial cues to solve the maze. Remember that neither strategy works better than the other; whichever is adopted results in fifty percent errors. Maze-bright rats attended to spatial cues, which is not surprising because they were selectively bred on this basis. Maze-dull rats, on the other hand, attended to the visual cues. Further research, using a variety of other learning tasks, proved that only in learning situations in which food reinforcement was used and/or in which spatial cues led to success were the maze-bright animals significantly brighter than the maze-dull animals. Thus the rats had been bred for a specific ability, not for their general intelligence.

Consider carefully the conditions under which the animals in the Tryon experiment were selected. They were selected for performance in a complex T-maze, each unit of which was identical. To learn the maze, the rats had to depend on *spatial cues* (they had to "remember" from trial to trial to turn right, then left, left again, now right, and so on). The animals were also hungry when put into the maze and were rewarded with food after they had successfully run the maze. Thus they were selected on the basis of their ability to learn spatial cues under conditions of hunger motivation with food reinforcement.

At this point, we may ask: Were the maze-bright rats bright under all conditions, or did they perform efficiently only when hungry and when forced to use spatial cues? One way of answering this question is as follows: Suppose maze-bright and maze-dull rats are tested in a maze in which one arm is painted black, the other white (of course, one arm is still on the right side and the other on the left side). Suppose also, that the maze is made unsolvable by changing the contingencies randomly from trial to trial (now right-black is correct, next right-white is correct, next white-left is correct, and so forth).

Another question that Tryon asked was whether the bright rats learned more efficiently because they were brighter or because they were hungrier—more motivated. To obtain an answer, four groups of rats were tested under the following motivational conditions: (1) maze-bright animals, standard degree of hunger, (2) maze-bright animals, less than standard degree of hunger, (3) maze-dull animals, standard degree of hunger, and, (4) maze-dull animals, more than standard degree of hunger. If differences in performance between bright and dull rats were related to differences in motivation, then the experimental results should have revealed this fact. The actual results of this experiment were as follows: (1) the degree of hunger did not significantly affect the number of errors made by either bright or dull rats in learning the maze, (2) the time it took the animals to run the maze varied as a function of how hungry they were (i.e., the more motivated animals took less time to run the maze), (3) the more motivated maze-bright rats made fewer errors than the less hungry maze-bright rats; however, both groups made fewer errors than the two maze-dull groups, and (4) there were no significant differences in terms of errors in the two maze-dull groups, although these animals differed considerably in terms of motivation. Thus the differences in performance between maze-dull and maze-bright rats could not be attributed to differences in hunger.

Tryon's experiment is not the only example of selective breeding for differential learning ability. Animals have also been selectively bred on the basis of other learning tasks as well as other behavioral phenotypes. For instance, animals have been selectively bred for their degree of "emotionality," locomotor activity, susceptibility to experimentally induced seizures, preference for alcohol, and responsiveness to gravity and light. Every case in which selective breeding for behavioral traits has been attempted has been successful. Therefore, psychologists are no longer surprised when another success is reported. Again, there are two important points to keep in mind about selective breeding. First, the ability to select is proof that the trait selected for is determined, partially at least, by genetic factors. Second, the animals obtained through selected breeding for a particular behavioral trait are tremendously useful for subsequent research designed to answer questions about the genetic causes underlying the behavior.

Summary

In this chapter we have tried to provide you with an introductory overview of behavioral genetics. The most important point to learn is that behavioral traits are in part determined by genetic factors and that the evidence which corroborates this statement has been obtained by applying classical genetic, quantitative genetic, and molecular genetic concepts and techniques to the analysis of behavioral phenotypes.

First, we illustrated the scope of behavioral genetics by providing a brief introduction to classical, quantitative, and molecular genetics. Next, we illustrated how the concepts and techniques from each of these branches of genetics is applied to the study of behavior. To familiarize you with classical genetics we described phenylketonuria (PKU)—a disease that results in mental retardation. To illustrate quantitative genetics, we discussed some of the research concerning the inheritance of I.Q. test scores and how selective breeding is used as a tool in behavioral genetic research.

If you are interested in the genetic approach to the study of behavior, we urge you to take courses in biology and chemistry in addition to psychology. Work in behavioral genetics is continuing at an ever-accelerating pace, and many important theoretical and practical developments will result from future work in this field.

3

The Nervous System

In Chapter 2 we discussed the genetic mechanisms of inheritance, which are found in all cells of the body. This chapter is devoted to the specialized cells that make perception and behavior possible—the cells of the nervous system. Although every psychologist is interested in the nervous system directly or indirectly, the structure and functions of this amazing system are the physiological psychologist's primary interest. Thus the physiological psychologist shares many concerns with scientists from other disciplines, such as neurophysiology, neuroanatomy, and neurochemistry.

In this chapter we will discuss three topics: (1) the techniques that physiological psychologists use to learn about the nervous system, (2) the physiology of the nerve cell—the fundamental unit of the nervous system and (3) the overall organization of the nervous system.

Techniques in Physiological Psychology

Ablation and Lesion Techniques

Perhaps the most commonly used methods of investigating the organization and functions of the nervous system are the *ablation and lesion techniques.* The rationale for these methods is quite simple. After surgically disconnecting (the ablation technique) or removing or destroying (the lesion technique) a portion of an animal's nervous system, the psychologist can observe the animal to determine whether the procedure has affected some aspect of its behavior. In humans, this kind of brain damage occurs accidentally or during removal of a tumor or other brain disorder. Most of our knowledge about where the functional areas of the human brain are located comes from studies of brain-damaged individuals. For example, damage to the back of the brain, which might occur in a severe blow to the back of the head, may result in blindness. Removal of this posterior portion of the brain will result in complete blindness in humans and varying degrees of blindness in different experimental animals. Thus the conclusion that this region of the brain is important in vision is a reasonable one, and in fact a variety of investigations have produced results that are consistent with this view. We now know, for instance, that the regions of the cerebral cortex located at the back of the brain correspond to *visual cortex,* which receives information that originates in the retina of each eye. We also know, from observing the effects of brain damage in humans, the approximate locations of areas of the brain that are involved in a variety of other functions such as speech, hearing, memory storage, movement, and so forth (e.g., see fig. 3.17).

Similarly, much of what we know about the localization of function in animal brains comes from studying the effects of localized brain lesions. An experiment in which the lesion technique was used to study eating behavior in rats is described in box 3.1.

Box 3.1

The Lesion Technique

In the experiment illustrated here, the *ventromedial nucleus* of the *hypothalamus* was destroyed bilaterally (on both sides of the brain) in a rat, using the lesion technique (Teitelbaum, 1964). (The lesions or damaged areas are outlined in black on the schematic cross section of the rat brain.) The ventromedial nuclei are suspected of controlling some aspects of feeding behavior in rats and other animals. Thus, by making a lesion bilaterally in this area, the experimenter sought to eliminate its normal function.

As you can see in box figure 3.1, the experiment produced dramatic results. The rat with the hypothalamic lesions ate much more food than the normal animal and became obese. This syndrome of overeating and obesity is termed *hyperphagia.* The results of this experiment as well as many others using stimulation, recording, and biochemical techniques, indicate that the ventromedial nucleus or fibers passing through this area are part of an important series of circuits in the brain which regulate food intake.

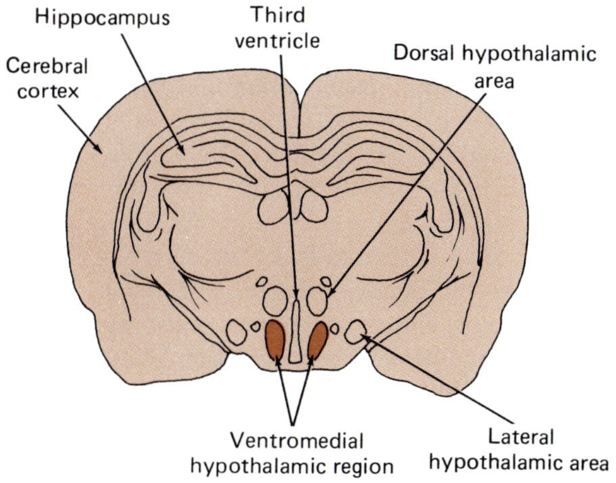

(a)

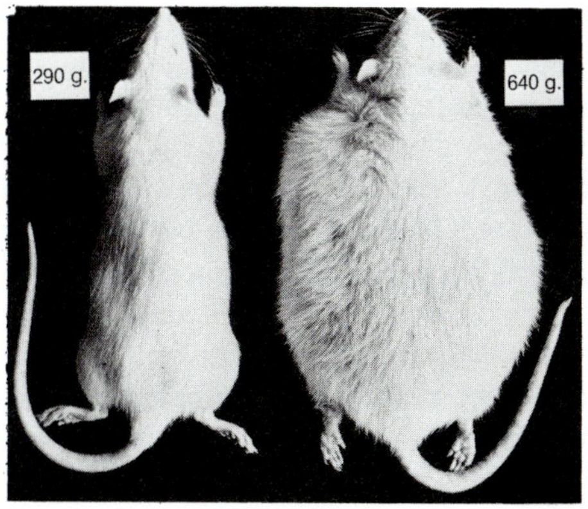

Box Figure 3.1 Destruction of the ventromedial hypothalamic region (the area outlined in black in the cross section of the rat brain) leads to overeating and obesity, as shown in the photograph on the right. (From Krech, David, et al. *Elements of Psychology.* New York: Alfred A. Knopf, Inc., 1969, p. 570. Reprinted by permission. Photo courtesy of Philip Teitelbaum.)

Although the lesion and ablation techniques are extremely useful in understanding the structural basis of behavior, they cannot be relied on exclusively. The reasons are as follows: First, a particular behavior involves a complex, interconnected chain of systems. If one link in the chain is broken, the entire group of systems may become inoperative. This does not mean that only the broken or missing link was doing all the work; all the links are important. Thus it is difficult or impossible to assign the effects of damage to a specific area within the brain. Second, in experimental brain damage, everything within the selected area is destroyed, including nerve fibers which may carry information between structures that are far removed from the destroyed area. Thus, despite careful microscopic analysis of the brain, which is essential for locating and describing experimental brain damage, the fibers passing through the damaged area may go unnoticed, although their destruction may be partially or entirely responsible for the behavioral effects seen by the investigator. Other techniques must be combined with the lesion or ablation technique to reveal the complete function of any area or group of areas in the brain.

Stimulation Techniques

Another powerful tool that has been used to understand the brain is the stimulation method. There are two techniques for stimulating the brain. In the electrical stimulation technique, a metal *electrode,* or wire, is surgically placed in a specific area of the brain. Electrical current is then passed through the electrode to artificially stimulate the neural tissue surrounding its tip. The animal or human subject can then be observed to determine whether the electrical stimulation produces behavioral responses or alters some ongoing behavioral act. An X-ray photograph of stimulating electrodes implanted in a rat's brain is shown in figure 3.1.

Electrical stimulation of certain areas of the brain in human patients undergoing brain surgery has evoked memories, movements of the limbs, speech, and many other behaviors. In this way, many parts of the brain have been "mapped" to indicate the location of functional areas. For example, we noted previously that destruction of the visual cortex will produce blindness. Stimulation of the visual cortex, on the other hand, often produces visual sensations in human patients. A blow to the head can produce similar effects, often referred to as "seeing stars." An example of what a person may perceive when the brain is stimulated artificially is provided in box 3.2.

However, electrical stimulation of one area may, because of its connections with other parts of the nervous system, activate some other area indirectly. Furthermore, stimula-

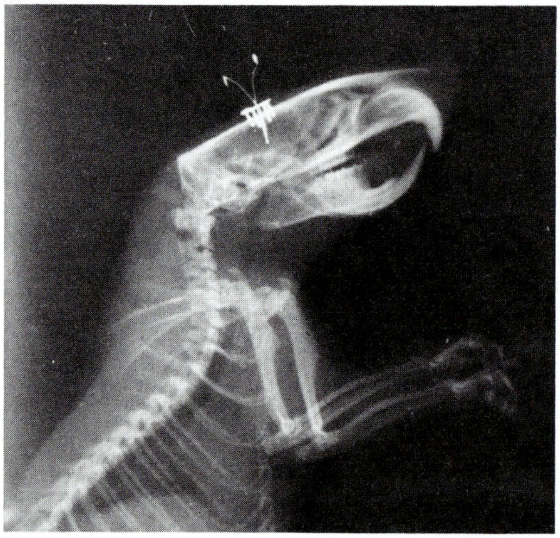

Figure 3.1 Electrodes implanted in the brain of a rat are shown in this X-ray photograph. The electrodes are held in place by a plastic carrier that is screwed to the skull. These can be used either to give an electrical stimulus to the brain or to record electrical impulses generated by the brain. (From Olds, James, "Pleasure Centers in the Brain," *Scientific American,* October, 1956. Reprinted by permission of the author.)

Box 3.2

Electrical Stimulation of the Brain

During the series of observations listed below, a twelve-year-old boy was undergoing brain surgery to locate the area responsible for the severe convulsions he had experienced for three years. (Plate 6 is a photograph of the brain taken during surgery.) The surgeons were stimulating the visual cortex—the area of the cerebral hemispheres where visual information is processed—and another region that borders it. Each number below corresponds to the numbered area in the drawing and the unnumbered regions in plate 6. The boy's own verbal reports are enclosed in quotation marks. Because there are no pain receptors in the brain, only local anesthetic is required during this kind of operation. Thus the boy was completely conscious.

Response to Stimulation

Area Stimulated

19. *. . . "Color flashes" said to be in front of him.*

18. *The patient was asked to fix his gaze on Dr. Everitt's finger, which was held to his right. During stimulation, his eye moved slowly back to the midline, and a little across to the left.*

    He said he saw "lights." On questioning, he answered, "The light started by your finger, and then went over to the left."

24. *"Yes, the robbers; they are coming after me."*

15. *. . . "Colored glasses. They were in front of me and then off to the left." His eyes were central, but he shut them toward the end of stimulation.*

25. *Colored flashes.*

26. *"Colored flashes again—and two people with guns, a girl and a boy." He said he knew them. The girl was his cousin.*

26. *Repeated without warning. The patient said nothing. When asked, he said he had seen the "colored flashes again, nothing else."*

    The patient was warned that he was to be stimulated, but stimulation was withheld. On inquiry, he replied he had noticed "nothing."

30. *"I heard someone speaking, my mother telling one of my aunts to come up tonight."*

31. *"Would you do it again, please?"*

31. *Repeated. After a pause, he said, "The same as before. My mother telling my aunt over the telephone to come up and visit us tonight." When asked how he knew she was talking on the telephone, he said he did not see her, but from the way his aunt's voice sounded when she answered, he knew it was over the telephone.*

    Stimulations nearer the inferior surface of the temporal lobe caused him to have a headache, nothing else.

32. *"My mother is telling my brother he has got his coat on backwards. I can just hear them." He was asked if he remembered this, and he replied, "Oh yes, just before I came here." When asked if he thought these things were like dreams, he said, "No." He was then asked what it was like, and he replied, "It is just like I go into a daze." (Penfield & Jasper, 1954).*

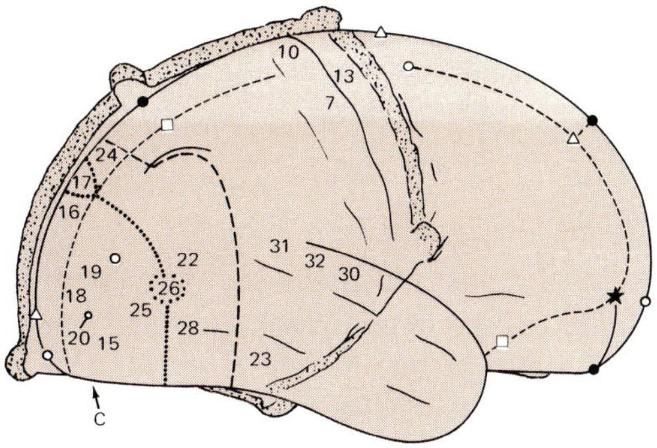

Box Figure 3.2 The schematic diagram on the right illustrates where electrical stimulation was applied to the brain. Stimulation at different points, each indicated by a number, produced different effects. (From Penfield, W., and Jasper, H., *Epilepsy and the Functional Anatomy of the Human Brain.* Copyright 1954 by Little, Brown and Company, pp. 118–120. Reprinted by permission of publisher and authors.)

tion of one region may activate not only that region but fibers which are simply passing through or near it. Thus, although electrical stimulation of the brain can provide suggestive evidence, it must, like the lesion and ablation methods, be combined with other techniques to produce an accurate and reliable picture of the organization and function of the brain.

A more recent technique for stimulating the brain involves the use of *chemical substances* rather than electrical current. In the chemical method, small cylinders (cannulae) are implanted into specific areas of the brain and minute amounts of chemicals are applied directly. By using this technique, we have learned much about how and where certain chemicals can alter the brain's activity and thereby alter behavior.

There are also objections to this technique. For example, if the substance injected into the brain is not present and active under normal conditions, it may not be acting by normal physiological means. And even if the substance is normally present in the brain, the addition of more may produce spurious results. In addition, the problems of indirect action that exist when other techniques are used are still present. That is, chemical stimulation of one area may cause indirect stimulation of another and so forth. However, by using this technique, in combination with many others, physiological psychologists and scientists from other fields have enhanced their understanding of the neural and chemical substrates of behavior.

Recording Techniques

A third means of studying the nervous system are the recording techniques. Although the brain generates many different kinds of electrical signals, all the techniques used to record this electrical activity have certain things in common. For example, they all require that an electrode be placed near or in direct contact with the brain or other nervous structures from which one wishes to record. These electrodes can be rather large. For example, a dime-sized metal electrode is placed on the surface of the scalp to record the electroencephalogram (EEG), which involves the activity of millions of nerve cells. (The absence of this activity is one of the criteria defining death.) Smaller electrodes (or wires) can be inserted deep into the brain to record the electrical activity in obscure areas. Both surface electrodes and these large wires are termed *gross electrodes,* because they are relatively large compared with the size of nerve cells.

A third type of recording technique involves extremely fine wires, which are sharpened to a microscopic tip and insulated with glass or some other substance so that the electrode will only conduct electricity at the tip. These microelectrodes are used to record the electrical activity of single nerve cells.

When combined with the lesion, stimulation, and other techniques, electrical recording can provide detailed and valuable information about how different elements of the nervous system respond during perceptual and behavioral processes. Because electrical activity is one of the fundamental mechanisms by which nerve cells communicate, the ability to record this activity has provided important knowledge about how the nervous system operates.

Figure 3.2 illustrates several types of electrical activity that can be recorded from the brain. The first is the spontaneous *electroencephalogram* or *EEG*—the ongoing electrical activity of the living brain. The second type is an *evoked potential,* recorded from the visual cortex. Unlike the EEG, evoked potentials are not considered spontaneous; they occur in response to sensory stimuli (here, a visual stimulus). However, both kinds of electrical activity are produced by large populations of

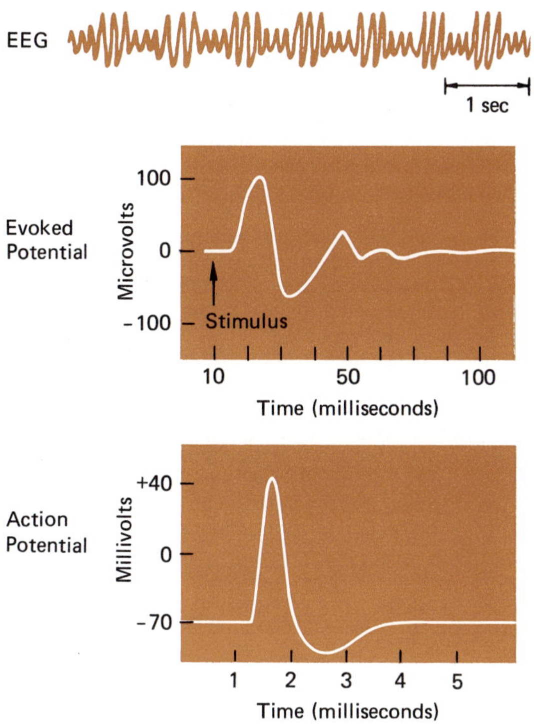

Figure 3.2 Three types of electrical signals that can be recorded from the brain. At the top is the electroencephalogram or EEG. In the middle is an evoked potential to some sensory stimulus. At the bottom is the action potential of a single nerve cell. (From Penfield, W., and Jasper, H., *Epilepsy and the Functional Anatomy of the Human Brain.* Copyright 1954 by Little, Brown and Company. Reprinted by permission of the publisher and authors.)

nerve cells near the recording electrode. Note the difference in the time scales between evoked potentials and the EEG. The third type of electrical response is recorded from the brain with microelectrodes and represents the *electrical discharge* of a single nerve cell. Note the time scale. These signals are much briefer than the other types of electrical activity shown in figure 3.2.

All electrical responses recorded from the nervous system are expressed as changes in voltage as a function of time. In addition, although these responses differ dramatically in size, the changes in voltage in each case are quite small and must be amplified many times before they can be seen on a recording instrument. Finally, the investigator needs a device that will display these changes. In the case of the EEG, the changes in voltage are often amplified and written out by an ink pen on a narrow strip of chart paper. Evoked potentials and single cell discharges can also be written out on strips of chart paper, but more often they are displayed on an *oscilloscope,* one of the most common recording instruments in the biological laboratory. Box 3.3 describes how the oscilloscope works.

Many other techniques have been used to study the nervous system. Some of them will be mentioned in other sections of this chapter and in other chapters of this book. The important point to remember is that only by using all the existing techniques in combination will we obtain the answers to our questions about the biological mechanisms of behavior. We can now turn our attention to the building block of the nervous system, the nerve cell or neuron.

The Neuron

Like all other cells, the neuron must carry out the processes necessary to maintain life. But unlike other cells, the neuron is functionally specialized to *conduct* and *transmit* information. The human nervous system contains many billions of neurons, as well as many times this number of nonneural cells that serve important support functions for the nervous system. Some of these nonneural cells are the so-called glial cells, blood cells, etc. Thus understanding how these cells behave and how they are interconnected is a formidable task. Fortunately, although there are many types of neurons and although some may do entirely different things for the organism than others, most of them appear to operate in similar ways.

Box 3.3
The Oscilloscope

Box figure 3.3 illustrates the principal features of the oscilloscope, which operates (and looks) somewhat like a television set. The major component of the oscilloscope is the *cathode-ray tube* shown below. The cathode-ray tube contains a source of electrons. Because electrons possess a single negative electrical charge and have virtually no mass, they can move very rapidly. The beam of electrons is passed between two sets of plates. The X plates are electrically charged in such a way that they force the beam of electrons from one side of the tube to the other. The X plate on the right becomes slowly positive relative to the X plate on the left, so that the electrons are pulled from left to right across the screen of the oscilloscope. Because the screen is coated with a substance that glows when struck by electrons, a light trace can be seen as the electrons move across it. The Y plates are connected through an amplifier to the source from which the experimenter is recording. As the source changes voltage, the Y plates change voltage with respect to each other and produce vertical deflections of the electron beam as it sweeps across the oscilloscope screen. Thus the X plates generate the time axis by sweeping the beam of electrons horizontally across the cathode-ray tube at a constant rate. The Y plates generate the voltage axis by deflecting the beam vertically whenever the source changes in voltage. The record that appears on the screen can be photographed on film for permanent storage.

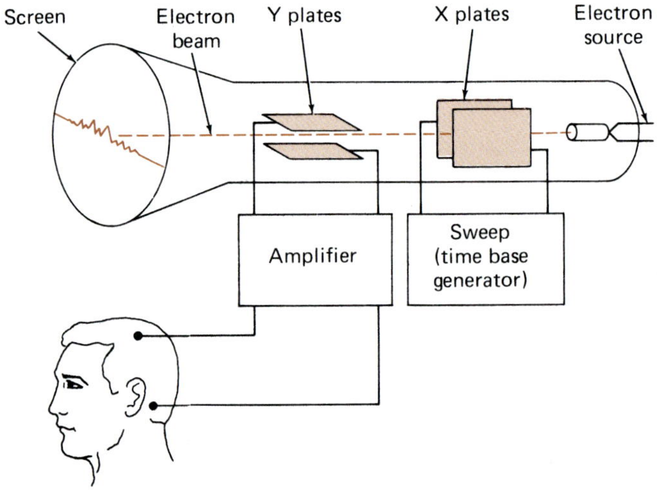

Box Figure 3.3 Basic operation of the oscilloscope. The electron beam is moved across the screen by the X plates, and the incoming signal (here, a human EEG) is displayed as vertical deflections produced by the Y plates. (From *Foundations of Physiological Psychology,* R. F. Thompson. Copyright © 1967 Richard F. Thompson. Reprinted by permission of Harper & Row Publishers.)

Basically, the nerve cell is composed of three major portions, as shown in figure 3.3. The *cell body* and its *nucleus* control all cellular activities, as they do in all other cells. But unlike other cells, the nerve cell possesses extensions from the cell body, which may extend several feet or more before reaching their destinations. The *axon* is a long slender extension that conducts information away from the cell body. It is joined to the cell body at a point called the *axon hillock. Dendrites,* of which there may be from several to several hundred per cell, are generally shorter than the axon and typically conduct information toward the cell body.

Many axons are encased in an insulating, lipid (fat) substance called *myelin.* Myelin is of a relatively recent origin in evolution and

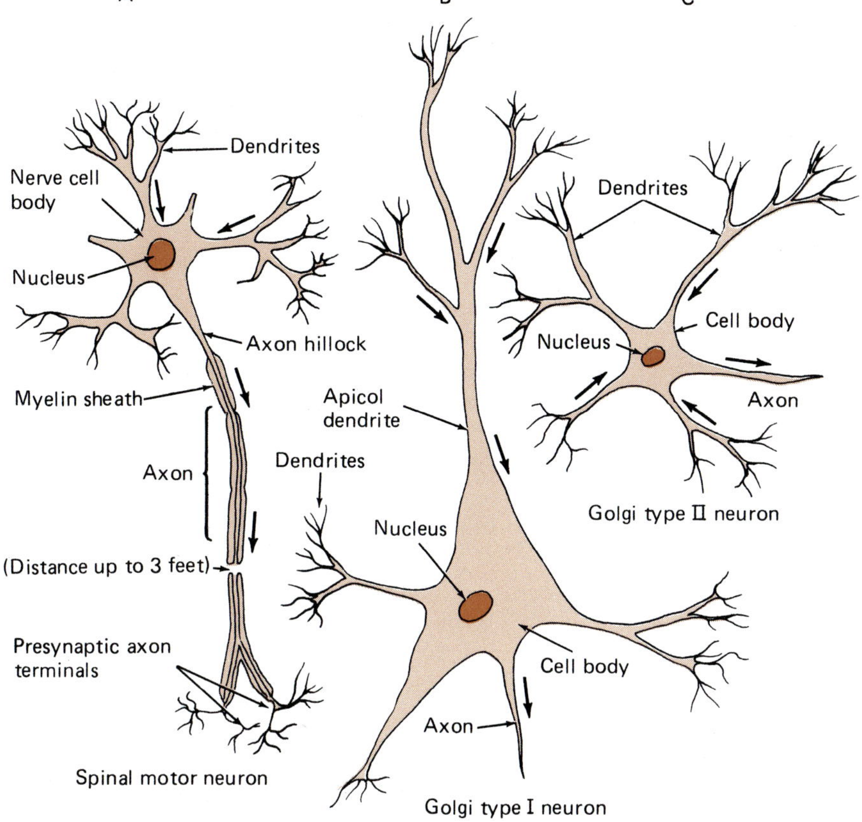

Figure 3.3 Several types of neurons illustrating the basic components that virtually all neurons have in common. The motor neuron (A) is found in the spinal cord, and carries information out to muscles and other effectors. The Golgi type I neuron (B) generally possesses an extremely long axon (not shown in full length in this diagram), while the Golgi type II neuron (C) has a short axon. (From *Foundations of Physiological Psychology,* R. F. Thompson. Copyright © 1967 Richard F. Thompson. Reprinted by permission of Harper & Row, Publishers.)

serves the important function of increasing the speed at which axons can conduct information. This myelin sheath, as it is called, has small gaps along its length called *Nodes of Ranvier.* The axon hillock, cell body, and dendrites are not myelinated. Some of the other structural features of the neuron include axon collaterals—branches of the axon that act as additional axons to conduct information to more than one place—and axon terminals, or *endings.* The axon terminals represent the end of one nerve cell and are the last point at which conduction of information in a neuron can take place.

To transfer information from one cell to another, the axon terminals form *synapses* with the dendrites; cell bodies, or sometimes axons of other cells. In other words, synapses are the functional contacts between separate neurons. At the synapse, the cells do not actually touch one another; the axon terminals of one cell simply come very close to some part of another cell. The transmission of information across synapses is achieved by means of small *chemical packets,* which are discharged from the axon terminals and move across the small space between the cells to act on the next nerve cell. The mechanisms by which transmission at the synapse takes place will be discussed shortly. First, however, we must describe how information is conducted from the cell body down the axon to the axon terminals.

Conduction in Nerve Cells: The Action Potential

As far as we know today, the means by which neurons conduct information are essentially the same for all nerve cells. Like most living cells, the neuron possesses a *resting membrane* potential, which can be recorded by penetrating the cell with a microelectrode. The resting membrane potential is a voltage difference that exists across the cell membrane. These differences result from a distribution of electrically charged particles (ions) on either side of the cell membrane. A schematic illustration of the resting membrane potential as well as the electrically charged molecules that produce it are shown in figure 3.4. The actual mechanisms by which the resting membrane potential is generated are too complex to outline in detail here; briefly, they can be described as follows: some electrically charged particles that exist in the body fluid can pass readily into the cell—notably, potassium (K^+), which in solution possesses a positive charge, and chloride (Cl^-), which possesses a negative charge. Certain other particles are unable to pass into or out of the cell —notably sodium (Na^+), which is highly concentrated outside the cell and possesses a positive electrical charge, and certain large proteins, which exist in high concentration inside the cells and possess negative charges. Because only some ions, as these electrically charged particles are called, can pass through the cell membrane freely, the nerve cell membrane is referred to as a semipermeable membrane. The end result of a differential distribution of charged particles across a semipermeable membrane is a voltage difference across the membrane, which for neurons is negative inside the cell and positive outside. The value of this separation of charge is approximately seventy millivolts (or 70 thousandths of a volt)—about 1/20 the voltage of a common flashlight battery. The separation of charge is called polarization. If the charge increases—becomes more negative inside—the membrane is said to be *hyperpolarized.* If the charge decreases—becomes less negative inside—the membrane is said to be *depolarized.*

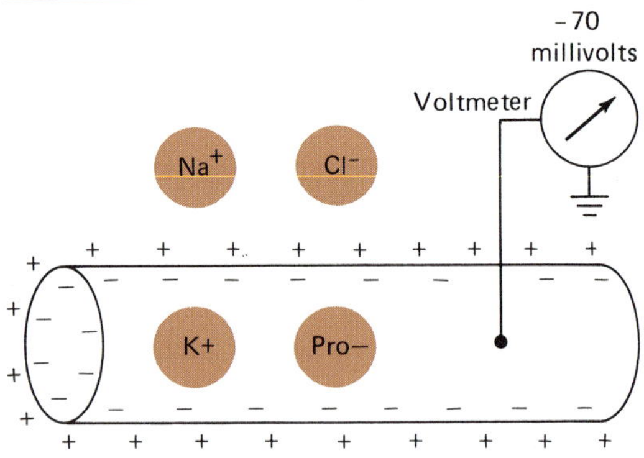

Figure 3.4 A schematic illustration of an axon and its resting membrane potential. The potential exists across the cell membrane and is produced by a differential distribution of charged particles or ions. These include sodium (Na+) and chloride (Cl−), which are highly concentrated outside the cell, and potassium (K+) and large protein ions (Pro−), which are highly concentrated inside the cell. Although sodium and chloride also exist inside the cell and potassium is found outside, the concentrations in each case are much lower.

Although all cells have a resting membrane potential, only neurons (and muscle cells) are capable of altering their membrane potential. This capacity to alter the membrane potential is what allows the neuron to conduct information. The means by which information is conducted is the *action potential* (see fig. 3.5). The action potential represents a temporary reversal of the resting membrane potential, which, because of the specialized nature of the nerve cell's membrane, can travel or *propagate* down the axon of a nerve cell. Action potentials originate in or near the cell body of a neuron. Once initiated, they travel down the entire length of the axon, like the lighted portion of a fuse, at a constant size and speed until they reach the axon terminals. For this reason, they are called *all-or-none* responses.

The basic principles of the action potential are not difficult to understand. Normally, sodium ions are highly concentrated in the fluid surrounding nerve cells. The all-or-none action potential is generated by a temporary breakdown in the cell membrane's normal barrier to sodium ions. Opening the cell membrane to sodium ions results in a rapid inward movement of a small proportion of these charged particles toward the inside of the cell, producing a rapid but temporary change

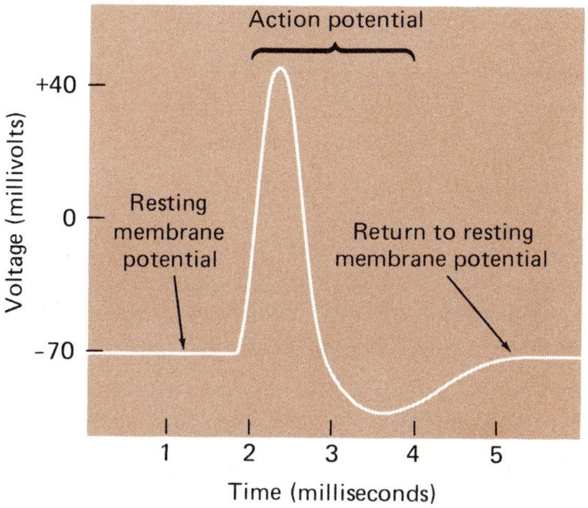

Figure 3.5 The action potential is a temporary change in the membrane potential of the neuron which travels down the axon.

in the resting membrane potential—the inside becomes positive for a brief period. Thus, if we record an action potential with a microelectrode inside the cell, the resting membrane potential, which was initially 70 millivolts negative inside, will suddenly become positive inside to a value of about 40 millivolts—a 110 millivolt change (see fig. 3.5).

Potassium ions, which are also positively charged, are normally highly concentrated inside the cell. When sodium ions rush into the cell during the action potential and make the inside temporarily positive, potassium ions tend to move outside the cell. This movement results in the second phase of the action potential. As you might expect, following the transient depolarization of the cell membrane created by the inward movement of sodium, the potassium moving outward causes the membrane to become hyperpolarized. Thus, the second phase of the action potential is a brief hyperpolarization of the membrane potential, pushing the value of the membrane potential to around seventy-five millivolts negative inside, which is slightly higher than the normal value of seventy millivolts. Once the membrane approaches its original resting value, it resumes its original semipermeable state, and the potential returns to its normal resting value of seventy millivolts negative inside relative to outside.

In other words, the two phases of the action potential—the initial depolarization followed by a brief hyperpolarization—are produced primarily by the movement of sodium ions rushing into the cell and subsequently by potassium ions moving out of the cell. This is illustrated schematically in figure 3.6. Any positive ion moving into the cell will produce a depolarization of the cell membrane potential, and any positive ion moving out of the cell will produce a hyperpolarization. A similar situation exists for negatively charged particles, although the effects are precisely the opposite. When negatively charged mole-

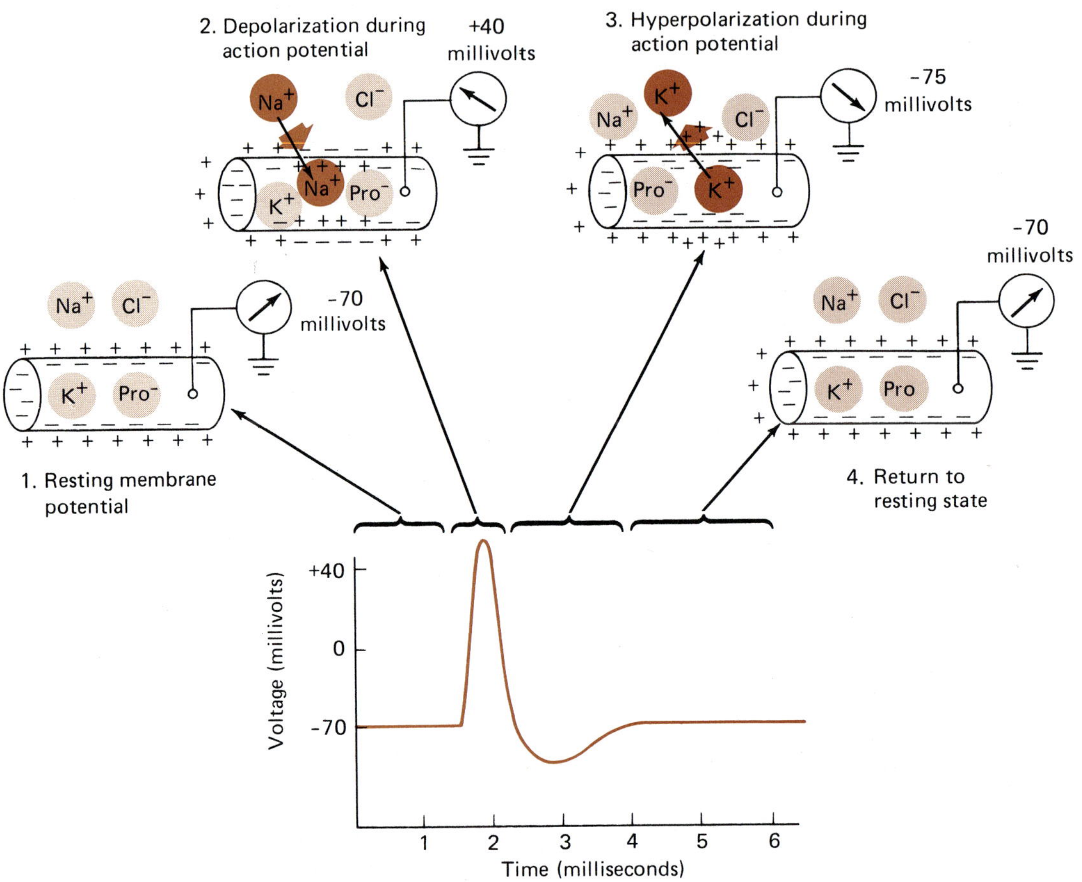

Figure 3.6 The events that produce the action potential. In the resting state (1 and 4), sodium (Na+) and chloride (Cl−) are highly concentrated outside, and potassium (K+) and large protein ions (Pro−) are highly concentrated inside the cell. During the first phase of the action potential (depolarization), sodium flows into the cell. During the second phase (hyperpolarization), potassium moves out of the cell. The concentrations are restored by the sodium-potassium pump.

cules (such as chloride) move out of the cell, they produce a depolarization; when they move into the cell, they produce a hyperpolarization. Although action potentials are produced primarily by the inward movement of sodium and the outward movement of potassium, other types of electrical activity found in neurons often depend, in addition, on the movement of other charged particles such as negatively charged chloride ions.

Because virtually all neurons conduct information by means of action potentials, an understanding of this mechanism is basic to understanding how the nervous system operates. Thus several additional features of the action potential merit special discussion. First, all neurons have a *threshold* which must be passed by the membrane potential for the neuron to initiate an action potential. If the resting membrane potential is altered, the alteration must reach a minimum of several millivolts or more below its normal resting value before the depolarization will reach the threshold and the action potential will be initiated. Second, each time an action potential occurs, the neuron is incapable of initiating another action potential for a fraction of a millisecond. This period is called the absolute refractory period. For one or several milliseconds after the absolute refractory period, the neuron can fire another action potential, but a stronger stimulus than normal will be required. This second period is termed the relative refractory period. Some neurons are more excitable for a time following an action potential; this interval is termed a supernormal period. Once a nerve cell returns to its original state, however, action potentials can again be initiated normally. And finally, the action potential, once initiated, must be propagated down the axon to its destination.

In the unmyelinated nerve, the localized inward rush of sodium ions is sufficient to produce another action potential in the region of axon adjacent to the point at which the action potential occurred. This is termed a *self-regenerative process,* because each action potential produces sufficient depolarization in the next region of the membrane to reach threshold and initiate an action potential there. Because of myelin's insulating properties, action potentials in myelinated axons are generated only at the small gaps in the myelin sheath, the Nodes of Ranvier. Thus myelin vastly increases the speed of conduction because the action potential can jump from one Node of Ranvier to the next, skipping over the insulated portions of axon between the nodes. This phenomenon is called *saltatory conduction.*

If neurons remain active for the duration of a human lifetime and if action potentials involve an influx of sodium ions and efflux of potassium ions, what keeps neurons from eventually running out of potassium and filling up with sodium? The answer is that the membranes of all neurons contain a special mechanism called the *sodium-potassium pump,* which forces sodium back out of the cell, into the extracellular fluid and pumps potassium back into the cell. Because an action potential depends on the movement of only a small number of sodium and potassium ions, the normal balance of these ions is easily restored by the sodium-potassium pump. See box 3.4.

You will appreciate the importance of the action potential in the operation of the nervous system if you realize that everything you perceive in your environment must be translated by your sensory receptors into action potentials, which in turn carry the information to your central nervous system, where the resulting patterns of electrical and chemical activity correspond in some unknown way to your perception of images, sounds, and so forth. By the same token, all of your responses to the environment are the result of action potentials initiated in your central nervous system, which travel out to and trigger the actions of your muscles and glands.

Synaptic Transmission

The entire nervous system consists of billions of separate cells. Thus in order for the nervous system to function these independent cells must be able to communicate with each other. The means by which one nerve cell communicates with another is called synaptic transmission. In the mammalian nervous system, synaptic transmission takes place by means of chemical substances that are released by one cell to act on another. The point where this activity takes place is the synapse. Some of the most important features of the synapse are shown in figure 3.7.

You will recall that as an axon approaches its destination, it branches into many fine strands that end in small swellings called axon terminals or terminal buttons. Each terminal contains tiny packets of *chemical transmitter substance*. When the action potential reaches an axon terminal, it triggers the release of these chemical transmitters, which are stored in *synaptic vesicles* (see fig. 3.7) into the small gap or *synaptic cleft* between the synaptic ending and the membrane of another cell. The chemical diffuses across the synaptic cleft and attaches to specialized receptors on the membrane of the next cell. This usually alters the permeability of the second cell and therefore its membrane potential. If the change in membrane potential reaches the threshold, it may produce an action potential, which will then be propagated down the axon of the cell and initiate the process of synaptic transmission again farther down the line. After the synaptic transmitter substance has altered the permeability of an adjacent cell membrane, it is broken down by other chemical substances in or near the synaptic cleft, a process called *degradation;* or it can be taken up into the synaptic terminal to be used again, a process called *re-uptake*.

Although most forms of synaptic transmission involve the basic processes of release, diffusion, receptor attachment, and breakdown or re-uptake, the effects on the postsynaptic cell can be quite different, depending on the function of the synapse.

There are two functional types of synapses: excitatory and inhibitory. Excitatory synapses initiate action potentials in the postsynaptic neuron, while inhibitory synapses prevent another cell from firing. The ability of one cell to inhibit the activity of another is equally if not more important than excitatory synaptic activity.

In *excitatory synaptic transmission,* the action potential of the initiating or presynaptic cell invades the cell's axon terminals and triggers the release of the *excitatory synaptic transmitter substance*. This substance diffuses across the synaptic cleft and attaches to receptor sites on the receiving or postsynaptic

Box 3.4

The Giant Axon of the Squid

Many properties of the action potential were discovered during experiments on the giant nerve cells of the squid. Squids possess several of these extremely large nerve cells; two of them are illustrated in box figure 3.4a. When confronted with a dangerous obstacle, the squid is capable of propelling itself backwards very rapidly. This escape response is controlled by these large neurons.

The axons of these nerve cells, as seen under the microscope and illustrated in box figure 3.4b, can be as large as a millimeter in diameter. They can be dissected completely out of the squid, and if placed in a special water bath, they will remain alive and function for as long as twelve hours. The substance inside the axon can be squeezed out like toothpaste out of a tube and be replaced with a medium of any chemical constitution, to study the effects of removing specific ions, adding special radioactive particles, and so forth. Similarly, a variety of chemical substances can be added to the extracellular bath to assess the effects of various substances outside the cell. Because the axon is so large, it is unnecessary to use the extremely tiny microelectrodes that are needed to record the electrical activity of small mammalian nerve cells. The substitution of different chemical environments both inside and outside the giant axon of the squid led to the conclusion that the action potential was generated by a breakdown of the cell membrane's barrier to external sodium ions (Na^+). Thus sodium ions were able to pass into the cell, and subsequently potassium ions (K^+) moved out of the cell. It was also shown that following an action potential, an active *metabolic pump* (sodium-potassium pump) forced the excess sodium ions out of the cell and drew potassium ions back into the cell.

Organisms such as the squid have been used as models for understanding phenomena such as the action potential throughout the history of biology and psychology.

Box Figure 3.4 Giant nerve cells of the squid (top). The approximate location of two giant nerve cells and their axons is shown on the left from the top of the squid. The photomicrograph (bottom) illustrates the size of the giant axons. In each case, an electrode is inserted into the axon. (Top from R. Keynes, *Scientific American,* December, 1958; A. Hodgkin and A. Huxley, "Action potentials recorded from inside nerve fiber," *Nature,* 144, 1939, pp. 710–711; bottom, A. Hodgkin and R. Keynes, "Experiments on the injection of substances into squid giant axons by means of a microsyringe," *The Journal of Physiology,* 131, 1956, pp. 592–616. Reprinted by permission.)

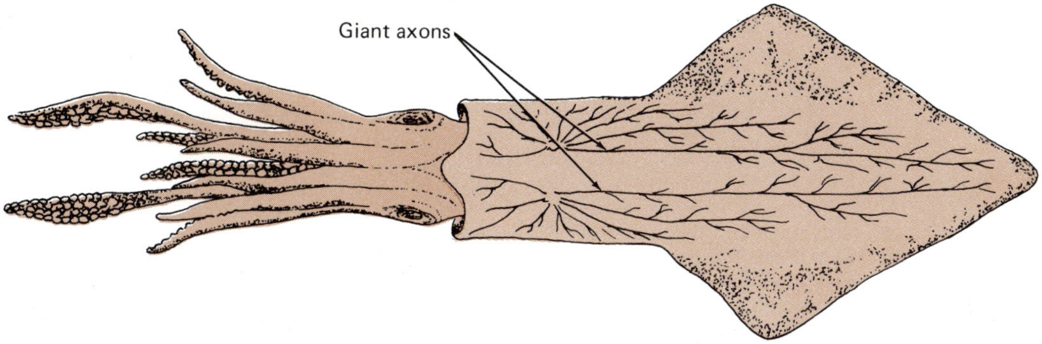

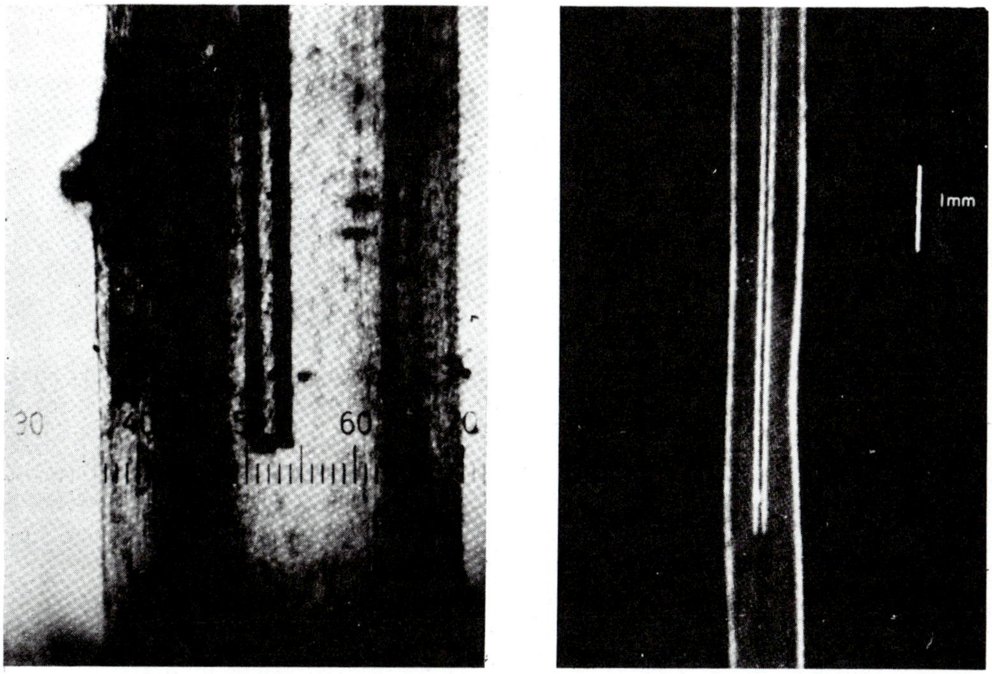

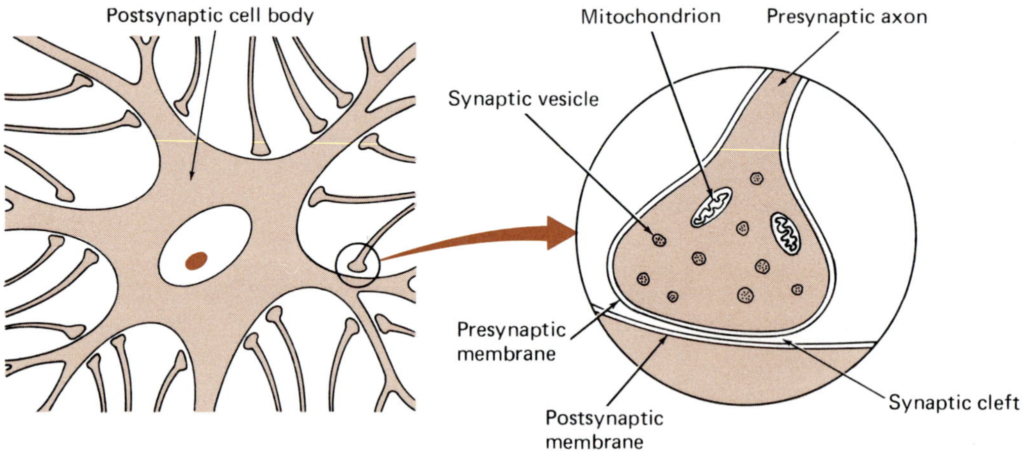

Figure 3.7 The cell body and dendrites of a neuron covered with synaptic endings. One of these endings is shown schematically on the right. Synaptic terminals deliver short bursts of synaptic transmitter substance, which is stored in the synaptic vesicles and released during synaptic transmission into the synaptic cleft. *Mitochondria* are specialized structures that help to supply the cell with energy. (From E. Peter Volpe, *Man, Nature, and Society.*

cell. The excitatory synaptic transmitter alters the permeability of the postsynaptic cell membrane and this in turn results in a slight depolarization of the postsynaptic cell membrane; this depolarization may range from a few to as many as ten or twenty millivolts or more. The important fact is that excitatory synaptic transmission involves a depolarization of the postsynaptic cell, called an excitatory postsynaptic potential or EPSP, which is illustrated schematically in figure 3.8. If the depolarization caused by synaptic transmission is large enough to pass discharge threshold in the postsynaptic neuron, an action potential will be initiated. This action potential can then be propagated to its appropriate destination. Unlike the all-or-none potential, EPSP's do not travel down the axon, and their size depends on how many synaptic endings are activated within a short period of time. If only a few excitatory synapses are active, the EPSP will be small and will not reach discharge threshold, and the postsynaptic neuron will not fire an action potential. However, if many excitatory synapses are active at one time, the EPSP will be large and reach firing threshold, and the postsynaptic cell will fire (see fig. 3.8).

The mechanism by which excitatory synaptic transmission takes place is a depolarization of the cell membrane toward firing threshold. Inhibitory synaptic transmission is characterized by the opposite action: a hyperpolarization of the cell membrane. Again, the release, diffusion, and attachment of the synaptic transmitter substance are essentially the same as in the excitatory synapse. However, because a different type of chemical substance is released, or because the postsynaptic receptors are different, the postsynaptic cell becomes permeable to a different pattern of ions, which results in a resting membrane potential that becomes more negative inside than is normal. This brief hyperpolarization of the membrane potential is called an *inhibitory postsynaptic potential,* or IPSP. In essence, *inhibitory synaptic transmission* moves the value of the resting membrane potential away from firing threshold, so that the postsynaptic cell is unlikely or unable to fire an action potential. The IPSP is illustrated in figure 3.9. Again, the IPSP, like the EPSP, is a graded potential; its size depends on the number of inhibitory synapses and the rapidity with which they are activated.

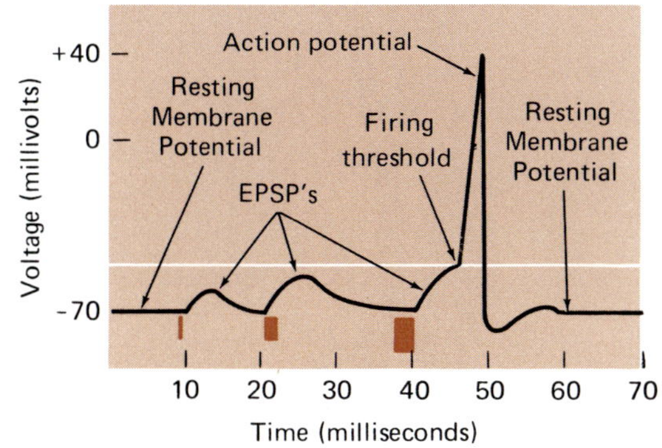

Figure 3.8 Schematic illustrations of excitatory postsynaptic potentials (EPSPs). The vertical bar that appears immediately before each EPSP represents the amount of synaptic activity producing the EPSP. Note that as the synaptic input increases, the EPSP increases. If enough synaptic activity bombards the neuron, the EPSP will reach firing threshold and an action potential will be initiated, as shown on the extreme right.

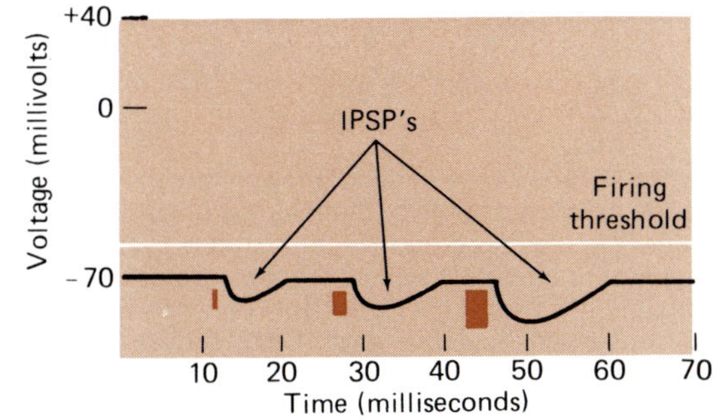

Figure 3.9 Schematic illustrations of inhibitory postsynaptic potentials (IPSPs). The vertical bar that appears immediately before each IPSP represents the amount of inhibitory synaptic activity producing the IPSP. As the amount of inhibitory synaptic activity increases, the IPSP increases (i.e., becomes more negative). The larger the IPSP the less likely that the neuron will fire an action potential.

Each nerve cell in the nervous system is constantly receiving excitatory, inhibitory, or, more commonly, some combination of these synaptic effects. Thus each cell acts as an individual computer, combining and weighing excitatory and inhibitory actions and determining when and when not to fire an action potential. Given the complexity of individual nerve cells, and given that there are many billions of cells in our nervous systems, it would be impossible to build a computer that would do all the myriad operations that our brains are not only capable of carrying out but actually do carry out every minute of our lives.

Synaptic Transmitter Substances

Some of the chemical transmitter substances that exist in the nervous system have been identified and are being studied extensively. Although we cannot cover all of these substances, a few examples will illustrate the nature of these chemical messengers.

Acetylcholine (ACh) is the chemical transmitter at the neuromuscular junction—the synapse between motor neurons passing out of the central nervous system and body muscles. Release of ACh from presynaptic endings of these motor neurons causes muscles to contract; in other words, its action is excitatory. ACh is also present in the central nervous system and is presumed to act there as a synaptic transmitter substance, although the precise details of its action are not completely understood. In the central nervous system, it may be excitatory in some cases and inhibitory in others.

Another group of transmitter substances, known collectively as the *biogenic amines,* are assumed to be active in the peripheral and central nervous system. These include *norepinephrine, serotonin,* and *dopamine.* Norepinephrine acts at synapses between neurons of the sympathetic division of the autonomic nervous system and its peripheral targets, such as smooth muscles and glands. A recent theory has implicated the biogenic amines in emotional states such as depression. Like ACh, the biogenic amines may be excitatory or inhibitory, depending on where and the mechanisms by which they act.

The Structure of the Nervous System

Now that you are familiar with some of the cells that make up the nervous system, we can discuss the overall organization of this complicated and amazing organ. The nervous system is comprised of functional groups of neurons and their fibers and is schematically illustrated in figure 3.10.

Note first that the nervous system is composed of two major portions: (1) the central nervous system, including the brain and spinal cord, which is encased entirely within the bones of the skull and vertebrae of the spinal column; and (2) the peripheral nervous system, which includes all nervous tissue lying outside the skull and spine. Another obvious feature of the nervous system is that it is *bilaterally symmetrical*—that is, a structure on one side is virtually always duplicated on the other. Thus, there are two cerebral hemispheres, two of each functional nucleus in the brain, and similar groups of nerves on both sides of the peripheral nervous system.

Any functional group of cell bodies within the central nervous system is called a *nucleus* (plural: nuclei). A group of fibers in the central nervous system is called a *tract.* If a group of cell bodies occurs in the peripheral nervous system, it is called a *ganglion* (plural:

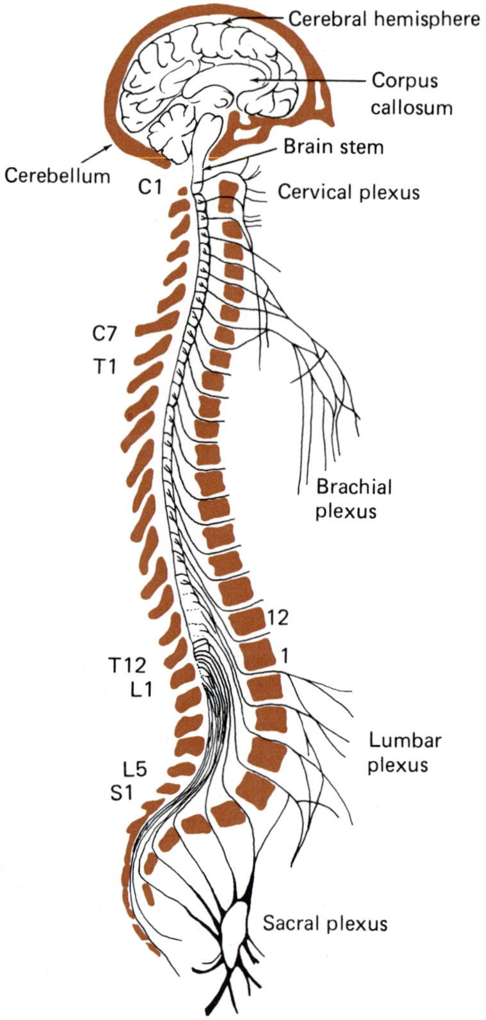

Figure 3.10 A cross section through the brain, spinal cord, and some of the major groups of spinal nerves that comprise the nervous system. The letters along the spinal column indicate cervical (C), thoracic (T), lumbar (L), and sacral (S) regions of the spinal cord. The numbers correspond to the position of each vertebra within each region. Similarly, the major bundles of spinal nerves are named according to their origin along the spinal column. *Plexus* refers to a bundle of nerves. These nerves continue to branch and reach out to innervate sensory receptors, muscles, and various internal organs. (From E. Gardner, *Fundamentals of Neurology* (5th ed.) Philadelphia: W. B. Saunders Company, 1968. Reprinted by permission of author and publisher.)

ganglia). A group of nerve fibers in the peripheral nervous system is referred to as a *nerve.*

Peripheral Nervous System

The peripheral nervous system brings information from the body and external environment to the central nervous system and carries information from the central nervous system out to the muscles and glands to produce behavior. Thus it primarily consists of bundles of nerve fibers that come into and go out of the central nervous system to the rest of the body. These are the *peripheral nerves.* Nerve fibers that carry information toward the central nervous system—for example, those carrying pain, temperature, and other sensory information—are called *sensory* or *afferent nerves.* Nerve fibers that carry information away from the central nervous system to muscles or glands are called *motor* or *efferent nerves.* Although most nerves in the body contain sensory *and* motor fibers, both classes of fibers segregate as they enter the central nervous system. Peripheral nerves that enter the spinal cord (most peripheral nerves enter the central nervous system through the spinal cord) separate just before they pass into the spinal column. Sensory nerves pass into the spinal cord through the *dorsal roots,* and motor nerves leave the cord in large bundles called *ventral roots.* If you were lying on your stomach, the dorsal roots would be toward the top of the spinal cord (dorsal means toward the top or back), and the ventral roots would be at the bottom (ventral means toward the bottom). We will mention this arrangement again later when we deal with the central nervous system.

Although most peripheral nerves either enter or exit from the spinal cord, there are twelve special peripheral nerves that enter or leave from the brain directly. These are called *cranial nerves* and they bring sensory information from the head—from the eyes, ears, nose, and mouth—and carry out movements of the head and face, such as chewing, speaking, and so forth.

Divisions of the Peripheral Nervous System

The peripheral nervous system is divided into two major divisions or functional groups of nerves and their associated cell bodies: the *somatic division* and the *autonomic division.* The somatic division handles sensory and motor information such as touch, temperature, control of muscles that produce body movement, and so forth. The somatic division is *not* concerned primarily with the activities of glands and smooth muscles, which do not produce bodily movement. In general, the autonomic division controls glandular activities and emotional behavior, such as heart rate, sweating, crying, and so forth.

As shown in figure 3.11, the autonomic nervous system also consists of two separate divisions, the sympathetic division and the parasympathetic division. Apparently, these two divisions fulfill different functions for the organism. Although both are active to some degree at all times, the sympathetic division becomes dominant during emergencies or stress. When you are confronted with an emergency, the sympathetic division prepares your body to cope with the emergency by speeding up your heart, dilating your pupils, inhibiting the activity of your gastrointestinal tract, and activating your adrenal glands. The adrenal glands produce *epinephrine* (sometimes termed *adrenaline*), a substance that flows to all parts of the body to produce effects which mimic and therefore reinforce the actions of the sympathetic nervous system. The sympathetic division also diverts blood from your internal organs to your muscles to prepare them for action.

Generally speaking, the actions of the parasympathetic division are the opposite of those of the sympathetic division. The parasympathetic division is more concerned with the vegetative functions of the body, such as digestion and the conservation of energy. For example, activation of the parasympathetic division stimulates the activity of the gastrointestinal system and slows the heart. Under normal circumstances, however, the two divisions of the autonomic nervous system maintain a balance or tone, so that normal body functions operate smoothly and effectively.

Central Nervous System

As we mentioned earlier, the central nervous system is composed of the brain and spinal cord. Most information coming from the internal and external environment, as well as all commands to the muscles and glands, are

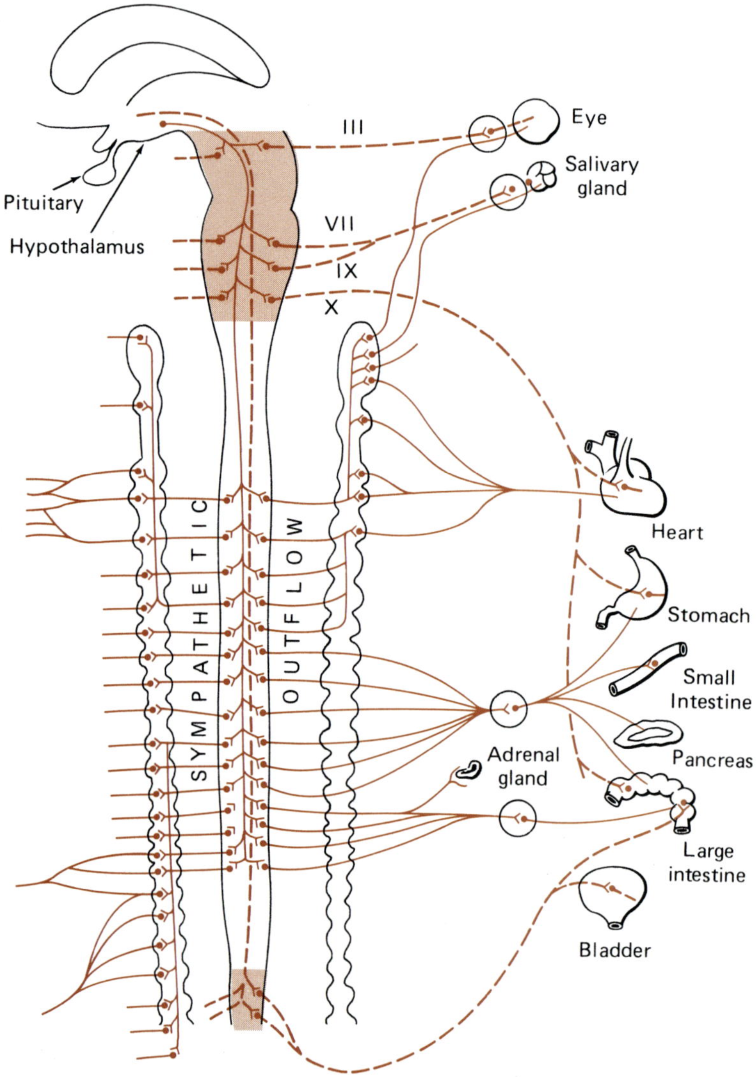

Figure 3.11 The general arrangement of the autonomic nervous system. The fibers from the hypothalamus that control the pituitary gland have been omitted; those to lower centers are shown in solid lines (sympathetic division) and broken lines (parasympathetic division). The portions of the brain stem and sacral cord from which the parasympathetic preganglionic fibers leave are shaded, and the sympathetic outflow from the thoracic and upper lumbar cord is labeled. Autonomic fibers to organs of the head and trunk are shown on the right side, while those on the left side represent the sympathetic outflow to blood vessels, sweat glands, and smooth muscle fibers attached to hairs. The roman numerals indicate cranial nerves. (From E. Gardner, *Fundamentals of Neurology* (5th ed.) Philadelphia: W. B. Saunders Company, 1968, p. 232. Reprinted by permission of author and publisher.)

transmitted by way of the peripheral nerves to and from the spinal cord. (Although cranial nerves enter and exit from the brain directly, all information coming from nerves below the level of the neck must relay through the spinal cord.)

In humans, the tissue making up the spinal cord is about the diameter of a little finger. A cross section of the spinal cord is shown schematically in figure 3.12. Note the butterfly-shaped area that forms the central portion. This area, called the spinal grey matter, is predominantly composed of cell bodies and small, unmyelinated nerve fibers. It is called grey matter to distinguish it from the so-called white matter that forms the outer portion of the spinal cord. White matter consists almost exclusively of myelinated nerve fibers, which give it a whitish appearance. Also shown are the dorsal roots through which afferent fibers enter the spinal cord, and the ventral roots through which motor or efferent fibers leave the spinal cord. These two roots eventually combine and branch out to form the peripheral nerves. The cell bodies of the dorsal root fibers are contained in the dorsal root ganglia at the periphery of the cord; the cell bodies of the ventral root fibers lie within the grey matter of the spinal cord. At the center of the spinal cord is the small *central canal,* which runs the length of the spinal cord and is connected to cavities in the brain. This canal is filled with a semiclear liquid known as *cerebrospinal fluid.*

The white matter of the spinal cord is a mass of nerve fiber bundles or *tracts* that connect the spinal cord and peripheral nerves to the many areas of the brain which receive sensory information and transmit messages to the muscles and glands. However, the spinal cord is also capable of controlling numerous important functions independently of the brain. These are called spinal reflexes. Simplified circuit diagrams of several spinal reflexes are described in box 3.5. These relatively simple behaviors mediated by the spinal cord have been used extensively as models for the more complicated behaviors mediated by the brain. Much of what we know about the activity of nerve cells and control of behavior has been derived from preliminary research on *spinal reflexes* and the neural connections that produce them.

The Brain

Figure 3.13 illustrates some of the important divisions and structures of the brain. During embryological development, the nervous system begins as an elongated tube. During de-

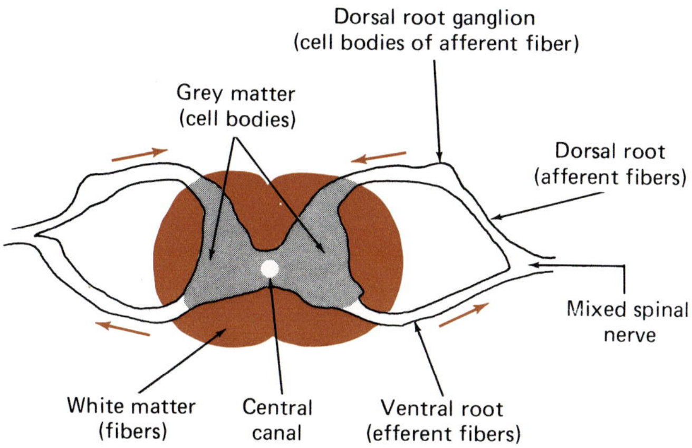

Figure 3.12 A diagrammatic cross section through the spinal cord illustrating its obvious features. Sensory information enters by way of the dorsal roots and motor information exits by way of the ventral roots.

Box 3.5
Spinal Reflexes

Schematic "wiring diagrams" of two spinal reflexes are illustrated in box figure 3.5. The one on the left is the *stretch reflex,* and the one on the right is the *flexion reflex.*

The stretch reflex involves only two neurons and is therefore the simplest of all the spinal reflexes. Because there is only one synapse between the sensory and motor fibers that participate in this reflex, it is called a *monosynaptic reflex.* The mechanisms by which the stretch reflex operates are fairly well understood. When a muscle is stretched slightly, as it is when a physician taps the tendon below your knee with a small hammer, sensory receptors in the muscle respond by producing action potentials in the afferent fibers. Afferent fibers from the muscle then synapse directly on motoneurons, and synaptic transmission takes place in response to these action potentials. The motor neurons then generate action potentials, which travel out the motor nerve, activate synaptic transmission between motor nerve fibers and the stretched muscle, and produce contraction. This entire chain of events usually takes place in a few milliseconds.

The flexion reflex has more than one synaptic connection in its circuit and is therefore called a *polysynaptic reflex.* The basic events in the flexion reflex are as follows: Some painful stimulus causes sensory fibers in the skin to respond. This information is transmitted to *interneurons* in the grey matter of the spinal cord, which relay the information to motoneurons. In turn, the motoneurons fire to produce withdrawal of the limb from the painful stimulus even before the information has reached the higher levels of the nervous system to be experienced as pain.

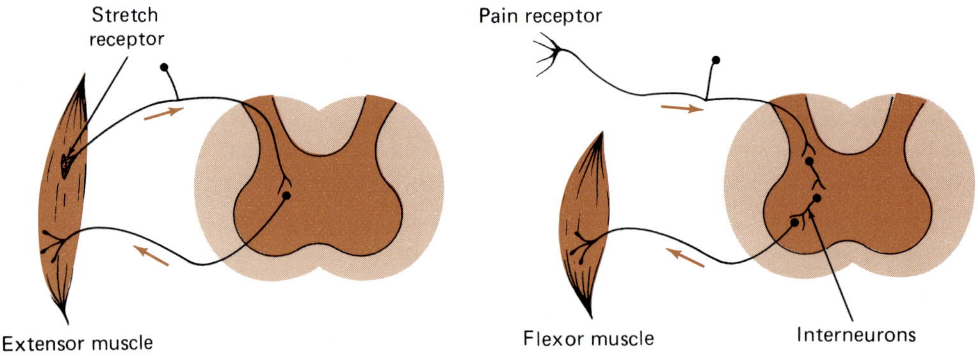

Box Figure 3.5 Spinal reflexes.

velopment, some areas of the nervous system expand more rapidly than others and eventually become the large, complicated, distorted structure you see in figure 3.13a. However, even in its mature state, the brain retains some of the characteristics of a long hollow tube. What was originally a central canal, running the length of the immature nervous system, becomes a series of distorted but interconnected cavities or *ventricles* at the center of the nervous system. These ventricles are interconnected along the length of the brain as well as to the central canal of the spinal cord. All of them contain cerebrospinal fluid.

Beginning with the lowest portion of the brain adjacent to the spinal cord, one can identify the medulla oblongata (or simply, medulla), which contains a number of important nuclei, including sensory and motor nuclei that receive or transmit information by way of the cranial nerves. Several of these nuclei are responsible for the automatic con-

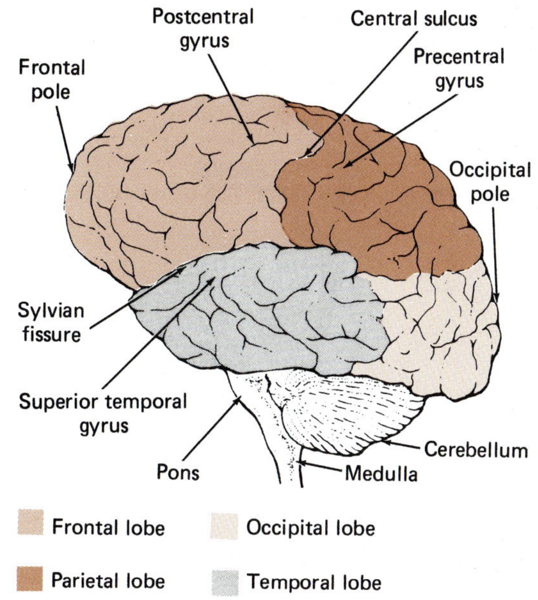

Figure 3.13a Surface views of the brain.

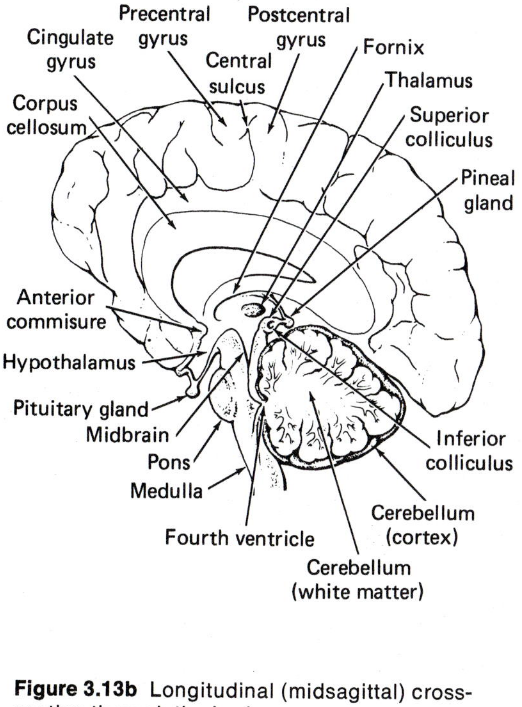

Figure 3.13b Longitudinal (midsagittal) cross-section through the brain.

trol of respiration, heart rate, and other vital functions. In addition, all nerve fibers that connect the spinal cord and the brain must pass through the medulla. On both sides of the medulla's central core, note the *reticular formation,* a central network of cells and fibers that runs the length of the *brain stem* (which includes all of the brain except the cerebral cortex). The reticular formation plays an important role in wakefulness and sleep as well as other behaviors.

The pons, which lies in front of the medulla, contains several cranial nerve nuclei as well as ascending and descending fibers that interconnect the brain and other structures in the nervous system. Notice the unique appearance of the pons in figure 3.13b: it bulges out at the bottom, forming a distinct bump along the length of the brain stem. This bump is formed by large numbers of fibers that wrap around the region of the pons some of which connect the *cerebellum* with the rest of the central nervous system. Some fibers passing downward from the cerebral cortex to the spinal cord also run through the pons. The derivation of the name of this area comes from its bulging appearance (pons is derived from the Latin word meaning bridge). The reticular formation forms the central core of the pons on both sides of the brain, as it does in the medulla.

The cerebellum, lying on top of the pons, is a large structure with a *cortex* or covering consisting of cell bodies that form regularly repeating convolutions and underlying white matter consisting of fibers that go to and from the cerebellar cortex. Deep within the cerebellum are the *cerebellar nuclei,* through which the information from the cerebellum must relay. Although it is not obvious in figure 3.13a, the cerebellum is composed of two large *lobes* that are connected to one another by the white matter within the cerebellum. The behavioral functions of the cerebellum are not well understood. For many years, the cerebellum was thought to be primarily a motor structure, responsible in part for the maintenance of coordination. Damage to the cerebellum in humans, for example, produces uncoordinated and jerky movements. However, recent evidence suggests that in addition to its role in bodily movement and coordination, the cerebellum may be involved in other kinds of behavior, including certain kinds of learning.

The traditional name for the region adjacent to the pons is the *midbrain.* The midbrain, like the medulla and the pons, contains many important nuclei and fiber systems. The most obvious nuclei are the *superior* and *inferior colliculi* (see fig. 3.13b). These four large nuclei, two on each side of the brain, form the top of the midbrain. The superior colliculi relay visual information and may play a role in certain types of visually guided behaviors. The inferior colliculi, lying just behind the superior colliculi, relay auditory information and may be involved in various types of auditory reflex functions such as turning the head toward the source of a sound. The *pineal gland,* which lies above the superior colliculi on the midline of the brain, is one of the few structures in the central nervous system that is not duplicated on both sides. Actually, it is a gland rather than a neural structure.

The reticular formation (shown in diagrammatic form in fig. 3.14) forms the central core of the brain on both sides of the entire brain stem. This central network of cells and fibers sends information upward toward the cerebral cortex and downward toward the spinal cord. It also has connections with many other parts of the brain, including the cerebellum, thalamus, hypothalamus, and limbic system. The reticular formation has been implicated as a control center for sleep and wakefulness since 1949, when Morruzzi and Magoun demonstrated that electrical stimulation of this structure produced not only modifications of motor behavior through its connections to the spinal cord but modifications of the electrical and behavioral signs of sleep and wakefulness through its ascending connections toward the cerebral cortex.

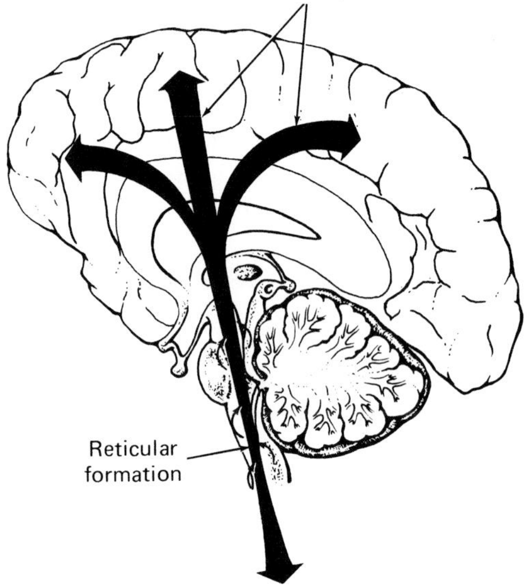

Figure 3.14 The reticular formation. The small arrows along the length of the reticular formation indicate that ascending and descending sensory and motor information is in part relayed into the reticular formation. The large arrows indicate that the reticular formation has widespread influences on the cerebral cortex (ascending projections) as well as influences on motor activity and spinal reflexes (descending projections).

Another important structure that runs along the length of the lower brain stem is the *raphé* or the so-called raphé nuclei. Lying very close to the midline of the brain stem, this group of nuclei contains the neurotransmitter serotonin, a chemical that is believed to be important in producing sleep.

The hypothalamus, located above the midbrain, is a small compact area that contains a number of nuclei, which, singly or in combination, appear to be involved in hunger and thirst, sexual behavior, sleep and wakefulness, temperature regulation, and other important behavioral functions. In addition, the hypothalamus plays an important role in the cen-

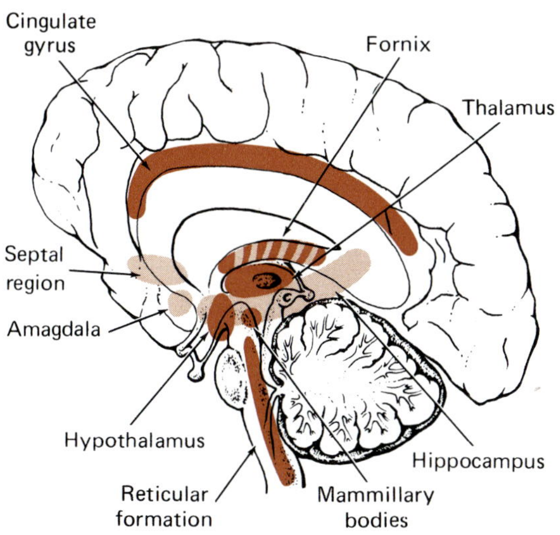

Figure 3.15 Some of the interconnected structures that make up the limbic system. Lighter shaded structures are behind darker shaded areas.

tral control of the autonomic nervous system. The pituitary gland, which lies just below the hypothalamus, is the master endocrine gland of the body. This gland mediates many physiological and behavioral functions, for example, sexual and maternal behavior; and, its activity is controlled by the hypothalamus. The functions of this important gland are discussed in more detail in Chapter 4.

The thalamus is buried in the center of the brain at the top of the brain stem, underneath the cerebral hemispheres. It contains three kinds of nuclei. (1) The sensory relay nuclei that relay sensory information to specific regions of the cerebral cortex from the spinal cord, the cranial nerves, and the lower portions of the brain. Thus, the thalamus is an extremely important relay center. (2) The association nuclei also relay information to the cerebral cortex but not to specific sensory areas (which we will describe in a moment). Instead they connect diffusely to regions of the cortex called *association areas,* which apparently are not involved in the reception of specific sensory information. (3) The intrinsic nuclei do not connect to the cerebral cortex but appear to have important functions apart from direct cortical connections. For example, they may be part of the system involved in the maintenance of sleep.

Limbic System

The major structures in the limbic system (pictured diagrammatically in fig. 3.15) include components from several different levels of the brain. For many years, the limbic system has been implicated in the control of motivated behavior such as emotion, aggressive behavior, sexual behavior, and the like. The limbic system includes many structures such as the *hippocampus* and *amygdala, septal region* and hypothalamus, as well as other nuclei and fibers that interconnect them. The human limbic system has also been implicated in the memory storage process. Removal of the temporal lobes, which include a major portion of the hippocampus on both sides, results in a specific and dramatic impairment of memory. Patients who have had their temporal lobes removed are unable to store new information in their long-term memories. In addition, research on aggression in animals and humans indicates that removal or stimulation of certain portions of the limbic system can produce a ferocious animal or a docile animal, depending on which area is treated.

The Cerebral Hemispheres

The cerebral hemispheres are the largest and most highly developed divisions of the mammalian brain. This is particularly obvious in the picture of the human brain shown in figure 3.14. Among other structures, the cerebral hemispheres contain the *basal ganglia* and the enormous cerebral cortex.

Although the nuclei that make up the basal ganglia are in the central nervous system, they have been called the basal ganglia by convention (you will recall that the term ganglion is usually applied to a group of cell bodies in the peripheral nervous system). The basal ganglia, which include three major nuclei on each side (the caudate nucleus, the putamen, and the globus pallidus, as illustrated diagrammatically in fig. 3.16), are buried within the large cerebral hemispheres. These ganglia are generally considered to have motor functions and are now believed to be involved in Parkinson's disease as well as Huntington's chorea (an inherited disease that was discussed in Chapter 2). The jerky (choreic), uncoordinated movements that characterize parkinsonism and Huntington's chorea apparently result in part from deterioration of the basal ganglia and certain nuclei that are connected to them.

The cerebral hemispheres are the most obvious structures in the human brain. In man they virtually cover the rest of the brain. In figure 3.13, note that the cerebral cortex in humans is highly convoluted—that is, it consists of small lobules or *gyri* (singular: gyrus) that are separated by grooves or *sulci* (singular: sulcus). All these sulci and gyri have specific names; several are indicated in figure 3.13. The entire outer surface of the cerebral hemispheres is grey matter consisting of cell bodies and some fibers. (As you view the surface of the brain, you can only see about one-third of the surface of the cerebral cortex; the other two-thirds are buried within the convolutions.) The inner portions of the cerebral hemispheres are composed of white matter or myelinated fibers. The two symmetrical cerebral hemispheres are connected by a large band of fibers termed the *corpus callosum,* which lies at the base of the longitudinal fissure separating the two hemispheres. Severing the corpus callosum in animals and humans produces some startling effects, as you will see later.

Some areas of the cerebral cortex receive direct sensory information and are presumed to underlie many aspects of sensory perception. These areas and their functional labels are shown in figure 3.17. The visual cortex,

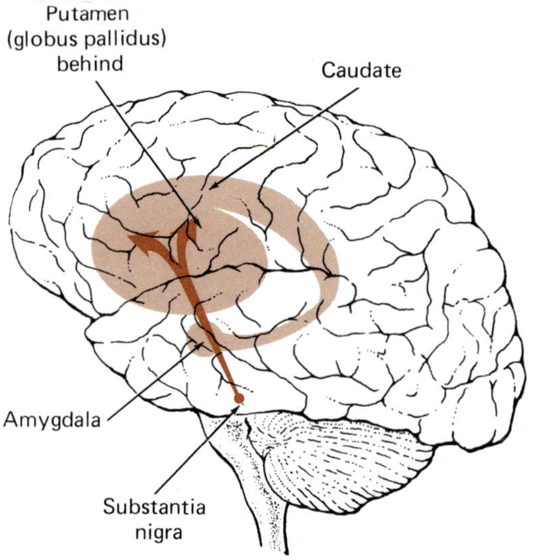

Figure 3.16 The basal ganglia, including the *putamen, globus pallidus,* and *caudate nucleus* and their connection to the amygdala. Degeneration of connections to the basal ganglia from the *substantia nigra* is involved in Parkinson's disease.

located at the back of the brain, receives its information from the *lateral geniculate nuclei* of the thalamus, which in turn, relays sensory information from the optic nerves. The auditory cortex, which lies along the *sylvian fissure,* receives information directly from the *medial geniculate nuclei,* the specific sensory relay nuclei in the thalamus that relay auditory information. The somatosensory cortex receives fiber projections from its relay nuclei in the thalamus which transmit somatic sensory information such as touch, pain, temperature, pressure, and the like.

The motor cortex gives rise to the so-called *pyramidal tracts.* These tracts descend through the entire brain and end in the opposite side of the spinal cord on interneurons and motoneurons, which ultimately control the muscles. Thus the left hemisphere controls the right side of the body, and vice versa.

One important feature of the sensory and motor areas of the cerebral cortex is their topographical organization. For the sensory

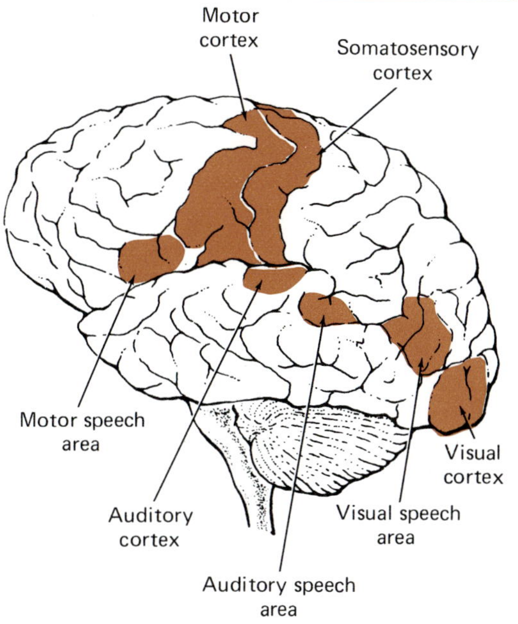

Figure 3.17 Localization of function on the cerebral cortex. In addition to the major sensory and motor areas, note the areas involved in speech and language.

areas, this means that the receptor surfaces on the body are mapped out spatially on the cerebral cortex. For example, the receptor surface for the visual cortex would be the *retina* of the eye. Thus for each point on the retina, there is a corresponding point or set of points on the visual cortex to which information is projected from the retina (with intermediate connections in the thalamus). Similarly, for each point on the body surface, there is a specific point or set of points on the somatosensory cortex, to which information from a specific point on the body surface is carried. And finally, the muscles of the body are represented spatially in the motor cortex. Thus, each muscle or group of muscles is represented at a corresponding point on the motor cortex. This topographic organization of the cerebral cortex is illustrated in box 3.6.

The bulk of the cerebral cortex is neither sensory nor motor cortex but *association cortex.* It is called association cortex because it does not appear to be strictly sensory nor motor. Although a wealth of information is available on the association cortex, we have a long way to go before we will fully understand its functions. However, the following features may provide us with some insights. The amount of the association cortex, relative to the other cortex, increases as the apparent learning ability of different species increases. Humans appear to have the most, while lower organisms have less. This seems to have been a trend in the evolution of primates.

In humans, there are a number of fairly well defined functional areas within the association cortex. For example, speech and language appear to be represented in several association areas. Interestingly, speech appears to be localized in the dominant hemisphere, which in humans is usually the left one. Stimulation as well as accidental or surgical lesion in the speech areas will produce a variety of problems, ranging from the inability to name common objects properly to a complete inability to speak or write. One preparation that has proved to be particularly useful in determining functional differences between the dominant and nondominant hemispheres is the split-brain animal or human. In most cases the corpus callosum, which connects the two hemispheres, is surgically severed for medical reasons; a few individuals are born without a corpus callosum. In both instances, information from the eyes or hands, under carefully controlled experimental conditions, may be channelled to only one side of the brain. Because the corpus callosum is cut, this information does not pass into the other hemisphere. Thus one hemisphere can be trained to recognize an item and the other hemisphere will not know what it is. The trick in this technique is to be sure that only one side of the brain receives this

Box 3.6

Sensory and Motor Homunculi

Box figure 3.6 illustrates the topographical organization of the *motor cortex* (top) and the *somatosensory cortex* (bottom). As shown in figure 3.13a the motor cortex lies just anterior to (in front of) the central *sulcus* while the somatosensory cortex lies immediately behind the central sulcus. Note in the cross section of the motor cortex that the muscles in different parts of the body are controlled by different regions. For example, the muscles of the toes, ankles, and legs are controlled by the area at the top of the motor cortex, whereas the muscles of the face and neck are controlled by the region farthest from the top. In other words, the areas of the motor cortex that control the muscles in different parts of the body are arranged in a definite sequence: stimulation of the area controlling the hands will produce movements of the hands, stimulation of the area controlling the lips will produce movements of the lips, and so forth. A similar situation exists in the somatosensory cortex. Thus tactile stimulation of the toes or feet will be received by neurons in the upper portion of the somatosensory cortex, whereas touching the lips or face will activate lower regions of the somatosensory cortex.

These examples illustrate several important general principles with regard to the way the nervous system is organized. First, the parts of the nervous system that control different parts of the body's musculature and represent different areas of a receptor surface such as the surface of the body are spatially organized. Second, in general the finer the control you have over a particular region of musculature, the greater is the area of the motor cortex needed to control it. Similarly, the more a particular receptor surface of the body is used and the more sensitive it is to sensory stimulation, the greater is the area of the sensory cortex devoted to receiving sensory information from it. Note, for instance, that the area of the motor cortex controlling the hands is much larger than the area controlling the hip. Also notice that a much larger amount of the somatosensory cortex is devoted to receiving sensory information from the hands and lips than from the leg, for example.

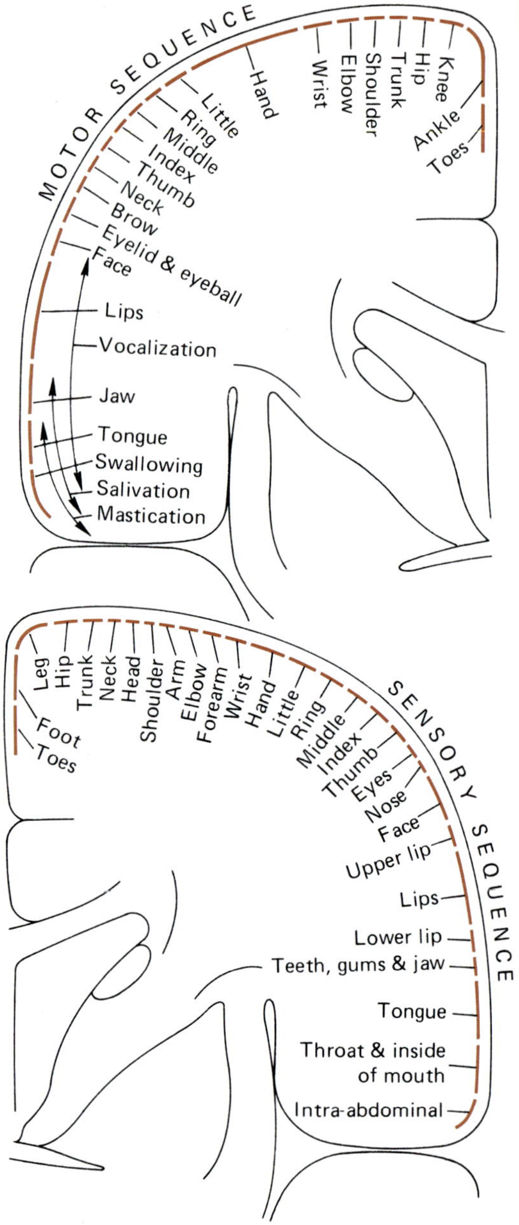

Box Figure 3.6 The motor sequence represents a cross-sectional view through the precentral gyrus. The sensory sequence is a cross-sectional view through the post central gyrus. (From Rasmussen and Penfield. Reprinted from FEDERATION PROCEEDINGS *6:* 452–460, 1947 by permission.)

information. Thus, the subject must use one hand to perform a task, and he is then asked to repeat the task with the other hand. Depending upon the task, he often may not be able to transfer the information to the other hemisphere. It is almost like having two separate brains that operate independently of one another. Because the information that goes into one eye or one hand is, under normal circumstances, also available to the other eye or hand, a split-brain individual is indistinguishable from a normal person. However, under carefully controlled laboratory conditions, differences can be observed. (See box 3.7.)

Box 3.7

The Split Brain

To obtain a split-brain preparation, the corpus callosum and the optic chiasm are severed. Sperry (1964) and Gazzaniga (1967) have begun working with humans whose corpus callosums have been cut during surgery. The results indicate that certain functions are localized in either the dominant or nondominant hemisphere. The following illustrates data obtained during carefully controlled experiments.

> *When the information (visual or tactile) was presented to the dominant left hemisphere, the patients were able to deal with and describe it quite normally, both orally and in writing. For example, when a picture of a spoon was shown in the right visual field or a spoon was placed in the right hand, all the patients readily identified and described it. They were able to read out written messages, and to perform problems in calculation, that were presented to the left hemisphere. . . .*
>
> *In contrast when the same information was presented to the right hemisphere it failed to elicit such spoken or written responses. . . .*
>
> *Yet, the right hemisphere is not in all respects inferior or subordinate to the left. Tests have demonstrated that it excells the left in some specialized functions. As an example, tests by us and by Bogen, have shown that in these patients, the left hand is capable of arranging blocks to match a pictured design, and of drawing a cube in three dimensions, whereas the right hand, deprived of instructions from the right hemisphere, could not perform either of these tasks. . . .*
>
> *All the evidence indicates that separation of the hemisphere created two independent spheres of consciousness within a single cranium. . . . There is, to be sure, hemispheric inequality in the present cases. . . . It is entirely possible that if a human brain were divided in a very young person, both hemispheres could . . . separately and independently develop mental functions of a high order. . . . (Gazzaniga, 1967)*

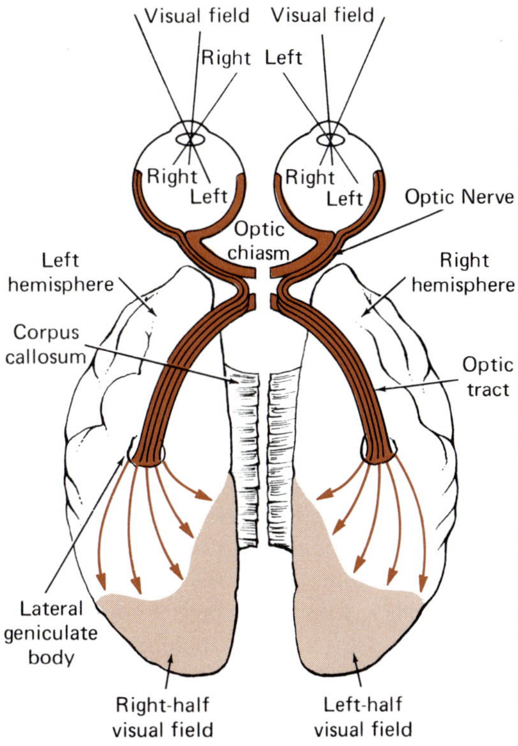

Box Figure 3.7 Visual fields and the visual centers of the brain are related, as illustrated in this diagram of the monkey brain. If the optic chiasm and corpus callosum are cut, the normal overlap of visual fields is eliminated, and each eye is capable of feeding information to only one side of the brain. (From "The great cerebral commisure," by R. Sperry. Copyright 1964 by Scientific American, Inc. All rights reserved.)

Summary

In this chapter we have presented an overview of the nervous system, including a discussion of some of the techniques commonly used to study it, the principal elements of the nervous system—the nerve cells—and the structural features of the nervous system.

To study the nervous system, physiological psychologists rely on a number of standard techniques as well as many that are derived from other disciplines. With the time-honored ablation and lesion techniques, in which some area of the nervous system is disconnected or destroyed, the psychologist seeks to elucidate the functions of the area. He can also use electrical or chemical stimulation techniques to discover the principal functions of different areas of the nervous system. And by using the recording techniques, he can take advantage of the fact that the nervous system generates a variety of electrical signals, such as the spontaneous EEG, evoked potentials, and the electrical discharges of single cells.

The neuron or nerve cell is the building block of the nervous system. Although neurons come in a wide variety of forms, they possess similar characteristics. For example, all neurons have cell bodies as well as extensions that either conduct information toward the cell (dendrites) or away from the cell body (axons). Like other cells found in the body, they possess a resting membrane potential, which results from a differential distribution of charged molecules (ions) that exist in the fluids inside and outside the neuron. However, unlike most cells, neurons are able to alter this resting membrane potential—that is, to generate action potentials, which are the means by which information is conducted from the cell body along the axon to the axon terminals. Invasion of the axon terminals by an action potential then triggers synaptic transmission, during which small packets of a chemical transmitter substance are released from the axon terminals to diffuse across the synaptic cleft between the terminal of one neuron and the receptive portion of another and alter the permeability of the postsynaptic neuron, such that synaptic excitation or inhibition can occur. Excitation usually involves a depolarization of the membrane of the postsynaptic cell, while inhibition involves a hyperpolarization of the postsynaptic cell. Depolarization (called an excitatory postsynaptic potential or EPSP), if it reaches the threshold of the postsynaptic cell, will cause it to fire an action potential; hyperpolarization (termed an IPSP) on the other hand, will prevent the neuron from firing.

Groups of cell bodies and nerve fibers and associated nonneural elements (e.g., blood cells and glia) make up the structure of the nervous system. The vertebrate brain begins as a long, segmented, hollow tube. But during the process of development, the tube becomes a large complicated organ with several large subdivisions. The nervous tissue of the central nervous system is encased within the bones of the skull and spine, whereas the nervous tissue of the peripheral nervous system lies outside these bony encasements. The peripheral nervous system is made up of groups of cell bodies (ganglia) and nerves and has two major divisions. The somatic division carries sensory information from the external world to the central nervous system and carries commands out to the muscles that control bodily movement. The autonomic division, which is concerned with sensory and motor functions of the glands and smooth muscles and is involved in emotional behavior, also has two divisions: the sympathetic branch, which prepares the organism for stress and the parasympathetic branch, which serves more vegetative functions and conserves bodily energy.

The central nervous system includes the

brain and spinal cord. The spinal cord carries information to and from the brain and is the point of entry and exit for the spinal nerves. The twelve cranial nerves enter and exit from the brain directly. The spinal cord is also capable of certain elementary behaviors called spinal reflexes. The medulla oblongata, the most posterior division of the brain, contains a number of important nuclei and fiber systems that connect the spinal cord with the rest of the brain. Adjacent to the medulla are the cerebellum, which is in part responsible for bodily coordination, and the pons, which serves as a bridge between the cerebellum and the rest of the nervous system as well as between the brain and the spinal cord. The midbrain contains the superior and inferior colliculi, which relay visual and auditory information. Between the midbrain and the large cerebral hemispheres are the thalamus, hypothalamus, and the pituitary gland.

The largest part of the human brain consists of the cerebral hemispheres, which contain the basal ganglia and cerebral cortex. The two hemispheres are connected to one another by the corpus callosum, the largest single bundle of fibers in the nervous system. The human cerebral cortex is made up of sensory, motor, and association areas. It is the cerebral cortex that makes man uniquely human—that is, capable of language, speech, and other complicated behaviors. The reticular formation, important for sleep and wakefulness, makes up the core of the brain from the medulla to the midbrain. The limbic system is another interconnected group of structures, including the hypothalamus, hippocampus, septal nuclei, amygdala, and others, all interconnected in complex ways to form an important structural circuit that may be involved in motivation, emotion, and perhaps memory.

4

Hormones and Behavior

When asked to define a hormone, a student once said: "A hormone is, well, like a female hormone. It causes menstruation and cramps and female troubles." We now know that the lack of a hormone which was previously present is a more likely explanation for these "troubles," but the student was correct in thinking that hormones were involved. Let us try to refine our understanding of hormones somewhat.

The word hormone comes from the Greek *hormon,* meaning messenger. But to be useful, the word must be more narrowly defined. First, a *hormone* is a *chemical* messenger. Second, it is secreted, or released by an organ into the blood. And third, it is carried by the blood to a target organ, where its message is received and acted upon. This process of secreting a specific chemical messenger into the blood is also called an *endocrine function*—as opposed to the *exocrine function* of organs such as the tear glands or sweat glands, which do not secrete their products into the blood. Some organs have both an endocrine and an exocrine function. The pancreas, for example, releases insulin into the blood as well as digestive enzymes into the gut. The testis not only secretes male hormones into the blood but manufactures spermatozoa and releases them into the genital tract.

The idea that a specific organ can manufacture a chemical substance that has widespread effects on the body has existed for a long time, as evidenced by the centuries-old practice of removing the gonads of (castrating) male animals that are not needed for breeding. The desired effect is a less aggressive, more tractable animal, although this is not invariable. At various times in history, the operation has also been performed on boys, who thus become eunuchs. In some instances, this was done to produce harem guards who would pose no threat to their master's rights and prerogatives concerning the women in the harem. In other instances, boys with good soprano voices were castrated so that their voices would not deepen at puberty. Apparently such men, although infertile, were not always incapable of copulation. And at least one eunuch became a soldier and eventually rose to the rank of general, a profession and position not ordinarily associated with timidity.

These early practices, experiments, or outrages (as you will) had little effect on the development of the science of endocrinology during the late 1800s and early 1900s. Although surgical ablation of a gland continued to be an important technique, experimenters began to develop other useful procedures such as (1) transplanting a gland to another location in the body where its function could be studied more closely—for example, attaching a bit of uterine tissue to the back of the eye where it could be observed through the pupil, (2) preparing extracts from certain glands (obtained from slaughterhouses) and administering these extracts to experimental subjects while observing them carefully for possible reactions, and (3) connecting the blood systems of two animals so that the effects of stimulating one could be studied in the other.

Unfortunately, early investigators worked with animals in which the nerves had been cut or destroyed to avoid the possibility that the effects they observed could be caused by the action of nervous tissue rather than glandular tissue. Because of this experimental practice, we still tend to think of the nervous system and the endocrine system as separate integrative communication systems, when in reality they usually do not work alone or at cross purposes. Thus to say that one system functions independently of the other is nearly always erroneous. Different kinds of communicative tasks may be allocated unequally to each system, but both are engaged in coordinating a series of responses.

Let's examine some of the similarities and differences in the two systems. First, the nervous system is specialized for *speed of response;* it can transmit a message from the brain to the big toe in less than one-tenth of a second. The endocrine system, on the other hand, is specialized for *sustained response,* and its actions are usually slower. Because the endocrine system depends on the blood to transmit its chemical messengers, it is limited to the speed of circulation. Note, however, that this is a *relative* slowness. Endocrine responses can be elicited rather quickly; for instance, the letdown of milk in response to a suckling stimulus occurs in a matter of seconds.

Second, both systems use chemical mediators or messengers. Sometimes it is the same chemical. For example, some neurons release norepinephrine during synaptic transmission. Norepinephrine is also a product of one of the endocrine glands, the adrenal medulla, which is located next to the kidneys and is derived, embryologically, from nervous tissue.

Two additional phenomena—*neuroendocrine reflexes* and *neurosecretion*—further emphasize the interaction between the two systems. We have already mentioned one neuroendocrine reflex: the letdown of milk. Stimulation of the nipples by the suckling young is coded into neural impulses that reach the brain through neural pathways. The brain integrates this information and instructs the pituitary gland to release *oxytocin* into the blood. When the oxytocin makes its way to the mammary tissue and causes the release, or letdown of milk, the neuroendocrine reflex is completed. This process also illustrates neurosecretion because the oxytocin that is released from the pituitary has been manufactured by *neurons* in the hypothalamus, transported down the axons of these neurons into the pituitary, and stored there awaiting a release signal.

Another example of a neuroendocrine reflex is temperature control in birds and mammals. As outside temperatures drop, this information is sent to the brain through neural pathways. Again, the brain integrates the information and signals the hypothalamus to release a hormone that causes the pituitary to release a *thyroid stimulating hormone.* This thyroid stimulating hormone is carried to the thyroid gland in the neck, where it triggers the release of thyroid hormones. The thyroid hormones are then carried by the blood to all parts of the body, where they cause the rate of cellular metabolism to increase. As a result, the body generates more heat and body temperature is maintained. Although other processes, such as shivering, muscular activity, or even standing near a radiator may be involved, the point is clear: the endocrine and nervous systems *cooperate* rather than conflict with one another.

Ordinarily, when we think about the endocrine system, we think in terms of hormone release, which is followed by a number of physiological changes, including behavioral ones. However, the reverse is equally true—that is, a behavior can lead to the release of a hormone. Quite often it is the behavior of another individual that triggers this release. If an airline pilot is suddenly confronted by a hijacker, the danger he perceives may cause his adrenal medulla to release adrenalin (epinephrine) and noradrenalin (norepinephrine) into his blood and thus prepare his body to cope with the emergency by affecting his behavior and other physiological responses.

Ring doves, smaller-sized relatives of the pigeon, exhibit a complex and striking reproductive pattern in which a veritable chain of behavior-endocrine links is forged, as you will notice in box 4.1.

In the examples of hormonal actions we have described thus far, a certain degree of oversimplification has been necessary. Hormones seldom work alone; they are influenced not only by the nervous system but by the actions of other hormones as well. There is usually a complex interplay among these elements.

Later in this chapter, we will return to a detailed discussion of the relationship between hormones and behavior. But first, you will need to become familiar with some of the major endocrine glands of the body and the hormones they produce.

The Endocrine Glands and Their Products

Pituitary Gland

The *pituitary gland,* or *hypophysis,* is located just under the brain, immediately in front of the optic chiasm and above the bony, hard palate of the mouth. Despite its inaccessible location, malfunctions of the pituitary gland quickly become apparent because of the gland's important role in controlling many other endocrine glands in the body. For many years, the pituitary was called the "master gland" since it appeared to control all endocrine functions. We now know, however, that essentially all pituitary functions are closely controlled by the hypothalamus, which in turn is responsive to higher neural centers and to levels of hormones in the blood.

The adult pituitary gland of mammals consists of an anterior portion, the *adenohypophysis,* and a posterior portion, the *neurohypophysis.* During embryonic development, the adenohypophysis grows upward from the tissue forming the roof of the mouth, while the neurohypophysis descends from the base of the developing brain. Because of its location at the roof of the mouth, the ancient Greeks thought the pituitary was the source of phlegm, one of the four humors of the body. Remnants of these outmoded concepts are still with us in the form of the name pituitary (from "pituita," meaning mucus) and the use of the adjective "humoral" to refer to endocrine products.

In figure 4.1 you will notice that the neurohypophysis is divided into two parts, the pars

Box 4.1

The Reproductive Behavior of Ring Doves

If a male or female ring dove is placed alone in a cage with nesting material, nothing much in the way of reproductive behavior takes place: the female does not build a nest or lay eggs; the male does not show courting behavior. Place the birds together, however, and changes soon become evident. The sight and sound of the female stimulate the male to begin a characteristic behavior toward her, the bow-coo, intermixed with strutting about. After several hours of this, the couple announces it has selected a nest site by crouching in a particular place and uttering a distinctive coo.

Both birds participate in building the nest: the male's main job is to fetch nest material and bring it to the female, who stands in place and weaves the nest. During the week or so of nest building, the birds copulate. The female becomes "broody" near the end of this period. She remains in the nest and is difficult to dislodge should this be tried. After seven to eleven days, she lays one egg, usually in the late afternoon, followed by a second the next morning. The birds then take turns sitting on the eggs, with the female assuming about seventy-five percent of the duty. In about fourteen days the eggs hatch, and both parents begin regurgitating a cheesy substance ("crop milk") from their crops to feed the squabs until they are about two weeks old. Gradually, the parents become less willing to feed them, and the whole reproductive cycle may begin anew.

Analysis of this reproductive sequence has revealed a number of relationships between hormones and behavior. The bow-coo and strutting of the male are dependent on the presence of his male hormones. If he is castrated, he does not respond in this way. The response of the female, in turn, depends not so much on the male's presence as on his display. If his display is adequate, her pituitary begins to release gonadotrophic hormones that cause her ovaries to develop the eggs and secrete the female hormones, estrogen and progesterone. Under the influence of these hormones, chiefly progesterone, she becomes "broody" and ready to incubate eggs. These events and behaviors are augmented by the presence of the nesting material and perhaps by the act of nest building itself. The sight of his mate sitting on the nest, both before and after there are eggs in it, stimulates release of the pituitary hormone *prolactin* in the male. The same hormone is being produced by the female at about this time. With the rising level of prolactin in the blood, the lining of the crop proliferates until the crop may be triple its usual weight. This lining is sloughed off and remains in the crop until it is regurgitated for feeding the squabs. The *behaviors* of regurgitation and squab-feeding are also largely dependent on prolactin.

After the squabs are hatched, visual and contact stimuli from them serve to help maintain prolactin levels in their parents for the necessary period. As the squabs mature, they become less effective stimuli for their parents, and if temperature and other environmental conditions are right, the parents may begin another reproductive sequence that culminates in another family.

nervosa and the median eminence, while the adenohypophysis consists of three parts, the pars tuberalis, pars intermedia, and pars distalis. Only the *pars nervosa, pars distalis* and *median eminence* are relevant to our present discussion.

The pars nervosa of the neurohypophysis contains hormones that raise blood pressure (pressor factors), retain fluids in the body (antidiuretic factors), and induce contractions of the uterus as well as the letdown of milk (oxytocic factors). We have already mentioned oxytocin's role in the letdown of milk in the mammary glands. By causing uterine contractions, oxytocin aids in expelling the fetus during the process of birth, or *parturition,* and may help to transport spermatozoa after copulation. These oxytocic effects differ somewhat in different animals and are modulated by the presence of other

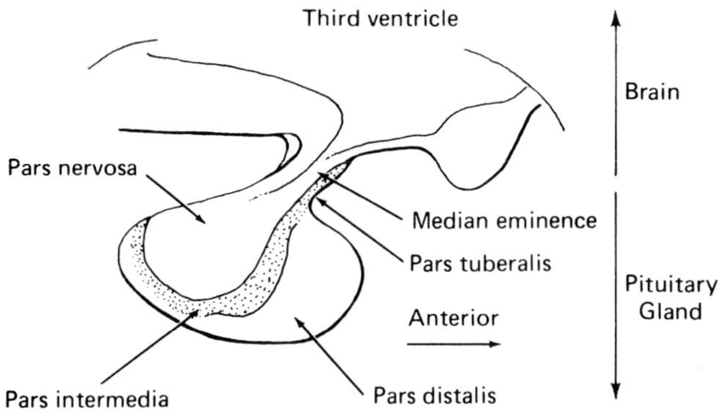

Figure 4.1 Diagram of the human pituitary gland showing relationship of parts derived from neural tissue (pars nervosa and median eminence) and parts derived from buccal (mouth) tissue (pars intermedia, pars tuberalis, and pars distalis). (From *A Textbook of Comparative Endocrinology,* Gorbman, G., and Bern, H. A. Copyright 1962 by John Wiley & Sons Inc. Reprinted by permission of John Wiley & Sons Inc.)

hormones. The hormones released from the pars nervosa are not manufactured by the pituitary but by nerve cells within the hypothalamus. They are then transported within the axons of these neurons to the pars nervosa, where they are stored. Neurons from the hypothalamus transmit the control signal for release of these hormones from the pituitary into the blood.

The pars distalis region of the adenohypophysis is the largest single area in the pituitary and secretes the most hormones (six). Three of these hormones act on the gonads, or sex glands, and are therefore called *gonadotropins.* The fourth is a growth (or *somatotrophic*) hormone; the fifth is a thyroid-stimulating (or *thyrotrophic*) hormone, and the sixth, which acts on the adrenal glands, is called an *adrenocorticotrophic hormone.* Although descriptive, the names of these hormones do not necessarily indicate all their important functions.

One of the three gonadotropins is called *follicle stimulating hormone,* or FSH. FSH stimulates the growth and maturation of the Graafian (egg) follicles in the female ovary. In the male testis, it acts synergistically with a second gonadotropin—*luteinizing hormone* (LH)—to stimulate production of spermatozoa. In females of most species, a surge of LH released from the pituitary will cause the Graafian follicles to enlarge and rupture—the process of ovulation. Under the influence of LH, the resulting cavity refills with a yellowish (luteal) material and becomes a temporary endocrine gland called a *corpus luteum.* The corpus luteum secretes the hormone called progesterone which is important in maintaining pregnancy.

Together, FSH and LH are also important factors in the synthesis and release of ovarian hormones, the *estrogens.* In the male, LH stimulates interstitial cells in the testes to produce male hormones, or *androgens.* For this reason, LH is sometimes called interstitial cell stimulating hormone (ICSH). These androgens are necessary for development of male characteristics and for maturation of spermatozoa.

In some species, the existence of the corpus luteum, as well as its progesterone-secreting function, depend on the third gonadotropin, the *luteotrophic* hormone (LTH or *prolactin*). In addition to maintaining the corpus luteum, LTH acts synergistically with estrogen to promote growth of the duct system of the mammary glands and, together with progesterone, on the lobular-alveolar system of the mammary glands. And together with hormones produced by other glands, it initiates and maintains milk secretion from the mammary tissue. The function of LTH in male mammals remains to be established. In some birds, LTH stimulates the development of "crop milk," a cheesy mass of cells developed from the epithelial lining of the crop, which both parents feed their young (see box 4.1).

Growth hormone (STH), as its name implies, stimulates growth, chiefly of skeletal and muscular structures. Lack of STH in childhood results in a stunting of growth, or *dwarfism*. If additional growth hormone can be administered to the child, he will often develop normally. Excessive STH in childhood causes *gigantism,* a condition characterized by excessive tallness (without correspondingly greater strength) and decreased life expectancy. Sometimes the secretion of excess STH begins in adult life, perhaps as a result of a pituitary tumor. In this situation, a condition known as *acromegaly* develops, and results in the disfigurement shown in figure 4.2.

The major target of the thyrotrophic hormone (TSH) is the thyroid gland. TSH controls the function of secretory cells in the thyroid in three ways: it causes them to proliferate—to the extent of tumorous overgrowth or *goiter* under certain circumstances, it causes them to take up iodine and synthesize thyroid hormones, and it stimulates release of thyroid hormones into the blood. The chief result of these actions is to speed up cellular metabolism by way of the thyroid hormones. As we mentioned earlier, warm-blooded animals will utilize this mechanism to speed up cellular metabolism as a means of maintaining body temperature.

The adrenocorticotrophic hormone (ACTH) stimulates production of steroid (fat soluble) hormones by parts of the adrenal glands. These steroid hormones, in turn, are involved in a number of activities, including anti-inflammatory actions, protection from bacterial invasion, and perhaps even sex drive, or libido.

Like the hormones of the pars nervosa in the neurohypophysis, those of the adenohypophysis are also controlled by the brain. However, it took some good detective work to find out how because for all practical purposes, no neural connections exist between the hypothalamus and the anterior pituitary. It is now established that the hormones secreted by the adenohypophysis are controlled by yet other hormones, or factors, which are secreted by cells in the *median eminence* of the neurohypophysis and nearby hypothalamic areas. These hormones are released into the blood and carried about one inch to

Figure 4.2 Acromegaly. The patient is shown at age 24 (**a**), before the onset of the malady, (**b**) at age 29, at the time of onset, (**c**) at age 37, and (**d**) at age 42, when acromegalic changes are evident. (From A. Grollman, *Essentials of Endocrinology,* Philadelphia: J. P. Lippincott, 2nd ed. 1947, p. 212.)

the adenohypophysis. By this means the brain controls adenohypophyseal function just as surely as if it had direct neural connections. Evidence indicates that at least nine substances (hormones or factors) from the median eminence and hypothalamus are involved in controlling the functions of the adenohypophysis. Some of these substances cause synthesis or release of a particular pituitary hormone and are called releasing factors (−RF) or releasing hormones (−RH). LH-RH, for example, leads to the release of luteinizing hormone by the pituitary. Others inhibit or prevent release of a particular hormone and are called inhibitory factors or hormones; for example, LTH-IH inhibits the release of prolactin.

Thyroid

The *thyroid gland,* in most species, is located in the neck region, and in mammals it is a bilobed or H-shaped structure. Its interior is made up of a large number of follicles that are filled with thyroid hormones. The thyroid is the only endocrine gland that stores its hormone product in an extracellular space or follicle. There are two principal thyroid hormones, *thyroxin* and *triiodotyrosine;* both are built up from iodine and the amino acid tyrosine. The thyroid is essentially the only place in the body where iodine is accumulated and it has even been defined as "that tissue which accumulates iodine."

In some parts of the world so little iodine occurs in nature that *goiter* is a frequent problem. Goiter is the proliferation of thyroid tissue caused by iodine deficiency. It has been known since the twelfth century that feeding burnt seaweed to persons suffering from goiter alleviates the problem. Today we know that the seaweed contained large amounts of iodine and we now avoid goiter by using iodized salt at the table.

Although thyroid hormones have a vast array of effects on bodily processes, a most important one is the speedup of metabolism. As mentioned previously, the rate of metabolism can be increased by lowering the environmental temperature until TSH and thyroid hormones are brought into play to cause increased oxygen consumption and generation of more cellular heat. Thyroid hormones are also intimately involved in the following processes:

1. *Metamorphosis of amphibian larvae.* If tadpoles are fed thyroid hormones, they develop prematurely into tiny frogs. Alternatively, if thyroid tissue is removed from tadpoles, giant tadpoles result.
2. *General growth.* Thyroid hormones act in synergy with STH to promote growth. The thyroid hormones probably aid chiefly in differentiation of tissue. For example, they may cause the ossification and maturation of the epiphysis (end part) of bone, rather than affect its length. The growth and eruption of teeth are responsive to thyroid hormones, as are the horns of sheep and antlers of deer.
3. *Reproduction.* Adult reproductive behavior is delayed or missing if thyroid hormone is lacking. In females, estrous cycles, fertility, and lactation are adversely affected; in males, testicular growth, accessory gland growth, and fertility are likewise affected.
4. *Development and functioning of the nervous system.* Neural tissue probably is directly responsive to thyroid hormones. If these hormones are missing or in short supply, the result is a smaller brain, delayed maturation, fewer neurons, and a reduced amount of myelin. Neural function is, of course, depressed. An insufficient supply of thyroid hormones in the growing child may result in dwarfism and mental retardation, or *cretinism* (see fig. 4.3a). Hypofunction in the adult leads to a condition known as *myxedema,* characterized by slow mental activity, lowered basal metabolic rate, lack of energy, and puffy facial skin. This condition responds well

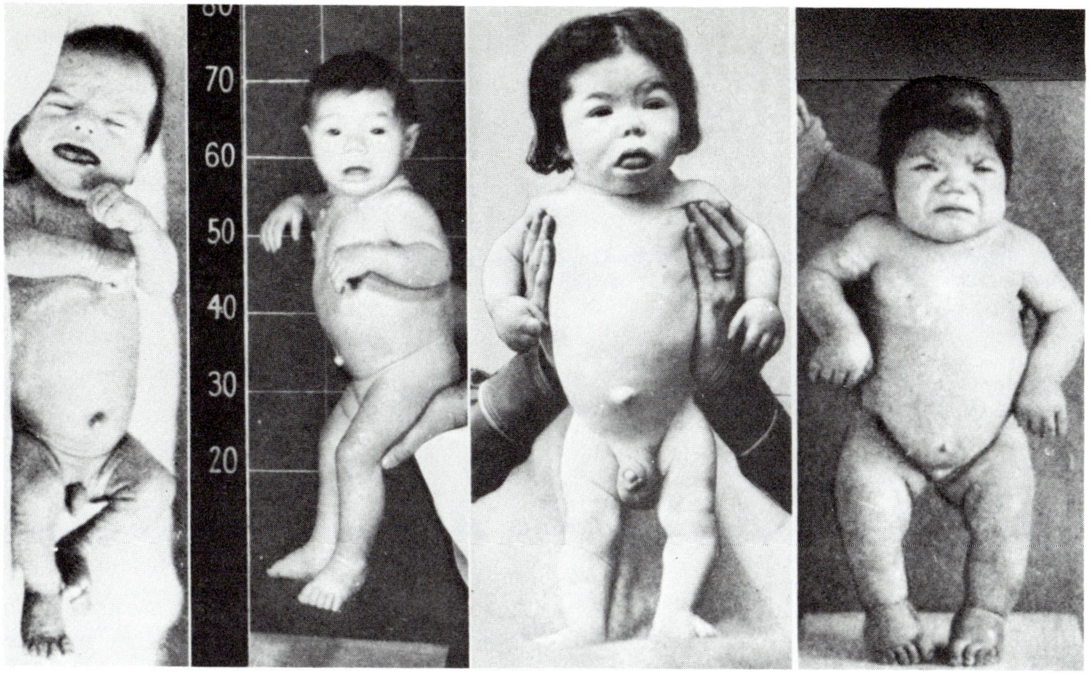

Figure 4.3a Cretin children. Cases of arrested physical and mental development caused by an early deficiency of thyroid hormones. (From Wilkins and Lawson, *Endocrine Disorders in Childhood and Adolescence,* 3rd Ed. Courtesy of Charles C Thomas, Publisher, Springfield, Ill.)

to treatment with thyroid hormones. Sometimes excess hormone is produced, resulting in a condition called *hyperthyroidism.* This is characterized by nervousness, anxiety, high pulse rate, heightened blood pressure, feelings of fatigue, and, sometimes, protruding eyes. (See fig. 4.3b.)

Parathyroid

The *parathyroid* gland is usually located on the surface of the thyroid; in some cases, it is embedded in the thyroid tissue. This small gland, through its product, *parathormone,* is an important regulator of calcium metabolism—so much so that its removal results in the death of the individual. For some time it was thought that the thyroid was necessary to sustain life; now it is known that the deaths which occurred after the thyroid was removed were actually caused by the inadvertent removal of the parathyroid. A typical sequence of events after parathyroidectomy is as follows: On the first day, the subject becomes restless and excitable. On succeeding days, his muscle tonus increases and some spasticity is observed. This is followed by *tetany,* in which opposing muscles contract. Tetany tends to be produced by smaller and smaller stimuli until the subject dies, often from a sudden constriction of the larynx.

The effects of removing the parathyroid are similar to those produced by calcium deficiency and can be avoided or at least ameliorated if additional calcium is supplied. Parathormone maintains blood calcium at functional levels by its demineralizing action on bone salts. Despite the striking effects of

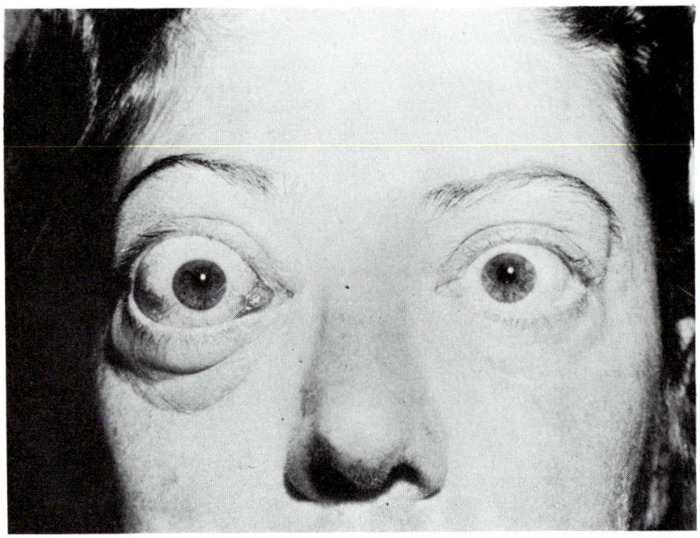

Figure 4.3b A case of hyperthyroidism. Note the protruding eyes in this patient. (Photo courtesy of Camera M. D. Studios.)

parathormone deficiency, relatively little is known about the behavioral effects of the condition.

Adrenal Glands

The *adrenal glands,* located on the kidneys, actually consist of two glands, an inner portion or *medulla* and an outer portion or *cortex*. The cells of the medulla arise during embryologic development from nervous tissue and are actually modified neurons. Their source is reflected in their hormonal products —adrenalin (epinephrine) and noradrenalin (norepinephrine), which are also produced by neurons—and in the method by which they are controlled—by direct innervation from the central nervous system. Adrenalin and noradrenalin have many similar functions. But because different amounts of the hormones are released under certain conditions, their synthesis and release may be controlled by separate neural pathways. Both are "emergency" hormones, that is, they increase blood pressure and blood sugar and cause the diversion of blood from the smooth muscle of the internal organs to the large striate muscles, which are used when fighting or running. However, they mediate these effects to different degrees and sometimes by different mechanisms. Adrenalin, for example, is a strong inhibitor of smooth muscle, and although it dilates the blood vessels (which would reduce blood pressure), it causes an increase in blood pressure by speeding up heart action. Noradrenalin inhibits smooth muscle only slightly and causes an increase in blood pressure by constricting the blood vessels. There is some evidence that in humans, the secretion of adrenalin is likely to be associated with feelings of fear, while the secretion of noradrenalin is likely to be associated with anger.

The *adrenal cortex* secretes as many as twenty different hormonal products. Some of them are so vital for salt metabolism that removal of the adrenal glands will lead to death if the subject is untreated. During embryologic development, the cortex is derived from tissue associated with the kidney and the fetal gonad. Thus it is not surprising that some of the hormonal products of the developed adrenal cortex are identical with or similar to gonadal hormones.

The adrenal cortex can be divided into three layers, each of which produces a different class of hormones. The outermost layer, the *zona glomerulosa,* mainly produces hormones called *mineralocorticoids,* which maintain the proper levels of sodium, chloride, and bicarbonate ions in the blood. If the adrenal glands are removed, these ions are excreted along with water and their concentrations in the blood are decreased. Death will usually result from an increased concentration of cells and solids in the blood caused by water loss unless mineralocorticoids are administered. Death can also be avoided by drinking saline solution rather than pure water, as this tends to keep sodium and chloride ions closer to normal limits and causes retention of water in the body.

The middle layer, the *zona fasciculata,* mainly produces hormones known as *glucocorticoids,* which lead to the breakdown of proteins to glycogen and sugar. Thus, the presence of excess glucocorticoids can lead to elevated blood sugar, or *steroid diabetes.* In addition, these hormones are good anti-inflammatory agents and, among other things, increase the number of cells that fight invading organisms.

The innermost layer, the *zona reticularis,* seems to be the main source of gonadlike steroids, especially *weak androgens.* These androgens are referred to as "weak" because they do not usually cause masculinizing effects in females. However, hyperactivity of the adrenal cortex—often caused by a secreting tumor—may lead to a condition that is especially noticeable in women because the muscle structure becomes more masculine, the voice deepens, the amount of facial and body hair increases, and the clitoris becomes enlarged (see fig. 4.4). The "bearded ladies" of the circus were sometimes victims of an overactive adrenal cortex. A similar tumor of the adrenal cortex in a young boy may lead to early puberty, with essentially adult-sized

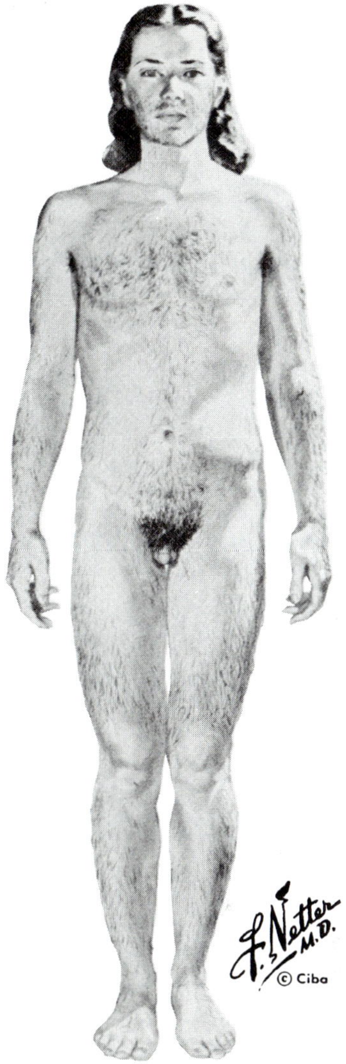

Figure 4.4 Adrenogenital syndrome showing marked virilization related to excess production of hormones from the adrenal cortex. (© Copyright 1954, 1965 CIBA Pharmaceutical Company, Division of CIBA-GEIGY Corporation. Reproduced with permission from THE CIBA COLLECTION OF MEDICAL ILLUSTRATIONS by Frank H. Netter, M.D. All rights reserved.)

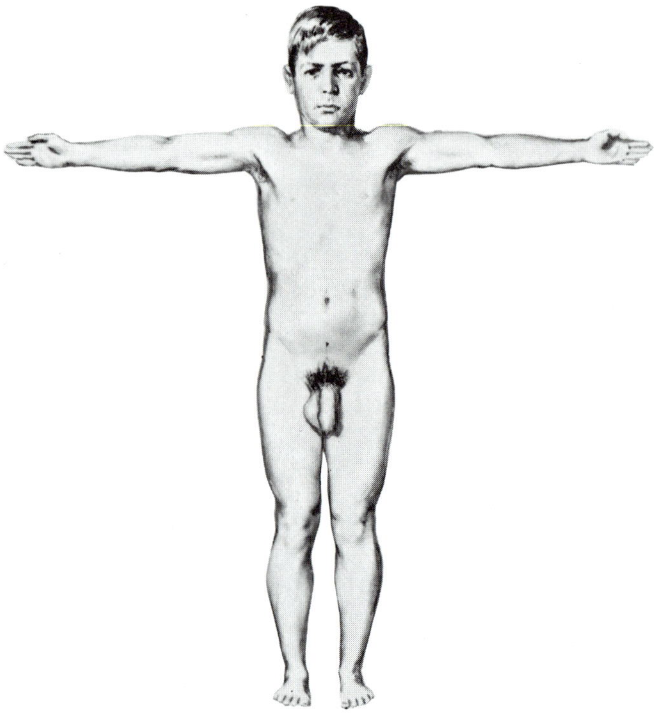

Figure 4.5 A case of precocious puberty caused by excess production of adrenocortical hormones in a boy. (© Copyright 1954, 1965 CIBA Pharmaceutical Company, Division of CIBA-GEIGY Corporation. Reproduced with permission from THE CIBA COLLECTION OF MEDICAL ILLUSTRATIONS by Frank H. Netter, M.D. All rights reserved.)

genitalia and often with adult sexual desires (see fig. 4.5).

The middle and innermost layers of the adrenal cortex are responsive to pituitary ACTH, but the outer layer is not. Thus, the secretion of mineralocorticoids is not regulated by the pituitary but instead seems to be controlled by a hormone from the kidney.

Gonads

There are both male and female sex glands, or *gonads*. Because most gonadotrophic hormones were named for their functions in the female, let us consider the *ovary* first. In the course of female embryological development of the Müllerian duct system, the "indifferent" gonad becomes an ovary. In the adult female, the ovary serves an exocrine function (development of eggs, or ova) and an endocrine function (secretion of female hormones). Before puberty, the ovary is relatively quiescent, although most of the egg cells (oogonia) are present from birth or shortly after. As puberty approaches, however, the levels of FSH rise, stimulating growth of the Graafian follicles that contain the eggs, as well as stimulating the interstitial cells that produce female hormones known as *estrogens*. LH also may be implicated in estrogen production. The estrogens stimulate the development of female characteristics that are appropriate to the species. In birds, for example, estrogens lead to the formation of feathers with female markings; in mammals, estrogens (in combination with STH and thyroid and adrenal hormones) lead to the development of functional mammary tissue (in humans, they also lead to the pattern of fat distribution and bodily form that is characteristic of the female). And, in most mammals, estrogens lead to fusion of the end-cap, or epiphysis, of growing bones and thereby curtail development of stature in females.

At puberty, other ovarian functions become evident. A principal one is *cyclicity*. Between puberty and menopause (some ovarian cyclicity may persist after menopause), the ovary functions in a regular cycle. This cyclicity has been traced to the hypothalamus; it only occurs when the hypothalamus of the developing fetus has not been exposed to large amounts of androgens. At puberty, the hypothalamus of the female begins to stimulate a regular cycle of FSH (and LH and LTH) production by the pituitary, which leads to regular changes in the production of ovarian hormones. The ovarian hormones in turn stimulate the cyclic changes characteristic of the species. In most species, females exhibit *estrous* cycles with a follicular phase and a luteal phase. During the *follicular* phase, the eggs, under the influence of FSH and estrogens, reach maturity and anatomical and physiological changes occur that prepare the female for copulation—and perhaps signal this readiness. These changes may include changes in coloration and the supply of blood vessels in the genital area, the development and release of odoriferous substances that signal the female's breeding condition, or any other signals and preparations characteristic of the species. Increased levels of estrogen lead not only to these changes but also to increased LH production by the pituitary. A sudden surge of LH stimulates ovulation and the secretion of progesterone by the cells lining the egg follicle. At about this time, levels of estrogens and progesterone that are characteristic of a particular species now lead to an important behavioral change in the female: she becomes *receptive* to the male's advances and will allow copulation. Thus she is said to be in estrus or in heat. Although estrus may last hours or days, depending on the species, it is soon followed either by pregnancy (if the ova were fertilized) or by anestrus or quiescent phase of the cycle (if they were not). In either case, the female will no longer receive the male.

Usually (keep in mind the species differences we discussed earlier), the *luteal* phase of ovarian activity now begins. The follicular cavity becomes the functioning corpus luteum and secretes large amounts of progesterone. The progesterone depresses further estrous cycles and causes a thickening of the lining of the uterus. This thickening and the concomitant increase in the supply of blood vessels in the uterine wall furnish an appropriate site for implantation of the fertilized ova after they traverse the fallopian tubes and arrive in the uterus. After the fertilized ova implant in the uterus, a placenta gradually forms and begins to assume an endocrine function. If there are no fertilized eggs, the lining of the uterus is resorbed, the regression of the corpus luteum signals another follicular phase, and so on (see fig. 4.6).

Several primates, including humans, have evolved a slightly different pattern: They have menstrual cycles rather than estrous cycles. In the menstrual cycle, the uterine lining that has been prepared for the fetus is not resorbed in the absence of fertilized eggs but is sloughed off, along with some blood, through the vagina—the process of menstruation. Cycles of receptivity may be somewhat less apparent in these species. Females of many primate species may receive the male at any time in the cycle, although copulation at nonovulatory times may serve to appease male aggression. Several attempts have been made to correlate the menstrual cycle with sex drive in the human female, but sexual behavior in humans is complicated by social factors to such a degree that no definitive conclusion seems warranted.

There are many estrogens, including *estradiol, estriol,* and *estrone.* (Some estrogens are also natural products of plants, which

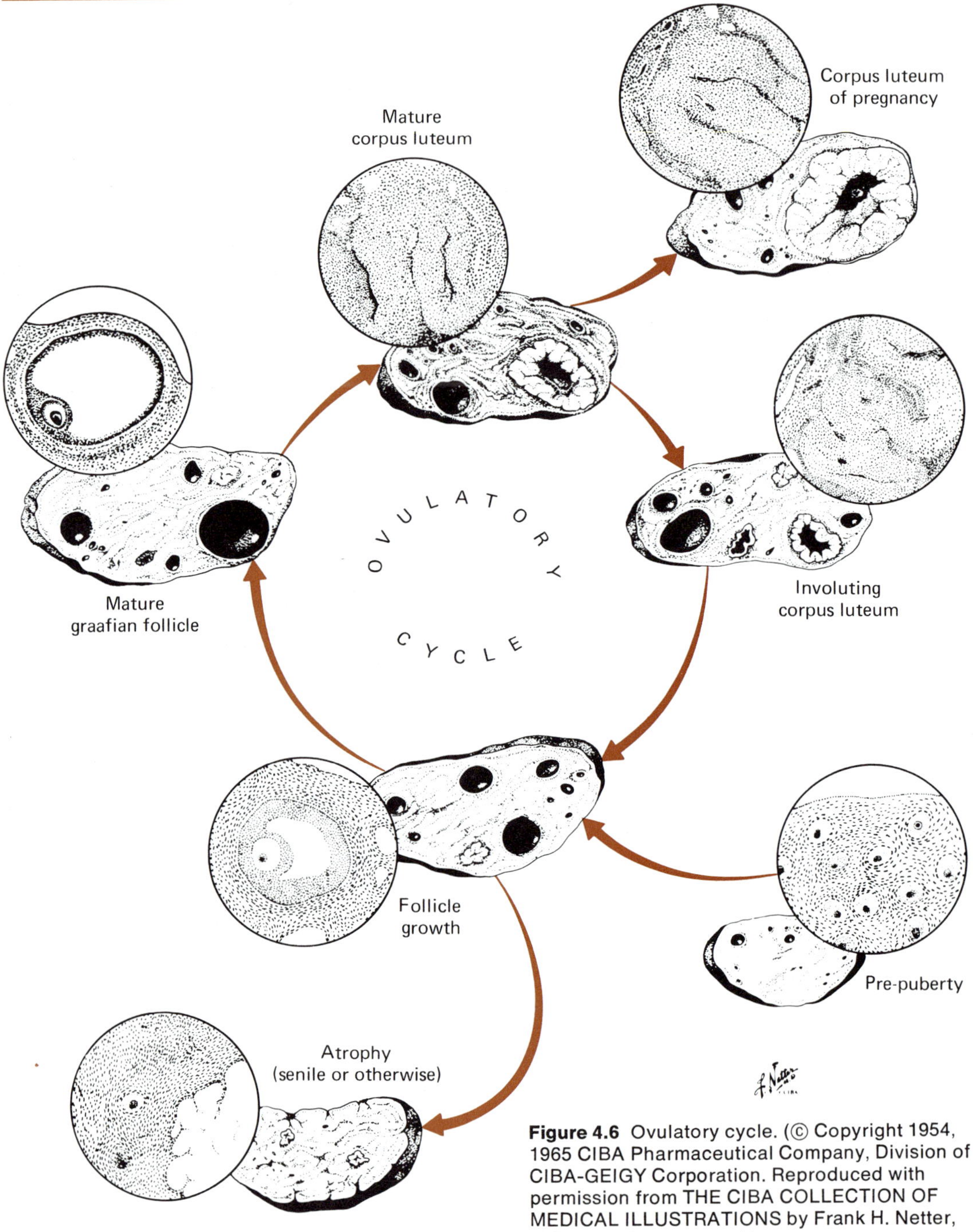

Figure 4.6 Ovulatory cycle. (© Copyright 1954, 1965 CIBA Pharmaceutical Company, Division of CIBA-GEIGY Corporation. Reproduced with permission from THE CIBA COLLECTION OF MEDICAL ILLUSTRATIONS by Frank H. Netter, M.D. All rights reserved.)

can cause troublesome feminization of a rancher's bulls.) All these hormones exhibit typical estrogenic properties, but in varying degrees. Different estrogens may have fairly specific tasks. Many compounds with estrogenic action have been synthesized in the laboratory; some of them are apparently the same as naturally occurring hormones, while others are quite different. Most birth control pills contain a fixed ratio of estrogens and progesterone, which serves to "lock" the cycle in one phase and prevent the ebb and flow of hormones necessary for pregnancy.

In addition to estrogens and progesterone, the ovary also produces androgens, but usually "weak" ones. These androgens, along with those from the adrenal cortex, probably serve as synergists for muscle development. Because they are typically "weak," they may be able to circulate freely without masculinizing the female and then be metabolized into a more potent form in the tissue where they are needed. Androgens may also serve as libido hormones in the female. This provocative hypothesis, which has been espoused by John Money, is reviewed in box 4.2.

Males produce some estrogens, chiefly in the testes and the adrenal cortex. These apparently have a physiological function—perhaps in maintaining skin moisture and pliability. Surprisingly, stallions produce vast amounts of estrogens. In most species, however, excessive amounts of estrogen in a male, whether from internal or outside sources, usually produces some feminization; for example, breast development, redistribution of body fat, and so forth. In addition, the male pituitary responds to an increase in estrogen by stopping the release of FSH, which in turn stops spermatogenesis and results in sterility. Because of its effect on the production of spermatozoa, estrogen treatment is said to cause functional castration. In the *testicular feminizing syndrome,* testicular estrogen production may be so high that a genetic male develops a strikingly female morphology (see fig. 4.7). More commonly, however, the cells of such persons are unable to respond to androgens in the usual way for some unknown genetic reason and respond instead to the testicular estrogens. As a result, a large amount of female differentiation takes place.

Box 4.2

Androgen: The Libido Hormone

Libido, or sex drive, in males of most species that have been studied is closely associated with the availability of testicular androgen. Loss of these androgens through castration or other means usually results in a substantial diminution of sex drive, even though the ability to copulate is not always lost. In the human male, castration or gonadal malfunction leads to a reported decrease in sexual desire and frequency of coitus; potency may be impaired as well. Normal levels of desire and function can be recovered with androgen therapy.

Human females, however, show no clear-cut changes in sex drive when estrogen levels are reduced. After ovariectomy or menopause, when estrogen levels fall, there is no consistent decrease in sexual drive, activity, or response; in fact, desire may increase. Of course, there may be vaginal dryness and tenderness in the absence of estrogens, which promote vaginal lubrication, and this may require estrogen therapy, *but libido remains* in the absence of estrogen. How can this be?

The answer seems to be that androgens function as libido hormones in women as well as men. The evidence for this statement is twofold: (1) women treated with androgens for medical reasons often report a definite increase in sex drive, and (2) removal of the adrenal glands, the chief source of androgens in females, results in a clear-cut diminution or loss of sex drive. Although this rather surprising relationship needs further exploration, evidence from clinical studies and from experimental investigations using rhesus monkeys leads to the same conclusion: in man and some other primates, androgen is the libido hormone for both sexes (Money, 1961).

Note in figure 4.7 that although the testes are present, they are undescended and located in the groin, or inguinal region.

In addition to its *exocrine* function of producing spermatozoa, the *testis,* or male gonad has the *endocrine* function of producing steroid hormones. During the active breeding season, the paired testes of most mammals are located outside the abdomen in a loose sac called the scrotum. Marine mammals, and some other vertebrates, retain the testes within the abdomen, and in some species males withdraw the testes into the abdominal cavity during the nonbreeding season or on other occasions (e.g., during fights). The ability to withdraw the testes into the abdomen has been lost in man, although in some individuals one or both testes may, on occasion, temporarily slip back up the inguinal canal. Among those mammals (including man) in which the testes are located in the scrotum, spermatogenesis is dependent on the lower temperatures to be found there and is impaired at abdominal temperatures. (It has been jokingly suggested that men should take advantage of this temperature sensitivity to accomplish birth control by taking a very hot bath before intercourse. This method is *not* recommended.) Failure of the testes to descend normally into the scrotum is a pathological condition that can often be relieved with hormonal treatments and/or surgery.

During embryonic development, the indifferent gonad becomes a testis if the genetic sex is male. Most of the genital tract in the male differentiates from the *Wolffian* ducts under the influence of fetal androgens, while the Müllerian ducts (from which the female tract is formed) are caused to regress by a substance called *Müllerian inhibiting substance* (MIS). If MIS is not produced, the fetus may be born with ambiguous-looking genitalia containing parts appropriate to each sex.

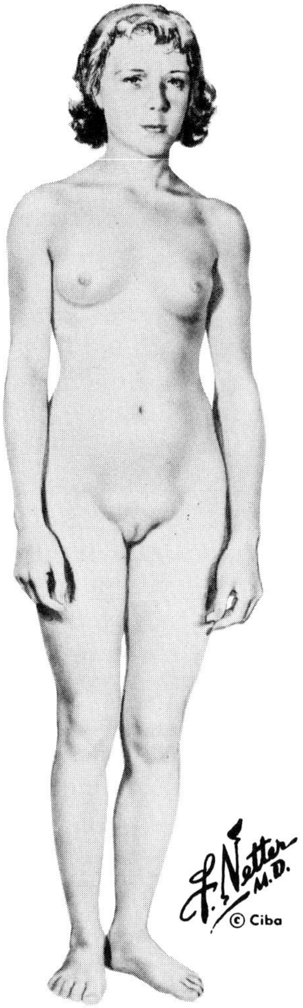

Figure 4.7 A case of androgen insensitivity—also called Testicular Feminizing Syndrome—caused by a congenital insensitivity to androgen. Note the testes located as inguinal hernias. (© Copyright 1954, 1965 CIBA Pharmaceutical Company, Division of CIBA-GEIGY Corporation. Reproduced with permission from THE CIBA COLLECTION OF MEDICAL ILLUSTRATIONS by Frank H. Netter, M.D. All rights reserved.)

Before puberty, the testes are relatively quiescent and the sexual organs remain small. At puberty, pituitary FSH and LH stimulate interstitial cells in the testes to begin producing steroid hormones, which are mainly *androgens.* Under the influence of androgens, further male differentiation takes place: the penis, testes, and male sexual tract grow in size, spermatogenesis begins, the musculature becomes heavier and typical of the male of the species; male-specific structures (such as antlers, tusks, rooster combs, or manes) develop; and sex drive, or libido, becomes more intense and usually leads to successful copulation. Many of these changes are seen in man and are accompanied by a deeper voice related to enlargement of the larynx, growth of pubic and axillary hair and beard, and, often though not invariably, chest hair (and sometimes a receding hairline!).

After puberty, hypothalamic release factors and pituitary gonadotropins are produced at nearly constant rates in males and lead to the release of relatively constant amounts of male hormone from the testes. However, recent evidence indicates that the amount of male hormones may increase dramatically during sexual excitement (see fig. 4.8). In other words, although males do not show estruslike cyclicity, the levels of male hormone can and do rise in response to appropriate stimulation. Males of some species (for example, deer, camels, and goats) do show another kind of cyclicity in that they have regular breeding seasons *(rut)*—often once or twice a year. At other times, the gonads may become smaller and withdraw into the abdomen, and spermatogenesis and androgen production may cease. In these species, male characteristics and especially the male duct system and accessory glands are thought to be maintained during the interval by adrenal androgens.

There are several known androgens, including *testosterone, dehydroepiandrosterone, androstenedione,* and *dihydrotestosterone.* Dehydroepiandrosterone and androstenedione are weak masculinizing agents and may function only after being converted into a more

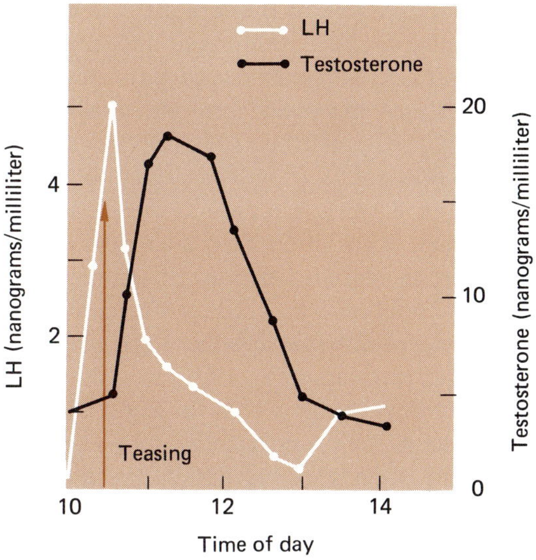

Figure 4.8 The effect of sexual excitement on the blood LH and testosterone levels in a bull. (From Katongole, C. B., Naftolin, F., and Short, R. V., *Journal of Endocrinology,* 50, 1971. Reprinted by permission of J. P. Lippincott Company.)

potent form in the target tissue. Testosterone, a potent androgenic product of the testes in many species, may be changed into the even more potent dihydrotestosterone in target tissues such as the prostate. Androgens can be metabolized into estrogens by several endocrine organs and other tissues (e.g., the skin). Because of the similarities among these compounds and the possibility that they are able to convert into one another, it is sometimes difficult to ascertain exactly what compound is producing certain effects, even though a carefully measured dose of a specific hormone has been given.

The *placenta* secretes steroid hormones, and protein hormones as well. Hormones from the placenta supplement those of the pituitary and the ovary. Two hormones which act as pituitary supplements are *human chorionic gonadotropin* (HCG) and *human chorionic somatomammotropin* (HCS). HCG is similar to LH, but has a much longer half-life. HCS is most similar to growth hormone; it is known to promote breast development and, together with HCG, to maintain the corpus luteum of pregnancy. A placental hormone with strong FSH properties can be obtained from mares and is known as *pregnant mare serum gonadotropin,* or PMSG. Because of its FSH-like properties, it has often been used in research to stimulate ovarian function. HCG may stimulate the fetal testis to produce the androgens necessary for differentiation as a male. Therefore, underproduction of HCG would be one cause of development of a male pseudohermaphrodite with imperfectly formed male genitalia. Because of the difficulties involved in surgical construction of functional male genitalia, most babies born with this problem are surgically and hormonally treated so that they become normal-appearing (but nonfertile) females. Socialization and acceptance of a female role seem to be complete in such cases.

Pineal Gland

We will end this section on endocrine glands by returning to the head and describing the *pineal gland,* or *epiphysis cerebri.* This small gland, located above the midbrain and weighing about 0.1 gram in man, has a long but confused history (Wurtman and Axelrod, 1965). In the second century, the Greek scholar Galen concluded that it regulated the flow of thought from its storage bin in the lateral ventricles of the brain! In the seventeenth century, the French philosopher Descartes announced that the pineal gland was the seat of the soul, the point of interaction between events of the mind and events in the outer world. The gland mediated these events by tilting this way or that, thereby controlling the flow of humors down the hollow nerve tubes to the muscles, which would expand and do work. Although these Greek and Cartesian ideas have had some effect on the development of scientific methodology (e.g., by furnishing a model that could be tested), they had no influence on the correct interpretation of the gland's function.

The pineal gland seems to operate as a biological clock in man and other animals. Information about the amount of light that exists during day and night is relayed to the pineal gland, which in turn influences the pituitary and probably other parts of the body to adopt a daily cycle of activity. If anything, the pineal contains *two* "clocks." One, the so-called "endogenous" or free-running clock, uses serotonin, a hormone and neurotransmitter, to impose two rough *circadian* (from the Latin *circa diem,* meaning "about a day") rhythm on bodily processes, even in the absence of external light cues, such as in blindness or when working in a deep mineshaft. The "exogenous" clock uses the hormone *melatonin* to incorporate circadian processes in tempo with the solar day. If an individual is unable to process information about the light cycle (e.g., if he is blind), the exogenous function is lost, and the individual usually shows a very rough cycle of twenty-two to twenty-eight hours under the influence of the endogenous clock. Just how these mechanisms integrate or summate information about the light cycle over a number of years to time the onset of puberty is as yet unknown. But other timing processes are almost certainly involved.

Integrated Patterns of Behavior

Sexual Behavior

In *Homo sapiens,* as well as a vast number of other species, there is a *dimorphism,* or distinct difference between male and female members, not only in terms of bodily conformation, but in terms of behavior and other physiological functions. In mammals these differences begin during embryonic development. In Chapter 2, we said that female fetuses carry two X-chromosomes, one from each parent, while male fetuses have an XY chromosomal complement, an X from the mother and a Y from the father. Somehow the genetic information carried on these sex chromosomes or on the autosomes allows development of primordial sexual structures that are appropriate to the individual's sex.

In the female, the indifferent gonads become ovaries and the Müllerian ducts become the oviducts, uterus, vagina, and other internal structures of the female genital tract. Externally, the genital tubercle becomes the clitoris and the labioscrotal swelling becomes the labia. The brain also undergoes sexual differentiation and will eventually be seen to control the *cyclic* release of pituitary hormones, which in turn will effect the changes seen in estrous or menstrual cycles.

The Y-chromosome of the male carries one or more potent male-determining genes that cause the indifferent gonads to differentiate into fetal testes. The fetal testes respond to gonadotropins in the placenta by manufacturing and releasing androgens (male hormones) and Müllerian inhibiting substance (MIS). Under the influence of MIS, the Müllerian ducts regress until they become only small remnants of tissue in the adult male. Under the influence of fetal androgens, the Wolffian ducts differentiate and become the male genital tract and its associated structures (discussed in more detail in Chapter 10). The fetal androgens also affect brain structures. If endogenous or exogenous androgens are present during fetal development, brain mechanisms differentiate to control sustained release of pituitary gonadotropins. It has been proved by exchanging pituitary glands in male and female animals that it is the brain, and not the pituitary, which controls cyclicity or tonicity. If a male pituitary is transplanted into a female, it begins the cyclic release of gonadotropins, and vice versa.

Between birth and puberty, pituitary gonadotropins and gonadal hormones are produced at low levels, apparently because of the inhibitory action of pineal hormones (and perhaps other mechanisms). Although this is a relatively quiet period, some behavioral aspects of sexual dimorphism are usually present. Young males are somewhat more muscular than females and they often engage in more rough play and perhaps more fighting. Young males of nonhuman species often show more sexual *mounting* behavior, even though complete copulation is usually impossible. In some primitive human societies where there are relatively few sanctions against sex play among children, boys are observed to initiate physical contacts more often than are girls. This observation agrees with the behavior observed in other mammalian species, but we must always consider the additional effects of learning and social expectations on male and female roles in human societies.

Shortly before puberty—at about age 10 in girls and age 11 in boys—pituitary gonadotropins begin to be released in much larger amounts than previously. In response to these gonadotropins, the gonads produce and release increased amounts of steroid hormones, which are largely sex-specific—that is, estrogens from ovaries and androgens from testes. These steroid hormones complete the process of sexual differentiation as we outlined in the section on gonadal hormones. Behavioral changes also become apparent. Males of many species become more aggressive and may struggle to achieve and maintain a high position in the male-dominance hierarchy or to capture and hold a geographic area known as a *territory*. Often, these activities are necessary preliminaries to successful breeding: A male with no territory will probably be unable to mate; a male with an inferior position in the dominance hierarchy may have little or no opportunity for complete copulation. Various mechanisms underlie these generalities.

For example, a male with no territory near the breeding grounds will have no place in which to copulate because all the available space is held by other males. A male that is low in the dominance hierarchy may be less acceptable to females or may be attacked by dominant males if he ventures near the females.

At puberty, the sex drive intensifies. Although this drive is usually directed toward a reproductively suitable individual, it may on occasion be directed toward the wrong species or the wrong sex. Lorenz (1937) has described *"imprinting"* in graylag geese, which oriented their mating display to a human being if they were denied sight of their parents for a few hours after hatching and saw human beings during this period. Bestiality (sexual acts between a human being and an animal) is another example. Although this behavior is quite rare, it does occur.

Sexual orientation toward a member of the same sex (homosexuality) is not so rare in our species (about 1 to 8%, according to Kinsey et al., 1948, 1953), although it seems to be virtually nonexistent in other species. Sometimes, components of an animal's sexual behavior, especially mounting behavior, are the subject of uncritical focus, and an investigator jokingly says that homosexual behavior has occurred in his animal subjects. In a sense, his statement is true. Such mounting behavior is widespread and may even have important signalling functions to alert selection of a more appropriate mate. Also, the males of some species (e.g., frogs and elephant seals) will mount almost any appropriately sized individual, and they depend on the other individual's behavior to indicate its sex and, if female, its state of estrus. In general, however, it does not seem useful to classify this behavior as homosexual because these animals show no prolonged orientation to like-sexed individuals and they do not fail to reproduce.

Whatever its object, the increase in libido that occurs at puberty is a rather direct effect of gonadal hormones on brain tissue. As the production of gonadal hormones increases, these hormones are taken up by relatively specific cell groups in the hypothalamus (and probably other sites in the brain), and this leads to an increased propensity to mate. Small amounts of hormone can effect this change. For instance, receptivity in ovariectomized females and mounting behavior in castrated males can be stimulated by implanting minute amounts of gonadal hormones into appropriate areas of the brain—amounts far too small to have any effects elsewhere in the body (Michael, 1965; Barfield, 1964). Because the relevant sites are usually located in the hypothalamus and because the hypothalamus is responsible for releasing hormones that control pituitary and in turn gonadal functions, a complete endocrine loop is formed. This loop can be affected by other endocrine systems, especially those of the thyroid and the adrenal cortex. It can also be affected by neural and hormonal systems within the brain, including hormonal influences from the pineal gland and neural influences from the basal ganglia and limbic system.

After puberty, the species-specific reproductive pattern is usually present in complete form. In addition to the example of ring doves, which was described in box 4.1, we will discuss three additional examples—rats, baboons, and humans. We will begin with the rat, as its pattern has been most completely worked out, chiefly by Frank Beach and his students (e.g., Beach, 1941; 1951).

Sexual Behavior in Rats

Prior to puberty, rats of both sexes often mount one another, but the males are unable to achieve penile penetration (intromission). After puberty, males often achieve intromission but only if the female is in heat. The male will mount the female from the rear and clasp her around the lower abdomen with his forelegs. Often he will squeeze or "palpate" the female's abdomen rapidly and repetitively while thrusting with his penis at the same time. If the female is in estrus, she will stand still, raise her hindquarters, avert her tail, and allow entry by the male. Her posture usually includes a mild concavity of the back (*lordosis* posture, see box fig. 1.1a) and a tightening of the neck muscles so that her head points almost straight up rather than forward. Before the mount, the female and male will probably have indulged in some precoital sniffing and exploration of each other, after which the female leaves the male and runs a short distance away *(darts)* then crouches and shakes her head rapidly from side to side. Her actions seem to stimulate the male and orient him to mount from the rear. If he now succeeds in penetrating the female, he thrusts once deeply and dismounts rapidly by lunging backwards. This pattern of intromission is repeated at one-minute intervals until, finally, after about ten such intromissions the male *ejaculates.* During ejaculation the male remains deeply intromitted, clasping the female tightly, and shakes convulsively for several seconds. He may fall on his side, carrying the female over with him. He then dismounts, and raises his forelegs from the female in a slow, distinctive fashion.

When a sexually experienced male rat is castrated, he loses his sexual abilities in a predictable way. First, it takes a longer time and more intromissions before he ejaculates, or he may not ejaculate at all. Next, he seems to have more and more difficulty achieving intromission, until this ability too may be lost. After several weeks, he may still mount the female but usually with decreased frequency. If he is injected with androgen, he will be able to intromit again within a few days and, in a short time, will again be able to ejaculate. These procedures emphasize the importance of testicular hormones for sexual behavior in the male rat, and the pattern points out the sequence of development—mount, intromission, ejaculation.

A female rat, similarly castrated, shows a loss of estrous cycle almost immediately and will not accept the male. If she is injected with an estrogen such as estradiol benzoate, she tends to show some receptivity about two days later. In most cases, her receptivity will improve if she also receives an injection of progesterone a few hours before testing. Estrogen and progesterone are said to have a *synergistic* effect on her behavior because together they stimulate better estrus than either does when used alone. Presumably, the period of one or two days is needed for the hypothalamus to take up the estrogen and in turn stimulate other neural and endocrine systems underlying estrus. The female does not need any cerebral cortical tissue to display lordosis posture and receive the male (Beach, 1943). Apparently, the lordosis reflex is organized at the spinal level, but it is inhibited by higher neural (brain) centers until hormonal conditions are met. Then the inhibition is lifted and lordosis can be elicited, even without participation by cortical areas. However, females whose cortexes have been removed are barely able to mate; they do not investigate the male or dart, nor do they show any malelike mounting behavior. If their eggs are fertilized, these females can carry a litter to term, but they do not show appropriate maternal behavior.

Because of the drastic loss of sexual behavior in the female rat after ovariectomy, we can conclude that female receptivity in this species is critically dependent on ovarian hormones. Previous sexual experience seems to have no effect. The case for the male rat is somewhat different. If he is sexually experienced, he may continue to mount (and occasionally intromit). Thus the male's sexual behavior may not be completely dependent on gonadal hormones; it may simply be a matter of degree. Retention of mounting behavior may be related to the continued presence of adrenal hormones, or perhaps this behavior is neurally organized to such an extent that hormonal support is not needed.

The rather complex and time-consuming copulatory pattern in the rat is necessary to assure implantation of the fertilized ova in the wall of the uterus. Unless there has been sufficient vaginal and cervical stimulation by the male's penis, there is a failure of a neuroendocrine reflex involving the release of prolactin from the anterior pituitary. Without prolactin, the corpora lutea are not formed, insufficient progesterone is produced, and the uterine lining does not proliferate. As a result, the eggs cannot implant and are instead resorbed. Having skipped the luteal phase of her ovarian cycle, the female will come back into estrus in four or five days, ovulate, and again allow copulation. Alternatively, if the female has received adequate copulatory stimulation but her ova are not fertilized (perhaps because the male is infertile), she will enter the luteal phase and will not come into estrus again for twelve to fourteen days, although she is not really pregnant. This condition is called *pseudopregnancy,* and its hormonal basis is essentially the same as in true pregnancy.

If both fertilization and stimulation of the luteal phase have been successful, the female will remain pregnant and deliver her pups in about 21 days. The hormonal changes that occur during pregnancy and lactation will be discussed in the section on parental care.

Sexual Behavior in Baboons

The sexual behavior of the baboon, a species of ape, has been studied extensively by Irven DeVore in the Royal Nairobi National Park and the Amboseli National Reserve in Africa. DeVore's studies indicate that sexual behavior in free-ranging baboon troops is strongly influenced by the female's reproductive cycle. The female is receptive only once during her monthly (35-day) estrous cycle; she is not receptive at any other times, including during pregnancy or lactation. During the early phase of her cycle, there is a marked swelling (tumescence) of her *sexual skin*—a large bare area on her rump. This swelling and a concomitant brightening of color, is caused by the action of estrogen. Swelling begins after menstruation and continues for about nineteen days, after which ovulation occurs. The female is sexually receptive during the latter two-thirds of this phase. After ovulation, detumescence occurs within two days and lasts about eight days longer. Menstrual flow occurs during the latter part of the detumescence phase.

Although female baboons are reproductively functional by the time they are five years old, male baboons take considerably longer because they must become large enough and strong enough to attain a sufficiently high position in the male *dominance hierarchy.* Until they achieve this status, either individually or as part of a mutually supportive group, they are kept away from estrous females by higher ranking males.

In the early phase of her tumescence, a female will approach adult males. Dominant males do not attempt to mount her at this time, but juvenile males and subdominant adults do mount during this period. Later, when the swelling of her sexual skin is maximum and ovulation is imminent, the dominant males become interested and compete with each other for access to her. In these free-ranging troops, most females are either pregnant or lactating (and therefore not estrous); thus an estrous female is an object of fierce competition, and only the winners have access to her. DeVore found a strong correlation between dominance status and breeding success in this species. Only a strong and dominant male (or one supported by comrades) can repel the attacks of other males successfully enough to complete copulation.

Actual copulation involves mounting by the male, insertion of the penis accompanied by about fifteen pelvic thrusts, and ejaculation in about seven to eight seconds. This sequence may be repeated several times in a matter of hours, especially if a male and female have formed a consort pair. Sometimes a pair may be harassed so effectively by a dominant male that they are unable to complete copulation. The female may react to this aggression or threat of aggression by losing tumescence of her sexual skin for several hours.

Although DeVore was unable to investigate the effects of castration in these studies, laboratory experiments have shown that male primates are likely to be incapable of ejaculation after castration (even though an experienced male may continue to mount and sometimes intromit). Thus we can conclude that the sexual behavior of the male primate is importantly dependent on an adequate supply of testicular hormones. Similarly, the female primate's sexual behavior is almost totally dependent on levels of ovarian hormones. Although female monkeys do "present" their rear to a male when not in estrus, this is probably a gesture of appeasement rather than sexual behavior for its own sake.

Human Sexual Behavior

Accurate data on human sexual behavior have been comparatively sparse. There are probably many reasons for this, including the desire for privacy, modification of behavior through learning, and the difficulty of correlating behavior to hormone levels without manipulating hormone levels experimentally. Every human society has a set of taboos or mores concerning sexual behavior. Even in some primitive societies, where little or no clothing is worn and where sex play among children is accepted, adults tend to seek privacy for actual coitus. Such a society is also likely to have a set of taboos pertaining to menstruation, pregnancy, lactation, or other sex-related behaviors. Many societies are even more restrictive. Until recently, one could almost conclude that coitus didn't exist in European-American societies if it weren't for their substantial birthrates. Cultural anthropologists, through comparative studies of scores of human societies all over the world, have done much to define our essential humanity in the sexual as well as other spheres.

The landmark studies of Alfred Kinsey and his associates (1948; 1953) did much to dispel the aura of secrecy surrounding sex and made public a vast array of relevant data, such as the frequency of many sexual behaviors, including masturbation, petting to orgasm, coitus, and bestiality. More recently, Masters and Johnson (1966) have studied the anatomical and physiological changes that transpire during human sexual behaviors (especially coitus and masturbation) which lead to orgasm. After suitable counseling of their volunteer subjects, Masters and Johnson were able to photograph or electrically record responses such as the following: nipple and mammary tissue tumescence in both males and females; erection of the penis and clitoris; tumescence of the labia; changes in vaginal conformation during arousal and coitus; vaginal lubrication; patterns of skin flushing in both sexes; and changes in blood pressure and heart rate before, during, and after coitus. Based on their studies, these investigators determined that sexual behaviors leading to orgasm could be divided into three phases: excitement, a plateau, and orgasm. Figure 4.9 shows these phases for men and women. Note that males tend to proceed from plateau to orgasm and then go through a refractory period. Females, on the other hand, may either remain at a plateau level or proceed to single or multiple orgasms. A moderately detailed comparison of male and female sexual responses is presented in table 4.1. Behavioral and physiological responses during coitus are but one aspect of the important sex-related behaviors that will be discussed extensively in Chapter 10.

There is no absolute relationship between genetic sex, anatomical sex, and sexual behavior, as evidenced by conditions such as transsexualism, homosexuality, or by deviant behaviors such as sexual interest in children or animals. Despite many attempts, no hormonal basis has been discovered for these behaviors. The prevailing view at the moment is that these behaviors are caused by faulty learning and socialization, probably early in life.

Parental Behavior

In man as well as many other species, there is an intimate and prolonged relationship between parents and their young. Many aspects of this relationship seem to be influenced by the endocrine status of the parents—as demonstrated, for example, by the effects of prolactin in both male and female ring doves (see box 4.1). Because the female is usually more involved with the young than the male, parental behavior is often called *maternal behavior.* But to avoid denigrating the male's role, we shall use the term *parental behavior,* although we recognize that most available data pertain to the female's role.

Parental care is most striking just after birth of the young, but some aspects of parenting are evident so long before parturition that it is

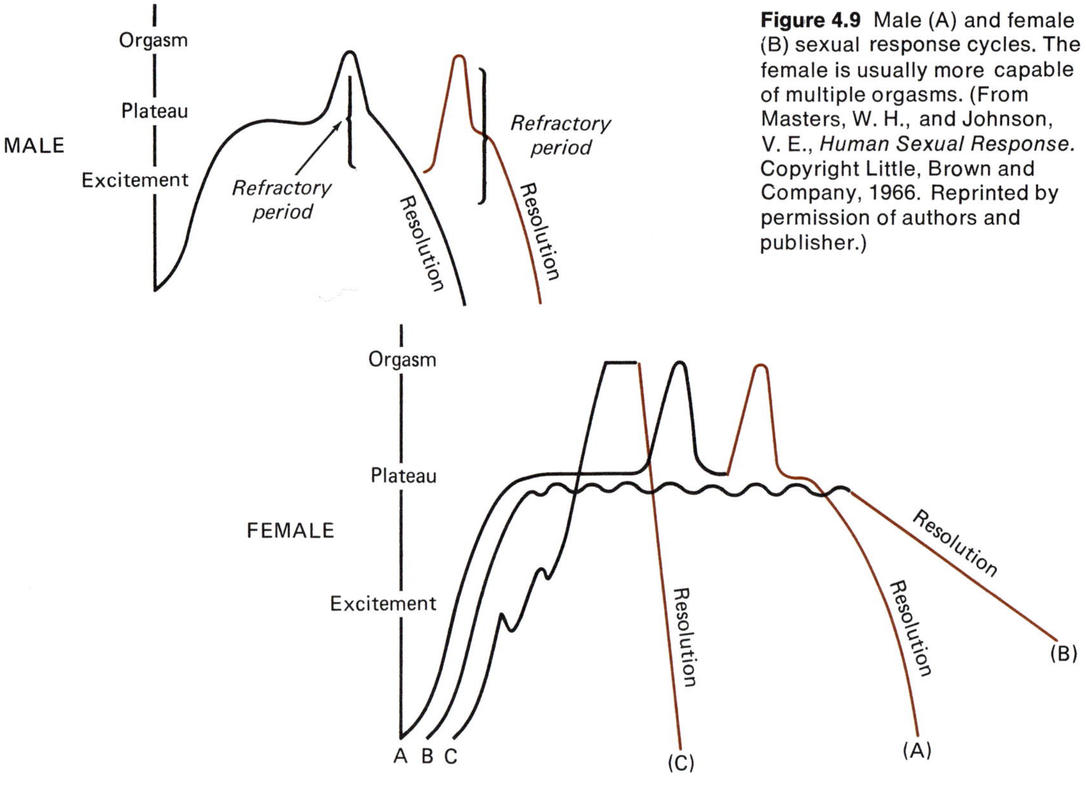

Figure 4.9 Male (A) and female (B) sexual response cycles. The female is usually more capable of multiple orgasms. (From Masters, W. H., and Johnson, V. E., *Human Sexual Response.* Copyright Little, Brown and Company, 1966. Reprinted by permission of authors and publisher.)

Table 4.1 Sexual responses observed in males and females during coitus[a].

Males	Females
Excitement Phase	
Nipple erection (30%)	Nipple erection
	Sex-tension flush (25%)
Plateau Phase	
Sex-tension flush (25%)	Sex-tension flush (75%)
Carpopedal spasm[b]	Carpopedal spasm
Generalized skeletal muscle tension	Generalized skeletal muscle tension
Hyperventilation	Hyperventilation
Tachycardia[c] (100 to 160/min.)	Tachycardia (100 to 160/min.)
Orgasmic Phase	
Specific skeletal muscle contractions	Specific skeletal muscle contractions
Hyperventilation	Hyperventilation
Tachycardia (100 to 180/min.)	Tachycardia (110 to 180/min.)
Resolution Phase	
Sweating reaction (30 to 40%)	Sweating reaction (30 to 40%)
Hyperventilation	Hyperventilation
Tachycardia (150 to 180/min.)	Tachycardia (150 to 180/min.)

[a]The percentages in parentheses indicate the proportion of subjects who exhibited the response.

[b]Spasmodic contractions of the muscles in the hands and feet.

[c]Rapid heart action. Normal heart rate is 70–75 beats per minute.

Source: From *Human Sexual Response* by W.H. Masters and V.E. Johnson, by permission of Little, Brown and Co. in association with the Atlantic Monthly Press.

difficult to determine the time of onset. Can we say that when little girls (and little boys) play with dolls, they are exhibiting a type of preparental behavior? Or how about being a "mommy" or "daddy" while playing house? If these behaviors seem too remote, how about the actual child care a teenage babysitter undertakes? Clearly, many young people practice a parental role long before they are parents themselves. The same is true of many other mammals. For example, young female rats that have been restrained from licking their own bodies and carrying objects about their cages seem to be defective in maternal licking and carrying behavior when they have their own young.

Although it is difficult to determine when studies of parental behavior should begin, it is somewhat easier to focus on hormonal correlates. In this case, we may begin with hormonal changes before and after copulation in adults. For obvious reasons, hormone levels have usually been manipulated in animals such as rats, dogs, and so forth rather than humans. Thus, we will review some of the evidence gathered during animal experiments and extract any principles we can concerning hormonal involvement.

Many rodents and rabbits build nests. These nests can be used for protection and warmth, and nest building can be stimulated by lowering the temperature, shaving the animal, or by removing the thyroid (which lowers the body temperature). During pregnancy, however, other hormones come into play. In rats, the decrease of progesterone and increase of estrogen near the end of pregnancy are probably involved in stimulating the female to build a special, more complicated (often covered) maternal nest. The mouse constructs a maternal nest during pregnancy, and this behavior is probably associated with *rising* levels of progesterone. Female rabbits build a special maternal nest near the end of pregnancy and line it with hair plucked from their own bodies. These events seem to be associated with the shift in the estrogen-progesterone ratio that occurs late in pregnancy; also, pituitary prolactin may be involved because pregnant rabbits whose pituitary glands have been removed do not build maternal nests. The principle here seems to be that one or more of the hormonal shifts that occur during pregnancy stimulate the building of a special maternal nest for the protection of the young.

During the later stages of pregnancy, females of many species lick their mammary glands and vaginal region. The licking stimuli may assist the development of functional mammary tissue, and it may furnish practice in licking and cleaning skills that will be used later in cleaning the fetal membranes and blood from the newborn young and in inducing the young to defecate and urinate by licking their abdomens. During this period, female lions have been observed to clear the area around their nipples of hair by pulling it out with their incisor teeth. The endocrine correlates of these behaviors are not so clear. Pregnancy hormones are undoubtedly involved in the sensitivity of the mammary and vaginal tissues, but stretching and distention of the skin by the developing fetuses may also be important stimuli.

Near the end of pregnancy, females often become more responsive to the young of others. A near-term ewe, for example, may "adopt" an alien lamb and attempt to drive its mother away. A rat or mouse in late pregnancy may steal young pups from other nests and carry them to her own. These behaviors seem to be early manifestations of what will be maternal reactions to her own young. Many attempts have been made to correlate these reactions with changes in the level of prolactin because there is an intriguing correlation between onset of milk production and maternal behavior as well as between maintenance of milk production and maternal behavior. In most of the species studied, however, injections of prolactin do not lead directly to maternal responses such as retrieving (carrying the young back to the nest) or crouching (nursing posture). Even when combined with injections of estrogens and progesterone (to mimic the endocrine status of parturition), prolactin does not seem to stimulate these behaviors directly. However, it does tend to decrease the time it takes for these responses to develop. Surgical removal of the uterus also tends to decrease the latency of development of maternal responses by causing a drastic reduction of placental hormones, including estrogens and progesterone. Perhaps this reduction in steroid hormones, in conjunction with an increase in prolactin (and other hormones), leads to an increase in maternal responsiveness. Thus these internal changes, along with the sight, sound, taste, and smell of her young, may stimulate a female to display the maternal responses appropriate to her species.

Some years ago, Wiesner and Sheard (1933) demonstrated that these associated stimuli can lead to parental responses even in the absence of pregnancy. They placed newborn rat pups overnight in a test female's cage, and, after several days, observed that even virgin females retrieved the pups and crouched over them. These findings emphasize the importance of stimuli from the young; subsequent responses may be mediated by the endocrine system. A useful generalization here is that hormonal events associated with pregnancy and perhaps with termination of pregnancy cause the female rat to be increasingly responsive to the young, chiefly to the young of her own species but occasionally to those of other species as well. This increased maternal responsiveness is variable, for example, some female rats spend their days retrieving anything that is portable—pups, food pellets, fecal material, reluctant mates, and even their own tails; others would rather eat their young than care for them. (There are other reasons for cannibalizing young, e.g., dietary deficiencies.) In time, some of these females stop eating their newborn pups and begin caring for them.

The interaction between endogenous hormonal factors and the experiences associated with developing and newborn young seems to be important in many species, perhaps including our own. The vast majority of pregnant women look forward to having their baby and caring for it. A few, however, apparently do not develop these maternal feelings and may desert (or even kill) their newborn child. Given the complexities of learning and socialization in our species and the difficulties of manipulating hormone levels experimentally, it is difficult to ascribe these differences to different hormonal states. Yet the evidence from other species furnishes a provocative model for possible endocrine involvement.

During the period in which the mother is nursing the young, there may be several physiological and behavioral correlates. The mother may be fiercely protective of her young, keeping away all others of her species including her mate. She may spend a great deal of time with her young, either in the nest or while carrying them about, and her estrous cycles will probably be delayed or missing altogether. In many primitive human societies, a mother may nurse a child for two to four years and is less likely to become pregnant again during this time. All these related factors are likely to be mediated, partially at least, by the hormonal conditions of nursing. As lactation ends, many of these correlates change: The female will be less protective, will spend less time with her young, and will come into estrus again or (in the case of humans) may become pregnant again. Because of the many correlates between maternal behaviors and duration of lactation, both processes may depend to an important degree on many of the same hormonal events. In some species and for some behaviors, these links are established; for others, they remain as possibilities.

Some interesting facets of parent-offspring interaction occur after the cessation of lactation. These include play, training to hunt or otherwise obtain food, development of language, socialization, assistance during competition for dominance, and many other things. In general, these behaviors do not seem to be associated with specific hormonal events; the young are probably treated differently simply because they are sexually immature. For example, adult males often tolerate and indulge young males until puberty; then, with the increase in androgens associated with puberty, the young males seem to become objects of competition and may be attacked or driven away.

Agonistic Behavior

Agonistic behavior can be defined as hostile or aggressive behavior such as fighting or threat of fighting, but excluding killing for food. Some aggressive behavior is observed in virtually all species and may serve a variety of functions, such as achieving *dominance* over other individuals, obtaining and maintaining a *territory,* and *protection* of the young. Man's agonistic behaviors range from mild verbal competition in social situations to overt fighting.

A number of conditions are known to increase the probability of aggressive displays among many species. These include competition for food, space, or mates; frustration and pain; early experiences such as isolation or lack of normal contacts; learning—especially a history of winning in agonistic competition; and hormonal status. Here, of course, we will focus on hormonal correlates.

One consistent finding is that the degree of aggression is related to androgen levels. Generally speaking, males have higher androgen levels than females do and are more aggressive. Castration of males, especially if done early, leads to a decrease in aggressive behaviors. As we mentioned at the beginning of this chapter, one reason that farm and ranch animals are castrated is to make them easier to handle. There is also a correlation between level of aggression and seasonal breeding. In many species, renewed activity of the testes after a period of inactivity is associated with a dramatic increase in male aggression, along with sexual displays and breeding.

Because of these obvious associations, many investigators have tried to explore the relationship further. Castration has been shown to reduce aggression in disparate animals such as swordtail fish, lizards, turkeys, rats, and chimpanzees, while treatment with testosterone or other androgens leads to an increase in aggressive behavior (Beach, 1948). Exogenous estrogen usually leads to decreased aggression in the female, while removal of the ovaries often leads to an increase which is probably related to an increase in adrenal androgen after the loss of ovarian estrogens.

These effects can be magnified if hormonal treatments are begun at an early age. Male mice injected with a single dose of estradiol benzoate at three days of age tend to fight with other males less often after reaching adulthood, and baby female mice injected with a single dose of testosterone propionate fail to come into behavioral estrus as adults and tend to attack their male partners (Bronson and Desjardins, 1968). This androgenic effect in female mice can be obtained by injecting them with testosterone anytime between birth and thirty days of age. When these females are given exogenous androgen as adults, they are much more prone to fight than are control females who were not primed with testosterone as infants. One possible explanation is that the neural systems which predispose this species to aggression are present in both sexes but are developed only under the influence of circulating androgens (Edwards, 1968).

Males of many species fight for territory or social status. Those that fight for territory are most prone to do so when they are in breeding condition. This behavior seems to serve the purpose of furnishing the necessary physical and psychological space for mating displays and for breeding, sometimes with a number of females. Thus territorial behavior may also be an effective means of population control.

In some species, males are more intent on establishing their dominance over rivals than on defending a particular territory. Sometimes this leads to a "pecking order" from the strongest to the weakest, with the strongest getting first choice of food, mates, nesting sites, and other amenities. For instance, DeFries and McClearn (1970) have shown that if three male and three female mice are placed together in a cage, the dominant male will sire more than ninety percent of the litters. Despite free access to the females, the subordinate males seldom mate. Again, this may be a population control mechanism.

The baboons studied by DeVore (1965) establish dominance hierarchies on the basis of fights and threats. Males have impressive canine teeth, and a threatening display of teeth is nearly as effective as fighting (see fig. 4.10).

In most species that form dominance hierarchies, castration of a high-ranking male will lead to loss of rank—sometimes all the way to the bottom. If hormone therapy is initiated quickly enough, he may recover his rank. If

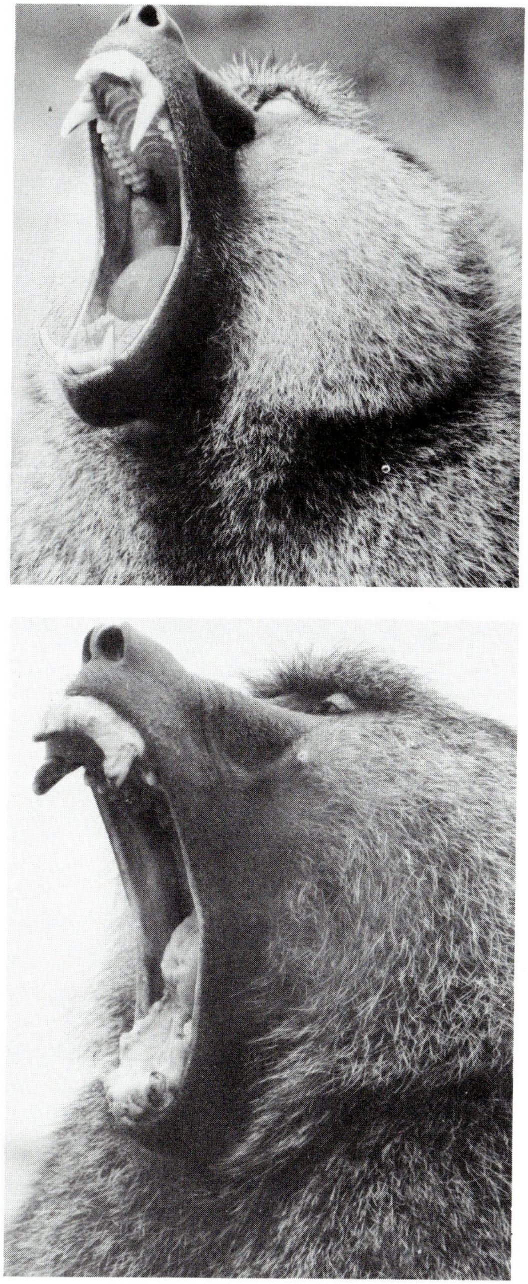

Figure 4.10 Canine display in male baboons, (a) a young male baboon, (b) an old male baboon. (From Beach, F. A. (ed.), R. E. Krieger Pub. Co., Inc., Huntington, N.Y. 1974. Photo credit I. DeVore.)

therapy is delayed, however, he may never recover his former rank.

Females usually do not enter the males' hierarchy, although they may have their own. In some species with a strong male hierarchy, the female seems to share the rank of her consort and has the same privileges. A ranking female may even, through her behavior and support, be able to "pass on" rank to her sons.

The fact that human males, young and old, display more overt, physical aggression than females do is well confirmed. It seems clear that this phenomenon is related to androgens, including those produced by the fetus. Boys tend to use their large muscle groups and engage in rough play, while girls, who are not as strong physically, do not engage in as much rough play and do not get into as many physical fights. However, girls may be quite aggressive verbally. Thus the difference in sex hormones seems to lead to different expressions of aggression—that is, physical for males and verbal for females. This difference is observed most clearly in young children before social inhibitions are well established.

Men whose testes failed to descend normally produce little or no androgenic hormones, and they tend to be mild and unaggressive. Males who have been castrated (therapeutically, for prostate cancer, for instance) tend to become less aggressive and may have trouble maintaining their social and business status. If these men receive a skin implant of androgens or injections of long-acting androgens, they tend to recover their competitive ability and status (Masters and Johnson, 1966).

Hormonal correlates of human female aggression are not so clear-cut. Women tend to be less aggressive during the follicular (high estrogen) phase of their menstrual cycle and more aggressive during the luteal (high progesterone) phase and menstruation. However, the dramatic hormonal shifts that occur during menstruation have many physiological effects, and it is not clear whether the increase in aggression is related to levels of a particular hormone or to physiological stress.

Learning

A number of hormones have been implicated in learning processes. We will discuss four classes: thyroid hormones, gonadal hormones, adrenal medulla hormones, and adrenocortical hormones.

The presence of thyroid hormones is crucial to proper development of the nervous system, especially during the "critical" or (in newer terminology) "sensitive" period of fetal development and early infancy. If thyroid hormones are absent or deficient during this period of human development, the child will be a severely retarded and dwarfed cretin. If the deficiency is discovered early enough, most of the damage can be avoided by treatment with thyroid hormones. Treatment is much less effective if begun later. Eayrs and Levine (1963), through experiments with animals, have determined that the learning deficit associated with insufficient thyroid hormone reflects underdevelopment of the brain. Individuals who lack thyroid hormones during the sensitive period of development have smaller brains containing fewer neurons. Their learning deficit is particularly evident when they are faced with relatively complex tasks. Because the damage has already been done, thyroid therapy is ineffective. These effects apparently reflect a direct influence of thyroid hormones on developing neural tissue, not an indirect effect mediated by the general influences of thyroid hormones on metabolism and growth.

Gonadal hormones are involved in learning processes in two general ways, motivation and arousal. Motivational effects have been recognized for some time. Young males of many species seem to be motivated to engage in sex- and species-specific behaviors, such as rough play, mock fighting, threat displays, and mounting, as a consequence of fetal androgens. If males are estrogenized or do not respond to androgens, these behaviors tend to be reduced significantly. If genetic females are androgenized, through experimental procedures or perhaps because of progesterone treatments to the mother, they tend to show male-like levels of these behaviors (Money and Erhardt, 1972). Sex-specific behaviors in adults seem to be quite directly motivated by the presence of androgens—certainly in males and perhaps also in females (see box 4.2). Very rarely does the loss of androgens through surgical ablation of the gonads or adrenals (or both) or use of a specific androgen antagonist leave development of sex and aggressive behaviors unaffected. The same learning opportunities are present, but the motivation to learn is missing. Rats who have been trained to press a bar for a rewarding electrical stimulus to the brain stop pressing after castration, but resume if treated with androgens—another example of a motivational component (Olds, 1956).

A newer and more puzzling correlation between learning and a gonadal hormone involves progesterone. If progesterone is administered to a female rat while she is learning a new response, learning is delayed. Apparently this delay is mediated by the direct effect of the progesterone on the posterior thalamic nuclei of the brain (Van Wimersma Greidanus et al., 1973). However, much remains to be learned about this phenomenon.

Adrenal medulla hormones (epinephrine and norepinephrine) act in conjunction with the sympathetic branch of the autonomic nervous system and help to activate and mobilize bodily resources in times of excitement or danger. Many experiments have shown slower learning of a conditioned avoidance response after surgical removal of the adrenal medulla and consequent loss of its hormones. Overactivation leads to equally poor learning, perhaps due to "freezing" from fear or to panicked running.

During training to establish a conditioned avoidance response, administration of ACTH may, under certain conditions, facilitate acquisition (learning) and retard extinction (loss) of the response. This seems to be a direct effect of ACTH because administration of a physiological or synthetic glucocorticosteroid tends to *facilitate* extinction of the avoidance response. Since glucocorticosteroids are released in response to pituitary ACTH, this opposition of response is rather puzzling. Several hypotheses have been developed to explain these findings, but general agreement has not been reached (Levine, 1969; Weiss et al., 1969). In 1973 Van Wimersma Greidanus and his colleagues pointed out the molecular similarities among corticosteroids that facilitate extinction and progesterone, which also facilitates extinction, and have suggested that the similarity of effect is related to the structural similarity, with the receptors being located in specific posterior thalamic nuclei of the brain. This is but one instance where we need to know more about cellular and molecular effects of hormones as well as the significance of these effects for behavior.

Summary

The ancient idea that there are four fluids or "humors" in the body was never very helpful as a scientific explanation for natural phenomena. The early use of the castration technique did, however, lead to the concept of blood-borne chemical messengers.

In the past three-quarters of a century much has been learned about these chemical messengers in the blood—where they come from, where they go, and what they do. During this time literally dozens of hormones have been discovered, and hundreds if not thousands of their effects have been studied. Most of this work has been done by endocrinologists and physiologists who have tended to concentrate on anatomical and physiological correlates of hormone release. There has been less emphasis on behavior, the traditional domain of the psychologist, but a few gifted workers have, nevertheless, left us a considerable legacy in this respect.

We now know in considerable detail the effects of gonadal hormones on many different aspects of sexual functioning in both males and females of several species, and we know many of their effects on aggressive behavior, parental behaviors, and even in learning. Information is building about the behavioral effects of other hormones, chiefly from the thyroid and adrenals.

New studies relating hormones and behavior cannot fail to benefit enormously from technical advances made within the last few years. Modern chemical techniques can detect miniscule quantities of a hormone, sometimes only a few molecules. No longer will crude extracts of "dried thyroid" or "ground-up pituitary" be used: Chemically pure extracts can be prepared, or hormones for which the precise molecular structure is known can be synthesized. No longer will locus of action be a mystery: Hormones can be labeled with radioactive tracers so that the site of uptake can be ascertained from tracer concentration.

Along with improvements in technique, there will be advances resulting from a broadening of understanding. For example, we are already aware of relatively simple effects of behavior on endocrine function, such as copulatory stimulation leading to LH secretion in rabbits. We are becoming more aware of what could be called "social" stimulation, such as the effects of crowding on ACTH secretion, with resultant reproductive difficulties and population loss. Thus, the expectation that endocrine changes will lead to behavioral changes has been broadened with the understanding that behavior can affect endocrine function. A two-way street has been established, and we can expect heavier traffic and new models. One guess might be that many emotions will prove to have a strong hormonal component or basis. We already have several hints of this—in sex, in anger, in fear, and in maternal feelings. Perception of these emotions could lead to hormonal and emotional changes in others, perhaps furnishing a basis for nonverbal communication—since the messages in such a context seem to be feelings, not ideas.

Whatever may be the outcome of this particular speculation, we may be sure that the study of hormone-behavior interactions is well begun and should remain as an important interface between psychology and biology.

5

Drugs, The Nervous System, and Behavior

Psychologists study the effects of drugs on behavior for a number of reasons. First, certain drugs act primarily on the nervous system and affect behavior; therefore, the psychologist can use them to gain some understanding of how the nervous system mediates behavior. Second, the pharmaceutical industry throughout the world synthesizes thousands of new drugs each year, which must be screened for their behavioral effects before being placed on the market. Third, some drugs are used to treat mental illness, and their effects and therapeutic value must be evaluated. Fourth, abuse of certain drugs has become a serious social problem in some cultures. Because these drugs have psychological effects on the user and a profound impact on the society in which they are used, their psychological and social effects must be studied and understood. Fifth, some drugs induce behaviors that are interesting in themselves: for example, a few drugs apparently affect creativity and alter states of consciousness; others induce symptoms that mimic those observed in certain mental illnesses. Creativity, consciousness, and mental illness are of great interest to psychologists, and experimentation with these drugs may shed some light on these behavioral phenomena.

For the reasons just mentioned, a new area of specialization, *psychopharmacology* (sometimes called *behavioral pharmacology*), has developed within psychology for the study of the effects of drugs on behavior. Psychopharmacology can also be defined as a subfield of psychology that uses the tools and concepts of psychology and pharmacology to explore the behavioral action of drugs (Thompson and Schuster, 1968). This chapter will present examples of work that is typical in this field of study. Since psychopharmacology is a hybrid discipline, drawing heavily on concepts and techniques of pharmacology as well as psychology, we will begin our discussion by defining certain terms and ideas used in pharmacology.

Basic Concepts of Pharmacology

Pharmacology is often defined as the study of how animals respond to chemical stimuli. The chemical stimuli referred to are drugs—substances that because of their chemical nature alter either the structure or function of a living organism. Within this broad definition, even food and water could be classified as drugs. So to restrict our definition somewhat, we can say that a drug is a chemical compound which has *selective biological activity*. By biological activity, we mean that cellular processes are affected; when we call it "selective," we mean that at low concentrations, one effect of a drug predominates.

If drugs show selective activity, then there must be something unique about the cells on which they act. In other words, cells must have some method of "recognizing" a drug. And, indeed, cells contain molecules called *receptors,* the site where a drug becomes attached to the cell membrane. Although the chemical structure of receptor molecules is largely unknown, it is nevertheless convenient to talk about the action of a drug in terms of its attachment to specific receptors. A drug's propensity to attach itself to a receptor molecule is called its *affinity*. Once a drug is bound to its receptor, it can initiate its biological activity, and the degree to which it is biologically active is termed its *intrinsic activity*.

Not all of a drug's specificity is necessarily related to the interactions between the drug and receptors in certain types of cells. If a drug is to affect a certain cell population, it must be accessible to those cells. For example, some drugs affect the central nervous system. But to do so, they must first get into the brain, and they may not get there if injected into muscle tissue. Therefore, although a drug is known to affect nerve cells if injected directly into the brain, it may exhibit specific biological activity only on muscle cells if injected intramuscularly.

Because pharmacology is intimately associated with the field of medicine, drugs are most commonly used in the treatment and prevention of disease. This aspect of pharmacology is referred to as *therapeutics*. In general, the more selective the action of a drug, the more useful it is in therapeutics; this is also true when drugs are used as research tools. One difficulty with using drugs in research is that a drug may act on either the central nervous system or the peripheral nervous system. Thus one is not always certain which action caused the behavior being studied.

The effect of one compound on certain cells may be blocked by the effect of another. For example, *acetylcholine* acts as a *neurotransmitter* at the *neuromuscular junction* (the synapse between nerve cell axons and muscles). The drug *curare,* used by some South American Indians as an arrow poison, blocks the action of acetylcholine at this site, thereby producing paralysis. A drug (chemical compound) that acts selectively on a certain structure is called an *agonist*. A chemical compound which blocks the action of another chemical compound is called an *antagonist*. Thus curare is an acetylcholine antagonist.

In a quantitative sense, the actions of a drug depend on how much of it reaches the site of action per unit of time. If a drug is to have any effect, it must first be absorbed, and the rate of absorption depends on the form in which the drug is introduced (e.g., as a solid or a liquid), the method by which it is taken (e.g., by injection or by mouth), the rate at which it is administered, and so forth. Once a drug has been absorbed, it is distributed from the site of administration, where it is highly concentrated, to areas of lower concentration. The distribution of a drug also depends on a variety of factors, including its solubility in different kinds of tissue, the supply of blood to the tissue, and the like. Absorption of a drug is considered complete when its concentration in the blood equals its concentration at the site of administration.

Once it is absorbed and distributed, the drug must be excreted. Some drugs are excreted in the form in which they were absorbed. Others undergo a chemical change called *biotransformation* before they are excreted. The inhalent anaesthetics such as ether do not undergo biotransformation before they are excreted; barbiturates do. The biotransformation of many drugs, including the barbiturates, involves the action of liver enzymes. One measure commonly used to determine the fate of a drug is the rate of its elimination, or *biological half-life*—the amount of time required for the elimination of one half of the amount administered. The rate at which lysergic acid diethylamide (LSD) is eliminated from two types of tissue is shown in figure 5.1.

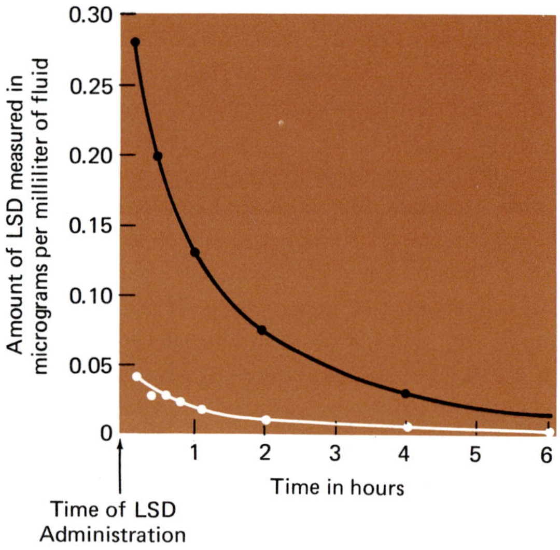

Figure 5.1 Rate at which LSD is eliminated after a single dose of 20 mg./kg. is injected into a monkey's bloodstream. The solid line represents the rate of elimination from the blood; the dotted line, the rate of elimination from the cerebrospinal fluid. (From Axelrod, J., Brady, R. O., Witkop, B. and Evarts, E. V. "The distribution and metabolism of lysergic acid diethylamide." Annual of New York Academy of Science 1957, 66:435.)

The effects of drugs vary from individual to individual and from species to species. The quantity of a drug required to produce a response or effect is termed the *dose*. The relationship between the dose and the size of the response is called the dose-response relation. Examples of dose-response relations are given in figures 5.2a and 5.2b. The curve in figure 5.2a demonstrates the relationship between the dose of the drug and the magnitude of the response, while the curve in figure 5.2b relates the dosage of a drug and the percentage of animals that respond to the drug. With such a curve it is possible to ascertain the dosage that affects fifty percent of the animals (the ED50). It is also possible to ascertain the dose that is lethal to fifty percent of the animals (the LD50). The ratio of these two numbers (LD50/ED50) is known as the *therapeutic index,* which is conventionally used to express the safe dosage of a drug; the larger the therapeutic index, the greater the margin of safety.

Drugs can be administered by several routes. However, the two routes commonly used to introduce a drug into the body are the *oral* and *parenteral* routes; the latter refers to a method of administration that does not involve the alimentary canal. A drug that is administered parenterally is usually injected subcutaneously (under the skin), intramuscularly (into muscle tissue), intravenously (into the blood stream), intraperitoneally (into the peritoneal cavity), or intracranially (into the brain).

Drugs That Affect the Nervous System and Behavior

Drugs can be classified in a variety of ways. For example, they can be distinguished from one another in terms of the principal tissue on which they act or in terms of their major action. Because our concern here is with drugs

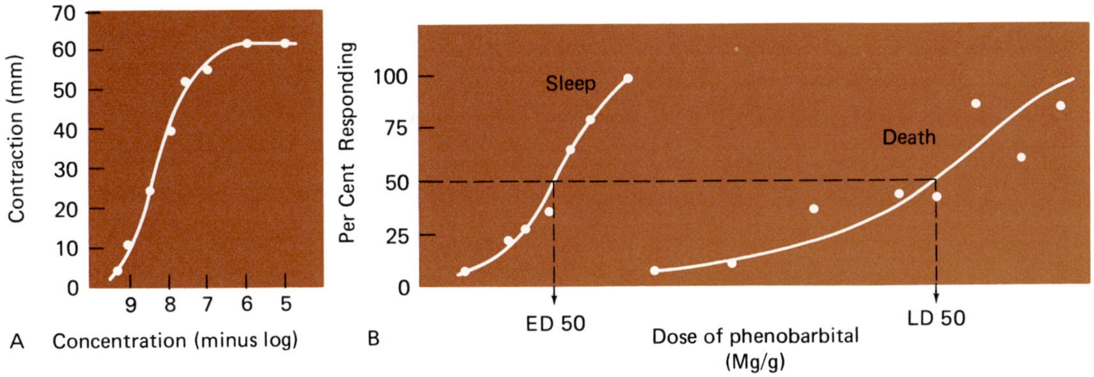

Figure 5.2 *Part A.* Hypothetical dose response curve in which the magnitude of the response (e.g., a muscle contraction measured in arbitrary units) is measured as a function of the dose of the drug injected. *Part B.* Actual dose-response curve obtained by measuring the "righting reflex" of mice in response to increasing doses (ED50) of phenobarbital (animals not showing this response were considered asleep). If the animals died within twenty-four hours, the dose was considered lethal and these data are plotted as a dose-response curve to the right of the illustration. (Part A after George A. Condouris in *Drill's Pharmacology in Medicine,* J. R. DiPalma (ed.) from R. F. Furchgott, S. F. Kippehar, M. Reiker and A. Schwab; Part B after George A. Condouris in *Drill's Pharmacology in Medicine,* J. R. DiPalma (ed.). McGraw-Hill Book Company. Reprinted by permission.)

that affect the nervous system, we should distinguish between drugs that act primarily on either the *autonomic nervous system* or the *central nervous system* (although many drugs act on both systems). Drugs that act on the central nervous system can also be classified further in terms of their principal pharmacological characteristics; for instance, certain drugs are neural *depressants* while others are neural *stimulants.*

Another way to classify drugs that affect the nervous system is according to their use. For instance, *anticonvulsants* are effective in the treatment of convulsive disorders such as epilepsy, while tranquilizers are used to treat psychiatric disorders. In the next section, several of the drugs listed in table 5.1 will be discussed.

Autonomic Nervous System

In Chapter 3 we noted that the autonomic nervous system is comprised of two divisions, the *sympathetic* and the *parasympathetic.* These divisions can be distinguished on the basis of *anatomical, biochemical, pharmacological,* and *functional* considerations. We also mentioned in Chapter 3 that the sympathetic and parasympathetic divisions of the autonomic nervous system often produce opposite effects on the organs they innervate. The sympathetic division increases heart rate, for example, while the parasympathetic division decreases heart rate. Because we will consider drugs that affect the autonomic as well as the central nervous system, it will be helpful to review some of the major anatomical differences between the sympathetic and parasympathetic divisions of the autonomic nervous system, which are illustrated schematically in figure 5.3.

Anatomical Differences

The nerves of the sympathetic division of the autonomic nervous system exit from the central nervous system, as do other efferent fibers,

Table 5.1 Drugs which act on the nervous system.

Category of Drugs	Effects
1. *DEPRESSANTS*	
A. *Barbiturates*	
i. Phenobarbital:	long-acting hypnotic and sedative
ii. Pentobarbital:	intermediate-acting hypnotic and sedative
B. *Aliphatic Alcohols*	
i. Ethyl alcohol:	intoxicant, slowing of brain wave rhythm
ii. Methyl alcohol:	
C. *Narcotic Analgesics*	
i. Morphine:	analgesic
ii. Codeine:	analgesic
2. *STIMULANTS*	
A. *Analeptics*	
i. Strychnine:	convulsant
ii. Pentenetetrazol:	convulsant
B. *Xanthines*	
i. Caffeine:	cerebral cortex stimulant
C. *Amphetamines*	
i. Amphetamine:	central stimulant
ii. Methamphetamine:	central stimulant
D. *Cocaine*	
i. Cocaine:	central stimulant, local anesthetic
ii. Procaine:	central stimulant, local anesthetic
3. *ANTIEPILEPTIC COMPOUNDS*	
A. Diphenylhydantoin:	anticonvulsant
B. Barbiturates (e.g., phenobarbital):	anticonvulsant
4. *MAJOR TRANQUILIZERS*	
A. Diphenylhydantoin:	antipsychotic
B. Reserpine:	antipsychotic
5. *MINOR TRANQUILIZERS*	
A. Meprobamate (Miltown):	antineurotic
B. Chlordiazepoxide (Librium):	antineurotic

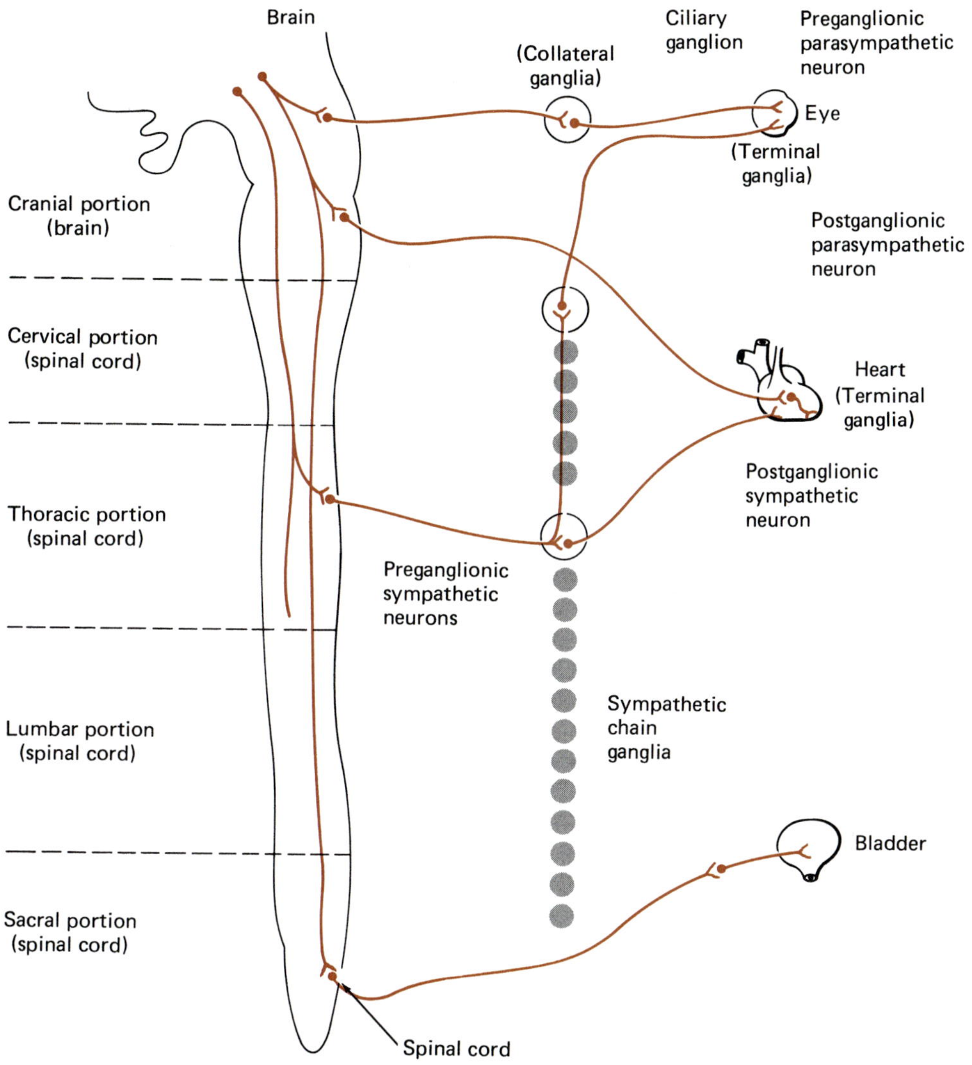

Figure 5.3 Schematic illustration of the autonomic nervous system. In the parasympathetic nervous system the preganglionic fibers leave the central nervous system at the level of the brain or the sacral portion of the spinal cord; typically the fibers terminate either in collateral or terminal ganglia. In the sympathetic division the preganglionic fibers leave the central nervous system at the level of the thoracic or lumbar portion of the spinal cord; then the fibers terminate in the sympathetic chain ganglia. Note: Many end organs, for example the eye and heart, are dually innervated. Parasympathetic stimulation results in constriction of the iris and deceleration of the heart. Sympathetic stimulation results in dilation of the iris and acceleration of the heart. In many instances the two branches of the autonomic nervous system have opposing functions.

by way of the ventral roots of the spinal cord. These efferent sympathetic fibers, however, terminate in a long interconnected chain of ganglia called the *sympathetic ganglionic chain,* as illustrated in figure 5.3. Efferent fibers of the parasympathetic division, on the other hand, typically end in either *collateral* or *terminal* ganglia. Whereas the sympathetic ganglia lie in a long chain next to the spinal column, collateral or terminal ganglia lie farther away from the spinal cord. In both branches of the autonomic nervous system, these nerves, or *preganglionic neurons,* synapse on the nerve cells that make up the sympathetic ganglionic chain, the collateral ganglia, or the terminal ganglia. In turn, the cells of the collateral and terminal ganglia leave the peripheral ganglia and terminate on or *innervate* target organs such as smooth muscles that line the blood vessels, heart, or glands. Cells that leave the peripheral ganglia to innervate these end organs are termed *postganglionic neurons.* Therefore, with few exceptions, the preganglionic nerve fibers of the sympathetic division are relatively short because they end in the sympathetic ganglionic chain close to the spinal cord; the postganglionic nerve fibers of the sympathetic division are relatively long because they must pass from the sympathetic ganglionic chain to the various target organs. Preganglionic fibers of the parasympathetic division are also relatively long since they must pass from the spinal cord to outlying collateral or terminal ganglia, while postganglionic fibers of the parasympathetic division are somewhat shorter.

In addition to these anatomical differences between the sympathetic and parasympathetic divisions, there is an important difference in the location of the cell bodies that give rise to preganglionic fibers in the two divisions. In the sympathetic division, efferent nerve cell bodies are located within the *thoracic* and *lumbar* regions of the spinal cord (see fig. 5.3). In the parasympathetic division, the nerve cell bodies giving rise to preganglionic fibers are located either in the *brain stem* and *cervical* region of the spinal cord or in the lowest segments of the spinal column, the *sacral* region.

Interestingly, the sympathetic division activates the adrenal glands, which in turn release epinephrine, a hormone with effects similar to those of norepinephrine. By activating the adrenal glands, the sympathetic division increases its effects on target organs because norepinephrine, which is released by postganglionic neurons, and epinephrine, which is released by the adrenal glands into the blood stream, produce similar effects such as increased heart rate, dilation of the pupils, and so forth.

Biochemical Differences

The sympathetic and parasympathetic divisions of the autonomic nervous system can also be distinguished in terms of the neurotransmitter substances that are released at synapses formed by the nerve fibers contained in these two systems. In the sympathetic system, the transmitter released by the preganglionic neurons is acetylcholine (ACh); the transmitter released by most postganglionic neurons of this system is norepinephrine (NE). Sites at which ACh is the transmitter are called *cholinergic* synapses, while sites where NE is the neurotransmitter are referred to as *adrenergic* synapses.

In the parasympathetic division, the transmitter released by both the pre- and postganglionic neurons is ACh. Figure 5.4 illustrates these important chemical differences between the two branches of the autonomic nervous system. It also shows that ACh is the transmitter released by spinal motor neurons, which innervate skeletal muscles and are not part of the autonomic nervous system.

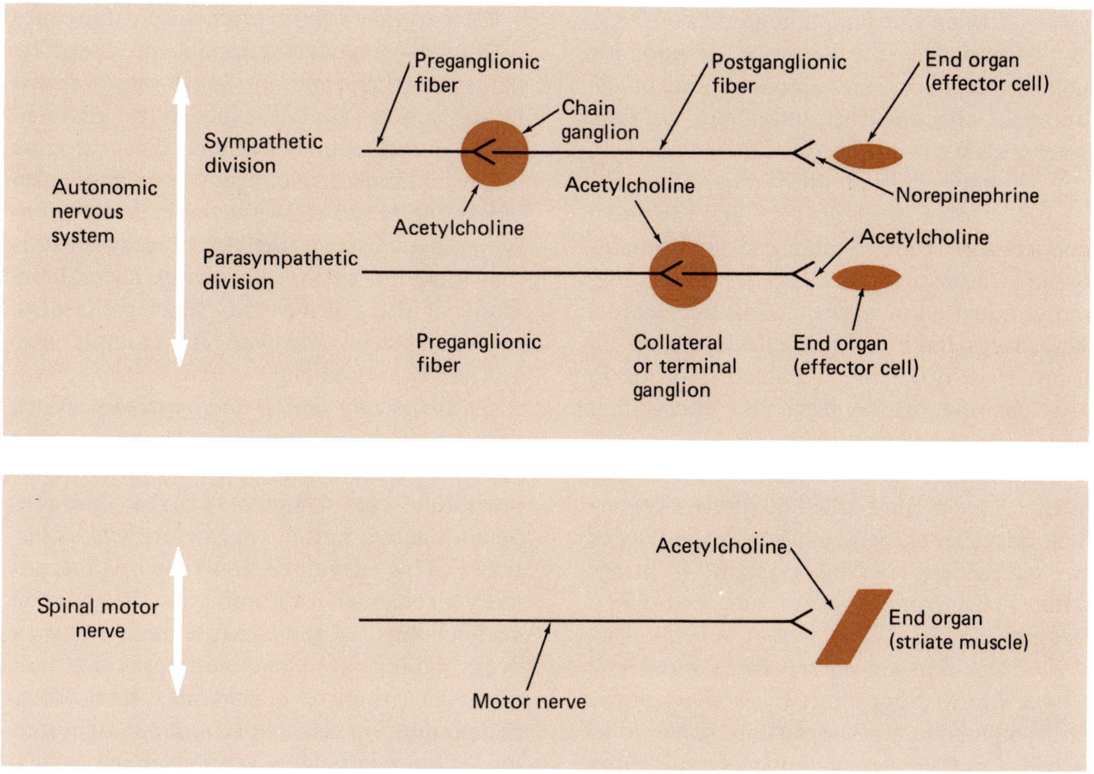

Figure 5.4 The transmitters at different junctions of the autonomic nervous system and at the *neuromuscular junction* of the spinal motor neurons.

Pharmacological Differences

Drugs may act selectively on either division of the autonomic nervous system. Some drugs tend to mimic the action of norepinephrine, released by the postganglionic neurons of the sympathetic division. Others block the action of this transmitter substance. Similarly, some drugs mimic the action of acetylcholine, released by both pre- and postganglionic fibers of the parasympathetic division, while others inhibit or block the action of acetylcholine. Examples of drugs that affect the autonomic nervous system are discussed below:

1. *Drugs that act on the sympathetic system.* As already suggested, drugs that act on the sympathetic system may be of two types. Some mimic the action of the sympathetic division of the autonomic nervous system and are collectively called sympathomimetic agents. Others inhibit normal sympathetic activity and are known as adrenergic blocking agents.

One class of sympathomimetic drugs, because of their chemical similarities, is collectively called *catecholamines:* examples are epinephrine, norepinephrine, and isoproterenol. A sympathomimetic drug that is not a catecholamine is *amphetamine.* All these drugs mimic activity of the sympathetic nervous system to some extent. For instance, epinephrine increases heart rate, dilates the pupils, and the like; these reactions are also observed when the sympathetic nervous system is activated. Furthermore, compounds such as epinephrine and amphetamine, in addition to affecting the autonomic nervous system, also act on the central nervous system. Humans injected with epinephrine, for example, often feel restless and anxious; amphetamine leads to increased motor activity and restlessness, feelings of well-being, and a reduction of appetite. In other words, these drugs have multiple effects, as do all drugs. How drugs are classified depends in large measure on the particular effects that interest the investigator.

An example of an adrenergic-blocking agent is a compound called dichloroisoproterenol. Because this drug inhibits the activity of the sympathetic nervous system, it brings about a decrease in heart rate and blood pressure.

2. *Drugs that act on the parasympathetic system.* Many drugs affect the activity of the parasympathetic nervous system; some do so by acting at the postganglionic synaptic junction. Drugs that stimulate the activity of the parasympathetic postganglionic junction are referred to as muscarinic agents, whereas those that are inhibitory at this site are called antimuscarinic agents.

In general, it is customary to distinguish between two types of cholinergic synapses (synapses at which acetylcholine is the neurotransmitter): (1) *muscarinic synapses,* at which ACh and *muscartine* are agonists and which are blocked by atropine and, if stimulated, produce postganglionic parasympathetic action on smooth muscles, the heart, and so forth; and (2) *nicotinic synapses,* at which ACh and nicotine are agonists, and that are antagonized by curare and, if stimulated, produce sympathetic stimulation and striate muscle activity. In other words, at muscarinic synapses, ACh and muscarine are agonists, and atropine is an antagonist. At nicotinic synapses, ACh and nicotine are agonists, and curare is an antagonist.

Pilocarpine, a muscarinic agent, stimulates salivation—an effect normally produced by parasympathetic activity. Salivation produced by the action of pilocarpine can be inhibited by the introduction of atropine. Thus atropine is an antimuscarinic agent. Atropine also blocks the action of acetylcholine in the parasympathetic system, thereby suppressing normal secretion of the mucous glands. Again, many of these drugs also affect the central nervous system. Atropine, for example, acts as a (CNS) stimulant.

3. *Drugs that inhibit cholinesterase.* When acetylcholine is released by a neuron into the synaptic space, it affects the postsynaptic membrane (see Chapter 3) and is then rendered inactive by the enzyme *acetylcholinesterase.* This enzymatic breakdown is the primary mechanism for terminating the action of acetylcholine at the synapse. A variety of drugs inhibit acetylcholinesterase and thus affect the activity of the nervous system. These compounds are referred to as *anticholinesterases.* One example is physostigmine, which inhibits the action of acetylcholinesterase by preventing its breakdown and allowing ACh to accumulate on the postsynaptic membrane. Thus physostigmine enhances the normal action of acetylcholine. Anticholinesterases affect both the autonomic and central nervous systems.

Central Nervous System (CNS)

A number of drugs affect the central nervous system, that is, they act on either the brain or the spinal cord. Many of them may be classified as *depressants* or *stimulants* depending on how they affect the central nervous system.

CNS Depressants

One class of CNS depressants are the so-called *hypnotics* and *sedatives,* such as barbiturates, which are commonly used to induce drowsiness and sleep. The degree of depression caused by the barbiturates depends on the kind that is used, the dose, route of administration, the organism's tolerance to the drug, and so forth.

Another familiar CNS depressant is *ethyl alcohol.* The depressive effects of alcohol, at least initially, are thought to be mediated by the drug's action on the *reticular activating system,* which has been implicated in the control of wakefulness and vigilance. Electrical stimulation of this system produces heightened attentiveness and arousal. When this system becomes depressed, the behavior of humans and animals becomes lethargic or depressed and this also affects mood, emotions, and motor coordination. When the concentration of alcohol in the blood is 0.06 percent (roughly the equivalent of two cocktails) the average person feels relaxed, "high," and so on. At a concentration of 0.10 percent (approximately three cocktails), a person is defined as legally drunk in California and is forbidden to drive. At concentrations of 0.15 percent (approximately five cocktails), the average individual becomes unsteady, his mental functioning suffers, and he looks drunk to an observer. Keep in mind that individuals vary widely in their tolerance to alcohol.

A third class of CNS depressants is made up of narcotic analgesics, such as morphine and heroin. Morphine, perhaps the oldest known narcotic analgesic, is used medically to alleviate severe pain. It also produces drowsiness and changes in mood.

CNS Stimulants

One class of drugs with excitatory effects on the central nervous system are the *convulsant stimulants* such as *strychnine* and *pentylenetetrazol (metrazol).* The convulsant stimulants are a diverse group of compounds in terms of both their chemical structure and their mechanisms of action. Collectively, they have been called *analeptic* drugs because they cause seizures. This effect, in the case of strychnine, is mediated in part by a blockade of inhibitory neural pathways.

A second class of CNS stimulants are the *xanthines.* Caffeine is probably the most familiar example of this group. A number of experimental studies have found that caffeine facilitates motor performance and mental activity, even at doses as low as those found in a single cup of coffee.

The *amphetamines* also stimulate the central nervous system, in addition to affecting the autonomic nervous system as noted earlier. Amphetamines have a variety of effects including anorexia (loss of appetite), hyperthermia (increased body temperature), lessening of fatigue, elation and so forth. If taken continuously for periods of days or weeks in high doses, as is common among abusers of this drug, amphetamine may lead to a condition termed "amphetamine psychosis." This condition is nearly identical to paranoid schizophrenia. The study of the mechanisms by which amphetamine acts is currently believed to be one way of understanding the mechanisms underlying psychotic disorders. Amphetamine appears to act in part by releasing the biogenic amines from synapses in the central and peripheral nervous system, which you will recall from Chapter 3 include norepinephrine, dopamine, and serotonin. The basis for its psychotic effects is not yet fully understood, although it may be in part related to changes in transmission at these synapses.

Another CNS stimulant is *cocaine,* a drug obtained from the leaves of trees indigenous to South America. Cocaine is an interesting drug because it affects the peripheral and central nervous systems differently. When applied locally, it prevents sensations in the areas by blocking neural conduction. Thus *novocaine,* a synthetic variety of cocaine, is used as an anaesthetic in dentistry. In the central nervous system, however, cocaine acts as a stimulant, similar in many respects to amphetamine, and as such has an excitatory effect on behavior. In man, these effects include an increased ability to perform hard physical labor, restlessness, excitement and talkativeness, and an increased ability to do certain types of mental work, according to the results of some experiments! At high doses, the drug causes seizures.

Cocaine also affects the sympathetic nervous system. As we noted earlier, norepinephrine (NE) is the neurotransmitter released by the postganglionic nerves in the sympathetic nervous system. NE's effects are terminated by a re-uptake mechanism through which the transmitter is reabsorbed into the presynaptic terminal. Because cocaine enhances the release of NE and inhibits the re-uptake mechanism, NE persists for longer periods in the synaptic space. In this manner, the drug increases the activity of the end organs innervated by postganglionic sympathetic neurons.

Sigmund Freud was among the first to study the clinical actions of cocaine. The accounts of his work and his experiences with the drug in the late nineteenth century are fascinating to read, as you will see in box 5.1.

The Use of Drugs in Behavioral Research

Psychologists have used many kinds of drugs as aids to understand various aspects of behavior. In this section we will discuss the use of analeptic drugs in research on the learning and memory storage processes—specifically, the use of these drugs to study time-dependent processes involved in memory storage.

Very early in the history of research on memory storage, the hypothesis was formulated that experience is not stored permanently in memory until some time after it had occurred. In its original form, this hypothesis was proposed to account for the observation that the acquisition of new information interferes with the retention, or memory of previously learned material. Muller and Pilzecker (1900) were the first to propose that some neural process which underlies memory continues or perseverates for some time after learning. More precisely, they suggested that memory exists in an unstable form after learning and becomes fixed or consolidated only after some time has elapsed. In other words, the formation of permanent memories, sometimes referred to as *long-term memory,* depends on some time-dependent process. This idea is known as the *perseveration-consolidation hypothesis.* You will read about this as well as other theories of memory in Chapter 12.

The perseveration-consolidation hypothesis also attempts to explain retrograde *amnesia*—the loss of memory for recently acquired information—which is often observed in victims of head injuries. Russell and Nathan (1946), for example, found that seventy-five percent of these cases suffered amnesia for events that occurred half an hour before the injury. Hebb (1949) is credited with formulating the modern version of this idea, the so-called *dual-trace hypothesis,* which states that the neural activity initiated by an experience persists for some time afterward. This activity, which he hypothesized to be *reverberatory activity* in certain neural circuits, sustains the memory in some form until it is changed into a long-term memory. The reverberatory neural activity is also assumed to produce the neural changes necessary for consolidation to occur.

Many techniques exist for interfering with memory storage, and it is assumed that this is caused by disruption of the consolidation process. (This research will be covered in some detail in Chapter 13.) In this section, we will consider the opposite proposition: that if techniques were available to increase the rate of consolidation, then the rate of memory storage should be facilitated.

A vast amount of research literature has been accumulated on the effects of pharma-

Box 5.1
Sigmund Freud and Cocaine

In his biography, *The Life and Work of Sigmund Freud,* Vol. 1 (1953), Ernest Jones devotes an entire chapter to Freud's experiences with cocaine (see "The Cocaine Episode").

Between 1884 and 1887, Freud was preoccupied with two thoughts: his fiancé, Martha Bernays, and achieving a distinguished reputation in clinical medicine. To achieve his professional reputation, which would enable him to marry Martha, he decided to work on the drug cocaine, thinking that it might be useful in a number of ways, either as a substitute for morphine in medical practice or as a method of treating morphine addicts. Although his work did not proceed without difficulties, Freud became enthusiastic about it and expressed his enthusiasm in a letter to Martha:

> *If all goes well, I will write an essay on . . . [cocaine], and I expect it will win its place in therapeutics, by the side of morphium and superior to it. I have other hopes and intentions about it. I take very small doses of it regularly against depression and against indigestion, and with the most brilliant success. I hope it will be able to abolish the most intractable vomiting, even when this is due to severe pain; in short, it is only now that I feel I am a doctor, since I have helped one patient and hope to help more. If things go on in this way, we need have no concerns about being able to come together and stay in Vienna.*

Freud even sent some cocaine to Martha—"to make her strong and give her cheeks a red color." When he heard that Martha did not look well and lacked appetite, he wrote: "Woe to you, my Princess, when I come. I will kiss you until you are quite red and feed you till you are plump. And if you are froward, you shall see who is the stronger, a gentle little girl who doesn't eat enough, or a big wild man who has cocaine in his body."

However, it was Carl Koller, an intern in ophthalmology, not Freud, who discovered the clinical use of cocaine. After trying several drugs to anesthetize the surface of the eye during surgery, Koller finally tried cocaine and was successful. Because Freud had introduced Koller to cocaine, a dispute arose between the two men about whom should receive credit for this pharmacological discovery. Koller received credit for discovering the local anesthetic action of cocaine while Freud went on to discover psychoanalysis.

cological agents on memory storage: certain types of drugs appear to enhance memory. (For a complete review of the effects of analeptic drugs on memory processes, see McGaugh and Petrinovich, 1965, who studied the effects of analeptic drugs on memory storage processes extensively.)

McGaugh and Thompson (1962) injected rats with either strychnine or saline solution (control injections) and studied the animals' ability to learn a maze. The animals used in this study were descendents of Tryon's maze-bright and maze-dull rats, which were discussed in Chapter 2. To learn the maze, the animals had to solve a problem involving visual discrimination and were given massed trials, that is, the intervals between trials were quite short. During training, the rats received foot shocks for making incorrect responses. Some were injected with strychnine, others with saline solution a few minutes *before* the learning trials. The animals were then placed in the maze, and the number of errors they made in learning the maze was recorded. Table 5.2 shows the results of this experiment; the number of errors on trials 2 through 7 are included for maze-bright and maze-dull rats. In general, rats injected with strychnine learned the maze more rapidly and made fewer errors than those injected with saline solution. The degree of facilitation was related to the dose of the drug.

Table 5.2 Effects of strychnine on the number of errors made by maze-bright (S_1) and maze-dull (S_3) rats while learning. Strychnine facilitated learning, especially in S_3 animals.

	Control Group 0.9% Saline			High-Dose 1.25 Mg./Kg.		
Strain	N	M	S.D.	N	M	S.D.
S_1	10	26.5	4.48	12	20.2	5.35
S_3	10	22.2	2.99	11	13.8	4.57

Source: J.L. McGaugh and C.W. Thompson, "Facilitation of simultaneous discrimination learning with strychnine sulphate," *Psychopharmacologia*, 1962, pp. 166–172. Used by permission of Springer-Verlag, New York, Inc., Publishers.

How do we interpret the results of this experiment? One possible interpretation is that strychnine somehow facilitates the neural mechanisms underlying the learning process. On the other hand, it is difficult to rule out other interpretations on the basis of one experiment. An alternative explanation might be that strychnine somehow lowers the pain threshold and that the animals injected with the drug learned the maze more efficiently because they felt the pain of the foot shock more severely. If this was the case, then we can explain McGaugh's and Thompson's results in terms of motivational variables. Perhaps strychnine enhanced the animals' vision or made them more attentive. If so, then we can explain the results on the basis of sensory or attentional variables. In other words, on the basis of this experiment alone, it is difficult to say that strychnine facilitates learning or memory processes *per se*.

The results of other experiments make this interpretation seem more likely, however. For example, an experiment conducted by Breen and McGaugh (1961) differed in at least four respects from that of McGaugh and Thompson. For instance, they used a different neural stimulant, *picrotoxin;* a more complex maze; positive reinforcement in the form of food; and most important, they injected the neural stimulant *after* rather than before the learning trials.

Breen and McGaugh used maze-bright and maze-dull rats in their experiment. All animals were deprived of food before the learning trials. Each animal had one trial per day in the maze and was rewarded with food. Thus, the learning trials were distributed rather than massed. Immediately after each trial, half the animals were injected with picrotoxin; the other half were injected with saline solution. The results indicated that the animals injected with picrotoxin made significantly fewer errors than the control rats, with the number of errors decreasing as the dose was increased. Furthermore, the degree of improvement was significantly greater among maze-dull rats.

What conclusions can be drawn on the basis of Breen's and McGaugh's experiment? First, the effect of neural stimulants in terms of improving the performance of animals in learning situations is probably the result of the action of these compounds on memory storage processes *per se*. In this experiment, the drug was given *after* each trial. Thus, during the actual trial, the animals were free of the drug. The next trial was not given until twenty-four hours after the drug had been administered; this was sufficient time for the drug to be completely metabolized and eliminated. Therefore, motivational, perceptual, or attentive mechanisms that were operative during the trial could not be influenced by the drug. (See box 5.2.) Second, a variety of neural stimulants have a similar effect on the performance of animals in these situa-

Box 5.2

Effects of Analeptic Drugs on Latent Learning

Westbrook and McGaugh (1964) used a synthetic strychninelike neural stimulant in an experiment that is especially interesting because it investigated a phenomenon called latent learning. Latent learning refers to the acquisition of new information in the absence of reinforcement and is important in the history of psychology because it addresses the question of whether reinforcement is both a necessary and sufficient condition for learning to occur. There is little doubt that reinforcement is sufficient for learning, because animals do learn when they are reinforced. However, whether reinforcement is necessary for learning to occur was a question much debated in psychological theories of the 1940s and 1950s. For example, does an animal learn anything when it merely explores a maze on its own. The results of experiments on latent learning suggest that it does, although the results of this type of acquisition are not observable until reinforcement is introduced into the situation.

In the experiment described here, maze-dull and maze-bright rats were taught a six-unit T-maze, one trial per day for five days. Half the animals were rewarded after each trial; the other half were not. Each group was then divided into two subgroups; some animals were injected with the neural stimulant after each trial, the others were injected with saline solution. The results of the first half of this experiment are summarized in box figure 5.2a. The animals that were reinforced made significantly fewer errors than those which were not rewarded. Within the reinforced group, those that received the drug made significantly fewer errors than the control animals.

During the second phase of the experiment (trials 6 through 10), all animals were reinforced after each trial. The results are plotted in box figure 5.2b. Notice that the animals which had not been rewarded during the first phase did as well as those which had been rewarded. This suggests that the nonreinforced group did acquire some knowledge about the maze during the first half of the experiment, but it was not observed until reinforcement was introduced. Thus the experiment illustrates that latent learning did indeed take place.
In addition, the animals injected with the neural stimulant made significantly fewer errors than did the animals injected with saline solution.

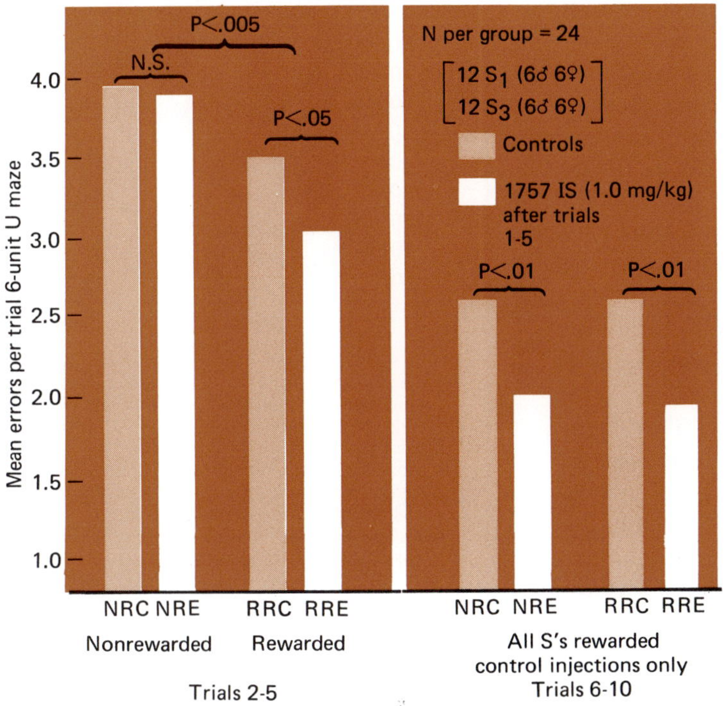

Box Figure 5.2 Effect of 1775 I.S., an analeptic drug, and reinforcement on learning and performance in rats. There were four groups of rats in each experiment: nonrewarded controls (saline injected) (NRC), nonrewarded experimental (drug injected) (NRE), rewarded controls (RRC), and rewarded experimental (RRE) animals. (From McGaugh, J. L. "Facilitation and Impairment of Memory Storage Processes." In D. P. Kimble (ed.) THE ANATOMY OF MEMORY. Palo Alto, California: Science and Behavior Books, 1965.)

tions. Third, neither the type of learning nor the motivational condition under which the experiment is performed, is important; that is, these drugs have the same effect in simple or complex learning situations, whether the animal is rewarded by negative or positive reinforcements.

These experiments and many others indicate that neural stimulants facilitate learning or memory, regardless of the stimulant used, the species of animal being tested, or the type of learning being studied. Precisely how these drugs act, in terms of their facilatory effects on learning, remains to be determined. One tentative explanation is that neural stimulants enhance learning by speeding up the consolidation process.

We have cited these experiments to illustrate how psychologists use drugs as tools to study behavior. Several additional examples are offered in box 5.3.

Drugs of Abuse and Drug Addiction

It is difficult to define precisely what we mean by the term *drugs of abuse* for several reasons: first, because the term can be defined in a variety of ways and, second, because words such as "drug addict," "heroin," and "cocaine" carry emotional overtones. In the following paragraphs, we will offer several definitions of the term drugs of abuse and point out some of the difficulties associated with them.

In the social context, drugs of abuse are defined as drugs that are taken in ways and in quantities which are disapproved of by the majority in a particular society. This definition has certain inherent problems, not the least of which is that it is too broad. For example, many people in our society consume vitamins and headache remedies in quantities that most people would consider excessive.

Box 5.3

Effects of Amphetamines on Food Intake and on Electrical Activity in the Hypothalamus

As we mentioned earlier, the amphetamines are classified as stimulants because they tend to increase the excitability of the central nervous system, as reflected in increased locomotor activity, reduced fatigue, and the like. However, amphetamines may also exhibit depressant properties, depending in part on the frequency of certain behaviors at the time the drug is administered and the type of behavior being studied. An example of the latter phenomenon is observed in hyperactive children who have been treated with amphetamines to reduce their activity. An example of the latter phenomenon is the way amphetamines affect eating behavior.

Box figure 5.3a illustrates the effects of various doses of two molecular forms of amphetamine, d- and 1-amphetamine, on food consumption in adult rats. The data are plotted as percentage food intake as a function of the dose of the amphetamines

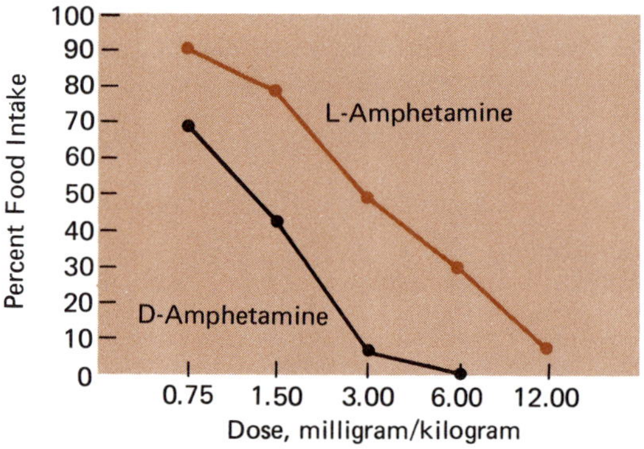

Box Figure 5.3a The effect of d- and 1-amphetamine on food intake in rats. The dose-response relation is given for both the d- and 1-form of the drug. Note that the d-form is much more potent than the 1-form. (From L. A. Baez. "Role of catecholamines in the anorectic effects of amphetamines in rats." *Psychopharmacoligia* 35:95. Reprinted by permission of Springer-Verlag, Berlin Heidelberg, New York.)

that were administered. Animals injected with saline were used as controls. Both forms of the drug reduced the food consumption of these animals. If we determine the dose of each form that is necessary to reduce the animals' food intake by fifty percent, the proportion is 1.38 milligram per kilogram of d-amphetamine to 3.80 milligrams per kilogram of 1-amphetamine. Thus the d- form of the drug is approximately three times more potent than the 1- form; the only difference in their molecular structure is that they are mirror images of each other.

One possible explanation for the amphetamines' ability to depress appetite can be deduced from their action on cells of the hypothalamus. The effects of ventromedial hypothalamic lesions on eating behavior in rats were discussed in Chapter 3. Because these lesions caused a substantial increase in food consumption, it appears that the ventromedial nuclei of the hypothalamus—or fiber tracts passing through it—are inhibitory with respect to eating behavior. Box figure 5.3b illustrates the findings of Brobeck, Larsson, and Reyes (1956), who investigated the effects of amphetamine on the electrical activity of cells in the ventromedial hypothalamic region.

According to these data, amphetamine decreased neural activity in most areas of the hypothalamus, a result which is analogous to that observed during barbiturate anesthesia. However, cells in the ventromedial hypothalamic nucleus responded to amphetamine by increased electrical activity.

These results are predictable, based on the belief that this nucleus inhibits eating behavior. One interpretation of the effects of amphetamines as appetite depressants might be in terms of their *excitatory* actions on an *inhibitory* mechanism in the ventromedial hypothalamic nuclei.

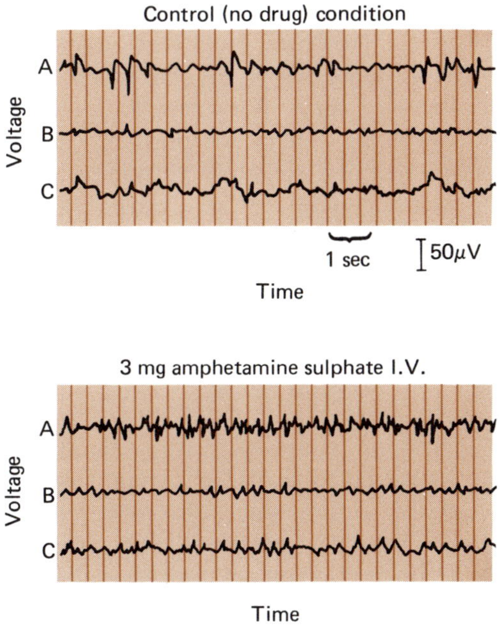

Box Figure 5.3b Electrical activity in various parts of the hypothalamus under controlled conditions and after intravenous injection of amphetamine sulphate. A = activity in ventromedial hypothalamus; B = activity in rostrolateral hypothalamus; C = activity in caudal hypothalamus. Note the increased activity in A after amphetamine. (From J. R. Brobeck, S. Larsson, and E. Reyes, "A study of the electrical activity of the hypothalamic feeding mechanism." *Journal of Physiology* (London) 132, 1956, pp. 358–364. Reprinted by permission of Cambridge University Press and J. R. Brobeck.)

Scale: Horizontal axis = time, where ⏟ = 1 second. Vertical axis = voltage where I = 50μV.

Are these compounds drugs of abuse? In our society the answer is no; headache remedies or "across the counter drugs" are not considered drugs of abuse.

If we look at the list of drugs that are classified as drugs of abuse, we are struck by the fact that they affect mood and behavior. However, even this restricted definition causes problems. For example, is morphine—a drug that affects mood and behavior—a drug of abuse? Not if a physician prescribes it for relieving a patient's pain. On the other hand, if a person takes morphine simply because it makes him feel good, then it is considered a drug of abuse.

Finally, it is important to realize that what is classified as a drug of abuse in one society or culture is not necessarily classified as such in another. In our society, cocaine is considered a drug of abuse. However, this is not the case among the natives of some South American cultures.

Drugs of abuse can also be defined in behavioral terms because they lead to addiction. But in the behavioral context, we must also define what we mean by addiction, and this is not an easy task. The word addiction can be used to refer to a compulsive search for and use of a particular drug. This behavior is often antisocial because the drug that is sought is illegal.

Addiction can also refer to the use of drugs that harm the user or other people. Finally, the use of many drugs of abuse result in the development of *tolerance* and *physical dependence,* phenomena that will be discussed in the next section.

Table 5.3 lists the common drugs of abuse, the slang terms used to identify them, the symptoms commonly associated with their use, and the common methods of administering them. However, keep in mind that the symptoms attributed to each drug will not necessarily occur in every individual.

In the next section, we will briefly consider the different categories of drugs of abuse, their behavioral effects, and some experiments in which these compounds were used.

Categories of Drugs of Abuse

Drugs of abuse are commonly separated into three classifications: (1) the *narcotic analgesics,* which include the opiates such as morphine, codeine, heroin, and methadone and their antagonists such as nalorphine, (2) the *central nervous system depressants* such as the barbiturates and ethyl alcohol, and (3) the *central nervous system stimulants* such as amphetamines and cocaine. The so-called psychoactive drugs—LSD and marihuana—are often placed in the third category because of their excitatory properties.

This system of classifying drugs of abuse is based on whether a drug's effects on the central nervous system are predominantly excitatory or inhibitory. These terms are useful because drugs classified under these headings do indeed have either depressant or stimulant effects. However, drugs that are classified as depressants may have some excitatory effects and vice versa. For example, high doses of morphine, which is a depressant, can produce seizures (an excitatory phenomenon) in animals of some species. Conversely, the amphetamines, which are stimulants, can depress appetite; cocaine, a stimulant, also acts as a local anesthetic. In other words, although these categories are useful, you should keep these qualifications in mind.

Narcotic Analgesics

As we noted earlier, the major medical use of the narcotic analgesics is to relieve pain. For example, morphine and codeine, both derivatives of opium, are generally used for this purpose. One advantage these drugs have over other analgesics is that in moderate doses they relieve pain without inducing sleep. High doses, however, do result in drowsiness and sleep. The subjective sensation of pain is a complex sensory modality; it can be induced by stimulating certain sensory nerves, which when excited do not produce any other sensation. This aspect of pain is usually referred to as a sensory attribute. However, the degree to which the stimulation of these nerves elicits the experience of pain can be modulated by other factors, including other sensory stimuli. This aspect of pain is usually referred to as a perceptual or "psychological" attribute. The narcotic analgesics appear to affect both the sensory and the perceptual aspects of pain. Morphine, for example, raises the threshold of excitation of pain fibers, but not to a pronounced degree. Morphine also affects the perception of pain: Thus, individuals who have been treated with morphine report that they can still feel pain but are indifferent to it.

The behavioral effects of the narcotic analgesics are varied and depend on a number of factors. One factor is the individual's experience with these drugs. Few people, including confirmed addicts, report that their first experience with these drugs was pleasurable. After some experience with the drugs, however, they feel euphoric after the drug is administered. Addicts report that these drugs reduce their anxieties associated with social interactions as well as their desire for food and sex. The more pronounced physiological effects of these drugs are nausea and vomiting, pupillary constriction, constipation, changes in body temperature, and so forth.

The abuse of the narcotic analgesics is a problem of staggering proportions in the United States. More than 600,000 people are estimated to abuse these drugs. The most frequently abused narcotic analgesic is heroin, which is synthesized from opium. Heroin passes into brain tissue much more readily than does morphine, but once there it changes into morphine. Heroin is obtained through an illegal drug traffic that is centered largely in the metropolitan areas. The following sociological data have been obtained on drug addicts: (1) Until recently, a large proportion of drug users came from the lower socioeconomic groups, but drugs are now being used increasingly by more affluent groups. (2) Male users outnumber female users. (3) Most individuals who abuse the narcotic analgesics have had previous experience with other drugs, such as tranquilizers or marihuana. However, there are no reliable data to indicate that there is a relationship between use of these drugs and abuse of the narcotic analgesics. (4) Addicts were first enticed to try drugs by other addicts, not, as is popularly believed, by professional pushers.

Why do some people become addicted to drugs such as heroin? There are no clear-cut answers to this important question, although a number of theories address the problem. One theory suggests that users of the narcotic analgesics suffer from long-standing psychiatric problems and begin taking drugs to relieve the anxieties associated with these problems. If this theory is correct, we would expect to find common personality traits among users of these drugs, and according to some research findings, this is indeed the case. As a group, narcotic addicts find it difficult to cope with their aggressive, dependent, and sexual feelings. Furthermore, they tend to handle these feelings by avoiding situations in which they might arise.

Other theories suggest that learning is involved in addiction; in other words, addicts learn to appreciate the euphoria produced by the drugs. Thus an individual may become addicted through a chain of events similar to the following: At first he may be reinforced by the pain-reducing qualities of these drugs. Later he may find that the social and behavioral consequences of using drugs are reward-

Table 5.3 Terms and symptoms of drug abuse.

BUREAU OF NARCOTICS

Terms & Symptoms of Drug Abuse

This chart indicates the most common symptoms of drug abuse. However, all of the signs are not always evident, nor are they the only ones that may occur. Any drug's reaction will usually depend on the person, his mood, his environment, the dosage of the drug and how the drug interacts with other drugs the abuser has taken or contaminants within the drug.

	SLANG TERMS	DROWSINESS	EXCITATION & HYPERACTIVITY	IRRITABILITY & RESTLESSNESS	BELLIGERENCE	ANXIETY	EUPHORIA	DEPRESSION	HALLUCINATIONS	PANIC	IRRATIONAL BEHAVIOR	CONFUSION	TALKATIVENESS	RAMBLING SPEECH	SLURRED SPEECH	LAUGHTER
MORPHINE	M, dreamer, white stuff, hard stuff, morpho, Miss Emma, monkey	●		○		○ ●	●	○	●	○		○			●	
HEROIN	H, snow, junk, horse, dope, smack, skag	●		○		○ ●	●	○		○		○			●	
CODEINE	Schoolboy	●		○		○ ●	●	○		○		○			●	
HYDROMORPHONE	Dilaudid, Lords	●		○		○ ●	●	○		○		○			●	
MEPERIDINE	Demerol, Isonipecaine, Dolantol, Pethidine	●		○		○ ●	●	○	●	○		○			●	
METHADONE	Dolophine, Dollies, dolls, amidone	●		○		○ ●	●	○		○		○			●	
EXEMPT PREPARATIONS	P.G., P.O., blue velvet (Paregoric with antihistamine), red water, bitter, licorice	●		○		○	●	○		○		○				
COCAINE	The leaf, dynamite, gold dust, coke, flake, speedball (when mixed with Heroin)		●	●		●	●		●				●			
MARIHUANA	Smoke, weed, grass, pot, Mary Jane, joint, reefer, tea, hash, roach	●	●	●		●	●	●	●	●			●			●
AMPHETAMINES	A's, pep pills, bennies, uppers, whites		●	●		●	●		●	●			●			
METHAMPHETAMINE	Speed, meth, splash, crystal, methedrine		●	●		●	●		●	●			●			
OTHER STIMULANTS	Pep pills, uppers		●	●			●		●				●			
BARBITURATES	Yellow jackets, reds, seccy, pink ladies, blues, red & blues, barbs, phennies	●		○ ●	●	○	●	●	○		●	●			●	●
OTHER DEPRESSANTS	Candy, goofballs, sleeping pills	●		○ ●	●	○	●	●	○		●	●			●	
LYSERGIC ACID DIETHLAMIDE (LSD)	Acid, cubes, sugar, instant Zen		●			●	●	●	●	●	●			●		
STP	Serenity, tranquility, peace, DOM, syndicate acid						●	●	●		●			●		
PHENCYCLIDINE (PCP)	PCP, peace pill, synthetic marihuana	●				●				●		●				●
PEYOTE	P, Mescal button, cactus, Mesc.		●	●		●			●					●		
PSILOCYBIN	Sacred mushrooms, mushroom		●	●		●	●	●	●		●			●		
DIMETHLTRYPTAMINE (DMT)	DMT, 45-minute psychosis, businessman's special		●			●	●	●	●		●			●		

● SYMPTOMS OF ABUSE

AND DANGEROUS DRUGS

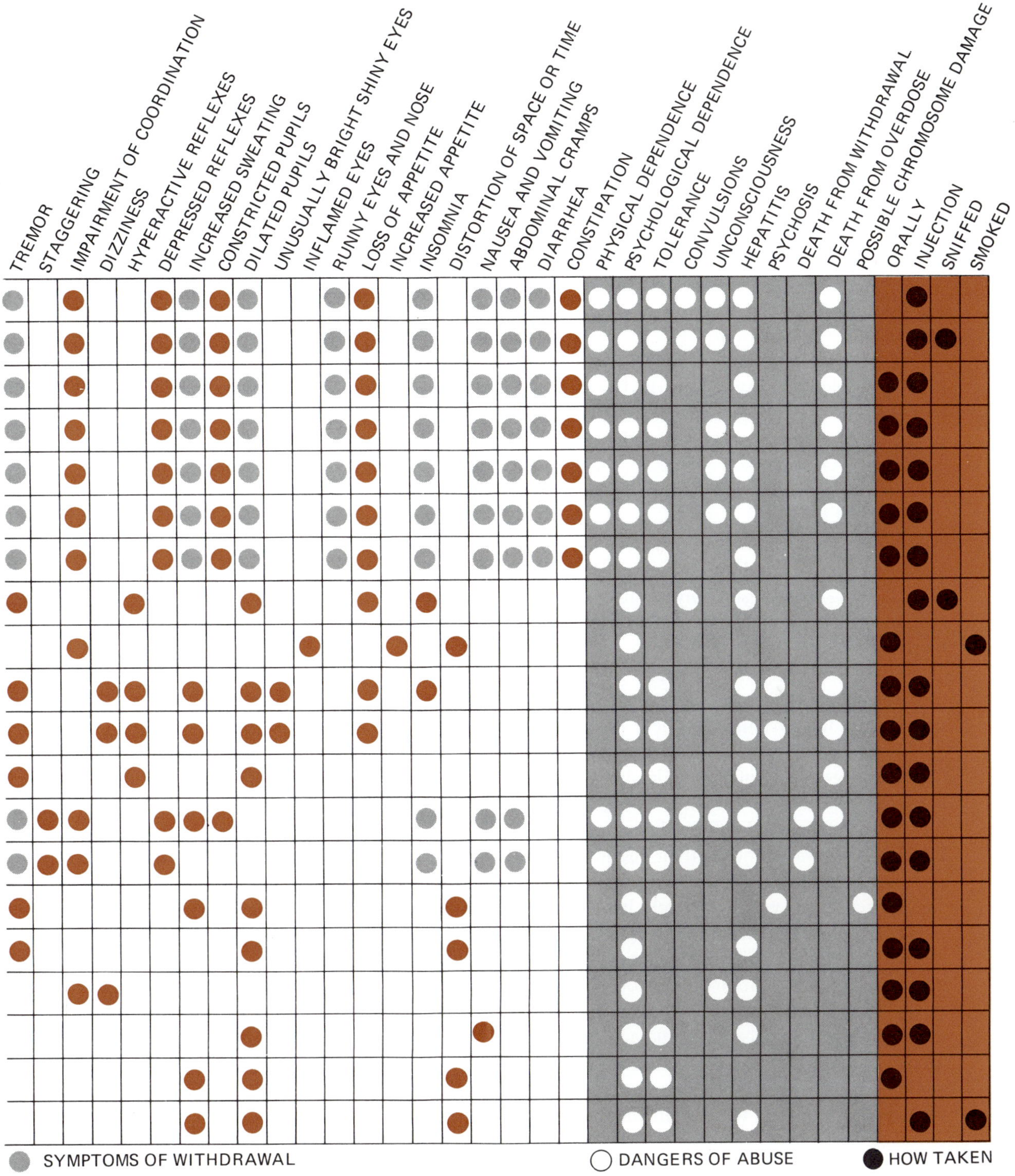
TREMOR
STAGGERING
IMPAIRMENT OF COORDINATION
DIZZINESS
HYPERACTIVE REFLEXES
DEPRESSED REFLEXES
INCREASED SWEATING
CONSTRICTED PUPILS
DILATED PUPILS
UNUSUALLY BRIGHT SHINY EYES
INFLAMED EYES
RUNNY EYES AND NOSE
LOSS OF APPETITE
INCREASED APPETITE
INSOMNIA
DISTORTION OF SPACE OR TIME
NAUSEA AND VOMITING
ABDOMINAL CRAMPS
DIARRHEA
CONSTIPATION
PHYSICAL DEPENDENCE
PSYCHOLOGICAL DEPENDENCE
TOLERANCE
CONVULSIONS
UNCONSCIOUSNESS
HEPATITIS
PSYCHOSIS
DEATH FROM WITHDRAWAL
DEATH FROM OVERDOSE
POSSIBLE CHROMOSOME DAMAGE
ORALLY
INJECTION
SNIFFED
SMOKED
SYMPTOMS OF WITHDRAWAL
DANGERS OF ABUSE
HOW TAKEN

ing. Finally, he may continue using drugs because he is afraid of what will happen if he withdraws from them.

There are many problems associated with this theory. For example, why do individuals use the drugs the first few times if the experience is extremely unpleasant? Once an individual becomes addicted, however, there is little doubt that these drugs possess reinforcing properties. These properties have been studied in animal research, some examples of which are summarized in box 5.4.

CNS Depressants

The most widely used and abused CNS depressant is alcohol. Excessive drinking causes more serious psychological, social, and physiological consequences than all other drugs combined. Although some investigators consider alcoholism a *behavior disorder,* others consider it a disease.

In small doses, alcohol may have some excitatory effects, including a transient feeling of well-being that presumably results from a release of inhibition. Some individuals, particularly creative artists, appear to do better work when slightly intoxicated. Objective assessments of their performance also indicate some improvement, which has been explained as a release from intellectual inhibitions. Larger doses of alcohol lead to intoxication and sedation. At such concentrations, individuals find it difficult to distinguish between wishes and actions, their judgment is seriously impaired, and their motor coordination decreases. Even at relatively low doses, psychomotor skills such as driving an automobile are impaired. The physiological effects of alcohol include dilation of the blood vessels in the skin (the face appears flushed, for example), increased pulse rate, and accelerated breathing.

Genetic, psychoanalytic, and social theories have been proposed to explain alcoholism.

Box 5.4

The Rewarding Properties of Drugs

The experiments discussed here (Thompson and Schuster, 1968; Schuster, 1970) demonstrate that certain types of behavior can be reinforced and maintained in experimental animals by administering drugs of abuse.

In one experiment, catheters were inserted into the jugular veins of monkeys. The animals were then placed in restraining chairs (see box fig. 5.4a) and were injected with morphine through the catheter four times a day for thirty days.

After thirty days, the actual experiment began. A white stimulus light and a telegraph key were presented to the animals; the light was illuminated every six hours for fifteen minutes. During the initial phases of the experiment, the animals were injected with morphine during the fifteen-minute intervals, whether or not they

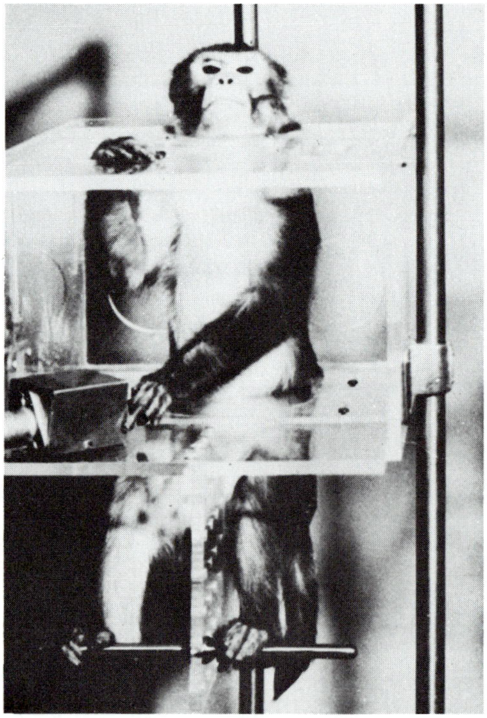

a

pressed the lever. Within one week, the animals were administering morphine to themselves during the fifteen minute intervals by pressing the lever. The period between the onset of the light stimulus and the response of pressing the lever decreased with training. Thus monkeys learned to make a response, pressing the lever, reinforced by the administration of morphine.

The results of a similar experiment by Schuster (1970) are reproduced in box figure 5.4b. In this experiment, monkeys pressed a lever for saline injections during the first phase of the experiment and received morphine for the last thirty days of the experiment. Although saline did not increase the frequency of lever pressing, the number of morphine injections the monkeys gave themselves increased with training.

The phenomenon of *tolerance* has also been investigated using these techniques. Tolerance means that after repeated administration of certain drugs such as morphine, greater amounts are required to produce the same effect. Schuster and Thompson (1969) asked whether monkeys would infuse themselves with more and more morphine as their tolerance to its effects increased. The answer to this question was yes. If given the opportunity, the animals did inject themselves with more and more morphine, presumably to produce the same effect.

These experiments demonstrate that morphine has reinforcing or rewarding properties which can lead to the acquisition of new behaviors. Similar experiments with other drugs have demonstrated that animals will abuse virtually every drug abused by man, with the exception of LSD (Schuster and Thompson, 1969).

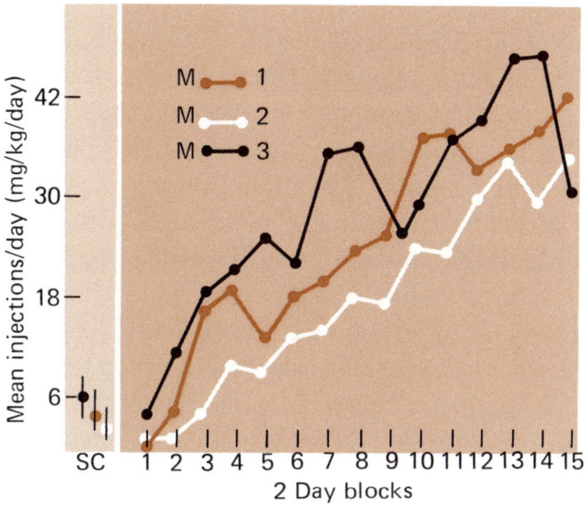

b

Box Figure 5.4a A monkey in a restraining seat. Other equipment consists of a telegraph key on which the animal makes its response. (Photo courtesy of Department of the Army. Walter Reed Army Institute of Research.)

Box Figure 5.4b. Lever pressing by three monkeys for morphine reinforcement. The data at the bottom left (SC) represent the responses made while the animals received saline injections. The rest of the data were obtained during the following thirty days (plotted in blocks of two days), when the animals were injected with morphine. It is important to remember that all injections were contingent upon the monkey's lever-press response. (From Schuster, C. R., "Psychological approaches to opiate dependence and self-administration by laboratory animals," *Federation Proceedings* 29, 1970, pp. 2–5. Reprinted by permission of of Federation of America Societies for Experimental Biology and C. R. Schuster.)

For instance, Jessor, Graves, Hanson, and Jessor (1968) suggested that a number of psychological and social factors are conducive to deviant behavior. These factors are pertinent in this context because alcoholism is viewed as a form of deviance. Psychological factors that may predispose an individual to deviancy, in this case alcoholism, are dissatisfaction with one's lot and feelings of failure and despair; a sense of helplessness, isolation, and meaninglessness in one's life; and a belief that deviant behavior is not only necessary to achieve certain desirable ends but rarely results in punishment. Two social factors that contribute to deviant behavior are (1) a discrepancy between the value placed on success and socially patterned access to opportunities to achieve success and, (2) opportunities to observe other individuals engaging in deviant behavior (alcoholism) and to engage in these behaviors oneself without being punished.

Barbiturates comprise another large class of CNS depressants. The principal medical uses of the barbiturates are as sedatives and hypnotics—sleep-inducing and calming agents. The degree and duration of the depression induced by the barbiturates depend on the type of barbiturate used, the dose, the route of administration, the individual's experience with the drug, and so forth. Some of the barbiturates have also been used medically to relieve anxiety. In box 5.5 several studies on the effects of barbiturates are summarized.

CNS Stimulants

Earlier in this chapter, we described several studies involving CNS stimulants, including cocaine. We also noted that the amphetamines are widely abused stimulant drugs, and that if taken for periods of days or weeks, may result in the condition "amphetamine psychosis." This condition is sufficiently similar to paranoid schizophrenia that misdiagnosis has not been uncommon without a knowledge of the history of drug abuse.

Interestingly, antipsychotic drugs, such as chlorpromazine, are used to treat both of these mental disorders, thus reinforcing the possibility that amphetamine psychosis and paranoid schizophrenia may have common underlying mechanisms. Furthermore, amphetamine administration will worsen the condition of a paranoid schizophrenic patient.

Death from an overdose of amphetamine is not rare, especially when other drugs are taken in conjunction with it, such as alcohol. It has been established that in many cases, one drug will affect the metabolism of another. In this case, alcohol inhibits liver enzymes that metabolize ("detoxify") amphetamine, so that what would under other circumstances be a nonlethal dose of the latter drug becomes deadly.

Psychedelic or Psychotomimetic Drugs

Psychedelic drugs are compounds that induce altered states of consciousness, change feelings, and affect thought. Compounds such as LSD, mescaline, psilocybin, dimethyltryptamine, and cannabis (marihuana) are examples of these drugs. Some psychedelic drugs —for example, mescaline, LSD, and psilocybin—induce behaviors that resemble those observed in psychotic patients. These psychotic-like states are transient, and drugs that induce them are referred to as psychotomimetic compounds. Other drugs with effects similar to those induced by the psychedelic agents—that is, compounds such as *nitrous oxide,* which induce altered states of consciousness and affect mood—are not usually classified in this category.

Several experiences are commonly associated with the use of psychedelic drugs: The individual focuses on his "inner experiences"; his sensations and thoughts seem more meaningful to him; his apparent awareness of sensory stimuli is increased; he often feels

Box 5.5

Effects of Barbiturates on Animals

The effects of drugs on different organisms depend on a number of variables, including genotype and sex. For example, when Yaffe, Krasner, and Catz (1968) injected male and female mice of several inbred strains with hexobarbital and observed how long the animals slept, they obtained the results illustrated in box figure 5.5. The length of time the animals slept varied tremendously, depending on their genotype. Furthermore, the male mice of all strains slept much longer than did female mice injected with the same dose of the drug. This sex difference is related to the fact that the male hormone testosterone acts *synergistically,* that is, in combination with barbiturates, to prolong the action of these drugs.

Masserman (1962) used the following experimental design to study the effects of barbiturates on anxiety in cats. First, he trained the cats to press a lever for food. After they had learned to make this response, he gave them an electric shock whenever they pressed the lever. In other words, to obtain food the animals had to tolerate pain, which created a conflict. After a while, the animals exhibited abnormal behaviors, including a disorganization of previously learned behaviors, stereotyped behaviors, sexual abnormalities, gastrointestinal difficulties, and so forth. Masserman called this syndrome an "experimental neurosis." When he injected the animals with barbiturates, their behavior improved markedly, to an extent greater than the improvement achieved with alcohol, for example.

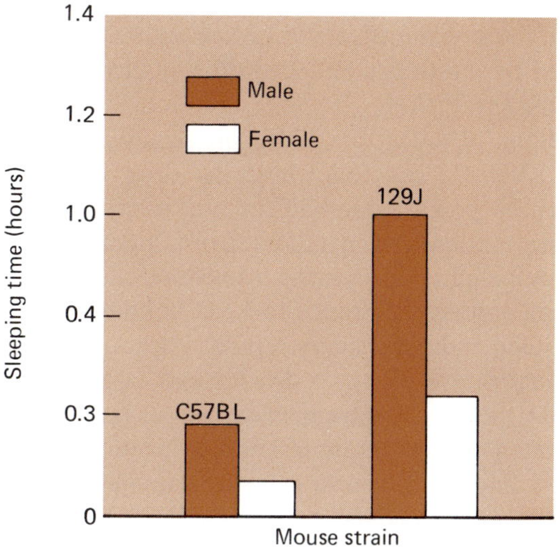

Box Figure 5.5 Duration of sleeping time in male and female mice of two inbred strains after injection with 100 mg./kg. of hexobarbital. (Yaffe, S. J., Krasner, J., & Catz. Variations in detoxification enzymes during mammallian development. *Annals of the New York Academy of Sciences,* 1968, *151,* 887–899. Reprinted by permission.)

that his self is split—one part assumes the passive role of onlooker while the other is actively involved in the experience; and many aspects of his environment assume novel and often beautiful or ugly qualities. For these reasons, psychedelic drugs are sometimes called mind-expanding drugs. Two psychedelic agents, LSD and cannabis, will be discussed briefly in the next section.

LSD

The pharmacological effects of LSD usually fall into four general categories: (1) "psychic" phenomena such as general excitation, disturbed perceptions, hallucinations, and changes in mood, which may be either euphoric or depressive, depending in part on the user's personality and the situation in which the drug is used, (2) disturbances in other processes mediated by the central nervous system, for example, ataxia (loss of muscular coordination) and spastic paralysis, (3) disturbances in the functioning of the autonomic nervous system, such as an increase in heart rate, elevation in body temperature, respiratory depression, and the like, and (4) effects on peripheral structures such as constriction of muscles associated with the bronchia and blood vessels. Obviously, these effects do not occur independently; for example, the psychic effects of LSD are also mediated by the drug's action on the central nervous system.

Some of the more striking physical features of LSD are the following: the drug is extremely potent; one-half to one microgram (one millionth of a gram) per kilogram of body weight represents an average effective human dose. Tolerance to LSD is known to develop and occurs very rapidly. Although no humans have died as a direct result of taking LSD, the drug is extremely dangerous because it often causes paranoia and confusion. It is also known to cause genetic damage, but whether this occurs at doses typically taken by humans is unclear.

Structurally, LSD resembles 5-hydroxytryptamine (serotonin), a molecule that is thought to be a neurotransmitter in the central nervous system. Many experiments have shown that LSD can either activate or inhibit the action of serotonin in peripheral structures. These findings have given rise to the hypothesis that LSD's effects on the central nervous system are mediated in part by its antagonistic action on serotonin. The d-isomer of LSD does not produce the same psychotomimetic effects as another molecular form, the 1-isomer, although the effects of both compounds on peripheral structures are equally pronounced. Recently, it was discovered that only the 1-isomer inhibits the action of serotonin in the central nervous system. However, the precise mechanisms of action of LSD, especially in terms of its psychotomimetic properties, remain to be explained.

Cannabis

Cannabis, also known as marihuana, hashish, "grass," and "pot," contains an active ingredient called *tetrahydrocannabinol.*

The effects of marihuana vary from individual to individual and are dependent on environmental circumstances. Effects become noticeable within minutes after the drug has been smoked—somewhat longer if ingested —and may last as long as five hours.

Under the influence of marihuana, an indidual experiences free and disconnected ideas; his perception of time is altered, he feels intense cravings for food, especially sweets; his behavior may become impulsive; he may talk constantly or become extremely quiet; and after high doses, he may have hallucinations. Although some experimental evidence indicates that individuals develop a tolerance to marihuana effects, they neither seek the drug compulsively nor experience withdrawal symptoms, even after prolonged use.

It is commonly believed in the United States that marihuana decreases the motivation to work and be productive in society. Thus, for example, students who use the drug leave school, lose their desire to pursue careers, or reject society completely. It is also believed by many that chronic marihuana use leads to serious medical and psychological consequences. These beliefs have been challenged by more recent and careful experimental and observational investigations. One significant fact is that the society or culture in which a drug is used may determine, at least in part, the nature of its effects. In the case of the student leaving school, however, it could equally be the case that marihuana use is an excuse rather than the cause for the student's desire to leave school or reject society. Jamaican laborers who smoke many times the amount daily that the average heavy user in the United States smokes, do so in order to increase their motivation and to enable them to work harder and longer than they might otherwise do. In a recent extensive study of the use of marihuana in Jamaica (*Ganja in Jamaica. A Medical Anthropological Study of Chronic Marihuana Use.* V. Rubin & L. Comitas, Mouton, The Hague) medical and anthropological investigators were unable to confirm any of the few, scattered reports of ill medical or psychological effects of chronic marihuana use.

In terms of its chemical structure, tetrahydrocannabinol does not resemble other psychotomimetic drugs or any of the known neurotransmitters, and no pharmacological antagonists for the drug have been discovered. For these reasons, its mechanisms of action remain a mystery.

Tolerance, Physical Dependence, and Withdrawal

One feature shared by many drugs of abuse is that users develop a *tolerance* to and a *physical dependence* on these drugs. Tolerance, as noted previously, refers to the fact that after repeated use of a drug, an individual needs more and more of it to produce the same effects. Or conversely, a dose that was previously effective no longer produces the desired effects.

One important point you should keep in mind is that an individual does not necessarily develop a tolerance to all of a drug's effects to the same degree. For example, tolerance to the hypnotic effects of the barbiturates does develop, but tolerance to the depressant effect of these drugs on the respiratory system develops much more slowly, if at all. This phenomenon no doubt underlies many cases of overdose reported for the barbiturates. Another phenomenon that occurs is *cross-tolerance,* which means that repeated administration of one drug may result in tolerance to another. Cross-tolerance between the barbiturates and alcohol is well known, and anesthesiologists know that it is sometimes difficult to put alcoholic patients to sleep with barbiturates, even at doses that would kill a nonalcoholic.

A person is considered to be physically dependent on a drug when, after repeated use, abrupt withdrawal results in great discomfort —*withdrawal symptoms.* Traditionally, the terms physical dependence and withdrawal have been used to describe the symptoms of withdrawal from drugs that depress the central nervous system. The symptoms of withdrawal from depressants such as the narcotic analgesics, barbiturates, and alcohol are severe and may in fact be life-threatening because convulsions are not unusual after these drugs are discontinued. Although withdrawal symptoms vary, depending on which drug has been used, their general nature can be predicted if the action of the drug is understood. If the drug acts as a CNS depressant, the nature of the withdrawal symptoms will be excitatory. Morphine users for example, suffer from constipation, whereas withdrawal causes diarrhea. Because the narcotic analgesics also suppress the activity of the autonomic nervous system, the activity of this system increases during withdrawal—a result called an *autonomic storm.* In other words, withdrawal from the CNS depressants causes excitatory symptoms, the exact nature of which varies from drug to drug.

Withdrawal from drugs that stimulate the central nervous system does not produce the dramatic symptoms associated with withdrawal from the depressants. On the other hand, calling these symptoms "withdrawal symptoms" seems justified. As Jaffe (1970) has pointed out:

> It is still true that abrupt discontinuance of sympathomimetic amines does not cause major, grossly observable, physiological disruptions that would necessitate the gradual reduction of the drug. But the prolonged sleep, lassitude, fatigue and hyperphagia, as well as the occasionally reported profound depression that follow discontinuation of these drugs, are difficult to attribute merely to the preceding loss of sleep and weight.

As this statement suggests, withdrawal from cocaine seems to result in lethargy, and withdrawal from the amphetamines can induce severe depression. This suggests that symptoms which occur after the use of stimulant drugs is discontinued are depressive in character.

Several theories have been proposed to account for the phenomenon of tolerance. For example, tolerance may develop as a consequence of an increase of enzymes that degrade the drug. Thus, after repeated use a drug may be degraded more rapidly and the individual may become tolerant to its effects. This type of tolerance is referred to as *drug dispositional tolerance* and is known to occur with respect to the barbiturates; repeated use of the barbiturates induces liver enzymes that metabolize these drugs. Prolonged use of alcohol also induces these drug-metabolizing enzymes, for which reason it is difficult to anesthetize the alcoholic patient with barbiturates. On the other hand, nerve cells themselves may develop a resistance to a drug's effects; this type of tolerance is called *functional tolerance.*

One functional theory that attempts to explain the symptoms associated with withdrawal of the CNS depressants (Jaffe and Sharpless, 1968) is called the *supersensitivity of disuse theory.* According to this theory, depressant drugs such as heroin, the barbiturates, and alcohol reduce neural input to certain cells in the central nervous system. If these drugs are chronically used, the reduction in the activity of these cells is prolonged, and the cells are not used for long periods. If the drug is suddenly withdrawn, the disused neurons become hyperexcitable, and withdrawal symptoms occur. Functional theories such as this are attractive because they attempt to explain the major withdrawal symptoms observed for a wide variety of drugs.

Some organisms, including humans, will return to addictive drugs again months, sometimes even years after being completely free of them. *Repetitive relapses* are not at all uncommon. Although no clear-cut explanations exist for this behavior, two hypotheses have been proposed. The first is based on the observation that addictive drugs have effects which persist long after use of the drugs has been discontinued. A number of these effects have been identified, but how they may lead to a relapse is not understood. The second hypothesis is more behavioral in orientation and relies on the idea that the reinforcements or the circumstances associated with drug use remain desirable for long periods. Animal experiments have demonstrated that circumstances associated with drug use can themselves become reinforcing. For example, rats will drink water containing anise if morphine is dissolved in the water and if the animals are addicted to morphine. Long after withdrawal from morphine, the rats will continue to drink water containing anise, although normal rats will not. In all likelihood, phychological as well as physiological variables contribute to the phenomenon known as repetitive relapse.

Drug-Induced Behavior

We have already said that some drugs induce certain kinds of behavior, ranging from religious experiences or enhanced creativity to behaviors that resemble symptoms commonly associated with mental illness. This section contains a description of one individual's experiences while under the influence of a drug and a summary of a study which suggests that psychedelic drugs may enhance creative problem solving.

William James (1882), one of America's greatest philosophers and psychologists, described his experiences with nitrous oxide as follows:

> Some observations of the effects of nitrous-oxide-gas-intoxication, which I was prompted to make by reading the pamphlet called *The anaesthetic revelation and the gist of philosophy* (Blood, 1847), have made me understand better than ever before the strength and the weakness of Hegel's philosophy. I strongly urge others to repeat the experiment, which with pure gas is

short and harmless enough. The effects will, of course, vary with the individual, just as they vary in the same individual from time to time; but it is probable that in the former case, as in the latter, a generic resemblance will obtain. With me, as with every other person of whom I have heard, the keynote of the experience is the tremendously exciting sense of an intense metaphysical illumination. Truth lies open to the view in depth beneath depth of almost blinding evidence. The mind sees all the logical relations of being with an apparent subtlety and instantaneity to which its normal consciousness offers no parallel; only as sobriety returns, the feeling of insight fades, and one is left staring vacantly at a few disjointed words and phrases, as one stares at a cadaverous-looking snow peak from which the sunset glow has just fled, or at the black cinder left by an extinguished brand.

The immense emotional sense of *reconciliation* which characterizes the "maudlin" stage of alcohol drunkenness—a stage which seems silly to the lookers-on—but the subjective rapture of which probably constitutes a chief part of the temptation of the vice—is well known. The center and periphery of things seem to come together. The ego and its objects, the *meum* and the *tuum,* are one. Now this, only a thousandfold enhanced, was the effect upon me of the gas; and its first result was to make peal through me with unutterable power the conviction that Hegelism was true after all, and that the deepest conflictions of my intellect hitherto were wrong.

Clearly, James believed that the drug enabled him to have flashes of insight and understanding that he normally did not have. It was as if his mind had been expanded to grasp ideas that were previously beyond him—as though his creative powers of understanding had been enlarged.

Other reports of a more experimental nature contain similar results. In 1966 Harman, McKim, Mogar, Fadiman, and Stolaroff (Tart, 1969) studied the effects of mescaline on creative problem solving. Twenty-seven professional men (engineers, physicists, mathematicians, architects, furniture designers, and commercial artists) were selected as subjects because their work involved problem solving, they appeared to be normal on the basis of psychiatric examinations, and they were well motivated to participate in the experiment. During the first of three sessions, the investigators described the "psychedelic experience" quite positively and told the men that after some initial disturbances, they would be able to work more effectively than usual. The investigators then introduced the men to one another, gave them certain tests of creativity, and asked them to bring some problems which they had been working on to the next session.

Immediately after arriving at the second session, the men were given mescaline. They then listened to music for several hours, took several more tests of creativity, and finally began working on the problems they had brought with them. Some weeks later, the men were asked to comment on how the experience had affected their creative ability and whether, in their opinion, the solutions to the problems they had brought with them to the second session were valid and acceptable.

The results of the experiment can be summarized as follows: The men obtained higher scores on the objective tests of creativity while under the influence of the drug than they had obtained in the first session. One of these tests, the *Witkin Embedded Figures Test,* required them to distinguish a simple geometric figure that was embedded in a more complex colored figure. Because the men performed better on this test while under the influence of mescaline, the drug apparently enhanced their ability, not only to recognize patterns, but to isolate and minimize visual distractions. The results of the problem-solving tasks the subjects brought with them to the second session were also interesting. Some of the men had been trying to solve these problems for weeks prior to taking the drug. Many of them were able to solve their problem during the drug session. Some solutions were practical: One man designed a building that was accepted by a client, another designed a linear electron accelerator beam-steering device during the session, a third designed a letterhead that was later approved by a client, a fourth completed the designs for a line of furniture.

What can we conclude from this experiment? Although one would like to conclude that the drug enhanced creative problem solving, particularly during the so-called "illumination phase" produced by the drug, flaws in the experimental design make positive conclusions hazardous. First, no placebo control group was used, and as we explained in Chapter 1, proper control procedures of this type are extremely important in this kind of research. Thus it is difficult to determine whether the results were produced by the drug itself or by the subjects' expectations of what the drug would enable them to do. Second, it is important to remember that the subjects were told before the experiment that the drug would help them solve problems. Since these subjects were willing and well-motivated participants, perhaps their performance can be attributed to motivation alone. If an equally well motivated control group had received the same instructions as the experimental group but had been given a placebo rather than mescaline, the experiment would have been more meaningful. As it is, we can say that the results, although preliminary, are interesting and should be confirmed in a more carefully designed experiment.

For a long time, it was believed, or at least hoped, that investigators could produce experimental models for the study of certain mental disorders (particularly schizophrenia) by using psychotomimetic drugs. However, after some experimental studies, it became obvious that the behaviors observed in mental illness and those induced with these drugs were quite different. To be sure, LSD does produce a variety of bizzare behaviors, including hallucinations, that bear a superficial resemblance to those exhibited by schizophrenic patients. However, the hallucinations produced by LSD are predominantly visual—the individual "sees" things that are not actually present—while the hallucinations of the schizophrenic patient are usually auditory—he "hears" voices that are not there. Another distinction, perhaps a fundamental one, is that the individual experiencing the bizzare effects of LSD knows he is being influenced by a drug. The schizophrenic, on the other hand, usually does not realize that he is ill.

Summary

Although the study of drugs is relevant for a number of reasons, including the treatment and prevention of disease, psychologists use drugs as tools to study behavior. The hybrid discipline of psychopharmacology uses the tools and concepts of both pharmacology and psychology to explore the behavioral actions of drugs.

Drugs may be regarded as chemical stimuli that have selective biological activity: in other words, they act on some cells or cell processes but do not act on all cells. In this chapter we have limited our discussion to drugs that act on the nervous system because these drugs produce profound effects upon behavior. Within this broad classification, drugs can be separated into two subclasses on the basis of whether they act principally on the peripheral or central nervous system.

The effects of a drug depend on its intrinsic activity and the rate at which it is absorbed, which in turn depends on the route of administration and the quantity or dose administered. Following their action, most drugs are excreted, either in their original form or after undergoing biotransformation.

Perhaps the best understood drugs, in terms of their effects on nervous tissue, are those that affect the autonomic nervous system. For example, drugs such as epinephrine and the amphetamines are sympathomimetic agents, that is, they mimic the normal activity of the sympathetic division of the autonomic nervous system. Adrenergic blocking agents block the normal activity of the sympathetic division of the autonomic nervous system. Similar classes of drugs may be defined with respect to the parasympathetic division of the autonomic nervous system; for example muscarinic agents stimulate the activity of postganglionic synapses in the parasympathetic division.

Drugs that act on the central nervous system can also be classified in different ways. For example, CNS depressants, such as barbiturates or alcohol, usually produce drowsiness, lethargy, or sleep. CNS stimulants, such as amphetamines, analeptics (which produce convulsions), or caffeine, usually produce excitation of behavior and associated changes in mood and activity. One particularly interesting example of drugs that have been used in psychological research are the analeptics or convulsants. A variety of experiments has shown that in subconvulsive doses, analeptics may enhance learning and memory in animals. This suggests that memory involves some time-dependent process which is more rapid following the administration of low doses of these neural excitants.

Many drugs that affect the central nervous system can be classified as drugs of abuse because those who use them deviate from society's norms. Drug abuse constitutes a serious social problem in the United States. The most commonly abused drugs include the narcotic analgesics such as heroin and morphine, CNS depressants such as alcohol and the barbiturates, and many CNS stimulants such as the amphetamines and related compounds. Psychedelic drugs such as marihuana, LSD, psilocybin, and mescaline are also commonly abused. These drugs usually affect a person's state of consciousness, mood, and thought. In many cases, psychedelic drugs produce symptoms that resemble mental illness, although the similarity is only partial. For this reason, psychedelic drugs are often called psychotomimetic agents.

Ernst H. Weber (1795-1858)
Weber was a professor of anatomy and physiology at the University of Leipzig. His early experiments on the psychophysiology of touch and hearing led to the formulation of Weber's Law, relating perceptual thresholds to the magnitude of the physical stimulus.

Floyd Ratliff (1919-)
A professor of psychology at Rockefeller University, Dr. Ratliff together with Professor H. K. Hartline pioneered the quantitative description of the process of lateral inhibition in visual perception.

Gustav T. Fechner (1801-1887)
Recognized as one of the fathers of experimental psychology, Fechner trained in medicine at the University of Leipzig but became well-known as a physicist and philosopher. His experimental and theoretical findings, including Fechner's Law, were instrumental in founding the field of psychophysiology.

Section

3

Sensory Processes and Perception

6

Sensory Information Processing

One of the most important questions in the history of human thought has been how we are able to perceive the external world. How do external events inform us about the objects, patterns, sights, and sounds that make up perception? Most of us take for granted that perception depends, at least in part, on stimulation of the sense organs by physical energy such as light or sound. Therefore, the study of perception requires a knowledge of the physical characteristics of the external world. However, a moment's reflection will reveal that a physical description of the world around us is not enough to account for our perception of it. Indeed, perceptual psychologists are fond of using examples, such as those shown in figure 6.1, to illustrate the difference between physics and perception.

Figure 6.1a illustrates a reversible figure, the Necker cube. Although nothing changes physically on the page, we see one corner coming out of the page at one time and the same corner receding into the page at another. Similarly, although the physical characteristics of the small gray square do not change, the square seems brighter against a dark background than a light background (see fig. 6.1b). Although nothing changes in the pattern of light striking our eyes from the painting shown in figure 6.1c, we can see either the skull or the woman viewing herself in the mirror. There are many examples in the visual arts of such ambiguous figures which illustrate that our perceptions can vary when nothing changes in physical terms. (See box 6.1.)

On the other hand, it is possible for our perception of events in the world to remain constant, even though their physical characteristics vary—a phenomenon termed *perceptual constancy*. For example, we perceive the shape of this book as rectangular whether we look straight at it or whether it is tilted, despite the fact that the image produced on the retina at the back of the eye is quite different in each case. If we did not have the capacity

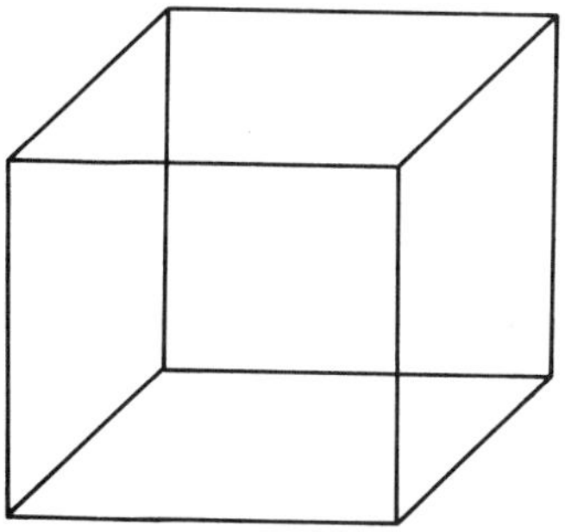

a

b

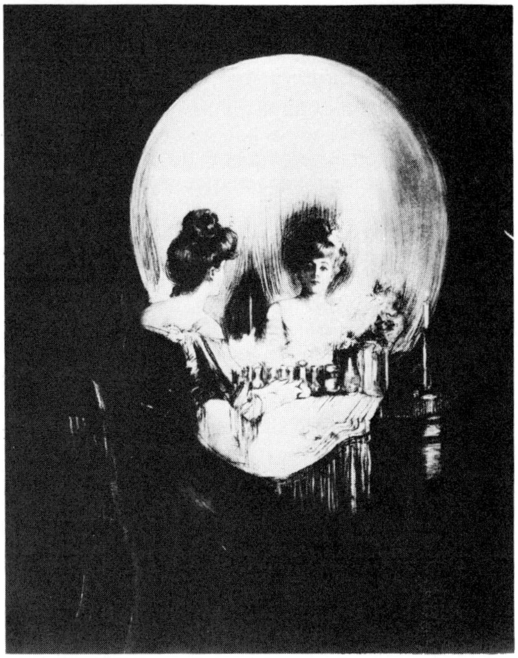

c

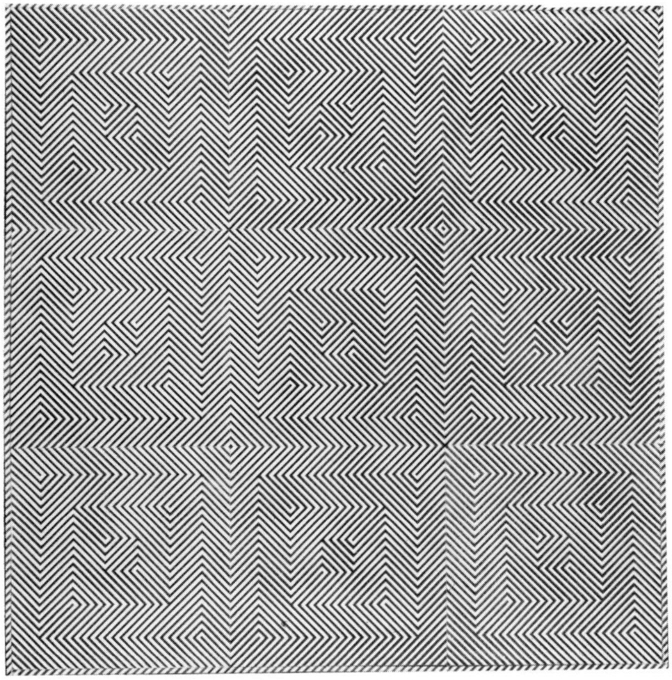

d

Figure 6.1a The Necker Cube.

Figure 6.1b Gray squares.

Figure 6.1c *Vanity.* (Courtesy of The Bettmann Archive.)

Figure 6.1d Square of *Three, Yellow and Black* by Reginald Neal. (By permission of NEW JERSEY STATE MUSEUM COLLECTION, TRENTON.)

Box 6.1

The Mach-Eben Illusion

A remarkable example of the difference between the physical and perceptual world is illustrated in box figure 6.1. Fold a 3 x 5 card into the shape of a "W," as shown in box figure 6.1. Place the card on a flat surface and, while covering one eye, fixate the card steadily with the other eye. After a short time, the card will appear to stand up. By moving your head slowly back and forth, you will notice changes in the pattern of brightness and the size and shape of this "standing W shape." Some understanding of the basis for this illusion will be provided in Chapter 7.

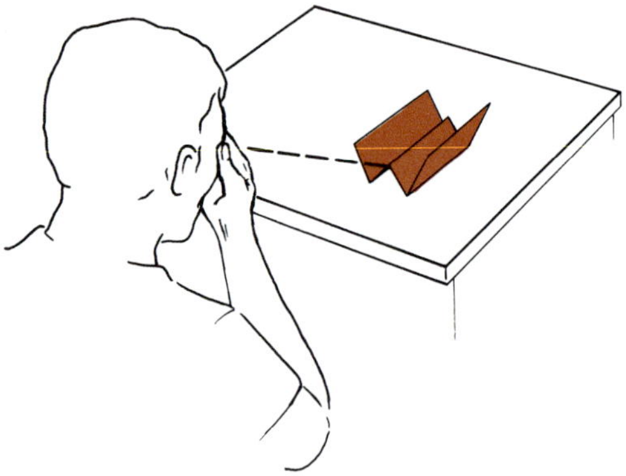

Box Figure 6.1 The Mach-Eben illusion.

for perceptual constancy, objects would have to be exactly the same in relation to our sense organs each time we encountered them or they would be unfamiliar to us.

One major emphasis in the study of perception is to understand the relationship between physical events and our perception of them. We can make progress toward this understanding by examining the physiological processes that result from stimulation of the sense organs. At a simple level, it is clear that not all forms of physical energy affect our sense organs. We cannot see X-rays or hear the sound of a dog whistle, for instance.

In this chapter, we will consider some of the basic relationships between the physical, physiological, and perceptual events involved in vision and hearing. In the next chapter, we will expand our focus to include a discussion of how knowledge and experience influence perception. We will describe some theoretical attempts to account for perception.

Vision

Physical Dimensions of Light

Imagine that you are looking at a small spot of light. Emitted from the light source are small wavelike packages or *quanta* of energy. Because these packets have wavelike characteristics, they can be distinguished on the basis of their wavelengths, as shown in figure 6.2. The range of wavelengths may cover the entire electromagnetic spectrum, as depicted schematically in plate 3.

Plate 3 also demonstrates that only a small range of wavelengths will be sensed by the

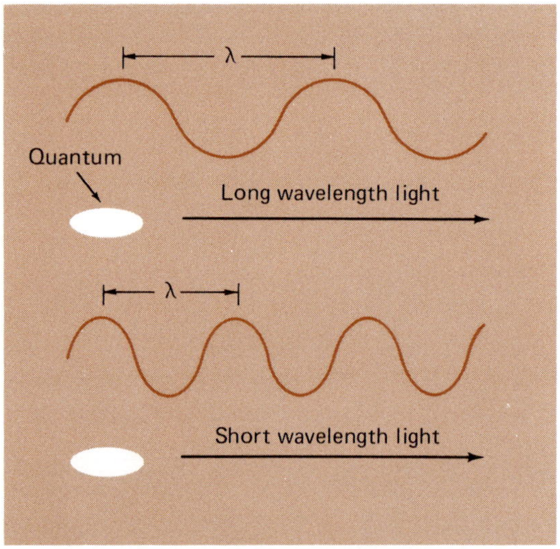

Figure 6.2 As a light quantum travels through space at 186,000 miles/sec., its energy pulsates according to the curve shown above. The distance between pulsations is the wavelength (λ) of the quantum. Quanta that pulsate more rapidly have shorter wavelengths.

human observer as light. Quanta with wavelengths ranging from 400 to 700 nanometers (a nanometer or nm is one billionth of a meter) are visible, while the vast remainder of the electromagnetic spectrum is invisible and contains radio waves, X-rays, and other forms of electromagnetic energy. Therefore, the only dimension on which light differs from other forms of electromagnetic energy is that we can see it. If a light source emits a narrow range of wavelengths—ideally a single wavelength—it is referred to as *monochromatic*. A monochromatic light will appear to have a particular color, depending on the wavelength. As shown in the diagram of the electromagnetic spectrum, the colors will range from violet (about 400 nm) to blue (about 440 nm) to green (about 510 nm) to yellow (about 580 nm) to the longest wavelength of visible light, slightly yellowish red (700 nm). Again considering monochromatic light, the greater the number of quanta emitted during some period of time, the greater the energy of the light. The higher the energy of the light, the brighter it will appear.

Most lights, such as common house lamps, are not monochromatic, but emit many wavelengths of light simultaneously. To describe such a *complex* light source, we must measure the energy of each wavelength emitted by it. A graph of these energy values is termed the emission spectrum of the light source, two examples of which are shown in figure 6.3. The color of a complex light depends on its emission spectrum. Roughly speaking, the *hue*, or color depends on which wavelength region is dominant in energy and how sensitive the eye is to different wavelengths of light. In the case of the household lamp, yellow and red wavelengths predominate, but because we are more sensitive to yellow wavelengths the light appears yellowish. The color's *saturation* will depend on how much a given wavelength predominates. Saturation refers to the "purity" of the color, or hue. Highly saturated colors are much more vibrant in appearance than less saturated colors; for example, a red, which is saturated, is more vibrant than a pink, which is a less saturated red. The *brightness* of a complex light will depend on the number of quanta emitted at all its wavelengths as well as the eye's sensitivity to each wavelength emitted.

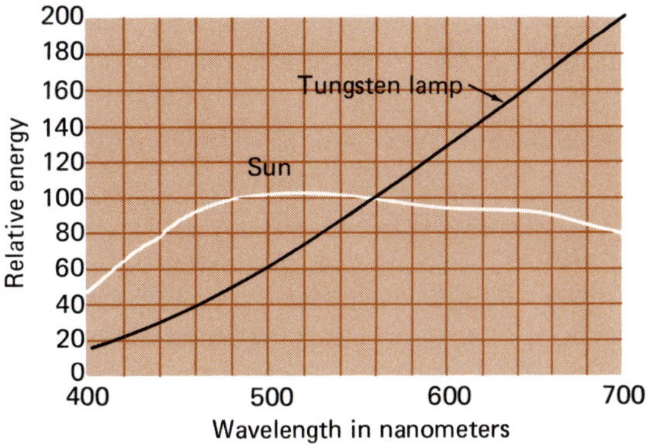

Figure 6.3 The emission spectra of sunlight (top) and an incandescent light (bottom).

Most visible objects are not sources of light. We see them because they are illuminated by sources of light, and their appearance depends not only on the characteristics of the light source but on the way the object *reflects* light. When light strikes a surface such as a piece of paper, some light is absorbed and some is reflected, and we see the paper by the light that is reflected into our eyes. Thus the appearance of an illuminated object depends on the wavelengths of the reflected light. Given a light source such as the sun, which emits many visible wavelengths (see fig. 6.3), a green object will appear green because it reflects wavelengths of approximately 510 nm and absorbs others. A piece of paper that appears white when illuminated by sunlight reflects all wavelengths of light. If the light source emitted wavelengths only in the green portion of the spectrum (i.e., it would then be a green light) the same piece of paper would appear green, and so forth. If the paper reflected only wavelengths within the red portion of the spectrum and if it were illuminated by a light source that emitted only shorter wavelengths in the blue or violet range of the spectrum, the paper would not reflect the light and would appear black. In other words, the appearance of an illuminated object depends on the wavelength composition of the light reflected by it, which in turn is dependent upon the spectral characteristics of the light source and the absorption-reflection characteristics of the object's surface.

We have just described the characteristics that a physicist uses to describe a point of light as well as the perceptual dimensions that are related to these characteristics. Most things we see, however, are not single points of light but patterns of light, and to understand the effects of patterns of light, we must discuss the nature of the eye—the visual receptor apparatus.

The Eye

Figure 6.4 is a diagram of the human eye. Note that the eyeball is surrounded by a tough tissue called the *sclera,* which becomes the clear *cornea* at the front of the eyeball. The cornea is an amazing structure comprised of layers of cells which are aligned in such a way that light can pass through with a minimal amount of disruption. After light passes through the cornea and a watery substance called the *aqueous humor,* it goes through the pupil, a hole formed by a ring of muscles called the *iris.* The outer, pigmented, layer of the iris gives our eyes their color. Changes in the contraction of the iris will open or close the pupil. Light then passes through the lens and a jellylike material, the *vitreous humor,* and strikes the *retina,* the light-sensitive receptor surface at the back of the eye, where it is absorbed by specialized receptor cells. The absorption of light initiates a complex series of physiological processes which result in action potentials, conducted to the brain by axons of nerve cells in the retina that make up the optic nerve.

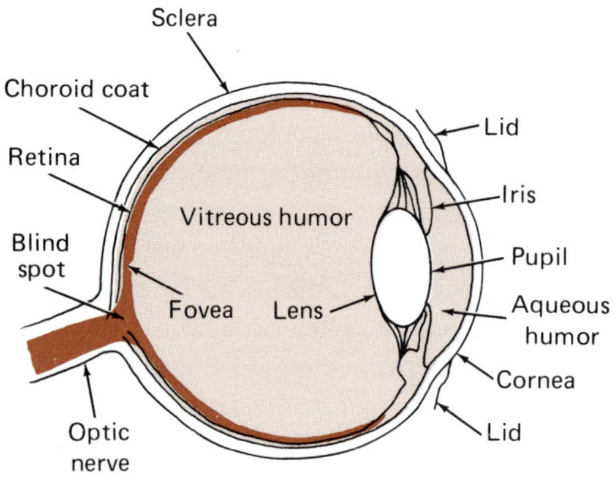

Figure 6.4 The human eye.

Optical Properties

Now that we have a rough idea of the path of light through the eye as well as structures through which it passes, we will consider what occurs when a person looks at an object. This process is illustrated in figure 6.5a. Imagine that the arrow consists of many points of light and let us consider the light coming from a point at the very tip of the arrow. The light arising from this point will strike the entire surface of the eye, as will light from all other points comprising the arrow. However, when we are properly focused on the arrow, the cornea and the lens bend, or *refract* the light in such a way that the points of light are reformed at the back of the eye into an image of the arrow in a manner similar to the image made by a camera on photographic film. Curiously, the image is upside down and reversed left to right on the retina. In the human retina, this refraction of light is accomplished primarily by the cornea and to a lesser extent by the lens. Figure 6.5a illustrates that the degree of refraction required to form an image of an object depends on its distance from the eye. The closer the object, the more refraction required to focus the object's image on the retina. The amount of refraction is controlled by the curvature of the lens. When

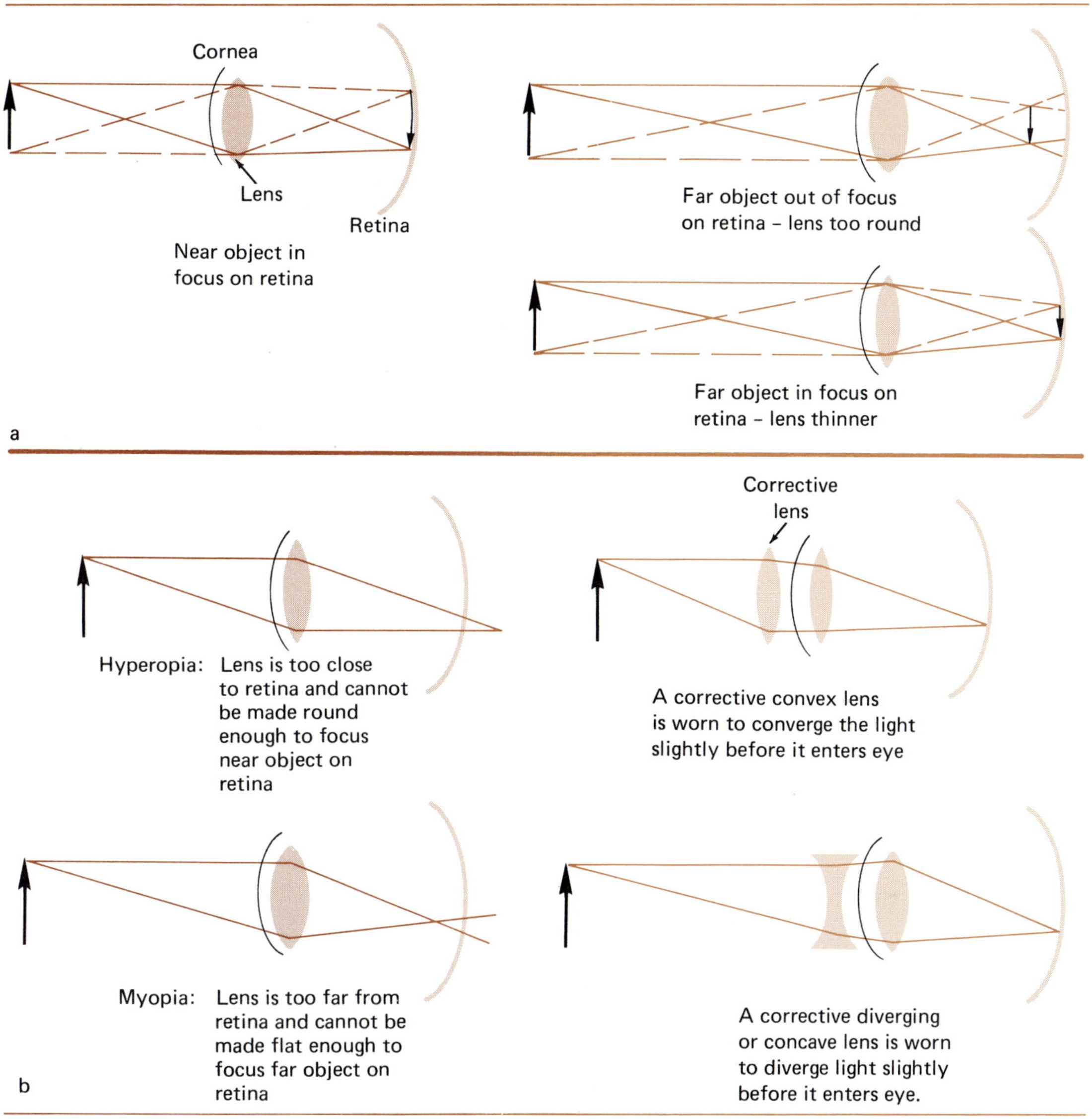

Figure 6.5 Accommodation and optical defects.

a far object is focused, the lens is relatively flat; to focus near objects, the lens must be relatively more curved. The process by which the curvature of the lens is altered to focus objects at different distances from the eye is referred to as accommodation (see box 6.2 and fig. 6.5). Certain common defects in vision, depicted in figure 6.5b, can be traced to problems in accommodation. These defects occur because the shape of the eyeball is such that the lens is either too close or too far from the retina. The condition in which the lens is too close to the retina is called hyperopia, or farsightedness; the opposite condition is called myopia, or nearsightedness. Eyeglasses can correct either condition by refracting the light before it enters the eye (see fig. 6.5b).

Box 6.2

Accommodation

An examination of figure 6.5a reveals that if the lens of the eye remains *constant* in curvature, objects at different distances from the eye will be in focus at different distances from the lens. If the shape of the lens remains constant, then it must be at different distances from the retina to focus near or far objects properly: that is, to focus far objects, the retina must be closer to the lens; to focus near objects, it must be farther away. On the other hand, the distance between the lens and retina can remain constant, and the curvature of the lens can be changed; made flatter for far objects and more convex for near objects. The second method of accommodation is used by humans (see fig. 6.5a).

Other organisms, however, have evolved different mechanisms of accommodation. Fish, for example, use the first method of accommodation described above; in other words, the lens moves back and forth in the eye to accommodate, as shown in box figure 6.2a. Horses and manta rays utilize a "ramped retina" (box fig. 6.2b) in which parts of the retina are at different distances from the lens. By rotating their eyes, these animals can focus properly on objects at different distances. This same principle is used by the flying fruit bat, although this animal's retina is corrogated, as shown in box figure 6.2c. Near objects are in focus on those portions of the retina farthest from the lens, while far objects are in focus on points of the retina nearer the lens (Walls, 1942).

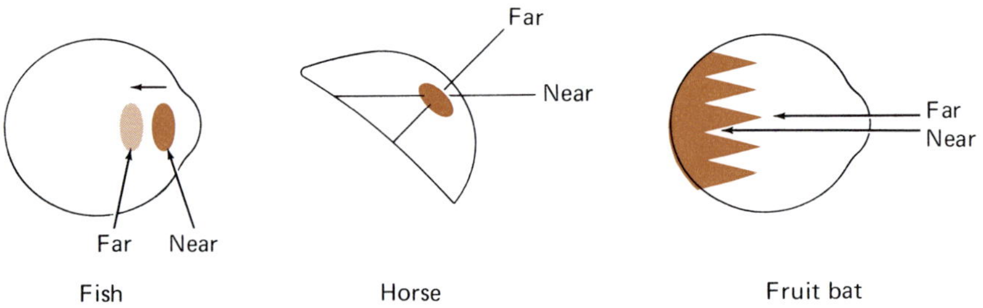

Box Figure 6.2 Different ways to accommodate.

Because of the eye's optical properties, the size of an image produced by an object will vary with its distance from the eye: Far objects will cast smaller images on the retina than will near objects. This relationship is such that as the distance of an object from the eye doubles, the size of the image produced by the object is halved.

Retina

Figure 6.6 illustrates the structure of the retina. The retina is a complex multilayered organ. Studies of embryological development indicate that the retina is derived from the same structures that ultimately form the central nervous system; thus in reality it is an extruded portion of the brain. The retina is composed of six major kinds of cells: rods, cones, bipolar cells, amacrine cells, horizontal cells, and ganglion cells.

Starting at the back of the eye, there is the receptor layer, consisting of the two classes of cells that are sensitive to light: the *rods* and *cones*. There are approximately 6 million cones and about 125 million rods in the human retina. These receptor cells are not evenly distributed across the retina. The cones are most dense (approximately 147,000 per square millimeter) in the region termed the *fovea,* where rods are virtually absent. Out-

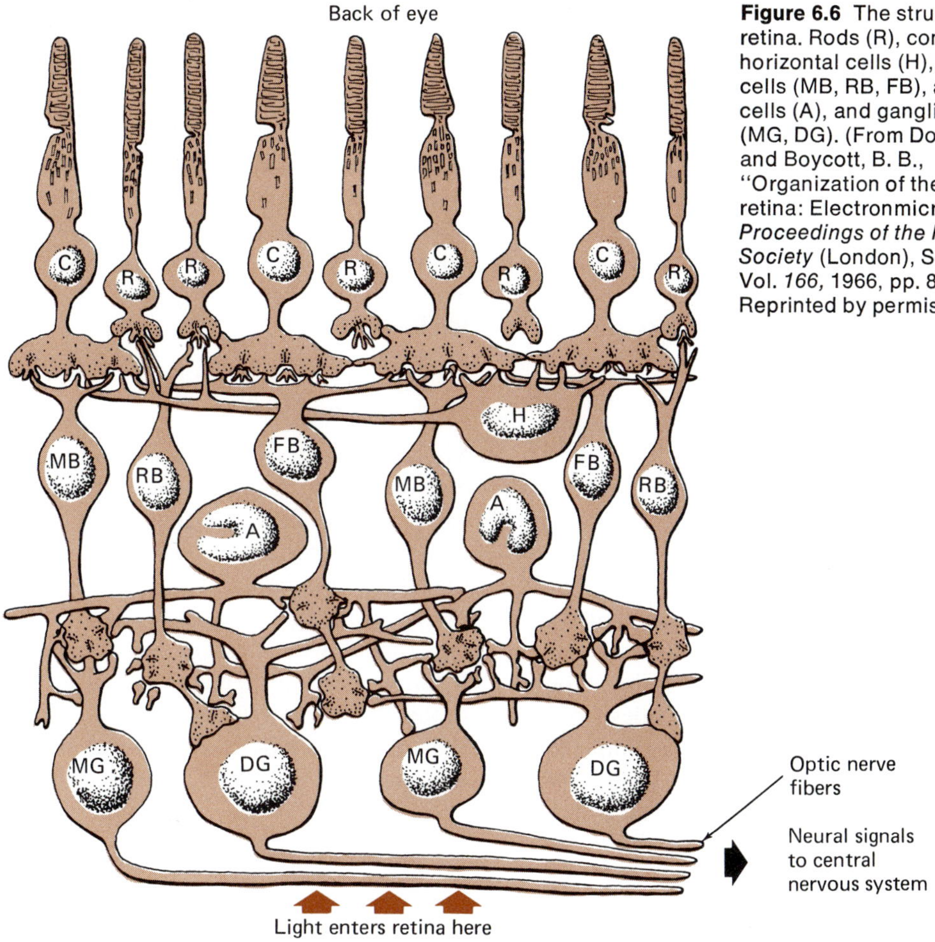

Figure 6.6 The structure of the retina. Rods (R), cones (C), horizontal cells (H), bipolar cells (MB, RB, FB), amacrine cells (A), and ganglion cells (MG, DG). (From Dowling, J. E., and Boycott, B. B., "Organization of the primate retina: Electronmicroscopy," *Proceedings of the Royal Society* (London), Serial B., Vol. *166,* 1966, pp. 80–111. Reprinted by permission.)

side the fovea, the density of cones drops drastically and remains low out to the retina's peripheral portions. The rods are greatest in number (approximately 160,000 per square millimeter) some distance away from the fovea, and they too decrease in number toward the periphery, although more rods exist in the periphery than cones.

When light falls on the rods and cones, they send signals to *bipolar* and *horizontal* cells. Horizontal cells send their information to other receptor and bipolar cells. The signals arising from stimulation of the bipolar cells are transmitted to *amacrine cells* and *ganglion cells.* Amacrine cells, in turn, communicate with other amacrine cells, bipolar cells, and ganglion cells. This rather confusing line of communication can be clarified if we first imagine a pattern of light making up an image lying across the receptors. Each receptor is stimulated by a point of light on the pattern. A receptor signal concerning one point in the pattern flows *vertically* through the retina from receptors to bipolar cells to ganglion cells, while at the same time it affects and is affected by information arising from *other points* in the pattern by means of the *horizontal flow* of information across the retina through the horizontal and amacrine cells. As we shall see, the interactions between the horizontal and vertical flow of information modify and enhance the "picture" of the image which the eye presents to the central nervous system.

Information leaves the eye by means of the axons of the ganglion cells that make up the *optic nerve*. In the region of the fovea, optic nerve fibers are pulled to the side so that they do not interfere with the transmission of light to the receptors in this region. In all other areas of the retina, light must pass through the network of nerve fibers and cells in the retina before striking the receptors; thus, in a sense, the retina is backwards with respect to light entering the eye.

Approximately 800,000 nerve fibers leave the eyeball in the region termed the optic disc, which is devoid of receptors and is therefore called the blind spot. You can find your blind spot by viewing the two small spots shown in figure 6.7a. If you drew two imaginary lines connecting these spots to the pupil of your eye, the angle formed by the two lines would be approximately fifteen degrees. Similarly, the angle formed by the images of the two spots from the retina to the pupil of your eye would also be about fifteen degrees, as illustrated schematically in figure 6.7b. Therefore, when discussing the distances between points in an image or the retina or distances between points on an object, it is useful to talk in terms of degrees—a measure termed *visual angle*. For example, the region in the retina where the rods are most numerous is about seventeen degrees from the center of the fovea.

Rod and Cone Vision

Many elementary characteristics of visual perception can be related to the structure of the retina and the flow of signals through this remarkable organ. First, let's consider the fact that the retina contains two different classes of receptors, the rods and cones. A simple experiment will illustrate several important features of visual perception that are related to this duplicity in visual receptors.

Suppose we place a person in a dark room and give him sufficient time for his eyes to

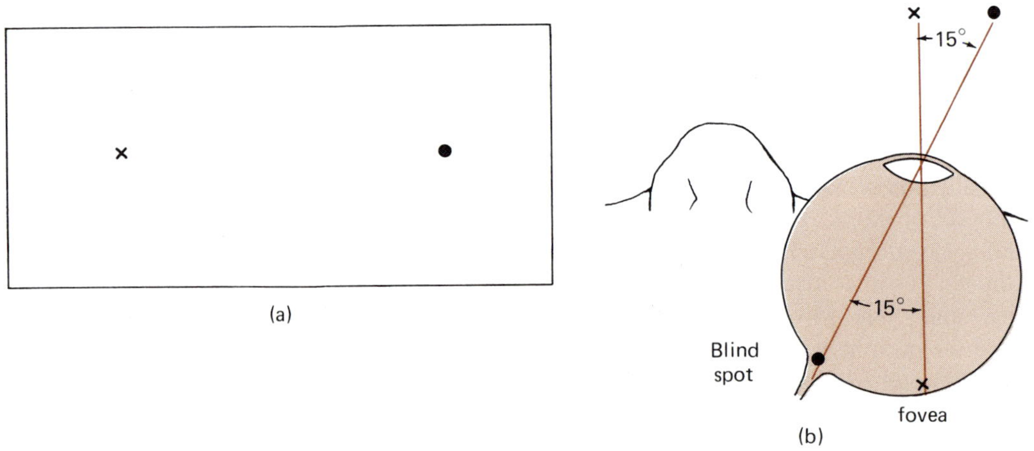

Figure 6.7 The blind spot. Close your left eye and view the *x* with your right eye. While maintaining fixation on the *x*, move the page back and forth. At one distance, the dot will disappear. At this distance the image of the dot is falling on the blind spot as shown in b.

adapt to the dark. We now present a small spot of light of a particular wavelength, and we determine the minimum amount of light energy emitted by the spot that allows the person to detect the spot of light. This minimum amount of energy would be termed his *absolute threshold.* We would find that his absolute threshold would vary, depending on the wavelength of the light and its location on the retina. Some of the techniques for determining absolute thresholds and other perceptual measurements are described in box 6.3.

Suppose that the image of the light falls in the region of the retina where the rods are most numerous, and we determine the minimum amount of energy necessary for the observer to detect the light at different wavelengths. We will find that the least amount of energy is required for a wavelength of about 510 nm and that all other wavelengths will require more energy to be detected. This relationship between the threshold for rod vision and wavelength, called the *scotopic threshold curve,* is illustrated in figure 6.8. We are more sensitive to some wavelengths of light than others because the photochemical substance in the rods, *rhodopsin,* absorbs some wavelengths of light better than others. It is possible to extract rhodopsin and measure how much light of any given wavelength it absorbs. In fact it has been shown that this *spectral absorption curve* of rhodopsin parallels exactly our sensitivity to light under the conditions of the simple experiment we just described. Interestingly enough, however, under the conditions of faint light described in the experiment, we would not observe differences in color between different wavelengths of light. The rod visual system can detect dim light, but it cannot provide information about color. Thus if we observed extremely dim lights of equal energy, a light of 510 nm would appear to be brighter than other wavelengths of light, but all wavelengths would appear gray in color.

Now suppose that we move the spot of light onto the center of the fovea, which contains only cones, still using the same simple experimental example. For the observer to see the light, its intensity would generally have to be increased—as much as a thousandfold for some wavelengths. With a light of sufficient energy for detection, the observer would now perceive different colors as the wavelength was varied. We could again determine the absolute threshold at different wavelengths of light. This relationship for cone vision is referred to as the *photopic threshold curve,* which is also shown in figure 6.8.

Several interesting phenomena can be related to the curves shown in figure 6.8. First, as we have already suggested, scotopic, or rod vision is considerably more sensitive to most wavelengths of light than is photopic, or cone vision. Indeed the rod system is so sensitive to light that at 510 nm, approximately six quanta of light, each absorbed by a different rod, are sufficient to produce a visual sensation. You will also note in figure 6.8 that the maximal sensitivity of cones occurs at a higher wavelength of light (555 nm) than that of rods (510 nm). In general, rods are more sensitive toward the blue end of the spectrum, whereas cones are more sensitive toward the red end. A Belgian physiologist, Purkinje, was the first to notice that two objects, one red and one blue, which appeared to be equally bright under high (photopic) illumination, differed in brightness under dim (scotopic) illumination: the blue object appeared to be brighter under dim illumination. We now know that this phenomenon is attributable to the shift in sensitivity from cone to rod vision. Thus it is appropriately called the *Purkinje shift.*

Most of us have stumbled around in a dark movie theater while our eyes become accustomed to the dim level of illumination. This process of adjustment is termed *dark adaptation,* and it occurs in part because the recep-

Box 6.3

Psychophysical Measurement

One of the most common procedures used to understand the relations between perception and physical dimensions (or *psychophysical relations*) is to determine the minimum change in some physical dimension which can just produce a change in an observer's perception. For example, one could determine the minimum change in light energy that would produce a just perceptible change or difference in brightness. Such minimum changes are termed *thresholds.*

One interesting feature of thresholds is that they vary from one moment to the next —a difference in energy that is just barely detected during one observation may be easily detected or undetectable during the next. Because of this variability, thresholds must be defined statistically. In many experiments, thresholds are determined as follows: an observer is given one stimulus, say a light, termed the *standard,* which is maintained at a constant level, and another stimulus, termed the *comparison* or *test stimulus,* which is varied from trial to trial. On each trial, the subject is asked whether he can detect a difference between the two lights. The small *physical* difference between the two lights that the subject can just barely detect on fifty percent of the trials would define the subject's *difference threshold* for brightness. A special case of the difference threshold, called the *absolute threshold,* would be the minimum energy necessary for the subject to simply detect the presence of a stimulus fifty percent of the time.

One of the earliest discoveries made concerning difference thresholds was that they depend on the energy level or physical magnitude of the standard. The higher the level of the standard, the greater the difference between the standard and the comparison stimuli required to detect that they differ. An example of this relationship can be obtained by considering the level of lighting in a room to be the standard and considering the room lighting plus the light from a match as the comparison. The match produces a large difference in the brightness of a dark room (low-level standard) but no change in brightness in a lighted room. E. H. Weber first noted this relationship in the nineteenth century and described it in terms of the following mathematical formula, later called *Weber's law:*

$$\Delta I = KI$$

ΔI is the difference in energy between the standard and comparison stimuli that can be perceived fifty percent of the time; that is, the difference threshold. I is the energy of the standard stimulus. And K is a constant that depends on the particular perceptual (e.g., brightness) and physical (light energy) dimensions. The value of K, called Weber's fraction, summarizes our ability to resolve change along a particular perceptual-physical dimension. The smaller the value of K, the better our resolution. In the case of brightness, K is equal to about 1/62, which means that brightness differences can be perceived when the difference in light energy between the comparison and standard is about 1.6 percent of the standard's energy level. In the case of weight, K is about 1/53, which means that a difference of about 2 percent can be detected between the standard and comparison stimuli.

In addition to determining minimum physical changes necessary for perception, it has also been of interest to determine how our perception varies as a stimulus changes more than threshold amounts. One method for investigating this relationship is called the *magnitude estimation procedure.* In this procedure, the observer is required to assign an arbitrary value to the standard stimulus, and comparison stimuli are estimated relative to this arbitrary standard value. For example, if the observer assigned a value of 100 to represent the brightness of a standard light stimulus, a comparison stimulus that appeared to be half as bright would be assigned a value of 50, and so forth. Such numerical estimates are termed *magnitude estimates.* By using a set of comparison stimuli that differ in physical magnitude, we can generate a graph in which the magnitude estimates are a function of the physical magnitude of the comparison stimulus (see box fig. 6.3). One general fact illustrated by these graphs is that perception, as indicated by magnitude estimates, does not always increase uniformly as the physical value increases. Thus in the case of physical energy and loudness or brightness, changes in energy at low levels lead to greater perceptual changes than equivalent energy changes at higher levels. In the case of perceived heaviness and its relation to weight, heaviness increases less with changes at low weights than at higher weights. S. S. Stevens (1961) noted that all these functions could be described by the same general equation: M.E. $= kI^a$. The equation is called a *power* function and is known as Steven's law. M.E. is the magnitude estimation, k is a constant depending on the arbitrary units, I is the appropriate energy value of the comparison stimulus, and *a* is an exponent determined by the particular perceptual and physical dimensions being evaluated. If *a* is greater than 1, the curve will have a form such as that shown for heaviness and weight. If less than 1, the curve will be similar to the one that describes the relationship between light energy and brightness. If equal to 1, the curve will be a straight line, like the one obtained for the relationship between physical length and the perception of length.

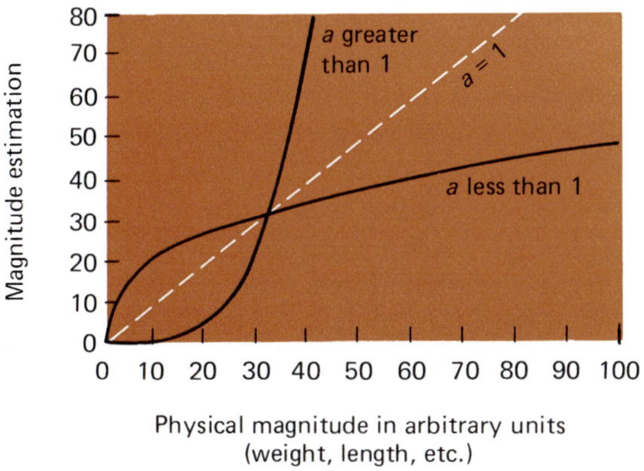

Box Figure 6.3 Magnitude estimations for various physical dimensions. The curve in which *a* is greater than 1 is similar to that obtained between heaviness and weight. The curve for *a* equal to 1 represents the relationship between perceived and physical length. The curve for *a* less than 1 resembles the relationship between brightness and light intensity or between loudness and sound intensity.

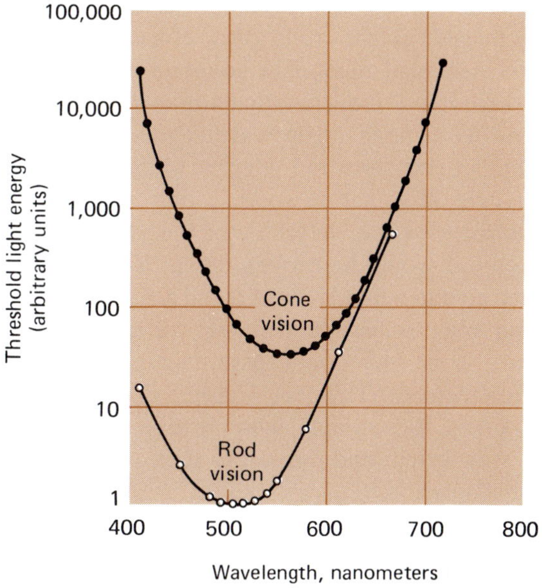

Figure 6.8 Threshold curves for photopic (cone) and scotopic (rod) vision. The lower the threshold, the more sensitive we are to the wavelength. (From *The Human Senses,* F. A. Geldard. Copyright 1972 John Wiley & Sons, Inc. Reprinted by permission of John Wiley & Sons, Inc.)

tors need time to achieve maximum sensitivity after exposure to daylight.

The absorption of light by the photochemical (pigment) in a receptor produces a chemical reaction in which some portion of the pigment is converted or broken down into other chemical products that are not sensitive to light. It is this conversion process that initiates the physiological signal about light. Under high general levels of illumination, such as daylight, a large portion of the photochemical within a receptor is broken down; therefore, there is less photochemical to respond to (absorb) the light striking the receptor. If light is removed from the eye, the chemical products recombine as time passes, so that more photochemical is present to absorb light. This increase in the receptors' absorption capacity accounts in part for our ability to detect dimmer lights as time goes by in the movie theater.

In addition to the regeneration of photochemicals in the rods and cones, neural processes also affect dark adaptation.

Figure 6.8 indicates that the rods are insensitive to long (red) wavelengths of light. Thus, if you wore red goggles while viewing daylight illumination so that only red light entered your eye, very little of the rod photochemical would be broken down. You could then go into a faintly illuminated area, remove your goggles, and immediately see quite well because the rods would contain a high level of photopigment. This fact is used to advantage by pilots, for example, who must be prepared to view bright and dim areas with little time for adaptation.

If, after entering a dark movie theater from normal daylight, we were to measure the minimum amount of light energy we could detect at various times, we would obtain a *dark adaptation curve* such as the one labelled W in figure 6.9. This curve indicates that the eyes become progressively more sensitive (i.e., we can see dimmer lights) in the dark. Furthermore, the curve appears to be divided into two distinct phases.

The first phase, which lasts approximately ten minutes, can be attributed to the cone system. We can establish this fact by using red light (which was the case for the adaptation curve marked R in fig. 6.9) because the rods are insensitive to red light. Thus the initial phase represents an increase in the cones' sensitivity, a process that is virtually complete within about ten minutes. Therefore, the R curve shows no further increase in sensitivity after this time. In the W curve, white light was used to test sensitivity. Because white light is composed of wavelengths to which both rods and cones are sensitive, the second phase, which represents the adaptation of the rods is apparent. This process lasts for a considerably longer period of time.

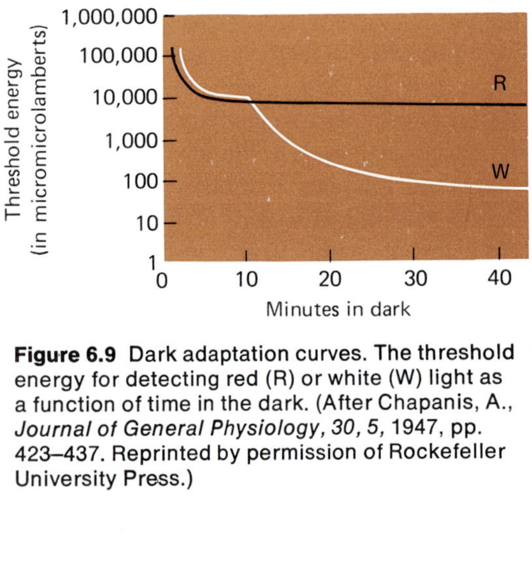

Figure 6.9 Dark adaptation curves. The threshold energy for detecting red (R) or white (W) light as a function of time in the dark. (After Chapanis, A., *Journal of General Physiology*, *30*, 5, 1947, pp. 423–437. Reprinted by permission of Rockefeller University Press.)

Why is rod vision more sensitive than cone vision? Part of the answer may be related to the fact that the rods contain a larger amount of photopigment, and therefore, have a greater opportunity to absorb the light striking them. Another reason for the difference in scotopic and photopic sensitivity can be understood if we consider the connections of the rods and cones to other neural elements in the retina, as was illustrated in figure 6.6. In the center of the fovea, a single cone is connected to its own set of bipolar cells. This is sometimes called a "private line" connection. As we move toward the periphery of the fovea, several cones will be connected to a single bipolar cell. This is termed *convergence* or a "party line" connection because the information about light from several cones is brought together at the bipolar cell. The greater the number of receptors giving information to the same bipolar cell, the greater the convergence.

Rods generally demonstrate much greater convergence than cones. This greater convergence also contributes to the greater sensitivity of the rod visual system to dim illumination. A dim light may have only a slight effect on a particular rod. But because many rods stimulate the same bipolar cell, their combined effects will be enough to produce a signal in the bipolar cells that is sufficient for visual detection. Convergence is also a structural property of many neural systems in the brain. In general, convergence provides a means for combining many weak signals into a stimulus that is strong enough to produce an effect.

In the retina, convergence enhances sensitivity to weak light; however, information about the pattern of light in the image is sacrificed. If receptors pick up information from different points in a pattern and combine this information at the bipolar cell, then the differences between these points will no longer be maintained. For example, imagine that you are looking at two points of light which are close together. If these points of light stimulate a group of rods that converge on a bipolar cell, the effects of the two points will sum and the signal produced by them will be as great as the signal produced by a single point of greater intensity. On the other hand, if the two points were stimulating cones in the center of the fovea, the difference between the two points and a single point could be distinguished. In this case, the two points of light would stimulate cones connected to different bipolar cells, and information about each of them would remain segregated.

Because the cone system displays less convergence than the rod system, the cone system is better suited to resolving the *details* of an image, while the rod system, as we have indicated is better suited to detecting the *presence* of light. This explains why we are able to see finer detail in bright light, that is, when the cone system is operating. In addition, it also explains why our ability to see fine detail, or our *visual spatial acuity* is best when we look directly at an object. In this case, you will recall, the image falls directly on the fovea, where there is the least convergence.

Thus far, we have covered a number of important visual functions that can be attributed to the processes and structure of the retina. Specifically, we have discovered that we possess a dual visual system. The cone system is responsible for fine, detailed color vision under high levels of illumination. The rod system is designed for maximum sensitivity to the presence of light. This concept of a dual visual system has been formalized as the *duplicity theory* of vision and is now a fundamental theoretical framework of visual perception.

Color Vision

Why does the cone visual system provide us with color information while the rod visual system does not? Suppose that you are looking at two spots of light of the same wavelength with your rod vision alone. If one spot is higher in energy than the other, the rods illuminated by the high energy spot would give a stronger response while the rods illuminated by the lower energy spot would give a weaker response. Now suppose that both spots are *equal* in energy but have different wavelengths. The rods illuminated by the wavelength that is absorbed to a greater extent by rhodopsin would give a greater response. Thus the same difference in the rods' responses to the two spots of light could mean that the spots differ either in wavelength or in energy. Therefore, the rod visual system cannot distinguish differences in wavelength from differences in energy.

In contrast with the rods, all of which contain the same photopigment, there are several different types of cones containing different photopigments. When you view a spot of light with the cones, the spot illuminates each type of cone. As we will see, there are three types of cones: those will be termed "R," which absorb best in the "red" or long wavelength region of the spectrum; "G," which absorb best in the "green" or medium wavelength region; and "B," which absorb best in "blue" or short wavelengths of light. Figure 6.10 illustrates the responses of cones when they are illuminated by different wavelengths of light.

Stimulus	Receptor	Receptor response	Visual effect	Stimulus	Receptor	Receptor response	Visual effect
(a) $\lambda = 680$ nm	C_1 C_2 C_3		"Red"	(d) $\lambda = 570$ nm	C_1 C_2 C_3		"Yellow"
(b) $\lambda = 530$ nm	C_1 C_2 C_3		"Green"	(e) $\lambda = 680$ nm $\lambda = 530$ nm	C_1 C_2 C_3		"Yellow"
(c) $\lambda = 460$ nm	C_1 C_2 C_3		"Blue"	(f) $\lambda = 680$ nm $\lambda = 530$ nm $\lambda = 460$ nm	C_1 C_2 C_3		"White"

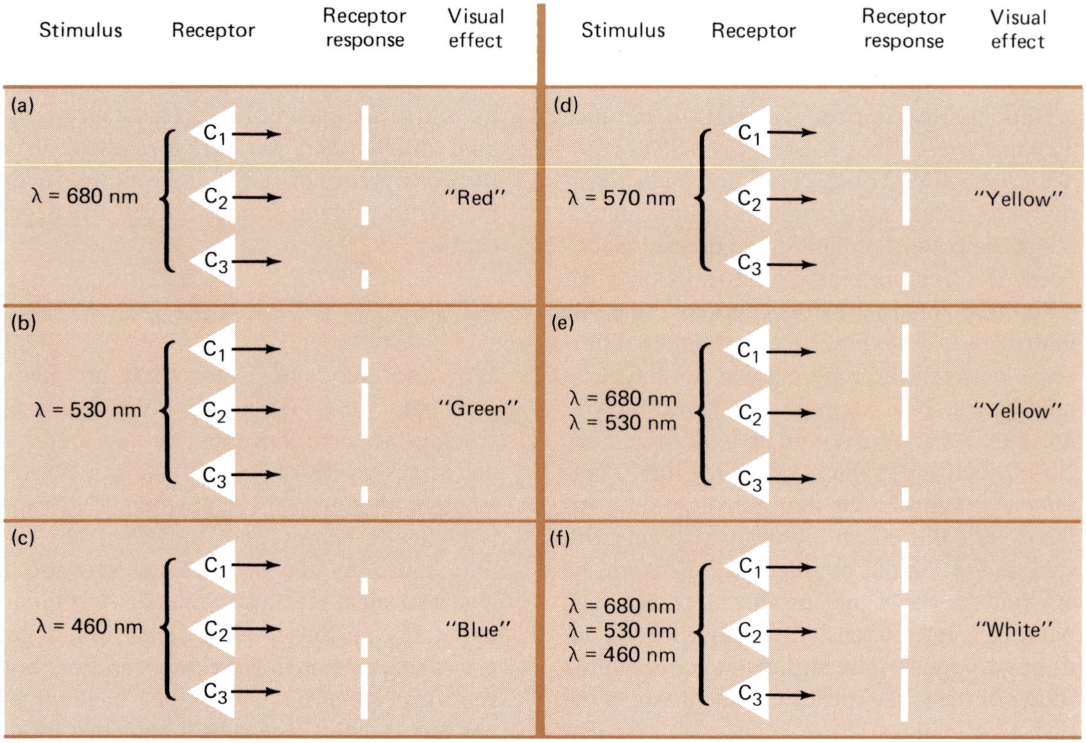

Figure 6.10 Each figure illustrates the response pattern produced by illuminating the three types of cones (C_1, C_2, C_3) with the wavelengths (λ) of light designated. The visual effect produced by stimulating is indicated.

Figure 6.10a indicates that when we view a light in the red region of the spectrum the R cones give the maximum response, while the other two types of cones give minimal responses. If we vary the energy of this light, the *pattern* obtained from the three cone types will remain the same. That is, with less energy, each cone type will be less responsive, but the responses of R cones will continue to predominate. Figures 6.10b and 6.10c indicate that a different pattern of response would be obtained with a green or blue light respectively. Again, varying the energy of the green or blue light would alter the responses of all the cones, but in the case of green light the G cones would still predominate, and similarly in the case of blue light, the B cones would still predominate, thus providing the same *pattern* of response at different energy levels.

Because the cone system produces different patterns of response to different wavelengths, it is capable of distinguishing between minor changes in energy and in wavelength. However, not all differences in the composition of wavelength can be discriminated. As shown in figure 6.10d and 6.10e, in the case of a yellow light the red and green systems respond equally and to a greater extent than does the blue system. Notice that this pattern of response can be produced by a monochromatic yellow light (fig. 6.10d) or a combination of long (red) and medium (green) wavelengths (fig. 6.10e). Thus different wavelengths can produce the same pattern of response. If you will reflect for a moment, you will realize that the larger the number of different types of cones, the more wavelength combinations we would be able to distinguish.

How many different photopigments we possess and how many different wavelength combinations we can distinguish have been questions of major interest in the theory of color vision. The classic color-matching experiment, first performed by significant figures in the history of science such as Isaac Newton, Herman von Helmholtz, Thomas Young, and James Maxwell, provides the answers to these questions. In this experiment an observer was asked to match the color of one spot of light by superimposing different lights to form a second spot. (See box 6.4 for a discussion of light mixing.) It was found that many lights could be matched by mixing the appropriate amounts of three other lights, called *primary* lights. This is the principle behind the color television set. Each of the small spots of light on the television screen, which together form an entire image, is actually composed of three different spots, each of which consists of a different phosphor that, when struck by a beam of electrons, produces either red, green, or blue. These three phosphor spots are so small and close together that the light produced by them is blended in the retinal image. Therefore, all the colors on the television screen are produced by electrically exciting these basic phosphor spots to produce the particular amounts of red, green, and blue light that, when mixed on the retina, produce the color we see.

The color-matching experiment suggests that three photopigments which respond differently to these three primary colors would be adequate to produce the range of colors that we perceive. Inferences such as these resulted in the trichromatic (three-color) theory of color vision.

Trichromatic Theory

Although the trichromatic theory of color vision was formulated by Helmholtz in the nineteenth century, direct physiological confirmation of the theory has only been obtained

Box 6.4

Mixing of Lights and Paints: Additive and Subtractive Mixtures

Why is it that when a blue and yellow light are mixed, we perceive white, despite the fact that mixing blue and yellow paint yields green? Plate 5a illustrates what happens when two lights are mixed. Two projectors are shown: one is projecting a blue wavelength of light; the other is projecting a yellow wavelength of light onto the same area. Note that this area now reflects light of both wavelengths. Thus the wavelength composition of the reflected light represents the addition of the two projected lights. This is termed an *additive* mixture. Because both the yellow and blue wavelengths are stimulating the same area of the eye, we see white.

Plate 5b illustrates the result of projecting a light containing all visible wavelengths (white light) onto a painted surface. The upper portion of the figure shows blue and yellow painted surfaces. Generally speaking, the blue paint reflects short wavelengths and absorbs longer wavelengths, while the yellow paint reflects long wavelengths and absorbs shorter wavelengths. The reflection and absorption characteristics of the two paints are illustrated graphically. When yellow and blue paint are mixed, as shown in the lower portion of Plate 5b, each paint in the mixture behaves as it did before. Because the blue paint absorbs primarily long wavelengths while the yellow paint in the mixture absorbs primarily short wavelengths, the reflected light mainly consists of the intermediate wavelengths, which are perceived as green.

Thus when viewing a painted surface, we see the wavelengths that are reflected rather than those that are absorbed. Those wavelengths that are absorbed by the painted surface can be considered as having been subtracted from the original wavelength composition of the light source. The color resulting from such paint mixtures is often referred to as resulting from a *subtractive* mixture.

within the last twenty years. We now know that three different types of cones have maximum absorptions at wavelengths of approximately 445, 535, and 570 nm. The spectral sensitivity curves of the photopigments contained in the three types of cones resemble those shown in figure 6.11. Notice that although each photopigment is sensitive to a *range* of wavelengths, one is most sensitive to green, another is most sensitive to blue, while a third is most sensitive to red. All the colors we see result from the different patterns of response of these three types of cones. Figure 6.10 illustrates schematically how, according to the trichromatic theory, we can

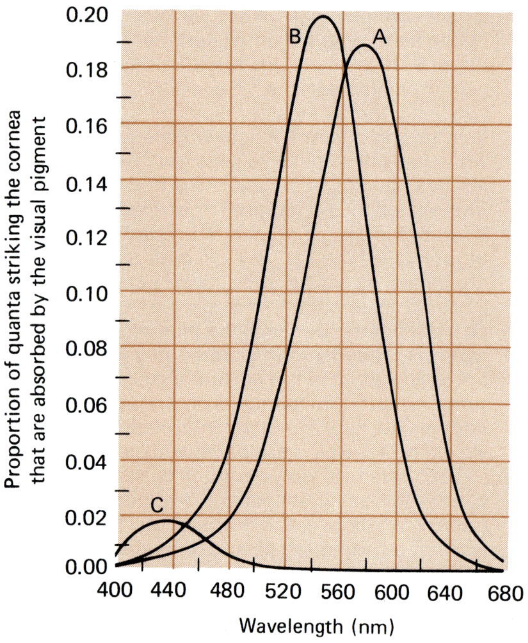

Figure 6.11 Idealized spectral sensitivities of the three color systems of the human retina. The curve labelled A illustrates receptors most sensitive to "red," B illustrates receptors most sensitive to "green," and C illustrates receptors most sensitive to "blue." (From "The receptors for human color vision," G. Wald, *Science, 145,* 1964, 1007–1017. Fig., 4 September 1964. Copyright 1964 by the American Association for the Advancement of Science.)

account for the three basic perceptual dimensions of color: hue, saturation, and brightness. *Hue,* as we noted earlier, depends on the pattern of response obtained from the three types of cones. White, an *achromatic* or hueless color, is produced by any combination of wavelengths that elicit equal responses in the three cone systems. This can occur when all three wavelengths elicit equal responses, as shown in figure 6.10f, or it can be produced by a combination of two monochromatic lights—for example, blue and yellow. Any two colored lights that, when combined, generate white are called *complementary* colors. *Saturation,* the intensity of a color, is determined by the extent to which the pattern produced by the color deviates from a pattern characteristic of white. Pink, for example, which is a relatively unsaturated red, is produced by only a slight predominance of the red system over the blue and green cone systems. The *brightness* of the light will depend on how strongly all the systems are responding. In this case, the pattern remains the same, but the overall magnitude of the responses increases or decreases to produce a brighter or dimmer color response. Individuals who do not possess a complete three-color system exhibit some form of color blindness. This interesting phenomenon is discussed in box 6.5.

Opponent Process Theory

Although the trichromatic theory summarizes the basic facts about color mixture, there are additional phenomena in color vision that cannot be explained by the trichromatic theory alone. Around the time that Helmholtz postulated his trichromatic theory, a German physiologist, Ewald Hering, attempted to develop a theory that would explain some of these other phenomena. For instance, he noted that observers considered some colors to be compounds: Orange, for example, was viewed as a mixture of yellow and red. Other colors could not be viewed as compounds and

Box 6.5

Color Blindness

About eight percent of the male population and one percent of the female population have defective color vision. The most common defect is red-green color blindness. Individuals who are truly red-green color-blind cannot distinguish between red or green wavelengths or any mixture of the two; that is, they will perceive all combinations of red and green as the same color. Other individuals are color anomalous, or color weak and require more red or more green in a red-green mixture than individuals with normal color vision require to perceive yellow. Normal viewers will see the number 42 in plate 2.

A rare defect characterized by an inability to differentiate between blue and yellow is termed tritanopia. Tritanopia is usually caused by a disease, whereas red-green color blindness is typically an inherited, sex-linked defect. The physiological basis for color blindness is still a subject of research and controversy. Most theories postulate that one of the photopigments in the cones of color-blind individuals has an abnormal spectral absorption, or that, in contrast with normal individuals, both the red and green color systems contain the same photopigment. Some individuals (called monochromats) lack cones in the retina and are entirely color-blind.

were considered "pure." Observers routinely arrived at four pure colors; blue, yellow, green, and red. Other colors were reported to consist of combinations of these basic colors.

In addition to noting the existence of the pure hues, Hering also observed that some combinations of these hues were impossible; such as a "reddish green" or a "bluish yellow." Therefore, he proposed that there must be some process in color vision that led to an opposition of color responses. This would account for the fact that when looking at a mixture of pure blue and yellow, depending on the amounts, one can see yellow, blue, or white, but not a "bluish yellow." In other words, apparently the pure blue and yellow processes opposed each other. Similarly, it appeared that pure red and green were in opposition. This led to Hering's four-color, or *opponent process theory* of color vision, which assumed the existence of four-color processes, one for each pure hue, arranged in opposing pairs of blue versus yellow and red versus green. Interestingly enough, physiological evidence for the opponent process theory and the trichromatic theory began to appear at about the same time.

To understand the evidence supporting the opponent process theory of color vision, we must investigate the processing of visual information above the retinal level. Refer to box figure 3.7 and note that each optic nerve sends one half of its fibers to each side of the brain. This crossing over of optic nerve fibers occurs at the optic chiasm and has the effect of relaying information from the left visual field (the right half of each retina) to the right side of the brain and sending information from the right visual field (the left half of each retina) to the left side of the brain. Once past the optic chiasm, the optic nerve fibers synapse with cells in the lateral geniculate nuclei of the thalamus (one of the specific sensory relay nuclei of the thalamus discussed in Chapter 3). After this synaptic relay, information is carried by the axons of cells in the lateral geniculate nuclei to the visual cortex.

Physiological evidence that supports the opponent process theory comes in part from recordings of the responses of neurons in the lateral geniculate nuclei (e.g., DeValois and Jacobs, 1968). In these experiments, different wavelengths of light were shone into the eyes of experimental animals (monkeys) and the responses of single neurons in the lateral geniculate nuclei to these different wavelengths of light were recorded. One class of neurons was termed *opponent neurons.* These cells increased their rate of firing maximally to one wavelength and decreased their firing

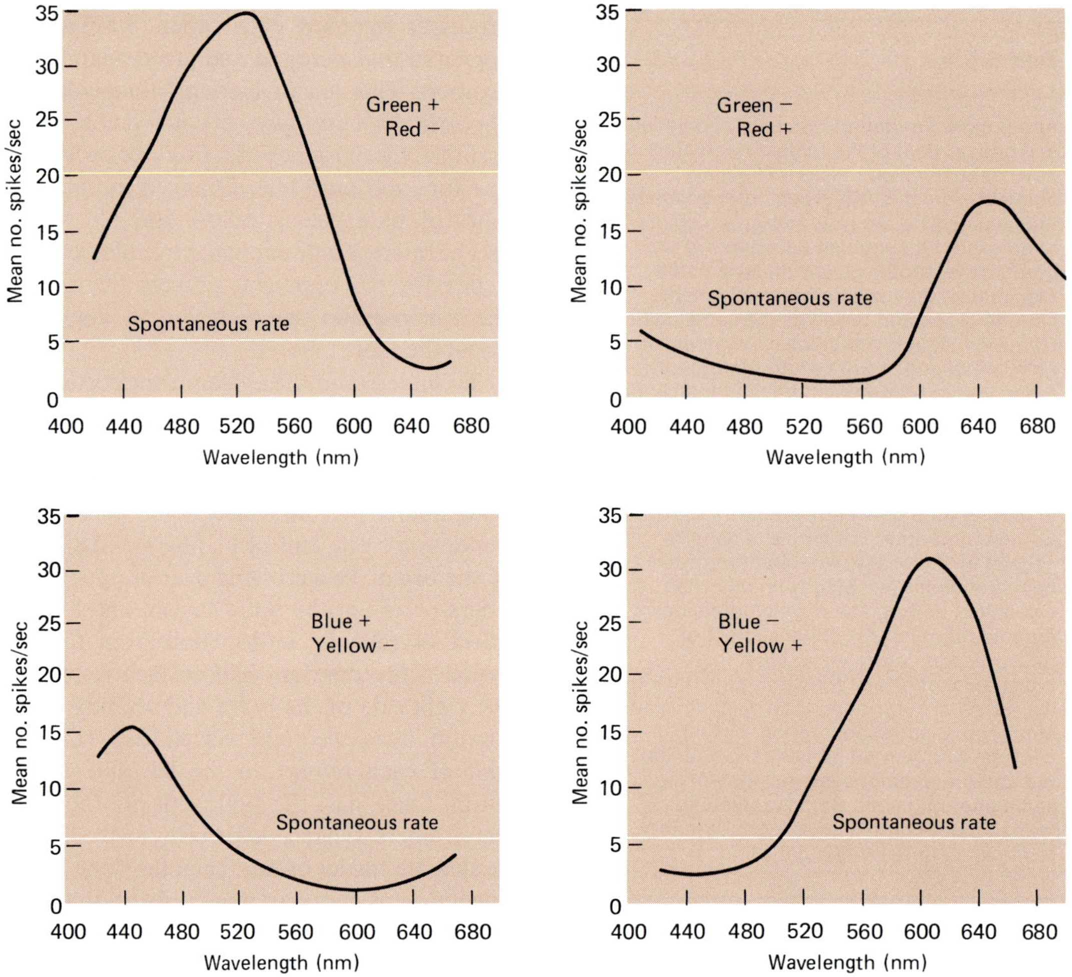

Figure 6.12 Responses of opponent cells in the lateral geniculate nuclei to different wavelengths of light. One class of opponent cells was maximally excited by green wavelengths and inhibited by red, or vice versa (top). Another class was maximally excited by yellow and inhibited by blue, or vice versa (bottom), (After DeValois, R., et al., "Analysis of response patterns of LGN cells," *Journal of Optical Society of America, 56,* 1966, pp. 966–977. Reprinted by permission of American Institute of Physics.)

maximally to the presentation of another, as illustrated in figure 6.12. In one type of opponent neuron, maximum response was produced by presenting a wavelength in the green region of the spectrum, while a maximal decrease in firing rate was produced by a wavelength of light in the red region of the spectrum. This category of opponent response is abbreviated green + red −. Presentation of both wavelengths simultaneously would, in this case, produce no change in response (i.e., the responses to green and red would "oppose" each other). Other opponent cells exhibited an opposition of yellow and blue wavelengths. The opponent responses of these neurons correspond to Hering's notion of op-

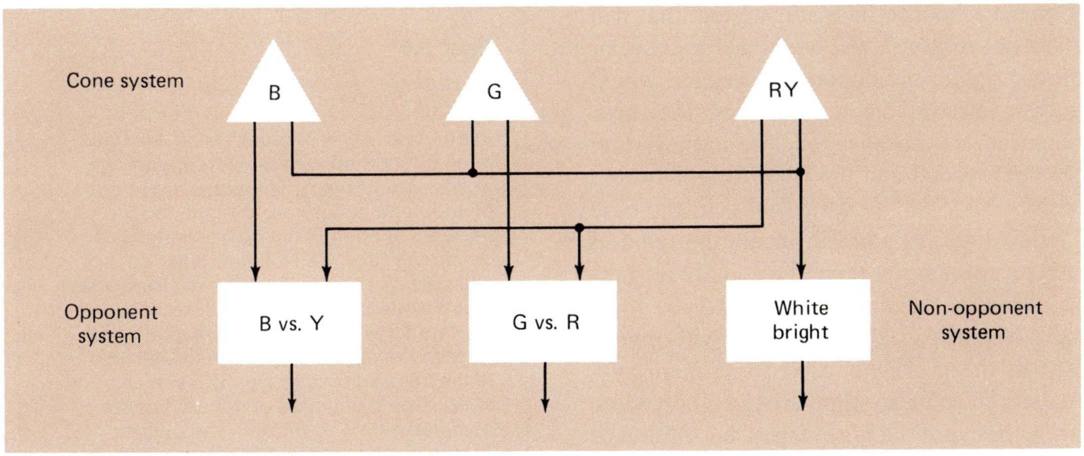

Figure 6.13 Model of color vision. The responses of the three types of cones (B absorbs best in blue wavelength region; G absorbs best in green wavelength region; RY absorbs best in red region) are fed to an opponent system and a nonopponent or white-bright system. Imagine that the three types of cones are grouped closely in a small area of the retina so that they all "view" the same point of light.

posing red-green and yellow-blue processes in color vision.

DeValois and Jacobs observed another major class of cells that were termed *nonopponent neurons*. One type of nonopponent neuron was excited to varying degrees by all wavelengths. In fact, the responses of these neurons, when taken as a whole, mirrored the photopic spectral sensitivity curve shown in figure 6.8. Thus nonopponent neurons appear to reflect the differences in brightness related to different wavelengths of light.

Combined Theory of Color Vision

A descriptive model of color vision that incorporates both the trichromatic and opponent process theories is illustrated in figure 6.13. In this view, color vision starts with the three cone systems specified by the trichromatic theory. The response patterns of these three classes of receptors are interpreted by higher neural systems in an opponent process fashion. In other words, the outputs of the green and red receptors interact at a higher level to form the green-red opponent process system. Similarly, the outputs of the blue and red receptors interact to form the blue-yellow system. The combined output of the three receptors forms the basis for a brightness system. Although one might easily conclude that the "higher level" systems are located in the lateral geniculate nuclei of the thalamus, the interactions between different receptors probably occur in the retina, although they are accurately reflected by responses of neurons in the lateral geniculate nuclei.

Let's examine how this model could account for two specific cases, white and yellow. When a white light is viewed, the responses of the three types of receptors will be equal. The responses of the red and green receptors will completely oppose each other in the green-versus-red system shown in Plate 4 (see box 6.6). Therefore, there will be no response from the green-versus-red opponent system. Similarly, the equal responses of the red and blue receptors will oppose each other completely in the blue-versus-yellow opponent system, producing no net response. The only system that will have a net response will be the achromatic or "white-bright" nonopponent system, which simply combines the responses of the three receptor types. Because the chromatic system does not respond and the white-bright system does respond, we see white light. In the case of yellow light, as you will recall, the red and green receptor systems will be equally responsive, whereas the blue receptor will be minimally responsive. Therefore, red will oppose green in the green-versus-red opponent system, but red will also stimulate the blue-yellow system. Because the blue response is minimal, yellow will predominate in the blue-versus-yellow opponent system and the visual effect will be yellow, the brightness of the effect will be determined by the degree to which the achromatic, or white-bright system is activated. The saturation of a color will depend on the relative amounts of opponent and nonopponent responses. Roughly, the greater the ratio of opponent to nonopponent responses, the greater the saturation. These illustrations should enable you to work out the appearances of other color mixtures and account for the color aftereffects described in box 6.6.

The study of color vision provides an excellent example of the interrelationships between perceptual, physiological, and physical analyses of visual phenomena. In many cases, scientists studying the relationship between the perception of color and the physics of light were led to postulate physiological mechanisms many years before they were actually discovered. In fact, we can argue that without these early perceptual studies, scientists would not have known what to look for when they began to explore the nervous system. Their explorations in turn have provided important insights into the study of perception. A similar pattern of interaction has occurred in other fields of perception, as you will see in the following discussion of pattern vision.

Box 6.6

Spatial and Temporal Color Contrast Effects

In our discussion of color vision, we have been concerned with the perception of a single spot of color. There are important phenomena in color vision that depend on patterns of color in space or changes of color over time. Plate 4 illustrates an example of a temporal color-contrast effect. If you fixate the dot in the colored picture in Plate 4a for a while and then shift your gaze to the dot on the white surface next to the colored picture, you will see *an afterimage* composed of colors that are complementary to those in the picture. This temporal contrast effect is understandable if we assume that the color receptors stimulated by the colored picture have "fatigued" or "adapted" as a result of prolonged stimulation. Thus when a white surface is viewed, the color receptor systems that were not adapted are temporarily unopposed and produce an afterimage of complementary color.

Plate 4b illustrates a spatial color-contrast effect. Notice that the light areas in the pattern appear pink as a result of their juxtaposition to the green areas. Apparently, the green pattern "induces" a color in the lighter area; otherwise this area would appear white. This effect is usually interpreted, in terms of the opponent process theory, as follows: a particular color process operating in one retinal area opposes the identical process in another retinal area. Presumably, the green region of the stimulus pattern produces green activity in the red-green system, which in turn opposes green activity in the nearby regions. Therefore, in the light regions of the pattern, where green and red would normally be balanced, red dominates and produces a pink appearance.

Pattern Vision

The spatial color-contrast effect described in box 6.6 illustrates that the color of one region of a pattern of light can be affected by other colors near it. Like colors generally oppose one another in nearby regions. Opposition of neighboring regions can also be observed for black-and-white patterns. For example, as demonstrated in figure 6.1b, the brightness of a gray square can be affected by the surrounding light. The brighter the surrounding light, the darker the figure; an effect termed *brightness contrast.* Thus, although the brightness of a point of light within a pattern is partly determined by its own intensity, the brightness of any given point is also partly determined by the intensity of points surrounding it. The basis for this important interaction between points of light in a pattern has been found to depend, in part, on the physiological processes of the retina.

Receptive Fields

Kuffler and others (see Ratliff, 1965) have measured the neural responses of a single fiber of the optic nerve while stimulating the eye of an experimental animal (e.g., a cat) with a small spot of light. By moving the spot of light around so that it stimulated different regions of the retina, Kuffler was able to determine the area of the retina that, when stimulated by the spot of light, produced changes in the response of a single optic nerve fiber. Keep in mind that the optic nerve fibers are the axons of retinal ganglion cells. Kuffler found that the ganglion cell response could be changed by light stimulation over a small, well-circumscribed area of the retina. Because this area was the region of the retina from which a single ganglion cell received information about light, it was termed the *receptive field* of the ganglion cell. Each ganglion cell had its own receptive field centered around some point on the retina. Receptive fields of different ganglion cells could overlap considerably, as shown in figure 6.14a and b. In addition, the receptive field for a particular ganglion cell could be subdivided into two areas, a *center* and a *surround,* which when stimulated with light produced opposing effects on the ganglion cell's response. Stimulating the center of the receptive field produced an increase in the firing rate of one type of ganglion cell, and the increase in firing was related to the intensity of the light stimulus. The effect of this center stimulus could then be opposed by stimulating the surround re-

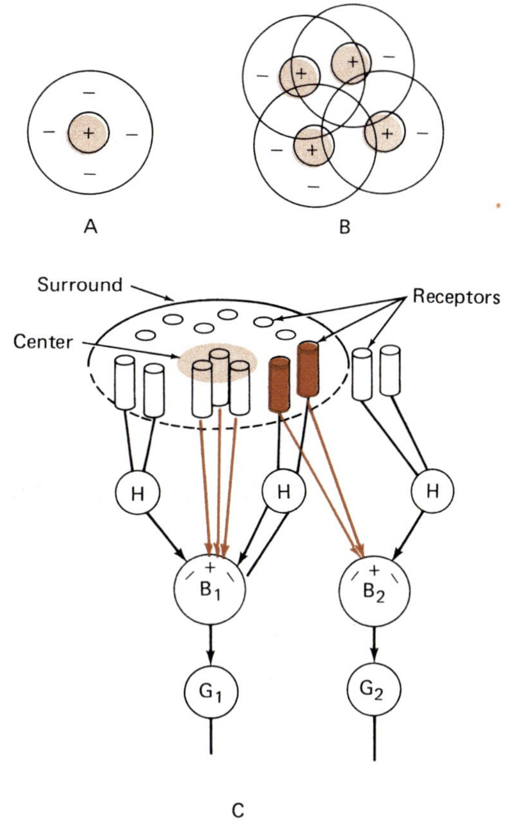

Figure 6.14 Receptive field organization of retinal ganglion cells. The center and surround regions oppose each other (A), and the receptive fields of different ganglion cells will overlap considerably (B). Possible neural connections leading to receptive field organization (C). Receptors in the center region send signals (red lines) to bipolar cells (B). These signals are opposed by those from the horizontal cells (H), which are stimulated by receptors in the surround region. The signal from the bipolar cell to the ganglion cell (G) reflects the positive and negative signals it receives. The shaded receptors show how the receptors in the surround of one ganglion cell (G_1) can form the center of another (G_2).

gion. The greater the illumination of the surround region, the greater the opposition. This type of receptive field organization can probably be explained by the vertical and horizontal flow of information in the retina, described on page 156. Center responses would be produced by information flowing in vertically oriented elements—the receptors, bipolar cells, and ganglion cells—while surround effects would be produced by information relayed in the horizontally oriented cell types—the amacrine and horizontal cells. (See fig. 6.14c.) The form of opposition found between center and surround is referred to as *lateral* (across) *inhibition* because the opposition derives from the lateral, or crossing elements in the retina.

To understand the effect of this organization of receptive fields, one can think of the "neural picture" produced when the image on the retina is translated into the pattern of ganglion cell responses. Each point in this neural picture is represented by the response of a single ganglion cell. For the sake of simplicity, let's assume that the greater the ganglion cell response, the "brighter" the neural picture. Each ganglion cell will receive information from the region of the image that corresponds to its receptive field. Thus a point in the neural picture will depend on a collection of points in the image. We can now ask what this neural picture will look like, given that each point in the neural picture is contingent upon the interaction of a collection of points in the visual image. Generally speaking, differences in the intensity of light within the visual image will be exaggerated in the neural picture. This phenomenon can be explained by considering the response of a single ganglion cell to the pattern of light falling on its receptive field, as shown in figure 6.14. If the entire receptive field is evenly illuminated, the center and surround oppose each other, and little net response will be produced. On the other hand, if the pattern of light changes over the receptive field—for example, if the center is illuminated at one level and the surround is illuminated at another—then a response will be produced. The greater the difference in illumination, the greater the response. Thus the function of the retina's receptive field organization is to respond to and enhance differences in illumination.

Mach Bands

A striking outcome of this neural picture can be seen in figure 6.15, which illustrates a phenomenon first discovered by Ernst Mach in the last century. If you look at the pattern of light shown in figure 6.15a, you will perceive (near the center of the picture) a bright band at B and a dark band at D. These are called Mach bands. What you see is indicated by the colored line in the graph of figure 6.15b. The solid line is the actual physical intensity of light, as measured by a light meter moved along the pattern from left to right. This line would also represent the distribution of light intensity across the image of this pattern on your retina. Notice that what you see does not correspond to the physical intensity distribution of your retinal image. The pattern you perceive exaggerates the abrupt transitions in the physical intensity pattern. We can relate your perception of this pattern to the translation of the pattern of the physical image into the neural picture, as illustrated in figure 6.15c. Consider ganglion cells A and B, which are stimulated by points along a horizontal line in the pattern. The receptive field of each ganglion cell is represented by a circle containing a dot. If we compare the responses of ganglion cells A and B, both cells receive the same illumination in the center (dot). However, the surround of ganglion cell B is illuminated, partly by a high intensity region of the pattern and partly by a low intensity region of the pattern. The surround of ganglion cell A on the other hand, is entirely illuminated by a high intensity region of the pattern. Thus center stimulation of ganglion cell B is opposed to a lesser degree than center stimulation of ganglion cell A, as shown in the graph in figure 6.15d. If we compare the responses of ganglion cells C and D, we note that the centers are equally stimulated by low levels of illumination, although C receives a higher degree of illumination in its surround region. Therefore, the center response of C is opposed to a greater degree than the center response of ganglion cell D. This is also illustrated in the graph of figure 6.15d.

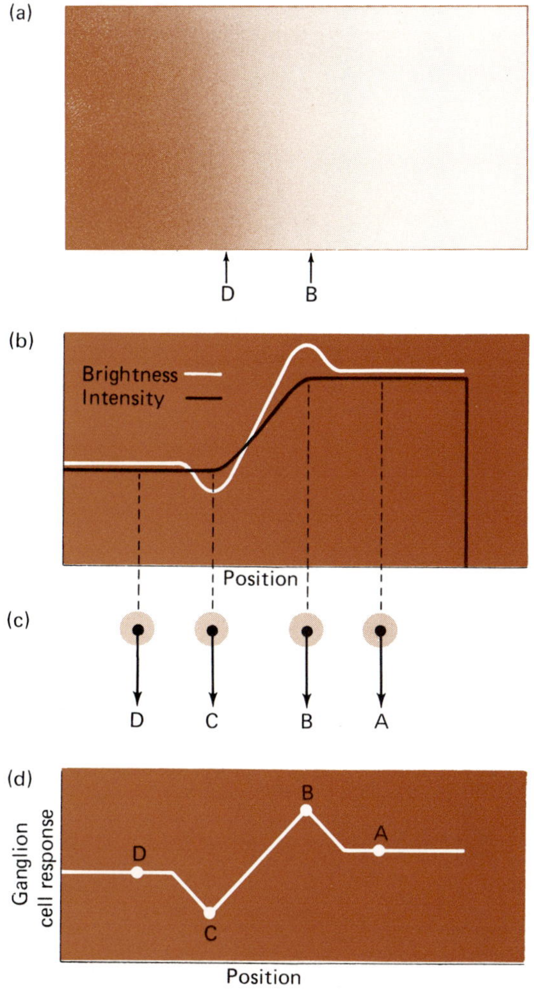

Figure 6.15 (a) A pattern of light which produces Mach Bands at D and B. (b) A graph of the physical intensity (solid line) and the brightness perceived across the pattern. (c) Receptive fields of some selected ganglion cells which would receive light at various points along the pattern. (d) The response or "neural" picture produced by these ganglion cells. (From *Visual Perception*, T. Cornsweet. Copyright 1970, Academic Press, p. 277 for parts a and b. Reprinted by permission of Academic Press, Inc.)

The neural picture illustrated by the graph in figure 6.15d closely resembles what is perceived, as represented by the broken line in the graph in figure 6.15b. Thus our perceptions of patterns of light are imposed on us in part by the center-surround organization of the retina's receptive fields and by the effect of lateral inhibition operating in these receptive fields.

Lateral Inhibition

Lateral inhibition emphasizes certain changes in a pattern of light over space (such as those shown in fig. 6.15b) more than others. Gradual changes, such as those that might occur within a shadow, are not usually perceived; neither are subtle, extremely fine, rapid changes such as those making up the "grain" of a photograph. In other senses as well as in other aspects of vision, lateral inhibition also serves to facilitate, or enhance certain types of change. For example, what we see varies not only over space but over time as well. Let's examine the role of lateral inhibition when light is changed over time.

Imagine that you are looking at a spot of light which alternates in intensity over time—that is, flickers—as shown graphically in figures 6.16a and 6.16b. The alternating light can be varied in two ways. First we can vary the *amplitude,* or amount of change from maximum to minimum. Second, we can vary the *frequency,* or rapidity with which the light alternates from maximum to minimum intensity. If you were observing the light flickering at a constant frequency, a certain minimum amplitude would be required to see the flicker.

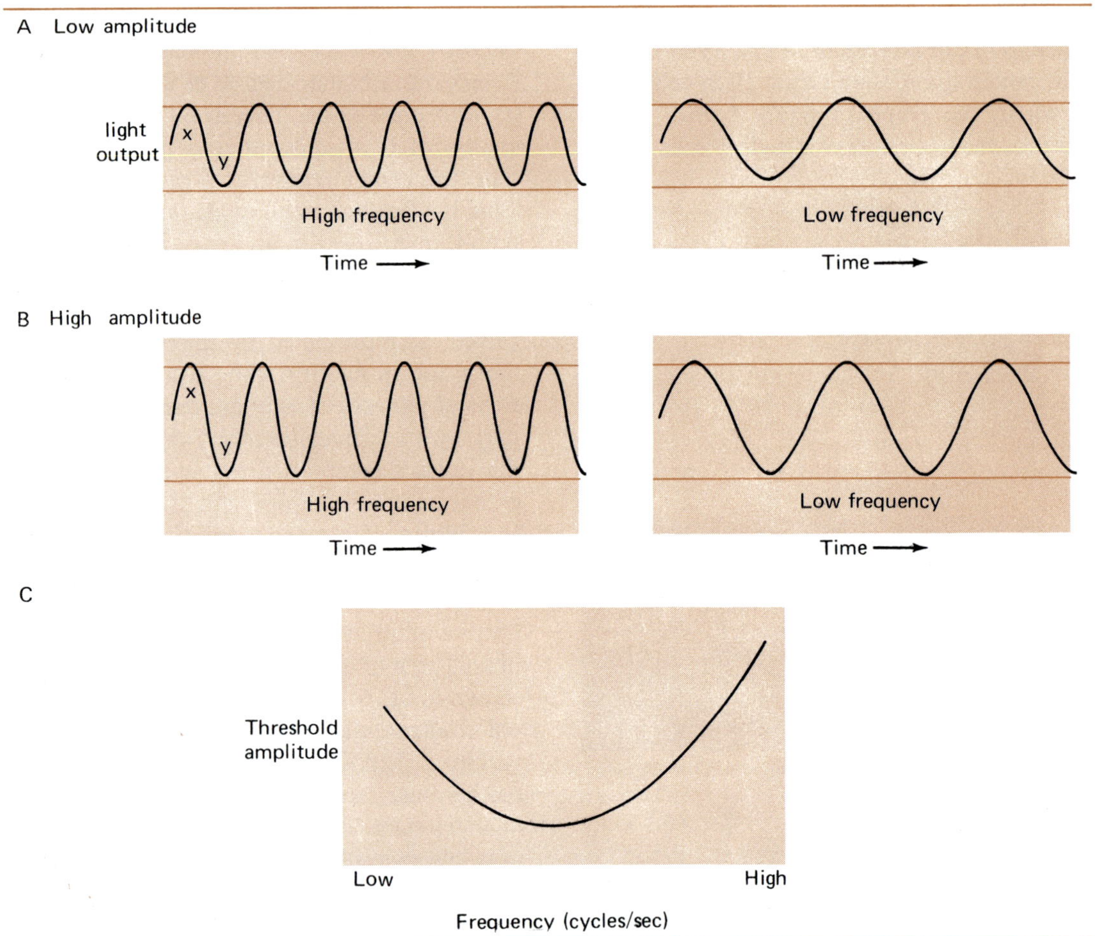

Figure 6.16 A and B illustrate a light changing in intensity over time (flicker). The light is maximally bright at point x and minimally intense at a later time, y. High frequency graphs illustrate a light varying more rapidly over time. The lights in A change less from maximum to minimum (low amplitude) than those in B (high amplitude). The graph in C portrays the minimum amount of amplitude to perceive flickering lights at different frequencies. We are less sensitive to extremely low or high frequencies of flicker than to intermediate frequencies.

The minimum amplitude required for detection depends on how rapidly the light is flickering. Figure 6.16c illustrates this effect, in which greater amplitudes are required to detect rapidly flickering light and, interestingly enough, extremely low frequencies of flicker. Lesser amplitudes are required to detect intermediate frequencies of flicker. For example, we cannot ordinarily perceive the rapid flicker of fluorescent lights, although the light goes on and off 120 times per second. Similarly, we do not ordinarily perceive the extremely slow changes in illumination that occur as the sun rises.

Again, there is a relationship between our perception of changes in light over time and the operation of lateral inhibition. This can be related to physiological processing if we consider that the flickering light is illuminating the receptive field of a ganglion cell. To perceive that the light is flickering, the ganglion cell's response must change over time in a parallel fashion. We know that the ganglion cell's response to stimulation of its surround is more "sluggish"—requires more time—than a response to stimulation of the center region. If the change in light is gradual over time, the response of both the center and the surround are able to follow this change. Because center and surround stimulation oppose each other, the net effect is a minimal response to this low frequency change. At intermediate frequencies of flicker, the surround is no longer capable of following the change in light over time, so its response remains essentially constant, although the light is changing. The far more agile center continues to respond to the change in light, now unopposed by changes in the surround response, producing a parallel change in the response of the ganglion cell. But even the center cannot follow extremely high frequencies of flicker; therefore, there is no change in the ganglion cell's response to these rapid changes in light intensity. For these reasons, we are most sensitive to intermediate rates of change in light over time.

The fact that the eye is insensitive to certain frequencies of change in light over time makes possible the continuous motion we observe in moving pictures and on television. For example, a standard motion picture camera projects about thirty frames per second; that is, a new picture is shown every thirtieth of a second. The light in the projector is actually blocked out as the frames are changed. If this was all that occurred, you would perceive an annoying, flickering picture. To avoid this problem, each frame is interrupted by the projector several times, so that the light is interrupted, not only when the frames are changed, but during the presentation of a single frame. This rate of flicker is too rapid to perceive.

Visual Processing in the Cortex

In addition to the amazing number of visual phenomena that can be related to the intricate mechanisms of the retina, there are still more perceptual effects in vision that require examination. Some can be related to visual processing at higher levels of the nervous system, and we will conclude this discussion of the visual system by briefly examining the central mechanisms of visual perception.

Higher Level Receptive Fields

As was illustrated in box figure 3.7, the neural picture produced by the processes of the retina is sent by way of the optic nerves to the lateral geniculate nuclei of the thalamus. From the lateral geniculate nuclei, this information is carried to the visual cortex. A vast amount of research has been done to determine the receptive field characteristics of neurons in the lateral geniculate nuclei and the visual cortex. Interestingly, receptive fields of neurons in the lateral geniculate body are similar to receptive fields of ganglion cells in the retina; in other words, they are concentric, having opposing center and surround regions. Receptive fields of neurons in the visual cortex, however, are quite different from those of ganglion cells and cells in the lateral geniculate nuclei.

According to extensive experiments by Hubel and Weisel (1963, 1965, 1968) and many others, the cells in the visual cortex respond to details of the neural picture originating from the retina. Hubel and Weisel's experiments were similar in many respects to Kuffler's experiments with regard to ganglion cells. However, Hubel and Weisel recorded the responses of single cells in the visual cortex to light falling on the retina.

They found that unlike ganglion cells, neurons in the visual cortex did not respond much to small spots of light, but instead responded to bars or slits of light falling onto restricted regions of the retina. One category of neurons, termed *simple cortical cells,* responded best to a bar of light falling on a specific place on the retina and having a specific width and orientation (see fig. 6.17a). For example, one simple cortical neuron might respond only to a vertical bar of a certain width falling in the center of the fovea. Another simple cortical cell might also respond to a bar of light of similar width in the same location, except that it would have to be tilted forty-five degrees off the vertical. A second category of cells, termed *complex cortical cells,* also required a slit of light of a certain width and orientation to respond; however, these cells did not require a specific location (see fig. 6.17b). Thus the bar of light could fall anywhere within a certain region of the retina. In fact, these cells responded best when the bar was moved around within this region. Frequently, there was an optimal direction and rate of movement. Finally, there were other cells in the visual cortex that responded to more complex features of visual stimuli. These were called *hypercomplex* or *higher order hypercomplex cells.*

The way in which the neural picture produced by the retina is translated into these more complex receptive fields in the visual cortex is a subject of current research and debate. One commonly held view, initially proposed by Hubel and Weisel, is that the more complex receptive fields are produced by combinations of simple receptive fields, which in turn represent combinations of the concentric receptive fields characteristic of the retina and lateral geniculate nuclei. Although substantial revisions of this early model are now being formulated, this view is probably partially correct. The organization appears to be considerably more complicated. For one thing, cortical visual cells evidently affect lower level cells, such as those in the lateral geniculate nucleus.

Aftereffects

In our discussion of color vision, we noted that there were certain aftereffects that could be related to the adaptation or "fatigue" of a particular color process (see box 6.6). An analagous aftereffect may occur in cortical cells. Several studies (e.g., Blakemore and Nachmias, 1971) have shown that when a pattern of bars of a specific width and orientation are viewed for a period of time, the viewer's sensitivity to this pattern is reduced, while patterns of other orientations and widths are not affected. Some of these effects are demonstrated in box 6.7. These effects suggest that when one views a pattern of bars of a specific width and orientation, cortical cells that respond best to the width of orientation viewed are adapted or fatigued, whereas cells that respond to other orientations and widths are unaffected. Therefore, it appears that perception is related to the behavior of these cortical cells and that one of the processes in perception involves an analysis of the visual scene into elementary *features* such as lines, bars, edges, orientations, and so forth.

Another interesting example of the correspondence between the behavior of cortical cells and perception comes from studies of *stabilized images.* Under ordinary conditions, even when you fixate steadily on a spot of light, your eye moves very slightly and rapidly. Thus the image of the spot vibrates about on the retina. In experiments on stabilized images, it is possible, by various means, to eliminate the effect of these eye movements on the image falling on the retina, so that the image is stabilized on a specific group of receptors. One method of stabilizing the image

Figure 6.17 Receptive field characteristics of some neurons in the visual cortex of the cat. In A, the neuron responds to a horizontal bar in its receptive field. In B, the neuron responds best to downward movement of a horizontal bar and less to upward movement of the same bar. It does not respond to a vertical bar. In C, the neuron responds best to certain stimulus angles moved into its receptive field, but not to other angles. (A and B from Hubel, D., and Wiesel, T. N. *Journal to Physiology 160,* 1962, Figures 7 and 8, pp. 120 and 121. Reprinted by permission of Cambridge University Press; C from Hubel, D., and Wiesel, T. N. *J. Neuro-Physiology 28,* 1965, Fig. 9, p. 245. Reprinted by permission of American Physiological Society.)

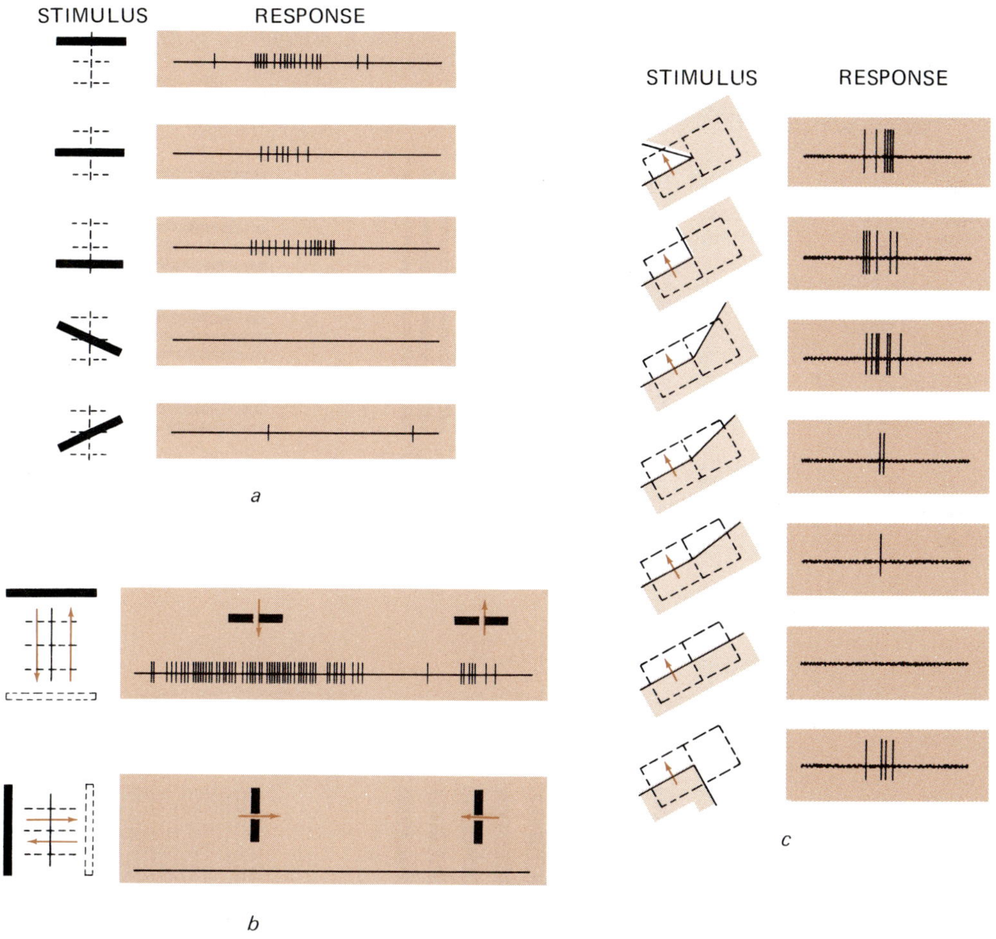

Box 6.7

Perceptual Adaptation to Gratings

The gratings in the upper-left corner and center of box figure 6.7 have the same bar width and orientation, although the central grating is of much lower contrast. If one adapts to the upper-left grating by moving his eyes around the small circle for a minute and then looks at the central grating, the bars will not be visible for a short time. However, perception of the central grating will not be affected, by adapting to any of the other gratings, which differ from the central grating either in bar width (bottom) or orientation (upper right). All the gratings are effective stimuli for cortical cells that are responsive to their specific widths and orientations. According to current physiological evidence, cortical cells that would respond to the grating on the upper left would also be responsive to the central grating because the bar widths and orientations of both gratings are the same. The other gratings would affect cortical cells that are responsive to their particular bar widths and orientations. Viewing the upper-left grating, therefore, adapts the same neurons that are required to perceive the central grating, whereas viewing the other three gratings would adapt other populations of neurons, leaving perception of the central grating unaffected. Thus this demonstration suggests that different details of perception are processed by different mechanisms (cells).

Box Figure 6.7 Perceptual adaptation to gratings. (From Maffei, L., Fiorentini, A., and Bisti, S., "Neural correlate of perceptual adaptation to gratings," *Science*, 182, 1973, pp. 1036–1038. Copyright 1973 by the American Association for the Advancement of Science. Photo Courtesy of L. Maffei.)

Plate 1 The orange square on different colored backgrounds illustrates the same principle as Figure 6.1b. (© 1961 and 1973 Otto Maier Verlag Ravensburg. American Edition © 1973 Van Nostrand Reinhold Company, New York.)

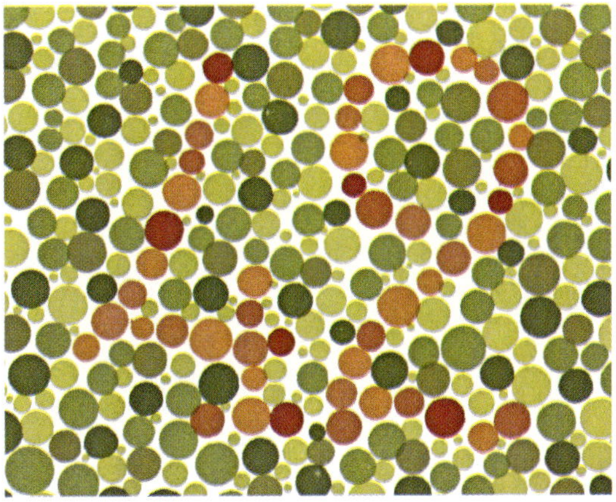

Plate 2 An illustration of the general configuration of a test for red-green color blindness. A. O. Pseudo-Isochromatic Color Test. (Courtesy of American Optical Corporation.)

FREQUENCY SPECTRA

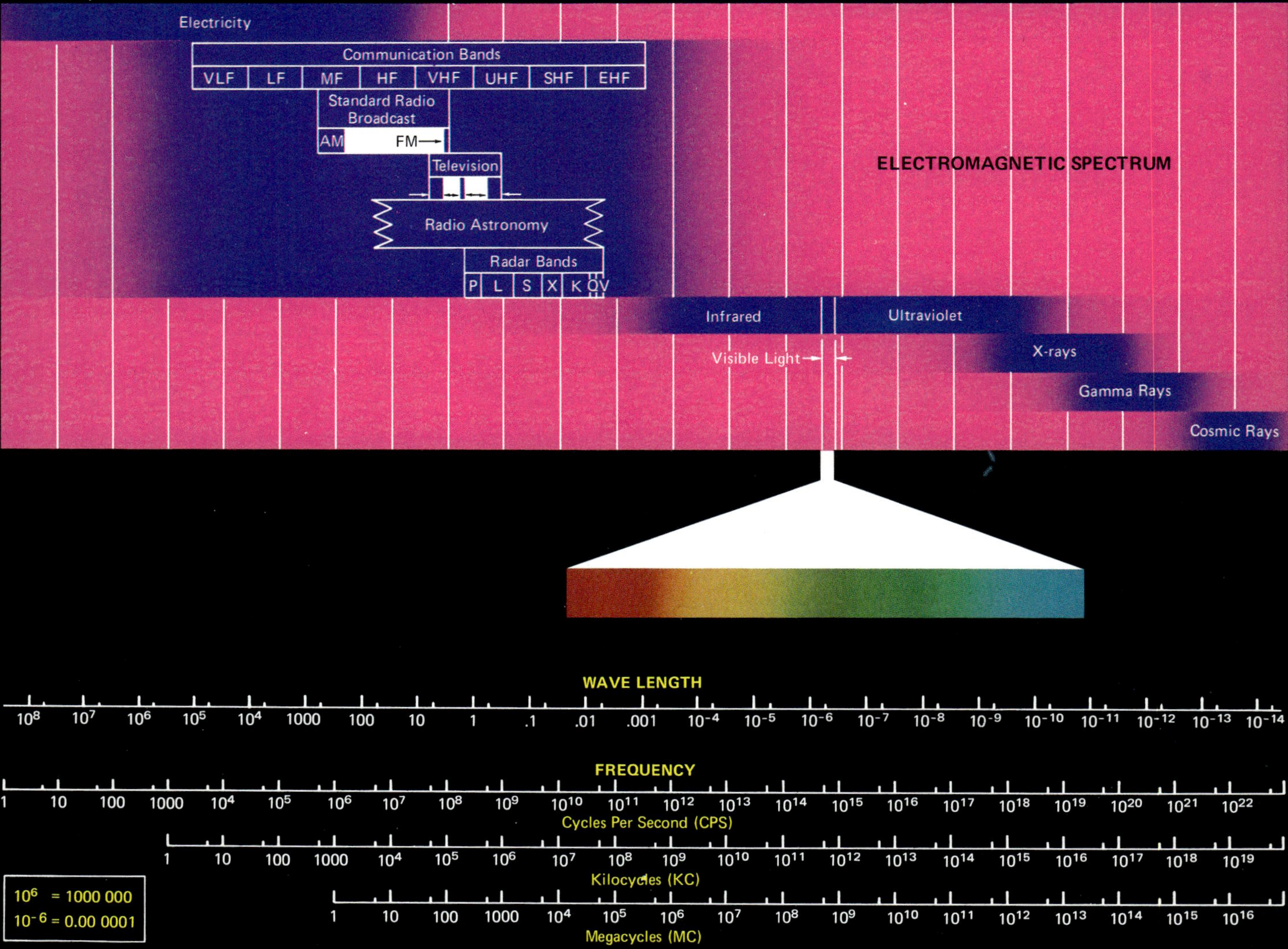

Plate 4 Examples of temporal (a) and spatial (b) color contrast effects. (From Lindsay, P., and Norman, D., *Human Information Processing: An Introduction to Psychology,* New York: Academic Press, 1972, p. 216 a and d. From *The Color Tree,* Inmont Corp., New York, 1965. Reprinted by permission of the publishers.)

Plate 3 The electromagnetic spectrum, showing the relatively small region visible to the human eye. The colors illustrate how these wavelengths appear to us. (Courtesy McDonnell Douglas Astronautics.)

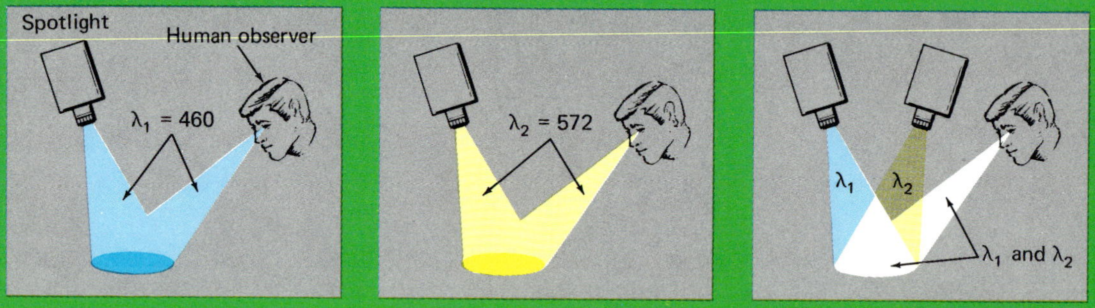

A. MIXING LIGHTS

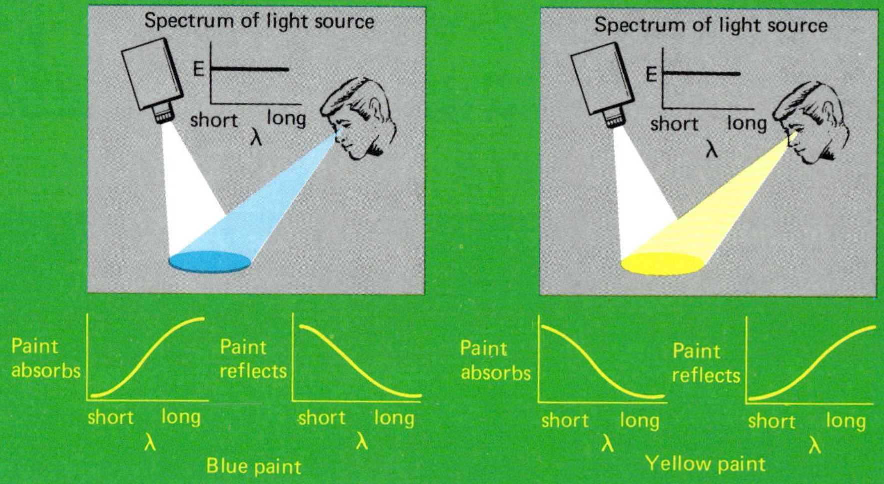

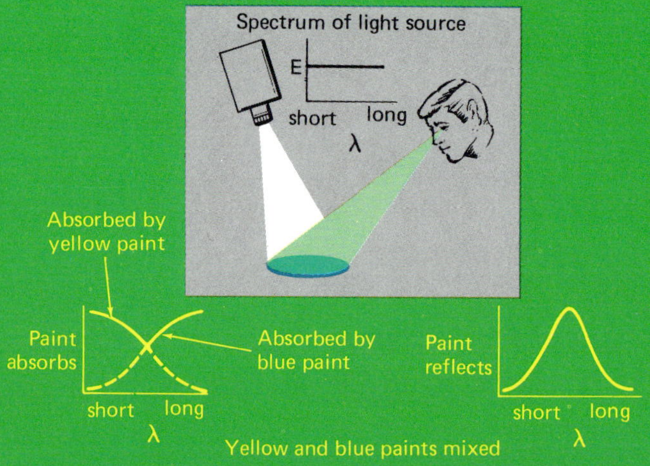

B. MIXING PAINTS

Plate 5 (A) Wavelength composition and appearance of a blue spotlight shone onto a surface (left), and yellow spotlight shone onto a surface (middle) and when these two lights are mixed (right). (B) Wavelength composition and appearance of a spot painted blue (left), a spot painted yellow (right), and a spot painted with a mixture of blue and yellow (bottom). (From *The Color Tree,* 1965. Reprinted by permission of Inmont Corporation.)

is to affix a tiny slide projector to a contact lens; whenever the eye moves, the lens moves and the image remains in the same position on the retina (Pritchard, 1961). When images are stabilized on the retina in this way, they are no longer perceived after a short time. Interestingly, before the image disappears completely, parts of it will disappear together, such as whole lines. Presumably, this happens because many cells respond best to a moving image. This is especially true of the cortical cells just described. The fact that features of the image, such as lines or edges, tend to fade out as a unit suggests that complex cortical cells responsive to these features are no longer responding.

Recent experimental evidence suggests still another function of these cortical cells in relation to visual perception; that of determining how far an object is from the observer. Figure 6.18 illustrates that identical images could occur by looking at two lines of different lengths, with the longer one farther away. One problem posed by this illustration is how a person can perceive that an object is small and close or large and far away. This problem raises the general question of the perception of size and distance. Apparently some information other than the size of the image must be used. We will discuss one important source of information, termed binocular disparity, which can be related to the apparent functions of these cortical cells. Other aspects of this important topic will be discussed in Chapter 7.

Binocular Disparity

Binocular disparity derives from the obvious fact that our eyes are not located in the same position on the head. Figure 6.19 shows that when we fixate on a point (F) both eyes are oriented so that the image of that point falls on the center of the fovea in each eye. Images from other objects, at other distances from the eyes—for example, a point on the tree in figure 6.19—will fall onto different locations in relation to the foveas. This occurs because the two eyes have different angles of view. Images of points or objects inside or outside the circle shown in figure 6.19 will fall differently on the two retinas. This is *binocular* (two-eyed) *disparity* (difference). The degree of difference between the two eyes is a source of information about

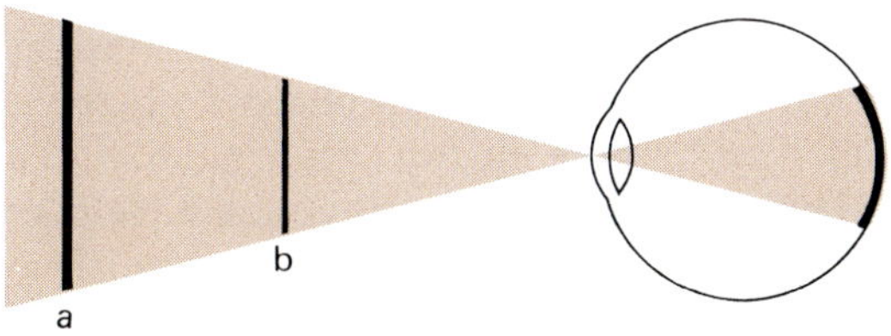

Figure 6.18 Two lines—a tall wide one (a) or a short thinner one (b) cast identical images on the retina.

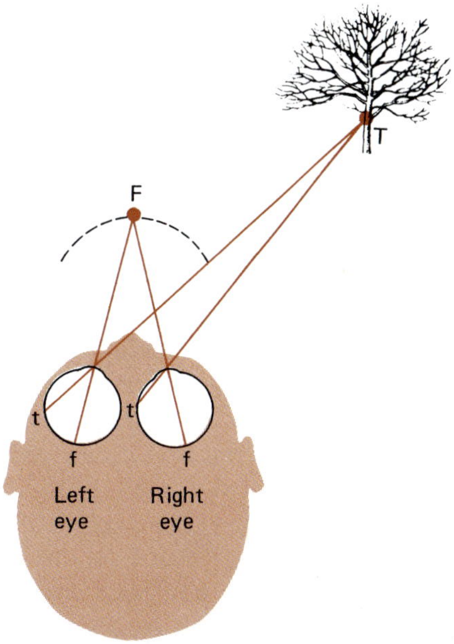

Figure 6.19 Binocular disparity. The point of fixation, point F in this case, is imaged on the center of the fovea in both eyes (f). A point on an object that lies off the broken line, such as T, will form images (t) in the two eyes in noncorresponding positions. Thus, t is closer to F in the left eye than in the right eye. The noncorrespondence (disparity) is greater the farther the point departs from the broken line.

how far in front of or behind the fixation point an object is from the eyes.

You will recall that nerve fibers from both eyes are sorted out at the optic chiasm, so that information from the left half of each retina goes to the left lateral geniculate nucleus and then to the visual cortex, while information from the right half of both retinas goes to the right lateral geniculate nucleus and then to the visual cortex (see box fig. 3.7). And you may have wondered where the information from the two eyes is put together. Many of the cells in visual cortex have been found to be influenced by both eyes. Thus the information from corresponding halves of both retinas appears to come together in the visual cortex. Some cells in the visual cortex respond best to stimuli falling on exactly corresponding places on the two retinas. Others, however, respond best when one stimulus is shifted slightly in retinal location with respect to the other eye; that is, when there is a disparity of a certain magnitude. These cells may be involved in providing us with information about binocular disparity and, therefore, our perception of distance (Blakemore, 1970; Pettigrew, 1972).

The study of the physical and physiological aspects of vision and their relation to visual perception provides an exciting, but as yet incomplete story. Many questions about the relationship between perception and the physiology of vision remain unanswered, and we have little idea about how to provide an answer. For example, we have seen that some perceptual effects are related to the neural processes of the retina and their consequent exaggerated neural picture. And we have seen that in the cortex, details of the neural picture appear to be analyzed. Yet, when we view the world, we do not see it in terms of lines, bars, or edges or in terms of neuronal discharges, for that matter. The problem of how all these physiological analyses eventually produce a coherent perceptual world remains a challenging and, in some respects, mysterious problem for contemporary and future study. As we turn our attention to the problem of auditory perception, we will see that it is possible to relate some aspects of what we hear to the physical and physiological analyses of sound. Yet, like the story of vision, the story of audition, although fascinating, is still incomplete.

Audition

Physical Dimensions of Sound

Before we begin our discussion of auditory perception, we must examine the physical characteristics of sound. When one plucks a string on a guitar, it vibrates back and forth, and as it moves toward the listener, it compresses the air in the small region of air with which it makes contact. When it moves away, it moves the air in the opposite direction, creating a subtle region of decompression. As the string moves back and forth, it creates a momentary increase and then a momentary decrease in air pressure. These alternate increases and decreases travel through the air at the speed of sound (approximately 740 miles per hour) and eventually arrive at the ear, where the tympanic membrane, or eardrum moves back and forth in synchrony with the pulsations of air pressure.

The simplest pattern of pressure pulsations is generated for a "pure" tone, or sine wave (see fig. 6.20). One important characteristic of a pure tone is its *frequency,* or the number of high to low variations in pressure per second, called *cycles*. The units of frequency are cycles per second, or *Hertz* (Hz). A graph of one low and one high frequency tone is shown in figure 6.20. Another important characteristic of pure tones is the degree of change from maximum to minimum pressure, which is termed the *amplitude,* or *intensity*. These changes in pressure are typ-

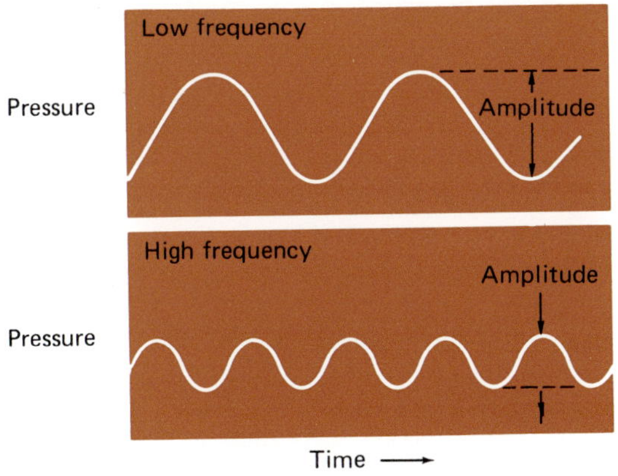

Figure 6.20 Two different sine waves representing pure tones of different frequencies. Frequency is a measure of the variations in pressure over time, while amplitude is a measure of the difference between maximum and minimum changes in pressure.

ically measured in dynes per square centimeter, a measure of force per unit area. This parameter of sound is also illustrated in figure 6.20.

From a physical point of view, sine wave tones are pure because any sound can be described as a combination of sine waves of specific frequencies and amplitudes. This fact was initially demonstrated by the French mathematician Jean Fourier. Thus the physical representation of sounds bears a certain resemblance to that of light. In the case of light, we said that a light source could be characterized in terms of the spectrum, or combination of wavelengths of particular intensities. Similarly, a sound can be described in terms of its sound spectrum, as illustrated in figure 6.21. A sound comprised of more than a single sine wave is termed a *complex sound*. Most sounds are complex sounds.

Some general relationships between these physical dimensions of sound and perception can be described. We can hear air pressure variations within a range of about 20 to 20,000 Hz. But this range diminishes with age; few people over the age of eighteen can hear above approximately 17,000 Hz. As the frequency of sound is increased within the range of from 20 to 20,000 Hz, we perceive an increase in the sound's pitch. For example, the lowest note on a piano (an A), corresponds to around 27 Hz; the highest note (a C), to about 4,186 Hz. It is interesting that our perception of pitch does not increase in exactly the same way as frequency does. For example, we would perceive the same note in successive octaves on the piano as roughly equal steps in pitch. Yet, for each octave increase the frequency doubles. Therefore, as we listen to the successive increases in pitch when playing middle C, one octave above middle C, and two octaves above middle C, the frequency of the notes increases from 262 to 534 to 1,048 Hz; but the change in pitch we perceive between the first and second C is about the same as that between the second and third C.

As the intensity of a sound of a particular frequency is increased, its loudness increases. The range of intensities we can hear is enormous. Because of this, sound intensities are typically reported in terms of logarithmic units called *decibels.* In the section on vision, we asked how sensitive we are to different wavelengths of monochromatic light; here we can inquire about our sensitivity to pure tones of different frequencies. The broken line in figure 6.22 shows that different intensities are required for the human listener to just detect different frequencies. As indicated in the figure, we are most sensitive to sounds in the range of between 1,000 and 4,000 Hz, and our sensitivity to higher and lower frequencies declines. This curve indicates that sounds of different frequencies require different amounts of energy to be barely loud enough to hear. The other curves shown in figure 6.21 were obtained by requiring a listener to adjust the intensity of a pure tone of a particular frequency to match the *loudness* of another tone at a specific level of intensity called the *standard.* The standard was always a tone of

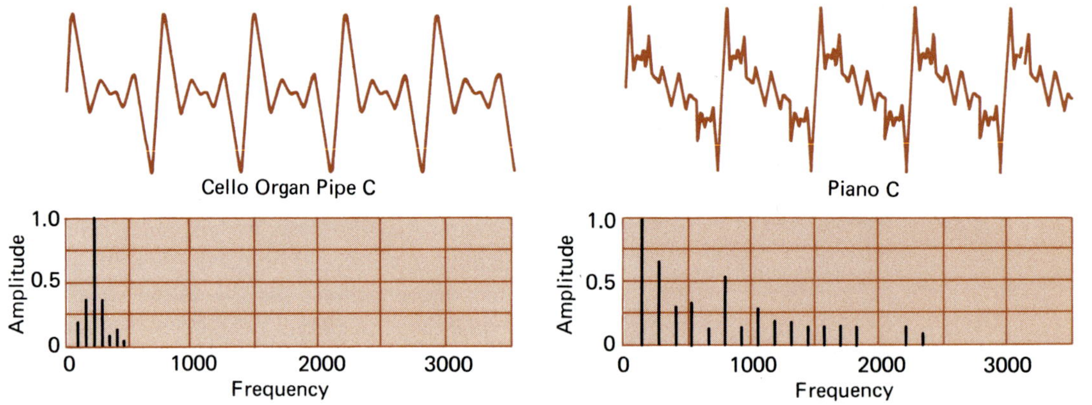

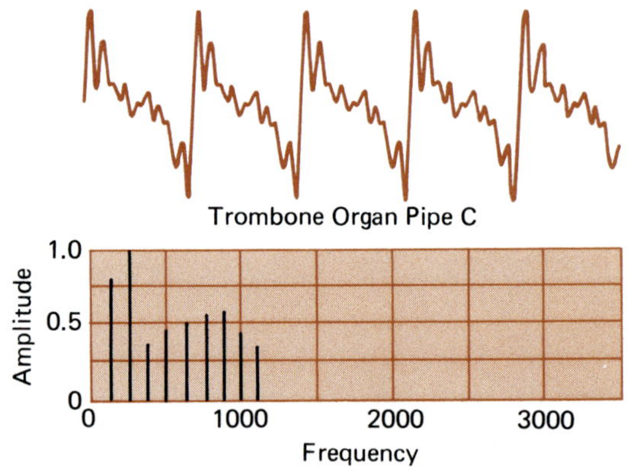

Figure 6.21 Complex sounds. When a musical instrument plays a particular note, it generates a complex tone consisting of a combination of frequencies. The upper graphs show the air pressure changes produced by various instruments playing the notes indicated. The lower graphs are the frequency compositions of these changes. (From *Speech and Hearing* by H. Fletcher, © 1952. Reprinted by permission of D. Van Nostrand Company.)

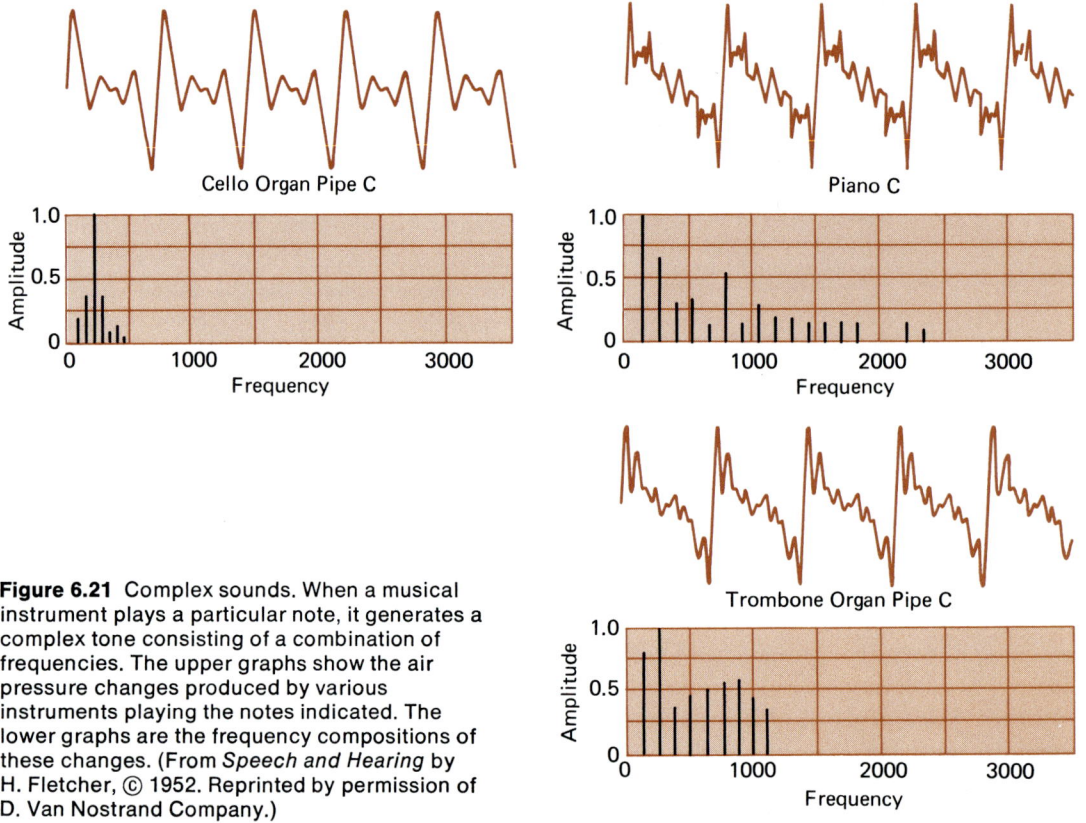

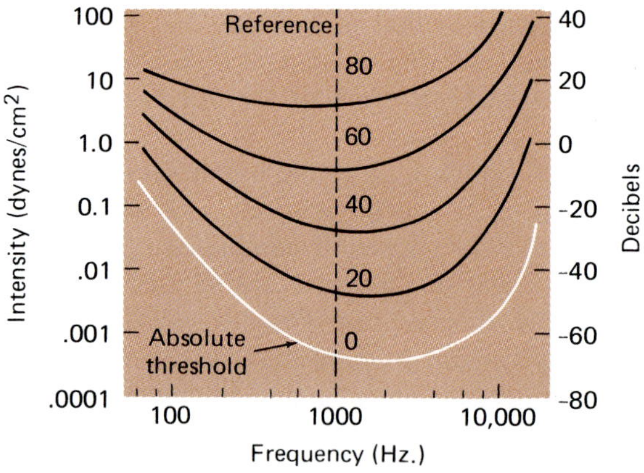

Figure 6.22 Equiloudness contours. The lowest line indicates the threshold amount of energy required to detect pure tones of different frequencies. The other curves show the amount of energy required for a listener to match the loudness of a 1,000 Hz standard, played at the intensity indicated by the number on the curve. (After Fletcher, H., Munson, W. A., "Loudness, its definition, measurement and calculation," *Journal of the Acoustical Society of America, 5,* 1933, pp. 82–108. Reprinted by permission of American Institute of Physics.)

1,000 Hz. For example, the curve labeled 20 indicates the intensity required to make tones of different frequencies as loud as the standard (1,000 Hz), which had an intensity of 20 decibels. Again, we see that different intensities are required to make different frequencies seem equally loud. These curves are called *equiloudness contours,* and they indicate that at extremely low levels of sound intensity, we are much more sensitive to intermediate frequencies of sound than to extremes in frequency. However, when sounds are loud, this difference in sensitivity diminishes. Thus, as in the case of vision, in which our sensitivity to different wavelengths of light depended on the level of illumination (photopic versus scotopic sensitivity), our sensitivity in terms of loudness is contingent upon the frequency of sound in a way that changes with the level of sound intensity.

You have probably experienced this phenomenon when listening to music. If you listen to the same piece of music at high and low volumes, you will notice that the bass and treble become much more noticeable at the higher volume. Some high fidelity systems attempt to compensate for this change by providing a loudness control that boosts the bass and treble at low volume. The relationship between loudness and frequency is another example of the fact that physical and perceptual descriptions are not identical; that is, the loudness of a tone depends not only on its intensity but on its frequency.

It is also true that pitch does not depend solely on frequency, but on intensity as well. If we increase the intensity of a low frequency sound, its pitch will decrease. If we increase the intensity of a high frequency sound, its pitch will increase.

Thus far, we have been considering the perception of pure tones. As we noted earlier, most sounds consist of combinations of pure tones. Typically, the pitch of a complex sound will correspond to the pitch of the lowest frequency component in the sound. This component is called the *fundamental.* Higher frequency components, termed harmonics, will affect the quality or *timbre* of the sound. For example, two musical instruments, such as a trumpet and piano, playing the same note, will be generating the same lowest frequency component, or fundamental. However, the higher frequency components, or *harmonics* will differ, as was shown in figure 6.21. These harmonics produce the characteristic difference in quality between different instruments. If we were to remove all the harmonics, leaving only the fundamental, a trumpet and piano playing the same note would sound identical.

An interesting comparison can be made between our perception of complex sounds and complex lights. When we listen to complex sounds, we can hear to some extent the different frequency components in the sound. Thus a musician, for example, can perceive the different notes in a chord. To some degree then, our perception is capable of a frequency analysis of a complex tone. In the case of complex lights, however, you will recall that two or more identically colored lights can be produced by *different* combinations of wavelengths. Thus it is impossible to analyze the wavelength composition of a light on the basis of our perception.

Now that we have described some of the basic relationships between the physical and perceptual characteristics of sound, we are ready to examine how these characteristics are related to the physiological processes of audition in the ear and brain.

The Ear

Earlier we said that the variations of air pressure, which form the physical basis of sound, travel through the air and create air pressure changes at the eardrum, or *tympanic membrane.* The tympanic membrane moves back and forth, corresponding to the variations in air pressure reaching it. Figure 6.23 illustrates that the tympanic membrane is connected to three tiny bones, the ossicles, which are located within the middle ear. These bones couple the movement of the tympanic membrane to a diaphragmlike membrane, the oval window. The oval window is located on a boney, snail-shaped structure, the *cochlea,* which is the receptor organ for hearing. Figure 6.24 is a schematic diagram of how the cochlea would look if it were uncoiled. The fluid-filled cochlea is divided into an upper and lower chamber by a complex structure called the organ of corti. Vibrations of the tympanic membrane are conducted by the ossicles to the oval window and create instantaneous changes of pressure in the fluid within the cochlea. These changes are transmitted throughout the cochlear fluid and are relieved by the flexibility of another small membrane, the round window, located below the oval window.

The organ of corti consists of two major structures, as shown in cross section in figure 6.25; the *tectorial membrane,* a rather stiff membrane attached to the bone of the cochlea at one side, and the *basilar membrane.* Between these two membranes are the *hair cells* of the organ of corti—the receptor cells of the auditory system—and a number of supporting cells. Hair cells, as the name implies, have small hairlike extensions that project from the cell through a delicate membrane, the *reticular lamina,* and onto the tectorial membrane above. There are two groups of hair cells, the *inner* and *outer* hair cells. The human ear contains about 3,400 inner and 12,000 outer hair cells. The two groups are separated by a structure referred to as the *rods and tunnel of corti.*

Mechanisms of Sound Conduction

The basilar membrane increases in width and decreases in stiffness along its length from the base (nearest the oval window) to the apex. When a pressure change occurs in the cochlea, the different regions of the basilar membrane flex to different extents and at different times. The resulting distortion of the membrane appears to travel away from the round window along the basilar membrane. As the distortion moves, it changes in size, reaching a maximum at a point along the membrane that depends on the frequency of the sound. The distortion then declines in size after this point, as shown in figure 6.26. As a result of the traveling distortion, the basilar membrane, and the hair cells lying on top of it, flex in relation to the tectorial membrane. As the basilar membrane moves upward, the tectorial membrane moves upward and to the side, producing a "shearing" movement. This shearing force bends the hairs of the hair cells. It is this shearing, or bending of the hairs that initiates signals in the hair cells and the auditory nerve that will be carried to the brain and will ultimately be perceived as sound.

The traveling distortion or wave, which begins at the oval window, creates a pattern of deflection of the basilar membrane which depends on the frequency of the sound producing it, as shown in figure 6.26. Extremely high frequency sounds distort the basilar membrane maximally over a narrow region at its base near the oval window. As the frequency of sound *decreases,* the maximal point of distortion moves away from the oval window toward the apex of the basilar membrane. The area over which this distortion occurs increases, until, for very low frequency sounds, the entire membrane is distorted. Maximal distortion, however, still occurs closer to the apex.

Place Theory

Because the hair cells in a given region along the length of the basilar membrane will be stimulated to a maximum degree by a fre-

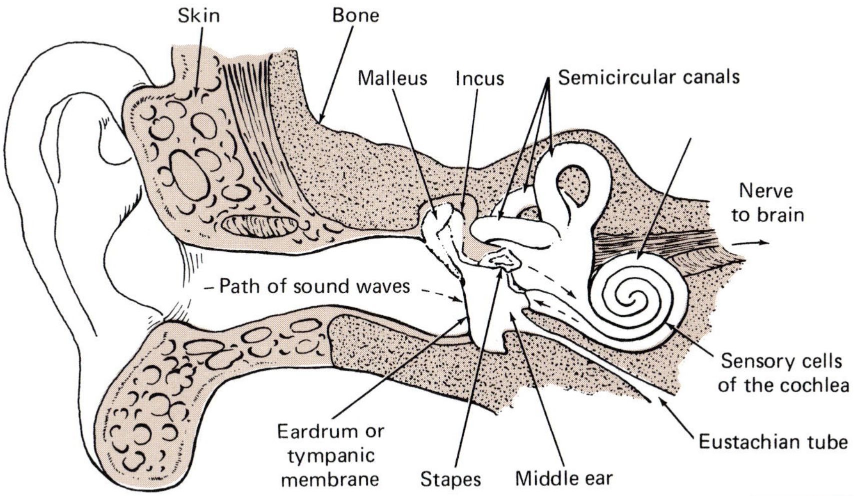

Figure 6.23 Gross anatomy of the human ear. The bones of the middle ear (malleus, incus, and stapes) transmit vibrations of the tympanic membrane to the oval window of the cochlea. (From Geldard, F. A., *The Human Senses,* 2nd ed. Copyright 1972 by John Wiley & Sons, Inc. Reprinted by permission of John Wiley & Sons, Inc.)

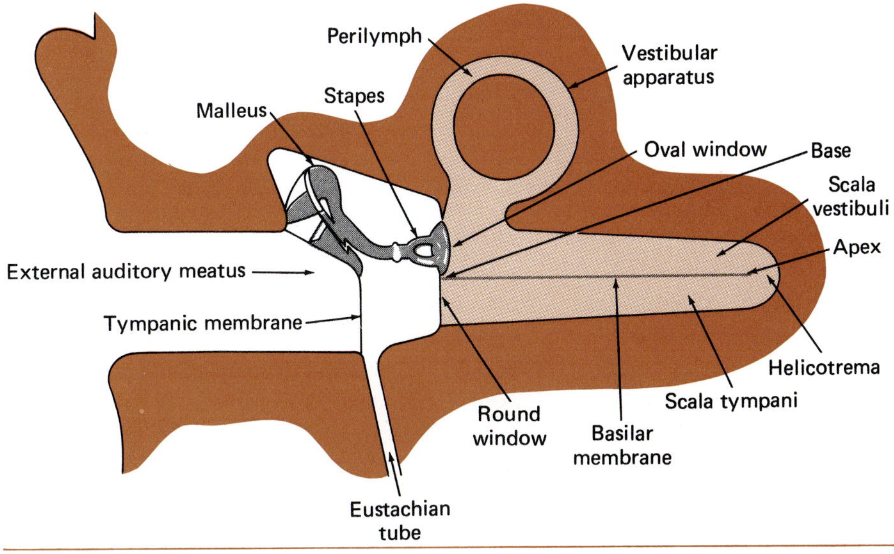

Figure 6.24 A schematic drawing of the pathway of vibrations from the external ear to the cochlea. The cochlea is shown uncoiled. (From von Bekesy, G. and Rosenblith, W. A. "The mechanical properties of the ear." In S. S. Stevens (ed.) *Handbook of Experimental Psychology.* Copyright 1951 by John Wiley & Sons, Inc. Reprinted by permission of John Wiley & Sons, Inc.)

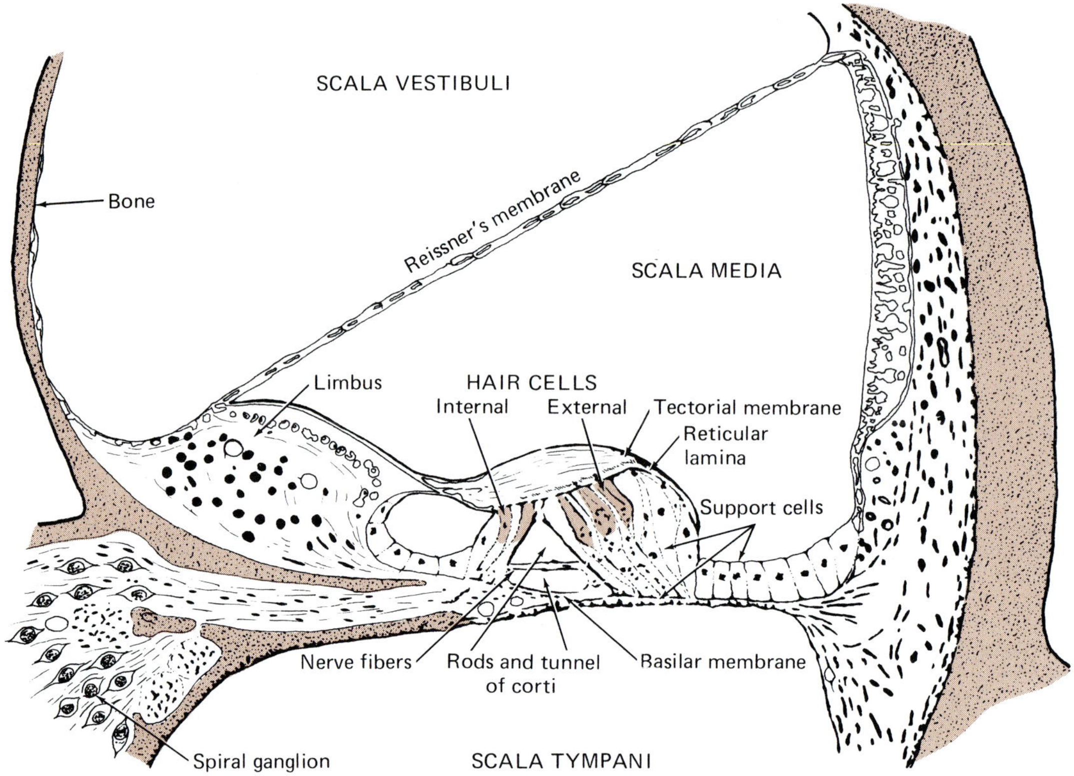

Figure 6.25 A diagrammatic illustration of the Organ of Corti. This is a single cross section through one coil of the cochlea. The Organ of Corti is contained within a fluid-filled duct (scala media) and is bordered above by the tectorial membrane and below by the basilar membrane. (After Davis, H. et al., "Acoustic trauma in the guinea pig," *Journal of Acoustical Society of America, 25,* 1953, pp. 1180–1189. Reprinted by permission of American Institute of Physics.)

quency that maximally distorts the basilar membrane in that region, it is possible that the *place* of stimulation along the basilar membrane determines the pitch of the sound that we hear. This idea, first proposed by Helmholtz over one hundred years ago, is called the place theory of hearing. It is, in fact, possible to record from a nerve fiber in the auditory nerve that receives its input from a small group of hair cells in a particular region of the basilar membrane.

According to the place theory, different frequencies of sound correspond to different places of stimulation along the basilar membrane; these in turn correspond to different nerve fibers having "receptive fields" in these different places. As the intensity of the sound is increased, while its frequency is held constant, the pattern of distortion of the basilar membrane is amplified. Thus hair cells in this region are stimulated more effectively, and hair cells around this region that did not previously respond may also be stimulated. This increased stimulation, which results in a greater firing rate of the nerve fibers receiving information from a given place, is presumed

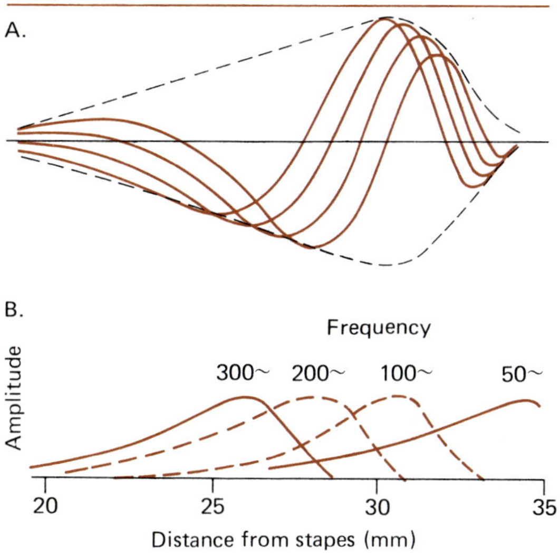

Figure 6.26 Traveling waves on the basilar membrane. A shows the pattern of deflection as it travels along the basilar membrane, reaching a maximum and then declining. The dotted lines indicate the amplitude of the deflection as it moves along the membrane. B illustrates that for different frequencies of sound, the maximal amplitude of distortion is reached at different points along the basilar membrane. Note that higher frequencies of sound reach maximum amplitude at shorter distances from the base of the cochlea. (After von Bekesy, G., "Variation of phase along the basilar membrane with sinusoidal vibrations," *Journal of the Acoustical Society of America, 19,* pp. 452–460; and "Description of some mechanical properties of the organ of corti," *Journal of the Acoustical Society of America, 25,* 1953, pp. 770–785. Reprinted by permission of America Institute of Physics and author.)

to relate to the intensity and therefore the loudness of sound.

Based on this explanation of loudness, the threshold intensity required to detect a tone of a particular frequency (the dotted line in fig. 6.22) should depend on the magnitude of the maximum distortion of the basilar membrane produced by that frequency. And frequencies that produce sufficient distortions with less energy should require less energy to be detected. Indeed, if the fact that some frequencies are transmitted to the cochlea better than others is taken into account, the magnitude of maximum distortion does relate well to our thresholds for detecting different frequencies of sound (Zwislocki, 1965).

The place theory appears to explain the physiological translation of frequency and intensity, with the exception of extremely low frequencies. For low frequencies, the place of distortion of the basilar membrane is not well localized. Thus it is difficult to imagine how such a wide range of distortion could allow for our discrimination of pitch in the lower frequency range.

Frequency Theory

Another theory of hearing, the frequency theory, which at one time was considered to be an alternative to the place theory, appears to account for our hearing in the low frequency range. This theory derives from the fact that the distortion of the basilar membrane pulsates according to the frequency of the sound transmitted to it. These pulsations produce bursts of firing in the auditory nerve fibers. The higher the frequency of sound, the more rapid the frequency of bursts. According to the frequency theory, it is the number of bursts per second in the auditory nerve that determines the frequency we hear and the number of impulses per burst that determines the intensity. In contrast with the place theory, the frequency theory does not require that stimulation in a particular place along the basilar membrane correspond to a particular frequency. No matter what region along the membrane is stimulated, the rate of pulsation transmitted in the auditory nerve determines the pitch that we hear.

Whereas the place theory has difficulty accounting for pitch at low frequencies, the frequency theory has difficulty accounting for pitch at high frequencies. According to the frequency theory, pitch is determined by the pulsations of firing in auditory nerve fibers.

Therefore, it is difficult to account for our perception of high frequencies of sound when pulsations can be as high as 20,000 Hz because nerve fibers cannot fire more than about 1,000 times per second. The frequency theorists have pointed out, however, that several neurons may fire "out of phase"; in other words, while some fibers are recovering, others fire and vice versa. This is termed the *volley effect*. Thus, although a high rate of periodic pulsations cannot be conveyed by one fiber alone, they may be conveyed if the firing occurs in an array of auditory nerve fibers. If the activity of the entire auditory nerve is recorded, one can indeed detect bursts of activity corresponding to the frequency of sounds up to about 4,000 Hz. Therefore, the volley principle extends the range of applicability of the frequency theory, but it does not sufficiently account for our ability to discriminate pitches higher than about 4,000 Hz.

A Combined Theory

Scientists have also attempted to extend the place theory's range by considering the possibility that the pattern of distortion may be sharpened in the "neural picture" of the basilar membrane produced in the auditory nerve or higher auditory centers. This sharpening could arise by a process of lateral inhibition, not unlike that of the visual system. In the auditory system, regions surrounding the point of maximal distortion of the basilar membrane could oppose stimulation at the point of maximal distortion. Thus, even if two low frequency tones produced maximal distortion of the basilar membrane in about the same place, the pattern of stimulation around this point, which could differ for the two tones, might sharpen the neural picture in the auditory nerve. This kind of sharpening process has been observed. (See box 6.8.)

At progressively higher levels in the auditory system, sharpening apparently increases.

Box 6.8

Difference Tones and Missing Fundamentals

If two sine waves of different frequencies are played simultaneously, a third low frequency tone (the difference tone) that corresponds to the difference in frequency between the two tones can be heard. No such frequency is physically present in the sound, yet it can be heard. A similar effect occurs when listening to a complex sound such as that produced by playing a low note on a piano. If the volume of the note is reduced to the point where the fundamental is below threshold or if the fundamental frequency is eliminated electronically, we still hear the note as though it were there. This is the problem of the *missing fundamental.* You will recall that complex sounds, such as those produced by musical instruments, have sound components, or harmonics, that are higher in frequency than the fundamental. These harmonic frequencies will typically be at whole number multiples of the fundamental. Thus when the low A on a piano is played, the fundamental will be 27.5 Hz, with harmonics at 55 Hz, 82.5 Hz, 110 Hz, and so forth. Notice that the difference in Hz between successive harmonics is 27.5, which is the frequency of the fundamental. Thus, as in the case of the *difference tone,* we hear a tone corresponding to the differ-

Box Figure 6.8 When two pure tones 1000 and 1100 Hz, are combined, the composite sound fluctuates in amplitude at a frequency of 100 Hz, although no 100 Hz tone is present in the original mixture. (From *An Introduction to Psychology,* P. H. Lindsay and D. A. Norman (eds.), New York and London: Academic Press, 1972, p. 265, Figure 7–15. Reprinted by permission of Academic Press.)

ence between successive harmonics, even in the absence of the fundamental.

These mysterious tones present difficulties for the place theory of hearing because no frequency is present to stimulate a particular place along the basilar membrane. To account for this phenomenon, the place theorists have postulated that distortions in the transmission of sound produce these missing frequencies. Although distortions do occur with extremely loud intensities of sound, the evidence strongly suggests that they do not occur at low levels where we still can perceive missing fundamentals and difference tones. The frequency theorists account for these missing tones by applying a different principle. As shown in box figure 6.8, when two simultaneous tones are played, the amplitude of the composite sound fluctuates periodically at the frequency corresponding to the difference between the two tones. This fluctuation is conveyed as a fluctuation in the firing pattern of auditory nerve fibers, which is the basis for frequency and intensity information in the frequency theory.

The results of an ingenious experiment support the frequency theory interpretation. The experiment is based on the fact that our perception of a pure tone can be masked by simultaneously playing a noise consisting of many frequencies within and around the frequency range of the pure tone. Suppose that a 1000 and 1100 Hz tone are played simultaneously, thus producing a difference tone of 100 Hz. If noise in the range of 1000 to 1100 Hz is presented, no difference tone can be heard; i.e., the difference tone is masked. On the other hand, if the noise is played in the range of 100 Hz, the difference tone is still heard. This result indicates that the frequency theory is correct because if a tone created by distortion were present, as the place theory presumes, and if this tone were stimulating a particular place along the basilar membrane, the 100 Hz masking noise should obscure its presence.

The frequency theory proposes that the 100 Hz tone results from the firing pattern of auditory nerve fibers, independent of the specific place of stimulation along the basilar membrane. Presentation of the 100 Hz masking noise does not alter the effect of the 1000 and 1100 Hz tones, so the difference tone is still present. On the other hand, when the masking noise is presented in the 1000 to 1100 range, this pattern is lost and no difference tone is heard.

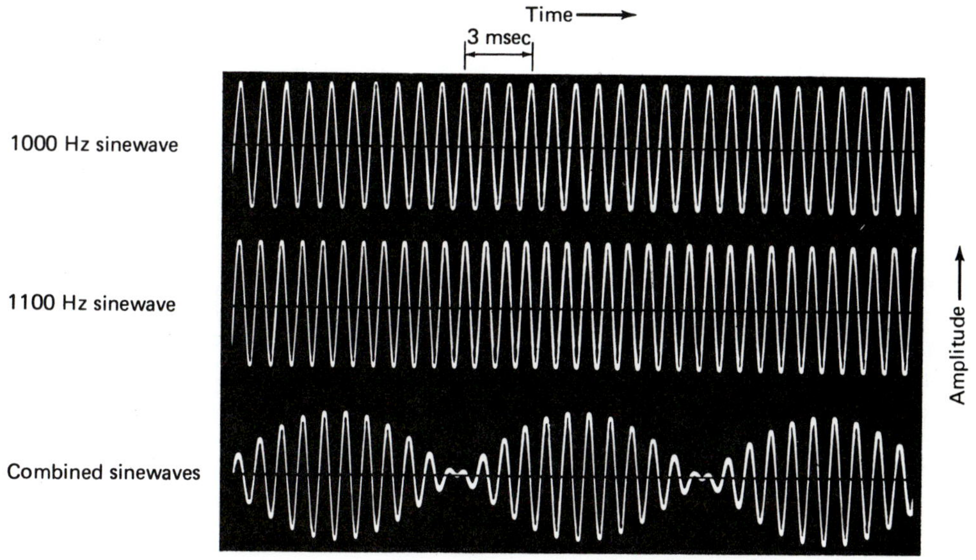

This process does extend the range over which the place theory could be applied. But, thus far, even the sharpening process has not provided a means of distinguishing between extremely low frequency tones, where it is clear that we can still discriminate. Thus, it appears that both theories are needed to account for hearing. As we have seen in box 6.8, an interesting difference between the place and frequency theories becomes apparent when we try to account for "difference tones" and "missing fundamentals."

It may be instructive to note, at this point, some similarities between the characteristics of the visual and auditory receptor systems, especially with regard to the way the pattern of stimulation in the receptors is translated into a neural picture to be carried to the central nervous system. Recall that in the visual system, the pattern of light, or image that stimulates the receptors is transformed into a neural pattern in which variations in the image are emphasized by the process of lateral inhibition. In the auditory system, there is also a receptor surface—the basilar membrane and associated hair cells. Now the image is the pattern of stimulation over this surface, representing the combinations of frequencies and their intensities being transmitted to the ear and ultimately producing the mechanical pattern of distortion along the basilar membrane. Here too, the neural picture of the sound results when each nerve fiber receives information about an area of the receptor surface in a way that emphasizes differences within and between these areas. In the auditory system, however, some emphasis is produced by the mechanical properties of the ear, especially the organ of corti. The neural picture is also sharpened at higher levels of the auditory system, as you will see in the next section.

Higher Level Auditory Processing

Figure 6.27 illustrates the major anatomical pathways from the cochlea to higher centers

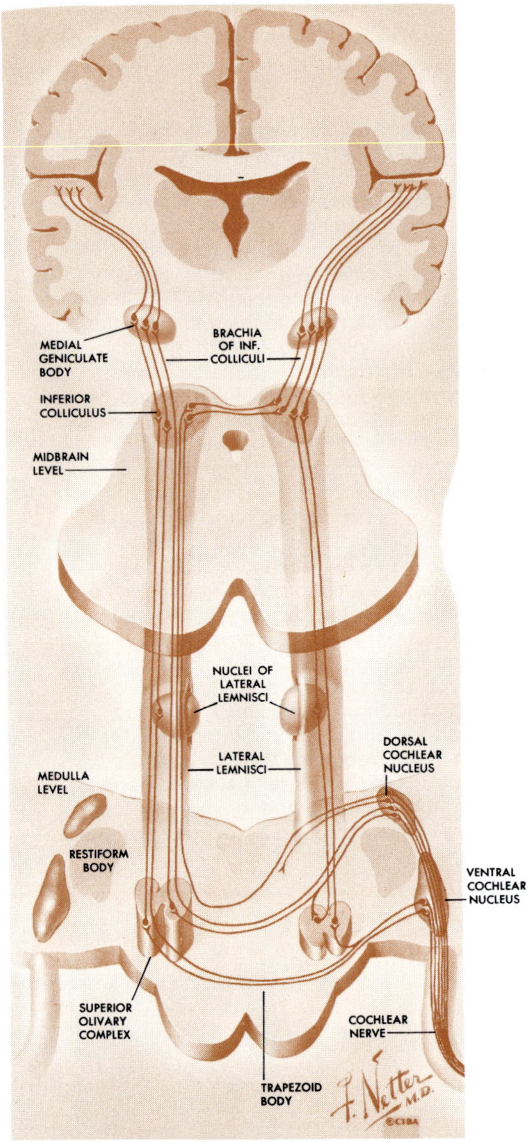

Figure 6.27 The major anatomical pathways from the cochlea to the auditory cortex. (Copyright 1953, 1972 CIBA Pharmaceutical Company, Division of CIBA-GEIGY Corporation. Reproduced with permission from the CIBA COLLECTION OF MEDICAL ILLUSTRATIONS by Frank H. Netter, M.D. All rights reserved.)

in the auditory system. From the cochlea, information is carried by the auditory nerve to the cochlear nucleus and several other nuclei in the brain stem. Information from these centers is carried to the inferior colliculus, the medial geniculate nucleus of the thalamus and ultimately to the auditory cortex.

Figure 6.28 illustrates one characteristic of the way neurons in these major auditory relay stations respond to different frequencies of sound. In these experiments, the activity of single neurons at various levels of the auditory system was recorded in response to various frequencies of sound. Typically, single neurons in the auditory system required the least amount of energy to respond to particular frequencies and were less responsive to other frequencies. In other words, different neurons are "tuned" to different frequencies. The curves shown in figure 6.28 are often called *tuning curves.* We noted earlier that the range of response of single neurons becomes narrower for cells progressively higher in the auditory pathways; that is, the tuning curves become narrower. In a sense, then, cells at the higher levels of the auditory system are examining finer details of the auditory neural picture. In fact, as in the visual system, where at higher levels we encountered cells having more specific stimulus requirements, neurons higher in the auditory system respond to more specific auditory information. Not only do the tuning curves of these neurons become narrower, but some cells may respond only to the onset or offset of a tone within their frequency range. Other neurons at higher levels may respond only to an increase or decrease in frequency within their response range rather than to a steady tone. In fact many cells in the auditory cortex will not respond at all to pure tones presented in any of these ways, but they will respond to more complex sounds.

Many neurons in the auditory system receive input from both ears as was the case for the two eyes in vision. One important kind of information derived from the fact that we have two ears is the location of a sound in space. Sound from a single source arriving at the two ears can differ in two ways. Suppose a tone is sounded directly on your left, as shown in figure 6.29. The intensity of high frequency sounds will be less in the right ear

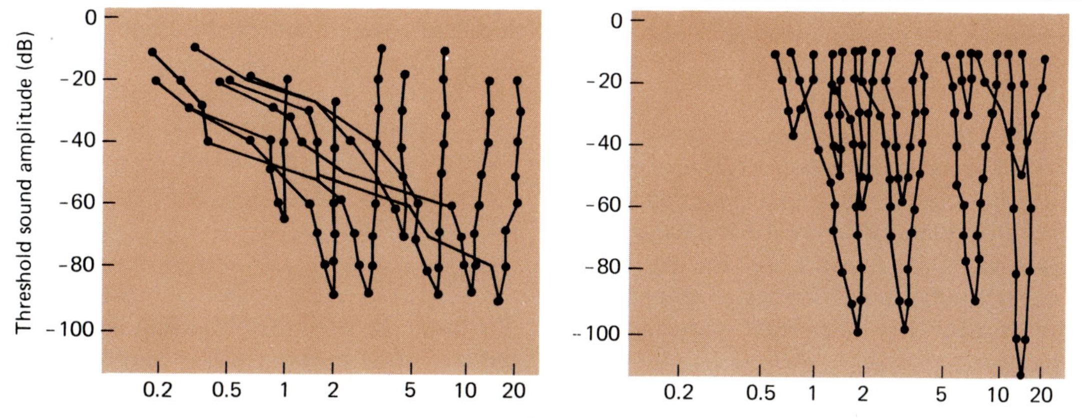

Figure 6.28 Tuning curves. Each curve illustrates the threshold energy required for a nerve fiber or nerve cell to respond at different frequencies. The tuning curves on the left are from fibers of the auditory nerve; those on the right are from the inferior colliculus. (Reprinted by permission of MIT Press, Cambridge, Mass.)

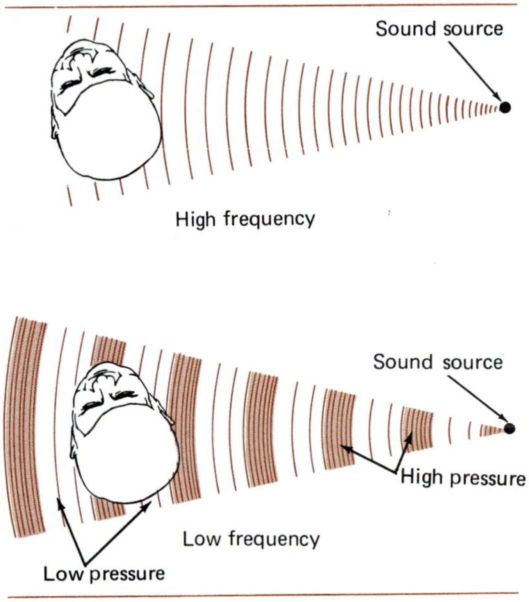

Figure 6.29 Auditory localization. High and low frequency sound waves emanating from a source to the right of a person's head are shown arriving at his two ears. Because high frequency sounds are blocked to some degree by the head (top figure), there is an intensity difference between the two ears. Low frequency tones (bottom) are not blocked, but high (dark) and low (light) pressure variations arrive at the two ears at different times. High frequency sounds provide ambiguous time information because the same pressure difference between the two ears could represent time differences of one, two, or an undetermined number of cycles.

than the left because it is blocked by the head before it reaches the right ear. The opposite would be true if the sound were on your right. This *intensity difference* will exist only for sounds above about 1,200 Hz. At lower frequencies, the sound can travel around the head without any significant reduction in intensity.

The degree of intensity difference for high frequency sounds will depend on the location of the source in relation to the two ears. The greatest difference will exist if the sound is directly on the right or left, whereas there will be no difference if the sound is directly in front or behind the listener. Therefore, the intensity difference is a source of information about the location of the sound. Intensity differences provide the information we get about location of sound when listening to stereo records, for example. The fact that the stereo effect occurs mainly at higher frequencies is consistent with this explanation of intensity differences.

A second source of information about the location of a sound source results from the fact that when a sound must travel farther to reach one ear or the other, a *time difference* exists between the arrival of the sound at both ears. Thus if we imagine the pulsations in air pressure arriving at the two ears and if the sound source is closer to one ear, a high pressure variation will arrive first at one ear and later at the other. Interestingly enough, this source of information is only useful for low frequency sounds because phase (time) differences become ambiguous when the distance between pulsations of air pressure is shorter than the distance between the two ears. This phenomenon is illustrated diagrammatically in figure 6.29.

A time difference as small as 30 microseconds between the two ears can be used to localize a sound source. Neurophysiologists have found cells in the olivary nucleus and the inferior colliculus (see fig. 6.27) that respond quite precisely to time and intensity differences between the two ears (Somjen, 1972, Gulick, 1971).

Other Senses

We have discussed the physiological and perceptual phenomena of vision and hearing in some detail. Of course, we have a variety of other senses. For example, our sense of *equilibrium,* or vestibular sense, is governed by specialized receptors in the semicircular canals of the inner ear that respond to displacement of our head and body and help to control balance. Our kinesthetic sense provides us with information about the state and position of our limbs received from receptors in the muscles and joints. We are often unaware of this information. The senses of *taste* and *smell* rely on specialized receptors in the mouth and nasal passages that are capable of responding selectively to different classes of molecules in our food and in the air. And our *skin* provides us with information about pain and temperature, for example.

We know a great deal more about the kinesthetic and skin senses than about the chemical senses of taste and smell. In the peripheral nervous system, for example, information from receptors that respond to stretch or contraction of the muscles is carried by large, rapidly conducting sensory fibers, while sensations such as pain and temperature are carried by much smaller fibers in the peripheral nerves. For many years, scientists believed that there were specialized receptors in the skin for the traditional somatosensory sensations of touch, warmth, cold, and pain. However, we now know that human observers are capable of distinguishing these four basic sensory experiences even in the cornea, where so-called "free" nerve endings are the only type of receptors that can be identified.

The skin contains specialized receptors that are especially sensitive to certain types of stimulation. For instance, the *Pacinian corpuscle* is a small capsule-like receptor containing nerve endings that are especially responsive to pressure. However, specialized receptors do not seem to be essential to distinguish between the traditional varieties of somatosensory stimulation noted above.

In the central nervous system, information is segregated according to the kind of sensory stimulus being applied as well as its location on the body surface. We noted in Chapter 3 that the surface of the body is topographically represented in the somatosensory cortex. In other words, if one area of the skin is stimulated, the information is carried to a specific region of the somatosensory cortex, information from a different point is carried to a different region, and so forth. The same principle applies to the visual and auditory systems. Information from one point on the retina is carried to a specific region in the visual cortex, while information from the hair cells in a restricted region of the basilar membrane is carried to a specific point in the auditory cortex. In addition to this spatial representation of information, single neurons in the thalamus and cerebral cortex may respond selectively to specific types of somatosensory and kinesthetic information in a way that is analogous to the selective responses of specialized neurons in the visual and auditory systems. For example, the ventrobasal nuclear complex of the thalamus, the specific sensory relay nuclei for somatosensory information, contains neurons that respond selectively to the angle of the joints, to light touch on limited portions of the skin surface, or to deep pressure stimulation. Neurons in other regions of the thalamus and brain stem respond selectively to pain. Thus the coding of specific features of kinesthetic and skin stimulation is apparently accomplished by different groups of single neurons within these sensory systems in the same way that coding of features of visual or auditory stimuli seems to be accomplished.

Summary

In this chapter we have discussed some of the basic relationships between the physical, physiological, and perceptual dimensions of vision and audition.

A point of light may be described in terms of the energy it emits within each of the visible wavelengths of light, that is, its spectrum. The spectrum of the light striking the eye is determined by the light source and the reflection and absorption characteristics of the object being viewed. The three perceptual dimensions of color—hue, saturation, and brightness—can be related to the spectral composition of a small spot of light.

Light enters the eye, passing through the cornea, anterior chamber, lens, and posterior chamber and strikes the retina. The image of an object on the retina is formed through the refraction of light rays by the cornea and the lens. To focus objects at different distances from the eye, refraction is varied by the process of accommodation. The image thus formed on the retina consists of points of light corresponding to points of light on the object. Light is absorbed by the receptors in the retina, the rods and cones, and is then processed by other kinds of cells within the retina: the bipolar, horizontal, amacrine, and ganglion cells.

According to the duplicity theory of vision, several characteristics of vision are related to the dual receptor system in the retina. The cone system (photopic vision) is responsible for fine, detailed, color vision under high levels of illumination. The rod system (scotopic vision) is organized for maximum sensitivity to the presence of light and functions under dim illumination.

The three perceptual dimensions of color are related to the spectral composition of light and to the physiological processes underlying cone vision. An integration of the two theories of color vision—the trichromatic theory and the opponent process theory—relates well to the physiology and perception of color. The responses of three types of cones (trichromatic theory) interact (opponent process theory) in opponent and nonopponent ways to form all the colors we see from points of light. In addition, perception of a point of light within a pattern can be affected, in terms of its color and brightness, by surrounding points; for example, spatial color contrast and Mach bands.

These effects of points near each other within a pattern were related to the general physiological phenomenon of lateral inhibition, as expressed by the organization of neurons into receptive fields within the visual system. The receptive fields of retinal ganglion cells produce a "neural picture" of the image that enhances differences between points of light in a pattern. Details or features of the neural picture are analyzed by the simple, complex, and hypercomplex organization of neurons into receptive fields in the visual cortex. Cells in the visual cortex also integrate information from both eyes, and their responses are related to our use of binocular disparity in depth perception.

Sounds, or variations in air pressure that reach the ear, can be described in terms of the amplitude of the pure tone frequencies that they contain, that is, their sound spectrum. The pitch and loudness of a sound—its perceptual dimensions—relate to the frequency and amplitude variations in air pressure. The specific manner in which these perceptual and physical dimensions relate involves the mechanical properties of the ear and the physiological processes in the receptor apparatus, or cochlea of the ear.

The two major theories of pitch and loudness perception, the place theory and the frequency theory, are both necessary to account for our perception of pitch and loudness and the neural events related to them. According to the place theory, different frequencies of sound stimulate hair cells at different places along the basilar membrane, while the amplitude of a sound affects the magnitude of stimulation at that place. In the frequency theory, the vibrations of the basilar membrane are transmitted by the hair cells to the auditory nerve, which fires in synchrony with these vibrations. The magnitude of each synchronous burst is determined by the amplitude of the sound. The neural picture produced by these processes of transduction is sharpened at successively higher stations in the auditory system, as was the case for vision. The response of neurons in lower auditory relay nuclei (e.g., in the cochlear nucleus, inferior colliculus, or medial geniculate body) are characterized by tuning curves, each neuron responding best to a specific range of frequencies. Many neurons in the auditory cortex respond to more complex features of auditory stimuli. Time and intensity differences between sounds arriving at the two ears provide information about the location of a sound in space. Information from the two ears is integrated in the central auditory pathways.

Many of the principles that were elaborated for vision and hearing, such as topographic organization of information, specialized receptive fields, and single neuron coding of stimulus features are also relevant for our understanding of sensory processes and perception in the other senses. These include somesthesis, the skin senses; kinesthesis, our sense of position and posture; the vestibular sense, which governs balance; as well as the chemical senses, smell and taste.

In the next chapter, we will turn to an overview of perception that will include the concept of "feature analysis" by sensory systems —an important theme that emerged in this chapter.

7

General Models in Perception

In Chapter 6 we considered the physical description of stimulus energy and its arrival to and processing by the visual and auditory systems. We are now in a position to look at some of the implications of the dominant themes and principles discussed in Chapter 6 as we develop a more complete view of perception.

One theme stands out even in the simplest cases of perception, we must consider *patterns* of stimulation. When we investigated the perception of a simple spot of light, we found that its appearance and physiological effects involved the pattern of wavelengths and surrounding illumination. That is, the color of the spot depended on its wavelength composition and that of the surrounding area. Thus it is evident that developing a general view concerning the perception of patterns will be important if we are to increase our understanding of perception. Let's examine the pervasive and important concept of patterns in perception more closely.

Templates and Features

We can begin our consideration of pattern perception by asking how we perceive the shapes in figure 7.1 as squares and rectangles. The problem is this: We have no difficulty in recognizing the varieties of squares as squares or in recognizing the wide variety of rectangles as rectangles. Furthermore, we can distinguish between rectangles and squares. But suppose we want to formulate some general set of processes, perhaps in physiological terms, that could perform these distinctions. How should we go about it?

Template Model

One possibility would be to imagine that inside the head there are representations or *templates* of every conceivable square and rectangle that can be perceived. When we view a particular form, such as one of those in figure 7.1, the pattern of stimulation would be sent simultaneously to each of these representations. If it matched one of the representations of a particular square, it would be perceived as such. If it matched one of the rectangles depicted in figure 7.1, then it would be recognized as a rectangle.

This view of perception treats the process of recognition as a matching of templates or representations against the incoming pattern of stimulation. The template method of pattern recognition is used by certain machines, such as those that "read" the numbers on bank checks. In the case of the check-reading machine, however, the check is precisely aligned with the machine's sensing device, and each symbol is uniquely designed so that only one matches a particular template. Thus there are only a few symbols and, in contrast with the problem of recognizing all possible squares and rectangles, there is only one version of each of the possible check symbols. Clearly, then, the template model is untenable for human pattern recognition because we would require a template for every distinguishable square and rectangle. Furthermore, from our discussion in Chapter 6 about the formation of the image on the retina, we know that the shape of the image of a square will change with our angle of view. Thus, even for one particular square, we would need an inordinate number of templates to recognize all the possible orientations of that square.

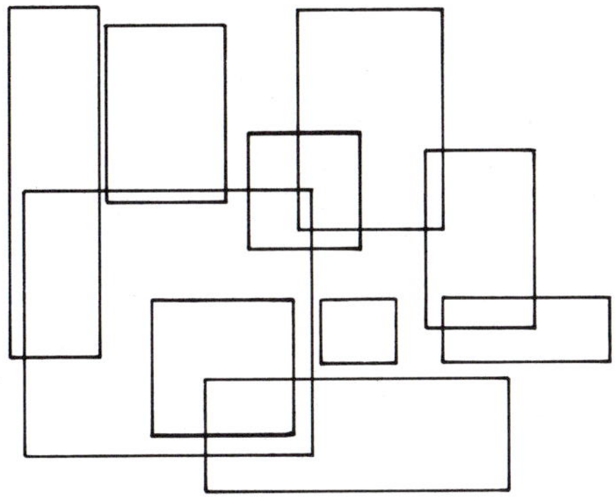

Figure 7.1 Squares and rectangles.

Feature Analysis Models

It is obvious that squares and rectangles generally contain a similar, basic set of elements or *features;* for example, straight lines, parallel lines, right angles, and an enclosed space. Therefore, it might be possible to find a small set of features that, when combined in one way, would represent all squares and, when combined in another, would represent all rectangles. These combinations would, in effect, be a set of *rules* relating the features together to represent squares on the one hand and rectangles on the other. This idea could be extended to develop a scheme in which several different types of forms could be distinguished by using a relatively small set of features along with different rules for combining them. This model of pattern recognition describes a general class of models called *feature analysis models* of pattern perception.

One form of the feature analysis concept, the *pandemonium model,* was developed by Selfridge and Neisser (1960) to describe the perception of letters. The problem of distinguishing between letters is similar to the problem of distinguishing different forms. In other words, although we readily recognize different versions of the same letter, we can distinguish between different letters at the same time. A diagram illustrating some of the characteristics of the pandemonium model is shown in figure 7.2.

Visual information from a letter is simultaneously analyzed by a set of feature analyzers or "feature demons," a term coined by the model's originators. In part, the term "demons" is used because many of the mechanisms to which these stages of analysis might correspond are hypothetical. The feature

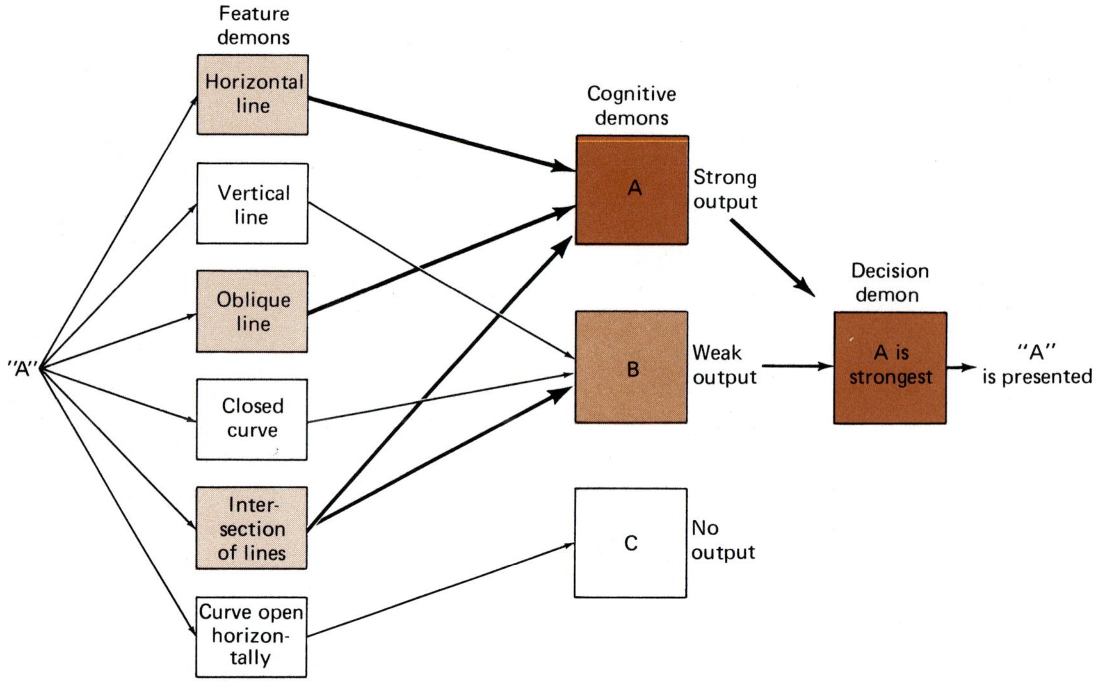

Figure 7.2 The pandemonium model of letter recognition. When the letter *A* is presented, as shown, certain feature demons respond (heavy lines) because their characteristics are present in *A*. The outputs of the feature demons are collected by various cognitive demons. In this case, all feature demons connected to the *A* cognitive demon respond, while only one feature demon connected to the *B* cognitive demon and none connected to the *C* cognitive demon are responding. Therefore, the *A* cognitive demon has the strongest output. The decision demon selects the cognitive demon with the strongest response to determine which letter is presented.

demons are somewhat like templates. Each feature demon represents a potential characteristic or feature of the incoming information. A feature demon responds when the incoming information contains its particular characteristic. One set of possible features, proposed by Gibson (1965), is shown in figure 7.3. Notice that some of these features resemble the receptive field characteristics of visual cortical cells described in the previous chapter, such as vertical and oblique lines. Therefore, these neurons are possible candidates for feature demons at a physiological level. However, other features shown in figure 7.3 do not correspond to the types of visual cortical neurons described in Chapter 6, including features such as type of curvature and cyclic change.

The important point here is that the physiological interconnections which bring about the responses of cortical neurons to features of visual stimuli suggest the way in which more complex feature demons could be created. Thus the receptive field properties of complex visual cortical cells were in part derived from the combination of simpler receptive field properties of simple cortical neurons. Perhaps some of the more complex fea-

Features	A	B	C	E	K	L	N	U	X	Z
Straight segment										
Horizontal	+			+		+				+
Vertical		+		+	+	+	+			
Oblique /	+				+				+	+
Oblique \	+				+		+		+	
Curve										
Closed		+								
Open vertically								+		
Open horizontally			+							
Intersection	+	+		+	+				+	
Redundancy										
Cyclic change		+		+						
Symmetry	+	+	+	+	+			+	+	
Discontinuity										
Vertical	+				+				+	
Horizontal				+		+	+			+

Figure 7.3 A set of features that could be used to characterize different letters of the alphabet. Each letter contains those features marked by a "+" below it. (From Learning to read. Gibson, E. J. *Science,* Vol. 148, pp. 1066–1072, Fig. 3, 21 May 1965. Copyright 1965 by the American Association for the Advancement of Science.)

tures in Gibson's list result from combinations of complex or perhaps hypercomplex receptive field characteristics, although at the present time such suggestions are only interesting speculations.

To return to the pandemonium model illustrated in figure 7.2, the reports (signals or outputs) from feature demons that characterize a particular letter are sent to *"cognitive demons"* at the next higher level of analysis. Thus all feature demons that respond to features in the letter *A* send their signals to the *A* cognitive demon. Similarly, feature demons responding to the letter *B* send their outputs to the *B* cognitive demon, and so forth. Notice that some of the features that characterize *B*'s are also found in *A*'s. Thus when an *A* is examined, both the *A* and the *B* cognitive demons will receive input, and therefore, both will indicate the fact with some signal or output. However, when *A* is presented to this system, *all* the features in the letter *A* will be present, while only a few of the *B* features will be present. A cognitive demon will respond to the extent that all the feature demons which feed to it are responding. Thus, when the *A* is presented, the signal or output from the *A* cognitive demon will be greater than that from the *B* cognitive demon.

The final stage of analysis in the pandemonium model is represented in figure 7.2 by the "decision demon." This demon determines which cognitive demon is responding most strongly and thereby "decides" which letter has been viewed.

Advantages of the Feature Analysis Model

The feature analysis model has several advantages over the template model. Whereas the template model requires a different template for every possible version of a given letter, the feature analysis model represents different letters in terms of particular combinations of a relatively small set of features. Also, the method of representing a form such as a letter as a combination of features represents our notion that a particular form is best described as a certain relationship between or a combination of elements.

Another advantage of the feature analysis model is that it can deal with somewhat distorted or only partially complete forms. Suppose, for example, that we looked at a letter *A,* which had a slightly curved side (like this; "A"). We might recognize the letter correctly because more features of the letter *A* are present than those of any other letter. Thus the output from the *A* cognitive demon in the pandemonium model would be the strongest output. Other kinds of distortions or "noise" could lead to the same result because the letter *A* is represented by a set of features rather than a single template, and no single feature would be absolutely essential for recognition. Of course, some distortions of a letter would lead to confusion. We do in fact confuse letters on occasion, especially as children, and a useful model of perception must include a means of explaining why certain letters are confused more often than others.

Figure 7.4 illustrates the results of one study in which confusion of letters was studied. In this experiment, subjects were very briefly presented different letters and asked to identify them. Figure 7.4 shows how

Character called (columns); Character shown (rows)

	A	B	C	D	E	F	G	H	I	J	K	L	M	N	O	P	Q	R	S	T	U	V	W	X	Y	Z	1	2	3	4	5	6	7	8	9	Ø
A																		1																		1
B				1														1								1								10		2
C		1					21								6																				1	
D		2					3						1		4		3																		1	
E		1				1																														
F																2											1									
G			1															1														7			1	1
H													5										1													
I																				2				1			4		2				1			
J									1								1										1			2			1			
K														3				2						1	1											
L									1																											
M														1			1						1													
N								4			1						1																			1
O		1	4	1			8										4																			
P						2												1																		1
Q	1			5			3								4																					
R	1													1		4																				
S		2																				1									3			2	5	
T									1																2								1			
U							1								1							3														
V																							1		3											
W																																				
X																									1											
Y																						2											1			
Z																									1			4					3			
1									2																											
2																		1								2										1
3																															1					
4	2																																			
5																			3										3			4		2		2
6		1					3																						1					3		1
7																									1											
8	1	10					1												2										1			3			1	2
9		1		1												1	2		1										1					1		2
Ø		1															1																	1		

Figure 7.4 The results of an experiment on letter and number confusion. The letter shown to the subject is on the left side of the table (A–Z and 1–0). The number in each box indicates the number of times the subject confused the letter or number shown with the letter or number at the top of that column. (From Kinney, G. C., Marsetta, M., and Showman, D. J. *Studies in display symbol legibility, part XII. The legibility of alphanumeric symbols for digitalized television.* Bedford, Mass.: The Mitre Corporation, November 1966, ESD–TR–66–117. Used by permission of the publisher, The Mitre Corporation.)

often a particular letter was reported correctly, or incorrectly as another letter. Notice that some letters, *R* for example, were mistakenly identified as another letter, in this instance *P,* and that some confusions were more frequent than others. According to the pandemonium model, a brief presentation of a letter may not provide sufficient time for all the feature analyzers to accurately assess the pattern (letter) presented. Thus a particular feature analyzer may inaccurately report the presence of a feature when, in fact, it is not present in a letter; or the feature analyzer may fail to signal a feature that is present. Because two letters such as *R* and *P* have several features in common, incomplete analysis would lead to confusion in recognition. Thus if the "oblique line" feature demon failed to report the presence of this line in the letter *R*, while all other features were accurately reported, the set of features reported would be consistent with the presence of the letter *P*. In general, we would expect the letter to be misidentified as another letter that contained all but a few of *R*'s features—the letter *P*. A perusal of the data in figure 7.4 will demonstrate that this is indeed the case.

Indeed, *R*'s are often mistakenly identified as *P*'s. It is interesting to note that this basis for errors of confusion would not necessarily predict that *P* would be mistaken as often for *R* as *R* would be mistaken for *P*. As we indicated previously, misidentification of the letter *P* may occur because (1) some of the *P* features are not reported or (2) some feature analyzer falsely reports the presence of a feature not contained in the letter *P*. The first type of error may lead to the misidentification of the letter *P* as the letter *F*. The second error may lead to reporting a *P* as an *R*. As shown in figure 7.4, both confusions occur. The frequency with which particular letters will be confused depends on how often the two kinds of errors are made and on the particular features that are incorrectly included or deleted. Errors may occur more often with some features than others.

The study of confusions is one way in which the potential features and rules involved in recognizing a particular pattern in a perceptual task can be discovered. Other clues can be obtained by using phenomena discussed in Chapter 6. For example, the experiments on stabilized images suggest the possibility that when particular portions of a pattern fade as a unit, a particular feature demon ceases to respond and the elements within the pattern detected by that feature demon are no longer seen.

As we noted earlier, the receptive field characteristics of neurons in the visual system also suggest potential features in pattern perception. These studies have led to several investigations of specific adaptation effects such as those described for orientation and size in Chapter 6 (e.g., box 6.7). The fact that prolonged viewing of one pattern can affect the subsequent perception of only some of the characteristics of another pattern is consistent with the notion that we are adapting specific feature analyzers involved in the perception of patterns. On the basis of studies such as these, we are beginning to develop ideas about what the features and rules of form perception might be.

A great deal of insight into the rules of form perception was furnished in the first half of this century by the work of Gestalt psychologists, who emphasized the importance of relationships between elements in perception. These psychologists formulated what they considered to be fundamental rules of organization in perception. Some of these rules are discussed in box 7.1.

Features in Speech Perception

When we apply the feature analysis point of view to the problem of how we recognize speech, we encounter a number of interesting

Box 7.1

Principles of Organization in Form Perception

In one sense, the picture in box figure 7.1a is nothing more than a collection of line elements and dots scattered on a surface. It is clear, however, that this is not the way the picture is perceived. Rather than a chaos of line elements, these elements form figures and shapes, indicating that there is substantial order or organization in perception.

Several principles of organization in form perception have been developed. One of the first principles, explored initially by Rubin (see Woodworth and Schlosberg, 1954), is that, typically, certain regions of a picture will be the background for other regions that form the figure. The figure is generally better defined than the background, which is more diffuse.

What are the necessary requirements for the organization or grouping of portions of the pattern that form figures? First, the figure must have some kind of edge or contour. That is, one must be able to discern differences in the illumination of the surface. In Chapter 6 we discussed several physiological processes related to the enhancement of changes in illumination and to the specific analyses of lines and edges. These processes make it possible for us to see the line elements in the picture but do not provide insight into why these line elements are grouped in the particular way that we perceive them. Thus we usually see a square rather than four separate lines. Some lines appear as part of one figure, while others form a different figure within the same picture.

Max Wertheimer, a Gestalt psychologist, attempted to formulate several principles by which such grouping takes place. Some of them are illustrated in box figure 7.1b. Elements that are relatively close to each other, for example, tend to form a group and thus illustrate the principle of nearness or proximity. Elements that move or change in size, for instance, tend to be grouped together, illustrating the principle of common fate. This is probably an example of a more general principle in which elements that share some common attribute are grouped together (the principle of similarity). Elements also tend to form closed figures with continuous rather than broken contours.

The Gestalt rules of form perception can be incorporated into a more general theoretical framework derived from *information theory.* One of the basic concepts in information theory is *uncertainty.* One gains information about a set of events if the uncertainty about that set of events is reduced in some way. For example, if someone told you your name, you would gain no information because you are not uncertain about your name in the first place; that is, your uncertainty would not be reduced. On the other hand, if you did not know someone's name and were given this information, your uncertainty would be reduced and you would therefore gain information. The extent to which uncertainty is reduced is a measure of the amount of information gained. This concept can be illustrated by an experiment performed by Attneave (1954). Subjects were asked to place ten dots on a shape, such as the one shown in box figure 7.1c, so that the configuration of dots would, if seen alone, resemble the shape as closely as possible. Presumably the subjects located the dots in such a way that they were maximally informative about the shape they represented. In other words, the configuration of dots reduced the viewer's uncertainty about the shape the dots represented and therefore provided him with maximum information about the shape. In Attneave's experiment, the dots tended to be located most frequently where the contour changed direction, as indicated by the length of the lines surrounding the shape in box figure 7.1c.

Because the perceptual system is limited in terms of the number of events it can process at a given time, we tend to process a limited set of characteristics that will provide us with maximum information about a pattern. That is, we process only those events that will reduce our uncertainty to a maximum degree. Some characteristics of patterns can summarize large amounts of information. For example, when all the elements forming a figure are dots and all those forming the background are dashes, we only need to process the fact that the figure contains dots and the background contains dashes; we do not need to separate each dot and dash. Similarly, if a pattern is symmetrical, (i.e., one half is identical to the other) the perceptual system can reduce the uncertainty about the entire pattern by processing the configuration of elements in half the pattern and applying a rule of symmetry. Generally speaking, if the perceptual system can assess a common characteristic among elements in a pattern, it can process the information in the pattern more economically. The Gestalt rules represent potential ways in which elements can be organized by the perceptual system to achieve economies in perception. One problem with these rules of organization is that although they appear to describe kinds of organization that occur in perception, they do not provide any insight into why other potential organizations are not used nor how those that are used are achieved in perception. However, these principles suggest ways in which a pattern's informative characteristics can be discovered, as illustrated by Attneave's experiment.

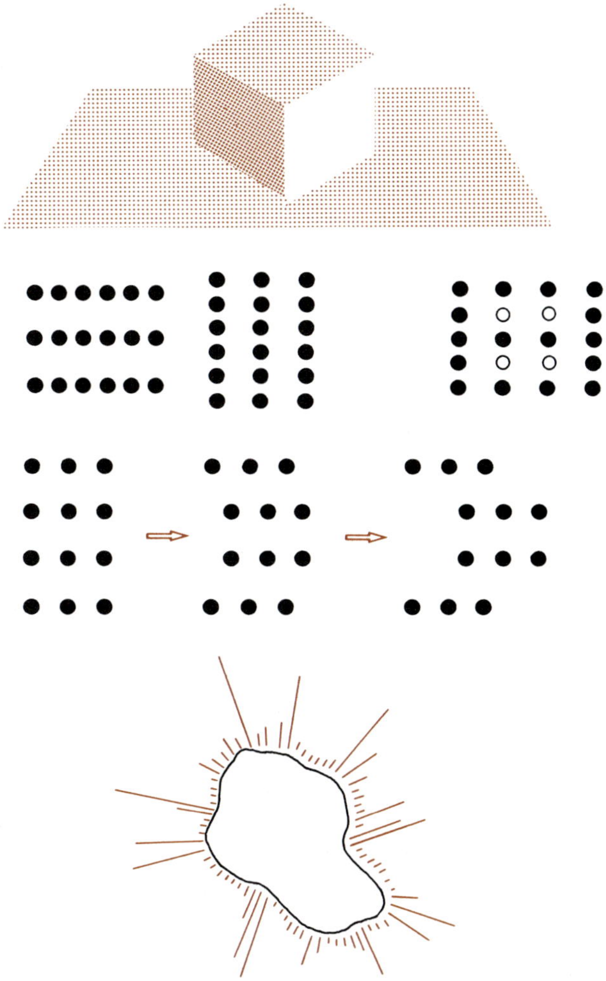

Box Figure 7.1 (a) Figure and ground. (b) Gestalt principles of organization. (c) An example of information theory analysis of perceptual organization. (From Attneave, F. "Some informational aspects of visual perception." *Psychological Review*, 1954, *61*, 183–193. Copyright 1954 by the American Psychological Association. Reprinted by permission.)

issues. We do not find it difficult to perceive spoken words in a sentence as distinct units. But how this is done becomes a mystery when we examine the physical characteristics of speech.

Physical Characteristics of Speech

Speech is a complex sound, and as you will recall from Chapter 6, complex sounds consist of many frequencies. In the case of speech, the frequency spectrum changes from moment to moment, depending on what is said. Thus to specify speech sounds physically, we must obtain a graph that indicates the amount of each frequency occurring in speech over time. Such a graph is called a *sound spectrogram,* and an example is shown in figure 7.5a. In this graph the presence of sound energy within a particular range of frequencies is shown by a dark area. The darker the area, the more energy within a given frequency range is present. Clearly, the pattern of frequencies changes in an extremely complex way throughout the sentence.

One surprising aspect of the sound spectrogram of a sentence is that often there are no obvious gaps in the energy pattern between words. This is especially puzzling because, although there are no physical gaps, we nevertheless hear the words in the sentence as distinct units separated by breaks or gaps. Ap-

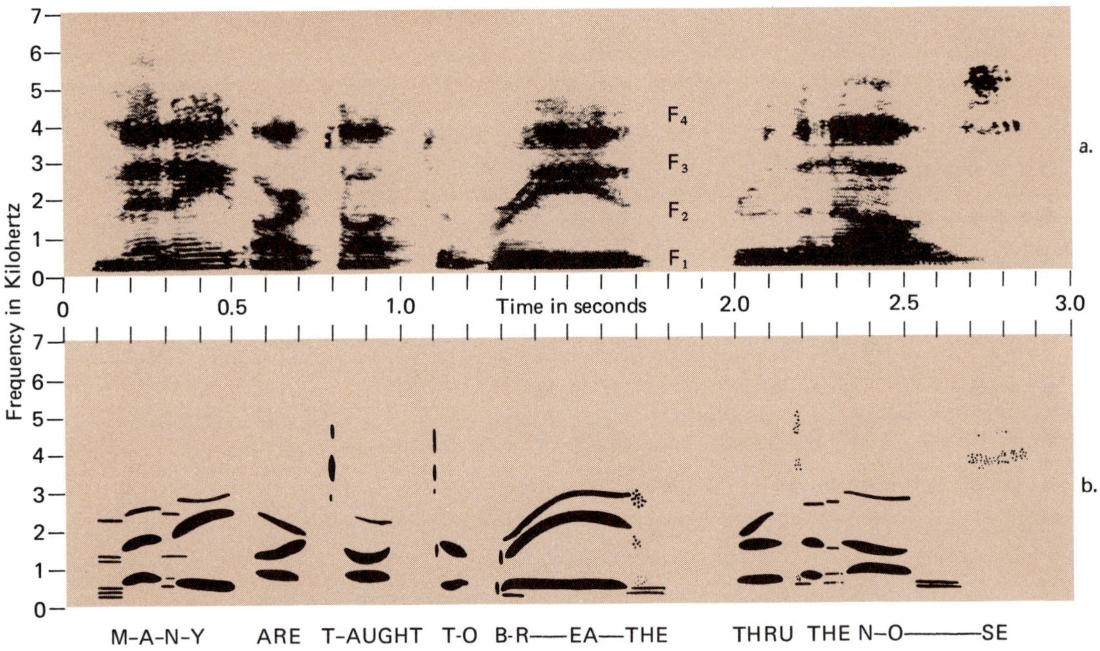

Figure 7.5 (a) The sound spectrogram of a naturally produced sentence: "Many are taught to breathe through the nose." (b) Illustrates a synthetic pattern, using only the first three formants which can be played to produce the sentence. The formants occurring in the naturally produced word, "breathe" are labelled. (From THE SPEECH/CHAIN by Peter B. Denis and E. W. Pinson. Copyright © 1963 by Bell Telephone Labs. Reprinted by permission of Doubleday & Co., Inc.)

parently, we are able to extract the units of speech from the relatively continuous physical stream of sound in much the same way that we can see the distorted patterns produced by an individual's handwriting as distinct letters. This comparison between letters and speech raises the possibility that a feature analysis model is applicable to speech perception.

Features of Speech Sounds

A large amount of experimental and theoretical work has been devoted to discovering the features of speech sounds. An early conception was that perhaps each small time-segment of the speech signal conveyed some specific sound or feature—part of a word. This conception had great appeal because linguists had successfully broken down spoken words into smaller sounds termed *phonemes.* For example, the *d* sound in diner, dune, and handle is one phoneme of spoken English.

Basically, a phoneme is a speech sound that can affect the meaning of what you hear. Thus we hear the spoken words *bit* and *bat* differently because they have different vowel phonemes, *ih* and *ah.* Note that we are talking about basic sounds here, not letters. Different letters can correspond to the same phoneme in different words; for example, the *k* sound in candle and kill. There are about forty phonemes in spoken English and these include the vowel sounds. Other languages have different numbers of phonemes, but typically not more than about forty. One might expect, as did earlier researchers who dealt with speech, that the phonemes occurring in a particular sentence would be laid out in a sequence in the speech stream. Thus, if we recorded a sentence on tape, we could simply slice the tape into small segments to find each phoneme. To our amazement, however, we would find that for a large class of phonemes, no small piece of tape can be found which corresponds to a single phoneme. Although we could reduce the tape to include only syllables, it would be impossible to reduce the tape in most cases to single phonemes within a syllable. In fact, the pieces become unintelligible and do not even sound like speech sounds!

This kind of research led scientists to examine the sound patterns within single syllables. Most of these experiments have been concerned with syllables consisting of consonant-vowel sounds; for example, *da, ba,* and *pa.* When the sound spectrograms for speech sounds are examined, it is generally found that, at any time, the energy in the speech signal is not spread evenly over the entire sound spectrum but instead is concentrated within four limited frequency regions or bands, as shown in figure 7.5b. These bands are called *formants.* For many phonemes, including the vowels, only the two lowest frequency bands—that is, the first and second formants—are required to provide intelligible speech, although some phonemes such as the *r* and *l* sounds require the third formant. Some examples of first and second formants for various consonant-vowel combinations are shown in figure 7.6. These examples were generated artificially by a machine called a pattern playback, using a specific pattern of changes in frequency within the range of the first and second formants.

By using such synthetic speech sounds, we can now attempt to slice various syllables into smaller pieces to determine which parts correspond to particular phonemes. Note that in a sense, the syllables in figure 7.6 consist of two halves. In the first half, the second formant undergoes a shift in frequency, a so-called *formant transition.* In the second half of each syllable, the formant frequencies do not change significantly. We might presume that the second half of each syllable corresponds to a vowel sound, while the first half

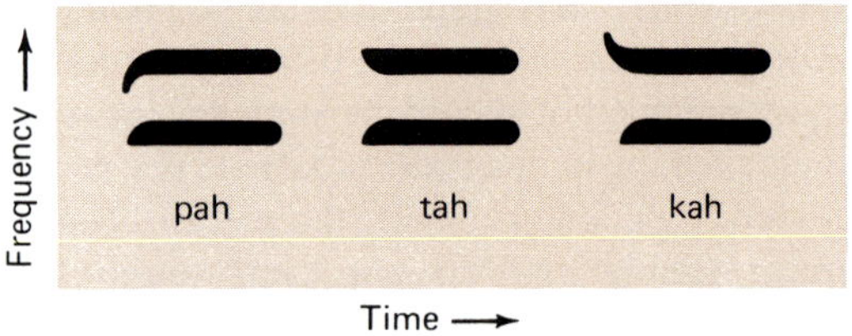

Figure 7.6 First and second formant combinations, generated artificially, which produce the consonant-vowel sounds shown. (From THE SPEECH/CHAIN by Peter B. Denis and E. W. Pinson. Copyright © 1963 by Bell Telephone Labs. Reprinted by permission of Doubleday & Co., Inc.)

corresponds to the sound of a consonant (e.g., *p, t,* and *k*). And indeed, we would be half correct! If we listened to the second half or, more specifically, the unchanging region of the formant frequencies, we would perceive the vowel sound. But if we listened to the first half alone, we would hear a sound totally alien to speech—a rising or falling whistle or chirp. This result is entirely consistent with our discussion about the difficulties involved in finding a single phoneme by slicing taped words into units smaller than a single syllable. Therefore, perhaps it is true that the consonant phoneme is represented by the entire pattern of sound in the examples given in figure 7.6. Perhaps the features that are required for recognition of the consonant phoneme are distributed throughout the syllable's sound pattern. Thus we might expect to find the same pattern every time we hear the same consonant; that is, we might expect the same type of formant transition to appear. Unfortunately, even this is not the case. Figure 7.7 shows that the same consonant sound may correspond to different energy patterns, depending on the vowel sound with which it is combined.

Production of Speech

In the search for some common pattern in all cases of the same consonant phoneme, the *production* of speech has been the subject of a large amount of research. In other words, what sequence of movements of the lips, tongue, vocal cords, and so forth leads to production of a specific consonant phoneme?

It is rather remarkable that we do in fact go through a specific sequence of movements when uttering a given phoneme. For example, *stop consonants* (*ba, pa, da, ta, ga, ka*) involve a sequence of articulation in which air is momentarily held (stopped) and then abruptly let out—a characteristic that distinguishes them from other consonant phonemes. The *s* sound in *sweet* is produced by letting air out continuously rather than abruptly. Stop consonants differ from each other in terms of other characteristics of articulation.

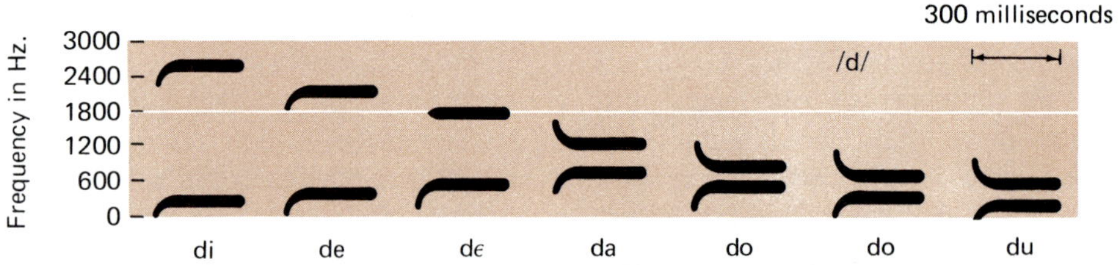

Figure 7.7 Schematic sound spectrographic patterns illustrating that the same consonant sound may correspond to quite different energy patterns, depending on the vowel sound with which it is combined. (From Liberman, A. M., Cooper, F. S., Shankweiler, D. P., and Studdert-Kennedy, M. Perception of the speech code. *Psychological Review, 74,* 1967, 431–461. Figure 2. Copyright 1967 by the American Psychological Association. Reprinted by permission.)

One of these differences is the position of the tongue prior to uttering the consonant. Say *ta* and *ga* and compare where your tongue is placed.

Another important difference for our upcoming discussion is called *voice onset time.* Activation of the vocal cords occurs virtually simultaneously with the expulsion of air in *ba* but is delayed for the syllable *pa.* You can determine this yourself by placing your hand on your throat while saying these two syllables and comparing the time when your vocal cords begin to vibrate with the time when your lips open to expel air. Interestingly enough, voice onset time is the only difference in articulation between these two sounds. Similarly, voice onset time is the only variable that distinguishes between *da* and *ta* and between *ga* and *ka.* These pairs differ from each other in terms of where the tongue is located during their articulation. Thus it appears that a small set of articulatory features (e.g., different voice onset times and places of tongue) is all that is necessary to distinguish between these six consonant phonemes.

All consonants can be characterized in terms of a small set of articulatory features, and it has been proposed that the commands for producing a particular speech sound consist of instructions to the vocal apparatus about voice onset time, tongue position, or other features. In normal speech, however, the articulation of these commands is blended. Although feature commands to the mechanism of articulation for specific phonemes are distinct, the articulatory apparatus blends the sound produced by these distinct phonemes because the mouth, tongue, lips, and so forth must make the transition from the position dictated by one set of commands to that dictated by the next. For example, when you say *dee,* your lips begin to form in anticipation of the *ee* sound while you are uttering the *d* sound. Thus the physical sound produced in making a consonant is influenced by the vowel sound that will follow it. In fact if a computer relays feature commands to a mechanical model of the vocal apparatus, the model will produce intelligible speech.

Recognition of Speech

You may wonder, at this point, what has happened to our original discussion of the *recognition* of speech. One theory of speech recognition, called the *motor theory of speech perception* (Liberman, 1970), postulates that the recognition of speech sounds involves an analysis of the incoming sound to determine which articulatory feature would produce the sound being heard. If the articulatory features are the features of speech perception, we should be able to apply some of the procedures discussed earlier for uncovering the features of visual perception; for example, the adaptation procedure.

Eimas and Corbit (1973) adapted subjects to a particular stop consonant-vowel such as *ba* by having them listen to its sound as it was played repetitively for several minutes. Before and after adaptation, the investigators played a tape containing the computer-generated sounds schematically illustrated in figure 7.8. The sounds represented by the spectrograms in figure 7.8 range from the physical sound spectrum for *ba* to that for *pa.* In other words, the voice onset time is graded from that for *ba* to that for *pa,* increasing a small amount for each sound from left to right. Eimas and Corbit then asked the subjects to indicate which speech sound they heard for each of the speech sounds presented to them. Interestingly, when listening to these different sounds, the subjects did not hear a continuously changing sound pattern. On the contrary, as indicated in the figure, one group of sounds was heard as *ba*—that is, the sounds were indistinguishable from one another—while another group was heard as *pa.* Only a few sounds fell in an indeterminant

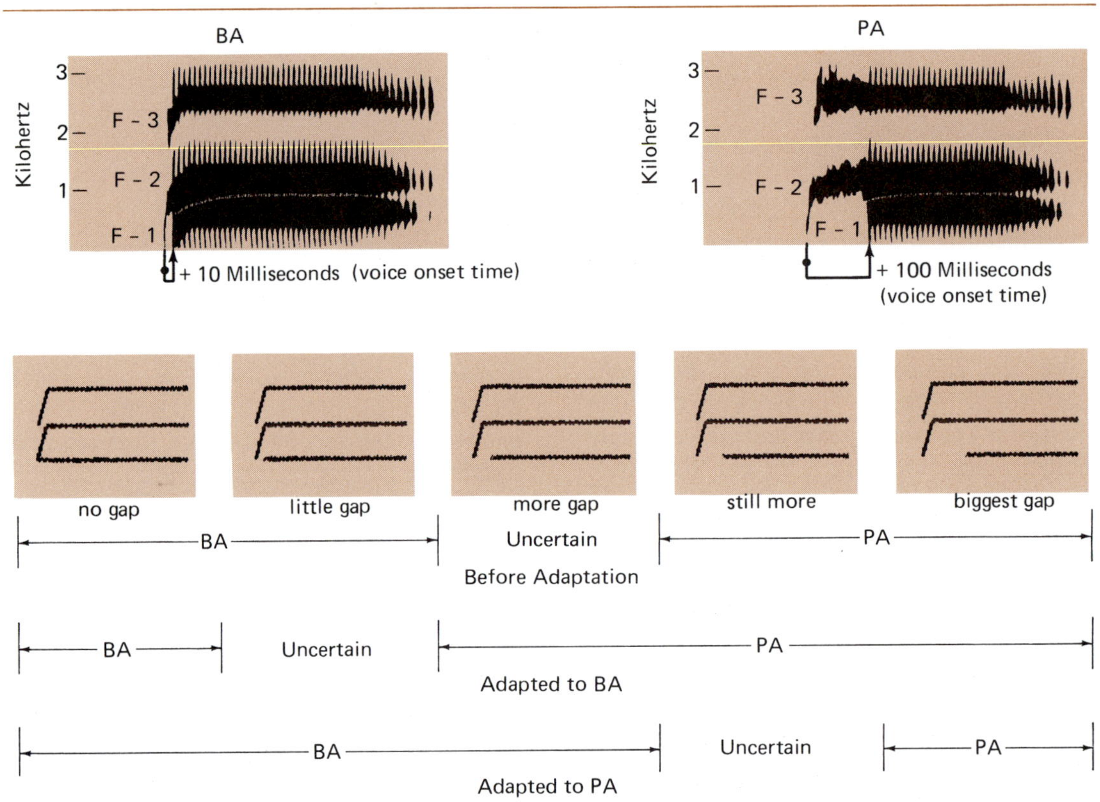

Figure 7.8 An illustration of the results of Eimas and Corbit's speech adaptation experiment. The sound spectrograms for the sounds "ba" and "pa" are illustrated at the top. Schematic illustrations of the sounds presented to subjects, with voice onset time graded from short (ba) to long (pa), are shown below the synthesized sound spectrograms for "ba" and "pa." Below these graphs, the results of the experiment are shown. Before adaptation, sounds with intermediate voice onset times were not identified with certainty. After adaptation to "ba," only sounds with short voice onset time were identified as "ba." After adaptation to "pa," only sounds with long voice onset times were identified as "pa." (From Eimas, P. D., and Corbit, J. D., Selective adaptation of linguistic feature detectors. *Cognitive Psychology,* 1973, *4,* 99–109. Figure 1. Reprinted by permission of Academic Press.)

category. Thus, although the physical characteristics of the sounds changed continuously in terms of voice onset time, most of them could be categorized into two groups. This phenomenon is termed *categorical perception.* After adapting to *ba,* the subjects required a sound that was closer to *ba* to categorize it as such. A similar effect in the opposite direction was obtained when subjects were adapted to the sound *pa* (see fig. 7.8). These results suggest that when a subject listens to *ba* many times, a feature demon or analyzer which is responsive to the voice onset time of *ba* is adapted (i.e., made less sensitive); thus a sound closer to *ba* in voice onset time must be played for it to be perceived as such. Similarly, a feature analyzer sensitive to the *pa* voice onset time is desensitized after *pa* is heard repeatedly. It appears, therefore, that voice onset time characterizes some of the features in speech recognition.

Experiments such as these provide support for the motor theory of speech perception. However, since the various features are blended in the production of speech, it is unclear how information about a particular articulatory feature can be extracted from the sound that arrives at the ear. Apparently, information about these features is contained in the speech signal, probably within the time segments corresponding to syllables. But given that the same phoneme occurring in different syllables produces different patterns of sound (see fig. 7.7) and this phoneme should contain the same set of features in the different syllables, the problem of how the same feature can be extracted from different patterns of sound still remains unsolved.

Some General Themes in Feature Analysis

After this discussion of form and speech perception you probably feel that the story is incomplete. Although we have suggested that patterns, whether visual or auditory, are processed by analyzing them for specific features, we have said that in many cases we are ignorant about the specific nature of these features. In the case of speech sounds, for example, it is not clear what information in the physical stimulus should be analyzed to inform us about a given feature. Finally, we have indicated that the rules by which features are combined are closely tied to the nature of the features themselves. Thus our uncertainty about features also applies to the nature of the rules for combining them. Perhaps we should view the concept of feature analysis as a general outline or sketch of what needs to be studied to understand pattern perception. The pandemonium model is only one example of this general conceptual model.

Some general themes of the feature analysis model seem especially well suited when attempting to understand pattern perception. One important theme is that information is subject to multiple levels of analysis. The first stage might consist of elementary features, which would then be combined according to certain rules to form the next level of analysis, and so forth. For example, although we represented the analysis of letters in terms of two stages—feature demons and cognitive demons of the pandemonium model—a more accurate picture might be that the feature demon represents a particular combination of even more elementary features of written letters. In some cases we may be able to use or "assess" information at each stage in the analysis. For instance, we have discussed a case in which we can recognize two different versions of the same letter as the same—for example, two handwritten *a*'s. Yet, at the same time we can perceive that the two letters are not physically identical. Thus we have access to a high level of analysis which indicates that both letters are *a*'s, but we also have access to a lower level at which differences between these two versions of the same letter are recognizable. Our consideration of speech perception, on the other hand, indicates that we do not always have access to all the different levels of analysis. We are unable to perceive the differences between different physical patterns of sound producing the same phoneme, although these differences must be represented at some lower level in our processing in speech. In other words, we know we can perceive some of the physical differences that make up speech; yet when these differences are part of a speech pattern, they sound identical. The question of how and when we can assess different levels of analysis is an important one, and we will return to it when we discuss the topic of selective attention later in this chapter.

Perception of Size and Distance

In Chapter 6 we discussed the problem of perceiving size and distance. As you will recall, two objects of different sizes at different distances from the eyes can cast images of identical size and shape on the retina. Yet we can quite accurately perceive one to be small and close and the other to be large and far away. The problem is this: Given that the two objects cast retinal images of identical size, what additional information do we use to perceive them accurately? We must have either additional information about physical distance or physical size. Thus, if we have additional information that one object is farther away than another, this information, combined with the size of the image, will inform us about the actual size of the object. Similarly, if we have a source of information about an object's actual size, we can combine this information with that concerning the size of the image to determine the actual distance.

We encounter another aspect of the same problem when we consider the fact that as an object changes position with respect to us, either because it is moving or because we are moving relative to it, the retinal image formed by the object continuously changes shape and size, depending on its distance and our angle of view. Thus as the object moves away from us, the size of its retinal image continuously decreases. An object such as a square may be imaged as a square, a rectangle, or a trapezoid depending on the angle of view. The amazing fact is that although its retinal image undergoes these contortions, our perception of the object's shape and size remains relatively constant. These constancies of perception, termed *shape* and *size constancy,* also mean that we need sources of information about distance, not only with respect to the distances of objects in relation to each other, but with respect to the distances between points on the same object. It is important to realize that we are usually unaware of these sources of information when perceiving size and distance; we use them automatically.

Depth Perception

Several sources of visual information for distance have been determined. They are classically divided into *binocular* sources, those that rely on information from two eyes, and *monocular* sources, those that rely on information from one eye.

Binocular Sources

The most important source of binocular information, *binocular disparity,* was introduced in Chapter 6. As you will recall, this source of information derives from the fact that points in the image of the same object lie in different places on the two retinas, depending how far away the object is from the point of the observer's fixation. One might assume that to use this disparate information, the shapes and forms present in the two eyes would be perceived first, and then these two visual images would be compared to determine the manner in which they exhibited disparity. The lack of correspondence between the two visual images would then be used to provide distance information. This sequence suggests that we would have to perceive form before we could perceive distance by means of binocular disparity. Although this notion is a reasonable one, it appears to be incorrect, largely because of the results obtained from an ingenious experiment performed by Julesz (1965). Julesz presented patterns such as those shown in figure 7.9 to his subjects. Notice that neither pattern contains any recognizable form. However, if you look at one

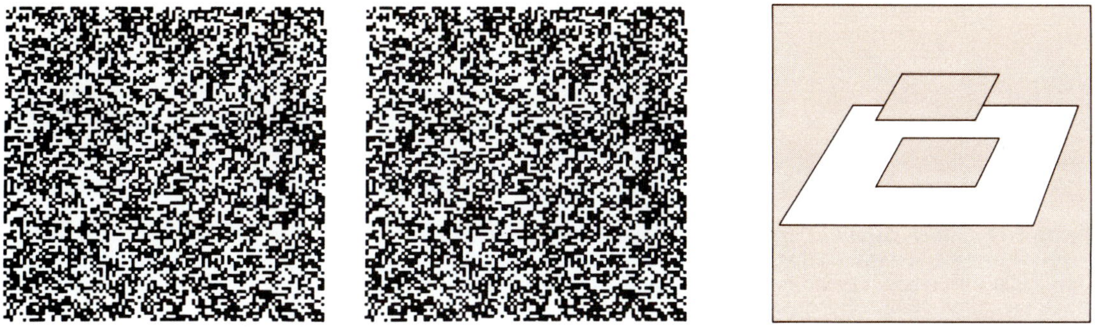

Figure 7.9 Stereoscopic images investigated by Julesz consist of random-dot patterns generated by a computer. When these two images are viewed with a stereoscope or with a prism held in front of one eye, a center panel should be seen floating above the background, as illustrated at the far right. You can try this effect by placing a 12-inch piece of cardboard or paper between the two patterns perpendicular to the page. By looking at one pattern with the left eye and the other with the right eye, the effect should occur. Your eyes should be focused so that the two patterns "fuse" into a single pattern. (From B. Julesz.)

with your right eye and the other with your left, so that the two patterns fuse into one, you will see a square in the center of the pattern that is closer to you than the background. (You will find it helpful to follow the instructions in the figure caption.) These patterns were constructed by generating the same random pattern of dots in the pictures for the right and left eye, except that in the center portion where the square appears, a square of light and dark spots is shifted slightly in the right as compared with the left picture. Thus, when you view the pictures with both eyes, binocular disparity exists between the dots within the square region, and the square appears to be closer to you than is the background. The important point here is that if either pattern is viewed alone, no square is seen. The only way that the square can be perceived is to obtain the disparity information and analyze it. Then the form becomes visible. Thus, contrary to our initial hypothesis, binocular disparity depth analysis appears to precede perception of form, not the other way around. A few of you will be unable to perceive this effect. About twelve percent of the population lacks the ability to use information on binocular disparity.

Another source of distance information dependent on two eyes is *convergence* as you will recall, when we fixate on an object, the object is imaged on the fovea of both eyes. If the point of fixation is closer to us, our eyes must rotate or converge toward the nose. The degree of convergence of the two eyes is another potential source of information about distance, although some controversy exists over whether this information is actually used.

Monocular Sources

Many sources of information are available from a single eye. A discussion of several of these sources follows.

Motion Parallax When a person is moving —riding in a car, for example—objects other than the one directly fixated change their angle with respect to the eye. Near objects undergo greater angular change than far objects do, and therefore near objects sweep

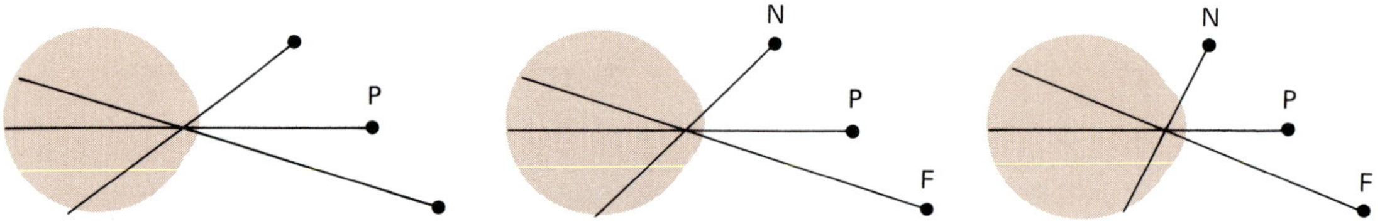

Figure 7.10 Motion parallax. The circle represents the eye of an observer moving toward point P. Objects such as N and F change their angle with respect to the eye. Near objects (N) will undergo greater angular change than far objects (F). Therefore, near objects sweep across the eye faster than far objects as the observer moves forward.

across the retina more rapidly, as illustrated in figure 7.10. Objects that are extremely close to the moving observer move so rapidly that they tend to blur as they sweep across the retina. This difference in the rate of movement of near and far objects, or motion parallax, is probably the most important monocular source of information about distance. As you will discover in Chapter 8, research indicates that young organisms can use both binocular disparity and motion parallax as sources of distance information. Thus the ability to use such sources may be present at birth.

Interposition The fact that objects located or interposed between the observer and objects farther away will block portions of the far objects from view also provides information about the relative distances of objects. As in our discussion of binocular disparity, we might assume that familiarity with the shape of objects would be necessary to use interposition information. For example, it might be necessary to know that houses are rectangular to perceive that a large tree disrupts this shape and is therefore interposed between the observer and the house. Evidently this knowledge is not always necessary. Figures 7.11a and 7.11b illustrate a situation in which one form is typically seen as being in front of the other. Because we have no basis for assuming that either form should have a particular shape, the fact that one appears to obstruct the other from view cannot be explained on the basis of familiarity with their forms. One of the basic processes of form perception appears to be involved in this effect. The form that contains the least number of changes in the direction of its border, or contour is seen as being in front of the other form. When both forms have an equal number of changes in the direction of their contours, there is an ambiguity as to which form is in front of the other, as illustrated in figure 7.11c. It is interesting to note here that we have encountered two cases in which the perception of form and distance are

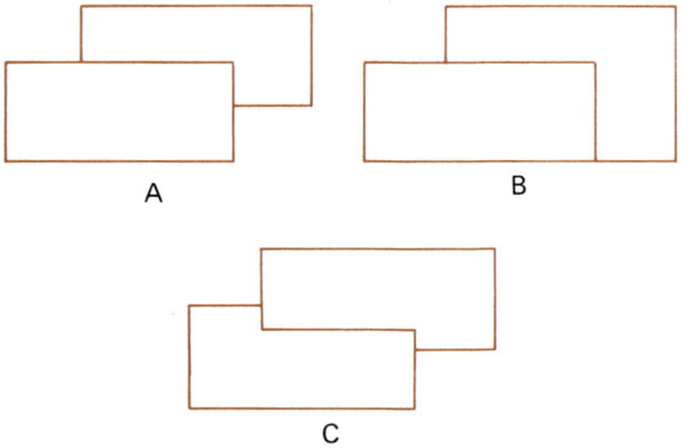

Figure 7.11 Examples of interposition as a source of information for the perception of relative distance. *A* and *B* give definite information; *C* gives ambiguous information. (From Ratoosh, P. On interposition as a cue for the perception of distance. *Proceedings of the National Academy of Sciences.* 1949, *35,* 257–259. Reprinted by permission.)

interrelated. In the case of binocular disparity, it was necessary to assess depth information before form became evident. In the case of interposition, an analysis of contours (i.e., form) appears to be necessary to obtain the depth information provided by interposition.

Linear Perspective and Texture When you look at a set of parallel lines, such as railroad tracks going off into the distance in figure 7.12a, the retinal images of these lines will converge because the visual angle formed by two points across from one another decreases as the points are farther away. Similarly, if you were viewing a textured surface such as a lawn, two blades of grass the same distance apart would be separated by a smaller distance in the retinal image the farther away they were because they would cover a smaller visual angle. Thus parallel lines converge and textures become finer the farther away they are. These optical character-

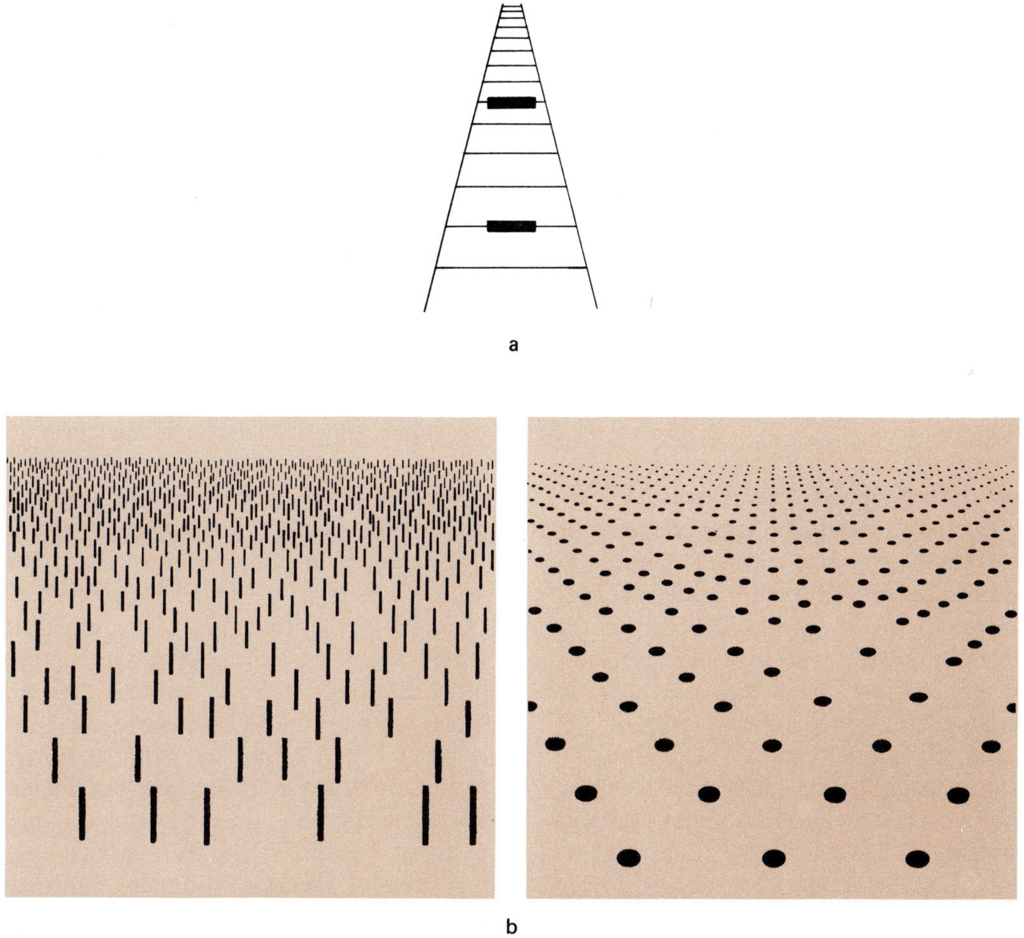

Figure 7.12 Linear perspective (Top) and textured surfaces (Bottom) can both convey depth and size information and can be used to gauge the size of objects. Heavy lines illustrate an illusion produced by misinformation about depth (see text discussion).

istics of images provide important sources of information for depth perception. Perspective is extremely important in artistic renditions of depth. Indeed, many basic rules of perspective were first elaborated by artists such as Leonardo da Vinci. On a two-dimensional canvas, the artist paints forms which produce retinal images that are identical with those produced by three-dimensional objects. Thus railroad tracks drawn as converging lines (see fig. 7.12a) produce the same image that would be obtained by looking at actual railroad tracks going off into the distance. Similarly, textures drawn on a two-dimensional surface (see fig. 7.12b) can simulate the same retinal images produced by three-dimensional textured surfaces.

Shading Patterns of brightness and darkness produced by overhead lighting such as the sun provide information about depth. For example, the surface around a hole in the ground is brighter than the center or bottom of the hole. Brightness differences are also used extensively in artistic portrayals of depth.

Familiar Size When objects are far away from us, the processes of size constancy do not seem adequate to assess or integrate distance information. Thus, at great distances—for example, when viewing objects on the ground from an airplane—we perceive them to be smaller than when they are near. In these situations, our familiarity with an object and, therefore, our knowledge that it remains constant in size can serve as a source of information about distance. Although from an airplane a house appears to be smaller than it would be if we were close to it, our knowledge about the size of houses informs us that the house is not actually smaller but is only far away.

Typically, all these sources of information about distance will be used in our perception of distance and size. But some are more important under certain conditions than others. It is also important to remember that there are nonvisual sources of information about distance. For example, we receive information from what we hear, and we may derive kinesthetic information from the fact that we must reach farther for some objects than others.

The preceding discussion indicates that there are relationships between the perception of size, shape, brightness, and the perception of distance. One might anticipate that when we are misinformed about distance, our size, shape, and brightness perception will be affected. Indeed, there are several cases where this appears to be true. You have probably noticed, for instance, that the moon appears to be larger when it is close to the horizon than when it is high in the evening sky. The change in the moon's appearance is only slightly affected by atmospheric phenomena. Although the atmosphere causes some smearing of the light from the moon when it is on the horizon, by far the greatest effect is perceptual. The moon is, in fact, the same physical size and distance away when viewed in these two positions. Because the atmospheric effect is minor and because the moon is virtually equidistant from the observer in both positions, it produces retinal images of the same size in both positions. You can prove this by holding at arms length an object that is just large enough to block the moon from view. This object will block the moon, whether it is on the horizon or at its zenith, which indicates that in each case it produces a retinal image of the same size. The illusion of a difference in size appears to be caused by the fact that we do not obtain accurate distance information about objects which are as far away as the moon. Because there are intervening objects on the earth's surface when we view the moon on the horizon, our distance analyzers apparently analyze the moon as though it is farther away than is the case when it is at its zenith, that is, when no objects intervene. An object that is analyzed as more distant would have to be larger to produce an image of the same size. Thus we perceive the moon as larger on the horizon than when it is at its zenith.

Given this basis for the moon illusion, we might expect an individual to judge the moon as farther away when it is on the horizon than when it is at its zenith. In fact, the horizon moon is judged to be closer than the zenith moon. It has been suggested that this occurs because we know that the moon's size is constant, and on the basis of this knowledge, as in the case of familiar size, we perceive the moon as closer on the horizon because it seems larger. In this illusion, we have resorted to two different levels or stages of analysis in the perceptual system. In the first instance, our distance analyzers do not obtain adequate information about distance. This insufficient information produces a perception of a larger horizon moon, which in turn produces a judgment that the horizon moon is closer to us.

The relationship between our size and distance analyzers has also been proposed to account for geometric illusions, such as the Müller-Lyer illusion shown in figure 7.13a. Notice that the line with fins pointed inward (a) looks shorter than the line with fins pointed outward (b), although both lines are actually the same length. Gregory (1966) proposed that this illusion occurs because our distance system interprets these figures in depth—as if they were three-dimensional—although they are in fact two-dimensional—on a plane surface. In other words, the retinal images cast by these lines are equivalent to those produced when we look at the outside corner of a building on the one hand or the intersection of walls in a room on the other, as illustrated in figure 7.13b. Thus, in relation to the direction of the fins, the line is interpreted by depth analyzers to be farther away in one case and closer in the other. As in the moon illusion, if one line is interpreted as being farther away, while the retinal image is the same for both, it is perceived as longer. Again, two levels of analysis are required to produce this illusion: one that produces mis-

Figure 7.13 (a) The Müller-Lyer illusion. (b) Theory of Müller-Lyer.

information about distance by processing a two-dimensional figure as though it were three-dimensional, and another that interprets depth analysis to indicate a difference in length. A similar effect was illustrated in figure 7.12a. The information about perspective indicates that the railroad tracks are going off into the distance, when in fact they are on a two-dimensional surface. Thus two lines of equal length (the heavy lines in fig. 7.12a) that cast identical retinal images are perceived to be of different lengths.

Other illusions are produced, not by misinformation but by inadequate or incomplete information, such as the Mach-Eben illusion described in Chapter 6. When the W-shaped card is viewed with both eyes, there is no ambiguity in its appearance because we receive binocular distance information. When viewed with one eye, however, this binocular information is not available, and the remaining information is consistent with two different appearances of the object; one in which it is in its normal position, flat on a table, and another in which it appears to be upright. Again, we notice that, depending on the view we obtain, the size, shape, and brightness of the object can also be affected. The necker cube, also discussed in Chapter 6, is another case in which the distance information is inadequate to distinguish between two alternative views of the same geometrical figure.

Analysis by Synthesis: Learning and Context

The fact that we can obtain multiple views of an object raises some interesting questions which will lead us to an elaboration of the feature analysis model. For example, how can we explain the fact that at one time the necker cube is seen in one configuration while at other times it appears in a different configuration? In the previous section, we concluded that we obtain the multiple views because the information available to us is consistent with two different views of the object. The question we are now raising is why, at any given time, we see one view as opposed to the other.

One possibility, which would still be consistent with models such as the pandemonium model, is that the two views are represented by two different cognitive demons and that the feature analyzers feeding into these cognitive demons fluctuate in their sensitivities over time. Thus at one time one cognitive demon gives the strongest signal because the feature demons signalling it are more sensitive at that time. At another time, a different cognitive demon gives the strongest signal, and these changes in output lead to the view that we perceive.

Learning and Context

Another possibility is that some system other than the feature analysis model receives the information from the cognitive demons, indicating that there are two possible views. This system then either chooses the view that we perceive at any time, or it modifies the features and rules to be more consistent with one view or the other. For example, when you tried the Mach-Eben illusion, you may have noticed that it is easier to obtain the effect of this illusion after you have been able to see it once. Presumably you have learned how to activate the feature analyzers and rules that produce the illusion. There are cases, in which your knowledge of the possibilities affects what you perceive. We must ultimately develop a view of perception that incorporates these other sources of knowledge. To accomplish this, we must consider two general categories of such effects. First, in many cases what we see depends on our general knowledge or the *context* of what we are viewing. There are many examples of this kind of contextual effect, some of which are shown in figure 7.14. At the top of this figure, the same

Figure 7.14 Three effects of context in perception. In the first example, the same symbol is perceived as the letter "B" or the number "13," depending on the context of surrounding symbols. In the second example, the context is your knowledge of language and the way that the sentence is printed, and this context prevents immediate recognition of the redundant word (the). (Adapted from Carson, G. *One for a Man, Two for a Horse,* Doubleday, 1961, and from SCIENCE PUZZLERS by Martin Gardner, illustrated by Anthony Ravielli. Copyright © 1960 by Martin Gardner and Anthony Ravielli. Reprinted by permission of the Viking Press, Inc. and Macmillan & Co., London.)

symbol may be seen as a letter (*B*) in one context or a number (*13*) in another. An example of this kind of contextual effect in speech is *ice cream* (*I scream* or *ice cream*). A complete model of perception would require a way for the feature analyzers to be directed or controlled and integrated somehow by the context; otherwise, alternative perceptions of the same physical pattern would be impossible.

The second category of perceptual phenomena that must be considered is illustrated in figure 7.15. What is figure 7.15? It probably seems to be some chaotic unintelligible pattern. However, suppose we tell you that it is a highly magnified view of synapses in the retina. For some individuals, this additional information would be sufficient for recognition of the subject of this figure. Most people, however, need *practice,* which might include viewing a schematic illustration of this photograph, such as the one shown in figure 7.16. A veteran electron microscopist could recognize the elements in figure 7.15 without difficulty. Apparently, then, we can learn to perceive things that were initially imperceptible. A more complete view of perception must include some method of modifying the way we perceive by learning.

The Analysis-By-Synthesis Model

Figure 7.17 is a model that incorporates the additional characteristics of perception we have discussed. In contrast with the model of feature analysis shown in figure 7.2 the present model contains a major addition; a representation of the way our knowledge of

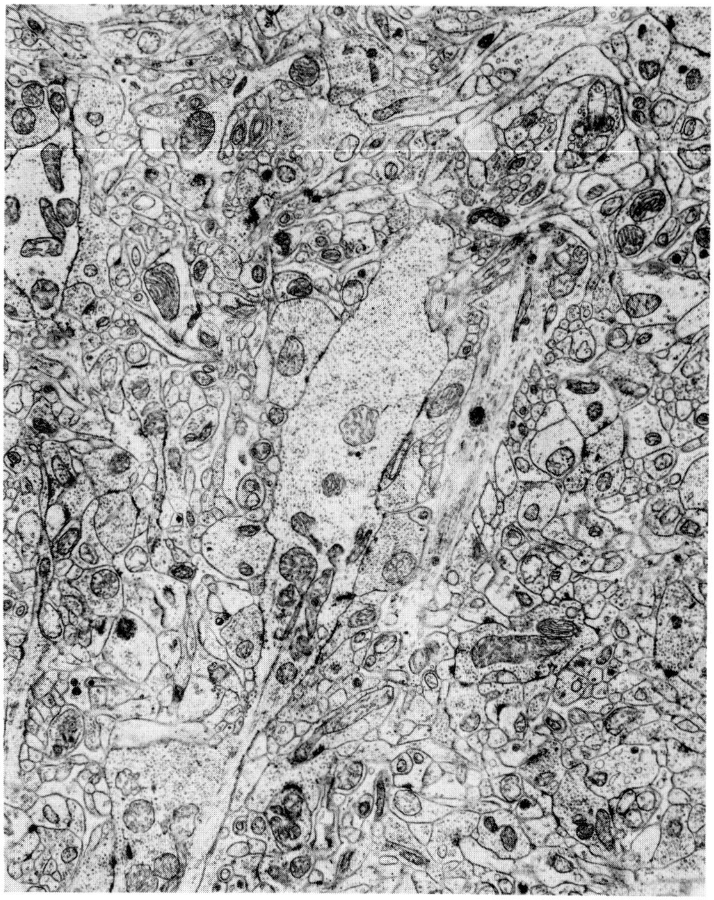

Figure 7.15 A picture of various structures, including synapses, in the retina taken with the electron microscope. Can you identify any parts of retinal cells or regions of synaptic contact? (Courtesy of Dr. Mark Dubin, Department of Molecular, Cellular and Developmental Biology, University of Colorado.)

the world can affect the features, rules, and decisions we use at any given time. This figure illustrates what is called an *analysis-by-synthesis model* of perception (Neisser, 1967).

In the analysis-by-synthesis model, we use information received immediately before and after incoming information, as well as our knowledge of what has occurred in similar situations in the past to analyze that input. Therefore, what we perceive in the present is integrated or synthesized with immediately preceding and future events as well as our construction of the world based on past experience. By means of our knowledge and previous information, we formulate expectations or hypotheses about incoming information. These expectations serve as a context or background against which new information can be compared and analyzed. If new information is not consistent with our expectations, our analysis of that information, our expectations, or both are modified. Thus perception results from a construction of the world based on the synthesis of our expectations and incoming information. For example, while you are reading this page, you are constantly anticipating what you will perceive next and testing it against your knowledge of language and the view of the subject matter that you have developed up to this time. At times your per-

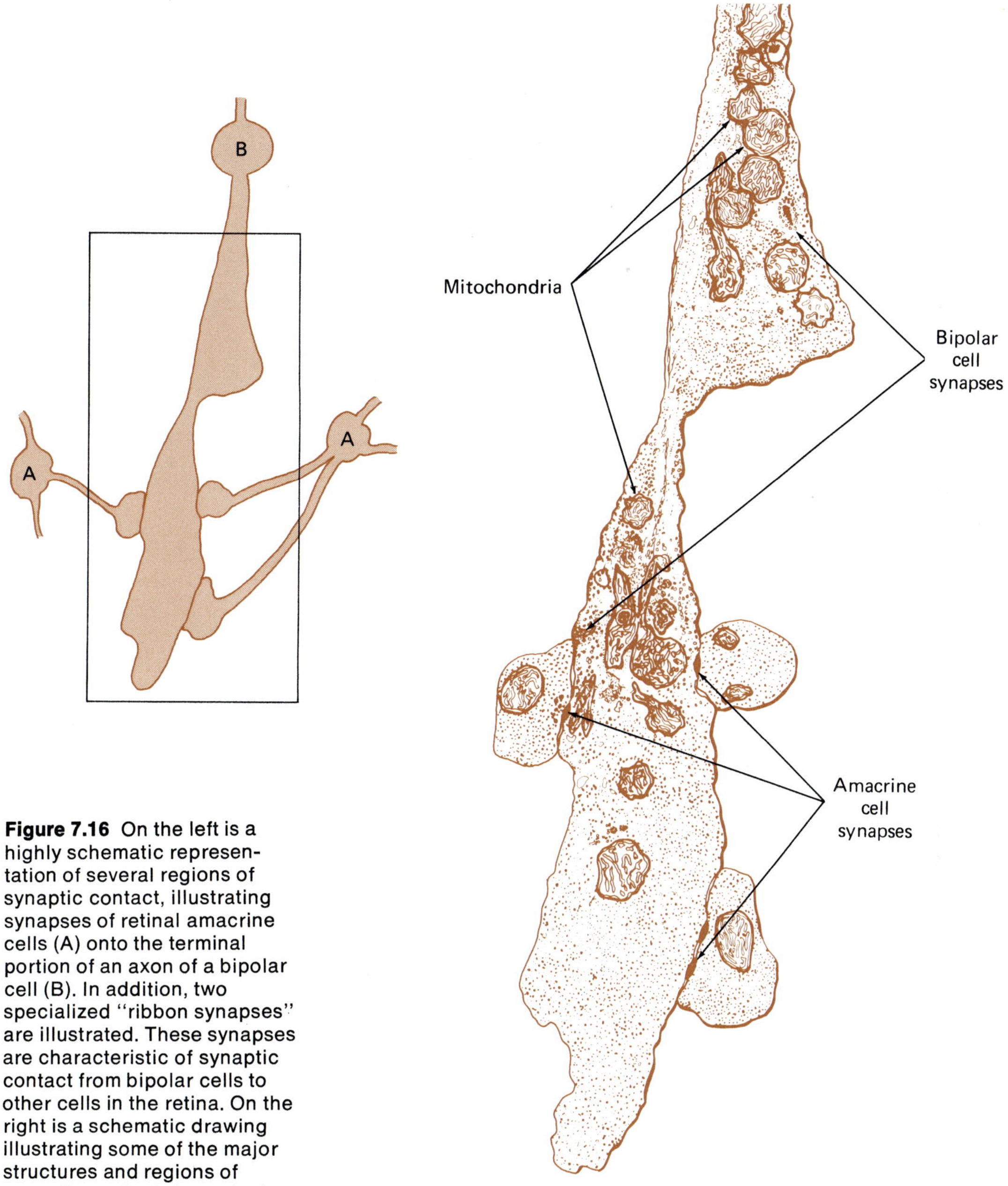

Figure 7.16 On the left is a highly schematic representation of several regions of synaptic contact, illustrating synapses of retinal amacrine cells (A) onto the terminal portion of an axon of a bipolar cell (B). In addition, two specialized "ribbon synapses" are illustrated. These synapses are characteristic of synaptic contact from bipolar cells to other cells in the retina. On the right is a schematic drawing illustrating some of the major structures and regions of synaptic contact shown in the electron micrograph in figure 7.15.

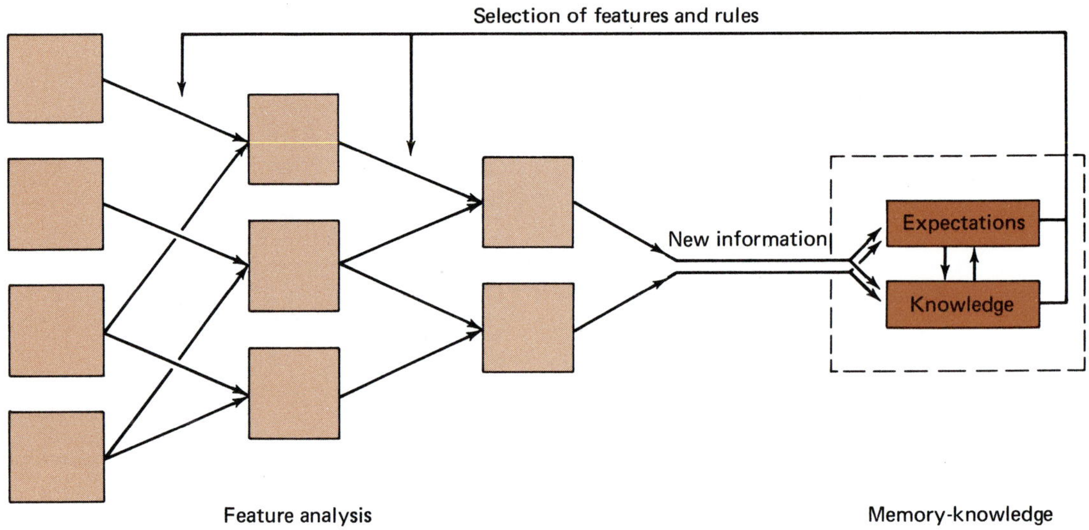

Figure 7.17 The analysis-by-synthesis model. Incoming information is analyzed by means of features and rules. The results of these analyses are sent to higher systems where they are integrated or synthesized with expectations and previous knowledge. On the basis of this synthesis, the rules and features used may be modified for processing future information.

ceptual expectations are so strong that you overlook inconsistencies in what you are perceiving, such as the redundant word in the sentence in figure 7.14.

On many occasions, overlooking information makes the observer more efficient, because it is unnecessary to analyze all the details of incoming information to perceive accurately what is going on. On other occasions, we find that our knowledge of the world and the analyses of incoming information are inadequate; for example, when interpreting the electron micrograph in figure 7.15. In such cases, we can learn to modify our view of the world so that we will be able to perceive information that was previously unintelligible to us. Even in a situation where we are simply trying to detect the presence or absence of a stimulus, we must account for our behavior with an analysis-by-synthesis approach, as illustrated in the discussion of signal detection theory in box 7.2.

Sensory Memory

To analyze incoming information and compare it with previous occurrences, it is necessary to retain information for a brief period. Retention also appears to be necessary because, as we noted earlier, critical information may occur over a period of time, for example, in speech perception. This is also true in vision because we must relate what we see as we move our eyes, fixating first one point, then another. Thus what we see at one point must be retained and, after a brief time, integrated with the next point, and so forth.

Experimental evidence indicates that we do have visual and auditory memories that can retain large amounts of incoming information for brief periods. A classic series of studies in this area was done by Sperling (1960). In one of these experiments, three rows of four letters each were flashed briefly on a screen, and observers were asked to

Box 7.2

Signal Detection Theory

Imagine that you are performing a task in which a trial consists of the following events: During each trial a tone is presented, and immediately afterward a dim (low energy) spot of light may or may not appear on a screen in front of you. In half the trials, the light is flashed on the screen; in the other half, no light is flashed. You must simply indicate whether or not you saw the light.

Box table 7.2 indicates the possible outcomes of this procedure. As you might expect from our discussion of thresholds in Chapter 6, there will be trials when the light is flashed but you will not see it. This response is called a *miss*. Interestingly enough, there will also be occasions when no light is flashed, and yet you will report that it was present. These responses are termed *false alarms*. Of course, on many occasions you will correctly report the presence of the spot (called a *hit*) and on others you will correctly report that the stimulus was not present (called a *correct rejection*).

A full account of these behaviors should predict the frequency with which each of the four responses will occur in a specific set of circumstances. *Signal detection theory* attempts to provide such a theoretical account. We shall develop this theory within the context of the analysis-by-synthesis model discussed in the text.

Let's assume that the subject uses a particular set of features and rules (i.e., a feature analysis system) that is appropriate for detecting the presence of the signal—the light stimulus in our previous example. We know that outputs of this feature analysis system can be produced by internal fluctuations in the feature analyzers and by stimuli other than the light signal. These other stimuli that produce outputs are termed *noise*.

Now let's consider those trials in which no signal is presented to the subject. During these trials, the subject will obtain an output from the feature analysis system because of the noise present in that trial. The particular noise will vary from trial to trial; therefore, output produced by *noise alone* will vary in strength from trial to trial. Some outputs will occur more frequently than others. Extremely strong or weak outputs, for example, will occur less frequently than outputs of intermediate strength. This can be illustrated by graphing how often trials with particular outputs will occur, when the output is caused by noise alone. This graph is illustrated in box figure 7.2a and is termed a *noise distribution*.

Thus far, we have considered outputs related solely to noise, that is, outputs during trials in which no signal is presented. During trials in which a signal is presented, the stimulation caused by the signal is *added* to that caused by the ongoing noise to produce the output of the feature analysis system. Thus signal trials are actually *signal-plus-noise* trials. On these trials, the output of the feature analysis system that would have been produced by noise alone is increased by the effect of the signal. Because the output related to noise varies from trial to trial, the output related to signal plus noise will also vary from trial to trial. This is illustrated in box figure 7.2b, in which outputs caused by signal plus noise on different trials are graphed. Notice that the most frequent output related to signal-plus-noise (box fig. 7.2b) has a higher value than the most frequent output caused by noise alone (box fig. 7.2a), because of the signal's added effect.

We are now in a position to consider an important point in signal detection theory. The same output may be produced during a trial in which no signal is present—that

Subject presented	Subject says: Saw the light	Subject says: Saw no light
Light (signal)	Hit	Miss
No light	False alarm	Correct rejection

Box Table 7.2 Possible outcomes in a signal detection task.

Continued on Page 222

Box 7.2 cont.

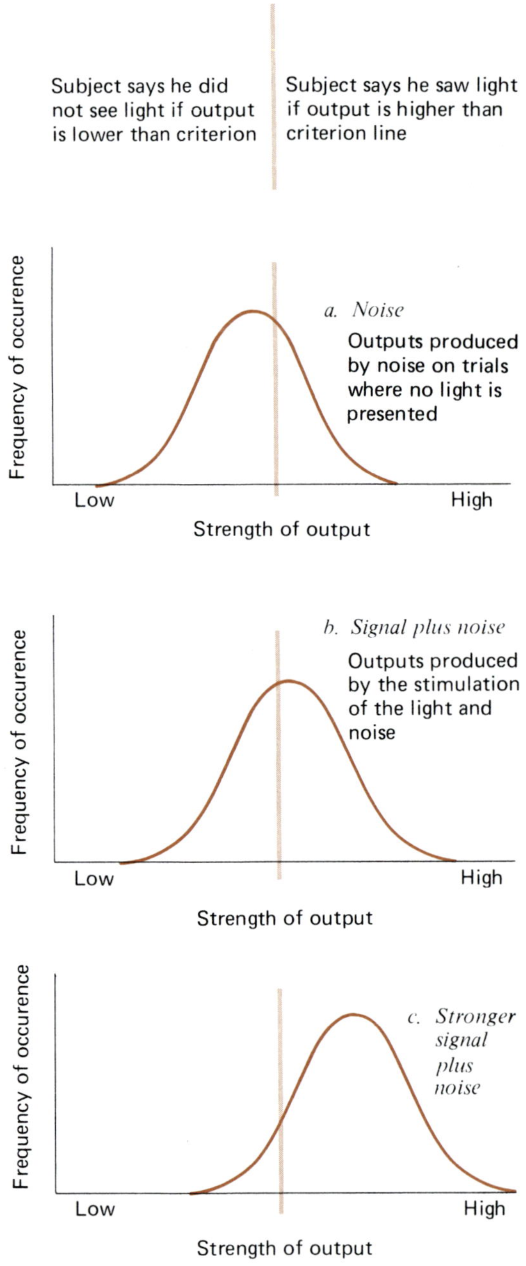

Box Figure 7.2 Output distributions.

is, a noise-alone trial—or during a trial in which a signal is present—that is, a signal-plus-noise trial. If the same output can be produced in these two kinds of trials, how do we decide whether the light was presented? Generally, as shown in the graphs, signal-plus-noise produces a stronger output than noise alone. We assume that the subject selects a minimally strong output to make a decision about whether the light is present. This is termed the *criterion output.* If the output of the feature analysis system during a given trial is above this criterion, the subject will report having seen the signal; if it is below this criterion, the subject will report that he has not seen the light. We have represented a particular criterion that a subject might select as the thick, vertical line in box figure 7.2. Notice that during some trials in which the light was absent (box fig. 7.2a), the output produced by the noise alone will be higher than the criterion. Thus if a subject uses this criterion, he will sometimes say that the light was present when it was not—he will make a false alarm response. Also, in some trials when the light is present (box fig. 7.2b), the output will be lower than criterion, and the subject will fail to detect the light—make a miss response.

Suppose that the subject wished to make fewer false alarms and therefore more correct rejections. To do this, he would have to adopt a higher criterion so that the noise-alone outputs would exceed it less frequently. Interestingly, if the subject did this, it would also increase the number of trials in which he missed seeing the light when it was presented—hits would become less frequent. Therefore, the theory of signal detection predicts that there will be a trade-off between hits and false alarms. This in fact occurs. The relationship between hits and false alarms provides a way of measuring the criterion that a particular subject adopts. When the effect of the signal remains constant, a relatively low frequency of hits and false alarms indicates a high or cautious criterion, whereas a high frequency of hits and false alarms indicates a relatively low or incautious criterion. Subjects tend to select high or low criteria depending on their personalities (e.g., how cautious they are), on the likelihood of getting a signal or a no-signal trial, and on the importance of hits, misses, false alarms, and correct rejections. A radiologist for example, may have to decide, on the basis of detecting subtle patterns in an X-ray, whether a patient should undergo a dangerous operation for cancer. In this case, the radiologist will probably adopt a high criterion to minimize the chances of a false alarm.

Is it possible for a subject to increase the frequency of hits while maintaining the same frequency of false alarms? The answer is yes. If there is some way to increase the signal's effect, it would be possible to shift the signal-plus-noise distribution farther away from the noise distribution, as shown in box figure 7.2c. The signal's effect could be increased by increasing its intensity or by modifying the feature analysis system used so that it would be more responsive to the signal. This could be produced by some artificial agent, such as a drug, or by learning a more effective set of rules and features for the task. In fact, subjects who receive feedback immediately after each trial as to whether or not a signal was presented do improve their performance as a result. Anything that increases the effect of the signal produces an increase in *sensitivity*. This increase in sensitivity is reflected by the shift of the signal-plus-noise distribution farther away from the noise distribution.

It is interesting to note that signal detection theory provides us with two means of determining how the observer's knowledge and experience influences his ability to detect a stimulus: First, knowledge of the importance of the outcome affects the selection of a criterion. Second, experience and practice can determine which feature analysis system will be used in the task and therefore determine the observer's sensitivity.

report as many letters as possible. Most observers could only report about four letters accurately. One interpretation of this result would be that because the letters were displayed briefly, only four letters scattered within the twelve-letter display were processed by the subject. Sperling, however, suggested another possibility: for a brief period, the observer had an image-like memory (a sensory memory) of all the letters on the screen, but the process of analyzing the information in the image required more time per letter than the image lasted. The subject's analysis was adequate to recognize only four of the letters scattered among the twelve letters flashed on the screen before the image faded.

To test the idea that all twelve letters were briefly available to the observer, Sperling performed what is called the *partial report experiment*. Shortly after the letters were flashed on the screen, a tone was sounded. The pitch of the tone indicated which row of letters was to be reported. Under these conditions the observer could report all four letters in the appropriate row correctly, provided that the tone immediately followed the visual stimulus. If the tone occurred much later than the visual display, the subject could not report all four letters in a row correctly.

What does the partial report experiment show? Sperling argued that if the subject had an image of all twelve letters for a brief period and if a tone, presented immediately after the visual display, told him which row he would have to report, he could then analyze all four letters in that row indicated by the tone, as opposed to four letters scattered throughout the twelve-letter display. If there were no momentary image of the entire display, and only those four scattered letters reported by the subject were seen, then the partial report experiment would not have improved performance. Thus Sperling's experiment suggests the existence of a visual memory that can briefly retain a large amount of information.

This brief visual memory has been termed an *iconic memory*. In addition, the experiment indicates that we can selectively attend to a particular portion of the information in sensory memory (e.g., a row of letters).

Selective Attention

Earlier studies of our ability to select information from iconic memory indicated that this kind of selection occurred along physical dimensions such as the row of letters in Sperling's experiment. Later research suggests that other dimensions of the information in the stimulus are used in selective processing. Studies by Mewhort et al. (1967, 1969) indicate that our knowledge of language can facilitate the extraction of information from sensory memory. These studies show that if the letters in an array form words, many more letters can be recognized correctly. These studies raise two important points. First, because higher analyses require more time, only a limited portion of the information received by the senses can be analyzed at any one time. Second, as suggested in the discussion of the analysis-by-synthesis model, the information that is selected and the quantity of information that can be handled at any given time depend on higher levels of processing which use our expectations and our ability to organize the incoming sensory events.

A similar view has been developed for auditory processing. One interesting approach in auditory studies uses what has been called the *shadowing technique*. In this paradigm, the subject hears two different messages delivered simultaneously through earphones, one to each ear, and is instructed to report or "shadow" the information coming into one ear as it is received. Usually the messages are presented rapidly enough so that he makes errors in reporting the shadowed message, which indicates that the task is difficult. Under these conditions, it appears that the subject must attend to or process the information coming into the shadowed ear at the expense of information arriving at the unattended ear. But what is he able to report about information arriving at the unattended ear after having shadowed information arriving at the other ear? He will be able to remember whether a voice was present and whether it changed from male to female, for example, and to recall unique sounds such as a whistle. However, he will usually be unable to recall the language used in the unattended ear, the content of the message, whether the language changed, or whether the message contained unintelligible sounds.

On the basis of these results, we could hypothesize that such selective listening operated very early in the processing of auditory information so that all but perhaps general physical characteristics of the unattended message were excluded from higher analysis and were therefore unavailable to the subject. However, if only one word is presented to one ear and another word to the other, and if the subject is asked to recall the unattended word soon after the listening experience, accurate recall is possible (Broadbent, 1958; 1962). This suggests that more than the general physical characteristics of the unattended message are available to the subject, for a moment at least. Perhaps the information in both ears reaches auditory sensory memory, and the selection of information represents the transfer of one of the messages from sensory memory to higher stages of analysis. Thus, during the short period over which sensory memory can retain the unattended message, information from both sources is available. During the shadowing task the subject must continuously and rapidly analyze information arriving at the attended ear; therefore, he does not have sufficient time to transfer information arriving at the unattended ear. As a result, later recall of the unattended information is extremely poor, consisting of only the most general physical characteristics of the message.

Other questions further complicate this picture. For example, how is it that we can recall even the gross physical characteristics of the unattended message if there is insufficient time to analyze the unattended information in sensory memory? A similar problem is created by experimental evidence which demonstrates that if a coherent message is transferred from the shadowed to the unshadowed ear, the subject will still follow it. Thus, if the subject is asked to shadow a sentence presented to his right ear and, unknown to him, the sentence is completed in his left ear, while an incoherent sequence of words is delivered to his right ear, the subject will report the entire sentence correctly, although a portion of it was completed in the unshadowed ear. This result would be impossible if the subject were transferring from sensory memory only that information arriving at the attended ear. Apparently, the subject performs a partial analysis of the information arriving at both ears. This partial analysis is based upon his general knowledge and expectations relating to information he received earlier; that is, from the initial portion of the sentence. The information most consistent with his knowledge and expectations is then transferred from sensory memory to higher levels of analysis. In other words, selective processing of information appears to be consistent with the view that perception is guided by and is a result of a synthesis of incoming information with our previous knowledge and expectations. Here again, we find that perception involves an interplay between multiple levels of analysis.

The analysis-by-synthesis model of perception provides us with a useful overview of the many facets of perception. It provides a means of relating the initial analysis of sensory input into features and rules, and it enables the simultaneous selection of features and rules by higher level processes that express our knowledge and experience. Furthermore, it provides a place for the important influence of learning on perception.

Summary

In this chapter we have developed a general view of perception that incorporates a number of its important aspects. Even in the simplest case, perception involves patterns of stimulation. Our ability to perceive different configurations of elements as the same pattern—for example, the sides of a square or different forms of the letter *a*—provide support for a feature analysis model of perception rather than one in which templates exist for every conceivable perceptual event. The feature analysis model proposes that perception occurs by the analysis of basic characteristics or features of patterns which are combined according to rules in which each combination represents a different pattern. Some features in visual pattern perception have been suggested by the use of the adaptation and stabilized-image techniques and by the kinds of errors made in confusion studies.

Several principles of the organization of or rules for combining features stem from the work of Gestalt psychologists and more recent concepts from information theory. The feature-analysis model of perception has also been applied to the problem of speech perception. Here one of the questions that is still under investigation is: What are the features of the speech signal and the rules by which different features are combined that allow us to recognize the basic units of speech, the phonemes? The motor theory of speech perception suggests that the features of speech recognition are those required for the production or articulation of speech. These articulatory features of speech may be speech-onset time, place of articulation, placement of the tongue, and so forth. The fact that two patterns may be perceived as the same letter, and yet differences between these two patterns can also be seen, suggests that there are multiple levels of analysis in perception. Although these levels are available to us in some cases, such as versions of the same letter, they are inaccessible in other cases, such as the case of categorical perception in speech.

Our perception of size and distance results from the integration of several sources of information, including binocular sources such as binocular disparity and convergence of the eyes and monocular sources such as motion parallax, interposition, linear perspective and texture, shading, and familiar size. Illusions result when analyzers that pick up these sources of information provide either inadequate or inaccurate information about actual size or distance.

Perception does not result merely from combinations of features and rules. It involves the synthesis or integration of incoming information, our expectations about future and immediately preceding events, and the context resulting from past experience. This analysis-by-synthesis view of perception also provides a means for considering the importance of learning, sensory memory, and selective attention in perception. Therefore, in some cases we must learn to use the appropriate set of features and rules before we can perceive certain patterns. Perception also requires information to be retained for some period in sensory memory so that there is sufficient time for it to be analyzed. Studies such as Sperling's have provided good support for sensory memory. In addition, these studies indicate that we can selectively process or attend to some portion of the information in sensory memory, but only at the expense of other information contained in it.

Jean Piaget (1896-   )
Piaget is a Swiss psychologist and philosopher who has contributed more than any other individual to our understanding of child development. Beginning with his fascinating observations of his own children in the 1920's, he has gone on to provide an elaborate theory of development which has become a major focus for child research around the world.

Alfred Binet (1857-1911)
A French psychologist, Binet initiated a systematic approach to the testing of intelligence in children. His pioneering efforts led to the development of the Stanford-Binet Intelligence Tests.

Arnold Gesell (1880-1961)
Gesell was an American psychologist who provided the first detailed normative description of behavioral development from week to week in infancy and year to year in the older child. He emphasized that individual children develop at their own pace.

Section

4

Developmental Processes and Behavior

8

Perceptual and Cognitive Development

"The child is parent of the adult" is a nonsexist paraphrase of a famous quotation from Wordsworth. It suggests that any complete understanding of adult behavior and human nature must include a knowledge of their developmental origins.

Most areas of psychology are explicitly or implicitly concerned with development. Freud's theory of personality (see Chapter 17) is actually one of personality development. Theories of perception (Chapter 7) have struggled with the developmental question of nature versus nurture since the time of such philosophers as Immanuel Kant and John Locke in the seventeenth century. Locke believed that man achieves his perceptual and conceptual capacities primarily through experience and learning; thus he characterized the mind of the newborn as a "tabula rasa," or blank slate, awaiting impressions from the world of experience. Kant believed that man is born with certain "innate categories." This view, later supported by Darwin's work on the theory of evolution, suggests that the newborn begins his life as an intelligently functioning organism, already tuned to important properties of the world in which his species evolved. We will see how developmental studies of infants emphasize the contributions of heredity in human behavior.

Jean Piaget, one of the first developmental psychologists, entered the study of child development through a philosophical interest in the nature of knowledge. However, he soon realized that the answers he sought lay in the *development* of knowledge systems and, therefore, began the first systematic study of the child's cognitive development. Thus, one of developmental psychology's basic orientations is the general *nature* of man, the forces that control his behavioral development, and the general principles by which these forces operate.

Developmental psychologists are also interested in the child for his own sake. Much of the knowledge gained from general theoretical studies may have implications for the way we raise and educate our children and deal with problems in development. For example, we know that attempts to accelerate a young child's perceptual and cognitive development are likely to fail because he is not biologically ready to understand advanced concepts or perceptual operations. We also know that inadequate intellectual and social stimulation in early childhood is likely to cause serious problems in adulthood. However, given a *normally* stimulating and supportive environment, most children grow to be healthy adults.

A considerable amount of data has been collected about American children, and average ages have been calculated for the onset of a variety of behavioral milestones such as walking and talking. We will present some of these data in Chapters 9 and 10. The most significant aspect of early behaviors is the variability in the time at which they appear in different individuals. Furthermore, the age when these behaviors appear bears little relation to the person's competence in later life. Parents who hover over their young children, anxiously marking each stage of progress, can relax. Again, given a normally supportive environment, the child is biologically programmed to grow and develop at his own rate.

The three chapters that make up this section on the development of behavior will acquaint you with the basic mechanisms and characteristics of several important foci of developmental psychology; physical, perceptual, and cognitive development; personality and social development; and psychosexual development. In addition they will provide you with some knowledge concerning an adequate environment for healthy growth. These chapters will *not* provide all you should know as parents. However, several excellent books have been written explicitly for parents; Spock's *Baby and Child Care,* for example, is a classic and still a popular book on this topic.

The developmental functions described in Chapters 9 and 10 are dependent on social interaction to a relatively large degree, while the functions reviewed in this chapter are controlled to a greater extent by genetic factors and interaction with the nonsocial, physical world. The distinction is not clear-cut, however. Some aspects of cognitive development, such as language and cognitive style, are very much dependent on the child's interactions with his parents, siblings, peers, and the larger society—the same forces that are so important for the development of his personality and socialization.

Physical Development

The infant enters the world with a variety of inborn functional capacities. He is not, as William James (1890) once believed, a totally naive organism, viewing the world as a "booming, buzzing confusion." Some of the infant's perceptual functions become surprisingly sophisticated within two months. He can perceive the distance and shape of objects. His auditory system is already tuned to deal with the sounds of language. His motor functions develop on a schedule, from reflexive behavior at birth to voluntary walking around one year of age. More advanced cognitive functions become apparent when the infant begins to talk. Basic patterns of thought continue to develop through *qualitatively* different stages as he progresses through childhood and adolescence. But, let's begin at the beginning.

Prenatal Development

The Chinese designate a person's age as the time since his birthday, plus one year. This method of calculating age reflects the notion that an individual's life begins at conception, long before he trades the intrauterine environment for the external world. Between conception and birth, all the basic organs have developed to an advanced state, capable of supporting the infant in his new world. His motor behavior, although still relatively reflexive, began to develop long before birth.

A survey of the major stages of prenatal physical and behavioral growth reveals several important developmental principles. After the egg is fertilized to form the zygote, it divides by the process of mitosis (described in Chapter 2) as it migrates down the mother's fallopian tube. After about seven days of cell division and growth, the zygote attaches to the uterine wall, thus beginning the *embryonic stage* of development. Two fluid-filled protective membranes, the *amnion* and *chorion,* surround the embryo. Life-giving oxygen and nutrients from the maternal *placenta* are passed to the embryo through the *umbilical cord,* and the stage is set for rapid development. Genetically programmed *differentiation* of bodily structures occurs during the embryo's first two months. By the end of the second month, all the major organs have begun to develop, and sexual differentiation occurs with the secretion of *androgen* (sex hormones).

The embryonic stage of development is a *critical period.* Certain drugs and diseases that have little or no effect if introduced at later stages may have catastrophic effects at this time. A tragic example is the drug *Thalidomide,* which was widely used during the early 1960s in European countries as a sleeping pill and nausea preventive. Women who took the drug between the fourth and sixth weeks of pregnancy often had severely deformed children; however, no deformities resulted if the drug was introduced after the third month, after the critical period of development. Similarly, if a woman has German measles (rubella) during the first two or three months of pregnancy, the infant may show a variety of defects, including blindness and deafness. The particular defect depends on the time of infection because the critical period varies for different organs. Generally speaking, the probability of defects decreases if the disease is contracted later in pregnancy; usually no damaging effects result after the fourth month. (See box 8.1 for a further discussion of prenatal environment.)

Organs continue to grow and become more finely differentiated, and motor behavior begins to emerge during the third month, thus beginning the *fetal stage.* At the beginning of the third month, the fetus is only about an inch long, its hands and feet are stubby, its fingers and toes are not fully developed, and its first motor behavior is reflexive. When touched the nine-week-old fetus will respond by flexing the trunk and extending the head. At the end of three months, the fetus is about three inches long and weighs about three quarters of an ounce. Spontaneous movements begin to occur and may be noticed by the mother in the fourth month. Plate 8 shows the development of the fetus from four weeks to over four months.

Seven months after conception, the fetus weighs about 2½ pounds and is roughly fifteen inches long. Infants born at this age have about a fifty-fifty chance of surviving if placed in the protective environment of an incubator because the systems that regulate some of the basic bodily functions, such as temperature maintenance, have not yet fully matured. Although the premature infant will continue to develop, following the same pattern as if he had remained in the uterus for the full term, most infants that are born prematurely fall behind in their early physical and behavioral growth rates. Most of them will catch up by the end of the first year after birth.

Box 8.1

Prenatal Environment

The bloodstreams of the fetus and mother do not mix. They are separated by the placenta, which acts as a semipermeable membrane. Pores in the placental barrier are too small for the blood cells but are large enough to pass the molecules of needed substances such as oxygen and food.

Drugs also pass from mother to fetus through the placental barrier. The effects of Thalidomide, as discussed, were disastrous, but other more commonly used drugs affect the fetus in more subtle ways. Nicotine, for example, accelerates the fetal heart rate. Pregnant women who are heavy smokers show a much higher incidence of premature births (18.6 percent versus 11.2 percent for nonsmokers), and their infants generally weigh less than those of nonsmokers. Women who are addicted to drugs such as heroin and methodone, may also have premature or underweight babies. After birth, the addicted infant must be withdrawn from these drugs gradually. The effects of psychedelic drugs, such as LSD and Mescaline, are as yet unknown but could be dangerous.

The *nutritional* needs of the fetus are supplied from the mother's blood and, therefore, her nutritional state affects that of the fetus. Poor nutrition is particularly detrimental during the last three months of pregnancy, when the fetus is growing rapidly and the mother's reserves may be exhausted. Well-nourished mothers generally have fewer complications during pregnancy and their infants are healthier and grow taller.

Although the fetus has no direct neural attachments to the mother, he may be influenced by her *emotional state.* When strong emotions are aroused in the mother, her endocrine glands secrete adrenalin and other hormones into the bloodstream. These substances enter the fetus's blood and affect his nervous system. Prolonged and severe emotional stress during the embryonic stage of development may result in harelip and cleft palate. Later in pregnancy, the fetus responds to the mother's stress with increased movement. Infants born to stressful mothers tend to be irritable and overactive. Because hormonal effects should wear off after the infant is separated from his mother's blood supply, the cause of postnatal problems is not clear. The infant's nervous system may have been altered prenatally, or he may learn to be irritable after birth from an overanxious parent or caretaker.

Birth

Nine months is the normal period of intrauterine development. The average full-term infant weighs about 7½ pounds and is twenty inches long. The birth process itself may have critical effects on the individual. Otto Rank's fanciful theory of personality suggests that the infant suffers great trauma when he is introduced into the external world and that life then becomes a search for the lost comfort of the womb. But when you see how well prepared and eager the infant is to interact with the world, you will understand why Rank's theory has been severely criticized. The one major potential danger of childbirth is the loss of life-supporting oxygen. The fetus receives oxygen from the mother by way of the umbilical cord. If the birth process is difficult and the supply of oxygen through the cord is cut off for even a few minutes, the infant may die or suffer serious brain damage. Even mild *anoxia* (oxygen deficiency) may affect later development. Infants who have had difficult births tend to develop more slowly during the first few years of life. Although most of them catch up as they grow older, some continue to lag behind in intellectual and physical development. Fortunately, modern medical practices have reduced the incidence of this problem to a minimum. Also, increased use of natural childbirth methods is reducing the complications that can be caused by administering powerful anesthetics to the mother during birth.

Infant Reflexes

The infant's first cries are ample proof that one of his basic life-support reflexes—breathing—is operating. Other basic reflexes necessary for his survival include sucking, digestion, and elimination. The *rooting reflex* plays an important role in the infant's early feeding behavior. If touched on the side of the cheek, the infant will turn his head in the appropriate direction to contact the object with his mouth (see fig. 8.1 a-c). His first efforts are clumsy, but within a few days, he zeroes in quite accurately on the bottle or mother's nipple. This is one of the first clear signs of learning in his natural environment.

Several interesting infant reflexes have no obvious survival value but may have been functionally important in man's evolutionary history. The *grasping,* or *"Darwinian"* reflex is so strong that the newborn can almost support his own weight with his hands wrapped around a rod. The *moro* reflex occurs when the infant is moved suddenly or dropped on his back. His body tenses, he reaches out, and then draws his arms in toward his body as if he was hugging something. The behavior of our tree-dwelling ancestors indicates a possible reason for these reflexes in our evolutionary history. Monkey infants must cling to their mother's abdomen soon after birth.

As the human cortex develops control over behavior, the more primitive reflexes disappear in favor of voluntary motor behavior (e.g., the moro and "Darwinian" reflexes, which seem to be controlled by lower brain centers, usually disappear by the time the infant is six months old). However, primitive reflexes may reappear under certain conditions. For instance, the presence of the *Babinsky reflex*—a fanning of the toes when the sole of the foot is stimulated—is commonly

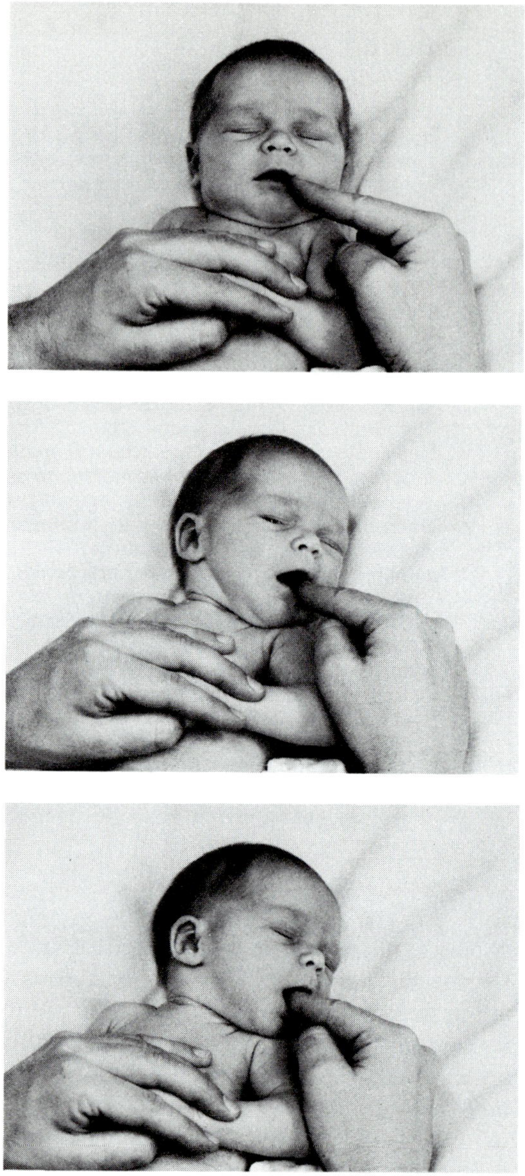

Figure 8.1 The *rooting* response is observed when the infant's cheek is touched. He turns his head and tries to contact the object with his mouth. (From Prechtl, H. and Beintema, D., "The neurological examination of the fullterm newborn infant." *Little Club Clinics in Developmental Medicine* 12, 41. London: Spastics Society Medical Information Unit and William Neinemann Medical Books, Ltd., 1964. Reprinted by permission of Spastics International Medical Publications and H. Prechtl.)

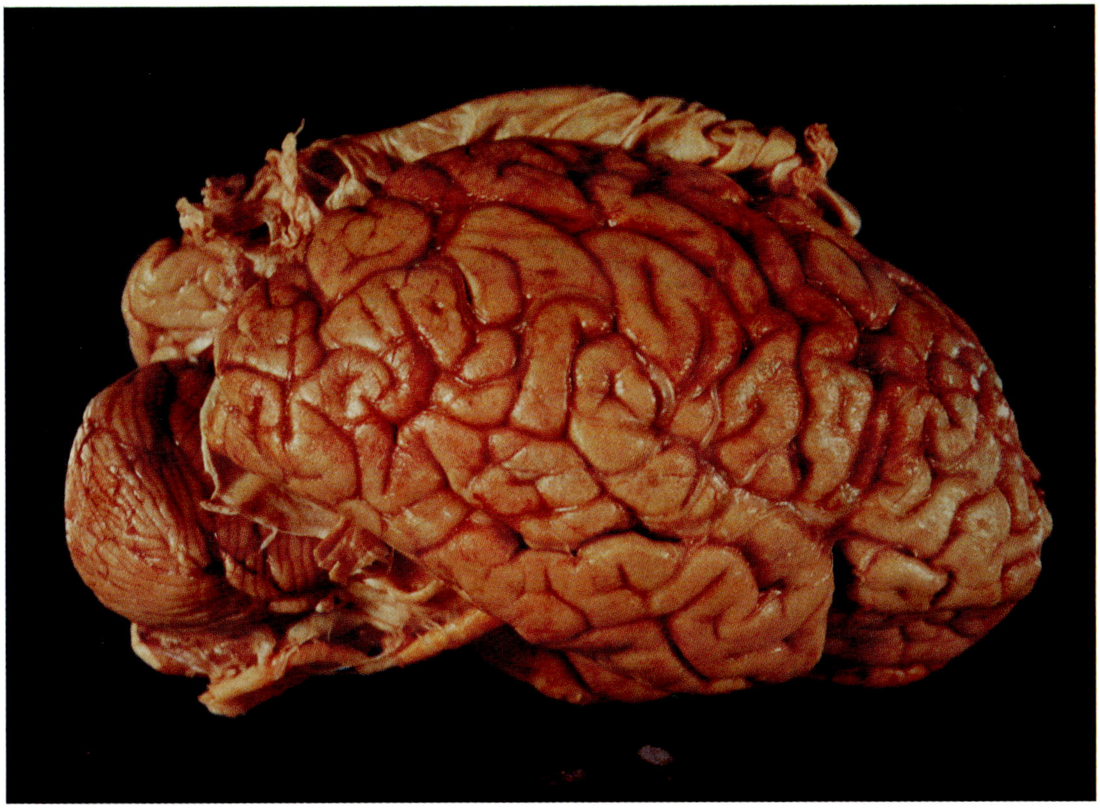

Plate 6 The human brain.
(Photo courtesy Camera M. D.
Studio.)

Plate 7 Perception of depth in pictures. Although the picture's surface is flat, we use information such as "overlap" and "height in the field" to determine that the green house is farther away than the red house. Children raised in Western cultures do quite well at this by age three. (Photo by R. Olson.)

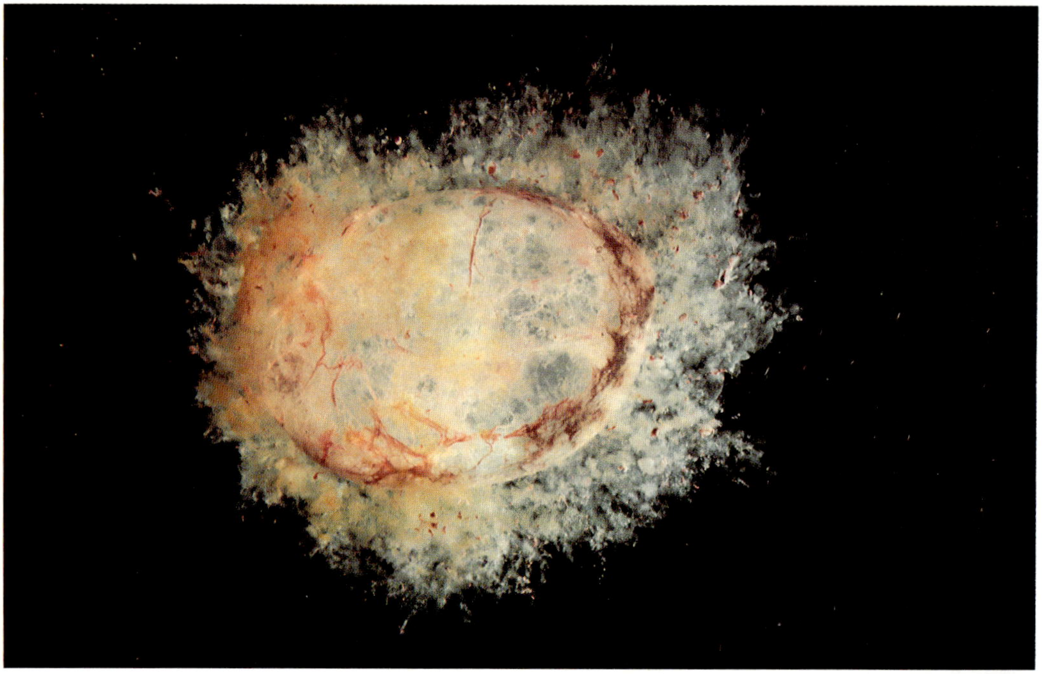

a. 4 weeks

Plate 8 Various stages of fetal development. (Photos a, d—Carlo Bevilacqua Scala. Photos b, c, e, © Donald Yeager, 1975.)

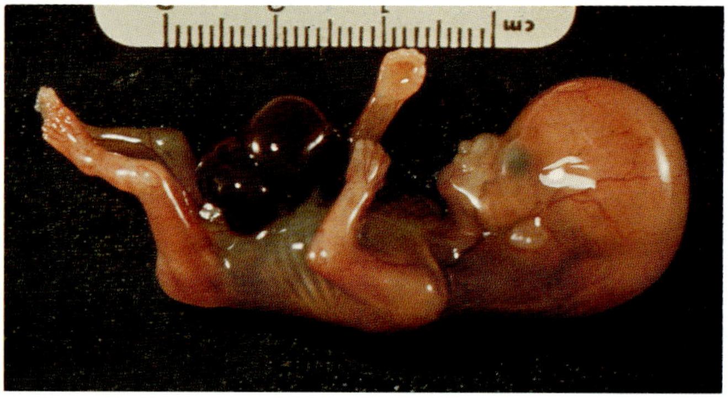

b. 5 weeks

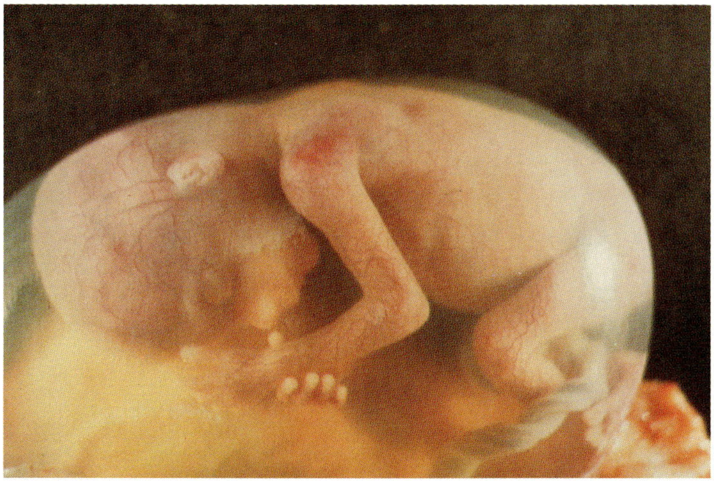

c. 12 weeks

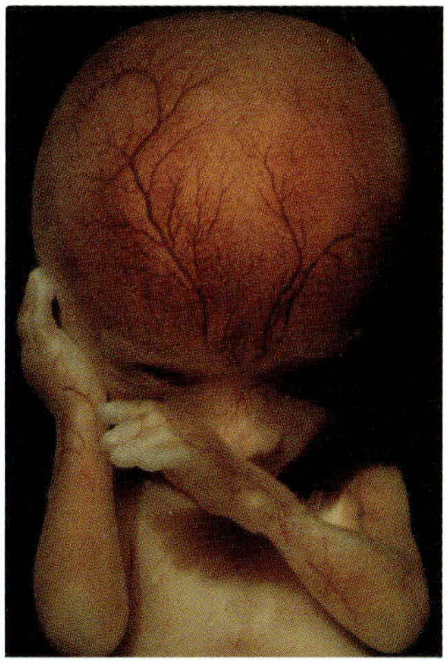

d. 14 weeks

e. facial close-up, age unspecified

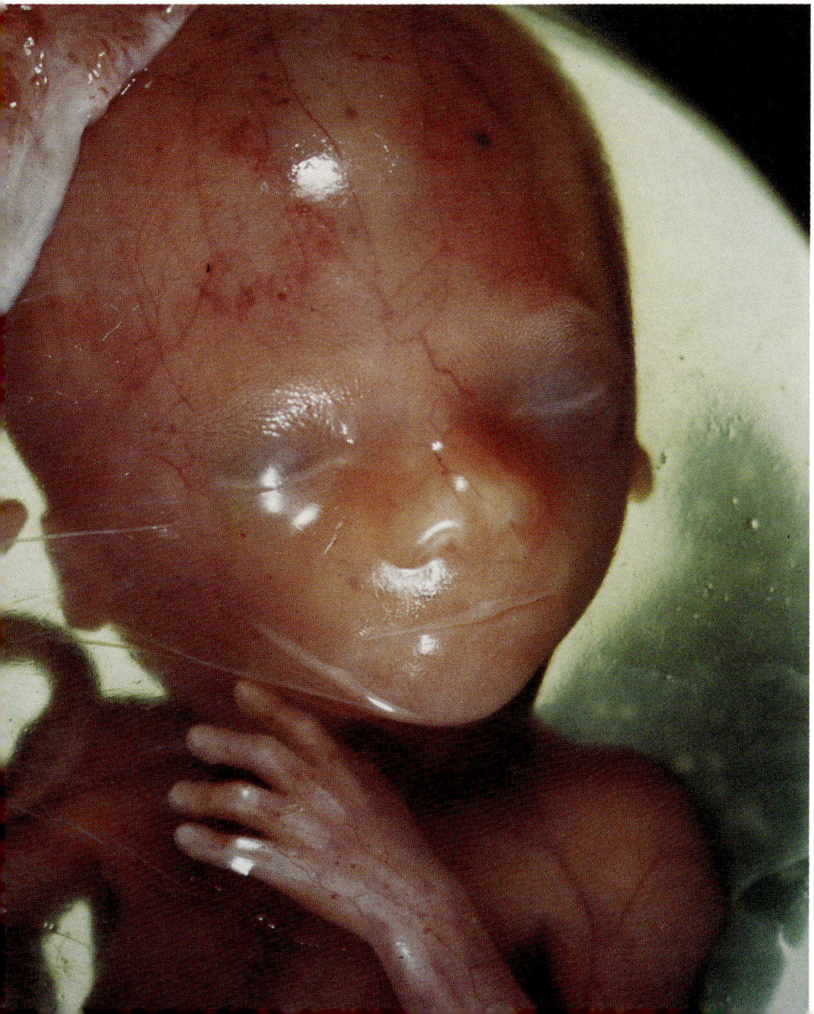

Plate 9 The Chinese Moon Goddess, Kwan-Yin. (Courtesy Nelson Gallery-Atkins Museum, Kansas City, Mo. Nelson Fund.)

used to indicate cortical brain damage in adults.

One set of reflexes that the parents or caretakers would be happy to see disappear earlier involves the excretory functions. Infants urinate reflexively to pressure in the bladder until they are about eighteen months old (on the average). Although they can be conditioned much earlier to urinate when set on the pot, they will be unable to withhold urination voluntarily until the neural mechanisms for control have sufficiently matured.

Learning in the Newborn

Because the newborn infant's rapid modification of the rooting reflex suggests that he is able to learn as soon as he enters the world, it is surprising that developmental psychologists have often failed to demonstrate learning in young infants. The problem seems to lie in the kind of learning they have studied. *Classical conditioning* procedures pair a new stimulus with a stimulus that is already capable of eliciting a response. Repeated pairings may then lead to a response when the new stimulus is presented alone. For example, after repeated pairings of a bottle of milk and the sound of a bell, sometimes the newborn will show a conditioned sucking response to the sound of the bell alone. Many studies, however, fail to show classical conditioning in infants.

Recent studies of infant learning have focused on another type of learning situation, *instrumental or operant conditioning*. Here, the contingencies to be learned shift from a simple relation between external events as in classical conditioning to a relation between the infant's *behavior* and an *external event*. Papousek (1969) presented two-month-old infants with a situation where they could turn on a light by moving their heads to the left. The initial response occurred by accident, but one accident was usually enough for the infant to learn this response. He would then make a few more responses and, apparently, lose interest. One way of reinstating responding was to make the light contingent on turning his head to the right. Only by changing the behavior-stimulus contingencies could the infant's responses be maintained. The infants learned fairly complex sequences such as right-right-left-left by actively trying different sequences until they discovered the correct one. Then after a few correct responses, they again lost interest. These studies have helped change our view of the infant as a passive nonlearning organism to one that regards him as an active and remarkably intelligent tester of hypotheses about his behavior and the external world. Lipsit (1969) has even suggested that some kinds of learning occur more rapidly in infants than in adults! The young infant's learning ability has recently been used to ask fascinating questions about his perceptual and cognitive views of the world. We will consider some of these questions in a later section.

Voluntary Motor Behavior and Maturation

As the infant becomes more capable of *differentiating* and *integrating* his movements, voluntary motor behavior gradually develops. At first, the arms move together. The prone infant at three months will reach toward an object with both hands. Control appears first over the upper arms and gradually extends to the lower arms, hands, and fingers. Independent movement of the fingers is not achieved until about the eighth month, when the forefinger will curl around an object. This trend in which control progresses from central (proximal) to more peripheral (distal) regions of the body is called *proximodistal development*. These increases in *differentiation* of motor control are complemented by an increase in ability to *integrate* and coordinate different bodily movements (see fig. 8.2).

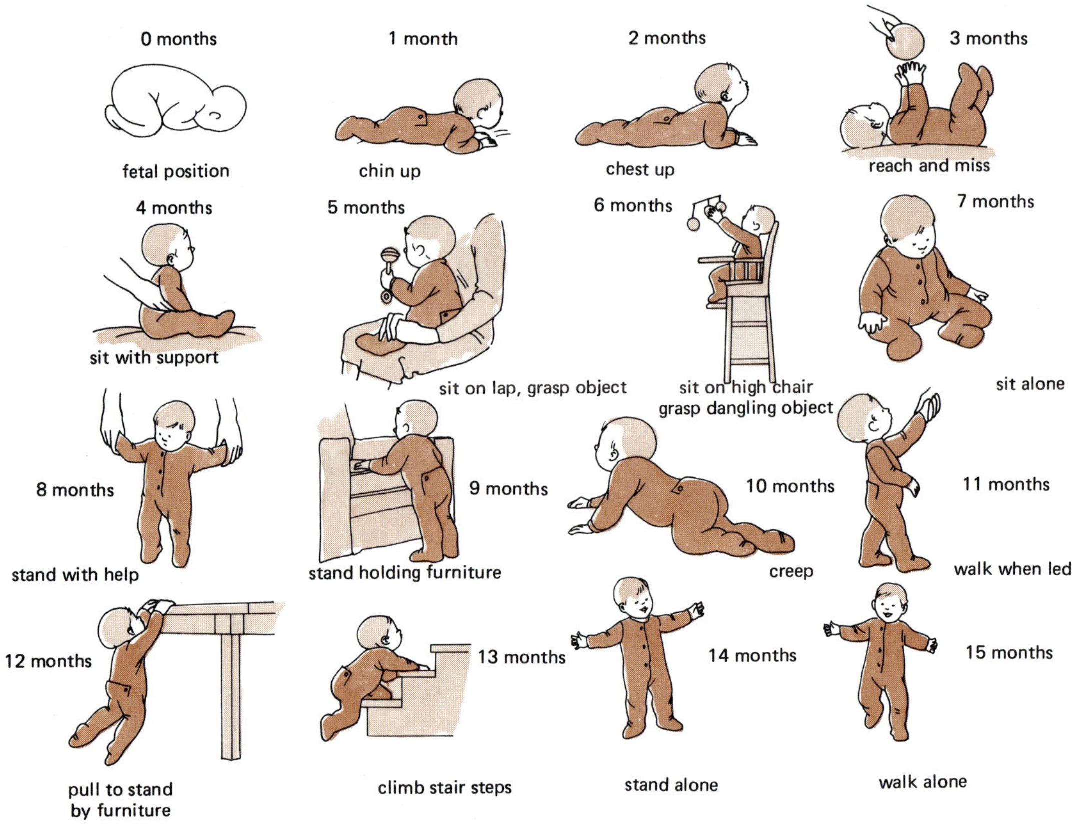

Figure 8.2 Stages of motor behavior leading to walking. The ages noted for each behavioral milestone are averages. Later studies reveal that the average ages at which these behaviors occur are now slightly younger. (Adapted from Shirley, M.M., *The First Two Years,* Institute of Child Welfare Monograph, No. 7. Copyright 1933 University of Minnesota Press; renewed copyright 1961 University of Minnesota Press. By permission of the publisher.)

The older the child, the more capable he is of complex motor activities, such as those involved in playing baseball or driving a car.

Walking is one of the most notable milestones in the development of motor behavior. Parents often look forward to the infant's first steps and try to teach him to walk by holding him upright by his hands. One interesting cross-cultural study suggests that special training and experience have little influence on the infant's walking behavior. For centuries, the Hopi Indians of North America confined their infants on cradle boards until around nine months of age (see fig. 8.3). Despite their confinement and lack of practice, Hopi infants walk at about the same age as infants from other cultures. A study *within* the Hopi culture compared two groups of

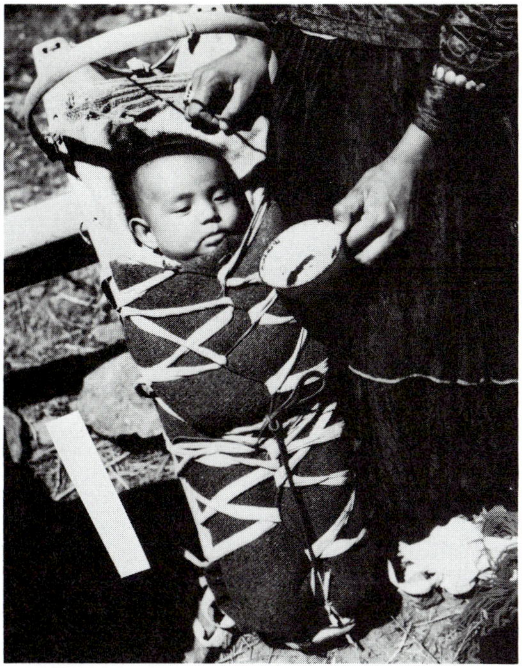

Figure 8.3 The Hopi cradleboard. Although restricted to the cradleboard until they are about nine months old, Hopi infants walk at approximately the same age as other infants. (From Photoworld-FPG.)

infants—one raised in the traditional cradle boards, the other without restraint. Both groups walked at virtually the same age (Dennis and Dennis, 1940). Thus development of a motor function as basic as walking apparently follows a *biological maturational* schedule based on genetic programming, and is surprisingly independent of environmental variations. Many other stages in infant motor behavior, such as rolling over, sitting up, and the disappearance of primitive reflexes, also seem to follow a biologically set sequence. The individual differences in the age at which these behaviors emerge also seem to be largely controlled by genetics. Identical twins, reared apart or together, will reach these milestones of motor behavior at about the same age. Although more complex and specialized motor tasks are dependent on specialized learning, the child's *readiness* to learn them may also depend on his *maturational level.*

What precisely do we mean by *maturational level? Both* genetics and environment are important factors in development, and genetic propensities are expressed only through their *interaction* with environmental variables. This is true for all aspects of development. The challenge to developmental psychologists is to discover the nature of this interaction. As we discussed in the context of walking, the term *maturation* is used when the occurrence of developmental changes seems relatively independent of *normal* environmental variation and when most of the individual variation in the time of emergence is closely associated with genetic programming. Keep in mind that large variations in the environment can have a marked influence on the maturational rate of physical growth and behavior. The *secular trend* (historical changes in adult height) described in box 8.2 is one example.

Physical Growth

Maturational factors are most clearly present in physical development. Comparisons of identical twins provide ample evidence that even minute physical characteristics are based on genetic makeup and that the milestones of physical development generally follow a tight maturational schedule. Ossification (hardening) of the bones, appearance of teeth, and the onset of puberty all emerge with biological regularity and show genetically based individual differences. Some infants have their first tooth at birth; others may not cut one until they are a year old. The average age is about seven months.

In extensive studies on growth curves for physical variables such as height, Tanner (1970) found that individual growth follows a definite *trajectory* (see figs. 8.4, 8.5, and 8.6). Large deviations from this maturational path may be produced by a severe environ-

Box 8.2

The Secular Trend

Variability in rates of maturation is largely controlled by genetic factors, if environmental influences are held fairly constant. Under such conditions, identical female twins usually reach puberty within two months of one another, while the average difference is ten months for nonidentical sisters.

Environmental influences on rates of maturation are reflected in the secular *trend* (see box fig. 8.2). For example, we know that the average ages for onset of menstruation and pubertal growth have been steadily decreasing since 1830, when the first reliable data were obtained. In the United States, for example, the average age of onset of menstruation shifted from 14.2 years in 1905 to 12.6 years in 1960. In addition, there has been a change in average adult height; individuals born relatively recently tend to be slightly taller.

Although the causes of the secular trend have not been precisely specified, there are some likely possibilities. First, and perhaps most important, is the improvement in nutrition, particularly with respect to increased protein and calorie intake during early infancy. Second, growth-inhibiting childhood diseases are less frequent. Geneticists suggest that the increase in average height may be related to an increase in outbreeding (mating with an individual from outside one's own group), which in turn has enhanced the expression of dominant genes for stature.

Trends toward increased height are still continuing in Europe, but there is some evidence that the trend is leveling off in America's affluent populations.

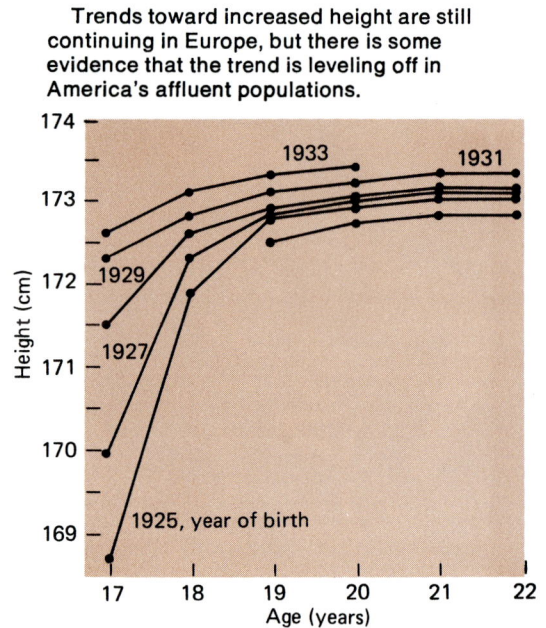

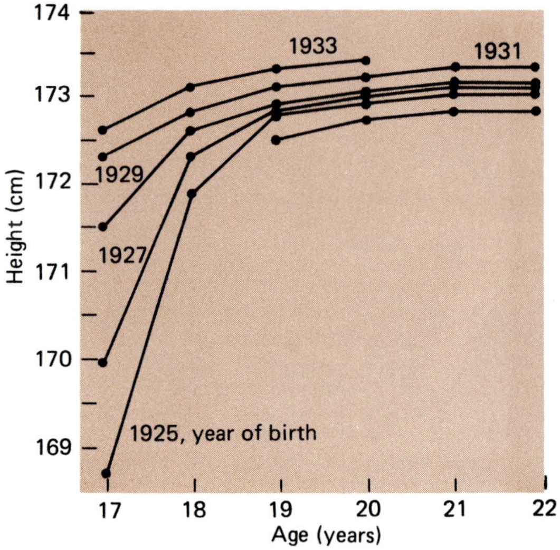

Box Figure 8.2 The secular trend. These curves show growth patterns of French university students born in different years. Note that the students who were born more recently achieved maximum height earlier and were slightly taller than those born earlier. (From Tanner, J. M., "Physical growth" in *Carmichael's manual of child psychology, Vol. 1,* 3rd edition, P. H. Mussen (Ed.). Copyright 1970 by John Wiley and Sons, Inc.)

mental insult, such as malnutrition or serious illness, but afterward, the pattern of growth tends to return to the original trajectory, a process referred to as *canalization.*

The anxious parent should be reassured that the time of emergence of early infant behaviors such as walking and even early physical growth patterns does not predict later development to any significant degree. The child who walks at thirteen months is likely to be as coordinated and physically competent as the child who walked at ten months.

Perceptual Development

How does the world look, feel, and sound to the infant? This is a difficult question to answer because the human infant's means of communication are rather limited. At least a year will pass before he can tell us much through language, and his voluntary motor responses generally consist of poorly coordinated movements of his arms, legs, and head. Superficially, the infant appears to be making little sense of his world. Until recently, James's description of the infant's experience as a

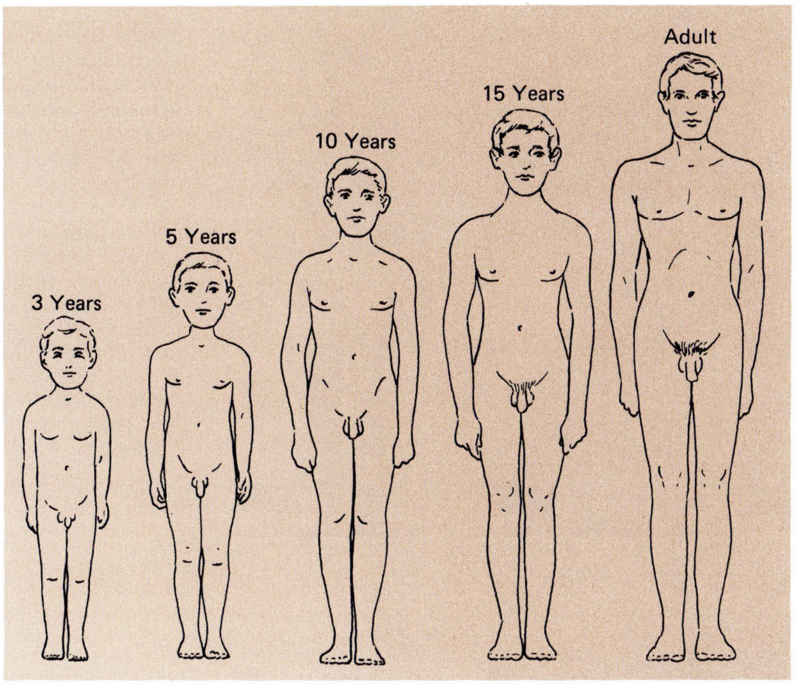

Figure 8.4 The same boy at six different ages. Note that although his head is proportionately much larger than the rest of his body initially, its actual size increases at a much slower rate over the years. (Courtesy of Hubbard Scientific Company. © 1968 by Hubbard Scientific.)

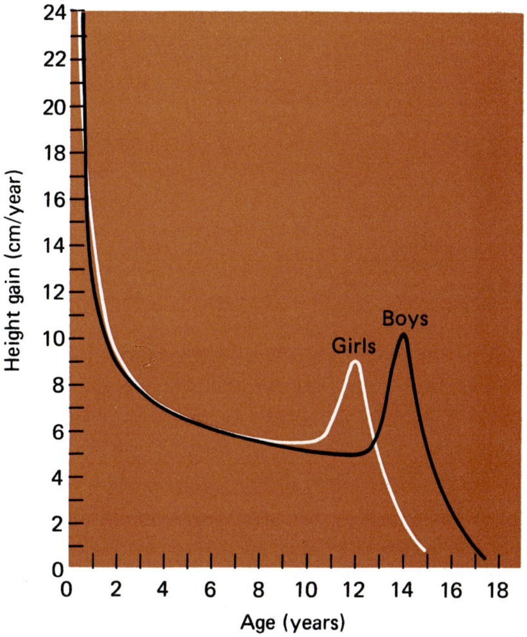

Figure 8.5 Growth curves. These curves are for average individuals. The peaks in the boys' and girls' growth curves coincide with approximate times of puberty. Note that the most rapid changes in height occur during infancy. (From Tanner, J.M., "Physical growth," in *Carmichael's manual of child psychology. Vol. 1,* 3rd edition, P.H. Mussen (Ed.). Copyright 1970 by John Wiley & Sons, Inc. Reprinted by permission.)

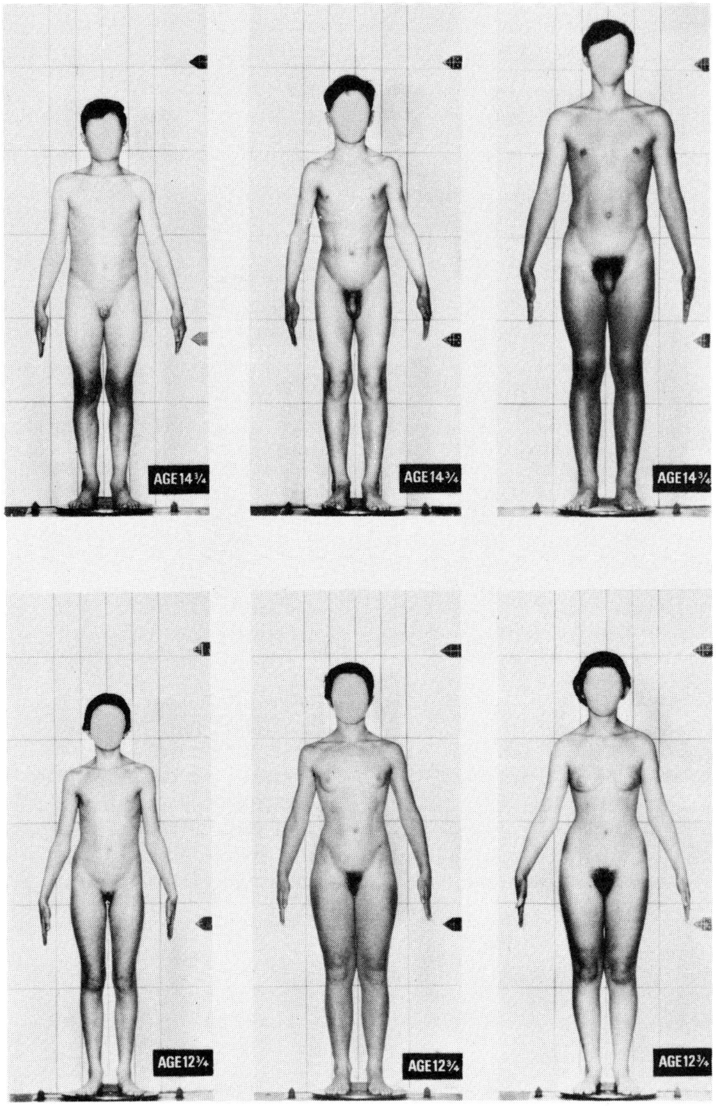

Figure 8.6 Individual differences in physical maturity. Although these children are the same chronological age, their physical maturity varies considerably. The range of differences pictured here are not unusual, and such variability may have important social and emotional consequences. (From Tanner, J.M., "Physical growth" in *Carmichael's manual of child psychology, Vol. 1,* 3rd edition, P.H. Mussen (Ed.). Copyright 1970 by John Wiley & Sons, Inc. Photo courtesy of J.M. Tanner.)

"booming, buzzing confusion" seemed quite reasonable. His view also fit well with the traditional theoretical orientations of English and American psychology, which placed a heavy emphasis on learning to account for human behavior development. How then could the inexperienced infant "know" anything? His mind had to be, in Locke's words, a "tabula rasa," or blank tablet.

Although there always was ample evidence that this view of behavioral development had to be wrong, the remarkable capacities of human infants were not generally recognized until new theoretical orientations and research methods were developed, largely within the past fifteen years. During this time, articles on infant behavior have occupied a major portion of developmental psychology journals, and new and exciting discoveries are being reported all the time (e.g., Bower, 1974).

Perception in Infancy

The behavior of many animals during infancy suggests that we should not underestimate the human infant's perceptual sophistication. The mountain goat is a striking example of precocious sensory and motor behavior. Because he is born on precarious cliffs and ledges and is able to walk the first day of life, his perceptual system must be tuned to the dangers of falling off a cliff. The fact that this species survives attests to an advanced level of perceptual development at birth.

Gibson and Walk (1961) have tested a variety of animals on a laboratory version of a cliff. It is called the "visual cliff" because the deep side is covered with a sheet of glass (see fig. 8.7). Animals can be tested for their responses to the cliff without danger of injury. As we would expect from his behavior in the natural environment, a day-old mountain goat will not step on the glass covering the deep side. The behavior of other newborn animals, however, varies in apparent relation to their natural environment. Kittens, for example, will wander over the cliff when their eyes have first opened, but they will avoid the cliff after a few days of visual experience. This experience need not include a fall, as might be predicted by those who explain perceptual development in terms of learning. Like the mountain goat, the kitten's apparatus for visual perception is highly developed, but its natural environment does not require such precocious behavior at birth.

What do these experimental results say about the behavior of human infants? We should not make the mistake of drawing direct parallels, but the biological view of evolution and the similarities among species suggest that we should take a closer look at the human infant's seemingly naive behavior.

Figure 8.7 The visual cliff. The baby willingly crawls to his mother over the shallow side, but he will not crawl over the glass-covered deep side. (Photo courtesy Monkmeyer Press Photo Service.)

Gibson and Walk (1961) did so, using the same basic apparatus used for testing animals. Infants six months and older (about crawling age) were placed on the center board of the visual cliff. Their mothers then called to them from either the deep or shallow side of the cliff. Twenty-four out of twenty-seven infants crawled to their mothers across the shallow side, but only three would crawl over the deep side. In other words, the infants were sensitive, not only to the visual depth, but to its potential danger. It is interesting to note that their motor behavior did not always match their perceptual sophistication. In turning themselves around to go across the shallow side, many infants would allow their legs to rest on the glass over the deep side, a sure fall without the glass.

This fascinating demonstration of the infant's perceptual abilities leaves several important questions unanswered. It does not tell us, for example, which perceptual functions are present at birth or how the six-month-old infant's abilities are related to experience. Certainly most, if not all, of Gibson's and Walk's subjects had experienced some sort of fall, so perhaps they learned to avoid the deep side in the "school of hard knocks." It is also possible that their very ability to see the difference between the deep and shallow sides was based largely on learning. Unfortunately, it is difficult to test such questions about perceptual sensitivity because the motor behavior of infants younger than six months is limited. A three-month-old infant would be unable to crawl off the center board.

In 1970, a research team at Denver University (Campos et al.) devised an ingenious method of testing a group of two-month-old infants; they simply placed their subjects over the deep or shallow side and monitored changes in heart rate. They predicted that if the infants were sensitive to depth, heart rate should go up over the deep side because they would be fearful and aroused. The actual result was surprising and informative. The in-

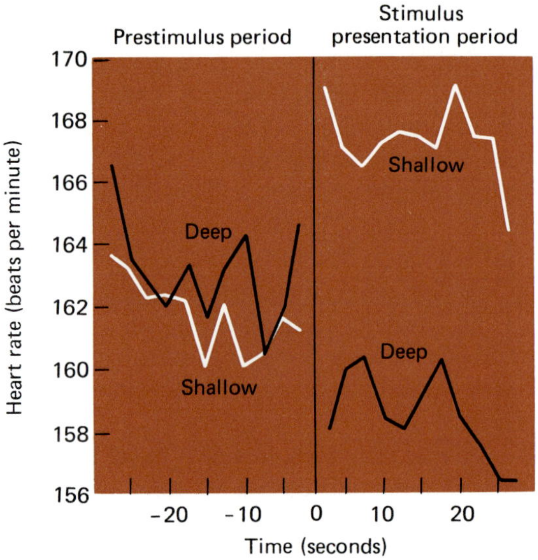

Figure 8.8 When 55-day-old infants were placed on their stomachs over the visual cliff, their heart rates went up over the shallow side and down on the deep side. Apparently they could see the depth, but were not afraid of it. (From "Cardiac Responses on the Visual Cliff in Prelocomotor Human Infants," Campos, J. J. et al., *Science* Vol. 170, pp. 196–197, Fig. 1, 9 October 1970. Copyright 1970 by the American Association for the Advancement of Science.)

fants' heart rates went *down* on the deep side and *up* on the shallow side (see fig. 8.8). Observation of the infants' general behavior suggested a likely reason for the unexpected results. Infants on the shallow side were on an uninteresting sheet of glass with a textured surface immediately beneath. Thus they soon became bored, restless, and agitated, and their heart rates increased. Because the deep side was novel and therefore much more interesting, the infants were attentive, not frightened, and their heart rates went down. (This is also a common reaction in attentive adults.) The infants' physiological responses to the two sides indicated sensitivity to the difference in depth. Their interest and apparent lack of fear over the deep side suggested that infants need to take a few falls and *learn* their fear of depth. However, this fear could be biologically programmed to emerge when the infant begins to crawl. So far, no controlled experiments have been done to resolve this issue.

Visual Depth and Size Constancy

The ability of human infants to perceive depth in visual space has a more important function than the avoidance of falls. Before six months of age, they are not mobile enough to be in much danger anyway. What could be the functional significance of visual depth in a preambulatory infant? The answer is perceptual *constancy.*

The ability to perceive the size of an object accurately, despite variations in the distance from which you observe the object, is something you take for granted. As you approach an object, its *image* on your retina increases in size proportionately with the change in distance (see fig. 8.9). However, your perceptual experience is generally one of a *constant-sized* object at varying distances. Under normal conditions, your perceptual system automatically evaluates information for visual depth and enables you to perceive a constant world, despite the changing images on your retina. Earlier views of perceptual development held that size constancy had to be *learned* by moving closer to and away from objects, then confirming their actual size by touch. Because the young infant could not have such experiences with objects beyond his reach, his visual world had to be a constantly changing flux of visual images and objects; a "booming, buzzing confusion." However, recent evidence indicates that the infant's visual world is far more orderly than the learning hypothesis suggests.

In an ingenious series of studies, Bower (1966) showed that two-month-old infants have size constancy and several other basic perceptual functions. He demonstrated the existence of these abilities by using a procedure borrowed from learning theory—*instrumental conditioning.* The problem was how to get the infant to tell what he saw. Bower's solution was to take a fairly simple response, a turn of the head, and to train the infant to make that response in the experiment. Training proceeded as follows: The infant was placed in a baby chair, and a thirty-centimeter cube was placed on the table one meter in front of him. When this stimulus was present *and* when the baby turned his head, the experimenter jumped up from beneath the table and said "peek-a-boo." (Head turning was not rewarded when the cube was absent.) The infants apparently appreciated the "peek-a-boo" game, because they soon learned to turn their heads rapidly when the cube was present.

The next step was to test for *size constancy.* Bower did this by presenting each infant with a thirty-centimeter cube, nine feet away (*same object,* different distance, different retinal image); a ninety-centimeter cube, three meters away (different object, different distance, *same retinal image*); and a ninety-centimeter cube, one meter away (different object, *same distance,* different retinal image). Bower's two-month-old subjects gen-

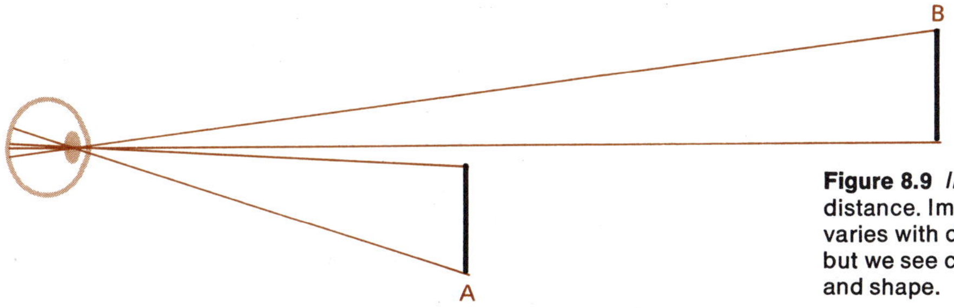

Figure 8.9 *Image* size and distance. Image size and shape varies with distance and slant, but we see constant *object* size and shape.

eralized their head-turning response most often to the same object (fifty-eight turns), next most often to the same distance (fifty-four turns), and least often to the same image (twenty-two turns). In other words, two-month-old babies use their ability to perceive depth to perceive a constant world where an object's size and identity do not change with distance and the size of the image. Bower then did another study using rectangles viewed at different angles and again found that infants usually generalize their responses to the same object rather than to a different object with the same retinal image. Further tests indicated that the sources of depth information necessary for perceptual constancy were *motion parallax* and *binocular disparity,* which were described in Chapter 6.

Rather than total confusion, infants see some degree of consistency in their world and after very little experience. Although they certainly learn some things during the first two months of life, it seems likely that much of their early perceptual capacity to deal with visual space is based on genetically programmed structures and operations. Along with other species of animals, we have evolved in a world where we must deal with visual space, sounds, smells, and so forth. Given a limited life span, there would not be enough time to "learn" important functions, such as the perception of space, that are necessary for survival. As a result, our nervous systems and perceptual apparatus have already developed to an advanced state by the time we are born.

Space Perception

If some basic mechanisms of space perception are operative at two months of age, what is left for learning and the influence of environment? One major aspect of perceptual learning is an increase in *precision* of spatial judgments. Another is the ability to use the information to perceive depth in pictures (see plate 7). Cross-cultural studies have shown that persons raised in pictureless cultures have difficulty interpreting and seeing depth in pictures. When this ability develops in our picture-rich culture is also being investigated. The evidence suggests that two- and three-year-old American children—already exposed extensively to television and picture books—have developed the ability to see pictorial depth (Olson, 1975). A third example of developmental changes in space perception is an increase in the child's ability to perform *abstract* spatial operations. The youngest children are quite good at operating on *direct* spatial information and seeing where things are from their own point of view. However, *imagining* how a scene might look from *another* point of view requires the ability to manipulate space abstractly, and children younger than five are not very good at this. Piaget, in his original experiments on this problem termed the young child's behavior "egocentric"; that is, he is unable to take a point of view other than his own. The concept of *egocentrism* will reappear in somewhat different forms when we consider Piaget's views of cognitive and social development.

Pattern Perception

In addition to knowing *where* things are (space perception), we need to know *what* they are (pattern perception). The newborn's ability to see and discriminate patterns is somewhat limited. His eyes focus at a point about seven inches from his face (about right for looking at his hands). He can track a moving object with jerky eye movements, but does not do much systematic or voluntary visual searching. Visual contours are fixated, but the infant appears to "lock" on to them. His nervous system is already uniquely sensitive to contours, but he is not yet ready to fixate on successive parts of a pattern. The newborn's visual system seems basically reflexive. After two months, he has a reasonably good range of focus; his eyes move together in smooth sweeps to follow an object and his gaze will shift to different parts of a figure that interest him. But what does he see?

One common method of testing an infant's pattern perception is to observe his *fixation preferences.* Two patterns are presented side by side, and the experimenter observes which one the baby is looking at. If he fixates on one pattern more than the other, the experimenter infers that the infant must notice some difference.

Investigators have focused on two major aspects of infant pattern perception: responses to *complexity* and *human faces.* Generally, the optimal amount of complexity an infant prefers to look at increases with age. Perhaps this reflects an increase in the amount of information he can process effectively. Another developmental trend, probably related to processing capacity, is found in the infant's fixation of faces. Around two months of age, a simple oval shape with two black eye spots will elicit fixation and smiling. The two-month-old has not yet developed a capacity to discriminate schematic from real faces or real faces from one another. Thus a stranger's face is as effective as his mother's in eliciting a smile. Later on, the schematic face must have more detail to cause smiling, but the eyes remain a preferred point of fixation. Finally, at around six to seven months, individual faces are discriminated, and some infants begin to respond negatively to strangers. Interestingly, the eyes remain a major point of visual contact, and the infant's tendency to fixate eyes increases when the target begins to talk. In the chapter on social and personality development, you will see that eye contact is a critical variable in the relationship between mother and infant.

Perceptual Learning

The ability to recognize and discriminate patterns increases rapidly during the early years. By seven or eight months of age, the infant recognizes different facial expressions. A variety of objects also capture his attention and he learns to identify his favorite toys. Two major developmental changes are related to this rapid increase in perceptual learning. First, the absolute amount of visual information that children can process increases with age. Second, children become increasingly efficient in processing available information. When Zinchenko (1963), a Russian psychologist, examined the development of object discrimination in relation to visual and tactile scan patterns, he found that three-year-olds fixate or touch relatively few areas of an object, and these areas may not reveal the object's critical characteristics or features. At age four or five, however, children carefully trace the contours of an object and discover the important features by taking in more information. Although the number of fixations *declines* in older children, they go directly to the characteristics that enable them to discriminate the object. Thus, there is a developmental change in both quantity and efficiency of perceptual information processing. A similar change will be noted in the cognitive realm.

Perceptual learning occurs throughout the life of the individual. Gibson (1969) characterized this learning as a process of *differentiation* and increasing of sensitivity to *critical features.* When we first approach a group of somewhat similar and unfamiliar objects, we may have great difficulty in telling them apart; for example, to the uninitiated, one white wine tastes much like another. With experience, however, we learn to discriminate between the members of a group of objects. Gibson demonstrates the nature of this learning with an amusing illustration. Suppose you have to learn to discriminate and name ten goats. At first, they all look the same. After you have been with them for a while, they start looking different from one another, and you can name them without error. What exactly have you learned? One possibility is that you have learned a precise image of each goat face and attached the name. Another is that you have learned something about the unique dimensions of differences that discriminate goats, such as the length of the nose or distance between the eyes. If the first explanation is true, learning a new group of goat faces would be equally difficult and would take just as long because you would have to form a complete new set of precise images. If the second explanation is correct, learning to discriminate the members of the new group should take less time. With the first group, you learned which dimensions or features of goats are relevant when discriminating between them. The outcome of such experiments is clear. If the second group can be differentiated on the same basis as the first, i.e., by using the same features, there are considerable savings in learning.

Differentiation and Integration

So far, we have characterized the development of pattern perception as a general increase in differentiation. However, the ability to differentiate some perceptual dimensions appears before others. Gibson et al. (1962) compared childrens' ability to discriminate between letter-like forms, which varied on several different dimensions such as orientation and line curvature. They found that children under the age of five had little trouble discriminating forms with differences in line curvature (e.g., ⧐ versus ), but they could not discriminate between identical forms which were simply rotated about the vertical axis (e.g., ⧐ versus ⧏). Teachers encounter this problem when teaching young children to discriminate between letters such as b and d. Letters that differ in rotation about the horizontal axis (e.g., p versus b) are much easier to discriminate. Gibson and her colleagues noticed a sudden improvement in discrimination of vertical axis rotations in six-year-olds and related this to training in reading.

The relatively late development of discrimination in vertical rotation may seem puzzling until we realize that in the natural environment, b is the same object as d when seen from the other side. Until the child learns to read, or is trained to discriminate right from left, he is not required to attach a different name to these letters. The fact that many adults have difficulty discriminating between right and left suggests that our perceptual system has evolved with some lack of sensitivity to differences in right-left orientation.

Another aspect of differentiation is its opposite—*integration.* We have already seen that the members of a group of objects, such as goats, can be discriminated on the basis of certain dimensions. However, each goat also possesses a set of features that characterize the whole group of goats and *differentiate* them from other animals. Thus, a set of features may be *integrated* to define a *class* of objects. This process also shows interesting developmental trends. We will take a close look at these in the section on cognitive development.

Speech Sounds and "Recognition"

One important area of pattern recognition and production is language. Let's look at the *production* side of language first. Infant babbling contains many of the basic speech sounds called *phonemes,* as we discussed in Chapter 7. These phonemes are a sort of alphabetic base for the words we speak in our natural language. Different languages use most of the available phonemes, although a few are used in some languages, and not in others. Two important points can be made about the content of infant speech. First, the sounds emitted during the early months are quite similar for babies in different countries. Second, deaf infants and normal infants emit the same sounds during their first three months (Lenneberg, 1969). Apparently the speech apparatus and the neural mechanisms associated with them are at least partially functional in the first three months, do not depend on experience with language, and emerge according to a maturational schedule. Here, we are referring to the *elements* of speech, not the later combining of those elements into words. (See box 8.3 for a discussion of the importance of early infant crying sounds.)

Recent evidence indicates that the infant's babbling is mirrored by an even earlier perceptual ability to discriminate these sounds. This would not seem to be such a remarkable achievement, except that perceptually dissimilar speech sounds are based on *extremely* similar sound energy patterns.

Box 8.3

Infant Crying and Speech Sounds

The first sounds an infant makes are crying sounds, alternating with occasional gurgles and coughs. At about three weeks of age these sounds are supplemented with pseudo cries, which include more complicated changes in pitch, duration, and articulation. At about five months of age, the infant begins to make babbling sounds, which contain many components of later speech, such as vowels and consonants, and often include patterns of intonation that are remarkably similar to those of adult speech. Approximately one year after birth, these speech sounds are finally combined to form the first words (Kaplan and Kaplan, 1970).

Recent research on the earliest crying sounds suggests that the infant's cries may convey information about his comfort and general physiological state. Spectrographic analysis of these sounds (see box 8.4) has shown that the fundamental frequency of a normal infant cry lies within a band of between 400 and 600 Hertz. When the infant is in pain, the fundamental frequency rises to more than 1,000 Hz. Thus mothers can use this information to tell when their babies are in distress. Extremely high-pitched cries can indicate a serious pathological condition in the infant. Ostwald and Peltzmon (1974) found that infants with a variety of disorders such as hypoglycemia emitted cries in a range of pitch that was far above the range for normal infants in distress.

Researchers have concluded that adults must possess specialized speech sound detectors, or feature analyzers, which enable them to make such precise discriminations. Eimas (1971) tested the sensitivity of one-month-old infants to the subtle sound energy differences that distinguish the speech sounds *ba* and *pa* for adults and found that the infants were *uniquely* sensitive to the minute differences between these sounds. Eimas then argued that these categories were probably innate, considering the one-month infants' limited exposure to experiences involving auditory differentiation. Thus a predominantly biological view of early language development has emerged over the past ten years, adding one more set of functions to the list of innate categories. (See box 8.4 on the spectrographic analysis of speech sounds.)

Elaborate auditory language is a uniquely human ability, and its existence attests to the importance of verbal communication for our survival as a species. Although chimpanzees are able to reach cognitive levels comparable to those of a three-year-old child and construct three word sentences with sign language or form symbols, their ability to produce *auditory* language and understand it will not progress much beyond that of a one-year-old child, even after special training.

Critical Stages in Speech and Vision

One interesting and basic effect of different language environments is individual variation in sensitivity to certain categories of speech sounds. The Japanese language, for example, does not distinguish between *ra* and *la* sounds, and individuals who have lived *exclusively* in a Japanese language environment since birth will not be able to discriminate those sounds. This is not a genetic difference, because Japanese individuals raised in an English language environment have no difficulty in discriminating *ra* and *la*. Furthermore, there seems to be a *critical period* for learning to

Box 8.4

Spectrographic Analysis of Speech Sounds

The sounds emitted by our vocal apparatus consist of unique patterns of frequency and intensity. For example, the consonant sound *b* contains three major sound energy bands (*formants,* see Chapter 7), at around 2,700, 1,400, and 800 Hz.

The sound spectrograph (see box fig. 8.4) is a visual record of the energy pattern of sound in which frequency is represented on the vertical axis and time is represented on the horizontal axis.

The first spectrograph below is for the sound ba. Note that all three frequency bands are simultaneously present in the energy pattern. However, there is a lag of 10 msec. in the onset of the lowest frequency band. Very different sounds may be generated by such slight changes. Thus if the onset lag for the lowest frequency is enlarged to about 100 msec., as shown in the second graph, the sound shifts abruptly for the adult listener from ba to pa.

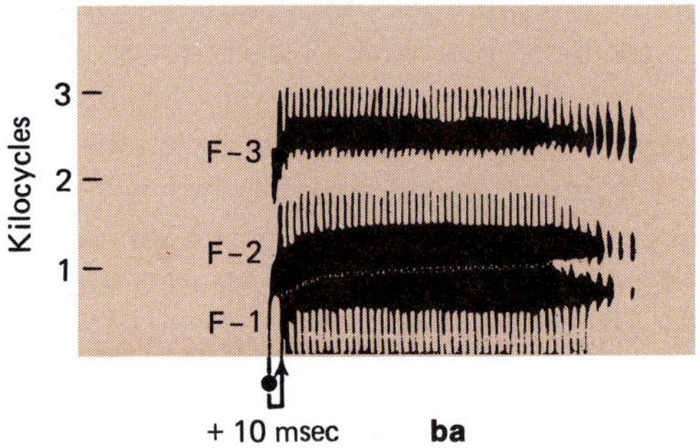

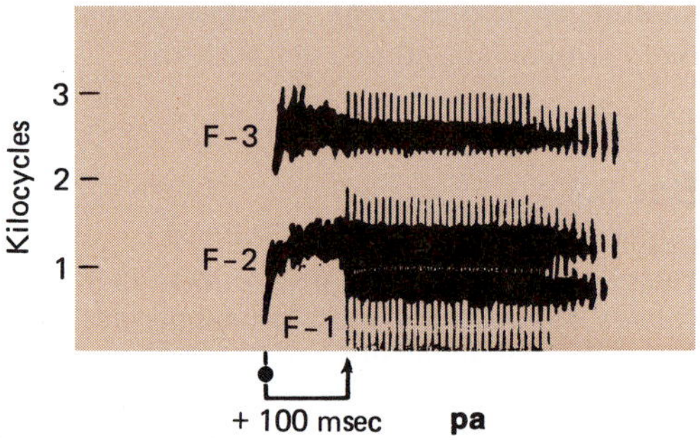

distinguish these sounds. Although the genetically programmed perceptual apparatus for discriminating *ra* and *la* is present in Japanese children, unless it is exercised during childhood, the perceptual analyzer for these sounds disappears and may not be recovered in adulthood. This broad critical period for language development is probably one reason why adults often have great difficulty learning to speak certain foreign languages fluently and why children should learn a second language early if they will have to use it later in life.

The visual system also depends on *early* use for its later functional integrity, and the critical period is a great deal more narrow than in the auditory system. Evidence of this in humans comes from patients who either were born with cataracts or developed them within a few years after birth. Surgical techniques have been used to replace the clouded cornea with a piece from a normal eye. Unfortunately, these operations are generally not too successful in producing normal vision if the cataract appeared before the patient was a year old. Prognosis for recovery improves if the patient had several years of visual experience before he went blind. We now know, from studies with blindfolded kittens, that the neural mechanisms responsible for vision, although present at birth, will be lost if they are not exercised early in life. An equal period of blindness in the adult cat has relatively little neurological or behavioral effects. Thus the maturation and maintenance of genetically programmed perceptual systems depends on normal experience during the early critical period. The concept of critical period will come up again when we discuss social and personality development.

Cognitive Development

Language, memory, understanding, learning, and perception are interrelated components of cognitive development. We discussed perception separately in the previous section, not because it is an independent function but because it is more directly tuned to the physical world of space and objects. Perception brings the world into the mind and provides the material for operations generally referred to as cognition or "thinking."

Differentiation and Integration

Cognitive development can be described along some of the perceptual dimensions considered in the previous section. Werner (1948) noted that almost all aspects of development can be considered complementary changes in *differentiation* and *integration*. As the child grows, he makes finer and finer discriminations. At first, he may call all four-legged animals "dog." Gradually, he learns to apply the term to a more restricted class of animals. Similarly, a child may call all adult women "mother." Later he discovers that some women are mothers and some are not and only applies the term to females with children.

Sometimes the problem in differentiating categories may be perceptual; for example, when the differences between objects are so minute that they are literally not seen at first (recall the example of goats in our discussion of perceptual learning). At a cognitive level, the problem tends to be one of deciding which perceived characteristics are relevant to the class. The two-year-old child visiting a zoo sees differences between the dog, lion, and elephant, but he does not yet know that their differences define different classes of animals. By the age of four, he has probably learned the different animals quite well and would not call the lion a dog. Much of the developmental changes that occur in the early years involve increased differentiation at the motor, perceptual, and cognitive levels.

At the same time, *integration* is occurring as a complementary process. A conceptual world, broken down into finer and finer pieces, would soon have no meaning if the pieces were not combined into larger classes and concepts. We can view the process at both the perceptual and conceptual levels. Individual goats might easily be included in a common category because they are perceptually so similar. But what about variation between a fox terrier and an Irish wolfhound? Here, some obvious perceptual differences must be ignored in favor of a few critical characteristics that define the dog family. Other object classes may be purely conceptual with no perceptual characteristics in common. The class of "living things," for example, has a wide range of shapes, colors, sizes, and mobility. Other concepts, such as justice, are so abstract that they have no physical reference.

Young children prefer to deal with the *concrete* characteristics of objects as dimensions for differentiation and integration. The basis of children's cognitive organization is inferred from experiments in which they are required to separate a cluster of objects into two or more piles. Three-year-old children tend to choose dimensions such as general size, color, or shape to separate objects. These choices suggest a preference for concrete classifications. Later, they may classify objects in terms of the *thematic* and *functional* relationships between them. For example, when presented with a "businessman," an "Indian," a "horse," and a "dog," the typical American five-year-old will place the horse with the Indian. The child may agree that there are two "humans" and two "animals," but he will resist the experimenter's suggestion to separate the Indian and horse (see fig. 8.10). Whenever there is a good functional, or thematic, relationship between objects, the more abstract relationships between objects tend

Figure 8.10 Three bases for cognitive organization. Children are asked to put the objects into two piles. The two-year-old groups the objects on the basis of perceptual dimension such as color. The five-year-old groups them according to a functional or thematic relationship. The eight-year-old may use the abstract categories of "man" and "animal."

to be ignored. However, older children and adults reverse this order of preference and usually focus on abstract groupings (e.g., "humans"), although they will also use some functional relationships.

Hierarchic Integration

One important aspect of behavior, from the physical to the cognitive level, is its *hierarchic* integration. In the adult mind, individual classes of objects and concepts stand in certain relationships to each other. A Japanese rose, the class of roses, flowers, plants, and living things are all sequential steps in a hierarchical classification system. Jean Piaget's experiments on *class inclusion* show that although young children may be somewhat familiar with the different levels of classification, they are often unaware of *relative positions* in the hierarchy. Thus, when a five-year-old separates round and polygon forms, then further separates the polygons into squares and triangles, he may be unaware that there are more polygons than squares.

There is a general developmental trend toward increased hierarchic integration. Part of this integration is externally imposed on us through the classification systems we learn in school, but much of our mental organization seems spontaneous. Individual differences in mental organization are quite evident among college students. Some students actively organize and understand relationships in an area of knowledge, while others take in information more passively. Unfortunately, we have little hard evidence concerning the influences that account for different integrative intellectual styles.

Egocentrism

Piaget suggests that at first, a young infant does not have the cognitive structures to differentiate himself from the external world. Gradually he learns that he has a separate identity and direct control over his own body space. After infancy, the young child often fails to differentiate his own views of the world from those of other people. As we mentioned previously, Piaget called this behavior *egocentric*. We have already considered one aspect of egocentrism in perception: the inability to imagine a visual scene from another point of view. The child believes that others see things as he sees them; often he believes that the contents of his dreams and imagination are available to other people. Furthermore, he may fail to differentiate his wishes from external reality. Parents are sometimes disturbed when their children come to them with far-fetched stories, especially when the story is contradicted by an immediately present reality. Although some persons would view such behavior as "lying," the concept of lying includes a deliberate falsification of truth. Because the young child cannot differentiate his wishes from reality, he does not have the cognitive sophistication to lie.

Children may express egocentrism in different ways. Christmas shopping with a five-year-old is quite revealing. Presents he considers appropriate for his mother or father may include a red truck or a doll. Children are so involved in their own worlds that they think other people will like what they like.

It is also fascinating to watch a group of six-year-olds play a game "together." Each child understands the rules in his own way, and the game may be played in absolute chaos. Piaget found that children do not completely lose their egocentric view of game rules until they are about eleven years old. Then they may become so preoccupied with the rules that the game never gets played. For example, children can spend an entire afternoon discussing the rules for a snowball fight, then find it too dark to play. Of course, their actual interest is rulemaking and they are quite satisfied with the day's activities.

Piaget's Cognitive Stages

Piaget's view of cognitive development is currently having a great impact in psychology. Psychologists regarded the development of intelligence as a simple matter of knowing more, until Piaget suggested that cognitive development proceeds through qualitatively different stages—that children know the world in qualitatively different ways as they develop. The first evidence for this view came from Piaget's early work on the standardization of Alfred Binet's intelligence test for children, which involved giving the test to many children and scoring the number of right and wrong answers. A theoretical breakthrough occurred when Piaget noticed that there was a certain *consistency* in the *wrong* answers. In other words, although the children did not give the right adult answer, they gave the view of the problem that seemed right to them. We will turn to some examples of this discovery in a moment.

Sensorimotor Intelligence

Piaget's elaboration of the first developmental stage came primarily from observing his own children. In *The Origins of Intelligence in the Child* he has recorded many fascinating and insightful observations of infant behavior. He calls the first stage, extending from birth to two years, *sensorimotor* because much of the infant's thought seems to be represented in his overt motor activities. Bower (1971) has presented a striking example of the dominance of motor behavior in infant thought. The toy train in figure 8.11 was moved several times, from in front of the infant to his right side and back again. Then, when the train moved to the left for the first time, the infant did not follow it but made the same turn to the right. Apparently his mental representation of the toy train was closely related to his original motor behavior.

Infant motor patterns, or *schemes* as Piaget calls them, become more and more elaborate and innovative. Between twelve and eighteen months of age, the infant greatly accelerates his activities and becomes a sort of miniature

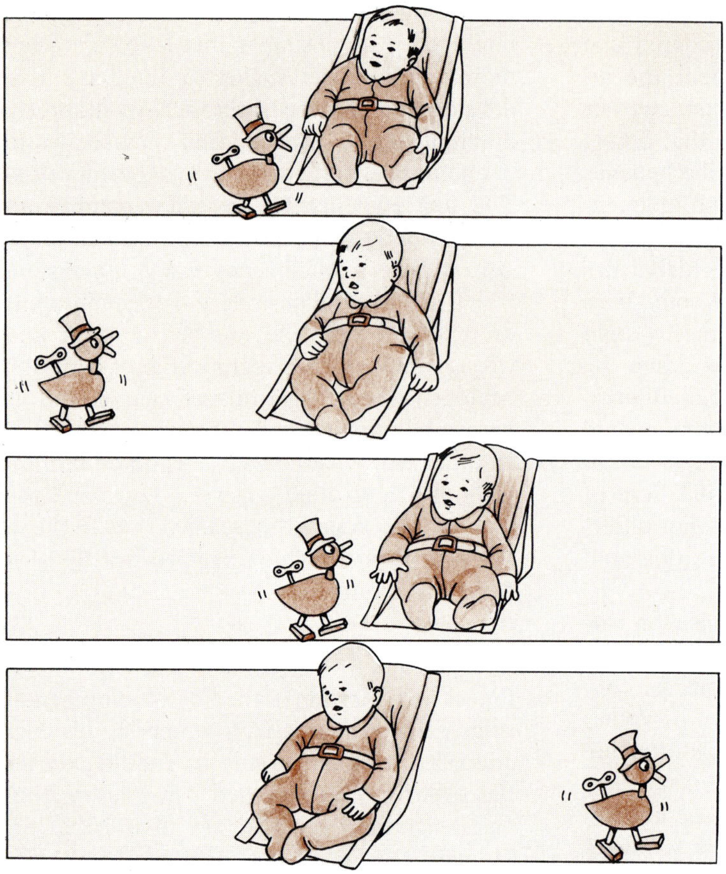

Figure 8.11 Objects may be partly represented in the infant by his motor responses. The toy duck was repeatedly moved from in front of the infant to his right. Then it was moved to his left. Instead of following the visual object, the infant repeated his previous motor pattern in looking to the right. (Adapted from T. J. R. Bower, "The object in the world of the infant." *Scientific American,* 1971, *225.*)

scientist, experimenting with almost any object he can get his hands on. One expression of this is the "dropping" stage that many infants go through. When less than a year old, they frequently knock objects off their high chair or table, either accidently or when waving their arms in frustration, but pay little attention to the resulting "splat" on the floor. Then suddenly, they become much more interested in the event. Such actions should not be construed as "misbehavior." The baby is just finding out more about his world; parents, on the other hand, may want to limit his opportunities for such mess-making.

One of the most striking characteristics of twelve- to eighteen-month-old infants is their tremendous curiosity. They will pull open every drawer and play with every available object. Why?

Psychologists have long been fascinated with the issue of *motivation* in behavior. According to some early theorists, behavior was largely motivated by the basic drives of hunger, thirst, and sex. Other theorists, such as Piaget, believe that children have a fundamental curiosity and need to learn about their world. The new concepts in education reflect this view. Many schools are now providing children with more opportunities for free exploration and are imposing less regimentation in the belief that the self-motivated child will be a better learner.

The Emergence of Language

Around the age of two, children's mental representations become more abstract. The most overt sign of this shift into what Piaget calls the *preoperational stage* is the emergence of *language*. Language development has been the focus of much research over the past few years, and some interesting general principles have been discovered. First, the emergence of single words around twelve months of age, two-word phrases around eighteen months, and successively more complicated grammatical constructions follows a similar sequence in all cultures studied (Slobin, 1971). Psycholinguists believe that as the infant develops in a normal linguistic environment, his cognitive structures mature, and he becomes biologically capable of incorporating the language of his culture. Second, children seem to be self-motivated in learning language. Specific training and rewards are unnecessary. Although "reward-oriented" approaches to language learning might suggest that children's early and grammatically incorrect utterances should be corrected, this seems to make little difference in their progress. Brown, Cozden, and Bellugi-Klima (1969) analyzed parental reinforcement patterns for children's speech and found that parents often rewarded grammatically incorrect utterances if they were correct statements of fact. For example, if the child says "All gone milk," he would be rewarded for his grammatically incorrect but factually correct statement. However, if he makes the grammatically correct statement "See the milk" while pointing to the sugar, he would probably be corrected.

A third principle concerns the general issue of *what* the child learns during language development. Eventually the child learns the grammatical structure of his language. All he seems to need are adult models who speak correctly. However, language development is *not* a simple matter of *imitating* either word patterns or grammatical rules in the environment. Let us turn our attention to the question of what is learned.

If imitation accounted for the learning of language, then children would learn particular word combinations by copying adult speech. However, such learning would be quite tedious and would not reflect the *generative* nature of language in the production of novel words and sentences (Chomsky, 1968). A clear example of generation rather than imitation can be found in childrens' use of plural endings. Most English nouns can be pluralized by adding *s*. However, certain nouns such as foot and mouse have irregular plural endings. Children initially give the correct plural forms of these nouns but tend to give incorrect forms when they become aware of the general rule for plurals. Thus mice becomes mouses and feet become foots. The generative aspect is clear because the child says these words although he has not heard them in his environment. A similar phenomenon has been noted in childrens' tendency to generalize the common past tense ending to all verbs; for example, "do" becomes "doed" in the past tense.

The generative nature of language is most clearly evident in the child's production of sentences according to grammatical rules. The early rules for two-word sentences are unique to childrens' language and obviously are not learned from adults. In one type of two-word sentence, the first word is called a *pivot* word and has a fixed position relative to the second word. A typical first-position pivot word is "more." Other vocabulary words such as milk or hot can be placed in the second position to express the desired meaning. "Come" is a second-position pivot word (Mommy come, plane come).

Around two years of age, children begin

producing sentences composed of more than two words and using the grammatical constraints of the adult language. They gradually learn to transform simple positive statements into questions and negative statements. Initially the child can make only one transformation in a sentence; for example, "He is going" can be transformed into the question "Is he going?" A child capable of this single transformation may not be able to make a second transformation such as adding "why" to the question ("Why is he going?"). With further linguistic development, the child becomes capable of handling two or three transformations ("Why is he not going?") (Bellugi-Klima, 1968). This second expansion of language skills heralds the child's entry into Piaget's second stage of cognitive development, *concrete operations.*

Concrete Operations

Children in the preoperational stage, between the ages of two and seven years, show a great deal of intelligent behavior. The size of their vocabulary expands from about fifty words to three thousand words, and they can carry on meaningful conversations and read children's books. However, Piaget's experiments suggested that the child under age seven also thinks in basically different ways from the older child and adult. One difference in mental function is the child's ability to perform *concrete operations.*

Conservation problems are used to test for the presence of concrete operations. The child's task is to recognize certain qualities that remain constant in spite of various transformations. In the *quantity* conservation problem, two equal-sized containers, A and B, are filled with equal amounts of water and set side by side. Once the child has agreed that both containers have equal amounts of water, the contents of B are poured into a taller, narrower container C, bringing the waterline up to a higher level. Then the child is asked whether containers A and C hold equal amounts of water. Before age seven, most children are distracted by the higher water level and insist there is *more* water in container C; that is, they fail to *conserve* the actual constant quantity. Another task most children fail before age seven is the conservation of *substance.* Here they are shown two equal-sized clay balls. Then one of the balls is rolled into a sausage shape. When asked which object contains more clay, the child points to the sausage shape. At about age seven, however, the child realizes that by using the same operation that led to changing the clay ball, it can be made into a ball again. This critical mental operation, known as reversibility, helps him recognize the identity of substance (see fig. 8.12).

Formal Operations

During the concrete operational period, between ages seven and eleven, children can solve the conservation problems when the materials needed to solve them are present and can be manipulated. However, they typically fail to solve problems that require much abstract thinking until they are about eleven years old—the stage of *formal operations.* The deficit is not so much in quantity of knowledge as it is in the available mental operations. At the stage of formal operations the child can solve a problem by formulating various hypotheses and working out their solutions "in his head." This is the highest stage of mental operations considered in Piaget's theory, and even adults do not always function at this level.

Stages and Ages

Piaget has included several important qualifications in his theory of cognitive stages. One is that the ages at which the different mental operations emerge are only approximate; they vary between individuals and within the same individual at different times. Furthermore, the

Figure 8.12 Conservation of substance and reversibility. After the five-year-old agrees that two equal size balls contain the same amount of clay, the experimenter rolls one of them into a sausage shape and asks the same question. The child insists there is more clay in the sausage shape because of its greater length; that is, he has failed to conserve substance. At about age six or seven the child *will* conserve substance, perhaps because a new mental operation, *reversibility,* has emerged.

transition from one stage to the next is gradual. For example, a child in the concrete operational stage is likely to show some behavioral characteristics of adjacent stages.

One constant in Piaget's theory is the *sequence* of stages. Each stage of mental operations lays the groundwork for the next. Thus the preoperational child cannot suddenly jump to formal operations without first going through the concrete operational stage.

Piaget views the progression of stages as an unfolding of a maturational sequence in *interaction* with the environment. The average ages at which the transitions between stages occur have been compared cross-culturally and have been found to be remarkably similar up to the level of formal operations. When educated and uneducated children from the southern United States were compared, little difference was found in the age at which they could perform concrete operations. Apparently these basic mental abilities develop in the normal course of biological growth and interaction with the physical world and do not require special training. In fact, experiments that attempt to train young children to perform advanced operations have met with little success. This has led educators to be more concerned with the child's mental readiness to deal with various kinds of knowledge.

Assimilation and Accommodation

So far, we have said nothing about the actual mechanism of cognitive growth. What causes a change in mental contents and operations during development? As the child grows, he must *adapt* to new aspects of his environment. Often the set of mental operations and knowledge he has at a particular stage are adequate to understand new aspects in the environment. The five-year-old, for instance, can deal with a new brand of candy bar without significantly modifying his view of the world.

Piaget uses the term *assimilation* when objects or events can be understood and dealt with through existing mental structures. Thus, the candy bar can be physically and mentally assimilated by the child.

But, sometimes an event is novel enough so that none of the currently available mental structures can deal with it adequately. At about age 3½, my son began to go along on downtown shopping expeditions (see fig. 8.14). This involved parking the car and putting a nickel in the parking meter. He was curious about this funny little machine and asked what it was. When told it was a "parking meter," he looked perplexed. As I was in a hurry, I offered no further explanation. On several subsequent shopping trips, the child watched the meter take nickels with some interest. Finally, one day he had a flash of insight and yelled out "parking eater." This example is more than humorous; it demonstrates two complimentary processes: *assimilation* and *accommodation*. The child already understood the concepts of "parking" and "eating." All he had to do was combine them. By using available concepts, he was demonstrating *assimilation*. The *new* association of these concepts demonstrated a partial *accommodation*, or change in his understanding of the originally incomprehensible park-

Figure 8.13 Because the child has no way of mentally representing the concept "parking meter," he *assimilates* it with concepts that are already in his repertoire: "parking" and "eating."

ing meter. Eventually, he realized that "parking eater" was not right, and the concept of meters as timing devices emerged. Accommodation was then complete.

Children are constantly probing and pushing the limits of their knowledge as they interact with the environment. When they do not understand something, they actively seek solutions through assimilation and accommodation. However, the ability and drive to accommodate varies considerably between individuals. Some children show an intense drive to learn as much as they can about the world, while others seem less eager. Although we know that there are differences in intelligence between children, they probably do not completely account for individual differences in intellectual enthusiasm. Most likely, some of these differences are related to attitudes expressed in the home and school. If the child's parents are intellectually active and share their interest with him and if the school provides a stimulating approach to learning, the child is likely to be enthusiastic about learning.

Summary

There have been several common themes in our consideration of physical, perceptual, and cognitive development. The strongest has been a biological emphasis on genetics and the process of maturation, in which heredity and environment interact. All development takes place in an *environment,* but many aspects of development show a regularity in their emergence and are relatively independent of a normal amount of environmental variation. This was true for physical development, from the prenatal stages to infancy, to puberty, and finally adult stature. The emergence of motor functions showed a similar regularity in maturation schedule, from prenatal and infant reflexes to walking.

Perceptual development includes some remarkably complex mental operations. The infant's capacity to see depth allows him to achieve perceptual constancy. His auditory system is uniquely sensitive to the specialized speech sounds made by other humans. Thus he begins his life with a remarkably broad set of functions, which are already tuned to some important characteristics of his world. These basic perceptual mechanisms are further developed with experience. His spatial perceptions become more accurate and generalized, and he learns to differentiate the various contents of his perceptual experience. His specific skills will vary, depending on his individual experiences.

The contents of the child's perceptual experience must be cognitively ordered, and this ordering varies considerably with age. A general change occurs in the levels of differentiation and integration as the child grows older; for example, his ability to classify objects becomes more finely differentiated, and he begins to realize their relationships as he hierarchically integrates the contents of his experience. Jean Piaget has made some major contributions to our view of how this happens. According to his theory of development, the child's mental operations go through qualitatively different stages. His first thoughts are based on his direct sensory and motor operations. Later, with language and images, he internalizes these overt operations. Each stage of development brings new qualitative changes in mental ability, until at about age eleven or twelve the child reaches the final stage and is capable of formal operations and abstract thought.

9

Personality and Social Development

Within a broad range of physical, perceptual, and cognitive competence, the thing that differentiates us most as individuals is the cluster of traits called personality. We often think of personality in a rather nonspecific way. For example, the statement "She has a nice personality" expresses a general feeling of positive regard toward a person. In the systematic study of personality, however, we must go beyond these general characterizations and attempt to specify the components of personality. Each of us has our own unique clustering of characteristics such as sociability, activity level, and personal mannerisms. Furthermore, our responses to the characteristics of others vary; for instance, some of us find extremely active people exciting while others find them irritating. Psychologists must also be objective when assessing personality variables rather than view individual expressions of personality as desirable or undesirable.

In this chapter we will consider some of these characteristics and the forces that produce them, without passing judgment on their value or suggesting that they should be changed. On the other hand, most of us would agree that the value of some personality traits is greater than others. For example, a sense of security and confidence is more desirable than its opposite. There is also a relatively broad consensus about the desirability of a certain degree of conformity to society's rules. Specific aspects of the environment affect these areas of socialization, and we will consider them in this chapter.

There are several major theoretical orientations toward the development of personality. In the first part of this chapter we will present these different views and assess their contribution to general knowledge about the growth of personality. In the second section, we will consider some of the forces and mechanisms of personality development at different age levels and apply an integrated theoretical approach to areas such as attachment to the mother in infancy, modeling of parents in early childhood, and integration into society in late childhood and adolescence.

Theories of Personality Development

There are four major theoretical orientations to the development of personality: the *biological, cognitive developmental, Freudian psychoanalytic,* and *social learning* approaches. Each is based on somewhat different views of the important mechanisms involved in the child's personality development, and each has its proponents who argue that their perspective on child development is more complete or "true" than others. The relative validity of these theories is the subject of frequent debate and numerous experiments. Yet despite theoretical infighting, each view continues to have significant influence.

Psychological theories that seem to be at odds may turn out to be different and equally valid perspectives on the nature of a very complex organism. To use a simple analogy, if a blind man is asked to evaluate the nature of an elephant, he might grab hold of the tail and say an elephant is like a rope. Another, who comes in contact with the animal's leg, would disagree and say an elephant is like a tree. The point is that each opinion may have some validity from its particular perspective. Thus instead of arguing about the general truth or falsity of the theories of personality development, we will present different aspects of child development that are relevant to each. By combining these different perspectives, we can hope to arrive at an overall view of the major forces and mechanisms in personality development.

Biologically Based Theories

Genetic and ethological approaches to the development of personality share a common biological emphasis. However, the genetic approach applies the techniques of behavioral genetics to a wide range of measurable human characteristics, while the ethological approach, although recognizing its biological basis in genetics, selectively views certain aspects of behavior that occur consistently across species.

Genetic Approach

The methods of behavioral genetics described in Chapter 2 have been applied to a wide range of human behaviors. For example, the behavioral differences between monozygotic (identical) twins are compared with behavioral differences between dizygotic (fraternal) twins, based on the assumption that environmental influences contribute equally to variation within pairs. If the assumptions of the twin-comparison method are correct, we can calculate the relative amounts of variability contributed by genetic and environmental differences.

Performance on intelligence tests shows a rather high proportion of variability contributed by genetics, but estimates for personality variables are typically smaller. Let's consider the few characteristics of personality that seem to show a strong genetic component. Recall from Chapter 2 (box 2.3, p. 38) that Vandenberg (1962) used the twin-comparison method to study *stability,* a characteristic measured with the Thurstone Temperament Scale. The percentage of individual variability related to genetic differences in stability was calculated to be approximately forty percent.

Another aspect of personality that seems to be partly under genetic control is called *introversion-extroversion.* A person on the extroverted side of the scale tends to be outgoing, social, and active. The introverted person is timid and less socially active. Scarr (1969) reviewed several studies which showed that identical twins tend to be more similar than fraternal twins on this dimension. Also there is some experimental evidence that even in infancy, identical and fraternal twin infants differ in ways that may be related to the introversion-extroversion dimension. For instance, identical twins tend to be similar in terms of their smiling behavior and fear of strangers, whereas fraternal twins tend to vary as much as ordinary siblings. So far, there has been little research on the stability of these early personality characteristics, although one longitudinal study by Kagan and Moss (1962) showed that three-year-olds who tend to be inhibited in their relationships with others are likely to respond this way in adulthood. Scarr (1965) found that infants who avoid social contacts tend to behave the same way in childhood.

One interesting study by Juel-Nielson (1965) compared twelve pairs of identical twin adults who were separated early in life and reared apart. Little commonality was found within pairs in matters such as political views, style of dress, fields of interest, and aggressiveness. However, they were very similar in terms of facial gestures, expressive movements, and neurotic symptoms.

Research on the contribution of genetics to personality is still relatively new and incomplete. Measures of the relative contributions of genes and environment depend to a large degree on the range of environmental variation. Environmental differences are held to a minimum in most studies that compare identical and fraternal twin pairs reared in the *same* family. This situation is most sensitive to genetic variation. Estimates of genetic contributions to variance in personality might be considerably lower if environmental differences between twins were as large as they are between families. We can clarify this point by considering an example of extreme environmental variation. Suppose that identical twins are separated at birth, and one is placed with parents who are cold and harsh disciplinarians while the other is adopted by warm, loving parents. These different environments would be likely to lead to the development of very different personalities, *despite* the twins' genetic identity. Although evidence suggests that identical twins raised in radically different environments would be more alike than fraternal twins, a much larger portion of the variation in their personalities would be attributable to environmental influences than would be true if they had been raised together.

Estimates of genetic control tell us nothing about the *mechanisms* by which the genes contribute to personality development. We know that environment and heredity *interact;* the question is how. The complexity of the interaction between heredity and environment will be illustrated later in a discussion of early infant-mother relationships.

In spite of these limitations, the results of research in behavioral genetics have served notice to developmental psychologists that their explanations of personality must consider more than the environment. Traditional views of infants as a homogeneous population waiting to be molded by their environment are giving way to the view long held by many parents—that infants are unique individuals from birth. Therefore, the developmental process should be viewed in part as one of *actualizing the potential* of each child, rather than simply *molding* him into one form or another.

Ethological Approach

Ethologists, many of whom study the behavior of animals in their natural environments, have made important contributions to our thinking about social development. Most important is the concept of *attachment,* the bond formed between an infant and its mother. In many species this bond is quite strong, and signs of disturbance occur if it is broken. Ethologists believe that attachment behavior is derived from the species' genetic base.

The traditional view of mother-infant attachment emphasized the act of feeding. The infant received food from his mother, thus gratifying his most basic need. This was presumed to be the basis for infant attachment, until Harlow and Zimmerman (1959) conducted several fascinating studies with monkeys that suggested otherwise.

Infant monkeys were raised with two surrogate "mothers." (See fig. 9.1.) One mother was made of wire mesh and had a nipple for feeding. The other mother was of the same general shape but was covered with soft terry cloth and had no feeding nipple. Surprisingly, although the infants ate from the wire mother, they spent most of their time cuddling against the terry cloth mother. In other words, their attachment seemed to be based on *contact comfort* rather than feeding. The monkey infants also relied on the terry cloth mother for security. When frightened by a mechanical toy, they always ran to the terry cloth mother. (See fig. 9.2.) Eventually, however, they would leave the cloth mother and tentatively explore the strange object. If they were frightened, and only the wire feeding mother was present, their behavior was markedly different. They would cry and crouch in a corner and would not explore the strange object.

Although terry cloth mothers provided the infant monkeys with contact comfort and security, they failed to provide for some of the infant's more complex needs. Monkeys raised for six months with terry cloth mothers displayed abnormal social and sexual behavior and only approached normalcy after a year of living with other monkeys. Abnormal behavior was more pronounced and lasting if the period of deprivation was lengthened to twelve months. Behavior in human infants that is possibly related to these phenomena will be considered in the section on human infancy.

The ethological approach has also been used to study group social behavior related to *dominance hierarchies*. One of the first

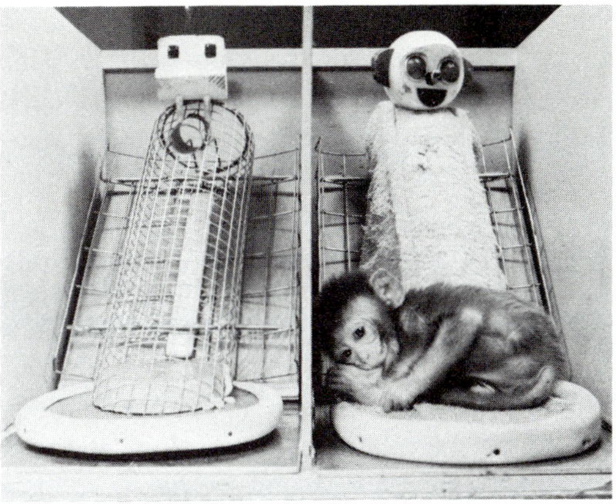

Figure 9.1 Terry cloth and wire mother surrogates. Although the infant monkey is fed from the wire mother, he prefers to remain in contact with the more comfortable terry cloth mother. (From Harlow, H. F. and Zimmerman, R. R. "Affectional Responses in the Infant Monkey," *Science,* Vol. 130, pp. 421–432, Fig. 23, Fig. 1, 21 August 1959. Copyright 1959 by the American Association for the Advancement of Science. Photo courtesy of Harry F. Harlow, University of Wisconsin Primate Laboratory.)

Figure 9.2 The infant monkey clings to his terry cloth mother for security when frightened by a strange object. (From Harlow, H. F. and Zimmerman, R. R. "Affectional Responses in the Infant Monkey," *Science,* Vol. 130, pp. 421–432, Fig. 23, Fig. 1, 21 August 1959. Copyright 1959 by the American Association for the Advancement of Science. Photo courtesy of Harry F. Harlow, University of Wisconsin Primate Laboratory.)

things that monkeys do when placed in a group is establish a "pecking order." This may involve a period of fighting and threats, but soon the order of dominance is established from top to bottom. This social structure is remarkably stable. Similar behavior in children will be discussed later.

The ethological approach has led us to view human social behavior in the context of evolutionary development. Ethologists point out that humans have certain social conventions which may be related to the biological needs and predispositions of our species.

Cognitive Developmental Theory

Another relatively recent view of social and personality development was sparked by Jean Piaget's work on cognitive development. The cognitive developmental theory proposes that a child's personality and social behavior vary as a function of his level of cognitive development. In Chapter 8 we said that the child progresses through different age-related stages of cognitive function. During the earlier stages, his cognitive abilities are relatively undifferentiated. Thus his social relations and personality will also be relatively undifferentiated. This theory is unique in its account of differences in personality and social behavior as related to differences in age.

Because the young child is often unable to view things from another individual's perspective and automatically assumes that his view corresponds with that of others, Piaget describes him as *egocentric* in his social relations. In 1926, Piaget recorded the conversational interactions of young children and found that many could only be described as "collective monologues." In other words, although children often talk together in a group, they do not actually listen to or understand each other.

Kohlberg's (1964) theory of moral development relates cognitive development and *moral judgment*. Kohlberg found that the level of sophistication in the child's moral judgments parallels his cognitive development. The seven-year-old child will judge his behavior as right or wrong on the basis of whether the personal consequences are desirable or undesirable; for example, whether it will result in physical punishment. At approximately eleven years of age, the child begins to rely on authority and conform to conventional rules. In adolescence, the frequency of judgments based on individually generated principles of conscience increases, although conformity to conventional rules remains the dominant mode of judgment throughout adulthood. In other words, the young child has little conception of rules formed by consensus or of distant authority because he does not have the necessary cognitive base for this type of representation. Since he is incapable of adopting another's perspective, he responds egocentrically in terms of his own rewards and punishments. Similarly, in middle childhood, the child does not have the level of abstract thinking needed to develop individual principles of conscience.

Kohlberg (1966) also applied the cognitive developmental approach to sex typing. The child's self-categorization as boy or girl begins very early in life, long before the child really *understands* the different sex roles. By age five or six, the choice is stabilized, and the development of the conception of the appropriate sex role parallels the general changes in cognitive sophistication. The environment also plays an important role, but instead of being passively shaped by social expectations, the child actively seeks out the sex role defined by society as appropriate. This self-directed view of social and personality development parallels Piaget's view of self-motivated cognitive development.

Cognitive developmental theory accounts for some differences in personality and social behavior that are dependent on age, but it does not account for specific environmental effects or individual differences within each age group. The genetic approach gives a general view of the relative contributions of heredity and environment, but it does not specify the developmental processes involved. The two theories we will describe next—the Freudian psychoanalytic and the social learning approaches—direct themselves specifically to the environmental influences that result in individual differences.

Freudian Psychoanalytic Theory

Freud's theory is certainly the most imaginative and detailed account of personality development. We could not hope to summarize the content of this theory adequately here; a more complete description of Freud's theory will appear, however, in Chapter 17.

Freudian psychoanalytic theory describes two major mechanisms for personality development, *prototype reactions* and *identification.* Prototype reactions develop from the young child's experiences during the oral and anal phases of gratification. During the first year, the infant's major focus is on oral gratification. Freud postulated that general *personality types* developed from these early experiences, especially if the infant was deprived or gratified to an *excessive* degree. Similarly, the anal area becomes a major focus during the second year, and excessively strict or lenient toilet training may also affect the child's personality development.

Freud's theory is unique in its emphasis on these early experiences as a basis for personality development. Psychoanalytic theory is rather pessimistic in this respect. If things go wrong in the early stages of development, the pattern is set and difficult to change; thus the prescription for maladjusted adults is a prolonged period of psychoanalysis. Actually, there is little experimental evidence to support the connection between early oral-anal experience and later personality. Furthermore, the evidence for general *personality types* predicted in Freud's theory is also rather limited, and although correlations between supposedly related adult personality characteristics have been reported, they are usually rather low (Mischel, 1968).

Identification

Freud's second major mechanism of personality development occurs at approximately five years of age in connection with the repression of Oedipal impulses toward the parent of the opposite sex (Chapter 17). The male child's identification with his father consists of emulating the father's behavior and internalizing the father's attitudes toward him. Freud conceived of identification as a general mechanism that goes beyond the resolution of psychosexual conflicts into adulthood. For example, as adults we may identify with and internalize the values of a powerful and successful leader. This process will be considered again in connection with *modeling* and the social learning theory of development.

Freud was a prime mover in our thinking about personality. Although many of his speculations have either been rejected or ignored for lack of evidence, he stimulated the field of psychology and inspired explorations into the mechanisms of personality development. Two developmental psychologists who have been heavily influenced by Freud are Alfred Adler and Eric Erikson. Adler viewed the relationships between siblings as an important force in personality development. For instance, the relationship between the firstborn and the younger children in the family consisted of a power struggle in which the younger child tried to topple the older, more powerful child (see fig. 9.3). This theory became an impetus for the later exploration of other variables related to sibling interaction and birth order. Erikson developed a broad theory of psychological growth from birth to adulthood; the

Figure 9.3 Sibling rivalry. Relationships between brothers and sisters are powerful forces in personality development. (© 1967 United Features Syndicate, Inc.)

early states are closely related to those in Freud's theory. Erikson is best known for his discussion of adolescent strivings for identity (see fig. 9.4 and Chapter 17).

Freudian psychoanalytic theory presents a view of the organism that is part social and part biological in orientation. The oral and anal phases are *instinctual,* genetically determined stages of development, but development emerges from the *interaction* of these stages with *environmental* events. These early events and their supposed influence on general personality traits are the primary focus of the theory; later socializing forces in the home, school, and community receive little consideration.

Social Learning Theory

Because a detailed account of learning theory will be presented in Chapter 11, we will only touch on the basic principles and their developmental applications here. Early learning theorists scrupulously avoided mentioning abstract concepts such as personality, preferring to confine their considerations to overt and *directly observable behavior.* They also preferred to view the causes of behavior in terms of *observable environmental events,* and proposed a few simple "laws" of learning to account for the relationship between environment (stimuli) and behavior (responses). In general, if a response is rewarded, the probability that it will reoccur in a similar situation is increased. If the response is punished or unrewarded, its frequency tends to decrease. This and other basic laws of learning apply to children, adults, rats, pigeons, and college sophomores. They presumably allow the behavior theorist to predict, control, and, at a rather primitive level, understand behavior without looking inside the organism.

These behavioral "laws" have considerable intuitive appeal. If a child misbehaves, "punishment" can be applied in the hope that it will curb the offending response. If the child does something the parents consider desirable, they may reward the response to increase the behavior. The results often correspond to expectations. All parents and social controllers are aware of this kind of practical psychology. Furthermore, the principles apply to specific instances, whereas other theories do not. How do you get Johnny to mow the lawn or do his homework? Reward him for doing it or punish him for not doing it. How do you toilet train Johnny's little sister? Praise her for having a bowel movement on the toilet. But should you punish her for having it in her pants? Most social learning theorists would *not* advocate spanking a child for toileting accidents.

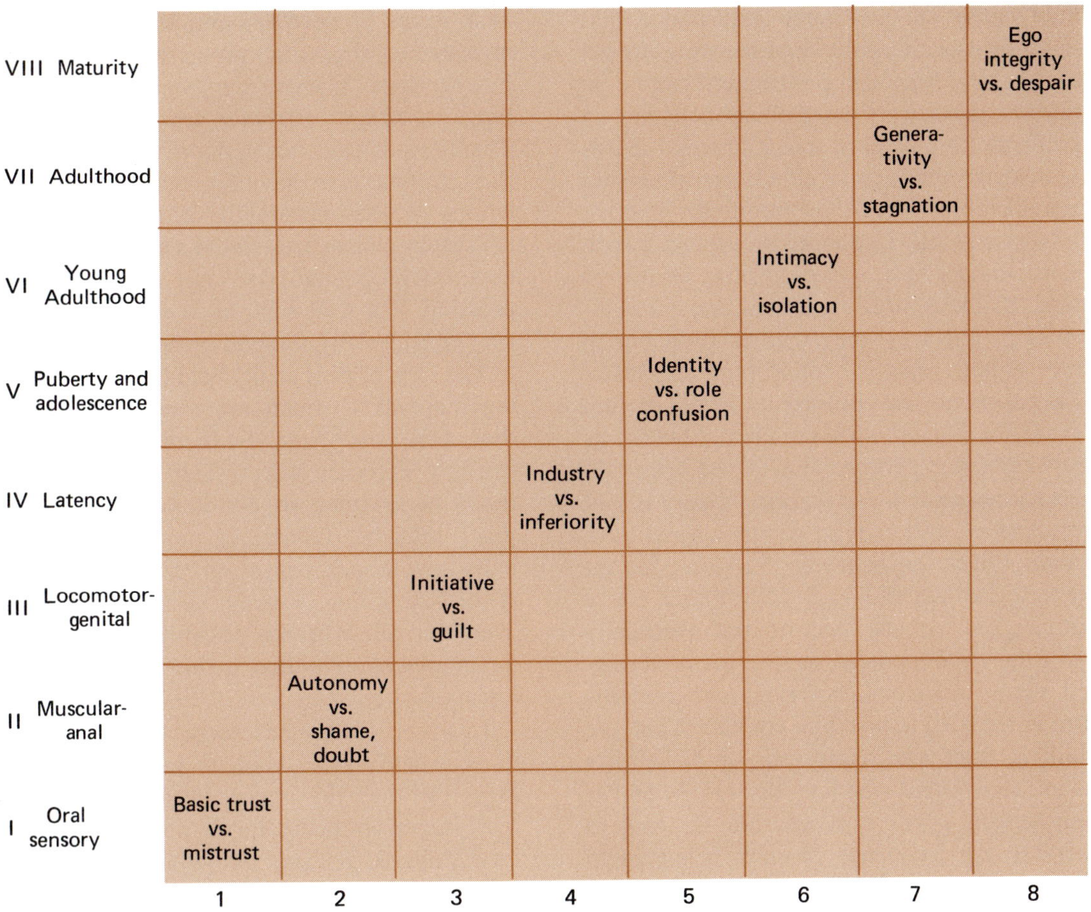
VIII Maturity
VII Adulthood
VI Young Adulthood
V Puberty and adolescence
IV Latency
III Locomotor-genital
II Muscular-anal
I Oral sensory
Ego integrity vs. despair
Genera-tivity vs. stagnation
Intimacy vs. isolation
Identity vs. role confusion
Industry vs. inferiority
Initiative vs. guilt
Autonomy vs. shame, doubt
Basic trust vs. mistrust
1
2
3
4
5
6
7
8

Figure 9.4 Erikson's psychosocial stages of development, a stage theory of development that is partially related to Freud's ideas but also includes many novel contributions. Erikson's theory focuses on areas of personality development specific to different ages, from infancy to old age. (Reprinted from CHILDHOOD AND SOCIETY, Second Edition, Revised, by Erik H. Erikson. By permission of W. W. Norton & Co., Inc. and The Hogarth Press, LTD. Copyright 1950, © 1963 by W. W. Norton & Co., Inc.)

Many parents would not hesitate to punish an older child but might balk at punishing an infant. Actually, learning theory has specific things to say about the effects of punishment that are particularly relevant to child development. Punishment may suppress a response temporarily, but often the response will reappear unless some *new* response is learned in that situation. Punishment does not necessarily establish new responses and, if severe, may actually inhibit learning. For example, spanking a two-year-old child for soiling his pants *may* speed up the process of toilet training *if* it is accompanied with positively reinforced responses on the toilet. On the other hand, severe punishment alone could cause an emotional disturbance that would disrupt the process of learning proper toilet habits. Although punishment can be an effective method of controlling behavior in certain situations, most developmental learning theorists find that its effects are somewhat unpredictable. Thus they frequently suggest that undesirable responses be replaced with desirable ones by means of positive reinforcement. If undesirable responses are not reinforced in any way, they tend to drop out in favor of new, positively reinforced responses. This notion may be contrary to the old dictum "spare the rod and spoil the child," but it has the weight of experimental evidence behind it.

Another principle of learning theory is that *intermittent schedules of reinforcement* have unique effects on behavior. Suppose, for instance, that a child nags his mother for a cookie. At first she says no but eventually gives the child a cookie to stop his pestering. On other occasions, however, she remains firm in refusing to give him cookies. Thus the child is positively reinforced for his efforts on an intermittent schedule. Because he learns that begging pays off on occasion, he tends to increase the frequency of such behavior to maximize the payoffs. The consistent mother, on the other hand, saves herself a great deal of trouble. If her "no" means just that, the child quickly learns about this regularity in his environment and realizes that further requests will be futile. He may still make frequent requests if his environment has not been specified well enough so that he knows *when* a cookie is likely to be forthcoming. Children look for consistency in their environment and respond accordingly. Much of the strife between parents and children is related to parental *inconsistencies* in patterns of reinforcement and social interaction.

The social learning theory view of personality is quite different from the psychoanalytic approach. Instead of focusing on general traits derived from early experiences in the oral and anal stages of development, learning theory investigates the total range of experience. Furthermore, it views personality as a wide range of *situation-specific* learned behavior. Two lines of evidence support this approach. First, most studies have found that the correlations between personality traits that Freudian theory claims are related are either low or nonexistent. Second, for most people the expression of a trait such as honesty seems to vary considerably, depending on the situation.

The view of personality held by social learning theorists is much more optimistic than that of the psychoanalytic theorists. Although learning theorists acknowledge that certain kinds of learning in childhood (e.g., phobias) may be difficult to modify, they usually give equal weight to the child's total range of learning experiences as he develops. They also allow for the possibility of "behavior modification"—that is, old habits can be replaced by learning new habits.

Learning theory has some serious limitations. Some early theorists ignored certain aspects of the behaving organism, perhaps the most important being the child's maturational level. John B. Watson, one of the founders of behaviorism, wrote in 1928 that infants should be toilet trained at six months of age. Apparently, he did not realize that the neural mechanisms for *voluntary* control of excretory functions are not completely mature until the child is approximately eighteen months old. Young infants can be conditioned to excrete when set on the toilet at approximately six months of age, but no amount of training will enable them to *inhibit* excretion until they are maturationally ready. Contemporary social learning theorists are aware of the importance of physical maturation and also recognize that the older child's cognitive development often depends on his level of cognitive maturity. Thus other aspects of the child must be considered, in addition to his previous learning history.

The principles of social learning theory just described suggest that the child is a *passive* organism, shaped by specific environmental reinforcement patterns. Although this may be the case in many instances, a large amount of learning and new behavior emerge without specific reinforcement, as we noted in the previous chapter in the context of cognitive and language development. This is also probably true for many aspects of social and personality development. Piaget accounts for the emergence of nonreinforced behavior by viewing the child's attempts to understand his world as *self-motivated.*

Modern social learning theory also recognizes the emergence of behavior that does not seem to be associated with direct reinforcement contingencies. Much of this behavior has been placed under the general label of *modeling,* that is, the child "learns" new behavior by copying the behavior of someone else. Social learning theorists have shown that a child is more likely to follow a model whose behavior is rewarded, and thus they have tried to ground the concept of modeling in the basic laws of learning. However, a considerable amount of modeling behavior may occur *without* any such vicarious reinforcement. Perhaps Piaget's view of the child's development as self-motivated is more appropriate in many cases.

Whatever the precise mechanisms involved in modeling, it is clear that children emulate the behavior of significant people in their social environment—parents, siblings, and peers. In fact, modeling may be the *most* important contributing factor to social and personality development. We will consider the nature of these influences in more detail in the following section.

Each of the four theoretical approaches described here has a different perspective on the organism, and each makes its unique contribution to our understanding of child development. We can now apply these theories to specific aspects of child development at different age levels.

Major Aspects of Development at Different Age Levels

As the child progresses through infancy, early childhood, late childhood, and adolescence, the major forces of socialization change. In infancy the major social force is the mother. In early childhood the social forces broaden to include the father, siblings, and neighborhood playmates. In late childhood and adolescence, the school and peers become dominant forces. The aspects of personality development that are most prominent vary, depending on the age level and social context. Because a thorough treatment of this topic would require more than a full-length book, we will narrow our focus to a few important components of development at each age level.

Infancy

Infant studies are relatively recent in contributing to our understanding of personality development. Freud recognized that experiences in infancy were a major force in development, but he never supported his speculations with experimental evidence. Although recent studies offer little support for Freud's speculations, they have demonstrated that infancy is a unique and important stage in which we can view the beginning of social behaviors and further assess the interaction of heredity and environment.

Individual Differences at Birth

Mothers of several children typically report that each child behaved differently as an infant. Some of these differences are probably related to differences in the intrauterine environment, but many of them are associated with genetic variables. For example, in early infancy, identical twins are much more alike than fraternal twins in terms of activity and irritability (Scarr, 1969). Individual differences in the temperament of newborns can be readily observed during a visit to the nursery in your local hospital.

Let us consider how these genetic differences might affect the infant's developing personality. Some characteristics, such as *level of activity,* may be expressed in a fairly direct way throughout one's life. However, the effects of genetically controlled behavioral differences should not be considered separately from the child's environment. Consider the mother-infant relationship in infancy. Early studies of mother-infant interactions focused on the mother's effect on the child. Recent research, however, has focused on how the infant's behavior affects the mother or caretaker.

Ethologists have gathered considerable evidence from other mammals to show that an infant's behavior has powerful effects on the mother's behavior. But relatively little research of this kind has been done on human infant-mother interactions. The anecdotal observation that mothers respond differently to different children has been supplemented by studies of foster mothers in foster homes, which indicate that the care given by these women varies with different infants. Moss (1967) found that male infants tend to be more irritable than females at three weeks of age and that this factor is later correlated with less frequent social stimulation of males by the mother. Although research on the effects of the infant-mother relationship is still rather fragmentary, it has forced us to revise our views of the infant as a *passive recipient* of environmental input to an *active shaper* of his environment.

Smiling and Early Social Experience

Smiling is one of the infant's major modes of social interaction. By three months of age, infants vary considerably in their propensity to smile and coo. The effects of this behavior are bidirectional: The happy, smiling infant elicits more social attention than the passive one does. The more social attention the infant receives, the more he smiles. Rheingold (1956) spent two months talking, smiling, and handling eight institutionalized six-month-old infants. At the end of this period these babies were significantly more socially responsive (they smiled and babbled more) than the other infants in the institution (see fig. 9.5). However, the improvement was

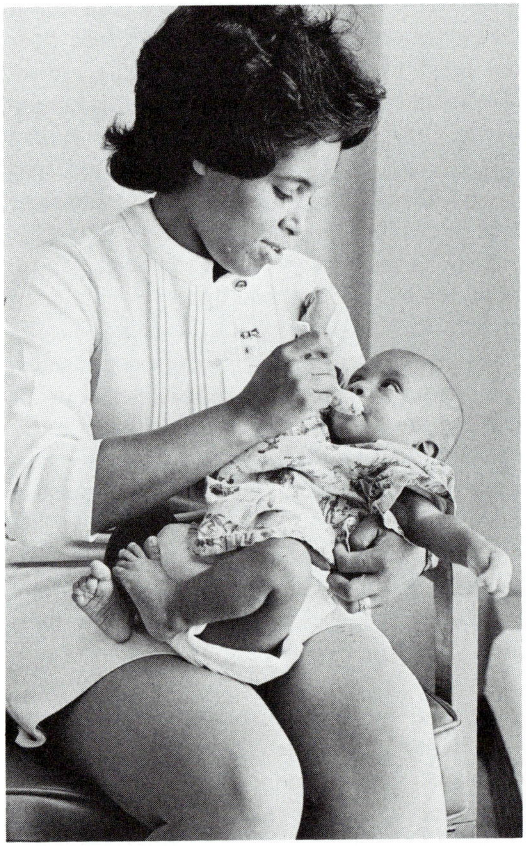

Figure 9.5 Infant smiling at a caretaker in an institution. If the caretaker does not respond, the child's smiling will decrease. (Courtesy University of Chicago Hospitals.)

temporary; when the children were retested at age two, little or no difference was found between experimental and control groups. Apparently the treatment was too brief to establish permanent behavior patterns.

Environmental differences of *long duration* in infancy tend to have more lasting and pronounced effects. Gewirtz (1965) studied the frequency of smiling among infants raised in Israel under three different conditions. Children in one group received institutional care with little social interaction; those in the second group were raised in a Kibbutz nursery and had some daily contact with their parents. The third group was raised in a normal family environment. Figure 9.6 shows the rather large differences among the groups' frequency of smiling between the ages of ten and eighteen months.

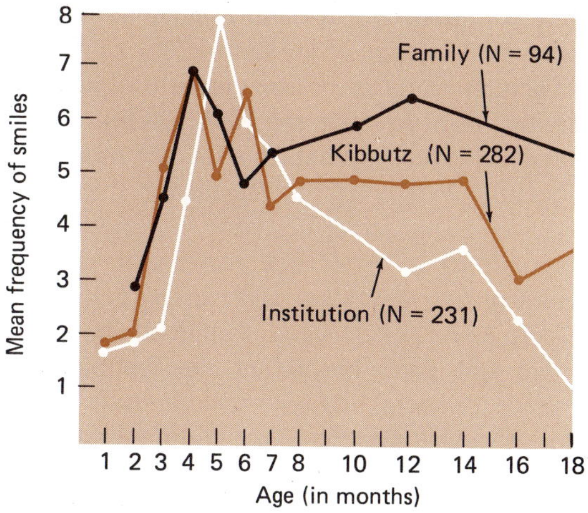

Figure 9.6 Frequency of smiling among infants in three different environments. Initially, the frequency is similar in all three environments. Later, its frequency varies, depending on the environment.

Mother-Infant Interaction

Patterns of mother-infant interaction influence many aspects of child development, including motor, cognitive, and social competence. *Specific* caretaking practices, such as breast or bottle feeding, do not seem to have much influence. Most important is the mother's overall attitude and behavior toward the infant. Infants of severely rejecting mothers tend to be retarded in cognitive and social development, while infants of accepting mothers tend to develop normally.

Maternal behavior that is *contingent* upon the infant's behavior is one of the most important general components of maternal stimulation. For example, when physically handling the infant, the mother should be responsive to his movements. During verbal expression, and eye contact, she should be responsive to behavior initiated by the infant. Toys are likely to be ineffective stimuli unless the mother plays *with* the infant.

Clarke-Stewart (1973) describes the "optimal mother" as follows:

> [She] . . . is aware of her infant's needs and wishes—hunger, fatigue, desire for physical or social contact—and . . . responds to behavioral expressions of these needs and desires immediately and contingently. She gives care or stimulation which is appropriate for her infant according to his state, individual capacities, and developmental level. She is affectionate, accepting, and nonrestrictive.

Clarke-Stewart also points out that the infant's behavior has a strong effect on the mother, especially during the first few months. The infant who looks and smiles at his mother is more likely to receive those responses from his mother. The fact that these behavioral sequences can be initiated and terminated by the infant as well as the mother means that a balance of social control can be reached.

The bidirectional nature of mother-infant interactions makes it difficult to predict how a particular woman will respond to the mothering task. Suppose that a young mother is at first ambiguous about her new role, and her early interactions with the baby are somewhat distant. Fortunately, the baby's temperament is calm and nondemanding, so the early stages of mothering go smoothly. Then, around two or three months of age, the baby begins to smile and babble at his mother and achieve eye contact with her more frequently. Whatever the reason for the emergence of this social behavior, the mother responds to it. And as a pattern of positive interaction develops and strengthens, she feels more positive and confident about her role and gives her infant the feedback he needs for social and emotional growth. These positive attitudes may then continue throughout the parent-child relationship. Note that it was the *infant* who initiated this positive chain of events. Thus the hypothetical pattern of interaction could be negative if the infant initially tended to be irritable and asocial.

Social Deprivation

Relatively little is known about the long-term effects of social deprivation in infancy. Follow-up studies of children raised in institutions tend to show that as adults, these individuals have problems in the area of social and personal adjustment. However, the maladjustment tends to be less severe if the children are adopted before the age of two or three. Thus the child's social development is not confined exclusively to a *critical period* in the early years. This fact was demonstrated by the study mentioned in Chapter 2 in which thirteen children under the age of three were transferred from a poorly staffed orphanage to an institution for the retarded, where they received a large amount of personal attention and affection from retarded adults. Although these children had been classified as socially and intellectually retarded, remarkable improvement was noted after a period of close personal care. Later, when it was established that these children were *not* retarded, most of them were placed in adoptive homes. At age 30 the subjects in the experimental group were functioning normally and independently in society. Most of the subjects in the control group remained in institutions and were classified as retarded or mentally disturbed (Skeels, 1966).

Attachment

"Attachment" is a concept derived from ethological observations of maternal behavior in animals. In some species that are mobile shortly after birth, the infant becomes attached to, or *imprints* on its mother and attempts to maintain physical proximity with her. During early infancy, separations of only a few days can seriously disrupt attachment and mothering behavior in some species such as goats and sheep. The ethological conception of attachment as a special bond between mother and infant can be extended to the study of human mother-infant relationships.

The phenomenon of attachment in humans is evidenced by two types of infant behavior: fear of strangers (often called "stranger anxiety") and separation anxiety. *Stranger anxiety* emerges in *some* infants at approximately seven months of age and may continue for several months. When a stranger approaches the infant, he sobers and eventually cries. The explanation for his behavior may be partially *perceptual,* because the anxiety emerges shortly after the infant's perceptual sophistication develops to the point where he can discriminate different faces. However, some infants do not show such disturbance, which indicates that additional factors are involved. For example, if the infant's social contacts have been limited to those with his mother, the discrepancy between her and strangers is likely to trigger an anxiety reaction. The infant who has had frequent contact with siblings and others is unlikely to be disturbed by the presence of a new face.

Separation anxiety has been studied in situations similar to those used by Harlow and Zimmerman in their work with monkeys and the results have been comparable. In strange and unfamiliar situations, the year-old infant clings to his mother for security. Later, however, he will begin to explore the new environment and may even crawl into an adjoining room, out of his mother's sight. However, he will check on her frequently to restore his confidence (see fig. 9.7). This *detachment* and exploration depend on the infant's attachment to the mother as a base of security.

The effects of separation from the mother or caretaker vary widely among infants, and the reasons for these differences are unclear. After separations of only a few days, some infants exhibit an increase in attachment behavior and tend to cling to their mothers; others may react with ambivalent, rejecting, and angry responses. Prolonged separations can lead to a general detachment and lack of response when the mother returns, and considerable time may pass before the infant reattaches to her.

The ethological view of attachment emphasizes the bond between the *biological* mother and infant. However, the results of several social experiments cast doubt on the importance of this particular bond. Box 9.1 describes the methods of raising children in Israel's Kibbutz settlements, where infants have relatively little contact with their parents. Bettleheim (1969) has suggested that the lack of contact between infant and mother has led to problems in forming intimate adult relationships. Other researchers, however, do not agree. They find that adults who were raised in the Kibbutzim have a strong sense of group affiliation and confidence, and they form intimate relationships as well as people reared in other societies.

Infant Needs

Erikson (1963) views infancy as a period in which the child establishes a sense of basic trust in the world. Part of this trust depends on satisfaction of bodily needs, such as food and warmth. Erikson emphasizes the *infant need-adult response contingency* and recommends that parents avoid imposing schedules of feeding and play on their infants.

Figure 9.7 Infant detachment. The infant will explore an adjoining room if he can return to his mother for security. (From Rheingold, H. L. & Eckerman, C. O. "The infant separates himself from his mother." *Science,* Vol. 168, pp. 78–83, Fig. 5, 3 April 1970. Copyright 1970 by The American Association for the Advancement of Science.)

In our culture, most infants are adequately cared for in terms of their bodily needs. The major variability is in the quality of social interaction. Most parents, however, will adequately fill their child's social needs without the advice of "experts." Benjamin Spock (1945) offers the following advice to parents:

Don't be overawed by what the experts say. Don't be afraid to trust your own common sense. Bringing up your child won't be a complicated job if you take it easy, trust your own instincts, and follow the directions that your doctor gives you. We know for a fact that the natural loving care that kindly parents give their children is a hundred times more valuable than their knowing how to pin a diaper on just right or how to make a formula expertly. Every time you pick your baby up, even if you do it a little awkwardly at first, every time you change him, bathe him, feed

Box 9.1

Child Rearing in the Kibbutz

Most children in the United States are reared primarily by their parents and live with them at least through high school. Thus it may seem surprising that the children of the Kibbutz settlements in Israel are raised with other children, in houses away from their parents, by an unrelated adult caretaker. The children progress by age through a series of five "childrens houses": four days to one year in the infant house, one year to four years in the toddlers house, four years to seven years in the kindergarten house, seven to twelve in the child's house, and thirteen to eighteen in the youth house. Caretakers remain with a particular house and thus are closely associated with the children only during a particular age range. By most accounts, children do not become particularly attached to the caretakers. Parents typically visit with their children for some time in the evenings, but most of the child's social contact is with his peers. They eat, go to school, play, and sleep together. From infancy, the children rely on each other for most of their security and companionship.

him, smile at him, he's getting a feeling that he belongs to you and that you belong to him. Nobody else in the world, no matter how skillful, can give that to him.

Early Childhood

The majority of two- to five-year-olds in American society spend most of their time with and are most controlled by the *family.* Several important aspects of personality begin to form in this context. One is the need to conform to social demands. During toilet training, the child learns that there are certain restrictions on his behavior and rules to follow. Another aspect of his personality develops as he strives to deal with his expanding world, while remaining dependent on adult guidance and support. Much of his personality development evolves from modeling his parents' behavior.

Early Socialization Demands

The first rules children learn involve the inhibition and control of natural impulses to urinate, defecate, explore, and aggress or cry when frustrated. The methods for social control of these impulses include punishment, reward, and the establishment of primitive concepts of what behavior is "good" or "bad."

Toilet training has been the subject of considerable research and speculation with regard to the appropriate age, methods, and subsequent effects on personality (Sears, Maccoby, and Levin, 1957). Most American mothers begin toilet training when their infants are about twelve months old and complete it within six months. Training usually consists of reward and praise for bowel movements on the toilet and some form of negative reaction for accidents in the pants. Many theorists believe that the major mechanism of control —particularly for children who are less than eighteen months old—is anxiety induced by punishment. After the child has been punished several times for an "accident," he tends to associate the sensations that *precede* urination and defecation with memories of previous punishment and anxiety. This leads him to inhibit the punished response and substitute the rewarded toilet response. Older children are cognitively differentiated enough to want to please their mothers and may learn toilet habits primarily through positive reinforcement. In some cultures, such as the Kwoma of New Guinea, there is no toilet training (Whiting and Child, 1953). When the child is old enough to understand, his parents simply tell him what to do, or he does it by modeling because he is motivated by a desire to conform to the cultural patterns of his family. Many American children, however, are probably trained by partially punitive methods.

Freudian theorists suggest that a cluster of personality traits are associated with strict toilet training, and they ascribe special evils to harsh training. For instance, consistently harsh training may make the child feel fearful, anxious, and powerless; he has no choice but to submit to his parents' will and obsessively follows their demands. As a result, his personality is likely to be characterized by a generalized inhibition of independent action, compulsive orderliness, and a negative self-concept.

In fact, these personality traits *do* tend to occur together. But rather than being directly related to harsh toilet training, as claimed by Freudian-psychoanalytic theory, the extent to which these traits are correlated in the child's personality may depend on a similar correlation in the mother. Mothers who practice strict toilet training also tend to be compulsive, orderly, and generally restrictive. In other words, the child may learn these traits from his mother rather than develop them in response to her harsh methods of toilet training. This view is more congruent with the social learning approach.

Other areas of impulse control involve similar methods and possible effects on personality. The child's drive to explore is often a major inconvenience to parents and dangerous to the child. The destruction that the eighteen-month-old leaves in his wake as a result of exploring his mother's collection of china certainly is not malicious, and parents should realize this and place fragile items out of his reach. Ideally, the environment should contain many objects that the child can explore freely without danger of destruction. Of course, some restrictions on a child's exploratory behavior are necessary. However, harsh restriction of his exploratory drives can lead to fearful, inhibited interactions with the environment and a lack of spontaneity.

Need for Rules and Consistency

In an ideal world, rules might be unnecessary. In the imperfect world we actually live in, however, a certain amount of conformity to society's rules is vital. Futhermore, regardless of society's need for rules, children may need rules for healthy development. The range of possible behavior is almost infinite, and parentally imposed rules for behavior may serve to reduce a child's uncertainty about his own behavior to manageable levels. Baumrind (1970) found that children of *permissive,* warm parents tend to lack self-reliance and inquisitiveness, while *authoritarian* parents, who control through harsh punishment, tend to produce children who are discontent, withdrawn, and distrustful. In Baumrind's opinion the ideal parent is one who exerts a high degree of control but encourages the child's striving for autonomy in appropriate areas. Children raised in this environment tend to be self-reliant, self-controlled, and inquisitive.

Because of the child's need for consistency, an inconsistent environment often leads to behavior problems. When an undesirable behavior is punished inconsistently, the child may deliberately repeat the behavior to find out what the consequence will be this time. In other words, his need to discover the contingencies in his environment may override his fear of potential punishment. Families in which there is constant conflict between parent and child typically show a pattern of inconsistency in their interactions. The parents are sometimes overwhelmed by their children's bad behavior and feel helpless. Thus they may become even more inconsistent, and the child's behavior may become worse. If this pattern is not modified, the child may develop a manipulative personality and feel alienated from his parents. A behavior-oriented treatment that stresses the child's need for consistency and makes specific recommendations for behavior control is usually effective with this kind of problem.

Modeling and Identification

Although punishment and reward continue to be used throughout childhood as methods of controlling behavior, a new kind of behavioral control emerges when the child is about three or four years old. Freudian-psychoanalytic theory calls it identification; social learning theorists call it modeling. A primitive form of identification with the parents occurs when the two- or three-year-old tries to be a "good boy" in his parents' eyes. The child's motivation, however, is still closely tied to rewards for "good" behavior and punishment for "bad" behavior.

Between the ages of three and five the child begins to learn by observing his parents' behavior, for reasons less directly associated with punishment and reward. This shift relies, somewhat in part, on cognitive development, because parental behavior patterns and values are complex and the child must outgrow his egocentrism before he can be sensitive to them.

What are the differences between psychoanalytic and learning theory with regard to the cause of identification and modeling? Freudian psychoanalytic theory suggests that identification with the parent of the same sex and adoption of his values and behavior is based in part on fear of punishment, particularly in the male child (see Chapter 17), and in part on the desire to obtain the parent's affection. This identification goes a step beyond the concepts of "good boy"/"bad boy" associated with direct punishment. The child adopts a broad range of behavior and values from his parents without reward or punishment of *specific* behaviors. He understands explicitly or implicitly, that by being more like his parents he will gain their love.

Modeling, the term used in the social learning approach to imitative behavior, is almost identical in meaning to identification—that is, children adopt the behavior of others. However, there are some important theoretical differences in the way the terms are used. Social learning theory views modeling in a broad social context that ranges from parents to characters in television programs. Second, it emphatically rejects the Freudian psychosexual interpretation of identification. However, the two theories do have one point in common. When the social learning or psychoanalytic theorist considers the reason for modeling or identification, he typically states that the child perceives probable rewards for himself, based on what happened to the model as a consequence of the model's actions. Stretching this notion to include a cognitive interpretation, we can say that the child models his parents because he recognizes their power and competence and wants these qualities himself. Bandura, Ross, and Ross (1963) demonstrated that mere exposure to a model is sufficient to induce learning. For example, watching an aggressive model in a movie may increase a child's aggressiveness (see fig. 10.1). However, whether a child will imitate the model depends on several variables: If the model has previously been nurturant toward the observing child in real life or is perceived as powerful and able to dispense favors, the probability of modeling increases. A similar increase occurs when the model is rewarded for his behavior.

A *cognitive developmental* view of modeling has been proposed by Kagan (1971), who believes that four- and five-year-olds begin to *perceive similarities* between themselves and their parent of the same sex. This self-concept of being like the parent leads to a feeling of sharing in the parent's successes and failures. Kagan demonstrated that when observing a contest between the parent and a stranger, children are excited and elated when the parent wins. This was viewed as evidence that children identify with their parents and share in their affective states. Further strengthening of identification occurs when children perceive the parent's attributes, such as power and skill, as desirable and believe that by acting more like him, they will attain these attributes for themselves.

The motivational basis for modeling in Freudian and social learning theory is also partly shared by cognitive developmental theory. Changes in identification and modeling after Kagan's perceived similarity stage are motivated by the child's perception of possible benefits. Several aspects of modeling behavior suggest that all three theoretical explanations are incomplete. Children and parents often exhibit similar personality traits, which may be either positive or *negative* with respect to successful adjustment (see fig. 9.8). From the motivational point of view, it is difficult to understand why children would model themselves after a neurotic and anxious adult, for example.

A fourth view of modeling stresses the range of behavior present in the child's social environment and the child's need to *interact* and grow in that environment. In the American family, the preschool child usually interacts most often with his parents; thus the range of behavior that he can model is limited.

At least some of the behavior within the available range will be modeled for two reasons and in two different ways. First, the child interacts with his parents partly because he is biologically programmed as a social being. We have already seen that the child actually initiates the majority of social interactions during early infancy. We have also seen that the infant's social behavior continues to develop *within* a pattern of interaction that is strongly influenced by the way the parents treat the infant. One personality variable that seems to be correlated between parents and children is "social distance": that is, cold, distant parents tend to be unresponsive to the child and do little to reinforce warm social behavior. The child then becomes like his parents, because they set the limits of his behavior through their own responses.

Although some theorists would hesitate to call this behavior modeling or identification, we will do so because we are trying to dis-

Figure 9.8 Modeling of personality. Feiffer's rather grim view of "like father, like son." Modeling of positive traits also occurs. (Feiffer, September 17, 1973, *Colorado Daily*. Reprinted by permission of Publishers-Hall Syndicate.)

cover how children become similar to their parents or other significant figures in the social environment. Here, the term modeling will be used when referring to the presence of similarities; it will not be used to imply a specific mechanism.

A second basis for modeling the parents involves less direct social interaction. As the child's motor and cognitive functions develop, he begins to live in a context that increasingly overlaps with the parents' world. For example, he may go to the store or take trips with them. The presence of the parents during these forays into the world again defines the range of behavior that can be modeled, and the parents' reactions to the world may be a major aspect of personality that the child will model. Some parents are confident and comfortable with their lives, while others are less so. In either case, the parent shows the child how to live in the outside world, and the child looks to the parent for the lesson. Because children respond directly to the affective states of their parents *and* to the contingencies between these affective states and relevant events in the environment, they learn from the parents how to respond in various situations. Their motivation may not involve a desire to be like the parents or to gain their affection or their power; they may simply want to *learn* how to respond to the world, to learn what things are happy or sad, dangerous or safe. This view of social and personality modeling is close to Piaget's conception of the motivation underlying cognitive development. The one-and-a-half-year-old child explores his environment intensely because he wants to learn about the world and exercise his expanding cognitive capacity; thus he will extract his information from the environment that is available to him.

To the extent that parents dominate the social environment of their young children, they will be the major force in shaping their children's early personality. Much of this shaping occurs unintentionally through the parents' pattern of living. This view of personality development places less emphasis on specific training. No doubt, parents may shape certain specific characteristics by specific training, but the child's basic social skills, adjustment, and confidence may in part be acquired from the parents in much more subtle ways. This view is both disturbing and challenging because parents are responsible for being good examples of how to live.

Late Childhood

Most five- and six-year-old children in our culture move into a new and broadened social context when they enter kindergarten or grade school. Here they encounter teachers and other children, who will have a powerful influence on their social and personality development. How a child develops in this new context will depend in part on his previous social experiences within the family.

The family will continue to exert a powerful influence on the child, through modeling of parent behavior and more direct controls over the child. This influence will be greater if the family is warm and emotionally supportive. Brothers and sisters may supplement parental influences in many ways. Siblings may help the child learn patterns of intimate social cooperation and interaction. They can also teach the child that interaction with others is based on competition.

We will now consider how the interaction between the school and expanded neighborhood environment on the one hand and the family on the other affect two major areas of development; *social interactions*—involving friendship, cooperation, competition, dominance and the like, and *socialized values*—involving society's general view of desirable behavior.

Social Interaction

Children are well on their way toward greater social participation by the time they reach school. Parten (1933) compared the amounts of onlooking, solitary play, parallel play, cooperative play, and associative group play observed in children ages two to four and a half. As shown in figure 9.9, he found that the amount of associative group play and cooperative play increased dramatically during this period, while onlooker and solitary play diminished sharply.

On their first day of school, many children are confronted for the first time with a large group of strange children and an authority figure other than their parents. Some children enjoy these new encounters, while others react with silence and fear. Teachers are well aware of the broad range of reactions exhibited by children attending school for the first time, patterns of which will have important consequences for socialization in the new context.

Early social interactions in the classroom and on the playground are in part competitive, involving the establishment of dominance hierarchies, and in part cooperative, involving friendships and group play.

The tendency of children to sort themselves into a *hierarchy of dominance* may be partly based on our evolutionary heritage as mentioned earlier. Social organization in other primates is clearly marked by dominance hierarchies. Goodall's (1971) studies of chimpanzee colonies in their natural habitat reveal a rather distinct and stable dominance hierarchy. Although battles for dominance do occur occasionally, as younger males challenge the older ones for control of the troop, observation on any given day usually reveals a stable and cooperative social group. Relative positions of dominance are usually related to size, strength, and aggressiveness. However, one smaller chimp rose to the top position when he discovered that he could make a tremendous racket by kicking two

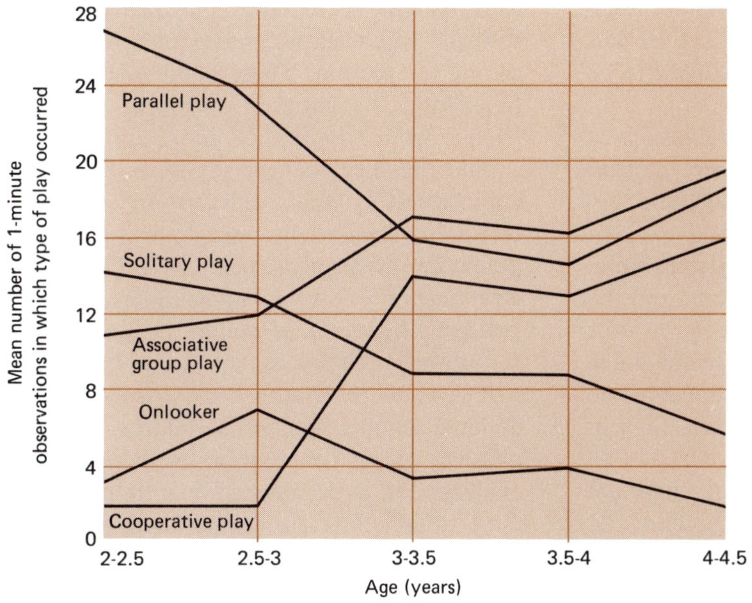

Figure 9.9 Play patterns as a function of age. Note the increase in group and cooperative play with increasing age. (From Parten, M. B., "Social participation among preschool children," *Journal of Abnormal and Social Psychology* 27, 1933, pp. 243–269. Copyright 1933 by the American Psychological Association. Reprinted by permission.)

empty gasoline cans as he ran along. This remarkable bit of intelligent behavior so intimidated the larger males that they yielded to the can-kicker without a direct physical contest.

Physical size, strength, and aggressiveness are also important factors among children, although somewhat less so than in our primate relatives. Some direct physical aggression may be involved in the settling of children's arguments, but general athletic skills probably contribute more to prestige and dominance, particularly among boys. "Choosing up sides" is an age-old formula for picking two balanced teams, and it also defines the order of social preference more or less directly. As this ritual is repeated children develop a strong sense of their relative position because the order of choices tends to be somewhat consistent. Athletic skills are highly valued in our society (witness the parental frenzy over Little League baseball games), and the child who does well athletically may reap advantages beyond the athletic field—the admiration of his peers and a general sense of confidence. Many other factors will ultimately contribute to adult prestige, but boys who are physically advanced *tend* to be more dominant as adults.

Other factors may also contribute to a child's relative prestige. For instance, intellectual competence is highly valued in some segments of our society. Family prestige and socioeconomic level may also contribute, through both the child's self-concept and the group's respect for such status. Perhaps *most* important are the child's general social skills. If he is friendly, outgoing, and confident, he will be respected by others and rank high in general popularity.

Competitiveness, with its ethic of individual achievement, has been considered one of the most significant characteristics of American society. The struggle for social dominance is based on the assumption that everyone has an equal chance to "make it to the top," and that those who strive hardest will win. Children learn this at home, in the school, and in the community. In each new social situation, they strive for approval and prestige. The game is repeated over and over again as the child's social groups change from grade to grade. Some children become good at the game and identify themselves as winners; others perceive themselves as losers. These *self-concepts* may in turn influence the child's physical, intellectual, and social achievements in the future. In other words, self-concepts can become self-fulfilling prophecies. Although self-defined winners benefit from the competitive struggle, they often pay the price of anxiety. But the real tragedy for our society may be the lost potential of self-defined losers.

No society can survive unless its children are trained to *cooperate*. Doing things together, being part of the "team," is highly valued, even in extremely competitive societies. During late childhood there is much practice of cooperative social skills in games and various group projects, such as building forts, forming secret clubs, playing house, and so forth. Friendships can be clearly identified during this period. These childhood interactions form the patterns of cooperation and friendship in adolescence and adulthood.

The balance between cooperation and competition is quite different in other societies. In England the child's position is often defined by his family's social class. This social stratification limits the opportunities for competitive interaction, as well as the possibilities for upward mobility.

The Israeli Kibbutz system discourages individual competition in its children and emphasizes group cooperation. Although some evidence of a dominance hierarchy exists, most interactions are cooperative; the children literally take care of each other. Individual achievement is allowed as long as it contributes to the group's welfare, but being a good comrade is most important. The children of this social experiment tend to grow into "well-adjusted" adolescents and adults. The incidence of psychosis, neurosis, and delinquency is low compared with American norms. Much of this difference is undoubtedly related to the security, stability, and control in a highly structured society. Part of this security and stability derives from the emphasis on comradeship and cooperation and the downgrading of competition. Thus the Kibbutz system avoids generating groups of self-defined losers and neurotic winners.

Social Values

Each society seeks to instill values in its children. Competitiveness and individual achievement are valued in America and are encouraged in its school system. Group orientation and comradeship are encouraged in Kibbutz children. These different orientations not only prepare children to live in their society but perpetuate the social order and prepare the next generation. Thus we see a good deal of stability in national character, as long as radical revolution does not intervene.

However, the U.S.S.R. and China, which did undergo radical revolution, have managed to establish a new, stable social order relatively quickly. Both countries accomplished this by intensively training their children, as described in box 9.2.

American society, on the other hand, may be somewhat less stable and is faced with a number of extremely serious social problems that are rapidly becoming worse. The rate of juvenile delinquency, including violent crimes such as murder, has nearly doubled over the past ten years. And there is a general feeling of helplessness and lack of purpose. Why? Let's take a look at our methods of socializing children.

At their best, the American family, school, peer group, and economic system integrate reasonably well; they provide structure and continuity in the socialization process. However, a number of cracks have appeared in the system over the past thirty years. Many parents have delegated the responsibility for instilling values in their children to the schools; at the same time, the schools are less able than ever before to perform this function. Today's schools have considerably less control over children than they had in the past. Part of this change has been intentional, based on the notion that a child's potential will be best realized in a free environment. However, a large amount of the schools' loss of control can be attributed to the fact that things have sometimes gotten "out of hand."

The disintegration of the schools' authority would not be so serious if the same thing were not happening in many families. Box 9.3 details some relatively recent disruptive changes in family structure and society. In an estimated six million American families, both parents work or, for some other reason, are not at home when the children come home from school. As a result, the peer group takes over the major socializing function, with potentially dangerous results. Peer groups have always been an important factor in socialization, but in the past they were relatively continuous with the rest of society. Now there is a difference. Now many of them are distinctly noncontinuous with the rest of society and may promote values that conflict directly with prevailing social norms. Some of these groups have attempted to be constructive, offering visions of a better society. The so-called "counterculture" of the 1960s cited corruption in the "American way of life" and challenged traditional values. However, other groups that emerged from the new-found freedom would be considered destructive by any society. The result for many children of the 1960s has been disillusionment and alienation: Some have found that their values are incompatible with those of the larger society and economy; others are totally unprepared

Box 9.2

Socialization in the U.S.S.R. and China

Both Russia and China have undergone major social revolution in the last half century. Even though the Chinese revolution is only about twenty-five years old, it has resulted in a remarkably stable social order. Both Russia and China have focused much of their energy toward the education of their children.

Russian children are instilled with three major values, work, cooperative group interaction, and social control of behavior. Even very young children are required to perform chores within the limits of their ability. (See box fig. 9.2a.)

> *Beginning in the second year of nursery and continuing through kindergarten, children are expected to take on ever increasing communal responsibilities, such as helping others, serving at table, cleaning up, gardening, caring for animals, and shoveling snow. The effects of these socializing experiences are reflected in the youngster's behavior, with many children giving an impression of self-confidence and comradery. (Bronfenbrenner, 1970, p. 25).*

Competition is encouraged in the schools, but always between groups rather than individuals. In grade schools, a group may consist of children seated in a row. The overall standing of each row of children in quality of recitations, personal cleanliness, and so forth is recorded on charts in the classroom. Individual entries are never made, but the group is encouraged to exert considerable pressure on individuals who do not contribute their share to the group effort. Manuals of Soviet education refer to this as "socialist competition."

Social control is exerted primarily by the group rather than the teacher. Her main duty is to set standards for performance, teach, and evaluate the group's behavior. When a child needs prodding, the teacher encourages the group to exert pressure on and evaluate him. (See box fig. 9.2b.) If she must refer to an individual child's behavior, she is likely to suggest that he has failed his comrades.

Bronfenbrenner (1970) evaluated the consequences of Soviet training in social control in terms of two types of behavior; the children's willingness to misbehave and their reactions to misbehavior in others. Ten hypothetical situations that involved actions such as cheating and denying responsibility for property damage were presented to Soviet grade school children under three different assumed conditions: (1) no one would know of their actions, (2) adults would know, and (3) classmates would know. Bronfenbrenner found that Russian children were far less willing to misbehave under all three conditions than an American control group. Soviet children were most likely to misbehave if no one would know; adults and classmates exerted equal control. The highest rates of hypothetical misbehavior among American children occurred if peers would know about it.

Bronfenbrenner also demonstrated the relative strength of peer control over Soviet children's behavior by presenting the children with a series of hypothetical misdeeds. Each child was asked how he would respond to another child's misbehavior: (1) tell an adult, (2) tell other children, (3) talk to the offending child, or (4) do nothing. The choices for Soviet children were 11, 12, 75, and 1 percent, respectively. Swiss children's responses were 39, 6, 33, and 20 percent, respectively. In other words, Soviet children are much more likely to play an active role in the social control of others, less likely to rely on authority figures, and less likely to take a do-nothing attitude than Swiss children.

Chinese socializing practices are similar to those in the U.S.S.R., but if anything, even more widely and systematically applied. Although little hard experimental data are available on the effects of these practices, Bronfenbrenner and several other American psychologists were recently allowed to travel in China for three weeks. It was Bronfenbrenner's (1974a) impression that Chinese children have thoroughly incorporated Mao's teachings with regard to the value of work, cooperation, and selfless service to the people. (See box fig. 9.2c.) Misbehavior and aggression, common among Western children, were never observed in Chinese children.

Teachers indicated that these problems almost never arise. One might think that only severe punishment—perhaps in the form of social ostracism, which is common in Russian schools—would bring about such proper behavior. However, the lack of social deviance in China is paralleled by a lack of punitive methods of control. This does not mean there are no controls, simply a different kind. In China, there is only one way—the teachings of Mao—and his words have been raised to the level of a religion. Children are constantly drilled, verbally and in practice, in Maoist values. Because they grow up knowing no other way, deviance is virtually unthinkable.

Social control and training in values is observed most clearly in Chinese schools, but the remarkable effectiveness of the schools is probably based on their continuity with the rest of the culture. Parents participate in the socialization process by providing additional support and training in Mao's thoughts. Children learn the value and nature of work by participating directly in productive activity; for example, they may be responsible for growing vegetables or manufacturing simple items. As adults they will be required to do manual labor during part of the year, regardless of their occupation. All these factors contribute to a cultural stability and homogeneity of values that is unparalleled in Western society.

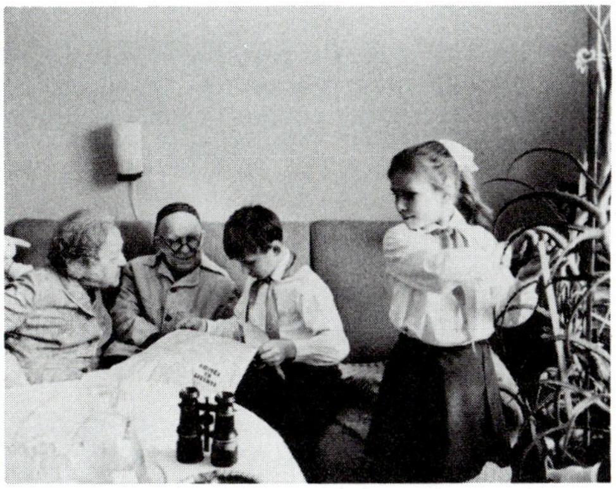

a

Box Figure 9.2a Russian children visiting elderly relatives. (Courtesy Sorfoto.)

Box Figure 9.2b Russian children encouraging fellow student. (Courtesy Sorfoto.)

Box Figure 9.2c Chinese children participating in productive labor. They spend twenty minutes of their school day making boxes for the factory next door. (From the personal collection of Urie Bronfenbrenner's, 1974. Reprinted by permission of Dr. Bronfenbrenner.)

b

c

Box 9.3

Changes in the Family and Society

Many students reading this text come from stable middle class families with both parents in the home, enjoy an economic standard of living that is the highest in the world, and have a hard time relating to the fact that the United States is having some very serious and rapidly worsening social problems. Juvenile suicide has doubled since 1950. Rates of juvenile delinquency, including violent crimes such as murder, have nearly doubled over that in the past ten years. Why?

Urie Bronfenbrenner (1974b) believes that a major factor in these serious social problems is the increasing disintegration of family structure. Between 1960 and 1972, the divorce rate nearly doubled, leaving ten percent of our children with single-parent families. In addition there has been a rapid increase in the number of families with both parents working (presently 45%) and spending proportionately less time with their children. In earlier times, such changes might not have been so serious. Fifty years ago, about half of our households had at least one additional adult, usually a grandparent, who could care for the children. Today only four percent of our households have additional adults. Further, our communities have changed from relatively close-knit towns and neighborhoods to massive suburban sprawls where neighbors often don't know the names of children living three houses away. The schools are about all that is left for many children to provide a stable socializing force, but most present day schools restrict their role to one of academic education. Thus an increasing number of children must rely on the peer group to define their values and behavior. It is hardly surprising that many of these children feel bitter and alienated from the rest of society, with values that often lead to criminal behavior.

Bronfenbrenner notes that the changes in family structure result largely from outside conditions related to business, urban planning, and transportation. He proposes several changes in social policy to reverse the trends of family disintegration and alienation of our children. These include the establishment of day care centers which involve the participation of parents, increasing social responsibility of children, and reestablishing a healthy neighborhood ecology. These changes will happen only when people such as ourselves realize the seriousness of these problems and act on them.

to assume adult social roles in family, work, and education. Although most of these young people will make the transition without too much difficulty, many will not.

What shall we do? Provide even less structure? Lack of structure seems to be the cause of some of our social problems. If "freedom" and lack of social structure lead to disintegration and alienation, then we actually have *less* freedom in the long run. Should we move toward the extreme social regimentation of the Chinese? Few of us would accept the ideological dogma and loss of individual freedom involved. Perhaps we can find some compromise that will allow for the child's smooth passage in the social system and yet retain some of the freedoms we cherish.

One thing is certain. Our child-rearing practices are not solely to blame; they only reflect the values of the larger society. In the years ahead, we will have to make some far-reaching decisions about how to raise our children and how to live as adults.

Summary

Socialization and personality development of the child emerge through the interaction of biological and social forces. The wide variations in infants' behavior may be related to genetic influences. These biologically based differences interact with environmental forces to produce individual patterns of personality and social behavior.

The nature and effects of environmental forces vary, depending on the child's age. From one perspective, social development depends on cognitive development. In other words, as his cognitive sophistication increases, the child becomes capable of conceptualizing and incorporating adult values *(cognitive developmental theory).* From another perspective, the child's behavior reflects the available models and patterns of reinforcement *(social learning theory).*

The child's environmental context varies with age. In infancy the child's primary social contact is with his mother. Recent evidence suggests that the young infant *initiates* much of this social contact and that his social development depends on the contingency of the mother's or caretaker's social responses.

In early childhood the social environment expands to include other family members and the immediate neighborhood. During this time, the child learns to follow certain rules concerning toilet habits, aggression, and exploration. Basic aspects of his personality develop through modeling and identification, as he seeks ways of reacting to his expanding world.

Children in late childhood and adolescence come into direct contact with socializing forces in the larger society. Two major influences are the school and the peer group. In this new context, children learn patterns of social interaction such as friendship, cooperation, and competition. Recent trends in our society have resulted in a weakening of social control in the family and schools and in an increase in peer-group influences. The resulting social disorder has led many to question the trend toward even greater freedom and to look toward more structured methods of socialization.

10

Psychosexual Development

Males and females are different. In all mammalian species, the two sexes differ genetically, morphologically, and hormonally. They also differ psychologically in ways that are less easy to describe; in temperament and in specific abilities. These psychological differences are more evident among primate than subprimate species and are particularly marked among human primates. This chapter is concerned with the nature and development of psychological sex differences in human beings. We will begin by discussing the expectations and beliefs we humans share about the psychological characteristics of one sex or the other: that is, with our *stereotypes* of the male and the female. We will then inquire into the truth or falsity of these stereotypes. Are our beliefs about the attributes of men and women correct? Finally, we will consider the development of sex differences and the relative roles played by biological and environmental factors—the perennial problem of nature versus nurture.

Sex Stereotypes

Beliefs about sex differences, often expressed symbolically, pervade our culture, its literature, language, mythology, music, and art. Consider the following passage from George Eliot's *Silas Marner:*

> Silas meditated a little while in some perplexity. "I'll tie her to the leg o' the loom," he said at last—"tie her with a good long strip o' something."
>
> "Well, mayhap that'll do, as it's a little gell, for they're easier persuaded to sit i' one place nor the lads. I know what the lads are; for I've had four—four I've had, God knows—and if you was to take and tie 'em up, they'd make a fighting and a crying as if you was ringing the pigs. But I'll bring you my little chair, and some bits o' red rag and things for her to play wi'; an' she'll sit and chatter to 'em as if they was alive. Eh, if it wasn't a sin to the lads to wish 'em made different, bless 'em, I should ha'

been glad for one of 'em to be a little gell; and to think as I could ha' taught her to scour, and mend, and the knitting, and everything. But I can teach 'em this little un, Master Marner, when she gets old enough."

Here, the girl is described as passive, more easily persuaded to stay in one place than a boy, and more easily instructed in the domestic skills of scouring, mending, and knitting. Similar stereotypes are embodied in our everyday language. For example, a girl who is active, climbs trees, likes rough games, and shuns dolls may be called a tomboy because her behavior fits our stereotype of male behavior. On the other hand, the girl who prepares elaborate tea parties for her dolls, loves sewing and ironing, and seldom gets her clothes dirty is a "real girl" or "little lady." Her behavior coincides with our stereotype of how a girl should act. The boy who fits our stereotype of boys is "all boy," while the boy whose behavior coincides with what we expect of girls is a sissy. If it were not for the fact that we *do* have certain ideas about what constitutes masculine and feminine behavior, there would be no way of understanding how a little girl could be less than a "real girl" or a little boy less than "all boy" (Brown, 1965).

Sex stereotypes, whether true or false, determine, to a large extent, how we react to one another. Therefore, it would be extremely desirable to be able to express our stereotypes in more general terms; references to "climbing trees" and "giving tea parties" are too particular to be useful. What is masculine and what is feminine?

"Man does; woman is," says Robert Graves. This theme appears again and again: Man is the agent; while *being* (in the sense of being a part of) characterizes woman. Bakan (1966) views these characterizations as two universal modes of existence, two different aspects of living forms, one of which tends to be masculine, the other feminine:

I have adopted the terms "agency" and "communion" to characterize two fundamental modalities in the existence of living forms, agency for the existence of an organism as an individual and communion for the participation of the individual in some larger organism of which the individual is part. Agency manifests itself in self-protection, self-assertion, and self-expansion; communion manifests itself in the sense of being at one with other organisms. Agency manifests itself in the formation of separations; communion in the lack of separations. Agency manifests itself in isolation, alienation, and aloneness; communion in contract, openness, and union. Agency manifests itself in the urge to master; communion in noncontractual cooperation. Agency manifests itself in the repression of thought, feeling, and impulse; communion in the lack and removal of repression. (Bakan, 1966.)

Such formulas are appealing because they seem to capture some fundamental duality that we associate with sex. But do they really express our stereotypes?

One way of finding out is to ask people to what degree certain traits, such as self-assertion or openness, characterize the male or the female. Better yet, to avoid prejudicing the matter, we can have these individuals generate their own lists of masculine and feminine traits. This kind of experiment was carried out by Rosenkrantz et al. (1968) with college students—a group of subjects one would expect to be relatively critical of conventional social norms and categorical generalizations about people; in other words, a group in which one would not expect to find strong sex stereotypes. Students in undergraduate psychology classes were asked to list all the characteristics, attributes, and behaviors on which they thought men and women differed. One hundred twenty-two differences were mentioned at least twice by this group of subjects.

Subsequently, the 122 differences were listed in a questionnaire that took the form of rating scales ranging from zero to sixty for each characteristic. For example, one dimension of difference that was mentioned at least twice by the students was "competitiveness." Therefore, the questionnaire included a sixty point rating scale for the trait of competitiveness, labelled "very competitive" at one end and "not at all competitive" at the other. Similar rating scales were constructed for the other attributes. The questionnaire was then administered to other students, who were instructed to indicate the extent to which each item characterized an adult man and an adult woman. For 41 of the 122 items, there was substantial agreement (75 percent or higher) among subjects of each sex as to which pole was more descriptive of the average man or woman. These items are presented in table 10.1. There was no disagreement between men and women subjects as to which characteristics were masculine or feminine.

The psychologists also endeavored to assess the social desirability of each attribute by asking subjects to indicate that point on the scale which they considered most *desirable* for an adult, sex unspecified. For the twenty-nine "Male-Valued Items," the point considered most desirable was closer to the masculine pole; the most desirable point among the twelve "Female-Valued Items" was closer to the feminine pole. There was no disagreement between the sexes concerning the social desirability of the attributes.

In 1972 Broverman et al., administered the questionnaire to 599 men and 383 women, both married and single, who ranged in age from seventeen to sixty and in education from the elementary school level to the advanced degree level. Although the responses varied somewhat from group to group, there was strong consensus about the differing characteristics of men and women on a considerable number of items. The subjects' stereotypes were similar to those reported by other investigators.

The sense of table 10.1 is fairly well captured by Bakan's terms, agency and communion. More surprising, perhaps, is that men and women have virtually identical sex stereotypes.

It may be that the "sexual revolution" and the rebirth of activist women's movements will alter these stereotypes. For example, according to table 10.1, women are considered to be intellectually inferior to men (e.g., less logical). This belief, which is clearly incompatible with the feminist philosophy, was held by women themselves in 1967, as documented by Goldberg (1967), who asked female college students to evaluate a number of professional articles in terms of writing style, value, competence, persuasiveness, and so forth. In some cases, the author of the article was listed as a man (e.g., John T. McKay), and in other cases the identical article was attributed to a woman (Joan T. McKay). Goldberg found that the same article received a higher rating when it was attributed to a male author, even when the article dealt with a topic that was traditionally considered female, such as dietetics or elementary school education.

The prejudice against women by women that Goldberg reported was *not* found in a similar study of Swarthmore women carried out about six years later (Baruch, 1972). The Swarthmore women, as a group, did not downgrade articles they believed had been written by women. The discrepancy between Baruch's and Goldberg's results might be a function of the different populations studied (Goldberg's subjects were students at a traditional women's college). In support of this interpretation, some of the Swarthmore women—for example, those whose mothers had not worked—tended to rate the articles attributed to females lower than those attributed to males. The discrepancy might also indicate a general lessening of women's prejudices toward other women between 1967 and 1972.

Table 10.1 Male-valued and female-valued stereotypic traits. The 41 traits listed in this table are indicative of our stereotypes about males and females. Each is presented as a continuous dimension with the extremes of the dimension labelled on the left and right.

Feminine pole	Masculine pole
Male-valued items	
Not at all aggressive	Very aggressive
Not at all independent	Very independent
Very emotional	Not at all emotional
Does not hide emotions at all	Almost always hides emotions
Very easily influenced	Not at all easily influenced
Very subjective	Very objective
Very submissive	Very dominant
Dislikes math and science very much	Likes math and science very much
Very excitable in a minor crises	Not at all excitable in a minor crisis
Very passive	Very active
Not at all competitive	Very competitive
Very illogical	Very logical
Very home oriented	Very worldly
Not at all skilled in business	Very skilled in business
Very sneaky	Very direct
Does not know the way of the world	Knows the way of the world
Feelings easily hurt	Feelings not easily hurt
Not at all adventurous	Very adventurous
Has difficulty making decisions	Can make decisions easily
Cries very easily	Never cries
Almost never acts as a leader	Almost always acts as a leader
Not at all self-confident	Very self-confident
Very uncomfortable about being aggressive	Not at all uncomfortable about being aggressive
Not at all ambitious	Very ambitious
Unable to separate feelings from ideas	Easily able to separate feelings from ideas
Very dependent	Not at all dependent
Very conceited about appearance	Never conceited about appearance
Thinks women are always superior to men	Thinks men are always superior to women
Does not talk freely about sex with men	Talks freely about sex with men
Female-valued items	
Very talkative	Not at all talkative
Very tactful	Very blunt
Very gentle	Very rough
Very aware of feelings of others	Not at all aware of feelings of others
Very religious	Not at all religious
Very interested in own appearance	Not at all interested in own appearance
Very neat in habits	Very sloppy in habits
Very quiet	Very loud
Very strong need for security	Very little need for security
Enjoys art and literature very much	Does not enjoy are and literature at all
Easily expresses tender feelings	Does not express tender feelings at all
Doesn't use harsh language at all	Uses very harsh language

Source: From Broverman, I. K., Vogel, S. R., Broverman, D. M., Clarkson, F. E., and Rosenkrantz, P. S., "Sex-role stereotypes: A current appraisal," *Journal of Social Issues,* 1972, *28.* Copyright 1972 by the Society for the Psychological Study of Social Issues.

Are our stereotypes of male and female behavior peculiar to this culture and this age? Do they reflect passing modes of behavior? Doubtless some aspects of our stereotypes are transient (e.g., only girls wear their hair long), but other aspects seem resistant to change. Although the period from 1968 to 1972 was one of militant activity for women's rights and equality, individuals continued to depict the differences between the sexes in the most traditional terms.

The psychologist Carl Jung believed that our concepts of masculinity and femininity are deeply ingrained, part of the "collective unconscious" of mankind. Rather than viewing these concepts as stereotypes, he considered them to be archetypes—ideas that surface again and again in recurring symbols and myths. It is no accident to a Jungian psychologist that in ancient times, priestesses (e.g., the Greek Sibyls) interpreted the mysteries and kept in touch with the gods, for woman is seen as intuitive and prophetic, in touch with the nature and the powers of darkness. Masculine and feminine archetypes are personified in the deities of Greek and Roman myths. The sky—"the eternal thunderer"—is male, Jupiter; the night is female, Latona. The dalliance between them results in the sun, Apollo, the "lord of life and light," and his sister of darkness, Diana, the pale and inconstant moon goddess. The Chinese too associated the moon with a female, the goddess Kwan-Yin (see plate 9). For the Jungian psychologist, these recurrent themes are evidence of the primitive, enduring character of sexual archetypes.

Sex Differences

Differences in Temperament

Are the stereotypes true? Do men and women actually differ in temperament and intellect the way we think they do? We are not concerned here with how these differences arise, whether "by nature" or as a consequence of social pressures. That issue on which so much emotional energy has been expended will be left until later in this chapter. Here, we are concerned only with the question of accurately describing temperamental differences between the sexes.

It may seem simple to discover the real differences in the behavior of males and females. All we have to do is put males and females into well-defined, controlled, and comparable situations and describe, measure, or rate their behavior in some objective manner. However, we are immediately faced with two major problems: (1) we see the world through our own stereotypes and therefore find it difficult to obtain a truly objective picture of sex-typed behavior, and (2) even if we could describe sex-typed behavior more or less objectively, we would have to contrive situations that bring out subtle and possible unexpected differences in modes of reacting. Although neither problem is unique to the study of sex differences, both are especially acute in this area, perhaps because few beliefs are as important to us as our stereotypes of masculinity and femininity. The following sections describe these difficulties more fully.

Problem 1. Biased perception

Numerous investigations of differences in temperament between the sexes have relied on rating scales in which one person is asked to rate others with respect to traits on which the sexes may differ. Teachers for example, typically report that boys are more aggressive and less dependent than girls, that they threaten more, and are more destructive, noisier, and negativistic. It is impossible to say how accurate these reports are because they are subject to unconscious bias by the stereotypes themselves; that is, the same behavior may be judged differently depending on whether it is done by a male or a female. Clearly, the behavioral categories in such studies should be as specific as possible, and rather than ask how "dependent" a child is, investigators should ask how often a child seeks help from teachers or peers, resists separation, seeks cuddling, and the like. Unfortunately, even these more specific types of ratings call for the rater's *interpretation* of behavior. He must decide what constitutes "seeking cuddling" as opposed to "seeking to annoy." Particularly when these ratings are made from memory rather than during actual observation of behavior, they are subject to distortion by the rater's own stereotypes.

Occasionally, children are asked to evaluate their peers. For example, Tuddenham (1951) obtained evaluations from first, third, and fifth graders by using a "guess-who" reputation test, in which the children were asked questions such as: Who is wiggly and who is quiet? The typical girl was rated as quiet, popular, full of fun, not quarrelsome, a good sport, good-looking, not a show-off, tidy, friendly, and a little lady. The typical boy was rated as wiggly, quarrelsome, bossy, show-offish, takes chances, not bashful, good at games, and a "real boy."

One might suppose that stereotypes are more entrenched in adults than children and that children's ratings would be relatively unbiased. Whether children are *less* affected by sex stereotypes than adults is not known. Nonetheless, it is evident that children's perceptions of male–female behavior can be colored by stereotypes, just as adults' can be. This was shown in a study by Hartley (1959), who interviewed five-, eight-, and eleven-year-old children about working mothers. The results were clear: the children perceived the man as the agent or breadwinner and the woman as homemaker, regardless of what they actually did. The mother who worked outside the home was simply helping the father in his duties; the man, occupied with domestic duties, was helping the mother in her home-centered responsibilities. Even children, then, may perceive the same behaviors —working outside the home or doing domestic chores within the home—differently, depending on whether the chores are done by a male or a female.

Thus in describing the sex-typed behavior of others, neither adults nor children make reliable witnesses; their perceptions are colored by their stereotypes. The problem even afflicts our perception of ourselves. A woman may or may not behave according to her own stereotype of female behavior, but she will usually see herself as doing so. This phenomenon may help explain results obtained by Levanthal et al. (1966) in a study of sex differences in persuasibility. In this investigation, college students were exposed to communications designed to alter their attitudes about taking tetanus shots. In contrast to men, women reported being strongly affected by the communication. They took the threat of tetanus more seriously and felt more vulnerable to the disease and more favorable toward the shots. However, the investigators also found that the women were no more likely to take the shots than the men. Possibly the women felt more influenced in accordance with the stereotype of the female as being easily persuaded (see table 10.1). Nonetheless, their *behavior* did not differ from men's. Mischel (1962) found a similar phenomenon among children. When asked whether they would prefer an immediate reward, or a delayed reward that would be of greater value, girls more often said that they would rather wait for the larger reward. But in an actual choice situation, no differences between the sexes were found.

One line of research begun in recent years promises to minimize the problems involved in rating the behavior of others. This is the application of ethological techniques to human behavior, exemplified by the work of

Blurton-Jones and Konner (1973). In this type of research, the observer approaches the rating of human behavior as he would the rating of animal behavior. Small, easy-to-describe items are rated and no *a priori* attempt is made to label the behavior as aggressive, dependent, emotional, and so on. Instead, behavior is scored in almost anatomical terms; for example, "red face," "run," "grab-tug-take." The strategy here is to determine which behaviors tend to occur with which other behaviors and only then to apply a label to the empirically determined cluster of behaviors. In this way the label is less likely to bias the observation. The data from these studies are not easy to summarize; in general, however, the pattern of results does not appear to contradict the sex stereotypes in any major way.

Problem 2. Choosing the situation

The second problem in studying sex differences in temperament is to find situations in which males and females will react in different and perhaps unexpected ways. Clearly, the kinds of behaviors that occur in one situation may be different from those that occur in another. A child who displays a large amount of aggression at home may not do so at school, and vice versa. Temperament is best described with reference to behaviors in specific situations. For example, in a detailed analysis of 200 quarrels among nursery school children, Dawe (1934), reported that not only did boys engage in more quarrels than girls, but the nature of their quarrels was different. Boys quarreled more over possessions; girls quarreled more over interference with an activity. Boys usually instigated quarrels, while girls took a more retaliatory role. Physical aggression was also expressed differently; boys hit while girls were more likely to pinch and pull. It is clear from these data that whether one will observe sex differences in aggression depends to a considerable extent on the situation in which aggression is studied.

One commonly used stimulus for aggressive behavior is the inflatable Bobo doll shown in figure 10.1. When placed with a Bobo doll, boys display much more aggression than girls. It is also obvious that the Bobo doll is a much more effective stimulus for eliciting male-type aggression (punches and slaps) than female-type aggression (pinches and pulls). However, as figure 10.3 shows, both sexes will imitate the behavior of a model who kicks, hammers, and otherwise abuses Bobo (Bandura et al., 1963).

Aggression may also be verbal, subtle, and nevertheless destructive. Many studies find no difference in the amount of verbal aggression expressed by preschool boys and girls in the classroom, whether it be verbal quarrelling, verbal disapproval, or tattling (Mischel, 1970). Thus in situations that elicit primarily verbal aggression, boys and girls would not be expected to differ in aggressiveness.

The value of seeking out an appropriate situation to reveal differences between the sexes is further illustrated by an experiment undertaken by Feshbach and Feshbach (1973). First-grade children were grouped into "clubs," each of which consisted of two same-sex children. An in-group feeling was established by giving each pair of children a name and a badge. The clubs met in a special room that contained a variety of toys and games. At the second club meeting, the experimenters introduced a third child into each club and observed the children through a one-way mirror to see how the newcomer was treated. In half the clubs, the third child was of the same sex as the club members; in half, the third child was of opposite sex. In this situation, the girls initially displayed *more* aggression toward the newcomer than the boys did, especially when the newcomer was of the opposite sex. Almost all the aggression of both boys and girls, however, was ex-

Figure 10.1 Imitation of aggressive behavior toward a Bobo doll by boys and girls. (From Bandura, A., Ross, D., and Ross, S. A. "Imitation of film mediated aggressive models," *Journal of Abnormal and Social Psychology*, 66, 1963. Copyright 1963 by the American Psychological Association. Reprinted by permission. Photo courtesy A. Bandura.)

pressed indirectly rather than directly. Acts of indirect aggression against new club members included the following: not responding to the child's overtures; moving away when the child attempted to initiate contact; denying a request for help, play, or information; and stating that the child could not be a member of the club.

Twenty-five of the forty girl club members committed one or more acts of indirect aggression toward the newcomer, whereas only fifteen of the forty-four boys responded in this way. Rejection of the newcomer reached a peak of expression when one girl attempted to terrorize a boy by stalking him around the room with a pointed pick-up stick, saying something about a "strange feeling" that sometimes came over her. In contrast, one of the boys' clubs prepared a musical fanfare to welcome their new member. The Feshbachs found the same kinds of sex differences in a comparable experiment with junior high school students.

The kinds of situations that evoke aggression in girls may differ from those that provoke aggression in boys. Also, girls may express aggression differently than boys. To bring out these differences requires some ingenuity and imagination on the investigator's part.

One approach to providing a situation in which sex differences are likely to be expressed is to use a *projective* test. For instance, an adult may be asked to describe what he sees in a series of inkblots, or a child may be provided with a dollhouse and a family of dolls and asked to tell a story about them. Although this relatively unstructured situation provides many opportunities for misinterpretation by the observer, it also offers rich potentialities for the expression of differences in temperament.

Sears (1965) presented the following statements as examples of children's "aggressive" responses in a doll play situation.

"The boy spills his milk all over the floor."
"The girl goes in the toilet and locks the door."
"The daddy turns on the television and the mommy turns it off."
"The baby falls down and hurts himself."

Occasionally, there is a stronger expression of aggression; for example, "And so he puts the mommy on the stove and fries her in the frying pan until she's all burned up." These responses seem to illustrate quite different modes of expression of aggression. Sears summarized the sex differences in aggression he observed as follows:

> Boys' aggression is usually hurtful and destructive. It is likely to involve large muscles and the bringing together of bodies in blunt contact. This need not be a matter of hitting between 2 dolls, but it may simply be the boys' jumping on the living room sofa or tipping over the baby's high chair or spilling the water in the bathtub, or simply having somebody fall down and hurt himself. Girls, on the other hand, do not bring bodies, animate or inanimate, into contact nearly so much. They are more likely to have the child dolls hide in the closets when the mother calls, or be disobedient, as exemplified by turning off the television when the mother has told her not to, or be sassy or just plain unpleasant. Girls include more verbal or nonphysical forms of aggression, and display relatively little of the contact form. This is true with one exception—spanking. Girls take a more disciplinary attitude than do boys.

These results agree with those obtained by Feshbach and Feshbach in demonstrating that girls rely on indirect forms of aggression to a greater degree than do boys. The "disciplinary attitude" taken by girls foreshadows another distinction between types of aggressive acts that becomes important among older children; the distinction between prosocial and antisocial aggression. *Prosocial* aggression may be defined as aggression in the name of the "establishment"; that is, when an individual threatens aggression or actually engages in an aggressive act to uphold some rule or law. Spanking and tattling could be considered acts of prosocial aggression. Acts of *antisocial* aggression are acts of aggression against the established system of order. In late childhood and in adulthood, males express more antisocial aggression than females do, but females express more prosocial aggression. This is true of responses to attitude scales as well as in behavior. Men are more often convicted of antisocial crimes than women, although it is difficult to determine how much of this difference is related to differences in the actual behavior of males and females, and how much is related to the stereotypes of police, judges, and juries. In other words, because of the stereotypes, it is possible that a man is more likely to be arrested and convicted than is a woman who commits an identical offense.

In this section, we have dwelled more on the problems of evaluating sex differences in temperament than on the differences themselves; that is, on the problem of seeing through one's stereotypes and the problem of arranging situations that are appropriate for eliciting the rich variety and nuances of behavior of which human beings are capable. However, even on the basis of the few investigations discussed here, we can say two things. First, sex differences in temperament do exist. And, second, the nature of these differences is not surprising. On the other hand, some of the empirical results of these studies expose the rather sketchy nature of the stereotypic adjectives in describing temperamental differences between males and females. For example, in the Feshbachs' study of sex differences in aggression toward a newcomer, girls were not less aggressive than boys, nor were they more nurturant and passive. Thus the stereotypic adjectives we use to describe sex differences in temperament are in need of refinement. Although these words may pinpoint dimensions of difference, they do not completely describe our store of knowledge about the sexes.

Differences in Intellectual Abilities

The question of which sex is more intelligent must be asked in terms of differences in I.Q. test scores because these scores provide our only measure of intelligence. But, in this context, the question is meaningless because most commonly used I.Q. tests were specifically designed to eliminate sex differences. The creators of these tests assumed that intelligence was something that both sexes were endowed with equally. Therefore, they excluded items on which there was a large sex difference and selected the remaining ones so that items tending to favor girls were balanced by those favoring boys. Theoretically, then, there should be no sex differences in I.Q. Nonetheless, a number of studies do report differences; some find that girls are superior; others find boys superior.

Sex differences in I.Q. may arise for a variety of reasons. For instance, the sample selected for testing is often biased in favor of one sex or the other. Achieving a nonbiased sample is not an easy task, however. If we test every senior in a large high school, for example, the sample is likely to be biased because the dropout rate is greater for boys than for girls. In other words, the boys in the sample would be a more highly selected group than the girls with respect to intelligence, and we would therefore expect to find that the average I.Q. of the boys was higher.

As the preceding discussion implies, there are often sex differences on certain types of test items; for example, on subtests of an I.Q. instrument. The pattern of differences in cognitive abilities that is usually, but not always found is briefly outlined below. (See Maccoby (1966) or Garai and Scheinfeld (1968) for a more extensive discussion.)

Spatial Ability

Boys tend to outperform girls on spatial tasks, beginning in the early school years, and this difference continues into adulthod. In general, such tasks assess a person's ability to comprehend relations between objects in space and the ability to visualize and mentally manipulate objects. An example of a test that presumably measures the latter ability is Thurstone's Paper Folding Test, in which the subject is asked to decide where holes punched in a folded piece of paper will appear if the paper is unfolded.

Number Ability

Beginning in high school, fairly consistent sex differences in favor of boys are found on tests of arithmetical reasoning and in the solution of problems involving numbers.

Verbal Ability

Girls are usually ahead of boys in developing language skills. They say their first words sooner, articulate more clearly at an earlier age, and use longer, often more complex sentences. Girls are also typically ahead in developing reading skills. However, the only types of verbal tests on which girls show consistent superiority throughout the school years are tests of grammar, spelling, and word fluency. No consistent differences are found in vocabulary, comprehension, or tests of verbal reasoning.

Mechanical Ability

Perhaps the most sizable differences are found in "mechanical ability." For example, a subject might be shown a picture of an automobile transmission and asked which direction a particular gear will move when the drive shaft turns. Beginning in adolescence, boys score considerably higher than girls do and tend to show superiority at a much younger age, depending on the kinds of skills that presumably reflect mechanical ability. Particularly large differences are obtained on tests in which subjects must assemble common objects from component parts. Male superiority is especially striking in this instance because females tend to have greater manual dexterity, which is also involved in assembling objects. You probably recognize that assembling objects, like other tests of mechanical ability, may also be tapping "spatial ability." The two are difficult to separate conceptually as well.

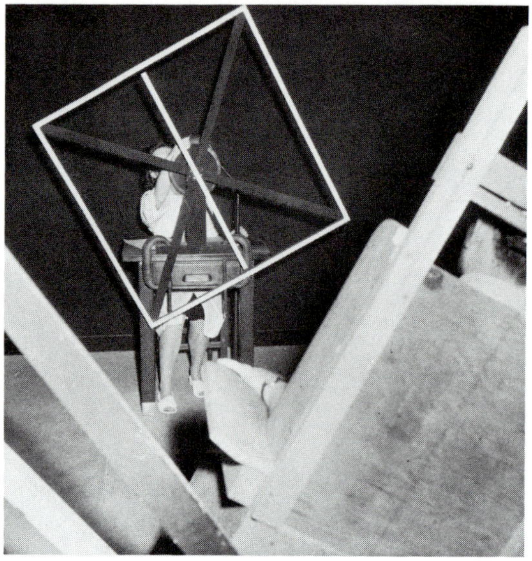

Figure 10.2 The rod and frame test. (From Personality Through Perception, H. A. Witkin et al. Copyright © 1954 by H. A. Witkin et al. Reprinted by permission by Harper & Row Publishers.)

"Analytic" Ability

One recurrent problem in investigating sex differences in cognitive abilities involves determining the particular cognitive skills that are being measured by any given test. We just alluded to this problem when discussing mechanical ability. The same problem is involved in interpreting differences in performance on tests of "field dependence." For example, in the rod and frame test, the subject is asked to adjust a rod to a vertical position despite the presence of misleading cues in the background or field on some trials. These cues are provided by a frame, which is tilted in such a way that when the rod is vertical with respect to gravity, it is crooked with respect to the frame (see fig. 10.2). Females are more distracted by the frame than are males; that is, the difference in performance during trials when the frame is present and when it is absent (or does not provide conflicting cues) is greater for females.

Another task believed to be measuring the same cognitive ability is the embedded figures problem, familiar to most readers of the Sunday comics. In this situation, the subject is asked to find a figure that is camouflaged by its surrounding field (see fig. 10.3). Men do better at this than women do, and performance in this situation is correlated with performance on the rod and frame test; that is, subjects who do well in one tend to do well in the other.

Thus females tend to be more affected by cues in the background or field and are therefore considered more "field dependent" than men. This difference between the sexes is often found as early as elementary school. But what kind of ability is involved here? The most popular view is that these tests assess "analytic" ability—the ability to separate figure from ground and deal with each independently. In the rod and frame test, a subject must focus on the rod and ignore the sur-

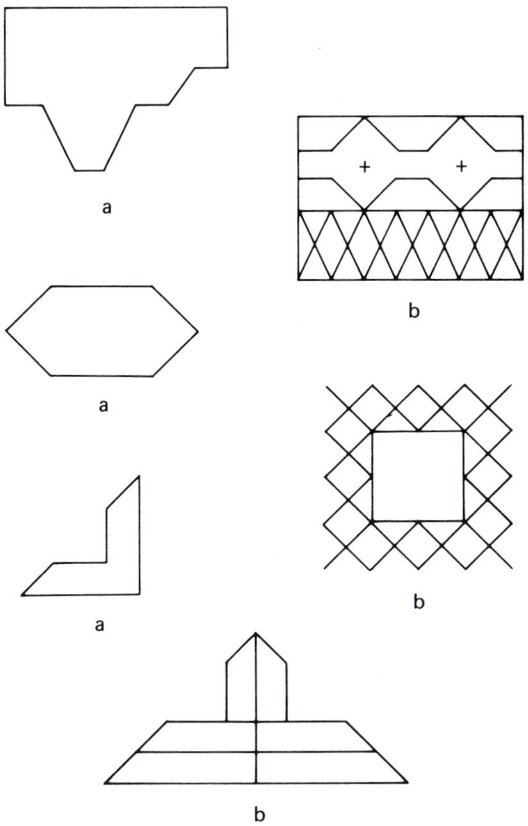

Figure 10.3 Examples of embedded figures. (From K. Gottschaldt, "Gestalt Factors and Repetition" In *A Source Book of Gestalt Psychology,* W. D. Ellis (Ed.), New Jersey: The Humanities Press, 1950.)

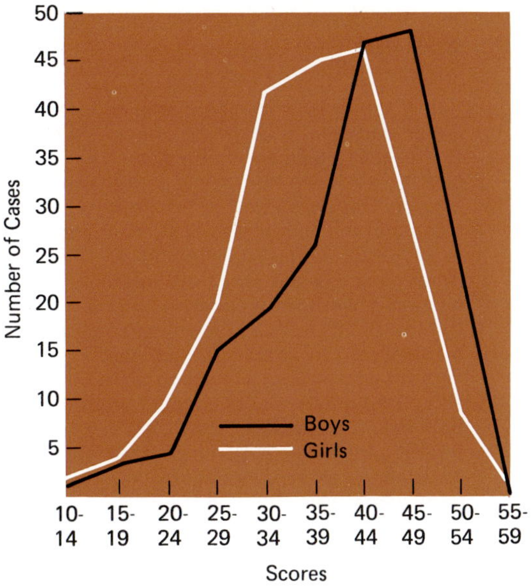

Figure 10.4 Distribution of scores made by boys and girls on a test of arithmetic reasoning. Notice how the distributions overlap. Twenty-eight percent of the girls reached or exceeded the median of boys. (From Anastasi, Anne. *Differential Psychology* (3rd Ed.) Copyright 1958 by Macmillan, Inc. Reprinted by permission.)

rounding field, while a similar cognitive skill is conceivably required to solve the embedded figures problem. Because females generally do not perform as well as males do on these tests, they are described as having less "analytic" ability than males. An alternative explanation, however, is that these tests measure something less general than analytic ability—that they assess a subject's ability to analyze relations between objects in space (Sherman, 1967). In other words, tests of field dependence may be actually tapping spatial ability.

The magnitude of all the differences discussed in this section varies to a great extent, depending on what is being assessed, the instrument used to assess it, the methods of testing, and the nature of the population being tested. In all cases, however, there is a considerable amount of overlap in the scores obtained by males and females. Figure 10.4 shows data obtained by Schiller (1934) on a test of arithmetic reasoning administered to third and fourth graders.

The magnitude of the sex differences in cognitive abilities also varies as a function of how often the subject is tested. In tests of spatial ability and field dependence, for example, females generally improve at a faster rate than males do, so that male superiority tends to decrease with repeated testing or repeated trials.

Box 10.1
Game Preferences

Informal play is universal across cultures. Organized games, however, are not (Sutton-Smith, 1961). Games can be viewed as offering a release from some of the tensions of socialization, as well as providing a means for the acquisition of skills needed in adulthood. Game preferences of American boys and girls have been changing over the last hundred years (Sutton-Smith, 1971). The preferred games involve less physical aggression and more indirect aggression, while singing, dialogue, and parlor games are less popular among both sexes. In addition, the difference between the sexes in game preferences has grown considerably smaller over the last thirty years. This situation is largely a result of changes in the preferences of girls. Girls are now interested in a wider range of games, many of which were traditionally considered boys' favorites. In contrast, boys are showing *less* preference for girls' games and a greater interest in a few major sports. One area of preference that has not changed is fantasy play. Boys still take fantasy roles involving great strength, adventure, status, and power while girls assume realistic roles with lower status and power, such as mother, nurse, teacher. Below are game preferences of fourth-, fifth-, and sixth-grade children studied by Rosenberg and Sutton-Smith (1961). (Games enjoyed by both sexes are not included.)

Games preferred by boys

Bandits	Building forts
Soldiers	Shooting bows and arrows
Cowboys	Throwing snowballs
Cops and Robbers	Throwing darts
Spacemen	Working machinery
Hunting	Making radios
Wrestling	Using tools
Basketball	Making model airplanes
Baseball	Shooting marbles
Football	Toy cars
Boxing	Toy trains
Fishing	
Climbing	

Games preferred by girls

House	Mother may I
Store	Ring around the rosy
School	London bridge
Church	Farmer in the dell
Actors	In and out the window
Actresses	Drop the handkerchief
Dancing	Mulberry bush
Playing dolls	Hopscotch
Sewing	Jump rope
Cooking	Jacks
Knitting	Cartwheels
Crocheting	Stoop tag

(The author wishes to thank Vicki Carlson for her help in preparing this box.)

Differences in Interests

Beginning in early childhood, the kinds of things boys do are likely to be different from the kinds of things girls do. The most salient difference between the sexes, from the viewpoint of parents or teachers, is level of activity. Boys use larger play areas and engage in rougher, more vigorous play; girls' play is usually more sedentary.

Throughout the school years, boys and girls tend to spend their leisure time differently. They read different books, go to different movies, watch different television programs, and read different sections of the newspaper. Boys tend to read less than girls and prefer mystery, sports, travel, exploration, and adventure stories. Girls prefer emotional fiction and stories about romance, home, and school life. Boys usually read the sports pages of the newspaper; girls tend to read the society page. There are also marked sex differences in game preferences (see box 10.1).

In all these activities, girls usually have a wider range of interests than boys. Their game preferences have grown wider over the years, while boys' game preferences have become

Table 10.2 Percentages of boys and girls reading various types of books during a two-month period. (Based on reading records kept by 511 gifted children and 808 control children studied by Terman and Lima, 1926.)

	Boys	Girls
Stories of adventure or mystery.	56	18
Stories of home or school life.	2.5	32
Emotional fiction.	3.5	16
Informational fiction, including the classics.	15	11
Fairy tales, folk tales and legends.	7	10

Source: From Terman, L.M. and Tyler, L.E., "Psychological sex differences" in *Carmichael's manual of child psychology*, Leonard Carmichael (Ed.), p. 1079. Copyright 1964 by John Wiley & Sons, Inc. Reprinted by permission of John Wiley & Sons, Inc.

narrower. Girls are now interested in activities that are considered masculine, while boys rarely engage in "feminine" activities. This is illustrated by data on sex differences in reading shown in table 10.2. Girls' reading choices are less focused than boys'. Although a small percentage of boys read emotional fiction or stories about home and school life, a much larger percentage of the girls read stories of adventure or mystery, the boys' favorites. One reason may be that society is more accepting of girls who display "masculine" interests than of boys who have "feminine" interests. The tomboy is censured less than the sissy.

The two sexes also differ in their preference for school subjects. Girls generally prefer courses in English and language arts; boys generally prefer science and mathematics. These different interests are reflected in occupational preferences later in life (Terman and Tyler, 1954).

The different patterns of interests displayed by boys and girls have important implications for the development of other sex differences. Because of their different interests, both in school and out, the two are likely to have very different experiences as they grow up.

Development of Sex Differences

It is clear from the previous section that aside from obvious and indisputable differences in structure, males and females differ psychologically, although the psychological differences are admittedly often difficult to describe. The remainder of this chapter will discuss the origin of these differences.

In discussing psychological development, there is a tendency to set up a dichotomy between characteristics that are somehow inherent in the nature of the organism and those that are attributable to the environment. We have already seen the futility of this dichotomy in several previous chapters (e.g., Chapter 2, "Behavioral Genetics"). In discussions of sex differences, the inclination to pit nature against nurture is particularly strong, and the appeal to nurture is by far the more popular. Not only does this approach seem more compatible with an egalitarian philosophy, but it is clear that children are not insulated from adult sex stereotypes and that these could easily influence their development. (See fig. 10.5.)

Even more compelling for an environmental explanation of sex differences is the fact that the two sexes are treated differently at home and at school, by parents and peers, and by the social environment in general. Hoffman (1972) has summarized a large amount of evidence which indicates that girls receive less encouragement for independence and more parental protection and experience less pressure to establish an identity separate from their mothers. In one study (Collard, 1964), mothers of four-year-olds were asked at what ages they thought parents should permit children to engage in certain activities; for example, playing away from home without letting their parents know where they would be. Mothers of girls believed that this kind of independence should be granted at a later age than did mothers of boys; the differ-

Figure 10.5 The "apron syndrome" affects not only mothers but their children too. (Courtesy Ken Heyman.)

ence was particularly apparent among middle-class mothers. If we recall that in many ways women are less independent and achieve less, it is indeed tempting to attribute these differences entirely to differences in socialization. However, one might also wonder what causes the differences in socialization. *Why* are girls and boys treated differently? At least part of the answer may lie in the different "natures" of males and females. We will begin our discussion of the origin of sex differences by discussing the development of physical differences between the sexes.

Differentiation of Reproductive Structures

In the human species, as in most mammalian species, the reproductive system is already differentiated as male or female at birth. Until about the sixth week of gestation, the human male and female are morphologically identical, and by the time they are born, there are unmistakable differences between boys and girls (see fig. 10.6). In this section we will consider the processes by which an infant becomes sexually differentiated. While reading, you will find it helpful to refer to figures 10.6 and 10.7. In addition, you may want to refresh your memory by reviewing some sections of Chapter 4.

Role of the Genes

The sexual structures include the gonads (sex glands: in the male, the *testes;* in the female, the *ovaries*), the accessory structures (internal structures such as the *vas deferens* and *epididymus* in the male; the *uterus* and *Fallopian tubes* in the female), and the genitals. The gonads of both sexes develop from embryological structures sometimes called *ovotestes,* each of which consists of two portions, an inner core and an outer rind. In the development of a female, the outer portion of each ovotestis develops into an ovary, while the inner portions grow smaller and all but disappear. The opposite happens in male development; that is, the core of each ovotestis develops into a testis, and the rind disappears. Thus male and female structures develop from separate embryological tissue, and the embryological foundations for both types of structures are present in both sexes.

A similar pattern is followed in the differentiation of the accessory structures. Male structures are formed largely from the embryologi-

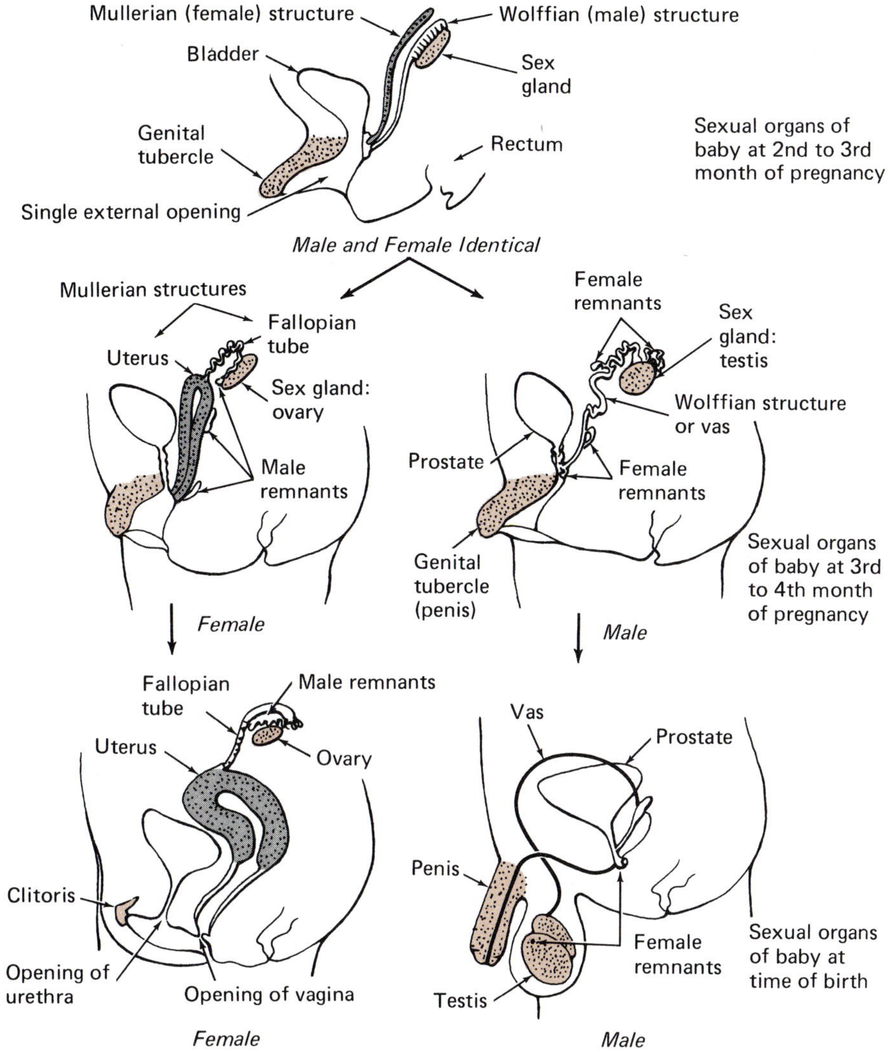

Figure 10.6 Sexual differentiation in the human fetus. Three stages in the differentiation of the sexual system, internal and external. Note the early parallelism of the Müllerian and Wolffian ducts, with the ultimate vestigation of one and the development of the other. (From Money, John and Ehrhardt, Anke A. *Man and Woman, Boy and Girl,* page 42. Copyright 1972 The Johns Hopkins University Press, Baltimore, Md. Reprinted by permission.)

cal *Wolffian duct,* and female structures from the *Müllerian duct.* Both ducts are present, side by side, in the embryo. In the male, the Wolffian duct proliferates to form male accessory structures, while at the same time, the Müllerian duct grows smaller. In the female, the Müllerian duct proliferates and the Wolffian duct regresses.

Genital development proceeds according to a different plan. In this case, male and female organs develop out of the *same* embryological tissue. In other words, a single embryological

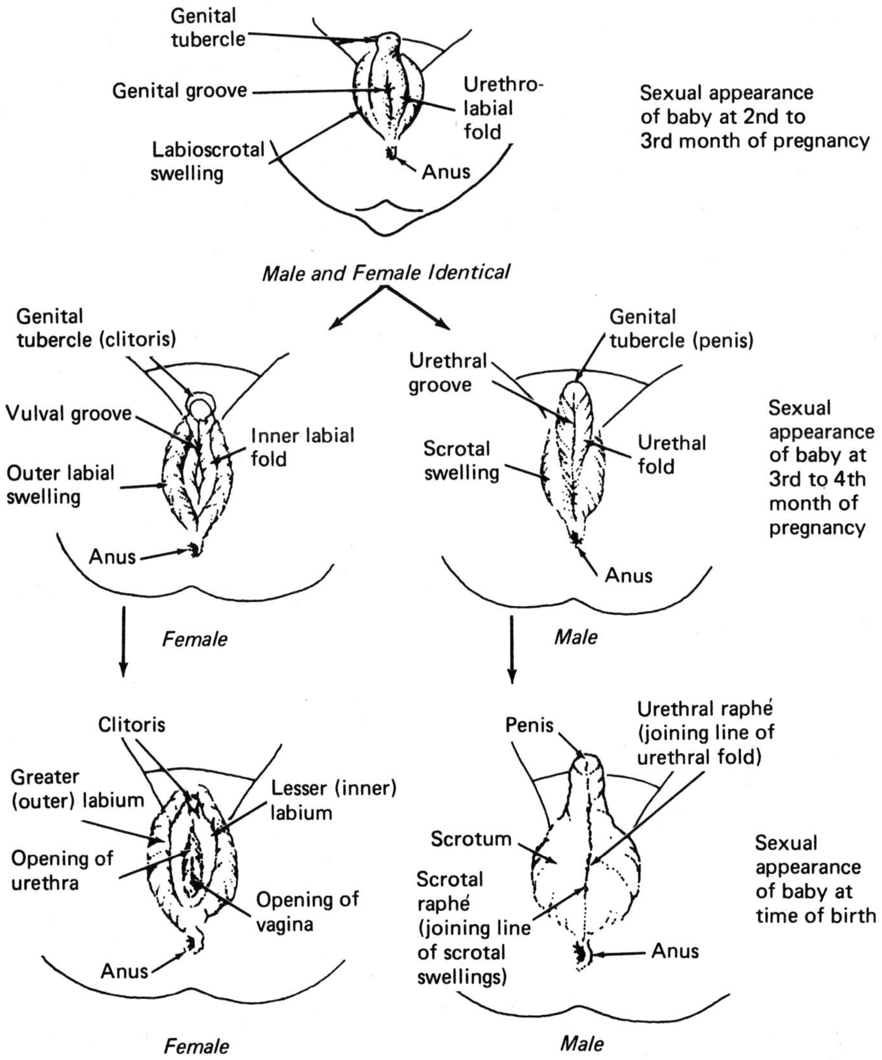

Figure 10.7 External genital differentiation in the human fetus. Three stages in the differentiation of the sexual system. Male and female organs have the same beginnings and are homologous with each other. (From Money, John and Ehrhardt, Anke A. *Man and Woman, Boy and Girl,* page 45. Copyright 1972 The Johns Hopkins University Press, Baltimore, Md. Reprinted by permission.)

structure, the *genital tubercle,* develops differently in each sex (see fig. 10.7). Because the same tissue is involved, differentiation in a male direction is to some extent incompatible with differentiation in a female direction. This is not the case for either the gonads or the accessory structures, where it is theoretically possible for development to proceed in both directions simultaneously.

The gonads are the first structures to differentiate. In the human embryo, differentiation of the testes begins after the sixth week of gestation, and differentiation of the ovaries begins at about the twelfth week. The next step is differentiation of the accessory structures from the primitive duct systems, and, finally, development of the genitals. Normally, the testes descend shortly before the male infant is born.

It is interesting to speculate about which of the two different patterns of structural differentiation provides a more appropriate model for psychological differentiation. Does the development of masculine attributes preclude the development of feminine attributes, as suggested by the process of genital differentiation? Or is a more appropriate model provided by the gonads and accessory structures, whose development suggests that an individual could develop along *both* masculine and feminine lines? Most psychologists adopted the first model without much question. Masculinity and femininity were treated as opposite ends of a continuum; that is, a high degree of "masculinity" automatically meant a low degree of "femininity." Recently, however, it has been suggested that this model may be inappropriate and that an individual may develop strong masculine traits as well as strong feminine traits (Constantinople, 1974).

Role of Prenatal Hormones.

In mammalian species, adults of both sexes produce the same types of hormones but in decidedly different proportions. For example, the male testes secrete some estrogen as well as larger quantities of androgen, while the female produces relatively small amounts of androgen along with larger amounts of estrogen. Another difference is that in the male, hormones are not secreted cyclically, whereas estrogen and progesterone are secreted cyclically in the female.

Hormones, specifically those produced by the male testes during fetal development, play an important role in structural differentiation. Soon after they develop, the testes begin to produce certain hormones. Although these secretions have not yet been studied directly, their existence has been inferred from experiments such as those we will describe below. When these testicular hormones are present in the organism, the reproductive system differentiates as male; when they are absent, differentiation is female. This generalization is true regardless of the individual's genotype—XX or XY. To make a male, something is added; otherwise development proceeds in a female direction.

In 1947 Jost observed that if the testes of a male rabbit were removed on the nineteenth fetal day, subsequent structural development was female. In other words, the animal developed female accessory structures and female genitalia, despite the fact that it was genetically male. An individual that is part male and part female is known technically as a pseudohermaphrodite. (The simpler term "hermaphrodite" is usually applied only to individuals of mixed *gonadal* sex; that is, to organisms that have both ovarian and testicular tissue. These cases will not concern us here.) Jost observed this extreme degree of feminization only if the testes were removed during a brief period of fetal development; that is, there was a *critical period* for these effects. If the testes were removed during the critical period, three things happened: the Wolffian duct regressed, the Müllerian duct differentiated into female structures, and the primitive genital developed as female. Removal of the testes shortly after the critical period produced a lesser degree of feminization. Jost thus demonstrated that the male testes or, more likely, something normally produced by the testes is necessary for normal male development. The nature of the critical substance or substances remained to be determined.

Because the testes produce androgen later in life, an obvious possibility was that the critical substance produced by the fetal testes was an androgen. One source of support for this hypothesis comes from experiments in which genetically female animals have been masculinized as a result of androgen administered during the critical period. Experiments of this type have been performed with a variety of species, including rhesus monkeys (Young, Goy, and Phoenix, 1965). Although the critical period varies with the species, in most species it occurs prior to birth. When the critical period occurs prenatally, androgen may be simply injected into the mother during pregnancy. The hormone does not appear to affect genetically male offspring, whose testes presumably are already producing it, but has striking effects on genetic females. These females develop along male lines, the degree of masculinization depending on factors such as the dose, the time of administration, and the particular androgen used.

In cases of extreme masculinization, genetic females, exposed prenatally to androgen, develop a phallus which is almost indistinguishable from that of a male. They also develop male accessory structures formed from the embryological Wolffian duct. However, *in addition* to male internal organs, the animal also develops female accessory structures. The fact that these structures are present in the androgenized female but not in the castrated male suggests that in addition to androgen, the testes produce a substance which prevents the Müllerian system from developing. This substance has been termed Müllerian Inhibiting Substance (MIS). Müllerian structures develop in the *absence* of MIS, which is normally produced by the fetal testes.

In summary, then, sexual differentiation is a product of both genes and hormones. The developmental process is best conceptualized in terms of steps or stages. The first step—the formation of either ovaries or testes—is somehow dictated by the genes. Subsequent sexual differentiation, however, depends on the presence or absence of hormones that are normally secreted in the male by the newly formed testes. In the absence of these hormones, female development proceeds, regardless of the individual's genetic sex. In this way, stage two depends on the outcome of stage one. The normal XX individual develops ovaries rather than testes, and because testicular hormones are absent, the accessory structures and genitals also develop as female. The normal XY individual develops testes rather than ovaries, and these organs secrete androgen and MIS, which cause the accessory structures and genital tubercle to differentiate in a male rather than female fashion.

The process of structural development appears to be essentially the same in all mammals, including humans. Naturally, human sexual differentiation has never been tampered with intentionally. However, nature has produced a number of types of human pseudohermaphrodites that fit the developmental pattern we have considered. Before discussing humans of biologically mixed sex, it is important to point out that in lower animals prenatal androgen has important effects on the development of behavior in addition to its effects on structural development. Because this subject was discussed in Chapter 4 and because our prime focus here is human development, we will mention only a portion of the work with nonhuman primates.

Sex-typed Behavior in Monkeys

Among nonhuman primates as well as human ones, males and females behave differently beginning at an early age. For example, the young male rhesus monkey mounts other monkeys more often than the female does, makes more threatening gestures, and engages in more vigorous play (Goy and Resko, 1972). All these sex-typed behaviors depend on the presence or absence of prenatal androgen. Thus the genetic female rhesus who has been masculinized by prenatal androgen also shows play behavior that is more typical of the male than the female. She exhibits more mounting behavior, engages in more rough play, and makes more threatening gestures than do control females. Furthermore, display of these behaviors does not appear to be related to postnatal hormones. In the male, removal of the testes during the first three months of life does not result in play patterns that are less typically male. Nor does postnatal removal of the ovaries in the female change her behavior. Thus the critical factor for certain behaviors appears to be whether androgen has been present during prenatal development. The presence of the hormone prenatally not only governs the direction of structural development, but also has important effects on mechanisms in the central nervous system that mediate behavior.

Human Pseudohermaphrodites

Because prenatal hormones have important consequences for sex-typed behavior among nonhuman primates, it is reasonable to assume that these hormones may also play a part in human behavioral development. The existence of human beings of biologically mixed sex provides us with useful information on this question as well as more general issues concerning the relative roles of nature and nurture in psychosexual development. Most often, genetic, hormonal, and environmental factors all work in the same direction. Thus if an individual is a genetic male, he usually develops male gonads that produce male sex hormones and is reared as a male. In other words, he differs from a normal female in genes, in hormones, and in experience. It is therefore extremely difficult to ascertain the relative contributions of nature and nurture in the development of any psychological differences that might exist between the sexes. In the case of pseudohermaphrodites, however, these factors may be separated. (See fig. 10.8.) One might inquire, for example, about the psychological characteristics of a child who is genetically male but looks female and has been reared as a girl. Does she behave more like a normal boy or more like a normal girl? In addition, what is her gender identity; that is, what is her conception of her own sexuality? Does she view herself as female, or does she perhaps feel ambiguous about the feminine role assigned to her? Does she later marry and want children? What kind of a mother does she make?

Figure 10.8 Hermaphrodite symbol. Copyright Leyden University Library, Bibliotheeh der Rijksuniversitut to Leiden. Reprinted by permission of Leyden University Library.)

In the following sections, we shall consider the psychology of such individuals.

Most of our information concerning development in people of biologically mixed sex comes from a single source, the endocrine clinic at Johns Hopkins University, to which these people are usually referred for medical treatment and counseling. Investigators at Johns Hopkins have studied almost every conceivable type of sexual biology, including a number of cases in which there is a lack of congruence, for one reason or another, among the various indices of sex. Most researchers list six indices of maleness or femaleness, five biological and one psychological: (1) the sex of the genes, (2) the sex of the gonads, (3) the sex of the accessory structures, (4) the sex of the hormones, (5) the sex of the genitals, and (6) the perceived sex, or gender identity. Thus, to take a single example, an individual might be genetically female, but have male genitals and a masculine gender identity. Obviously, numerous combinations are possible.

Only two types of sexual ambiguity will be described in detail here: genetic females who have been exposed to prenatal androgen and genetic males who have developed in the absence of effective androgen.

The Androgenized Female

Occasionally, androgen is present in the system of a genetic female fetus during the critical period of prenatal life. One cause of this situation is a defect of the adrenal glands, which results in the secretion of relatively large amounts of androgen. If the situation is medically unattended, it will continue after the baby has been born. Thus the syndrome in the human infant parallels that of the genetic female animal who has been masculinized in the laboratory, although in the human, the hormone usually arrives too late to result in male accessory structures. The genitals, however, are masculinized; the degree of masculinization varies from case to case. Androgenized XX individuals may be reared either as boys or as girls. Hormonal or surgical intervention is often initiated in either case.

Another cause of masculinization of the human genetic female has been *progestins*. These hormones, chemically related to androgens, were given to several women about twenty-five years ago to prevent miscarriage and had the unintended and unfortunate side effect of masculinizing the XX fetus. The use of progestins during pregnancy has been discontinued, of course. The several cases of progestin-induced pseudohermaphroditism provide the closest approximation to the genetic female animals who have been exposed to prenatal androgen. In both instances the masculinizing agent is present only during prenatal life. The human infants born with this condition have been reared as either boys or girls, usually depending on the degree of masculinization of the external genitals.

Testicular Feminization

The syndrome known as *testicular feminization* involves a genetic male whose testes develop normally and begin to secrete androgen and MIS. The problem arises because the cells of the body are unable to respond to the androgens being produced, which results in an effective absence of androgen during prenatal development. As a result of the absence of androgen, the individual develops female rather than male genitalia, the testes do not descend, and the baby is reared as a girl on the basis of the appearance of the external genitals. At puberty these individuals develop extremely feminine bodies with smooth, almost hairless skin (the result of a total absence of effective androgen, unusual even in the normal genetic female). The feminization is caused by estrogen, which is produced by the testes in amounts characteristic of the normal male. In the absence of androgen, these small amounts of estrogen are usually sufficient to produce a very feminine body type. It is this feminizing action of the testes that gives the syndrome its name; the individual is feminized by testicular estrogens. (See fig. 4.7.)

Gender Identity

It is difficult to exaggerate the sharpness of the line we have drawn between male and female. An individual is either one sex or the other. Few of us know anyone who is the least bit confused about which sex he or she is. The lack of ambiguity has nothing whatsoever to do with erotic preferences or direction of erotic inclination; homosexuals, bisexuals, and even transvestites have the same definite feeling of being either one sex or the other as do heterosexuals. Although some adults may experience a strong desire to be the opposite sex, they know which sex they *are*. (Among children, the desire to be the opposite sex is fairly common, particularly among girls (Brown, 1958), but this also does not indicate any ambiguity.) It is tempting to attribute feelings of sexual ambiguity to the transsexual who, although biologically of one sex, has a gender identity of the opposite sex. Even transsexuals, however, do not report feeling ambiguous about their gender: They have a solid sense of identity as a member of one sex (usually female) but feel trapped in the body of the other (usually male). The first question one might ask about the individuals who are biologically *both* male and female is whether they are ambiguous about their gender. According to the Johns Hopkins studies, the answer is a definite and unambiguous "no."* Almost all the biologically ambiguous individuals studied at the clinic were found to have completely unambiguous concepts of themselves as members of one sex or the other. Few expressed uncertainty about which was their real or proper sex. What determines this clear-cut perception of gender? Does an individual of mixed sexual biology adopt the gender of his or her genes, gonads, hormones, accessory structures, or genitals? Or are none of these factors consistently related to the sense of sexual identity that these people clearly have?

A major investigation into the determinants of gender identity in the Johns Hopkins sample was conducted by Hampson and Hampson (1961). They reported that gender identity was not consistently related to *any* of the biological indices of sex. Instead, in almost all cases, the individual perceived himself or herself to be a member of the sex in which he or she was reared. For each of the five biological indices of sex, the Hampsons listed all individuals who had been reared in a sex which conflicted with that aspect of their biology. For example, twenty individuals had been reared contrary to their genetic sex, thirty had been reared in conflict with their gonadal sex, and so on. These data are shown in table 10.3. In each instance, the investigators asked whether the gender identity of the individual agreed with the way he or she had been brought up or whether it agreed with the particular aspect of the individual's biology. Note in table 10.3 that there were few instances in which gender identity conflicted with the sex of rearing. (In fact, the table is somewhat misleading because some of the individuals who developed a gender identity that opposed the one in which they were raised are listed more than once.) Particularly noteworthy are the cases in which the individual developed a gender identity that conflicted with hormonal sex or the sex of the external genitals.

All thirty-one individuals whose hormonal sex conflicted with sex of rearing went into or

* Note that this conclusion, as well as others reached by the Johns Hopkins investigators, has been questioned on a number of grounds. (See Diamond, 1968, and Zuger, 1970.) One important question is whether the individuals studied at Johns Hopkins are indeed as they are described. For example, has their sense of gender been assessed adequately, or would more sensitive probing reveal some disturbances in this area?

Table 10.3 The relation between gender identity and sex of rearing among pseudohermaphrodites.

Sex of rearing Conflicts with Sex of:	Number of Cases	Number of cases in which Gender identity agrees With sex of rearing
Genes	20	20
Gonads	30	27
Hormones	31	26
Accessory Structures	25	22
Genitals	25	23

Source: From J.L. Hampson and J.G. Hampson "The ontogenesis of sexual behavior in man," in W.C. Young, Ed., *Sex and internal secretions* (3rd ed.). Copyright 1961 by the Williams & Wilkins Co., Baltimore.

beyond puberty with hormones contrary to the sex in which they were being reared. All of them developed some secondary sex characteristics of the opposite sex, yet only five became ambivalent about their gender. The other twenty-six developed an unambiguous sense of themselves as male or female in accordance with the way they were brought up. Among the twenty-five individuals who were reared in a sex opposite to that of their genitals, sixteen remained in this situation at least until they were teenagers and all but two developed gender roles that were undeniably in accord with their sex of rearing. However, the Hampsons noted that the individual who is brought up in the sex that conflicts with the visible external indices of sex is in a particularly difficult situation: The quantitative data do not "document the enormity of the problem these people had to surmount in coming to terms psychologically with their paradoxical appearance." Many of these individuals were moderately disturbed psychologically, although none was psychotic.

The Hampsons' data thus demonstrate that a strong unambiguous gender identity may develop in individuals despite the opposition of genes, hormones, gonads, accessory structures, or even genitals. In most cases of biological ambiguity, *experience* is the most important determinant of a sense of gender. These studies provide strong support for an environmental explanation of sex differences. On the other hand, although the Hampsons' studies clearly show that experience can override biological forces, they do not indicate that it is easy. The organism, by its biological nature, will be inclined to react to some types of experiences rather than others, or to some experiences *differently* than others. It is no doubt easier to raise a biological boy as a boy than to raise a biological girl as a boy and vice versa, as illustrated dramatically in box 10.2.

In cases of testicular feminization, we have already introduced the feminine pronoun, despite the sex of the genes and gonads. These individuals, although genetically male, are reared as girls and consider themselves female. Money and Ehrhardt (1972) have summarized their studies of ten such women. With one exception—an extremely troubled individual from an exceptionally troubled home background—these women conformed to traditional stereotypes of femininity and described themselves as fully content with the female role. Although physically incapable of bearing children, all entertained fantasies of raising a family. Two women had adopted children and proved to be good mothers. Most enjoyed homecraft and preferred being a wife to being a career woman. Their erotic inclinations tended to be exclusively heterosexual, and their sexual activities were quite normal. As children they had played primarily with dolls and other girls' toys.

When Money and Ehrhardt compared these women with women who had been exposed to androgen or related masculinizing substances during prenatal life, they found that the majority of the androgenized females

Box 10.2

A Case of Mistaken Sexual Identity

Stoller (1968) reports the case of an individual who, by every biological index (genes, gonads, and so forth) was male. However, because the testes had not descended and the penis was abnormally small, the child had the appearance of a normal girl. And she was reared as one, without questioning. The term tomboy seems mild to describe the childhood of this individual.

> *In all games with other children, the child seemed to take male roles. Her bicycle was her pride and joy and was constantly kept polished. She could scarcely be forced into girls' clothes. The family finally compromised and permitted her to dress as a cowboy or in jeans and T-shirt, except on rare occasions, such as Christmas or Easter, when she grudgingly consented to wear dresses. Her companions were boys, with whom she played boys' games—hiking, jumping, exploring, football. In the course of these, she was bruised and cut, continually tearing her clothes, but never complaining, enjoying the roughness and tension of these games. She did average work throughout school, but well below what psychological tests had measured as her potential.*

The mother recalled that even as a young child, her daughter did not behave like a little girl. She ate too fast, she moved too fast, she was too violent, too rough.

The child was first seen by a psychiatrist at the age of fourteen, after a medical examination (prompted no doubt by her failure to show any of the usual physiological signs of female adolescence) had revealed the nature of her condition. During this first visit, she wore a bandana and dress and, according to the psychiatrist, looked grotesque and miserable. The child was said to have developed a cold during early adolescence, which had left her with a persisting "hoarseness."

For a number of reasons, most of them already obvious, the child was finally told that she was a boy. The psychiatrist described her reaction to this news as follows:

> *She acted as though she were being told something of which she had always been dimly aware, of which she had no doubt. She did not show the sense of relief of someone who has struggled to prove a point, or the sense of triumph of one who has won after strenuous opposition, or the sense of shock of one given some astonishing information. Rather her attitude was as if to say, "Yes. Very good. Thank you. I am not surprised."*

The family moved to a new neighborhood, and the child began a new and highly satisfactory life as a boy. He began to take part in sports, to be attracted to girls (and to be found attractive by them), and was even first in his math class, a subject in which he had done poorly as a girl! (Of course, this latter change must be interpreted in the context of a reduction in emotional stress as well as a sex change.) Although these cases are extremely rare, they indicate that we are not totally the products of our environment.

described themselves (and were described by their mothers and friends) as tomboys and were proud of this status. They differed from control women and from women feminized by testicular hormones in terms of a higher level of physical activity, a preference for tailored clothing rather than more fluffy styles, and their feeling that a career was more important than marriage. As children they preferred cars, trucks, and guns to dolls.

None of these behaviors is unusual in a female; the unusual part is simply the number of androgenized females who displayed them. However, despite the greater prevalence of tomboyishness in these individuals, they adjusted quite successfully to the female role. Therefore, although the early hormones did exert a noticeable effect on their temperament and behavior, they did not by any means preclude development according to sex of upbringing. Additional evidence for the plasticity of the human organism is the fact that other individuals who had been exposed to prenatal androgens but had been reared as boys usually made successful adjustments to the masculine role.

It is clear from these studies of individuals of biologically ambiguous sex that both biological and social factors are important in psychosexual development. First, these individuals almost always develop an unambiguous gender identity of the sex in which they are brought up. Second, they usually adjust remarkably well to the sex role assigned to them. Both observations attest to the power of social forces in shaping an individual in either a male or female direction.

On the other hand, Stoller's report (see box 10.2) of the biological male who was reared as a girl is a dramatic reminder that biology also exerts a force. Further evidence is provided by comparing individuals who were exposed to androgen during prenatal development and were reared as girls with cases of testicular feminization. Both develop female gender identities. However, the individuals who developed in the presence of androgen were more tomboyish than those who developed in the absence of androgen. This result suggests that androgen exerts an effect on psychological as well as structural development.

Sex Differences in Other Societies

> Back of the word "man" stands in my mind a phalanx of images, men with white skins and brown skins and yellow skins and black skins; men with crew-cuts and shaved heads and great psyche knots; men in evening-dress in contemporary society and men wearing nothing but gleaming pearl-shell crescent ornaments on their chests; men with muscles that bulge and ripple and men with arms as slender as a girl's; men whose fingers are too clumsy to hold a tool smaller than an adze and men who sit threading tiny beads on a string; men whose manhood is offended by the smell of a baby and men who cradle an infant gently in a steady arm; men whose hands are always ready to fling upward and backward as if to throw a spear and men whose hands press easily palm to palm in a gesture of apology and entreaty; men of six feet six and men of five feet one. And beside them stand women, again with many-coloured skins; some with bald pates and some with long flowing hair; women with breasts that hang very low or can sometimes even be trained to a form which can be thrown over their shoulders and women with small high breasts like the figures on the Medici tombs in Florence; women who swish their grass skirts as they walk and women who handle these same grass skirts as if they were sheets of iron, protecting their virtue; women whose arms look empty without a child in them and women who hold their children at arm's length as if they were clawing little wild cats; women who are readier to fight than their husbands and women who scatter like leaves before the sound of a brawl; women whose hands are never still and women who sit after a heavy day's work with hands flaccid in their laps (Mead, 1949).

Sex differences of one form or another appear to be universal (Mead, 1949). However, the *particular* sex differences that are found across cultures are not universal—but they are not random either. That is, there is a pattern of differences that characterizes most societies, but not all of them. For temperamental differences, the modal pattern is for males to be more sexually active, more dominant, more deferred to, more aggressive, less responsible, less nurturant, and less emotionally expressive than females (D'Andrade, 1966). The magnitude of the difference varies with the culture, and there are exceptions to almost every rule.

The kinds of results that are typically obtained in cross-cultural studies may be illustrated by Stephens's (1963) findings concerning sex differences in authority between husband and wife. In a study of thirty-one societies, Stephens found twenty-one in which the husband exercised "considerable authority" over his wife; six in which husbands were "mildly dominant," and five in which authority was shared fairly equally. In six other societies, husbands and wives exercised authority in different spheres. In only four societies did women appear to have more authority within the family than did men—the people of Jodjokuta, Indonesia (formerly the island of Java), the Tchambuli of New Guinea, the Jivarvo of South America, and the Berbers of North Africa. Thus there is a modal pattern—husbands have more authority than wives—but there are also a few exceptions to this pattern, as well as a number of instances in which the difference is small. In the case of authority, even in the four societies in which women had more authority within the family, men had more control outside the family. For example, among the Tchambuli, the men, not the women, do the fighting in war. Stephens speculated that with respect to power over groups larger than the family, it is likely that all societies would be found to be male-controlled.

Many researchers have been impressed with the uniformity of the differences across cultures; other researchers, by the variety of patterns expressed. Mead emphasizes the exceptions rather than the rule; for example, she places considerable emphasis on the Tchambuli of New Guinea. Among the Tchambuli, a people of only about 600 in number, the modal pattern of sex differences is reversed in many respects. An aggressive dominating temperament is considered feminine, whereas the masculine ideal is artistic, sensitive, and emotionally dependent. Mead described two other societies in the South Sea Islands in which there are no apparent temperamental differences along these dimensions. In one, the Arapesh society, a gentle temperament is considered ideal for both sexes. In the other, the cannibalistic Mundugumor society, it is desirable for both sexes to have an aggressive suspicious nature. Thus the Tchambuli, the Arapesh, and the Mundugumor exemplify every possible type of deviation from the modal pattern.

Data such as these are open to a variety of interpretations, depending on whether one focuses on the uniformity of the cross-cultural differences or the exceptions from the uniform pattern. For Mead (1935) the exceptions are critical:

> If those temperamental attitudes which we have traditionally regarded as feminine—such as passivity, responsiveness, and a willingness to cherish children—can so easily be set up as the masculine pattern in one tribe, and in another to be outlawed for the majority of men, we no longer have any basis for regarding such aspects of behavior as sex-linked.

She concludes that differences in temperament between males and females are appropriately viewed as "cultural creations"—a product of the different social experiences of males and females.

In most societies, males and females are indeed socialized differently. Again, there is a modal cross-cultural pattern, and there are deviations from this pattern. In a survey of socialization practices in 110 societies, Barry, Bacon, and Child (1957) found that the modal pattern is for boys to be trained in self-reliance and achievement, while girls are trained to be nurturant, responsible, and obedient. These data are summarized in table 10.4. The results fit nicely with the fact that in most societies, males are more dominant, more self-reliant, and less nurturant.

Some Conclusions

Sex differences are found in other cultures as well as our own. It is also clear from cross-cultural data that the two sexes are treated differently by the social environment. Although it is tempting to attribute sex differences entirely to differences in the social experiences of males and females, we must

Table 10.4 Cross-cultural ratings for sex differences on five variables of childhood socialization pressure.

Variable	Number of Cultures with Ratable Information	Percentage of Cultures with Evidence of Sex Difference in Direction of		
		boys	neither	girls
Nurturance	33	0	18	82
Responsibility	84	11	28	61
Obedience	69	3	62	35
Achievement	31	87	10	3
Self-reliance	82	85	15	0

Source: From H. Barry III et al., "A cross-cultural survey of some sex differences in socialization." *Journal of Abnormal and Social Psychology,* 1957, *55,* p. 328, table 1. Copyright 1957 by the American Psychological Association. Reprinted by permission.

again raise the question of why males and females are socialized differently. And further, what accounts for the cross-cultural standardization of socialization practices? Why is it that in so many different societies, girls are trained in nurturance, responsibility, and obedience, while boys are trained in self-reliance and achievement? At least part of the answer appears to lie in the different biological natures of men and women. For example, one line of reasoning attributes the differences in socialization to the division of labor by sex. Because men and women perform different types of economic activities, it is appropriate that they be socialized differently. The sex-typing of jobs may be considered to have its origins in certain biological differences between the sexes, specifically in the greater physical strength of the male and the cyclic functioning of the female. In discussing the contemporary evolution of an Israeli Kibbutz society, Spiro (1965) develops this idea:

When the vattkim [pioneer settlers] first settled on the land, there was no sexual division of labor. Women, like men, worked in the fields and drove tractors; men, like women, worked in the kitchen and in the laundry. Men and women, it was assumed, were equal and could perform their jobs equally well. It was soon discovered, however, that men and women were not equal. For obvious biological reasons, women could not undertake many of the physical tasks of which men were capable; tractor driving, harvesting and other heavy labor proved too difficult for them. Moreover, women were compelled at times to take temporary leave from that physical labor of which they were capable. A pregnant woman, for example, could not work too long, even in the vegetable garden, and a nursing mother had to work near the Infants House in order to be able to feed her child. Hence, as the Kibbutz grew older and the birth rate increased, more and more women were forced to leave the "productive" branches of the economy and enter its "service" branches. But as they left the "productive" branches, it was necessary that their places be filled and they were filled by men. The result was that the women found themselves in the same jobs from which they were supposed to have been emancipated—cooking, cleaning, laundering, teaching, caring for children, etc.

Although these considerations are no doubt important, it seems likely that biological factors also exert a more direct effect on psychological development. In part, boys and girls may be socialized differently because they react differently. For example, during the first five days of life, newborn girls exhibit a greater tactile sensitivity than newborn boys and react more strongly to pain (Garai and Scheinfeeld, 1968). Between one and three months of age, boy babies spend more time awake and more time fussing and crying than do girl babies (Moss, 1967). These differences may result in differences in the way the parents respond to infants. When the child is older, the differential treatment is exaggerated in accordance with society's stereotypes of what is appropriate behavior for males and females. This explanation is compatible with the data on pseudohermaphrodites, which suggest that at least some differences between males and females have a biological basis.

In conclusion, in the area of sex differences, as in other areas of psychological development, it seems reasonable again to attribute the differences to the interaction of nature and nurture. By this, we do not mean to say that both nature and nurture influence equally all aspects of sex differences. For example, the fact that females typically show greater improvement during repeated tests of spatial ability or field dependence would suggest that whatever these tests are measuring, the initially observed sex differences are attributable in part to the lesser degree of experience females have in these areas. Other differences, however, may be based to a greater degree on differences in the nature of male and female organisms. For example, the aspects of personality we associate with tomboyishness may be an example of psychological attributes that are more deeply rooted in biology.

Summary

Males and females differ in temperament, interests, and specific abilities. The magnitude of the difference depends on the specific area being investigated, but in all cases there is considerable overlap in the behavior of the two sexes. Psychological differences are more difficult to evaluate than physical differences for a number of reasons. First, it is difficult to overcome our stereotypes about masculinity and femininity and classify behavior objectively. Second, considerable ingenuity is required to construct situations or tests that will clarify the nature of the differences between the sexes; psychologists have only begun to explore the range of situations that must be examined before the differences can be described adequately. Third, males and females clearly differ in their performance on certain kinds of tests, but the problem of describing the nature of the difference remains. For example, does the rod and frame test measure analytic ability or spatial ability? What component skills are tapped in tests of mechanical ability?

The results of studies of sex differences indicate that the differences observed usually do not conflict with our knowledge of males and females, but they do conflict with our verbalized stereotypes. For example, the generalization that girls are less aggressive than boys clearly does not hold for all types of aggression or for all situations in which aggression may be expressed.

The process of sexual differentiation is initially determined by the chromosomal sex of the individual, but the direction of subsequent development depends on the presence or absence of hormones normally produced by the fetal testes. A number of errors in sexual development is possible, resulting in the development of individuals of biologically ambiguous sex. Despite their biological ambiguity, however, these individuals almost always develop an unambiguous gender identity as male or female in accordance with the sex in which they are reared. However, the effects of prenatal hormones may be discerned in the higher incidence of tomboyishness among individuals who are reared as girls, but who have been masculinized by fetal hormones.

Sex differences of some kind appear in all cultures. Furthermore, the pattern of sex differences is similar in a variety of cultures, although there are exceptions. These differences, like those in our own society, are associated with the different social experiences of males and females. However, one cannot attribute sex differences entirely to environment. They appear to result from the interaction of biological and environmental factors over the course of an individual's development.

Ivan T. Pavlov (1849-1936) Pavlov was the first to systematically study classical conditioning and elaborate its laws. His pioneering work is as important today as it was in the early 20th century.

Hermann Ebbinghaus (1850-1909) Ebbinghaus was the first to apply experimental methods to the study of memory. His associationistic orientation gave direction to the study of memory until the middle 1960s.

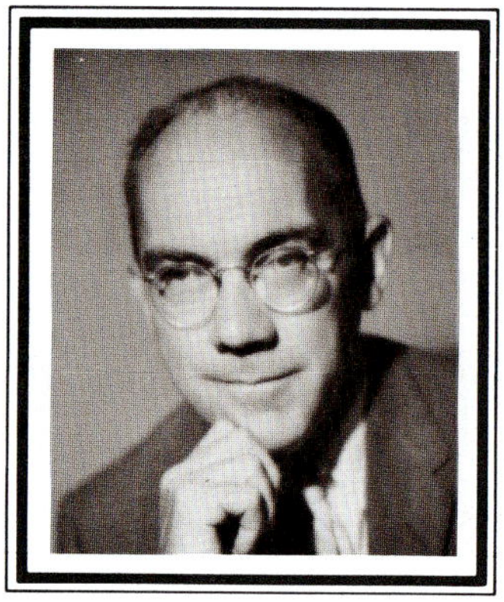

Edward Lee Thorndike (1874-1949) Thorndike was the first to systematically study instrumental learning and proposed some of its guiding principles. His Law of Effect is a cornerstone of psychology and is still involved in much current thinking.

B. F. Skinner (1904-   ) For four decades, Skinner has been the leading figure in the study of learning. He has pioneered a functional, analytic approach to the investigation of learning and continues to take controversial stands on important societal issues.

Section

5

Adaptive Behavior

11

Conditioning and Learning

A dog stands quietly in the middle of a small cubicle, restrained by a leather harness. Suddenly a bell sounds. The dog startles and orients toward it. A few seconds later, meat powder is injected into the dog's mouth, the dog salivates and consumes the food. A few minutes later, the bell again sounds and is again closely followed by food. As these pairings of the bell and food continue, the dog's behavior in response to the bell changes radically. Now when the bell sounds, the dog moves restlessly about, saliva dripping from its mouth. As the trials continue, more and more saliva flows from the dog's mouth in response to the bell. This saliva is collected by a tube attached to the dog's cheek and flows into an adjoining room, where the amount is measured (see fig. 11.1). What is so interesting about this change in the dog's behavior?

All goes well for a boy called "little Hans" until the age of five, when he develops an overpowering fear of horses. Little Hans is taken to Sigmund Freud for treatment of his horse phobia. Freud interprets Hans' fear of horses as an outcome of the Oedipal conflict: Hans desires his mother sexually, is therefore afraid of retribution by his father (castration), and displaces this fear onto horses—a horse being a symbolic representation of his father. What does Hans have in common with the dog that salivates to the bell?

A hungry cat is placed into a wooden enclosure called a puzzle box. It can escape the puzzle box by some simple act such as pulling at a loop of cord (see fig. 11.2). Outside the puzzle box, where the cat can easily see it, is food. If the cat pulls the loop of string, it is released from the box and allowed to eat the food. After it finishes eating, the cat is put back in the box and more food is placed outside. The cat learns to pull the string to escape the box. What is so important about this change in the cat's behavior?

The parents of a two-year-old boy visit a therapist because their son has developed a

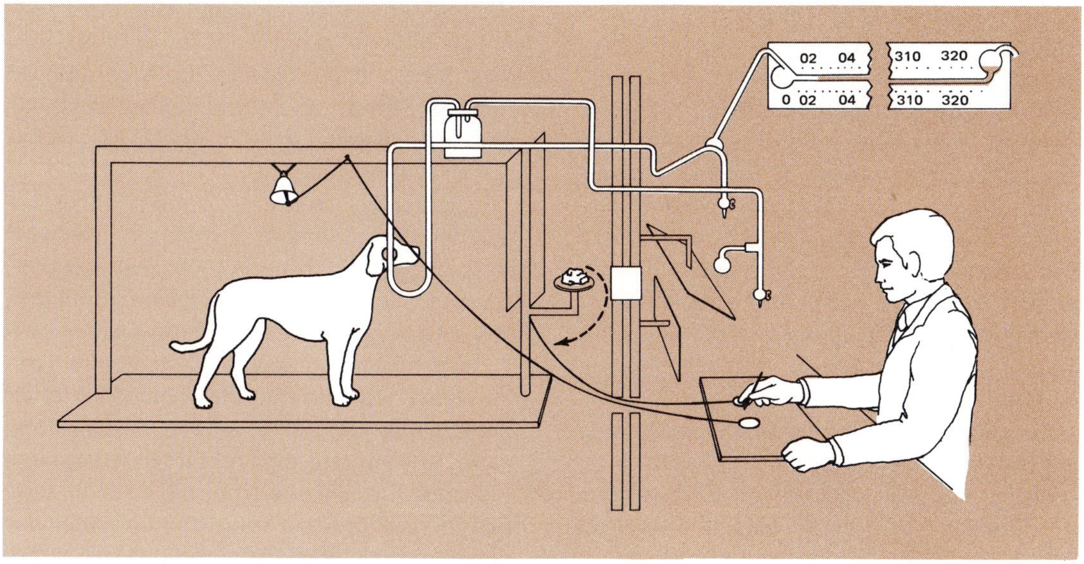

Figure 11.1 Pavlov's apparatus for studying the conditioning of salivation. The dog is isolated in a soundproof room, with a one-way vision window between the experimenter and the dog. The tube is attached to the dog's salivary glands and allows the experimenter to measure the magnitude of salivary flow. The experimenter can present the bell and food by remote control. (From Morgan, C. T. and King, R. A. *Introduction to Psychology* (4th Ed.), p. 69. Copyright 1971 McGraw-Hill, Inc.)

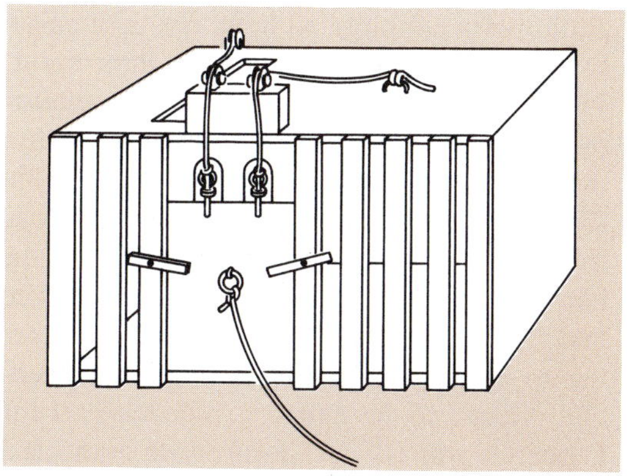

Figure 11.2 Thorndike's puzzle box. Cats were placed inside this enclosure, and if they pulled the string, the cage opened and gave them access to the food outside. (E. L. Thorndike, *Animal Intelligence.* Copyright 1965 by Macmillan Publishing Co.)

serious behavioral problem. He demands continual attention from his parents and has a severe tantrum whenever it is not immediately forthcoming. The therapist discovers that the boy was extremely ill for the first eighteen months of his life, but has now fully recovered. Naturally, however, the parents were extremely responsive to the child's demands during his illness. What does this child's behavior have in common with the cat's behavior in the puzzle box?

The experiments just described—the first performed by Ivan Petrovitch Pavlov in about 1890, and the second performed by Edward

Lee Thorndike in 1898—are two of the most important experiments ever performed in psychology. The topic of this chapter is learning, the role of experience in modifying behavior. However, our discussion in this chapter will be limited almost entirely to these two examples of learning; *Pavlovian conditioning* (often called *classical conditioning*) and *Thorndikian learning* (often called *instrumental learning*). Furthermore most of the experiments that will be described in this chapter use animal rather than human subjects.

To understand why classical conditioning and instrumental learning are sufficiently interesting and profound enough to determine the direction of an entire field of study, we must delve briefly into the history of Western intellectual thought.

Historical Foundations of the Psychology of Learning

Early explanations of behavior were generally religious in nature: Man's behavior was not causally determined because he had free will. Therefore, his behavior was unpredictable and not amenable to scientific study.

Cartesian Dualism

Rene Descartes (1596–1650) was the first to deviate from this religious theme with his publication of *The Passions of The Soul* in 1650. However, he did not make a complete break with theological doctrine (he was about 20 years old when the Church began to punish Galileo for deviating from Church doctrine). To reconcile his views with theological doctrine, Descartes divided human behavior into two classes—voluntary and involuntary. Man's voluntary behavior was governed in a manner consistent with Church doctrine, by a mind and soul, both of which were nonphysical in nature. However, man's involuntary behavior, like the behavior of lower organisms, was mechanically governed. According to theology, lower organisms had no souls, so Descartes viewed their behavior as mechanistically determined.

Apparently, Descartes' notions about the mechanistic control of involuntary behavior were strongly influenced by his observations of mechanical statues, which were popular in the seventeenth century. These statues performed various actions and were often unknowingly set into motion when an observer accidentally tripped a hidden switch. Descartes was impressed by the fact that the statue responded to a signal from the environment, and he reasoned that some of man's behavior (involuntary) could also be viewed as responses to some aspect of the environment rather than as the result of divine inspiration.

Descartes' view of the control of involuntary behavior is illustrated in figure 11.3. In this example, a boy's hand touched a fire and was withdrawn. Descartes argued that this response was not determined by the operation of a nonphysical mind but by a physical mechanism, operating through a nerve. The lower end of the nerve was put in motion by the fire, and this motion was transmitted to the brain. At the brain, a substance that Descartes called "animal spirits" was released from a cavity, and flowed back down the nerve to the muscle. When the liquid flowed into the muscle, it swelled and thus caused the leg to retract. This chain of events eventually came to be called a *reflex arc.* Thus Descartes was the first to propose a physical *deterministic* basis for at least some of man's behavior.

Descartes' views were important for psychology because of their *dualism;* the division into voluntary and involuntary behavior. This dualistic view implied that at least some of man's behavior could be studied, using the methods of science. Thus involuntary behav-

Figure 11.3 Descartes' representation of how the hand comes to be withdrawn when placed in a fire. (Courtesy of National Library of Medicine, Bethesda, Maryland.)

ior began to be studied by physiologists, while voluntary behavior remained the province of philosophy.

Empiricism and Associationism

As mentioned, Descartes' dualism left the study of the mind to philosophy. But how was the mind to be studied if it was impossible to observe the mind of another individual directly? The *behavior* of another individual could be observed, but behavior was not viewed as a reflection of the mind—involuntary behavior was a reflection of the brain's operations, not the mind's, and voluntary behavior was considered unpredictable and determined by free will. If it was impossible to study the mind by studying behavior or the minds of others, the only course left open was to observe one's own mind, to look inward. This method was called *introspection* and became the favored technique in the study of the mind.

One major question about the mind concerned the degree to which its contents were derived from experience; that is, from information entering the mind through the sense organs. Although Descartes acknowledged that experience must play a role in the development of ideas contained in the mind, he held that many of our most basic ideas are innate. For obvious reasons, this view is called the *doctrine of innate ideas*. Descartes maintained this position because he believed that certain ideas were qualities of the soul and thus divine.

The next step was taken by a British physician and scholar named John Locke, who rejected Descartes' notion that man is born with innate ideas and argued that all knowledge must come from the senses, or experience. The view that knowledge comes from experience with the outside world is called empiricism. In 1690 Locke clearly stated this view in *An Essay Concerning Human Understanding:*

> Let us then suppose the Mind to be, as we say, white paper, void of all character, without any ideas. How comes it to be furnished? Whence comes it by that vast store, which the busie and boundless Fancy of Man has painted on it, with an almost endless variety? Whence has it all the materials of Reason and Knowledge? To this I answer, in one word, from Experience: In that, all our knowledge is founded; and from that it ultimately derives it self.

The notion that all knowledge comes from the senses entails certain problems. By themselves, the senses can only provide sensations, not organized ideas. The contents of the mind are not just a meaningless jumble of remembered sensations; they are organized into meaningful units. Thus Locke and other British empiricists had to explain how this organization of ideas was achieved. The explanation they proposed was that some kind of "mental string" tied together the sensations that form a particular idea. This imaginary string was called an *association*. Any two sensations that frequently occur together will become associated; thus when one sensation occurs again later, it will invariably evoke the memory of the other. For example, a stone produces a variety of sensations, and because these sensations are always experienced together, they become associated. This compound sensation forms our idea of a stone. James Mill, in *Analysis of the Phenomena of the Human Mind* (1829), described this process as follows:

> From a stone I have had, (simultaneously), the sensation of colour, the sensation of hardness, the sensation of shape, and size, the sensation of weight, when the idea of one of these sensations occurs, the ideas of all of them occur. They exist in my mind; and their (simultaneous) existence is called the idea of the stone.

In addition to the idea that simultaneously occurring sensations became associated, associations were also said to form between successive sensations. Thus the order in which ideas occurred, as well as their existence, was explained by associations. A variety of laws of association was developed to specify the conditions in which associations would be formed and the factors that were important in determining their strength. The major factors that determined whether two sensations would become associated were *contiguity* and *similarity*. That is, if two sensations occurred together in space or time or if they had elements in common, they would become associated. The major factors influencing the strength of an association were thought to be the frequency with which the sensations occurred contiguously and the intensity of the sensations. The impact of the British empiricists' thinking can be felt to the present day.

Early Physiologists

The early physiologists accepted Descartes' dualistic division: they would study the body with the methods of science, while philosophers studied the mind with the method of introspection. However, as physiological knowledge began to accumulate, it became clear that physiology could account for some behaviors that were previously thought to be controlled by the mind. As time passed, mechanistic explanations were found for a wide range of these behaviors. This eventually led to the notion that *all* behavior might be causally determined and amenable to scientific study. In other words, perhaps Descartes' dualism was false.

The most important physiological investigations concerned reflexes. The list of known reflexes was extended, and by the middle of the nineteenth century, reflex mechanisms accounted for a wide range of behaviors.

However, an entire class of behaviors could not be explained in terms of the reflex and were therefore classified as voluntary acts. Learned behavior is behavior that is modified by experience; that is, it represents an adjustment to the environment. But reflexes are fixed, inborn mechanisms and cannot account for behaviors that developed as a function of experience. Thus reflexes could only account for innate behavioral responses. For example, a reflex can account for a person's reaction to being touched by fire, but it cannot account for a person's reaction to the sight of fire or to the word fire.

Pavlov

Let's consider Pavlov's experiment. A bell was sounded and the dog showed no particular response other than a brief orientation toward it. Food followed and elicited salivation as a reflex. After the bell and food had been paired together a number of times, the bell alone elicited salivation. It was as if a *new* reflex had been formed as a result of the contiguous presentation of the bell and food, as if the salivary reflex had been transferred to a new stimulus, or as if a *learned connection* had been formed. Note that this new reflex (called a conditioned reflex) provided a means of extending the reflex mechanism to *learned* behavior. That is, Pavlov's experiment showed how learning, a process believed to be a faculty of the mind that could be studied only by introspection, could be investigated by the scientific method. It allowed the mechanist to extend his domain to *all* behavior and signalled the end of Cartesian Dualism. Note also that the conditioned reflex resembled the concept of association. The bell and food were presented *contiguously* and seemed to become associated. However, in this case the strength of the association could be measured by the amount of salivation, the latency to salivate, and the frequency of salivation. Thus many considered the conditioned reflex to be an "objective" procedure that could be used to study associations.

Is it any wonder that Pavlovian conditioning became the center of the psychology of learning?

Functionalism

To understand the importance of Thorndike's experiment, we must consider another historical trend, *functionalism*. This school of thought was influenced by Charles Darwin (1809–1882), the originator of the theory of evolution, and emphasized the *functions* served by behavior rather than the elements that make up behavior. Furthermore, the functionalists were interested in continuities between men and lower animals, and one question they were interested in was whether animals could reason.

Thorndike set out to answer the question concerning animals' ability to reason. To this end, he constructed the puzzle box illustrated in figure 11.2 and began observing the course of learning. Figure 11.4a depicts the results of his experiment. Notice that the *learning curve* progressed gradually rather than suddenly; that is, the cat became a little more proficient on each trial. This suggested to Thorndike that animals did not learn by

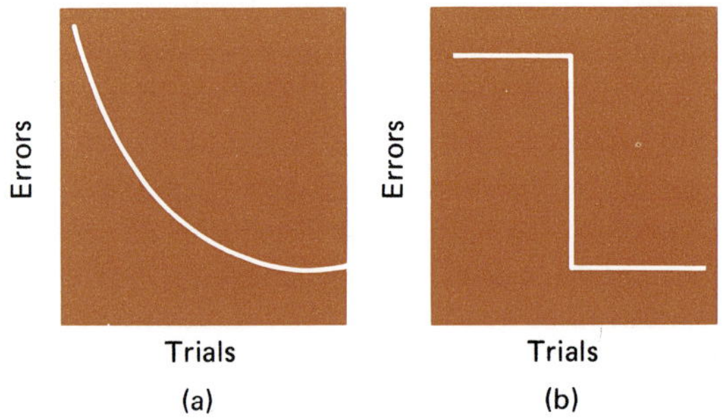

Figure 11.4 Thorndike's results are shown in (a). The learning curve showed only gradual improvement; the number of errors made on a trial decreased gradually as trials progressed. (b) Represents what Thorndike believed the results would look like if reasoning was involved in the learning in the puzzle box; there would be no improvement until the cat reasoned out the problem, and then a sudden and sharp improvement would appear at the point where correct reasoning occurred.

reasoning. If reason had been involved, the cat's performance should have improved suddenly (as shown in fig. 11.4b) at the point when the cat reached the correct solution to the problem. Therefore, Thorndike concluded that learning was a process in which the connection between a stimulus and a response was gradually stamped in.

Although the cat responded in a variety of ways in the puzzle box, not all of its responses were learned. Only the response that led to reward was learned. Thus Thorndike concluded that the *effects* of a response determined its connection to stimuli. He expressed this *law of effect* as follows:

> Of several responses made to the same situation, those which are accompanied or closely followed by satisfaction to the animal will, other things being equal, be more firmly connected with the situation, so that, when it recurs, they will be more likely to recur; those which are accompanied or closely followed by discomfort to the animal will, other things being equal, have their connections with that situation weakened, so that when it recurs, they will be less likely to occur. The greater the satisfaction or discomfort, the greater the strengthening or weakening of the bond. (1911)

In other words, Thorndike maintained that rewarded responses were repeated, and punished responses were weakened. It was not long until his law of effect was extended to include human as well as animal behavior. Note that Thorndike said that the *function* of responses determines their fate and that reasoning is not essential to the determination of behavioral adaptations to the environment. As a result, psychologists who were interested in the functions of learning seized on his experiment as their basic paradigm.

Behaviorism

All the influences described so far culminated in the tradition known as *behaviorism.* Its founder, John B. Watson became disenchanted with introspection primarily because introspectionists frequently failed to agree on their introspections. According to Watson, before any progress could be made, all observers would have to agree on what the observations or data would be. Because they could not observe mental events, which were private, they would be unable to agree on the contents of introspections. However, because different investigators could observe overt behavior, they would be able to agree on what the behavior was (e.g., the cat either pulls the string or it does not).

As a result of Watson's arguments, the focus of psychology shifted to the study of overt behavior. Naturally, the obvious methods to use in this study were those of Pavlov and Thorndike. Therefore, psychologists of learning set themselves the task of studying classical conditioning and instrumental learning and determining how these two processes could account for seemingly more complex learned behaviors.

The initial phase of this endeavor was characterized by the development of very broad theories designed to account for all or at least most learning phenomena. The most influential theorists were Edwin R. Guthrie, Clark L. Hull, B. F. Skinner, and Edward Chace Tolman. Guthrie attempted to explain learned behavior on the basis of one basic principle—*contiguity*. This principle states that if a response occurs in the presence of some stimulus, it will become connected to that stimulus. Thus the simple contiguous occurrence of a stimulus and a response was said to lead to learning.

Hull developed a much more elaborate theory to account for learned behavior. Hull agreed that connections are formed between stimuli and responses, but he did not feel that contiguity was a sufficient condition to promote the development of the connection. Instead Hull believed that the response must be accompanied or followed by a reduction in drive for a connection to be formed. Hull added numerous postulates to this basic proposition and developed an elaborate system to account for learning.

Tolman developed a different theory of learning. Guthrie and Hull both believed that learning consisted of the establishment of associations between stimuli and responses. Tolman disagreed and argued that organisms learn what leads to what in the environment, a cognitive representation of the world and of the relationship between the organisms' behavior and events in the environment. Again, Tolman developed a detailed system around this principle in an attempt to account for all of learning.

Skinner did not develop a theory of learning in the usual sense, but he did develop a system of thought. Skinner has argued that the best way to study learning is to measure how observable responses vary with changes in environmental conditions rather than by developing elaborate theories which specify unobservable entities. That is, Skinner argued that psychologists should stress the *description* of observable relations rather than seek explanation through theoretical processes.

Much of the work in the psychology of learning from about 1930–1960 was involved with testing these positions. A clear resolution did not occur and more recently psychologists of learning have shifted away from the development of broad global theories to the development of more limited explanations of only circumscribed phenomena.

Classical Conditioning

Pavlovian or *classical conditioning* is a procedure in which a behavior occurs in response to a stimulus as a consequence of the temporal sequencing of this and another stimulus. The behavioral change is categorized as a learned change because it depends on the organism's experience with the sequence of stimuli. Some "neutral" stimulus such as a bell, which evokes no special reaction, is followed closely by a stimulus such as food, which does elicit a response, for example, salivation. In time, the neutral stimulus evokes a reaction that is similar to the one evoked by the stimulus that followed it. The stimulus that elicits the target response from the outset is called the *unconditioned stimulus* (US), and the response it elicits is called the *unconditioned response* (UR). The initially neutral stimulus is called the *conditioned stimulus* (CS), and the response it comes to produce as a function of the conditioning procedure is called the *conditioned response* (CR). The CR represents a change in behavior to the CS as a result of pairing the CS and the US and is thus a learned response. The chain of events is illustrated diagrammatically in figure 11.5.

Generality

At this point, we know that if a dog is presented with a bell, followed by food, a num-

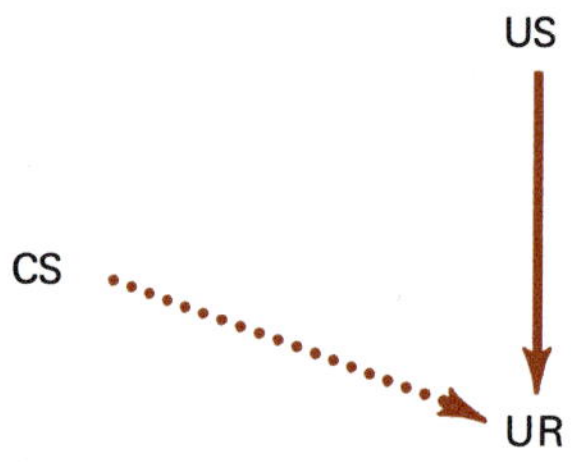

Figure 11.5 In classical conditioning, a CS occurs and is followed in time by an US. The US elicits an UR through an innate connection, symbolized by the solid arrow. As a result of pairing of the CS and US, a new connection is formed, so that the CS now elicits a response that is similar to the UR. This learned connection is symbolized by the dotted arrow.

ber of times, the bell will come to evoke salivation in the absence of food. But how general is this process? Is it restricted to dogs, bells, food, and salivation?

Unconditioned and Conditioned Stimuli

A wide variety of stimuli can serve as US. Effective stimuli are not restricted to *appetitive* stimuli—stimuli such as food, which the organism will seek out and approach—but also include *aversive* stimuli such as shock, which the organism will avoid. For example, in one popular technique for studying classical conditioning in human subjects, a noxious puff of air delivered to the subject's eye is the US. The UR is, if course, an eye blink, and this response becomes conditioned to stimuli that precede the air puff. Another example is called the *galvanic skin response* (GSR) conditioning. The GSR is a decrease in the electrical resistance of the skin which typically occurs when a person anticipates the occurrence of a painful event. If a tone or some other neutral stimulus is followed by an US such as electric shock, a GSR will become conditioned to the tone.

The US we have discussed so far have been *exteroceptive,* or delivered to the outside of the body. An US can also emanate from inside the body. These *interoceptive* US have been investigated extensively by Russian psychologists (e.g., Bykov, 1957). An example of an interoceptive US that has been investigated by American psychologists is the gastrointestinal symptoms induced by exposure to large doses of X-rays. Although we cannot see or hear X-rays, gastrointestinal distress such as nausea will follow some time after exposure to them. If a neutral stimulus, such as a particular taste, precedes the onset of nausea, the organism will develop a *conditioned aversion* to the taste; that is, it will avoid ingesting any substance with that taste.

Not only can a wide range of stimuli serve as the US, but a wide range of stimuli can also serve as the CS. There is nothing special about a bell. In fact, a US can even serve as a CS when paired with a "stronger" US. For example, if the presentation of food is followed by electric shock, food will come to elicit fear.

Responses

What kinds of responses can be classically conditioned? That is, what kinds of new behaviors will be evoked by a CS as a consequence of pairing it with an US? So far, most of our examples have involved the conditioning of relatively distinct, or discrete changes controlled by the autonomic nervous system (see Chapter 3). Salivation and the GSR are, in part at least, controlled by the autonomic nervous system. However, less discrete, more global kinds of responses can also be conditioned. If a neutral stimulus such as a tone is followed by a strong aversive stimulus such as electric shock, *fear* becomes conditioned to the tone. Fear has traditionally been defined as a *pattern* of changes in a large number of autonomically controlled response systems rather than as a change in a single response system. Thus fear is described physiologically in terms of increased heart rate, dilation of the peripheral blood vessels, increased activity of the adrenal glands, and so forth. More recently, it has been proposed that conditioned fear is actually a conditioned state in the central nervous system, rather than a pattern of peripheral changes (Rescorla and Solomon, 1967), but this question need not concern us here. For present purposes, it is enough to note that *emotional states* (whether controlled by the peripheral or central nervous system) can be conditioned.

Thus far, we have seen that responses controlled by the autonomic nervous system can be conditioned. Although it is still a matter of some dispute, responses controlled by the somatic (skeletal) division of the peripheral nervous system can also be classically conditioned. A recently discovered example of great theoretical interest is a phenomenon called autoshaping. (The reason why it is called *autoshaping* will become apparent later in this chapter.) A hungry pigeon is placed into an enclosure called a Skinner box (see fig. 11.6), and every minute or so, a small disc located in the front wall of the enclosure is illuminated. The disc, or key remains illuminated for eight seconds. After eight seconds, food is presented to the pigeon by raising a food hopper, also located in the front wall. In other words, the illumination of the key is followed by food, a classical conditioning arrangement. The result of pairing illumination of the key with food is that the pigeon starts to peck at the key as a CR. Because the pecks depress a microswitch located behind the key, they are easily recorded. Pigeons approach and peck food as an unconditioned response to food and thus begin to approach and peck the CS that is paired with food. This approach and pecking is controlled by the somatic division of the peripheral nervous system.

Figure 11.6 A pigeon in a Skinner box. The response measured is the pecking of the key; food reinforcement can be given by raising the food tray. The key is translucent and can be illuminated from behind by different lights. (From Morgan, C. T. and King, R. A. *Introduction to Psychology.* Adapted from C. B. Ferster and B. F. Skinner, *Schedules of Reinforcement.* Copyright 1971 McGraw-Hill Inc. Reprinted by permission.)

Classical Conditioning in Species and Stages

Although it is not clear whether one-celled organisms show evidence of classical conditioning, definite examples of classical conditioning can be found in organisms ranging from flatworms to man. This should not be surprising because even isolated ganglia can be conditioned (see Chapter 3).

In addition, classical conditioning is not restricted to adult organisms. For example, sucking can be conditioned in human babies who are three days old. Kaye (1967) presented babies with a tone followed by a nipple. After a number of pairings, the babies began to suck in response to the tone alone. It has even been demonstrated that some conditioning occurs in the human fetus. For example, pressure on the mother's abdomen (the US) produces movement of the fetus as a UR, and if this US is preceded by a loud sound, the fetus comes to move in response to the sound.

Basic Phenomena

Many phenomena are associated with classical conditioning. However, only the most important ones will be mentioned here.

Acquisition

One pairing of a CS and an US is usually not enough to establish the CR. Frequently, a large number of pairings is required. The strength of the CR usually increases gradually as the number of pairings increases. Furthermore, increments in the strength of the CR tend to be large during early trials, when the CR is still weak, and tend to be small on later trials, when CR strength is greater. Changes in the strength of a CR as a function of continued pairings of CS and US (trials are shown in figure 11.7a.

Many details of the conditioning procedure influence the rate at which acquisition of the CR occurs. The *temporal relationship* between the CS and the US is the most important factor. In the examples of conditioning that we have discussed, the CS must *precede* the US. In addition, *contiguity* is generally of great importance. Contiguity of the CS and US often facilitates conditioning. Thus the most effective arrangement of CS and US is one in which the CS is initiated before the US and remains until the US is presented.

Optimal conditioning occurs when the CS precedes the US and remains present until the US occurs, but what is the best interval between the two? A massive amount of research has been directed at this question, and the answer seems to be that there is *no* generally optimal interval between the CS and US. Apparently, different response systems have different optimal intervals. In general, the more sluggish the UR, the longer will be the optimal CS-US interval. An eye blink in response to a puff of air occurs with a short latency, and the optimal CS-US interval for eye blink conditioning is also short, around 0.5 seconds. Changes in heart rate caused by an electric shock have much longer latencies. Therefore, the optimal CS-US interval for conditioning of heart rate is much longer, perhaps between 5 and 10 seconds. Fear conditioning is quite effective with CS-US intervals on the order of minutes.

Extinction

Can conditioned responses be eliminated once they have been established? A moment's reflection will indicate that elimination of a CR should certainly be possible. It would be highly maladaptive for an organism to continue to respond to a CS that is no longer followed by a US. Presentations of a CS that are followed by an US are called *reinforced* presentations of the CS, and just as reinforced presentations increase the strength of the CR, *nonreinforced* presentations of the CS reduce

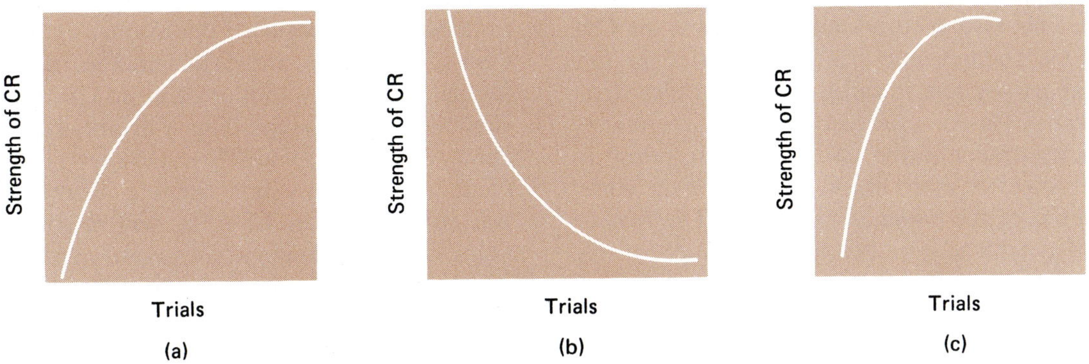

Figure 11.7 (a) Represents a typical acquisition curve. Here the CS and US are paired on each trial, and CR's strength increases gradually from trial to trial. Notice that the size of the increment in CR strength from a trial decreases as the trials progress. (b) Is a typical extinction curve. Here the CS is not followed by the US, and the CR's strength decreases gradually. Note that the size of the decrement from a nonreinforced CS presentation decreases as trials progress. (c) Represents a typical reconditioning curve. Here again the CS is followed by the US. Note how quickly the strength of the CR increases.

the strength of the CR. That is, CRs can be eliminated by presentation of the CS alone, without the usually accompanying US. This process of reducing CR strength through nonreinforced presentations of the CS is called *extinction.*

Just as one reinforced presentation of a CS is usually not sufficient to produce acquisition, one nonreinforced presentation of a CS is usually not sufficient to cause extinction. In addition, the decrement in strength of a CR which results from a nonreinforced presentation of a CS depends on the strength of the CR on that trial, just as does the increment in strength of a CR which results from a reinforced trial. The greater the strength of the CR, the larger the decrement that results from a nonreinforced presentation of a CS. An example of the resulting extinction curve is shown in figure 11.7b.

A phenomenon called *spontaneous recovery* is frequently observed following the extinction of a response. If an interval of time is allowed to elapse following extinction, and the CS is again presented, an appreciable CR often occurs. If the CR is repeatedly extinguished each time spontaneous recovery occurs, a point can be reached at which spontaneous recovery will no longer occur. It should be noted, however, that even though extinction can be carried to the point where spontaneous recovery no longer occurs, the preceding conditioning still may leave a residue in the organism. If the CS is again followed by the US after extended extinction, *reconditioning* will frequently occur more rapidly than did original conditioning (see fig. 11.7c). Although nonreinforced presentations of the CS extinguish the CR, a trace of the conditioning experience still remains.

Generalization and discrimination

Although it is possible to control stimuli accurately in the laboratory, *identical* stimuli rarely occur repeatedly in real life. Thus it appears likely that a CR occurs not only to the precise CS that has been paired with a US but also to other stimuli similar to the CS. This phenomenon has been studied in the laboratory and is called *stimulus generalization*. CRs do occur to stimuli that are physically similar to the CS. And the response is stronger or more likely, the greater the similarity of the stimulus to the CS. The results of a typical stimulus generalization experiment are presented in figure 11.8.

Organisms should not only be able to generalize a CR to a stimulus that is similar to the CS, they should also be able to learn to *discriminate* between a stimulus that is followed by the US and a stimulus that is not followed by the US. This kind of discriminative learning does indeed occur. If one stimulus called CS+ is followed by an US, and another stimulus called CS– is not followed by an US but is presented alone, responding will initially occur to both CS+ and CS–. However, with continued discrimination training, responses will continue to the CS+ but will disappear to the CS–. At this point, the organism is said to have formed a discrimination. Note that the CS– does not merely become neutral, it becomes actively inhibitory (see box 11.1).

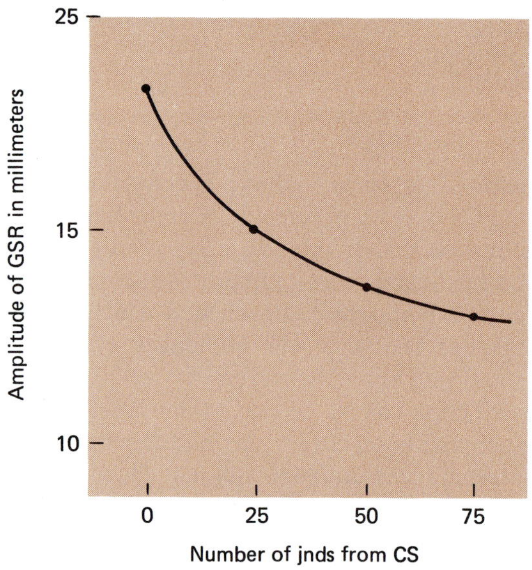

Figure 11.8 The GSR was conditioned to a tone represented as zero on the stimulus scale. Then tones differing from the CS by 25, 50, or 75 just noticeable differences in frequency (see Chapter 6) were presented and the GSR response was measured. Note that the further the tone is from the CS, the lower the level of responding. (From Hovland, C. I. "The generalization of conditioned responses. I. The sensory generalization of conditioned responses with varying frequencies of tone," *Journal of General Psychology, 17,* 1937. Reprinted by permission of The Journal Press.)

What Processes Are Involved?

Now that we have described some of the phenomena associated with classical conditioning, we will inquire into the nature of the *processes* involved. We should mention at the outset, however, that our understanding of the conditioning process is far from complete. Furthermore, psychologists disagree sharply about even the few issues that will be discussed here. So keep in mind that the views expressed in this section would not meet with unanimous agreement.

What is Learned?

What does the organism actually learn during exposure to a classical conditioning procedure? The first opinion on this issue was stated by Pavlov himself and was expressed in terms of the physiological knowledge of his day. Pavlov argued that a "cortical center" represents each different stimulus. He further argued that if two cortical centers are active at the same time, neural excitation will flow from the cortical center that has less excitation to the center that has more excitation. During conditioning the cortical centers corresponding to the particular CS and US will be activated at the same time. Because the US is generally a more powerful stimulus than the CS, excitation should flow from the CS to the US center. This flow of excitation

Box 11.1

Inhibition

In the discussion on discrimination, it was stated that a CS— (a stimulus not followed by the US but by the *absence* of the US) eventually comes to elicit no response. In other words, a CS— either may become neutral or may become actively *inhibitory.* In either case, it elicits no response. The simple observation that a CS— comes to evoke no response, however, does not help us decide whether a CS— merely lacks *excitatory* power or becomes actively inhibitory.

The distinction between a stimulus that lacks excitatory power and a stimulus that is inhibitory is a subtle one. Neither will elicit a response, but an inhibitory stimulus should actively suppress the response, whereas a neutral stimulus should have no suppressive power. Inhibition is considered a force that exerts an influence in the opposite direction from excitation. Thus it should be possible to tell whether a CS— is inhibitory by examining whether it will reduce the response produced by a CS+, an excitatory stimulus. This kind of test is called a *summation test,* and it reveals that CSs— are in fact inhibitory. If a well-established CS— is introduced during presentation of a CS+, responding is drastically reduced. A neutral stimulus that merely leads to no excitation should not suppress the responses produced by a CS+.

Discriminative conditioning is not the only procedure that leads to the development of inhibition to a CS. We defined a CS— as a stimulus that is followed by the absence of the US. It is possible to arrange such conditions without the presence of a discrimination. For example, a sequence of CSs and USs could be presented in a way that would always cause the US to occur long after the preceding CS. Thus the CS will be a CS— and, under these conditions, the CS will become inhibitory.

Whenever the US is more likely to occur in the absence of the CS than in its presence, the CS will become inhibitory. Thus conditioning is a bipolar affair; excitatory conditioning results when the CS predicts the occurrence of the US, and inhibitory conditioning results when the CS predicts the absence of the US.

will occur during every trial, and Pavlov argued that this would, in a sense, wear a path between the CS and US centers. Finally, a point is reached where the path is so strong that excitation flows from the CS to the US center even if the US center is not activated directly. Thus, if a CS is presented alone after many pairings with the US, the CS naturally excites the CS center, and now excitation flows to the US center and activates it. Activation of the US center elicits the UR, since the UR is held to be a reflex response to the US; that is, it is activated by an innate connection. Thus, in Pavlov's view, the CR is just the UR, but now it is activated through a connection that has been formed between the CS and US. It should be apparent that Pavlov believed that what is actually learned as a result of CS-US pairings is a connection between the CS and US. The CR is not learned or conditioned *per se;* it occurs because the CS and US have become connected. For these reasons, Pavlov's theory has been called a stimulus-substitution or S-S theory.

Early students of conditioning in the United States, however, quickly reached a different interpretation than Pavlov's. John B. Watson argued that because CS and US centers cannot be observed directly, they are unverifiable entities and thus should not be offered as an explanation. Instead, Watson argued, a *direct connection* is formed between the CS and UR; that is, between the observable stimulus and the observable response. The contiguity between the CS and the response was said to form a direct connection between them. This early theoretical position, called a *S-R* or stimulus-response position, was adopted by most, though not all, American psychologists and came to be the dominant view.

Pavlov's S-S (stimulus-stimulus connections) view differs from the S-R view in several respects. The most obvious differences concern the role of the US and the role of the UR. According to the S-R position, an association forms between the CS and the overt response (or UR) as a consequence of their contiguity. The role of the US is merely one of eliciting the response, so that the response can be contiguous with the CS. If some other means for eliciting a response could be found, S-R theory would predict that the US would not be required at all.

According to Pavlov, however, the association forms between the CS and US; therefore, the occurrence of the US is crucial. The occurrence of the UR during conditioning is not crucial, however. As long as activation of the US center can produce a response during *testing* of the CS, response to the CS should occur.

We have seen that, according to the S-R theory, the overt response must occur during conditioning for learning to be successful. According to S-S theory, however, the overt response is not required because the association is thought to occur between CS and US. A number of investigators have tested these predictions by pharmacologically and surgically immobilizing the response mechanism during conditioning. The CS and US are paired, but the UR is prevented from occurring. In subsequent test sessions, the response is no longer blocked, the CS is presented alone, and whether conditioning has or has not occurred is observed. Although the results of early studies of this kind are conflicting, the results of more recent experiments (Beck and Doty, 1957) seem consistent and show successful conditioning.

If it was possible to elicit a response directly following a CS, without presenting an US, S-R theory would predict successful conditioning and S-S theory would not. A motor response can be elicited directly by electrical stimulation of the motor cortex, the area of the brain that sends commands to the muscles. Thus we could present a CS and then elicit a motor response, such as a leg flexion, by stimulating the appropriate spot on the motor cortex. The results of such experiments have been inconsistent (Thomas, 1971). In general the results of these experiments suggest that such conditioning appears to be *unsuccessful.*

The weight of the evidence supports Pavlov's S-S view of conditioning. Apparently, conditioning is a process whereby the CS and US become connected in some fashion. However, we must still account for the occurrence of the CR. This was a simple matter for S-R theory: S and R became connected directly. However, we have seen that S and R do not become directly connected, so why does the CR occur? Pavlov believed that a US center in the brain was activated by the CS after conditioning. In his view, the CR was merely the UR transferred to the CS, or a *conditioned reflex.*

In Pavlov's view of CR production, the CR and UR must be identical or highly similar because the CR is viewed as the UR, elicited through a connection between CS and US. However, the CR and UR are rarely identical and in fact are often quite different. For example, electric shock often elicits an increase in heart rate, but a CS that is arranged to precede such a US often comes to elicit a *decrease* in heart rate as a CR. We have seen that if a stimulus precedes food, the organism will not only salivate to the stimulus but will approach it and direct food-related behaviors toward it. Furthermore, the organism's level of activity increases during this kind of CS (Zamble, 1967). Thus a broad range of behaviors is elicited by a CS, and only some of these behaviors can be interpreted as transferred reflexes. Approaching and ingesting food is not a reflex response to food, it is *motivated* behavior; that is, it occurs only when the organism is hungry. Reflexes do not depend on such motivational conditions for their occurrence.

If the CR is not directly connected to the CS and if the CR is not a transferred reflex or

UR, what can be said? It is only a small step from saying that conditioning involves the formation of a connection between CS and US to saying that what is learned is an *anticipation* or *expectation* of the US in the presence of the CS. That is, perhaps what is acquired is a *state* in the central nervous system induced by the CS as a result of its pairing with the US. And, perhaps this state can be described as an anticipation of the US. The advantage of this view is that an expectation of the US should have motivational consequences. Anticipation of the US can produce autonomic changes, such as changes in heart rate and salivation, but it can also lead to motivated behaviors that the organism uses in dealing with the US. In addition, this view does not require that the CR and UR be identical.

Contiguity and Contingency

We have seen that the relation between CS and US is the crucial one. But which aspect of the relationship between CS and US governs conditioning? The traditional view has been that the contiguity—the pairing in time of the CS and US—is the most important factor. A different view has been proposed by Rescorla (1967), who has argued that the *contingency* between CS and US, not the pairing between CS and US, is crucial.

To define the meaning of contingency, two terms will be required. The first is the *conditional probability* that a US will occur, given that the CS has recently occurred. This is abbreviated as P(US/CS) and is a statement of the likelihood or percentage of the time that the US follows the CS. If P(US/CS) equals .5, the US closely follows the CS fifty percent of the time. The second term is the *conditional probability* that a US will occur when the CS has *not* recently occurred. This concept is abbreviated as $P(US/\overline{CS})$ and indicates how likely a US is to occur if the CS has not just recently been presented.

These two probabilities form a *contingency space*, as shown in figure 11.9. The old contiguity view of conditioning maintains that conditioning is determined only by P(US/CS) because this term expresses the degree of pairing of CS and US. The contingency view says that the degree and direction of conditioning are determined, not only by the absolute value of P(US/CS), but by the value of $P(US/\overline{CS})$ and by the *difference* between P(US/CS) and $P(US/\overline{CS})$. If P(US/CS) is greater than $P(US/\overline{CS})$, excitatory conditioning should result. In other words, if the US is more likely to occur in the presence of the CS than in its absence, the CS should acquire excitatory power. Furthermore, the larger the difference

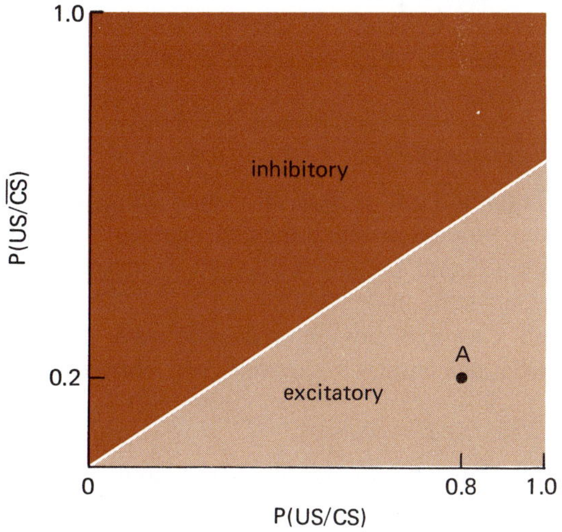

Figure 11.9 The contingency space representing possible relationships between a CS and an US. Any simple conditioning procedure can be localized as a point in this space. For example, if the US occurs following 8 out of every 10 CSs, but also occurs 20 percent of the time that the CS is not presented, the procedure can be represented by the point labeled A in the figure. Any point below the diagonal represents excitatory conditioning; the US is more likely in the presence of the CS than in the absence of the CS. Any point above the diagonal represents inhibitory conditioning; the US is more likely in the absence of the CS than in the presence of the CS.

between the two probabilities, the greater should be the degree of conditioning. If $P(US/\overline{CS})$ is greater than $P(US/CS)$, then conditioning should be inhibitory. In other words, if the US is more likely to occur in the absence of the CS than in its presence, inhibition should result. We have already seen that this is the case. If $P(US/CS)$ is equal to $P(US/\overline{CS})$, no conditioning should occur. To put it another way, if the relation between CS and US is random—that is, if the US is equally likely to occur whether or not a CS has occurred—conditioning should not take place.

Rescorla's evidence for the contingency position is beyond the scope of this chapter. However, we can say it strongly favors the contingency view. Thus it is the contingency between CS and US, or the *predictive* power of the CS, that determines the degree of conditioning.

Internalization of the Contingency

Thus far, our picture of conditioning is that of a process in which the contingency between the CS and US is internalized as an expectational state in the central nervous system. Are all contingencies internalized, and, if not, what determines which ones are learned?

Blocking Experiment

An experiment performed by Kamin (1969) suggests that organisms do not condition to all stimuli involved in a contingency. Kamin studied the conditioning of fear by pairing CSs with electric shock and assessing the degree of fear conditioning. His technique for measuring the amount of fear conditioned to the CSs is called a *conditioned emotional response* (CER) technique. In this procedure, an organism such as a rat is trained to perform a response like pressing a lever to obtain food. Once the animal has learned this response well, classical conditioning between a CS such as a tone and a shock (US) is initiated. The degree of fear conditioned to the tone is assessed by introducing the tone while the rat is pressing the lever. If the tone elicits fear, lever pressing will be suppressed. The greater the decrease in the rate of lever pressing, the greater is the amount of conditioned fear.

Kamin began by pairing a *compound* CS composed of a tone *and* a light with electric shock. When he assessed the amount of fear conditioning that occurred to each stimulus tested alone, he found that strong fear conditioning had occurred to each. Another group of rats also received the tone-light compound CS paired with shock, but first they received conditioning between just the tone and the shock. When the tone and the light were tested following the compound conditioning, the rats in the second group showed no evidence of fear conditioning to the light, they only showed fear of the tone. Thus previous conditioning to one element of a compound stimulus (the tone) *blocked* conditioning to a new superimposed element (the light). Conditioning to the light was successful if the tone-light conditioning trials were not preceded by tone conditioning. Conditioning to the light was not successful, however, if the tone-light trials were preceded by tone conditioning.

Kamin went on to perform a variety of experiments in an attempt to explain the results of his blocking experiment and arrived at the following conclusion:

> Perhaps for an increment in an associative connection to occur, it is necessary that the UCS instigate some mental work on the part of the animal. This mental work will occur only if the UCS is unpredicted, if it in some sense surprises the animal. Thus, in the early trials of a normal conditioning experiment, the UCS is an unpredicted, surprising event of motivational significance and the CS-UCS association is formed. . . . Precisely what mental work is instigated by a surprising UCS? . . . Suppose that for an increment in an associative connection to occur, it is necessary that the UCS provoke the animal into a backward scanning

of its memory store of recent stimulus input; only as the result of such a scan can an association between CS and UCS be formed, and the scan is prompted only by an unpredicted UCS, the occurrence of which is surprising (p. 293).

Thus Kamin argued that a contingency between a CS and a US is learned only when the occurrence of the US is a surprise to the organism; that is, when the US is not predicted by another CS. When the organism is surprised, it scans backward through its memory to find a stimulus that predicted the US. In the blocking experiment, the occurrence of the shock after presentation of a tone and a light was not surprising if tone and shock had previously been paired. Therefore, the rat did not scan backwards and thus showed no conditioning to the light.

This view suggests that much of the learning that occurs in classical conditioning takes place *after* the trial is over. A CS-US sequence occurs, and if the US is surprising (unpredicted), the organism then scans backward in its memory. In other words, it *rehearses* the CS-US sequence. If this is a correct picture—if the organism processes the trial sequence after the trial is over—it should be possible to influence conditioning by manipulating events that occur *after* a trial.

Specifically, it should be possible to retard conditioning to a stimulus by presenting a surprising event shortly after each conditioning trial. The surprising event should command rehearsal and thus decrease the likelihood that the subject will rehearse the preceding CS-US sequence. Precisely this result was reported by Wagner, Rudy, and Whitlow (1973).

Preparedness

To this point, we have discussed conditioning as though it were a unitary process. In other words, we have been talking about the learning of CS-US relation as though it does not matter what the CS and the US are; we have been implicitly assuming that the same thing happens, regardless of the stimulus we choose as a CS or US. This kind of assumption is a common one and it is the one made by Pavlov.

Most psychologists have followed Pavlov and have assumed that the same laws apply to the learning of all CS-US relationships. From an evolutionary point of view, however, it seems unlikely that organisms will learn all the different CS-US relations equally well. Seligman (1970) has argued for the existence of a dimension he calls *preparedness:* some organisms may have evolved prepared to learn some CS-US contingencies, unprepared to learn others, and contraprepared to learn still others. That is, the organism will rapidly make associations between events that it is prepared to associate, and will form other associations for which it is unprepared only with great difficulty.

To understand this concept, consider how a rat lives in the wild. The animal is a scavenger and lives on an ever-changing food supply. Thus to survive it must be able to learn which new foods in its environment are safe and which are poisonous. Because the physical location of food changes, the rat must be able to learn which foods are safe and which are dangerous on the basis of their taste and smell. Furthermore, it must be able to learn these associations rapidly. If repeated trials are required, the animal will die. Moreover, it must be able to learn, despite a long delay between the CS (the taste of the food) and the US (the gastrointestinal consequences of the food, e.g., poisoning). The effects of ingesting a poisoned food often do not occur until several hours after eating. We have seen that the optimal CS-US interval in many conditioning situations ranges from a fraction of a second to a minute or two. However, if the rat were restricted to these short CS-US intervals when it learns of the relationship between a food and its consequences, it would not be likely to survive.

There is ample empirical support for these conjectures. Rats develop a conditioned aversion to the taste of a food that causes illness after just one pairing of the taste and illness. In a typical experiment, a rat might be offered a substance with a distinctive taste, such as a saccharin solution. Some time later, the animal is injected with a substance that induces illness. After just one sequence, the animal develops an aversion to the taste of saccharin, and it will later refuse to ingest the saccharin solution, even when it is extremely thirsty. Furthermore, this conditioning will occur even if six or more *hours* intervene between ingestion of the saccharin solution and the administration of the illness-inducing agent. We should point out, however, that the rat does not develop a generalized aversion to *any* taste by this method; it avoids only the specific taste that preceded the onset of the illness. In addition, this kind of aversion can be extinguished only with great difficulty.

It is also crucial to recognize that the rat does not form an aversion to *any* stimulus that precedes illness, but only to tastes and smells. This has been demonstrated in a series of experiments by Garcia. In one experiment (Garcia and Koelling, 1966), the induction of illness was preceded by a light, a noise, and a taste. The rat did not develop an aversion to the light and noise, only to the taste. Thus it is prepared *selectively* to associate tastes with illness. Garcia and Koelling went on to show that this result is not related to the fact that tastes are "better" CSs than are lights and noises. A second group of rats also received a light, noise, and taste as a CS. However, the compound CS was followed by electric shock rather than illness. In this case, the rats developed a conditioned fear response to the light and noise, but did not develop a fear response to the taste.

Thus the *relationship* between the CS and US is the crucial element. When the US is illness, the rats develop a conditioned aversion to tastes that precede it; when the US is an exteroceptive US such as electric shock, the rats develop a conditioned aversion to preceding external stimuli. In nature, rats are made ill by food, not by external events such as visual and auditory signals. Conversely, external pain is induced by events that have distinctive visual and auditory features, for example, predators. The rat's conditioning mechanism has apparently evolved to reflect these cause and effect relationships that have occurred during the history of the species. In other words, the conditioning mechanism is selective; it does not simply hook together any two stimuli that occur together. This point is illustrated in the discussion of phobias in box 11.2.

Instrumental Learning

You will recall that in Thorndike's puzzle box experiment, a cat was allowed to escape from the box and obtain food if it pulled a string. As a result, the cat *learned* to pull the string. String pulling occurred infrequently at the beginning of the experiment and very frequently at the end. In classical conditioning, the learned behavior is produced by making a US contingent upon a CS; in *instrumental learning,* or operant conditioning, as it is sometimes called, the learned behavior is produced by making a US contingent on the subject's behavior. In Thorndike's experiment, food did not follow a tone or a light; the cat received food only after it pulled the string. Thus in instrumental learning, the behavior to be learned procures reward; in classical conditioning, on the other hand, the learned behavior has no influence on the occurrence of reward. In Pavlov's experiment, the dog received the food US following a CS *whether*

Box 11.2

How About "Little Hans"?

We are now in a position to confront the question raised at the beginning of the chapter. What does Hans' phobic fear of horses have to do with the fact that dogs will salivate to a bell paired with food?

Although Freud interpreted Hans' fear of horses as a result of the Oedipal conflict, another interpretation is possible. A little more information about Hans might help. Hans was an extremely sensitive child who was easily frightened. One day he went to a merry-go-round and one of the horses fell, producing a loud noise that scared Hans severely. Thus Hans' fear of horses might have resulted from classical conditioning—Hans saw horses at the same time that he was frightened (CS and US).

An experiment by Watson and Raynor (1920) supports this interpretation. Watson and Raynor showed a furry white rabbit to a little boy named Albert. They followed this with a loud noise behind Albert. As a result, Albert developed a fear of rabbits, which generalized to similar stimuli such as men with white beards. Thus Albert showed what appears to be a phobic reaction to men with white beards, but the cause was clearly classical conditioning.

Phobias can therefore be viewed as a case of classical conditioning. However, several features of most phobias should be noted. They develop extremely quickly; repeated pairings are unnecessary. Furthermore, phobias do not extinguish readily. If someone has a phobic fear of cats, every time he sees a cat and experiences no adverse consequence, the occasion constitutes an extinction trial. These two factors have often been taken as evidence against the assertion that phobias could be classically conditioned reactions. Classical conditioning has usually been thought to require repeated trials, and most classically conditioned responses extinguish readily. However, we have seen that *prepared* conditioning has the characteristics required for phobias. It is interesting to note that phobias do not generally develop to arbitrary objects, but instead seem to develop to stimuli that have been important in the history of man; for example, snakes, heights, fire, water, open spaces, and so forth. People do not usually develop phobias to chairs, cars, and flowers. Just as the poisoned rat developed an aversion to tastes and not lights when poisoned, Albert developed a fear of rabbits, not a fear of Watson or Raynor!

Therefore, it is likely that classical conditioning plays a large role in determining our emotional reactions. As we have seen, emotional states can be conditioned, and it is possible that many of our reactions to objects can be traced to the pairing of these objects with positive or negative events.

or not it responded (salivated); in Thorndike's experiment, however, the cat received food *only if it did* respond (pull the string).

The stimulus that promotes instrumental learning is called a *reinforcer,* and the process by which such a stimulus leads to the strengthening of responses is called *reinforcement.* There are four basic instrumental learning situations, defined by the type of reinforcer used and the relationship between the response to be learned and the reinforcer. These four basic paradigms are illustrated in figure 11.10. Reinforcers can be either pleasant stimuli, *rewards,* or aversive stimuli, *punishers.* Furthermore, reinforcers can follow a response or can be removed following a response.

In Thorndike's experiment, the cat received a pleasant stimulus following a response. This procedure increases the probability of the response and is called *positive reinforcement.* However, one could also remove a positive stimulus after a response. This is called *omission training,* and it reduces the probability of the response. It is also possible to present an aversive stimulus following a response. This is called *punishment* and weakens the response. Finally, an aversive

	Stimulus presented	Stimulus removed
Pleasant stimulus	Positive reinforcement	Omission
Aversion stimulus	Punishment	Escape (negative reinforcement)

Figure 11.10 The instrumental learning paradigms that occur by either presenting or removing pleasant or aversive stimuli.

stimulus can be removed following a response. This strengthens the response and is called *escape* or *negative reinforcement.*

Thus in instrumental learning responses are strengthened or weakened by the presentation or removal of pleasant or aversive stimuli after the response. This kind of learning seems to have the same kind of generality that was described for classical conditioning.

Basic Phenomena

Acquisition

Instrumental responses are acquired in much the same fashion as classically conditioned responses are acquired. However, there are some additional considerations. For example, how can a complex response be learned instrumentally? If a response cannot be reinforced until it occurs, how can one that occurs infrequently be strengthened? A device called a *Skinner box* is often used to study operant conditioning. A Skinner box for a pigeon was shown in figure 11.6. When this device is used to study instrumental learning, food is delivered only if the pigeon pecks the key. A Skinner box for a rat is shown in figure 11.11. Here, there is a lever that can be pressed instead of a key that can be pecked. If the lever is pressed, food drops into the tray.

But if a rat is placed into the box, it will not simply walk over and press the lever. If it does not press the lever, how can we reinforce lever pressing? The answer is that instrumental responses often involve *shaping,* a process in which behavior that resembles the desired response is reinforced. In other words, responses that the organism does make are reinforced; in this way, the responses can be shifted gradually toward the desired response. For example, as the rat initially explores the Skinner box, it might be reinforced whenever it comes close to the lever. After the rat has learned to stay near the lever, it might be reinforced only when it touches the lever. This process would be continued until the rat actually presses the lever. This shaping technique can be used to train extremely complex responses and is the basis for much everyday learning. If you have watched a mother train a child, you will realize that shaping was clearly in evidence.

Once the desired response is established, it is unnecessary to reinforce every response. Our behaviors are not reinforced every time they occur; in general they are only *partially* reinforced.

Partial reinforcement is ordinarily administered according to some plan or schedule. There are many different kinds of *reinforcement schedules.* Sometimes reinforcement is delivered only after a certain number of responses has occurred. This is called a *ratio* schedule. If the same number of responses is always required to obtain the reinforcer, the schedule is called *a fixed ratio.* If the number

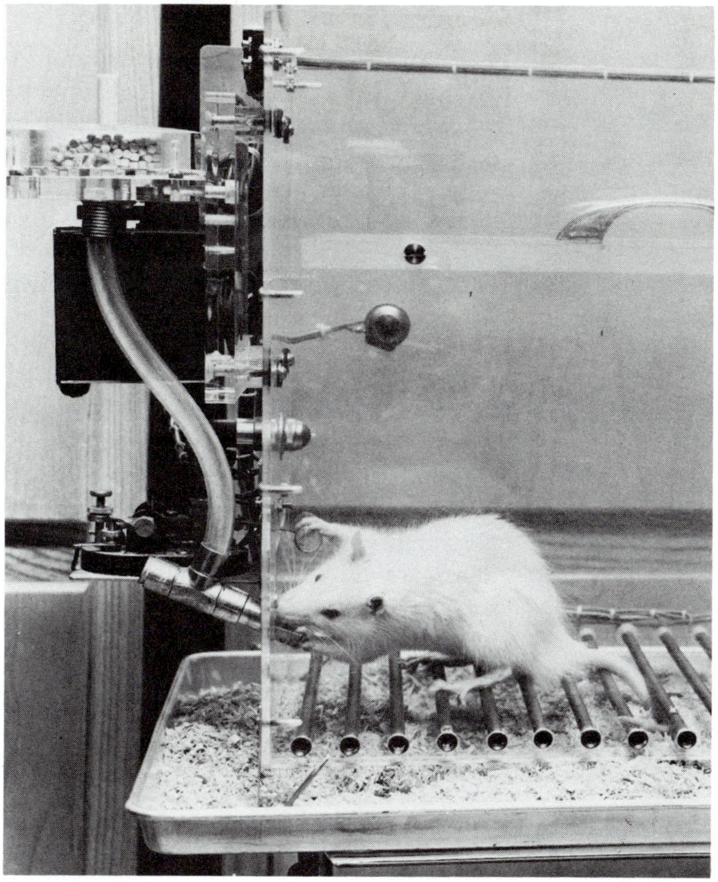

Figure 11.11 A rat in a Skinner box. When the rat depresses the lever, food is delivered in the round opening. (Reprinted by permission of B. F. Skinner. Photo courtesy Pfizer Inc.)

of responses that is required varies, the schedule is called a *variable ratio.* Reinforcers can also be delivered for responses that occur at a certain time after a previous reinforcement rather than for a given number of responses. These time-based schedules are called *interval* schedules. For example, the first response that occurs one minute after the preceding reinforcement might be reinforced. If the time interval is constant, the schedule is called a *fixed interval.* If the time interval varies, the schedule is called a *variable interval.*

Each schedule of reinforcement generates its own pattern of responding. For example, ratio schedules generate high rates of responding, while interval schedules generate somewhat lower rates. The reason for this difference is apparent. With ratio schedules, reinforcement will occur more frequently the more rapidly the organism responds; with interval schedules, this is not the case.

As was true of classical conditioning, many temporal variables influence the acquisition of instrumental responses. The most important is the delay of reinforcement—that is, the time interval between the occurrence of the response and the delivery of the reinforcer. The longer this interval is, the poorer the learning that will result.

Extinction

If reinforcement is discontinued, the response will extinguish. As a general rule, behavior that is established through partial reinforcement is much more persistent and difficult to extinguish than is behavior that has been established by continuous reinforcement.

Generalization and Discrimination

The reinforcement of instrumental responses always occurs in the presence of a variety of stimuli. In the Skinner box, for example, many cues are present, and reinforcement apparently builds up a connection between these stimuli and the response. As was the case with classical conditioning, the instrumentally trained response generalizes to similar stimuli. For example, if a pigeon must peck a key illuminated with a particular color to obtain food, it will also peck if another color is put on the key. However, the greater the difference between the new color and the color that was present during training, the weaker will be the pecking response to the new color.

A response is rarely reinforced under all circumstances. Usually a given response leads to reinforcement only under a specific set of circumstances. To study this situation in the laboratory, we might reinforce the pigeon's pecking behavior only when there is a red light on the key, not when a green light is present. This procedure is called discrimination training, as it was called in classical conditioning. However, the positive stimulus here is typically called an S+ rather than a CS+, and the negative stimulus is called an S− rather than a CS−. Under these conditions, the organism learns to respond in the presence of S+ and learns not to respond in the presence of S−. Furthermore, this kind of discrimination training tends to reduce the range of stimuli to which the organism will generalize its responses.

Secondary Reinforcement

Thus far, we have discussed examples of instrumental learning that have used *primary reinforcers*—stimuli that do not depend on previous learning for their ability to reinforce responses, for example, food. However, many of our responses are reinforced by events that are not inherently reinforcing (e.g., money) but depend on prior learning for their power. These events are called *secondary reinforcers*—stimuli that are originally neutral but can become reinforcers by being paired with a primary reinforcer. For example, if a tone is followed by food a number of times, it will acquire the ability to reinforce responses.

Stimuli paired with rewards are not the only stimuli that acquire the ability to promote learning. Neutral stimuli paired with aversive events also acquire reinforcing power. For instance, presentation of a tone that has been paired with shock can punish responses, and the removal of such a tone can reinforce responses.

What Processes Are Involved?

In his law of effect, Thorndike stated that instrumental learning is a process in which the connection between stimuli and responses is strengthened as a consequence of reinforcement. He viewed reinforcement as an agent that automatically strengthens the connection of the response which precedes reinforcement to whatever stimuli are present. By a response, Thorndike meant the movement of a muscle; by a stimulus, he meant the physical energies that stimulate the receptors of the body. Thus Thorndike argued that in insrumental learning a *direct connection* was established between a *physical stimulus* and *a motor movement*. The processes of thinking, insight, the development of expectations, and so on, were viewed to be irrelevant to instrumental learning—stimuli and responses simply become directly connected without any intervening processes.

The notion that instrumental learning involves only the connection of stimuli and responses was accepted and pushed forward by the early behaviorists, especially Watson. This position has come to be called *S-R theory*. As with classical conditioning, this view was attractive because stimuli and responses seemed to be observable, and thus the theory seemed testable.

Response

Do organisms actually learn muscle movements, or do they learn something more general that then produces movements? Does a rat that receives food reinforcement for pressing a lever learn the muscle movements involved in pressing the lever, or does it learn to expect that depressing the lever will lead to food?

Changed Response Experiments

The question of whether what is learned can be described as a series of muscle movements was effectively addressed by Lashley (1924). In one experiment, he trained monkeys to open a box to obtain food. The box was closed by a gate hasp and staple, with a wooden pin through the staple (see fig. 11.12). The monkeys had to learn a precise sequence of responses to open the box: (1) remove the pin, (2) lift the hasp, and (3) hold up the lid. After the task was well learned, Lashley removed part of each monkey's motor cortex, an area of the brain involved with the control of muscle movements. Although the surgery produced an initial paralysis, the monkeys gradually recovered their muscular movement. However, a residual minor paralysis remained, and this forced the animals to use a different set of muscle movements to open the box. If they had learned a series of muscle movements while learning to open the box, they should have been unable

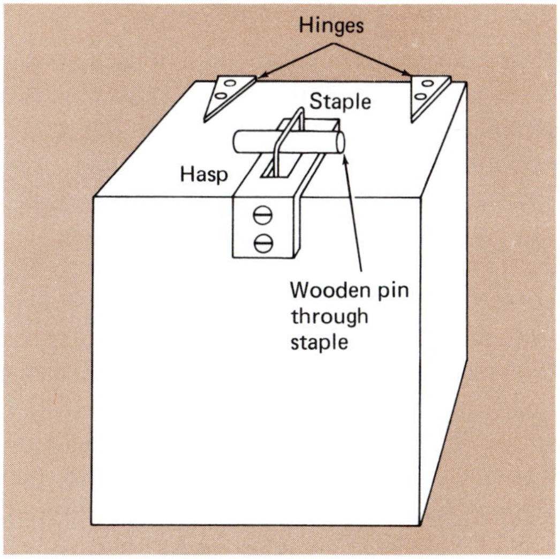

Figure 11.12 Diagram of a hasp box that is similar to the one used by Lashley. To obtain food, the monkey had to pull out the pin, lift the hasp, and lift the lid. (From Morgan, C. T., and King, R. A. *Introduction to Psychology* (4th Ed.), p. 88. Copyright 1971 by McGraw-Hill, Inc.)

to open the box after the operation without further training. Yet, after the operation, the monkeys opened the box without difficulty. Thus what they learned during training had to consist of more than a pattern of muscle movements.

The behavior of one monkey was particularly revealing. Before the operation, this monkey had been right-handed and thus learned to open the box with its right hand. After surgery, the monkey was permanently paralyzed on the right side of its body. However, it quickly opened the box with its *left* hand and arm. In other words, the animal was able to use a completely different set of muscles than it had when learning to open the box. Clearly, these monkeys did not learn a sequence of muscle movements; they seemed to learn a *sensorimotor schema*—the relationship between environmental stimuli (including reinforcement) and behavior.

Place Learning

If organisms learn more than muscular responses, it might be possible to show that instrumental learning occurs, even when the opportunity to perform the muscular responses during learning is absent. For example, an organism might be able to learn the path through a maze by mere exposure to the correct path. An example of a maze is shown in figure 11.13. The subject is released from the starting box and is rewarded when it enters the goal box. At each choice point, the subject must learn whether to turn right or left, and learning consists of eliminating the errors. Indeed, experiments by Gleitman (1955) and McNamara, Long, and Wike (1956) suggest that mazes can be learned in the absence of muscular responding. In both experiments, rats were exposed to maze-like situations by being wheeled through them in something like a trolley car; thus they did not run, turn, or perform overt muscular reactions. Later, when the rats were placed in the maze situation, they showed that they had learned the maze simply by riding through it. Thus, organisms seem to be able to learn the *location* of food and to use this learning to direct their overt responses. This does not mean that they do not learn muscular responses; it means that they learn other things in addition.

Learning Sets

We now know that organisms sometimes learn the relationship between their own behavior and reinforcement and sometimes learn the place where reinforcement occurs. Can they also learn a *strategy* to solve instrumental learning tasks? Consider the following experiment performed by Harlow (1949). Monkeys were given a series of two-choice problems. On each problem the monkeys were presented with two objects, such as a toy whistle and a ball. If a monkey picked up the correct object, it received a reward. A specific problem was continued until the monkeys made a certain number of correct choices in sequence. When one problem was solved, the monkeys were confronted with two new objects, one of which arbitrarily became the correct one. When presented with the first few problems, the monkeys required many trials to learn. However, as they received more and more problems, they began to solve the problems more and more quickly and usually reached a point at which they could solve a given problem in *one* trial. If they were rewarded for the object they happened to choose on the first trial, they continued to choose that object on subsequent trials. If they were not rewarded on the first trial, they chose the other object in subsequent trials. In other words, the monkeys learned a strategy for solving the problems; continue to choose the object that is rewarded, switch to the other one if there is no reward. Harlow called this process the formation of a *learning set,* a general solution to a problem. A learning set cannot be described as a muscular response.

Learned Helplessness

If organisms can learn the relation between their own behavior and reinforcement and also form learning sets, what should happen if an organism is exposed to a situation in which there is *no* relation between its behavior and reinforcement? This question was investigated by exposing dogs to electric shocks that were unrelated to the dogs' behavior (Overmier and Seligman, 1967; Maier, Seligman, and Solomon, 1969). The dogs could not escape or avoid these shocks in any way; thus their responses did not make any difference. After this experience, the dogs were put into another situation, where they could terminate the shock by performing a response. These dogs did not learn to escape shock in the new situation. Other dogs, who had not been exposed to inescapable shock, learned the escape response quite readily. The explanation for the first group's failure to learn was that during exposure to inescapable shock, the dogs learned that there was no relationship between their responses and escape from shock; that is, that they had no *control* over shock. This set was said to transfer to the new situation, thus preventing learning. If the organism has a set that the problem has no solution, none will be found.

The phenomenon of *learned helplessness* seems to have a wide range of applicability. For example, Engberg, et al., (1972) found that if pigeons are exposed to food independently of their behavior, they are subsequently retarded in their ability to acquire a response that procures food. That is, pigeons that receive food whether they respond or not learn to make a response that produces food only with great difficulty in subsequent situations. Seligman (1969) has found that learned helplessness can be demonstrated in man, and he believes it is involved in the development of depression. In addition, Dweck and Reppucci (1973) have studied the possibility that learned helplessness may be one reason why some children do poorly in school. Apparently, organisms can form fairly general sets, and these sets can have wide impact.

Stimulus

Just as the early behaviorists viewed the response acquired during instrumental learning in simple terms, the stimulus was also viewed in simple terms. Early behaviorists proposed that responses were connected to all physical energies that stimulated the organisms' receptors at the time of the response and reinforcement. For instance, if a red light, a loud tone, and a slight vibration were present at the time of response and reinforcement, the response was said to be connected to each stimulus. However, this assumption is in error. Organisms in fact are able to attach their responses to some stimuli and not others.

One mechanism that has been proposed to explain such selective associations is *attention.* The concept of attention has a long and complex history. At its core is the conviction that the number of stimuli which impinge on an organism at any given time far exceeds the organism's capacity to process stimuli. Thus the organism must select only a subset of these stimuli for processing; that is, because all the stimuli cannot be processed, some must be rejected. It has been argued that this selection is accomplished by a central process called attention: organisms attend to some stimuli and not to others. A corollary of this position is that responses only become attached to stimuli that the organism pays attention to, rather than to all the stimuli that reach its receptors.

There seems to be little doubt that a process of attention does exist. Nor is there any doubt that selectivity occurs in learning situations. However, the role of attention in accounting for selectivity in simple learning situations is in doubt (Thomas, 1970; Wagner, 1969). But it is clear that all stimuli which are present at the moment of reinforcement are *not* associated with the response (recall Kamin's blocking experiment, a similar instance in classical conditioning). Thus there must be a selective mechanism.

Reinforcement

Rewards do lead to an increase in the probability of responses that they follow, and punishers do lead to a decrease in the probability of responses that they follow. But why? Thorndike's answer was that reinforcers directly strengthen (or weaken) the connection between stimulus and response. That is, learning will not occur unless a reinforcer is presented, and reinforcers automatically strengthen the connection between preceding S-R sequences.

An alternative view was offered by Edward Chace Tolman who proposed that learning is a continuous process; it does not come into operation only when a reinforcer occurs. Tolman argued that organisms constantly learn the relationships between environmental events to which they are exposed and that reinforcement only affects the *performance* of responses, not the learning of responses. In this view, learning can occur in the absence of any overt change in behavior, and the role of reinforcement is to *motivate* the organism to perform the behavior it has learned. In other words, reinforcement is an agent that functions as an *incentive* for the organism to translate what it has learned into overt performance.

Latent Learning

Tolman provided a large body of research in support of his view. Consider the following experiment (Tolman and Honzik, 1930) in which three groups of rats were run in a maze similar to that shown in figure 11.13. Each rat was placed in the starting box and allowed to traverse the maze. As the rat came to a choice point, a door closed behind the animal, preventing it from going back where it had come from. In this way, each rat eventually reached the goal box. However, one group of animals received food reward in the goal box, while the other two groups did not.

The rats were given one trial every day for ten days. Each entry into a blind alley at a choice point was counted as an error, and by the end of ten days, the rewarded rats were making fewer errors than the unrewarded rats. Does this mean that the rewarded rats learned the correct path through the maze better than did the unrewarded rats? Or does this difference in errors merely reflect the fact that the rewarded rats had an incentive to perform correctly, whereas the unrewarded rats did not?

To answer this question, Tolman and Honzik introduced reward in the goal box on Day 11 for one of the unrewarded groups. If these

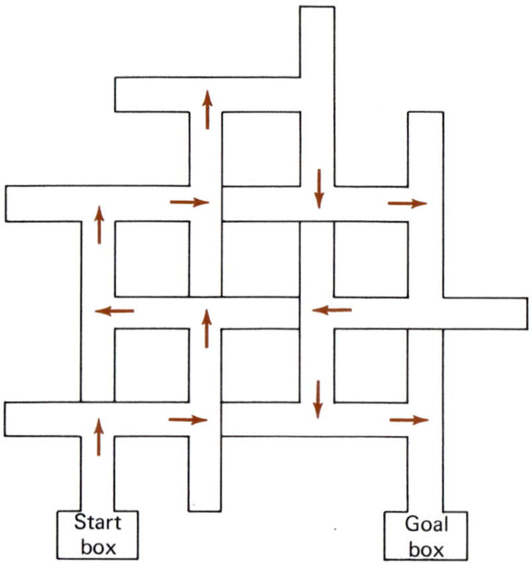

Figure 11.13 Diagram of a maze used to study learning in the rat. The rat is released in the start box and receives food in the goal box. The rat must learn to make the correct turn at each choice point to reach the goal box. (Reprinted by permission of the Publisher from C. Mussen, M. Rosinzwieg et al.: *Psychology: An Introduction,* Lexington, Mass.: D. C. Heath & Company, 1973.)

rats had learned the maze during the first ten days, but merely lacked the incentive to demonstrate their learning in overt performance, then they should have shown an immediate improvement in performance on Day 12, the first day after the reward was introduced. If these rats had not learned during the first ten days because the reward was absent, then their performance should have improved gradually beginning on Day 11—the point when reinforcement was introduced. The results of the experiment are shown in figure 11.14. As you can see, the rats' performance improved suddenly and dramatically when reinforcement was introduced. Thus they had learned before reward was introduced, but the learning was *latent* and was not revealed in their performance until reward

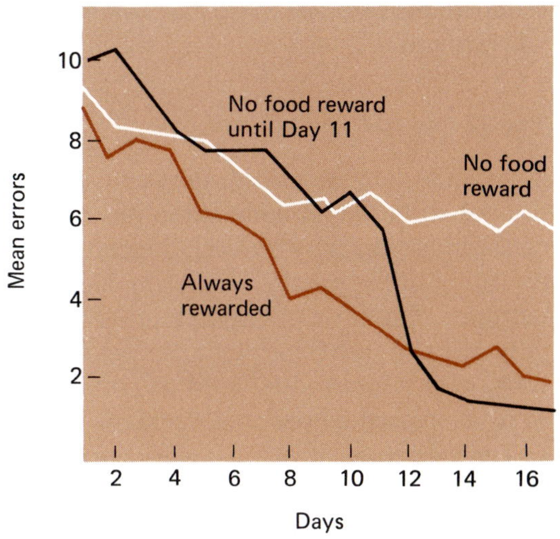

Figure 11.14 The results of the Tolman and Honzik experiment. The "always rewarded" group of rats were rewarded with food on every trial, the "no food reward" group never received a reward, and the "no food rewarded until Day 11" group began receiving rewards on Day 11. The group that was rewarded beginning on Day 11 showed marked improvement in performance between Day 11 and Day 12. These rats rapidly performed as well as the rats rewarded all along. (Reprinted by permission of the Publisher from C. Mussen, M. Rosinzwieg et al.: *Psychology: An Introduction,* Lexington, Mass.: D. C. Heath & Company, 1973.)

was introduced. For this reason, experiments such as this are called *latent learning experiments.*

Although the results of latent learning experiments can be interpreted in other ways, they do suggest that although reinforcement plays a primary role in motivating the performance of learned responses, learning will occur without it. This does not mean that reinforcement plays no role in promoting learning, only that it is unnecessary. At a minimum, the presence of reinforcers will cause the organism to pay attention to events. If no reinforcers are present, the organism may not attend to events that are occurring and will thus fail to learn.

Relativity of Reinforcement

We have been talking about the response–reinforcement relationship as though there is a fixed class of events called responses and a fixed class of events called reinforcers and as though any reinforcer is capable of increasing the probability of any response, if a contingency is arranged between them.

However, a series of experiments conducted by Premack (e.g., 1955) suggested that the response–reinforcement relationship is *relative* rather than fixed. In Premack's work, reinforcers were not viewed as stimuli, but rather as the opportunity to engage in a behavior. Thus, the opportunity to eat, for example, was viewed as a reinforcer, not food itself. In a typical experiment, Premack began with five responses that a monkey could perform, for example, pulling a chain or pushing a lever. We will call these responses A, B, C, D, and E. Premack set out to discover which response would be reinforced by the opportunity to engage in the others. To discover whether B reinforced A, for instance, the opportunity to perform B was made contingent on A. That is, the monkey was only allowed access to B if it performed A for a specific period of time. If B did reinforce A, then the frequency of A should have increased as a result of the contingency. But to know whether the contingency did increase the frequency of A, Premack had to know how frequent A was without the contingency. Thus he began the experiment by making all five responses available and simply measured the time the monkeys spent engaging in each.

To discover which responses would reinforce which of the other responses, Premack investigated all possible combinations of A, B, C, D, and E. If there was such a thing as a fixed class of reinforcers, then a response that reinforced one should have reinforced *all* the others. The outcome of the experiment was that the opportunity to perform one response often reinforced some of the other responses, but not all others. For example, B might reinforce A and D, but not C.

What determines which responses reinforce which? Recall that Premack began by measuring how likely the monkeys were to engage in each activity when they had a free choice (i.e., no contingency). Therefore, he was able to arrange the responses in the order of how likely the monkeys were to engage in them. Let's say that the order was B, C, A, E, D from most likely to least likely. Premack found that the opportunity to engage in a response would reinforce all those responses that were less likely to be engaged in than itself. However, a given response did not reinforce a response that was more likely than itself. Thus, in our example, A would reinforce E and D, but would not reinforce B and C. This outcome is depicted in figure 11.15.

This means that the power to reinforce is a relative matter. An event can reinforce less probable events but not more probable events. Therefore, reinforcement is not a property of the event but a property of the *relationship* between the response event and the contingent event. If the contingent event is more probable than the response event in a free-choice situation, then the contingent event will reinforce the response event, but not the other way around.

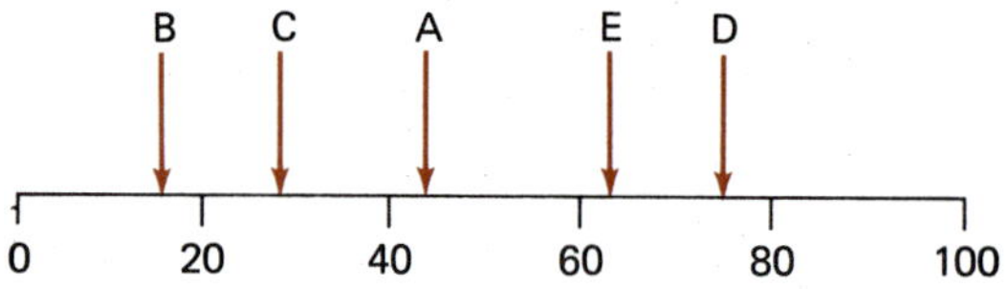

Figure 11.15 The percentage of the time that each of five activities is engaged in when a monkey is free to choose any of the activities. B is engaged in least often, and D is engaged in most frequently. Premack's (1965) results show that D would then be able to reinforce B, C, A, and E; E would be able to reinforce B, C, and A; A would be able to reinforce B and C, and so on.

The Crying Boy

We should now be able to answer the question raised in the introduction to this chapter concerning similarity between the cat pulling the string in the puzzle box and the boy with tantrums. Both were displaying instrumentally learned behavior; that is, pulling the string was reinforced by food and crying fits were reinforced by parental attention.

The relevance of instrumental learning to our everyday existence should also be apparent. Many behaviors we engage in are instrumentally learned responses, and reinforcers govern much of our behavior. Reinforcement should be able to strengthen not only behaviors that we judge as normal but also behaviors that we judge as abnormal. What if the little boy in our example had discovered that "acting crazy" brings parental attention as rapidly as do crying fits? A variety of behavior therapies are, in fact, based on the notion that abnormal behavior occurs because it has been instrumentally reinforced (see Chapter 19).

Interaction of Classical Conditioning and Instrumental Learning

Almost all instrumental learning situations contain the necessary conditions for the occurrence of classical conditioning. Most reinforcers used in instrumental learning situations are also effective Pavlovian USs, and if any stimuli reliably precede the reinforcer, classical conditioning of these stimuli should occur. For example, in an instrumental discrimination, the S+ is paired with the reinforcer, typically food, and the S− is paired with the absence of food. Thus a Pavlovian discrimination should form during an instru-

Box 11.3

The Importance of the Biological Relationship Between Response and Reinforcement

It has typically been assumed that any reinforcer can strengthen any response, assuming the reinforcer is more probable than the response, regardless of the relationship between them. This is false.

In general, a reinforcer can readily strengthen only those responses that are activated by the motivational system that is activated by the reinforcer. For example, Bolles (1970) has studied the kinds of behaviors that rats can learn as responses to avoid electric shock. An avoidance response prevents the occurrence of the noxious stimulus. In a typical procedure, some stimulus such as a tone might occur five or ten seconds before a shock. If the animal performs the designated response during this interval, the tone is terminated and no shock occurs. If the animal fails to respond, the shock comes on, and goes off when the response occurs. A response that occurs before the shock and prevents the shock from occurring is called an *avoidance response;* a response that occurs once the shock is present is called an *escape response.*

When a rat is frightened or subjected to a painful stimulus, it generally tries to flee. If flight is impossible, it usually freezes. Bolles has shown that rats will readily learn only behaviors that involve flight or freezing as avoidance responses. If a rat is required to press a lever to avoid shock, it will learn only with great difficulty, if at all. However, it will learn to run from a box as an avoidance response in just a few trials.

Similarly, pigeons do not readily learn to peck a key to avoid shock (Hoffman and Fleshler, 1959), but will rapidly learn to fly to a perch (Bedford and Anger, 1968) as an avoidance response. Pigeons peck when they are hungry and there is food; they do not peck when they are afraid. By analogy, it is easy to train a pigeon to peck a key for food reward, but it is difficult to train it to press a treadle with its foot (Moore, 1973).

Not only is it often difficult to reinforce a response that is not elicited by the same motivational system as is involved with the reinforcer, but even when successful, the reinforced behavior often breaks down and drifts to the behavior patterns that are elicited by the motivational system activated. This phenomenon was first noted by Breland and Breland (1961), who were educated as academic psychologists, but left the academic world to train animals for commercial exhibits. They trained animals to perform various complex acts, but frequently the reinforced behavior disintegrated and drifted toward the animal's instinctive behaviors normally directed toward the reinforcer used. For example, a bank hired the Brelands to train a raccoon to pick up a coin, carry it over to a piggy bank, and drop it in. By using food reinforcement, the Brelands managed to build up this chain of behavior. However, the raccoon soon developed a tendency to hold onto the coin. It would start to lower it into the piggy bank, but then lift it out and rub it between its hands. A point was reached where the raccoon would not even release the coin, even though this prevented the delivery of food. However, because raccoons always rub or wash potential food, there is a similarity between this change in behavior and what would be expected from classical conditioning. In other words, raccoons wash food (US) and now wash the coin (CS).

In addition, a behavior that is built up with one reinforcer will often disintegrate if the reinforcer is switched to one involving a different motivational system. For example, Schwartz and Coulter (1973) trained pigeons to peck a key for food. After pecking was well established, electric shock was introduced and by pecking the pigeons could escape or avoid the shock. But pecking disappeared!

It should be easy to see that, as in classical conditioning, the relationship between the events in the instrumental learning situation with respect to the evolution of the species is crucial. Responses that are biologically appropriate to the reinforcer are easily acquired, while responses that are not biologically appropriate are learned only with great difficulty.

mental discrimination. It is important to recognize that Pavlovian conditioning does not require a regular relationship between CS and US in which the CS occurs first and the US occurs at the end of the CS. As long as there is a contingency between the CS and US, conditioning should occur.

Even though there are no obvious external discriminative stimuli in an instrumental task, conditioning may still occur. For example, if a rat learns to press a bar for food, but no exteroceptive stimuli are correlated with food, lever pressing will lead to a distinctive pattern of interoceptive feedback, and this internal stimulus pattern will precede the food US in a reliable manner. Furthermore, because the external stimuli located at the lever and near the device for delivering food will be also correlated with the food US, classical conditioning to these stimuli should also occur. Thus there is ample opportunity for classical conditioning to occur, even in instrumental situations where the reinforcer is not correlated with obvious stimuli.

By analogy, it is possible for instrumental learning to occur in classical conditioning situations. Recall that a classical conditioning situation is defined as one in which a contingency exists between a CS and a US, while in instrumental learning, there is a contingency between the response and the US or reinforcer. If the CR in a classical conditioning situation alters the effective characteristics of the US, then there is a response-US contingency. Consider the ordinary salivary conditioning situation; CS is presented to the dog and is followed by an US, and salivation to the CS is measured as the CR. But what if it is easier to eat the food if some salivation occurs before the food? Or what if food tastes better after a little salivation? If salivation does have these effects, then there is an instrumental contingency—the response produces a consequence. A little thought will reveal analogous possibilities for an instrumental contingency in most of the classical conditioning situations we have discussed.

The obvious questions are: What is the role of the classical conditioning that must inevitably occur in most instrumental learning situations and, what is the role of the instrumental learning that might occur in classical conditioning situations? Although the second question has received some attention (Perkins, 1968), far more research has focused on the first question.

Two-Process Theory

A theory called *two-process theory* has been developed in an attempt to explain the relationship between the Pavlovian and instrumental processes that must both occur in most learning situations. This theory, developed primarily by Mowrer (1947) and Solomon (1953), asserts that both processes not only occur in most situations, but that they *interact;* that is, one influences the other. Specifically, the two-process theory argues that classically conditioned states motivate and reinforce learned instrumental responses. It argues that emotional states are conditioned to the cues that precede reinforcement or presentation of an US and that these emotional states motivate and help to reinforce the instrumental behavior.

To understand what this means, let's consider the avoidance learning situation discussed earlier. This kind of learning is often studied in a shuttle box (see fig. 11.16), where the instrumental response is jumping over a hurdle into the other side of the box.

What reinforces and motivates the avoidance response? Two-process theory would argue as follows: During early trials, the organism does not respond to a warning stimulus (e.g., a tone), so the warning stimulus is consistently followed by shock. In other words, conditioned fear should be established to the tone through a straightforward classical con-

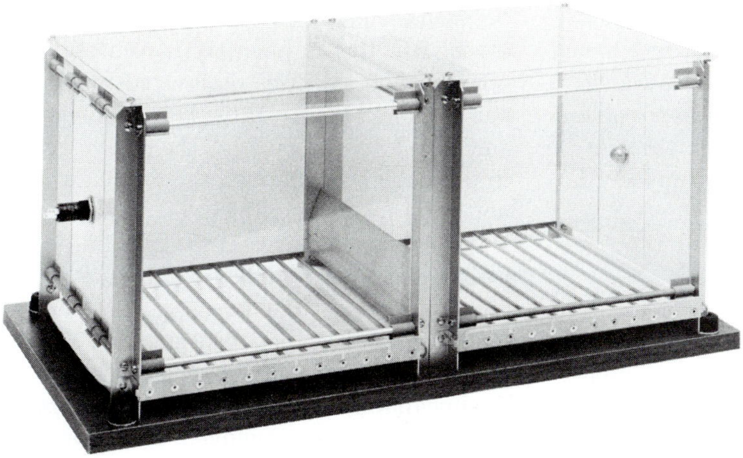

Figure 11.16 Shuttle box. The subject must run from one compartment to the other to escape or avoid shock. (From BRS/LVE, Division of Tech Serv Inc.)

ditioning process. Therefore, onset of the tone should be followed by an increase in the organism's level of fear, and termination of the tone should lead to a decrease in the level of fear. Thus the onset of the tone should motivate the organism to respond. Recall that the avoidance response is followed by the termination of the tone. Therefore the avoidance response, jumping over the hurdle, should be followed by a *reduction* in conditioned fear, and this should reinforce the avoidance response.

Two-process theory argues that the classically conditioned fear state *mediates* or controls the instrumental response. The onset of the classically conditioned fear state motivates, and the termination of the fear state reinforces the instrumental response.

Although two-process theory is not without its critics (e.g., Herrnstein, 1969), it seems clear that classically conditioned responses *can* control instrumental behavior. But whether such control is *necessary* for instrumental learning is a matter of some debate.

To see that Pavlovian processes can control instrumental behavior, consider the following experiment by Rescorla and LoLordo (1965). First, dogs were trained to avoid shock in a shuttle box. Then they were taught to avoid the shock by jumping over the hurdle at a steady rate. Second, in a different situation, the dogs were given Pavlovian fear conditioning. One stimulus, a CS+, was paired with shock, and another stimulus, a CS−, was followed by the absence of shock. The second situation was Pavlovian: the dogs could not escape or avoid the shock. According to Pavlovian principles, the CS+ should have elicited fear and the CS− should have inhibited fear. In the third and final phase of the experiment, the dogs were put back in the shuttle box. While they were responding and avoiding in the shuttle box, the CS+ and CS− from the classical conditioning phase were presented on separate occasions. If the two-process theory were correct, what should have happened? The theory asserts that the avoidance response is controlled by classically conditioned fear. The CS+ from the classical conditioning phase of the experiment should elicit fear, and the CS− should inhibit fear. Thus if two-process theory were correct, the dogs should have responded faster than usual when CS+ was presented and slower than usual when CS− was presented. This was in fact the result: the Pavlovian CSs were able to control the instrumental avoidance response. Thus the two processes can indeed interact.

Autoshaping

Because classical conditioning and instrumental learning can occur in the same situation, we might believe we are studying one process when in reality, we are studying the other. That is, we might believe that we are observing an instrumentally learned response when in fact we are observing a classically conditioned response or vice versa. This possibility is particularly serious when the instrumental response being learned is similar to the organism's UR to the reinforcer being used.

Let's consider the Skinner box for pigeons (see fig. 11.6), which is one of the most popular methods of studying instrumental learning. A pigeon is typically trained to peck a key when it is illuminated to obtain food. Because food is delivered only if the pigeon pecks, we could logically assume that this response is learned through an instrumental process.

However, a little thought will reveal a CS-US contingency as well as the response–reinforcer contingency. The pigeon receives food only if it pecks, and it can only peck when it looks at the key. Thus the sight of the illuminated key is often followed by food, a CS-US contingency. Could this Pavlovian contingency lead to pecking the key? The pigeon's UR to food does include pecking, so it is possible that the pecking of the key is a classically conditioned response.

If pecking the key is a Pavlovian response, it should occur even if a response–reinforcement contingency is lacking. That is, it should occur in the presence of a CS-US contingency alone. But this is precisely the autoshaping phenomenon that was discovered by Brown and Jenkins (1968). If the key is illuminated and then followed by food, the pigeon begins to peck the key although this behavior does not bring food any sooner.

This response suggests the possibility that many phenomena studied by the use of the pigeon's peck of the key for food may be Pavlovian rather than instrumental. Generally speaking, organisms seem to approach Pavlovian CS+s for USs related to appetite and withdraw from Pavlovian CS+s for aversive USs. And these reactions may account for a number of phenomena that have been considered instrumental.

By this, we do not mean that no response is learned through a true instrumental process. Undoubtedly, many responses are learned. However, when a response is not "arbitrary" and is intimately related to the organism's UR to the reinforcer, Pavlovian processes are likely to be involved in its acquisition. Pavlovian conditioning is perhaps the more primitive and widespread process and may be the first to come into play.

Summary

In this chapter, we have examined how behavior changes as a consequence of experience. We have discussed learned changes in behavior produced by contingencies between stimuli in the environment (classical conditioning), and those produced by contingencies between the organism's behavior and stimuli in the environment (instrumental learning).

We began by examining classical conditioning. We saw that Pavlov's ideas about learning were readily accepted and that his experimental paradigms became a cornerstone of the psychology of learning given the historical context of the times. The discovery of classical conditioning allowed the mechanists to extend their domain to the area of learned behavior, which formerly had been the exclusive property of the mentalists. This was so because the major process available to the mechanists of those days was the reflex, and Pavlov seemed to have discovered learned reflexes. Although the reflex is not the only possible mechanistic concept, it was the only one extensively studied in the nineteenth century. Therefore, Pavlov's work fit in beautifully. In addition, classical conditioning strongly resembled the associations discussed by the British empiricists and thus offered what was believed to be a more objective way of studying associations.

We considered the phenomena that occur during classical conditioning—e.g., acquisition, extinction, generalization and discrimination, and inhibition. Next, we discussed the processes involved. The first question was: What is learned during classical conditioning? Is a connection formed between the CS and US, as Pavlov maintained, or between the CS and the response, as many of the early behaviorists believed? The burden of the evidence indicated that the learned connection occurred between the CS and US. But if the connection or learned relationship is between the CS and US, why does the CR occur? The most likely answer was that what is learned in classical conditioning is a state best described as an expectation of the US in the presence of the CS. The CR was viewed as a reaction to this central state.

Once we found that what is learned is the relationship between the CS and the US, we asked which relationship is learned; the contiguity between CS and US or the contingency between CS and US? The evidence favored the second possibility.

Given that the contingency between CS and US is internalized, we then asked what promotes such internalization? We concluded that a surprising, unexpected US promotes rehearsal and thus internalization of the previous CS-US sequence.

Finally, we asked whether conditioning proceeds in the same fashion for different CSs and USs and found that it does not. A dimension of preparedness is involved. In other words, we discovered that the conditioning mechanism is selective; that is, it preferentially hooks together stimuli that have belonged together in the history of the species.

In our discussion of Thorndikian or instrumental learning, we saw that Thorndike's views became influential because they fitted into a functional tradition. Some of the phenomena that occur in instrumental learning—in addition to those in classical conditioning—are shaping, partial schedules of reinforcement, and secondary reinforcement.

Next we inquired into the nature of the processes involved in instrumental learning. The response, stimulus, and reinforcement were considered separately. According to S-R theorists, a muscular response is learned. However, changed-response, place learning, learning set, and learned helplessness experiments made it difficult to argue that a muscular response is all that is learned. With regard to the stimulus, the simple conception that responses become attached to all stimulus elements present at the moment of reinforcement was found to be untenable. Organisms learn about the relationships between stimuli as well as their absolute properties. Furthermore, selectivity seems to occur; that is, responses become attached to some stimuli that are present and not to others.

We also discovered that the reinforcement process was different than that proposed by the early S-R theorists. First, reinforcement does not seem to strengthen responses directly, rather it provides the incentive or motivation for the performance of learned responses. In addition, reinforcement does not appear to be an absolute property of a class of objects, but a relative property. Any activity can only reinforce a less probable activity. Finally, we saw that the biological relationship between a particular response and a particular reinforcer will determine the course of learning.

After discussing the differences between classical conditioning and instrumental learning, we described the relationship between the two. Both occur in most situations, and the *two-process learning theory* proposes that classically conditioned states motivate and reinforce instrumental responses. Furthermore, it is possible that some apparently instrumental responses are actually Pavlovian in nature.

12

Remembering and Forgetting

The nature of memory has been an intellectual puzzle for centuries. How do we remember? What do we remember? Do we remember different things differently? Questions such as these have been raised since the times of the early Greeks, and the answers are still largely unknown. However, rapid progress in the study of memory has been made in recent years, and the purpose of this chapter is to describe this progress.

It is obvious that learning and memory are closely related. In fact, memory has often been defined as the retention of what is learned. Thus theorists have commonly attempted to explain memory through principles of learning. For example, William James, the great American philosopher and psychologist, argued that memories are simply reexcited associations; in other words, if learning could be understood, memory would also be largely understood.

It is now recognized that memory involves far more than the simple retention of what is learned. Memory is a highly structured system that enables organisms to record facts about the world and use this knowledge to guide their behavior. If we can understand the structure of memory—how and in what form incoming information is stored in and retrieved from memory—we may understand the processes that occur during learning.

Historical Background

The experimental study of memory was begun by Hermann Ebbinghaus. In the late 1870s, Ebbinghaus became impressed by the fact that no one had yet applied experimental methods to study "higher mental processes" and decided to apply them in the study of memory.

Ebbinghaus's ideas about memory reflected those of the British empiricists. You will recall that the British empiricists argued that the mind was made up of ideas which were merely lasting copies of incoming sensations. These ideas were held together by associations, direct links, or connections formed between contiguously occurring sensations. Ebbinghaus adopted the notion that memory consists of stored associations between contiguously occurring events. Thus, he assigned no special *structure* or *organization* to memory; it simply contained *independent* associations between ideas or elements.

Given these assumptions, Ebbinghaus chose to investigate the retention or memory of associations. Thus Ebbinghaus's strategy was to associate two events by presenting them contiguously and, later, to test the retention of the association by presenting the first event and then ascertaining whether the subject could remember the second. For example, two words might be presented one after the other. After a *retention interval,* the first word would be presented again, and the subject's task would be to recall the second word.

The problem with this procedure was that items such as words differed in difficulty and were sometimes associated together in the subject's mind before the experiment started. Therefore it was difficult to know how to interpret the retention of any given association in the experiment. To solve this problem, Ebbinghaus developed a set of materials composed of three-letter, consonant-vowel-consonant, combinations such as ZUP, XEH, or RIF. Ebbinghaus presumed that these *nonsense syllables* were free of meaning and previous associations among themselves.

Rather than study the retention of associations between just one pair at a time, Ebbinghaus studied the retention of entire lists of nonsense syllables. For instance, in a list of ten syllables, adjacent syllables in the list would become associated, and therefore Ebbinghaus could study the retention of many associations at the same time.

This kind of learning is called *serial learning* and is still studied today, although the items are often words or numbers rather than nonsense syllables. Two general methods are often used. The first is called the *study-test* method (see fig. 12.1): here, the subject is exposed to the entire list, one item at a time, and is then asked to recall as many items as he can in the proper order. This procedure is repeated as many times as desired. In the *anticipation* method, the items are shown to the subject one at a time, and as the subject reads each item, he must try to anticipate the next item. The list is scored correct when the subject successfully anticipates all the items.

You will recall that the early behaviorists viewed learning as the formation of connections between a stimulus and a response. They argued that in serial learning, each item could be viewed as a response connected to the preceding item, which acted as a stimulus. Thus the learning of a serial list was viewed as the formation of a chain of S-R connections. To reveal the operation of S-R connections more clearly, however, the behaviorists developed a procedure called *paired-associate* learning, in which the subject is presented with a series of *pairs* of items. The first item of each pair was called the stimulus and the second item was termed the response. The subject's task was to learn to give the response item when the stimulus item was presented. Between trials, the order of the pairs was usually changed, but the items that were paired together remained the same. As in serial learning, either the study-test or anticipation method could be used (see fig. 12.1).

Ebbinghaus went on to study many aspects of memory using these techniques; for example, how the memory of a list is influenced by how well the list is learned, how memory varies with the passage of time, and how the

1. SERIAL LEARNING

A. *Study-test method:* Memorize this list of words in the correct order.

Study trial:	book	Test trial:	write down the words in the correct order.
	green		
	chair		
	radio		
	child		
	light		

B. *Anticipation method:* A list of words will be shown one at a time, always in the same order. As each word is presented, guess the next word and say it out loud before the next word is presented.

book → (guess) green → (guess) chair → (guess) radio → (guess) child → (guess) light

2. PAIRED-ASSOCIATE LEARNING

A. *Study-test method:* Remember the following pairs of words, so that when the left member of each pair is presented you can give the right member. First the pairs will be shown, and then there will be a test.

Study trial:	book-fence	Test trial:	book → ?
	green-phone		green → ?
	chair-sun		chair → ?
	radio-paper		radio → ?
	child-staple		child → ?
	light-eagle		light → ?

B. *Anticipation method:* After each stimulus is presented, guess the response, and then the correct response will be shown.

book → ?
book fence
green → ?
green phone
chair → ?
chair sun
radio → ?
radio paper
child → ?
child staple
light → ?
light eagle

Figure 12.1 Schematic representation of serial and paired associates learning. (Adapted from Bourne and Ekstrand. *Psychology: Its Meanings and Principles*, p. 109. Copyright 1973 Dryden Press. Reprinted by permission.)

amount of material to be remembered influences memory. Experimental psychologists of the early 1900s who were interested in memory elaborated on Ebbinghaus's work. The conception that memory was a passive repository for independent associations was not changed but merely extended. (This does not mean that everyone agreed with this view of memory, only that this view was dominant. For instance, Bartlett, 1932, and Kohler, 1938, dissented from this view.)

Interference Theory

One of Ebbinghaus's most striking findings was that forgetting, the loss of memory, occurred extremely rapidly and in massive amounts. Ebbinghaus measured forgetting by a *savings* method. The subject (in most cases, Ebbinghaus himself) learned a list to some criterion of performance, such as one perfect repetition. After a retention interval, the subject was asked to relearn the same list to the same criterion of performance. If relearning the list took as many trials or repetitions as did original learning, there was obviously complete forgetting. If the subject was able to recite the list correctly during the first relearning trial, then no forgetting had occurred. The measure of savings was the percentage of original trials that were saved when the subject relearned the list. Thus if a list took ten trials to learn and only five trials to relearn, the saving was five trials, or fifty percent. The dramatic results of these experiments are shown in figure 12.2. Ebbinghaus found that after one hour, the savings were only forty-four percent; after one day, only thirty-four percent. In other words, forgetting occurred extremely quickly and large amounts of learned material were forgotten in these brief intervals.

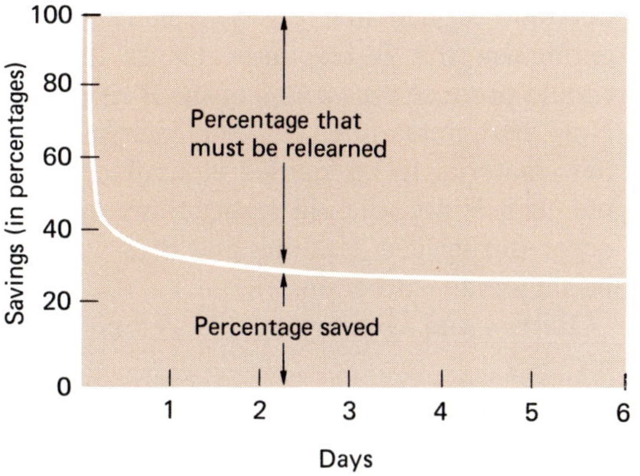

Figure 12.2 Ebbinghaus' curve of forgetting. The curve shows the percentage of savings as a function of the retention interval. (Adapted from Dember, W. M., and Jenkins, J. J. *General Psychology,* Copyright 1970 by the American Psychological Association. Reprinted by permission of the American Psychological Association and Prentice-Hall, Inc. Englewood Cliffs, N.J.)

Retroactive Interference

There was nothing in the ideas of the British empiricists to explain why forgetting occurs, let alone why it should be so great. An answer was provided by McGeoch (1942). McGeoch pointed out that in Ebbinghaus's experiments, the subject (again usually Ebbinghaus himself) would learn a list, and during the retention interval, he would learn other lists. Then at the appropriate time, he would try to recall the initial list. McGeoch argued that the initial list may have been forgotten because learning of the later lists *interfered* with the retention of the original list. That is, forgetting might be caused by the interference created by the new learning that occurred during the interval between the learning of the material to be remembered and the recall test.

Consider a list of paired stimulus and response items, or paired associates. These pairs might be nonsense syllable-word pairs such as ZUP-clean, RIF-house, and XEH-dog. The subject's task is to learn to say "clean" when ZUP is presented, "house" when RIF is presented, and so on. Let's call this list an A-B list; A stands for all the stimuli, and B stands for all the responses. Now assume that the subject must learn a second list after learning the A-B list and assume that the stimuli in the second list are identical with those in the original list but the responses are different. For example, ZUP is now paired with book; RIF, with dark; XEH, with train; and so on. Because the stimuli on this second list are the same as those on the first, but the responses differ, the second list is called an A-C list.

According to McGeoch, learning the A-C list after the A-B list should interfere with the subject's ability to recall the B responses to the A stimuli; that is, the *interpolated list* should *retroactively interfere* with the retention of the *original list* because now two responses, B and C, are connected to A. Therefore, when A is presented, and the subject is asked to recall B, both B and C should occur and compete with each other. Thus McGeoch ascribed *retroactive interference* (RI)—the interfering effects of new learning on the retention of old learning—to *response competition*. In other words, forgetting was ascribed to RI, and RI was attributed to response competition. Note that for response competition to occur, the stimuli used in the two lists had to be the same or similar. If they were not, competition would not occur.

RI does indeed exist. The demonstration of RI requires a design that compares the retention of a list by groups of subjects who do, and do not receive interpolated learning (see fig. 12.3). Many experiments of this kind have been performed, and interpolated learning does indeed reduce the retention of previously learned items.

However, Melton and Irwin (1940) raised some questions concerning the mechanism of response competition. In their experiment an RI design was used. Here too, the subjects learned list 1 (A-B) and then list 2 (A-C). But the degree to which list 2 was learned was varied by giving different groups of subjects different numbers of trials with list 2. As expected, Melton and Irwin found that the amount of RI (as measured by decreases in B responses) increased as a function of how thoroughly list 2 had been learned. In other words, as C became stronger and stronger, B was pushed out of memory more and more.

However, if RI increased because of increased response competition between B and C, then the increase in forgetting of B should have been related to the fact that the subject gave the C response instead of the B response. That is, the subject was asked to give B. Forgetting and RI mean that the subject made errors and did not give B. If the amount of RI was related to the amount of response competition, there should have been a rise in the number of errors because the subject said C instead of B. This was *not* the case. Errors in the recall of B did increase as a function of the thoroughness of A-C learning, but C responses to the stimuli during the recall test for B did *not* increase. Therefore, RI cannot be completely attributable to response competition. But what is the additional factor?

In 1948 Underwood provided an answer to this question. During the learning of list 2, the list 1 responses are extinguished. That is, the subject has learned A-B, he is again given A, but now B is incorrect and C is correct. Underwood argued that this procedure should extinguish the B responses to A; that is, should produce *unlearning* of the B response. Note that unlearning can only occur if the new material to be learned is similar to the old. If it is not, the old associations will not occur during new learning and thus will not be subject to extinction.

Barnes and Underwood (1959) provided

RETROACTIVE INTERFERENCE DESIGN

	I	II	III
Experimental Group	Learn List 1	Learn List 2	Test List 1
Control Group	Learn List 1	No learning	Test List 1

PROACTIVE INTERFERENCE DESIGN

	I	II	III
Experimental Group	Learn List 1	Learn List 2	Test List 2
Control Group	No learning	Learn List 2	Test List 2

Figure 12.3 Retroactive interference and proactive interference designs. The experimental group's poorer performance on the test indicates interference.

strong support for this position in the following experiment. Subjects were asked to learn the usual A-B and A-C lists and the number of trials with the A-C list was varied. The only novel aspect of this experiment was the type of retention test used. Again, the subjects were presented with A, but instead of being asked for one reaction to A, they were asked to give *both* the B and the C responses and were allowed as much time as they needed. Here, forgetting of B could not be caused by response competition because the subjects were allowed to give both responses. Thus if a subject could not give B, B must have been *unavailable,* which to Barnes and Underwood meant *unlearned.* As you can see in figure 12.4, the greater the number of list 2 trials, the more available C was and the less available B was.

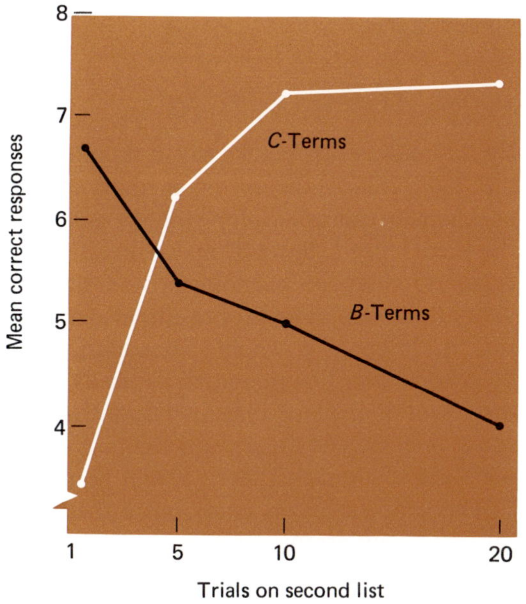

Figure 12.4 Results of the Barnes and Underwood's (1959) study. With increased training on the A–C list, C became more available and B became less available. (From Barnes, J. M. and Underwood, B. J., " 'Fate' of first-line associations in transfer theory," pp. 97–105, *Journal of Experimental Psychology* 58, 1959. Copyright 1959 by the American Psychological Association. Reprinted by permission.)

Thus by the early 1960s, the explanation of forgetting had progressed to the following point. Forgetting was attributed to RI, the interference produced by new learning. Forgetting increased over time because there was more new learning. RI was produced through two mechanisms: (1) response competition and (2) unlearning, or extinction of old material produced by new learning.

Proactive Interference

Problems with the notion that forgetting could be explained entirely by RI soon emerged. The basic problem was that too much forgetting occurred in the absence of an explicit interfering task. For example, in experiments in which subjects learned a series of lists containing paired-associate nonsense syllables, it was found that if subjects were tested immediately after learning the lists, their retention was quite high. But after a few days, forgetting was massive, often around seventy-five percent. In the few days between learning the lists and the recall test, no interpolated lists that produced RI had been given, so why did forgetting occur? If the subjects learned many things during the retention interval, RI would occur. However, if both mechanisms of RI—response competition and unlearning—require that the interpolated learning materials be similar to the original learning materials, what could the subjects have experienced during the retention interval that was so similar to nonsense syllables? Nothing!

In 1957 Underwood solved this problem by demonstrating that forgetting was great in these experiments because the subjects learned a number of lists before going away for the retention interval. They remembered the first few lists in the series rather well; it was only when the lists were averaged together that the amount of forgetting was as high as seventy-five percent. In other words, learning of the first lists interfered with retention of the later lists, a *proactive interference,* or PI (see fig. 12.3). Note that PI is similar to RI in that two lists are learned. However, in PI the focus of interest is the effect of learning list 1 on retention of list 2, whereas in RI, the focus is on the effects of learning list 2 on the retention of list 1.

Underwood had already proposed a mechanism that could account for such a PI effect: if a subject is given an A-B list followed by an A-C list, the A-B association should be extinguished. What phenomena are associated with extinction? In Chapter 11, we found that extinguished responses *recover spontaneously;* that is, they regain strength with the passage of time. Thus if the subject is tested for recall of the *second* list immediately after learning lists 1 and 2, his list 1 responses will be weak and should not compete with his list 2 responses. Underwood argued that if a time interval was allowed to pass before testing for retention of list 2, the list 1 responses would recover spontaneously and thus would compete with the list 2 responses, thereby producing a retention decrement.

In addition, Underwood demonstrated that if PI was eliminated by having the subject learn only one list of nonsense syllables or words, after a few days forgetting was only about twenty-five percent instead of seventy-five percent. This twenty-five percent was ascribed to RI and to sources of interference that were unrelated to the experiment. The extraexperimental sources of interference can be illustrated as follows: The learning of the nonsense syllable list requires the extinction of associations that accumulate during the normal course of the individual's life. For example, if the word "horse" was an item on a list, the association "horse-back" must be extinguished before the list can be learned. However, the association spontaneously recovers and causes PI. In the case of a nonsense syllable such as QAP, the normal association between Q and U would have to be extinguished.

By the early 1960s, interference theory was able to account for many aspects of memory and forgetting. Memory was viewed as the retention of associations, and forgetting was viewed as a result of RI and PI. We forget things because new learning competes with and causes unlearning of the old responses and because responses extinguished during the learning of new material recover over time and therefore compete. At this point, interference theory was powerful indeed, and it ruled the study of memory. Some psychologists, of course, disagreed with interference theory and with the entire associationistic tradition, but they were a small minority in the United States.

Decline of Interference Theory

By the mid-1960s, cracks began to appear in the interference theory of memory. First, problems began to develop with the details of the theory itself. Second, many investigators began to discover phenomena and develop views that were at odds with the associationistic tradition as a whole. Abandonment of the associationistic orientation naturally led to the abandonment of interference theory because interference theory was the best developed associationistic theory at that time.

The problems with interference theory itself revolved around the mechanisms proposed to account for RI and PI. RI and PI were reliable phenomena in experiments involving rote memory—in other words, interpolated learning did interfere with the retention of previous learning and previous learning did interfere with the retention of new learning. However, these phenomena could *not* be explained by unlearning and spontaneous recovery. Associations established outside the laboratory did not seem to extinguish during new learning. Therefore, it was unclear how PI could handle ordinary forgetting outside the laboratory. In addition, even those associations that were established in the laboratory, and extinguished during new learning, did not seem to recover spontaneously, as the theory maintained.

Although the interference theory has since been modified in an attempt to explain these facts (Postman and Stark, 1969), these modifications have not been entirely successful, and there has been a move away from interference theory. Interference is still recognized as an important source of forgetting, but the mechanisms proposed by interference theory are no longer widely accepted.

As we mentioned previously, disenchantment with interference theory also arose because of a general move away from the associationistic point of view laid down by the British empiricists. This move arose from several sources. First, a variety of investigators began to discover phenomena that were difficult to put into a simple associationistic framework. One of these phenomena was the importance of *organizational* and *reconstructive* processes in memory. The other factor was the discovery that there was more than one memory system. Finally, a number of investigators began to develop a new approach to problems of memory called an *information processing* approach.

Information Processing

The development of sophisticated electronic computers has had a tremendous impact on how psychological processes, especially memory are viewed. Computers accept information, code and transform the information in various ways, send the information through a series of stages, store information, retrieve information, and so on. In short, computers are able to engage in operations that are more complex than the simple association of events. Therefore, why can't human beings do the same?

Some psychologists began to think of the human mind as a computer and of memory as a system that processes information through a series of stages. This view led them to ask questions such as the following: What information is taken in from the environment? Through what stages does this information pass? How is the information represented in the different stages? What transformations occur at the junctions between different stages?

Information processing, as it applies to perception, has been discussed in Chapters 6 and 7. In this chapter, the information processing approach will be applied to the study of memory. Three stages of memory have been isolated; *sensory memory, short-term memory,* and *long-term memory.* Although other systems, such as intermediate memory have been postulated, the first three are generally agreed on, and they form the basis for many theoretical systems (e.g., Atkinson and Shiffrin, 1968).

Sensory Memory

Because sensory memory has already been discussed in the context of perception (see Chapter 6), only a brief review is required here. Visual information that is taken in by the organism is registered in a brief sensory memory called the *iconic store.* Three characteristics of iconic memory should be noted here. First, iconic memory is extremely brief, fading in less than a second. Second, the information in iconic memory is represented visually. We know this because a subsequent visual stimulus is able to interfere with the information stored in iconic memory. A flash of light, for example, is able to "erase" the information in iconic memory as soon as the flash is presented. And third, the capacity of iconic memory to store information is large.

Many items can be briefly held in iconic memory. In addition, we should point out that an analogous sensory memory called *echoic memory* apparently exists for auditory input.

Short-Term Memory

We just said that the information stored in iconic memory fades in less than a second. Information in iconic memory that is attended to is passed along to short-term memory (STM). Information that is not attended to disappears. Before discussing STM, however, we must confront the question of whether STM exists as a separate system from long-term memory (LTM). Indeed, until about ten years ago, most theorists believed that existing evidence did not justify the supposition of two different systems.

Are There Two Systems?

Intuitively, it has always seemed as if there were qualitatively different sorts of memories. Many years ago, William James distinguished between two kinds of memory: primary memory and secondary memory. His distinction was similar to the modern distinction between STM and LTM. James defined primary memory as the memory of events that have never left consciousness and described secondary memory as the memory of events that have not been in consciousness for some time and are stored permanently. If you look up a phone number and keep it in mind briefly until you have dialed, you will probably forget it quickly—this is James' primary memory and present-day STM. If you recall your own telephone number, you are using James's secondary memory and present-day LTM.

Although it is intuitively reasonable to assume that remembering a new phone number briefly and recalling your own phone number are qualitatively different activities, this assumption is not sufficient grounds for postulating the existence of two different memory systems. In the following paragraphs, we will describe some neurological and psychological evidence for the existence of a dual memory system.

A fascinating series of investigations has been conducted on neurological patients who have suffered damage to an area of the brain called the *hippocampus*. Milner, for instance, discovered a striking memory deficit in these patients. In the following excerpt she describes a man whose hippocampus was unavoidably damaged during surgery to stop his epileptic seizures.

> As far as we can tell, this man has retained little, if anything, subsequent to [the] operation, although his I-Q rating is actually slightly higher than before. Ten months before I examined him, his family had moved from their old house to one a few blocks away on the same street. He still has not learned the new address, though remembering the old one perfectly, nor can he be trusted to find his way home alone. He does not know where objects constantly in use are kept; for example, his mother still has to tell him where to find the lawn-mower, even though he may have . . . [used it] the day before. She also states that he will do the same jigsaw puzzles day after day without showing any practice effect, and that he will read the same magazines over and over again without finding their contents familiar (1959).

What is striking about this patient and other patients with similar damage is that they can remember events that happened before hippocampal damage occurred, and they can remember events that occurred after the operation for a brief period of time. However, they seem unable to remember new events for a *long* period of time. The patient Milner described could remember his old address, and he could remember new things briefly. We know that he could remember new things briefly because he could read a magazine. (If you were unable to remember the first sentence when you get to the second, it would be impossible for you to derive any meaning from what you are reading. However, he could not remember what he read from one day to the next, where the lawnmower was kept, and so forth.)

If there were only one kind of memory, this set of symptoms would be extremely difficult to explain. However, these symptoms fit in quite well with the notion that there are separate STM and LTM systems. If we assume that the hippocampus is involved in transferring information from STM to LTM, the patient's symptoms make sense. Retrieval from LTM is still intact, so the patient remembers events before the damage. STM is still intact, so he remembers new material briefly. However, because this material cannot get from STM to LTM for permanent storage, it is not retained for a long period of time.

Before considering the next line of evidence, we should mention several characteristics that have been proposed for STM. Theorists now believe that unless the information stored in STM is *rehearsed,* it *decays* fairly rapidly. In this sense, rehearsal is a process of keeping one's attention on the item. In addition, our rehearsal capacity is *limited;* thus we can rehearse only four or five items at any one time. Moreover, theorists believe that rehearsal is the process that is responsible for transferring information from STM to LTM. These factors will be considered in more detail later.

Suppose a list of twenty words is read to a subject, one at a time, and he is immediately asked to recall as many as possible in any order he chooses. Now suppose that the probability that he will recall a word is plotted against the word's position in the list—first position, second position, and so forth, up to the twentieth position. This curve is called a *serial position curve,* and a typical result is shown in figure 12.5. The first and last few words in the list are remembered best; the words in the middle of the list are recalled

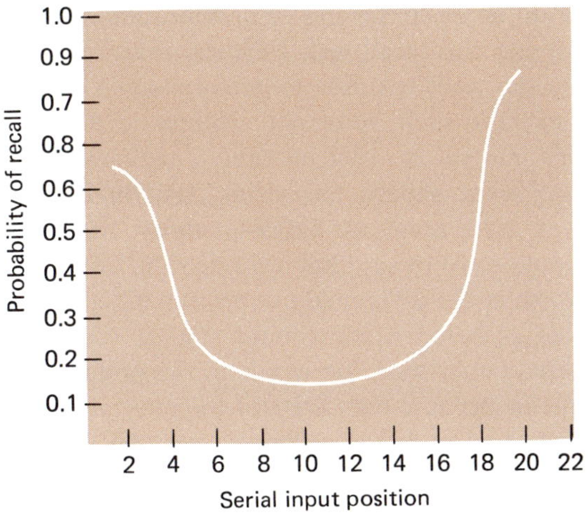

Figure 12.5 A typical serial position curve. The curve shows the probability that a word will be recalled as a function of its position in the list. Words at the beginning and end of the list are recalled best, while words in the middle are recalled least often. (From Gazzaniga, Michael, *Fundamentals of Psychology: An Introduction,* p. 415. Copyright 1973 Academic Press, Inc. Reprinted by permission.)

most poorly. This is called the *serial position effect.*

For the moment, let's consider why the subject recalls the last few words so well. A theorist who believes that there is only one memory system would argue that the most recently presented items are naturally remembered best. However, a proponent of a two-system memory would argue that words which are still in STM at the time of recall should be recalled very well; whereas words that are not in STM should be recalled less well because they may not have been stored in LTM when they left STM. Since words at the end of the list are most recent, they have the highest probability of still being in STM at the time of the recall test, and thus should be remembered best.

A number of experiments have been performed to test the validity of these views. Suppose that a delay of thirty seconds is interposed between the end of presentation of the list and the recall test. Further, assume that the subject is required to perform some complex task such as mental arithmetic during this interval, so that he cannot rehearse the list. What should the serial position curve look like now? A single-memory theorist would have to say that although the last few words in the list should not be remembered as well as before, they should still be remembered better than the words in the middle of the list because they are still the most recent. The dual-memory theorists, on the other hand, would argue that the mental activity during the interval should prevent the subject from rehearsing the last few items. Therefore, at the time of the recall test, no items from the list should remain in STM. As a result, all items would have to be recalled from LTM, and thus recall of the last few items should no longer be superior. The results of an experiment of this kind (Glanzer and Cunitz, 1966) are shown in figure 12.6, and they clearly support the two-system theory.

When we talk about two different memory systems, or memory stores, we are not implying that items are stored in two different places. Psychologists often talk in terms of separate "bins" for long-term and short-term memories, but this may be misleading. A subject who learns a list of words (or nonsense syllables) does not learn these words from scratch. They are already represented in his memory, and all he has to do is tag the words that are already in memory to indicate that they are on the list. One might conceive of two different ways to tag a word or item in memory, one temporary (STM), and the other permanent (LTM). One requires continued rehearsal to prevent loss, the other does not.

Acoustic Encoding

STM receives input from sensory memory. We know that information in iconic memory is visual. If information is transferred from iconic memory to STM, does it maintain its visual representation, or is it transformed? We also know that the *meaning* or *semantic properties* of items are represented in LTM. Is this also true of STM? Current knowledge seems to indicate that the *acoustic* or *auditory* prop-

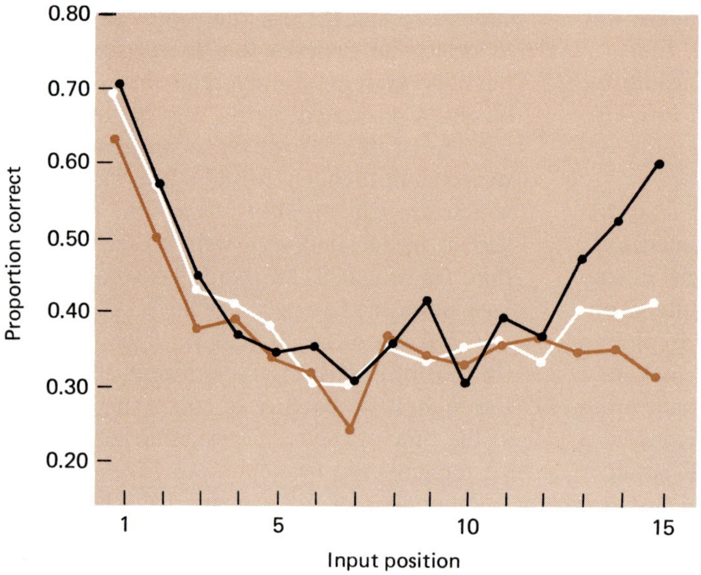

Figure 12.6 Results of the Glanzer and Cunitz (1966) study. The last words in the list were not recalled better than the words in the middle of the list, when a delay of 30 seconds was interposed between the end of the list and the recall test. (From Glanzer, M. and Cunitz, A. R., "Two storage mechanisms in free recall," *Journal of Verbal Learning and Verbal Behavior* 5, 1966, pp. 351–370. Reprinted by permission of Academic Press, Inc.)

erties of events are stored in STM. That is, the information coming in from iconic memory is transformed from a visual to an auditory mode. The following is a sample of the evidence that leads to this view. Perhaps the first hint at such a conclusion came from an experiment by Conrad and Hull (1964), who showed that STM was better for acoustically distinct (different sounding) lists of letters than for lists of acoustically similar (similar sounding) letters. This result occurred even though the letters were presented visually. For example, STM for E R T W Q M X was better than for C D E G P U V.

Even more convincing evidence for acoustic encoding in STM was provided by Conrad (1964). He began by measuring which letters sounded alike. Subjects were given auditory presentations of letters through headphones. The letters were presented at a low volume, and because auditory noise was present, the letters were barely distinguishable. The subjects' task was to say what letter they had heard. Because the letters were barely audible, the subjects made many errors, and the errors indicated which letters sounded alike. For example, if the letter was E, the subject would often say C, but never R.

Next, the subjects were visually presented with a list of letters for a STM test. The question was: If the subject made an error in memory recall, would the error be a letter that sounded like the letter on the memory list? If this was the case, then the letters on the list had to be represented, or encoded acoustically. Otherwise why would the error be another letter that sounded like the to-be-remembered letter? Because Conrad had discovered earlier which letters sounded like which other letters, it was easy to tell whether the errors of memory involved letters that sounded similar to the letters to be remembered. This was indeed the case. The correlation between the errors in auditory perception and memory was extremely high.

One final point, you will recall that we said RI is produced in LTM by the learning of new items similar to the old. However, we did not mention that maximal RI in LTM is produced by the learning of new material which has a similar *meaning* to the old material. In STM, on the other hand, maximal RI is produced by material that sounds similar (Wickelgren, 1965).

Thus it seems that material is acoustically represented in STM. This does not mean that STM can utilize *only* an acoustic encoding. Although subjects prefer the acoustic mode, they may be able to use others. We mentioned that material can be held in STM by rehearsing it; thus it may simply be easier to rehearse in the acoustic mode. It is much easier to "say" a letter to oneself over and over again than it is to visualize the letter repeatedly.

Chunking

We mentioned that sensory memory has a large capacity: it can store many items, although only briefly. However, at several points, we have alluded to the fact that STM has a limited capacity. But exactly how limited is the capacity of STM, and what is the unit in which this capacity can be measured?

Because we have been talking about information processing, the most obvious possibility is that the capacity of STM can be measured in terms of the unit of information specified by information theory (see page 359). Recall that the information provided by an item is measured in terms of uncertainty. In a situation where many alternative outcomes are possible and equally likely, uncertainty is great, and a message about the actual outcome provides much information. But if there are only a few alternatives, uncertainty is low, and thus a message about the actual outcome provides little information.

The transmission of information is measured in terms of *bits*. A bit is the amount of information contained in a message that gives the actual outcome, when there are only two equally likely alternatives. If four alternatives are equally likely, the message contains two bits, and so on.

Suppose we do a STM experiment and see how many binary digits a subject can remember after he is presented with a string of these digits. That is, suppose we investigate the size of the *memory span* for binary digits. We will find that the subject can remember about seven of them. Now, a binary digit can be either a zero or a one, and so each conveys one bit; that is, there are only two alternatives. Because the subject can remember seven of them, the total information retained by the subjects is seven bits. So, it seems that the capacity of STM is seven bits. A decimal digit contains 3.3 bits because there are ten alternatives that it could be, 0–9. If STM capacity is limited to seven bits, a subject should only be able to recall about two decimal digits after one exposure to a series of decimal digits. But the results of this experiment will reveal that the subject can recall about seven decimal digits. Each letter of the alphabet contains about 4.7 bits, but the memory span for letters is also about seven letters. The memory span for words is almost seven words! This situation is depicted in figure 12.7.

Thus it seems that the capacity of STM is not limited or fixed with regard to bits. STM seems to be able to hold almost any number of bits. However, it seems to be limited with regard to how many "things" it can hold. STM can hold seven things, and it does not seem to matter much what those things are. Miller has coined the term "chunk" to stand for what STM can hold. A chunk seems to be a meaningful unit, or integrated whole. A word contains a number of letters, but because the set of letters forms a meaningful whole, the memory system treats the sequence of letters as one unit.

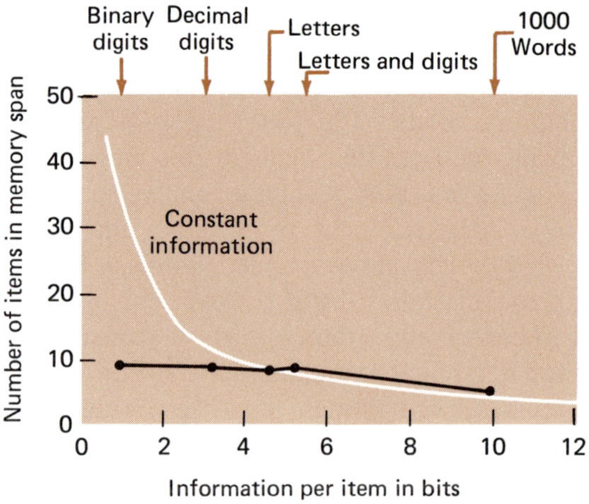

Figure 12.7 Number of items that can be kept in the memory span, for different kinds of items. The solid line shows the actual size of the memory span for the different items, and it is reasonably constant at seven items. The dotted line shows what the memory span should be for the different items, if memory span is limited by the number of bits. (From Miller, G. A., "The magical number seven, plus or minus two: Some limits on our capacity for processing information," *Psychological Review* 63, 1956, pp. 81–97. Copyright 1956 by the American Psychological Association. Reprinted by permission.)

Chunking seems to be partly determined by the subject's perceptual coding mechanisms. Stimuli can be arranged to facilitate particular chunking patterns, which in turn can strongly influence memory. For example, Muller and Schumann (1894) found that if a series of nonsense syllables is read in a rhythmic pattern, the subject will chunk and remember the syllables in keeping with the rhythm.

Chunking should not only be determined by the properties of perceptual mechanisms, it should also be possible to learn how to organize material together into a chunk. This should allow an increase in the amount of material that can be held in STM. In an experiment performed by Smith (cited by

Miller, 1956), subjects were taught to recode strings of binary digits into larger chunks. Suppose a subject is told to call the binary digit pair 00 a 1, the pair 01 a 2, the pair 10 a 3, and the pair 11 a 4. Most individuals recall about seven binary digits after one presentation. But if a subject recodes the binary digits into the above decimal digit code, he should be able to remember seven of the decimal digits and thus fourteen of the binary digits. For example, if a subject were given the string 0 1 0 0 1 1 0 1 0 1 1 0 1 0, he could recode it as 2 1 4 2 2 3 3, keep the recoded message in STM, and decode back to the binary digits at the time of recall. Well-practiced subjects are indeed capable of using schemes such as these.

However, these recoding schemes make the capacity of STM an elusive quantity. The recoding scheme is stored in LTM and combines with information in STM to produce recall performance. Thus it is sometimes difficult to know whether to ascribe recall performance entirely to STM, and interactions like this can be difficult to unravel. STM can hold seven organized entities, but what an organized entity is cannot yet be specified.

How long does STM last?

It has already been stated that information can be kept in STM for an indefinite period of time by rehearsal. As long as an item is rehearsed, it will stay in STM and will not be forgotten. It has also been implied that unrehearsed items are forgotten from STM fairly rapidly. How rapidly?

This question was answered by Peterson and Peterson (1959), who presented a single three-consonant nonsense syllable (e.g., QRT) for two seconds and then asked for recall of the syllable some time later. Because the object was to see how long it would take the subject to forget the syllable, the retention interval was varied from zero to thirty-two seconds from trial to trial.

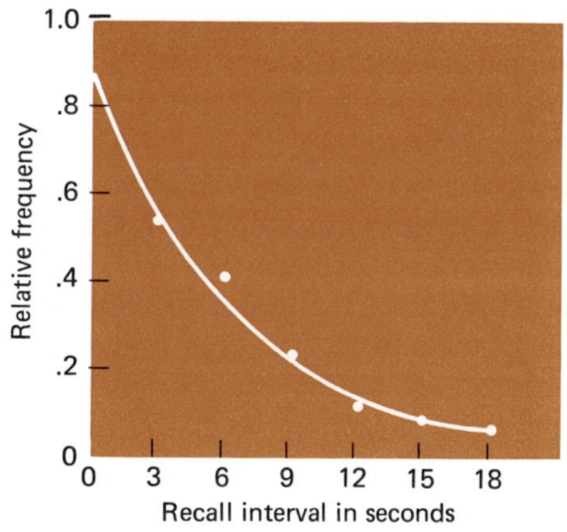

Figure 12.8 Results of a study by Petersen and Petersen (1959). The curve shows the probability of recalling a single trigram, as a function of the retention interval. (Adapted from Petersen, L. R. and Petersen, M. J., "Short-term retention of individual items," *Journal of Experimental Psychology* 58, 1959, pp. 193–198, Fig. 3, p. 195. Copyright 1959 by the American Psychological Association. Reprinted by permission.)

The interesting question was how rapidly forgetting occurs when the item is not rehearsed. Thus it was necessary to prevent rehearsal of the syllable during the retention interval. To accomplish this, Peterson and Peterson required the subjects to count backwards by three during the retention interval. Immediately after the nonsense syllable was presented, a number appeared and the subject was required to count backwards by three from this number at a rapid rate until the experimenters asked him to recall the syllable. The presumption was that people cannot count backwards by three and rehearse nonsense syllables at the same time.

The results of this experiment can be seen in figure 12.8. Recall of the syllable was quite high when no time was allowed to elapse, but forgetting was almost complete after eighteen seconds! After eighteen seconds, the likelihood of recalling the single syllable was less than ten percent. The fact that the likelihood of recall did not go much below ten percent can probably be explained as a combination of two factors: (1) the subject occasionally made a correct guess and (2) there was a small amount of transfer to LTM. This should illustrate the power of rehearsal. Although the subject had only one syllable to remember, he forgot it almost completely in eighteen seconds if he was unable to rehearse.

Why Is Information Forgotten?

The loss of information from STM has been explained in two ways. The first notion is simple *decay*—nonrehearsed material fades away of its own accord, much like an echo that grows dimmer and dimmer. The second notion is that material in STM does not simply decay but is *interfered* with by new incoming items. If STM has a limited capacity, then for new information to get in, an old piece of information must be pushed out. In other words, new items interfere with old items. The interference hypothesis can explain the Petersons' results by simply assuming that counting backwards requires the use of the STM system and thus pushes out the syllable to be remembered. After all, to count backwards by three, the subject must remember the preceding number.

An experiment performed by Reitman (1971) tested between these two ideas about forgetting in STM. She reasoned that if a subject was given a nonsense syllable to remember, as in the Petersons' design, and was then given a task that prevented rehearsal but did *not* require the use of STM, then the two hypotheses would make different predictions. The decay notion would still predict rapid forgetting—that is, if the task prevented rehearsal, then the item would decay. The interference theory, however, would make a different prediction. If the task that prevented rehearsal did not require the use of STM, then no new information would enter STM, and the syllable would not be pushed out. Thus the syllable should not be forgotten.

The task that Reitman used to prevent rehearsal was a signal detection task. The subject was given a nonsense syllable, and during the retention interval, from zero to five tones were presented. The tones were played at a volume so low that they could only be heard about half the time. The subject's only task was to press a button every time he heard a tone. However, because the tones were so low in volume, the subject had to concentrate deeply to hear the tones and thus could not rehearse the nonsense syllable. Simply listening for a tone and pressing a button does not require the subject to remember anything, so new information should not have entered into STM.

The results of Reitman's experiment were quite clear. Whereas Peterson and Peterson found that forgetting was almost complete after eighteen seconds, Reitman found that recall was ninety-eight percent accurate after fifteen seconds. When the task that prevented rehearsal did not require the entry of new information into STM, *no* forgetting occurred.

Thus items evidently do not decay from STM of their own accord but are interfered with—that is, pushed out—by new items.

To determine the kinds of activities that interfered with STM, Posner and Rossman (1965) tested a variety of activities for their ability to interfere with the retention of previous information in STM. They concluded that the more difficult the interpolated activity, the more it interfered with recall. One possible explanation for this phenomenon was that difficult activities require the entry of more information into STM, and thus they have a greater tendency to displace items in STM. Another important factor is the element of surprise, as described in box 12.1.

In summary, forgetting in STM is produced by interference; that is, new items bump old

Box 12.1

Unexpected Items Produce Interference

To find a more precise answer to what produces interference, Waugh and Norman (1968) constructed strings of items according to a variety of rules. The subjects listened to a string of items, and then were presented one item as a test. Their task was to say which item in the list came right after the test item. With this procedure, Waugh and Norman were able to pose many different questions. For example, is interference with an item determined by the sheer number of succeeding items or by the number of new succeeding items? Subjects could be given the two strings of numbers shown in box figure 12.1. On the test, the subject is given the number 8, and in both cases the correct response is 6. If interference is controlled by the sheer number of intervening items, the subjects should have been equally good at recalling 6 for both strings because the same number (four) of items intervened between exposure to 8, followed by 6 and the test in both strings. However, if the number of new items was crucial, the subject should have done better with the second string because it contained only two new items (5 and 3); whereas the first string contained four new items (5, 4, 3, and 7). It was found that the number of new items was crucial.

Waugh and Norman went on to test many different possibilities with this procedure. Their conclusion was that only *unexpected* items produced interference. New items seemed to displace old items from STM only if they were *not* redundant. A redundant item is one that the subject expects to occur at a given place in a series. For instance, 5 is expected after 1, 2, 3, 4, and it will not produce interference with the preceding items. Regularly occurring, predictable items produced no interference. (Note the similarity between this effect and the work on animal conditioning discussed in Chapter 11.)

String 1:	8	6	5	4	3	7	Test:	8
String 2:	8	6	5	5	3	3	Test:	8

Box Figure 12.1 An example of two strings used by Waugh and Norman (1968). (From Waugh, N. C., and Norman, D. A., "The measurement of interference in primary memory," *Journal of Verbal Learning and Verbal Behavior* 7, 1968, pp. 617–626. Reprinted by permission from Academic Press, Inc.)

items out of STM because STM has a limited capacity. Furthermore, only unexpected items (see box 12.1) can perform this function. However, note that these interference effects are not like those proposed by the older interference theory. The old theory claimed that new items interfered because they were similar to old items—that is, they had similar stimuli. Thus the responses interfered with each other associatively. Here we are saying that similarity is unimportant, and the interference is not associative in character. In other words, anything that requires mental work and cannot be predicted easily, interfered in STM.

Although we have discussed forgetting several times in this chapter, we have not yet distinguished between two possible reasons for it, *storage failure* and *retrieval failure*. Failure to recall an item may occur because it has been lost from storage. Or failure to recall may occur if the item is still in memory, but for some reason it cannot be retrieved. For example, suppose you are searching for a book in a library. If the book cannot be found, the reason could be that it is no longer in the library. On the other hand, the book may still be there, but either it has been filed or looked for in the wrong place.

Failures of memory are often retrieval failures rather than storage failures. If a subject cannot recall an item, the failure to recall might be caused by either process. However, a *recognition* test can distinguish between the two possibilities. Recognition is the process of discriminating something one has seen or learned from that something one has not seen or learned. In a typical recognition procedure, a subject is given some items to remember and is then tested for memory of those items by looking at those items together with new "distractor" items. The subject's task is to say which items were those he was asked to remember.

In this situation, the subject is not required to produce the item to be remembered, as he must in a recall test; therefore, retrieval is thought to be assured. That is, any failure to recognize an item must be related to a failure of storage rather than retrieval. A recall test reveals a memory failure, a recognition test can be used to assess whether the memory loss was caused by a storage or a retrieval process.

What do we know about how information is retrieved from STM? Suppose there are seven items in STM, and we want to retrieve a specific item. How can we accomplish this? Do we go through each of the seven items in STM one at a time until we find the correct one? Or can we simply pull the desired item out? That is, can we look at all the items in STM at once, or is the system restricted to looking at one item at a time?

Sternberg (1966) provided some answers to these questions. In his experiment, a subject was shown a set of digits to remember, called a *memory set*. The number of digits ranged from 0 to 6, and differed from trial to trial. On some trials, the subject was given one digit to remember, on some trials two digits, and so on. Soon afterward, a *target digit* was shown to the subject. All he had to do was indicate whether the target digit had been a member of the memory set by pressing one button if his answer was yes (target is in the memory set) and another button if his answer was no (target not in the memory set). Of course, sometimes the target was a member of the memory set, and sometimes it was not. Sternberg simply measured the subject's *reaction time*—how long it took the subject to say yes or no.

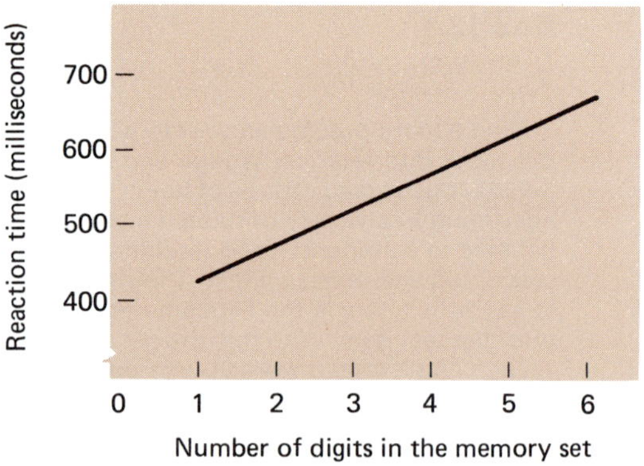

Figure 12.9 The time it takes the subject to decide whether a test digit is a member of the memory set, as a function of the size of the memory set. (From "High-Speed Scanning in Human Memory," Sternburg, S., *Science,* Vol. 153, pp. 652–654, Fig. 1, 5 August 1966. Copyright 1966 by the American Association for the Advancement of Science.)

The results of Sternberg's experiment are shown in figure 12.9. The figure plots how long it took the subject to say yes or no to the test digit, as a function of how many digits there were in the memory set during a particular trial. Remember that the number of digits in the memory set varied from trial to trial. It should be clear from the figure that for each item in the memory set, it took the subject a little longer to decide whether the target digit was in that set. The reaction time seemed to increase by thirty-eight milliseconds (38 thousandths of a second) for each item. That is, it took the subject thirty-eight milliseconds longer to decide whether the target was in the memory set for each item that was added to the memory set. (See fig. 12.10.)

If the subject can look at all the items in STM at once, it should not take him any longer to find an item in STM whether there are more or fewer items in STM. However, Sternberg's results indicate that it takes thirty-eight milliseconds longer for each item that is

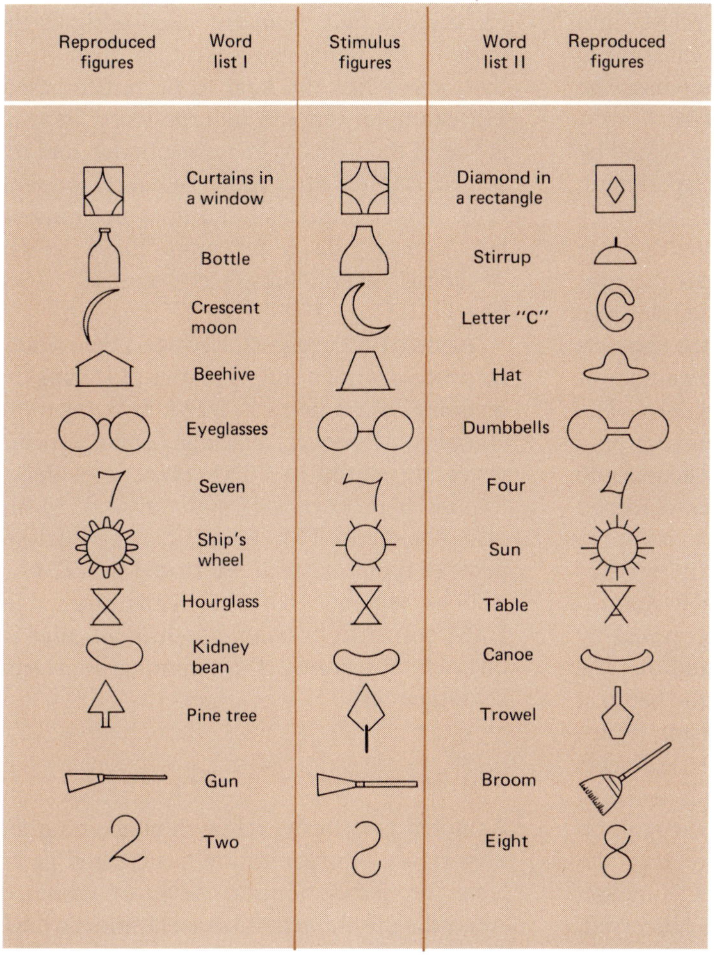

Reproduced figures
Word list I
Stimulus figures
Word list II
Reproduced figures
Curtains in a window
Diamond in a rectangle
Bottle
Stirrup
Crescent moon
Letter "C"
Beehive
Hat
Eyeglasses
Dumbbells
Seven
Four
Ship's wheel
Sun
Hourglass
Table
Kidney bean
Canoe
Pine tree
Trowel
Gun
Broom
Two
Eight

Figure 12.10 The stimulus materials and typical results of a study by Carmichael, Hogan, and Walter (1932). The subjects were shown the stimulus figures to remember and were given either Word List 1 or Word List 2 with the figures. When the subjects were later asked to reproduce the figures, their reproductions were frequently shifted toward the figure described by the verbal label. (Adapted from Carmichael, Hogan, and Walter, "An experimental study of the effect of language on the reproduction of visually perceived forms," *Journal of Experimental Psychology* 15, 1932, pp. 73–86. Copyright 1932 by the American Psychological Association. Reprinted by permission.)

added; thus rather than examining all items in STM at the same time, we must go through them one at a time. It seems to take thirty-eight milliseconds to go over each item.

This concludes our discussion of short-term memory. Although investigations of this process only began recently, progress has been rapid and should continue to be so.

Long-Term Memory

We will now return to long-term memory. First, we will examine recent developments in the study of LTM and then inquire into the implications of these findings for the general doctrine of association. Finally, we will briefly consider some recent attempts to handle these findings within an associationistic framework.

We have already seen that information passes from sensory memory to STM. From STM, information passes to LTM. However, not all of the information that passes through STM enters LTM, some is lost. If only some of the information that is in STM goes into LTM, some process must control what information enters and what information is lost.

Atkinson and Shiffrin (1968) have proposed a theory of memory which postulates that rehearsal is the process responsible for transferring information from STM into LTM. They argue that rehearsing an item not only keeps it in STM but also increases the likelihood that it will pass into LTM.

Support for this view has been provided by Rundus (1971). In Rundus's experiment, subjects were shown lists of words that they would later have to recall. The words were presented slowly, one at a time, and the subjects were told to rehearse out loud. Because the words were presented slowly, the subjects had ample time to rehearse a large number of items between successive presentations. The subject was not restricted to rehearsing only the last word presented; he could rehearse any words he desired. Because Rundus recorded this rehearsal on tape, he was able to compare how well a given word from the list was recalled as a function of how often it was rehearsed. In line with the model proposed by Atkinson and Shiffrin, Rundus found that the more a given item was rehearsed, the better it was recalled. In a similar experiment (Rundus, Loftus, and Atkinson, 1970), subjects were called back three weeks after learning the word list and were given a recognition memory test for the words. Here too, the memory for the words was a direct function of how frequently the words were rehearsed.

We know that when information is transferred from sensory memory to STM, it is encoded in STM in primarily acoustic form. What happens when information goes from STM to LTM? Does it remain acoustic, or is it again recoded? Theorists have frequently argued that the information which enters LTM is recoded to *semantic* form. That is, the *meaning* of the acoustic information in STM is extracted and stored in LTM.

The primary evidence for believing that LTM involves semantic encoding is similar in form to the evidence that favored the notion that STM involved acoustic encoding. When people make errors in LTM, the errors tend to be items that *mean* the same thing as the item to be remembered, rather than items that *sound* like the item to be remembered. For example, suppose that the word "house" is one of the items to be remembered, and the subject is tested after a long retention interval. If he makes a mistake and does not remember "house," he is far more likely to say "building" than "louse" or "mouse." (See box 12.2.)

As box 12.2 suggests, however, the semantic process is not a simple matter of storing the meaning of the items in STM. It is far more complex. Moreover, although semantic properties are stored in LTM, there is evidence that other properties of material in STM are also stored in LTM. Acoustic and visual aspects of input material are stored in LTM, as well as semantic features. Thus storage in LTM seems to be *multidimensional;* that is, a variety of features of the stimulus are stored simultaneously.

The Importance of Organization

As noted previously, research concerning the importance of organization has created problems for associationistic views of memory. According to the general associationistic position, the contents of memory consist of independent associations among items, and memory recall is simply a reexcitation of an existing association. Repeated presentations of the material to be remembered improve recall because the trace of each individual item is strengthened.

However, research on organizational factors in memory reveals that items in memory do not act as independent units which simply increase or decrease in strength. Instead, it seems that the *relationships* among items are important. The characteristics of a list as a whole, not the characteristics of individual items, seem to determine recall. Recall in-

Box 12.2

Semantic Encoding in LTM

An experiment by Bransford and Franks (1971) suggests that if the items in STM form a meaningful whole, the general idea of the *whole* is stored in LTM, not the meanings of the individual units. In their experiment, the materials to be remembered by the subject were groups of sentences on a related topic rather than lists of nonsense syllables or words. The group of sentences could be presented as a single sentence, with four elements expressing the whole idea. For example, the entire idea might be: "The rock that rolled down the mountain crushed the tiny hut at the edge of the woods." The four components would be the following: (1) the rock rolled down the mountain, (2) the rock crushed the hut, (3) the hut was tiny, and (4) the hut was at the edge of the woods.

The subjects were given a variety of sentences to remember. Some sentences contained three elements of the entire idea; others contained two or one element of the entire idea. However, the subjects were never given a sentence that contained the entire idea, that is, one that contained all four elements. An example of a three-element sentence would be "The rock rolled down the mountain and crushed the tiny hut." A two-element sentence would be "The tiny hut was at the edge of the woods." A one-element sentence would be "The hut was tiny." The four-element sentence that expresses the entire idea is given in the preceding paragraph.

After exposure to the sentences, the subjects were given a recognition memory test to see which sentences they remembered. An innovation in this experiment was that the subjects were not only required to say which sentences they had seen before, but also had to indicate how confident they were of their answer. The recognition test contained the three-, two-, and one-element sentences to which the subjects had been exposed. It also contained three-, two-, and one-element sentences to which the subjects had not been exposed. Finally, it contained the four-element sentence that expressed the entire idea of the component sentences, a sentence the subjects had not seen before.

The surprising result of the experiment was that the subjects believed they had been exposed to the four-element sentence. In fact, they were more confident about seeing this sentence than any of the sentences to which they had actually been exposed! In other words, they were more certain they had seen the sentence that expressed the entire idea than the sentences they had actually seen. This outcome suggests that while hearing the three-element, two-element, and one-element sentences, the subjects were abstracting the meaning of the whole idea and storing that meaning in memory.

volves a search and retrieval process, and whether this process will be efficient depends on how well the material has been organized in memory. The structure of material to be learned and the relationship of this material to what is already in memory partly determine how well the material can be stored. The importance of structure is difficult to deal with in associationistic terms, because the items are treated as independent units—sensations come in and associations are formed between contiguous ones.

Several lines of evidence point to the importance of organization in memory. First, lists of words that fall into categories are remembered better than lists of unrelated words. For example, a list of sixty words that is composed of fifteen animals, fifteen professions, fifteen items of furniture, and fifteen kinds of flowers will be recalled better than a list of sixty unrelated words of equal difficulty. Moreover, variations in how well categorized lists are recalled is related to how many categories are remembered, not how many items in a category are recalled. Cohen (1966) found that if one word from a category is recalled, subjects will recall a fairly constant percentage of the other words in the category. That is, subjects either forget to recall a category completely, or recall a fairly fixed number of words from a category.

Why is organization of the material to be remembered so beneficial? The answer seems to be that organization facilitates retrieval of information from LTM. Tulving and Pearlstone (1966) exposed subjects to categorized word lists that differed in length (12, 24, and 48 words), and in the number of words per category (1, 2, and 4). The items in each category were grouped together in the list, and each group of items was preceded by its category name (e.g., birds, cities, and the like). The subjects were told that they were to remember the words; they would not be tested on the categories and thus did not have to remember them.

The subjects were later separated into two groups. One group was asked to write as many words as they could remember on a blank piece of paper. The other group was also asked to write the words on a piece of paper, but the answer sheet had the category names printed on it. The group that was given the category names recalled many more words than did the group that was not given the category names. For example, in a list containing four categories of twelve words each, the subjects who were not given the category names recalled about twenty words, while the subjects who did receive the category names remembered about thirty words. This difference in recall was attributable to facilitation of the retrieval process by the category names. Because the groups were treated identically during the initial presentation of the words, each group of subjects must have stored an equivalent number of words. However, because the groups were treated differently on the recall test, the differences in recall must have been caused by more efficient retrieval by the group given the category names. Thus, the category names functioned as *retrieval cues*—cues that facilitated finding the groupings in memory.

After the first recall test, all subjects were given another recall test that included the category names. The subjects who had previously recalled twenty words were now able to recall about twenty-eight words. This result also points to the retrieval process as the source of the effect. The extra eight words that were recalled on the second test must have been in memory during the first test; otherwise, how could they have been recalled during the second test? In other words, the poor recall on the first test must have been produced by a failure of retrieval.

An additional finding of interest in the Tulving and Pearlstone experiment was that the subjects who received the retrieval cues recalled more words because they recalled words from more categories, not because they recalled more words per category. All subjects recalled about the same number of words per category. For example, the subjects with the 48-word list composed of 12 four-word categories recalled words from 11.5 categories when given the category names but only from 7.3 categories when not given the names. The mean number of words recalled per category, however, was 2.61 and 2.65, respectively. If at least one word from a category was recalled, a constant proportion of the remainder was recalled. Note that these results confirm Cohen's finding discussed earlier, and imply that the category name helps the subject find the group in memory.

The fact that organization seems to facilitate retrieval does not mean that organization and memory storage are unrelated. Retrieval cues such as category names can only facilitate recall if the material has been stored in an organized fashion. That is, if the items in a category are not stored together, retrieval of these items cannot be facilitated by providing the category names. Tulving and Osler (1968) presented different word lists to two groups of subjects. One list contained isolated words; in the other list, each word was paired with a retrieval cue that was a word weakly related to the word to be remembered. For example, the second list might consist of leg-MUTTON, girl-SHORT, soar-EAGLE, and so on. The words to be remembered were MUTTON, SHORT, and EAGLE. The subjects were told that they only had to remember the capitalized words. Half the subjects in each group were given the retrieval cues during the recall test and half were not. The retrieval cues facilitated recall only if they were present *both* at the time of storage (learning of the list) and at the time of recall. Thus retrieval cues aided recall only when they were relevant to the way in which the material was stored. Information about the retrieval cue had to be stored with the material to be remembered for retrieval cues to be effective.

This last point is illustrated by an additional feature of Tulving's and Osler's experiment. The subjects who were given the paired cues at the time of storage were helped more during recall by the paired cues than by words that were closely related to the word to be recalled. Recall of SHORT was facilitated more by the paired cue word girl, than by words such as small or tall. Thus, for a retrieval cue to be effective, it apparently must be stored with the target at the time of encoding.

Thus far, we have been discussing memory for lists that are organized or categorized by the experimenter. What does a subject do if the material to be learned is not organized by the experimenter? What, for example, does he do with a list of seemingly unrelated words? Mandler (1967) suggested that subjects develop organizations and groupings of their own and that these groupings form the basis for recall. Subjects seem to retrieve the groupings as a whole at the time of recall, so that they either recall all items from a grouping or none of the items. Repetition seems to serve the function of allowing subjects to add more and more items to the groupings rather than increase the strength of the individual items (see box 12.3).

Memory formation does not seem to be a simple process that involves the strengthening of the memory representation of individual items or associations. It seems to involve complex organizations that form the basis for the retrieval of items from memory. In other words, items do not operate independently, they are structured; and the structures themselves seem to be retrieved. Recall of individual items seems to depend on the structures retrieved and it is difficult to explain these structures on the basis of simple associations.

Reconstructive Processes

Earlier we mentioned evidence which indicated that the general idea contained in a set of sentences telling a story is stored, not the individual sentences presented. If something like a general idea is stored, how does a subject formulate a precise response on a memory test? If a subject is given a story to remember and is asked to recall it, he will give a statement made up of a precise set of words. But if only the general idea is stored, where does the exact response come from? An obvious answer is that the subject *reconstructs* the details from the general idea he remembers. That is, recall is more than the reappearance of a stored trace, it is an active construction.

This notion was first proposed by Bartlett (1932), who studied how people recall stories. His results indicated that people remember the general outline of a story rather than specific words or details, and they generate the details from the remembered outline when recall is required. Thus memory is not

Box 12.3

Subjective Groupings

The power of subjective groupings was beautifully illustrated by Tulving (1966). In this experiment, subjects were first taught a list of nine words. Then all the subjects received a list of eighteen words to learn and remember. For half the subjects, all eighteen words were new; for the other half, the list was composed of nine old words and nine new words. If learning and memory consist of building and storing inter-item associations, then the list of eighteen words should have been learned and remembered better by subjects who were familiar with nine of the words. However, if the process involved is not simply a matter of strengthening inter-item associations but one of building up organizations, then the eighteen-word list that contained no old words might be the easier of the two. The subjective organization imposed on the original nine-word list might not be appropriate for the eighteen-word list; the nine new words might not fit into the old organization. The results of Tulving's experiment can be seen in box figure 12.3. Not only did the repetition of the nine old items in the new list not help, it actually retarded performance. Perhaps the subjects found it difficult to abandon their old organization when the old items were repeated in the new list. The demonstration that the repetition of well-learned items does not help recall if new items which do not fit in are added is a powerful one indeed.

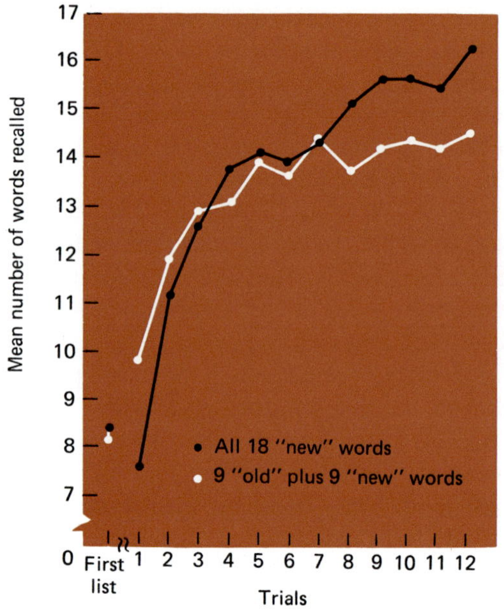

Box Figure 12.3 The results of Tulving's (1966) experiment. The list composed of nine new items and nine old items is recalled no better than a list of eighteen new items. In fact, its recall is somewhat worse. (From Tulving, Endel, "Subjective organization and effects of repetition in multi-trial free recall," *Journal of Verbal Learning and Verbal Behavior* 5, 1966, pp. 193–197. Reprinted by permission of Academic Press, Inc.)

simply the storage of input information, it involves an active construction of the recalled material from the outline that is stored.

Given that reconstruction is involved in recalling information, what principles govern the reconstruction? One principle seems to be that people reconstruct a plausible memory, that is, one that seems usual. Thus, if a person is asked to remember a story containing some unusual details, the details may be replaced by more usual ones at the time of recall. If the person stores only the outline of the story and reconstructs a plausible scenario around the outline, the unusual details should be replaced by more plausible ones. This effect occurred quite frequently in Bartlett's studies. For example, he asked subjects to remember a story about two Indians who went down to a river to hunt seals. At the river, the Indians had a variety of adventures, which were the core of the story. When the subjects were asked to recall the story, they recalled the essence of the story correctly, but almost all said that the Indians had gone down to hunt fish, not seals. One normally goes to a river for fish, not seals, and the subjects reconstructed the more plausible detail.

Storing the theme of a story does seem to have some advantages over storing individual items. The theme of a story does not seem to be as susceptible to interference effects as are individual items. Bower and Clark (1969) gave one group of subjects ten unrelated nouns and asked them to invent a story, using all ten words. Although the subjects could take all the time they needed to make up the story, they usually took about 2½ minutes. A control group was then given the same list of nouns for 2½ minutes, but these subjects were not asked to make up a story using the words; they were only asked to memorize the words. A recall test, conducted immediately after exposure to the list, indicated that both groups could remember the ten words perfectly. Both groups were then given eleven more word lists, with one group making up stories and the other memorizing. After all twelve lists had been learned, the subjects were asked to recall the ten words from each list for a total of 120 words. As expected, the subjects who had been asked to memorize the words did poorly: after twelve lists, RI and PI were large, and recall was only fourteen percent. However, the subjects who had made up stories recalled ninety-three percent of the words because they were able to remember the stories and reconstructed the words from them. The stories did not seem to suffer from large RI and PI effects, perhaps because each operated as a single organized chunk.

Retrieval from memory is not a process of simply finding something in memory; it is not like finding a book in a library. It seems to be a more active process, one of constructing a probable response on the basis of whatever information is available in memory. In other words, themes are easy to remember, and details are constructed from them.

Neoassociationism

It should be obvious by now that many findings discussed in this chapter do not fit well with the doctrines of the British empiricists. For example, if a person is asked what class of objects the word "chair" belongs to (superordinate), he will quickly respond with "furniture." If he is asked to name an object that is a subclass of "chair" (subordinate), he will quickly say "rocking chair." If the concepts contained in the mind were tied together by independent associations, a person should not be able to do this. Associations are not *labeled;* there is no superordinate and subordinate association. If the contents of the mind are tied together only by associations, how can a person get from "chair" to "furniture" when asked to give the superordinate? He should be just as likely to say "rocking chair."

The mind's contents seem structured and organized. There have been a number of recent attempts to specify mental organizations within an associationistic framework. These attempts all stress the *hierarchical* nature of the contents of the mind. An example of a scheme proposed by Collins and Quillian (1969) is shown in figure 12.11. These investigators proposed that semantic information in memory is structured into hierarchies, not independent associations. An important assumption in this scheme is that a property characterizing a particular class of things is stored only at the place in the hierarchy that corresponds to that class. For example, all animals "eat," so "eats" is stored only at the level of "animals," not at the level of "birds," "fish," and so forth. Similarly, "flies" is stored with "birds," not at the level of particular birds, for example, canary and bluebird.

Note that here there is some structure or organization, not haphazard associations. Also note that retrieval of information here

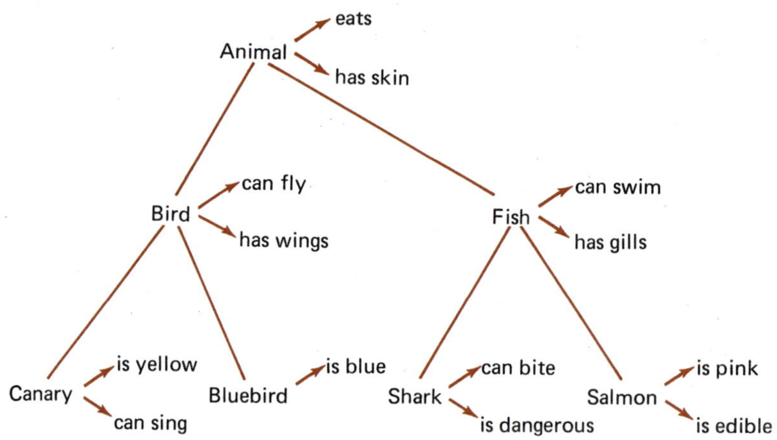

Figure 12.11 An example of the kind of hierarchical memory structure proposed by Collins and Quillian (1969). Note that information is stored as high in the hierarchy as possible. (Adapted from Collins, A., and Quillian, M. R., "Retrieval time from semantic memory," *Journal of Verbal Learning and Verbal Behavior* 8, 1969, pp. 240–247. Reprinted by permission of Academic Press, Inc.)

would have to follow a definite scheme. To find some piece of information about a topic, the hierarchy would be entered at the level of the topic, and the search would proceed from there. Thus, if a person were asked whether a canary was yellow, entry would occur at the level of "canary," and right there would be stored the fact that a canary is yellow. However, what would happen if someone were asked whether a canary has wings. Entry would occur at the level of "canary," but there is no information about wings there. The person would have to move to the next level in the hierarchy, "bird," to answer the question. What if the person were asked whether canaries have skins? He would have to move two levels up the hierarchy to "animal."

If the sort of memory structure proposed by Collins and Quillian is correct, it should take a person longer to answer the question "Does a canary have skin?" than the question "Does a canary fly?" Similary, it should take longer to answer whether a canary flies, than whether a canary is yellow. This is true because moving up each level of the hierarchy takes time, however brief. The results of this experiment are shown in figure 12.12.

An even more recent account of memory structure has been offered by Anderson and Bower (1973). Although their conception is also hierarchical in character, the connecting links are labeled; that is, the arrows or associations that hold items together differ in character from one to another. For example, some associations are labeled "subject" and some are labeled "object," which results in a high degree of structure. It is too early to tell whether this kind of approach will successfully handle the phenomena discussed in this chapter. Moreover, it may not be appropriate to call these models associationistic. Although Anderson and Bower argue that their model is indeed associationistic in spirit, there is room for disagreement. Their model may be consistent with the spirit of Aristotle's associationism (which was not discussed in this book), but perhaps not with the associationism of the British empiricists, whose central

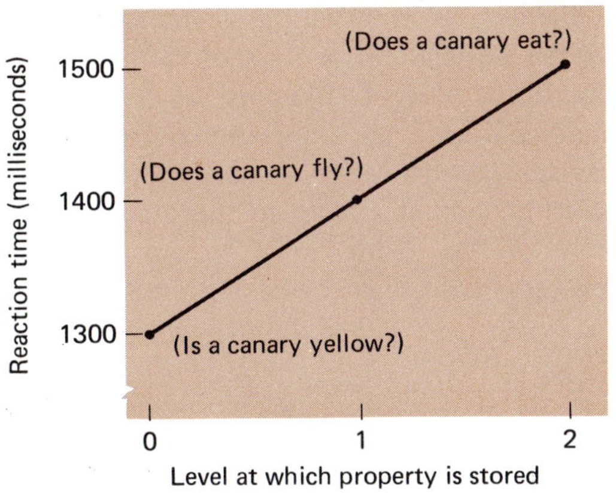

Figure 12.12 The reaction time to answer various questions about the objects depicted in the hierarchy (shown in figure 12.11). The reaction time is plotted against the number of levels in the hierarchy the subject should have to search to find the answer. (Adapted from Collins, A., and Quillian, M. R., "Retrieval time from semantic memory," *Journal of Verbal Learning and Verbal Behavior* 8, 1969, pp. 240–247. Reprinted by permission of Academic Press, Inc.)

assertion was that the contents of the mind are lasting copies of raw sensations, tied together by associations. The Anderson and Bower model contains perceptual processing stages before the memory stages, so raw sensations are not emphasized. Furthermore, whether labeled links in hierarchical structures can be viewed as similar to what the British empiricists meant by an association is open to question. Nevertheless, "network" models, such as Anderson's and Bower's, are exciting, and it will be interesting to see how successful they will be.

Summary

This chapter has considered what is known about memory. We began by discussing the associationistic view of memory put forth by the British empiricists and the experimental study of memory by Ebbinghaus.

We saw that the first real advance after Ebbinghaus was the interference theory of forgetting. According to this theory, forgetting was attributable to the interaction between successively learned associations. Associations acquired after the association to be remembered produced unlearning of and response competition with the remembered association (retroactive interference, or RI). Associations acquired before the association to be remembered were unlearned during the acquisition of the association to be remembered and spontaneously recovered. Thus they later competed with the association to be remembered (proactive interference, or PI).

We saw that by the early 1960s, interference theory was widely accepted but has since declined. The decline was caused by problems with the theory itself as well as by the development of new approaches to the study of memory.

One new approach was information processing. This approach stressed stages of memory and the flow of information from stage to stage. Three stages were isolated: sensory memory, short-term memory, and long-term memory. Sensory memory was discussed in a preceding chapter. Short-term memory was described as a system for holding information for a short period of time while the information was being processed for storage in LTM. A number of characteristics of STM were noted. First, information in STM is represented largely in acoustic form. Second, the capacity of STM is seven chunks, or seven organized entities. Third, forgetting from STM is a product of this limited capacity. Incoming information pushes old items out of STM. Only unexpected pieces of information seem to be able to do this. Finally, retrieval from STM involves going through the contents of STM, one item at a time.

The entry of information into LTM is governed by rehearsal. The more an item in STM is rehearsed, the more likely is its storage in LTM. Storage in LTM is multidimensional—that is, semantic, acoustic, and visual representations are stored. The importance of organization in LTM was also noted. People organize materials to be remembered into groupings and retrieve these groupings at the time of recall. The specific material seems to be reconstructed from the groupings.

Finally, the implications of these findings for the associationistic view of memory were examined. Recent attempts to handle the findings within an associational framework have proposed a variety of schemes for adding structure and flexibility to the associational view of the contents of memory. These schemes hold a high degree of promise.

13

Biological Correlates of Learning and Memory

This chapter concludes our discussion of learning and memory by examining some of the biological mechanisms that may underlie these important processes. We have already considered several important features of the biological foundations of learning and memory in earlier chapters. In Chapter 5, for example, we noted that learning and memory storage can be manipulated by certain pharmacological agents, such as convulsant drugs. In Chapter 12 we suggested that the *hippocampus* in humans may be involved in the transfer of information from STM to LTM. In this chapter, we will expand these topics and discuss a variety of other biological approaches to understanding the nature of learning and memory.

First, we will explore what is known about the memory storage process. How long does it take for information to be stored in LTM? Can this process be altered by drugs or other experimental intervention? Are memories stored in a single place in the brain? What are some of the anatomical correlates of STM and LTM storage processes? We will also examine electrical and biochemical events that seem to correlate with learning and memory storage. Finally, we will investigate the "model systems" approach, which utilizes the nervous systems of lower organisms or simplified portions of more complex nervous systems to study the cellular processes involved in learning and memory. Although we can give only the briefest account of the biological processes that are currently being studied in relation to learning and memory, we hope to convey some of the flavor of this exciting and new frontier in psychology and the neurosciences.

Experimental Modification of Memory

In Chapter 12 we said that under certain circumstances, one can interfere with memory retroactively. That is, new learning, especially when the new material is similar to that learned originally, can produce *retroactive interference.* A more general phenomenon, not unlike retroactive interference, is *retrograde amnesia.* As discussed in Chapter 5, this is a clinical symptom that may occur after a severe head injury or an epileptic seizure. The patient suffering from retrograde amnesia has a loss of memory for events that preceded the trauma, and the amnesia may be either relatively permanent or transient. The most interesting aspect of the syndrome is that amnesia is restricted to events that immediately preceded the injury, whereas events that occurred long before the trauma are remembered as well as ever. The following case history of a gunner who suffered a head injury during World War II illustrates several features of retrograde amnesia:

> Gunner J.W.T. was injured in an air raid on 28 November 1940. When first seen he was deeply comatose with flaccid limbs. Recovery of consciousness was very slow, and he did not begin to talk until a month later. On 11 March 1941 his mental state was still greatly retarded. The . . . [retrograde amnesia lasted] for about six months, and he had no recollection of three months in the army. He now remembered coming to himself in a hospital in January 1941, when he found two women and a man sitting at his bed. These people told him they were his wife, mother, and a close friend. He remembers arguing with them and saying he was not even married, and that he was certain he had never seen the man before. He was now correctly orientated, but was still very uncertain on the main facts concerning himself. He did all intelligence tests badly, and had difficulty in reading. He was very cheerful and friendly.
>
> By 16 April 1941 the . . . [amnesia] had shrunk to a few minutes, and he remembers standing by the guns on the night he was injured, and that a few shells had been fired, but he does not remember any bombs . . . (Russel, 1959)

Note that initially this patient was unable to remember a large chunk of his life preceding the injury, but eventually he was amnesic only for the few minutes that preceded the trauma. This clinical course is typical for retrograde amnesia. Very often, islands of memory will appear when the patient returns to familiar surroundings or discusses forgotten events with friends and relatives. Eventually, the gaps will be filled in until only the few moments before the injury are permanently forgotten.

Electrically Induced Amnesia

Several decades ago, it was demonstrated that retrograde amnesia could be produced experimentally by electroconvulsive shock—a strong electric current that is usually delivered through electrodes placed on the head. It is termed *electroconvulsive shock* because the severe shock to the brain usually produces convulsions; these convulsions are controlled to some extent in human patients by drugs and other devices that prevent the patient from injuring himself. In one early experiment by Zubin and Barrera (1941), patients were taught paired-associate words, and after some time had elapsed, they were asked to relearn the original material. As expected, relearning occurred more rapidly, demonstrating considerable savings. However, the investigators found that if an electroconvulsive shock intervened between original learning and relearning, less savings occurred. Most important, they discovered that the shorter the interval between the original learning and the administration of the electroconvulsive shock, the greater the amnesic effects. In other words, the amount of amnesia produced depended on the time that elapsed between the original learning and the interfering electroconvulsive stimulation.

Duncan (1949) demonstrated that similar retrograde amnesia could be produced in experimental animals. In a classic experiment, Duncan trained rats to run a maze. Each rat was given one trial per day and was rewarded with food for running through the maze. Although several groups of animals were involved in this experiment, the groups that received shocks at different intervals are the important ones for the present discussion. The results of this early experiment, which have been verified time and again, were that animals that were given an electroconvulsive shock shortly after a learning trial performed significantly more poorly than animals that either were not convulsed or had been given electroconvulsive shock long after the learning trial. The data from this experiment are shown in figure 13.1. Note the importance of the time at which electroconvulsive shock was administered; the longer the time interval after learning, the less effective was electroconvulsive shock in producing retrograde amnesia.

On the basis of data such as these and the existence of retroactive interference, a theory of memory termed *consolidation theory* has emerged. As we noted in the previous paragraph, the time that elapsed between original learning and administration of electroconvulsive shock is critical in producing retrograde amnesia. The longer the interval between original learning and electroconvulsive shock or other interference, the less memory is affected. This effect is called a *retrograde amnesia gradient,* and its existence—as well as the existence of other forms of retroactive interference—-suggest that memory storage is

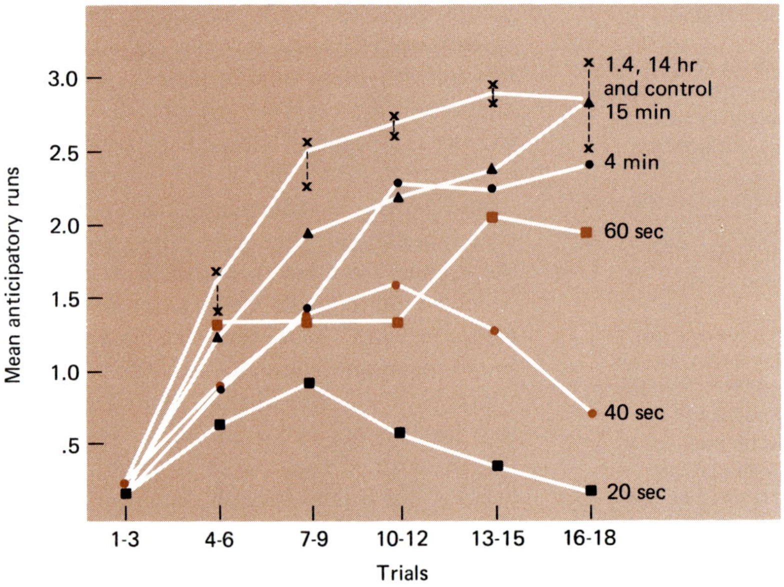

Figure 13.1 The effects of electroconvulsive shock on the acquisition of a T-maze task. Animals were given electroconvulsive shock 20 sec., 40 sec., 60 sec., 4 min., and 15 min. or 1, 4, or 14 hours after the learning trials. Note that the closer in time that the electroconvulsive shock was administered after each learning trial, the poorer the performance. (After Duncan, C. P., "The retroactive effect of electroshock on learning," *Journal of Comparative Physiological Psychology, 42,* 1949, pp. 32–44. Copyright 1949 by the American Psychological Association. Reprinted by permission.)

time dependent (McGaugh, 1966). In other words, memory storage does not occur immediately after learning takes place. The time required for memory storage reveals the time for the consolidation of memory and forms the basis for consolidation theory. A second important feature of these and other experiments is that memory is not a single process, as we noted in Chapter 12. Retrograde amnesia occurs for events that immediately precede brain trauma (or another interfering event). Therefore, memory must pass through a phase during which it is *labile,* or susceptible to interference. But once memory is consolidated, a trauma to the brain may have little effect.

More recent evidence suggests that retrograde amnesia following electroconvulsive shock may not be complete because certain experimental treatments can "reinstate" the lost memory. For example, Lewis et al. (1968) administered footshocks to rats for stepping off of a raised platform. When electroconvulsive shock was administered shortly after this experience, amnesia was produced, as revealed by subsequent retests of the animals. However, another footshock given four hours after training and in an entirely different compartment reinstated the memory. This "reminder" effect can be produced by a variety of treatments following the training and electroconvulsive shock. The effect does not involve retraining because the animals are not exposed again to the training situation but are simply given a shock or other, often noxious stimulus outside of the training situation. The mechanisms by which "reminder" effects are capable of reinstating a memory following its disruption by electroconvulsive shock are not yet understood. However, taken together, experiments such as these suggest that in many instances, some memory for the task remains following electroconvulsive treatment and that perhaps the treatment disrupts the *retrieval* of the memory from storage rather than merely impairing the storage process. This disruption of the retrieval process may be partially responsible for the apparent experimental amnesia.

Within the past few years, experimenters have attempted to determine which areas in the brain are important in producing experimental retrograde amnesia. Although electroconvulsive stimulation of any area of the brain can produce retrograde amnesia, Gold, Macri, and McGaugh (1973) and others have shown that relatively low electric current, which ordinarily does not produce seizures, can also cause amnesia if placed in specific areas of the cerebral cortex, amygdala, hippocampus, substantia nigra, and the caudate nucleus. Kesner and Connor (1972), for example, trained rats to press a bar in a Skinner box for sugar water reward. The rats were later given a footshock after each bar press. In an attempt to disrupt memory for the punishing shock, subcortical electrical stimulation was administered to the midbrain reticular formation of some rats and to the hippocampus of other rats four seconds after each footshock. The rats were then tested for memory of the footshock either sixty-four seconds or twenty-four hours after training. The rats that received electrical stimulation of the midbrain reticular formation remembered the footshock twenty-four hours after the trial but not after sixty-four seconds, while the rats receiving electrical stimulation of the hippocampus remembered the footshock sixty-four seconds but not twenty-four hours after training. These results are depicted in figure 13.2. Kesner and Connor suggest that their results support the notion that memory consists of at least two different phases which develop simultaneously. One phase, a STM phase, must be dependent on the reticular formation and structures associated with it because electrical stimulation in this area interfered with STM (64 seconds after training) but not LTM (24 hours after training). The hippocampus and related structures are important for the LTM phase because stimulation in this area interfered with long-term retention but not short-term performance. The dissection of memory storage processes by electrical stimulation of specific regions of the brain promises to provide us with additional information about memory processes as well as the circuits in the brain that may mediate them.

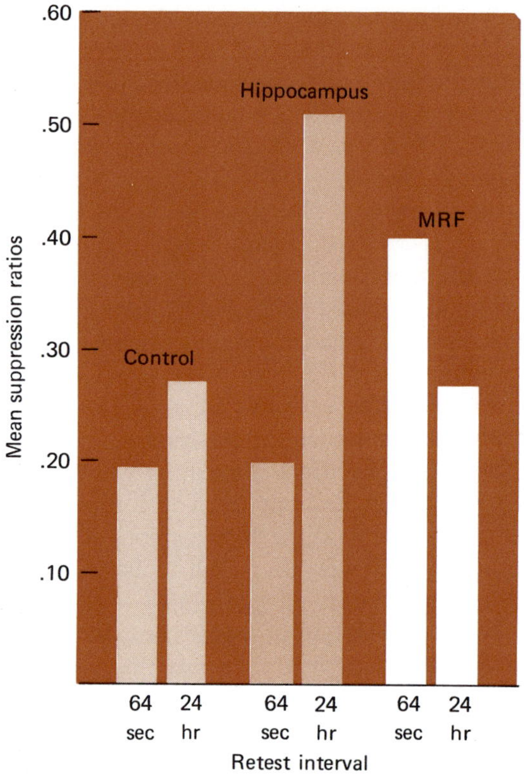

Figure 13.2 Suppression of bar pressing 64 seconds and 24 hours after a punishing footshock contingent upon bar pressing. The ratio measure on the ordinate is a measure of memory for the footshock. A low ratio means that the animal remembered the shock and did not press the bar very often, whereas a high ratio indicates little memory for the footshock and relatively more bar pressing. Experimental animals received electrical stimulation to the hippocampus or midbrain reticular formation (MRF) after the learning experience. Control animals did not receive interfering brain stimulation. (From "Independence of short- and long-term memory: a neural system analysis." Kesner, R. P., and Connor, H. S. *Science, 176,* pp. 432–434, Fig. 1, 28 April 1972. Copyright 1972 by the American Association for the Advancement of Science.)

Drug-Induced Amnesia

If memory is susceptible to interference by electrical stimulation for a period of time after learning, then it should be susceptible to interference by a variety of other means. We noted in Chapter 5 that certain convulsant drugs, if administered in low, or subconvulsive doses, appear to improve memory and increase the speed with which memories are stored. It is important, as well as interesting to note that these analeptic agents need not be administered during learning. If injected immediately after the learning experience, these compounds facilitate memory storage. Thus, rather than acting on the acquisition or initial learning of material, analeptic agents appear to act on the storage process that occurs after original learning—or, in theoretical terms, they affect the consolidation of memory.

Although we cannot cover the entire range of effects that the different drugs have on learning and memory we can mention a few important ones. For example, if you acquire information while in a particular drug state, you may find that you are unable to recall the information later when you are no longer in that state. This is called *state-dependent* learning, and is described in box 13.1. Disruption and facilitation of memory have been achieved with a variety of drugs. Anticholinergics, for instance, which interfere with synaptic transmission mediated by acetylcholine, have been reported to block both LTM (Deutsch, 1971) and STM (e.g., Alpern and Marriott, 1973). Although these and other experiments suggest that certain neural transmitters are important in learning and memory, the precise mechanisms by which these transmitters produce their effects are not well understood.

Box 13.1

State-Dependent Learning

Drugs can affect learning and memory in many ways. For example, if you learn something while under the influence of a drug, you may find that, in a nondrugged state, you may be unable to recall that information. A number of experiments have shown that when animals are trained to make a certain response while in a particular physiological state, they will perform poorly or as if they are naive when retested for retention of the same task while in a different state. This phenomenon has been termed dissociated, or *state-dependent* learning.

In one experiment (Overton, 1964), rats were trained to turn to the right in a T-maze while under the influence of sodium pentobarbital, a barbiturate (dark circles in box fig. 13.1) and were later tested in a nondrugged condition (light circles). As shown in the upper graphs of box figure 13.1, the subjects learned the correct response under the influence of the drug, but when tested in a nondrugged state, they had to learn the maze again as if they had never been exposed to it. That is, their performance dropped to random levels when they were tested without the drug. Furthermore, it took the experimental animals as long to relearn the task as it took a nondrugged control group (bottom graph) to learn the task initially. Overton also demonstrated that the amount of learning that was transferred from the drugged to the nondrugged conditions depended on the dose of the drug administered to the animals. Small doses produced less dissociation than did high doses.

Other experiments indicate that state-dependent learning can occur in humans. For instance, Goodwin et al. (1969) studied male volunteers who performed several memory tasks while sober or intoxicated with alcohol. As one might expect, the sober subjects performed better. However, when the subjects were tested later, those who had memorized sentences while drunk were also able to recall the material better when intoxicated rather than sober!

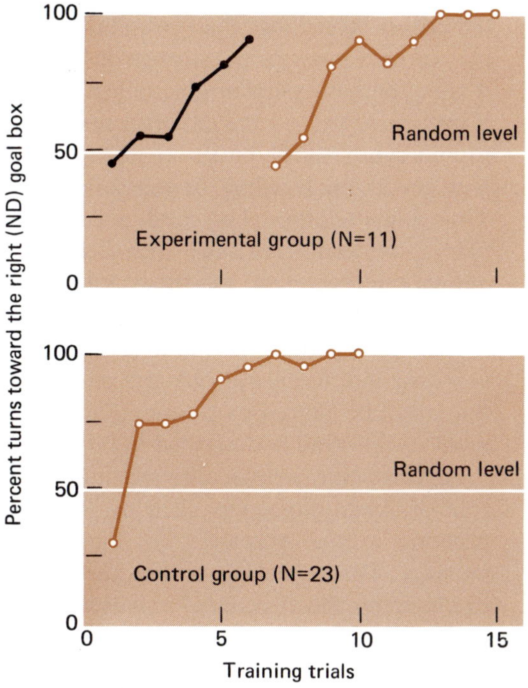

Box Figure 13.1 Performance in a T-maze by rats under the influence of the general anesthetic, sodium pentobarbital (dark circles). When tested later in a nondrugged condition (light circles), the animals had to relearn the correct response and took just as long as a nondrugged group of control animals (bottom graph). (From Overton, D. A. "State-dependent or 'dissociated' learning produced with pentobarbital," *Journal of Comparative and Physiological Psychology, 57,* 1964. Copyright 1964 by the American Psychological Association. Reprinted by permission.)

Perhaps the most significant outcome of all this work is the knowledge that memory is indeed time-dependent, and that a variety of experimental treatments can alter the memory storage process during its labile period. The most significant question yet to be answered is the nature of the biological process or processes that are altered by these treatments.

Several experimental attempts to answer this question have involved the use of antibiotics that inhibit the synthesis of RNA or proteins in the brain. A variety of evidence suggests that learning and memory involve alterations in the brain's manufacture, storage, or other biochemical processing of certain large molecules. For example, under some circumstances, drugs that inhibit the synthesis of RNA appear to produce a loss of memory. Similarly, certain antibiotics that inhibit the synthesis of new proteins in the brain can also cause memory loss. These results suggest that both of these important macromolecules may be involved in learning and memory storage.

Using this approach, Barondes and Cohen (1966) studied the effects of puromycin—a powerful protein synthesis inhibitor—on learning and memory storage in mice. Five hours before training, one group of mice received bilateral injections of puromycin directly into the temporal regions of the cerebral cortex. All the animals were then trained to choose one arm of a Y-maze to avoid a footshock. The results were that the puromycin-treated mice learned the response as quickly as did normal control animals. When tested for retention fifteen minutes later, puromycin-treated animals still remembered. However, when the mice were tested for retention forty-five minutes, ninety minutes, or three hours after training, the puromycin-treated animals exhibited a marked amnesia (see fig. 13.3).

Because puromycin has such a pronounced inhibitory effect on protein synthesis, we can

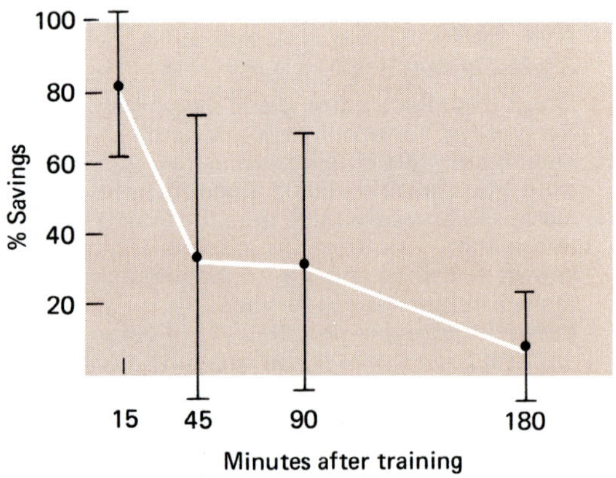

Figure 13.3 Amnesia in mice for a Y-maze during inhibition of protein synthesis produced by injections of puromycin directly into the temporal regions of the brain. Three hours after training, inhibition of protein synthesis was pronounced, as was the amnesia accompanying it. (From Barondes, S. H., and Cohen, H. D. "Puromycin effect on successive phases of memory storage," *Science, 151,* 1966, pp. 594–595, Figure 1, February 1966. Copyright 1966 by the American Association for the Advancement of Science.)

tentatively conclude that protein synthesis may be necessary for the storage of LTM, but it is not necessary for original learning or for STM. However, all the experiments that use protein synthesis inhibitors do not find equivalent effects on learning or memory storage. Thus much additional research must be done before we can draw any firm conclusions about the necessity of these biochemical changes for learning or memory. Some research findings indicate that in the absence of any drug interference, RNA and protein synthesis can be altered by training. One experiment of this kind is described in box 13.2.

At this point, we can only speculate on the role of macromolecules such as RNA and proteins in the processes of learning and memory. They may be involved, for example, in changing the functional relationships between neurons in the brain, either by altering connections between neurons or by making some connections or processes more or less efficient than others. There is also evidence

Box 13.2

Experience Can Alter RNA and Protein Synthesis in the Brain

Zemp et al. (1966) measured changes in RNA in the brains of rats who had been trained in a simple avoidance task. Two groups of mice were injected with radioactively labelled uridine, one of the basic molecules found in RNA. Subsequently, one group was trained in a conditioned avoidance task that required them to jump up onto an escape shelf in an experimental chamber whenever a buzzer was sounded. The control group was also exposed to this situation and was shocked precisely the same amount of times as the experimental animals; however, the animals in the control group were not provided with an escape shelf so they could not learn the conditioned response. After training, the brains of these animals were removed, homogenized, and separated into four different fractions: one contained nuclei; one, mitochondria; a third, primarily ribosomes (where protein synthesis takes place); and a fourth fraction, containing the residue. Upon analysis, it was found that the trained animals synthesized more RNA than the control animals did, but only in the nuclear and ribosomal portions of the brain tissue. These results suggested that some aspect of conditioning altered RNA and possibly protein synthesis in the brain.

Although many similar experiments have been and are currently being pursued, we can only speculate that changes in the synthesis of macromolecules like RNA and proteins may be involved in learning and memory.

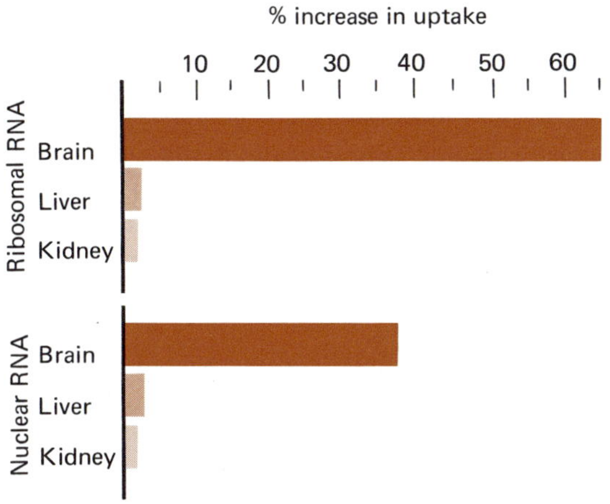

Box Figure 13.2 Average percentage increase in the uptake of radioactively labelled RNA precursors consequent to learning. (From Zemp, J. W., Wilson, J. E., Schlesinger, K., Boggan, W. O., and Glassman, E. "Brain function and macromolecules. I. Incorporation of uridine into RNA of mouse brain during short-term training experience." After Grossman, S. P., ***Essentials of Physiological Psychology.*** Copyright 1973 John Wiley and Sons, Inc. Reprinted by permission of John Wiley and Sons, Inc.)

that the activity of neurons is altered during learning and memory, and we turn to this research approach in the next section.

Neural Activity in the Brain During Learning and Memory

In Chapter 3, we described several forms of electrical activity that are generated by nervous tissue, including the electroencephalogram (EEG); evoked potentials in response to sensory stimuli; postsynaptic potentials, which are presumed to underlie these "gross" forms of electrical potentials in the brain; and the action potentials of individual neurons, which comprise one of the important mechanisms by which information is conveyed from place to place in the nervous system. We now know that all these forms of electrical activity can be altered in some way during learning. Furthermore, the alterations are not restricted to a single structure in the brain, and they may not be entirely similar in different areas or occur simultaneously during the learning process. Although we are a long way from understanding the relative importance of these changes or, indeed, whether any single change is essential to learning or memory, a few examples will illustrate this important work.

Electroencephalogram

The EEG, as we noted in earlier chapters, is a record of the brain's ongoing electrical activity and is often recorded from the surface of the cerebral cortex. We also noted that in a relaxed human subject, the ongoing electrical activity of the cerebral cortex is characterized by large, regular variations in voltage at a frequency of about ten cycles per second, termed *alpha waves.* If a sensory stimulus is presented to a relaxed subject, these highly synchronized waves of electrical activity become smaller, irregular, and rapidly fluctuating in voltage. This phenomenon is termed "alpha blocking" or the "EEG arousal response." Figure 13.4a illustrates this phenomenon in a cat.

Sharpless and Jasper (1956) studied the arousal response during habituation training. *Habituation* is defined as a decrease in the response to a repetitive stimulus, and it is an important means by which organisms learn to ignore repetitive but insignificant changes in their environment. In this experiment, loud tones were presented repeatedly to sleeping cats. At first, each tone produced a characteristic EEG arousal response and awakened the animals. After each tone, the animals were allowed to lapse into sleep again until the next tone was presented. After a number of presentations, the tone no longer awakened the cats and no longer produced EEG arousal, as shown in figure 13.4b.

Habituation is perhaps the simplest and most widespread form of learning in the animal kingdom. It is not unlike the phenomenon of *extinction.* However, during extinction, as noted in Chapter 11, learned responses decrease whereas habituation is a decrease in an unlearned response. Thus despite their similarities, we cannot equate the two processes.

The EEG arousal response can also be conditioned by using the classical, or Pavlovian conditioning paradigm described in Chapter 11. For example, Jasper and Shagass (1941) conducted an experiment in which college students who showed good alpha activity in the EEG served as subjects. In this experiment, a tone was the conditioned stimulus (CS), and a flash of light was the unconditioned stimulus (US). After habituation training with the CS so that it would not produce the EEG arousal response, the CS was paired with the US for approximately ten trials until the tone evoked an EEG arousal response. Thus the EEG arousal response, like many behavioral responses, could be classically conditioned. Many similar experiments, using different stimuli for both CS and US, demonstrate unequivocally that the EEG —at least in these learning paradigms—may change as a result of training.

Evoked Potentials

Like the EEG, evoked potentials may also change during learning. One of the most extensive analyses of evoked potentials and memory has been done by John (1967). In his experiments, cats were implanted with recording electrodes in a variety of sites in the brain. The animals were then trained, by operant conditioning (instrumental learning) techniques, to respond to a flickering light stimulus. In one intriguing experiment, cats were trained to make one response (CR1) to one flickering light (CS1) and another response (CR2) to a light that flickered at a different frequency (CS2). As shown in fig-

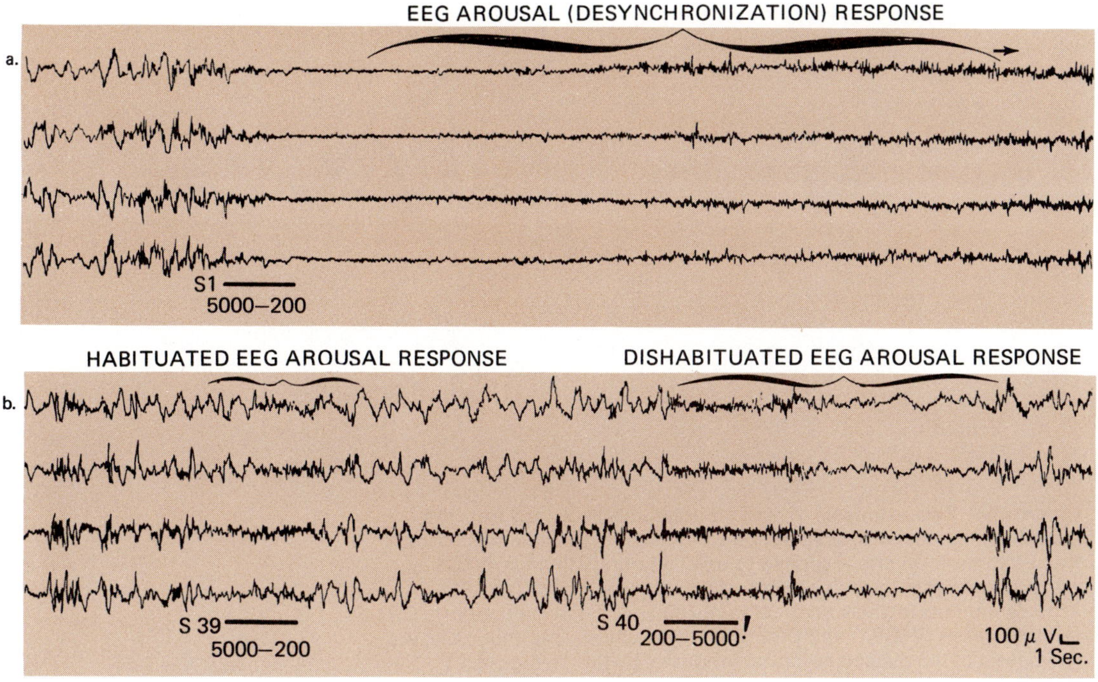

Figure 13.4 The upper four tracings (a) illustrate cortical electroencephalograms from different regions of the cortex to a "sliding" tone (labelled S1) falling in frequency from 5000 to 200 Hertz. As shown in the lower four tracings (b), when the tone is presented for the 39th time (S39) the EEG arousal response is much less pronounced, demonstrating marked habituation. When the tone is changed so that it now slides in the reverse direction (i.e., from 200–5000 hz., labelled S40), the EEG arousal response becomes dishabituated, responding to a greater extent to the novel tone than to the tone used for habituation training. (From Sharpless, S., and Jasper, H., "Habituation of the arousal reaction," *Brain,* 79, 1956, pp. 655–680. Reprinted by permission of the Editor of *Brain.*)

ure 13.5, the evoked response that was recorded after these animals were well trained looked quite different when CS1 was presented than it did when CS2 was presented. This suggested to John that the wave shape of the evoked potential might be a mechanism that could correlate with information in memory; that is, the evoked response might represent a "neural readout" of memory. In an attempt to correlate the wave shape of the evoked response with memory, John presented the cats with a third, flickering light (CS3), one which they had not seen before. In some cases the animals responded as though the novel flicker were CS1 and thus performed a CR1; in others, they responded to CS3 as if it were CS2 and performed a CR2. As shown in figure 13.5, the wave shape of the potential evoked by CS3 looked like that evoked by CS1 if the animals performed CR1. However, it looked like the potential evoked by CS2 if the animals performed CR2. Thus whatever meaning the animals attached to CS3, as demonstrated by their response to it, the wave shape of the evoked potential seemed to reflect that meaning (John, Bart-

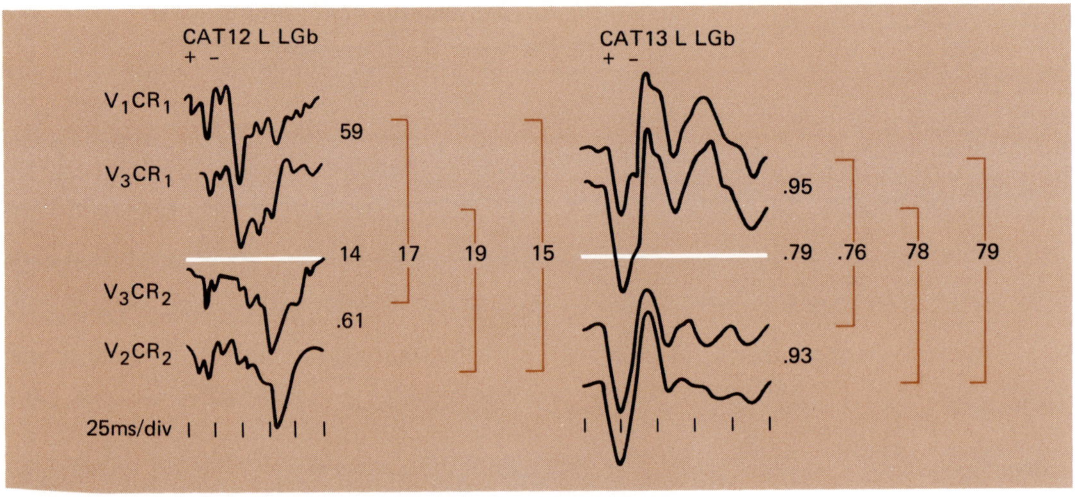

Figure 13.5 Two examples of evoked potentials recorded from the lateral geniculate body (a visual relay nucleus in the thalamus) in cats trained to perform one response to one flickering stimulus (V1CR1) and a second response to a different flickering stimulus (V2CR2). When an animal is given an ambiguous flicker (V3), it may perform CR1 in some cases (V3CR1) and CR2 (V3CR2) in others. In either case, the wave form of the evoked potential produced by the ambiguous stimulus looks like that evoked by one of the training stimuli, depending on how the animal interprets the ambiguous stimulus. Thus the same physical stimulus produces different wave forms depending on its meaning, as shown by the animal's response to it. (From John, E. R., Bartlett, F., Shimokochi, M., and Kleinman, D., "Neural readout from memory," *Journal of Neurophysiology,* 36, 1973. Reprinted by permission of the American Physiological Association.)

lett, Shimokochi, and Kleinman, 1973). We now know that this characteristic of the evoked potential can be demonstrated in humans as well as animals. The wave shape of the evoked potential can correlate, not only with the physical characteristics of the stimulus, but with its learned meaning as well. Evoked potentials to different stimuli may look alike if the stimuli mean the same thing to the subject. For example, evoked potentials to an auditory and a visual stimulus come to look similar if both stimuli are used in the same conditioning paradigm; that is, if they mean the same thing (John, 1967). And finally, these changes can occur in widespread regions of the brain; they are not restricted to specific sensory regions or to one level of the nervous system such as the cerebral cortex.

These experiments, and many others like them, do indeed suggest that the evoked potential is more than a response to the physical characteristics of a sensory stimulus. Furthermore, they indicate that, like the EEG, evoked potentials also reflect the occurrence of learning and memory. Whether they are necessary or sufficient for these processes, however, is still a matter of vigorous debate.

Activity of Single Neurons

One extremely active area of research on the mechanisms underlying learning and memory concerns the activity of single neurons in the brain during these phenomena. Here again, the evidence indicates that the activity of individual neurons or populations of neurons can be altered by training and that these changes take place during the learning and memory processes.

In one sense, it is obvious that changes in the activity of neurons must occur during learning because most glandular and muscular responses depend on the activity of neurons in the spinal cord, which in turn are controlled by the balance of excitation and inhibition imposed on them by higher levels of the nervous system. Thus the most significant questions concern how the changes in neural activity that occur during learning are produced and where these changes take place, rather than whether changes take place at all.

Buchwald, Halas, and Schramm (1966) recorded the activity of small populations of neurons in a variety of different brain areas during conditioning of leg flexion in the cat. The CS was a tone, and the US was an electrical shock to the hindlimb, which resulted in withdrawal of the hindlimb. An example of the development of conditioned neuronal activity recorded from the inferior colliculus is shown in figure 13.6. Note that between training sessions 1 and 9, there was a marked increase in neural activity when the CS was presented; this increase disappeared with extinction and then reappeared during retraining. The behavioral response also showed conditioning, as indicated by the electrical activity of the muscles of the hindlimb. According to the results of this experiment, and a number of others in which the activity of neurons in several areas of the brain was recorded during classical conditioning, there seem to be characteristic differences in the development of conditioned neural activity during training. Initially, neuronal responses to the CS develop in the reticular formation and lower relay nuclei of the sensory pathway of the conditioned stimulus. Thus in Buchwald's experiment, conditioned responses would presumably develop first in the reticular formation, inferior colliculus, and medial geniculate body—the latter two being relay nuclei in the auditory pathways (see Chapter 6). Later in training, conditioned neuronal activity seems to develop in the cerebral cortex, often first in the projection cortex of the CS (auditory cortex in the example above) and somewhat later in the projection pathway of the US (somatosensory cortex in the example above). Finally, conditioned neuronal activity develops in the motor cortex and associated motor nuclei involved in producing the behavioral response. Although this sequence of development of conditioned alterations in neuronal activity does not invariably occur it appears to represent a close first approximation to the development of conditioned neuronal activity during classical conditioning.

Olds and Olds (1961) reported operant conditioning of single neuron activity. In these experiments, microelectrodes were inserted into the brain in several areas, and the firing rate of single neurons in these areas was determined. A change in the rate of spontaneous firing, such as a temporary increase, was then "rewarded" with electrical stimulation of the medial forebrain bundle, an area of the brain that when electrically stimulated is rewarding to rats (see Chapter 3). Thus the investigators attempted to "reinforce" the firing of single cells in the brain by stimulating a "pleasure center" in the brain. Interestingly, Olds and Olds were able to alter the firing rate of these neurons using this operant conditioning technique. Cells in the hippocampus and certain subcortical areas were especially susceptible while some cells in the neocortex seemed resistant to this conditioning paradigm. Similar experiments have confirmed that neuronal activity may be altered by operant conditioning using conventional reinforcements such as food and water (Fetz, 1969).

Thus far, we have discussed the nature of changes in the activity of single cells during learning. We will turn our attention to re-

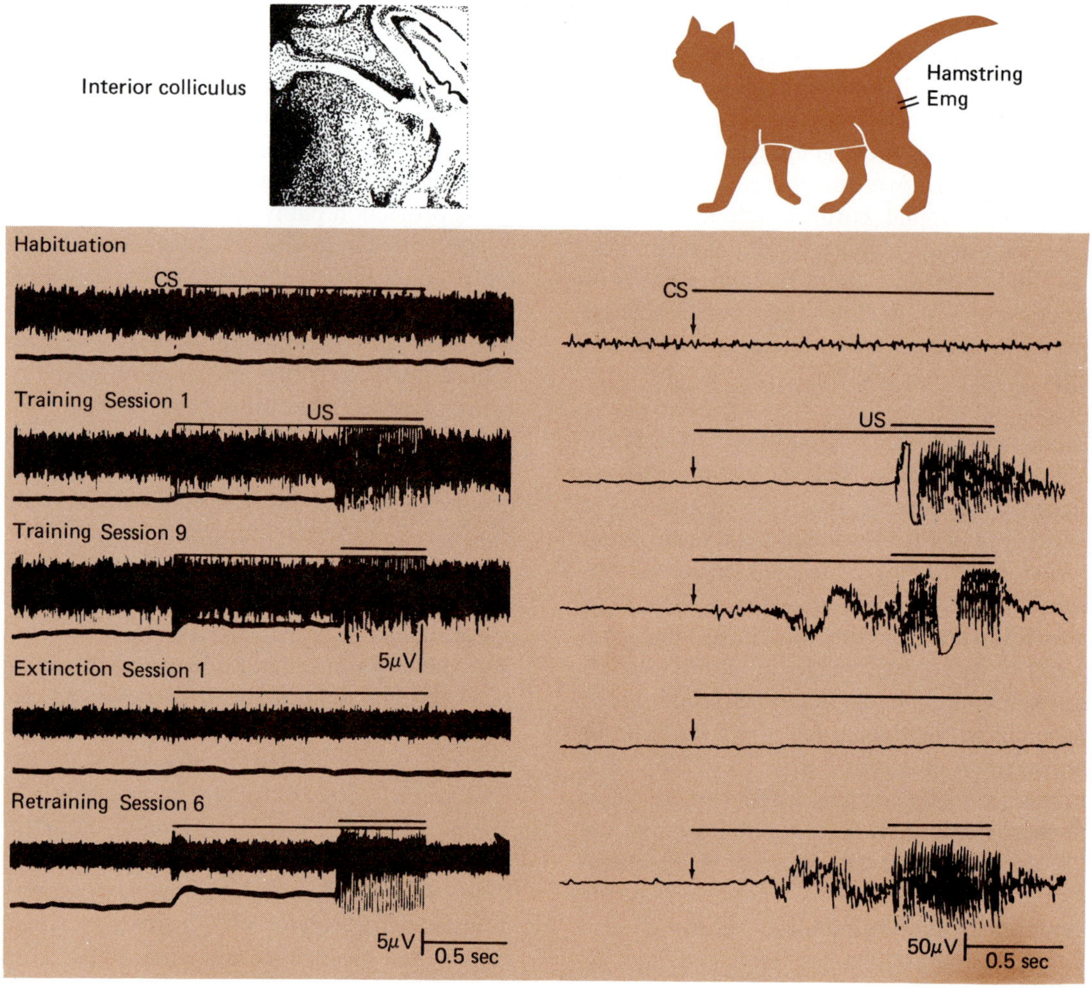

Figure 13.6 Classical conditioning of multiple neuronal activity in the inferior colliculus. On the left are examples of the neuronal activity during presentation of the conditioned stimulus (CS) and the unconditioned stimulus (US). On the right are electrical recordings from muscles of the hindlimb that demonstrate simultaneous conditioning of the behavioral response. Before pairing (habituation), there was little or no neuronal response to the conditioned stimulus, nor was there any behavioral response. During training sessions 1 and 9, however, both the neuronal activity and the behavioral response became conditioned. The solid line beneath each tracing is a measure of the total multiple unit activity. The neuronal and behavioral conditioned responses disappeared during extinction and reappeared during reconditioning. (From Buchwald, J. S., Halas, E. S., and Schramm, S., "Changes in cortical and subcortical unit activity during behavioral conditioning," *Physiology and Behavior, 1,* 1966, pp. 11–22. Reprinted by permission of Pergamon Press.)

Figure 13.7 Firing of a prefrontal cortex neuron (indicated by vertical lines) in five consecutive trials of a delayed response task, with delay intervals of 32, 32, 32, 67, and 65 seconds respectively, from top to bottom. The cue is indicated by a solid line. The delay interval on each trial follows the cue and ends at the arrow. Note that the neuron fires more during the delay interval than before the trial. (From Fuster, J. M., and Alexander, G. E., "Neuron activity related to short-term memory," *Science, 173,* pp. 652–654, Figure 3, 13 August 1971. Copyright 1971 by the American Association for the Advancement of Science.)

search in which recording the electrical activity of neurons was done not only during but after animals are well trained. In this context, we can assume that alterations in neural activity which persist once animals are well trained may be correlated with memory or memory retrieval.

Fuster and Alexander (1971) attempted to record the activity of neurons that might be involved in STM by training monkeys to perform a delayed-response task. In this task, monkeys were presented with several objects on a tray, and the experimenter hid a reward under one of the objects. The animals had to remember the correct object for a certain interval, then respond by moving the appropriate object and retrieving the reward. Fuster and Alexander recorded the activity of neurons in the prefrontal cortex and the nucleus medialis dorsalis of the thalamus, both of which are believed to be involved in the retention of information in STM, and found that the firing rates of the cells in these two areas usually increased during the delay interval. This suggested that the cells might be involved in the short-term retention of information. An example of Fuster and Alexander's results is shown in figure 13.7.

Olds et al. (1971) tried to find neural correlates of LTM by recording the activity of single neurons in rats that were trained to retrieve a food pellet shortly after presentation of a tone stimulus. The investigators were interested in the possibility that because the animals were well trained, changes in rates of firing that occurred when the tone (CS) was presented might represent memory or the retrieval of memory. They found that the activity of single neurons had been modified by this training procedure in a number of areas, including the hippocampus, pontine reticular formation, and posterior nucleus of the thalamus. The hope of this kind of research is to specify which areas show altered neuronal responses to the CS in trained animals and ultimately to specify the relationship of these changes to memory storage or memory retrieval.

Recordings of the brain's electrical activity have revealed that virtually all known forms of nervous activity can be altered by learning, and a variety of excellent candidates for the neural substrates of learning and memory has been discovered. Although we have only begun this important search and thus cannot specify whether any or all of these altered forms of electrical activity are necessary for learning and memory, this question is certain to become an even more important one in future research.

Anatomical Correlates of Learning and Memory

In Chapter 12, we noted that bilateral destruction of the hippocampus in humans produces a severe impairment of memory. Individuals whose temporal lobes have been removed on both sides of the brain, which in these operations also removes the hippocampi, are unable to transfer information in STM to long-term storage. This syndrome was critical in the development of theories that postulated the existence of two memory processes; one of short duration and the other of much longer duration. Yet it does not necessarily suggest that memories are stored in the hippocampus or the temporal lobes. The question of where memories are stored has been an important one, and despite many attempts, we still cannot specify the locus of memory storage in the brain. As you will see, however, the search for a single precise region where memories are stored may not be the most fruitful focus of research on this important question.

The localization of memory traces or *engrams* was one of Karl Lashley's major pursuits during his productive career in the first half of this century. Using the lesion and ablation techniques, Lashley systematically explored the effects of lesions in sensory, motor, and association areas of the cerebral cortex in animals on a variety of learning tasks such as sensory discrimination problems, maze problems, and Thorndike's latch box task. His work led to the formulation of the *principle of equipotentiality* and the *principle of mass action.*

The principle of equipotentiality suggested that, within limits, regions of the cerebral cortex had an equal potential with respect to the storage or location of memory. In other words, memories were not stored in a single place in the cerebral cortex because damage to specific and limited regions of cortex did not eliminate memories for various tasks or because animals could easily be retained if a deficit was produced by the lesion. The law of mass action suggested that it was the *amount* of cortex removed, not which area was removed, that was the critical factor in determining the severity of a deficit in performance. Thus the more cortex destroyed by a lesion, the greater the deficit in a learned habit. Lashley noted the following in a classic theoretical paper titled "In Search of the Engram" (1950):

> It is not possible to demonstrate the isolated localization of memory traces anywhere within the nervous system. Limited regions may be essential for learning or retention of a particular activity, but within such regions the parts are functionally equivalent. The engram is represented throughout the region. . . . The equivalence of different regions of the cortex for retention of memories points to multiple representation.

The statements Lashley made about memory storage more than two decades ago are still useful today. Most research on memory suggests that memories are not well localized in the brain and that the ability to remember a specific experience may involve a significant portion of the entire nervous system.

Although we cannot say that a memory is stored in a specific place in the brain, there is evidence that the cerebral hemispheres play a critical role in memory storage, especially in higher animals. (For example, see the discussion of split-brain experiments in Chapter 3.)

If the corpus callosum is severed, each hemisphere seems capable of learning and memory storage independently of the other. This *"split-brain" technique,* developed and explored in large part by Sperry (1961) and his students and colleagues, involves the severing of the major fiber systems that interconnect the two cerebral hemispheres. (See box fig. 13.3.) This procedure usually severs the large corpus callosum, which connects the two cerebral hemispheres to each other, as well as a number of smaller junctions. If the optic chiasm is severed in addition, then, as you will recall, visual input from the right eye is restricted to the right cerebral hemisphere, while input from the left eye goes only to the left cerebral hemisphere. Using this preparation, Sperry and others have demonstrated that if animals are taught a visual task with one eye covered they will be unable to perform the task if the trained eye is then covered while the opposite eye is uncovered. Even more intriguing is the fact that animals can be trained to learn two different tasks, one with each eye, without one side of the brain knowing what the other is doing. It is almost as if there were two separate brains, each of which learns and remembers independently of the other. Using a different technique, the ability of one cerebral hemisphere to acquire and remember information independently has also been verified. This method, termed *spreading depression,* is described in box 13.3.

Despite evidence that under most circumstances memories are not stored in a single, easily specified area in the brain, a great many research findings indicate that certain structures or circuits in the brain may be critical for some kinds of learning. Earlier we noted that electrical stimulation of certain areas in the brain, for example, can disrupt STM or LTM. Specific sensory areas of the cerebral cortex are often necessary for animals to be able to perform sensory discrimination problems, but removal of these areas seems to impair an animal's ability to receive sensory information rather than impair its ability to learn or remember. Unless their visual cortex is intact, rats are unable to learn complicated visual discrimination problems. Similarly, the ability to perform complex auditory discrimination tasks will be impaired by removal of the primary auditory cortex. In humans, complete blindness or deafness results if these sensory areas of the cerebral cortex are removed. However, when certain other areas of the brain are destroyed, there do appear to be effects on learning and memory that cannot be ascribed simply to deficits in the animals' ability to perceive the stimuli used in the learning task. Perhaps one of the most well known effects occurs after removal of the frontal cortex or certain areas to which it is connected. Specifically, removal of frontal cortex in many animals, such as dogs and monkeys, seems to impair the ability of these organisms to perform delayed-response problems.

Recall that in a delayed-response problem, the experimental animal is confronted with a set of several objects on a tray. The experimenter hides a raisin or other reward under one of the objects while the animal watches. A screen is then lowered in front of the objects, and during this delay interval, the animal must remember which object was baited. After the delay, the screen is raised and the animal responds by lifting the correct object and retrieving the reward. In most cases, monkeys are unable to perform this delayed-response problem if their frontal cortex has been removed, which suggests that the frontal cortex and certain other areas to which it is connected may be critical for this type of STM (Jacobsen, 1935). As we noted earlier, the activity of neurons in frontal cortex and certain other areas is also altered during the performance of delayed response problems in monkeys. This result provides additional evidence that the frontal region or

Box 13.3
Spreading Depression

"Spreading depression" refers to the fact that nervous tissue can be made functionally inactive by the application of a variety of agents, although the most common agent is some form of salt solution. For example, when a solution of potassium chloride is applied directly to the cerebral cortex, it will produce a profound depression of the tissue for several hours. This method is similar in some ways to the lesion technique, except that the "lesion" may be removed by removing the salt solution, after which the tissue appears to return to its normal functional state. By means of the spreading depression technique, one cerebral hemisphere can be made nonfunctional, while the other is left undisturbed. This method has also been called the "reversible split brain."

The results of one experiment of this type are illustrated in box figure 13.3. Rats were trained to perform an active avoidance task while one cerebral hemisphere was depressed with potassium chloride. In this task, the animals were required to make some response to avoid an electric shock to the feet. After the animals had learned the response, the opposite hemisphere was depressed, and the previously depressed hemisphere was allowed to return to normal. It took the rats approximately the same number of trials to learn the task the second time, although they had already been thoroughly trained, as shown in the figure. Thus, in the first training session, the right hemisphere was involved in learning and remembering the task while the left hemisphere was depressed. In the second session, the animals showed no evidence of memory because the trained hemisphere was depressed and the right hemisphere had to learn the task as though the animals had never been trained. The spreading depression technique has revealed that some types of training are effective even when both hemispheres are depressed. Similarly, some forms of training may be transferred in the "split-brain" preparation despite the fact that information cannot be transferred to the other hemisphere by way of the corpus callosum. Thus some types of learning and memory do not require a functional cerebral cortex; indeed, many kinds of learning can occur in animals whose cortex has been removed (Buchwald and Humphrey, 1973).

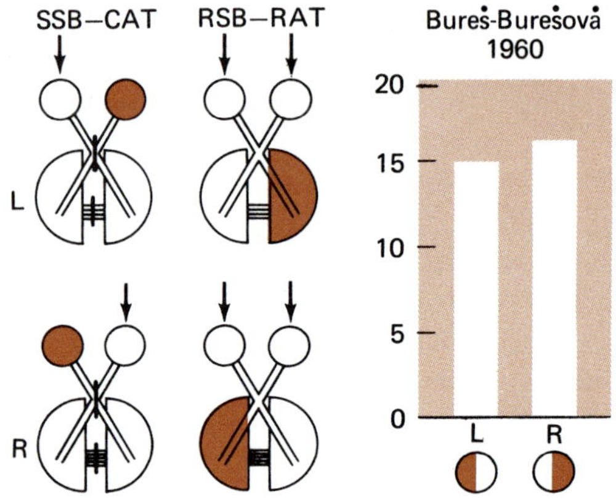

Box Figure 13.3 The figures on the left show the conditions of learning (L) and retention (R) in the surgical split-brain preparation (SSB) and the so-called reversible split-brain preparation (RSB). In the surgical split brain, learning is carried out using one eye while retention is tested using the other. In the reversible split brain, no surgical disconnection is required and both eyes may be used. But because one hemisphere is depressed, information can be learned and processed in the other hemisphere only, making the animal functionally similar to the surgical split-brain preparation. On the right are results of one experiment demonstrating that learning and memory for an avoidance task were localized to a single hemisphere. (From Bures, J., and Buresova, O., "Learning and memory." In *The Neural Control of Behavior,* Whalen, R., Thompson, R. F., Verzeano, M., and Weinberger, N. (Eds.), 1970. Reprinted by permission of Academic Press and author.)

areas to which it is connected may be important in the short-term retention of information required by delayed-response tasks.

Another approach to understanding the possible anatomical correlates of memory storage involves the kinds of anatomical changes that occur when animals are reared in different environments. We now know that differences in the conditions under which animals are reared may produce dramatic differ-

Box 13.4

Different Environments Can Alter the Anatomy of the Brain

Some of the first reports of possible changes in the anatomy of the cerebral cortex as a result of rearing rats in different kinds of environments were those of Krech, Rosenzweig, and Bennet (e.g., 1962). The examples shown in box figure 13.4 are taken from Volkmar and Greenough (1972) who extended the early observations of Krech et al. In these experiments, rats were raised in several different environments beginning at the time of weaning. In one case, rats were reared alone in stark cages and dimly lit surroundings (IC). In another, they were raised in pairs but still in stark, dimly lit cages (SC). In the third case, however, rats were reared in groups in what has been called an "enriched environment" (EC); that is, the environment contained many toys and other devices that could be manipulated, the cages were well lit, the animals were allowed to explore the environment fully, and the toys and other devices were changed regularly. The brains of the animals were then analyzed to determine the amount of branching that was displayed by the dendrites of certain types of neurons in the cerebral cortex. Box figure 13.4 shows the results of this experiment. The dendritic branching of some cortical neurons was more complex in the animals reared in the enriched environment than in those reared in pairs or in isolation. Although at present we cannot say whether these changes reflect mechanisms underlying memory, results such as these suggest the exciting possibility that neuroanatomical changes do occur in the brain as a result of differences in the environments in which animals are reared.

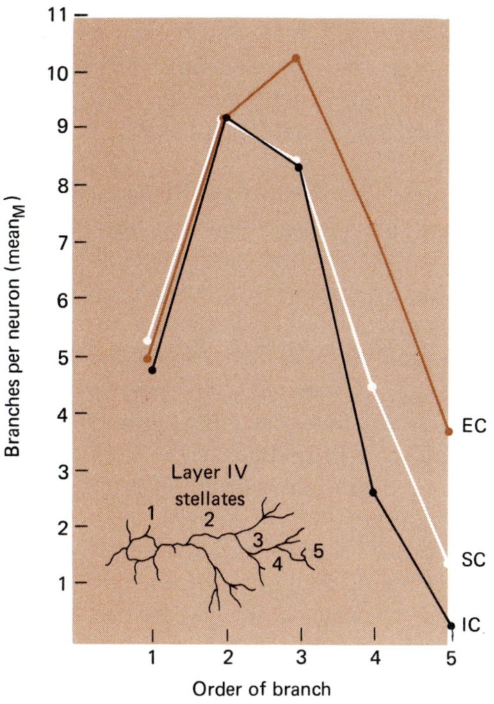

Box Figure 13.4 Branches per layer IV stellate cell of rats in three rearing groups: EC, enriched; SC, social; and IC, isolated. Differences between groups are confined to higher-order (3, 4, 5) branches. The diagram of the cells indicates the scoring procedure. (From Volkmar, F. R., and Greenough, W. T., "Rearing complexity affects branching of dendrites in the visual cortex of the rat," *Science, 176,* pp. 1445–1447, 30 June 1972. Copyright 1972 by the American Association for the Advancement of Science.)

ences in the anatomy of the brain. An experiment of this kind is described in box 13.4.

Simple Systems

Thus far, we have talked about the nature of biological changes in the brains of complicated animals, such as the rat, cat, monkey, and human, during learning and memory storage. Another approach to the study of the biological mechanisms of learning and memory is the *"model systems"* or *"simple systems"* analysis. This approach uses the nervous systems of lower organisms such as an invertebrate or a portion of the nervous system (e.g., the spinal cord) of a higher organism. Because this approach has provided numerous insights, it should be included in any discussion of the biological mechanisms of learning and memory.

Simple systems analysis is based on certain assumptions and requirements. Perhaps the most fundamental one is that the system used as a model must be less complicated than the entire nervous system of higher organisms. The simple system must also be amenable to the kind of analysis that the investigator wishes to use, whether it is anatomical, neurophysiological, biochemical, and so forth. Several examples of model systems or simple systems analyses will demonstrate the usefulness of this approach as well as provide additional information about the underlying assumptions and aspirations of those who use it to understand the mechanisms of learning and memory.

The use of "simple" organisms to study the possible mechanisms of learning and memory has involved every variety of animal imaginable—single-celled organisms as well as more complicated invertebrates. One example of the kind of analysis currently being carried out on single-celled organisms is illustrated in box 13.5. Another example of a model system is a marine invertebrate that lives in warm, coastal tidal waters and can often be found washed up on the beach. This organism, the *Aplysia* or sea slug, is capable of several simple forms of learning, including habituation, which we defined previously as a decrease in response to a repetitive stimulus. The Aplysia is especially interesting and useful because its nervous system is relatively uncomplicated, compared to those of most vertebrates, and is made up of separate and readily identified ganglia (small, distinct groups of nerve cells). Many of its nerve cells are so large that they can be seen without the aid of a microscope. Therefore, this organism meets the most significant requirements of a simple system approach to understanding the physiological mechanisms of learning and memory. It is capable of habituation, and because of the relative size and number of neurons in its nervous system, it is considerably more amenable to analysis than are more complicated animals. A schematic diagram of the Aplysia and one of the ganglia comprising its nervous system are shown in figure 13.8.

Over the past several years, Kandel et al. (1970) have been analyzing the cellular mechanisms in the Aplysia that might underlie habituation of the gill-withdrawal reflex—a defensive reflex in which the organism withdraws its gills when they are stimulated. If

Box 13.5

Learning and Memory in a Protozoan

Box figure 13.5 is a schematic drawing of a single-celled organism, *stentor coeruleus*. Although incapable of many complex forms of learning exhibited by higher organisms, this simple creature is capable of habituation.

When the substrate to which the organism is attached is vibrated the animal contracts abruptly to less than one-half its body length. If the stimulus is repeated, say, at one-minute intervals, the strength of contraction wanes, demonstrating marked habituation. Thus the organism "learns to ignore" the vibratory stimulus. The results of a series of experiments in which Wood (1970) delivered vibratory stimuli to these organisms at different rates are shown in the right-hand portion of the figure.

Although this form of learning is present in all higher organisms, at first glance you may see little obvious relationship between habituation in this simple protozoan and more complex organisms. However, the detailed analysis of the physiological mechanisms of habituation that is made possible by using an organism comprised of a single cell may enable us to gain some understanding of the fundamental properties of these mechanisms in higher organisms. In addition, these studies may inspire other lines of investigation into the more general area of how the behavior of higher organisms evolved from lower forms.

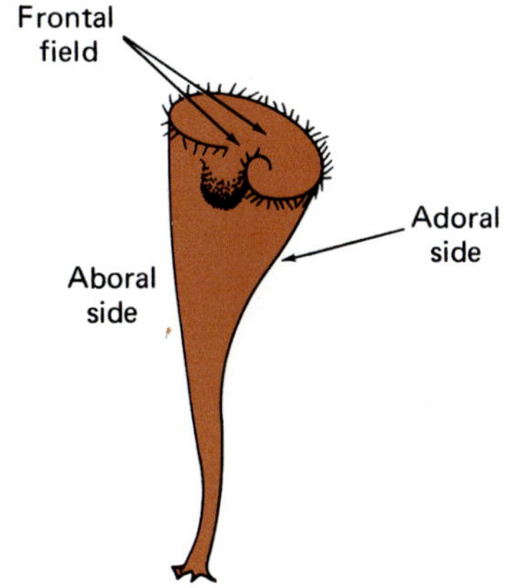

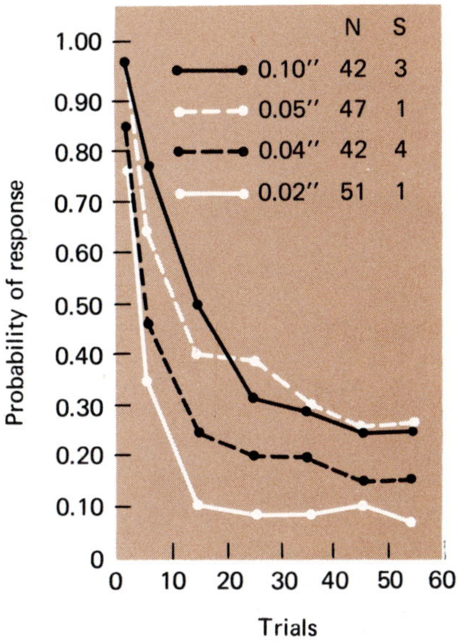

Box Figure 13.5 *Stentor Coeruleus,* a single-celled organism, is shown on the left. When a vibratory stimulus occurs, the organism contracts. On the right are a series of experimental results in which the vibratory stimuli were delivered repetitively at different rates. In each case, as the vibratory stimulus was repeated, a decrease in the probability of contraction occurred, thus illustrating habituation, one of the simplest forms of learning. (From Wood, D. C., "Generalization of habituation between different receptor surfaces of Stentor," *Physiology and Behavior, 9,* 1972, pp. 161–165. Reprinted by permission. Wood, D. C., "Parametric studies of the response decrement produced by mechanical stimuli in the protozoan, Stentor coeruleus," *Journal of Neurobiology, 1,* 1970, pp. 345–360. Reprinted by permission of Wiley-Interscience, a division of John Wiley & Sons, Inc.)

the gills are stimulated repetitively, they demonstrate marked habituation. Kandel and his associates have been able to isolate the most important neurons that produce this reflex behavior and, by a variety of neurophysiological techniques, have shown that habituation of the gill-withdrawal reflex is caused by a decrease in the effectiveness of certain excitatory synapses between the sensory nerve fibers which carry information into the nervous system and motor nerve cells that activate the gills to produce withdrawal.

An example of habituation of the gill-withdrawal reflex is shown in figure 13.9. This example is especially interesting because, in this experiment (Carew, Pinsker, and Kandel, 1972), habituation training was carried out for five days and the animals were maintained and tested for many days after the original training sessions. Note that each day, the strength of the gill-withdrawal reflex decreased as the stimulus (a jet of water applied near the gill) was repeated. But, even more important with each day's training the gill-withdrawal reflex habituated more rapidly and to a greater extent. After twelve days, this savings of habituation training, or "memory" of habituation, was still present. There

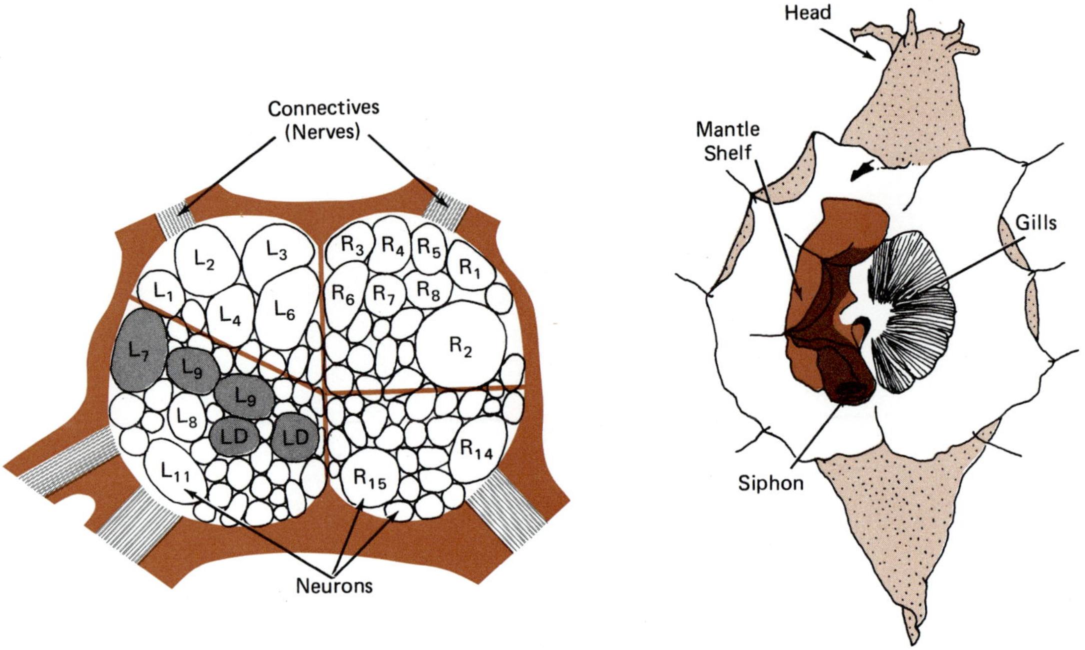

Figure 13.8 A schematic drawing of the *Aplysia* (left) and one of the ganglia that make up its nervous system (right). Some of the cells have been identified and numbered (LI, RI, LD, etc.) by investigators working on this organism. (From Kandel, E. R., Castellucci, V., Pinsker, H., and Kupfermann, I., "The role of synaptic plasticity in the short-term modification of behaviour." In Horn, G., and Hinde, R. A. (Eds.), *Short-term Changes in Neural Activity and Behaviour.* Reprinted by permission of University Press, London.)

was even evidence of some memory for original training twenty-six days after the initial learning, spanning a significant portion of this organism's lifetime. The fact that the effects of training were evident for an extended period demonstrates a clear memory-like process in this organism. After extended analysis of the neuronal processes that are at work in this memory-like phenomenon, these investigators may find some clue about the kinds of processes that are involved in memory storage in higher organisms.

A recent series of experiments suggests that a close relative of the Aplysia, the *Pleurobranchea,* may be capable of classical and instrumental conditioning (Mpitsos and Davis, 1973). An analysis of the neuronal processes involved in these phenomena may also provide important insights into the kinds of processes that mediate these forms of learning in higher organisms.

Literally hundreds of simple systems are currently being studied, not only in relation to the processes of learning and memory, but to many other physiological, biochemical, and behavioral processes as well. The ultimate hope in all of this work is that the knowledge gained from these simple systems approaches will help us explore and understand the biological substrates of learning and memory in all organisms, including one of the most complicated—ourselves.

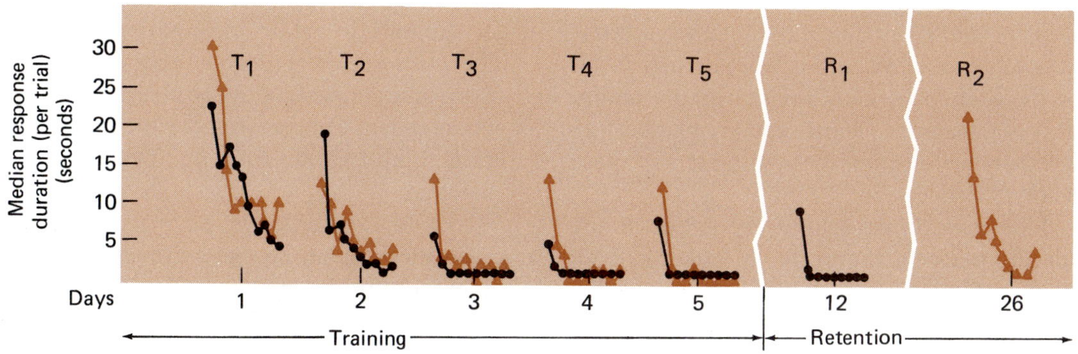

Figure 13.9 Habituation of the gill-withdrawal reflex in *Aplysia.* Animals were given habituation training, consisting of repeated tactile stimulation of the gills, for five consecutive days (T1, T2, etc.) and were tested for retention 12 (R1) and 26 (R2) days later. (From Carew, T. J., Pinsker, H. M., and Kandel, E. R., "Long-term habituation of a defensive withdrawal reflex in Aplysia," *Science, 175,* pp. 451–454. Copyright 1972 by the American Association for the Advancement of Science.)

Summary

Because learning and remembering are fundamental processes that allow organisms to adapt to their environments, the attempt to understand the biological mechanisms which allow us to learn and remember information is one of the greatest and most fascinating frontiers of science.

We know that memory storage is a time-dependent process. The existence of retroactive interference and retrograde amnesia both suggest that for some period of time after learning, memory is labile and susceptible to interference. The consolidation theory of memory is based on this information and its fundamental tenet is that memory takes time to become permanently stored in the brain, and this is termed the consolidation of memory. Head injury, electroconvulsive shock, direct electrical stimulation of the brain, and a variety of other experimental treatments may disrupt the consolidation of memory during this labile period. In addition, a variety of drugs may also alter the storage of memory, if administered during or shortly after learning. Low doses of convulsant drugs, for example, seem to facilitate memory storage, while other drugs, such as anticholinergic agents may disrupt the memory storage process. Learning in a particular drug state may also affect later recall of information if the subject is in a different state when recall is attempted, a phenomenon termed state-dependent learning. Although we do not know how memories are stored, there is evidence that learning and memory may involve alterations in certain macromolecules such as RNA and brain protein. Drugs that inhibit the synthesis of RNA or proteins in the brain often produce a loss of memory.

All known forms of electrical activity generated by the nervous system can be altered by training, including the electroencephalogram, evoked potentials, and the firing of action potentials by individual neurons in the brain. In addition, many of these changes seem to occur at different times during training, in some instances they may only be transient, and they may not be similar in different areas of the brain. The most significant question yet to be answered is whether any or all of these changes are essential to the ability of organisms to learn and remember or whether they are simply by-products of these or other processes.

Memories do not seem to be stored in any specific place in the brain. It was Lashley's heroic attempt to find the location of the engram that provided us with this important concept. His principle of equipotentiality suggested that, within limits, different regions of the cerebral cortex had equal potential for memory storage. And, in the context of the effects of brain damage on memory, his principle of mass action suggested that under most conditions, the amount of cerebral cortex destroyed in an experimental animal was more important than which area was destroyed.

Despite the fact that we cannot specify a given locus for memory storage, there is evidence that certain areas of the brain are especially important in specific types of learning or memory. The hippocampus in humans seems to be an important structure for the transfer of information from STM to LTM. The frontal cortex seems to be important for animals to retain information in STM. The corpus callosum and other bundles of fibers interconnecting the two cerebral hemispheres seem to be critical for the transfer of learned information from one hemisphere to the other.

In addition, different environmental circumstances in an animal's life may lead to differences in the anatomy of its brain. Rats reared in an enriched environment, for example, have cells in the cerebral cortex that are more complex in their dendritic branching properties than do rats reared in relatively impoverished environments.

Many investigators use a "simple systems" approach to exploring the biological processes underlying learning and memory. In this approach, simple organisms such as protozoans or other invertebrates, or isolated portions of the nervous systems of higher organisms, such as the isolated spinal cord, are used. By using simple systems to analyze the cellular processes involved in learning, scientists hope to gain insight into the mechanisms that underlie learning and memory in more complicated systems, such as man.

Harry Helson (1902-   ) For many years, Helson contributed importantly to both research and theory in psychology. Among his best-known contributions is his adaptation level theory, important for our current understanding and conceptualization of motivational and behavioral processes.

Walter B. Cannon (1871-1945) Cannon was an outstanding neurophysicist. His work on the biological mechanisms of behavior contributed enormously to our understanding of peripheral and central neural processes in motivation and in emotional behavior.

Abraham P. Maslow (1908-1970) Maslow was one of the principle figures in humanistic psychology. His research in personality and motivational processes spanned many years. Perhaps best known for his hierarchical theory of human motives and his contribution to the development of the concept of self-actualization.

Hans Selye (1907-   ) Eminent physician and neuroscientist. Selye is well known for his work on the hypothalamic-pituitary-adrenal axis. He also developed the concept of the General Adaptation Syndrome in response to stress.

David McClelland (1917-   ) Over the many years, McClelland has made significant contributions, both in terms of research and theory, to the areas of social psychology, personality, and motivation. His work on achievement motivation has won international recognition.

Section

6

Consciousness, Motives, and Emotions

14

States of Consciousness

The influence of states of consciousness on our behavior is so profound, and yet so much a part of our daily lives, that we simply take the different states of consciousness for granted. However, when we consider how much our behavior depends on whether we are awake or asleep, alert or drowsy, we realize immediately that these states of consciousness influence nearly everything we do and feel. This chapter describes some of the states of consciousness that pervade the lives of humans and other animals.

The alternation of sleep and wakefulness—two of the most obvious and profound categories of states of consciousness—is an example of a *circadian rhythm* or twenty-four-hour cycle. Most behavior of humans and other animals shows the presence of circadian rhythms. Not only sleep and wakefulness, but other activities as well, occur in definite cycles, which may be generally referred to as *biological rhythms.* Figure 14.1 illustrates the rhythmic behavior of two rats (Richter, 1967) that were monitored for two months. The behavior in this case was spontaneous running activity. Note that one animal began running every day at 6:00 P.M., the exact time when the lights were turned off in its living quarters. Although the other animal began running somewhat later, it also started at approximately the same time each day (about 8:00 P.M.). Your own experience will indicate that the sleep-wakefulness cycle in humans shows the same twenty-four-hour periodicity. Interestingly, if rats are completely blinded, so that they cannot determine whether lights are on or off, the circadian rhythm still occurs. However, figure 14.2 shows that under this *free-running* condition, the cycle begins a little later with the passage of each twenty-four hours at an average rate of about twenty minutes per day. Therefore, these rhythms, although they are often tied to external cues such as the light-dark cycle, are not entirely dependent on external control and may occur

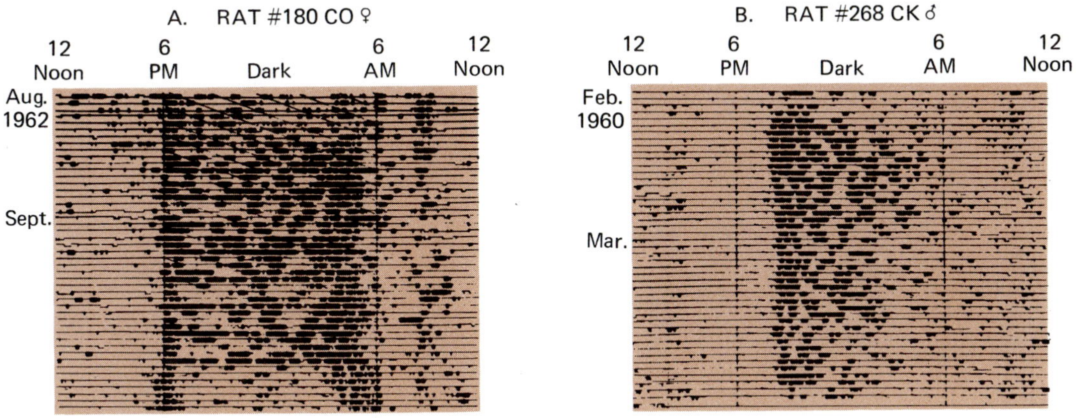

Figure 14.1 The distribution of activity for two rats monitored for forty-seven days. Both animals show spontaneous running activity at specific times each day. The dates are shown at the left of each figure. Darkness occurred between 6 P.M. and 6 A.M. each day. Running activity is indicated by the darkened lines. (From Curt P. Richter, "Sleep and activity: Their relation to the 24-hour clock," in *Sleep and Altered States of Consciousness*. Copyright Association for Research in Nervous and Mental Disease, New York.)

in the absence of external environmental events, as was the case for the blinded rats. This suggests that circadian rhythms may be produced and controlled by cyclic neural activity in the brain. Neurons in the nervous systems of some organisms have indeed been shown to have the remarkable property of circadian periodicity (see box 14.1). As you will see, sleep and wakefulness are also controlled by the brain, and although states of consciousness are often tied to external environmental events, such as light and darkness, the mechanisms of sleep and wakefulness are not solely dependent on such environmental cues.

The circadian rhythms of human and animal behavior can be disrupted by altering the normal light-dark cycle. In humans, sudden alteration of the "circadian clock" by changing the onset of light and dark during the normal twenty-four-hour day can have significant effects on behavior and mood. If you have traveled to a different time zone, you have experienced the effects of having your circadian clock disrupted. It may take a person days or weeks to readjust to a new time zone, during which he may experience fatigue, changes in mood, and other symptoms of "traveler's fatigue," or "jet lag."

One question that has intrigued scientists for many years is whether man is capable of adjusting to a regular sleep-wakefulness cycle that is substantially different from the normal circadian rhythm. Recent experiments suggest that it is possible for man to function well on a bicircadian or forty-eight-hour sleep-wakefulness cycle. In one experiment, two young male volunteers agreed to live in a cave for several months so that the onset of light and darkness could be completely controlled (Jouvet et al., 1974). Initially, they were studied in a free-running condition in which no light-dark cycle was established. Under these circumstances, one volunteer slowly altered his sleep-wakefulness cycle to a bicircadian rhythm (48 hours), in which he spent

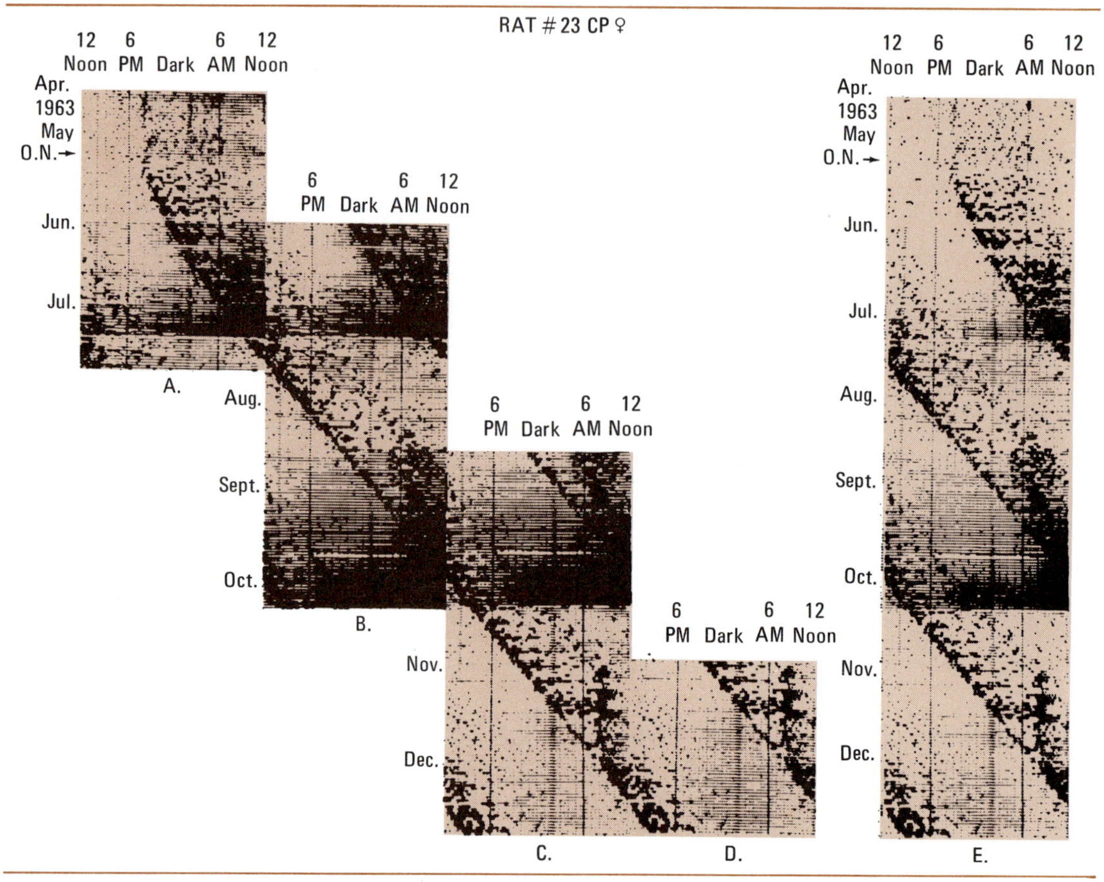

Figure 14.2 The distribution of a rat's spontaneous running activity for approximately seven months after it was blinded (indicated by O. N., to the left of the chart). The months are indicated to the left of each chart. Running activity is indicated by the darkened lines. (From Curt P. Richter, "Sleep and activity: Their relation to the 24-hour clock," in *Sleep and Altered States of Consciousness.* Copyright Association for Research in Nervous and Mental Disease, New York.)

approximately thirty-four hours awake, and fourteen hours sleeping. He maintained this sleep-wakefulness cycle for only nine cycles under the free-running condition, however. The other volunteer did not demonstrate this rhythm under these conditions. However when a light-dark cycle of thirty-four hours of light and fourteen hours of darkness was initiated, both volunteers were able not only to adapt to this bicircadian cycle, but to maintain it for two months without any obvious physiological or psychological problems. Thus man may be capable of living and functioning in a forty-eight-hour day! An interesting aspect of this experiment was that the forty-eight-hour day established by these individuals felt subjectively like a twenty-four-hour day, despite the fact that it was actually twice the length of their normal circadian light-dark cycle of twenty-four hours.

Box 14.1

The Pacemaker Neuron

The graphs in box figure 14.1 illustrate the activity of a single nerve cell recorded from the nervous system of the sea slug, *Aplysia.* In this experiment the sea slug was removed from its natural environment along coastal tidewaters and was exposed to nine successive days of twelve hours of light and twelve hours of darkness. On the tenth day, one portion of its nervous system was removed, and the activity of a single cell was recorded for forty-eight hours. Note the remarkable increase in activity at the time when the light cycle would normally occur, even during the second day of recording.

This is an example of a "pacemaker neuron." A variety of behaviors in the sea slug may be governed by such neurons, which serve as "internal clocks" to regulate the appearance of circadian rhythms in behavior. Similar neurons have been postulated to exist in the nervous systems of higher organisms, including man.

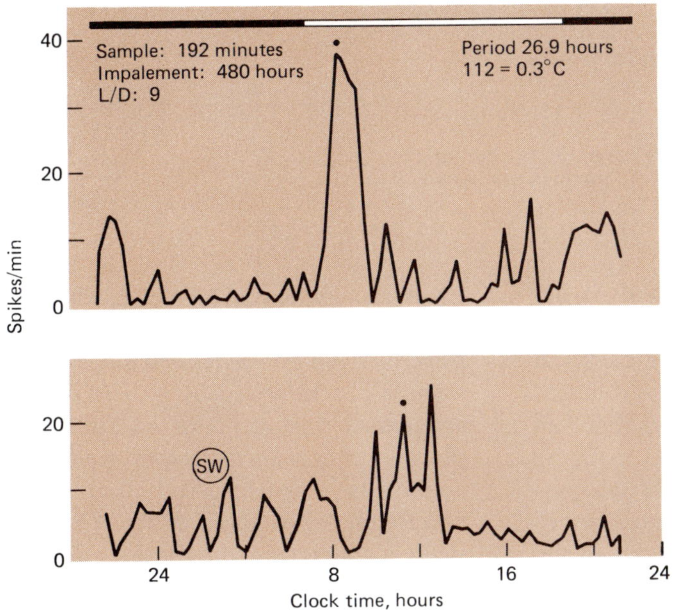

Box Figure 14.1 Circadian rhythm in a single neuron. (From Felix Strumwasser, "The demonstration and manipulation of a circadian rhythm in a single neuron." In *Circadian Clocks*, J. Aschoff (ed.), Amsterdam: ASP Biological and Medical Press, North-Holland Division, 1965, p. 445.)

Sleep and Wakefulness

Stages of Sleep

Although sleep and wakefulness are often viewed as a single continuum, with deep sleep at one end and extreme alertness at the other, both sleep and wakefulness are characterized by distinct stages, or levels of consciousness. The stages of sleep are defined by the electroencephalogram (EEG), the record of spontaneous changes in electrical activity that occur in the brain. The characteristic patterns in the EEG corresponding to various behavioral states ranging from excited to coma and the EEG patterns characteristic of the stages of wakefulness and sleep are illustrated in figures 14.3a and 14.3b respectively.

The EEG represents the activity of millions of neurons. In the awake, alert human sub-

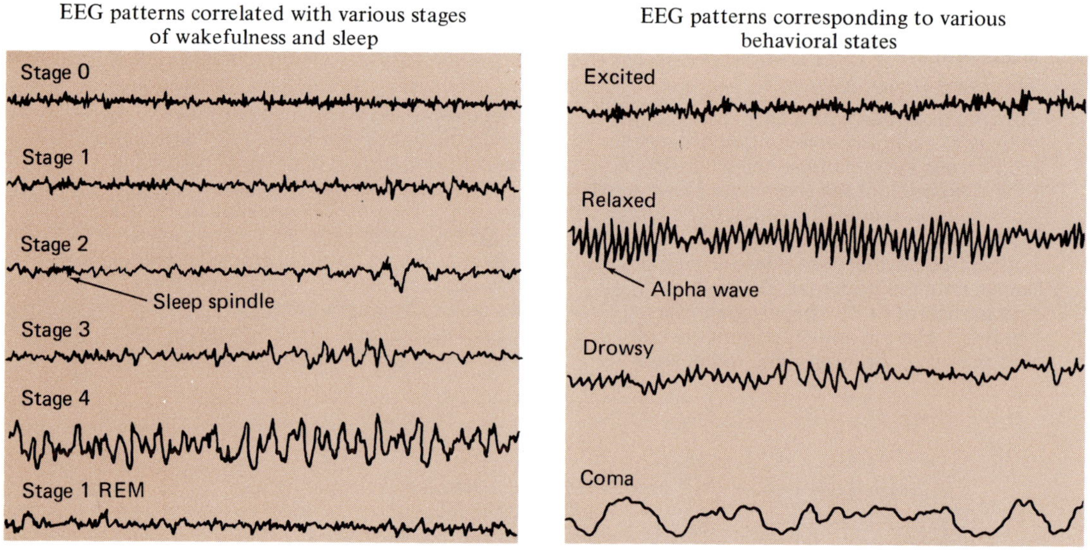

Figure 14.3 Illustrations of the electroencephalogram during different stages of wakefulness and sleep. All tracings are drawn approximately to scale.

ject, the many kinds of electrical activity occurring in the brain produce a "desynchronized" EEG pattern, in which the electrical activity of different neurons occurs at different times, producing small, rapid changes in voltage in the EEG, as illustrated in figure 14.3. As the subject becomes relaxed, perhaps closing his eyes, the EEG becomes synchronized, in other words, alterations in the membrane potentials of many neurons occur together, producing large regular changes in voltage called *alpha waves.* Alpha waves occur at an average frequency of about 10 Hertz (Hz), but may be disrupted if the subject opens his eyes and returns to a state of alertness. This phenomenon is called *alpha blocking* and is part of a complex set of behavioral and physiological responses called the *orienting* reflex, which may be provoked by any novel stimulus.

As the subject lapses into a state of light sleep, the EEG again changes to a pattern of small, rapid changes in voltage, which resembles the waking EEG pattern. This is the first stage of sleep and is termed *stage 1. Stage 2* sleep is characterized by an EEG of similar appearance that contains occasional groups of waves called *sleep spindles,* which are sudden bursts of synchronized electrical activity at a frequency of about 10 to 14 Hz. *Stage 3* sleep is characterized by large, slow changes in voltage (approximately 1 to 3 Hz) that are mixed with some characteristics of stage 2. *Stage 4* is dominated by these large slow waves called *delta waves.* For this reason, stage 4 is often called slow-wave sleep.

The final stage of sleep shown in figure 14.3 is called *stage-1 REM,* or sleep in which rapid eye movements (REMs) occur. During this stage, the EEG resembles stage-1 sleep or wakefulness. For this reason, stage-1 REM sleep is also called *paradoxical sleep.* It is easily distinguished from either stage 1 sleep or wakefulness because of the occurrence of rapid movements of the eyes and because a marked decrease in muscle tone accompanies it. This is the stage of sleep during which most dreaming takes place, and it is discussed in some detail below.

A final state of consciousness that shows a distinct EEG pattern is *coma,* during which the EEG is somewhat irregular and relatively inactive. The complete disappearance of the EEG and cessation of brain function is now the single most important criterion for defining death.

With this valuable and rigorous method for defining stages of sleep, it is possible to study problems such as the depth of the different stages of sleep and the effects of depriving subjects of sleep. Figure 14.4 illustrates the results of an experiment on the depth of sleep during the different stages. The investigators required human subjects to press a key whenever they detected a sound. The sound was presented at a variety of intensities during different stages of sleep, as defined by the EEG, and the subjects' responses were tabulated. Subjects made the most responses to the sound during stage 2 sleep, detected fewer tones during stage 3, and made the least number of responses during stage 4. Thus, based on the criterion of being able to respond to an auditory stimulus, stages 2, 3, and 4 represent successively deeper stages of sleep. Stage-1 REM is also a deep stage of sleep according to this criterion because the subjects made approximately the same number of responses during stage-1 REM sleep as they did during stage 4 sleep. This is not always the case, however. The depth of stage-1 REM sleep may resemble lighter stages if the arousing stimulus has some special significance to the subject; an important name, for instance (Williams et al., 1966).

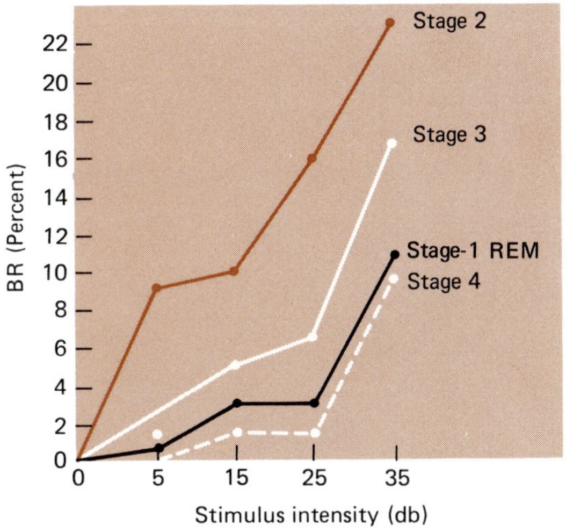

Figure 14.4 The effect of different intensities of auditory stimulation on behavior during four stages of sleep. (From Harold L. Williams, "The problem of defining depth of sleep" in *Sleep and Altered States of Consciousness.* Copyright Association for Research in Nervous and Mental Disease, New York.)

We spend different amounts of time in each stage of sleep. The average young adult, for example, spends about twenty-five percent of his sleep time in stage-1 REM sleep, about fifteen percent in stage 4 sleep, and most of the remainder in stages 2 and 3 (Webb, 1973). Furthermore, the amount of time we spend in each stage of sleep will vary, depending on our age. Newborn infants spend between fifty and eighty percent of their sleep time in stage-1 REM sleep, while individuals who are over thirty spend progressively less time in stage-1 REM and stage 4 sleep.

The occurrence of the different stages of sleep during the night is not random. Different stages occur in different amounts over the course of a night's sleep, and stage-1 REM occurs in definite cycles. Box 14.2 illustrates some of the patterns of sleep that occur over the course of a typical, uninterrupted night's sleep.

Is Sleep Necessary?

Although some people claim that sleep is a bad and unnecessary habit, it is in fact a bio-

Box 14.2

A Typical Night's Sleep

Box figure 14.2 shows the stages of sleep that occur over a typical six to seven hours of sleep for two different individuals. At the left of each graph are the various stages of sleep, as defined by the EEG, eye movements, and other measures. Both subjects begin in the awake state (A), but rapidly fall asleep, passing progressively from stage 1 to stage 4 sleep. This begins a cycle during which the subjects pass from stage 1 to stage 4 and back again to stage-1 REM (indicated by the solid bars). In both cases, the REM cycle takes about ninety minutes, and is repeated throughout the night until the subjects awaken.

Several consistent features emerge from this kind of analysis of sleep time. For example, most of stage 4 sleep occurs during the first half of the night, while episodes of stage-1 REM occupy more and more time as the night passes. In these subjects, each REM cycle took about ninety minutes, as indicated in the figure by the dotted lines. It is interesting to note that children and adults spend different amounts of time in the different stages of sleep. Furthermore, children generally have shorter REM cycles than adults. In the adult, a single REM cycle takes about ninety minutes; in children, the cycle may last less than sixty minutes. The vertical lines beneath each graph indicate times at which bodily movements occurred; the longer lines indicate major movements, the shorter lines indicate small movements.

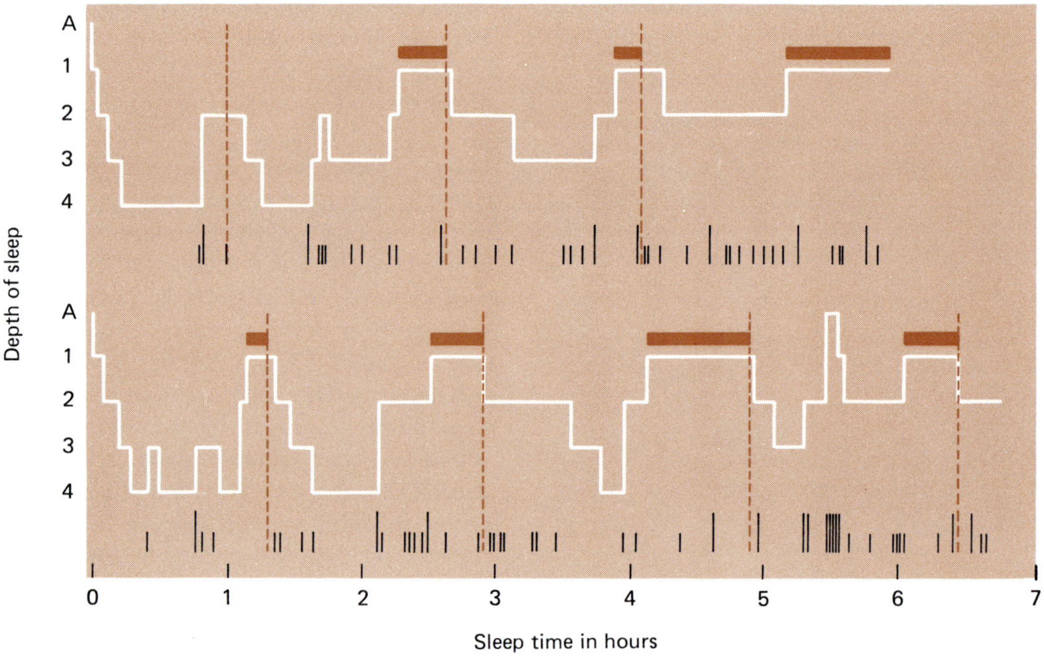

Box Figure 14.2 Cyclic variations in the sleep of two normal adults over a period of six to seven hours. (From "Patterns of dreaming," N. Kleitman. Copyright © 1960 by Scientific American. All rights reserved.)

logical necessity. As all of us have found out at one time or another that being deprived of sleep can produce profound changes in mood and adversely affect our performance in a variety of daily activities. Figure 14.5 illustrates the results of an experiment designed to determine how loss of sleep affects performance. Human subjects were required to perform the simple task of detecting a stimulus that appeared on a screen in front of them and ignoring irrelevant stimuli. After a normal amount of sleep, the subjects made few errors in this task over a ten-minute testing period. However, after thirty-one hours of sleep deprivation, they performed efficiently for about seven minutes and then began making errors. After fifty-four hours of sleep loss, the subjects performed efficiently for only two minutes, and their errors increased dramatically over the remaining eight minutes. Thus efficient performance of even the simplest tasks may be affected by the loss of a single night's sleep. Even relatively short periods without sleep can result in a number of problems in addition to decreased efficiency. Headaches, crankiness, muscular weakness and trembling, backache, overeating, and many other problems may be caused or aggravated by loss of sleep.

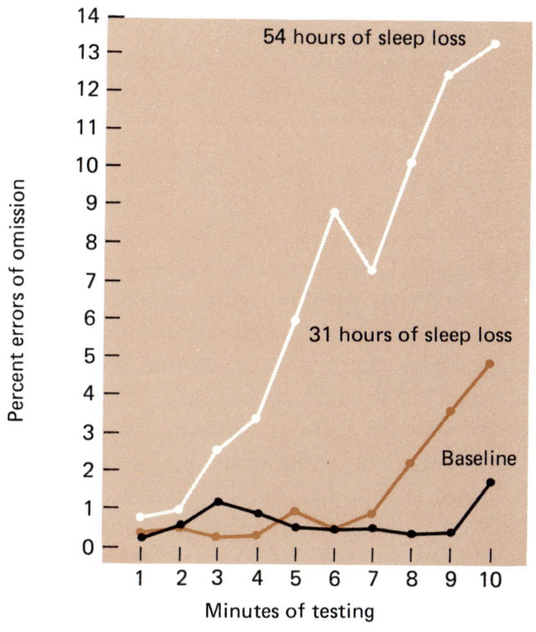

Figure 14.5 The effects of varying amounts of sleep loss on behavioral performance. (From Ardie Lubin, "Performance under sleep loss and fatigue," in *Sleep and Altered States of Consciousness.* Copyright Association for Research in Nervous and Mental Disease, New York.)

Although sleep deprivation produces different symptoms in different individuals to a greater or lesser extent, one universal effect of sleep loss is the need to make up the loss when the individual finally does sleep. If we lose a single night's sleep, for example, we tend to sleep more on subsequent nights to make up this "sleep debt." Experimental subjects deprived of sleep commonly spend a greater than average proportion of their first sleep period in stage 4 sleep. In addition, the amount of stage-1 REM sleep may increase on subsequent nights. However, the most dramatic increase in stage-1 REM sleep is produced when an individual is selectively deprived of stage-1 REM sleep alone. Thus there seems to be a specific need for stage-1 REM sleep, and some investigators believe that in humans this may represent a specific need for dreaming.

Stage-1 REM Sleep

As we mentioned earlier, the term stage-1 REM sleep was coined because of the rapid eye movements (REM) that clearly set it apart from other stages of sleep. Even more intriguing is the fact that much of our dreaming occurs during stage-1 REM sleep (Aserinsky and Kleitman, 1953). We have already noted that stage-1 REM sleep occurs in definite cycles throughout the night. Figure 14.6 illustrates the occurrence of rapid eye movements in a human subject averaged over thirteen successive nights of sleep. Note the

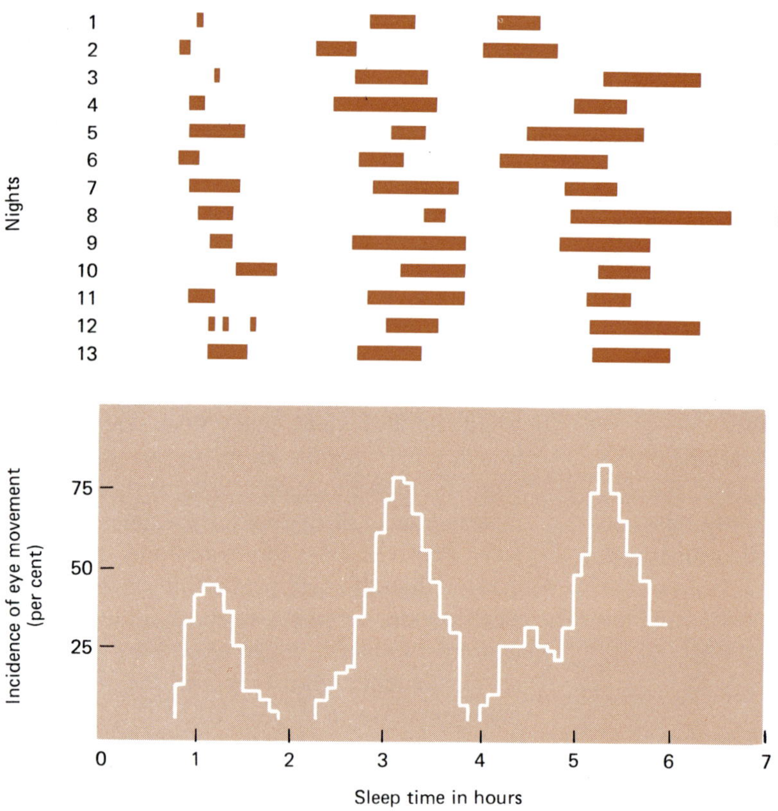

Figure 14.6 Rapid eye movements in a normal adult over a period of thirteen nights. The histogram represents a summary of these movements over the entire period. (From "Patterns of dreaming," N. Kleitman. Copyright © 1960 by Scientific American, Inc. All rights reserved.)

definite cycle of REMs and the increase in the duration of each episode over the course of the night. Man has long been fascinated by dreams, and the discovery of REM sleep has made it possible to study dreams in more detail than ever before.

One interesting fact that has been suggested by studies of REM sleep is that everyone dreams every night. Although some individuals do not remember their dreams and therefore claim they do not dream, the pattern of their rapid eye movements is the one normally found in REM sleep (Goodenough et al., 1959). Furthermore, if these individuals are awakened immediately following an episode of REM sleep, they can often recall their dreams quite well.

Perhaps the most intriguing aspect of REM sleep is the dreams that occur during this stage. What do dreams mean, and how is the content of dreams determined? Freud believed that the content of dreams was significant in the life of the individual and that, if properly interpreted, the subject matter would be found analogous to episodes in real life or would represent the fulfillment of unconscious desires and motives. Thus in his famous book, *The Interpretation of Dreams,* he noted that "there is a psychological technique which makes it possible to interpret dreams, and that on the application of this technique, every dream will reveal itself as a psychological structure, full of significance, and one which may be assigned to a specific place in the psychic activities of the waking state." Freud believed that dreams provided an outlet for sexual, aggressive, and other types of motives which would be unacceptable if acted out in real life. Box 14.3 contains an interesting example of the interpretation of a dream.

More recent attempts to determine the nature of dreams have shown that, on occasion, external stimuli which impinge on a sleeping subject may be incorporated into his dreams. For example, Dement and Wolpert (1958) found that if water was dropped on the skin of dreaming subjects, the subjects would sometimes incorporate the image of water into their dreams in some form, such as a waterfall. When Berger (1963) played names

Box 14.3

The Interpretation of a Dream

The following case history illustrates how the interpretation of dreams can be used in psychotherapy:

A young actor in his early twenties came to analysis because, although he felt he was pleasant to people, he did not get along very well socially and had no close friends. He had had mistresses, but no real love affairs.

In the initial interview it began to appear that, although outwardly always a gentleman and good-natured, he was condescending and scornful toward people, and was a skillful practitioner of sly, undermining wit. He felt [he was] far above the common male standards in his "considerateness" toward women, who nevertheless always turned out . . . to be difficult, rejecting, or inadequate for him. He spoke of a current sexually unconsummated attachment for an unhappily married young woman about whom he felt "very concerned." Speaking of her gave him even more surprise and confusion [because] his concern appeared . . . to refute the idea of himself as distant and disdainful, which I had tentatively proposed. He was asked if he could recall any dreams, and he said at once that he had had one just before coming to this first session.

> *"I am seated on a grassy hillside with Roberta. On the slope below us I see twenty or thirty people. It's a pleasant, warm day and everyone seems to be enjoying himself, strolling around, playing and talking. The girl is someone of 'noble birth.' (She's a European girl whom I really tried to cultivate, but with little success.) I see a bird approaching. It hovers in midair directly above the group of people below us and, because of our elevation, it is just at my eye level.* The bird has a cold, cruel, inhuman eye that frightens me. *I think that its intention is to attack Roberta, not by moving, but by becoming even more vivid and* frightening. *So I jump to my feet, seize some stones, and begin throwing them at the bird to make it go away, but I don't think it's frightened. I think it stays, but at this moment I awoke."*

He was puzzled by the dream, and particularly by the bird. He tried to connect the dream with his "concern" for the unhappily married woman with whom, at the moment, he was involved. The bird, he felt, represented some danger to this young woman, and his fear in the dream he ascribed to his protectiveness toward her.

The interpretive hypothesis was offered that the bird was not an outside force from which he was trying to protect her, but symbolized *an aspect of his own personality,* an attribute that it frightened him to observe. Perhaps he was something of a "bird of prey," like any of the wolfish, ordinary men whom he scorned! He considered this possibility and was able to see some relevance in his immediate situation.

Then he suddenly remembered an involvement with a girl about two years earlier. "I became engaged to her just . . . to get what I wanted. Of course, this created a hell of a lot of anxiety." The possibility of danger then from that young girl's family, and in the present situation from the woman's husband, were realistic sources of fear. Anxiety, however, could be attributed to a different and additional jeopardy—the undermining of his picture of himself: the dream threatened to expose to him that he was not one of God's noblemen, a protector of women, above the common crowd, but instead a rather "cold, cruel, inhuman," predatory sort of bird.

(W. Bonime, *The Clinical Use of Dreams,* New York: Basic Books, 1962.)

to dreaming subjects, he found that the names could be incorporated into the subjects' dreams. A familiar name might provoke the appearance of the individual in the dream, or the name might be heard in the dream.

In 1958 Griffith et al. analyzed the dreams of 250 American college students and found that the content of the students' dreams was remarkably similar (see table 14.1). When the dreams of the males and females were compared, some interesting differences emerged as summarized in table 14.1! Griffith and his colleagues also analyzed the dreams of Japanese college students and found that they were similar in content to those of the American students. This suggests that there is some universality of dream content among different cultures.

It is also interesting to note that REM sleep occurs in animals. In fact, much of our knowledge about the neural mechanisms that underlie sleep and wakefulness has come from studies of experimental animals. One wonders whether animals dream in the same sense that humans dream. If rapid eye movements and the electroencephalogram are used as the criteria, many animals do "dream" (see box 14.4).

Processing Information During Sleep

Although our ability to interact with the environment is considerably reduced during sleep, it is not totally absent. A number of experiments has shown that we are able to process sensory information while sleeping and even may be able to perform learned tasks. Furthermore, an enormous amount of anecdotal evidence supports the contention that we can respond to certain environmental events during sleep. The soft cry of an infant, for example, will awaken the new mother, whereas other, louder noises will not. If experimental subjects are instructed to awaken to a specific stimulus such as a name or a

Table 14.1 The content of typical dreams.

Dream	Male %	Female %
Have you ever dreamed of . . . ?	(*N*–134)	(*N*–110)
1. being attacked or pursued	76.6	77.6
2. falling	80.4	85.4
3. trying again and again to do something	67.9	75.0
4. school, teachers, studying	60.4	83.6
5. being frozen with fright	33.0	63.8
6. sexual experiences	92.5	36.2
7. eating delicious food	36.7	67.2
8. falling, with fear	62.4	73.3
9. arriving too late, e.g., missing train	60.4	67.2
10. fire	32.8	50.0
11. swimming	47.0	57.8
12. dead people as though alive	39.6	63.4
13. being locked up	55.2	57.8
14. loved person to be dead	48.5	67.2
15. snakes	43.3	55.2
16. being on verge of falling	51.9	40.3
17. finding money	61.0	50.0
18. failing on examination	34.3	44.0
19. flying or soaring through air	32.3	35.4
20. being smothered, unable to breathe	41.8	47.4
21. falling, without fear	33.1	33.6
22. wild, violent beasts	32.8	26.7
23. being inappropriately dressed	33.8	54.3
24. seeing self as dead	32.8	33.6
25. being nude	47.8	37.1
26. killing someone	38.1	11.2
27. being tied, unable to move	27.6	33.6
28. having superior knowledge or mental ability	27.6	23.3
29. lunatics or insane people	22.4	29.0
30. your teeth falling out	12.7	30.2
31. creatures, part animal, part human	18.7	10.3
32. being buried alive	34.9	14.7
33. seeing self in mirror	8.2	17.2
34. being hanged by neck	4.5	0.9

Source: From R.M. Griffith, O. Miyagi, and A. Tago, "The universality of typical dreams: Japanese vs. Americans," *American Anthropologist*, 60, 1958, p. 1777. Reprinted by permission of the American Anthropological Association from the *American Anthropologist* 60:1777, 1958.

Box 14.4

Do Animals Dream?

We have all watched dogs and cats twitch and yelp during sleep, and most of us assume that the animals are "dreaming." The discovery of REM sleep and the physiological correlates used to define it has made it possible to determine how much REM sleep different animals exhibit, despite the fact that they cannot tell us about the content of their dreams. The graph in box figure 14.4 illustrates the approximate percentage of time different animals spend in REM sleep. The data are summarized from Freemon (1972), Snyder (1967), and Williams et al. (1973). Adult humans spend about as much, or more time in REM sleep as any of the other animals, calculated on the basis of percentage of total sleep time. However, the opossum and the cat, for example, sleep more during a twenty-four-hour period than humans do and, therefore, spend a greater total amount of time in REM sleep than do humans (Snyder, 1967).

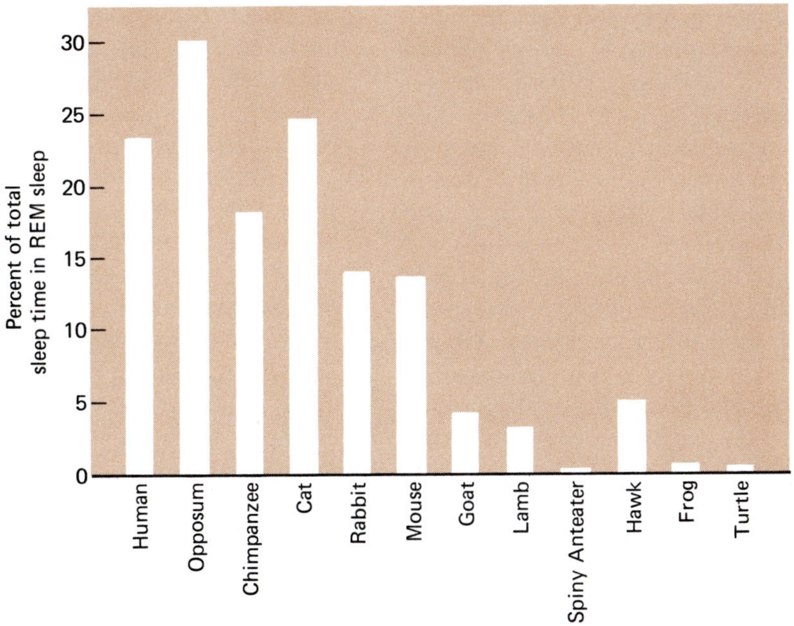

Box Figure 14.4 Percentage of total sleep time that humans and a variety of other animals appear to spend in REM sleep.

sound, they will often be able to do so (Oswald et al., 1960; Wilson and Zung, 1966). Williams et al. (1966) trained individuals to press a switch whenever a tone was sounded. If the switch was not pressed, the subjects would be awakened by loud noises and electric shocks. After training, sleeping subjects were able to press the switch to avoid being awakened. A similar kind of learned response was performed by subjects whenever a light was flashed (Okuma, 1966).

One especially interesting question is whether subjects can learn while sleeping. Industrious businessmen in past decades capitalized on this possibility by selling phonograph records containing lessons in foreign languages and other topics to be learned during sleep. It now appears, however, that subjects cannot learn this kind of material during sleep, and individuals who report they have done so were probably awakened while the record was playing. If novel verbal material is presented only during deep sleep, as defined by the EEG, no learning takes place (Bruce et al., 1970). Our ability to respond to significant environmental events during sleep is frequently better during REM sleep than during non-REM sleep.

Although the evidence suggests that subjects cannot learn significantly while sleeping, it is known that sleep-deprivation can adversely affect memory for previously learned information. For example, Yaroush, Sullivan, and Ekstrand (1972) studied the effects of sleep on memory for verbal material. Two groups of subjects learned a list of word pairs and after a period of time, eight hours, the subjects were tested for their memory of the words. One group of subjects slept during this eight-hour retention interval and the other group carried out normal daytime activities. The sleep group remembered more than the awake group. The traditional interpretation of such findings has been that sleep prevents new learning which might interfere with memory for the word pairs from taking place during the retention interval. Yaroush et al., however, demonstrated that memory over an interval filled mainly with non-REM sleep was better than over an interval consisting mainly of REM sleep. Thus, while memory is better if sleep rather than other activities intervenes between learning and retention, the stage of sleep that intervenes may also be a significant factor in such effects.

There is evidence that our behavior and that of other animals may manifest some kind of fundamental *rest-activity cycle* that is similar in duration and occurrence to the REM sleep cycle. On the basis of Kleitman's (1963) suggestion that the periodic occurrence of REM sleep may represent the operation of a basic rest-activity cycle, Sterman et al. (1972) studied the performance and sleeping habits of cats over extended periods and found that the REM cycle in these animals lasted approximately twenty minutes. Especially intriguing, however, was the fact that the cats' performance during the day showed a subtle cycle of about twenty minutes as well! For example, when the animals were taught to press a bar to obtain food or other reward, there were small fluctuations in the rate or pattern of bar pressing every twenty minutes. These fluctuations suggested that behavioral performance while awake as well as the occurrence of REM sleep might be related to this more basic twenty-minute rest-activity cycle. The suggestion that a similar periodic rest-activity cycle might occur in humans is both plausible and provocative.

Wakefulness

Intuitively at least, we know that there seem to be different stages or levels of arousal or wakefulness. We have already noted in Chapter 12 that individuals can selectively attend to environmental events. In other words, while in the general state called wakefulness, we can selectively process or reject incoming information. In a sense, this process of selective attention corresponds to selective alteration of our state of wakefulness. It is clear, however, that we are sometimes highly excited or aroused without such selective attention, while at other times we are awake but relatively unaroused, and our mental faculties are sluggish. The late Elizabeth Duffy (1972) used the term "activation" to refer to behavioral arousal or intensity and suggested that this construct could "account for the fact that an organism as a whole is sometimes excited, sometimes relaxed, and sometimes in one of a variety of intermediate conditions, even though the various systems of the organism may not be equally activated at a given moment."

Early interest in levels of arousal or "activation" focused on providing an adequate measure of various stages or levels of arousal, such as the relatively clear-cut EEG and other criteria used to define the different stages of sleep. Unfortunately, different levels of arousal did not seem to have correspondingly distinct patterns in the EEG; thus investigators were forced to devise two new strategies for measuring the different degrees of arousal. One strategy was to use some operational situation that could produce adequate differences in level of arousal. For example, performing a simple task was considered less "arousing" than performing a more difficult task. Forced exercise was also used to produce an increase in level of arousal. By defining levels of arousal in terms of these operational criteria, researchers could then relate different degrees of arousal to behavior in a variety of situations.

The second strategy was to use operational situations to define levels of arousal and then attempt to correlate the different levels with some physiological measure. For example, experimenters could be reasonably certain that unavoidable electrical shock would produce an increase in their subjects' level of arousal. Thus, by recording a host of physiological indicators, investigators hoped to obtain a suitable measure for different levels of arousal, such as EEG pattern. Although differences in the EEG did correlate with extremely high and low levels of arousal (relaxed wakefulness is characterized by alpha waves, while excited wakefulness is characterized by desynchronization of the EEG), levels of arousal between these extremes could not be specified adequately by the EEG alone. Other measures were explored at some length, and most of these were correlates of activity in the autonomic nervous system. (For a discussion of the autonomic nervous system, see Chapter 3.) It was noted that increased levels of arousal were often accompanied by activation of the sympathetic division of the autonomic nervous system, which produces dilation of the pupils, an increase in the output of epinephrine from the adrenal glands, an increase in heart rate and activity of the sweat glands, and a decrease in the electrical resistance of the skin. These effects are often accompanied by an increase in muscle tone in the neck and elsewhere. The result of this concerted effort was that although no single measure could accurately define different levels of arousal, many measures, taken simultaneously, could provide an approximate index of different levels of behavioral excitation.

Having found a variety of indicators that could be used to monitor level of arousal, and armed with a number of experimental procedures, such as forced exercise or the threat of electrical shock that would produce variations in arousal, investigators then asked the following question: What is the relation between level of arousal and behavior? Hebb

(1955) attempted to answer this question by suggesting a theoretical relationship between behavioral performance or efficiency and the level of arousal (see fig. 14.7). This relationship can be described as an inverted U-shaped function, in which behavioral performance, or efficiency is poor during low or high levels of arousal, and is best at some intermediate level. Thus there may be an *optimal level of arousal* for optimum behavioral efficiency. It may also be true, however, that the optimal level of arousal varies from one task to the next, and that in some cases, optimal behavioral performance may occur despite large fluctuations in level of arousal. Therefore, even if we have precise knowledge about a subject's level of arousal from moment to moment, we cannot predict in advance the optimal level of arousal necessary for a specific task or activity.

Fiske and Maddi (1961) extended the notion of optimal level of arousal to encompass the entire sleep-wakefulness cycle. They proposed that organisms actively sought the optimal level of arousal and that, in part, the purpose of the behaviors which occur during the entire sleep-wakefulness cycle is to achieve an appropriate level of arousal for each period in this cycle. Thus, they suggested that

> the organism's level of activation will decline when stimulation does not change very much, and when there, also, is no pressing task or strong need which can sustain a high level. In such situations, the organism must maintain activation at the level characteristic for it at that point on its sleep-wakefulness cycle, if it is to remain alert and is to avoid negative or displeasurable feelings. A particularly effective way of maintaining characteristic level of activation is to seek out or produce variation in stimulation. . . . The organism we describe is more than simply reactive: it behaves in such a way that it receives stimulation with impact appropriate for the level of activation required by the particular situation or demanded by its own organic functions (pp. 16–17).

An example of this behavior is exploration of the environment, which is presumably prompted in part by the requirement for an appropriate level of arousal (Berlyne, 1963). Indeed, the evidence suggests that organisms do behave in ways which will achieve an optimal level of arousal in relation to the particular stage of their sleep-wakefulness cycle. If an organism is deprived of sleep or activity, it tends to behave in a way that will compensate for this deprivation. Humans, monkeys, rats, and other animals will explore their environment, manipulate novel objects, and solve puzzles for no reward other than the activity itself. Like sleep, then, arousal or activation has a pervasive influence on behavior, and the sleep-wakefulness cycle is one of the most significant factors that determines how, when, and why we behave as we do.

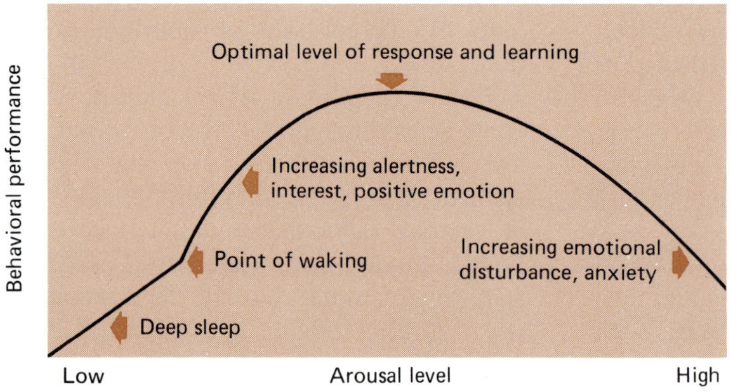

Figure 14.7 The effects of different levels of behavioral arousal on performance. (From D. O. Hebb, "Drives and the CNS [conceptual nervous system]." *Psychological Review*, vol. 62, 1955, pp. 243–254. Copyright 1955 by the American Psychology Association. Reprinted by permission.)

Sleep and Wakefulness, Active or Passive

The evidence we have discussed suggests that sensory stimulation plays an important role in determining whether we sleep or are highly aroused. Some of the earliest theories of sleep and wakefulness maintained that wakefulness was produced by sensory stimulation impinging on our sensory receptors, while sleep was the passive result of a loss of this sensory input. Although this view of the nature of sleep and wakefulness seemed reasonable, and there was little question that sensory stimulation can awaken us from the deepest sleep, research on the neural mechanisms of sleep and wakefulness has challenged this view. Evidence has now accumulated which suggests that both sleep and wakefulness are actively produced by the brain, rather than being the passive result of the presence or absence of environmental stimulation, although environmental stimulation can significantly affect both states.

The biological mechanisms that underlie sleep and wakefulness are the focus of intense research at the present time. Early in the history of research on the mechanisms of sleep and wakefulness, Morruzzi and Magoun (1949) demonstrated that electrical stimulation of the midbrain reticular formation produced the characteristic behavioral and electroencephalographic signs of wakefulness. It was subsequently demonstrated that large bilateral lesions in this region could produce permanent sleep. However, later evidence proved that this region of the brain was not the only area involved in maintaining wakefulness. If lesions were made in two stages, so that the animal could recover in between, even large lesions in the reticular formation did not result in permanent sleep (e.g., Adametz, 1959). Additional evidence suggested that the posterior hypothalamus as well as several other structures might also be involved in maintaining wakefulness (Gellhorn, 1967).

With respect to the onset and maintenance of sleep, the brain's mechanisms seem to be extensive. Figure 14.8 illustrates some of the structures in the brain that have been implicated in the onset, maintenance, and control of sleep. Although a variety of structures has been identified, many of the suggestions about their functions in sleep are

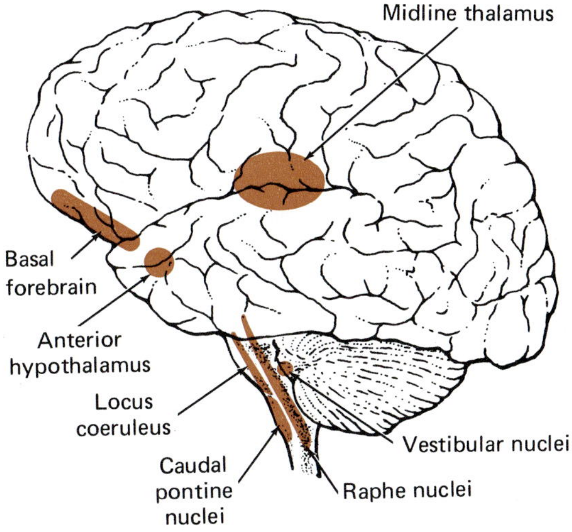

Figure 14.8 Areas of the brain that have been implicated in the onset, maintenance, or regulation of sleep.

speculative. Active research is still being done in this area, and the functions of many of these structures are being vigorously debated. It is also important to note that many of these structures are interconnected with each other and with other areas of the brain, which suggests that complex, interacting circuits are involved in the production and regulation of sleep. The following brief account will provide an overview of the structures and functions that may be involved in sleep.

Raphé nuclei This long group of nuclei runs along the center of the brain stem from the medulla, just above the spinal cord, up to the level of the midbrain reticular formation. The raphé nuclei are currently believed to be involved in the onset of sleep and in the maintenance of slow-wave sleep.

Midline thalamus The midline thalamus, which includes a group of nuclei in the center of the thalamus, may also be involved in the onset of sleep and the maintenance of slow-wave sleep.

Basal forebrain The basal forebrain, which lies at the base of the forebrain, includes the orbital cortex, located above the eyes, and the anterior hypothalamus. This region too may be involved in the onset of sleep and the maintenance of slow-wave sleep.

Caudal pontine nuclei These important nuclei of the reticular formation appear to be involved in the production and onset of REM sleep.

Locus coeruleus This group of nuclei lies along the midline of the pons and may have an important role in regulating the marked muscle relaxation and cortical desynchronization associated with REM sleep and its onset.

Vestibular nuclei The vestibular nuclei may be important in triggering the rapid eye movements as well as the phasic movements of the limbs and body that are characteristic of REM sleep.

This brief overview of some of the structures involved in producing and controlling sleep suggests several basic properties of sleep. First, both sleep and wakefulness are actively produced by the brain, and a number of different areas of the brain may be involved in one or more aspects of a given property of sleep, such as the onset of sleep and the EEGs associated with specific stages of sleep. Second, a fundamental difference may exist between the mechanisms responsible for slow-wave sleep and those responsible for REM sleep. Thus interactions of slow-wave sleep and REM sleep may involve interactions between several different regions of the nervous system.

In addition to these relationships between different nuclei and systems in the brain and stages of sleep, recent studies suggest that sleep and wakefulness may be mediated by systems with significantly different neurochemical characteristics. For example, we said that the raphé nuclei in the brain stem are associated with slow-wave sleep. These nuclei contain high concentrations of the neurotransmitter *serotonin,* and variations in the levels of this transmitter seem to be related to the production of slow-wave sleep. REM sleep appears to involve a combination of neurotransmitter agents, including serotonin and possibly norepinephrine (which is highly concentrated in the locus coeruleus and reticular formation) and acetylcholine. However, the precise roles of these agents are still unknown.

One neurochemical that has been implicated in wakefulness, on the other hand, is norepinephrine. High levels of norepinephrine in the brain have been associated with heightened arousal and can be produced by a variety of agents such as amphetamine and other stimulant drugs. One experiment that demonstrates a relationship between norepinephrine and behavioral arousal is described in box 14.5.

Altered States of Consciousness

Our intuition tells us that there are many different levels of awareness or states of consciousness within the waking state. Similarly, there are many ways in which our level of awareness can be altered. Disease states, or mental disturbance, for example, can often affect consciousness. We also know that drugs can alter our state of consciousness. Some of the effects of psychoactive drugs on mood and consciousness were reviewed in Chapter 5. Other methods for achieving alterations in awareness include hypnosis and meditation, which, at first glance, seem to produce some alteration in our state of consciousness and, indeed, are often used to achieve this end. In this section, we will briefly discuss some of these altered states of consciousness and some of the research that has been done to determine whether these states are in fact different from the levels of sleep and wakefulness that we have already described.

Disorders of Sleep and Wakefulness

Disorders of sleep and wakefulness not only disrupt the normal circadian rhythm and the pattern of sleeping and waking behavior, but dramatically affect the nature of consciousness and behavior as well. Understanding the nature of these disturbances is important from a practical standpoint because many individuals suffer from problems of sleep and wakefulness. It is also important from a theoretical standpoint because understanding disorders of sleep and wakefulness may provide insight into understanding the mechanisms of these states in the normal individual.

Disorders of sleep and wakefulness can be classified into several general categories. Three of these categories are: *insomnia,* in which affected individuals complain of too little sleep or an inability to obtain sound sleep; *hypersomnia,* characterized by attacks of sleepiness that sometimes are irresistible; and *parasomnia,* in which activity that is similar in some respects to waking behavior appears during sleep (Williams and Karacan, 1973). The causes of far too many of these disorders are unknown, and methods of treatment have yet to be determined.

Insomnia

Insomnia—the most common form of sleep disturbance—can be characterized in a number of ways; for instance, an inability to fall asleep, awakening during the night, or awakening early in the morning. The disorder sometimes accompanies aging and consists of a relative decrease in total sleep time with age. In other instances, however, insomnia may be related to some other disorder such as depression. Depressed patients sleep less than normal individuals do and show a particular decrease in the amount of stage 2 sleep. Insomnia is also a common early sign of developing psychosis.

Some individuals who complain bitterly about being unable to sleep do not, according to their EEGs, actually suffer marked disturbances in amount of sleep time or in the pattern of sleep. *Neurasthenic insomnia,* for instance, is characterized by subjective reports of poor sleep, an inability to fall asleep for a long time after going to bed, and many spontaneous awakenings during sleep. However, objective records of sleep onset time, total sleep time, distribution of different stages of sleep, and number of awakenings indicate that the neurasthenic insomniac's problem is not nearly as severe as his subjective reports would indicate. Apparently, this "subjective"

Box 14.5

Norepinephrine and Behavioral Arousal

For many years, scientists suspected that the level of norepinephrine in the brain—one of the biogenic amines and suspected to be a transmitter substance in the central nervous system—partly determined an organism's behavioral arousal and reactivity. Many stimulant drugs that produce hyperactivity, such as amphetamine, were known to release norepinephrine from certain nerve cells in the brain, whereas many depressant drugs decreased the release of this substance in the brain. However, many researchers injected norepinephrine directly into the brains of rats and found that it usually produced depression and lethargy, not hyperexcitability, as had been theoretically proposed. In the experimental situation illustrated in box figure 14.5, Segal and Mandell (1970) were able to demonstrate that norepinephrine could produce a hyperactive animal. They measured behavioral activity in the special apparatus shown on the left, which could detect the rat's movement. However, instead of injecting norepinephrine directly into the brain in one large injection, they used a slow pump, which enabled them to infuse the compound into the brain (inject continuously) over a much longer period of time. The result, as you can see in the graph, was dramatic. Infusion of norepinephrine into the brain over an extended period of time produced hyperexcitability and greatly increased the behavioral activity of these animals. Thus the hypothesis that norepinephrine might be involved in behavioral arousal was supported.

The key to this experiment was the infusion of norepinephrine over a long period of time. Earlier attempts to prove that norepinephrine was excitatory for behavior had relied on single large injections. As a result, the concentration of norepinephrine was apparently much larger than would normally exist, and thus it produced depression—the opposite of its effect in high, but normal physiological doses. Segal and Mandell managed to build up a concentration that was presumably more similar to concentrations under normal conditions, and hyperexcitability resulted.

This research is only one of many examples in which a particular transmitter substance or class of transmitter substances has been implicated in controlling specific types of behavior.

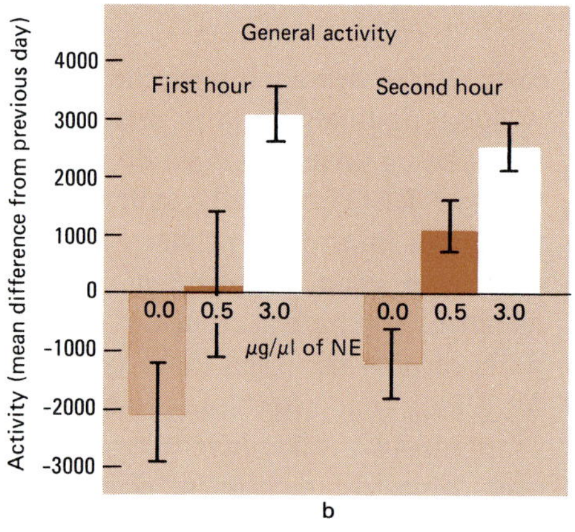

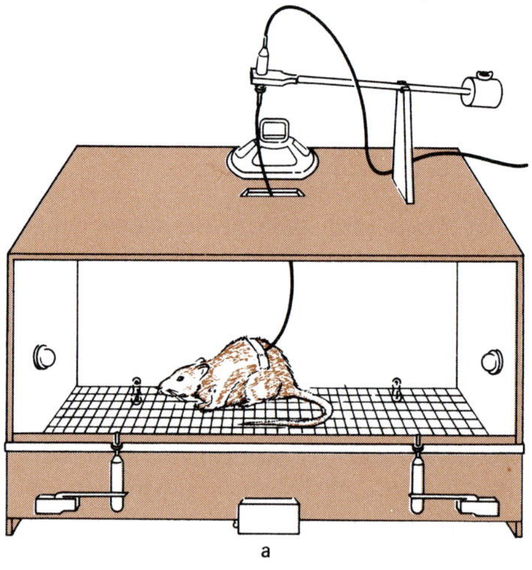

Box Figure 14.5 (a) Shows the experimental setup and figure. (b) Shows the effects of infused norepinephrine and saline on locomotor activity during a two-hour test period.

insomnia is produced by exaggerated worry about spontaneous awakenings (which normal individuals forget about) and about the somewhat longer than normal time it takes for these individuals to fall asleep.

Situational insomnia on the other hand, is experienced by everyone at one time or another. The symptoms of this disorder are produced by acute stress such as an emotionally disturbing event. It is interesting that situational insomnia is one of the few insomnias that can be treated effectively by hypnotic drugs ("sleeping pills").

Many forms of insomnia are aggravated rather than alleviated by sleeping pills. Many barbiturates, for example, which are frequently the main ingredient in sleeping tablets, alter the pattern of sleep by reducing the percentage of time spent in stage-1 REM sleep. Individuals who take barbiturates for extended periods may experience a *drug dependency insomnia* in which higher and higher doses become necessary to produce sleep. Because of the reduction in stage-1 REM sleep produced by the medication, withdrawal produces a rebound increase in stage-1 REM sleep, which is often accompanied by nightmares and insomnia! Alcohol appears to have a similar suppressive effect on stage-1 REM sleep. Thus, although sleeping pills may help an individual to fall asleep and stay asleep, they can alter the amount of time spent in different stages of sleep and therefore produce side effects that may hinder effective treatment of the insomnia. This is especially relevant to the long-term use of medication for insomnia.

Hypersomnia

Hypersomnia exists in many different varieties. The most powerful hypersomnia, *narcolepsy,* consists of uncontrollable and irresistible attacks of sleep. Individuals afflicted with this disorder may fall asleep at unpredictable times during the day, and the attacks can be precipitated by emotional stress as well as other situations. Narcolepsy is sometimes accompanied by other symptoms, such as *sleep paralysis,* in which the patient awakens from sleep but is unable to move; *cataplexy,* a sudden and marked muscular weakness; and *hypnogogic hallucinations,* auditory and visual hallucinations that occur at the onset of sleep. Other disorders that are not true narcolepsies are often called pseudonarcolepsies or simply "hypersomnias." These conditions can be chronic; for example, an individual may sleep well past noon or take lengthy naps, or he may have acute attacks of sleepiness during normal waking hours. Among the latter conditions are the Kleine-Levin Syndrome and the Pickwickian Syndrome. Both conditions involve attacks of sleep in the daytime, however, Pickwickian Syndrome is often associated with extreme obesity and with difficulty in obtaining adequate oxygen during respiration.

Parasomnia

Somnambulism, or sleepwalking is another interesting sleep disorder. It does not appear to occur during stage-1 REM sleep and is, therefore, not the "acting out of a dream" as legend would have us believe. Sleepwalking occurs primarily during stage 4 sleep, and the sleepwalker cannot remember the incident when he wakes. Although drugs have been used to alleviate sleepwalking, they are largely ineffective.

Other interesting disorders that occur during sleep include *night terrors* and *dream anxiety attacks,* both of which can be called nightmares. Night terrors can be frightening to the parent or other individual who witnesses them because the child who experiences them will awaken screaming and be terrified for up to half an hour. Eventually, the child falls asleep again and does not remember the episode when he awakens. Although one might assume that these attacks occur during stage-1 REM sleep, they actually happen primarily during stage 4 or slow-wave sleep. Fortunately, night terrors usually disappear spontaneously as children grow older. This is also true of other common sleep problems of childhood, such as enuresis (bed-wetting), nightmares (that do occur during stage-1 REM sleep), and somnambulism. Occasionally, however, these disorders occur in adults and can be serious problems for those afflicted with them. Although psychotherapy is probably the most common method of treatment for these disorders, universally effective cures are still not available.

Hypnosis

Many hypnotic-like states have been described in the history of man, but scientific interest in hypnotic phenomena has only been evident during the past one hundred years. Among the earliest investigators of hypnosis was Franz Mesmer, who believed that the hypnotic trance was caused by "animal magnetism," which originated from his own body. Although his theory of *"mesmerism"* was soon discredited, we still do not fully understand the nature of hypnotism nor can we adequately specify what the hypnotic state actually is or how it relates to "normal" states of wakefulness and sleep.

According to Hilgard (1965), the hypnotic state can be defined in terms of seven characteristics. As we will note later, however, one of the most significant questions in research on hypnosis is whether these characteristics in fact define a unique state of consciousness. Hilgard's seven characteristics of the hypnotic state are as follows:

1. *Subsidence of the planning function.* By this Hilgard means that the hypnotized subject does not have the desire to plan and carry out his own actions. Although the subject is still capable of initiating and carrying out such actions, he presumably relinquishes the "planning function" to the hypnotist.

2. *Redistribution of attention.* This characteristic does not suggest that the subject is more attentive, but that his attention is redistributed so it is directed primarily toward the hypnotist rather than toward other environmental events.

3. *Availability of visual memories from the past and heightened ability for production of fantasies.* This characteristic is self-evident. Hypnotists often ask a subject to recall events that occurred when the subject was a certain age. Subjects are also able to experience visual memories, dreams, or hallucinations more easily when hypnotized than when nonhypnotized.

4. *Reduction in reality testing and a tolerance for persistent distortion of reality.* Hypnotized subjects do not "test reality" as they might when in the normal waking state. The hypnotist can suggest distortions of reality and subjects will readily accept them.

5. *Increased suggestibility.* This characteristic is almost synonymous with the hypnotic state itself; in other words, the hypnotized subject will accept suggestions readily from the hypnotist.

6. *Role behavior.* The subject will accept a "role" suggested by the hypnotist and carry out the role enthusiastically.

7. *Amnesia for what transpired during the hypnotic state.* Amnesia commonly accompanies hypnosis, but it is not essential.

Although these seven criteria do not constitute the only definition of the hypnotic state, they do illustrate some of the fascinating experimental and theoretical controversies that have arisen in hypnosis research.

At the very heart of research on hypnosis is the question of whether the hypnotic state is in fact a unique state of consciousness; that is, different from what we might regard as normal wakefulness or sleep. A quotation from a lengthy treatise on hypnosis compiled by Fromm and Shorr (1972) summarizes the current state of affairs in research on the subject: "The hard fact is that, in the last decade of research in hypnosis, all claims made for the unique behavioral and physiological effects of hypnosis have proved unconvincing when subjected to careful experimental scrutiny."

The research to determine whether hypnosis is a unique state of consciousness has been of two major varieties. First, experimenters have tried to show that hypnotized subjects will behave in ways that are not characteristic of nonhypnotized individuals. Second, physiological researchers have attempted to find a unique set of physiological variables that can be used to differentiate the hypnotic state from other waking or sleeping states.

With respect to the experimental results concerning the behavior of hypnotized subjects, there is still great controversy. Despite a large body of evidence which indicates that hypnotized subjects will perform acts that differ from their normal behavior, it is also apparently true that *nonhypnotized* subjects will perform similar acts under appropriate circumstances. Orne (1959), for example showed that nonhypnotized subjects will perform seemingly dangerous acts in the laboratory when told to do so, as will hypnotized subjects. Apparently, subjects tend to obey the demands of the experimental situation whether they are hypnotized or not. Furthermore, it has been shown repeatedly that the experienced hypnotist cannot distinguish between a truly hypnotized subject and one who has merely been asked to "simulate" the condition. In terms of behavior then, nonhypnotized subjects do not seem remarkably different from hypnotized subjects.

With respect to physiological differences between the hypnotized and nonhypnotized states, there is little convincing evidence to suggest that the hypnotic state is unique. Although there have been reports of certain differences in the EEGs of hypnotized and nonhypnotized subjects, the differences are neither completely convincing nor completely distinct from what we would normally expect to see in the EEGs of nonhypnotized individuals.

Despite the lack of convincing evidence, however, many who deal with hypnotic phenomena are convinced that it is a distinct state of consciousness, unlike normal waking, sleeping, or unconscious states. The evidence to support such a belief is only suggestive. For example, hypnotized subjects are often unable to perform some requests made by the hypnotists, although nonhypnotized "simulators" often perform everything requested of them. In general, the subjective reports of hypnotized subjects are different from those of nonhypnotized control subjects. The most obvious difference is that although nonhypnotized subjects may perform "hypnotic" behaviors, they do not feel hypnotized. This is not the case for hypnotized subjects. As Orne noted: "Any subject who has experienced deep trance will unhesitatingly describe this state as basically different from his normal one. He may be unable to explicate this difference, but he will invariably be quite definite and certain about its presence." (1959)

In spite of the uncertainty and disagreement about the qualitative differences between the hypnotic state and the normal states of wakefulness and sleep, there are several interesting and seemingly unequivocal characteristics that make hypnotism a significant and fascinating area of scientific investigation. For example, not everyone is equally susceptible to hypnosis. Hilgard regards susceptibility to hypnosis as an ability that—like athletic ability, for instance—differs in different people and is relatively stable within a single individual. Many susceptibility scales have been developed and have proved useful in predicting both the ease with which subjects can be hypnotized and the depth of hypnosis they can achieve. For instance, susceptibility scales have verified the interesting fact that children are more easily hypnotized than adults.

Perhaps the most fascinating aspect of hypnosis is that it may prove to have a variety of valuable applications. It has already been used, for example, in dentistry and minor surgery as an alternative to anesthetics and in psychotherapy for temporary relief of symptoms and the elimination of certain undesirable habits, such as smoking. Although hypnotic techniques are not always successful, further research may demonstrate that hypnosis has a useful place in the science of psychology.

Meditation

Although Eastern cultures have believed in "higher" states of consciousness for centuries, these beliefs have been largely neglected in the western hemisphere. These states of consciousness differ—psychologically and physiologically—from wakefulness and from sleep states such as dreaming. In yoga, for instance, the body is fully relaxed and the mind is fully alert. In an effort to arrive at this state, practitioners of yoga use a variety of techniques, such as physical exercise, control of a particular bodily function such as heartbeat, or concentration and contemplation (Wallace and Benson, 1972). Scientific studies of these techniques and the psychological and physiological effects that accompany them have begun only recently.

A well-standardized meditative technique called *transcendental meditation,* was introduced from India by Maharishi Mahesh Yogi several years ago. Currently, more than 300,000 people in the United States practice this technique of meditation and many others utilize other meditative practices. During the practice of transcendental meditation, an individual sits comfortably with his eyes closed for about fifteen to twenty minutes, twice a day. By using a systematic technique for progressive refinement of mental activity, he is able to achieve the meditation state. Practitioners report that during meditation, the mind and body become progressively more calm and relaxed, although the mind remains completely alert. Thus the individual does not lose his awareness, as he does in sleep. Mahesh defines the technique as one of "turning the attention inwards toward the subtlest state of a thought, and . . . [arriving] at the source of thought" (1969). In this state of "pure" awareness, the mind is aware and alert, but has no object of awareness.

Physiological research suggests that during transcendental meditation, practitioners are indeed in a restful state (e.g., Wallace et al., 1972). For example, decreases in oxygen consumption, respiration rate, and heart rate indicate a drop in metabolic activity indicating that the body is in a relaxed, resting state. Figure 14.9 illustrates the decrease in rate of respiration that can occur during transcendental meditation. In addition, there may be changes in the EEG, particularly in the amount of alpha activity. Figure 14.9 indicates that alpha activity increases over the surface of the cerebral cortex. This result too suggests that the meditator is in a quiet and relaxed, although not sleeping state.

Can transcendental meditation produce beneficial changes in certain kinds of mental and physical activity? Several experimental attempts to answer this question suggest that this form of meditation may be useful for reducing stress, anxiety, and tension (Nidich, Seemen, and Seibert, 1973; Orme-Johnson, 1973). Furthermore, those who regularly practice transcendental meditation claim that

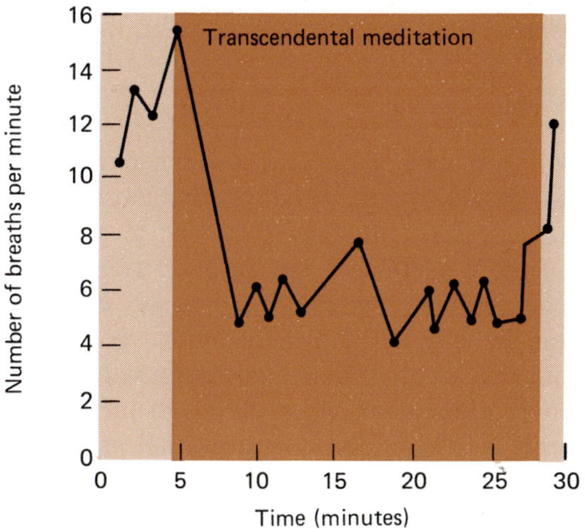

Figure 14.9 The effects of transcendental meditation on breathing rate. (From J.F.T. Allison, "Respiratory changes during transcendental meditation," *Lancet,* 1970, i, 833).

the technique is beneficial to their mental and physical health. Practitioners also claim that the state of consciousness produced is not unnatural; it simply refines one's ability to achieve a state of "restful alertness" that is potentially present in the daily lives of everyone.

Biofeedback

The final topic in our discussion of altered states of consciousness does not relate to a distinct state of consciousness but to a technique that can be used to control our state of consciousness or level of arousal. *Biofeedback,* as the name implies, is a technique in which biological signals such as heart rate, blood pressure, electroencephalographic activity, and muscular activity are "fed back" to the subject so that in addition to being consciously aware of these signals, he can attempt to bring them under voluntary control.

Under normal circumstances, we are virtually unaware of our own heartbeat, blood pressure, muscle tension, and similar biological phenomena. The biofeedback technique enables us to be aware of these normally subliminal signals. For example, the heart beat may be recorded, amplified, and played to the subject on a loudspeaker, so that the subject can hear his own heartbeat. And if appropriate instruments are used, blood pressure can be converted to a visual or auditory signal that changes when blood pressure changes. By monitoring the visual or auditory signal, a subject can often bring these functions under some degree of voluntary control—contrary to the belief that prevailed throughout much of psychology's history.

Many biological signals that are used in biofeedback are also indexes of level of arousal. Thus control of these signals is often accomplished by controlling the level of arousal, although subjects in such experiments may not be able to describe how they manage to control a particular function. The key to their ability to do so, however, seems to be an awareness of the biological process itself. Because we are normally unaware of our heart rate or blood pressure, we can hardly be expected to control them voluntarily. However, if we are provided with an obvious visual or auditory signal that is systematically related to the biological process, awareness of the process becomes possible.

An interesting application of the biofeedback technique involves the electrical activity generated by muscles over the forehead, which appears to be a major source of tension headaches. In an experiment by Budzynski et al. (1973), an electromyogram, or EMG (a record of the electrical activity of muscles) was taken from muscles overlying the forehead in one group of patients suffering from tension headaches. Electrodes attached to the forehead recorded the electrical activity, which was converted into a series of auditory clicks that were delivered to the patients through earphones. When these muscles were tense, the clicks were rapid; when they were relaxed, the clicks were infrequent. This first group, which actually received feedback of muscle activity, was designated group A. A second group (B) heard clicks that were not related to muscle activity. In other words, these subjects received pseudo-feedback and thus served as a control for simply being in the experimental situation. Another control group (C) did not receive any treatment at all. The feedback and the pseudo-feedback groups were told to practice the relaxation technique at home for fifteen to twenty minutes per day. In addition, participants in all three groups were asked to keep a record of the occurrence of their tension headaches.

Group A, which received actual feedback training, was able to reduce the activity of the muscles overlying the forehead to a significant degree. The control groups did not show this dramatic effect. The number of headaches experienced by members of group A—all of whom were able to reduce muscle tension over the forehead region—was reduced significantly for a period of three months following the biofeedback training.

Other biological functions that have been subjected to biofeedback include the alpha waves in the EEG. Alpha feedback became so popular for a while that commercial manufacturers began making "alpha feedback" machines. Whether these machines benefitted consumers in any way is questionable, although increases in alpha activity are generally related to a state of relaxation. In any case, there are less expensive ways to relax.

Biofeedback techniques may prove to be extremely valuable in a number of therapeutic settings. Currently, they are being used experimentally to relieve high blood pressure and other symptoms of hypertension. You can imagine how beneficial the ability to control these vital functions will be for individuals who have suffered heart attack or other diseases associated with hypertension.

Summary

The behavior of humans and other animals is dependent on their state of consciousness—for example, whether they are awake or asleep. Wakefulness and sleep are cyclic, appearing over definite circadian or twenty-four-hour cycles. Much of human behavior and that of other animals is governed by an internal circadian clock, although the clock itself is also often tied to external environmental cues such as light and darkness.

Sleep appears to consist of different stages, which may be best defined by certain characteristics of the EEG. During alert wakefulness, the EEG contains low amplitude, high frequency variations in voltage; as an individual becomes relaxed, the EEG is dominated by *alpha waves* of relatively high amplitude, with cyclic changes in voltage at frequencies of around 10 Hz. During stage 1, the first and lightest stage of sleep, the EEG is of low amplitude and somewhat irregular, consisting of voltage changes that are mixed but predominantly above the alpha frequency. During stage 2 sleep, the EEG is similar to that of stage 1; however it contains occasional sleep spindles—short bursts of waves within the 10 to 14 Hz. frequency range. Stage 3 sleep is characterized by occasional large slow changes in voltage of about 1 to 3 Hz. Stage 4 sleep, the deepest stage of sleep, is dominated by these large, slow waves called delta waves and thus is often termed slow-wave sleep. Stage-1 REM sleep is a distinct stage of sleep: the EEG looks like the EEG of stage 1 sleep or wakefulness and the stage is accompanied by rapid eye movements (REM) and dreaming. The discovery of stage-1 REM sleep has provided a great impetus to the study of dreams.

Wakefulness is also clearly not a single state, but is characterized by varying degrees of behavioral arousal or activation. Early interest in levels of arousal prompted attempts to find an adequate criterion for different levels of behavioral arousal, similar to the EEG criteria discovered for stages of sleep. Although heightened arousal is often accompanied by physiological activation of the sympathetic division of the autonomic nervous system, no single criterion is an adequate measure of level of arousal. Taken together, however, many physiological indexes may be used to obtain an approximate measure of level of arousal. Extremely high or low levels of behavioral arousal seem to be accompanied by a decrease in efficiency or performance, suggesting that there is an *optimal level of arousal.* Animals seem to behave in such a way that they arrive at the optimal level of arousal appropriate to their normal sleep-wakefulness cycle.

Although environmental stimulation may affect both, sleep and wakefulness are not simply the passive result of the absence or presence of environmental stimuli. They are actively produced by the brain.

Many altered states of consciousness have been described. Disorders of sleep and wakefulness, for example, produce marked alterations in our state of consciousness. Complaints of not being able to sleep fall within the class of disorders termed *insomnia,* which may be characterized by an inability to fall asleep, frequent awakenings during sleep, or early morning awakenings.

Hypersomnias are conditions in which individuals sleep too much. Narcolepsy is one such disorder characterized by irresistible attacks of sleep that can be accompanied by sleep paralysis, cataplexy, and hypnogogic hallucinations. There are also a variety of so-called pseudonarcolepsies such as the Kleine-Levin Syndrome or the Pickwickian Syndrome.

Parasomnias are disorders in which behavior similar to waking behavior occurs during sleep, such as somnambulism (sleep-walking). Other disorders of sleep include *enuresis* (bed-wetting), *night terrors, REM nightmares,* and other phenomena that affect the sleeping individual.

Hypnosis, another phenomenon that has been regarded as a distinct state of consciousness, has received a great deal of experimental and theoretical attention. Although definitions of the hypnotic state often suggest that the subject relinquishes his self-control to a large degree; is capable of heightened visual imagery, memory, and fantasy; becomes more suggestible; and tolerates distortions of reality, there is, as yet, no conclusive evidence that the hypnotic state is uniquely different from normal wakefulness or perhaps light sleep.

Other states of consciousness include the yoga state and the condition of relaxed but alert wakefulness achieved by practitioners of meditation. During *transcendental meditation,* one common technique of meditation practiced in the United States, breathing rate, oxygen consumption, and other indexes of metabolic rate decrease. Subjective reports indicate that the experience is a pleasurable one, and other evidence indicates that the practice may have beneficial side effects.

A recent technique termed biofeedback is being used to help individuals control their physiological and mental states. If any one of a variety of biological signals is converted into a visual or auditory stimulus, the subject is made aware of these physiological processes and is then frequently capable of controlling them to some extent. The results of recent experiments using this technique suggest that many individuals may be able to control heart rate, blood pressure, and certain characteristics of the EEG, such as alpha waves.

15

Drives and Motives

If one were to ask the average man on the street what he believes the central theme of psychology should be, he would most likely say *"motivation."* There are several reasons for this attitude. One involves the ordinary, everyday meaning of the word *motive,* which means an idea, need, emotion, or organic state that compels or incites an individual to action. Common synonyms are words such as impulse, inducement, and incentive. In other words, a motive is any stimulus that leads to behavior; thus if one understands motives, one necessarily understands the causes of behavior.

A second reason for the attitude that motivation is an important aspect of psychology is that psychoanalytic language and thought receive wide exposure in books, magazines, television programs, and so forth. Thus the general public knows that the goal of psychoanalytic treatment is to help the patient understand his motives.

Within psychology itself, the question of whether motivation is central to an understanding of all aspects of behavior is debatable. When E. G. Boring published his famous *History of Experimental Psychology* in 1929, he did not use the word motivation even once because the subject of motivation was the philosopher's domain and psychologists did little research on the subject. This climate has changed considerably. Today, much psychological research is conducted on motivational processes. No one could write a history of experimental psychology without devoting considerable space to a discussion of motivation. As Cofer (1972) has pointed out, the first half of the twentieth century could be termed the epoch of motivational research in psychology.

It might be instructive to trace briefly the history of the concept of motivation in philosophy, biology, and psychiatry as Cofer (1972) did in an excellent book on motivation. The following discussion is based on his analysis.

History of the Concept of Motivation

Philosophy

Within philosophy, two conceptions of the nature of man have and still do contend with one another. One conception holds that man is pushed and pulled by his inner needs and environmental forces and that he is largely unaware of the reasons for his actions and behavior. These ideas were most clearly enunciated by the French philosopher, *Rene Descartes* and by British empiricists such as *Hume, John Locke, James Mill,* and his son, *John Stuart Mill.* All these men had an enormous impact on psychology.

Descartes believed that animals were similar to machines because their behavior was guided by forces over which they had no control. Man, on the other hand, had a soul and therefore some of his behavior was more rational. The British empiricists went a step farther and, in a sense, took man's soul away from him. According to these philosophers, all of man's ideas (his mind) were shaped by experience. Human behavior could be explained entirely in terms of certain *laws of association,* which held that ideas come from experience and are combined into ever more complex ideas by association. These ideas are translated into behavior according to the principle of hedonism—that is, that man seeks to maximize pleasure and avoid pain.

The alternative conception of man's nature holds that the purpose of his behavior is to achieve certain ends and that one can often determine the motivation behind certain behaviors by simply asking the individual what guides them. Because, according to this view, behavior is guided by rational principles, the philosophy is termed *rationalism.* As psychology drifted away from earlier and purer forms of behaviorism, this philosophy became more and more important, until today, behavior is no longer explained as mechanically as it was in the early 1920s. Instead, perceptions, knowledge, and ideas are now believed to influence bodily needs and drives.

Because these two contending philosophies of man's nature are still very much alive in theories of motivation, one important and recurring issue in motivational theory is the question of *free will* versus *determinism.*

Psychiatry

Rationalistic philosophy has always found it difficult to explain the existence of mental illness. If man's behavior is rational, then how do we explain the bizzare and irrational symptoms that are characteristic of many types of mental disorders? The work of Sigmund Freud and his successors had a tremendous impact on psychology—especially on the study of motivational processes—because psychoanalytic theory is, in the main, a motivational theory. Psychoanalytic thought had its origins in the ideas Freud derived from his study of neurotic patients. According to these ideas, the characteristic symptoms of the neuroses can be explained in terms of motivational processes, irrational and unconscious, to be sure, but motives just the same.

Freud's ideas were greatly influenced by both philosophy and biology. He was well aware of Charles Darwin's work on evolution, and he attempted to use evolutionary principles to explain behavior in terms of instincts and drives. Freud postulated two major drives. The more important one, in terms of the emphasis it received, was the *libido,* Freud's term for the primitive biological drives; the other drive dealt with aggression. Motivation, in terms of psychoanalytic theory, can be considered a form of energy that leads to behavior. One of the great contributions of this theory to psychological work was its emphasis on unconscious drives, that is, forces that guide behavior but are largely unknown to the individual. Thus from psychoanalysis another important issue in the psychology of motivation was derived, that is, the distinction between conscious and unconscious motivation. According to psychoanalytic theory, behavior is largely the result of unconscious motives, and certain behaviors permit the discharge of these motivational energies. As such, the theory is deterministic in nature and stands in sharp contrast to more rationalistic philosophies.

Biology

Within psychology, thinking, theory, and research on motivation was influenced most directly by Darwin's theory of evolution, as elegantly presented in his epoch-making book, *The Origin of Species by Means of Natural Selection,* published in 1859. Central to the theory of evolution is the conception that animals *within* a species vary with respect to their morphological, physiological, and behavioral traits. Those traits that have adaptive value will survive by means of *natural selection,* whereas traits that lack adaptive value are lost. This idea can be expressed in terms of a trait's *fitness value*—that is, the number of offspring an individual produces who survive to reproductive age. From the viewpoint of psychology, it is important to realize that behavioral traits are also selected for in terms of fitness value; that is, whether they will contribute to the organism's survival in its environment. It is also important to realize that a behavioral trait may have fitness value in one environment and thus will be selected for; in another environment, however, it may lack fitness value and will not be selected for. The basic tenant of evolutionary theory is that through a process called *survival of the fittest,* one species slowly evolves or changes into another and that there is a continuum among all living forms. Thus evolutionary theory erased Descartes' distinction between animals and man. For the purposes of this chapter, one way to conceive of motivated behavior is to think of it as having adaptive value. An example of this kind of behavior is described in box 15.1.

Another of Darwin's books, *The Expression of the Emotions in Man and Animals,* published in 1872, had an immediate impact on motivational research in psychology. In this book, Darwin emphasized the behaviors that accompany emotions—how emotions are expressed—rather than the feelings that accompany them. This became an important trend in psychological research on emotions, a trend that will be illustrated in the next chapter.

Motivation as a Psychological Concept

How do psychologists explain the immense variety of behaviors they observe? How, for example, do we explain forty years of dedicated service to an academic discipline, a corporation, or a political philosophy or party? How do we explain murder, rioting, rape, or robbery? How do we explain the creative efforts of Albert Einstein or Pablo Picasso and the destructive behavior of Adolf Hitler or Joseph Stalin? How do we explain the fact that one individual has an enormous appetite, while another eats moderately?

It is now common practice, both among laymen and psychologists, to attempt to explain individual human behavior as well as human social behavior and interactions in terms of strivings based on love and hate, conflict and frustration, the need for social approval and achievement, curiosity, aggression, contact comfort, and so forth. And it is our purpose here to delineate what psycholo-

Box 15.1
Responses of Young Turkeys to the Silhouettes of Other Birds

Tinbergen (1951) studied the reactions of young turkeys as they observed the silhouette of a bird (see box fig. 15.1). In one case, the model was moved from left to right, which gave it the appearance of a bird with a short neck, such as a hawk; that is, the silhouette resembled a bird of prey. If moved in the other direction, from right to left, the model appeared to have a long neck and thus resembled a goose, for instance. In the first case, the young turkeys responded to the model by trying to run away. In the second case, the birds failed to respond to the model. According to Tinbergen, young ducks and geese respond similarly to such models. It should be pointed out, however, that several investigators have failed to obtain similar results; their findings indicate that the turkey's reaction depends in part on its experience with geese.

The young turkey's response to the silhouette of a bird of prey is of considerable adaptive value. Another issue that is illustrated by this demonstration is often raised with respect to motivated behavior: Is the motivated behavior innate, or is it influenced by learning and experience? This distinction between innate and learned influences on motivated behavior can be attributed directly to Darwin's influence on the psychology of motivation.

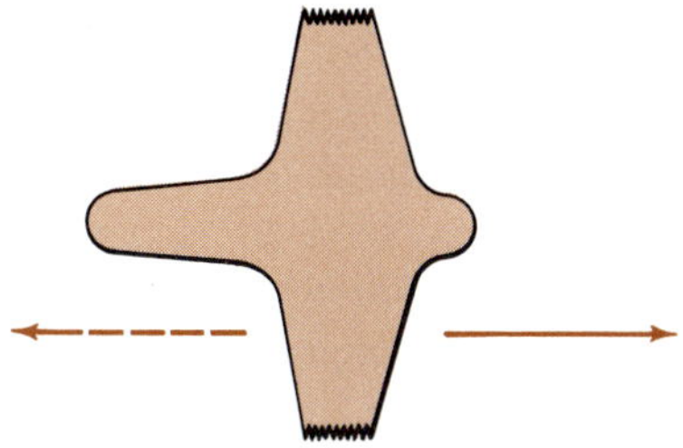

Box Figure 15.1 A model of a bird suspended on a wire. If moved to the right, the model looks like a short-necked bird of prey; if moved to the left, it gives the appearance of a long-necked and harmless bird. Moving the model to the right elicits alarm reactions in certain animals, whereas moving it to the left has no effect. (From N. Tinbergen. *The Study of Instinct*. Copyright 1951 Clarendon Press, Oxford, England.)

gists have learned about complex drives such as love, anxiety, and curiosity in empirical as well as theoretical terms.

Many behaviors are guided by internal stimuli—referred to by psychologists as *drives and motives*—that channel behavior in certain directions or toward particular goals. Until relatively recently, and for complex reasons, psychologists chose not to study motivational processes. As a consequence, many ideas that are relevant to motivation came, not from within psychology, but from biology, philosophy, and psychiatry. Today, however, many psychologists would agree that to understand behavior, one must understand *motivation*. By motivation we mean that which underlies the intensity and direction of behavior, that is, the energy necessary for behavior to occur.

For some time, psychologists have conceptualized drives—or "tissue needs," as they are sometimes called—as resulting from internal stimuli that energize behavior and give it direction. For example, a thirsty dog actively seeks water; a female cat in heat actively seeks a sexual partner. Motivated animals, a thirsty dog or a cat in heat, will behave in a way that will help them reach a goal. The behavior animals engage in to reach a goal is referred to as *consummatory* behavior or response.

Lashley is credited with setting the stage for many modern ideas concerning motivated behavior. In an article titled "An experimental analysis of instinctive behavior" (1938), he postulated the idea that all motivated behavior, from the simplest to the most complex, is controlled by the central nervous system, which responds to a variety of stimuli, both external and internal. His major contribution was to point out that behavior (1) depends on complex and interacting sets of stimuli and (2) does not consist of simple stimulus-response sequences. This idea helps us to understand the enormous richness of motivated behavior as well as the variability of motivated behavior within an organism over time and between different organisms of the same species.

It is not unusual to classify the stimuli that lead to motivated behavior into two categories; *biological drives,* which result from hunger, thirst, oxygen deprivation, and the like, and *psychological drives,* which result from stimuli associated with needs for achievement, social approval, self-esteem, and so on. But it is doubtful whether this distinction between biology and psychology, between body and mind, is useful. In this context, we should also point out that it is customary to think of biological drives as *innate* and psychological motives as *acquired.* This distinction too must be viewed with great suspicion because, as we noted in Chapter 2, hereditary and environmental factors continuously interact.

The distinction between drives and motives is not clear-cut. In a certain sense psychologists think of drives as being caused by deprivation, the organism being pushed in the direction of satisfying these drives. Motives is a more general concept which may subsume the concept of drives. Motivation includes states not induced by deprivation—such as a state induced by an external object which attracts or pulls the organism in its direction.

Regardless of the type of motivated behavior that is being discussed, all drives and motives share the following similarities:

1. Under certain conditions both activate behavior. This effect is probably mediated through some general arousal system in the central nervous system—most likely the reticular activating system discussed in several earlier chapters.

2. Both direct behavior. A thirsty dog is not only an aroused animal, but one which behaves in a way that will increase its likelihood of finding water.

3. Both reduce behaviors that are irrelevant to the motivational condition which exists at the time. For example, a cat in heat will stop engaging in activities that are unrelated to sexual behavior.

4. Both lead to persistent behavior. A motivated animal continues to engage actively in goal-directed behavior until a consummatory response has occurred.

5. Both are activated by internal and external stimuli. These stimuli activate behavior and, in addition, may serve as *cues;* that is, they may point in the direction of the goal. Smelling a steak on hot charcoals may lead to hunger *and* may point in the direction where food can be found.

6. Both interact with experience. Stimuli that previously were neutral may acquire motivational properties by association.

7. Both interact with performance. The strength of these interactions and indeed their directions depend on the strength of the drive and the complexity of the task, among other variables.

8. Both have an affective component; in other words, they lead to the expression of emotions. It is common to speak of emotions as the affective counterpart of motives.

Measuring the Strength of Motives

To study motivational processes, psychologists must have instruments with which to measure the intensity of motivation. Thus a number of techniques has been devised for measuring the relative strength of motives. Many of these techniques are based on a statement attributed to Morgan and known as "Morgan's Dictum," which says that the strength of a drive can be measured by the resistance it overcomes. Or, to quote Morgan, "The amount of inhibition necessary to overcome a tendency may be used as a measure of the strength of that tendency."

In this section, we will discuss four techniques used to measure motives; three of them are more appropriate for the study of motivation in experimental animals, the fourth is used to study motivation in human beings.

Techniques Used with Animal Subjects

One early technique that experimental psychologists used to measure the strength of motives is known as the *Columbia Obstruction Method.* It has this name because it was developed at Columbia University and because it places some obstacle, or obstruction between the motivated organism and the goal it wishes to reach. A Columbia Obstruction Box is shown in figure 15.1.

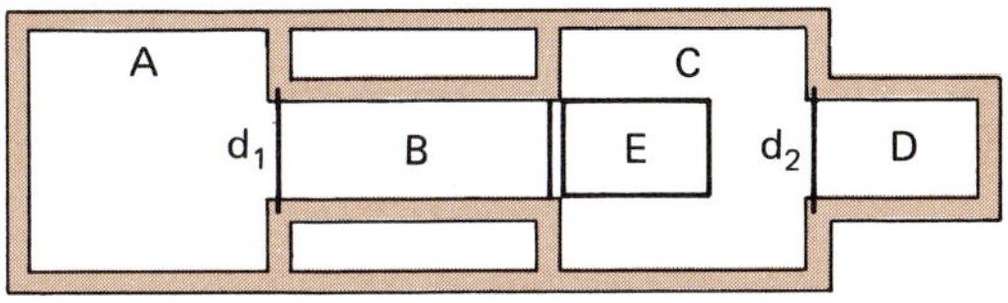

Figure 15.1 Floor plan for a Columbia Obstruction Box. A, entrance; B, obstruction (e.g., electric grid); C and D divided incentive chamber; E, release plate; d_1, manually operated door to grid; d_2, automatic door (which opens when the animal steps on the release plate) between two divisions of the incentive chamber.

The method involves the following procedure: A motivated animal such as a rat, which has been deprived of food for twenty-four hours, is placed in one corner of the obstruction box. The animal is separated from food by an electrified grid. The degree of the animal's motivation can then be measured by determining the number of times it will cross the electric grid per unit time. Alternatively, one can measure the degree of motivation by increasing the current through the grid floor and noting how much current the rat will tolerate to gain access to the food. If this technique measures the strength of a drive, hunger in this case, then we would expect an animal that has been deprived of food for forty-eight hours to cross the grid more often per unit of time or to tolerate a more intense current than one that has been deprived of food for only twenty-four hours. This is indeed the case. We can also use the Columbia Obstruction Box to measure the relative strength of two motives. If we place a hungry male rat into the middle of the box and separate it from two incentives, food and a female rat in heat, by two electric grids, we would be able to measure the relative strength of the hunger *versus* the sex drive.

Despite its apparent simplicity, the Columbia Obstruction Method is a useful technique for three reasons. First, it is almost infinitely variable. For example, we can substitute a variety of obstacles for the electric grid. We could separate the motivated animal from the incentive by a trough of water and make the water progressively colder. The degree of motivation could then be measured by how often per unit of time the animal would swim to the incentive as the temperature of the water decreased. A second reason why the method is useful is that it is a fairly reliable measuring instrument. That is, the same results tend to be obtained on the same animal under the same motivational conditions at different times. A third reason is that the method has been well validated. For example, if we determine the relative strength of a particular motive, using this method, then we are likely to obtain approximately the same result using some other method for measuring the strength of the same motive.

A second class of techniques that is frequently used by psychologists who study motivation are the so-called *free-choice methods*. For instance, if an investigator is interested in determining an animal's preference for sugar (sucrose) versus saccharin, he could place the animal in a cage supplied with all the food the animal needs and two drinking tubes. These drinking tubes could be attached to inverted graduated cylinders. One cylinder would be filled with a sucrose solution, the other with a saccharin solution. Every day the amount of fluid consumed from each bottle could be determined by simply looking at the amount of fluid taken from each bottle. could be determined by simply looking at the amount of fluid taken from each bottle. Empty cages might be set up as a control for evaporation and leakage. The animal's preference for sucrose could then be calculated by dividing the amount of fluid taken from the sucrose bottle by the amount of fluid taken from the sucrose plus the saccharin bottle. This preference ratio would vary between 1.0 and 0.0: if the animal drank only from the sucrose bottle, the ratio would be 1.0; if it drank only from the saccharin bottle, the ratio would be 0.0. Intermediate values would indicate intermediate preferences for sucrose. Note that because this preference ratio is unrelated to the *absolute amount* of fluid taken by an animal, large animals can be compared with small ones. Alcohol preference of mice, measured by this technique, has already been discussed in Chapter 5. There is no requirement that free-choice techniques must be restricted to measuring the preference for substances in solution. For instance, if the animal is given free access to dishes containing a variety of foods, we could determine its food preferences. Preferences for mates have also been determined in experimental animals, using free-choice methods. Like the Columbia Obstruction Method, free-choice preference tests have been shown to be both fairly reliable and valid. When using free-choice methods, it is not necessary to give the organism access to two stimuli; single stimuli have also been used.

A third technique that is useful in measuring motivation in animals is the Skinner box, which has been described in some detail in Chapter 11. It may surprise you to discover that the Skinner box is useful for measuring motives because it is more commonly associated with experiments on learning and memory. However, the apparatus can be used to measure the relative strength of motives in the following manner: An animal can learn to press a lever in a Skinner box if its performance is reinforced with food, for instance. After many reinforced trials, the animal's performance becomes stable, and it will press the lever a constant number of times per hour. In other words, under this set of conditions, the animal, in a sense, knows everything there is to know about pressing the lever. At that point, the instrument becomes useful for measuring motivation because the number of responses *per* unit of time will now vary as a function of how motivated the animal is—in this case, how long it has been deprived of food. Alternatively, the vigor with which the animal presses the bar can be measured; this behavior also varies as a function of the degree of deprivation. The experimenter could also attach weights to the lever and record the amount of effort the animal will exert to obtain food; this too will measure the degree of motivation.

Techniques Used with Human Subjects

Although the three techniques just described were designed primarily for research on experimental animals, the free-choice preference tests could, in principle at least, be used in research on humans. However, many techniques that are more directly applicable to research on human motives have been developed. One technique that is especially interesting was developed by McClelland in the 1940s (e.g., McClelland et al., 1953) to measure what must surely be a major human motive; the *need for achievement.*

McClelland showed human subjects certain portions of the *Thematic Apperception Test (TAT),* which was developed by Henry Murray in 1943. The TAT is one example of a class of psychological tests, collectively called *projective tests.* It consists of twenty stimulus cards, each containing a drawing, which are shown to the subject. (A sample card is shown in fig. 15.2.) All the drawings are somewhat ambiguous. The observer is then asked to tell a story about each drawing. Because the drawings are ambiguous, the individual presumably projects his own personality, motives, needs, and desires, into his stories.

To guide the subject, the person administering the test commonly asks him to describe (1) the identity of the individuals in the drawing, (2) the events leading up to the scene, (3) the present action, and (4) the end of the story, that is, what will ultimately happen to the characters in the scene. The subject's responses can then be used in a number of ways. Most often, the test is used clinically as a diagnostic device to draw inferences about

Figure 15.2 An example of one of the Thematic Apperception cards. (Courtesy Harvard University Press. Copyright © 1943 by the President and Fellows of Harvard College and 1971 by Henry A. Murray.)

the respondent's personality, feelings, and so forth. However, the test is also useful as a research tool. Before the TAT can be used to study the need for achievement, reliable scoring criteria must be developed so that two or more judges, looking at the same responses, will score them the same way. And in fact it is possible to train judges to score the results of the TAT so that the interjudge agreement is sufficiently high to make the test a reliable research instrument. However, to be useful, the test must also be checked with respect to its validity; that is, whether it indeed measures the need for achievement. This is a difficult undertaking. One approach is to develop and test certain hypotheses that have been formulated about the trait in question. For example, we might predict that the need to achieve should increase in competitive situations; thus we could measure the need in the same individual in competitive *versus* noncompetitive circumstances. This experiment has in fact been performed, and the results indicate that the need for achievement, as measured by responses to the TAT, increases in competitive situations. This suggests that the test is a valid measure of the need for achievement.

The TAT is only one of many techniques that psychologists have developed to measure motivational processes in human subjects. Many experimental psychologists prefer more direct methods of measuring the degree of motivation. An example of how instrumental and consummatory responses have been used to study human motivation will be discussed later in this chapter, for example, in Schacter's research on obesity.

Simple Behavioral Patterns

Beach (1950), one of the most eminent students of motivated behavior, pointed out that American psychologists generally restrict their investigations to a single trait—learning—and study it almost exclusively in one species, the rat. This statement was in the form of a lament for comparative psychology. According to Beach, far more progress would be made in understanding behavior if the behavior of a wide range of organisms was studied. Whether this criticism is as valid today as it was a quarter of a century ago is debatable; however, the general impression is that the situation has improved. If there has been a resurgence in comparative psychology, then this is partly due to the influence of a group of European zoologists known as ethologists. *Ethology* is the branch of zoology that is concerned with the study of animal behavior. Thus its subject matter is similar to that of psychology. However, there are some distinctions between the two. First, ethologists tend to study behavior in organisms from a wide spectrum of species. Although psychologists are not prohibited from comparative studies of behavior, they do tend to focus on a few species, as we just pointed out. Second, ethologists insist that a behavior cannot be understood unless it is viewed in the context of the entire behavioral repertoire of the species under study. Therefore, ethologists obtain as complete an understanding of the behavior of organisms of a species as is possible. Psychologists, on the other hand, tend to study a behavior in relative isolation. Third, ethologists insist that a given behavior must be observed and studied in circumstances that closely resemble the animal's natural habitat. Psychologists, on the other hand, have a penchant for studying behavior in the laboratory. Fourth, and perhaps most important, ethologists tend to study rather simple behavioral patterns, ones that are innate or instinctual and thus change little as a function of experience, whereas psychologists are interested in the effects of experience on behavior.

It is the distinction between innate and learned behavior that merits closer scrutiny here because it deals with one of the recurring issues in the study of motivated behavior; namely, whether motivated behaviors are influenced by experience or by heredity. This distinction greatly influences how we conceive of motivational processes, and therefore much research is devoted to this topic.

Little else in psychology has caused the same furor as this question. The word instinct has had a checkered career in psychology for several reasons. The early behaviorists, who had a tremendous impact on American psychology, wanted to write a psychology that did not involve heredity, in which instincts played no role. In other words, all behavior was the result of experience—a position best exemplified in the following statement by J. B. Watson, one of its leading advocates.

> Give me a dozen healthy infants, well formed, and my own specified world to bring them up in, and I'll guarantee to take any one at random and train him to become any type of specialist I might select—doctor, lawyer, artist, merchant-chief and, yes, even beggarman and thief, regardless of his talents, penchants, tendencies, abilities, vocations, and race of his ancestors. I am going beyond my facts and I admit it, but so have the advocates of the contrary, and they have been doing it for many thousands of years. (1930)

Other psychologists wrote books and articles bearing titles such as *Are There Any Instincts?* (Dunlap, 1919) or *A Psychology Without Heredity* (Kuo, 1924). Of course these are extreme positions, but the early behaviorists sincerely and passionately believed in them, and because of their influence, so did American psychology at large. Why? Certainly one reason is that the psychologists who preceded the early behaviorists had a tendency to publish long lists of instincts. What particularly annoyed the early behaviorists about these lists, and rightly so, was the ease with which they were turned into explanatory concepts. For example, it was postulated that *parenthood* was a primary instinct and that *tenderness* was the emotion that accompanied it. Having made this statement, it was easy to say that the nest-building behavior of a bird or a rat is *caused* by the parenthood instinct and that the bird retrieves its eggs when they roll out of the nest, or the rat retrieves its pups when they wander from the nest because of the tenderness engendered by the parenthood instinct. For this reason, among others, behaviorists rejected instincts; but, unfortunately, they overreacted.

What was the way out of this dilemma? According to Beach (1955), psychologists had to stop classifying behaviors as either learned or unlearned, at least long enough to make a careful analysis of the behavior in question. In Beach's view, behaviors were the result of interactions between genes and the environment; thus the development of the behavioral pattern in individual organisms warranted careful consideration. One example of what Beach meant, when translated into an actual scientific experiment, is given in box 15.2.

Imprinting

An illustration of imprinting is given in figure 15.3. The photograph shows a group of mallard ducklings following a man. The man in the photograph is *Konrad Lorenz,* winner of the Nobel prize for physiology and medicine in 1973, who gave imprinting its name and was among the first to recognize the importance of the phenomenon in animal behavior. Imprinting is a commonplace occurrence; it can be observed on any farm or in any city park where ducklings swim after their mother in a pond or chicks follow their mother in the barnyard. What is unusual about the photograph is that the ducklings are following a member of a different species. The reason for this rather strange behavior is that the ducks in the picture were exposed to Lorenz after hatching rather than to their natural parent. *Imprinting,* then, refers to certain early ex-

Box 15.2

The Mating Song of the Male Chaffinch: An Example of Evolutionary Determinants of Species-Specific Behavior

According to many investigators, comparative psychologists should extensively study *species-specific behaviors*—behaviors that occur in all, or almost all, members of a particular species who are of the appropriate age and sex. Species-specific behaviors are species predictable; that is, by observing the behavior, we can identify the species. A good example of these behaviors can be found in the songs of many species of birds. All birds of the same species will sing the same song, and an experienced observer can correctly identify the species on hearing the song. For research purposes, these songs are studied with an instrument known as a *sound spectrograph,* a machine that records the song and produces a printout of the frequency (pitch) of the sounds as a function of time. An example of a sound spectrograph of the song of the male chaffinch is shown in box figure 15.2a.

To the experienced observer, three characteristics of the song are obvious: (1) it lasts approximately 2.3 seconds, (2) it consists of three fairly distinct phrases, and (3) it ends with a fairly complex flourish. In a series of experiments, Thorpe (1956) studied the developmental determinants of this species-specific behavior.

Young chaffinches hatch during the spring, and remain in the nest through the summer. During this time, they continuously hear adult chaffinches singing the species-specific song, although the young birds cannot sing the song themselves. The following spring, when the birds become sexually mature (start to secrete sex hormones), they begin to sing the species-specific song, which is part of their mating ritual. Maturational factors are clearly important in this behavior because the sexually immature birds do not sing the song at all, whereas sexually mature adults do.

Box figure 15.2b illustrates this song in a bird that was raised in a soundproof cage, without an opportunity to hear other birds sing. When this bird became sexually mature, it too began to sing; however, its song was different from that of birds which had been reared normally. As you can see in box figure 15.2, the song was approximately 2.3 seconds long and tended to end on a high note. However, it was flat and the phrasing was largely absent. Once the bird has been allowed to sing this abnormal song for a few days, it becomes fixed, and exposing the bird to the normal chaffinch song has no effect.

How can we interpret the results of this experiment? If the entire song is taken as a unit of behavior, then it seems clear that both hereditary and experiential factors contribute to its expression. Namely, the bird sings a song of the appropriate duration, regardless of its experience with members of its species; however, for the song to have species-specific phrasing, the bird must hear members of its own kind sing the song. In other words, the opportunity to hear the song, as sung by other birds, is a necessary developmental determinant for the expression of this behavior. The question of whether the behavior is instinctual has little meaning; proper analysis of the behavior has shown that innate, maturational, and developmental determinants all contribute to the expression of this species-specific behavior.

Box Figure 15.2 a and b are sound spectographs of the mating songs of two wild chaffinches. c is the same song recorded from a hand-reared chaffinch. Notice the difference in the phraseology and the terminal flourish between the wild and hand-reared birds. (From Thorpe, W.H. *Learning and Instinct in Animals.* Copyright 1956 Methuen Pub's, London, England.)

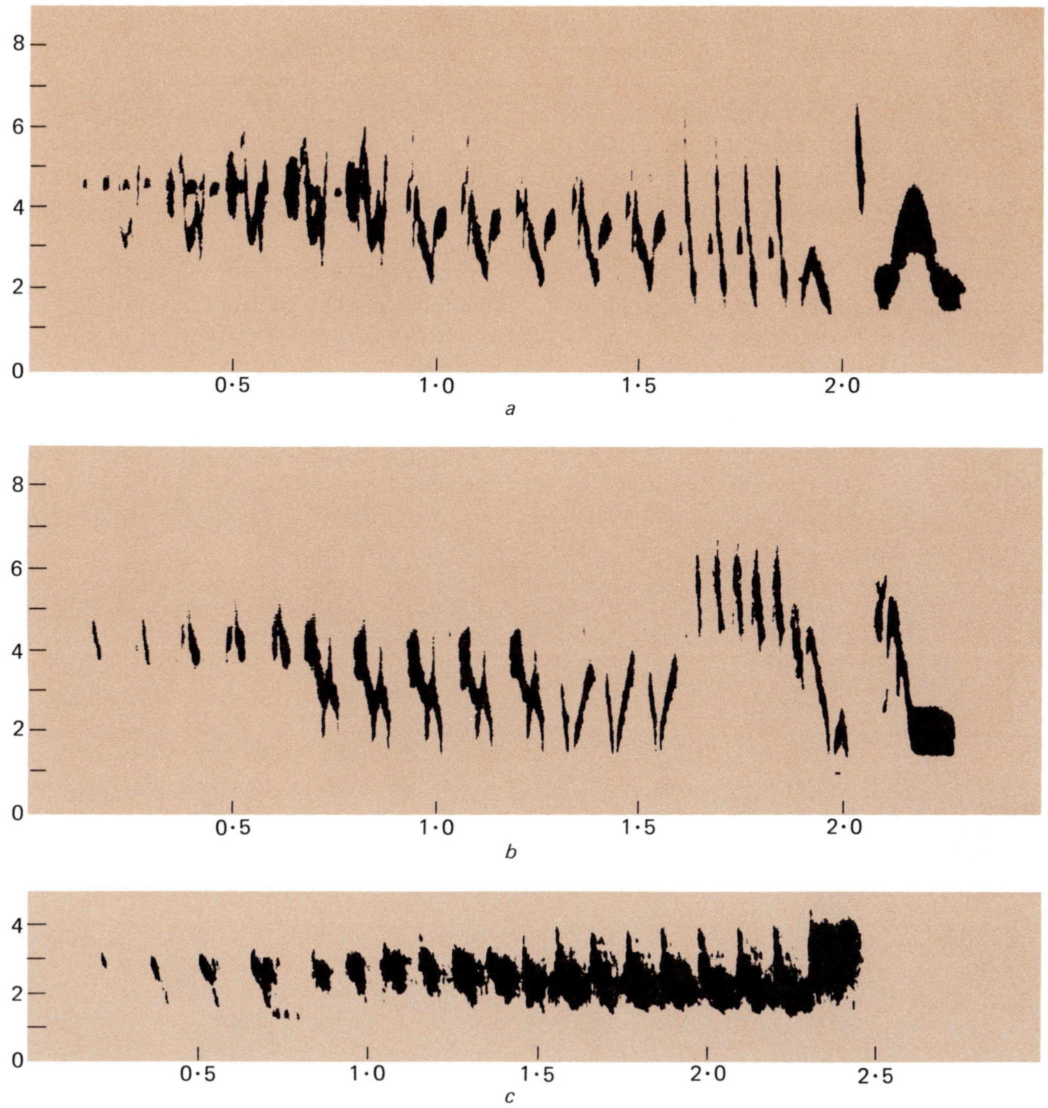
8
6
4
2
0
0·5
1·0
1·5
2·0
a
8
6
4
2
0
0·5
1·0
1·5
2·0
b
4
2
0
0·5
1·0
1·5
2·0
2·5
c

periences that have a profound effect on the organism's subsequent behavior. One fascinating aspect of imprinting is that it can occur only during a relatively short *critical period* during the animal's early development.

Figure 15.3 illustrates the so-called *following response:* The animal will follow the object it is first exposed to during the critical period. Because this object is usually the animal's biological parent, following it is a behavior of obvious adaptive value. However, the following response is not the only aspect of imprinting. According to Lorenz, the first object that elicits a social response, such as following, from the young animal will elicit the same response on subsequent occasions. Furthermore, not only will that particular response be elicited, but other related behaviors will also be elicited by the object. Of special importance, from the point of view of evolution, is the fact that sexual behaviors will be elicited by the object or type of object to which the animal was first imprinted. An interesting illustration of this phenomenon can be found in the mating behavior of wild pigeons. Normally, these birds will mate only with members of their own species. However, if wild pigeons are reared with another species of pigeon, they will not only mate with members of the other species, but will actually show a preference for them as sexual partners.

Figure 15.3 Ducks following Konrad Lorenz after being exposed to him during the critical imprinting period. (Nina Lein, Time-Life Picture Agency © Time, Inc.)

Imprinting has also been described in mammals, and when the criterion for assessing the occurrence of imprinting is the following response, then it seems to occur in animals that are relatively mobile almost from birth. An especially interesting phenomenon that is similar to imprinting has been reported for dogs. Apparently, dogs cannot be made into pets unless they have been exposed to humans early in life. The critical period for domesticating dogs appears to be between three and one-half to thirteen weeks of age, with seven weeks being the most important period. Cats also must be exposed to humans if they are to become pets; these animals must be handled by humans between the time when they first open their eyes and when they are weaned. If humans are absent during the critical period, dogs and cats tend to be wild and afraid of humans. It is also well known that human infants need extensive contact with other humans if they are to grow up normally (see Chapter 9). Infants need frequent handling and cuddling, and if they are deprived of this treatment, in an understaffed orphanage for instance, they experience profound difficulties in later life, especially in terms of establishing long-lasting relationships with other people.

Hess (1959) has reported an extensive series of experiments on imprinting in mallard ducks and chickens. Because his experiments illustrate many aspects of the imprinting phenomenon, they will be discussed in some detail. The laboratory setup he and his coworkers used is illustrated in figure 15.4. The imprinting object is a model of a male duck that circles the enclosure at a uniform rate of speed. The model is fitted with a heating element that emits some warmth and a loudspeaker that makes the sound of a male duck from time to time. At the beginning of the experiment, a duckling is exposed to this model for one hour. At some future time, it is again

Figure 15.4 The experimental setup Hess used to study the following responses of birds. (From "Imprinting" by Hess, E. H., *Science* Vol. 130, pp. 133–141, Figure 5, 17 July 1959.)

exposed to the model in retests that involve choices in four different situations. In one retest, the choice involves stationary, silent, male and female models; in another retest, the choices are between stationary and calling male and female models; in a third test, the choices are between a silent male and a calling female model, both of which are stationary; and in the fourth test, the choice is between a silent, stationary male model and a calling, moving female model. In all these tests, the duckling's following response to the model on which it was imprinted is measured. If, in all four tests it follows or stays with the model on which it was imprinted, its following behavior is scored as 100 percent.

Figure 15.5 illustrates the strength of imprinting (as measured by the following response) as a function of the age at which the animals were first exposed to the model of the male duck. Figure 15.5a gives the data as the average following scores of ducks in the various age groups. Figure 15.5b is simply another way of presenting the same data; it gives the percentage of animals in each age group that obtained a perfect following score

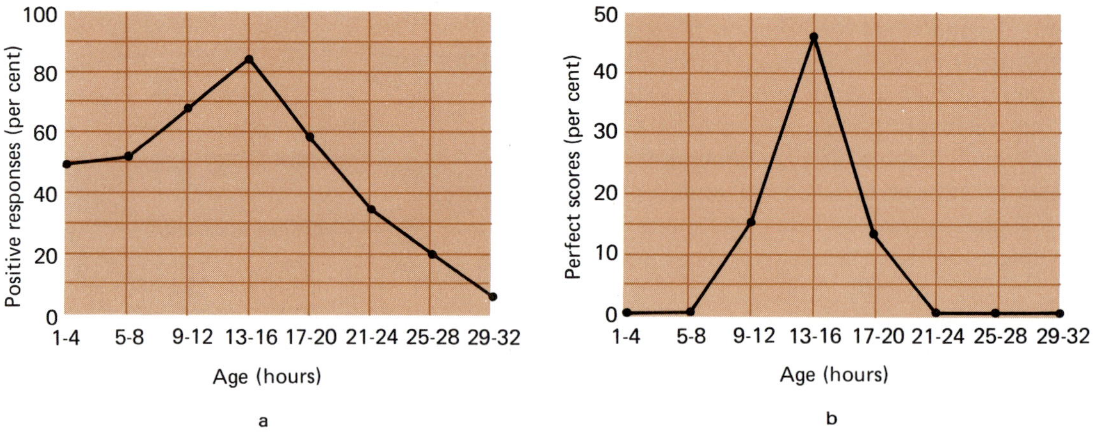

Figure 15.5 (a.) The following responses of birds imprinted on the model at different ages. The strength of imprinting is measured in terms of the percentage of positive responses. (b.) The following responses of birds imprinted on the model at different ages. The strength of imprinting is measured as a function of animals obtaining a perfect test score of 100 percent. Both graphs illustrate the sharply delineated critical period of imprintability in these animals. (From "Imprinting" by Hess, E. H. *Science* Vol. 130, pp. 133–141, Figure 5, 17 July 1959.)

of 100 percent. These data illustrate that imprinting occurs during a restricted, or critical period in the animal's development.

Hess and his coworkers also examined the effects of other experimental treatments on the strength of imprinting. For example, in one experiment, ducklings were exposed to the imprinting object for ten minutes. However, the distance that they followed the model during the first exposure was systematically varied between 1 and 100 feet and the effects of this treatment on the animal's subsequent performance were measured. The results of this experiment are illustrated in figure 15.6a, which shows the strength of imprinting as a function of the distance the animals followed the model during their first exposure. The results suggest that the strength of imprinting increases the more the animals follow the object, even though they were all exposed to the model for the same length of time. Thus it would appear that the amount of effort the animals expend during the imprinting period is positively correlated with the strength of imprinting.

Figure 15.6b summarizes the results of yet another experiment in which the animals were actually punished for following the imprinting object around the enclosure. Two groups of animals of four different ages were used. The control group was simply allowed to follow the model. Members of the experimental group received eleven footshocks during the imprinting period. When subsequently retested, it was found that the animals which had been punished during imprinting actually followed the model over greater distances than did the control subjects.

Imprinting modifies the behavior of organisms; exposure to the imprinting object during a critical period of development makes an animal's behavior different from what it would have been had it not been exposed to the model. Thus if a bird has imprinted, it tends to follow the model; if it is exposed to the model without having been imprinted, it tends to be fearful of the model. In other words, there are certain similarities between imprinting and the modifications in behavior that were called learning in Chapter 11. However, there are also some interesting differences between imprinting and the more common types of learning that the psychologist studies. For example, during discrimination learning—in which the animal learns to distinguish between two (or more) stimuli on the basis of being rewarded for responding to one or the other—if punishment is associated with the positive stimulus, learning is disrupted. On the other hand, as we have just seen, painful stimulation during the imprinting period does not have this effect; instead it tends to *strengthen* imprinting, as measured on a subsequent following test. A second difference is that imprinting occurs only during the so-called critical period, whereas other types of learning are not necessarily associated with critical periods.

Several hypotheses have been formulated to account for the critical period during which an animal can be imprinted. One, which for lack of a better name we will call the "fear-effort hypothesis," has been formulated by Hess (1959). An important factor in this hypothesis is that birds tend to be fearful of strange objects. This fear can be measured by recording the distress calls the bird utters when it is exposed to a novel stimulus. At birth, the birds do not seem afraid of novel stimuli, but they tend to become more and more fearful as they mature. On the other hand, birds cannot move quickly when they hatch; their speed of walking increases as they mature. According to Hess these two facts taken together—the development of the fear response and the development of locomotor skills—account for the critical period during which imprinting can occur. If the bird is exposed to be imprinting model for the first time when it is too old, it will be afraid

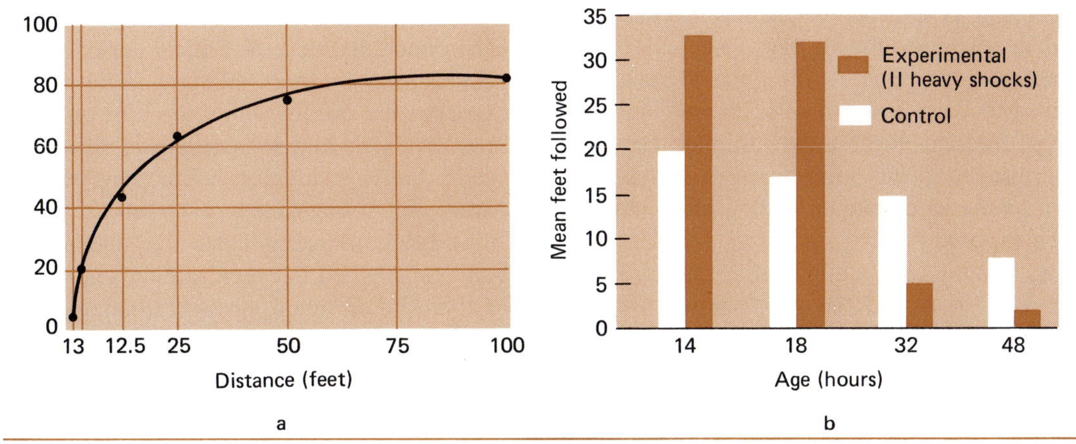

Figure 15.6 (a.) The following responses of birds measured as a function of the distance they followed the model during the imprinting period, which was identical for all animals. (b.) The following response in two groups of birds, measured in terms of the distance the bird followed the model. Experimental animals were punished during the imprinting period, whereas the animals in the control group were not. (From Hess, E. H., "The relationship between imprinting and motivation." Reprinted from *Nebraska Symposium on Motivation* by M. R. Jones (ed.) by permission of University of Nebraska Press. Copyright, 1959 University of Nebraska Press.)

of the model and will not follow it; if it is first exposed to the imprinting object when it is too young, it cannot follow the model vigorously because its locomotor behavior is not sufficiently developed. As we have already suggested, for imprinting to be most successful, the animal must follow the object. Therefore, to be imprinted, the animal cannot be too fearful of the model or it will not follow, and it must be able to walk well enough to follow the imprinting object around the enclosure. This hypothesis is only one example of several that have been formulated to account for the critical period during which imprinting can occur.

Most of the imprinting studies we have discussed are laboratory studies. However, Hess (1972) also conducted a fascinating series of experiments in the wild. Again, his subjects were ducks, but they were studied from afar in an undisturbed natural environment. He provided the ducks with two kinds of nests, a ground nest and an elevated nest. Hess discovered that birds which had been hatched in ground nests returned to ground nests to lay and incubate their own eggs, whereas birds which had been hatched in elevated nests returned to these nests to raise their offspring. These findings suggest that animals become imprinted to specific environments, that is, return to the same situation long after having been exposed to it.

By placing microphones in the nests, Hess was able to record the vocalizations of the parent birds during incubation, hatching, early brooding, and the ducklings' initial exodus from the nest. Both quantitative and qualitative changes in these vocalizations were observed. For example, during early incubation, the amount of vocalization was rather low. But as the time for hatching approached, the parent bird began to vocalize at a significantly higher rate. Furthermore, the unhatched bird responds to the parent's vocalization, both by becoming active in the egg and by vocalizing back. Therefore, it is possible that part of the imprinting process occurs before the animal has hatched. It is also possible that this communication between parent and egg explains a phenomenon termed *hatching synchrony;* that is, although some birds lay about half-a-dozen eggs at the rate of one egg per day, all the eggs, some of which are more mature than others, hatch at the same time. Perhaps the mother's vocalizations shortly before hatching make all the eggs active, and, therefore, all the ducklings break out of their eggs at the same time.

After hatching, there is also an intensive communication between the parent and the young; the parent vocalizes to them, squeezes them, pushes and scratches, and so forth. These behaviors may lead to the establishment of an extremely strong bond between offspring and parent, even before they leave the nest together for the first time. When the birds do leave the nest for the first time, they follow the mother over relatively long distances, and the social bonds may be further strengthened. In summarizing his findings, Hess concluded that the critical period of imprinting may be quite different in laboratory experiments, during which the bird only follows a model, and in naturalistic situations, where there is intense interaction between parent and young over a much longer period. In addition, it seems clear that the natural bond established between mother and young in the wild is much stronger than that observed in the laboratory because the amount of interaction appears to be much greater and lasts much longer.

Hunger and Thirst

The most basic motives are biological; in other words, based on an organism's need to maintain itself and survive. In this section, we will examine some of the information that is available about two basic behaviors, eating and drinking. In large measure, our discussion will concern what we know about the biological processes that may underlie the subjective experience of hunger and thirst. First, we will describe several theoretical positions that attempt to account for hunger and thirst; then, we will examine some of the evidence for and against these positions. It is customary to distinguish between what are called peripheral (or local) and central theories of motivation, including hunger and thirst. According to peripheral theories, the events that precipitate the motivational condition (that is, hunger and thirst) occur in structures which are not part of the central nervous system. For example, a peripheral theory of hunger might argue that stomach contractions lead to the subjective experience of hunger. A central theory, on the other hand, would state that an event in the central nervous system—activity of a circuit in the brain—leads to hunger. In this section, examples of both types of theories will be discussed. First, however, it might be instructive to consider what these theories attempt to explain. It is customary to state that any theoretical attempts to account for eating and drinking must come to grips with at least four issues (Rosenzweig, 1963): (1) the mechanism that initiates the motivated behavior, (2) the mechanism that stops the behavior, (3) the mechanism that regulates the amount of the behavior, that is, the amount of food or water ingested, and (4) the mechanism by which the opportunity to engage in motivated behavior reinforces other behaviors.

Cannon's Local Theory of Hunger and Thirst

Walter Cannon, an eminent neurophysiologist, proposed two local theories to explain hunger and thirst. Until the 1940s these theories were the most widely accepted theoretical accounts of these basic behaviors. They have several distinct virtues: They are simple, they are based on empirical evidence, and they explain some interesting observations.

In essence, Cannon's local theory of hunger states that there is a correlation between stomach contractions, on the one hand, and the subjective experience of hunger, on the other. The theory also states that this relationship is causal; that is, hunger pangs are caused by stomach contractions. However, it does not address itself to the question of how stomach contractions lead to the subjective experience of hunger. As evidence for this theory, Cannon performed the classic experiment illustrated in figure 15.7. He asked his subject to swallow a balloon which, when it reached the subject's stomach, was inflated; the balloon was attached to a recording device and thus could measure stomach contractions. In addition, the subject was placed before a bench and asked to press a telegraph key every time hunger pangs were experienced. When the data were analyzed, the results showed a correlation between the two events; in other words, stomach contractions were noted before the subject reported that hunger was felt. Using this relatively simple theory as an explanatory model, Cannon was able to account for several interesting phenomena associated with the subjective experience of hunger. First, he could explain the fact that the onset of hunger is sudden because the onset of stomach contractions is also sudden and the two events accompany one another. Second, he could explain the fact that there is a periodicity associated with the subjective experience of hunger because stomach contractions also occur periodically and the two events are correlated. Third, he was able to explain the fact that the subjective experience of hunger declines with severe starvation. Individuals who have not eaten for a long time feel sick, to be sure, but the sensation of hunger declines. With severe starvation, stomach contractions also decline.

Cannon also proposed a local theory of thirst, which states that the subjective sensation of thirst is associated with a feeling of

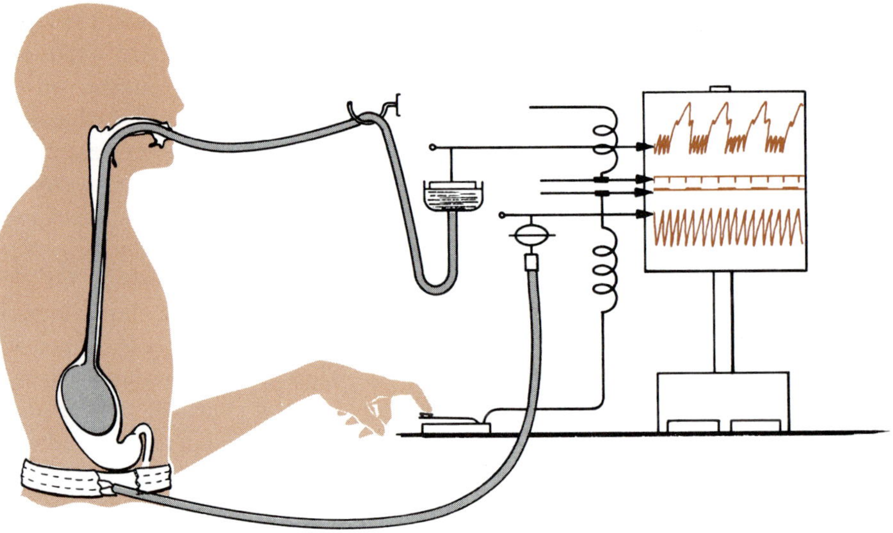

Figure 15.7 Diagrammatic illustration of the Cannon experiment illustrating the experimental arrangement and some sample results.

dryness in the mouth and throat and that the dryness causes the subjective sensation. Here again, Cannon does not deal with how the feeling of dryness in the area of the mouth and throat lead to the subjective experience of thirst. Some of the empirical data on which this theory is based were collected during experiments that Cannon performed on himself. For example, in his laboratory one day, Cannon attached himself to a device similar to the one Pavlov used in his experiments on salivation—a machine which measured his salivary flow. In addition, he sat at a bench and pressed a telegraph key every time he felt thirsty. When the data were analyzed, it became apparent that a sharp drop in salivary flow occurred before the subjective experience of thirst. On another occasion, Cannon injected himself with a drug, *pilocarpine,* which decreases salivary flow, and noted that this treatment resulted in thirst. However, if he injected himself with pilocarpine and also applied a local anesthetic, much as a dentist might, he did not experience thirst, presumably because he could not sense the dryness in his mouth and throat.

Today we no longer believe that local theories of hunger and thirst adequately account for eating and drinking, first, because a large amount of evidence has accumulated in favor of more central theories and, second, because we now have data that suggest these theories are incorrect. One example of such evidence is discussed in box 15.3.

Stellar's Central Theory of Motivation

Stellar (1954) has proposed a central theory of motivation, which locates the mechanisms that underlie motivational processes within the central nervous system. This theory is comprehensive in the sense that it attempts to explain all motivation. And, it is multifactorial in the sense that many sets of factors are presumed to control motivated behavior. The model for this theory is represented diagrammatically in figure 15.8.

As you can see in figure 15.8, the amount of motivated behavior an animal exhibits—

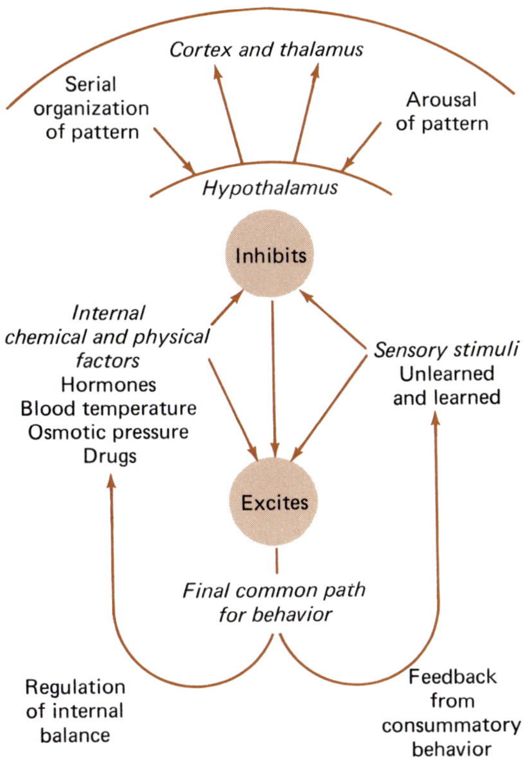

Figure 15.8 Schematic illustration of Stellar's motivational model, showing the physiological factors that are presumed to control the expression of motivated behavior. (From Stellar, E., "The physiology of motivation." *Psychological Review* 61, 1954, pp. 5–22. Copyright 1954 by the American Psychological Association. Reprinted by permission.)

how much it will eat or drink—depends on the activity of an "excitatory center" that is located within the *hypothalamus* of the brain. The more active the neurons within this excitatory center, the greater the amount of motivated behavior that the organism will exhibit. This is indicated by the arrow that links the activity within the excitatory site to the behavioral event, the *final common path* to the behavior.

Four sets of factors are presumed to control the activity of the excitatory hypothalamic nucleus: (1) activity within an inhibitory hypothalamic nucleus, which inhibits the excitatory nucleus, (2) conditions within the internal environment, such as levels of circulating hormones, blood sugar levels, and so on, (3) sensory stimulation, and (4) activity in other parts of the brain, such as the limbic system and the cortex. Within this scheme, the activity of the excitatory hypothalamic center is primary, and all other events affect motivated behavior by either exciting or inhibiting this nucleus. For example, activity in the inhibitory center would tend to suppress motivated behavior by inhibiting the excitatory site.

What is the evidence for this theory with respect to eating behavior? The results of a large number of experiments performed over the past two decades on a number of species suggest that the *lateral hypothalamus* may function as an excitatory area with respect to eating behavior. In general, this evidence demonstrates that bilateral lesions in the region of the lateral hypothalamus cause animals to stop eating. Animal subjects with such lesions refuse to eat, even when extremely palatable food is presented to them, and they must be fed artificially to be kept alive. Findings such as these suggest that the lateral hypothalamus serves as an excitatory site in the sense expressed in Stellar's theory because its destruction leads to a cessation of the motivated behavior in question.

The evidence also demonstrates that electrical stimulation in the area of the lateral hypothalamus, which would excite the nervous tissue in this region, results in an increase in food consumption which is often accompanied by licking and chewing movements. Furthermore, if procaine, a local anesthetic that blocks neural activity, is injected into the hypothalamus, eating is inhibited. Although this evidence suggests that the lateral hypothalamus is indeed involved in eating behavior, more recent evidence has called into question the role of this site in eating behavior

Box 15.3

Can Animals Regulate Their Body Weight if They Feed Themselves Through an Implanted Stomach Fistula?

It might be argued that it follows from Cannon's local theory of hunger that if an organism's stomach contractions are diminished or stopped, say by placing nonnutritive bulk into its stomach, it should feel less hungry, eat less, and as a consequence lose weight. In an ingenious experiment, Epstein and Teitelbaum (1962) provided some data that answer this question. Animals were first prepared with indwelling stomach fistulas which were attached to a pump so that a liquid diet could be administered directly into the animal's stomach. Box figure 15.3a illustrates this preparation. The rats were then placed into a chamber containing a lever, which was connected to a device that injected food into the animals' stomach every time the lever was pressed. The only way the animal could obtain food was to press the lever, and all food it received bypassed its mouth. The data obtained in this experiment are summarized in box figure 15.3b.

The data obtained before the operation indicated that rats were able to maintain a constant body weight over long periods if fed normally. During the immediate postoperative period, the animals tended to lose weight, which probably corresponded to the time required for them

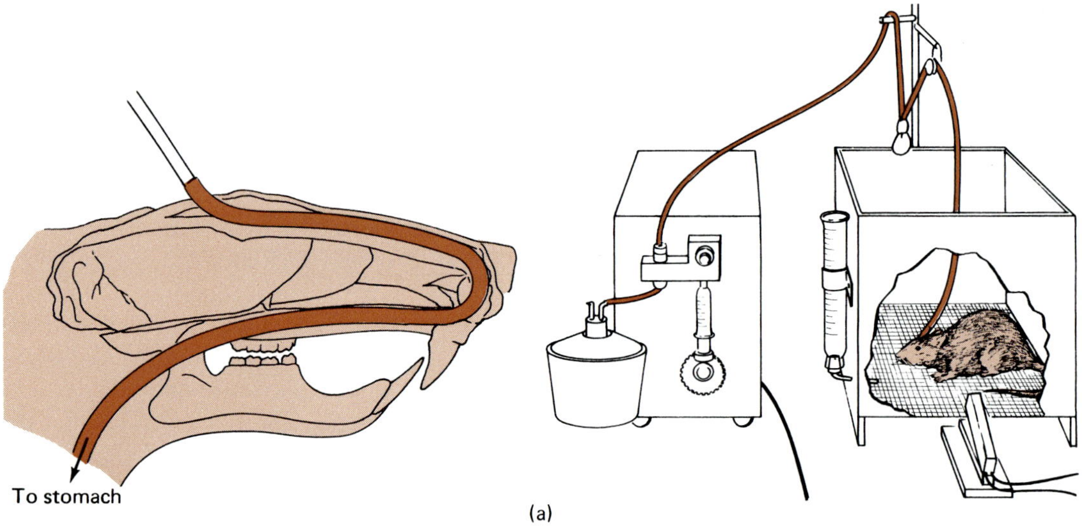

Box Figure 15.3 (a.) Illustrates the experimental preparation (the feeding tube) and the chamber in which the animal, by pressing the lever, feeds itself. (b.) Illustrates the results and shows that animals adjust their feedings if the diet is adulterated. (From Epstein, A. N. and Teitelbaum, P. "Regulation of food intake in the absence of taste, smell, and other oropharyngial sensations," *Journal of Comparative Physiology and Psychology,* 55, 1962, pp. 753–759. Copyright 1962 by the American Psychological Association. Reprinted by permission.)

to learn to press the lever. After this initial period, however, the animals regained their weight, maintained it accurately while feeding themselves only through the stomach fistula. The data also indicated that the animals pressed the feeding lever a fairly constant number of times during any given period. In the next phase of the experiment, the liquid diet was adulterated with fifty percent nonnutritive bulk (cellulose). Per lever press, however, the same volume of diet was injected, only it had less nutritive value. In response to this treatment, the animals pressed the lever more often and maintained their body weight accurately. If the nutritive value of the food was increased, the animals pressed the lever less often, and still maintained their body weight.

These data do not fit well with Cannon's local theory of hunger. Neither does the fact that patients whose stomachs have been removed because of cancer can still feel hunger, although obviously stomach contractions can no longer occur. There are also known cases of individuals who are born without salivary glands and whose mouth and throat are always dry, but who are not constantly thirsty. Thus Cannon's theory is no longer accepted.

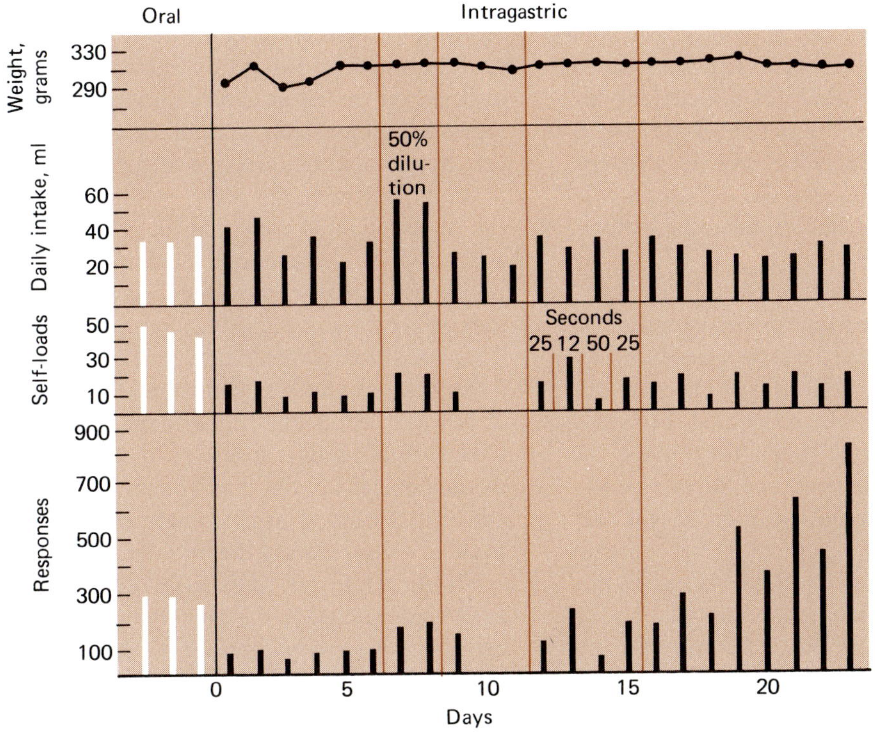

(b)

or, at the very least, indicates that other areas of the brain may be involved to a significant degree in the *lateral hypothalamic syndrome,* which includes a cessation of drinking as well as eating behavior. Zigmond and Stricker (1973), for example, have demonstrated that the destruction of certain fibers which pass near the lateral hypothalamus can duplicate the lateral hypothalamic syndrome to a large extent. These results suggest that the syndrome may be caused in part by damage to fibers originating in the *substantia nigra,* a nucleus far removed from the lateral hypothalamus. Additional evidence suggests that lesions or stimulation in the region of the lateral hypothalamus also affect fibers of the trigeminal nerve—the cranial nerve that supplies motor fibers to the mouth and jaws and carries sensory information from the face and teeth (e.g., Zeigler, 1973). Although there is still considerable disagreement about the specific regions of the brain that are affected by bilateral destruction in the region of the lateral hypothalamus, the critical cell or fiber groups that are affected still serve the excitatory role conceptualized in Stellar's scheme of motivational processes.

Teitelbaum and Epstein (1962) reported the results of a most interesting experiment. They have shown that the deficit produced by lateral hypothalamic lesions is not permanent, if the animal is carefully scheduled through a long recovery period. When they made bilateral lesions in the region of the lateral hypothalamus, the animals refused to eat *and* drink and had to be kept alive by artificial feeding for a prolonged period. After this period, however, the animals began to eat soft, palatable food such as chocolate milk. During the next recovery period, the animals began to eat other food, provided that it was wet and palatable, but they still refused ordinary food. During the last phase of recovery, the animals consumed enough ordinary food to sustain life. The results of this experiment, summarized in terms of the various recovery phases, are illustrated in figure 15.9. Interestingly, Zigmond and Stricker (1973) have shown that bilateral destruction of the substantia nigra is also followed by a similar pattern of recovery.

The results of the experiments in the preceding paragraph suggest that after a period of time, another part of the brain assumes the functions normally carried out by the region that was destroyed. Although we do not know exactly what area of the brain is involved, Teitelbaum and Cytawa (1965) published some data which indicated that the cerebral cortex might be this part of the brain. After the experimental animals had recovered from lesions in the region of the lateral hypothalamus, Teitelbaum and his colleague suppressed the activity of the cortex by means of spreading depression (see Chapter 13) and found that this treatment caused a decrease in food consumption. Cortical spreading depression in animals with an intact hypothalamus does not affect eating.

Small lesions in the ventromedial nuclei of the hypothalamus also seem to affect eating. Animals with these lesions increase their food intake enormously, provided that the food is soft and palatable, and become quite obese. This condition is referred to as *hypothalamic hyperphagia,* and was illustrated in Chapter 3, box 3.1. Brobeck, Teppermand, and Long (1943) made bilateral lesions in the ventromedial nuclei of rats, and observed that the animals consumed large amounts of food and became obese. During the initial phases of the syndrome (referred to as *dynamic* hypothalamic hyperphagia), the animals were ravenous and gained weight rapidly. Once they were extremely fat, however, their ravenous behavior disappeared, and they consumed only enough food, still a large amount, to maintain their excessive weight. This second phase of hypothalamic hyperphagia is referred to as the *static* period. If forced to diet, the animals lost

	Stage I Adipsia, aphagia	Stage II Adipsia, anorexia	Stage III Adipsia, dehydration-aphagia	Stage IV Recovery
Eats wet palatable foods	No	Yes	Yes	Yes
Regulates food intake and body weight on wet palatable foods	No	No	Yes	Yes
Eats dry foods (if hydrated)	No	No	Yes	Yes
Drinks water, survives on dry food and water	No	No	No	Yes

Figure 15.9 The stages of recovery from lateral hypothalamic lesions. The different stages of recovery are listed across the top and the behaviors that are characteristic of the stages are listed at the left of the diagram. (From Teitelbaum, P. and Epstein, A. N. "The lateral hypothalamic syndrome: Recovery of feeling and drinking after lateral hypothalamic lesions," *Psychological Review* 69, 1962, pp. 74–90. Copyright 1962 by the American Psychological Association. Reprinted by permission.)

weight, but when given free access to food later on, they would again go through the entire syndrome. These data suggest that the ventromedial nucleus of the hypothalamus or fibers which pass through or near this region inhibit eating behavior because of its removal results in overeating.

Other evidence in favor of this interpretation is that direct electrical stimulation of the ventromedial hypothalamic nuclei decreases food consumption and that drugs such as benzedrine and dexedrine, which suppress appetite, increase the electrical activity of the ventromedial hypothalamic nuclei. However, because many fibers pass through this region of the hypothalamus from other areas, these results may be related in part to destruction or stimulation of these fibers. Additional research on this important problem is still being carried out to establish whether this is in fact the case and to assess the degree to which the ventromedial hypothalamic syndrome is determined by these effects.

Stellar's model also states that sensory stimulation, extrahypothalamic areas of the brain, and conditions of the internal environment affect eating. Is there any evidence to suggest that this is the case?

1. *Sensory stimulation.* There is little doubt that sensory stimulation affects eating. How many people would claim that the smell of a broiling steak, for example, does not affect their appetite? There is also little doubt that individuals can learn to eat, and even like, foods they have not eaten before. This leads to an important conclusion concerning the effects of sensory stimulation on motivated behavior, namely, that these ef-

fects can be conditioned by association. Lazarus, Yousem, and Arenberg (1953) report the results of an experiment in which college students were shown slides, some of food and some of other items. These pictures were shown so briefly that it was difficult to recognize specific items. Approximately four hours after the students had had their last meal, they began to recognize the pictures of food more and more readily. But after another two or three hours had passed, the pictures of food were not as easily recognized. The results of this experiment can be related to the fact that individuals become extremely hungry as mealtime approaches, but their hunger tends to decrease after this time is passed. In other words, the sensory stimulation that indicates it is mealtime affects the subjective experience of hunger which makes individuals sensitive to food-related items in their environment.

2. *Conditions of the internal environment.* It has been shown that high levels of sugar (glucose) in the blood increase the electrical activity of the ventromedial hypothalamic nuclei and suppress the electrical activity of the lateral hypothalamus. Low levels of blood sugar have the opposite effect. Experiments with human subjects have demonstrated that high levels of glucose are normally associated with satiation, whereas low levels of glucose are generally associated with hunger. Thus it appears that levels of glucose, a condition of the internal environment, is related to hunger. This fact is not too surprising, because glucose is the primary fuel of cells. Levels of sugar in the blood affect not only the electrical activity of the hypothalamic areas we have described but the subjective experience of hunger.

3. *Extrahypothalamic control.* Many areas of the brain outside of the hypothalamus affect eating. For example, ablation of the tips of the temporal cortex results in a condition known as the *Klüver-Bucy Syndrome*. This Syndrome has been studied extensively in monkeys and other animals, and those exhibiting it are abnormal in a number of ways, one of which is related to eating. As a consequence of this experimental treatment, the animals will eat indiscriminately, consuming food that they would not normally eat. They will even place inedible objects into their mouth, chew them, and try to eat them. Furthermore, they will repeat this behavior over and over again, apparently unable to learn that certain things simply cannot be eaten.

On the basis of these data alone (there is much more), we can conclude that what we know about eating tends to fit quite nicely into Stellar's central theory of motivation, although the specific regions of the brain that control these excitatory and inhibitory functions are as yet unclear. Another interesting problem that has not been resolved is that rats suffering from hypothalamic hyperphagia consume large amounts of food, but only if the food is immediately available and palatable; in other words, these animals are finicky eaters for reasons we do not understand. An interesting series of experiments performed by Schachter demonstrates that this may also be the case for obese human subjects (see box 15.4).

Thirst can also be examined in the context of Stellar's model. For example, if lesions are made bilaterally in the *medial hypothalamus* of rats, the animals either drink far less or stop drinking altogether. However, lesions in the region of the *lateral hypothalamus* also reduce drinking behavior, a condition referred to as *adipsia.* These data suggest that both areas are excitatory with respect to drinking, in the sense of Stellar's model, because their destruction reduces drinking. Again, this interpretation has been strengthened by the use of other techniques. When these areas are stimulated electrically, for instance, drinking behavior occurs. Chemical stimulation of the same areas with saline solution has the same

Box 15.4

Stimulus-Bound Eating in Human Obesity

Experimental animals can be made to consume enormous quantities of food, which makes them exceedingly obese, if the region of ventromedial hypothalamic nuclei are destroyed bilaterally. However, these animals will not work hard for food, nor will they eat large amounts of food unless it is very tasty. If we test this phenomenon experimentally, we discover that rats with lesions of this kind will tolerate far less adulteration of their food, for example with quinine, than will normal animals. We could argue from these facts that obese rats are more sensitive to sensory cues concerning food than are normal rats. Schacter (1971) tested this hypothesis on a population of college students, approximately half of which were of normal weight and half overweight. All the subjects were brought into a room one at a time, and were asked to fill out a questionnaire, which was irrelevant to the experiment's actual purpose. On the desk was a bag of nuts, half of which had been shelled and the other half still in the shell. Sometime after a student began to fill out the questionnaire, the experimenter would help himself to a nut, excuse himself, and leave the room. To subjects who were of normal body weight, whether the nuts were shelled or not made no difference; about half ate the nuts regardless of their condition. However, only one out of twenty overweight subjects ate the unshelled nuts, while nineteen out of twenty ate the shelled ones.

Another experiment that illustrates the same point has also been reported by Schacter. In this case, the subjects were hospitalized patients who had come to the hospital to reduce. If the hospital food they were allowed to eat was extremely unappetizing, these overweight subjects reduced their food intake and lost weight. Under similar conditions, normal subjects will eat the same number of calories and maintain their body weight.

Thus both obese rats and obese humans appear to be stimulus-bound with respect to their eating habits; that is, eating seems to be strongly influenced by sensory stimulation. The eating behavior of normal rats and humans, on the other hand, seems to be influenced less by external conditions and more by internal events.

effect; that is, it can induce satiated animals to drink. Thus we can conclude that hypothalamic or other excitatory sites do exist which, when active, induce drinking. One complication that was unforeseen by the model was that more than one area of the hypothalamus is involved; the sites that appear to control drinking and eating overlap, at least anatomically. However eating and drinking seem to be controlled by two different systems. This discovery was reported by Grossman (1960), and the results of his experiments are shown in figure 15.10. Grossman implanted cannulae in the brains of rats and stimulated the lateral hypothalamus chemically. If this area was stimulated with acetylcholine, consumption of water increased for at least one hour after this neurotransmitter was administered; if the same area was stimulated with norepinephrine, no effects on water consumption were noted, but the animals consumed large amounts of food. These data suggest that drinking is controlled in part through a cholinergic system in the hypothalamus, whereas eating is controlled by an adrenergic system in the same region. Cholinergic and adreneric systems were discussed in Chapters 3 and 5.

Other areas of the hypothalamus appear to have inhibitory effects on drinking behavior. If animals receive bilateral lesions in that area of the hypothalamus immediately above the stalk of the pituitary, an area referred to as the *tuber cinerium,* the result is a substantial increase in the consumption of fluids (polydipsia) and the production of urine (polyurea). It is possible to demonstrate that the former effect is primary; for example, it is possible to prepare an animal surgically in such a way that anything it eats or drinks does not reach its stomach. This is done by cutting the esophagus and bringing the two ends to the surface of the body. The animal can then eat or drink as much as it wishes, but none of the food or water will reach its stom-

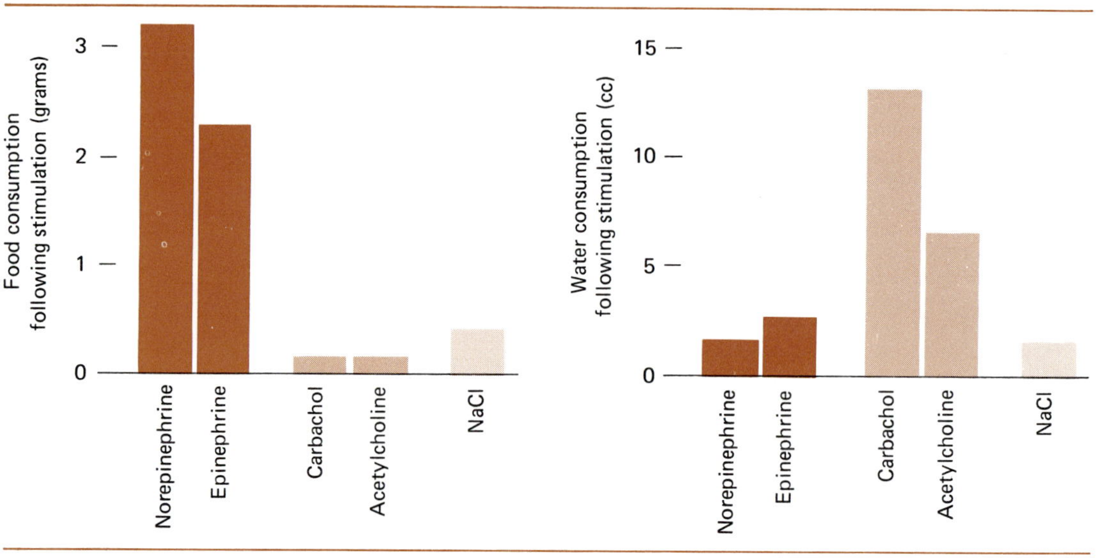

Figure 15.10 Eating and drinking behavior in rats, chemically stimulated with either cholinergic or adrenergic compounds. Notice that cholinergic stimulation increases water consumption, whereas adrenergic stimulation increases food consumption. (From "Eating and Drinking Elicited by Direct Adrenergic or Cholinergic Stimulation of Hypothalamus," Grossman, S. P., *Science,* Vol. 132, pp. 301–302, Figure 29, July 1960. Copyright 1960 by the American Association for the Advancement of Science.)

ach. The two ends of the esophagus can, however, be connected by a tube, so that the animal can eat and drink more or less normally. When lesions are made in the area of the tuber cinerium, the results are as follows: If the tube is not connected, only polydipsia is observed; when it is connected, both polydipsia and polyurea are observed. Therefore, it is possible to show that lesions of the tuber cinerium of the hypothalamus affect drinking behavior directly. Because this lesion causes an increase in fluid intake, the tuber cinerium is believed inhibitory in its control over drinking.

Conditions of the internal environment, sensory stimulation, and extrahypothalamic regions of the brain have all been shown to affect drinking. *Antidiuretic hormone* (ADH), a hormone secreted by the pituitary gland, increase the permeability of the renal collecting tubules to water. When ADH is present, water is retained and hydration of the body results. When it is absent, the body becomes dehydrated. Levels of ADH thus affect drinking. This hormone was discussed in Chapter 4, and its effects are mentioned here only to indicate that conditions of the internal environment do affect drinking behavior.

In summary, much of the available data on thirst and drinking can be summarized by Stellar's theory. The sexually motivated behavior discussed in Chapter 4 ("Hormones and Behavior") can also be interpreted using Stellar's model.

Reinforcement

An important principle in psychology is *reinforcement*. Much of the work done by psychologists, both in pure and applied research, deals with this principle. The question of whether reinforcement is both a necessary and sufficient condition for learning to occur has generated more debate among psychologists than almost any other issue. For the time being, this debate seems to have been laid to rest, and few psychologists today would argue with the statement that reinforcement is sufficient for learning to occur, although it may not be a necessary condition. Any theory that attempts to deal adequately with motivated behavior must come to grips with the issue of reinforcement. How does the execution of a motivated behavior—for example, eating and drinking—reinforce other behavior? Psychologists know almost nothing about how this all-important process occurs.

Olds and Milner (1954) began to unravel this mystery by showing that electrical stimulation of certain areas of the brain results in a phenomenon commonly referred to as *self-stimulation.* Their discovery was greeted with much acclaim because, for the first time in the history of psychology, it seemed that light might be shed on the mechanisms of reinforcement. What is self-stimulation? In some of their original and now classic experiments, Olds and Milner implanted electrodes in the brains of rats and then placed the animals in a Skinner box that was outfitted with a lever that animals could press. In the usual experiment using the Skinner box, the organism is reinforced with a bit of food or a drop of water every time it presses the lever. In Olds and Milner's experiments, however, the animals received brain stimulation every time they pressed the lever. The result of one such self-stimulation experiments is shown in figure 15.11. As you can see, the animals quickly learn to run a maze, apparently to receive the brain stimulation alone. In other words, their behavior, running the maze, can be reinforced by electric shocks to the brain.

When the stimulator is disconnected, the rat soon stops running the maze. This procedure is known as *extinction* (see Chapter 11; in other words, animals will stop responding if their behavior is not reinforced). Extinction will, of course, also occur in the more usual type of experiment, for example, if no food is delivered after the response. The difference in the two conditions—extinction of behavior after self-stimulation versus extinction after a more typical reward—appeared in the rate of extinction: the extinction that followed self-stimulation occurred more rapidly. Recently, however, even this difference has been challenged. The rates of extinction in hungry rats that have been reinforced with sugar water do not appear to be significantly different from the rates observed following self-stimulation.

What makes self-stimulation so interesting is the fact that animals will learn new behaviors when reinforced with it and will work hard to maintain it. Self-stimulation experiments have been done on human subjects who, when stimulated in areas similar to those just described for rats, report pleasurable feelings. Perhaps activity in these parts of the brain is the biological basis of reinforcement.

Not only will rats learn to press a lever in a Skinner box for self-stimulation, but they will also engage in other behaviors which suggest that activity in these regions of the brain has reinforcing properties. For example, animals will learn to run a maze for electrical stimulation, and they will run across an electric grid in an obstruction box to reach a lever which, when pressed, results in self-stimulation. They will even learn rather complex discriminatory behaviors when reinforced with electrical stimulation to the brain. In other words, all kinds of instrumental behavior can be reinforced with brain stimulation. The effects of fear-producing stimuli—for example, sounds that were previously associated with a painful foot shock—can be mitigated during self-stimulation; mild foot

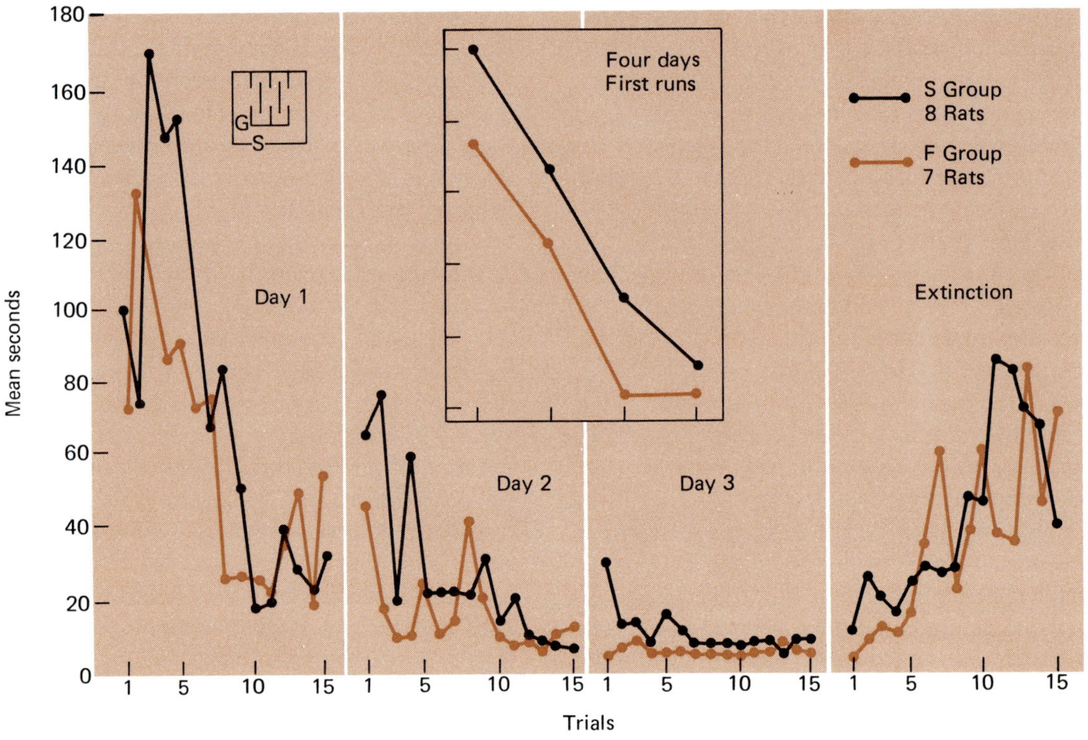

Figure 15.11 This figure illustrates the results of rats given brain stimulation as a reward for running the maze. The maze is shown in upper left corner. (S denotes the starting point and C+ the goal box.) Improvement is shown for the first three days, and extinction is shown by a decrease in performance during the fourth day, without brain stimulation. (From Olds, J. and Milner, P., "Positive reinforcement produced by electrical stimulation of septal area and other regions of rat brain," *Journal of Comparative Physiology and Psychology* 47, 1954, pp. 419–437. Copyright 1954 by the American Psychological Association. Reprinted by permission.)

shocks themselves are ignored during self-stimulation; and so forth.

The relationship between self-stimulation and other motivated behaviors such as eating, drinking, and sexual behavior, is not fully understood. However, self-stimulation can often be elicited from areas of the brain that, if stimulated, result in eating, drinking, and sexually motivated behavior. These events can be separated if certain aspects of the stimulating current are manipulated; for example, different behaviors will be elicited, depending on the intensity of stimulation and how long it lasts. Food and water deprivation, and manipulation of the sex drive through administration of the appropriate hormones, have small but significant effects on the performance of animals in self-stimulation experiments. Self-stimulation and other motivated behaviors may be related in the sense that they can often be elicited from similar structures in the brain and in the sense that one motivational condition affects the others.

Not all areas of the brain act in the way just described. Detailed anatomical research has shown that the highest rates of self-stimulation are obtained from structures that form the so-called *medial forebrain* bundle. This part of the brain is diagrammatically illustrated in figure 15.12.

Finally, some evidence suggests that the neural system underlying the self-stimulation phenomenon is adrenergic, that is, a system in which norepinephrine acts as the neural transmitter. This evidence was supplied by Stein (1967), who used pharmacological tools to investigate self-stimulation. He observed that drugs such as chlorpromazine and reserpine, which lower the levels of norepinephrine in the brain, decrease self-stimulation, in that more electric current is needed to produce self-stimulation in drugged animals than in control animals. Amphetamines, on the other hand, lower the thresholds for self-stimulation, and animals treated with these drugs tend to stimulate themselves without pause. Because amphetamines facilitate the release of norepinephrine from sites in the brain, these data suggest that self-stimulation is mediated by some adrenergic system, a hypothesis which is strengthened by the fact that adrenergic pathways in the medial forebrain bundle do in fact exist.

Self-stimulation has now been studied in many animals, including rats, cats, porpoises, pigeons, and man. In all these animals, the areas of the brain from which self-stimulation can be obtained are similar, and a variety of instrumental behaviors can be reinforced by stimulating the appropriate neural region. Whether the riddle of reinforcement will finally be solved through investigations of these so-called pleasure centers of the brain remains to be seen.

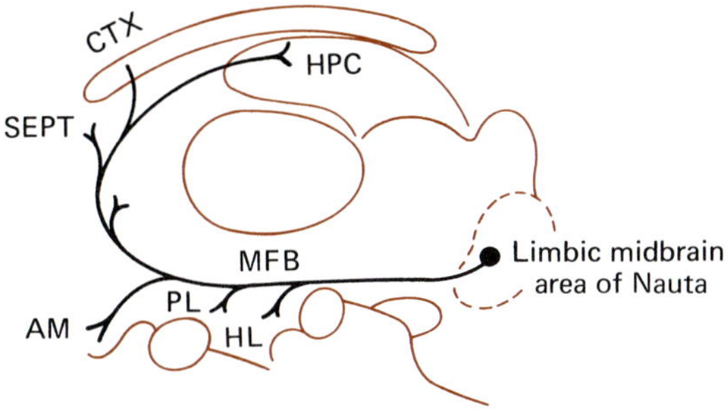

Figure 15.12 Medial forebrain bundle. Areas of the brain from which self-stimulation can be elicited. The system arises in the limbic midbrain area, ascends through the medial forebrain bundle (MFB) and terminates in the hypothalamus (HL), preoptic area (PL), amygdala (AM), septum (SEPT), hippocampus (HPC), and neocortex (CTX). (For a review of the anatomy of these areas, see Chapter 3).

Summary

We can think of motivation as the driving force behind our behavior. There were two dominant themes in the early philosophical concern with motivational processes: one presumed that motivation was governed by external events and was largely hedonistic in character; the other assumed that man's behavior was governed by rational thought and free will. Freud's early theories of behavior held that much of our behavior was governed by unconscious motives. And Darwin's evolutionary framework suggested that certain behaviors evolved through natural selection because of their adaptive, or fitness value. Thus from philosophy, the science of psychology inherited the vigorously debated controversy of free will versus determinism; from biology, the question of whether heredity or experience was the major factor in motivation; and from Freud's psychoanalytic theory, the question of whether conscious or unconscious processes were more important in guiding behavior.

Many techniques can be used to determine the strength of motives. The Columbia Obstruction Method, for example, measures the strength of an animal's motivation by making the animal cross an obstruction, such as an electrified grid, to obtain a goal. Free-choice methods, which allow an experimental subject to choose between several goal objects, provide some measure of the subject's relative preference for different goals, such as food, water, and the like. The Skinner box can also be used to determine the "strength" of motivation, either by determining the rate at which an animal will press a lever to obtain some goal or by determining the effort it will expend on pressing the lever. And finally, projective tests have been used with human subjects. In these tests, the subject looks at ambiguous scenes (or even inkblots) and constructs a story about each scene. It is presumed that the subject's own motives and desires will appear in the story, although they may not be apparent to the individual.

The field of ethology has played an important role in the development of theories concerning motivated behavior. Ethologists study the behavior of different species of organisms, usually in their natural environment. Imprinting, originally shown by Lorenz to be a powerful influence in the lives of many species, is a phenomenon that may have lasting effects on the behavior of many organisms. Ethology has demonstrated that both inheritance and early environment have significant effects on motivated behavior in animals.

Two widely studied forms of motivated behavior, from a biological perspective, are eating and drinking. Theories of eating and drinking can be classified into two broad categories that are representative of theories of motivation in general. Peripheral theories hold that factors outside the central nervous system are the primary determinants of motivation, while central theories emphasize the role of the central nervous system. Recent evidence favors central theories of hunger and thirst. Stellar's theory of motivation provides a general framework for central theories of motivation. Experimental evidence suggests that certain events in the central nervous system indeed underlie hunger, thirst, and other forms of motivation.

Both eating and drinking behavior may be affected if appropriate sites in the hypothalamus and related areas of the brain are stimulated electrically or chemically, or if these areas are damaged.

Perhaps one of the most important aspects of motivation is that animals (including man) learn and remember when rewarded or punished. That is, their behavior may be shaped by the process of reinforcement or reward. Although we have come a long way toward understanding the anatomical and physiological mechanisms that may underlie motivated behaviors such as eating and drinking, the question of how these events reinforce behavior is largely unanswered. However, Olds and Milner's discovery that direct stimulation of the brain can be reinforcing has begun the process of unravelling this important mystery. We now know that stimulation of certain areas of the brain of animals, including man, reinforces behavior in a manner that is similar to giving food or water to a hungry or thirsty rat. Stimulation of the medial forebrain bundle has been effective in producing this "self-stimulation" phenomenon, although we are still uncertain about whether this discovery will help us understand the neural basis of reinforcement and how behavior can be shaped according to the law of effect.

16

Motivation, Conflicts, and Emotions

In the previous chapter, we focused our attention on rather simple drives and motives. In this chapter we will discuss some more complex types of motivated behavior, several theories that have been proposed to explain them, and the emotions that are considered the affective counterparts of motives.

A good way to begin our discussion is to point out that all organisms are complex biological systems which function as integrated units and possess self-regulating mechanisms that maintain the internal equilibria necessary for life. These self-regulatory systems are termed *homeostatic mechanisms*. For example, under normal circumstances, all organisms regulate the concentrations of sodium in their body fluids within narrow limits. This is usually accomplished by hormones that are secreted by the adrenal glands and cause the kidneys to conserve sodium. But what happens when an animal's adrenal glands are nonfunctional or have been surgically removed? The animal loses its normal homeostatic control, and to stay alive it must replace the sodium through *behavioral* homeostatic mechanisms; in other words, it develops a specific appetite for salt (sodium chloride) and regulates the concentrations of sodium in its body behaviorally. In translating the physiological concept of homeostasis into psychological terms, we speak of *deficiency motivations*—behaviors that serve to regulate the needs of specific tissues.

Do human beings demonstrate these specific appetites? The answer is a qualified yes. Instances of this kind of behavior are more readily observed in infants than in adults living in Western cultures. One example of these specific appetites is described in box 16.1. Another example is our behavior when we consume large quantities of beer. In this case, we create a sodium deficiency by diluting our body fluids, and we attempt to regulate the deficiency by eating large quantities of salty peanuts or pretzels.

Box 16.1
The Wisdom of the Body

In 1932 the famous physiologist Walter Cannon, whose work on eating and drinking was discussed in Chapter 15, wrote a book titled *The Wisdom of the Body,* which had an enormous impact on psychologists who were working in the area of drives and motivation. In his book Cannon emphasized the fact that homeostatic mechanisms were commonplace and attempted to use these mechanisms to explain many motivated behaviors. As the title of his book suggests, he speculated that organisms will behave in a way that will maintain homeostasis. Is there any evidence to suggest that human bodies are indeed "wise" in the sense Cannon meant? Will humans select foods that are good for them, for example?

In 1928 Davis reported the results of an experiment that he performed on three newly weaned infants. These children were allowed to select their own food from a wide variety of nutritious alternatives; some of the foods were raw, some were cooked. Two of the infants selected their own food in this cafeteria fashion for six months, whereas the third infant fed itself in this way for one year. The results of this experiment were remarkable: All three infants would eat one food exclusively for a while; for example, only cereals, then only eggs, and so on. However, they ate balanced diets. All gained weight normally and showed no signs of nutritional disorders. One infant, in fact, cured himself of rickets—a nutritional disease caused by a deficiency in vitamin D—by selecting large quantities of cod-liver oil, which contains large amounts of vitamin D. After he had cured himself of the disease, he stopped eating cod-liver oil.

In view of this evidence, how seriously should we take Cannon's idea of the body's wisdom? Why do children and adults show such a penchant for soft drinks? Why do so many alcoholics suffer from malnutrition and specific vitamin deficiencies? The answer appears to be that our bodily wisdom can be affected by acquired tastes. Consider the following experiment. Rats are offered sucrose—a taste that they normally prefer—in some situations and not in others. All animals are then made protein deficient and are offered a choice between a solution rich in proteins and a solution of sucrose, in two situations. One situation is identical to that in which the animals had previous experience with sucrose, and the other situation is novel; that is, one in which the animals had had no previous experience with sucrose. In the first situation, the protein deficient animals will still select sucrose, whereas in the second situation the animals will show a preference for the protein solution. In other words, it appears that experience can seriously undermine what Cannon called the "wisdom of the body."

Adaptation Level Theory of Motivation

According to the British empiricists, especially John Locke, human beings behaved in ways that would maximize pleasure and minimize pain. In other words, behavior is governed by hedonistic principles. Modern psychological theories postulate in addition that drives and motives are caused by internal and external stimulation. Therefore, individuals behave in a way that will balance overstimulation and understimulation. If this is the case, then the question becomes one of determining what we mean by over- and understimulation.

Helson (1947) attempted to answer this question by proposing what he called *adaptation level theory.* According to this theory, the intensity of stimulation is determined, not only by the physical magnitude of the stimulus, but by the *context* in which the stimulus is applied. A common method of demonstrating the contextual nature of the perceived magnitude of a stimulus is to ask a subject to place his arm into a bucket of hot water and then transfer it to a container of tepid water. In this situation, the individual will say that the water in the second bucket is cold. If the same individual places his hand into a bucket of ice water and then transfers it to the container of tepid water, he will claim that the tepid water is warm. In other words, the individual judges the intensity of stimulation against the residue of previous stimulation. Levels of stimulation produce *adaptation,* and judgments about other stimuli are made against a reference point of the subject's *level of adaptation.* According to Helson, the magnitude of perceived stimulation is determined, not only by level of adaptation, but by *contextual stimuli.* Thus the temperature of tepid water will be perceived as different if one is reaching into a bucket of ice water or hot water. Levels of adaptation depend on previous stimulation and on contextual stimuli.

McClelland (1965) used the adaptation level theory to explain motivated behavior, claiming that a motive can be defined as an anticipated change in affect based on past experience. It is this anticipation of a change in affect that compels the individual to act; that is, the anticipation itself is the motive because it leads to behavior. Motivation, then, depends on two frames of reference, the contextual affective level (how the individual feels at the moment) and the anticipated change in feelings based on learned cues. Consequently, the motivational strength of stimulation depends on the discrepancy between the physical strength of the stimulus and the individual's level of adaptation. Individuals will seek either stimulation or its reduction, and both may have reinforcing properties. For example, after expending great mental effort on writing a term paper or studying for a final examination, an individual will often seek to reduce stimulation by taking a quiet stroll in the mountains or watching television. Conversely, many of us have experienced a desire to "get back to work" after a long vacation.

Animals of many species, and especially human beings, engage in large amounts of investigative behavior. They appear to be curious and to seek novel stimulation. Investigative behavior and curiosity-related behavior can be explained in part by adaptation level theories of motivation.

Curiosity

Look at the photograph of the monkey in figure 16.1. This animal is hard at work taking apart the latches and is not receiving any obvious rewards for its performance. Apparently, it works only to satisfy what has been termed a *manipulative motive.*

Is a reduction in sensory input experienced as unpleasant, and do animals seek stimulation by activity, curiosity, and manipulation? Box 16.2 illustrates how people feel when

Figure 16.1 Monkeys readily learn to unhook hasps on an apparatus such as this, even when they receive no obvious reward for successful performance. (From Harlow, H.F. and McClearn, G.E., H. Harlow, Wisconsin Primate Laboratory. Object discrimination learned by monkeys in the basis of manipulation motives. *Journal of Comparative and Physiological Psychology,* 1954, 47, 73–76. Copyright 1954 by the American Psychological Association. Reprinted by permission. Courtesy H.F. Harlow, University of Wisconsin Primate Laboratory.)

Box 16.2

The Unpleasantness of Boredom

College students were used as subjects in the following experiment reported by Heron, Doane, and Scott (1956) and Heron (1957). For participating in the experiment, the students were paid $20 per day, which was a handsome salary for a day's work in the 1950s, especially because they were being paid to do as little as possible.

The subjects lay in a small cubicle on a comfortable bed and were allowed to rise only to take their meals and go to the bathroom. Their sensory input was drastically reduced by the means illustrated in Box figure 16.2. Outside noises were masked by fans, the subjects wore goggles that prevented them from seeing, and they were prevented from touching objects by having their arms wrapped in cotton.

How did the students react to this situation? Initially, they slept most of the time. But after two or three days, they abandoned the experiment, which they were free to do at any time. The subjects reported that they had felt extremely bored and restless. They also said they had daydreamed a lot, and on occasion had hallucinated. Furthermore, their thought processes were disturbed, and their performance on standard intelligence tests was markedly reduced. In other words, the subjects felt so uncomfortable that they wanted to get out of the situation at all costs.

After reviewing many experiments on sensory deprivation, Zubeck (1969) concluded that although the extreme symptoms reported by Heron's subjects—for example, hallucinations—are rare, the general findings indicate that sensory deprivation is an extremely unpleasant experience.

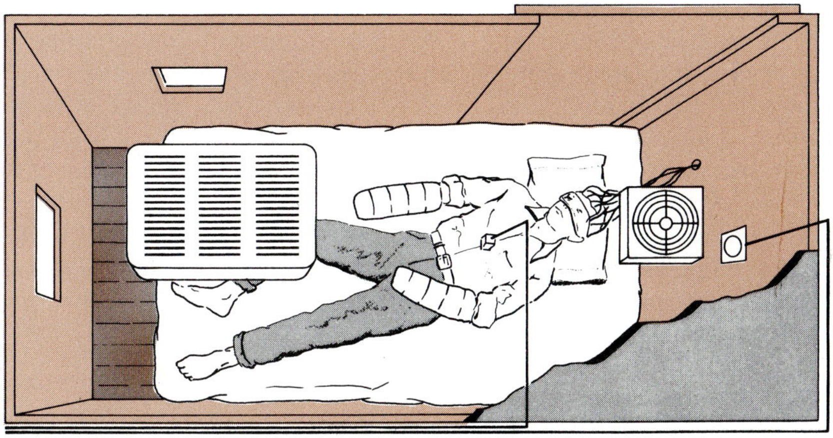

Box Figure 16.2 An experiment in sensory isolation. Subjects were asked to lie on a comfortable bed. The air conditioner and fan masked outside noises, and the subject's arms were taped in cotton to reduce their sensory input. The wires attached to the subject's head monitored the electrical activity of the brain. (From "The pathology of boredom," Heron, W. Copyright 1957 by Scientific American, Inc. All rights reserved.)

deprived of sensory stimulation. If the lack of sensory stimulation is unpleasant and a condition that human subjects seek to terminate, then we can ask the opposite question: Do animals seek stimulation? Many animals actively seek stimulation, and psychologists speak of curiosity and the need to manipulate and investigate the environment as motivational conditions. By this they mean that curiosity and the opportunity to manipulate the environment function as rewards, or reinforcement in learning situations.

Some of the classic research in the area of curiosity and environmental manipulation was done by Butler (1953, 1954), who used monkeys as his experimental subjects. Each animal was confined in an uninteresting enclosure in which stimulus display cards were mounted above doors. When the animal pushed the right card, the door over which it was mounted would swing open momentarily, and the animal was allowed a brief glimpse of the laboratory outside. The monkeys quickly learned this discrimination problem, reinforced apparently by nothing more than a look outside their enclosure. Furthermore, they worked for this reward over many, many trials.

Apparently, even rats will learn to perform tasks if rewarded with an opportunity to explore their environment. Consider the following experiment (Myers and Miller, 1954), in which three groups of rats were used: Animals in the first group were allowed to leave a black box and enter a white one if they pressed a bar in a Skinner box. Animals of the second group were allowed to leave a white box for a black one if they pressed a bar. Animals of the third group opened a door by pressing a bar but were prevented from going into the other compartment by a panel immediately behind the door. The first and second groups soon learned the bar-pressing response, reinforced only by the opportunity to explore their environment. The third group never learned the bar-pressing response.

It has also been shown that the opportunity to manipulate objects is reinforcing. For example, Harlow and McClearn (1954) presented monkeys with a test board into which screw eyes of different colors had been set. Screw eyes of one color could be removed, whereas those of another color could not. Over several trials, the animals soon learned to remove all the screws of one color without touching the others. The monkeys were presented with six of these problems, each consisting of a different color combination, and showed progressive improvement in solving the problems without any apparent decrease in motivation. The animals were allowed to rest, but their only reward was the opportunity to manipulate screw eyes of a particular color.

Humans engage in all kinds of behavior to satisfy their curiosity. They constantly manipulate objects in their environment as well as ideas in their minds. We study science, after all, to satisfy our curiosity about the world we live in. We gossip because we are intensely curious about our fellow human beings, particularly about the private affairs of our friends. We sail across huge oceans in small boats, and we climb the highest mountains. How do we explain these behaviors? Two explanations have been proposed: (1) We seek an optimal level of stimulation to relieve the kind of boredom that Heron's subjects (see box 16.2) found so unpleasant. This optimal level will vary from person to person. (2) Humans are afraid of the unknown. Thus they are curious about it, explore it, and, finding it largely harmless, feel less fearful. The reduction of fear is then reinforcing, and so we learn to be curious.

Contact Comfort

Harlow and his colleagues (1958, 1970) reported an extensive series of experiments in which they explored the needs of monkeys for what they termed *contact comfort.*

In Harlow's experiments, infant rhesus monkeys were reared with surrogate mothers made of either terry cloth or welded wire, as previously discussed in Chapter 9 and shown in figures 9.1, 9.2, and 16.2. Both types of surrogate mothers had long bodies so that the monkeys could easily cling to them. Some of the wire and cloth mothers

(a)

Figure 16.2 (a.) shows an infant rhesus monkey clinging to the soft terry cloth mother while feeding from the bottle in the wire surrogate mother. (b.) indicates the amount of time that monkeys spent with each surrogate. (From Harlow, H.F. The nature of love. *American Psychologist,* 1958, 13, 673–685. Copyright 1958 by the American Psychological Association. Reprinted by permission. Courtesy H.F. Harlow, University of Wisconsin Primate Laboratory.)

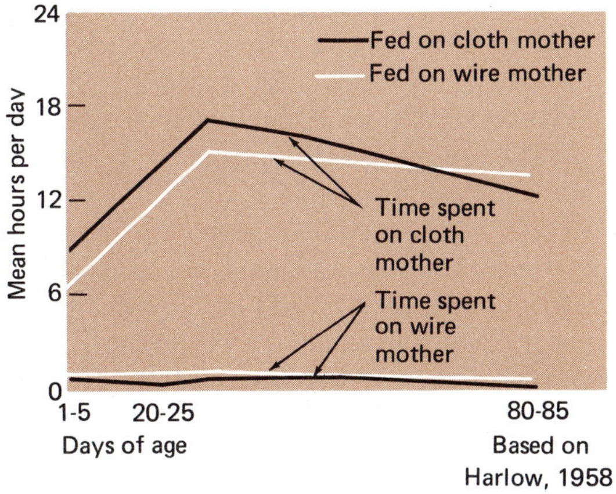

(b)

were provided with bottles on which the infants could feed.

Both a cloth and a wire surrogate mother were set up in a cubicle that was adjacent to the infants' cages. The animals were raised in groups, some with a nursing wire mother and others with a nursing cloth mother. The amount of time each monkey spent with the different surrogates was measured. The findings were rather astonishing: All the animals spent most of their time with the terry cloth mother, whether it provided food or not. Figure 16.2a shows a monkey clinging to the terry cloth surrogate while feeding from a bottle in the wire model; the actual data are reproduced in figure 16.2b.

On the basis of these results, Harlow argued that the infant's love for its mother was based on contact comfort rather than the reduction of drives such as hunger and thirst. In subsequent experiments, Harlow demonstrated that other stimuli are also important in forming infant-mother bonds. For example, if an infant rhesus monkey was offered a choice between a lactating and a nonlactating terry cloth mother, it preferred the one that provided food. Rhesus monkeys also preferred a rocking surrogate terry cloth mother over a stationary one, which may explain why a rocking cradle or a pacing mother soothes a human infant. Finally, given a choice between a warm wire surrogate and a cold terry cloth one, the monkeys preferred the warm model over the soft one until they were approximately twenty days old. After that they preferred the cold but soft surrogate.

Frustration

Most human beings have a deep-seated desire to be free and independent, not only politically and economically, but psychologically. In addition, most humans want to be self-fulfilled. We all hope that our children will be able to obtain the kind of education they desire—and they in turn hunger after a good education. In many societies even today, people strive for the kind of security which will ensure that their biological needs for food, water, clean air, and the like will be filled. In the more affluent parts of the world, people seek and work for certain luxuries. In other words, all individuals try to reach certain goals. When these attempts are blocked, we say they are frustrated. *Frustration* is defined as the blocking of ongoing goal-directed behavior. It appears to be a motivating condition because it is arousing and it leads to other behaviors.

The arousing nature of frustration has been illustrated in a number of experiments. For example, rats were trained to run down a straight alley to a goal box where they were rewarded with eight pellets of food. Then, they were trained to run down a second straight alley to another goal box for eight more pellets of food. The experiment was run over many trials, and the speed at which the animals ran down the alleys was used as a measure of performance until the animals learned the size of the reward. At this point the conditions of the experiment were changed so that the animals found either 0, 2, 4, 6, 8, 12, or 16 pellets of food in the first goal box. The speed of running down the second alley revealed that if an animal found less food in the first goal box than it had "expected," it ran faster. These results, it has been argued, demonstrate the energizing properties of frustration.

Another form of behavior that occurs in response to frustration has been termed *displacement activity*. This behavior has been studied extensively by animal behaviorists and is said to occur when an animal is blocked from reaching a goal or when one behavioral pattern conflicts with another. In the presence of a stimulus that normally elicits a particular response, the animal will engage in a particular action. When this action is thwarted, another type of behavior will occur.

Displacement activity has been observed in herring gulls, which are territorial and build nests. When engaged in a territorial dispute with a powerful rival, the gulls sometimes peck at, grasp, and toss bits of grass over their shoulder. This behavior is typical of nest building, but it is inappropriate when defending a territory. Ostensibly, the gull is simultaneously driven to attack the intruder and to flee from a stronger opponent, and this conflict is somehow channeled into nest-building behavior. The act of plucking up grass is similar to the fighting behavior of these birds because during fights, they pull out the plumage of opponents. Schaller (1965) described another form of displacement behavior, chest-beating by the gorilla, which occurs when the animal encounters man or other gorillas. In analyzing this behavior, Schaller pointed out that in these tension-producing situations, the gorilla is torn between the desire to attack and to flee. The animal "resolves" this conflict of motives by engaging in an inappropriate action, chest-beating.

Frustration has also been studied extensively from the viewpoint of aggression. In 1939, Dollard et al. postulated the theory that all aggression is caused by frustration. Whether this is true seems doubtful today; however, there is ample experimental evidence to indicate that under certain conditions, aggressive acts are indeed elicited by frustration. Consider the following experiment conducted by Azrin and his colleagues (1966). A pigeon was placed in a Skinner box and taught to press a key for food reinforcement. A second pigeon, an "innocent bystander," was put into the box and extinction procedures were initiated (pressing the key no longer produced a food reward). During these extinction trials, the first bird attacked the innocent bystander. In interpreting the results of this experiment, we can postulate that the pigeon's aggression was induced by frustration, brought about by the sudden withdrawal of reinforcement.

Figure 16.3 Displaced aggression. Rats that have learned to fight ignore the doll until one of the rats is removed; the remaining rat then displaces its aggression by attacking the doll. (Courtesy of Dr. N.E. Miller, Rockefeller University, New York.)

Displaced aggression is another phenomenon that can be demonstrated experimentally in animals. Figure 16.3 illustrates the behavior of two rats that have learned to fight with each other. Notice that the animals ignore the doll which is in the compartment. When one rat is removed from the compartment, however, the other animal displaces its aggression by attacking the doll.

These experiments support the frustration-aggression hypothesis proposed by Dollard et al. Because Azrin's results can be replicated with birds reared in isolation, it is possible to argue that frustration-induced aggression is mediated by innate mechanisms. Furthermore, we can cautiously speculate that similar innate mechanisms may exist in all animals, including humans. However, it should be carefully noted that all aggressive behavior should not be viewed as the result of frustration.

Conflicts

At the conceptual level, psychologists think of conflict as the result of competition among motives. An individual is described as being in a state of conflict when he wishes to attain two or more goals simultaneously but is unable to do so. Because motivated behavior is goal directed, we can think of it as either *approach* or *avoidance* behavior. Using this scheme of classification, we can identify four types of conflicts: (1) approach-approach conflicts, (2) approach-avoidance conflicts, (3) avoidance-avoidance conflicts, and (4) multiple approach-avoidance conflicts.

Approach-Approach Conflicts

This kind of conflict occurs when an individual must choose between two positive goals. Having to decide which of two countries to visit on a vacation when you only have the time and money to visit one country is an example. Another is the conflict that a customer in a restaurant sometimes experiences when reading the menu. Should he have steak or lobster? Many restaurants resolve this conflict for their customers by offering combination dishes that feature both lobster and steak. This illustrates the general proposition that approach-approach conflicts are easily resolved. One can, for instance, decide to have lobster on this occasion and steak the next time; or one can decide to visit one country on this trip and the other country on the next vacation. Approach-approach conflicts only cause serious problems when the motivation for both goals is extremely strong.

Approach-Avoidance Conflicts

Approach-avoidance conflicts occur when a single goal has both positive and negative properties. For example, those of us who smoke cigarettes often find ourselves in this kind of conflict. We enjoy cigarettes and are probably addicted to smoking; yet we know the serious consequences of this behavior to our health and are thus in conflict. An experienced poker player can be almost certain that he holds the winning hand, but he must make a substantial investment to win the pot and this creates a conflict. The psychological distance from the goal appears to be a major factor in approach-avoidance situations. That is, we enjoy the cigarette today and feel miserable today if we do not smoke; the potential health hazards are in the distant future and thus are not powerfully motivating.

Avoidance-Avoidance Conflicts

An avoidance-avoidance conflict arises when an individual must choose between two goals, both of which have negative qualities. Many individuals do not like to cook or houseclean, but the results of not cooking or housecleaning are also negative. Conflicts such as these are notoriously difficult to solve, especially if the alternative goals are strongly negative. Instead of cooking and cleaning, a person may watch television while eating an easily prepared frozen TV dinner. This behavior is sometimes referred to as "leaving the field" and is an easy way to reduce an avoidance-avoidance conflict. Leaving the field is less possible in the other types of conflict, in which the positive aspects of at least one alternative keep the individual in the situation.

Multiple Approach-Avoidance Conflicts

Individuals are frequently confronted with more than two choices, and any given goal is likely to have many negative and positive properties. In other words, life consists of a series of alternatives, each of which has many positive and negative properties. Choosing a career often involves a multiple approach-avoidance conflict. First, there are many careers to choose from, and each has unique advantages and disadvantages. But let's assume that you have drastically reduced your alternatives and have decided on a career in the health field. At this point, many choices still remain. For example, you may decide to become a physician because you want to help people, the income is attractive, the medical profession is prestigious, and so on. This choice also has its negative aspects; for example, your education will be lengthy and expensive, you will have to work extremely hard, and you will have little free time. Thus you may decide instead to become a medical technologist because you would still be working in the medical field and providing services to people, your training would be shorter and far less expensive, and so forth. However, this choice also has its negative aspects; for example, the job will bring you less prestige, you will have to work for someone else, and your income will be much lower.

Psychologists have attempted to provide theoretical and quantitative descriptions of conflict situations. One of these attempts is discussed in box 16.3.

Acquired Motives

The reasons people behave the way they do are often difficult to understand. Human motives are complex, and analyzing them has proved to be extraordinarily difficult. Some theorists believe that the term "human motives" is inadequate, that the only way to convey the complexity of human behavior is to speak of human motivational systems.

With respect to human motivational systems, two facts are obvious. First, much of what we call motivated behavior in human beings has little to do with satisfying biological drives such as hunger and thirst. For example, people continue to work hard for symbolic rewards such as money, although they already earn far more than they need to buy the products that will satisfy their basic biological drives. Second, learning and experience underlie much of what we call human motivation. In other words, we learn to want

Box 16.3

A Gradient Analysis of Conflicts

Box figure 16.3a is a diagrammatic illustration of how one might conceive of approach and avoidance conflicts. The vertical axes in these diagrams represent the strength of the tendency to approach or to avoid the goal object. The horizontal axes represent the distance from the goal object; in this sense, distance is conceived in terms of space, time, or similarity. Similarity is the degree to which a particular goal object, (e.g., a sculpture) resembles an actual object that is feared.

You should note two aspects concerning these gradients of approach and avoidance. (1) The absolute strength of the tendency to avoid is greater than the absolute strength of the tendency to approach. In other words, fears and anxieties are stronger motivating factors than positive goals. Experimental evidence suggests that this is the case. (2) The approach gradient is not as steep as the avoidance gradient. That is, at great distances from the goal object, the avoidance gradient exerts little negative force and the approach gradient does exert some force.

Box figure 16.3b illustrates this kind of gradient analysis in a situation involving an approach-avoidance conflict; a single goal object has positive and negative properties.

Notice that the two gradients—the tendency to approach and to avoid—intersect. At the point of intersection, the maximal degree of conflict can be expected to occur. This type of an approach-avoidance conflict can be demonstrated experimentally by training rats to run a maze to a goal box where both food and a punishing shock are given. The rats start out by running quickly and vigorously towards the goal box; as they get closer to it, however, they slow down. They may actually back away when they get very close to it. At the point where the two gradients intersect, the animals often freeze for long periods. This behavior can be observed in humans who have made an appointment with either a physician or dentist. Appointments such as these have both positive and negative properties, and they are often made many weeks or months in advance. At the time the appointment is made, the individual actually looks forward to it because he expects the physician to cure some disease or the dentist to fix his teeth. As the appointment approaches, however, the negative tendency becomes stronger, and as a result the individual may "forget" to keep the appointment.

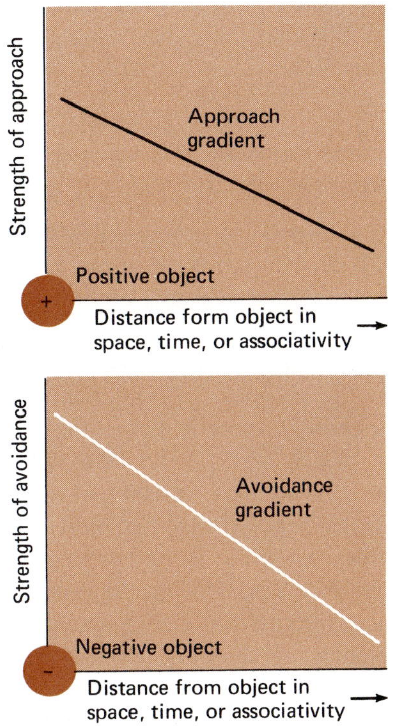

Box Figure 16.3a Approach and avoidance gradients. The tendency to approach positive objects or to avoid negative objects increases with nearness to the object and decreases with distance from the object. Distance may be defined in terms of time, space, or associativity. (From Kimble, G.A., Garmezy, N., & Zigler, E. *Principles of General Psychology.* Copyright 1974 by The Ronald Press Company.)

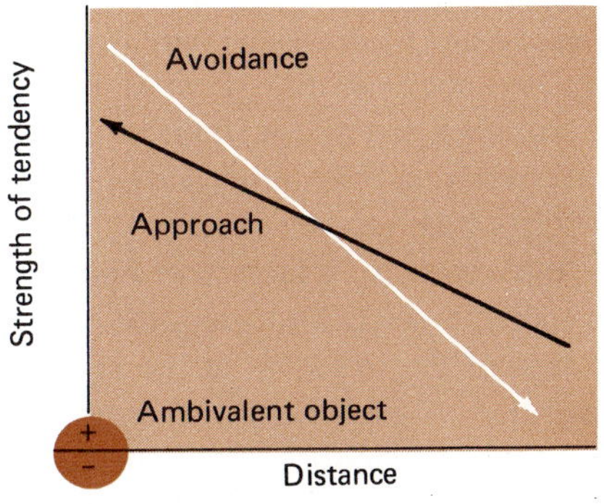

Box Figure 16.3b Combined approach and avoidance gradients: A model for conflict. Both approach and avoidance tendencies increase with nearness to the ambivalent object. However, the tendency to avoid has a higher absolute value and increases more rapidly. (From Kimble, G.A., Garmezy, N., & Zigler, E. *Principles of General Psychology.* Copyright 1974 by The Ronald Press Company.)

many of the things we work hard for. How learning or experience produce these motives is a question that has only been partially answered.

Acquired Motives Based on Negative Incentives

Figure 16.4 is a diagram of an apparatus that Miller (1951) used to study acquired fear. The apparatus consisted of a box containing two compartments—one white, one black—which were separated by a door. A rat was placed in the white compartment, given an electric shock through the grid floor, and allowed to run to the black compartment to escape the shock. The door was then closed, and the apparatus was arranged so that the door would open when the rat either turned a wheel or pressed a lever. When the animal was again placed into the white compartment, it learned to open the door by rotating the wheel. When the wheel was disconnected, the animal soon learned to press the lever to open the door. After turning the wheel or pressing the bar, the animal would run from the white into the black compartment. The point of the experiment was that after the first few trials, the electric shocks were discontinued, yet the animals continued to run from one compartment to the other and even learned two new ways of escaping from the compartment where they had received the shocks. These responses, running from one compartment to the other, persisted over hundreds of trials after the shocks had been discontinued. Furthermore, the rates at which the animals learned to turn the wheel and press the lever were functions of the intensity of the shocks given during the original trials; the more intense the shocks, the more quickly the animals learned to turn the wheel and press the lever.

In interpreting the results of his experiment, Miller proposed that the rats *learned*

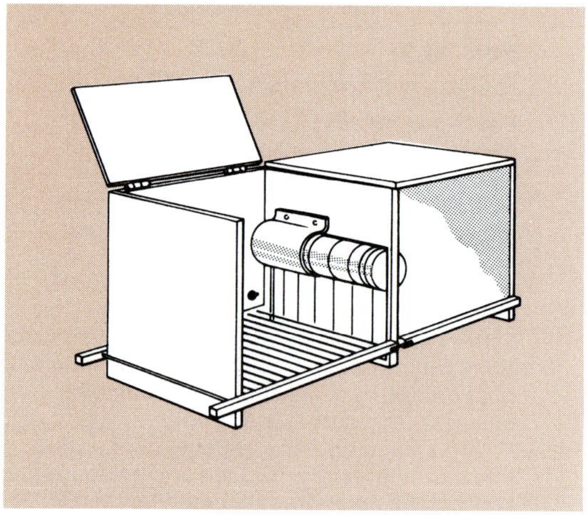

Figure 16.4 The instrument Miller used to study acquired fear. The left compartment is painted white, the right compartment is painted black. Shock was administered through the floor of the right compartment, and the striped door could be raised by the animal. (From Miller, N.E. Studies of fear as an acquired drive: I. Fear as motivation and fear-reduction as reinforcement in the learning of new responses. *Journal of Experimental Psychology,* 1948, *38,* 89–101. Copyright 1948 by the American Psychological Association. Reprinted by permission.)

to be afraid of the white compartment because it was there that they had experienced the painful electric shocks. The responses of turning the wheel and pressing the lever, according to this view, were motivated by fear, and gaining entrance to the black compartment reduced fear and was thus rewarding. In other words, the animals' behavior was motivated by an acquired drive; that is, one acquired through association with a biological drive—in this instance, pain.

Allport (1937) postulated that many motives develop under the impetus of biological drives. However, after some time these motives become independent of their biological source and persist as motives in their own right. To state this idea succinctly, Allport coined the term *functional autonomy;* meaning that motives, particularly human motives, become independent of their biological origins. However, these theorists have been unable to explain how functional autonomy is achieved.

Another way to interpret Miller's experiment is in terms of an *incentive condition*. The fear of the white compartment is, after all, aroused by the situation—the complex of stimuli associated with the white compartment. As such, this complex of stimuli is external to the animal and thus differs from hunger and thirst, which are internal. In this example, the incentive is negative, representing a condition that the animals learn to escape from or avoid.

Regardless of the interpretation—acquired drives based on negative incentives—there is ample experimental evidence to demonstrate these phenomena. It is easy to demonstrate that previously neutral stimuli can acquire motivational properties if they are associated with the reduction of fear. In principle, there is no reason to believe that similar experiments should not be successful when the initial source of motivation is the reduction of hunger or thirst.

Acquired Motives Based on Positive Incentives

As with learned negative incentives, or with learned drives based on reduction of fear, associating a neutral stimulus with food or water should lead to an acquired incentive. Consider the following experiment by Wolfe (1936), which is illustrated in figure 16.5. The apparatus shown in the figure has been termed a Chimpomat. The experimenter showed the chimpanzees that if they inserted a poker chip into the slot, a grape or a raisin would appear below. The animals quickly learned this behavior when rewarded with a grape or raisin. After working on the Chimpomat for some time, the animals learned to perform other behaviors that were rewarded with poker chips alone. For example, they quickly learned to pull heavy baskets into cages to obtain the poker chips hidden on the bottom. They would engage in this behavior for long periods to hoard the poker chips, which they were allowed to "spend" for grapes and raisins later. As the experiment progressed, the experimenter complicated the situation by teaching the chimps that red poker chips would get them food, blue would get water, and white ones would open the doors of their cages and let them run around outside. The animals soon learned to work hardest for the chips that would satisfy the need that was dominant at the moment.

Unfortunately, most experiments of this nature have not been as successful. The psychological literature is full of reports about

Figure 16.5 A chimpanzee inserting a poker chip into the chimpomat to obtain a bit of food. After learning the value of poker chips, the ape will learn complex tasks to obtain chips, which are of symbolic value to the animal. (Courtesy of Yerkes Regional Primate Center, Emory University, Atlanta, Georgia.)

experimental results that have been entirely negative. These failures have made it difficult to maintain that secondary acquired drives explain human behavior, unless one believes —as Brown does (1961)—that most human behavior is motivated by fear or anxiety.

Hierarchy of Motives

Most psychologists think of motives as having a hierarchical organization in the sense that psychological needs are based on physiological ones and so forth. Some psychological theorists think of this hierarchy of motives in terms of an emerging or unfolding of developmental sequences. Maslow (1943, 1970), for example, views human motives as developing in the following sequence:

1. *Biological needs.* According to Maslow, the lowest form of motivation derives from physiological needs; all other motives derive from these. However, because these needs are easily satisfied most of the time, they are not particularly important to adults. Most behaviors observed in adult humans are based on motives higher up in the hierarchy.

2. *Safety.* All humans want to feel safe from predators, extreme temperatures, criminals, and the like. But Maslow does not believe that these motives are important factors in adult human behavior because society provides environments where these needs are reasonably well satisfied. These motives are more important in children because their sense of security is related to an environment that is orderly and predictable. Children who grow up in environments they cannot understand because the consequences of their behavior are not predictable (that is, not consistent) often become insecure adults who are unable to cope with environmental demands.

3. *Love.* If biological and safety motives are satisfied, motives for love emerge. These are expressed as the need to affiliate with friends and groups, the need for acceptance and approval from friends and groups, and the need to belong. If these needs are satisfied, the individual will be able to get along well with friends, affiliate with groups and organizations, and become a spouse and parent. Maslow believes that the inability to express the need for love is the principal cause of neurosis in our society.

4. *Self-esteem.* People need to form a stable self-image. To satisfy this need, they will learn a skill or profession and engage in behaviors that will elicit praise from others and a feeling of self-respect.

5. *Self-actualization.* Maslow's writings on the motive of self-actualization have made him famous as a "humanistic" psychologist. In his motivational hierarchy, self-actualization is the highest form of motivation. Accordingly, an individual will attempt to satisfy this need after his biological needs and the desire for safety, love, and self-esteem have been satisfied. Self-actualization is defined as having become everything that one is capable of becoming. When an individual fills this need, he experiences a sense of fulfillment, is satisfied with his philosophy of life, and behaves in a manner that is consistent with these achievements. According to this view, an individual experiences a feeling of alienation when his desires for self-actualization conflict with society's values.

In his later writings, Maslow profoundly changed his position, stating that self-actualization does not follow automatically after satisfaction of the needs lower down in the hierarchy. Many individuals stop developing after they have achieved self-esteem. What distinguishes individuals who seek self-actualization from those who are satisfied with self-esteem? Maslow has devoted much research to this question but has found it difficult to identify self-actualizers. In this research, he has defined self-actualizers as individuals who do not manifest any psychopathology (i.e., symptoms of neurosis and psychosis are absent), who have satisfied their biological needs and their needs of safety, love, and self-esteem, *and* who have begun to develop a philosophy of life.

These studies led Maslow to the following conclusions about self-actualizing individuals: Self-actualizers are "healthy" individuals who differ qualitatively as well as quantitatively from the average person. He also suggested that the focus of psychological research has been off the mark and that the basis of the science of psychology should be the study of the motivations and personalities of self-actualizing human beings. Regardless of what one thinks of the particulars of Maslow's scheme of motivation, it does force one to focus on human strengths rather than weaknesses. In other words, it forces one to have an optimistic view about the human condition and human motivations.

Motivation to Achieve and Fear of Failure

According to McClelland and his colleagues, one of the major human motives is the need for achievement, which is defined as competition with some standard of excellence. In a long series of studies, McClelland and his collaborators studied the need to achieve using fantasy material derived from stories told in response to the Thematic Apperception Test (TAT), a method of measuring motivation which was discussed in Chapter 15.

How are subjects scored for need to achieve? They are shown TAT cards, typically those that depict one or more individuals in situations where some degree of achievement is necessary—such as a boy playing a violin—and the number of achievement-related statements is scored. The sum of these statements for all the pictures shown represents the degree of motivation for achievement. Individuals differ in terms of their need to achieve and can be classified as having a strong, intermediate, or weak need to achieve.

Lowell (1952) examined the performance of persons with strong or weak needs for achievement on an arithmetic and a scrambled-word test. He found that those with a strong need to achieve scored higher on the arithmetic test than did the other group. On the scrambled-word test, both groups started at approximately the same level of proficiency. However, the "strong need" group showed a significant improvement in their performance over trials, whereas subjects in the other group did not improve.

In another experiment, words that were clearly related to achievement (e.g., success and failure) or were neutral with respect to achievement were flashed briefly on a screen. The subjects represented a wide range of scores with respect to need for achievement. Subjects with high scores recognized words that denoted success much more quickly than did subjects with low scores. More interesting, however, words that denoted failure were recognized more quickly by subjects with high or low scores than by those with intermediate scores. This result suggests that subjects with a moderate need to achieve are motivated by a fear of failure rather than by a desire for success. Other studies tend to confirm this observation. Atkinson (1953) asked subjects to perform a task but only allowed them to complete half the tasks. These tasks were performed under three conditions, relaxed, task-oriented, and ego-involved. Ego-involvement was created by telling the subjects that the tasks were a measure of ability. Under these conditions, subjects with a strong need to achieve remembered more incomplete than complete tasks. Under the relaxed and the task-oriented conditions, they tended to remember completed and incompleted tasks about equally well. Subjects with low scores, however, remembered more of the completed tasks under the ego-involvement condition and more incompleted tasks under the other two experimental conditions. Thus we can argue that all the subjects viewed incompleted tasks as failures. If this assumption is correct, we can also speculate that subjects with a weak need to achieve are upset by failure. Subjects with a strong need for achievement, on the other hand, can be viewed as individuals who have a positive attitude toward success and are willing to work hard to achieve it.

Another interesting experiment was reported by Atkinson (1958), who asked college students to work on a task to obtain a reward of either \$1.25 or \$2.50. The students were also told that their chances of obtaining the rewards varied: in some instances their chances were 1 in 20; in others, 1 in 3, or 1 in 2, or 3 in 4. When working for a reward of \$1.25 subjects with a strong need to achieve performed best when the odds of obtaining a reward were intermediate, that is, 1 in 3 or 1 in 2. When the odds were extremely low (1 in 20) or high (3 in 4) these subjects did not work particularly hard. This outcome suggests that individuals with a strong need for achievement test themselves against a standard only when the odds of success are intermediate. When the odds are extreme, success seems to mean little to these individuals.

These experiments indicate that the need for achievement, as measured by fantasy, is indeed related to other behaviors. However, this relationship appears to be complex and depends on a number of variables. The need for achievement appears to interact with behavior, but the interaction depends on how the subject views the situation, whether he considers it evaluative or neutral. Subjects with low scores appear to be motivated by a fear of failure rather than by a need to succeed. The need to achieve also depends on whether the subject views the task as difficult or easy. In other words, research on the motivation to achieve indicates once again that motivational processes, especially in organisms as complex as humans, are determined by multiple factors.

Opponent-Process Theory of Motivation

Solomon and Corbit (1973) have proposed what they call an opponent-process theory of motivation. The underlying principle of this theory is that within the brain, there are multiple systems which suppress all deviations from what these authors term "hedonic neutrality," regardless of whether these departures are pleasant or unpleasant. In other words, these systems dampen emotions. Operant responses, which were discussed fully in the section on instrumental learning in Chapter 11, maximize the likelihood of positive reinforcement and minimize the probability of negative reinforcement; these opposing processes of the central nervous system function in a way that minimizes both positive and negative reinforcement. These systems are conceived of as fully automatic and function to return the organism to a homeostatic level of arousal. Sensory stimuli arouse affect and this is suppressed by these opposing systems, which reinstate a condition of emotional equilibrium.

As an analogy, the authors point to the following phenomenon in visual perception: When an intense red light is suddenly turned off, the subject experiences a quickly fading afterimage of redness. This experience in turn is followed by a green afterimage, which fades slowly. The analogy suggests several properties of opponent processes, namely, that these processes have a fast onset and a slow rate of decay.

To illustrate the meaning of their model, the authors discuss six examples of behavior, which are listed in table 16.1.

Table 16.1 Emotional situations and their effects during original and subsequent presentation of the motivational-affective stimuli.

Empirical examples of dynamics of "affect"	First few stimulations		Later stimulations	
	State A (input present)	State B (input gone)	State A′ (input present)	State B′ (input gone)
1. Dogs in Pavlov harness 10″ shocks → gross behavior	"Terror"	"Stealth" (subdued, cautious, inactive, hesitant)	"Unhappy" (annoyed, anxious, afraid)	"Joy" (euphoric, active, social, happy)
2. Dogs in Pavlov harness 10″ shocks → EKG responses	Large cardiac acceleration	Slow deceleration, small "overshoot"	Small acceleration or none	Quick deceleration, large overshoot
3. Epstein's parachutists Free fall → gross behavior → physiology	Terror, sympathetic arousal	Stunned, stony faced	Tense, expectant, not much arousal	Exhilaration, jubilation, "good feeling"
4. Opiate usage I.V. injection → moods, feelings	Euphoria, "rush," pleasure	Craving, irritating withdrawal symptoms	Loss of euphoria, normal feeling, "relief"	Intense craving, abstinence agony
5. Dogs and M & Ms	Pleasure, tail wagging, chewing	Tenseness, "focus," motionless		
6. Love Interpersonal stimulation → moods, feelings	Ecstasy, excitement, happiness	Loneliness	Normal, confortable, content	Grief, separation syndrome
7. Imprinting, the attachment of creatures to their "mothers"	Pleasure, cessation of fear, no distress	Loneliness, distress cries, short duration	Pleasure, no cries	Loneliness, intense cries, long duration

Source: From Solomon, R.L. and Corbit, J.D. "An opponent process theory of motivation: I. Temporal dynamics of affect." *Psychological Review*, 1974, *81*, p. 121. Copyright 1974 by the American Psychological Association. Reprinted by permission.

Several points must be raised with respect to this illustration. The table is divided into three columns. Column 1 contains a list of six affective states. Column 2 lists the behaviors elicited after the first few stimulations. And column 3 lists the behaviors that are elicited after the stimulation has been given many times; that is, when the animal is accustomed to the situation. Columns 2 and 3 are divided into two additional columns titled States A and B and States A′ and B′. States A and A′ are the behaviors observed when the stimulus is present; States B and B′ occur when the stimulus is no longer present.

Let's consider several of the emotional and motivational phenomena outlined in table 16.2. Example 1 concerns a dog in a classical conditioning harness in which it receives electric shocks—that is, intense aversive stimuli. During the first few shocks the dog yelps and thrashes about, its hair stands on end, its eyes bulge and the pupils dilate, its tail is curled between its legs, and so forth. The authors call these behaviors "terror," or state A.

When the dog is released from the harness, it is unfriendly, hesitant, and stealthy (state B). Thus the change from state A to state B is one of terror to stealthiness. State B disappears within a few minutes, and the entire sequence of behaviors can be described as state A, state B, and a return to normalcy. After the dog has become accustomed to the conditioning procedure, its behavior is dramatically altered. Now, when the shock is delivered, it whines rather than yelps, and it looks pained, anxious, and annoyed. This is state A′, which differs from state A; that is, the animal looks unhappy rather than terrified. When it is released from the harness, it jumps about, wags its tail, jumps up on people, and in general behaves in a way that Solomon and Corbit describe as a "fit of joy" (or state B′).

Example 3 illustrates the behavior of parachutists. When parachutists make their first few jumps, they are terrified and their sympathetic nervous system is aroused. These data have been obtained by monitoring the responses of the autonomic nervous system and by photographing the jumpers' facial expressions. When they land safely, they appear stunned, stony-faced, and quiet. These behaviors represent states A and B. After making many jumps, the behavioral sequence is altered dramatically. The parachutists are tense and expectant, but they are not terrified; on landing they are talkative and report that they feel exhilarated and jubilant. These behaviors characterize states A′ and B′.

Finally, consider example 6, which is meant to illustrate romantic love. When an individual sees the person he loves the first few times, he feels happy, excited, and ecstatic (state A). When the loved one is not present, he feels lonely (state B). Later, the loved person's presence elicits feelings of comfort and contentment (state A′). When the loved one is then removed, for example, by death or divorce, the individual feels an intense grief, which has been called a "separation syndrome." This characterizes state B′.

What general conclusions can we reach from these examples? First, some sensory stimuli arouse affect, which terminates when the stimulus terminates. Second, the individual does not return to normalcy when the stimulus terminates; he progresses to a new state that is different from the one that was present during stimulation. In other words, he reaches normalcy only after passing through a new state. Figure 16.6 illustrates these events.

After an individual is repeatedly aroused by a sensory stimulus, one can reach slightly different conclusions about his affect, as illustrated in figure 16.7. First, after the sensory stimulus has been presented repeatedly, the degree of arousal it elicits is much lower. Second, state B′ is far more intense than state B and it lasts much longer; that is, after repeated stimulation, state A becomes weaker and state B becomes stronger and longer lasting. Finally, these generalizations appear to be correct regardless of whether state A was pleasurable or aversive.

In conclusion, the opponent process model offers an explanation for the maintenance of certain hedonic behaviors. Although the pleasure of a situation may decrease with time, the behaviors associated with the situation are maintained because the aversive consequences of discontinuing them become greater. That is, the withdrawal of the stimulus in question leads to a highly aversive B′ state. This aversive state can be terminated by reexposure to the original stimulus. Thus there are now two motives to maintain behaviors—one, the pleasure associated with the stimulus and two, a reduction in the aversiveness produced by the absence of the stimulus. It is no wonder, therefore, that some acquired motives can be so powerful. In their original paper, Solomon and Corbit used this model to analyze addiction to cigarettes and suggested

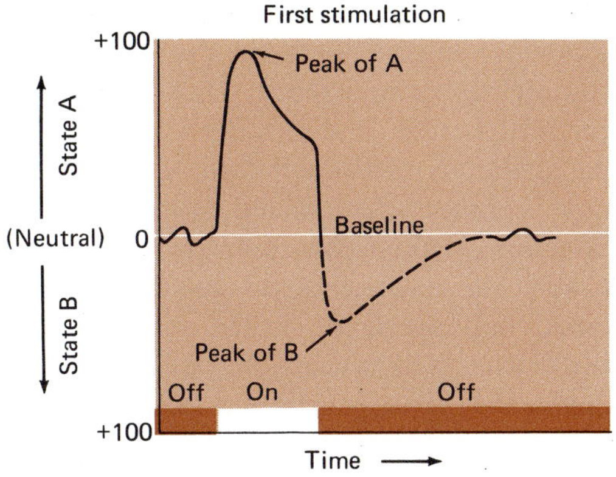

Figure 16.6 The conceptualized affective reactions of subjects after a few presentations of an emotional stimulus. (From Solomon, R.L. and Corbit, J.D. An opponent-process theory of motivation: II Cigarette addiction. *Journal of Abnormal Psychology,* 1973, 81, 158–171. Copyright 1973 by the American Psychological Association. Reprinted by permission.)

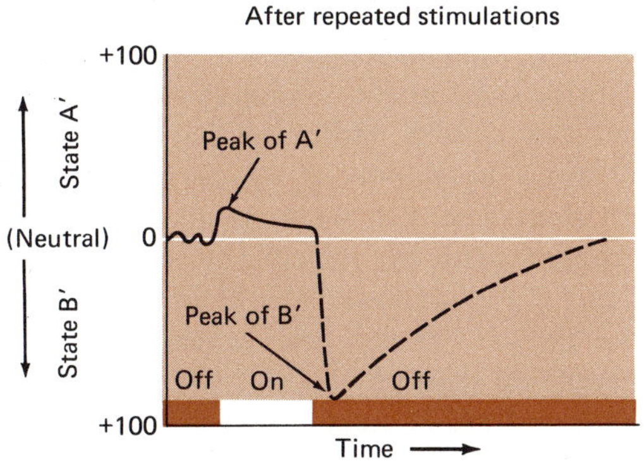

Figure 16.7 The conceptualized reactions of subjects after repeated exposure to emotional stimuli. (From Solomon, R.L. and Corbit, J.D. An opponent-process theory of motivation: II Cigarette addiction. *Journal of Abnormal Psychology,* 1973, 81, 158–171. Copyright 1973 by the American Psychological Association. Reprinted by permission.)

that to "cure" individuals of smoking it was necessary either to suppress or to antagonize the two opponent processes that are operative in this habit, the pleasure derived by individuals who have only recently taken up the habit and the acute distress that long-term smokers suffer when tobacco is withdrawn. The authors suggest that rather than look for quick and easy remedies for smoking, one should engage in psychological research on the opponent processes inherent in this and in all affective behaviors.

Emotions

Emotional experiences are certainly the richest aspects of our mental life. The diversity of these experiences is extremely great —a fact attested to by the large number of words in all languages that describe the emotions and their various shadings.

In this section we will consider some of the theories that have been proposed to explain emotional behavior. Then we will examine several classifications of emotional reactions and the facial and postural expressions associated with different emotional states. Finally, we will discuss some of the physiological correlates of the emotions.

Theories Concerning Emotions

James-Lange Theory

One early theory that was proposed to explain the emotions was suggested at about the same time by the American psychologist, William James, and the Danish physiologist, Carl Lange. According to these men, emotional situations are accompanied by certain characteristic bodily changes. These include increased tension in the skeletal musculature, contractions of the stomach and other viscera, perspiration, and vascular changes in which the blood is routed away from the viscera and toward the heart, muscles, and brain. Emotionally aroused individuals are aware of these physiological changes, and according to the James-Lange theory these physiological events constitute the emotion; that is, the bodily changes and the emotion are one and the same. The following example is often used to illustrate this theory: When a person encounters a bear while strolling through the woods, he runs away, physiological changes take place, and *then* he feels afraid.

There are several difficulties with this theory. First, humans can experience a vast range of emotions, whereas the physiological events that accompany emotional states are all pretty much the same. Second, emotional states can persist for long periods, whereas the accompanying bodily events last for a relatively short time. Third, the visceral changes that accompany emotions take a relatively long time to develop, whereas emotions can be induced very quickly. There is also a considerable body of experimental evidence that argues strongly against the James-Lange theory. For example, many physiological events that accompany emotional states can be mimicked by injecting human subjects with epinephrine, a neurotransmitter that was discussed in Chapters 3 and 5. However, although persons who have been injected with this compound say that they feel fearful, they also say the feeling differs from actual fear. There are also reports in the clinical literature of individuals who have suffered a broken neck and thus receive no sensory input from their viscera, but nevertheless feel all the normal emotions. When the sympathetic nervous system has been rendered nonfunctional in experimental animals by surgery, avoidance conditioning—presumably based on reduction of fear—is difficult to establish. But if the animals learned the avoidance response before the surgery, they will maintain their avoidance behavior for a long time (Wynne and Solomon, 1955).

Thalamic Theory

The objections to the James-Lange theory led W. Cannon and P. Bard to formulate an alternative theory to explain emotional behavior. According to their theory, sensory stimuli that are initiated by emotional situations reach the cerebral cortex by way of the classical sensory fibers. In the cortex these stimuli have two effects: They activate the cerebral cortex, and this activation releases the thalamus from inhibition. The thalamus now becomes activated and discharges in two directions. In one direction, the discharge is toward the cerebral cortex and results in the emotional experience. In the other direction, the discharge is toward the viscera and produces the physiological correlates of emotional experience. Thus, when one sees a bear, fear develops, the physiological changes occur, and one runs away. The James-Lange and thalamic theories are contrasted diagrammatically in figure 16.8.

Cannon's theory has sometimes been referred to as an *emergency theory* of emotions. According to this view, emotions facilitate the body's capacity to respond vigorously; that is, they prepare the body for either "fight" or "flight." Cannon suggests that emotions activate the sympathetic division of the autonomic nervous system while simultaneously suppressing the activity of the parasympathetic division. The net result is that metabolic energy is made available for muscular activity and for redistributing the blood away from the internal viscera and toward the brain, heart, and muscles.

Seyle (1950) suggested that similar metabolic reactions occur during stress and called the resulting effects the *general-adaptation syndrome* (see box 16.4).

Arousal Theory

According to the arousal theory, emotions fall along an "arousal continuum," from drowsiness and a low degree of emotional reactivity to strong emotions such as rage. The theory suggests that stimuli from the autonomic nervous system and viscera which accompany emotional states act on the midbrain reticular system (see Chapter 3), which activates the cerebral cortex through complex neural connections by way of the hypothal-

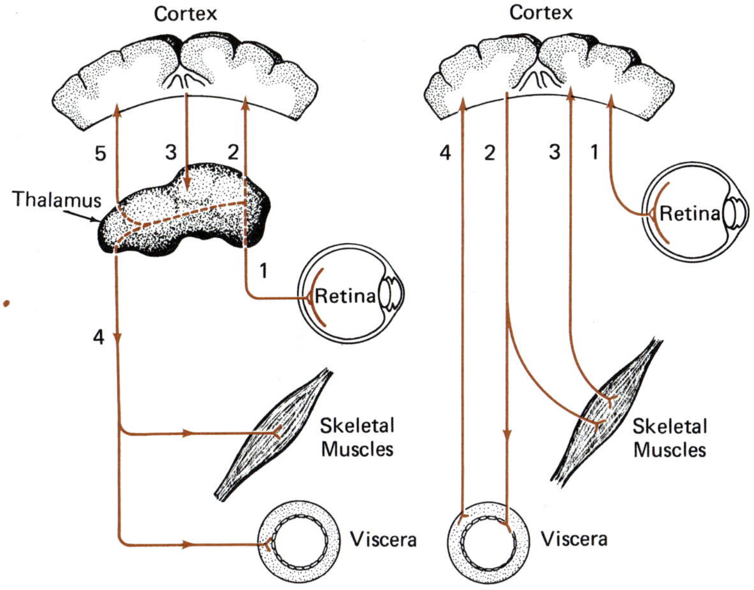

Figure 16.8 Illustration of the James-Lange and thalamic theories of emotions. From A. Schneider and B. Tarshis, *An Introduction to Physiological Psychology.* Copyright 1975 by Random House, Inc.)

amus and thalamus. Lindsley (1950) provided some support for this theory. He recorded the EEGs of relaxed and apprehensive subjects and noted some interesting differences. Among the more obvious effects of making subjects apprehensive was that the alpha rhythm of the EEG was reduced or blocked. (Recall that alpha activity is characteristic of relaxed human subjects, see figure 14.3.)

One difficulty with arousal theories of emotions is that cortical changes, namely EEG activity, do not distinguish one emotion from another. This problem has concerned many proponents of the arousal theory; some have suggested that the individual's knowledge of the situation in which the arousal is experienced forms the basis of experiencing a particular emotion (e.g., Duffy, 1962).

Situational Theories

Visceral changes (or physiological arousal) are indistinguishable from one emotional state to another. Nevertheless, people do know that they are aroused, and they are aware of the internal changes that are correlated with emotional states. According to situational theories of emotion, people interpret their physiological states in the context of the situation in which they find themselves. In other words, people label and interpret their condition in terms of contextual cues. Thus an individual becomes aware of emotional stimuli first, then he notices his aroused physiology, and, finally, he labels and interprets his bodily feelings according to the context in which he experiences these feelings.

Experiments by Schachter and Singer (1962) and by Schachter (1964) provide strong evidence for cognitive theories such as these. One such experiment is discussed in box 16.5.

Physiological Correlates of Emotions

Throughout this section on emotional behavior, we have referred to the fact that certain physiological processes are altered in animals when they experience intense emo-

Box 16.4
The General Adaptation Syndrome

Stress may be defined as a situation that mobilizes the body's resources and utilizes more energy than is normal. Prolonged exposure to extremes of temperature, overwork, pain, and the like can be defined as stressful under this definition. The body reacts to stress in three fairly well-defined stages, which Seyle (1950) called the general adaptation syndrome (GAS). The GAS is illustrated diagrammatically in box figure 16.4.

Stage 1: *The alarm reaction.* The changes that occur in the body immediately after stress are similar to those we have already described in connection with emotional states. They include an activation of the sympathetic nervous system, inhibition of the parasympathetic nervous system. These changes help the organism deal with the stressful situation.

Stage 2: *Resistance to stress.* During Stage 2 the individual recovers from Stage 1, the bodily processes return to normal, and the stress is endured. However, endurance puts a considerable strain on the individual's resources and he may enter the next phase of the syndrome.

Stage 3: *Exhaustion.* If the original stress continues for too long, the individual may exhaust his internal resources. If the stress continues beyond this point, the person may finally weaken and die. This third stage of the GAS is seen in connection with physiological stresses such as exposure to cold or heat; psychological stresses, however, seldom reach this final stage.

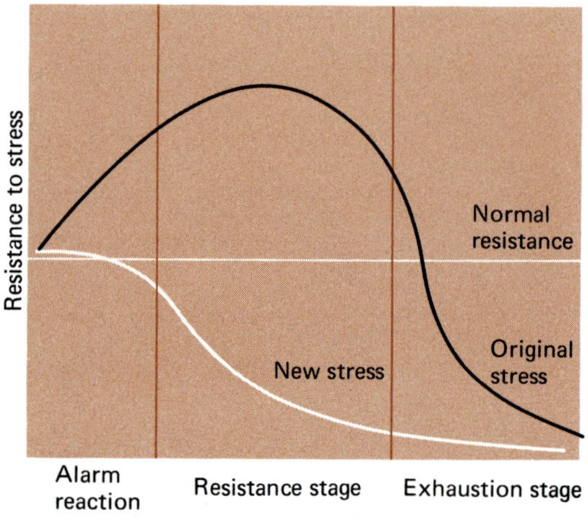

Box Figure 16.4 The general adaptation syndrome. Resistance to stress increases during the alarm and resistance stages. However, if the stress is too prolonged, the subject enters into the exhaustion stage and may die. If the subject is stressed again, resistance is lowered in all stages of the adaptation syndrome. (Adapted from Selye, H. *The physiology and pathology of exposure to stress.* 1950, ACTA, Montreal.)

tional reactions. In this section we will discuss some of the more frequently studied physiological correlates of emotional behavior.

Activity of the Vascular System

For any given organism, the amount of blood is a constant at any given moment. Nevertheless, organisms do possess mechanisms whereby they control blood circulation. These mechanisms are the action of the heart and the relative constriction of the blood vessels. When the heart expands, blood enters it from the venous system. This is referred to as the *diastolic phase* of the heart's action. The duration of the diastolic phase determines the amount of blood that will be pumped to the body during the next contraction. This contraction is referred to as the *systolic phase* of the action of the heart. The amount of blood circulating in the body, then, depends on the duration of the diastolic phase *and* on the heart rate, providing that the pump's capacity is not exceeded. The second factor which determines the amount of blood that will be available to certain structures is the relative

Box 16.5

We Feel Like What We See

One of the strongest pieces of evidence in favor of situational determinants of emotional experience was provided by Schachter and Singer (1962). These investigators injected one group of human subjects with epinephrine, a chemical compound that causes physiological arousal; another group was injected with saline solution (a placebo). All subjects were told they had been injected with Suproxin, a vitamin supplement, and that the purpose of the experiment was to test the effects of this drug on visual acuity. One-third of the subjects in both the experimental and control groups were informed that Suproxin would produce certain side effects (the effects described were actually the effects of epinephrine). Another third were told nothing about the drug's effects. A third group was misinformed about the effects of the drug; for example, they were told they would experience slight headaches, numbness, and itching (none of these symptoms is associated with epinephrine).

The subjects were then tested and observed in two different situations. One situation was designed to make the subjects joyful or euphoric: The subjects were placed into a room where a confederate of the experimenter acted as if he were in extremely high spirits, sent paper airplanes through the air, and so forth. Another situation was designed to make the subjects feel angry: They were placed in a room with a person who acted as though he were angry. All subjects were then asked to fill out a questionnaire on which they had to rate their mood.

The subjects who had been injected with epinephrine reacted as follows: Those in the informed group did not shift their mood to match that of the experimenter's accomplice, nor did they act like him. The ignorant and misinformed groups, however, did shift their moods and tended to act like the accomplice. These data indicate that our interpretations of how we feel, as determined by contextual cues, are important in leading us to experience different emotions.

In another experiment subjects were injected with either a placebo, epinephrine, or with chlorpromazine (a depressant). All subjects were then asked to watch a slapstick comedy. The subjects who had been injected with epinephrine reported that the movie was funnier than did control subjects, who in turn thought the movie was funnier than did the subjects injected with the depressant. The same situation thus induced different feelings and emotions in people whose emotional tone had been altered by drugs; in other words, emotions depend on situational cues *and* levels of arousal.

dilation or constriction of the blood vessels supplying the organs of the body. Changes in the diameter of the blood vessels are produced by smooth muscles that line the walls of these vessels.

Changes in emotional states have a variety of effects on human subjects. Individuals who are asleep or relaxed increase the amount of blood to their brain, with a compensatory decrease in volume of blood that is pumped to other organs. Exercise increases systolic pressure as well as the heart rate. Increased heart rate and constriction of the blood vessels have been reported to occur in subjects who are under psychological stress. Although these changes are quantitatively quite small, they are observed consistently. In certain emotional situations, individuals will either become pale or flushed; these changes are brought about by vasoconstriction and vasodilation, respectively.

In general, no systematic changes in the vascular system can be associated with specific emotional states. The changes that do occur in the vascular system can be attributed to general arousal.

Skin Conductance

Skin resistance, the electrical resistance of the skin to the flow of an electric current has been studied extensively in relation to emotional states. *Skin conductance* is the reciprocal of skin resistance. Many experiments have shown that skin resistance changes in subjects who are either aroused or attentive. Correlations between measures of skin resistance and specific emotional states are quite low. Measures of skin conductance during arousal has been referred to as the *galvanic skin response,* or GSR. Figure 16.9 illustrates the results of an experiment in which skin conductance was measured in a human subject in response to the suggestion of a pin prick and an actual pin prick.

Respiration

Emotional situations produce changes in respiration, which can be measured in terms of changes in the volume of air during inhalation and exhalation. Emotional states have been found to affect this ratio. In general, the changes in respiration that are correlated with emotional reactions can be ascribed to general excitation.

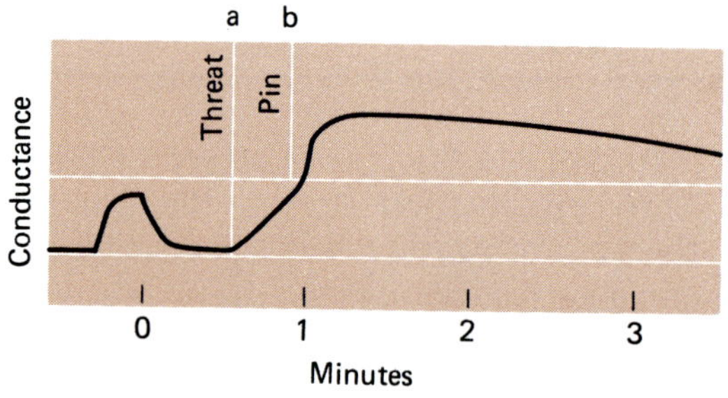

Figure 16.9 Skin conductance, or galvanic skin response, recorded over time. Point *a* represents the "threat" of a pin prick; point *b,* an actual pin prick. (From Waller, A.D. Concerning emotive phenomena: II Periodic variations of conductance of the palm of the human hand. *Proceedings of the Royal Society* (London) B, 1919–1920, 91, 17–32. Used by permission of the Royal Society.)

Hormonal Changes

During strong emotional reactions, the adrenal glands begin to secrete large amounts of epinephrine and norepinephrine. These compounds lead to an increase in the amount of stored sugar released by the liver, and an increase in blood pressure and heart beat. They also lead to perspiration, dilation of the pupils, and dilation of the lungs to allow for more vigorous respiration.

Other Physiological Changes

Many other physiological measures have been used as indexes of emotional states. For example, during emotional arousal, muscular tension increases and the temperature of the skin decreases. The general metabolic rate (i.e., the body's utilization of oxygen) also increases. Finally, in animals such as cats and dogs, certain emotional states produce piloerection—the hair rises on certain parts of the body. This response is produced by the contraction of smooth muscles located at the base of the hair cells.

Presumably, telling a lie arouses an emotional reaction in guilty individuals. If this is so, then we would expect these individuals to show the physiological concomitants of emotional arousal. In addition, because these reactions are involuntary, the guilty person would not be able to suppress them. This reasoning has led to the development of lie detection procedures. Individuals who submit to lie detection tests are presented with emotional stimuli, usually particular words, and a host of physiological measures are recorded. Deception, that is, telling a lie, is often accompanied by rapid inhalation and subsequent shallowness of breath and by changes in skin conductance, heart rate, and blood pressure. All these measures are taken during a lie detection test, which is nevertheless *not* an infallible index of the truth. Only an expert can properly interpret the results of these tests.

Dimensions of the Emotions

People's facial expressions, as well as their postures and gestures, vary as a function of their affective state. There is also a great diversity among the words we use to describe different emotions and different shadings of emotions. Several experimenters have addressed the question of whether all these facial expressions and descriptive words actually signify separate emotions or simply changes in the intensities of a few basic emotional states. Two classic experiments, one dealing with facial expressions and the other with emotional words, have been performed in an attempt to classify the emotions.

Schlosberg (1954) asked subjects to sort photographs of people's faces into groups, depending on which emotion they believed was being expressed. In addition, the subjects were asked to rate each picture along two dimensions; pleasantness-unpleasantness and attention-rejection. The results indicated that people do categorize emotional expressions and that these categories could be fitted onto an oval surface, the major coordinates of which were attention-rejection and pleasantness-unpleasantness (see fig. 16.10). Notice in the figure that the oval surface is tilted to accommodate a third dimension, "activation level," which was added to the dimensional analysis at a later time.

Davitz (1969) attempted to classify words that are used to describe emotional states. First, he asked a large number of subjects to describe their emotional experiences. From these descriptions, 556 statements were extracted and made into a checklist. Next, 50 words that represented a wide variety of emotional states were picked from the Thesaurus. Subjects were then asked to check items on the checklist that described experiences they had had with reference to the 50 words. One result of the experiment was that the 50 emotional words clustered themselves into groups according to the checked items that described them. Twelve clusters were obtained; for example, tension, inadequacy, and comfort. The descriptive phrases that corresponded to these clusters were "I'm wound up inside," "I feel vulnerable and totally helpless," and "A sense of well-being," respectively. Further analysis revealed that these clusters were interrelated and seemed to vary along four basic dimensions termed activation, relatedness, hedonic tone, and competence.

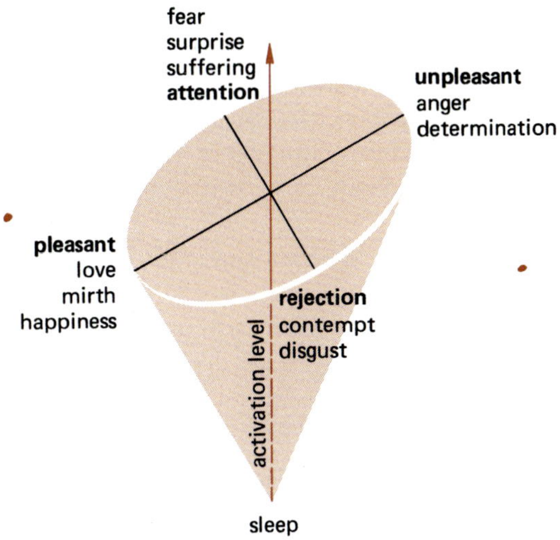

Figure 16.10 The dimensions of emotions. Affective states fit along the cone; the two major axes are pleasantness-unpleasantness and attention-rejection. The third axis represents activation. Note that the cone is tilted, indicating that unpleasant motions are more activating than pleasant affective states. (From Schlosberg, H. Three dimensions of emotion. *Psychological Review,* 1954, 61, 81–88. Copyright 1954 by the American Psychological Association. Reprinted by permission.)

Summary

Most organisms, but especially human beings, engage in a vast array of behaviors which are difficult to explain in terms of basic drives such as hunger, oxygen deprivation, thirst, etc. In this chapter we have considered some of the theories proposed by psychologists interested in understanding these more complex motivational conditions, and some of the research which these theories have generated.

Homeostatic mechanisms automatically regulate internal equilibria necessary for life. In some cases when these homeostatic mechanisms fail it is possible to demonstrate that organisms sustain life by engaging in behaviors which maintain these essential internal equilibria.

Human beings judge the intensity of external stimuli relative to some reference point which depends on the context in which such judgements are made. Such observations led Helson to propose his famous Adaptation Level Theory which McClelland used to propose that motivated behavior occurs within two frames of reference; the feelings of an individual at a particular moment in time, and the anticipated change in feelings an individual thinks will occur in response to some behavior. The individual judges the anticipated change on the basis of previous experience, that is, learned cues.

Many animals seem to be motivated by curiosity and manipulate objects in their environment. It has been possible to demonstrate that organisms will learn even complex tasks rewarded only by an opportunity to explore their environments or to obtain sensory stimulation.

A series of experiments performed by Harlow demonstrated that an infant's love for its mother is based largely on contact comfort.

The frustration-aggression hypothesis was discussed; that is, the theory which proposes that aggression is based on frustration. Within this context, frustration is defined as the blocking of ongoing goal-directed behavior. Many organisms exhibit displacement activity in response to frustration.

Conceptually, psychologists think of conflicts in terms of a competition among motives. Conflicts have been studied in terms of approach and avoidance behavior resulting in (1) approach-approach, (2) approach-avoidance, (3) avoidance-avoidance, and (4) multiple approach-avoidance conflicts. In everyday life, multiple approach-avoidance conflicts are most common, individuals having to choose between many alternatives each possessing both positive and negative attributes.

Psychologists have been interested in the fact that neutral stimuli can acquire motivational properties by association. This hypothesis has led to the formulation of the concept of acquired motives. Many experiments have shown that stimuli can acquire motivational properties if they are paired with negative reinforcement. However, in the laboratory it has been difficult to demonstrate the existence of acquired motives based on association with positive reinforcement.

Motives have been arranged into hierarchical orders by many theorists. Maslow devised one such hierarchy which begins with simple biological needs and ends with the need for self-actualization. Self-actualization is defined as becoming everything one is capable of and individuals who have fulfilled this need are thought of having a satisfactory philosophy of life and possessing a sense of fulfillment. In this context, alienation is thought of as a conflict between the need for self-actualization and societal values.

The need for achievement is considered as a major human motive. Individuals behave differently depending on how strong their needs for achievement are; for example, individuals with a strong need for achievement, under conditions of ego-involvement, remember tasks which they did not complete, whereas the opposite tends to be true for subjects with low levels of need achievement.

Several theories of the emotions were discussed; these included the James-Lange, the Cannon-Bard and the Arousal Theory. The physiological changes which accompany emotional states do not distinguish clearly between the various emotional states but are characteristic of all aroused animals. The various emotions also tend to depend on situational cues.

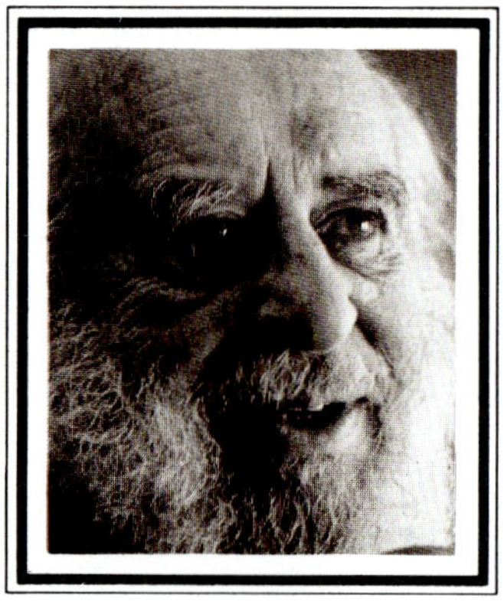

Frederick (Fritz) Perls (1893-1970) Perls was the developer of Gestalt psychotherapy, a form of therapy that focuses on bringing into awareness in the here-and-now the total experience of the individual. The therapy has a particular focus on nonverbal experiences and uses such techniques as role playing to take care of "unfinished business," that is, unresolved conflicts from the past.

Joseph Wolpe (1915-) Wolpe is a physician who originated the learning-theory-oriented therapy of systematic desensitization, a therapy involving imagined fearful scenes while in deep muscle relaxation. Wolpe used laboratory tests and experimental designs to develop and assess the effectiveness of this form of therapy. Systematic desensitization is one of the major forms of behavior motivation in use today.

Sigmund Freud (1856-1936) Freud was the founder of psychoanalytic theory. He proposed a theory involving unconscious conflicts in the development of neuroses. He added the concepts of sexual conflict and defense mechanisms to the vocabulary of everyday life. He also developed a comprehensive theory of normal development, abnormal psychology, and psychotherapy.

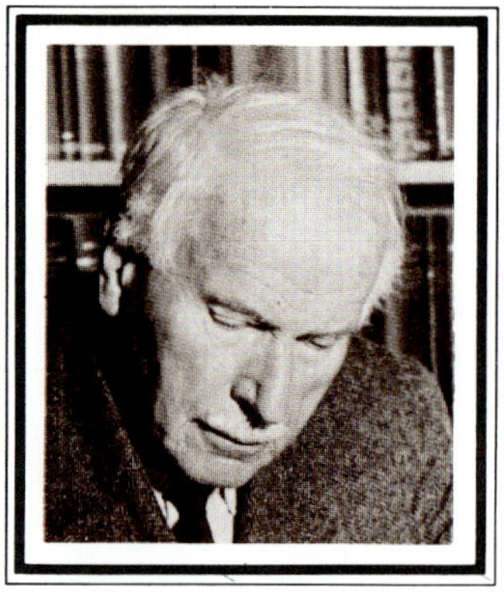

Carl Jung (1875-1961) A follower of Freud, Jung broke off to form his own school of analytic psychology. His theory de-emphasized the role of sex and aggression in the conflicts of mature adults and focused on the meaning of life and death. He introduced the Word Association Tests and the concepts of introversion and extroversion. Jung was particularly interested in the study of ancient myths, art, and rational memory as a way of understanding the symbolic content of the unconscious.

Section

7

Personality and Abnormal Behavior

17

Personality

The psychology of personality looks beyond particular behaviors and seeks to grasp the essential nature, inner organization, and capacity of the person as a whole. Personality is unique in the sense that no two individuals behave exactly alike in any one environment; thus the inner organization of each person must be unique to account for these differences.

What can we gain from the scientific study of personality? We can learn general principles of personality organization, which can then be applied to many different problems in daily life. For example, a personnel officer can determine which candidates for a particular job have the right profile of personality traits. A marriage counselor can help a client decide whether she wants to continue giving her husband the constant reassurance about his masculinity that he unconsciously seeks. A family therapist can help the parents of an adolescent son understand that he needs their unconditional positive regard. Or a clinical psychologist can use psychological tests to gain insight into his patient's underlying conflicts and recommend a course of treatment.

The central thrust of the psychology of personality during the first half of the twentieth century was made by Sigmund Freud and his associates in psychoanalytic work, which was almost entirely clinical. Freud and other psychoanalysts would treat patients most of the day and then would try to make theoretical sense of the patients' symptoms and events in their lives.

Since the 1930s, other investigators have made contributions that have furthered the development of Freud's theory or have led to different but nevertheless consistent theories. The work of Erik Erikson, Henry Murray, and Eric Berne represents developments in theory and research that are consistent with Freud's psychoanalytic theory.

Freud's views have provoked sharp opposition since they were first published in the early 1900s. Many thinkers of his day ridiculed his notions of infantile sexuality, for example. How could a baby possibly have sexual feelings! Some said that Freud's emphasis on the sexual instincts as prime drivers of personality dynamics was completely wrong. Carl Jung, for example, thought that many different kinds of forces influenced personality and that these forces were inherited as part of a collective unconscious. Other psychologists believed that the notion of an "unconscious mind" was not justified by the evidence. Among them was Carl Rogers, who developed a comprehensive theory of personality based on humanistic principles.

The psychology of personality has also benefitted from contributions made by other branches of psychology. The fields of psychological testing and experimental study of human behavior have been especially important. Raymond Cattell and Hans Eysenck have been leaders in this area.

All of these major approaches to personality theory and research are being vigorously pursued today. In addition, rather than focus their research on a specific theory, many scientists choose a particular problem and use elements of several theories to study it. These studies tend to continue over several decades, with successive researchers attempting to correct the methodological and conceptual problems discovered in earlier research. Examples of problems that have been studied in this way are aggression, locus of control, and anxiety.

Freud's Psychoanalytic Theory of Personality

Sigmund Freud was born in 1856 and spent most of his life in Vienna, Austria, where he graduated from medical school in 1881. In seeking to cure a mental disorder called hysteria, he first tried hypnosis but found it unsatisfactory. Gradually he perfected his own technique, known as *free association*. In this method the patient was to let his thoughts go along, one idea leading to the next, no matter how silly it might seem. By doing this, Freud believed, the patient would be led back to the root causes of his problems.

Conscious and Unconscious Parts of Personality

Freud found that in the course of free associating, patients would stumble on some event in early childhood that they had subsequently forgotten. Because patients only recalled these events after a great deal of anguish, Freud believed that the memory for these events had been active and had contributed to the patient's illness all along although the patient had not been consciously aware of it. After testing this hypothesis on himself through a prolonged self-analysis and talking it over with his colleagues, Freud proposed that everyone, normal people as well as patients, has two parts to his personality, an unconscious part and a conscious part.

Can you recall feeling terribly afraid when you were eight months old and a stranger entered your room? Can you recall some of the dreams you had when you were eleven years old? Can you recall wanting to climb into your mother's lap and cry sometimes when you were in high school because you felt defeated? Most people cannot remember these things; yet most of us were afraid as babies, had dreams during early adolescence (and at other times!), and have occasionally felt defeated and helpless. Usually we cannot bring memories of such matters to consciousness at will; that is, they are *unconscious*.

For a number of years, Freud worked with the notion of zones of consciousness and unconsciousness as his main framework for understanding personality, and he maintained that the major driving forces of personality were the sexual instincts. Representations of these instincts *could* become conscious; but because of social disapproval and punishment, sexual ideas were mainly kept unconscious. In an informal way, Freud thought that the ego, one of the components of personality, was conscious and that it defended itself against the onslaught of sexual impulses by repressing them; that is, keeping them from entering consciousness. But sometimes, as in cases of hysteria, these impulses would find a way out anyway—often in the form of neurotic symptoms. Freud also thought that if sexual energy was repressed, it was converted quite directly into anxiety.

This form of the theory did not fit all the facts, however. Freud (1923, 1962) himself described the problem as follows. In psychoanalytic treatment the patient is required to make free associations. That seems easy enough. But actually, patients often find it difficult to free associate; in fact, many come to a complete stop. Their mind goes blank. The stream of free association dries up.

Freud reasoned that there must be a dynamic cause for this impasse and proposed the concept of *resistance,* which is an unconscious, but extremely active opposition to continuing the free associations. However, the ego is the agent of repression, and the ego is supposed to be conscious. Therefore, because the patient has no idea why free associations cease to flow, either the opposition is not coming from the ego or the ego is not entirely conscious. Freud decided that the second answer—that the ego is not completely conscious—best fit the facts and revised his theory accordingly.

Id, Ego, and Superego

The result of Freud's revisions was modern psychoanalytic theory, so-called because it is based on the method of psychoanalysis (free association and so forth) that Freud invented. Psychoanalytic theory explains the functioning of personality as the interaction of forces. Typically, three groups of forces are in conflict, although for healthy personality development they should be working together in harmony. These forces are the *id,* the *ego,* and the *superego.*

The energy of these forces is viewed as *mental energy:* It is attached to the ideas that represent instincts or related strivings. Instincts have a biological source. The *aim* of an instinct is to reduce the tension associated with stimulation from this source. The *object* of an instinct is whatever becomes instrumental to achieving its aim. In hunger, the object would be food; in adult sexual behavior, it would be another person. Freud called all the instincts the *id.*

By 1923 Freud realized that aggression was also an instinctual force in human beings. The id, then, was composed of sexual and aggressive instincts. More precisely, it was that part of the personality which contained mental representations of instinctual impulses; that is, unconscious wishes, feelings, urges, and strivings for sexual and aggressive behavior. Many of these ideas were also *repressed,* in the sense that when they tried to come up into consciousness, they were thrust back by the ego because of the danger involved in expressing them.

Although thinking of the ego as conscious —that is, as the conscious will opposing the pressures of instinctual impulses—made things seem clear-cut, the evidence to the contrary forced Freud to abandon this view and accept the idea that the ego is partly conscious and partly unconscious. In its struggles against the id, then, the ego is involved in conflicts, some of which can be completely unconscious. The *ego* is the main executive of the personality, a mysterious mixture of conscious and unconscious ideas, representing both sensations and actions. The ego is also the main receiving station for perceptions of the outer world. Thinking and reasoning are also functions of the ego.

Freud was the first to realize the tremendously important role that parents play in forming the child's personality during the earliest years of life. Part of the child's ego becomes differentiated into a controlling force, which incorporates the commands and prohibitions his parents give him. Freud called this part of the structure of personality the *superego*. The superego is mainly unconscious and plays an especially important part in the formation of neuroses. It is responsible for the unconscious sense of guilt that underlies many of the self-punishing features of psychological disorders. For example, the person suffering from an *obsessive-compulsive* disorder is obsessed with ideas of his own unworthiness, uncleanness, or evil nature. Sometimes, he is compelled to keep washing his hands or tidying his room, thereby "cleansing" away the guilt.

The ego's overall task is to obtain satisfaction for the id's impulses in a way that not only meets the limitations of physical and social reality but does not violate the requirements of the superego. Freud said the ego could be compared to a person riding a horse: For the most part, the person is in control and guides the horse, but sometimes the horse is determined to go its own way, and then there is a struggle, a conflict.

What power does the ego really have? Like the rider using a bit and spurs, the ego controls by means of anxiety and guilt.

Anxiety and Guilt

Freud (1926, 1963) described anxiety as having three main characteristics; (1) a specific, unpleasant feeling, (2) autonomic responses such as an increase in heart rate, and (3) the perception of these feelings and responses. The first total reaction of anxiety, he believed, occurs at birth, with all the drastic physiological changes that birth entails. Compared with the comfort of the womb, birth portends danger. And thereafter, any dangerous situation arouses anxiety as a response.

Freud pointed out that intense stimulation is involved in birth and that the baby also experiences intense stimulation whenever hungry. This stimulation is calmed by the mother, whose presence signals relief from tension. But her absence can also signal danger—namely impending hunger, which the baby is helpless to satisfy alone. The ego notices her absence and calls up the memory of previous anxiety responses to actual hunger and helplessness. Now it is possible for the ego to trigger an anxiety response simply by anticipating danger. Freud called this "realistic anxiety," a response to external danger.

In contrast, "neurotic anxiety" is a response to internal danger. Typically, these responses begin when a mother punishes her child or becomes tense and anxious herself. This is likely to happen when the child does something that is offensive to her, such as biting her nipple, making messes on the floor with bowel movements, or masturbating. The child subsequently responds by becoming anxious when he feels the impulse to bite, make messes, or masturbate, thereby checking its expression in behavior. But at the same time, the impulse itself becomes a source of *internal* danger. And because it is instinctual, it will not simply go away, nor can the child escape from it. This produces an inescapable conflict between impulse and anxiety. This is neurotic anxiety.

Realistic anxiety and neurotic anxiety are associated with the ego; a third type of anxiety is associated with the superego. After the child has identified with his parents and has incorporated the parents' prohibitions in the form of conscience, he experiences this form of anxiety as *guilt*. The chief function of the superego is to maintain a critical appraisal of personal failings and unacceptable impulses. Therefore, by way of the superego, people blame themselves (feel guilty) for various actual and imagined offenses (Fenichel, 1945). The sense of guilt may be felt consciously or unconsciously. In melancholia (pervasive and persistent depression) the sense of guilt is overwhelmingly conscious, as Freud pointed out (1923, 1962). In hysteria, on the other hand, the patient is completely unaware of the sense of guilt. Can there possibly be such a thing as unconscious guilt? Freud reported that apparently, many of his patients had committed criminal offenses, largely because of a need to do something that would justify these unconscious feelings of guilt; that is, the guilt *preceded* the crime.

Defense Mechanisms

According to psychoanalytic theory, the ego opposes the id with the power of anxiety and guilt. This power is exerted through specific mechanisms of defense—repression, reaction formation, and projection.

Repression is a direct blocking of the instinctual impulse, and all conscious acknowledgment of the instinct is withdrawn by the ego.

In *reaction formation,* the ego changes, taking on character traits that oppose expression of the instinct. For example, a little girl who hates her mother for having another baby may rapidly discover how dangerous it is to express aggressiveness. At first, repression is enough, but then it weakens and the impulses threaten to break through. The little girl may then begin expressing extreme tenderness and concern for her mother, opposing the hatred (Anna Freud, 1966). This is reaction formation.

In *projection,* a curious displacement occurs; the person manages to experience his impulses consciously, but he attributes them to another person. Freud believed that male paranoia (intense preoccupation with suspicious thoughts) involved the projection of hostile and homosexual impulses. He also suggested that some wives become jealous because they project their own homosexual impulses on their husbands, who are then accused of being interested in other women!

Freud's Theory of Psychosexual Development

Freud is perhaps most widely known for his discovery of infantile sexuality (1905, 1938). He began by observing that many components of adult sexuality appeared to be present in the earliest years. In normal adults, for example, kissing and biting frequently accompany intercourse; their prototypes in infantile nursing and teething are quite evident. Adolescents often masturbate. Freud pointed out that small children also masturbate frequently (sometimes they are encouraged to do so by caretakers who want them to sleep). Therefore, it appeared that the genital sexuality of the adult was based on an integration of numerous partial instincts, such as sucking, looking, smelling, showing, holding, exciting the genitals, touching, and so on.

Freud then proposed that psychosexual development proceeds in five stages which begin at birth and last until full maturity is achieved. The stages are *oral, anal, phallic, latency,* and *genital*.

Fixation at an early psychosexual stage was believed to lead to specific personality traits in the adult. Summarizing the results of psychoanalytic research, Fenichel (1945) stated that early stages of development are never completely obliterated during progression to later stages. Indeed, in some cases, an early stage may persist with high potency and later stages never really mask its existence in the individual's personality. The process that enables an early stage of psychosexual organization to become so potent is called *fixation.* Fixation apparently occurs as a result of three types of parental handling: (1) excessive gratification of the impulses that are prevalent at the stage, (2) excessive frustration of those impulses, or (3) alternation between the first two.

The *oral stage* represents the earliest sexual instincts, which are focused on the mouth, lips, tongue, and ingestive processes. It occupies the first year of life, the period when the child is almost completely dependent on a caretaker, and consists of two substages: sucking in the first half of the year and biting in the second. The *oral character,* resulting from fixation in the oral stage, may be either optimistic or pessimistic. If a person experiences an unusual degree of oral satisfaction in infancy, he is apt to become optimistic and self-assured; if he experiences unusual deprivation, he tends to become dependent, clinging, and either passive or aggressive. If the fixation occurred in the first half of the oral stage, passivity is likely; if it occurred in the second half (where biting predominates), then an aggressive-dependent personality (demanding, complaining, blaming, and hostile) is the probable outcome (Fenichel, 1945).

During the second year of life, when bowel control begins, the child's interest focuses on elimination processes and the anus. This is the *anal stage,* which also has two substages; an early phase, when pleasure is derived mainly from expelling the feces, and a later phase, when pleasure is derived from retaining the stool in the bowel. Freud reported that many of his patients showed a combination of three traits as a result of fixation in this latter phase: obstinacy, frugality, and orderliness. Orderliness included punctuality, cleanliness, conscientiousness, and so forth. Obstinacy could be so extreme as to be persistent defiance and vindictiveness. Frugality might range from exceptional carefulness with money to outright avarice. Analysis showed that these patients were all fixated at the anal stage; hence the constellation of traits known as the *anal character.*

The *phallic stage* lasts from age 3 to 5. During this time the child is interested in his own genitals and those of other people, especially those of his parents and members of the opposite sex. At this time, the boy develops a strong emotional attachment to his mother, and the girl becomes attached to father. These attachments are known as the *Oedipus* and *Electra Complex,* respectively. The child resents the parent of the same sex as a rival and strives to have sole possession of the other parent, with more or less dimly realized sexual intent.

In the Oedipal Complex the most important and fateful factor in the boy is *castration anxiety*—the fear that his father will retaliate by castrating him. Boys are prepared for this fear by earlier losses (of the nipple at weaning, of stools in bowel training) and by threats of punishment for masturbation. When they see a person without a penis—a girl—the previously vague fear that their own penis will be removed now becomes a definite threat. The ensuing anxiety can be mastered only by repressing the Oedipal impulses. Repression is reinforced by ". . . identification with the father taken as a model" (Freud, 1923, 1962, p. 44). With this identification, the superego becomes fully developed.

Freud maintained that the course of development is different for girls. They too have a phallic stage, but it consists of envying the penis and wishing to have a child by the father. Freud believed that although the Electra Complex disappears for lack of gratification, the basic desire to possess a penis and bear a child remains as preparation for eventually becoming a mother.

Resolution of the Oedipus and Electra Complexes leaves the child's sexual instincts under repression and other controls, which are strong enough to last until puberty, with its upsurge of chemical changes. This intervening period is known as the *latency stage*.

During adolescence, a consolidation of all earlier instincts takes place, and they all become integrated into a unified drive toward adult sexual union. This final integration is known as the *genital stage*.

Experimental Studies of Psychoanalytic Theories

Freud's theories have generated great interest among experimental psychologists. In this section, we will describe some of the experimental studies that have been done on the theories of repression and psychosexual development.

Repression

Because of its prime role as an ego defense, repression is one of the most important concepts underlying psychoanalytic theory. Freud (1915) postulated that there were two forms of repression; "primal repression," the denial to consciousness of threatening impulses such as Oedipal wishes, and "after-repression," the denial to consciousness of ideas associated with repressed wishes. These hypotheses state that repression results in inattention and forgetting which are specifically designed to avoid anxiety. The question is: Can such processes be shown to exist? According to certain investigators a phenomenon termed "perceptual defense" exemplifies this form of inattention and "memory defense" represents this kind of forgetting.

Perceptual Defense

McGinnies (1949) did a well-known study in which students were shown emotional and neutral words by tachistoscope (an apparatus that exposes visual stimuli for brief periods). He expected that the students' recognition times for emotional words would be longer than for neutral words. He found that words such as whore, belly, raped, or Kotex required .12 seconds or more for recognition while words such as dance, broom, or music required .08 seconds or less. According to psychoanalytic theory, the emotional words aroused anxiety, and the ego attempted to defend itself (repression) by interfering with perception; that is, perceptual defense took place.

One criticism of McGinnies' study was that words on McGinnies' "emotional" list occurred less frequently in the English language than did the words in his "neutral" list. Thus the emotional words were likely to take longer to perceive simply because they were less familiar. Another criticism was that the students in this experiment could merely be anxious about saying the taboo words out loud.

In a study which avoids both of these criticisms, Dixon (1958) established a "closed loop" method of studying perceptual defense. Each subject looked through a stereoscope, and the two visual fields were separated. The left eye saw two spots of light. The subject had continuous control over the brightness of these spots and was instructed to adjust the apparatus so that he could only see the brighter spot. The right eye was presented with emotional words (e.g., penis, whore) of neutral words (e.g., rider, weave) at subliminal levels; that is, the subject was not aware of these words at any time and was not asked to report seeing them.

Dixon reasoned that if perceptual defense was generated by subliminal perception of threatening words, then it would result in a raising of visual thresholds. These thresholds would be manifested in the higher levels of brightness the subject required to continue seeing the brighter spot of light. This was found to be the case; emotional words raised the visual threshold for both male and female subjects.

Because the subjects did not have to report seeing the stimulus words or even recognize them, Dixon's results were *not* caused by conscious suppression of response. But did the stimuli actually elicit anxiety? Or were the differences in visual thresholds related to some other factor, such as differences in the familiarity of the stimuli? In another experiment, Dixon showed that the differences were not related to the familiarity of the words. Kline (1972) has concluded that Dixon's experiments provided a clear demonstration of "the phenomenon of perceptual defense" (p. 181).

Memory Defense

An excellent demonstration of dynamic forgetting was provided by Glucksberg and King (1967). Noting that psychoanalytic theory calls for the forgetting of ideas that are associated with dangerous wishes ("after-repression"), they designed their experiment accordingly. First, they assembled a number of association chains, such as the following:

stem → flower → smell
memory → mind → brain

Then they paired the first word of each chain with a nonsense syllable. For example:

CEF → stem
DAX → memory

Subjects were then required to learn the list of pairs so that they could produce the correct response to each nonsense syllable.

In a later session, subjects were presented with the end words in each chain. In some cases, the subjects received an electric shock. For example:

smell → (shock)
brain → (no shock)

In the final session, the subjects were retested for the original learning of paired associates. As predicted, the subjects were less likely to recall a word from a chain in which the end word had been paired with shock.

Psychosexual Stages and Personality Development

The general trend of the evidence obtained from studies of Freud's hypotheses concerning psychosexual development and character formation is that certain character types do exist, as Freud postulated. Furthermore, certain fantasies, typical of the various psychosexual stages, do exist and continue to affect our reactions to life. However, specific connections between childhood experiences and types of character in adulthood have not been demonstrated.

Character Types

Kline (1972) reviews several correlational studies of the anal character, in which traits of orderliness, thriftiness, obstinacy, etc., have been found to be positively correlated. These studies tend to confirm Freud's hypothesis that when a person exhibits one of these traits to a strong degree, the other traits also tend to be strong.

Using an experimental procedure, Noblin (1962) predicted that subjects with an anal character would learn better in an operant conditioning situation if the reinforcers used were pennies. This prediction was based on the psychoanalytic hypothesis that money is symbolic of feces. Noblin also predicted that oral characters would condition better when reinforced with gumballs. His results confirmed both predictions.

Psychosexual Fantasies

In one of the earliest studies relevant to the castration complex, Friedman (1952) asked children to complete the following story about a monkey who had a long curly tail: "The monkey had fun with his tail every day. One day, the monkey woke up to find that something was different. What had happened?" Only twenty-five percent of the story completions offered by five-year-old children involved loss of the tail; twelve-year-olds gave the next lowest percentage of these responses. However, almost seventy percent of the nine-year-olds completed the story with loss or damage to the tail. These results were consistent with the hypothesis that castration anxiety should be highest during the phallic stage (age 5) and next highest during puberty (age 12).

Spence and Gordon (1967) studied the effects of experimentally induced oral fantasies on recall and sensitivity to a subliminal stimulus. The withdrawal of love (rejection) can increase the need for food in some people because of the following chain of association:

mother's breast → food → love and acceptance

In the experiment, some subjects were made to feel rejected by making it seem as though their peers did not want them as friends. All subjects then rated how hungry they felt; those who had been rejected reported more hunger, as expected. Then the subjects were shown thirty words, including some that were associated with infantile feeding (e.g., suck or sleep) and some that were neutral. Although the rejected and nonrejected groups did *not* differ in the number of words they could recall immediately after exposure to the list, the rejected subjects recalled more words associated with infantile feedings, as predicted. In addition, half of the rejected subjects and half of the nonrejected subjects had been exposed to a subliminal stimulus word "milk" just before the learning task. Again, as predicted, the rejected subjects showed additional sensitivity to this subliminal stimulus because they were able to recall an even greater proportion of the infantile words. In other words, Spence and Gordon demonstrated that it is possible to arouse oral fantasies experimentally and thus produce specific constraints on immediate memory and sensitivity to subliminal stimuli.

You should not conclude that all of Freud's hypotheses have received unequivocal support from research data of the kind just described. Many studies have failed to support particular hypotheses or have challenged other results that seem to support them. However, after reviewing the evidence, Kline (1972) concludes that a substantial proportion of Freud's strictly *testable* hypotheses have been supported by the evidence of experimental research.

Subsequent Developments in Personality Theory

Erikson's Psychoanalytically Oriented Theory

Erik Erikson received his training at the Vienna Psychoanalytic Institute and subsequently worked with Henry Murray, Margaret Mead, Alfred Kroeber, and others at Harvard. The influence of these scholars is evident in his work on psychosocial development in several different cultures, and his work has continued to illuminate our understanding of the way each social organization contributes to the growth or distortion of individual identity.

Erikson's conception of the "eight ages of man" (1968) has received widespread attention. The first four parallel Freud's psychosexual stages, but Erikson focuses on the implications of each stage for the development of identity. The oral stage is the first *psychosocial crisis* through which all human beings must pass. All emerge from it either with a sense of basic *trust* and hope or basic *mistrust* and pessimism. These residues constitute the elements from which identity will be fashioned during adolescence.

The anal stage has implications for control. The child develops a sense of *autonomy* or a sense of *self-doubt* and *shame*. By autonomy Erikson means freely collaborative compliance; doubt is often coupled with jealousy or compulsiveness.

The phallic stage is accompanied by great strides in the child's ability to move about and get into things and in his ability to imagine what is going on or what the future holds. The psychosocial crisis of this stage may be resolved with a sense of *initiative* or *guilt;* that is, the child imagines either successful enterprises or frightful punishments for imagined sins (the castration complex).

The latency stage is also important for identity development, according to Erikson. From roughly 7 to 11 years of age, the child can develop a sense of *industry,* that is, a sense of being able to do things well, or a sense of *inferiority,* if his efforts do not turn out well. Notice the strictly social emphasis of inferiority. The child learns during this period that different people do different things (the division of labor) and that they do them well or poorly, and he gauges his own competence by comparing himself with others.

Adolescence is either the period of *identity* or the period of *role confusion.* At this time all the previously formed elements of identity are brought together, or they remain unintegrated, leaving the person with a sense of inner chaos. We shall return to the period of adolescence after briefly mentioning the last three stages. (See fig. 17.1.)

Once identity has been established, the individual faces the crisis of *intimacy* with others versus *isolation.* Friendship and marriage provide resolutions for this crisis. The next stage revolves around adult productivity. Society expects some pattern of *generativity* during the active years of adulthood. Failure to meet the expectations of others and of oneself is associated with a sense of *stagnation,* often accompanied by feelings of boredom. Finally, in old age the person can with dignity hand over the reins to others and accept the worth of his own contribution to society, which yields a sense of *integrity,* or hc may hide his feelings of *despair* behind expressions of contempt for people and society's institutions.

According to Erikson (1968), adolescence is a period during which the young person must reconstitute all the previously formed elements of his identity into a single or at least unified psychosocial identity. Not

Figure 17.1 Children, in adjusting to the world around them, pass through many stages.

only sexual maturity but also social maturity is upon the person. The end of childhood and family protection is signalled by the approaching end of school days and the looming potentials and threats of entering the labor market. Although this crisis may be delayed by entry into college, the youth must soon become a full social person who participates in the occupational, political, religious, and recreational institutions of his society. The elements of identity formed during the encounter between ego and family must now be integrated as the form and substance of the ego's encounter with society and be reshaped accordingly. Basic trust must be moulded into *faith* —faith in people and in ideas. Autonomy must be shaped into *freely chosen service* to others. Initiative must be transformed into *aspirations*—an imaginative sensing of the possibilities and goals for self-development. Industry must become *commitment to an occupation,* an assurance that one can function satisfactorily and with satisfaction in a chosen work role.

Erikson (1958) points out that the adolescent must have a *moratorium,* a period of delay in social demands during which to put all these elements together. Many young persons, especially the very gifted, need a longer moratorium in which to develop their true identity.

What do other investigators have to say about Erikson's theory of personality development? In a study of groups of 5-, 8-, and 11-year-old children, Ciaccio (1971) asked whether the ego stages actually progress in accordance with Erikson's theory. The children were asked to tell stories to pictures; the stories were then coded according to the percentage of statements reflecting each of the first five stages; for example, trust or mistrust, autonomy or shame, and so on. In figure 17.2 it is clear that the children's stories show a progression of concerns appropriate to their

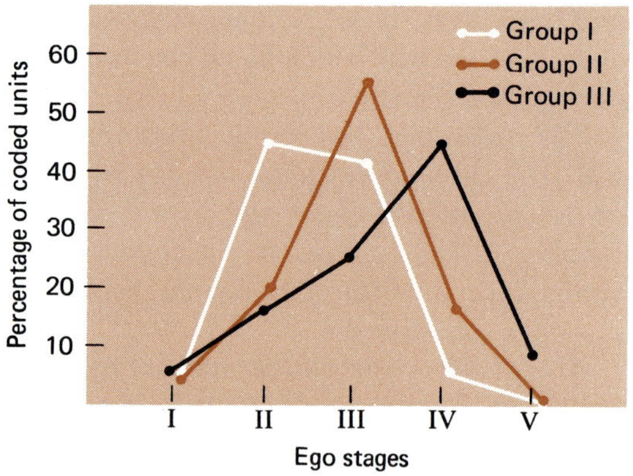

Figure 17.2 Frequency distributions in terms of percentage of coded units within ego stages for three age groups. (Group I, 5-year-olds; Group II, 8-year-olds; Group III, 11-year-olds. From Ciaccio, N.V. A test of Erikson's theory of ego epigenesis. *Developmental Psychology, 4,* 1971, pp. 306–311. Copyright 1971 by the American Psychological Association. Reprinted by permission.)

age group. Few have reached the stage of identity.

What are the implications of a successful resolution of the identity crisis? Using a self-rating scale, Constantinople (1969) showed that college students whose psychosocial development is relatively well advanced tend to be happier people. Reimanis (1973) replicated this result and found that college students who described themselves (on a check list of adjectives) as happier than other students were also more trusting and had fewer feelings of shame, doubt, inferiority, and isolation. Using the method of interviewing described in box 17.1, Toder and Marcia (1973) placed students with different identity status in an experimental situation in which several of their peers deliberately gave incorrect judgments when comparing the lengths of twelve pairs of lines and made correct judgments for six pairs. Would the experimental subjects yield to this pressure to conform and also give inaccurate judgments? Toder and

Box 17.1

Identity Status among College Students

In 1966 Marcia developed a brief interviewing technique for assessing the identity status of college students. The interviewer focuses on the student's occupational choice and on his ideological commitment, especially with regard to religion and politics. Independent judges then listen to recordings of the interviews and place each student in one of the following descriptive categories: *identity achievement*—the student has actively asked questions about a specific aspect of his identity (e.g., occupational choice) and has found answers; *moratorium*—the student is still asking the questions, is still in crisis, and is still seeking a meaningful personal commitment; *identity diffusion*—the student is not asking any questions and is neither committed nor striving for commitment; *foreclosure*—the student has committed himself but without consciously questioning the matter; often he simply incorporates identity elements from his parents.

Using Marcia's method, Waterman, Geary, and Waterman (1974) interviewed ninety-two male students at the end of their freshman year and then interviewed fifty-three of these students again at the end of their senior year. A significant number of the twenty-two students who left school before their senior year had originally been placed in the *moratorium* category. Box figure 17.1a shows the percentages of students in each category in the freshman and senior years. (Only students who remained in school are included.) It is evident that substantial changes took place during the interim with respect to the students' occupational identities because the percentage of students in the *moratorium* category dropped sharply while the percentage in the *identity achievement* category increased sharply.

Even greater changes occurred in the students' ideological status. As shown in box figure 17.1b, students who were placed in the *foreclosure* group as freshmen were likely to be jolted out of that status by the time they were seniors. As with occupational identity, many of the students changed to *identity achievement* status with regard to ideology by the time they were seniors.

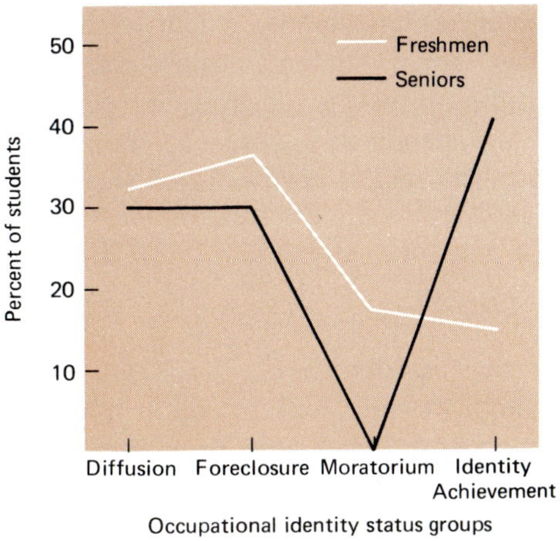

Box Figure 17.1a Percentage of students in each of four occupational identity status groups during freshman and senior years. (N = 53.) (Adapted from data in Waterman, A.S., Geary, P.S., and Waterman, C.K. Longitudinal study of changes in ego identity status from the freshman to the senior year at college. *Developmental Psychology*, 1974, *10*, 387–392. Copyright 1974 by the American Psychological Association. Reprinted by permission.)

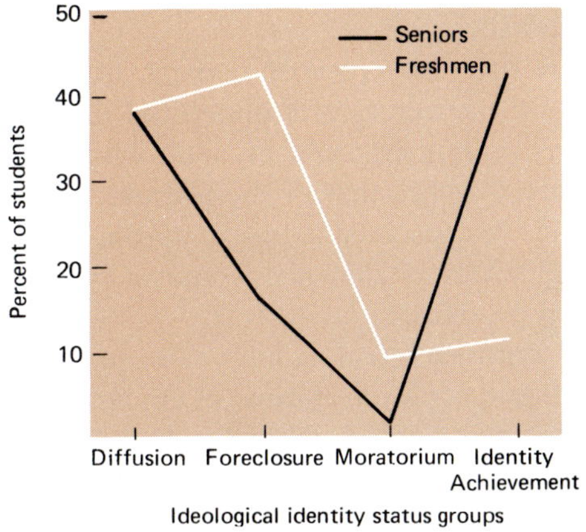

Box Figure 17.1b Percentage of students in each of four ideological identity status groups in freshman and senior years. (N = 53.) (Adapted from data in Waterman, A.S., Geary, P.S., and Waterman, C.K. Longitudinal study of changes in ego identity status from the freshman to the senior year at college. *Developmental Psychology*, 1974, *10*, 387–392. Copyright 1974 by the American Psychological Association. Reprinted by permission.)

Marcia expected that college students who had achieved their identity would resist such pressures, while students whose identities were diffuse—that is, lacking in personal values and standards—would be more conforming. The results corroborated their predictions.

Jung's Type Theory

Before we consider C. G. Jung's theory of personality, we must look briefly at type theories in general. Types have been highly successful conceptual tools in biology and botany, where classifications of plants and animals have been fundamental to scientific progress.

Are there types of human beings? Anthropologists have found it useful to classify races and people from different geographic areas into types; for example, the Nordic type has light skin, blond hair, and a long head. In this sense, a type is a particular combination of characteristics.

There are also types of persons with respect to the extremes of a dimension such as intelligence. For example, an adult whose intelligence matches that of the average eight-year-old child is classified as a moron, while an adult whose intelligence is unusually high is called a genius.

For centuries attempts have been made to categorize people in terms of their body build, temperament, or character. Kretschmer (1925) proposed that humans come in one of three basic shapes: broad trunk and short limbs, thin trunk and long limbs, and intermediate. The first type tends to be outgoing and sociable but cyclic in mood; thus Kretschmer called such persons *cycloid.* The second type of individual tends to be withdrawn, wrapped up in himself, and was termed *schizoid.* In cases of mental breakdown, the cycloid type would become manic-depressive while the schizoid type would become schizophrenic.

Typologies of these kinds have not been especially fruitful in psychology. Attractive as the idea may be, people rarely fit into neat categories. However, theories such as Jung's provide insight into complex patterns of human personality and suggest that many characteristics *tend* to be combined with one another.

Jung, a Swiss psychiatrist, was associated with Freud for many years but then developed his own theory of personality, which differed in important ways from psychoanalysis.

In his most famous book, *Psychological Types* (1923), Jung stated that there are four functions or ways of relating to the world: thinking, feeling, sensing, and intuiting. *Thinking* brings representations of objects and events into relatedness with each other. For instance, you might notice that one of your professors is more interested in the students than some others are, and you might relate this to the fact that she is younger than the others and less involved in administrative work. *Feeling* relates the ego to objects and events, primarily in evaluative terms. You might have positive feelings about the new professor, for example. *Sensing* simply means the receiving of impressions from objects and events, without conceptual or evaluative elaboration. For instance, you might sense the richness or softness of the professor's voice. *Intuiting* is a realization that something exists; but you are unaware of the sense channels involved. You might intuit that the new professor likes you or that she will teach a good course.

Jung also described two basic attitudes of mind, introversion and extroversion, meaning turned in and turned out. Consider your experience of looking at this book: You might say, "I see this book." The *introvert* focuses on the "I"; the *extrovert,* on the book. The extrovert is probably restless and wants to be having fun with his friends; the introvert is more likely to stay home alone, reading, thinking, and meditating. Extroverts are responsive to their environment; they enjoy the natural world, activity, parties. Introverts are more withdrawn and silent, seek new experiences within themselves, and analyze their dreams, beliefs, faith, or personal philosophy. Jung referred to the basic attitude of mind as a "central switchboard" for controlling external behavior as well as consciousness. *Consciousness,* for Jung, was that part of the mind with which the ego is in direct relationship. Indeed, the ego *is* consciousness. The rest of the mind is *unconscious.*

Because extroverted and introverted attitudes are one-sided and because, in fact, no experience can occur without both an "I" which experiences and a "that" which is being experienced, everyone is actually both extroverted and introverted. How then does one attitude come to dominate? Jung said that to cope with physical and social reality, one must have an extroverted attitude. Therefore, quite often the extroverted attitude becomes conscious in the individual while the introverted attitude becomes unconscious. In other words, a balance between the two attitudes exists; the more extroverted a person is in behavior and consciousness, the more introverted he is in his unconscious mind—a *compensation,* as Jung called it.

Similarly, one of the mental functions becomes dominant in the conscious. For example, if *thinking* becomes a student's primary way of relating to the world, then another function such as intuiting will become dominant in the unconscious. Ordinarily, just two of the functions are important in consciousness; the other two are important in the unconscious. Although Jung believed that any two could be dominant in consciousness, thinking and feeling are dominant in consciousness in the western world. All these concepts and relationships are illustrated in figure 17.3.

Now we come to the more controversial aspects of Jung's theory: the "racial unconscious" and the "archetypes." First, we must point out that Jung believed there are two realms in the unconscious: a realm of the "personal unconscious," which is produced largely by the repression of personal experiences in life, and a realm of the "racial unconscious," which is common to all persons

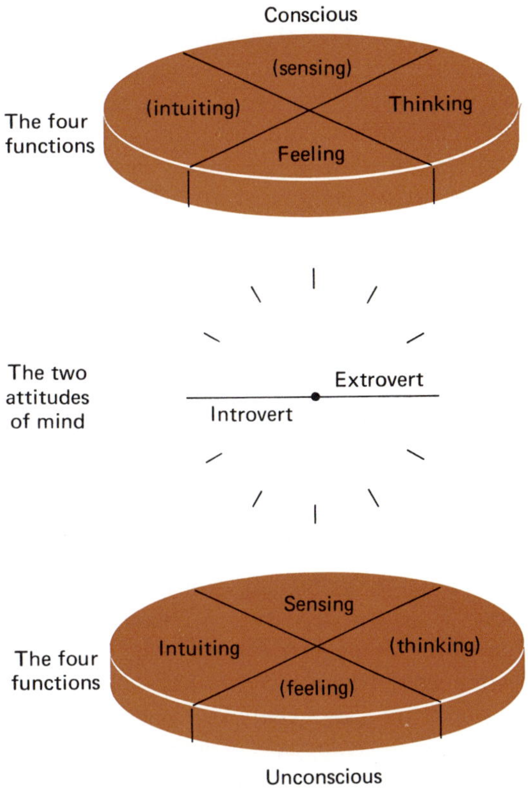

Figure 17.3 Diagram illustrating part of Jung's personality theory: Conscious and unconscious, the four functions, and the two attitudes. (From Cartwright, D.S., *Introduction to personality,* © 1974 Rand McNally, College Publishing Company, Chicago.)

and derives from the experiences of the human race over the eons. The racial unconscious never becomes conscious, but its contents produce images in conscious experience and in the personal unconscious. These images are the archetypes, or "primordial images" of certain predictable experiences within the lifetime of any human being. What experiences are common to all members of the human race? Birth, growth, social customs, a mother image, a father image, the sun, a wise old man, God, power, renewal or rebirth, and death. The archetype of a mother prepares all humans at birth to see and respond to a mothering figure. The archetype of rebirth prepares all humans to see the sun rise again each day after seeing it "die" the night before; it also prepares them for the rebirth they might experience during religious conversion.

The archetypes prepare the forms of personal development; that is, they hold the secret of all personality. There is an archetype for the *ego,* whereby an actual ego develops in the center of an individual's consciousness. There is an archetype for the *persona,* whereby an individual adapts to the wishes and demands placed on him by his society. The archetype for storing unwanted features of the personality is the *shadow,* which consists of all the experiences that have been repressed by the ego, the persona, or both. One important part of the personality, which has hitherto been subject to repression in society, is the feminine side of men (*anima*) and the masculine side of women (*animus*).

There are also archetypes for the person's long-term development, or *individuation.* Individuation involves the progressive differentiation and detailed development of all parts of the personality; that is, the development of all mental functions, both conscious and unconscious, extroverted and introverted, masculine and feminine. These functions must then be integrated into a smoothly working whole, or unity. The archetype for unity is also the archetype for the *self,* which lies midway between the ego and the collective unconscious. Unity cannot be attained while there are "complexes" in the mind, however. Complexes are concentrations of ideas, all highly charged, around a central archetypal image. Someone with a mother complex, for instance, would always be thinking about mother, wondering what mother would say about things, judging new acquaintances in comparison with mother, and so on. The more ideas that are attracted to this central complex, the stronger the complex. A person with many strong complexes (or one overwhelming complex) would need analytic treatment to dissolve them before proceeding toward individuation.

The symbol of the archetype for the self is often that of a *mandala,* a square shape within a circle, frequently containing four symbols of some kind. In figure 17.4 the self is represented as a mandala, and the archetype of unity has a similar representation. This representation of unity is taken from a dream sequence described by one of Jung's patients (1938), whose early dreams of circles, globes or balls, and squares, gardens, or town squares eventually fused into a complicated image of a vertical and horizontal circle, with a clock face on one circle and four little men on the other.

Unity refers particularly to a sense of unity between ego and the human race, or even nature as a whole. Jung reported that the patient who dreamed in the complex imagery just described had been raised as a Catholic but was not at all concerned with religion. Yet he had become subject to uncontrollable outbursts of primitive impulses, which made him worry about his sanity. Although the blending of science and religion seemed impossible, precisely such a blend was unconsciously

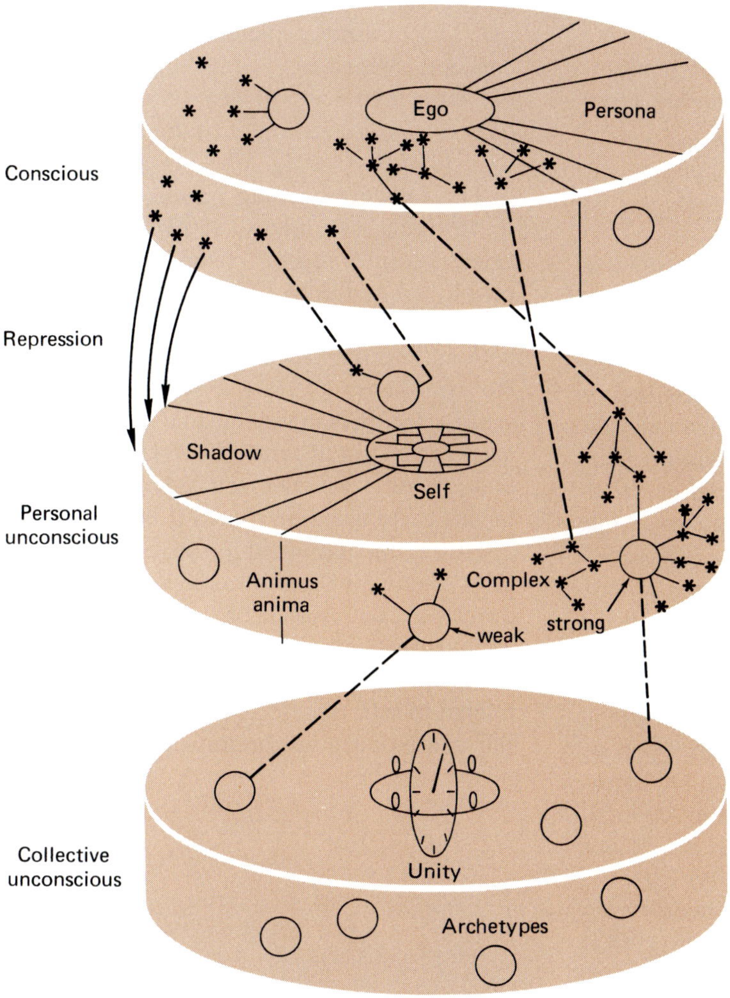

Figure 17.4 Diagram illustrating some of the main dynamics of personality according to Jung's theory. (From Cartwright, D.S., *Introduction to personality,* © 1974 Rand McNally, College Publishing Company, Chicago.)

being produced during this man's process of individuation. The symbol shown in figure 17.4 represents a "world clock" (vertical circle) and the Trinity together with the Virgin Mary (four persons rather than three). The horizontal circle shows the dream's solution to the problem of whether three or four persons should be represented (a problem that has greatly concerned the patient). The intersection of circles on a common center shows the unconscious tendency toward unity of scientific beliefs and practices (e.g., clock, time, measurement) and religious beliefs and faith (horizontal circle), with a common center in the self of this man.

Jung's theories have so far not generated much research in psychology departments, but there are indications that this will soon change. A questionnaire developed by Myers (1962) reliably measures a person's preferences for extroversion versus introversion, thinking versus feeling, and sensing versus intuiting. Business students tend to be predominantly extroverted, thinking, sensing types; science students tend to be predominantly introverted, thinking, intuiting types (Myers, 1962, Table D5).

Rogers' Humanistic Theory

The American psychologist Carl Rogers has formulated an influential new theory of personality, which, although based on subjective experience, is being tested in objective research. One basic proposition of this theory is that persons are born with a tendency to actualize themselves as fully functioning people, but deficiencies in their social environments prevent this self-actualization to a greater or lesser extent.

The fully functioning person evaluates experience on the basis of "organismic valuing processes." Like an infant's pleasure in food that tastes good and rejection of food that tastes bad, a person's organismic valuing process selects experiences that are good or helpful and rejects experiences that are harmful. This process involves definite visceral, physical reactions. In most people, it becomes distorted as they grow up and incorporate the values of their parents and other people concerning what is "good" for them and what things are "bad" and should be avoided. Rogers defines the organismic valuing process as the capacity of an organism ". . . continually to adjust its behavior and reactions so as to achieve the maximum possible self-enhancement" (Rogers and Stevens, 1971, p. 16). However, the process is effective only insofar as the person is *open to,* or able to become aware cf all or most of his experiences. Being *aware* means that the experience is symbolized in some way.

As the child develops, certain portions of his experience become differentiated as those that are himself in action, or are qualities of himself. He becomes aware of experiences relating to *my* body, *I* like, *I* am strong (lovable, pretty, or whatever), and mother loves *me*. There results a picture of self; the "self-concept," which is ". . . *an organized, fluid, but consistent conceptual pattern of perceptions of characteristics . . . of the 'I' or the 'me'* . . ." (1951) (see fig. 17.5).

The fully functioning person is one who, under ideal conditions, receives "unconditional positive regard" from the significant people around him. This means that they accept and prize him without question and without imposing their own values on him. In Rogers' theory (1959), certain basic needs govern the person's behavior: "positive regard" from significant others (such as parents) and "positive self-regard." Regard means acceptance or approval in either case.

Given unconditional positive regard, the fully functioning person accepts himself and develops a self-concept that is congruent with his self-experiences. This means that the person is open to his experiences, including those related to self; therefore, the symbolization of self can be accurate because the evidence is

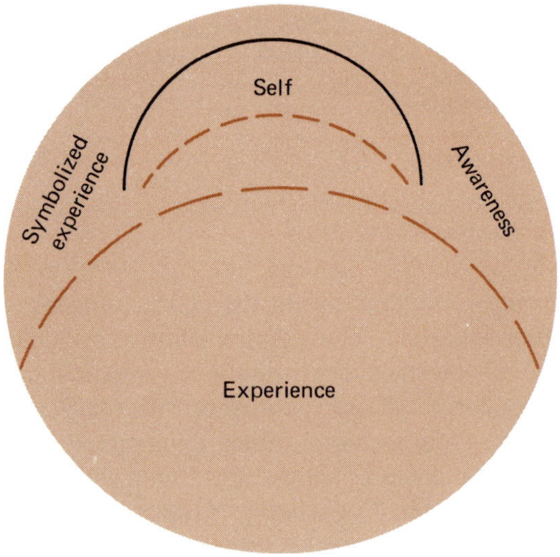

Figure 17.5 A portion of experience becomes differentiated and symbolized in awareness as the concept of self or self-structure. (From Cartwright, D.S., *Introduction to personality,* © 1974 Rand McNally, College Publishing Company, Chicago.)

allowed into awareness. Moreover, because experience keeps changing, the self-concept will be fluid. With freely flowing experience, the process of organismic valuing guides the person's behavior in the most adaptive and flexible manner, allowing creative response and satisfying expression in each new situation.

But when positive regard is not given unconditionally, distortions arise. The person develops "conditions of worth," which begin as conditions laid down by significant other people and end up as conditions for "self-worth." For example, parents may indicate to a girl that her sex is a disappointment to them and only boyish behaviors and expressions will meet with their approval. Soon the girl incorporates these values and only accepts herself in ways in which she seems more like a boy. Any new self-experience that threatens this boyish self-concept will not be admitted openly to awareness. If she wants to sob, for example, that wish will not be admitted to awareness, or it will be given a *distorted symbolization* in awareness. In other words, the self-concept is no longer congruent with experience; it is *incongruent,* or divided (see fig. 17.6).

Denying what they are, or trying to be what they are not, incongruent persons are always vulnerable, because some new threatening experience can always take them by surprise, break through, and make them anxious. They are psychologically maladjusted. Their defense against the experience of anxiety is to reinforce their denials of such experiences or to produce further distortions. Thus, incongruence is a self-sustaining process: it leads to vulnerability, which leads to anxiety and defense, which leads to further incongruence. However, psychotherapy can interrupt this process.

But does psychotherapy change the self-concept? Rogers and his colleagues have studied this question extensively, using a procedure called a *Q-sort* self-description, in which a subject describes himself by arranging one hundred cards in a particular way (Butler, 1972). Each card has one statement printed on it, such as those shown in figure 17.7. The subject arranges the cards in the order in which each statement most closely describes himself: "Most Like Me," "Least Like Me," or somewhere in between. A fixed number of cards must be placed in each of the nine piles, as shown in the figure.

Because each statement receives a score that equals the number of the pile in which it is placed, we have an array of one hundred scores each time a subject describes himself. This array can be correlated with the array of scores obtained on a later occasion. If there is no change in the self-concept, the correlation will be close to 1.00; if there is some change, it will be close to .50; if there is a large amount of change, it will be closer to .00. So

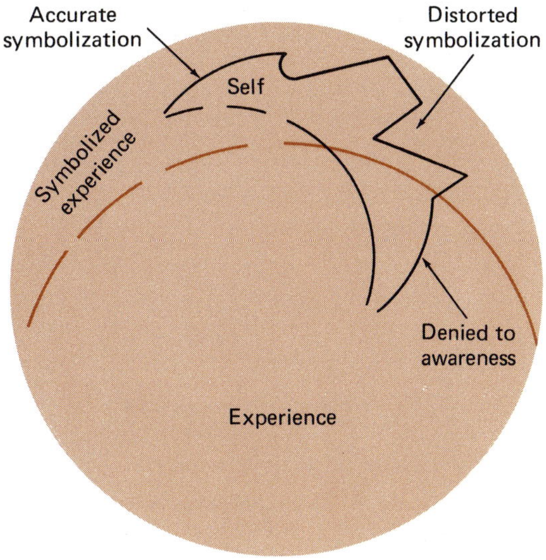

Figure 17.6 In the incongruent personality, the self-structure includes two portions: One portion accurately symbolizes self-experiences; the other contains distorted symbolizations of self-experiences. There are also portions of experience that should be symbolized and assimilated into the self-structure but are denied to awareness. (From Cartwright, D.S., *Introduction to personality,* © 1974 Rand McNally, College Publishing Company, Chicago.)

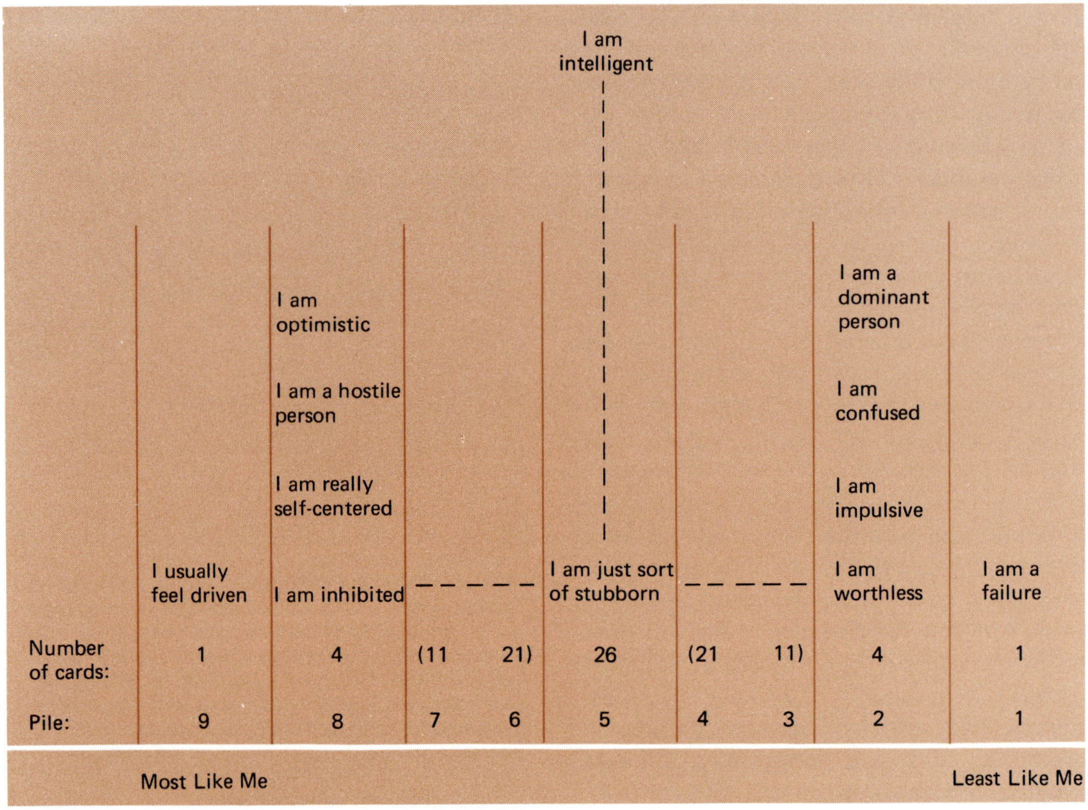
I am
intelligent
I am
optimistic
I am a hostile
person
I am really
self-centered
I am a
dominant
person
I am
confused
I am
impulsive
I usually
feel driven
I am inhibited
I am just sort
of stubborn
I am
worthless
I am a
failure
Number
of cards:
1
4
(11
21)
26
(21
11)
4
1
Pile:
9
8
7
6
5
4
3
2
1
Most Like Me
Least Like Me

Figure 17.7 A Q-sort self-description. Piles 1, 2, 8, and 9 are complete. In Pile 5 only the first and the 26th cards are shown. Piles 3, 4, 6, and 7 have been omitted.

if a client in therapy does Q-sort self-descriptions every few weeks, the changes can be plotted.

The self-descriptions of one client, taken before therapy began, had the following correlations with later Q-sorts: correlation between initial Q-sort and one obtained after the 7th interview, .50; after the 25th interview, .42; after therapy had ended, .39; and 12 months later, .30. In other words, the client's self-concept was continually changing from what it had been before therapy. In what direction was change taking place? Apparently, it was changing toward the client's own ideal of what she would like to be. When Q-sorts done both during and after therapy were compared with a Q-sort of her ideal self done twelve months after therapy had been terminated, the following correlations were obtained: Q-sort of ideal self and Q-sort after the 7th interview, .39; after the 25th interview, .41; after therapy, .67; and 12 months later, .79. The pattern of increasing correlational values revealed that the client's self-concept was progressing steadily toward her own ideal self.

Butler has shown that the average correlation between self and ideal among twenty-five clients changed from −.01 before therapy to +.31 twelve months after treatment was terminated, a highly significant result. Butler (1972) reported that the descriptions of ideal self obtained from samples of clients, control subjects, and other persons throughout the United States tend to agree very highly. The average Q-sort of control subjects, for instance, correlates +.90 with the average Q-sort of clients in therapy. The salient contents of this common ideal are shown in table 17.1. Notice in table 17.1 the prominence of precisely those characteristics Rogers has described for the fully functioning person: I understand myself, I am liked by most people who know me, and so forth. Evidently, Rogers' concept of the fully functioning person matches the ideal that most Americans hold up for themselves.

Theories Based on Psychological Measurement

Before proceeding to the work of Cattell and Eysenck, we must examine the nature of psychological testing and factor analysis.

Table 17.1 Items that are most like the ideal self described by clients.

Items that are Most Like the Ideal Self Described by Clients and Controls[a]
I am emotionally mature
I understand myself
I feel adequate
I am intelligent
I am self-reliant
I have warm emotional relationships with others
I am a responsible person
I usually like people
I can live comfortably with those around me
I am liked by most people who know me
I am tolerant
I take a positive attitude toward myself
I am an attractive person

Source: From Butler, J.M. "Self-concept change in psychotherapy." In Brown and Butler, *Science, Psychology, and Communication: Essays honoring William Stephenson.* Copyright 1972 by Teachers College Press, Columbia University. Reprinted by permission.

These procedures are important in personality research in general. But they have played a special role in the generating of data on which Cattell and Eysenck have based their theories.

Psychological tests are natural developments from the ordinary ways in which people know each other. For example, if you wrote down the outstanding characteristics of your best friend, you might say "John is bright, warm, and reliable." This statement would summarize numerous observations you have made of your friend. Think back to some experiences which showed that your friend is intelligent, for instance. Perhaps he solved a problem that stumped other people, learned how to fix a washing machine, or earned a high grade in math. How about another trait such as warm? Maybe your friend is easy to be with, makes other people feel liked, and expresses affection easily. Each of these behaviors would be called a *trait indicator*. Psychological tests are simply refinements of the ways we assemble the trait indicators about a person.

For example, if you were a trained rater, after some months of acquaintance with several people you could rate them on a scale such as the following:

Hard to be with. Makes you feel tense.				Easy to be with. Makes you feel at ease.
1	2	3	4	5

You would assign each person a number from 1 to 5 indicating how hard or easy he is to be with. Then you might rate each one in terms of whether he makes others feel liked or disliked, whether he expresses affection easily or with difficulty, and so on. Because your own judgment might not be perfect, it would be well to have other raters rate the same persons and then average the judgments of all raters on each scale for each person rated. This would yield a table of data such as the following:

Person Rated	Ease	Average Rating Liking	Affection
John	3.5	2.8	4.1
Sammy	4.3	3.9	4.1
Carlos	3.8	3.3	4.0
Peter	1.8	2.9	3.9

Trait indicators such as ease, liking, or affection are called *variables* as soon as it is possible to assign different numbers to different people indicating the degree to which they display the relevant behaviors. Is there an objective way of finding the *traits* indicated by these behaviors? The variables can be correlated and those variables that are highly related are presumed to indicate the same trait. For example, if ease, liking, and affection all had correlations with each other of more than .50, we would conclude that they all indicate the trait, *warm.*

Suppose we had rated six traits: speed of solving problems, amount of general information, memory for complex instructions and ease, liking, and affection. The three new variables are likely to have correlations of roughly .00 with the other three. In fact the whole set of correlation coefficients might appear as in table 17.2. Notice that the three new variables are all highly intercorrelated, but they each have correlations of about .00 with ease, liking, or affection. Thus it appears that we are actually dealing with two traits: warm versus cold, and bright versus dull.

Factor analysis is a mathematical procedure that is applied to correlation matrices like the one in table 17.2 so that we can objectively decide just how many traits are indicated. In this instance the factor analysis technique would give the same result that we can see: two traits. In a situation where the data are more complex—where we cannot see how many traits there are—factor analysis will provide the answer. It will also tell us how correlated the traits themselves are. In our last example, the correlations between ease, liking, and affection and the other three variables are roughly zero. But suppose those correlations had ranged from +.05 to +.27? We would still be dealing with the same two traits, but they would now be positively correlated to some extent, somewhere between +.05 and +.27 or perhaps a bit more. Factor analysis would tell us exactly how much the two traits are correlated.

So far, we have only spoken about ratings. There are other ways of obtaining measurements on trait indicators. Perhaps one of the most widely used techniques is the questionnaire. For example, instead of rating your friend, you might ask him to respond to items such as the following by choosing the alternative that best describes himself.

1. If something comes up at the last minute so that I have to change my plans
   a. I change them easily most of the time
   b. In between
   c. I tend to get upset
2. The best way to spend a vacation is
   a. Doing what I've always done on vacations
   b. Doing something entirely different from anything I've ever done before
   c. Neither *a* nor *b*

Table 17.2 Hypothetical correlations among six variables.

	Ease	Liking	Affection	Problems	Information	Memory
Ease		.65	.55	.05	−.05	.00
Liking			.50	−.01	.02	.01
Affection				−.04	.02	.00
Problems					.70	.67
Information						.59

These choices are assigned numbers to produce item-scores, such as a = 2, b = 1, c =0. Each item is a trait indicator, and correlations among the items reveal the traits that are being measured. For example, the two items in our illustration measure adaptability.

When people respond to questionnaires, they may be unable or unwilling to give a true picture of themselves. For this reason psychologists have attempted to devise tests that measure trait indicators even more objectively. One type of test uses the *projective technique,* in which the subject responds to more or less ambiguous stimuli such as inkblots or incomplete sentences. The idea is that the subject will project his inner needs and characteristics onto the stimuli and manifest them in his response. An example is Murray's *Thematic Apperception Test* (1943), in which the respondent looks at twenty pictures and is invited to tell a story about each one. One picture shows a man and a woman together in a room; the woman is looking out of a window and the man is gesturing and apparently speaking to her from across the room. What is going on? What are the people thinking and feeling? How will it all turn out? The respondent's story will indicate something about his relationships with other people; for example, does he try to control others, does he "go blank" whenever someone expresses a need for tenderness? If the respondent indicates the same tendencies in story after story, it would be a strong indication that a particular trait is part of the respondent's personality.

Actually, projective techniques have proved most useful in clinical work; in assisting the clinician to understand a patient and to help the patient understand his own problems better. Furthermore, projective tests are more useful when administered to individuals than to groups, that is, with just the subject and the administrator present. For personnel selection or research, it is usually better to give tests specifically designed for groups. Also, the data obtained with projective techniques are not very reliable.

Another kind of objective test calls for performance in some "miniature" situation, such as balancing on a rail or holding your leg up for as long as possible—a measure of persistence. An objective test that would assess whether a person gets upset easily is the Cursive Miniature Situation, described by Hundleby et al. (1965):

> S [subject] is presented with a highly speeded and complex cancellation task, asking for carefulness and fast speed of performance and quick decisions. The test consists of four parts or "runs", each comprising six sections. Each individual section is represented by a pathway inside which small lines are drawn in varying arrangements. S gains points from cancelling [circling] vertical or horizontal lines but loses points for erroneously cancelling slanting lines. S can increase his gain by not circling lines singly but encircling a mass of lines as a whole; however, he is only allowed six such circles per run. The test is further complicated as the pathway frequently divides; at such points S has to decide which "path" to choose in order to maximize his score (since the number of lines to be cancelled—and thus, the number of points to be gained—is different in the different alternative paths).
>
> The four successive runs increase in difficulty. In addition, less time is allowed per section on runs 3 and 4 than on runs 1 and 2.
>
> Because the task is difficult and the subject is under time pressure, individuals who are easily upset score lower than subjects who are not upset easily.

Cattell: Source Traits and Strata in Personality

The theories of Freud, Jung, Erikson, and Rogers were all based initially on observations made in the clinical setting. A different approach has been taken by Raymond B. Cattell. After graduating with a degree in physics in 1924, he entered academic psychology and has since devoted his life to the development of sound measurement techniques for personality research. Therefore, his theory is based on the data obtained from psychological measurement. Cattell's essential notion is that personality is made up of different layers or *strata* (1973). The higher the strata, the more general the set of tendencies or traits, as illustrated in figure 17.8.

At the lowest level are *behavior tendencies,* which are equivalent to what we called trait indicators in the previous section. Behavior tendencies are assessed by ratings or by responses to test items.

At the next level in the hierarchic structure shown in figure 17.8 are the *primary source traits,* which are higher order influences that bind together two or more behavior tendencies. Correlations between measures of the behavior tendencies would reveal the existence of the higher order influences, and factor analysis pinpoints how many primary source traits there are and the degree to which they correlate one with another. Cattell defines a factor as a mathematical representation of a unitary underlying source of influence. In figure 17.8, the factor immediately underlying a set of correlated behavior tendencies is shown as one of the primary source traits, F+, A+, and so forth.

Using a measure called the Sixteen Personality Factor Questionnaire (16PF), Cattell and his coworkers (Cattell et al., 1970) have established sixteen primary source traits: "affectia" (A+), meaning warm and outgoing as contrasted with cool and aloof; "ego strength" (C+), meaning emotional stability; "low ego strength" (C−) (note that C− is part of the higher-order anxiety pattern); "premsia" (I+), protected emotional sensitivity, easily hurt, fanciful; and "superego strength" (G+), conscientious, dependable, reliable, persistent; and so forth.

Because these factors have been obtained empirically from test data, in some cases they provide confirmation as well as measurement for the concepts of other workers; for example, ego strength and superego strength from Freud's theory, and affectia, which is similar to Kretschmer's concept of cycloid

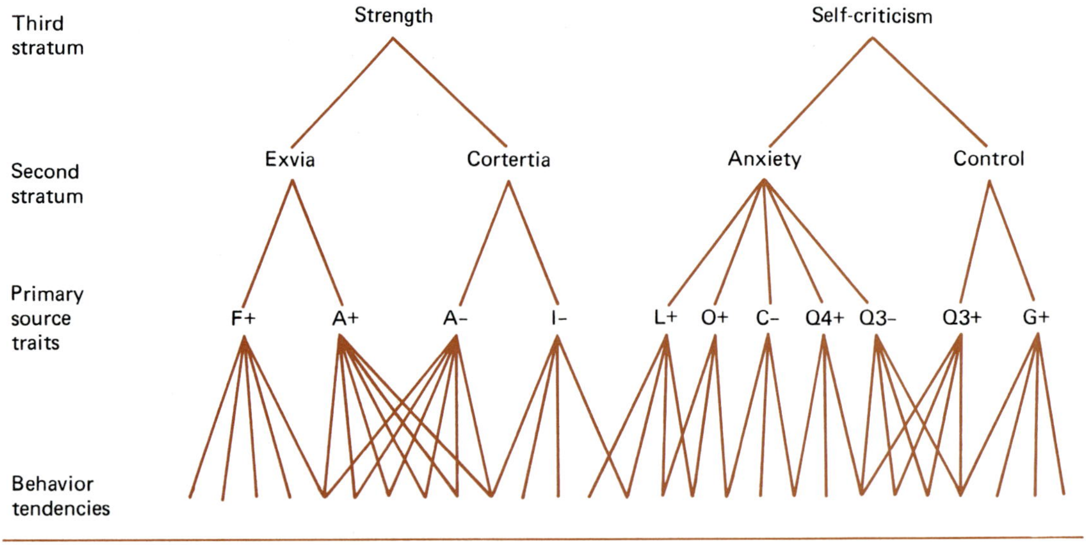

Figure 17.8 Illustration of Cattell's theory of source traits and strata in personality. (Basic data for this illustration were taken from Cattell, R.B., Eber, H.W., and Tatsuoka, M. *Handbook for the sixteen factor questionnaire,* Copyright 1970 Institute for Personality and Ability Testing, Champaign, Ill. Reprinted by permission.)

personality. In other cases (e.g., premsia) the factors point to new concepts.

Recall that the factors themselves may be correlated with one another, thus indicating the presence of influences of a still higher order, or those in the *second stratum*. Correlations among the primary source traits of the 16PF show several such influences in the second stratum, as you can see in figure 17.8. "Exvia" means outgoingness, adaptability, enthusiasm, and warmth of personality. Thus it brings together a number of primary traits in an overall pattern that is conceptually similar to Jung's concept of extroversion versus introversion. "Cortertia" means cortical alertness or mental alacrity; "Anxiety" is a pattern that brings together low ego strength (C−), high suspiciousness (L+), high guilt proneness (O+), high tension (Q4+, undischarged instinctual energy), and low self-sentiment control (Q3−). "Control" is a second stratum influence that means the ability to control impulses.

The influences in the *third stratum* arise from correlations between measures of the second stratum influences. As shown in figure 17.8, they are "strength" (of the nervous system) and "self-criticism." These two highest order influences seem to reflect the basic effectiveness of the biological organism on the one hand, and the central core of society's impact on the organism on the other.

Does the 16PF actually measure personality? Extensive research has shown that different occupational groups have typical profiles of scores on the sixteen source traits. For example, figure 17.9 contrasts the scores obtained by airline pilots with those obtained by

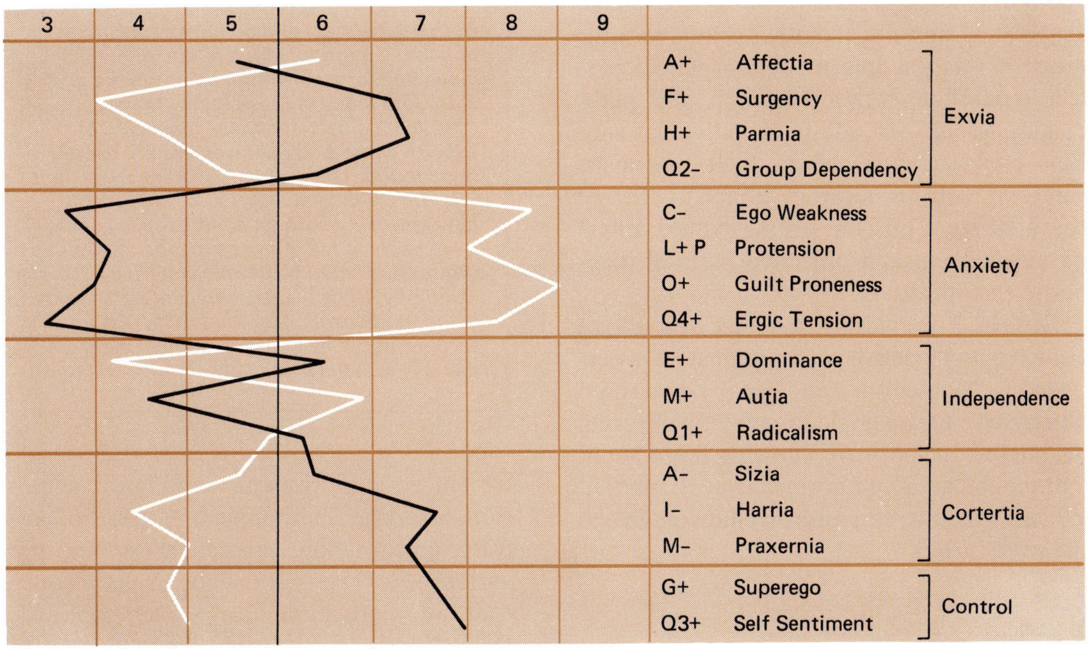

Figure 17.9 Mean profiles obtained for 360 airline pilots (solid black line) compared to patients suffering anxiety neurosis (white line) using the 16PF. (Adapted from Cattell, R.B., Eber, H.W., and Tatsuoka, M. *Handbook for the sixteen factor questionnaire,* Copyright 1970 Institute for Personality and Ability Testing, Champaign, Ill. Reprinted by permission.)

patients suffering from anxiety neurosis. You will be relieved to see how calm, alert, controlled, and adaptable pilots are! Data of this kind provide sound evidence for the validity of the 16PF in measuring personality.

Using objective tests as well as questionnaires to study the structure of personality, Cattell and his associates in the United States and other countries have discovered primary source traits such as anxiety, assertiveness, and exuberance. Many of these objective test factors have been found to differentiate clearly between normal and pathological groups. For example, when Cattell, Schmidt, and Bjerstedt (1972) measured exuberance in schizophrenic and normal subjects by speed of judgment, speed of letter comparison, fluency of ideas, and the like they found that the schizophrenics had significantly lower scores than normal subjects. By appropriately combining the scores obtained for assertiveness, exuberance, anxiety, and other primary source traits, it was possible to obtain almost perfect separation between normal and pathological groups. In addition, individual subjects could be assigned to their diagnostic category with an accuracy equal to that of psychiatrists. Thus the testing battery offers an independent and objective basis of diagnostic classification.

Box 17.2 provides a detailed account of Hundleby's objective measurement of assertiveness. Motivation can also be measured objectively; for example, a person will reveal his interest in sports by knowing more about that topic than about art or the stock market. Which of the two responses would you give to the word "Club"?

CLUB
a. Stick
b. Friends

The response of "friends" would suggest that you are gregarious and interested in being with other people.

Cattell et al. (1964) have found evidence for ten basic motives or "ergs": sex, aggression, assertion, fear, appeal, narcissism, curiosity, construction, protectiveness, and gregariousness. The ergs are the primary source traits of motivation, discovered empirically through factor analysis of correlations among objective motivation tests. In any given culture, ergs may become attached to specific objects or institutions; for example, parents, self, children, career, nation, and so on. Several ergs may become attached simultaneously

Box 17.2
Assertiveness

This trait [assertiveness] has been identified in a large number of factor analytic studies (Hundleby, Pawlik and Cattell, 1965). Among the tests that are associated with this factor, and which could be used to obtain a trait score are:

- *Preference for "unquestionable" and social acceptable book titles rather than "questionable" book titles.*
- *Faster speed of tapping (using a simple stylus and electrical recorder).*
- *Faster tempo of arm and leg circling.*
- *Faster speed of reading under instructions to read at one's usual rate.*
- *Higher score on a complex maze task (Cursive Miniature Situation).*
- *Higher ideomotor tempo (reading poetry and copying simple stick-figure drawings).*
- *Greater preference for objects or activities that appear sophisticated or "highbrow."*

Both educational and cultural sophistication and a generally high tempo of bodily movement and performance on simple tasks enter into many of these tests. Positive correlations between these measures of assertiveness and achievement are usually to be found. There are also rather consistent relations with clinical criteria; the person having a low score on Assertiveness being more likely to fall into a psychotic or neurotic group. Reprinted by permission from J. D. Hundleby, "The measurement of personality by objective tests." In: Paul Kline (Ed.), New approaches in psychological measurement, *N.Y.: Wiley, 1973, Ch. 4.*

to one object such as the family; protectiveness, gregariousness, and narcissism, for example.

Cattell et al. (1964) produced a convenient battery of tests to measure a number of ergs and sentiments, the *Motivational Analysis Test*. Interesting research can now be carried out on, for example, the vicissitudes of motivation in everyday life. Kline and Grindley (1973) report such a study for a young woman who took the test daily and kept a diary over a 28-day period. Sexual tension rose gradually and irregularly toward the time of ovulation, which also coincided with an important event in her life, however. Fear rose sharply on the twelfth day, when she was feeling rejected by a work group, and on the seventeenth day, after a trip in an "unsafe" automobile. Correlations between ergs showed that as her fear increased, her aggressiveness decreased and that as her sexual tension increased, so did her assertiveness. Furthermore, correlations between ergs and sentiments showed that as the strength of her superego decreased, her sexual tension increased.

Cattell's work has resulted in a vast array of tests and measuring devices, all of which are aimed at some part of the overall structure of personality. The primary purpose of his most recent work is to integrate motivational structure with learning and traits of temperament with changes in mood.

Eysenck: Biological Basis of Personality

H. J. Eysenck, one of Britain's foremost psychologists, obtained his doctoral degree from the University of London in 1940. He has proposed an economical theory of personality that integrates individual differences with the general principles of behavior established by experimental and physiological psychology.

According to Eysenck, individual differences in a wide range of traits are related to differences in two dimensions, *extroversion* and *neuroticism*. Each dimension is built up from the integration of *specific responses* to specific situations, which in turn results in *habits*. For example, the responses of going to a party, joining a committee, playing a game, and having fun with a friend may be integrated into habits of party-going, committee-joining, game-playing, and liking people. These habits are then found to be correlated together in the traits of sociability and liveliness. Sociability, liveliness, and other traits are then found to be grouped together in a *dimension*. The dimension illustrated in our examples would be extroversion (as opposed to introversion). Figure 17.10 not only illustrates Eysenck's total conception but demonstrates that *types* of personality can be found at the point where the dimensions of extroversion and neuroticism intersect.

Extroverted neurotic patients typically suffer from hysteria. They have a low level of aspiration, tend to do clerical tasks quickly but inaccurately, and lack persistence. Persistence is measured by having the person sit on one chair and hold his leg over another chair while keeping his heel about an inch above the seat of the second chair for as long as possible. Hysterics usually manage to maintain this position for approximately 14 seconds; introverted neurotics can hold it for about 31 seconds. Eysenck points out that these results agree with earlier psychiatric formulations that although hysterical subjects initially put great energy into a new task, they tire quickly and are unwilling to treat anything seriously or persist at it. Introverted neurotic patients, who typically show anxiety reactions and depression, have a high level of aspiration and tend to be accurate but slow when doing clerical tasks.

How do neurotic subjects differ from stable ones? Eysenck (1952) gave a large battery of tests to 200 normal subjects and 120 neurotic subjects and found many differences between the two groups. For example, when shown a list of potentially annoying situations, such as a squeaky door, normal sub-

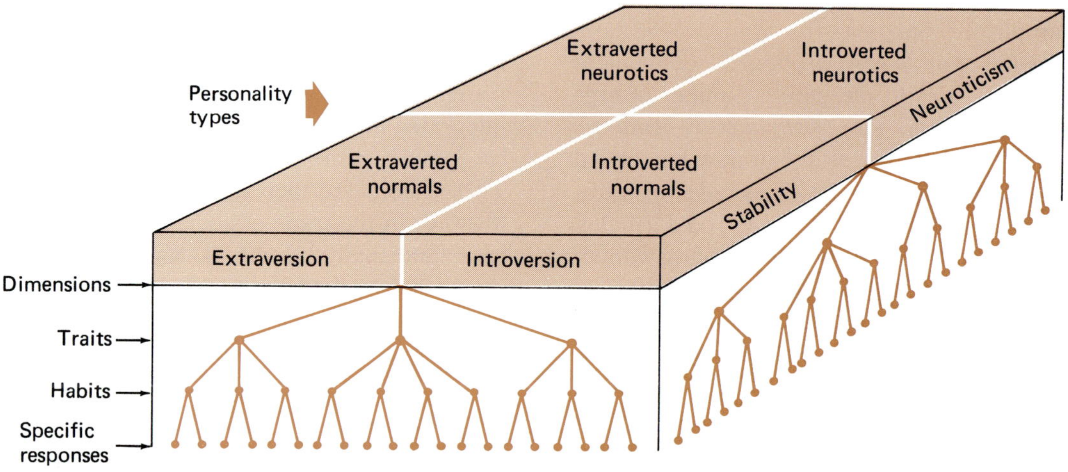

Figure 17.10 Eysenck's theory of the structure of personality. (From Cartwright, D.S., *Introduction to personality,* © 1974 Rand McNally, College Publishing Company, Chicago.)

jects indicated they would find twenty-three of the situations annoying, while neurotics said they would be annoyed by twenty-six items. Normal subjects were able to place about twenty-six small pegs in holes correctly, whereas neurotics could place only twenty-three during the same period. In other words, there are behavioral differences between extroverts and introverts and between normals and neurotics. But what does this mean?

Eysenck proposes (1967) that individual differences in extroversion are primarily related to differences in characteristic brain functions. Extremely extroverted persons characteristically have a weaker potential for cortical excitation than less extroverted persons. Because the cortex controls lower centers of excitability, a weakening of cortical excitation would result in a lessening of control and hence an increase in general behavioral excitability.

Eysenck cites the effects of alcohol as an illustration: by inhibiting the action of the cerebral cortex, alcohol releases the lower areas from cortical control and thereby produces excited behavior. Thus, extroversion is distinguished from introversion on the basis of the relative balance between inhibitory and excitatory potentials in the cortex, with extroversion being associated with a greater degree of cortical inhibition.

Several of Eysenck's experiments (1967) tend to support this theory. For example, in a tapping test, extroverted subjects tend to pause involuntarily more often as we would predict if their attention keeps wandering (i.e., if the inhibition builds up more rapidly in the cortical areas controlling mechanisms of attention). Also, evidence has accumulated over the years concerning the heritability of both neuroticism and extroversion. Eysenck's latest research shows that both traits are determined, in part, by genetic factors.

One excellent example of Eysenck's research (Howarth and Eysenck, 1968) is a study that relates extroversion to learning. If the theory of cortical excitation and inhibition is correct, then extroverts should show the same pattern of learning and retention as that shown by subjects who learn under experimentally induced conditions of *low* degree of arousal; introverts should show the pattern found under conditions of *high* degree of arousal.

Howarth and Eysenck established two groups of subjects, one highly extroverted and one with a low degree of extroversion, as determined by the Eysenck Personality Inventory, a questionnaire that measures extroversion and neuroticism. Subjects were required to learn a set of seven pairs of nonsense syllables, as shown in table 17.3. As trials progressed, the subjects were required to pronounce each stimulus word (e.g., SEP), as well as the response word (e.g., MOL), if they recalled it. The trials continued until one complete set could be recalled. Then, after different intervals of time, different subgroups

Table 17.3 Howarth and Eysenck's experiment on extroversion, arousal, and learning.

	Extraverts (Low arousal)	Introverts (High arousal)
	N = 55	N = 55
Procedures	Example:	
S is to learn paired nonsense syllables. He is to say each one aloud. There are seven pairs. As trials progress, S is to show that he has learned by calling out what the paired syllable will be before it appears.	SEP -------- MOL ZIL -------- PAF ⋮ NEF -------- VAB	
Mean number of trails to criterion of one complete set correct:	15.9	18.3
	(not significantly different)	
After a pause, the test of retention is given by asking S to print all the stimulus words. 14 is the maximum correct.		
There are five groups, each waiting a different length of time. The mean number of words recalled by each group was:		
Time of pause		
0 mins.	11.8	7.0
1 min.	9.3	7.9
5 mins.	8.9	8.1
30 mins.	7.0	10.0
24 hours	7.0	11.0
	(patterns significantly different $p < .001$)	

Source: Howarth and Eysenck, 1968.

of subjects wrote down all the stimulus and response words they could recall. Table 17.3 shows the results, which clearly confirm the hypothesis.

Eysenck continues to develop his theory from a biological point of view. In collaboration with geneticists at the University of Birmingham, he is currently developing large-scale studies on the inheritance of personality. Many of his ideas remain controversial and are constantly being studied by other investigators.

Problem-Focused Research: the Case of Aggression

We have examined a number of major theoretical positions in the study of personality and have described some of the research associated with each. As we said at the beginning of the chapter, however, many investigators focus on particular problems such as aggression, locus of control, or imagery, rather than on a major theory. Here, we will describe one example of such problem-focused research, emphasizing the progressive formulation of the problem. One scientist follows another with alternative hypotheses, experimental proofs, critiques of earlier work, new hypotheses, and new experiments. These problems are full of puzzles, and the scientist's challenge is to solve one puzzle after another.

You will recall that Freud considered aggression to be one of two basic human instincts and that Cattell found an aggression *erg* among the ten basic ergs or systems of energy in human motivation. And war, mob violence, and crime make aggression a current topic of interest and concern. Yet aggression formed only part of Freud's theory, and only one of Cattell's ten basic ergs. Therefore, even a comprehensive theory of aggression can only be a partial theory insofar as personality is concerned.

One of the earliest hypotheses about aggression was that aggression is always a consequence of frustration, the so-called frustration-aggression hypothesis discussed in Chapter 15. Subsequent research, however, has indicated that frustration can elicit other responses (e.g., regression) and that there are other causes of aggression as well. For example, Bandura, Ross, and Ross (1963) let children see an adult sit on a Bobo doll, punch it in the nose, hit it with a mallet, and so forth. Later, after being frustrated to arouse aggression, the children were allowed to do what they wanted with the Bobo doll and other things. Those who had watched the adult's aggressive behavior were much more likely to be aggressive themselves than were control subjects. Moreover, girls tended to imitate female models, while boys tended to imitate male models. Thus children may acquire the trait of aggressiveness by observing models, and the more similar the children are to the models, the more likely the children are to imitate them.

The next question was: Do television, movies, or comics produce aggressive behavior in the young by portraying aggressive models? In a careful field experiment, Feshbach and Singer (1971) gave groups of boys controlled diets of aggressive or nonaggressive television programs for a period of six weeks. Observers rated the boys aggressiveness and found that the boys who watched aggressive behavior on television were *less* aggressive toward peers and authorities. One explanation for this result is that watching aggressive films is a *catharsis,* or a freeing of aggressive emotion.

In a similar experiment, Hartmann (1969) showed delinquent boys one of three films: an aggressive film depicting the attacker's behavior, one depicting the victim's suffering, or one that lacked aggressive content. Prior to seeing the films, some of the boys had been angered by supposed insults from another participant in the experiment (actually a tape-recording). All the boys were then given an opportunity to give an electric shock to the "other participant," who was supposedly in another room. Would the aggressive film reduce the angered subjects' aggression, as measured by the intensity and duration of the shock delivered to the target? It did not. On the contrary, both angered and nonangered subjects delivered more shocks if they were exposed to aggressive films.

The controversy has not yet been resolved. Closely related to the process of catharsis, however, is the process of displacement, which, according to Freud's theory, meant the shifting of emotional charge from one object onto another. The hypothesis of catharsis through viewing aggressive films rests on the notion that the viewer's own aggressive impulses can be discharged vicariously on a symbolic object in the film. Numerous researchers have postulated that when aggression is displaced, the object of the displacement must closely resemble the original instigator on some dimension. However, Fenigstein and Buss (1974) have shown that, when given the opportunity to deliver shocks (for "errors" in learning tasks), angered subjects give more intense shocks, regardless of the relationship between the target of their aggression and its instigator. Thus it is the intensity of affect rather than the characteristics of the stimuli that controls displacement of aggression; in other words, the emotions of intense anger *can* be displaced by viewing aggressive films. But whether *watching* another person's aggressive behavior is as effective in discharging the affect as is actually delivering punitive shocks has not been determined.

Although Bandura (1973) points out that Hartmann's experiment with delinquent boys yielded results that are contrary to the catharsis hypothesis, Hartmann's subjects were not exposed long enough (only one minute) to allow any catharsis to take place. By contrast, Feshbach and Singer's subjects were exposed to a regular schedule of television viewing for six weeks! Thus Hartmann's experimental conditions were not really relevant to the catharsis hypothesis.

Another formulation would suggest that *instigation* (the impulse to act) must be accompanied by *facilitation* (the means to act) and *permission* (the sanction to act). Hartmann's experiment provided the instigation (by insulting the subject) and the facilitation (the shock machine), and his aggressive film probably provided the necessary permission to express aggression. And in their experiment using the Bobo doll, Bandura and his colleagues also found it necessary to frustrate their subjects (instigation) before placing them in the test room with the doll (target) and mallet (facilitation). Because the subjects in both experiments were shown films or models of aggressive behavior, the experimenter gave them tacit permission to express aggression.

An individual's predisposition to aggression, then, must be studied in the context of the immediate environmental situation, which can permit or otherwise trigger an aggressive response. Baldwin (1975) has shown that environmental cues like hostile graffiti or pictures of violent scenes hanging on the wall of the experimental room can raise the intensity of expressed aggressive behavior.

Clearly there remain many more interesting puzzles still to be solved in research on aggression.

Summary

In this chapter, some of the psychological thought about human personality as it has gathered momentum over the past seventy-five years, was reviewed.

Freud said that personality is composed of three major divisions: the id, ego, and superego. The id is undifferentiated and consists mainly of instinctual drives; the ego is a differentiated structure that seeks to cope with external reality; the superego is a structure that represents parental controls. The essence of personality can be seen in the ego's task of satisfying instinctual impulses in ways that do not conflict with external reality and the prohibitions of the superego (conscience).

Erikson has advanced our understanding of the ego in its encounter with society by postulating eight stages of psychosocial development. These stages parallel Freud's stages of psychosexual development to a substantial degree. His formulation of the problems related to the development of identity allows for a moratorium during adolescence, during which the person strives to bring all the elements of his identity together.

The concept of personality types has had a long history in psychology. For example, Kretschmer's theory postulated the existence of personality types known as cycloid and schizoid. Jung developed a theory of types he called extrovert and introvert. Jung also introduced the idea of a collective unconscious and argued that it was more important than the personal, dynamic unconscious stressed by Freud. The collective unconscious is shared by all people everywhere and is chiefly composed of archetypes, or racial memories, which control experience and development. Archetypes function in part by sensitizing the person to certain images from the outer world, such as a mother figure or a hero. They also produce certain parts of the personality, such as the ego and the persona (or public personality).

Rogers believes that the basic aim of every person is to actualize his potentialities. The basic relation to the world is achieved through an organismic valuing process, whereby the person decides what is good or bad for him. If the person is open to experience, his experiences will be symbolized in awareness, and so the person can symbolize experiences that pertain to his or her own body and characteristics, and thereby develop a concept of self.

Working from data provided by psychological tests, Cattell has developed a hierarchic theory of personality, which is organized into *strata* of increasingly general influence. The dimensions of influence within these strata are discovered by procedures of factor analysis. Cattell finds evidence for sixteen primary source traits of temperament and ten of motivation. Personality functions through these traits.

Eysenck combines measures of individual differences with the principles of general experimental psychology (such as learning and conditioning) to account for the dynamics of personality. From empirical research he has established two main dimensions of personality; emotional stability versus neuroticism, and extroversion versus introversion. People differ in their degree of neuroticism and extroversion based on differences in the way their nervous system functions.

Active research programs are currently being carried forward in connection with each of the major theoretical positions we have described. In addition, many researchers focus their studies on a specific problem such as aggression.

18

Psychopathology

In Chapter 17, we saw how several different theorists would explain the normal development of personality. There was also some discussion about how and why normal development can go awry, so that abnormalities of personality and behavior occur. In this chapter we will focus on *psychopathology,* the technical term for abnormalities of personality development.

You will recall from Chapter 1 that the clinical psychologist specializes in observing, studying, classifying, understanding, and treating the various kinds of psychopathology. The treatment of psychopathology will be the subject of the next chapter. Here, we will discuss (1) the definition of psychopathological or abnormal behavior, (2) the history of man's fascination with psychopathology, (3) the current models of psychopathology observed in adults and children, and (4) the different types or classifications of psychopathology.

Psychopathological Behavior

Consider for a moment the following examples of human behavior. A student stands up during a test and throws his textbook through the closed classroom window. A girl whose boyfriend has rejected her has cried every day for a month and has lost all interest in attending classes. A middle-aged woman walks into the emergency room of a hospital carrying the severed head of a pig in her shopping bag. An Iowa farmer blows up Voice of America radio transmitter with a 50-pound dynamite charge, then claims he was trying "to shut off the voices" in his head. A layman might label these people "crazy" or "nuts" or say they are suffering from a "nervous breakdown," a term that is meaningless to the clinical psychologist. Nerves do not break down, get jangled, or do any of the other things they have been accused of doing by people who are eager to explain the strange behavior that mentally abnormal people display. The psychologist might say that the individuals just described have in common the fact that their behavior deviated from the range of behaviors considered normal in our society. Because they were unable to behave in socially appropriate ways, the consequences were maladaptive for themselves and/or society. Thus they displayed *psychopathology.*

Characteristics of Psychopathological Behavior

If a person behaves in a psychopathological way, four things are usually true:

1. His behavior *deviates from normal* in a negative direction. People who deviate in the positive direction (Albert Einstein, for example) are more likely to be labeled as admirable, not pathological.

2. The *motivation* for his actions cannot be explained on a reasonable basis. The conscious or unconscious motives for his acts are thus irrational. For example, if the student who threw the book had been aiming at a dog that had bounded into the classroom and tried to bite a classmate, but the book had missed the dog and sailed through the window, his act would appear noble, not pathological.

3. The *context* in which the act occurs makes it inappropriate. In wartime, if any enemy blew up a Voice of America transmitter, he would be called a hero in his society; his behavior would certainly not be called psychopathological. In many contexts, the *lack* of a strong reaction is considered abnormal. For example, if a loved parent dies and his child shows no emotions, the psychologist would be concerned about the normality of the child's reaction.

4. The *majority* of the society in which the individual lives would define his behavior as psychopathological. Suppose the woman carrying the pig's head lived in Australia and dropped by an emergency room to have her cut hand bandaged while on her way to an aboriginal ritual that featured a dance around boars' heads placed on stakes. She would be viewed as making a valuable contribution to the ceremony and be sent on her way. Some remarkable behaviors are defined as normal in certain cultures, and what is considered normal can vary from year to year in any one culture.

Thus, deciding whether a behavior is normal or abnormal is not always easy. Parents and children often disagree about what is normal or abnormal (see fig. 18.1), and even psychologists do not always agree among themselves.

Degree of Abnormality

Not only does the psychologist want to define whether a person is behaving abnormally, he wants to determine the *degree* to which a person is abnormal. Because stress is ever

"My kid doesn't smoke pot, doesn't wear dirty jeans, and doesn't let his hair grow long. We're having him checked out by a psychiatrist." Courtesy: Medical Economics.

Figure 18.1 In the 1950s and 1960s, this joke would have had no point in America. It may have no point in the 1980s either. (Courtesy Al Kaufman.)

present in most people's lives, how we cope with stress determines how normal we are.

There are two major kinds of abnormal reactions to stress, *neurotic* and *psychotic*. Neurotic reactions can range from mildly to severely pathological; psychotic reactions are almost always judged to be severely pathological. Furthermore, people who have neurotic reactions to stress rarely become psychotic.

Although we will describe the differences between these two reactions in more detail later, we can use our book-throwing student to clarify the main differences now. Suppose the student had thrown the book because he was unable to answer the questions on the examination. The psychologist who observed his inability to control his anger and pick more appropriate ways of discharging tension or anxiety would have labeled his behavior neurotic and moderately abnormal. However, if the student had seen a threatening human face outside the third-floor window and voices in his head had told him to throw the book, his reaction would have been labeled psychotic and severely abnormal. Thus book throwing in response to taking an examination is more or less abnormal, depending on the degree of irrationality of the reasons behind it. Freud put it clearly when he said "Neurosis does not deny the existence of reality, it merely tries to ignore it; psychosis denies it and tries to substitute something else for it." (Noyes and Kolb, 1968.)

Historical Conceptions of Psychopathology

Humans have always attributed to the supernatural things they cannot explain in any other way. In early Egypt, Israel, and Greece, madness was viewed as punishment meted out by offended gods or as possession by evil spirits or demons.

In the fourth century B.C., Hippocrates, the great physician, argued that mental illness should not be attributed to the supernatural but to natural causes, such as a disease of the brain. Aristotle believed that man's mind is independent of the body and incapable of being psychologically diseased; therefore, mental disturbances were organic diseases of the brain. Thus he anticipated, by more than two thousand years, the modern dispute about whether functional (psychological) or organic (medical) causes are the primary reasons for psychopathology. In the second century B.C., Galen distinguished between two types of mental illnesses based on whether he thought their cause was mental or physical.

Greek thinking about psychopathology had not spread to the region where Christ was born, as illustrated in the following quotation from the Bible (Luke 8:26–37):

> . . . and when He [Jesus] had come out of the boat, there met Him out of the tombs a man with an unclean spirit, who lived among the tombs and no one could bind him anymore, even with a chain; for he had often been bound with fetters and chains, but the chains he wrenched apart, and the fetters he broke in pieces and no one had the strength to subdue him.
>
> Night and day among the tombs and on the mountains he was always crying out, and bruising himself with stones.
>
> . . . and Jesus asked him "What is your name?" He replied "My name is Legion; for we are many."

According to the Bible, Jesus drove out the "many unclean spirits" inhabiting the man and for his compassionate act was asked to "depart from their neighborhood."

The spread of Christianity paralleled the return to the demonology that had characterized the Dark Ages. Again, man was viewed as a pawn in the hands of the demons and spirits who fought for his soul. By the fifteenth century, two schools of thought about psychopathology predominated: One, the insane person was being punished for his sins, or two, he had voluntarily sold his soul to the devil, and in exchange for his soul he was given supernatural powers—that is, he became a witch. The treatment based on this faulty conception of psychopathology will be described in the next chapter. Only gradually did these notions of psychopathology give way to the more scientific views we will discuss next. However, demonology is still a fascinating topic—as illustrated by the fact that in 1974 many thousands of people were frightened by *The Exorcist,* a movie based on the premise that possession by the devil still occurs.

Modern Models of Psychopathology

Beginning in the late nineteenth century, demonological models of psychopathology gave way to those with a scientific orientation. Although today there are a number of models for explaining psychopathology, we shall describe five of the major ones—the medical, societal, psychodynamic, behavioral, and existential models. But first, we need a case history to which we can refer when discussing each one.

John D., a 27-year-old college senior majoring in speech pathology, was referred for therapy by a physician who was concerned that his high blood pressure might be related to psychological factors rather than any purely physical cause. John had had several attacks during which his blood pressure would rise, he would feel dizzy, see black spots before his eyes, and twice he had fainted briefly. After these attacks, he would have a pounding headache that would last for hours.

The attacks seemed to occur when John was required to speak up to anyone about anything—presenting a paper in class, asking a teacher for a letter of reference to graduate school, telling a friend to leave his room long after the friend should have taken mild hints to leave—all of these occasions called forth a violent physical reaction, and nothing was ever said. John spoke so quietly in talking of his problems that he could scarcely be heard. He had high expectations for perfect performance on his part and felt worried that he would not do well and people would criticize him. Although his grades were high and he was well liked by his teachers, he was convinced he was a failure.

When John was five years old, his father had died, leaving him in the care of a mother who was an aggressive and dominating person. She forbade him to talk back to her but gave him many orders to follow. He felt that no matter what he did, he couldn't please her because it was never good enough. He thought of himself as devoted to pleasing her and a failure because he couldn't. Even at 27, the only way he could handle his mother was to keep thousands of miles between them. If he tried to speak with her, one of his attacks was bound to occur and he would feel guilty and depressed for several days.

Medical Model

We have seen that physicians and philosophers of ancient Greece were the first to say that psychopathology had medical or organic causes. With the discovery in the nineteenth century that the abnormal thinking and behavior which characterized a disease called general paresis were caused by syphilis, it became fashionable to hunt for the physical causes of other mental problems. The terms mental disease and mental illness are a direct result of the belief that the symptoms, the causes, and ultimately the cures for psychopathology are biologically based.

The medical model has stimulated interesting research on biochemical and *genetic factors in psychopathology,* and breakthroughs in describing the biochemical disorders related to the psychoses are likely to occur soon. Although no one claims that all neurotic behavior can be explained in biochemical terms, many theorists believe that the capacity to tolerate stress is inherited. Individuals with a high tolerance to stress have autonomic nervous systems that respond slowly and produce relatively small amounts of the chemicals, for example, epinephrine that can cause symptoms such as anxiety. The autonomic systems of individuals with a low tolerance to stress react quickly and produce large amounts of the chemicals that are related to feelings of anxiety. Thus inherited temperamental differences predispose certain individuals to have more psychological troubles than others. Although a person may be anxious because he modeled himself after an anxious parent, he also may have inherited from that parent the predisposition to react strongly, even to low levels of stress.

In addition, evidence also indicates that an hereditary predisposition may influence the type of physical symptoms the anxious person has, or whether he has any physical symptoms at all. Physical problems such as migraine headaches, allergic asthma, ulcers, and skin rashes commonly run in families, and they all tend to become more severe when the individual experiences stress. The genetic theory predicts that if an individual inherits a tendency to secrete high levels of acid in the stomach during stress, he may develop an ulcer. Another individual may develop a headache if the blood vessels of his head dilate during stress. Although individuals with no genetically vulnerable organ systems experience stress and feel anxiety, they will not have severe physical (psychosomatic) symptoms.

The most active research in human behavioral genetics has involved the inheritance of psychotic disorders. After summarizing recent work on the subject, McClearn and DeFries (1973) concluded that the evidence clearly indicated that a genetic factor is involved in the two major psychoses that will be discussed later in this chapter.

How would the medical model explain the case of John D.?

First, John's psychosomatic symptom of high blood pressure would be considered an inherited predisposition to react in this way to stress. (His father and grandfather also had unexplained bouts of high blood pressure.) In addition, the medical model would attribute John's chronic anxiety to the fact that he has a low tolerance for stress.

Second, it would absolve John of any responsibility for his reactions. He is ill; his organs can't help responding the way they do to stress. He should consider himself a patient.

By explaining John's physical problems in biological terms alone, however, we would be unable to account for the fact that they only occur in a clearly definable social context, that is, when John is required to assert himself. Also, it is difficult to explain his poor self-concept, feeling of failure in school, and relationship to his mother as "illnesses" in a medical sense. However, the medical model does recognize a relationship between biological predispositions and environmental conditions that cause symptoms to appear. Thus John's mother would clearly be labeled as an environmental stress.

Historically, it was probably necessary to adopt a medical posture toward psychopathology. This approach removed behavior from the realm of superstition and tried to explain it with laws that could be scientifically tested. Although medical explanations took away personal responsibility for psychopathology, they at least paved the way for viewing the "mentally ill" as people with problems rather than as criminals or witches to be punished.

Societal Model

Theorists who attribute psychopathology to societal influences point to research findings such as the following: Greater psychopathology is consistently found among the lower socioeconomic classes (Srole et al., 1962; Hollingshead and Redlich, 1958). The problem with these findings is that they do not address the question of which came first, the poverty or the pathology. In other words, did these individuals begin their lives in this lower-class status or did the pathology interfere with their functioning to the point where they descended to the lower class? But it is not only the presence of serious problems in ghettos or other undesirable environments that concerns the societal theorists. They view modern man as inevitably trapped in the impersonal atmosphere of a mass mechanistic society. Fromm (1973) and Riesman (1969) have portrayed the alienation, loneliness, and isolation faced by man lost in the crowd of humanity. For example, student uprisings and unrest have been attributed, in part, to reactions to the large impersonal bureaucracies that some of our universities have become. The suspiciousness that led to Watergate and other corruption at the highest levels of government and big business have been viewed as the inevitable result of administrations which have become so large and complex that they have lost sight of individual rights and freedoms.

Societal theorists might argue that in a society organized for the benefit of people like John D. (whose father died when John was five), a social agency would have provided him with a strong male to help him become a man, his mother would have been given help in raising him, and he would not have become neurotic.

It is undoubtedly true that large organizations are impersonal, and individual needs are lost in bureaucratic inefficiency and red tape. It is also probably true that individuals in the lower strata of society must struggle harder to develop normally. Yet, blaming society for an individual's pathology leaves that individual as much of a helpless victim of circumstances as blaming biology does. What can a person like John do if society's failure to provide for him at age five is the reason he is "sick"? Even if society does change, it will be too late for him.

Psychoanalytic Model

Instead of reflecting a war between an individual and society, the psychoanalytic model locates the war within the person and talks about conflict between parts of his personality. Because Freud was thoroughly discussed in the previous chapter, only the main features of his theory of conflict will be reviewed here.

Freud proposed that the cause of psychopathology is a conflict between the individual's need or desire to express an impulse and the prohibition of parents or society against its expression. With the development of the superego or conscience, the prohibition against expressing the impulse becomes internalized as a part of the self. Now the conflict leads to open warfare within the self, and the wish to express the impulse leads the person to defend against the impulse that threatens to break through. But even if he is successful, some psychopathology will show itself. Sometimes obvious symptoms of anxiety and depression occur whenever the conflict is activated; at other times, defense mechanisms such as repression, denial, or reaction formation are brought into play. The individual tries in any way he can to defend against the wish to express the impulse. Most of the time he is not aware of his unconscious conflicts or that his reactions occur in response to them.

How would the psychoanalytic models explain John D.'s pathology? John's mother did not allow her son to express aggression towards her, which made him angry and frustrated, but he repressed these feelings and tried to please her. And because he internalized her prohibitions and demands, his superego forbade any expression of aggression toward anyone in any situation. Whenever his wish to speak out conflicted with the prohibition, he suffered a psychopathological symptom.

Again, the focus of responsibility for the pathology rests in the parent's mistakes, and with this model much time is spent in going over past experiences. Many people seem to believe that if character is set at the age of five and parents are to blame for their children's problems, one should simply understand and accept the inevitable pathology and try to live with it as comfortably as possible. Although the analytic model often allows the person to be more tolerant of his neurotic behaviors, hopefully, the patient takes responsibility for working through the conflicts so he no longer behaves maladaptively.

Behavioral Model

Classical behavior theorists, such as B. F. Skinner, say that both normal and abnormal behavior are related to the individual's reinforcement history. Behavior that was rewarded remains in a person's repertoire; behavior that was punished does not remain. All our behavior results from learning about the environment and what important people in our lives expect of us. Changing abnormal behavior is a matter of learning new, more appropriate responses to people or situations in our environment. Also, because man can manipulate his environment, he can make whatever changes in the environment are necessary or helpful. Anything that is learned can be unlearned. And because everything is learned, change is possible; it is never too late to learn to behave in new ways.

Critics accuse behaviorists of describing a mechanical man who responds automatically, as a pigeon does, to reinforcing stimuli. The richness of human thought and feeling is ignored, and only an empty organism is left. In response to that criticism, more and more behaviorists are adding cognitive and physical elements to their theories of psychopathology. Lazarus (1973), for example, believes the therapist must actively modify or change what the person thinks and feels about himself. At times, modification of a person's thinking must precede attempts to modify his behavior or no change will occur.

Behaviorists would say that John D.'s psychopathology is based partly on his mother's failure to reinforce appropriate assertive behavior. Because he generalized to all situations requiring assertive or aggressive behavior, John was unable to emit any assertive responses. His mother also reinforced faulty cognitions about what a failure he was when he was unable to do what she expected of him. His autonomic nervous system responded to the stress of dealing with her. Thus a faulty autonomic response (high blood pressure) was conditioned to situations that called forth his fear of failing or demanded assertive behavior.

Notice again that John's personal responsibility for his behavior is neglected by such theories. The reasons for his pathology are located outside himself; that is, faulty reinforcements by his mother and the lack of a father who might have reinforced more appropriate behavior. However, he can learn new ways of behaving. This model clearly defines what he must do to change and how he must go about it.

Existential Model

Several contemporary theorists attempt to place the responsibility for psychopathology as well as change on the person himself. These theories relate psychopathology to man's estrangement from his life and himself. Man is viewed as an active participant in life, vibrantly trying to become what his ability and potential would allow him to become. He does not succumb to faulty reinforcements; he frustrates himself, and ultimately, he despairs because he cannot conquer the inevitable problems of living. Because existential means to exist in the here and now, existential theorists describe man as a choice-maker—a free and responsible agent who often makes wrong decisions that cause him to despair.

The *moral* existentialists, such as Thomas Szasz (1960), may be thought of as having *moral models* of psychopathology. Szasz attacks the medical model in particular because it allows people to avoid responsibility for their acts. He says that people who exhibit psychopathology have "problems in living" everyday life and must take personal responsibility for their problems. O. Hobart Mowrer (1961) carries this position a step further and claims that man suffers guilt and despair because he actually is guilty of *sin.* In his attempts to confront life, he behaves immorally and despair is the price.

The *self-actualizing* existentialists (Carl Rogers and Abraham Maslow) take a brighter view of man's capacity to fulfill himself in a stress-filled world. Rogers believes that man is naturally disposed to be kind, self-accepting, and productive. If this potential is restricted in the ways discussed in Chapter 17, then he will become ineffective and disturbed. The motto "Today is the first day of the rest of your life" is a Rogerian exhortation to make the most of present opportunities and future possibilities rather than dwell in the past. In other words, man is responsible for identifying and overcoming his failures.

In the moral view then, John D. feels guilty and depressed when dealing with his mother because he fails to follow the commandment "honor thy mother." His problems in living include getting on with the job of becoming what he can become. He must take responsibility for going to a therapist who can help him discover the steps he must take to actualize himself. In Rogerian terms, he must bring his real self and ideal self into reasonable alignment so that he can do a better job of living his life. Because he is responsible for his own faulty choices and decisions, it is up to him to stop making them.

It is important to realize that the existential model assumes that the individual is responsible for making faulty choices and decisions that *cause* his problems. Psychopathology is not blamed on illness, society, parents, unconscious conflicts, reinforcement history, or any other impersonal factors.

There are several problems with the existential model. The moral theorists' concepts of sin and morality require value judgments about what is right and wrong. Because morality is a relative, not absolute concept, it is difficult to determine what is moral. Many would say, for example, that parents are honorable only to the extent that they treat their children honorably; that is, they must earn their children's respect instead of demanding it as a moral right. In the case of the self-actualizing theorists, problems arise because of the imprecise meaning of "being yourself and fulfilling your potential." How do you know what your potential is? Do you do what you feel like doing without worrying about how your acts will affect other people? Some would say there is too much self-actualizing and not enough consideration for others in today's world.

An Integrated Model for Psychopathology

When trying to explain a specific psychopathological syndrome, most psychologists draw from several of the models just discussed. No single model or theory is complete enough to be the only useful way of looking at psychopathology. In other words, no single approach is adequate to deal effectively with human psychopathology.

Models or theories that explain psychopathology are useful if they help to prevent or treat emotional disorders. Because each model contains ideas that are worth considering, the trained observer of psychopathology uses many different ideas when thinking about the cases he sees.

Biological and genetic factors are more important in some kinds of psychopathology than in others. However, the fact remains that each of us begins life with biophysical states that are unique to us. These states help to determine how we will interact with whatever we find in the world. We grow up in a society that provides us with certain opportunities and prohibits others. Furthermore, our parents and other important models have a profound impact on what we become as we mature. Although our parents cannot teach us anything they do not know, we can learn things they could not teach us. Thus change is always possible.

Psychopathology is characterized by disturbances in how a person *thinks, feels,* and *acts*. In some cases, the key to understanding pathology is to identify repressed material that is related to unresolved conflicts. In others, this approach is unnecessary, and a focus on present behavior will help us to understand what to do about it. For every type of psychopathology, there is some form of therapy that can help a person adapt more comfortably to life. In the final analysis, however, each individual is responsible for insuring that he will be at peace with himself and others in his life. Only if we take responsibility for changing ourselves will there be a significant reduction in the amount of psychopathology in the world. Often, taking responsibility means that we must recognize our need for professional help; sometimes it means taking medication or consulting a genetic counselor before having children. Understanding our responsibilities is the greatest challenge we face.

Now that we have defined what psychopathology is and have discussed both the historical and modern conceptions of what causes it, we are ready to talk about the different kinds of psychopathology the clinical psychologist observes.

Types of Psychopathology

It is estimated that one in every five Americans living today will seek professional help in understanding and changing his psychopathological behavior. This is roughly forty-two million people, or one member of every family. Approximately one in ten Americans will be hospitalized at some point in their lives for mental problems. In box 18.1, you will discover how two investigators attempted to explain why these numbers are so high.

Because change and the stress that results from change are ever present in our way of life, it is easy to understand why so many people seek help with their problems. A great range of problems and symptoms are represented in such a large group. Experienced observers of psychopathology believe they have seen all the psychopathologies that exist, until some new person with a unique combination of symptoms and problems comes for treatment. They are then reminded anew that the variations on human misery are endless. Major themes can be identified, however, and much effort has been devoted to refining systems of classifying and categorizing the types of psychological disorders.

The advantages of classifying psychopathology are fairly obvious. It is useful for record-keeping as well as research purposes. Most important, however, it serves as a shorthand system of communication between professional clinicians. If a psychologist says "she is an obsessive-compulsive neurotic" to

Box 18.1

Change as a Predictor of Physical or Emotional Problems

Holmes and Rahe (1967) report that if enough changes occur in your life over a two-year period, you can expect to get sick with either physical or emotional disorders. It does not matter whether a change is good or bad, whether it makes you happy or sad, or whether you like change or not. Any change is stressful and requires coping.

Below is a list of events and the Life Crisis Units points attached to them that a college student might experience.

Social Readjustment Rating Scale

Life Event	*Life Crisis Units*
Being in School	
Outstanding personal achievement or failure	28
Begin or end school	26
Change in living conditions	25
Revision of personal habits	24
Change in residence	20
Change in school	20
Change in recreation	20
Change in church activities	19
Change in social activities	18
Change in sleeping activities	15
Change in number of family get togethers	15
Change in eating habits	15
Vacation	13
Christmas	12
Marriage	
Death of spouse	100
Divorce	73
Marital separation	65
Marriage	50
Marital reconciliation	45
Pregnancy	40
Gain in new family member (e.g., baby)	39
Change in number of arguments with spouse	35
Trouble with in-laws	29
Working	
Wife begins or stops work	26
Fired at work	47
Change in financial state	38
Change to different line of work	36
Change in responsibilities at work	29
Trouble with boss	23
Change in working hours or conditions	20
Personal Experiences	
Death of close family member	63
Personal injury or illness	53
Change in health of family member	44
Sex difficulties	39
Death of close friend	37
Minor violations of the law	11

How to use the rating scale: Add up the value of the life crisis units for life events you have experienced during the last two years: 0 to 150, no significant problems; 150 to 199, mild life crisis (33 percent chance of physical or emotional problems); 200 to 299, moderate life crisis (50 percent chance of physical or emotional problems); 300 or more, major life crisis (80 percent chance of physical or emotional problems).

Four of every five persons with 300 or more life crisis units during the past two years will have physical or emotional problems this year. This scale has been used successfully to predict which football players are likely to be injured in the upcoming season, which bus drivers are likely to have accidents, and which university students are likely to make use of medical or psychiatric health services.

Many people find it reassuring to know that almost all human beings are likely to experience some kind of emotional or physical reaction to change.

If you feel fine but your total number of crisis points seems unusually high, you may have inflated the total by including minor variations as changes.

another psychologist, he avoids having to use several other descriptive phrases to communicate information about the person. Of course, the richness of that person's way of showing her problems is lost.

One problem with classification is that (except for the most obvious psychotic disorders) it is difficult for clinicians to agree about a diagnosis. Technically speaking, the reliability of the classification system currently in use is low. We can usually agree on the major categories, such as whether a person is neurotic or psychotic, but finer discriminations are sometimes unreliable. If we consider the validity of the current system of classification, we must recognize that if we place a person in a certain category, a therapist may see the evidence that supports his diagnosis and ignore evidence that would refute it. Another danger is that if a person is mislabeled, that label can follow him around for years, until even he begins to believe it.

The classification label often carries with it implications for treatment, how successful the treatment is likely to be, the severity of the problem, and how the problem came about. For example, to some psychologists, the label "schizophrenia" means "because schizophrenia involves a genetically caused, biochemical problem that can be controlled but not cured, relapses will probably occur, so certain drugs should be used." Schizophrenia may mean something else to other psychologists, although there is fairly general agreement that the prognosis or chance for complete recovery is not favorable. Yet this label is often applied carelessly to eighteen-year-olds who react strongly but temporarily to the overwhelming stress of suddenly leaving home to face the heavy pressure of college and life in a crowded dormitory. Therefore, any classification system carries with it the responsibility to use it carefully and wisely.

Because of the drawbacks of classification, the modern emphasis is to understand the psychopathology of each individual and use whatever treatment will work, rather than apply a name to the disorder. However, because you will encounter the major classification system over and over again, you should be familiar with it.

The American Psychiatric Association continues to revise a system called the Diagnostic and Statistical Manual-II (DSM-II Classification System) proposed by Kraeplin over seventy years ago. This system is based on the medical and psychoanalytic models of psychopathology. It uses terms such as "symptoms," which are medical in nature, and distinguishes disorders on the basis of their severity (e.g., psychosis or neurosis). It also distinguishes between *organic* disorders (such as mental retardation, brain trauma), which are caused strictly by biological malfunctions, and *functional* disorders, in which organic causes are unclear or minimal. The system also differentiates between disorders brought on by current stress (*transient situational disturbances*) and those that reflect long-standing problems (*personality or character disorders*). A wide variety of signs and symptoms that appear together in case after case are clustered under single labels, thus simplifying classifications. Obviously, people don't always fit neatly into categories, so there is much overlapping between diagnostic categories. However, the main classifications of psychopathology the psychologist deals with are transient situational reactions, neuroses, personality and character disorders, psychophysiological (or psychosomatic) disorders, and the psychoses. In the following pages, we will discuss each one of them.

Transient Situational Reactions to Stress

Transient situational reactions often represent the normal person's attempts to cope with overwhelming stress. For example, in battle, a soldier often has difficulty eating and sleeping and displays other symptoms that indicate high levels of anxiety. Traumatic situations in civilian life, such as auto accidents or rape, often provoke high levels of anxiety that disturb a person's functioning to some degree. The anxiety usually subsides with time, with short-term supportive therapy, or even through talking with sympathetic friends.

Final examinations often cause transient situational reactions among college students. Their level of anxiety is high, they have difficulty sleeping, their irritability increases, they eat more or less food than usual, and life is difficult indeed. Usually this reaction ends once the examinations are over. But final exams are only one of the stressful situations facing college students—being far away from home for long periods for the first time; constant pressure in classes; fights with roommates, boyfriends, or girlfriends; and the seemingly endless bureaucratic red tape are only a few. It's no wonder that you or someone you know suffers so often from transient stress reactions. What distinguishes these reactions from neurotic or psychotic reactions to stress is that transient reactions are short-lived, linked to fairly specific crises, and clear up with minimal support. The psychiatric division of the student health service at the University of Colorado (total enrollment, 20,000) saw about 1,000 students with situational crisis reactions in 1973, and thousands more were seen in the center's physical health division (see box 18.2). The following case history is fairly typical:

Jim B., an 18-year-old freshman, youngest of three children, complained about his "insomnia." Upon questioning, it turned out that he hadn't slept much the previous few nights after his parents had called to tell him they had decided on a divorce. He expressed concern that he had to get his thoughts together and call them about reality matters such as money for his education. He also admitted he had many anxious thoughts about not having a family unit, his parents'

Box 18.2

Why Students Seek Psychological Services

Data collected by the Psychiatric Division of the University of Colorado Student Health Service from 1965 through 1970 show that eighty to eighty-four percent of all students treated were classified as "transient situational disorder; adjustment reaction of adolescence." Beginning in 1971, the staff attempted to define the students' problems more precisely. From 1971 to 1973, there was little change in the types of problems reported. The following data were obtained from 1,093 students during the academic year 1973:

Major reason for seeking help	%
Difficulties with making or keeping close friends	10%
Crisis in a major personal relationship (e.g., parents, boyfriend or girlfriend, roommate)	24%
Academic concerns or problems	14%
Sexual concerns	13%
Psychosomatic illnesses	7%
Problems with self-identity (identity crisis)	5%
Major symptoms reported	
Depression	25%
Worry, fear, or anxiety	24%
Insomnia	10%
Psychotic symptoms	3%

During their college years, students are faced with the following questions: How can I survive in this environment? Who am I as a person, independent of my family? Where am I going next, and am I going there alone or with someone? If a student fails to solve the developmental issues inherent in these questions, he will experience discomfort and may seek help. Note that only three percent of the students reported serious psychotic symptoms, while the vast majority experienced mild to moderate problems in living with themselves or others.

plans to sell the house he'd been raised in, whom he should spend his holidays with, and how to keep from taking sides. He was also aware of feeling "guilty" because his leaving home seemed to have deprived his parents of their only remaining common interest. But he admitted with a rueful laugh that "It must not have been much of a marriage if I needed to be there to hold it together."

Typically, during a transient situational response the individual may not *think* of the things he must do to cope with the immediate crisis; he simply *feels* anxious and distressed. However, before long he begins to *act* appropriately or seeks help.

Neurotic Reactions to Stress

In general, neurotic reactions are characterized by pervasive and exaggerated doubts, fears, or anxieties. The neurotic person expends so much energy trying to control these strong feelings that he has little strength left for the joyful aspects of living. Although he is usually aware of his misery, he cannot stop feeling or doing things that make him miserable. Yet his personality is not disorganized: he does not lose contact with reality or have hallucinations or delusions.

There are several types of neurotic reactions to stress: anxiety reactions, phobias, obsessive-compulsive reactions, hysterical reactions, hypochondrical reactions, and neurotic depressions.

Anxiety Reactions

Anxiety reactions are probably the most common of all the neuroses. The individual feels mildly and chronically anxious, with occasional moments when his anxiety becomes so intense that it verges on panic. During periods of strong anxiety feelings, any or all of the physical symptoms associated with anxiety may be present—rapid heart beat, shaking and trembling, difficulties in breathing, excessive perspiration. This disorder is often called "free floating anxiety" because often the individual is unaware of what is causing it. His usual methods of defending himself against anxiety fail him, and he is at the mercy of a stress reaction over which he feels he has no control. A chronically anxious person often reacts with extreme panic in situations that (1) seem to threaten his status in life, (2) present him with occasions in which he might express feelings such as anger or sexuality, (3) provoke guilt and fear of punishment, or (4) reactivate responses to a prior trauma in his life.

The fourth type of reaction is illustrated in the following case:

Janet D., a 22-year-old junior, said she was anxious and nervous all the time. She came for treatment primarily because she was having extreme panic attacks in her history class. Though it was her favorite class, she had begun to skip it. The only other time such extreme reactions occurred were when her boyfriend arrived at their apartment later than he said he would. She had visions of terrible things happening to him and would be in a total panic until he walked in. About two years before these incidents, her much loved father had been killed suddenly in a car accident in a foreign country where he had been an ambassador. She dated her pervasive anxiety feelings from a few years before his death when she had learned he had a heart condition. During her first panic attack she feared that the plane in which she was traveling to his funeral might crash. Her father had been a professor of history before his government appointment and had delighted in taking her to museums and telling her about the history of her own country and all the countries they visited. Any situation that reminded her of his traumatic death, the possible loss of other loved ones, or the strong feelings about her father and his interests touched off panic attacks.

Thinking does not usually help the anxious neurotic discover the causes of his anxiety, unless he has help. His anxious *feelings* can turn into extreme emotional panic, with all the physical signs of anxiety, and his *actions* indicate he cannot control this response. Anxious neurotics often find relief with mild tranquilizers. They are also good candidates for therapy and usually do well after treatment.

Phobic Reactions

The person with phobias fears specific objects, acts, or situations to an inappropriate and unreasonable degree. These fears persist despite his realization that they are irrational. Phobias can be extremely incapacitating; for example, consider for a moment how a person with claustrophobia (fear of enclosed places) must live.

Vetter (1972) described a fifty-one-year-old woman who could not stay by herself in a room, a house, a movie, or a church or drive her car alone for more than three or four miles. Her son had to hold the doors of ladies rooms ajar because she was afraid to have them closed.

Perhaps the most famous phobia of all was that of "Little Hans," the classic case of Freud discussed in Chapter 11. Hans was a five-year-old who would not go into the street for fear he would be bitten by a horse. Freud concluded that the boy was afraid his father would castrate him because of his Oedipal attachment to his mother and that this fear was displaced onto the horse. Most psychoanalysts believe that all phobias represent a displacement of anxiety onto substitute objects or events. However, earlier in his life, Little Hans had almost been run over by a horse; thus it is not difficult to understand why he would imagine that even a horse standing still could hurt him by biting.

The phobic's *thinking* is distorted in that he makes fearful mountains out of molehills. His *feeling* is often an intense anxiety that catastrophic destruction will occur, and his *actions* almost always consist of avoiding the fear-producing stimuli. Phobic neurotics are treated successfully most often by behavior modification techniques, and the outcome of treatment is usually excellent.

Obsessive-Compulsive Reactions

In an effort to defend himself against overwhelming anxiety, a person may develop obsessions and compulsions. Obsessions are recurring thoughts, words, or impulses that the individual cannot control. Compulsions are repetitious acts that the individual feels an overwhelming need to carry out; often these are magical rituals which reassure him that what he fears is not true (see box 18.3).

Childish games such as "Step on a crack and break your mother's back" are examples of the child's ritual defenses against hostility toward his parents. Many of us followed some superstitious rituals as we grew up, and thoughts of a somewhat obsessive nature are common in adulthood—for example, a melody keeps going through our mind, or we go over and over the details of what happened on an important date. In the obsessive-compulsive person, however, these rituals and thoughts are extremely persistent and seriously interfere with other aspects of his life. For instance, a young college student felt compelled to take as many as twenty-five showers a day. Performance of this compulsive act brought temporary relief and satisfaction. If he tried to restrain himself from the act, he was overcome with anxiety. Such washing compulsions often stem from feelings of guilt. This boy's guilt was about masturbation, for example. But because he could never truly cleanse himself of guilt, he had to repeat the ritual over again and again in an effort to control his guilty anxiety.

The *thinking* of the obsessive-compulsive person is rigid and intellectual. His *feelings* of anxiety are minimal as long as he can maintain his rigid defenses. In fact, all his feelings are controlled, except perhaps for righteous anger. His *actions* are repetitive, driven attempts to keep his feelings under control. The obsessive-compulsive neurotic can be treated successfully if he can consciously acknowledge the anxiety against

Box 18.3
Suicide

> *Kent W. received his MA degree in Mathematics in the early afternoon of a June day, bright with promise for so many other graduates. At 5:00 p.m. that day, he drove to a remote area 15 miles from campus. Still dressed in his graduation robes, he shot and killed himself. A psychological autopsy showed that he had been a lonely student who had admitted feeling depressed because he felt he would never find anyone who would share his future with him.*

Kent was one of about 25,000 persons in the United States who committed suicide in 1973. Someone in this country tries to kill himself about once every minute; once every twenty-four minutes the attempt is successful, making suicide the ninth leading cause of death.

Black (1971) studied student suicides in five southwestern states and found that his results agreed with those of studies done at Berkeley, Harvard, and Yale as well as with those found among nonstudent populations. Black reported that although three times as many females as males attempt suicide, three times as many males as females succeed in killing themselves. Approximately one out of every 10,000 students will commit suicide; usually he is an older student who is lonely, friendless, and isolated. Rejection by the opposite sex (57 percent) was the most common reason for suicide; other reasons included academic problems (10 percent), homosexual problems (10 percent), and conflict with parents (10 percent). Most of these students were not in any academic difficulty, and their grades were similar to those who did not commit suicide. The most common time to commit suicide was during midterm examinations; another peak occurred around final examination time. Students majoring in science and math committed suicide three times as often as those majoring in social studies and the humanities. The "typical" undergraduate student who kills himself is twenty-three years old, single, in his junior year, and majoring in science or math. He has a 2.70 grade point average, and is not involved in any extracurricular activities. He kills himself with a gun in his off-campus residence on a November day, shortly after his girl rejects him. He never sought help from a campus counselor or psychiatrist for his problems.

which he is protecting himself. He can then learn to accept his forbidden wishes as characteristic of most humans and in turn accept himself. Certain behavior modification techniques that will be discussed in the next chapter are often used to help obsessive-compulsive patients bring their anxiety under control.

Hysterical Reactions

Most of us, at one time or another, have avoided participating in an activity by saying "I don't feel very well," even when completely healthy. (The classic example is the wife who has a "sick headache" at bedtime.) But the neurotic hysteric habitually resorts to disabling physical symptoms, which are entirely psychological in origin, when faced with stress he cannot cope with. He is not faking the symptoms: they are very real, and he is unaware that he is converting his anxiety into a physical symptom. In the old days, before television's "doctor shows" made everyone so medically sophisticated and when nice girls never expressed any sexual impulses, hysterical conversion reactions were far more common than they are today.

> Judy M. was an 18-year-old freshman drama major, only child of doting parents and particularly close to her "daddy." She was seen in the emergency room after the third fainting episode she had experienced in less than a week. With gestures and voice inflections that did credit to her major, she described fainting as she approached the stage at the theater where she had a part in a play. . . . It turns out her leading man had been trying to talk her into

some extracurricular sexual activities and the swooning occurred as she first caught sight of him. "I'm very *emotional*," she reported, "and I like me fine just the way I am. Life is a picnic and a continually joyful party. It's just not too convenient to keep fainting all the time."

Freud thought that conversion symptoms were expressions of repressed sexual energy. Modern theorists believe that they are an effort to help the individual avoid a fearful situation. Mucha and Reinhardt (1970) studied fifty-six student aviators who had conversion reactions to the stress of the flight training program. Most of these students had been successful athletes before enlisting in the Navy and could not admit failure by quitting outright. Physical symptoms, on the other hand, were acceptable excuses for being unable to continue in the program because these men had had many athletic injuries before, and their parents had physical symptoms that were similar to the ones the students developed. These men were completely unaware that they wanted to get out of the program and that their physical symptoms had no organic basis. They resorted to this unconscious mechanism to relieve stress and avoid failure, which was unacceptable to them.

Another type of hysterical response to stress is the dissociative reaction. The dissociative reactions include amnesia, fugue states, and multiple personalities (see fig. 18.2). Persons with these reactions share a common pattern of avoiding stress while gratifying their needs in such a way that they can deny personal responsibility for behavior that is unacceptable. Instead of becoming physically sick, as in conversion reactions, they avoid stress by dissociating themselves from situations that cause it.

In hysterical amnesia, the person has a partial or total loss of recall for his past. Typically, he cannot remember his name, age, address, or other identifying data and does not recognize his friends and relatives. Yet, neutral knowledge such as how to read and write remains intact. In the fugue state, the individual flees the scene of stress and may recover years later in a strange place, unable to figure out why he is there or remember what happened during the fugue or flight.

Figure 18.2 A famous case of multiple personality is the fictional Dr. Jekyll and Mr. Hyde. In the story, Jekyll's change was also physical rather than (as in reality) an inner, psychic state. Shown here are both Dr. Jekyll and Mr. Hyde. (Culver Pictures.)

Multiple personality reactions are fairly rare and represent an internal flight; that is, one part of the personality dissociates completely from the other part or parts. The person then possesses two or more complete and separate personalities, each with its own emotional and thought patterns. The personality which dominates at any one time is usually unaware of the other personality's existence. Most of us recognize the different sides of our own personalities—for example, the carefree side, the worried side, the sad side, the happy side—but we also recognize that they are all parts of the same person. In the pathological dissociation, the conflict between "good" and "bad" impulses is so intense that resolution can only be achieved by separating the conflicting sides from one another. The main character in the book *Sybil* had sixteen separate personalities, all of which reacted as entirely different people. After extensive therapy, Sybil's sixteen selves were integrated into one splendidly functioning person who became a successful artist (Schreiber, 1974).

The hysteric's *thinking* is almost deliberately nonintellectual and superficial. The individual places great emphasis on *feelings* but is unaware that his feelings have a superficial quality. His *acts* resemble dramatic acting, with florid, theatrical gestures and speech. These actions represent his attempts to escape from stress through sickness or flight of some kind. Treating a hysteric is sometimes a fairly simple matter of identifying the stresses that cause his reactions and either removing them or helping him to learn better ways of coping with stress. However, if the stress is related to deep-seated inadequacies or conflicts, the individual may need longer, more comprehensive therapy.

Neurotic Depressive Reactions

Most of us get the "blues" occasionally, but neurotic depression is characterized by a significant degree of chronic depression. In addition, the individual usually feels anxious. If his anxiety is severe, he may have difficulty falling asleep. More commonly, however, he wakes too early in the morning; for example, between four and five o'clock. Often some significant loss, either of an important person or status, precedes the depression (see fig. 18.3). About five percent of depressive neurotics are estimated to commit suicide (see box 18.3).

The neurotic depressive's *thinking* often slows down, and he has many misconceptions about his self-worth. His *feelings* are those of sadness. In fact, sad affect (feeling) gives this disorder its name. Because depressed persons are often unable to *act* in ways that would alleviate their depression, they are trapped in a vicious cycle of feeling bad and doing nothing about it. Neurotic depressives are usually quite responsive to therapeutic intervention and recover their coping responses once help is offered.

Figure 18.3 Ancient people grieved over loss. Shown is an Egyptian figurine representing mourning and found in a tomb. (Photo R. Guillemot—TOP Agency.)

This completes our discussion of neurotic responses to stress. At this point we will move to the next major diagnostic classification, psychophysiological reactions.

Psychophysiological (Psychosomatic) Reactions to Stress

The dominant feature in psychophysical reactions is an observable, pathological, physical response to stress. The case of John D. was an example of psychopathology in which psychosomatic symptoms predominate. In contrast to the hysteric or the hypochondriac, the person who reacts physically to stress actually has a physical problem—for example, insomnia, obesity, tension or migraine headaches, asthma, ulcers, skin problems, or heart palpitations—which becomes more frequent and severe when he is confronted with stress. These physical problems are termed psychosomatic symptoms to indicate that there is a relationship between the mental (psychic) and physical (somatic) systems that produce them. Individuals who suffer from them frequently share the following personality traits.

1. They are unable to express their feelings directly to other people. Occasionally, an individual who cannot inhibit his angry feelings will develop a physical symptom because his body is constantly secreting stress-related chemicals. Usually, however, these feelings are suppressed; it is as if the body expresses the feelings physically rather than verbally. Angry feelings are particularly difficult for psychosomatic personalities to deal with.

2. They are perfectionists. In other words, they are highly ambitious and demand much from themselves. Although the individual with a psychosomatic personality often feels dependent and insecure, he masks these feelings with independent, striving behavior. His inability to be as perfect as he wants to be creates tremendous tension, which seems to be discharged physically rather than verbally.

These observations do not completely explain why psychosomatic symptoms occur. But we do know that the psychosomatic individual's *thinking* is pervaded by demands for perfection, and productivity is very important. His *feelings* are inhibited, or at least they are not directed at the stimuli that elicited them. His *acts* have a driven quality, and it is extremely difficult for him to relax. Therapy with a psychosomatic individual is often prolonged because attention must be focused on both the psychological and physical aspects of the problem. Behavioral therapy techniques, such as assertive training and biofeedback procedures, have been successful in many cases.

Character or Personality Disorders

Character or personality disorders fall into two broad categories, each having a number of different types of disorders. In the first group of disorders, the individual may have symptoms that are similar to the psychoses or neuroses. For example, the obsessive-compulsive personality is characterized by rigidity, extreme orderliness and an excessive concern for "the rules." The paranoid personality includes unwarranted suspiciousness and imagined threats, and is often self-centered, unfriendly, and angry. The schizoid individual is generally extremely shy and introverted with an inability to have close, warm personal relationships with others. These and other personality or character disorders in this general category are more fixed and difficult to treat than are neurotic personalities. The main difference between neurotics and individuals with personality disorders seems to be that the latter are less aware of their anxious and uncomfortable feelings than are neurotics. Frequently they seek treatment only because their behavior gets them into trouble with society or other people. In other words, rather than being motivated to seek help by an internal sense of discomfort, motivation is imposed by external sources.

The second major subtype includes persons whose behavior frequently brings them into major conflict with society and the law. These include sociopathic personalities, individuals who are dependent on drugs, and persons with sexual problems. We shall discuss each of these personality types in turn.

Sociopathic Personalities

Sociopathic individuals lack a sense of morality and are unconcerned about the trouble their behavior causes for others. When they feel an impulse, they tend to act on it immediately; they only feel sorry if and because they are caught. Some feel anxious if prevented from expressing their impulses. Sociopaths can be very charming and appealing (con men are typical of this type). They lie convincingly, promise to reform their wicked ways, and then continue acting in the same self-seeking manner. Many sociopaths on the other hand, are not at all charming and can be ruthless, hostile, and cruel. Extremely sociopathic people are frightening because of their intense hatred and willingness to cause harm to others. (Box 18.5 contains the statement of a prisoner who expressed these attitudes.)

Apparently, the presence of a sociopathic male model is an important factor in the antisocial male's development. The sociopath's *thinking* is aimed at justifying his antisocial behavior by blaming others. His *feelings* are characterized by self-satisfaction and a lack of remorse, guilt, or anxiety—except when he is prevented from doing what he wants to do. His *acts* are self-seeking, impulsive, and harmful to other members of society. Because successful therapy depends on the patient's anxiety and motivation to change, antisocial personalities are extremely difficult to treat. Because they do not view the problem as internal, it is almost impossible to stop them from acting on their impulses long enough to feel any anxiety.

Drug Dependence

Although a large percentage of college students will try *marihuana* at least once during their college career, only a small percentage will become heavily dependent on it. Some researchers have noted that heavy use of marihuana is associated with "amotivation," meaning a lack of desire to do anything constructive. This lack of motivation interferes with students' ability to do their school work and thus they often seek counseling. Their amotivation seems to disappear about two weeks after they stop using marihuana. Typically, moderate use of the drug is associated with a sense of relaxation, mild euphoria, and enhanced sensory inputs. A musician described the effect of marihuana on perception of time by saying: "Your fingers can be flying over the keys, but the music floats along in a slow, dreamy, heavenly way." Occasionally, people who are extremely anxious to begin with become even more anxious as well as suspicious while using marihuana. In general, marihuana seems to intensify whatever mood the person was in before using the drug.

Lysergic acid diethylamide (LSD) is a potent drug that produces psychotic-like symptoms in some individuals; visual hallucinations and the loss of the boundary between self and environment have been described. The effects of this drug are different from person to person and from time to time, depending on the setting and the mood and personality of the individual involved. During the early 1970s, a typical student health service on a campus of 20,000 saw one or two "bad trips" a week, and a telephone crisis service dealt with at least that

Box 18.5

A Severely Sociopathic Personality

> *I started doing time when I was eleven years old and have been doing practically nothing else since then. . . .*
>
> *I have done as I was taught to do. . . . You taught me. If you continue teaching others as you taught me, then you as well as they must pay the price, and the price is very expensive. You lose your all, even life.*
>
> *Now, you who do not know me or my wishes, you decide without consulting me in any way; you start to try to revoke the judgment of a legally constituted court and the sentence that was pronounced on me. I tell you now that the only thanks you or your kind will ever get from me for your efforts on my behalf is that I wish you all had one neck and that I had my hands on it.*
>
> *I have no desire whatever to reform myself. My only desire is to reform people who try to reform me. And I believe that the only way to reform people is to kill 'em.*
>
> *In my lifetime I have murdered 21 human beings, I have committed thousands of burglaries, robberies, larcenies, arsons and last but not least I have committed sodomy on more than 1,000 male human beings. For all of these things I am not the least bit sorry. . . . I don't believe in man, God nor Devil. I hate the whole damned human race including myself.*
>
> *If you or anyone else will take the trouble . . . to follow and examine every one of my crimes, you will find that I have consistently followed one idea. . . . I preyed upon the weak, the harmless and the unsuspecting.*
>
> *This lesson I was taught by others: might makes right.*
>
> Carl Panzram 31614

In a letter to James Long about this prisoner, Karl Menninger wrote:

> *. . . I have chosen this dark day, June 6, 1968 (Robert Kennedy having died this morning), to tell you about a man who felt that he was too evil to live.*
>
> *I saw him at the request of a federal official. He sat in the anteroom of the federal court on a cold spring day in Topeka—his arms and legs in irons and five policemen standing around him. He was bald and burly, and in the impressionistic photo gallery of my memory, the skin of his scalp was mottled. I remember how brawny he was and how fiercely he talked.*
>
> *At one point I told him that in spite of how bad, terrible, vicious, ruthless and cruel he might be he really didn't frighten me: I didn't believe he would hurt me since I had done nothing to hurt him.*
>
> *His answer was characteristic of our interview. He leaped forward as far as his chains would allow him, he shook them and startled the police officers and me, too.*
>
> *"Take these off of me for three minutes," he said, "and I'll show you. I'll kill you right before their eyes, before they can stop me. You wouldn't have time to be scared. Take them off me and see."*
>
> *Without hesitation he told me of murder after murder that he had committed. Then he went on in further diatribe about the incurable evilness of mankind, justifying complete extinction, including himself.*
>
> *I carried away a vivid image of this earnest, very intense, very profane, very ugly, but obviously thoughtful individual faced with the problem of evil in himself and in the rest of us. He was a remarkable man in his fierceness, in his restless mental activity and his great embitteredness. I have always carried him in my mind as the logical product of our prison system. (From Addis, T., and Long, J.,* Killer: A Journal of Murder, *New York: Macmillan Co., 1970, pp. 9–13).*

Note that both the sociopath and the psychiatrist blame society and the prison system for the sociopath's problems. No one mentions the fact that his father deserted the family when Carl was seven or eight and his older brothers treated him so cruelly that he was determined to run away. He committed his first burglary just before leaving home at age eleven.

many. Currently, "bad trips" are extremely rare among students, which probably reflects the alarm caused by reports of flashbacks, possible chromosome damage, and long-term adverse effects on the mind. In any case, the use of LSD has declined.

The *amphetamines* (commonly called speed) produce feelings of euphoria, alertness, restlessness, increased motor and verbal activity, and wakefulness. Although the person feels he is being more productive (i.e., learning more and concentrating better), there is little evidence that this feeling is based on fact. When amphetamines are used excessively, the user becomes trapped in a vicious cycle of taking speed for the "up" and tranquilizers or barbiturates for the "down" part of the cycle. Amphetamine psychosis, characterized by the paranoid symptoms of suspiciousness and delusions of persecution, is common among heavy users. The use of amphetamines has declined on college campuses.

The use of *cocaine,* a central nervous stimulant, is increasing among middle- and upper-class drug users. Symptoms include talkativeness, euphoria, restlessness, excitement, alertness, and a feeling of increased capacity for mental and physical work. When overdoses of cocaine are taken, stimulation of the central nervous system is followed by depression, and death can result from respiratory failure. In one acute form of cocaine intoxication described in Goodman & Gilmann (1970), the patient collapses and dies before the physician can diagnose what is wrong with him. Such patients could have an abnormal tendency to absorb the drug very rapidly. The toxic psychosis that occurs with prolonged use of cocaine cannot be distinguished from the psychosis induced by the amphetamines. Indeed, there is no definite evidence that cocaine and the amphetamines differ significantly in terms of their subjective effects.

The *barbiturates,* sedative drugs such as Seconal or "reds," are severely addicting, and withdrawal can be dangerous. People have died from barbiturate withdrawal. People have also died—without intending to commit suicide—after combining barbiturates and alcohol. The chronic barbiturate user feels dull and sleepy, almost numb, and thus escapes from his anxiety.

No drug is more powerful than *heroin* in terms of producing relief from tension, pain, and anxiety. The euphoric "rush" produced by the drug is said to be the ultimate in the momentary experience of pleasure. However, physical addiction is dangerously rapid, and the subculture in which heroin users move is psychologically addicting as well. Because the habit costs up to fifty dollars a day to maintain, the addict often turns to criminal activities to support it. Furthermore, all his thoughts, conversations, and social activities —all of his energies, in fact—are devoted to obtaining his next fix (see fig. 18.4). Withdrawal symptoms begin from four to twelve hours after the last dose, and acute flu-like pains last from two to four days. Despite this discomfort, the rate of relapse is high. When such a powerful, pleasant, immediate escape is available, life often seems unbearably dull or painful without it. The long-term consequences seldom seem important to the impulsive user.

Alcohol is the most popular and socially acceptable drug in America today. Phrases such as "drowning one's sorrows" and "alcohol is a fluid that dissolves the superego" help to explain its popularity. Although the drug is a CNS *depressant,* many people believe it is a stimulant because they feel livelier after a few drinks. What often happens is that shyness, and sometimes even sexual inhibitions, disappear. Unfortunately, motor control is affected too; as Shakespeare said, "Alcohol provokoth the desire but taketh away the ability." Most tragic of all, judgment about what one can do is impaired. This fact, coupled with the loss of motor coordination, results in constant tragedy on the world's high-

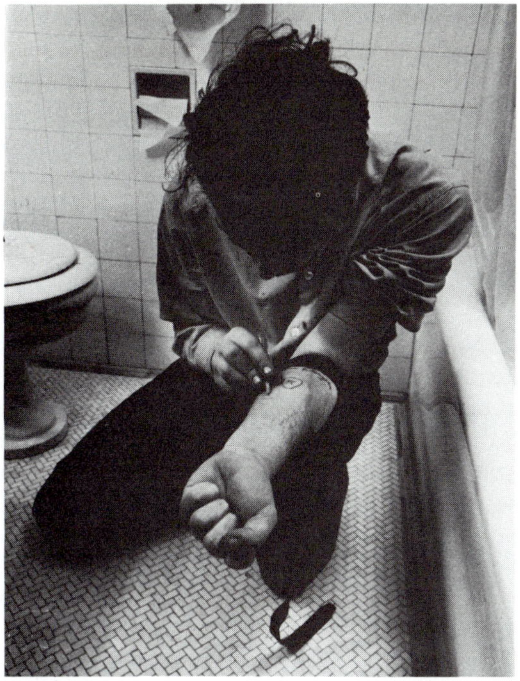

Figure 18.4 Unable to find any more functioning surface veins into which he can inject heroin, a young addict shoots the drug directly into skin tissue. (Courtesy Michael Hanulak, Magnum Photos.)

ways: Drunk drivers are the most common cause of fatal traffic accidents.

Alcohol is a poison. Excessive use over a long period of time can result in liver and brain damage and eventual psychosis. Alcoholics cannot control their drinking and their social and occupational performance suffers as a result. The following case illustrates the problems of an alcoholic student:

Sharon R., a 26-year-old graduate student in her final year of law school, began drinking as an undergraduate living in her parent's home "to drown out the sound of their fighting." She was dependent on her mother for affection and approval but said her mother was a "bitch" whom she couldn't please. Sharon had progressed to drinking steadily every day and had begun to suffer blackouts, after which she could not remember what she had said or done. When she tried to stop drinking, she got shaky and felt great anxiety that she might fail in school. During three years of law school she had never taken a final exam without being "bombed," but she had passed all her courses and nobody knew. When she came for treatment, she was drinking so heavily that she no longer went to classes. After quitting drinking, she found that when she took exams, she did not do as well as when she was drunk. She felt this was only partly related to increased anxiety, but mostly to impaired concentration and memory. Her friends at Alcoholics Anonymous told her that it takes up to a year of being dry before you can think clearly again, even if you are only a young person and haven't been drinking heavily for long. "Tell them not to start heavy drinking," she said when asked permission to use her story in a college textbook.

Many psychologists agree that alcoholics begin using alcohol to escape from anxiety caused by problems in living. They have a low tolerance for emotional and physical pain, and alcohol provides a release that can turn into a trap. Alcoholics drink to avoid pain in the present, despite their knowledge that they will feel worse in the future. Treatment can be highly effective *if* the individual is motivated to stop. Alcoholics Anonymous, an organization run by recovered alcoholics, has proved to be extremely helpful to many people who are addicted to alcohol. In recent years, behavior modification techniques have proved helpful in teaching the alcoholic how to keep his drinking within limits (Mills et al., 1971).

Sexual Problems

According to Masters and Johnson (1970), one of every two married couples is psychologically unable to enjoy a satisfying sexual relationship. A problem that is so common can hardly be called deviant. These investigators claim that problems such as premature ejaculation, impotence, and frigidity are usually caused by faulty learning or conditioning. In certain cases, unexpressed anger makes the partners unable to express their loving feelings. At times people are unaware of their own hostility and resentment, and this interferes with their ability to express warmth sexually. Therapy with sexual disorders of this type is usually highly successful. Most often, treatment focuses on improving the couple's overall marital relationship. When communication in other areas of the relationship improves, sexual communication often improves (Wyden and Wyden, 1971).

Prostitution and *rape* are defined as antisocial sexual activities because they are counter to the moral norms of our society. *The Happy Hooker* (1971) notwithstanding, prostitutes often hate themselves—many have made repeated suicide attempts. According to MacDonald (1971), most rapists are either sociopathic or extremely inadequate men who are afraid to relate to women and are often apologetic about taking what they believe they have no chance of obtaining in a normal way.

The American Psychiatric Association removed *homosexuality* from its list of personality disorders in 1974, largely because of the efforts of the Gay Liberation movement. The homosexual is now defined as abnormal only if he suffers from other symptoms or problems that would place him in a neurotic or psychotic classification.

Forms of sexual behavior that are defined as deviant include fetishism, voyeurism, and exhibitionism. The *fetishist* achieves sexual gratification through an attachment to objects such as gloves or shoes rather than to people. The *voyeur* becomes stimulated and experiences orgasm by peeping, usually at members of the opposite sex while they are nude or undressing. The *exhibitionist* attains sexual pleasure by exposing his sexual organs, usually to a person of the opposite sex. The case of a former football star's struggle with exhibitionism is discussed in box 18.6 .

With the exception of inability to perform sexually, the character and personality disorders are extremely difficult to treat. The actions associated with these disorders are usually so effective in relieving the individual's anxiety that he is not motivated to give them up. Because of the anxiety such individuals must tolerate when trying to change, their motivation often fails and the habitual anxiety-relieving actions occur again.

Psychotic Reactions to Stress

The person who reacts psychotically to stress can be described as follows: His *thinking* becomes bizarre, illogical, or distorted; he loses touch with reality; and he may experience hallucinations. In terms of *feeling,* psychosis is characterized by extreme mood swings, deep depressions, or even the absence of appropriate affect (feeling). The *acts* of the psychotic may include wandering aimlessly about, asking who, what, or where he is; talking nonsense to himself or others; or saying nothing for long periods of time. These extreme disturbances of personality and behavior frighten and repel others to the extent that the psychotic has difficulty keeping his job or friends. He becomes isolated from the social world and often feels isolated from himself—as if he were standing outside himself looking at a stranger who is behaving oddly. Psychotics often describe the terror of knowing that strange things are happening to them that they cannot control (Green, 1965). Psychotic disorders that are not organic in nature are usually chronic, although there may be periods when the individual seems symptom-free.

Toxic Psychoses

Toxic psychoses are often caused by ingestion of toxic substances such as alcohol or amphetamines over long periods of time or in toxic amounts. Some toxic psychoses can be brought about by an imbalance between chemical substances in the body.

Ten years ago, I was asked to test patients

Box 18.6
A Compulsive Act of Sexual Exhibitionism

In an unusually frank autobiography, former football star Lance Rentzel writes of the genesis of his compulsive sexual exhibitionism:

> *Many of the conflicts beneath the surface of my family life were not unusual, but certain relationships were perhaps out of balance: for example, a mother who was highly affectionate and perhaps overconcerned with me, and a father who was a powerful person but a somewhat remote figure because of his extensive travels.*
>
> *This unusual intimacy with an intensely devoted mother threatened me. I do know that I tried to resolve this ambivalence toward my mother by escaping from her, by pursuing a supermasculine image to prove to myself that I wouldn't always be a baby. In doing so, I also removed any fear of reprisal from my father; he simply had to approve of me if I excelled in all the ways that I felt were important to him. So I became a Superboy, who would presumably grow into a Superman. I did all the approved things: earned good grades in school, starred in athletics, and won the most beautiful girls.*
>
> *However, two emotionally immature patterns developed out of this. One was the need to prove my masculinity over and over. The other was an inability to establish a permanent, meaningful adult relationship with a woman. How could I allow myself to get that close to a woman? She would smother me, as I felt my mother did, and then I couldn't be a man.*
>
> *As I grew older, these conflicts resulted in a number of unconscious defenses for my emotional protection. They included a constant need for sexual conquests, a compulsion to be vigorously and continually active, and a demanding competitive drive to be a winner.*
>
> *However, at various times in my life, these defenses failed me. This happened when I could no longer repress the anxiety welling up from the conflicts within me, owing to a number of pressures building up at once, while at the same time I felt no reassurance in the Superman department, because I was losing instead of winning. I felt defeated, emasculated. At that point there would arise the necessity to resort to a very childish gesture to prove my masculinity: self-exposure. It derived from a feeling of power and excitement that had come from an accidental but sexually meaningful episode of exposure when I was around twelve years old, with a girl about the same age.*
>
> *In exposing myself as an adult, I was a halfgrown boy again, reverting in search of a gesture that would reassure me that I was, in fact, not emasculated after all. A girl the same age would symbolize that earlier incident, with all its innocence and importance; for a moment I was Superboy again, with my vital parts intact. Needless to say, there was no desire for actual contact with a female at that point. The act was more magical than sexual, a ritual to restore that all important sense of power that the defeats of life had temporarily destroyed.* (When All the Laughter Died in Sorrow, *New York: Saturday Review Press, 1972, pp. 238–239.)*

awaiting kidney transplants to reassure the surgeons that they had the psychological strength to withstand this difficult operation:

> Peggy F., a 27-year-old housewife with terminal renal (kidney) disease, received her transplant and within 12 hours the new kidney had produced over two gallons of fluid. She began to hallucinate and converse aloud with God and her dead mother. She thought the doctors were devils sent to persecute her and screamed whenever anyone in uniform came near. The surgeons thought the strain brought on by the operation had precipitated a psychological breakdown. The psychiatrist correctly diagnosed her problem as an imbalance in the sodium-potassium ratio in her body caused by rapid fluid loss. In one day of intravenous treatment with the proper chemicals, all symptoms disappeared. The psychologist was struck by the

similarity between these symptoms and those of many acutely psychotic patients. And in the following ten years, no instances of psychopathological behavior were observed in this patient.

Schizophrenia

The schizophrenic is usually a socially isolated individual whose thought, feelings, and actions indicate a loss of contact with reality. Over fifty percent of all hospital beds in the United States are occupied by schizophrenics, and more than two million Americans are or will become schizophrenic. The four major types of schizophrenia—simple, hebephrenic, catatonic, and paranoid—will be discussed next.

The *simple schizophrenic* gradually loses his ambition and interest in the external world. He becomes emotionally indifferent, and withdraws from social relationships. He no longer cares whether he works or passes in school and neglects his personal appearance and hygiene. Unless simple schizophrenics exhibit bizarre, intolerable behavior, they can live a fringe existence in society all their lives. The following case history illustrates a typical simple schizophrenic:

> The patient was hospitalized on the complaint of his sister-in-law, who stated that he had tried to force her at the point of a gun to have sexual relations with him. On admission to the hospital the patient appeared rather indifferent about the whole matter and explained that it must have been some "temporary impulse" which overcame him. Although 30 years of age, the patient had been living with his parents and was completely dependent upon them. . . . He made an A average in high school, but during his first year of college he lost interest in his studies and refused to attend classes, despite his parents' pleadings. His parents then did their best to help him achieve some vocational adjustment, but the patient seemed indifferent to their efforts and hopes for him. After leaving college he did take several part-time jobs, including one in a grocery store, which he soon lost because of his listless attitude and indifference to his duties. Thereafter he would not either look for or accept work and was quite content to remain dependent upon his parents. Although rather handsome, he had never gone out with girls. When questioned on this subject he stated that "I'm not interested in girls. All they ever do is get you in trouble." (Coleman, 1956.)

Hebephrenic schizophrenia usually occurs at an earlier age than the other types. Usually their behavior is silly and they laugh inappropriately. They hallucinate frequently, and the hallucinations are usually bizarre. The following quotation from a letter written by a hebephrenic shows the incoherent thinking that is common to these patients:

> Improper wave length-wave length changes, later visable death. That is a moving trollysis similar to circulation life action. Born high focussating action may die through wave length charge and still live until visable death takes place. (Millon, 1969.)

The *catatonic schizophrenic's* behavior usually alternates between stupor and excitement. In the excited phase, there is unceasing activity, inability to sleep, disorganization, and weird, incoherent speech. In the stuporous phase, the individual tends to remain in a fixed posture for hours or even days and does not respond or communicate for long peroids of time. It is interesting, however, that after the stupor passes, he can often recall things that were said and done to him. During both the excited and lethargic phases, the patient has hallucinations, consisting mainly of terrifying visions or apparitions with religious or mysterious meanings. The fixed postures that catatonics assume are often compulsive reactions to ward off the fearful consequences of not carrying out the orders given them by voices.

Paranoid schizophrenia can be of two types, paranoid state and paranoid schizophrenia. In the paranoid state, the individual's delusions of persecution and grandeur are well organized and do not intrude on all areas of functioning. For example,

A 46-year-old woman who ran a dress shop was absolutely convinced that the mafia was trying to take over her shop. On the rare occasions when a man in a hat and dark suit entered the shop, she became delusional and phoned the police with an incoherent story. Most of the time, no one was aware that she had any emotional problems.

In paranoid schizophrenia, the loss of contact with reality is more pervasive. The person's delusions are vague, bizarre, and unconvincing. Delusions of grandeur (thinking they are extremely important people) occur often (see fig. 18.5). Ideas of reference (that people are talking about them) are very common; so are hallucinations. The paranoid schizophrenic is emotionally involved with his delusions and may deliberately plan and carry out violent revenge against his imagined persecutors.

A 34-year-old rancher began to hear voices that accused him of having homosexual feelings for an 18-year-old ranch hand. He became convinced that the sheriff of a nearby town was monitoring his brain to read his thoughts and transmit them by radio to all the deputies. He became afraid to go into town because people looked at him so strangely they must know about the monitor. When the family doctor came to the ranch at the family's request, the patient was convinced the doctor was an FBI agent sent by the sheriff. He attacked the doctor with a table, breaking his glasses and knocking him out. The rancher was sedated and sent to the nearest psychiatric hospital 200 miles away, which he was convinced was a prison. He ran from the attendants (who were seen as guards) into a busy street. There he lept on the hoods of cars shouting, "Help, I am being unfairly jailed." On the ward, he would wander off searching for the sheriff who would then turn off the monitor. When he stopped police cars asking to be taken "to the sheriff immediately," they returned him to the hospital.

When we see great disorganization of personality and behavior, such as the schizophrenic suffers, we naturally want to know what is happening to him and why. Most researchers have noted that the schizophrenic's reaction time for all tasks is abnormally slow. Fenz and Vilnor (1970) explain this phenomenon by concluding that the schizophrenic's ability to process stimuli is impaired. In others words, because his thought-filtering process is flooded with unrelated, confusing ideas, it takes him a long time to select one thought as a response. If all thoughts are admitted for consideration, regardless of their logic, usefulness, value, or sense, the schizophrenic's slow reactions are understandable.

Explaining why this happens includes genetic factors. Kallman (1946) reported that sixty-nine percent of the identical twins whose co-twin was schizophrenic also developed schizophrenia. Among fraternal twins with a

Figure 18.5 The Madhouse, painted by Goya. Note the "King" and the "Bishop" on the right. These represent delusions of grandeur. (Courtesy Real Acadimia De Bellas Artes De San Fernando, Madrid, Spain.)

schizophrenic co-twin, only ten percent were schizophrenic. Kallman has been criticized for investigating only severe and chronic cases. Investigators who have studied the range of severity possible in this disorder find that degree of concordance is higher for severe schizophrenia than for mild schizophrenia. Although no one has found a concordance rate as high as Kallman's study, the average concordance rate from other studies is about forty percent for identical twins.

If we look at the presence of *any* disorder on the schizoid continuum—from the schizoid type of personality to actual schizophrenia—we find that almost fifty percent of the close relatives of schizophrenics (children, siblings, or parents) have either schizoid or schizophrenic disorders (Heston, 1970), as discussed in Chapter 2 (p. 51). If the person has a genetic predisposition to some disorder on the schizoid continuum, then environmental stress may well trigger the disorder. If either extreme environmental stress or the genetic factors are missing, the individual may escape these serious problems.

Some of the environmental factors that may be implicated in the development of schizophrenia in predisposed individuals are trauma and deprivation in early childhood, family disorganization, and faulty communication patterns from parent to child. For example, Bateson (1960) described a type of communication called the *double bind* in which the parent says one thing and does another. The mother may complain that the child is not loving enough but pushes the child away if he tries to express affection. Because these messages are extremely difficult for a child to interpret, he may develop a faulty sense of reality.

Whatever the cause, treatment of schizophrenia does not usually result in a "cure." During the acute phase of schizophrenic psychosis, the therapist tries to establish a relationship of some trust so that the individual will take the necessary medication and will return when relapses occur. However, when the psychotic process is in remission, supportive therapy will often help the person cope with everyday stress more adequately so that he feels better and can maintain the improved functioning.

Affective Disorders

The other major category of psychosis, psychotic affective disorders, includes conditions in which the individual's emotions, feelings, or moods are seriously disturbed. *Psychotic depression* can occur as a separate disorder, or depression can alternate with periods of extreme elation (*manic-depressive* psychosis). Approximately ten to twenty percent of severe depressives also show the manic pattern. In the depressive state, the person feels unworthy, hopeless, and apathetic. His thought processes and behavior can become extremely slow, or else he can be agitated, worried, and pace around continually, mumbling to himself about what a terrible person he is. Delusions of a hypochondrical nature are quite common; for example, the person may be convinced that he has syphyllis or that his insides are rotting away.

In contrast, the manic phase is characterized by grandiose denials of any misfortune. The manic person is more than just excited; he is under great pressure to express his ideas, which are extreme and irrational. Although people initially find the manic's enthusiasm attractive, they soon lose interest in associating with him because he is arrogant and angers easily when frustrated. The manic phase is often considered to be a defense against the patient's underlying depression. For example, box 18.7 contains an excerpt from a session between a forty-six-year-old manic woman and her therapist.

There is increasingly convincing evidence

Box 18.7

A Female Manic-Depressive Patient in the Manic Phase

Doctor. Hello, how are you today?

Patient. Fine, fine, and how are you, Doc? You're looking pretty good. I never felt better in my life. Could I go for a schnapps now? Say, you're new around here, I never saw you before—and not bad! How's about you and me stepping out tonight if I can get that sour old battleship of a nurse to give me back my dress. It's low cut and it'll wow 'em. Even in this old rag, all the doctors give me the eye. You know I'm a model. Yep, I was No. 1—used to dazzle them in New York, London and Paris. Hollywood has been angling with me for a contract.

Doctor. Is that what you did before you came here?

Patient. I was a society queen . . . entertainer of kings and presidents. I've got five grown sons and I wore out three husbands getting them . . . about ready for a couple of more now. There's no woman like me, smart, brainy, beautiful and sexy. You can see I don't believe in playing myself down. If you are good and know you're good you have to speak out, and I know what I've got.

Doctor. Why are you in this hospital?

Patient. That's just the trouble. My husbands never could understand me. I was too far above them. I need someone like me with savoir faire you know, somebody that can get around, intelligent, lots on the ball. Say, where can I get a schnapps here—always like one before dinner. Someday I'll cook you a meal. I've got special recipes like you never ate before . . . sauces, wines, desserts. Boy, it's making me hungry. Say have you got anything for me to do around here? I've been showing those slowpokes how to make up beds but I want something more in line with my talents.

Doctor. What would you like to do?

Patient. Well, I'm thinking of organizing a show, singing, dancing, jokes. I can do it all myself but I want to know what you think about it. I'll bet there's some schnapps in the kitchen, I'll look around later. You know what we need here . . . a dance at night. I could play the piano, and teach them the latest steps. Wherever I go I'm the life of the party. (Coleman, 1956)

that a genetic component is involved in the manic-depressive psychoses. Kallman (1950) found a concordance rate of ninety-six percent in identical twins and twenty-six percent in fraternal twins; but, again, his studies probably overestimated the factor of inheritance. Kringlen, who summarized all studies on the manic-depressive psychoses up to 1967, excluding Kallman's, found that the average concordance is sixty-one percent for identical twins and fourteen percent for fraternal twins. All the studies showed higher concordance rates for identical than fraternal twins, which supports a genetic hypothesis. Slater and Cowie (1971) presented evidence that when depression occurs alone, the genetic basis is different from that in the manic-depressive syndrome. Most of the evidence gathered in the 1970s is fairly convincing that the major psychoses require a genetic predisposition to biochemical abnormalities, which may be activated by certain stresses and in turn cause gross disturbances in thinking, feeling, and actions.

The environmental stresses that may precipitate psychotic disorders of affect in susceptible people include (1) death of a loved person, (2) failure in personal relationships, and (3) severe failure at important work. In other words, the loss of something valuable can precipitate affective disorders. Depressives often come from families in which the child learns to feel guilty for failing to achieve and develops a strong conscience so that he is unable to express angry or frustrated feelings. The combination of a restrictive environment and a genetic predisposition can bring about severe affective disorders.

Psychotherapy with manic-depressives has recently been successful since the discovery that the drug lithium carbonate will bring the episode under control and thus help the patient talk more rationally about the stresses in his life. For psychotic depressives, drugs or shock therapy can also be of help.

Before leaving the topic of psychopathology, let us briefly consider some of the psychopathologies found in children.

Psychopathology in Children

With the exception of childhood psychoses, the emotional disorders found in children are less deeply seated and therefore easier to treat than those found in adults. Perhaps this explains why people have found it harder to classify childhood problems. In a study of 1,220 child guidance clinics, Rosen et al. (1964) found that thirty-two percent of the children were undiagnosed and thirty percent were simply called "transient situational disorders: adjustment reaction of childhood." Dreger et al. (1964) studied seventeen clinics and found that forty percent of the children had been placed in the same category. They concluded that "after the elaborate diagnostic procedures used in most clinics are completed, the child is placed in a category which says exactly what we knew in the first place, that he has a problem." In an effort to remedy this situation, the Group for the Advancement of Psychiatry (GAP) published a manual (1966) that dealt exclusively with pathology in children. The student doing advanced work in childhood disorders will surely become familiar with this system, but we shall remain within the DSM-11 system, mentioned earlier in this chapter for our introductory look at child psychopathology.

First, we will discuss the psychotic disorders of autism and childhood schizophrenia. We will then consider more common behavioral disorders such as hyperactivity (hyperkinesis), overanxious and withdrawing reactions, runaway reaction, and unsocialized aggressive reactions.

Autism and Childhood Schizophrenia

The autistic child seems isolated and unresponsive to others from earliest infancy. Thus this disorder is often called infantile autism. Mothers state that their autistic babies are not "cuddly," do not reach out to be picked up, do not smile or laugh during the family's attempts to play, and are generally indifferent to people. Many autistic children do not talk at all, and in those who do speech is extremely limited. Bizarre movements, such as rocking or spinning, are repeated over and over. Bettleheim (1967) called these children "the empty fortress" because they lack the concept of self, or "I." Perhaps because people mean so little to these children, they are frequently preoccupied with objects (see fig. 18.6). One autistic child carried a little purse with her night and day; it contained several objects that she endlessly took out and put back. If she dropped one of these objects, she would cry and scream until someone returned it to her. During her tantrum, she would bite her hands and arms, often hard enough to draw blood, but was seemingly insensitive to pain. Such self-mutilating behavior is not uncommon, although some of these children are apathetic.

The childhood schizophrenic tends to present symptoms similar to those found in autistic children. Frequently, the only clues to a correct diagnosis are provided by the child's history. The schizophrenic child usually seems to develop normally and then begins to withdraw. Unlike the schizophrenic adult, the schizophrenic child rarely has hallucinations and delusions.

Figure 18.6 A typical position of an autistic child, seemingly unaware of the events surrounding him. (Courtesy Constantine Manos Magnum Photos.)

Most investigators believe that infantile autism is caused by some defect that renders the child unable to process incoming stimuli correctly. Some suggest that the innate defect is a basic inability to comprehend and organize sounds so there is no meaningful communication with language. Others talk about defects in forming social bonds. Because the autistic infant resists the intrusion of other people into his world, the mother feels rejected and rejects the infant in return. Although some claim that rejection by the mother is a primary cause of autism, they also recognize the difficulty any mother would have in relating warmly to an infant who fails to show any social responses.

Obviously there is still much to learn about infantile autism. All we know now is that whatever the cause and whatever the treatment, less than one-fourth of these children will achieve even a marginal adjustment in later life. Poor outcomes also appear to be the case for childhood schizophrenics.

Hyperactivity

Hyperactivity is a common problem at child guidance clinics. It occurs most frequently in boys under age eight and tends to disappear during the midteens. Parents often describe these children as "constantly on the go," restless, and unable to sit still long enough to be read to, do puzzles, or pay attention to anything. Their motor coordination is poor, and because their moods are changeable and unstable, tantrums are frequent. Often it is the school authorities who refer such children to clinics because parents can tolerate far more disruptive behavior than can a teacher, who must cope with thirty other children. A teacher describes the behavior of one student that she finally decided she needed help with.

> I found David up on the window sill pulling the shades off. He'd jump down, then jump up again despite my request that he stop. Then he ran up and down the rows of desks striking out at children in a random way. This hitting was hard enough to hurt the children, so half the class was in tears. The other half was frightened. In reading group, he would not stay on his chair and kept falling to the floor. His arms and legs constantly fidgeted, and he couldn't pay attention to the lesson long enough to learn to read.

Some investigators believe that hyperactivity is a sign of damage to the central nervous system so slight that it is sometimes called "minimal brain dysfunction." However, hyperactivity can occur in anxious or schizophrenic children too. But in any case, a thorough neurological and psychological workup is needed for a correct diagnosis.

Paradoxically, in about half to two-thirds of such cases, the administration of a *stimulant* drug (amphetamines) *calms* these children remarkably. As a result, they are better able to sit quietly and concentrate long enough to use their basic intelligence more effectively (NIMH, 1971). Often, therapy is indicated to help the child gain control of himself and improve his self-concept. Parents, teachers, and even classmates can learn to respond in ways that will help the hyperactive child.

Overanxious or Withdrawn Child

Overanxious and withdrawn children share the following patterns: shyness and timidity, nightmares, feelings of inadequacy, unusual sensitivity, and unrealistic fears. However, the overanxious child copes with his fears by clinging to others for support, while the withdrawn child tries to minimize his anxiety by turning inward and becomes the classroom daydreamer.

The following case of a "school phobic" boy is typical of overanxious children:

> Johnny was a highly sensitive six-year-old boy who suffered from myriad fears, nightmares, and chronic anxiety. He was terrified of being separated from his mother, even for a brief period. When the mother tried to enroll him in kindergarten, he became so upset when she left the room that the principal arranged for her to remain in the classroom. But after two weeks this had to be discontinued and Johnny had to be withdrawn from kindergarten, since his mother could not leave him even for a few minutes.
>
> Later when his mother attempted to enroll him in the first grade, Johnny manifested the same intense anxiety and unwillingness to be separated from her. At the suggestion of the school counselor, the mother brought Johnny to a community clinic for assistance with the problem. The therapist who initially saw Johnny and his mother was wearing a white clinic jacket, and this led to a severe panic reaction on Johnny's part. His mother had to hold him to keep him from running away, and he did not settle down until the therapist removed his jacket. Johnny's mother explained that "He is terrified of doctors, and it is almost impossible to get him to a physician even when he is sick." (Coleman, 1972)

These reactions are thought to be the result of a combination of a nervous system that responds to stress with high levels of anxiety and a home life that does not allow the child to develop mastery over his anxiety. For example, parents can be overprotective and communicate a lack of confidence in their child's ability to cope. Treatment for these problems is usually successful. Teachers are increasingly aware of ways to help these children. Behavior modification techniques involving both the child and his family currently show promise of success (Patterson, 1972).

Runaways

In 1970 an estimated 600,000 children ran away from home. This often represents an early to middle adolescent's attempt to escape from a home life they consider intolerable. Sometimes running away is a cry for help. If, for example, the parents' marriage is unstable and neither parent will go for counseling, the child hopes his act will force the parents to do something. If the child feels he cannot live up to his parents' expectations for social or academic success, he may give up by leaving home. Whatever the reason a child runs away, family therapy is usually the best treatment. In some cases, foster care may be necessary if the parents have abused the child or are uncooperative.

Unsocialized, Aggressive Children

Overly aggressive youngsters (usually boys) are sometimes called predelinquents when five to twelve years old and delinquents as teenagers. As adults, they are called sociopaths. Lying, stealing, overt sexual and aggressive acts, disobedience, vengefulness, and destructiveness are common symptoms. Frequently, and not surprisingly, these children have been subjected to severe beatings (see box 18.8). In studies of such boys in Philadelphia and Denver, eighty percent had been

Box 18.8

The Battered Child

Jody was four years old when this picture was taken upon her admission to the hospital. She weighed only seventeen pounds and was covered with bruises and open sores. X-rays revealed a fracture of the skull and arm and two fractures of her hands. She had been treated cruelly by her mother since her birth, and represents a classic case of the child abuse syndrome. (Helfer and Kempe, 1974, p. XV–XVI, Introduction.)

Sixty thousand cases of child abuse are reported in the United States each year. Half of these children are less than a year old and between 3,000 and 4,000 of them die of their injuries. In almost all cases, a parent inflicted the abuse.

What makes a parent inflict serious injuries on a helpless child? Three conditions are necessary for a parent to be a child abuser:

1. *The parent must have the potential.* Child abusers come from all levels of society and represent all levels of intelligence. They are lonely, isolated people who often were abused by their own parents. Whether they are male or female, child abusers have a limited capacity to mother; that is, they are unable to show tenderness, gentleness, or empathy; to view a baby as a person rather than a thing; and to value the child's needs more than their own. To be good at mothering, a person must have been mothered well himself. Abused and criticized by his own parents, the child abuser expects his baby to provide the love and comfort he never had. This reversal of roles (i.e., when the child is expected to mother the parent) places the baby at great risk.

2. *The child must fail to provide what the parent expects.* Some babies do not cry much, sleep most of the time, and are considered to be loving in every way by their parents. Thus even though their parents are potential child abusers, these babies may escape. But a child who is difficult in some way is in great danger if he lives with a potentially abusive parent.

3. *A crisis must trigger the abuse.* The crisis may consist of a broken washing machine or a spouse who walks out in anger. Either situation may make the vulnerable parent feel rejected. If the baby then begins to cry, the parent's feeling of rejection may deepen because the baby's cry is viewed as a sign that the parent has failed to satisfy it. For these emotionally needy parents, a crying baby can either be the final crisis in a series of small crises or be the only crisis. In any case, almost all infant abuse occurs while the baby is crying.

Child abuse is a serious problem that must be recognized, not only to protect children who are too small to protect themselves, but because recent evidence indicates that abused children tend to become violent adults. For example, convicted assassins Sirhan Sirhan and James Earl Ray were battered children (Steele, 1973). In other words, violence breeds violence from one generation to the next.

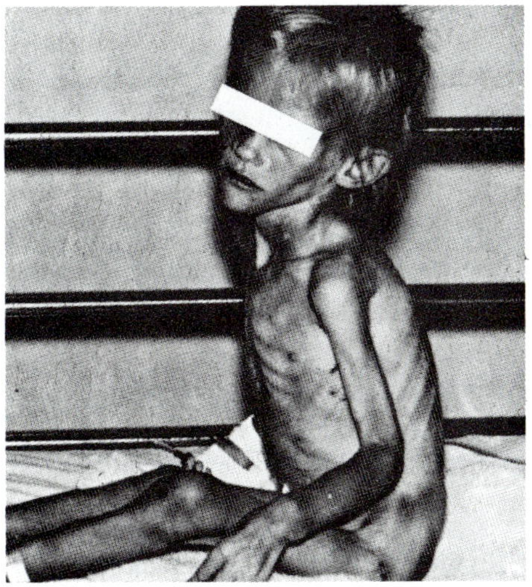

Box Figure 18.8 Jody. (Reprinted from *The Battered Child* by Ray E. Helfer and C. Henry Kempe by permission of University of Chicago Press.)

beaten severely; forty percent had been knocked unconscious at least once (Hopkins, 1970). Parents who abuse their children provide little consistent affection or guidance, and such disturbed family patterns often result in a child who is inadequately socialized and acts out his frustrations in antisocial ways.

Because the family situation must be modified, aggressive children are difficult to treat. But if the child is identified early and if the family cooperates, behavior modification techniques are successful in creating a happier environment for the child as well as his parents (Patterson, 1969). In the past, many aggressive children were removed from their homes, which made them feel even more rejected.

It is obvious from this brief discussion of childhood disorders that the seeds of adult pathology can be recognized early. And in the young child, these disorders are less fixed and often more amenable to modification. Thus the prevention of serious psychopathology in adulthood can best be accomplished by helping children overcome their problems in living and growing.

Summary

Psychopathology is defined as the inability to behave in socially adaptive ways. Disturbances in how a person thinks, feels, and acts are present.

For centuries, psychopathology was thought to be the result of possession by demons. In the nineteenth century, however, these ideas gave way to the medical model which viewed psychopathology as due to a disease process wherein the symptoms, causes, and cures are biologically based. In the twentieth century, a number of other models have been developed to explain psychopathology. Societal models, for example, attribute psychopathology to society because it does not meet the personal needs of its members. Psychoanalytic models assume that psychopathology is caused by conflict between conscious and unconscious wish to express an impulse and the need to defend against expressing that impulse. Behavioristic models explain psychopathology in terms of faulty learning. Existential models blame psychopathology on man, the choice-maker, who makes inappropriate, maladaptive choices.

Change and stress are ever-present facts of life, and both can cause anxiety, which is unpleasant to experience. Unfortunately, people sometimes cope with their anxiety in maladaptive ways. Neurotic coping patterns represent one pathologic means of dealing with anxiety. For instance, in the anxiety reaction, anxiety floods the person and cannot be controlled. In the phobic reaction, the individual has irrational fears of specific objects or situations and responds with acute anxiety when confronted with them. The obsessive-compulsive reaction is an attempt to close off feelings of anxiety by compulsive actions or obsessive thoughts. The individual with hysterical reactions uses physical symptoms, flight, or amnesia to escape from his anxiety. In neurotic depression, if the individual experiences a loss that is severe enough to disrupt his usual style of coping, he becomes extremely sad and is unable to do anything to help himself cope again.

Psychophysiologic reactions (or psychosomatic) in contrast to neurotic patterns, are actual physical illnesses, which occur more frequently and severely when the person is confronted with stress.

Personality disorders include constellations of character traits that are more fixed than in the neuroses and less disorganized than in the psychoses. Furthermore, the individuals with personality disorders are less aware of their anxiety than neurotics are. Included among these disorders are alcoholism, drug dependence, and sexual deviations—personality styles that often bring the individual into conflict with society's laws.

Psychosis refers to thoughts, feelings, and behavior that indicate a loss of contact with reality; hallucinations and delusions are often present. Psychoses can be organic, toxic, or functional (i.e., psychological) in origin. Genetic predisposition plays an important role in the genesis of psychologically based psychoses. Schizophrenia, the major psychotic reaction, can exist in four forms: simple, hebephrenic, catatonic, and paranoid. Depression is called psychotic when the individual's thoughts and behavior indicate that his contact with reality is affected. Manic-depressive mood swings are cyclic alterations between extreme depression and euphoria.

Prototypes of adult psychopathology are often seen in children. Childhood autism and schizophrenia are particularly baffling problems because their genesis or cure is not well understood. Hyperactivity is a fairly common problem reported by teachers, because the child's overactive behavior causes classroom control problems. Overanxious and withdrawn children cope with their anxieties in a preneurotic way. Runaway children are usually trying to escape from an anxiety-producing home situation or to give a cry for help to parents or authorities. Unsocialized, aggressive children can become delinquents or criminals in later life if not treated early.

All of us should view psychopathology as an understandable, predictable result of the stress that is present in all aspects of modern living. Seeking help to learn better ways of coping with stress is not only a sign of personal strength but an important indication that we are willing to take personal responsibility for solving our problems.

19

Psychotherapy

Although psychopathological symptoms are extremely varied, one feature they generally have in common is the distress, pain, and unhappiness they cause those who bear them. People with neurotic disorders, for example, may suffer from intolerable levels of anxiety or repeated disappointments in their personal or professional lives. Severe depressive states may be characterized by sleeplessness, crippling apathy, and, in some instances, frightening suicidal thoughts. An individual who is becoming psychotic may be terrorized by hallucinations or destructive fantasies.

In some cases, these feelings pass with little effort or intervention. For example, circumstances in a person's life may change, lowering the level of stress and associated discomfort, or an individual may make a conscious effort to improve his situations. In many cases, however, no effort at self-improvement seems to bring about desired changes. When people become "stuck" in this way, they often seek professional help in the form of psychotherapy. Psychotherapy is the general term for a relationship in which one individual (the patient or client) seeks help from another (the therapist), who provides treatment that is based primarily on psychological principles.

Until recently therapy was a somewhat stigmatizing experience. Seeing a "shrink" was often regarded as a sign of weakness or "craziness." It is now widely recognized that millions of people have received therapy. Surprisingly, however, most people who enter therapy do *not* suffer from phobias, character disorders, psychotic symptoms, or other classical conditions. They suffer instead from problems in the way they feel about themselves and conduct their lives—difficulties that trouble most of us at one time or another. Some of the reasons people enter therapy are discussed in box 19.1.

Box 19.1
Why Seek Help?

After learning about the categories of psychopathology and the classical symptoms in Chapter 18, you may be surprised by the complaints that people actually bring to therapy. You might expect the common complaints to be phobias, problems of sexual functioning, hallucinations, and the like.

In actual practice, however, peoples' problems do not fall into such neat categories. One study (Strupp, Fox and Lessler, 1969) revealed what is probably a typical distribution of problems. The frequencies with which problems were reported are summarized in box figure 19.1. Phobias, delusions, and obsessive-compulsive symptoms were relatively rare. The most common complaint was "Loss of Interest/Feel Overwhelmed": In other words, these clients felt that their lives were too stressful and too complicated to deal with effectively. Other common problems included physical symptoms, generalized anxiety, interpersonal difficulties, depression and suicidal thoughts, and negative feelings about oneself.

Therapists report that many of their patients complain of problems such as lack of purpose, vague anxieties, and personal alienation—in many instances, problems of personal identity that some therapists attribute to a society which increasingly makes individuals feel harried and anonymous.

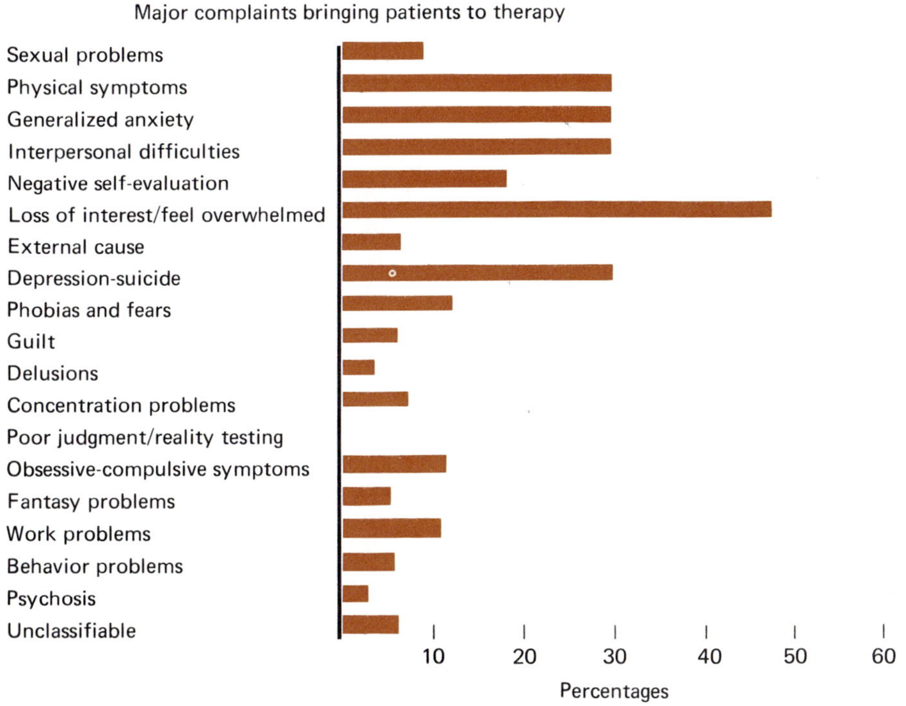

Box Figure 19.1 Problems reported by people seeking outpatient psychotherapy. (From Strupp, Fox and Lessler, *Patients View Their Psychotherapy*, Copyright 1969 Johns Hopkins University Press, Baltimore. Reprinted by permission.)

Who Does Psychotherapy?

A psychotherapist is usually trained in a profession such as the following:

Clinical Psychology A clinical psychologist generally has a Ph.D. degree in psychology, with specialized training in personality theory, psychopathology, and psychotherapy and a year's internship in a mental health setting. Doctoral programs in clinical psychology ordinarily require four to six years of training beyond the bachelor's degree.

Psychiatry A psychiatrist is an M.D. with specialized training—generally a three-year psychiatric residency—in addition to medical school and internship. Psychiatrists, unlike clinical psychologists, are licensed to prescribe drugs in conjunction with psychotherapy.

Psychoanalysis Although a psychoanalyst is usually a psychiatrist, he can also be a clinical psychologist or other mental health professional who has specialized in psychoanalytic treatment. Psychoanalytic training typically takes place in special institutes. The candidate becomes involved in seminars on psychoanalytic theory, undergoes psychoanalysis himself, and conducts a supervised "training analysis" (i.e., he treats someone else while undergoing his own analysis).

Counseling A counselor has typically an M.A. or Ph.D. from a guidance and counseling or counseling psychology program. Counselor training, which ordinarily takes place in graduate schools of education, emphasizes vocational and career counseling as well as therapy training.

Psychiatric Social Work A psychiatric social worker usually has an M.A. or M.S.W. degree from a graduate school of social work.

School Psychology A school psychologist usually has an M.A., Ph.D., or Ed.D. from a graduate school of education. This work usually involves training in diagnosis of children's problems, teacher consultation, remedial programs, etc.

Psychiatric Nursing A psychiatric nurse has specialized in mental health training in addition to his or her nursing degree.

Mental Health Work The mental health worker needs specific training in working with psychiatric populations. The job may require two to four years of college-level training but is sometimes open to people who lack college degrees. Such workers are sometimes called paraprofessionals and are discussed at greater length in Chapter 21.

Many people with psychological problems find help not from professionals, but from what Schofield (1964) calls invisible therapists: friends, relatives, bartenders, ministers, family physicians, and so forth. Often all a troubled person needs is an attentive, sympathetic listener, and many nonprofessionals are excellent at this. When a problem is severe or chronic, however, professional help is probably indicated.

What Happens in Psychotherapy?

Typically, someone with psychological problems either goes to a mental health clinic or counseling center where he will be assigned a therapist, or he seeks out a therapist on a private basis, often on a referral from another professional or a friend. Appointments generally last forty-five to sixty minutes, although group therapy sessions are usually longer. Psychoanalytic treatment may require three to five sessions per week, but most psychotherapy takes place once or twice a week. There is no typical length of therapy: it may last only a few sessions or go on for years. The length of time required for therapy is not necessarily an index of the severity of disturbance but rather of the treatment goals shared by the client and therapist. Psychoanalysis, for example, generally takes years, because its goal is thorough personality change.

A therapist in private practice generally charges fees that range from $15 to $40 per session; $20 to $30 is typical. There are less expensive ways to obtain treatment, however. Campus counseling services are generally free to students, and some industrial companies are now offering free or low-cost treatment to their employees. Community mental health centers, hospital outpatient clinics, family service agencies, and the like often tailor their fees to an individual's ability to pay. Thus fees may be only a few dollars or nothing at all.

Client and therapist usually sit facing one another, and the client is urged to discuss the problems for which he seeks help. The therapist's response can vary considerably, as you will see in the section on therapeutic approaches. Most therapists are eclectic; that is, they use a variety of approaches and techniques. On the one hand, the therapist may talk a great deal and share much of himself. On the other hand, he may talk very little. He may encourage the client to think about his problems carefully and rationally or to scream and yell with as much feeling as possible. Generally, a therapist tries to understand what is troubling his client and share his understanding with the client. He also encourages his clients to express what they are feeling and become aware of previously hidden thoughts and emotions. By and large, therapists do not give advice; they would rather help clients come to their own conclusions and implement them in their own way.

How Effective Is Psychotherapy?

Almost a century after the beginnings of psychotherapy, the question of how effective it is is still unanswered. Prior to the 1950s, it was generally assumed that personal reports or ratings by clients and therapists confirmed the procedure's usefulness. In the past twenty years, however, there has been some skepticism about this conclusion. H. J. Eysenck did much to open the discussion about psychotherapy's effectiveness. (See box 19.2.)

Although determining whether therapy has helped someone would seem to be a simple matter, in actual fact is it a difficult and puzzling problem to assess. Reports by clients, for example, may be biased. In many cases, the client is the most accurate judge of the degree to which his life has been changed for the better, but there are also potential sources of distortion in such reports. For instance, after spending years in treatment and a considerable sum of money, it may be difficult to admit to oneself that it was all wasted. A bad mood, or the sudden discovery of the existence of some previously concealed, distressing problem, may make one bias his report in a negative direction. Therapists' reports may be subject to similar biases. A therapist, for example, may find it difficult to admit a case was a failure because that would imply that he is a failure as a professional.

Researchers have also gathered data from objective and projective tests, ratings of in-therapy behavior, and ratings by intimates of clients. None of these procedures is generally recognized as providing "the truth" about the outcome of therapy, and researchers who try combinations of assessment procedures often find poor agreement among different ways of judging a client's gains.

Despite these difficulties, a general picture of psychotherapy effectiveness can be formed, and that picture is a favorable one. In reviewing one hundred carefully controlled studies of outcomes published before 1970, Meltzoff and Kornreich (1970) concluded that eighty percent of the cases demonstrated that therapy was superior to no therapy and that the best-designed studies offered even stronger evidence for therapy's effectiveness. Typically, clients who are relatively intact with good motivation for treatment can expect gains in self-esteem, contentment, interpersonal relationships, feelings of competence and pleasure in life, and the like.

Box 19.2

Does Psychotherapy Work?

Eysenck's paper, "The Effects of Psychotherapy" (1952), has been widely cited by researchers who are skeptical of therapy's usefulness, and it has made therapists sensitive to the need for empirical demonstrations that their procedures are effective.

Eysenck's finding was that about two-thirds of neurotic patients improve, *whether or not* they receive therapy—in fact, the evidence hinted at an "inverse correlation between recovery and psychotherapy"—that is, the more therapy a person received, the less likely he would improve.

Basically, Eysenck contended that the rate of "spontaneous remission" among neurotic patients did not increase when psychotherapy was introduced. Approximately seventy percent of the neurotic patients admitted to state hospitals in New York, for example, were discharged as "recovered" or "improved"; for the U.S. as a whole, the rate was approximately sixty-eight percent. Data from cases of "neurotic disability," as reported in life insurance company files, showed that seventy-two percent of the patients treated by general practitioners recovered. All these patients received were things like medicine, reassurance, and helpful suggestions—no psychotherapy as such.

The criterion for effective psychotherapy, Eysenck argued, is that it must improve on these base rates. He then reviewed nineteen studies concerning the effectiveness of psychotherapy and concluded that only sixty-two percent of the neurotics treated by "eclectic" psychotherapy improved substantially. Even more discouraging, the figure dropped to forty-four percent for patients treated by psychoanalysis.

Certainly, this is a pessimistic picture of psychotherapy. However, Eysenck's paper has been criticized extensively for various methodological shortcomings. Rosenzweig (1954), for example, points out

(1) The definition of "neurosis" to include cases of disability, which often seem to be related to malingering rather than to real neurotic conflict, would not be universally acceptable to practicing therapists,

(2) Eysenck used questionable procedures for determining the degree to which patients were helped and averaged the findings of disparate studies, much like adding apples and oranges,

(3) In all likelihood, the criteria of success for, say, the psychoanalytic patients were more stringent (e.g., successful interpersonal functioning in a variety of areas, or stable, satisfactory self-concept) than those of the disability cases, where "return to work" was often the only major criterion for evaluating gains.

(4) Finally, it is difficult to say whether the base rates Eysenck reported were really "base rates" at all. Hospital treatment presumably includes some psychotherapeutic elements, and treatment by family physicians with medicine, suggestions, and reassurance is similar to psychotherapy, especially for patients who have great confidence in their physicians. Under these circumstances, the statement that there was no treatment in these cases was questionable. Therefore, Eysenck did not demonstrate unequivocally that therapy was ineffective.

Early Therapeutic Approaches

Treatment of psychological abnormality has probably been in existence as long as abnormality itself, and methods of treatment have usually reflected people's understanding of the origin of the difficulties.

Thousands of years ago, people believed that psychopathological behaviors were caused by a devil or devils, which had taken up residence in someone's head. The task of the earliest "psychotherapists," then, was to drive or coax out the evil spirit. Medicines and incantations were probably used to accomplish that end, and there is even archaeological evidence that primitive brain surgery was performed to release the demons.

During the Dark Ages, the devil theory of psychological abnormality continued to prevail, but with a different twist. It was widely believed that bizarre behavior was a sign that a person had somehow entered into a covenant with the devil. Thus instead of being an innocent victim of invading spirits, the sufferer was considered a sinner or moral deviant. Treatment procedures were then directed primarily at purging the evil and only secondarily at helping the troubled person. Thus, psychologically disordered people were often tortured until they confessed their pact and renounced it. The end result was that many died during or after the "treatment."

The devil theory of psychopathology is widely discredited now, and medical and psychological approaches to the understanding and treatment of psychopathology predominate. However, there is still a religious or spiritual component to much psychological treatment, and many clergymen are skilled therapists.

Medical Approaches

As we saw in Chapter 18, the devil theories of abnormal behavior first gave way to medical explanations based on diseases or disorders of the brain and central nervous system. That change in conceptualization brought treatment approaches based on medical knowledge.

Prior to this development, people with severe psychological disorders had often been jailed, chained to the walls, or otherwise neglected. Within the last hundred years, however, the "snake pit" has, for the most part, given way to more humane hospitalization procedures. One major change has been the effort to create hospital settings that are themselves therapeutic. This approach is known as the "milieu therapy" (Cumming and Cumming, 1962) or "therapeutic community" (Jones, 1953) in which the mental hospital environment is consciously designed to provide important personal and social influences for its patients. A typical milieu therapy program in a mental hospital may include frequent group therapy meetings with patients and staff, occupational therapy, recreational therapy (arts, music, crafts), and so forth. By functioning responsibly, patients can earn progressive privileges (e.g., freedom of the grounds and home visits). One problem with this approach, however, is that a hospital, like all other institutions, may be so comfortable and secure an environment for some people that they find it increasingly difficult to leave and face the less predictable world outside. Such people are said to be "institutionalized"; they sometimes live out their lives in the back wards of mental hospitals.

Another implication of medical theories of psychopathology has been that surgery and drug therapy have been increasingly used. These procedures are generally called somatic or organic approaches. Although they are not psychotherapy in the usual sense, they are sometimes substituted for or used in conjunction with psychotherapy.

One organic technique is psychosurgery, or brain surgery to alleviate psychological problems. Forty years ago, the most common form of psychosurgery was lobotomy, which involves severing neural connections between the frontal regions of the cerebral cortex and other portions of the brain (see Chapter 3). Lobotomies were frequently performed on patients who were unusually anxious, confused, or violent. In many cases, patients benefited from this procedure; in some cases, however, lobotomies were performed relatively indiscriminately, which led to a public outcry and a subsequent reduction in the frequency with which the operations were performed. Recently, there has been a controversial resurgence of interest in more sophisticated techniques of psychosurgery, particularly cryosurgical and electrosurgical procedures, which make more limited and precise lesions. There is considerable controversy among scientists, physicians, and others concerning the efficacy and legality of these procedures. Opponents point to the possible secondary costs, such as irreversible personality changes that sometimes accompany such operations. Others are concerned that psychosurgery has frightening implications for control of behavior.

Another medical procedure used extensively with hospitalized mental hospital patients—and many nonhospitalized patients as well—has been electroconvulsive therapy (ECT) or electroshock therapy (EST). In the early 1930s, Sakel (1938) observed that psychiatric patients who were also diabetic sometimes improved markedly after an insulin coma. He and other investigators tried inducing such comas in nondiabetic patients and discovered that many of these patients also improved. Insulin shock therapy proved to be less than ideal. It was difficult to gauge effective but safe doses of insulin, and the comas were associated with violent convulsions that could result in broken bones.

Beginning in the late 1930s, electrical techniques were used to bring about the same convulsive effects. In ECT, a low-voltage, low-amperage current is passed through the patient's brain, resulting in a shorter, more controllable, and less violent seizure. ECT has proven to be effective with some patients, particularly those who are chronically depressed or severely confused. A recent vice-presidential candidate, for example, underwent ECT treatment with apparent success.

The greatest influence of medical procedures in psychopathology has probably been in the area of *chemotherapy* or *drug therapy*. Prior to the 1950s, mental patients were often given sedative drugs such as chloral hydrate to calm them. These drugs, however, often made patients drowsy and therefore less able to participate in individual or milieu therapy programs.

In the early 1950s reserpine, a derivative of the East Indian snake root, became the first of what are known as the "major tranquilizers." These drugs reduce anxiety and psychotic symptoms without significant drowsiness. More recently the phenothiazines, known by trade names such as Thorazine, Compazine, and Stelazine, and the butyrophenones, such as Haloperidol, have been used extensively as antipsychotic drugs. These drugs have revolutionized mental hospital treatment by shortening the length of institutional care and helping the patient maintain his gains once he is released.

Therapeutic drugs have also been widely used outside of mental hospitals. Less powerful tranquilizers, marketed under names such as Librium and Valium, have become useful adjuncts to psychotherapy or standard medical care. A heroin substitute known as methadone has proved useful in helping addicts break the cycle of crime associated with heroin use and, in some cases, eventually breaking the drug dependence altogether. Antidepressant drugs such as Elavil and Tofranil have been effective in alleviating deep depressions. Recently, Lithium carbonate has proved successful in the treatment of manic-depressive patients. The drug appears to calm manic patients and reduce the violent emotional swings common to this disorder.

These and other psychiatric drugs not only alleviate considerable suffering, they also enhance other therapeutic procedures. However, many mental health professionals are as skeptical of chemotherapy as they are of psychosurgery, arguing that the drugs have potentially harmful side effects or may serve as a temporary crutch which discourages patients from closely examining the basic stresses in their lives. Furthermore in some cases, these pharmacological techniques have been used to control the patients' behavior without consideration for their ultimate therapeutic value.

Psychological Approaches

As you saw in Chapter 18, there is considerable controversy in psychology about the causes of abnormal behavior. Thus it is not

surprising that the same controversy is mirrored in discussions about which therapeutic procedures are most effective. Each approach discussed in this section is derived from a different psychological principle or principles to explain psychopathological conditions and the ways in which they can be altered.

Psychoanalysis

Psychotherapy, as a practice distinct from medicine, probably began with a group of physicians known as the French hypnotists. In the late nineteenth century, French physicians began experimenting with the age-old phenomenon known as "Mesmerism" or *hypnotism* (see Chapter 10) and discovered that they could create hysterical conversion symptoms, such as paralysis or insensitivity to pain, through posthypnotic suggestion. They also discovered that the process could be reversed. When patients with real hysterical symptoms were hypnotized and were told their symptoms would disappear, the physicians found that sudden and dramatic changes occurred. Unfortunately, the cures were short-lived in most cases; the symptoms usually reappeared within a matter of days.

Freud had studied in France with Charcot and had seen these dramatic but ephermeral gains. He returned to Vienna puzzled by this, but determined to work with hysterical patients until he understood their problems better. At this time, he began his association with Joseph Breuer, a Viennese physician who worked with hysterical patients. One patient in particular, a young woman known as Anna O., caught Freud's interest.

Anna O. was being treated for a puzzling variety of conversion symptoms, including paralyses, visual problems, and anorexia (a severe reduction in eating). Breuer was using hypnosis with an interesting variation in his treatment of Anna. He would hypnotize her and suggest that she try to recall the time when a particular symptom had first appeared. He would then encourage her to talk in detail about the events surrounding the onset of the problem. When Anna had done so, usually with a great outpouring of emotion, Breuer would awaken her, usually to find the symptom had been relieved or removed altogether. Anna called these sessions "chimney sweeping."

It was experiences with patients like Anna that not only broadened Freud's idea of what must be done to effect lasting change in people, but eventually resulted in the deeper and longer treatment known as *psychoanalysis*. Like Breuer, Freud encouraged his patients to relive the traumatic circumstances under which the symptoms first appeared. At first, he relied on hypnosis, but gradually abandoned it when he discovered that the same ends could be achieved if the patient simply talked about these events. He eventually adopted the technique called *free association*, a basic principle of psychoanalysis. Recall from Chapter 17 that in free association, the patient is instructed to say everything that comes to his mind, no matter how unpleasant or shameful, without censoring anything.

Over the years, Freud's experiences with patients led him to different theories of psychopathology, and with them, different treatment approaches. By the early 1900s, he had abandoned the "trauma" theory of neurosis in favor of the "conflict" theory discussed in Chapters 17 and 18. The emphasis of psychoanalysis shifted from the reliving of critical traumatic incidents to a broader exploration of many facets of the patient's personality, in the hope that gains would be more firmly established.

Take, for example, the case of a patient who came to analysis with a conversion symptom such as a paralyzed arm. In his early practice, Freud would have worked on eliciting the painful feelings associated with the appearance of the paralysis. Later, however, he would have listened to the patient's free associations to understand such things as deep-seated hostilities and socialization experiences involving the control of aggression—all the feelings and prohibitions against feelings that might cause conflict in a person and subsequently result in neurotic symptoms.

"Classical" psychoanalytic therapy was lengthy. Patients (analysands) were often seen an hour a day, six days per week for years. They lay on a couch, with the analyst behind and out of their sight, and tried as best they could to free associate. (See fig. 19.1 of Freud's sitting room.) The analyst remained a shadowy figure, saying little. His basic task was thought to be the analysis of the patient's *resistances*—defenses against seeing things about himself that could be discerned by the analyst when free association became blocked or when slips of the tongue occurred.

Since Freud believed that neurotic symptoms resulted from repression of sexual and aggressive feelings, the task of psychoanalysis was to "make the unconscious conscious"; that is, to allow the client to gain *insight*. First, he would make his patients aware of their prohibitions or resistances and then the feelings which were being defended against. He went about this in several ways. One was the analysis of dreams, which psychoanalysts believe symbolize neurotic conflicts (see Chapter 10, box 10.3). He also offered his own ideas or impressions, a process called *interpretation*.

The major technique for facilitating insight, however, was the analysis of the patient's *transference*. Transference is often misunderstood. Some people believe that it means the patient sees the analyst as his father or mother; others believe it involves falling in love with the analyst. In actual fact, transference means seeing others partly as they are, but also partly on the basis of our own needs, feelings, and conflicts. These feelings may come from experiences with our parents, but they need not. Any human relationship may elicit them, especially if it has been unsatisfying in some way. It may leave as its transference residue a need to "re-create" that relationship in ones that follow in an unconscious effort to right the previous wrongs.

Psychotherapy seems to heighten transference feelings. If a patient has a "father transference" the analyst may be seen as cruel and depriving; or as someone important and perfect. In both instances, transference is important because it is an exaggeration of the dis-

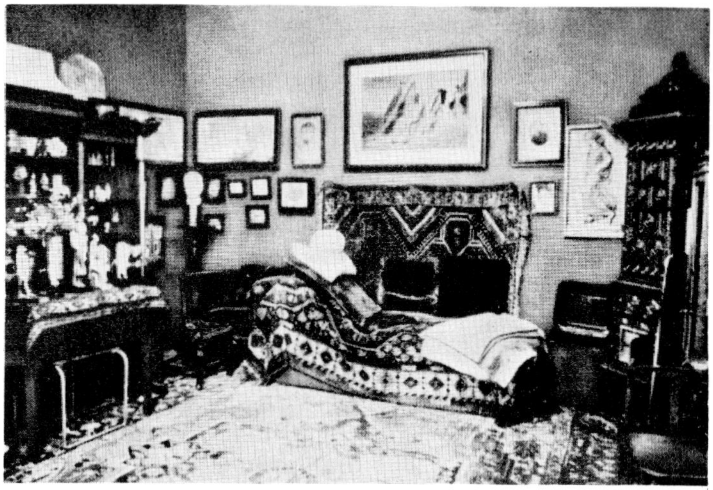

Figure 19.1 Freud's sitting room in his Vienna office. His patients lay on the couch at the right, and Freud sat behind them. (Courtesy Historical Pictures Services-Chicago.)

tortion the client brings to many relationships *outside of* therapy.

Ideally, then, the analyst can help the patient see his habitual ways of responding to people by pointing them out as they occur during therapy. Gradually the conflicts and unfulfilled needs can be elicited more directly, and dealt with. To facilitate this process, Freud recommended that analysts put aside their own feelings and personalities and instead appear as a "mirror" to their patients, reflecting back what the client presented, but adding little or nothing of their own. This stance is known as the "analytic incognito" or "blank screen." Under these circumstances, Freud believed, whatever the client felt about his analyst *must* come from the client himself rather than from any real characteristics of the therapist.

Although this position appears to make transference clearer and more understandable, it brings about its own problems. It is impossible for analysts to hide their own personalities completely. Some clients may experience the analyst as cold and disinterested. In part, of course, this may be the expression of transference (for example, in the form of denying the warmth and concern of one's parents). Realistically, however, the analyst's "blank screen" is, compared to other forms of therapy and counseling, a more remote stance.

Interestingly enough, Freud himself was not a good Freudian, if one judges him against the stereotypical picture of an analyst. The contrast between Freud's technical recommendations and actual therapeutic procedure is described in box 19.3.

Within psychoanalysis, there has been a gradual but unmistakable trend away from the conception of the analyst as a blank screen to one that embraces and makes use of his humanity. In modern psychoanalysis the analyst tends to be a more real and human figure (e.g., Greenson, 1967).

Box 19.3

Freud Was No "Freudian"

Freud the author, who wrote careful papers on psychoanalytic technique, and Freud the therapist seem like two different people. This is probably related in part to his concern for high ethical standards and technical competence among psychoanalysts. He was afraid that untrained or incompetent practitioners would radically alter his ideas and procedures. In 1912 he wrote:

> *I cannot recommend my colleagues emphatically enough to take as a model in psychoanalytic treatment the surgeon who put aside all his own feelings, including that of human sympathy, and concentrates his mind on one single purpose, that of performing the operation as skillfully as possible.*

The physician should be impenetrable to the patient, and like a mirror, reflect nothing but what is shown to him. This remote quality of the psychoanalytic technique has often been parodied and caricatured.

In actual practice, however, Freud neither behaved like a surgeon nor a mere mirror with his clients. Other analysts who were Freud's patients often speak of his warmth, concern, and interest.

One particularly interesting account is that of Wortis, who wrote a book about his analysis with Freud (1963). The picture that emerges of Freud is an enlightening one. Rather than allow Wortis to "free associate," Freud often turned his verbalizations in some more promising direction, changing the subject when necessary or dismissing a particular dream as insignificant.

Freud's dogs often sat in on their sessions, and the two men were as likely to discuss medicine, analytic research, telepathy, or politics as they were Wortis's neuroses. Furthermore, Wortis frequently argued with Freud about theory and technique. All in all, the therapy appears to have been informal, chatty, and friendly —a very different atmosphere than the one Freud described in his writings.

Client-Centered Therapy

Client-centered therapy was the first—and probably the best known—of the treatments that offered to "correct" the psychoanalytic approach. Where analysts emphasized insight, Carl Rogers—the originator of the client-centered approach—emphasized feeling and human growth. Where most analysts embraced the analytic "incognito" to a greater or lesser degree, Rogers stressed the importance of warm, caring concern on the therapist's part for his clients.

Rogers' theory, like Freud's, grew out of his own practice (Rogers, 1942, 1951). If there was a common denominator among the clients Rogers saw, it was that they seemed to have lost touch with themselves somehow. For various reasons, they had hidden their real feelings and ideas and replaced them with social facades. Presumably this happens in the process of growing up when the child discovers that certain things he says or does meet with the parents' approval whereas others do not. Gradually, the child begins to do what *others* want and expect of him and evaluates himself on the basis of meeting or not meeting their expectations. For example, a child may be angry about some real or imagined wrong, but he has learned that his parents disapprove of anger. Thus, he hides his angry feelings to keep the parents' approval, and builds a facade—the "nice" child—which is incompatible with anger. Gradually his anger is hidden away, not only from significant others, but from himself. As an adult, the person may be unable to deal with his angry feelings, partly because he has learned not to recognize or express them.

To Rogers, then, the therapist's task is to provide a therapeutic atmosphere within which this process can be reversed, thus allowing the client to "own" his feelings once again. The therapist can do this in several ways. For one, he can *reflect* what the client is feeling, thereby expanding the client's awareness. More important, however, the therapist must be a certain kind of person if this process is to take place.

Early in his work Rogers emphasized "nondirectiveness" (i.e., letting the client decide what topics to cover, free from the therapist's structure) and an attitude of "unconditional positive regard" toward the client. In recent years, he has shifted the emphasis to what is called the *therapeutic triad:* nonpossessive warmth, accurate empathy, and genuineness.

"Nonpossessive warmth" means that the therapist demonstrates a caring, concerned attitude toward the client, but in a way that fosters growth and independence rather than being viewed as smothering or possessive. It is also critical for the therapist to be "accurately empathic"; that is, to put himself in the client's shoes, to see the world in the client's terms, to understand deeply the client's feelings, and to communicate that understanding. The client often finds it deeply gratifying and moving to be understood and accepted in this fashion. Finally, the therapist must be genuine or "congruent"; in other words, he must be what he really is and communicate that to the client directly and honestly.

If the client-centered therapist comes across as warm, empathic, and real, he will presumably create a therapeutic atmosphere that helps the client be "real." Without parent-like judgmental comments and subtle coercions to be a certain way, the client hopefully begins to accept his hidden feelings and find ways to deal with them. Client-centered theorists believe that the more the therapist provides these conditions and the more the client perceives them, the better the results of the therapy. Extensive research—reviewed later in this chapter—has tended to support this contention.

Behavior Modification

Behavior modification or behavior therapy is a collection of therapeutic techniques based mainly on principles from learning theory (see Chapter 14). When Eysenck and other authors (box 19.2) raised serious questions about the effectiveness of traditional, insight-oriented therapies, many practitioners began to seek therapeutic methods based more directly on empirical research in psychology. Early results from such methods were encouraging, and, as a consequence, behavioral methods grew in popularity to become a major part of contemporary psychotherapy.

In general, behavioral therapists devalue insight in favor of observable behavioral change. Rather than being interested in the origins of symptoms, they tend to avoid making assumptions about causation and focus instead on mechanisms for change. Many of them view psychopathological symptoms, not as signs of underlying psychological conflict, but as maladaptive *habits* that have been learned because they initially reduced anxiety.

If abnormal behavior can be learned, then it should be possible to *unlearn* it with the assistance of psychological principles such as conditioning or extinction. Behavioral approaches vary considerably, but all are based to some degree on the systematic application of principles of learning to the elimination of certain maladaptive habits and, in most instances, the establishment of more adaptive ones in their place.

Systematic Desensitization

The best-known form of behavior modification is systematic desensitization, which is based on the "reciprocal inhibition" or "counterconditioning" therapy developed by Wolpe (1958). Wolpe contended that psychopathological behaviors, such as an exaggerated fear of heights, are motivated by anxiety. Anxiety is seen as a learned response, specifically a conditioned autonomic (usually visceral) response. Wolpe's therapeutic method attacks the anxiety directly through a process known as counterconditioning. The theory of counterconditioning is that an organism cannot display two contradictory internal states at the same time. Thus, if an individual can be conditioned to feel relaxed in a situation that currently makes him anxious, then the anxiety response itself eventually will not be elicited. The goal is to replace the anxious responses with relaxed responses. This is done in the following way: First, the patient is taught to relax deeply, often by Jacobson's method of progressive relaxation (Jacobson, 1938). When the relaxed responses are well learned, the therapist and client develop what is known as an anxiety hierarchy. The patient lists a number of situations that elicit anxiety; these are arranged in a hierarchy from least to most anxiety-arousing. Thus, if the patient is afraid of heights, the first item in the hierarchy might be something like "standing on a plain, looking up at a mountain." A middle item might be "watching a TV program of someone trapped on a ledge, high above traffic." Finally, "standing on a high ledge without a railing, looking down at the ground" might be at the top of the hierarchy.

Systematic desensitization begins with the patient relaxing. He is then instructed to imagine the first item on the hierarchy while maintaining his relaxed state. Therapy progresses as the client can imagine progressively more anxiety-arousing situations while remaining relaxed. If the client cannot stay relaxed, he signals the therapist, and the two go back to the last item in the hierarchy for which full relaxation was possible. The hierarchy is practiced until the client can imagine the previously most anxiety-arousing scenes without becoming anxious. If the treatment generalizes from the laboratory setting, with its imagining of the situations, to the actual situations—as it usually does—then the client should not experience anxiety at those times. Hence, pathological avoidance behaviors to reduce the anxiety will no longer be necessary; the abnormal "habit" will be gone. A typical desensitization study using college students is presented in box 19.4.

Box 19.4

Desensitization of a "Snake Phobia"

In 1963 Lang and Lazovik recruited twenty-four students from an undergraduate course in psychology and asked them to rate their fear of snakes. Because all the students rated their fears as "intense" and said they would avoid approaching a live snake, they were judged to be "snake phobic."

Subsequently, thirteen of the students were assigned to a desensitization treatment group and eleven were placed in a control group. The control group received no desensitization treatment. The experimental group received five training sessions of forty-five minutes each in which they practiced deep muscle relaxation and constructed a twenty-item hierarchy of their anxiety. Typical items that were low on the hierarchy included things such as "writing the word snake." Items that caused strong anxiety included "picking up a snake" or "stepping on a dead snake." After the experimental group had learned the deep muscle relaxation thoroughly and had assembled their individual anxiety hierarchies, they received eleven desensitization sessions lasting forty-five minutes each.

When the treatment had been completed, the experimental group claimed that their fears were far less intense and that they were less anxious about approaching a live snake. The fears of the control group were equally intense before and after the experiment. When the students were followed up six months later, the results were the same.

The procedures used in this study are typical of desensitization therapy, and the design—the use of treated and untreated subjects—is also common. What the results of this experiment mean, however, is not clear. For example, a nonbehaviorist might wonder why one introductory psychology class would contain twenty-four students who are snake phobic, when actual snake phobias are clinically rather rare. Thus the nonbehaviorist would contend that although Lang and Lazovik went to considerable trouble to find students with intense fears and patterns of avoidance, they were probably not successful. What they actually found were students who disliked snakes but were not truly phobic.

Although these distinctions may seem trivial, they are actually of some importance. Recent research has demonstrated that many individuals who describe themselves as snake phobic can be induced to approach snakes if the experimenter is persuasive and enlists their cooperation.

There is considerable controversy over the range of problems for which desensitization therapy is suited. It is clearly an effective therapeutic procedure with phobias, learned avoidance behaviors, and problems that have clear-cut anxiety components (e.g., public speaking anxiety). But whether it is the treatment of choice for more complex neurotic constellations, character disorders, or psychotic states is still unclear.

A variety of other therapeutic approaches have been derived from learning theory. *Implosive therapy,* for example, utilizes the principle of extinction (Stampfl and Levis, 1967). Psychopathological symptoms such as phobias are treated as learned habits, which under appropriate circumstances (such as repeated exposure to the feared object without consequent harm) may be extinguished, just as any other learned response. The principles of operant conditioning, in which certain behaviors are rewarded or punished in therapy, have also been used with some success. Operant conditioning techniques have been used in training autistic children to speak (e.g., Lovaas, 1968) and in mental hospitals where reinforcements for appropriate behaviors take the form of tokens that may be exchanged for goods or special privileges. Aversive conditioning is used in situations where undesirable habits are punished by electric shock or nausea-inducing drugs in an effort to reduce their frequency of expression and, perhaps, eliminate their occurrence.

Rational-Emotive Therapy

Albert Ellis's Rational-Emotive Therapy (1962) is specifically designed to alter people's misconceptions about themselves and the world. To Ellis, thoughts and feelings—the rational and the emotive—are opposite sides of a single coin; they inevitably go together. Feelings can generate inappropriate ideas, but inappropriate ideas can also generate unpleasant feelings. A person may *feel* depressed and subsequently *think* of himself as bad or worthless; but the same situation may result if he *thinks* he is bad, which thereby makes him *feel* depressed. Ellis believes that in growing up, people learn certain false premises, which in turn make it difficult to conduct their lives satisfactorily. For example, a child may quickly learn, in interactions with his parents concerning report cards or Little League baseball, that he must excel to gain their approval and gradually come to believe that he must do well at everything. If he performs badly, he may say to himself: "It's essential that I always do very well. I didn't do very well. Therefore, I'm bad."

The rational-emotive therapist mounts a direct, no-nonsense attack on his client's misconceptions. First, he tries to unmask the misconceptions or inappropriate philosophies that guide the client's life. Common misconceptions include ideas that one must be loved or approved of by everyone or that success is the only thing that makes a person worthwhile. Once the misconceptions are unmasked, the therapist engages the client in an active, argumentative dialogue about the validity of his ideas. By doing so, he hopes to persuade the client to see the logical and practical errors in his beliefs. The therapist's goal is to get the client to stop passing "good-bad" judgments on things, to accept what he cannot actively control, and stop dwelling on his fears. More than most other therapies, rational-emotive therapy emphasizes the importance of the client's *practice* outside of the therapy sessions.

Certainly, many people have been helped by rational-emotive therapists. The procedure is an especially appealing one to some clients, particularly those who want an active, assertive, confident therapist. Others, however, may consider rational-emotive therapists as nagging or overly intellectual.

Existential Therapies

As noted in box 19.1, the traditional problems—phobias, sexual disorders, obsessive-compulsive rituals—that led to the development of psychoanalytic therapies are no longer what therapists commonly treat. Instead, prospective clients complain of loss of interest, feeling overwhelmed, generalized anxiety, and the like. Complaints such as these, which emphasize subjective distress that lacks a clear focus, are sometimes referred to as "existential anxieties." Some therapists believe that they arise from unique human dilemmas and that unique therapeutic procedures—collectively referred to as "existential"—must be utilized to deal with them.

These theories of therapy have their roots in particular in the philosophies of Husserl, Kierkegaard, and Heidegger. These philosophies have subsequently been incorporated into specific "theories" of therapy, such as those developed by Binswanger (1956) as "Daseins analyse" or Frankl (1963) as "Logotherapy." To a large extent, they have been explained and popularized in America by Rollo May (1961) and his colleagues.

These theories hold that man is an insignificant figure in a hostile environment. He is alone in an immense, meaningless universe, and his insignificance is heightened by his mortality. Although everyone senses his own insignificance to some degree, people vary in the extent to which they will allow themselves to recognize these feelings. Partial awareness may lead to what is called "ontological anxiety" or "ontological insecurity"—a vague but discomforting dread about the meaninglessness and fragility of one's existence. This anxiety may lead the person to shut down much awareness of his functioning in the world. When this happens, the person's behavior becomes rigid, ritualistic, and ungratifying.

Existential therapists try to increase a person's awareness as well as his ability to make active, personally meaningful decisions. In a meaningless universe, they feel, the only meaning in one's life can come from self-directed acts of one's own free will. The person must develop a sense of self-awareness, of "being," and, with it, a sense of "being-in-the-world." He must seek active solutions and commitment to personally meaningful ideas and goals.

Partly because meaning is defined differently for each individual, the therapist's approach is basically "phenomenological"; that is, he attempts to understand the world as his client experiences it, not as some theory dictates that it should be experienced. The therapist displays a profound respect for the client and the decisions he makes, even if the therapist does not agree with those decisions. As the therapist gradually comes to understand the client, he can help the client gain the same understanding. In time, the client begins to understand the anxieties of which he was previously only partially aware. His sense of being-in-the-world is heightened, and active choices become more feasible.

Like rational-emotive therapies, existential therapies appeal to many people, possibly because they speak in a language (e.g., "dread") that accurately describes how many distressed people feel and because they emphasize free will and creative, self-directed solutions. Many, however, find them rather vague and abstract. There is little research on the effectiveness of existential therapies, partly because the outcomes are difficult to measure and partly because the actual procedures existential therapists use are so difficult to specify.

Gestalt Therapy

Gestalt therapy is one of the most popular of the newer therapeutic procedures. It is the most explicit in disavowing the importance of clients' past experiences (the phrase "here and now," meaning an emphasis on the present, comes from Gestalt therapy), and it is the only therapy based to any substantial extent on perceptual psychology—in this case, the Gestalt "school" of Kohler and Wertheimer (see Chapter 7). To some degree, it has become a rallying point for therapists who are disenchanted with what they view as the intellectualizing aspects of other therapies; for example, the endless discussions about the past in a futile search for reasons for present problems.

The late Fritz Perls, the predominant figure in this form of psychotherapy, chose the term gestalt to characterize his emphasis on perceptual integration as an attribute of well-functioning individuals. All situations consist of multiple, simultaneous components. At any given time, a person may be aware of something he is feeling or thinking—a sound, the look on someone else's face, or some other feature of the environment. Ideally, one's attention can shift readily, and these different components can be perceived. Under these circumstances—where everything a person is aware of forms a whole configuration or gestalt—a state of flexible perceptual balance has been achieved.

As with all ideal states, however, this balance is easily disrupted. Often, when someone is close to realizing something unpleasant, he may cut off awareness of that aspect of himself. For example, he may begin to sense how desperately he needs someone else's approval and quickly block off that recognition from his awareness. The gestalt thus cannot be completed, and a state of tension or discomfort arises. When people are separated from their feelings, there are gaps in their perceptions of themselves and the world, and neurotic behavior may be the result.

The Gestalt therapist's task is to help reintegrate the person by increasing his *awareness*—awareness is at the core of all Gestalt techniques. By listening carefully to the client's inflections as well as words, by observing his gestures and other body language, the therapist begins to understand what is missing from the client's gestalt—that is, what he is trying to avoid. The therapist then tries to break down the blocks, admit the missing element or elements to awareness, allow the client to integrate them, and thus complete the gestalt.

This is done partly by means of some ingenious techniques, but also by means of an atmosphere of honesty where clients' tendencies to fool or deceive themselves are dealt with quickly and straightforwardly. Dreams may also become the vehicle for such work. A person may describe a dream, and then play each person, animal, or object in it. All the characters in the dream presumably represent projected aspects of the self that may not have been fully integrated into awareness. And hopefully, the person begins to experience diverse aspects of himself, and integration in the form of a series of completed gestalts occurs. An example of Gestalt therapy appears in box 19.5. Gestalt therapy's emphasis on the "here and now" comes as a welcome relief to people who have tried more traditional forms of therapy and have found that delving into the past is not particularly profitable for them. The emphasis on feelings also appeals to many clients. Some therapists, on the other hand, criticize Gestalt therapy as being merely cathartic. Although it may arouse strong feelings, these feelings must then be integrated intellectually, in the form of insight and attitudinal change, if the treatment is to result in stable, long-term gains. Again, little research evidence exists to help settle this debate.

Box 19.5

Here and Now

The following excerpt from a Gestalt therapy session, which appears in a paper by Naranjo titled "Present-Centeredness" (Fagan and Shepherd, 1970), illustrates how the Gestalt therapist emphasizes here-and-now awareness of what the patient is feeling and the kind of completed gestalt that may result.

"P(atient): I don't know what to say now. . .
T(herapist): I notice that you are looking away from me.
P: (Giggle).

T: And now you cover up your face. ("Body Language")
P: You make me feel so awful!
T: And now you cover up your face with both hands.
P: Stop! This is unbearable!
T: What do you feel now?
P: I feel so embarrassed! Don't look at me!
T: Please stay with that embarrassment. ("Go with" feelings)
P: I have been living with it all my life! I am ashamed of everything I do! It is as if I don't even feel that I have the right to exist!"

In this instance, the therapist sticks with the immediate situation, despite the patient's efforts to distract him or to lead him to abandon his pursuit for reasons of social courtesy. Eventually, the unarticulated feeling leads the patient to a discussion of shameful feelings that may be central to the therapy.

Group Treatment

Over the last two decades, a variety of group methods have become increasingly popular. One reason is that these techniques are often more practical than individual therapy: because several clients share the therapist's time, the fees are usually lower. Groups also tend to counteract feelings of loneliness and interpersonal unrelatedness that characterize many who seek therapy today. Finally, groups seem to provide certain unique advantages or benefits that cannot be provided readily in individual therapy sessions.

Sensitivity Training and Encounter Groups

T-groups and *encounter groups* are often not actually therapy as such. T-groups (the T stands for *t*raining in sensitivity) are generally composed of people who wish to improve their interpersonal sensitivity and to learn how others view them. Clinical psychologists, for example, are often members of T-groups during their training.

Encounter groups (see fig. 19.2) are also likely to be sought out by people who would not be considered disturbed psychologically. For instance, encounter groups often consist of members of an organization, such as a large corporation, who need to improve their communication and interpersonal relationships within the organization, or with members of different groups (e.g., police and ghetto residents) that have problems in relating to one another.

The purpose of encounter groups, which are part of what is sometimes called the "Human Potential Movement," is to enhance personal growth rather than correct psychological or behavioral malfunctions. Group members accomplish this, with the assistance of a leader by interacting as openly and honestly as possible. Under these circumstances, they may begin to drop their social facades and allow others to know them as they really are.

Centers that specialize in human potential offerings, such as encounter groups, specialized therapies, meditation, massage, and so forth, have appeared throughout the United States; one of the best known is Esalen, on the Monterey peninsula in California. The honesty and openness that is emphasized in the human potential movement is extremely disconcerting to some people, particularly when it branches, for example, into nude encounter groups, which are designed in part to help individuals dealing with excessive modesty or shame about their bodies. For extended discussions of this trend, see Schultz (1967) or Howard (1970).

Some professionals are increasingly concerned about the possible harmful effects of such groups. Lieberman, Yalom, and Miles

Figure 19.2 A scene from an encounter group, with participants expressing angry feelings by pounding on pillows. (Courtesy Mimi Forsyth, Monkmeyer Press Photo Service.)

(1973) found that thirty-three percent of the participants in such groups changed in beneficial and apparently lasting ways. However, twenty percent seemed to have suffered to some degree, and nine percent were thought to be psychiatric "casualties." Encounter groups are probably most likely to be harmful if the leaders are insufficiently trained or uncertified or if potential clients are not screened to eliminate poor risks.

Group Therapy

Unlike encounter groups, therapy groups ordinarily include people who would define themselves as having psychological problems. A typical therapy group consists of one or two therapists and six to twelve clients. Here again, the emphasis is on openness and honesty, but with a greater expectation that members will deal with personal problems, that they will attempt to help one another find constructive solutions, and that the therapist or therapists will interact with clients in a more traditional fashion by offering interpretation and self-exploratory leads.

Group therapy appears to be an effective method of helping many people (e.g., Yalom, 1970). Some therapists argue that because the group therapist must divide his attention among several people, the group situation does not allow him to focus on individual clients who need help with severe problems. Proponents of group therapy, however, argue that these approaches have unique advantages over traditional one-to-one therapeutic relationships. For example, group therapy helps break down a client's sense that he is the only troubled person in the world; it allows the client to feel useful, because he acts in part as a therapist for other group members; and it provides a kind of laboratory for developing new interpersonal skills. Maladaptive patterns of relating can become obvious very quickly in groups. In addition, each client has several models of alternative behaviors and a relatively safe environment in which to experiment with them.

A variety of different forms of group therapy have emerged. Psychodrama, for example, requires individual group members to play roles in dramatic episodes that may center around the problems expressed by one member (see, for example, Moreno, 1946). Another form is family therapy, which emphasizes working with entire families rather than individual members (see, for example, Satir, 1967). Typically, if one person in a family is in pain, the interlocking of family members makes it likely that all of the family members are suffering in some way and therefore need some kind of help. In addition, many family therapists believe that family problems cannot be permanently resolved if the family situations that brought them about in the first place are left unaltered.

As in group therapy, the emphasis in family therapy is on openness and honesty. Most family therapists pay special attention to patterns of communication among family members because they believe that many problems are generated and maintained by the members' indirect or distorted messages to one another. When each family member's needs and feelings become clearer to the others, the family becomes a more satisfying and functional group, and a variety of stresses on its members are reduced.

Recent Innovations in Psychotherapy

Although new therapeutic approaches are constantly being developed, experience suggests that few of them will endure or become widespread. But it is difficult to predict which will last and which will not. Two contemporary procedures—transactional analysis and primal therapy—will be discussed in this section. Unfortunately, space prohibits a discussion of other interesting approaches; for example, spiritual philosophies, such as Zen,

Yoga, Buddhism, Sufism, Krishna Consciousness, and the like, which are growing in popularity in the United States.

Transactional Analysis

Transactional Analysis (T.A.) is a relatively new form of therapy that emphasizes the individual's understanding of his interactions (or transactions) with other people. It is probably the fastest-growing form of therapy in the early 1970s, branching extensively into education and religious counseling as well as traditional therapeutic settings. T.A.'s popularity probably is due to the fact that it describes personality in terms that people can readily grasp and apply to their own lives. Two best-selling books, Berne's *Games People Play* (1964) and Harris's *I'm OK—You're OK* (1967), have popularized Transactional Analysis.

As you discovered in previous chapters, Transactional Analysis suggests that personality exists in three "ego states," child, parent, and adult. In any transaction between people, a part of each person may predominate. Transactions may be complementary, for example, adult-adult, or they may be crossed, for example, adult-parent. Generally speaking, *complementary* transactions are regarded as satisfactory, while *crossed* transactions usually are not.

T.A. usually takes place in groups. The group gives individual members feedback suggesting they are really OK. It also monitors the individual's progress toward specific goals (e.g., holding a job, ceasing to drink heavily, communicating with spouse) set at the beginning of therapy. The major work of T.A., however, is to analyze each person's transactions, both within and outside the therapy group. As the individual becomes more and more aware of each aspect of his personality, child and parent transactions should diminish and adult transactions should begin to dominate.

Primal Therapy

Primal Therapy is the creation of Arthur Janov, whose first book, *The Primal Scream* (1970), was a best-seller because of the interesting procedures it advocates—principally, urging clients to scream for their parents—and its claim of striking therapeutic gains.

Janov, much like Rogers, contends that neurosis arises when an individual loses touch with his real feelings and erects unreal facades in their place. The child who is repeatedly disappointed in his efforts to receive love or approval from his parents begins to feel what Janov calls "Pain"—or intense psychobiologic distress. Because this feeling is overwhelmingly unpleasant, the child goes to great lengths to avoid it on subsequent occasions. Since the Pain is associated with unmet needs, however, the child must shut off feeling the need to truncate the pain itself. Gradually, the child "shuts down," thus becoming more and more "unreal." He begins to pursue what Janov calls symbolic satisfactions—for example, the need to be praised continually, which is symbolic gratification of the need to be loved by one's parents.

Janov sees his therapeutic task as helping the client get in touch with his infantile needs again and recognize that they will never be satisfied; then, presumably, the client will be free to have adult needs met in an adult fashion. For the client to experience these needs again, however, he must first reexperience the original Pain. To bring this about, the Primal therapist must sometimes be very provocative: attacking the client's system of defenses, prodding here, confronting there, until the Pain begins to break through. The experience of the Pain reentering awareness is called a "Primal," which is accompanied by a deep scream. Although it appears that this scream can be a deeply moving and relieving experience, Primal therapy and its many offshoots are so recent that they have not been investigated systematically.

Psychotherapy Research

Despite all the different approaches to psychotherapy and the many thousands of people who have experienced them we still know woefully little about what causes psychopathology, how it can be changed, or why this change takes place. Some patients seem to improve regardless of what is done to them; others work for years with experienced and otherwise successfully therapists to no avail.

Here, as in other areas of psychology we must turn to research in an effort to answer our questions. Psychotherapy research, however, is extremely complicated because it seeks to understand a complex interpersonal process that is not readily compartmentalized or controlled. Thousands of studies have attempted to define the "process" by which psychotherapy works. Some of the major findings from such research are described below and several comprehensive reviews of this research are available, such as those by Gardner (1964), Luborsky et al. (1971), or Meltzoff and Kornreich (1970).

Client Variables

We now know that clients with certain characteristics are more likely to profit from therapy than are those who lack them. The clients who seem to gain most from therapy are moderately anxious, highly motivated to change, and have positive expectations about the outcome of therapy. They are usually perceived by their therapists—and by others as well—as more likable, flexible, and self-aware. There is no evidence to suggest that either men or women usually gain more from therapy.

Schofield (1964) has described the ideal candidate for therapy as a YAVIS: Young, Attractive, Verbal, Intelligent, and Successful. In other words, the clients who seem to do best in therapy are those who need it *least*. This kind of bias has prompted an increasing interest among some professionals in working with non-YAVIS clients—older people, members of minority groups, and so forth.

Therapist Variables

Despite the emphasis on "schools" or approaches to psychotherapy, the affiliation or kind of training a therapist receives does not seem especially relevant to the outcome of his or her cases. Research indicates that experienced therapists become similar to one another over the years, regardless of the method or methods in which they were originally trained. Although it appears that some behavior modification techniques may be the treatments of choice for problems (such as phobias) that have clear-cut anxiety components, there is no convincing evidence that one approach is generally superior to any other.

There is evidence to suggest, however, that the therapist's *personality* is important to the outcome of therapy. The therapist who is well-adjusted and successful in his relationships outside of therapy, has positive expectations about his work, is actively involved in therapy sessions and is open, honest, and willing to be known by the clients is most likely to be successful. Conversely, the therapist who seems bored, passive, or remote is unlikely to be as effective.

The most extensive research on the characteristics of therapists that affect the outcome of therapy has been done within the Client-Centered school. As we discussed earlier, Client-Centered practitioners believe that the best therapist offers his clients the greatest amount of the facilitative attitudes known as the "therapeutic triad:" nonpossessive warmth, accurate empathy, and genuineness or congruence. Hundreds of studies support this conclusion; many of them are reviewed in Truax and Carkhuff (1967).

One study, summarized in box 19.6, shows how the deliberate manipulation of the therapeutic triad can dramatically alter at least one important aspect of the client's behavior within a single therapy session.

Relationship Variables

Research indicates that one of the best predictors of the outcomes of a given therapy is the *quality of the relationship* between client and therapist. Apparently most successful therapy occurs, for example, when patient and therapist are somewhat, but not too similar in terms of expectations, background, and important values. Mutual feelings of warmth and closeness and respect are similarly related to outcome (Strupp, Wallach and Wagan, 1964). In other words, the better the therapist and client relate to one another, the better the results.

Unfortunately, most of these findings are based on correlational studies, and correlational findings cannot tell us about cause and effect. Do clients get better in the best client-therapist relationships because, as Rogers believes, they feel freer to talk about what is troubling them and begin to reclaim hidden aspects of themselves? Or are those clients who are going to get better *anyhow* also the ones who get along best with their therapists?

Hopefully, future research in psychotherapy will answer these questions of cause and effect. In all likelihood, such studies will move further away from global studies of single therapeutic procedures. Strupp and Bergin (1969) have suggested that future research should concern itself with the following ques-

Box 19.6

A Study of Therapy Processes

Truax and Carkhuff (1965) were aware that a therapist's empathy, genuineness, and nonpossessive warmth were correlated with outcome of therapy, so they set out to see whether this was a long-term phenomenon, accruing over many hours of therapy, or whether it could be demonstrated within a single therapy session. To answer this question, they deliberately manipulated the conditions during the therapy sessions.

The subjects in this study were three hospitalized female schizophrenics. During the first twenty minutes of their individual therapy sessions, the therapist was warm and empathic. During the next twenty minutes, he deliberately withheld his comments and presumably seemed less warm and empathic to the patients. During the last twenty minutes, he again responded as he had during the first third of the session.

Independent raters, who were unaware of the experimental design or purpose, assessed two things from tapes of the therapy sessions: the therapist's warmth and empathy in each third of the session and the degree to which the client engaged in self-exploration in each third of the session. The results of these ratings appear in box figure 19.6.

During the first and last thirds of the session, when the therapist was warm and empathic the patients were able to explore their own feelings and behavior. During the middle third of the sessions the patients were less able to engage in self-exploration. These findings suggest that the degree to which the therapist offers facilitating circumstances has substantial, if not causal, bearing on the degree to which a client is able to engage in behaviors that will be beneficial to him.

In this study—as in most studies of therapy processes—one must be careful when generalizing the results. Truax's and Carkhuff's conclusions are based on only three subjects. In addition, the clients were schizophrenic, and some researchers would be hesitant about generalizing the findings to include neurotic clients. Only after research has been done by a number of different investigators with different clients in different settings will generally applicable and acceptable findings emerge.

tion: Given this particular client, with these problems, what would be the most effective technique to use? Research and practice in the future will probably focus to a greater degree on specific procedures for specific problems.

Summary

Most people enter psychotherapy, not because they are "crazy," or suffer from well-defined problems, but because they feel anxious or depressed, have difficulties in their relationships with others or persistent problems in meeting their day-to-day responsibilities.

There are many kinds of psychotherapists. Most professional therapists are helpful, well-trained people who are certified in most states to insure their competence and ethical behavior. The length, frequency, and cost of sessions, length of therapy, and specific treatment procedures vary from therapist to therapist. Although important questions have been raised about psychotherapy's effectiveness, many doubts appear to stem from methodological problems in assessing personality change. A survey of well-designed experiments suggests that psychotherapy is usually beneficial.

The ways in which people have treated psychological problems have grown from their ideas regarding the causes of those problems. When it was thought that abnormal behavior was caused by demonic possession, remedies included opening the victim's skull, rites aimed at driving the demon away, and

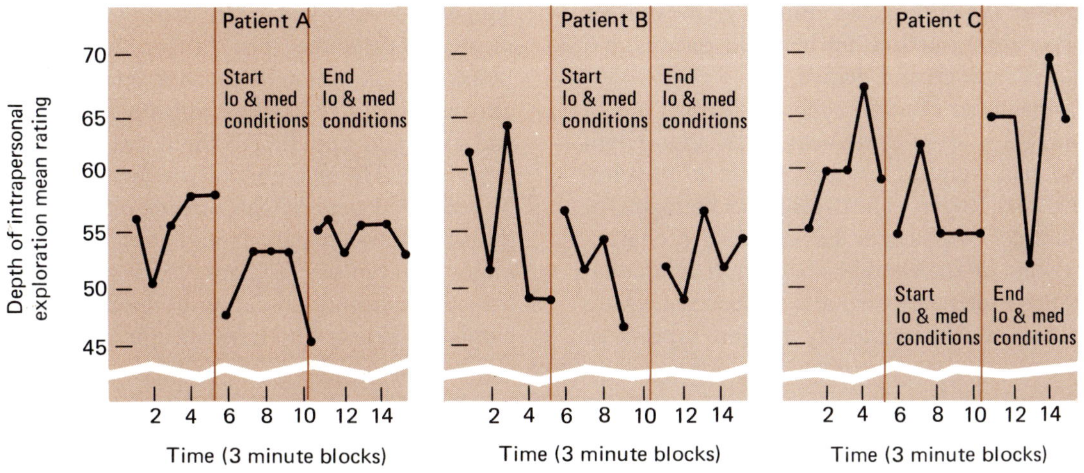

Box Figure 19.6 Three clients' responses to greater and lesser degrees of therapist warmth and empathy. In the first and last third of each interview, when the therapist expressed greater warmth and empathy, the clients engaged in the most self-exploration. In the middle third, when therapists withheld warmth and empathy, clients displayed the least self-exploration. (From Truax, C.B. and Carkhuff, R.R. Experimental manipulation of therapeutic conditions. *Journal of Consulting Psychology,* 1969, 29, pp. 119–124. Copyright 1969 by the American Psychological Association. Reprinted by permission.)

various forms of torture to compel an offender to renounce a satanic contract.

As medical interest in psychological problems grew during the latter part of the nineteenth century, a variety of disease-oriented treatments were developed. Reforms were brought about in mental hospitals, making them less custodial and potentially more therapeutic institutions. Surgical and electroshock techniques were refined, and an impressive array of tranquilizing, antipsychotic and antidepressant drugs was developed.

Psychologically-oriented treatment approaches began when hypnosis was used to treat conversion hysterics. As a result of his work with these patients, Freud gradually developed the psychoanalytic procedure. Psychoanalysts believe psychopathology is caused by unconscious conflicts and attempt to facilitate insight into these conflicts by interpreting their patients' free associations and the transference relationships their patients develop toward them. However, modern psychoanalytic approaches emphasize the real interpersonal relationship between patient and analyst to a greater degree.

A number of approaches has grown out of therapists' disenchantment with the length and relatively impersonal nature of psychoanalysis. Rogers' client-centered therapy, for example, emphasizes the way certain characteristics of the therapist (warmth, empathy, and genuineness) help a client become aware of and accept previously hidden aspects of himself. Behavior modification techniques, on the other hand, employ principles of learning theory to eliminate maladaptive habits. Such techniques have proved to be efficient and useful in many cases and have become increasingly widespread.

There are a great many other theories and therapeutic techniques, each with its own distinct features. For example, in Ellis's Rational-Emotive therapy, the therapist tries in various ways to alter the client's illogical and unrealistic ideas. Existential approaches emphasize that the client must become aware of and accept his deep-seated feelings of aloneness and mortality. Perls' Gestalt therapy stresses awareness of the ongoing flow of one's feelings. Transactional Analysis strives for an understanding of the elements of one's interpersonal relationships. A variety of group methods promote interpersonal honesty and feelings of connectedness with others.

Psychotherapeutic research suggests that clients who are young, intelligent, and articulate will profit most from therapy. For the most part, the therapist's theoretical orientation does not seem to be critical to success; apparently, the therapist's warmth, openness, and ability to understand the client are most important. The outcome of therapy seems to be predicted best by the quality of the relationship between patient and therapist. One major trend in psychotherapy research is the development and validation of specific treatments for clients who have specific problems.

20

Community Mental Health

Community mental health is a rather recent development for helping people who are in emotional distress. Whereas psychotherapy developed because of the need for nonmedical techniques to help people with their emotional problems, community mental health developed as the result of a need to find more efficient means of providing psychotherapy services *and* a need for nonpsychotherapeutic methods of helping people. These needs developed for several reasons: (1) there were not enough psychotherapists to treat all those who needed help, (2) psychotherapy was too expensive for many people, (3) psychotherapeutic treatment was least likely to be effective with those who could least afford to help themselves—the poor, and (4) psychotherapy usually focused on emotional pathology rather than on emotional health or positive functioning.

From a theoretical standpoint, community mental health is a branch of community psychology, a subfield of psychology that focuses on the individual in relation to his environment. Although both community psychologists and community mental health psychologists have a fundamental concern for the mental health of individuals, their general orientation tends to be somewhat different. Community psychologists tend to be concerned with broad issues such as social injustice, the unequal distribution of power and resources, and ways in which communities can support self-determination, self-competence, and a sense of belongingness. In other words, they view mental health in the context of broad social change.

Specialists in community mental health, on the other hand, generally focus on community-oriented strategies that will result in meeting the needs of community residents, reduce stress, and increase residents' happiness and sense of responsibility. Although the overall aim of the community mental health psychologist is to help individuals, programs that will have a broad impact on the entire community are given a higher priority than those designed to help people on a one-to-one basis.

To achieve these goals, the community mental health psychologist designs programs to include the following strategies:

1. *Outreach.* Many people who suffer from emotional problems, especially the poor, avoid psychotherapy or are unaware of it as a solution to their problems. Thus the psychologist attempts to initiate programs that reach those who do not ordinarily ask for help but have demonstrated a high risk for developing emotional problems. These groups can be identified through research. For example, the psychologist may discover that a large number of people from a certain section of town is sent to the state mental hospital, or come in contact with the mental health center, are likely to commit suicide, or are alcoholic. When these populations at risk are identified, programs can be implemented to help them.

The outreach function sometimes causes difficulties for the psychologist and the community mental health center. The center is a part of the community and yet its purpose is to change the community structure in a way that will enhance the mental health of residents. However, because groups or individuals in the community may not agree with the proposed changes or see the need for them, the center's staff is confronted by the ethical dilemma of either bringing about change against the wishes of some residents or sitting by and doing nothing when the staff sees the need for change.

2. *Indirect services.* Because there is a serious shortage of manpower in the mental health field, mental health problems may have to be solved by changing the community in some way. Individual therapy would not only be too expensive to provide to everyone in the community who might benefit from it, but many problems could not be solved through psychotherapy. There is a need to help professionals in community services to better serve the community's needs. Such help may involve changing the structure of the community to make communication easier, politicians more accessible, and help agencies to be more responsive to the people they serve. Community mental health consultation may be provided to community caregivers such as clergymen, nurses, teachers, and police to help them cope with the mental health needs of the public.

3. *More efficient services.* It is known that when an individual is suffering from severe stress, he is most likely to seek help and therapy is most likely to be effective. Thus the psychologist might set up a suicide prevention center or a crisis intervention center to help people at a time when they are especially open to therapeutic change.

4. *Prevention.* Although the prevention of emotional problems by anticipating their cause and changing the community in some way to eliminate that cause is the most important goal of community mental health strategies, it receives the least attention. As you will see, mental health professionals frequently support the idea of prevention, but they are often too overwhelmed by already-existing problems to devote adequate attention to prevention. Furthermore, they receive little support for their preventive efforts from the public, which has a difficult time anticipating future problems when there are so many immediate problems that concern them.

History of Community Mental Health

When the medical model became the dominant method of treating the mentally ill, the large state hospitals, although starting out with treatment in mind, quickly became overwhelmed by patients. Many deteriorated into custodial institutions that provided minimal treatment and functioned primarily to remove troublesome people from society. Schizophrenics who were hospitalized stayed an average of twelve years! By 1957 a total of 1.2 million people were occupying beds in public and private mental hospitals, and many were receiving little or no treatment because of inadequate funds for staff.

However, during World War II, several things began to occur that eventually brought about a change in the situation. These changes occurred within the mental health profession itself and with the federal government.

Developments Within the Mental Health Field

During World War II, mental health professionals learned how to handle victims of combat neurosis, or "shell shock" more effectively. Shell-shocked soldiers had previously been removed from the combat zone and had received psychiatric care, but they were rarely able to return to combat. Then mental health professionals found that if short-term treatment was provided to these men close to the battlefield and they were then returned to combat as soon as possible, fewer psychiatric casualties resulted (Menninger, 1948). This strategy became the basis for present-day intervention and short-term psychotherapeutic techniques. In addition, because there was a shortage of psychiatrists during the war, other mental health professionals such as psychologists, social workers, and psychiatric nurses, were used extensively as psychotherapists. This trend has continued to the present day.

When drugs began to be used in the mid-1950s to treat mental illness, the number of patients in state mental hospitals began to decline. Many patients could be maintained in the community as long as they took their medication.

Also in the mid-1950s, a new treatment strategy began to develop within mental hospitals themselves. Maxwell Jones (1953, 1958), a British psychiatrist, pointed out that traditional mental hospitals were organized for the staff's convenience rather than the patients'. According to Jones, the regimentation of these institutions turned patients into nonpersons who had little control over or responsibility for their own lives thus hindering their progress (see box 20.1). Thus he developed the first therapeutic community in London's Belmont Hospital, based on the philosophy that one of the mentally ill person's major problems was an inability to deal effectively with the social environment. Thus the best method of treatment would be to create a supportive social environment in the hospital. Among other changes, the patients and staff met regularly to discuss issues, approaches to treatment, and their problems. All patients were encouraged to retain their individuality and sense of responsibility, and most important they were active participants in decisions concerning their treatment and discharge plans.

In addition, other kinds of alternatives to the traditional state mental hospital began to emerge. One change during the 1950s and 1960s was geographic decentralization; this involved breaking up the large state hospital into smaller hospitals that were located in strategic areas around the state so that patients would be closer to their own communities. In the second alternative, the large state hospital was maintained, but the patients were assigned to wards according to the geographic area they came from. These changes enabled the patients to maintain their ties with their own communities, and enabled the staff on the particular ward to become familiar with a particular community and thus facilitate the patient's return to their communities after discharge.

Mental Health Planning at the Government Level

Shortly after World War II, the federal government began to become involved in mental health planning. In July, 1946 Congress passed the National Mental Health Act, which established the *National Institute of Mental Health* (NIMH), the first national agency whose sole responsibility was mental health. NIMH's mandate was to develop mental health services in the various states through grants and consultation and to support research and training in fields related to mental health. During this time the Veterans Administration became a major employer and trainer of mental health professionals.

In 1955 Congress formed the Joint Commission on Mental Illness and Health, to obtain "an objective, thorough and nationwide analysis and reevaluation of the human and economic problems of mental illness." After undertaking numerous studies concerning the magnitude of the problems and potential intervention strategies, the Commission published a report titled *Action for Mental Health,* in 1961. One of the Commission's major recommendations was that community-based mental health centers be set up across the nation. This report led to the passage of the Community Mental Health Centers Construction Act, in 1963.

Comprehensive Community Health Center Program

Under the act, much of the responsibility for treatment of the mentally ill was to be shifted from the huge state hospitals to comprehensive community mental health centers. The federal government and the states would share the costs of building and initially staffing of these facilities. Each state would be divided into *catchment areas,* geographic areas or populations served by an agency or institution. Each catchment area would have its own comprehensive community mental health center. These community–based centers would accomplish several things: (1) emotionally disturbed individuals could be identified and receive treatment before they needed to be hospitalized; and (2) if hospitalization was necessary, the community could be involved in the treatment and the patient could be returned to the community as quickly as possible. NIMH felt that the country could be divided into approximately 2,000 catchment areas, where everyone could be served by a community mental health center. Catchment areas were to have populations ranging from 75,000 to 200,000, areas that were felt to be large enough to be efficiently served and small enough that the center could be responsive to the needs of the individual communities.

To qualify for federal funds the centers had to provide five essential services:

1. Inpatient services for patients who needed to be hospitalized.
2. Outpatient services such as individual and group psychotherapy.
3. Emergency services such as crisis intervention, suicide prevention, and other forms of immediate help.
4. Partial hospitalization such as day care, in which the patient would live at the center during the day and return home at night, or night care, in which the person would work at his job during the day and return to the center at night.
5. Consultative and educational services to other caregivers in the community.

To be considered truly comprehensive, five additional services were considered highly desirable; however, they were not mandatory —diagnostic services; rehabilitation services such as vocational training; precare and aftercare (i.e., anticipating a person's needs

Box 20.1

The Inhumanity of the Mental Hospital

Rosenhan's (1973) extensive study of twelve mental hospitals paints a bleak picture of the care patients receive in the typical psychiatric ward. Eight sane people deliberately gained admission into these hospitals by claiming they heard voices saying the words "empty," "hollow," and "thud." In all other respects, excluding their name and occupation, they told the truth about themselves. Once on the ward, they behaved normally and openly kept extensive notes about their observations. Despite their obviously normal behavior, the only persons who identified them as normal were their fellow patients! All eight were discharged approximately nineteen days after admission with the diagnosis of schizophrenia or schizophrenia in remission (the disorder remains but the symptoms are no longer obvious).

The information these patients gathered during their hospitalization was startling. For example, ward attendants usually spent about 11.3 percent of their time on the wards and the remainder in the nurses' station. Day nurses left the nurses' station only 11.5 times per shift, and psychiatrists appeared on the ward only 6.7 times per day. The higher the staff member's status in the staff hierarchy, the less time he spent with patients.

To evaluate the staff's responsiveness to patients, the eight patient-researchers asked psychiatrists, attendants, and nurses the following questions: "Pardon me, Mr. (Dr., or Mrs.) X. Can you tell me when I will be

Box Table 20.1 Self-initiated contact by pseudopatients with psychiatrists and attendants, compared to contact with other groups.

Self-initiated contact by pseudopatients with psychiatrists and nurses and attendants, compared to contact with other groups.

Contact	Psychiatric hospitals		University campus (nonmedical)	University medical center: Physicians		
	(1) Psychiatrists	(2) Nurses and attendants	(3) Faculty	(4) "Looking for a psychiatrist"	(5) "Looking for an internist"	(6) No additional comment
Responses						
Moves on, head averted (%)	71	88	0	0	0	0
Makes eye contact (%)	23	10	0	11	0	0
Pauses and chats (%)	2	2	0	11	0	10
Stops and talks (%)	4	0.5	100	78	100	90
Mean number of questions answered (out of 6)	*	*	6	3.8	4.8	4.5
Respondents (No.)	13	47	14	18	15	10
Attempts (No.)	185	1283	14	18	15	10

*Not applicable.

Source: From "On being sane in insane places." Rosenhan, D.L. *Science,* Vol. 179, Table 1, pp. 250–258, 19 January 1973. Copyright 1973 by the American Association for the Advancement of Science.

eligible for grounds privileges (discharge, and the like)?" Although the content varied, their questions were always relevant and asked in a courteous way. Seventy-one percent of the psychiatrists completely ignored the question and moved on without making eye contact; 88 percent of the nurses and attendants also ignored the question. While a few made eye contact and moved on without answering, only 6 percent of the psychiatrists and 2.5 percent of the nurses and attendants paused or stopped and answered the question.

In a control study in which faculty members of a university were stopped on campus and asked a series of six questions, including the location of a nonexistent building, one hundred percent of them answered the questions. These depressing comparisons are summarized in box figure 20.1.

Minimal contact between staff and patients was only one indication of the inadequate care that patients received. In addition, attendants were frequently abusive. The patient's personal records could be read by any curious volunteer.

On many occasions, the staff behaved as though the patients were not there: for example, they would carry on an animated discussion about a particular patient in front of the entire ward.

Over five months the pseudopatients received almost 2,100 pills—two of which were actually swallowed. They also noticed that many patients on the ward did not take their medication.

Therapy was minimal (as might be expected given all of the above). Average daily contact with mental health professionals was 6.8 minutes. This time included intake interviews, ward meetings with staff members present, group and individual psychotherapy, case presentation conferences, and discharge meetings. Given these results for twelve different hospitals, it is not surprising that an alternative to hospitalization was needed!

and providing treatment before he needed hospitalization), and supportive help when he returned to the community after release from the hospital; training (i.e., providing continuing education for staff so that quality of care would be upgraded); and research and evaluation to determine the effectiveness of service.

Qualifications concerning treatment had to be the same for every single person. If an individual was eligible for one service, he was automatically eligible for all the other services the center provided. And the center had to be organized so that the individual could be transferred easily from one unit to another. For example, when a patient was discharged from the inpatient service, he was to be easily transferred to the outpatient service. Thus information about patients also had to be easily transmitted within the system so that different staff members would be able to follow a patient from one service to another for follow-up treatment. Finally, legal residency was not to be used as a means of excluding people from services. A person who had just moved into the catchment area was as eligible for services as a person who had lived in the catchment area for years.

Strengths and Weaknesses of the Program

Despite what some critics say about the comprehensive community mental health center concept, the program had several important new aspects. First, it was designed to provide care to a large segment of the population that previously had been denied this type of care, either because it simply did not exist or because it was too expensive. Centers typically use sliding fee scales, related to the patient's ability to pay. The cost of therapy sessions, for example, can be free or range from as little as fifty cents to thirty dollars per session. Second, until the program was initiated, many of the services we listed earlier—for example, emergency services, consultation, and evaluation—had been geographically scattered and controlled by separate administrative agencies. Now they were located under one roof and administered by one agency. Thus the services were convenient and administrative red tape was reduced. And third, whereas inpatient services were available only in the huge state hospitals that were often hundreds of miles away from the patient's home, they were now located in his own community.

In many ways, however, the critics' complaints are justified. One of the inherent problems of the community mental health centers is similar to early complaints registered against psychotherapy. In spite of minimal information about the effectiveness of psychotherapy, therapists continued to provide therapy. Much the same thing can be said of the comprehensive community mental health centers; although they provide a large number of services, little research has been done to determine whether the selection of these services and the exclusion of others is justified. In addition, because all centers are required to provide certain services to qualify for federal funds, individual centers are forced to ignore one of the most important concepts of community mental health—responsiveness to a particular community's needs.

Another major complaint concerns the size of the catchment areas. Many critics argue that arbitrarily designating catchment areas as consisting of 75,000 to 200,000 people makes them unresponsive to the natural size of individual communities. For instance, in rural areas, the center's catchment area must be enormous to include the requisite population, while in the cities, needless duplication of services often occurs. (What does a city with a population of 250,000 do? Have two centers?)

Although *prevention* of emotional disorders is one of the basic tenets of the community mental health philosophy, it is almost totally ignored by the comprehensive community mental health center program. As we pointed out earlier, it is an extremely difficult service to provide because of the enormous number of already existing problems, and the public's lack of interest. And we have also mentioned the fact that even if we have information about the causes of emotional problems, it is difficult to translate them into programs. For example, if data were available to indicate that divorce was a major cause of emotional problems in parents and children, preventing either the causes of divorce or eliminating the negative consequences is not easily accomplished. In addition, the stress that led to the divorce may be the source of the emotional problems rather than the divorce per se.

Finally, the comprehensive community mental health center program has been criticized because many centers are still dominated by the medical model of psychopathology. Initially, the federal guidelines specified that psychiatrists had to be the administrative directors of the centers. And because of their medical orientation, the attitude was often—wait until people ask for help. See patients only in your office and provide one-to-one, long-term psychotherapy. Do not advertise your services. Although some centers have avoided domination by the medical model, others have remained unobtrusive in their communities, unknown, and inaccessible. The federal guidelines with respect to administrative directors have now been changed and NIMH has funded a mental health center management training program to train mental health professionals from a number of fields to take over the job of administrating these centers. For obvious reasons, psychiatrists must be the medical directors of these centers.

At this point, we must differentiate between the comprehensive community mental health center program sponsored by the federal government and the community mental health philosophy. The overall philosophical or theoretical approach called community mental health includes a variety of strategies that are not necessarily included in the massive practical application of the theoretical approach that the federally sponsored program represents. We will now discuss three concepts that are basic to the community mental health philosophy—primary, secondary, and tertiary prevention.

Three Levels of Prevention

Primary Prevention

The term primary prevention refers to strategies that are designed to eliminate the *causes* of emotional problems and thus eventually reduce the incidence of these problems. Primary prevention of emotional disturbance is not new. As early as 1915, Adolf Meyer began talking about preventive measures that could be carried out by juvenile courts, schools, hospitals, and churches. However, as we indicated earlier, little work has been done in prevention at this level.

Bloom (1965) has pointed out that primary prevention in the field of mental health is at a stage of development that is similar to the stage that public health was in when it began. The medical model, which was based on germ theory of disease, was not influential in early public health. The initial model in public health was *miasma theory,* which claimed that all diseases were caused by a poisonous gas, or miasma, from soil that was polluted with waste materials. In other words, breathing this bad air was the cause of infectious diseases. Obviously, this theory was completely incorrect, but led to a number of important public health measures. For example, the polluted areas were cleaned up or removed from populated areas; and thus the breeding grounds for the minute living organisms that actually cause disease were inadvertently removed. The following is a classic example of how appropriate public health measures could be taken for the wrong reasons: During a cholera epidemic in London during the nineteenth century, a man named Snow observed that people who drew their water from a certain well developed the disease. Although he knew nothing about germ theory or contaminated water, he stopped the epidemic by simply removing the handle on the pump.

Thus the major strategy for prevention of disease that resulted from miasma theory was to *modify the environment* by removing the sources of the miasma. In this sense then, mental health professionals, who have a strong theoretical orientation toward the prevention of mental "disease," try to modify the environment by removing the sources of stress that lead to emotional problems. In other words, poverty, social injustice, unemployment, and other socioeconomic factors are "psychological miasmas" that cause emotional problems. Although this approach to preventing mental illness is as imprecise as the miasma theory was for the prevention of physical disease, it suggests the reasonable proposition that eliminating severe stresses such as poverty should reduce the amount of emotional disorders in society.

One major principle of public health is that early detection and treatment will not eliminate disease. The greatest strides in the field have come from eliminating the breeding grounds for the microorganisms that cause disease and immunizing people against diseases such as smallpox, diphtheria, measles, polio, and so on. When translated into mental health, the principle becomes: we cannot eliminate or even significantly reduce the "epidemic" of emotional problems in our society unless we remove the *cause.* Thus the two major strategies in primary prevention of emotional problems are (1) to reduce stress

Figure 20.1 Many community mental health professions have proposed that poverty is like a "miasma" or poisonous gas that, as a serious stress in people's lives, leads to emotional problems.

in the environment and (2) to "immunize," or reduce people's susceptibility to the stress that exists in the environment (Bloom, 1973). See figure 20.1.

Reduction of Stress

Reducing stress in the environment is no easy task. The sources of potential stresses are almost unlimited and people differ not only in terms of tolerance for stress but in terms of what they perceive as stressful. Because no one can avoid phenomena such as death, natural disasters, occasional difficulties with their interpersonal relationships, and other stresses that are the result of being alive, it would be impossible to eliminate stress completely. In fact, many theories of personality claim that learning to cope successfully with stress is necessary for emotional growth. A life devoid of stress would be extremely dull. Indeed, how do we explain the fact that mountain climbers, sky divers, and racers seem to deliberately seek out stress rather than avoid it? So we should probably limit our discussion to the reduction of *unnecessary* stress, which would enable people to focus their energies on coping successfully with unavoidable stress.

The effect of stress on performance seems to follow an inverted U-shaped curve, a characteristic discussed earlier in Chapter 13; that is, in small amounts, stress seems to improve performance while extreme stress impairs performance.

There are numerous examples of small-scale attempts to reduce stress that have implications for mental health. For instance, some colleges have adopted a pass-fail system of grading students in an attempt to facilitate learning by removing the stress caused by evaluation. Architects are beginning to design office buildings so that monotony and noise are reduced while communication is facilitated—all of these factors contribute to job satisfaction. And motorists can be spared the frustration of having to stop constantly for traffic lights if the lights are properly synchronized.

Sometimes the major source of stress in a community seems to be only remotely connected to mental health. In a trailer park with signs of serious marital and familial disruption and delinquency, the primary complaint of residents was dogs running loose and the trash in people's yards! It may not be clear to the mental health professional how his or her training helps to solve that problem. Community psychologists always start helping people by responding first to their perceived needs, whatever they might be. In this particular case, the interpersonal skills developed during training may help the mental health professional help the community to solve its own problems.

Large-scale attempts to reduce stress are represented by the War on Poverty, job training programs, guaranteed income plans, and the like. Although these programs were designed to alleviate social injustice and human suffering, many proponents believe that one major side effect would be a significant reduction in the amount of emotional disorder that is so prevalent in our society.

Obviously, some stresses are severe and others are minor and subtle and how they contribute to the development of emotional problems is as yet unclear. The important point to keep in mind is that stressors tend to interact with one another. Thus although no one would claim that poorly synchronized traffic lights are a cause of major emotional problems (with the possible exception of the traffic cop) you can easily see that if a person must drive through heavy traffic after a highly stressful day at an office, to reach a home that is filled with conflict, the accumulation of stresses could result in emotional disorder.

As you can see from the examples just listed, many of the environmental changes that would lead to a reduction of stress are not within the psychologist's area of expertise. Economists, political scientists, sociologists, city planners, public health specialists, architects, engineers, and other members of the community all have something to say about how to reduce stress.

Decreasing Vulnerability to Stress

Psychologists *have* been actively involved in programs designed to help people cope with the stresses of life. There have been three primary strategies in this approach: identification of life crises, identification of populations at risk, and modifying the system for populations at risk.

Following Potential Life Crises

There are major potential crises that occur in almost everyone's life: entering school, entering high school, entering college, dating, marriage, first baby, job, relocation, divorce, or death of spouse. Caplan (1964) proposed that people are especially vulnerable to the stress connected with these transitional phases of life and by helping people anticipate the stresses associated with these changes, we can help them cope more effectively. This strategy is known as *anticipatory guidance* or emotional *inoculation* (Caplan, 1964). In small group or individual discussions, the mental health specialists help people who may go through such stress in the near future to understand what is likely to happen, the feelings that commonly accompany the event, and possible ways of solving the problems that occur. In this way, the person is better able to handle the stress.

This approach is used in many hospitals to help children anticipate the stress of surgery and may include a picture book of all the things that are going to happen (including a picture of how the ceiling will look as the patient is rolled into the operating room). Janis (1958) indicates that the stress of surgery, the cooperation with the postoperative treatment, and recovery are best in the person who has a realistic picture of the risk and amount of discomfort to be experienced. Bloom (1971) developed an anticipatory guidance program for college freshmen by soliciting answers to questionnaires about the stresses of the transition to college and then giving this information back to the students. By helping them understand what other students are experiencing, and by being given information about helping agencies on the campus, Bloom hopes to reduce the number of nonacademic dropouts on campus (which are generally more common than academic failures). Evaluations of the pilot project indicate that participating students were more likely to survive in college than students in a control group with no contact.

Identification of Populations at Risk

A population at risk is an identifiable group of people with a higher than average probability of developing a particular problem. An example from psychopathology is the research done on the relationship between hereditary factors and schizophrenia. Perhaps ten to fifteen percent of the children who are born to a parent diagnosed as schizophrenic are likely to develop the disorder by the age of forty-five. Thus, we would call the children of schizophrenics a population at risk for the development of schizophrenia. If, as we suggested in Chapter 2, schizophrenia is caused by a combination of genetic predisposition and certain kinds of environmental stresses, knowing that a child has a schizophrenic parent could lead to intervention techniques designed to avoid the kinds of stresses that might precipitate a psychosis.

Social epidemiology refers to the study of social forces that lead to emotional problems. By careful research on the relationship between demographic characteristics, such as age, marital status, job status, income, sex, number of moves, household population density, and the development of emotional problems as measured by contact with mental health centers, police, state hospitals, ministers, or any caregiver, intervention programs can be designed (see box 20.2). For example, Kramer (1967) reported that first admission rates in state mental hospitals is four times as great among single and not previously married persons as for married persons and six times as great for separated or divorced than for married persons. Moreover, males are more likely than females to be first admissions only if they are single and not previously married. However, separated, divorced, and widowed women are a greater risk for psychiatric hospitalization. Of particular high risk were widowed, divorced, and separated women and men who live alone, and divorced and separated females who were head of families.

An example of intervention programs with populations at risk is Silverman's research with the widowed (see box 20.3). Death of a husband can be a strong stressor in our society, particularly if the husband was the sole wage earner in the family. Silverman (1967, 1972) hired widows to serve as counselors to recently widowed persons under sixty years of age. Sudden death requires a mourning process over the loss of the loved one. Sudden changes in financial status require help in coping with a new world. Loneliness is a major problem. Pathology was particularly strong in widows and widowers who could not give up the role of spouse, and who acted as though the dead spouse were still alive. Although research on the effectiveness of the program is not yet complete, new widowed individuals reported that the widow-counselors were very helpful to them in their crises.

Modification of the System

The third approach to decreasing vulnerability to stress as a primary prevention technique is to modify society to make it more responsive to potential problems. There are two social systems that touch the lives of almost everyone, the family and the school. The family is a small group, loosely organized with little formal organization between families. The schools are part of a social system with formal

Box 20.2

The Social Epidemiology of Emotional Problems

The interaction of social factors and psychopathology can lead to intervention programs involving social change. Early research in this area involved studies of the relationship between diagnostic categories of hospitalized psychiatric patients and social factors, such as place of residence, age, sex, and socioeconomic status. One early study in the area of the social epidemiology of emotional problems was done by Faris and Dunham (1938), who found that as one moves from the more affluent suburbs of a city to its poorer, more disorganized sections, the level of psychopathology increases. They proposed that social disorganization and isolation played a role in the cause of psychopathology.

In a much later study, Hollingshead and Redlich (1958) found that psychotic disorders are much more likely to occur in the lower classes than in the middle and upper classes. The prevalence rate (i.e., all known patients in treatment on a certain date) of schizophrenia in the lowest socioeconomic class was approximately eight times higher than that in the highest socioeconomic class. Neuroses were found to be more common in the higher socioeconomic classes.

In both studies, the investigators tried to determine whether the social drift hypothesis could account for the relationship. This hypothesis states that social disorganization is not the cause of schizophrenia, but the result of these disorders. People who have minimal social skills, and who are more comfortable being left alone, are more likely to migrate to the poor part of a city, where it is also easier to survive on minimal income. Both groups of investigators felt that they eliminated social drift as an explanation for the high rates of schizophrenia in the lower class. Wolman (1965), in summarizing several research studies, notes that the parents of schizophrenics seem to come from all classes, and psychosis in children occurs in all classes, again suggesting that the relationship could be a result of the disorder rather than a cause. Because of the extreme social mobility in our culture, particularly among the lower classes, the social drift hypothesis is particularly difficult to test.

Another problem in the interpretation of such results is revealed in the finding by Hollingshead and Redlich that people in the lower classes were much more likely to be coerced into treatment. Numerous people have noted that private hospitalization that occurs with upper-class psychiatric problems is more likely to result in a diagnosis with less social stigma attached to it. Thus, upper-class schizophrenics may simply not be labeled as such.

Community surveys of mental disorders were done in two groups of studies during the 1950s. In the Midtown Manhattan Study (Srole, Langner, Michael, Opler, and Rennie, 1962; Langner and Michael, 1963), the investigators interviewed 1,660 residents that represented a cross section of all adults in the area under study. One unique aspect of this study was that the data were obtained from community residents rather than from mental hospitals, which are usually used in such studies. After interviewing the community residents extensively, they rated the mental health of each person. They reported finding extraordinary levels of pathology. Forty percent of the residents were judged to have mild symptoms of psychopathology and twenty-one percent showed moderate symptoms, neither group at a level that would lead to a psychiatric diagnosis. Another twenty percent were judged to have serious emotional problems. Only eighteen percent were viewed as showing no signs of emotional disorder. When the researchers examined the data more closely, they found (as have other studies) that the severe emotional problems were more likely to be found among older residents and among those from lower socioeconomic groups.

Bloom (1974) provides us with an example of social epidemiological research that has implications for intervention strategies. Bloom found that in Pueblo, Colorado, 7.5 percent of all divorced men (and 2.3 percent of all divorced women) were hospitalized *each* year for psychiatric disability. This finding suggests that anticipatory guidance strategies for divorced men could possibly reduce the psychiatric risk for this population. However, Bloom points out that men with emotional problems may have more difficulty maintaining a stable marriage.

Box 20.3
Grief Crises: Two Case Histories

A woman, aged 40, the mother of a 10-year-old child, lost her husband in a fire. She had a history of good adjustment previously. When she heard about her husband's death she became extremely depressed, cried bitterly, did not want to live, and for three days showed a state of utter dejection.

When seen by the psychiatrist, she was glad to have assistance and described her painful preoccupation with memories of her husband and her fear that she might lose her mind. She had a vivid visual image of his presence, picturing him as going to work in the morning and herself as wondering whether he would return in the evening. . . . She gradually tried to accept the fact that he was not there any more. It was only after ten days that she succeeded in accepting his loss and then only after she had described in detail the remarkable qualities of her husband, the tragedy of his having to stop his activities at the pinnacle of his success, and his deep devotion to her.

In the subsequent interviews she explained with some distress that she had become very much attached to the examiner and that she waited eagerly for his coming. This reaction she considered disloyal to her husband but at the same time she could accept the fact that it was a hopeful sign of her ability to fill the gap his death had left in her life. She then showed a marked drive for activity, making plans for supporting herself and her little girl, mapping out the preliminary steps for resuming her former work as secretary, and making efforts to secure help from the occupational therapy department in reviewing her knowledge of French. Her convalescence, both emotional and somatic, progressed smoothly, and she made a good adjustment on her return home.

A successful businessman of 52 had lost his wife, with whom he had lived happily. He responded with a severe grief reaction with which he was unable to cope. He did not want to see visitors, was ashamed of breaking down, and asked to be permitted to stay in the hospital psychiatric service because he wanted further assistance. . . . Any mention of his wife produced a severe wave of depressive reaction, but with psychiatric assistance he gradually became willing to go through this painful process, and after three days on the psychiatric service he seemed well enough to go home. . . .

As soon as he returned home he took an active part in his business, assuming a post in which he had a great many telephone calls. He also took over the role of amateur psychiatrist to another bereaved person, spending time with him and comforting him for his loss. In his eagerness to start anew, he developed a plan to sell all his former holdings, including his home and furniture, and to give away anything that could remind him of his wife. Only after considerable discussion was he able to see that this would mean avoiding grief at the price of an act of poor judgment. Again he had to be encouraged to deal with his grief reactions in a more direct manner. He has made a good adjustment. (Lindemann, 1944)

lines of power and responsibility and bureaucratic structure. The greater the extent to which we can modify either of these institutions to be more responsive to potential problems, the greater the impact on all of our society. If we change the structure of the school, we have intervened at the level of stress reduction in the environment. There are several strategies for helping people that can be viewed as a combination of stress reduction and identification of populations at risk. Over a period of several years Cowen and his colleagues (Zax and Cowen, 1967) devised a method of identifying first graders who seemed to have a strong potential for developing emotional problems in the future. These investigators then trained housewives and undergraduate volunteers to work with these children during and after school in informal talks, recreation, or academic work, in a warm supportive environment. Children at risk who participated in the program experienced less anxiety, superior achievement, and were better liked by teachers and peers than children at risk who were not given an opportunity to participate in the program. Here is one of the few examples where intervention made a clear difference in preventing emotional problems.

The concept of primary prevention seems at first glance to be unattackable. Yet, when it is looked at more closely, several problems arise. Some people have argued that we simply do not have the technology at the present time to do anything major in primary prevention. The various interactions of causes are so complex that we do not know what variables to manipulate to produce change. When it comes to complex problems, like schizophrenia, with its genetic, familial, social, and biochemical causes, the criticism may be quite valid. However, as Zax and Cowen's studies demonstrate, when the problem can be narrowly defined and the degree of pathology is not great, intervention is possible.

A much more serious attack on the concept of primary intervention concerns the question of *who makes the decision* to intervene. Often we cannot obtain the permission to change the environment to reduce stress from those whose lives will be affected. For example, society has decided that children who are physically abused by their parents should be removed from the home. But suppose that society decides that children who are psychologically abused by their parents should also be removed from the home. Despite the obvious primary prevention implications of such a move, serious ethical questions are involved. Such a move goes against a strong value in our society that gives parents the right to rear their children any way they want, within broad limits. Can we predict with absolute certainty that psychological damage will occur? Because serious ethical problems may exist in the area of primary prevention, they should not be an excuse for avoiding primary prevention entirely.

Secondary Prevention

Secondary prevention refers to techniques that are designed to treat the symptoms of emotional problems. Traditional psychotherapy is an example of secondary prevention. Several intervention strategies have developed from a need to have more available, more efficient treatment procedures than one-to-one psychotherapy. One example is *crisis intervention*. (See fig. 20.2.)

Crisis Intervention

Caplan (1964) defined crisis as an "imbalance between the difficulty and the importance of the problem and resources immedi-

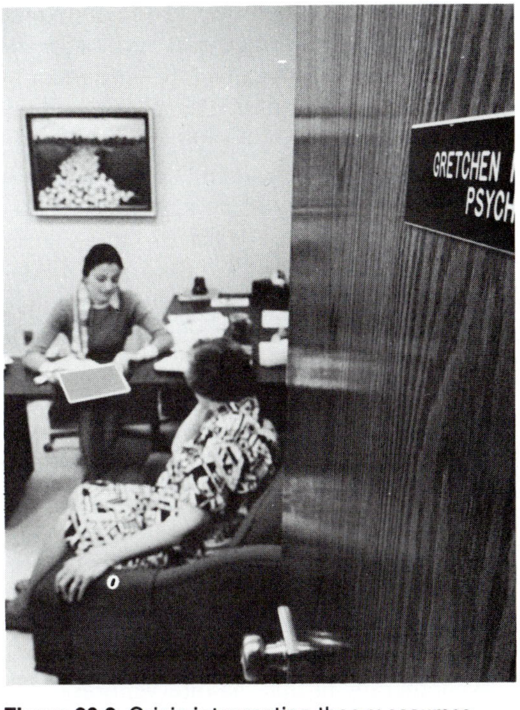

Figure 20.2 Crisis intervention theory assumes that a person is more open to change and growth in therapy when under stress than during non-stressful times in their lives.

ately available to deal with it" (p. 39). The person caught in this situation feels that he is faced with an insoluble problem and feels helpless and overwhelmed. In an attempt to cope with the crisis, he may try to lose himself in other activities or repeatedly try inadequate solutions to the problem. According to Caplan, an individual who faces a crisis goes through four stages.

1. His tension increases and he responds by applying his usual methods of solving problems.

2. When his typical method of problem-solving fails, his level of anxiety rises sharply.

3. This stress acts as a powerful stimulus for the mobilization of reserves and emergency problem-solving mechanisms. He then tries novel solutions to the problem—that is, a process of trial and error. Or he may give up.

4. If the crisis continues, the individual may reach the breaking point and major disorganization of his personality may occur.

The basic assumption of crisis intervention is that during a crisis, an individual is particularly receptive to treatment. With the proper experiences, he may learn new ways of coping. The person may learn to handle stress more appropriately in the future. Crisis intervention typically is time-limited, lasting anywhere from two to eight sessions. Usually, the sessions are held during one or two weeks, since crises are seldom so obliging as to wait for resolution for once-a-week sessions spread over two months. The intervention may be in a crisis center or over the telephone. Many mental health centers maintain twenty-four-hour telephone service to aid those who need immediate help or are too timid or cautious to come in to the center.

Crisis intervention differs from traditional psychotherapy in that the intervention is limited to the cause of the crisis. The therapist does not attempt to explore other areas or concern himself with the individual's overall psychological growth. The first task of the crisis intervention specialist is to help the person define the problem (see box 20.4). People in crisis are often confused about exactly what the problem is. Sometimes the crisis involves several problems and thus no single solution is possible. With some people, defining the problem may be ninety percent of the intervention. In most cases, however, once the problem is defined, the caregiver tries to help the individual explore alternative solutions. Sometimes solutions simply do not occur to the person, and frequently, they simply reject alternatives without thinking them through. We have all heard people who are upset make remarks such as the following "I couldn't tell him that!" "Divorce is out of the question." "If I can't get into graduate school, there is nothing else I want to do."

Once the alternatives have been explored, the individual may need help in deciding which alternative will bring the most benefits and the least negative effects. Once the individual has learned to use these techniques, he will be able to apply them to future crises. In addition, self-esteem increases because the problem is handled successfully.

One important form of crisis intervention involves the prevention of suicide. A person who considers suicide as a means of solving their problems is almost always in the midst of a crisis. Suicide prevention centers have been set up in many areas across the country since the late 1950s; the most well known and innovative center of this kind is the Suicide Prevention Center of Los Angeles.

There are several facts about suicide attempts that make a prevention center reasonable. Suicidal individuals are often highly *ambivalent* about killing themselves; that is, although they want to die, they also want to live and therefore are possible candidates for intervention. Thus the suicide prevention counselor attempts to align himself with that part of the person which wants to live. The

Box 20.4

Crisis Intervention

Margie, an extremely attractive young woman in the process of divorce from her third husband, was referred to a crisis intervention center for help because of severe depression and anxiety. This was manifested by insomnia, lack of appetite, tremulousness, inability to concentrate, and frequent crying spells. These symptoms had begun three weeks earlier when she was notified of the date of the divorce proceedings. She had lost her job because she was unable to control her crying spells and had subsequently developed bursitis in her shoulder, which further limited her ability to work. Her symptoms had intensified so much in the past three days that she felt she was losing complete control over her emotions and needed help.

During the initial session, Margie stated that she did not want a divorce and that she still loved her husband, even though he did not love her. When questioned about the increased intensity of symptoms that had begun three days ago, she stated that at that time she had been informed by her attorney that the only way she could receive alimony would be to countersue for divorce.

In Margie's previous two divorces she had remained a passive participant; her husbands had sued her for divorce. She had accepted these and had not contested. Now, for the first time, due to her inability to work she was forced to become an active participant in a divorce she did not want. She stated frequently that "something must be wrong with me if I can't hold a husband," and later commented, "I don't feel this is a good marriage—but I hate to fail again." This ambivalence and her expressed guilt feelings were felt to be part of the crisis-precipitating event, as was the necessity of being forced to take an active part in a divorce she did not want.

Margie had almost totally withdrawn from her social and family contacts. Her mother came occasionally to give her money for rent and bring her food. Beyond this social contact she remained isolated in the apartment she had previously shared with her husband, weeping at intervals, staring at her husband's picture, and unable to decide whether or not to contest the divorce.

The goal of intervention was established by the therapist to assist Margie to recognize and cope with her feelings of ambivalence and guilt. Unrecognized feelings about her marriage and the impending divorce would also be explored. In the next three weeks, through direct questioning and reflection of verbal and nonverbal clues to Margie, it became possible for her to view the present crisis and its effect upon her in relationship to her previous marriages and divorces.

Margie wanted desperately to marry in order to become a housewife and mother. Her usual social contacts and previous patterns of meeting men (bowling alleys and bars) and her impulsive marriages (Las Vegas, three times) and reasons for marriage ("I thought I could help him . . . he needed me") were not meeting this need. The men she had met and married, and who later divorced her, were men who did not want to "settle down" with a wife and children. Instead, they wanted a gay, attractive companion to show off to their friends. Margie always hoped that they would change after marriage. However, they remained unchanged and divorced Margie when she persistently suggested "starting a family." With each marriage and subsequent divorce her guilt feelings about her ability to be a good wife magnified. With the loss of her previous patterns of coping the third divorce precipitated this crisis.

After the third session Margie's depression and symptoms had lessened as she recognized the possibility that the failure of her marriages may not have been in her "inability to be a good wife" but in the disparity between what she wanted and expected from a marriage and what the men she had married wanted and expected. (Aguilera, Messick, and Farrell, 1970.)

part of the person that wants to live will frequently communicate the desire to commit suicide so that others will have an opportunity to stop it. This communication may consist of calling a suicide prevention center and talking to the counselor about suicidal wishes. Sometimes, these communications are more nonverbal, for example, suddenly writing a will or giving away prized possessions. Mental health professionals feel that even these subtle expressions of suicidal ideas indicate the wish for someone to intervene. Finally, suicidal wishes tend to be short-lived. Even short-term intervention can prevent people from killing themselves.

Recently, some humanistic psychologists have made a strong statement of the right of a person to decide to commit suicide. Is intervention then unethical? First, those who call a prevention center already want help. It is, in fact, ultimately impossible to prevent someone from committing suicide. All a prevention counselor can do is try to show an individual that, in almost all cases, there are other ways to solve a problem.

The suicide prevention counselor uses several criteria to determine the amount of suicide risk that exists:

1. *Sex.* For the country as a whole, males of all ages are three times more likely to *commit* suicide than are females. Females, on the other hand, are approximately three times as likely to *attempt* suicide. (Yolles, 1965)

2. *Age.* Generally the older the suicidal person, the more likely they will actually commit suicide. Black males between the ages of 20 and 35 are exceptions to this finding (Hendin, 1969).

3. *Marital status.* Married people are about half as likely to commit suicide as those who have never been married. Widowed persons are only slightly higher risks than singles. However, the risk of suicide for both divorced males and females is more than twice that of unmarried persons and almost four times that of married persons. In spite of the common belief that divorce is harder on women than on men, divorced men are three and one-half times as likely to kill themselves as divorced women (Yolles, 1965).

4. *Lethality of the suicide plan.* People who have vague ideas about how to kill themselves are at less risk than those who pick highly lethal means of killing themselves. Aspirin, while potentially lethal, is less likely to kill than a gun. Furthermore, if the means are available, the risk is greater than if the person must obtain the means.

5. *Emotional support.* What significant others does the person have in his or her life? What is the attitude of these other people toward the messages of suicide potential? Where other people exist whom the suicidal person depends on, developing such contacts can strongly reduce the suicide risk. It is not unusual, for whatever reason, for significant others to ignore the suicide hints. Such a response may be due to insensitivity, anxiety, and even approval. For example, if a husband "forgets" to follow the doctor's instructions to remove sleeping pills from the house after his wife was hospitalized for an overdose, his wife may interpret his behavior as a wish that she will kill herself.

The suicide counselor goes through several steps in working over the phone or in person with a suicidal person. How demanding and active the counselor is, and how much the counselor lets the suicidal person take responsibility depend on the counselor's perception of the suicide risk. If risk is low, the counselor can afford to be more passive, and turn over more of the responsibility to the person who is asking for help. (See fig. 20.3.)

First, the counselor establishes a relationship that indicates warmth, support, acceptance of the story and feelings of the suicidal person, and support for the act of calling for help. While establishing a relationship, the counselor helps the suicidal person define his

Figure 20.3 The suicide prevention counselor, "hot-line" or phone crisis worker is often a volunteer from the community who has undergone intensive training in active listening, evaluation of suicide potential, intervention and referral.

problem or problems. Frequently, this step alone greatly reduces the risk of suicide. People are often quite confused about what exactly the problem is, making it understandable why it was so difficult to find a solution. After determining what the problem is (which may take several sessions) the counselor tries to help the person find alternative solutions. Implicit in this solution is the attempt to help the person establish contact with someone in the community who can serve as a potential source of support, a doctor, minister, or friend.

A Study of Student Suicide

The leading causes of death among fifteen- to nineteen-year-olds are accidents, cancer, and suicide—in that order. Among college students, suicide is the second most common cause of death. Although the total number of *actual* suicides among college students is low compared with the rest of the population, the *risk* of suicide is extremely high (Yolles, 1965). Seiden (1966) studied twenty-three suicides that occurred at the University of California from 1952 to 1962. Although the size of Seiden's sample is small compared with those used in many research studies, he found several significant differences between suicidal students and the student body as a whole. Table 20.1 summarizes these results. It appears that the population at risk for suicide on the college campus are older, graduate, and foreign students who have had contact with the mental health service at some point during their college career.

It is also interesting to note Seiden's findings about when student suicides are most likely to occur. Oddly enough suicides are not likely to occur during final examination time. Suicides happened more often during holidays or on the first warm spring day. Most people are not surprised that they feel depressed during final week or when the weather is bad. But if they continue to be depressed after the weather or the situation improves, the risk of suicide increases.

Tertiary Prevention

Tertiary prevention refers to intervention strategies designed to correct for the *results* of emotional problems. This level of prevention is often referred to as *rehabilitation.* Many patients who are discharged from state hospitals need help in adjusting to life outside

Table 20.1 Demographic characteristics in which suicidal and nonsuicidal students differ for the University of California at Berkeley, 1952–1961.

Demographic Characteristics	Suicidal Students (percentage)	Total Student Body Population (percentage)
Age		
Under 25	39	70
25 and above	61	30
Class Standing		
Undergraduate	52	72
Graduate	48	28
Nationality		
U.S.A.	83	96
Foreign	17	4
Mental-health service		
Psychiatric Patient	34	10
Nonpatient	66	90

Note: Suicidal students did not differ from the total student body in terms of percentages by sex, race, religion, marital status.

Source: From Seiden, H.R. "Campus Tragedy: A study of student suicide." *Journal of Abnormal Psychology*, 1966, *71*, pp. 389–399. Copyright 1966 by the American Psychological Association. Reprinted by permission.

the hospital, and even nonhospitalized clients of mental health centers wish to learn new job skills or increase their social effectiveness. Rehabilitation can occur in the areas of vocational training, development of social skills, and residential rehabilitation (the ability to function by oneself or in the context of a family and to maintain basic and social needs).

Many ex-mental patients are overwhelmed by the prospect of returning to the outside world, which requires them to support themselves, assume the role of husband or wife, father or mother, and friend—a world that had adjusted to life without them. Vocational rehabilitation has perhaps received the greatest emphasis in tertiary prevention (see box 20.5). Many jobs are relatively easy roles to fill. The demands may be set forth in a relatively structured way as compared to the role of friend or parent. It has been estimated that around forty percent of ex-mental patients can rid themselves of the ex-patient identity and find jobs on their own in the outside world. However, not all mental patients need rehabilitation to obtain jobs. Olshansky (1968) refers to the belief that all ex-mental patients are incapable of assuming their former life roles as the "myth of transitionalism," which makes mental health professionals assume that all ex-patients need a network of transitional institutions to supply them with skills that are usable in the labor market. According to Olshansky's estimates, approximately twenty-five percent of patients who are discharged from mental hospitals are rehabilitated to the working world. Another

Box 20.5
The Sheltered Workshop

The Sheltered Workshop provides vocational rehabilitation for mental patients and ex-mental patients to give them training and to allow them to perform duties associated with typical job placements. In a Sheltered Workshop, a mental health clinic or mental hospital contracts with local businesses to provide a variety of simple work jobs that can be done in a Sheltered Workshop under the supervision of mental health professionals. In this protected setting the patients learn to get to work on time, gradually increasing the amount of work to the point where they can work an entire day, maintain their work over long periods of time, and behave appropriately with peers at the job and handle employee-employer relationships.

Typically, participants in a Sheltered Workshop are paid on a piece-work basis. Thus as their productivity approaches that of the average worker, their pay also approaches the appropriate level.

Working and supporting oneself are important values in American society. Self-esteem increases when a person becomes capable of being partially or totally self-supporting. Our culture does not encourage individuals to be dependent upon others for livelihood. It also allows individuals to move toward more appropriate roles that are defined as normal in our culture. Income gives an individual a new source of freedom of movement and of use of leisure time. The role of work in our society is one of the basic roles for defining appropriate behavior.

thirty-five to forty percent will require long-term services because they will never be able to return to work. Halfway houses are residential treatment centers that are designed to serve patients returning to the community. These homes are designed to provide support in a controlled environment to ex-mental patients and yet move from a sheltered environment in a group setting toward the more demanding world outside the hospital. Ex-patients have formed clubs for socialization purposes and ex-patient advocacy groups have been formed to demand their right to treatment and job opportunities.

Manpower

Since World War II, when Congress began to support the provision of services to people with emotional problems, the problem of adequate manpower has been a major concern. While the medical model predominated, most therapists were psychiatrists. But even after other mental health professionals began to provide therapy, it was clear that there were not enough therapists to go around. The population was growing faster than the number of therapists. Even when the federal government began providing funds to train mental health professionals, the field seemed hopelessly behind in satisfying the country's needs. And in the 1970s the government decided that it could no longer afford to provide major financial support for training mental health professionals and developing services. In addition, the development of mental health centers was severely curtailed and it seemed unlikely that a significantly greater number of centers would be built. The approximately 500 existing centers is far short of the 2,000 catchment areas originally identified for service.

The services that psychologists, psychiatrists, psychiatric nurses, and psychiatric social workers provide are expensive, and the federal government is becoming increasingly reluctant to spend tax dollars in this way. Thus it is clear that alternatives to the presently existing system of mental health care are necessary. We have already discussed several of these alternatives—crisis intervention and primary intervention. Two additional strategies to increase the means of providing for mental health needs involve using the skills of professionals more efficiently as consultants, and training people who lack formal

Box 20.6

Training Police Officers as Intervention Specialists in Family Crises

Police are in an unusual position to identify, advise, and refer people who have emotional problems; and the nature of the policeman's job often results in high levels of stress which could be effectively reduced.

An estimated seventy to ninety percent of the calls the police receive do not involve law enforcement. One kind of call that is especially dangerous for the officer who responds to it, is family disturbance. Thirty-five percent of all homicides in New York City in 1965 involved family members or close friends, and twenty-two percent of the policemen killed in the line of duty are on calls of disturbance, many of which are family disturbances. Such calls account for forty percent of the time lost to injuries (Bard, 1970).

The officer who enters a house during a family disturbance faces a potentially dangerous situation; anger is high, one or both persons do not want him there (the call may have been made by a neighbor), and violence can easily be displaced onto the officer. How the officer responds to this explosive situation may determine whether they or someone else will be injured and whether the family develops a better way of resolving their disagreements.

Bard (1970) devised a special program to train police officers to handle family crises. In a New York City police precinct serving a population of 85,000 people, eighteen officers volunteered for this program.

These officers received 160 hours of training, including instruction in the psychology and role-playing of family crisis situations. One patrol car was designated the Family Crisis Intervention Unit. Although this car was on regular patrol, whenever a call came in concerning a family crisis, this car was dispatched, regardless of where it was located at the time. During busy hours other officers were available on a backup basis. Consultation to the officers was provided on a continuous basis.

After the program had been in existence for twenty months, they found:

1. The number of requests for police intervention had risen sharply.
2. Homicides had increased (this may have been a random result).
3. Family homicides in the experimental precinct had also increased. However, there were no homicides in the 962 families that had received help from the crisis unit.
4. Family assaults decreased.
5. No officer was injured during a family crisis call.
6. The crisis unit's impression was that the community was much more receptive to the unit's patrol car than to other patrol cars because the officers noted that residents did not "freeze" when the car entered the neighborhood. This training program is an example of how a non-mental-health professional can be trained to handle more effectively the emotional problems of the people he or she serves.

training in the mental health field to provide mental health services as paraprofessionals.

Community Mental Health Consultation

Community mental health consultation refers to the consultation provided by mental health professionals to caregivers within a community, such as ministers, police, courts, public health nurses, welfare workers, politicians, and teachers, in order to help them respond more effectively to people who have emotional problems. Even bartenders and beauticians are potential mental health resources in the community. The mental health consultant does not try to change these people into psychotherapists, but helps them perform their roles better. For example, teachers who know how to reduce the level of aggression in the classroom will be more comfortable in their jobs and the children will learn better. (See figs. 20.4 and 20.5.)

Non-mental-health professionals are the people in contact with the hurting people in our society (see box 20.6). In a study sponsored by the Joint Commission on Mental Illness and Health, Gurin, Veroff and Feld (1960), found that less than twenty percent of the people who sought help with an emotional problem went to see a mental health professional. The largest number (42 percent) went to a clergyman; the second largest group (29 percent) went to nonpsychiatric physicians! By helping these people better respond to these requests for help, the need for long-term contact with mental health professionals can be reduced. More importantly, many people who would never have received help from a mental health professional benefit from the help from the caregiver. For some caregivers, it is not a question of giving advice to individuals, but how to help the person under their care. How does the teacher help the withdrawn child or aggressive child?

Figure 20.1 indicates how mental health consultation differs from medical consultation. If a physician needs help in diagnosing or treating a patient, this may be provided by a medical consultant, who independently diagnoses the patient and either assumes the responsibility for treating the patient or gives the referring physician suggestions for treatment. Typically, the mental health consultant receives a request for help from a caregiver in handling the problems the client presents. The consultant usually responds to the problem based on information provided by the consultee, although he may observe or interview the client himself. In other words, the consultant does not take over either the diagnosis or treatment but helps the consultees develop alternative solutions to the problem so that they can return to their jobs, hopefully better able to respond to the problem.

Figure 20.4 Mental health consultation with the police can lead to both the police and the mental health professional to lose stereotypes of each other. Riding in a patrol car during regular patrols can help the professional understand the policeman's job, encourage trust, and facilitate appropriate solutions to mental health problems.

Figure 20.5 A mental health consultant can provide a teacher with mental health principles that could affect his or her effectiveness as a teacher for years thus benefiting a large number of children.

Altrocchi (1972) has identified three sets of roles and functions for the mental health consultant: teaching and training, facilitating communication, and promoting new ideas. The teaching and training function refers to the transmission of specific skills and information about mental health problems. The skills may be given to the consultee by direct instruction or by example. The consultant may facilitate communication between consultee and client, may help with communication, either within a group receiving consultation or between agencies. Often the consultant finds it necessary to facilitate communication between an agency and the community, or between different groups in the community. As a promoter of new ideas, the consultant may try to develop new, novel solutions to community problems. Sometimes such solutions border on political activism.

This approach represents an efficient use of the consultant's time. This may involve a few hours developing a solution to the problem that will be carried out by the consultee, whereas if the consultant had seen the client individually in psychotherapy, positive results might take much time. The other major advantage of consultation is that the consultee not only learns to handle a particular problem, but hopefully, similar kinds of problems encountered in the future. When acting as consultant, the mental health professional keeps the following principles in mind: (1) allow the consultee to accept or reject advice, (2) do not attempt to adopt a supervisory role with the consultee, (3) try to develop solutions that are consistent with the requirements of the consultee's job, and (4) help the consultee learn *how* to solve the problems.

During a typical consultation, the consultant gathers as much information from the consultee as possible. Although many consultees can describe the behavior of their clients accurately, their interpretation of the behavior may be in error. Therefore, the consultant tries to understand why the consultee cannot solve the problem. Does the consultee simply lack information about how to solve these problems? Is he emotionally over–involved with the client? Does he lack self-confidence, that is, would he be able to solve the problem if he only trusted himself? Or is he struggling with what Caplan (1974) calls "theme interference" which means that his bias against the client or the client's behavior prevents him from being effective? For example, does he make remarks such as the following? "All unmarried pregnant girls are impulsive, sinful, and totally immoral." "All effeminate six-grade boys are homosexual. Homosexuals are basically different from other people." "People who talk too much are empty-headed." After the consultant has determined the reasons for the consultee's difficulties, a strategy can be devised to help him. If the consultee simply lacks information, a simple explanation will be all that is required. If theme interference occurs, the consultant may work for several short sessions to break up the theme and help the consultee see that such consequences are not inevitable.

Research on mental health consultation is in an early stage of development. Many of the early publications are case histories, developing the theory of consultation and the intervention techniques. Few studies have been done, and most of them have inadequate measures of effectiveness or poor controls. Two levels of effectiveness have been investigated, the behavior of the consultee and the behavior of the client. For the few studies that have been done, the pattern seems to indicate that the consultee appreciates the opportunities for consultation because he feels less anxiety about dealing with clients, feels more competent and effective. Positive changes in clients' behavior have been harder to document; some studies show changes, while others indicate little effect.

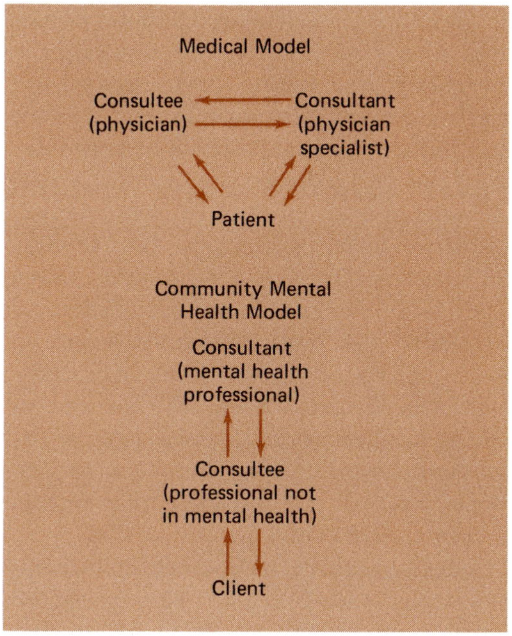

Figure 20.6 Consultation. In medical consultation, the consultant sees the client (patient) for diagnosis or may assume responsibility for treatment. In community mental health consultation, the consultant works only with the consultee to improve his or her effectiveness and may not see the client at all.

Paraprofessionals

The term *paraprofessional* refers to a person who is recruited from the community and trained to assume some of the professionals duties. When a paraprofessional is recruited from a poor neighborhood and is a member of a minority group, he is often called an *indigenous paraprofessional.* The term paraprofessional was coined because those who filled these jobs objected to being called "nonprofessional" because it somehow implied that they were less concerned or less prestigious. The term "psychiatric technician," which is sometimes used in mental health centers, may imply either a paraprofessional or someone who has more mental health training, but does not have a bachelors degree. (See fig. 20.7.)

Paraprofessionals are obviously one answer to the manpower problem. Because it is far less expensive to train paraprofessionals, the mental health center can provide less costly service. The indigenous paraprofessional is *not* just an undertrained mental health professional. Because his background

Figure 20.7 Paraprofessionals may help people to organize to protest unfair rents or insensitive public service agencies or even band together as a community to clean up trash in the area.

is poverty and because his language, ethnic origin, and interests are the same as the clients he serves, he has unique communication skills, which are generally unavailable to the mental health professional; he understands the problems of the poor, and is therefore in a position to develop solutions that would not occur to the average mental health professional. Of necessity, the indigenous paraprofessional, like his neighbors, has learned how to survive on welfare income, how to cope with bureaucratic red tape, and how to handle an insensitive and uncaring landlord. As we pointed out in Chapter 16, certain basic needs, such as nutrition and safety, must be satisfied before people can concentrate on more complex needs such as emotional satisfactions. Such a hierarchy of needs was developed by Maslow. It is precisely these basic needs that the poor must concentrate on fulfilling. Because most mental health professionals come from middle-class backgrounds, they have difficulty understanding the problems facing the poor. Thus the paraprofessional, perhaps a lower-class member himself, can serve as a bridge between the mental health professional and the lower-class client.

One paraprofessional described the reason for his choice of job in the following way: "Well, people have always come to me to talk about their problems. Now I get paid for it." By identifying the natural sources of help within a community and making them more available, the mental health center provides clients with someone who understands them and can expedite communications with community agencies by acting as an interpreter, negotiator, and instructor. (See box 20.7.)

As you probably realize, paraprofessionals do not need to be lower-class poor. Middle-class housewives with no graduate level training can be effective psychotherapists. One early example of using housewives as therapists was reported by Rioch et al. (1963), who developed a training program for housewives who were interested in developing a new career. She selected eight women, all middle-class mothers, from over fifty applicants. Selections were based on a short autobiography, group discussions, and interviews. The women were involved in both practical experience under supervision, and lectures and seminars. Training took two years with a large amount of experience in providing services during this time. Evaluation based on direct observation of their work indicated a high level of competence. The amount of training for these housewives was more extensive than is typical in the use of paraprofessionals, but their role was more traditional in the provision of psychotherapy services.

College students can also be effective therapists. Poser (1966) compared experienced mental health professionals with undergraduate women in a treatment program involving group psychotherapy for more than three hundred chronic schizophrenics. Some of the patients were treated in groups led by eighteen-year-old female undergraduates who had no special training; others were members of psychotherapy groups led by mental health professionals, the third group was designated as a control group. There were ten patients in each group, which met one hour a day, five days a week, for five months. In both treatment conditions, the patients showed greater improvement than in the nontreated control group. However, there was significantly greater improvement in the groups led by the young girls than in the groups of mental health professionals. It is clear that under certain conditions, nonprofessionals may have a greater impact than professionals. Whether the critical factors in this result are the age, sex, and degree of involvement and enthusiasm of the nontrained therapist is not known. But in any case, the paraprofessional can play a unique *and* effective role in helping people who have emotional problems.

Box 20.7

The Storefront Mental Health Center: The Neighborhood Service Center

One recent effort described by Zax and Specter (1974) at using paraprofessionals to aid neighborhoods is the Neighborhood Service Centers developed by Lincoln Hospital of the Albert Einstein College of Medicine (Riessman, 1967; Hallowitz and Riessman, 1967) in New York City. Lincoln Hospital had as its charge provision of mental health services to the South Bronx region of New York City, an area of 350,000 people. This area is one with high levels of emotional problems, homicide, suicide, crime, and unemployment. The first Neighborhood Service Center set up in 1965 was based in a storefront. Offices were, therefore, close to the people to be served and in a setting familiar to the community. Large sterile hospitals at some distance from parts of the community can leave the residents lost, fearful or angry at the difficulty at getting services, knowing who to ask, where to go, and what to do next.

The average Neighborhood Service Center had five to ten paraprofessionals who were from the neighborhood that was being served. In addition there might be one or two professional staff, who directed the center. Paraprofessionals were selected on the basis of being empathetic, comfortable in groups, good at communication, flexible, self-aware, handling stress well, having little personal pathology and having had relevant experiences.

The Neighborhood Service Center operations are described by Riessman (1967) as follows:

> The NSC (Neighborhood Service Center) escapes the office atmosphere, shortens intake procedures and makes them less formal, has no waiting lists, accepts any problem in any form, does not require continued visits, catches people at the point of crises, uses treatment agents recruited from the population itself who can be informal, personal, and friendly. It helps people with concrete, present-oriented problems and provides directive advice and assistance (i.e., it does not demand that the individual do it himself). Its staff is willing to make home visits at any time and participates in all types of activities including funerals, outings, helping people to move, and extinguishing fires in apartments. (Riessman, 1967.)

Much of what the Neighborhood Service Center takes on as projects has strong community social action implications. For example, such programs include: voter registration, block cleanups, antidrug campaigns, protests about local agency operations, and work in collaboration with schools, welfare and housing. In many ways such a program has a more community psychology orientation than community mental health. The focus of services is much broader than the frequency of neurosis in the community.

Obviously the paraprofessional is an extremely effective community resource because he can, with relatively little training, develop skills in crisis intervention and short-term psychotherapy. However, long-term therapy, which involves more complex problems, is more skillfully handled by professionals than paraprofessionals. This is not likely to be a major problem in most mental health centers, because the focus is on short-term treatment.

One major problem associated with the use of paraprofessionals is their tendency to identify with professionals. The status and power in a mental health center is centered on the trained mental health professionals, and the more training they have the more power they typically have. By looking toward the mental health professional as a model, the paraprofessional begins to acquire the professional jargon and orientation, and as a result loses the communication skills that made him valuable in the first place.

Some centers have tried to counter these tendencies by building in reward structures for the job that the paraprofessional is hired to do and by making him an expert consultant to the mental health professional when discussing the poor. As the paraprofessional obtains more and more experiences, his competence as a diagnostician and therapist also increases substantially. The paraprofessional movement has led to increased concern about the *skills* that a person has rather than the degrees obtained. Certification may in the future be based on competency rather than a diploma. Some schools are now using competency testing to give credit in areas that were previously limited to academic and professional training. The concern for competency has also led mental health centers to reduce the distinctions between professions as well as between professionals and nonprofessionals. Thus the emphasis is shifting toward skills and away from academic degrees.

Summary

Community mental health is defined as community-oriented strategies that are designed to improve the mental health and adaptive functioning of members of a community. Theoretically, community mental health is a subcategory of community psychology, which tends to focus on broad social, economic, and political issues, as a means of improving the quality of life. Community mental health is strongly oriented toward devising broad programs involving outreach, indirect services, and prevention rather than traditional psychotherapy.

With the treatment of shell shock during World War II, short-term psychotherapy approaches developed. At the same time, other mental health professionals began to deliver mental health services. Shortly after World War II, Congress established the National Institute of Mental Health to develop a nationwide system of mental health services. More recently (1963), comprehensive community mental health services were developed to provide services within each community of 75,000 to 200,000 people. Although such a program provides service under one roof, where none existed before, there is minimal research to support the effectiveness of those particular services, the guidelines are somewhat arbitrary, and prevention of emotional problems has been largely ignored.

We said that the community mental health philosophy advocates three different levels of prevention. Primary prevention refers to intervention strategies that attempt to eliminate or reduce the causes of emotional or behavioral problems. As was discovered by examining the early approaches used in the field of public health, it is not necessary to understand the stresses in the environment to eliminate them, and thereby reduce the number of emotional problems that exist in our society. There are two major strategies of primary prevention of emotional problems that are modeled after early public health efforts: Reduce the stress in the environment and immunize people to stress. One major principle of public health that applies to community health is that you cannot eliminate a medical or emotional problem in a society through early detection and treatment. *Secondary prevention* refers to intervention procedures that treat the symptoms of emotional problems. Crisis intervention—short-term help during a crisis—places emphasis on helping the client by defining the problem, developing alternative solutions, and choosing the best one. Suicide prevention is one example of crisis intervention. Tertiary prevention refers to rehabilitation of job and interpersonal related skills.

Because of severe shortages of trained manpower in the mental health field, a variety of alternative solutions has been developed. Consultation by mental health professionals to other caregivers in a community such as the police, physicians, clergymen, etc., about how to more effectively help the people they serve who have emotional problems, is one. The paraprofessional is also an efficient means of coping with the manpower problem because they receive a minimal amount of formal training. Furthermore, the paraprofessional provides skills that are not always available to the professional, such as an ability to communicate with the poor and to act as a liaison with other helping agencies.

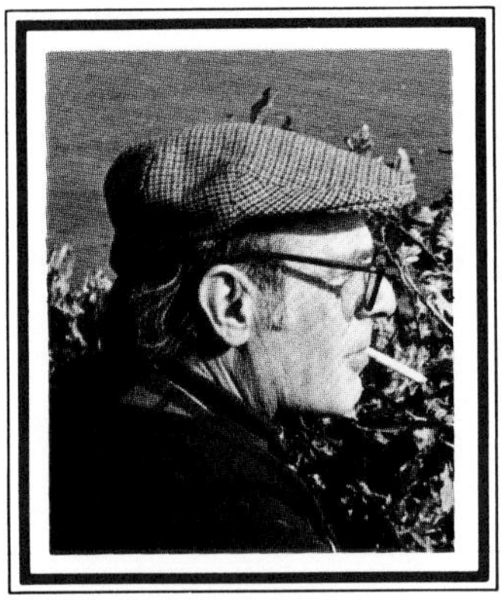

Stanley Schachter (1920-) Social psychologist whose work has had an enormous impact on our understanding of social, motivational, and emotional processes and how they affect and influence human behavior.

Stuart Cook (1913-) innovator and research contributor to the theory and practice of attitude change and intergroup relations. Cook also has made significant contributions to attitude measurement and to the study of ethics in social science research.

Section

8

Social Behavior

21

The Social Context of Behavior

In psychology, as in everyday life, we tend to think of behavior as determined primarily by individual factors. Basic acts, such as eating, sleeping, and drinking, are obviously related to an individual's biological needs. Many cognitive activities such as thinking, remembering, planning, and decision making are also closely identified with the individuals performing these activities. Even "social" activities such as sports, parties, or college classes are typically viewed as collections of individual actions rather than as systems of interaction or as group behaviors.

In society at large, a high value is placed on individualism—"being your own person" and "going it alone." Some of the most popular movies and filmstars (Mae West, Humphrey Bogart, John Wayne, and Paul Newman) have capitalized on the theme of being independent, tough, and not letting other people push you around. But is this really the case? Are people as free of social influence as they would like to have us believe?

A large proportion of our behavior takes place in the presence of others and in group settings. Even the basic acts of eating, drinking, and sleeping are often performed with other people. There is even evidence to show that a basic behavior such as eating can be influenced as much by social cues as by biological states of hunger (see box 21.1). Plans and decisions are rarely made outside the context of the needs and expectations of other people or the influence of groups we belong to, such as family, work groups, or friends. Certainly our social behavior, although it expresses our personal needs and motives, is heavily restrained and modified by social norms, expectations, and rules of conduct, and those who attempt to break out of these social constraints usually find themselves defined as eccentrics, deviants, criminals, or mentally disturbed. In this chapter, we will examine some of the social and group influences on human behavior.

Box 21.1

Obesity, Social Cues, and Eating Behavior

Why are some people fat and others skinny? Obviously, individual factors such as genetic constitution and learned habits are important. However, as you recall from Chapter 15, Schachter et al. (1968a) developed the hypothesis that people of normal weight pay attention to *internal cues* to regulate their eating behavior, while obese people are influenced more by *external social cues.*

Several studies have been conducted to test this hypothesis. One experiment assessed the amount of food that fat and normal individuals would consume under conditions of a high or low degree of fear. The normal subjects behaved as you might expect—fear resulted in less intake of food. But the obese subjects ate the same amount under both conditions, presumably because the external expectations for eating were more important to them than their internal states of hunger. In another study, clocks in a laboratory were preset to go slow or fast during an experiment conducted in late afternoon. Obese subjects ate much more when the clocks showed six p.m. (the conventional time for eating), whether it was actually before or after six o'clock. The food intake of normal subjects was regulated more by length of food deprivation than by apparent time (Schachter and Gross, 1968b). Other studies have shown that international airline pilots who are overweight adjust much better to time changes and disruptions of internal biological rhythms, apparently because they pay more attention to the external cultural cues for eating and sleeping than to length of deprivation, wherever they are. Furthermore, obese Jews adhere better to the rigors of religious fasting than do Jews of normal weight (Goldman et al., 1968).

Thus even with something as simple as eating, the influence of other people and the social environment cannot be overlooked as an important source of behavior.

Effects of Groups on Individual Behavior

One of the first systematic social psychological experiments concerned the effects of the presence of others on individual performance. In 1897 Triplett arranged a laboratory situation in which subjects wound fishing line as fast as they could. Some subjects worked alone, while others worked together in small groups. He found that persons working in the *coaction* setting (working with others) performed significantly better than those working alone. In subsequent variations of this study, individuals who had tried their best when working alone did even better when working with others.

What specific factors could account for Triplett's finding? Competition among group members was one obvious possibility. However, when Allport (1924) reduced the effects of competition by having other group members simply sit and watch the performer, the same improvement in performance occurred.

The effect of an audience on improving individual performance has been observed in many studies since Allport's. (See fig. 21.1.) However, some investigators have found that an audience leads to a *decrease* in individual performance, as compared with working alone. For example, when Pessin (1930) presented subjects with lists of nonsense syllables to be learned either alone or in front of an audience, subjects who worked in the presence of an audience took significantly longer to learn the list than did subjects working alone. What could account for these inconsistencies in the results?

Zajonc (1966) proposed an explanation based on the drive-habit theory of learning. The presence of other people is assumed to have an arousing or *energizing* effect on individual behavior. This effect is assumed to occur in all social situations, not only when in

Figure 21.1 One argument in favor of coed dormitories on college campuses may be that the presence of others is highly arousing and should enhance performance of well-learned responses. However, this effect might be hindered somewhat by the tendency for coaction to be converted into various forms of interaction. (Courtesy Hugh Rogers, Monkmeyer Press Photoservice.)

the presence of an exciting partner. Furthermore, heightened drive is assumed to increase the likelihood that the most *dominant* response in the *hierarchy* of learned habits will be emitted or performed. For example, if the best-learned response in the presence of your lover is to make love, the greater the level of arousal, the more likely you are to have sexual intercourse than to have some other less well-established response, such as reading poetry.

Thus this theory would apply very well to the situation where a dominant response, for example, winding fishing reels, was facilitated by the presence of others. But would the theory also apply to the inhibition effect for learning nonsense syllables? Yes, because in a situation where *learning,* rather than simple performance, takes place, the dominant response is likely to be an *incorrect* response rather than the correct one. The energizing effects of an audience are more likely to elicit errors in learning, and therefore it would take longer to complete the list. Or, take the case in which making love is not a well-learned response in the presence of your lover. Increased arousal is likely to lead to more fumbles and errors (some comical) than occur when the level of arousal is low. However, once the act of seduction is well-learned, a heightened state of arousal will bring about the objective much faster than would a low level of arousal.

To test the hypothesis that the presence of others facilitates the performance of well-learned tasks, but inhibits the learning of new tasks, Zajonc and Sales (1966) performed the following study. During the learning trials, each subject saw different syllables, one, two, four, eight, or sixteen times. Thus the syllables that were seen sixteen times were well-learned (or dominant) responses, whereas those seen only once, twice, or four times were less well learned (or subordinate). During the test trials for recall, the words were flashed on the screen so quickly that the subjects were forced to guess. The results showed that in the presence of others, subjects were more likely to give the well-learned or dominant responses, while in isolation, the guesses contained a greater range of responses, including subordinate as well as dominant responses. This study gives some support to the hypothesis that the presence of others will serve to heighten the emission of dominant responses on a well-learned task. One further example, closer to the lives of students, is given in box 21.2.

Although there is ample evidence to support Zajonc's theory, some researchers have questioned the nature of the level of arousal or drive in groups. Zajonc's theory implies that the arousal is physiologically based. On the other hand, Cottrell et al. (1968) have hypothesized that the arousal is more dependent on cognitive factors such as apprehension about being evaluated.

To test this possibility, Cottrell and his colleagues repeated Zajonc and Sales' experiment with nonsense words, but added two different kinds of audience conditions. In one of the audience conditions, the subject waited in a room with other individuals who were blindfolded and presumably waiting for a

Box 21.2
Social Facilitation and Examinations

The hypothesis put forward by Zajonc (1966) states that the presence of others will enhance individual performance on well-learned tasks but hinder performance on new tasks. What implications could this idea have for studying for and taking examinations? Should you (1) study alone and take the exam alone, (2) study alone and take the exam with others present, (3) study with others and take the exam alone, or (4) study with others and take the exam with others present? (See box fig. 21.2.)

Zajonc has suggested, somewhat lightheartedly, that the second alternative may be the most appropriate application of his theory. However, this assumes that by the time you take the exam, you will have thoroughly learned the correct responses. Therefore, if you are the kind of student who puts off studying until the night before the exam, it may be advisable for you, not only to study alone, but to take the exam alone, so that you will avoid the enhanced emission of *incorrect* dominant responses!

Box Figure 21.2 Should *you* study alone or with others? (Courtesy Ken Heyman.)

dark-adaptation study; in the other audience condition, people could watch how the subject was doing. Although the experimenters assumed that being observed would increase the subject's apprehension about being evaluated and thus increase arousal level, this result was obtained only in the regular audience condition, not when the observers were blindfolded. In a study by Henchy and Glass (1968), the effects of an audience on arousal were obtained only when the subject thought the observers were experts, not when they were described as nonexperts. Thus there is some evidence to suggest that the effects of others on facilitating well-learned tasks and inhibiting poorly learned tasks are caused by cognitive arousal, or anxiety about the performance being evaluated by others. Note that in all these studies, the effects of competition were minimized by having a passive, rather than a coactive audience. We will discuss the effects of competition later.

Voluntary Affiliation with Groups

The group situations examined thus far were mostly involuntary—that is, subjects were not always able to choose whether they would be in a group situation. We will now investigate several reasons why people may *choose* to be with others. Although there are numerous reasons for group affiliation, we will concentrate on a few that are not so obvious and have generated some unusual research: (1) to reduce fear and anxiety, (2) to provide a comparison group against which to evaluate oneself, and (3) to create or confirm a definition of social reality.

Reduction of Fear

In times of acute fear, people seek the company of other people. During disasters such as floods, mine cave-ins, or fire, even total strangers will form highly effective and cohesive groups in a short time. And during times of more long-term and global anxieties, such as the threat of nuclear war, economic recession, or invasions from outer space, church attendance and membership in volunteer organizations may rise. This impetus for group affiliation has been demonstrated dramatically by Schachter (1959).

For his study, Schachter recruited coeds from the University of Minnesota. Upon arriving at the laboratory, the women were greeted by a large stern man in a white lab coat who introduced himself as "Dr. Gregor Zilstein of the Medical School, Department of Neurology and Psychiatry." He then announced that the study they had agreed to participate in concerned the effects of electric shock on the nervous system. One group of subjects was taken into a room filled with banks of electrical equipment, monitors, flashing lights, and the like. Dr. Zilstein then announced that to make the study as realistic as possible, he would give them some strong, quite painful shocks. Another group of subjects were led into a room that did not contain threatening equipment and were told that they would receive mild shocks and had nothing to worry about.

All subjects were then told that there would be a delay, and they could wait in a room down the hall. A choice of rooms was offered—a room where several other people were waiting or a room where they could be alone. Which room would you choose after being told that you were going to get a series of severe shocks? In Schachter's study, sixty-three percent of the subjects who expected strong shocks chose to be with others, while only thirty-three percent of the other subjects chose to wait in a group setting. These results supported the hypothesis that a high degree of stress and fear leads to a greater tendency to affiliate with other people. In the words of the old adage, "misery loves company."

But does misery love any kind of company? Apparently not. In a similar study, Schachter varied the experiment by offering subjects the option of (1) waiting alone or with other participants in the same experiment or (2) waiting alone or with other students who were presumably waiting to talk with a professor. There was a clear-cut difference in the choices of the two groups. Sixty percent of the subjects who had the option of waiting alone or with others involved in the experiment chose to wait in a group. None of the subjects in the other group chose to wait with people who were waiting for the professor. As Schachter suggests, the old adage should be amended to read, "misery loves *miserable* company." Additional findings by Schachter on the effects of birth order on affiliation are found in box 21.3.

Basis of Comparison

The finding that similarity is important when choosing people with whom to affiliate points to an important reason for group affiliation. Whether anxiety is involved or not, people often join groups to compare their ideas, opinions, and performances with other people (e.g., Festinger, 1954; Morse and Gergen, 1970). For example, people use groups as a means of establishing their own relative position in the performance of skills such as playing chess, guitar, and basketball or even telling jokes. Also, a person will often define his religious or political attitudes within the context of a chosen group. For instance, he may define himself as a "political moderate" because he perceives himself as falling within the middle range of the opinions and attitudes represented by his friends and associates. However, outside this group, a radical may perceive him as highly conservative and a conservative may view him as a radical. But in his own evaluation of his political position, the person tends to use his chosen group as a frame of reference.

One central assumption of social comparison theory is that a person will choose comparison groups with attitudes and interests which are *similar* to his own. In some cases, initial similarities in attitudes may be a better predictor of long-term personal relationships than will initial feelings of attraction. To test this hypothesis, Newcomb (1963) recruited male students to live together in rent-free, cooperative housing for a period of sixteen weeks. In return the students agreed to par-

Box 21.3
Birth Order and Affiliation

One interesting finding in Schachter's (1959) studies on affiliative behavior in the face of increased stress was that subjects who were firstborn or only children showed a much stronger tendency to wait with others than did other subjects. When extremely anxious, sixty-seven percent of the subjects who were the oldest or only children in their families chose to wait with others, while only thirty-five percent of the subjects who had older brothers or sisters chose this alternative. Under less stressful conditions, no such differences were found.

What might account for the tendency of firstborn subjects to respond to stressful events with affiliative behavior? Two possibilities have been explored. One is that in the first year or so of life the firstborn or only child learns to depend on adults to a greater extent than do other children, whose mothers are busier. Perhaps this pattern persists, that is, the oldest child continues to cope with anxiety by depending on others, while the younger child has learned to depend more on his own resources. Another possibility is that firstborns have stronger needs for social comparison; that is, for checking out uncertain situations with others. Two further research studies, in which birth order, opportunities for reduction of anxiety, and social comparison were varied systematically, have supported both these interpretations (Wrightsman, 1960; Ring et al., 1965).

ticipate in research on the development of interpersonal and group relationships. Measures of interpersonal attraction and a variety of attitudinal and value measures were obtained at regular intervals throughout the sixteen-week period. Results show clearly that initial measures of liking (taken in the first two weeks) did not adequately predict the stable interpersonal relationships and coalitions that were established later. However, initial measures of attitudinal similarity did predict later social and subgroup memberships. The predictability based on early attitudinal similarity becomes even more impressive when we note that the students were generally unaware of one another's attitudes during the initial measurement period. (See table 21.1)

There is also strong evidence that similarity of attitudes may be more important than racial similarity in the choice of work groups or companions during coffee breaks (Rokeach, 1968; Rokeach and Mezei, 1966). The procedures for Rokeach's studies were identical, except that one study was done on a college campus and the other was conducted in an employment agency in a racially mixed section of a large city. In both studies, the subject (a student or an unemployed person) was engaged in conversation by four accomplices of the experimenter. Two accomplices were black and two were white. During the course of the conversation, the subject found that he agreed with one black and one white accomplice and disagreed with the other pair. Following the conversation, the subject was given the opportunity to choose two of the four as either companions for a coffee break (students), or members of a work group (employment office). Results showed that the subjects demonstrated a greater preference for the two persons whose opinions were similar to his own than for the two of his own race (Rokeach, 1968; Rokeach and Mezei, 1966).

Table 21.1 Summary of mean correlations between mutual attraction and actual agreement about other house members on the part of 136 pairs. Notice that the longer the time period, the greater the attitudinal similarity between pairs. This indicates that a sorting-out process occurred and that the people who ended up as friends shared common attitudes.

Week	Year I	Year II
0–1	.15	.18
2–5	.45	.37
6–9	.52	.40
10–13	.50	.43
14–15	.46	.58

Source: From Newcomb, T.M., "Stabilities underlying changes in interpersonal attraction." *Journal of Abnormal and Social Psychology*, 1963, *66*, p. 381. Copyright 1963 by the American Psychological Association. Reprinted by permission.

These systematic *field experiments* provide some support for the prediction that people will tend to join groups of persons whose attitudes are similar to their own to provide a context for social comparison and self-evaluation. It should be noted, however, that several factors may lead to a choice of *dissimilar* rather than similar people under conditions of social comparison. For example, Gordon (1966) found that an individual who is certain of his own attitudes and opinions may choose to be with dissimilar rather than similar persons because he finds it more exciting to argue with others than to agree with them all the time. Furthermore, if he wants to improve his performance in a specific activity such as playing the piano or selling more cars, he may associate with persons whose performance in these skills is superior to his own (Wheeler, 1966).

Thus far, we have looked at two reasons why people join groups—fear, and the need for social comparison and evaluation. In a study by Miller and Zimbardo (1966), both factors were studied at the same time. These investigators used a modified form of Schachter's "shock" study and gave subjects a greater variety of choices concerning whom they could wait with while the apparatus was being set up. Subjects were given the choice of (1) being alone, (2) waiting with someone in the same experiment who supposedly had dissimilar personality traits and interests, or (3) waiting with someone who had similar interests and personality traits but was not involved in the shock experiment. It was assumed that if reduction of fear was the most important variable, subjects would choose to wait with someone from the same experiment. If social comparison or evaluation was more important, subjects would choose to wait with someone who did not share the same threatening situation but who did share similar interests. The results showed that among those who decided to wait with others, forty-one percent chose to wait with another experimental subject and fifty-nine percent chose to wait with someone who was similar to themselves. Thus both fear and social comparison seem to be influential factors in affiliation, but in this case, the need for social comparison was somewhat more important than the direct reduction of fear.

Definition of Social Reality

Most of the situations for group affiliation we have discussed have been relatively unambiguous; that is, people knew what was happening. One further assumption of Festinger's (1956) social comparison theory is that the greater the *uncertainty* involved in a social situation, the stronger the tendency to affiliate with others to define some *social reality* for the situation. For example, if a meteor enters the atmosphere and falls to earth, people can pick it up, test it, and be fairly satisfied with the explanation that it is a meteor. In this case, there is some objective physical basis on which to establish a judgment with a high degree of certainty. But if a glowing, blinking, cigar-shaped object descends from the skies at dusk, people tend to join with others to create some definition of reality. Is the object an apparition, a Soviet spy ship, a helicopter, or creatures from outer space? (See box 21.4.)

A similar process takes place when there is uncertainty about which opinion or attitude is "correct," or what is the appropriate way to think or feel in a highly ambiguous situation. For example, when something unexpected happens—for example, when the vice-president of the country is charged with a criminal act or a model student goes berserk and shoots people—individuals look to their political parties, families, friends, work groups, or churches to establish some definition of what went wrong and what is the appropriate response. In the vice-president's case, his close friends and business associates and governors of his political party defined him as a victim of circumstances and decided that the appropriate response was to sympathize and offer help. Members of opposition groups tended to accept the news as confirmation of their belief that the man and his political party were inherently corrupt, and they responded with righteous indignation and, sometimes, glee. (See also fig. 21.2.)

Even in situations that call for an emotional response, individuals may depend on the surrounding group to define what the appropriate emotional expression should be for the situation. At first glance, this statement may seem silly; after all, emotions such as anger, happiness, and despair are surely *individual* reactions to situations. And didn't we say in an earlier chapter that internal neurophysiological states are the bases for emotions? You will recall, however, that researchers have found it difficult to differentiate emotional states on the basis of physiological indicators alone. Although a state of *general* physiological arousal may occur in emotional situations, what we need to *define* the specific emotion is some set of cues. These cues are often provided by the social or group context. For example, the physiological basis for a "high" gained from a moderate amount of alcohol or marihuana may be fairly diffuse and nonspecific, but the social surroundings will often specify the emotion that is expressed. Thus the predominant mood may be euphoria in one situation and gloom in another.

In summary, the research reviewed in this section has demonstrated that reduction of fear, social comparison, self-evaluation, and the need to define the appropriate attitudinal, social, or emotional response in an uncertain situation are all important bases for affiliative behavior among human beings. We now turn to some processes of interaction that are central to groups once they are established.

Cooperation and Competition Within Groups

The twin processes of competition and cooperation are fundamental to any ongoing group. Without some minimal amount of cooperation among members, no group would survive. On the other hand, without some degree of friendly rivalry, a group may lapse into lethargy, or at least lack a certain challenge and interest for its members. Despite the obvious importance of balancing these two aspects, many groups in our society attempt to operate almost exclusively on the basis of competition. One notable example is the classroom. In most school systems, rewards such as grades, teachers' praise, and

Figure 21.2 The importance of other people in providing a context for the support and development of new "definitions of social reality" is seen in the different kinds of communal living groups that have formed in recent years. These groups are vital to those who seek to develop alternatives to the current social, economic, and political realities of contemporary society. (Courtesy Dennis Stock © Magnum Photos, Inc.)

Box 21.4
Definition of Social Reality: A Case Study

One group's resistance to changing its definition of social reality was demonstrated dramatically in a field study by Festinger et al. (1956), who infiltrated a religious group that was convinced the end of the world was at hand. This group also believed that their own salvation had been provided for in the form of a space ship, which would come down to earth and save them on a specific date. The seriousness with which they held this unusual definition of reality was demonstrated by the fact that as the day of reckoning drew near, they gave away all their possessions and went to a certain hill to await their extraterrestrial visitors. However, the day came and went, and not only did the space ship not arrive, but the world did not end.

What did the group do in the face of this clear evidence that contradicted their beliefs? You might expect that they would give up this particular viewpoint in favor of a more reasonable one. But, in this case, the opposite occurred. Not only did they refuse to give up their ideas and beliefs (they simply changed the date), but they became much more militant and began a public crusade to recruit new members. Rather than modifying their definition of social reality in the face of contrary evidence, this group simply made a greater effort to reassure themselves that their beliefs were correct by attempting to recruit more people who would share them.

parental approval are based strictly on competitive individual efforts. Little attempt is made to structure learning experiences around cooperative and shared group processes. Even if this were possible, would requirements such as group projects or even group grades be feasible? Would anyone learn the material or achieve anything?

In a pioneering study of the effects of competitive versus cooperative structures of reward in a college classroom, Deutsch (1949) divided students in an introductory psychology course into ten groups of five students each. Half of the groups were assigned to a *cooperative* reward situation in which the best *group* received the highest grades. The other half were assigned to the usual *competitive* reward situation in which the best *individual* performances received the highest grades. To obtain ongoing measures of performance, all groups were required to work weekly on logical and visual puzzles and to solve complex problems in human relations. In addition to these measures of outcome, observers recorded the group interactions, and group members also rated their perceptions of group performance and interpersonal relations. At the end of the term, the most striking finding was the uniform superiority of the cooperative groups. For example, cooperative groups were superior to competitive groups in *performance,* as measured by productivity per unit of time, diversity of each member's contributions, and quality of solutions. Cooperative groups also were superior in terms of *coordination* of task activities, that is, subdividing tasks among the members, mutual understanding of instructions, and knowledge of each member's contributions. Finally, members of the cooperative groups evaluated their groups more positively in terms of friendliness during discussions and favorable effects on fellow members.

These results have been replicated in subsequent studies, although not in as great detail. When Haines and McKeachie (1967) compared competitive and cooperative discussion groups, they found that the competitive groups experienced higher levels of anxiety and tension, which disrupted individual performance. Using fifth and sixth grade girls, Fay (1970) found a better level of learning among cooperative project groups. Members of competitive groups, on the other hand, were likely to withhold rather than share ideas about how to improve performance.

Blau (1954) obtained similar results when he compared cooperative and competitive counseling sections in a public employment agency. The job security of counselors in the competitive section was dependent on individual productivity; that is, how many clients each one served and how many job openings he filled. In the cooperative section, the emphasis was placed on group rather than individual productivity. The results of this study showed that the cooperative section placed more job applicants than did the competitive section. One reason was the counselors' willingness to share job information with each other and to refer applicants to another counselor when appropriate. They also took their coffee breaks together and provided mutual support and encouragement. Counselors in competitive groups tended to stick to themselves and to "sit on" rather than share job openings with one another.

Despite all these results in favor of cooperative groups, you may well ask whether competitively based groups are not better, in some situations at least. The answer is yes—in situations where the group task is simple (well-learned) and easily divisible into individual components (Miller and Hamblin, 1963). This finding fits the general set of results we discussed earlier: That the presence of an audience (or competition) enhanced individual performance for well–learned tasks but inhibited performance for complex, less well learned tasks. Because education and a large part of business involve complex, learning–in–process kinds of tasks, more cooperative and fewer competitive reward systems might be beneficial, not only in terms of production but in terms of the satisfaction derived by students and workers. In other societies such as Japan and China, cooperative group structures are much more common in business and industry than they are in the highly individualistic, competitively oriented European and American societies.

Experimental Games

The field studies we have discussed provide us with valuable information about the effects of cooperative and competitive reward structures in groups in real life. However, as is often the case with field research, it is difficult to obtain precise measurements of the actual processes involved because people's lives cannot always be rearranged to suit the requirements of the research design. Fortunately, in the area of cooperation and competition, there has been a long tradition of controlled laboratory research.

Most of the laboratory research has utilized one or two forms of a *nonzero sum* game. The most popular form, "Prisoners' Dilemma," involves two players, who make simple joint binary choices to win as many points (or dollars) as possible in a given number of trials. The payoff matrix is shown in figure 21.3. To understand the game, imagine you are player A, your partner is player B, and you are sitting on either side of a partition. In each trial, you both make a choice by pressing either a red or blue switch. The experimenter, using feedback lights, then shows you the two choices made and indicates the

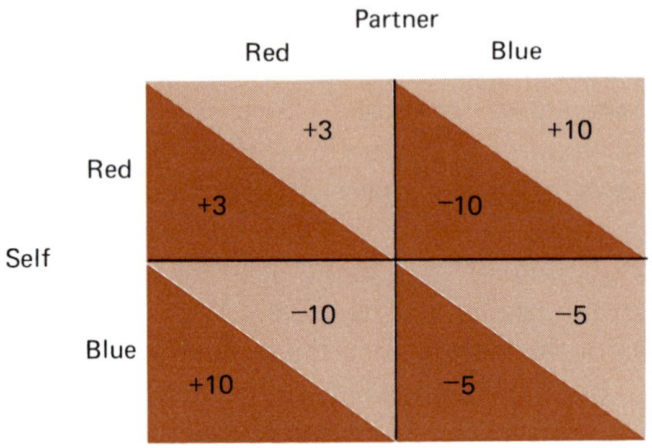

Figure 21.3 A typical matrix of Prisoners' Dilemma. Own payoffs for each set of joint responses are in light areas; the opponent's payoffs are in dark areas.

payoffs for you and your partner. For example, if you both choose red (see fig. 21.3), you and your partner each win three points (the *cooperative* response). What happens if you choose red, but your partner chooses blue? In this case, your partner wins ten points and you lose ten points (the *exploitive* response on the part of your partner). If you are clever enough, you might get your partner to choose red while you slip in a blue. Then he would lose ten points for his attempt to cooperate and you would win ten points for your exploitive efforts. If you both try to be competitive and both choose blue, you each lose five points. (The origins of this game are described in box 21.5.)

You can see that after a few trials, this game can become extremely interesting. For example, should you try to get your partner to cooperate consistently so that you both win moderate amounts? Or should you try to compete as much as you can to increase your own earnings, but at the same time risk losing a large amount? Because this particular form of the game involves a conflict, or mixture of cooperative and competitive motives, it is called a mixed-motive game. It is termed a *nonzero sum* game because both players can win simultaneously. In a *zero sum* game, when one player wins, the other loses something, so that only competitive strategies will lead to one player winning.

What are some of the factors that determine the cooperative or competitive strategies of players in mixed-motive, nonzero sum games such as Prisoners' Dilemma? We will consider three factors: communication among participants, strategies of partners, and incentives.

Communication

An early study by Sidowski, Wycott, and Tabory (1956) showed that a minimal amount of cooperation would develop between two players in a nonzero sum game, even when they were unaware of each other's presence. When they arrived at the laboratory, the subjects were kept apart and shown into separate rooms. They were seated in front of the apparatus and simply told to make choices. Although payoffs were posted for each subject, he was not told he was playing against another person. Despite the lack of communication, subjects eventually learned to play the mutually cooperative choices and to respond to the reinforcement contingencies in the game. However, later studies have shown that when subjects are aware of one

Box 21.5
Prisoners' Dilemma

The nonzero sum, mixed-motive game called Prisoners' Dilemma was developed on the basis of the following situation:

> *Two suspects are taken into custody and separated. The district attorney is certain they are guilty of a specific crime, but he does not have adequate evidence to convict them at trial. He points out to each prisoner that each has two alternatives: to confess to the crime the police are sure they have done, or not confess. If neither suspect confesses, then the district attorney states that he will book them both on some very minor, trumped-up charge. . . ; if they both confess, they will be prosecuted* [and] *he will recommend* [a rather severe] *sentence; however, if one confesses and the other does not, then the confessor will receive rather lenient treatment for turning state's evidence, whereas the latter will get the book slapped at him (Luce and Raiffa, 1957 p. 95).*

Compare this verbal description with the values of the outcomes or payoffs in figure 21.3 and translate "not confessing" as a cooperative response with a beneficial outcome for both prisoners. Trying to confess and hoping the other will not is defined as a competitive or exploitive response. If both partners try to exploit each other (i.e., they both confess), they each face a serious loss, but this loss is not as severe as the cost to the sucker who is exploited when the other turns state's evidence.

another's presence and have the opportunity to talk to each other, the cooperative strategy develops much more rapidly. For example, Deutsch (1960) found that subjects who were able to communicate showed significantly higher levels of cooperation than subjects who were not. (See table 21.2.)

The factor of direct, as opposed to indirect communication has some significance for actual mixed-motive situations. How many times have you had an argument with a friend, lover, or family member and refused to talk to him for a while? You probably watched his behavior closely for signs of continued conflict or signs that he was relenting and wanted to cooperate. The conflict might have been settled more quickly if you had argued it out at the beginning. Keeping the lines of communication open becomes even more critical in the area of international conflict—a topic we will consider in the next section.

Strategies of Partners

In any mixed-motive situation, the behavior of the other person will, in part at least, determine your own response. You will be watching to see whether your partner shows any intention of cooperating, whether he seems to be concentrating only on exploitation, or whether some kind of *reciprocity* is

Table 21.2 The effects of different motivational instruction on cooperative choices under two levels of communication. (Adapted from Deutsch, 1960.)

	Percentage of Cooperative Choices		
Motivation Instructions	No Communication	Communication	Avg.
Cooperative	89.1	96.9	93.0
Individualistic	35.0	70.6	52.8
Competitive	12.5	29.2	20.9

Source: From Freedman, J.L., J.M. Carlsmith, & D.G. Sears, *Social Psychology*. Copyright 1970, Prentice-Hall, Inc., Englewood Cliffs, N.J. Reprinted by permission.

developing. Controlled investigations of the effects of different strategies on the subject's competitiveness are possible in the laboratory simply by doing away with real partners and replacing them with a preprogrammed set of strategies. Of course, this can only be done under conditions of noncommunication. For example, McClintock et al. (1963) arranged preprogrammed strategies for subjects under three conditions. In the *highly cooperative* situation, the "partner" was programmed to cooperate during eighty-five percent of the trials. In the *moderately cooperative* condition, the partner cooperated 50 percent of the time, and in the *uncooperative* or competitive condition, only fifteen percent of the partner's choices were cooperative. Under which conditions do you think the real subject was most cooperative? The answer seems easy: it should be the highly cooperative condition. However, the results of this and several similar studies demonstrated that there was *no difference* in the amount of cooperation subjects showed under each condition. In all three situations they cooperated about fifty percent of the time.

One reason for this surprising result is that the real subjects seemed to be confused by the seemingly random behavior of their partner. Although the partner was programmed to make a certain percentage of cooperative responses, it did so without considering the real partner's responses. That is, the partner's strategy was *not* contingent upon the subject's behavior. It would be somewhat similar to playing with an irrational person who does things for no apparent reason.

Later studies attempted to set up more contingent, preprogrammed strategies. Oskamp (1972) arranged a situation in which the real subjects made their choices first, and the "partner" always responded with the same choice. For example, if the subject chose the cooperative response, the "partner" chose the cooperative response too. If the real subject chose a competitive response, the "partner" reciprocated. This was the *reciprocity* strategy. The study also included a strategy of *unconditional* cooperation in which the "partner" responded with a cooperative response no matter what kind of choice the real subject made. Which of these two simulated strategies elicited the most cooperation from the real subject? Again, the results might not be obvious because the highly cooperative strategy did *not* produce as much cooperation as did the reciprocity (or matching) strategy. Apparently, real subjects consider the partner who cooperates all the time to be a bit of a sucker or an "easy mark" and cannot resist exploiting him, at least part of the time (usually 50 percent). On the other hand, when the real subject is punished for competitive responses and rewarded for cooperative responses in the reciprocity strategy, he quickly learns that cooperation is the best policy. In some studies, the reciprocity strategy has produced rates of cooperation as high as eighty-five to ninety percent (e.g., Wrightsman et al., 1967). Cross-cultural differences may shed some light on these results (see box 21.6).

Box 21.6
Cultural Differences in Cooperation and Competition

Several studies have demonstrated that cultural groups in the United States vary in their dispositions toward competition and cooperation. For example, using a game similar to "Prisoners' Dilemma," Kagan and Madsen (1971) found that Anglo-American children were significantly more competitive than Mexican-American children, who in turn were more competitive than children in rural Mexico. These differences make sense in terms of the degree of urbanization (more highly competitive life-styles) of each culture as well as the relative cultural differences in the value placed on cooperation and competition.

However, it appears that competition may be overdone on some occasions. Using a form of a game that tested rivalry, Kagan and Madsen (1972) found that Anglo-American children chose irrational competitive responses more often than did Mexican-American children. That is, they overlooked a condition where both players could win six marbles each in favor of a condition where they won two marbles for themselves and their rival only won one marble. Apparently, the ethic of winning is so strong in Anglo-American culture that it blinds its members to more lucrative cooperative alternatives.

Size and Type of Incentive

Some people may believe that cooperating or competing for a few points or pennies in a laboratory situation is inconsequential compared with the seriousness of payoffs in real life. Would the same results be obtained if the payoffs or incentives for the Prisoners' Dilemma game were increased or made more realistic? Gallo (1966) used a game that was similar to Prisoners' Dilemma but included two conditions: one in which participants played for *points,* and one in which they played for *money* and could win or lose large sums. The results showed that playing for money increased the amount of cooperation and that the higher the stakes, the greater the cooperation. Other researchers, however, found no differences when they increased the size of the monetary payoffs. In a study by Knox and Douglas (1968), subjects could make up to sixty dollars by exploiting their partners. But no differences in the amount of cooperation were found between this high-payoff condition and one in which the maximum possible earnings were only sixty cents.

How can we explain these contradictory results about the effects of increasing the size of incentives? Some commentators have sought to explain these differences on the basis of the different payoff matrices or instructions used in these studies. However, a different explanation has been offered by Brown (1971), who contends that monetary incentives may not always be the most important incentive in the mixed-motive game situation. To some individuals, the excitement of the competition or the affiliative aspects of mutual cooperation are more important than winning money. Brown also suggests that the desire to "save face" may be a powerful factor in the choice of strategies. To test this possibility, he set up a special game situation in which subjects were opposed by a highly exploitive and insulting partner and were given the choice of (1) retaliating and thus avoiding the appearance of being a sucker, but also losing money, or (2) not retaliating (accepting the insults), but making a lot of money. Most of the humiliated subjects retaliated despite the loss of monetary gains.

Sometimes the costs of "losing face" are so great that people are willing to give up a great deal to avoid it. An example of this occurred in a law class at the University of Michigan. In this class, students were paired off as opponents in a simulated contract dispute. Their task was to negotiate a legal settlement. Because each participant's grade was based on whether the settlement was a favorable one for his prospective client, this was obviously a classical mixed-motive situation. A good individual grade was dependent on winning a good settlement from the opponent (competitive aspect). However, failure to reach a settlement by the end of the term would mean a negative outcome (a D grade) for both sides (cooperative aspect). Surprisingly, about twenty percent of the bargaining teams failed to reach a settlement by the end of the term and thus received poor grades. In each case, the conflict became so intense that both negotiators preferred to see both sides lose (get D grades) rather than give the other side a competitive advantage. This is similar to the situation that occurs in the Prisoners' Dilemma game when both players choose the competitive choice (and both lose points) over a series of trials rather than risk exploitation by making a unilateral cooperative move. The explanation the law students usually gave for their behavior was that they would rather receive a bad grade than risk "losing face" by finding themselves on the losing side of a contract dispute—even if the dispute was simulated! There are more optimistic signs of the possibility for more cooperation in our society. (See box 21.7.)

Generalizing from Laboratory Games to Real Life

From the few examples of research on mixed-motive games reviewed here, you can see that

Box 21.7

Encounter Groups: New Moves Toward Cooperation

A variety of new "group" movements, such as T-groups, encounter groups, and many communal living situations may be viewed as attempts to create small pockets of cooperation in a largely individualistic and competitive society. The importance of cooperation is illustrated in the following description of the goals of a form of encounter group called a "contract group" (Egan, 1970):

> *In the contract group, cooperation means getting into the community as quickly as possible. It means that members have come together, not to compete, but to grow. A cooperative style of group interaction will produce a distinctive type of interpersonal movement in the group. Three types of interpersonal movement may be indicated . . . :*
>
> *Type A self ⟵ other*
> *Type B self ⟶ other*
> *Type C self —— other*
>
> *In Type A, one member remains entrenched in himself, and makes the other capitulate or move toward him. In Type B, . . .* [one participant] *leaves himself in a movement that entails giving-in to the other. In Type C, which is characteristic of a cooperative group movement, both participants venture out of themselves, and each encourages the other to venture forth.*

experimental research has been able to throw considerable light on the processes of cooperation and competition in groups. In some cases, such as the effects of communication, or the research on "saving face" as an important motive, it is possible to make fairly direct applications from the laboratory to actual situations. However, one must be cautious about generalizing all the laboratory results to actual situations.

Several researchers (e.g., Gergen, 1969; Pruitt, 1967) have pointed out that the restrictions placed on laboratory games make it difficult to generalize the results to situations outside the laboratory. Three problems in particular deserve special mention:

1. The players, or subjects in laboratory studies are usually strangers and thus have little knowledge of each other other than their simple game choices. This is atypical of many actual situations involving cooperation or conflict because the other players may be family members, friends, work mates, or sports partners. On the other hand, the standard game situation in the laboratory may be fairly typical of mixed-motive interactions between strangers, or even between foreign countries, because little is known about the other party, and the possibilities for communication are minimal.

2. In the typical laboratory game, the choice of response is severely restricted—for example, a player can choose only the blue or red. In real life, a person may decide to choose other alternatives: for example, withdraw and not participate or adopt a superficial attitude of helpfulness or consideration while actually exploiting the other person. Options such as these are not available to participants in the laboratory game, but they may make a difference in real life.

3. The *social norms* that govern behavior in the laboratory may be quite different from those which exist outside it. For example, experimental participants may perceive the main social expectations in the laboratory to be winning the most points, or perhaps not appearing to be a sucker in the eyes of the other player or the experimenter. In many settings in real life, such as the family, there may be strong social expectations to reduce individual competition and increase cooperation on behalf of the group (see field studies at beginning of this section). Indeed, even in the laboratory, the competitive, cooperative, or individualistic expectations set up by the experimenter have produced marked differences in experimental behavior (e.g., Solomon, 1960).

Therefore, in this as well as other areas of social psychology, it is important to maintain a balance between laboratory and field research. Field studies test whether the behavioral principles discovered in the laboratory research can be generalized to settings in real life.

Conflict and Reduction of Conflict Between Groups

Many of the studies we described in the last section, particularly the field experiments, were concerned with the effects of cooperation or competition within groups and on individual behavior. We will now turn to a consideration of how conflict *between* groups affects the behavior of members.

Intergroup Conflict and Its Resolution

Competition over *scarce resources* is perhaps a universal source of conflict between groups and nations. In war, for example, the scarce resource has been land or natural resources. In sports events or debating teams, the resource may be a trophy. Here again, however, the goals of conflict or competition may be something intangible, such as saving face, maintaining prestige, or even preserving "national honor."

In a series of ingenious field studies, Sherif et al. (1961) used a summer camp for boys to demonstrate how intergroup conflict may develop and, more important, how it may be reduced. In the "Robbers Cave" experiment (named after the campsite), twenty-four boys from white, middle-class families were divided into two groups immediately after arriving at the camp. The groups were matched as evenly as possible in terms of size, strength, skills and were housed in separate cabins. For the first week, the boys engaged in camp activities in their separate groups, and there was little contact between them. By the second week, the boys had developed a strong sense of group solidarity, as evidenced by the fact that they had chosen group names—Eagles versus the Rattlers, and the experimenters arranged a sports tournament between the two groups. In addition to the tournament, they also arranged for one group to eat breakfast early and consume most of the food before the other group arrived. No other experimental manipulations of scarce resources were necessary. The friendly rivalry between the two groups rapidly deteriorated into forms that ranged from "hassling" (e.g., stealing the group flag, raids) to physical fights and modified gang warfare. The intensity of intergroup conflict that resulted from these simple manipulations of resources was difficult to believe. Furthermore, each group developed excessively high opinions of its skills and abilities and extremely negative opinions about those of the other group; that is, there was a strong differentiation between the in-group and out-group. This was demonstrated when the boys were asked to estimate the margins of defeat or victory in the contests. As you can see in box 21.8, in-group victories were vastly inflated, and out-group successes were denigrated and attributed to chance or luck. In addition, elements of out-group prejudice began to appear after a short time. For example, on measures of negative stereotypes (e.g., "weak," "sneaky," "stinkers"), seventy-seven percent of the Eagles rated *all* members of the Rattlers as having these characteristics, and fifty-three percent of the Rattlers reciprocated these blanket negative stereotypes. On the other hand, in-group ratings were almost universally positive (100 percent by Rattlers, 94 percent by Eagles). Furthermore, the amount of positive contacts between members of the respective groups fell to zero, and the only contacts that did occur were negative. This lack of opportunities for positive interaction naturally helped to strengthen the *in-group/out-group differentiation* and *negative stereotypes.*

Thus the experimenters, through a few fairly minor manipulations of scarce resources, were able to create two highly segregated and antagonistic groups of boys, who threw forks and garbage at each other during meals and spent the rest of the day (and night) planning and executing a form of war against each other. Obviously, something had to be done before the boys were returned to their parents.

In earlier studies in this series, Sherif and his colleagues had tried a number of approaches, but all of them had failed to reduce the level of conflict significantly. The fruitless attempts included the following: (1) Each group was given *accurate information* about the performances, skills, and backgrounds of the other. This approach is similar to trying to correct stereotypes about disliked racial groups by informational means alone. (2) Appeals were made to the *moral values* of brotherhood and friendship during Sunday morning "sermons." This approach is popular with many ministers, priests, rabbis, and politicians. (3) *Conferences* between the leaders of the two groups were organized along the lines of a "summit" meeting. And (4) A *common enemy* was introduced in the form of a group from another camp that "threatened" the experimental camp. Although this last solution worked better than the others, it was not used in the Robbers Cave experiment because it simply shifted the focus of the intergroup conflict from the small group to a larger group. However, this is a favorite tactic of national leaders who want to unite conflicting factions within their own borders and consolidate their own power.

In the Robbers Cave experiment, the strategy was to involve the Eagles and the Rattlers in a series of tasks with *common goals*. The experimenters arranged a series of crises that affected every boy in the camp. For example, a rag became "stuck" in the camp's water supply, and after a long search for the problem, both groups climbed on the water tank and found the rag. During a trip, the truck broke down, and everyone had to pull on the rope to get it going. On another occasion, everyone had to pool their money so that the entire camp could go to a movie. This series of joint goals and activities had the effect of gradually reducing the conflict, increasing the amount of positive contact between the two groups, and reducing the negative stereotyping. The important aspects of this successful method of resolving conflict were (1) the existence of *common goals,* (2) the need for *interdependent action* ("fun" activities alone did not work), and (3) opportunities for *positive contacts* between the two hostile groups. In Chapter 23, these factors will again be important when we examine the research that has been done on the reduction of racial conflict. Here, however, we will consider these factors in the context of reducing tension and conflict between nations.

International Conflict and Its Reduction

Many of the social psychological factors that Sherif studied in the experimentally induced conflict at the boys' camp are evident in conflicts between nations. For example, competition over territory, whether the territory is a piece of land or a set of missile sites, is still a common source of conflict. However, more potentially dangerous conflicts arise over nations' attempts to either gain or maintain national prestige, just as the Eagles and Rattlers were concerned with the prestige of their groups. Although the Cuban missile crisis was initially triggered by the threat that the presence of Soviet missiles on nearby territory posed to United States, the conflict quickly became a "test of wills" in the public mind; in other words, which side would back down first.

Another common aspect of the boys' conflict and international conflict is the development of mutually negative stereotypes by both sides. In a study of American and Russian attitudes, Bronfenbrenner (1961) discovered that, not only were the stereotypes of both sides negative, but they seemed to be almost identical. The Russian people believed they were peace-loving citizens of a progressive nation, while American citizens were dupes who lived under a tyrannical warlike regime that lied to and exploited them. Moreover, the Russians perceived the United States as highly expansionist and ready to take over the world at the first opportunity. A large number of Americans held almost identical attitudes toward the Russian people and government. To capture the similarity of the mutually negative stereotypes held by opposing sides, Bronfenbrenner referred to his results as the *mirror-image phenomenon.*

One final similarity between the boys' camp and international relations concerns the methods of reducing conflict and competition. The methods that failed in the boys' camp (information and cultural exchange, summit meetings, and moralistic statements) have also proved to be of limited value in reducing international tensions. However, the strategy of developing common goals and the necessity of interdependent efforts to reach them show

Box 21.8

The Psychological Effects of Group Conflict

In the following description of a tug-of-war between the two factions in Sherif's Robbers Cave experiment, note the differences in the Eagles' and Rattlers' perceptions and interpretations of events and, in particular, the distortions of time by the winning and losing groups after the event:

> *The Rattlers . . . won the first contest, whereupon the Eagles burned the Rattlers' flag. . . .* [The next day] *the Eagles devised a strategy to win the second tug-of-war. On a prearranged signal, the Eagles all sat down on the ground and dug in their feet. The confident Rattlers were pulling strenuously in an upright position, but rapidly losing ground and becoming exhausted. After seven minutes, the Rattlers adopted the enemy's strategy, and dug in, too* (see box fig. 21.8). *Tired by their initial pull in a standing position,*

the Rattlers were being pulled gradually across the line. . . . At the end of [the time] period, the Rattlers were still not all across the line, and the contest was declared a tie. The Eagles were indignant, but the Rattlers were relieved and satisfied. The Rattlers accused the Eagles of employing a dirty strategy. Privately, they remarked that it seemed that the contest would never end. The Eagles, on the other hand, were overheard to remark to one another that the . . . time flew too fast on the verge of their victory. On the day following the contest, observers of each group asked the members. . . . "How long did the tug-of-war last after both groups had sat down and dug in?" [Although] the actual duration was 48 minutes. . . . the Eagles gave their judgments in minutes (20–45), while the Rattlers gave theirs in hours (1–3½).

e.

f.

Box Figure 21.8 In the Robbers Cave experiment, Rattlers and Eagles had their first contact just before the phase of intergroup conflict. (a) Rattlers hang a banner on the backdrop of playing field, which they had improved and considered theirs. (b) Eagles arrive at the field for first contest as Rattlers look them over. (c) The two groups eye each other across the playing field. (d) Eagles around their banner in prayer huddle—a ritual before each contest. (e) Rattlers developed norms of toughness and rowdiness. Here they boldly march with banners near the area where Eagles (background at (left) are huddled in a quieter pursuit. (f) The tug-of-war between the Eagles and the Rattlers. (From *Social psychology,* by M. Sherif and C. W. Sherif. Harper & Row, 1969. Reprinted by permission.

more promise. In fact, the recent reduction in tension between the United States and the Soviet Union may be attributable to a large extent to the emergence of common goals. For example, building larger or better nuclear weapons to destroy each other with has reached a point of diminishing returns because both sides would be destroyed ten times over. Thus the common threats posed by nuclear energy have become more urgent in recent years. In the strategic arms limitation talks (or SALT talks), both sides made an initial commitment to devote mutual effort to reduce these threats. In the future, these joint goals may involve cooperative exchanges and mutual attempts to develop more constructive and peaceful uses of nuclear energy.

This strategy may sound good on paper, but how can it be initiated in an international atmosphere of distrust and suspicion? Who makes the first move? If one side takes the initiative and makes a unilateral move, will it be reciprocated? Or will it be considered a sign of weakness and, therefore, be exploited? You may recall that even in simple laboratory games, such as Prisoner's Dilemma, an unconditional cooperative move (like a unilateral move) was typically pounced on and exploited by an opponent. Why would it be any different in conflict at the international level, where so much more is at stake?

Osgood (1962) proposed a solution that involves small, unilateral, conciliatory moves, which can be quickly withdrawn if unreciprocated but can be used as a building block for further moves if reciprocated. Because this method is a gradual approach to the reduction of conflict and also makes continued progress contingent upon the other side's response, it is called the Graduated Reciprocation in Tension-Reduction plan (GRIT). In addition to the basic principle of small unilateral moves, GRIT has several other requirements: (1) the initial steps must involve a *low degree of risk* and not endanger national security, (2) the move must be *well publicized* in advance and publically *verifiable,* and (3) it must be *possible to withdraw* the offer if the other side does not respond. (See fig. 21.4.)

Etzioni (1967), who developed a similar plan, points out an example of the GRIT plan in President Kennedy's actions between June 10 and November 22, 1963. During a major speech at a large university, the president referred to the joint costs of nuclear escalation by the United States and the Soviet Union and then announced that American nuclear

Figure 21.4 Hopefully, as nations come to depend more and more on negotiation and diplomacy rather than war to settle their differences, the contributions of social psychologists (e.g., Osgood's GRIT plan) will become more widely used. (Courtesy United Nations/Y. Nagata.)

tests in the atmosphere would be suspended temporarily. In this speech, several conditions of the GRIT plan were met. First, the president invoked a common goal—the mutual advantages of not escalating the development of nuclear weapons. Second, the speech was well-publicized. Third, the low-risk, unilateral move was easily verifiable. And fourth, the ban on testing could be lifted if no reciprocal response was forthcoming from the U.S.S.R. In this particular case, the initiative seemed to be effective. Within a few months, several reciprocated moves were made to reduce tensions. The day after Kennedy's address, the Soviet Union agreed to a request by the United States to send United Nations observers to Yemen. This was followed by American support for seating a Hungarian delegation at the U.N. These events eventually led to a limited ban on nuclear tests, restricted production and development of strategic bombers, expanded trade agreements, and more cultural exchanges. Unfortunately, Kennedy's death and the escalation of the war in Viet Nam served to postpone the cycle of reciprocated actions until the SALT I pact and the new trade agreements were signed in 1972. Although the emphasis in this case study has been on developing common goals, some theorists believe the problem lies more in defining what are the best ways to obtain goals that are already held in common (see box 21.9).

Box 21.9
New Research on the Resolution of Conflict

Hammond (1965) perceives the nature of intergroup conflict as a gradual shifting from a "conflict of interests" to a "conflict of meanings": "My effort to look to the future, then, results in the forecast of an important change—a change from a world in which there has been conflict over ends (the spoils), but agreement as to means (political and economic pressure, including war), to a future in which there will be agreement over ends (world security), but cognitive conflict over means (how to get it)."

Hammond's message is that the attainment of common or superordinate goals among nations will not necessarily put an end to conflict. The problem of how to achieve these common goals will remain, and the differences in opinion may easily harden into "ideologies." Hammond not only pointed to the need for new directions in research on conflict but subsequently developed a sophisticated research paradigm to investigate the formation and resolution of the cognitive conflicts to which he refers (Hammond et al., 1966).

Because it is difficult to verify a theory or proposition such as Osgood's GRIT plan on the basis of news reports alone, two social psychologists, Gamson and Modigliani (1971) did a systematic and detailed *content analysis* of all available communications between the United States and the Soviet Union from 1946 to 1963. This analysis involved subtracting as much identifying material as possible from a message and having "blind" coders (persons who knew nothing about the study's purpose) rate it on certain categories. For example, was the tone of the message friendly or hostile? Did its content pose a challenge or did the content consist of a conciliatory offer or response. The findings showed that throughout this period, whenever one side made a conciliatory offer, the other side reciprocated; but long periods of time often elapsed between these moves. In the early 1960s, however, the rate of reciprocal actions increased rapidly, thus giving some support to the effectiveness of a plan that was similar to GRIT.

In an additional test of the GRIT plan, Pilisuk and Skolnick (1968) devised a complex simulation game in which subjects played the roles of political and military decision makers for a hypothetical country. To test the effects of various strategies, the experimenters presented different groups of subjects with different preprogrammed strategies. One was a matching, or *parity* strategy; that is, whenever the subject increased his supply of weapons, the "partner" would match this increase. This is similar to the arms race of recent years. In a *unilateral* strategy that was similar to GRIT, the programmed partner always completed a round of negotiations with one less missile than the real subject had. If the subject reciprocated by reducing his stock accordingly, the partner made a further reduction in the next game. If no reciprocal reduction was made, the "partner" maintained his weapons stock at that same level. In a third strategy called *natural pairs,* no preprogramming was used; the strategy consisted of a free-for-all between two real subjects. The results showed that both the parity and unilateral strategies were superior to the strategies of the natural pairs. At the end of the session, it was found that the least number of weapons was stocked by both sides when a strategy similar to GRIT was used. (See fig. 21.5.) However, the difference in the results when this strategy and the more conventional parity strategy was used was not statistically significant.

In other words, the research support for a program such as GRIT is mixed. Although some results seem to support its effectiveness in reducing intergroup or international conflict, the clear superiority of this approach over the conventional parity or matching strategy has not been convincingly demonstrated. Thus the conceptual approach needs to be refined and more and better research must be done.

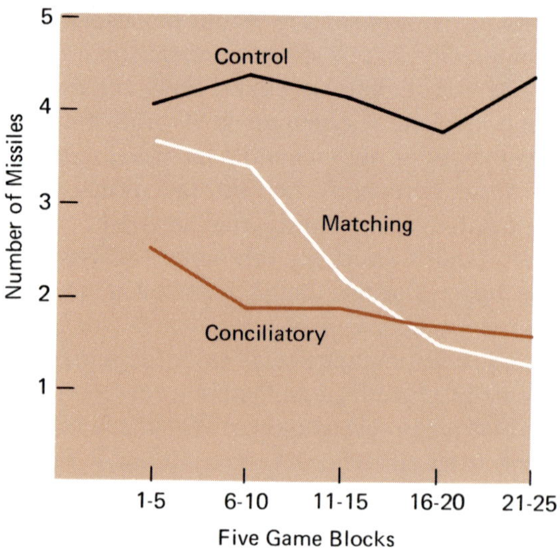

Figure 21.5 Number of missiles remaining after each block of trials for the conditions in the Pilisuk and Skolnick study. The three conditions are natural pairs (control), matching (or parity), and conciliatory (or the condition similar to the GRIT strategy). (From M. Pilisuk & P. Skolnick, "Inducing trust: A test of the Osgood proposal." *Journal of Personality and Social Psychology,* 1968, *8,* pp. 121–133. Copyright 1968 by the American Psychological Association. Reprinted by permission.)

Summary

Although the individual sources of behavior are a major focus in psychology, this chapter examined the social context of behavior. After describing the simplest source of social influence, the effects of the "mere presence" of others on behavior, we considered several sources of the motivation to affiliate with others. Finally, we examined the effects of competition and cooperation, both within and between groups.

When competition is controlled for, the presence of other people appears to have the effect of increasing individual drive or arousal level. If the individual is working on a well-learned task, performance will be facilitated. However, if the individual is working on a new, unlearned task, a decrement in performance will result.

Among the sources for peoples' tendencies to affiliate with others that we examined were the effects of fear or stress, the motive to compare oneself with a comparison group and the use of a group to provide some acceptable definition of social reality.

Although some balance between the processes of cooperation and competition is essential to the effective functioning of any group, most activities, especially in education and business, are structured on a purely competitive basis. Field research in these areas, however, has demonstrated the advantages of cooperative over competitive reward structures for group performances, communication and member satisfaction. More controlled laboratory research, using mixed-motive, nonzero sum games, has isolated several factors that affect the amount of cooperation or competition within groups: More open communication between members tends to increase the level of cooperation. The strategy of the partner makes a difference. Surprisingly, an unconditionally cooperative partner does not elicit maximum cooperation, and is exploited as much as he or she is appreciated. Maximum cooperation is elicited by the matched or reciprocity strategy, where cooperation is rewarded by cooperation, and exploitation punished by reciprocal exploitation. Some problems with generalizing directly from the results of laboratory games to real-life situations are: lack of knowledge of the other person in laboratory situations and frequent use of a noncommunication condition, restriction on choice of alternative responses to the mixed-motive situation in laboratory games, and the artificiality of social norms, and expectations for behaviors in experimental settings.

Most serious conflict between groups may be based on competition for scarce resources, whether these be territory, money, or prestige. The intensification of conflict has been characterized by such indicators as extreme ingroup differentiation and relative evaluations, mutual negative stereotypes, and the reduction of intergroup contacts. The most effective conflict-reduction strategy has been to create common group goals, where both factions are constrained to work together for their common good.

Research in international conflict has indicated some similarities with the intergroup conflict research. Conflict between nations is often based on scarce resources. Also, studies of United States and U.S.S.R. attitudes toward each other have demonstrated the existence of mutually negative stereotypes, called the mirror-image effect. A tension-reduction plan, called GRIT, incorporates the principle of common goals, but goes further to specify particular steps in the process: (1) that superordinate or common goals are stressed, (2) that an initial unilateral move be made by one side, (3) that the move be well publicized and verifiable, and (4) that the unilateral move can be withdrawn easily, if it is not reciprocated by the other side.

An analysis of United States and U.S.S.R. relations, as well as simulated international conflict research, has sought to test this approach. However, at present, the results do not show a consistent advantage for the GRIT plan over the more conventional parity strategies.

22

Attitudes and Attitudinal Change

Think for a moment about the following questions. Is a college education useful for anything? Is marijuana a potentially dangerous drug for long-term users? Do prisons produce more or less crime in society? Do you think tax loopholes should be closed? Is your mother always wrong in what she believes? For each question, you will have a response, even if it is "I don't know." But would your responses five years ago have been the same as those you would give today? Probably not because your feelings and thoughts about things have changed over the years.

Although psychologists have defined the word attitude in many different ways, all the definitions contain one or more of the following elements. (1) Attitudes have an *affective* or emotional component. For example, to have an attitude toward abortion is to have some kind of positive or negative feeling about it. (2) Attitudes also include a *cognitive* component; that is, some set of specific beliefs about the object of the attitude. (3) And, most important, attitudes consist of *dispositions toward behaving* in a certain way. When someone expresses a favorable attitude toward a political candidate, we would expect that person to be willing to talk about the candidate, campaign, even vote for him.

Now think of the attitude that has changed most in the last five years. What influenced that change? Was it more information on the topic, more experience with the object of the attitude, or a change in the reinforcements associated with the behavioral expression of the attitude? Perhaps the change was influenced more by moving away from home, changing friends, or joining a different religious, political, or social group. Maybe a variety of events or even arguments made it apparent that there were certain inconsistencies in your beliefs, attitudes, and behavior, and thus you felt obliged to change one or another of the inconsistent elements.

All these sources of attitude information, maintenance, and change will be examined in this chapter. In the field of social psychology, this topic occupies the major part of the psychologist's thinking, research, and writing.

Group Influence and Attitude Change

Reference Groups

One of the first major longitudinal field studies in social psychology (Newcomb, 1943) investigated the changes in the political and social attitudes of female students during the four years (1935–1939) they spent at Bennington College.

In this study, Newcomb found a strong connection between changes in attitude over time and choice of *reference group*. A reference group is defined as any group to which a person may look to develop, maintain, conform, or change his attitudes or opinions. Reference groups serve as frames of reference or anchors for the definition of social reality. If a person's reference group changes, it is almost certain that there will be subsequent changes or modifications in his beliefs, attitudes, and values. Some changes in reference groups are fairly constrained and difficult to avoid—for example, being drafted into the army or sent to prison. Other changes are more or less voluntary—for example, choosing a college. After women chose Bennington College, there was a classic conflict between parental values and attitudes and the "new" attitudes represented by a liberal college faculty and environment. (See fig. 22.1.)

Most students came from wealthy and conservative families (the study was done during the Great Depression, when only the rich could afford a college education). For example, more than two-thirds of the students' parents were registered in the Republican Party. Franklin Roosevelt's New Deal was about as popular with these parents as the idea of free distribution of cocaine by the federal government might be today. However, despite this conservative background, the amount of attitude change within the liberal college environment was dramatic. Although sixty-two percent of the students endorsed the Republican presidential candidate as freshmen, only fifteen percent en-

Figure 22.1 The face-to-face interaction with faculty and students at college is often the setting for a fundamental reevaluation of one's attitudes and values. For others, attitude change may simply be a conforming response to the perceived norms and pressures of the group. (Courtesy Hugh Rogers, Monkmeyer Press Photo Service.)

dorsed the Republican candidate four years later as seniors. On the other hand, as freshmen, only twenty-nine percent endorsed Democratic candidate Roosevelt, while fifty-four percent favored him as seniors. In addition, Newcomb found that the students who changed most in a liberal direction also became most popular and politically active among the student body. They were most often elected to student offices, chosen as friends, and were even rated as better adjusted according to medical reports.

But did the changes in attitude produced by moving from a conservative family to a liberal college environment persist? Apparently so. When Newcomb et al. (1967) made a follow-up study almost twenty-five years later, they found a much higher degree of liberalism among the Bennington alumnae than among non-Bennington women of the same age and socioeconomic background. For example, sixty percent of the Bennington graduates preferred Kennedy to Nixon in 1960, whereas only thirty percent of the comparison group made the same choice. In fact, the Bennington women had made choices subsequent to college that tended to reinforce and maintain their newly acquired liberal reference group. For example, compared with the conservative controls, they read many more liberally slanted newspapers and periodicals and many had married men or had chosen careers that supported their liberal beliefs. A more contemporary example of attitude change and reference groups may be found in box 22.1.

Although the long-term results of the Bennington study provide impressive evidence for the influence of reference groups on attitude formation and change, the exact processes that brought about these changes are not clear. Was the adoption of the faculty reference group a result of "thinking through" political issues and accepting the most "reasonable" position, or was it a matter of social conformity? There were many social rewards for girls who became more liberal, and there were some social, and perhaps even academic penalties for those who remained conservative. For some, both new insights and social approval may have been important, as demonstrated by the comment of one young

Box 22.1
The "Generation Gap" and Reference Groups

Newcomb's Bennington study showed the effects of changing from family to college reference groups on female students' attitudes in the late 1930s. Today, when so many students are coming from liberal rather than conservative families, is a generation gap still created by college attendance? Are the so-called student radicals moving from the liberal stance of their families toward more radical reference groups?

The answer depends on how we define a radical student. Block, Haan, and Smith (1969), in their study of student activism, made an important distinction between *dissenters* and *activists.* They found that while dissenters scored high on protest activities and low on humanitarian interests, activists tended to score high on both.

In examining the family backgrounds of these two groups, Block and her colleagues discovered different patterns of relationship to the family. The dissenters had divorced themselves completely from the family attitudes and values; that is, they had rejected the liberal values of their families as a source of attitudes. The activists, on the other hand, seemed to take the liberal values of their parents more seriously than before. The criticisms they directed toward their families were not against their liberal values as such, but against the hypocritical manner in which their parents held these values. The activists were determined that they would represent these values more honestly than did their parents.

Thus generation gaps may be created, as in the Bennington study, by giving up the family reference group in favor of another. On the other hand, as with the activists of today, generation gaps may also be created by simply trying to live up more fully to the reference group values of the family.

woman: "I became liberal, at first, because of its prestige value; I remain so because the problems around which my liberalism centers are important. What I want now is to be effective in solving the problems" (Newcomb, 1943, p. 136).

Are these changes in attitudes genuine, or are they merely rationalizations, or justifications for social conformity? A more highly controlled field experiment by Siegel and Siegel (1957) attempted to separate conformity from reference group change effects.

Siegel and Siegel conducted their field experiment at a large private coeducational university, where all freshmen were required to live in dormitories. In the second year, however, female students were given the choice of living in a high-status house on what had once been sorority row or continuing to live in smaller dormitories. Because there was more demand for space than was available in the former sorority houses, the dean of women conducted a drawing to determine which students would live in them. Thus the experimenters had a group of students who shared a common membership group for one year and then chose the same reference group for their second year (row house) but were not guaranteed their choice. In fact, in the second year, the experimenters *randomly assigned* the women students who chose row houses to either row houses or dormitories. This random assignment made the study a *field experiment* rather than a field study because it allowed far greater control over critical variables than was present in Newcomb's Bennington study.

At the end of the sophomore year, the women were again given a choice of where to live the third year. This created three groups of special interest to the investigators: group A, consisting of women who had chosen and lived in a row house the second year and chose to remain for the third year; group B, composed of women who had been assigned to a dormitory the second year but again chose the row house for the third year; and group C, which was made up of women who had been assigned to a dormitory the second year but reversed their earlier decision and chose the dormitory again for the third year.

To assess the effects of the reference group on attitude change under these three conditions, the experimenters took advantage of the previous finding that row-house women rated much higher on measures of *authoritarian* attitudes than did dormitory women. Based on this information they predicted that the least amount of attitude change would occur among students in group A, whose reference groups were row houses and whose attitudes had been maintained by actual membership in row houses. Attitude change in group B would be greater than in group A because group B's reference group (row houses) had not changed, but the membership group (dormitory) was different. The greatest attitude change was predicted for members of group C because during the second year, their reference group changed from row house to dormitory, while this change was reinforced by living in a dormitory. The results of the experiment supported these predictions (see table 22.1). The most change in attitude toward reduced authoritarianism occurred among members of group C, who changed their reference group, while the least amount of change occurred in group A, which had not changed reference group. Group B fell in between.

Because the students were randomly assigned to their living quarters, the Siegel study demonstrated the direct effects of reference groups on attitude change *per se*. By including group B, consisting of women who maintained a preference for row houses and also maintained their authoritarian attitudes, but *without the reinforcements* of row-house living—the effects of reference group and

Table 22.1 Mean Authoritarian Attitude Scores.

Group		Mean E-F Attitude Scores Freshman Year	Sophomore Year	Mean Change*
A (n=9)	Reference group SAME Membership SAME	103.0	99.1	3.9
B (n=11)	Reference group SAME Membership DIFFERENT	102.2	91.0	11.2
C (n=8)	Reference DIFFERENT Membership DIFFERENT	102.0	82.3	19.7

*Differences between groups significant at $P. < .025$ by the Jonckheere test for ordered group differences.

Source: Adapted from Siegel, A.E. & Siegel, S. "Reference groups, membership groups, and attitude change." *Journal of Abnormal and Social Psychology,* 1957, *55,* p. 363. Copyright 1957 by the American Psychological Association. Reprinted by permission.

group conformity could be separated. If group conformity were the sole factor in attitude change, the change in attitudes would only have occurred in group A, not in group B. On the other hand, group pressures to conform must have played some part in group A's attitudes because the amount of attitude change in this group was less than that found in group B. We will now examine the effects of conformity on attitude change in more detail.

Conformity to Group Norms

As we just discussed, attitudes may be influenced by reference groups because an individual genuinely accepts the value bases of the attitudes endorsed by the group. However, much so-called attitude change may simply be the consequence of *conformity to group norms.* For many people, being different or having a deviant opinion is uncomfortable, and they would rather go along with the group's opinion, even when they do not fully accept it. This effect was demonstrated by Asch (1951) in an experimental situation in which the opinion to be expressed involved nothing more than a simple judgment about the relative lengths of lines. Imagine that you have just arrived at the laboratory to take part in an experiment on vision and are seated with five others around a table. The experimenter explains that your task is to decide which of three lines on a piece of board is the same length as a standard line (see fig. 22.2). The first few trials seem easy—each person announces his judgment in turn, and you are the last person in the group to report. Everyone agrees on which line matches the standard line. However, during the third trial, the first person announces that a line which is clearly shorter than the standard is the same length as the standard line, and you suspect he has made a silly error. But then the next person makes the same judgment. Then the next person agrees! Your turn is coming up, so you think fast. Should you ask the experimenter about the rules? Maybe your own eyes are deceiving you. What should you do? Stick with your own judgment of what you see, or go along with what the others seem to see?

Of course, the other subjects in the experiment are accomplices who have been asked to give unanimous false judgments during several critical trials. The main measure is the degree to which the actual subject will abandon his own judgment and conform to the

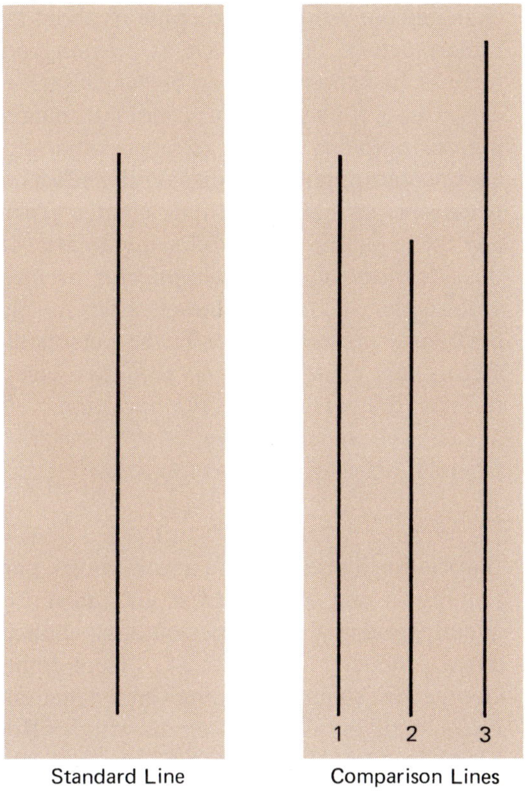

Figure 22.2 A sample set of lines for the judgment task in the Asch conformity experiment. The subjects' task was to indicate which line, 1, 2 or 3, was the same length as the standard line on the left. (From Asch, S.E., *Social psychology*. Copyright 1952, Prentice Hall, Inc. Reprinted by permission.)

false judgments of the group. Sixty-seven percent of the subjects in these early studies conformed to the unanimous but false group judgments. Furthermore, the same two-thirds of the subjects always made the conforming responses. The other one-third consistently refused to yield to the group's false judgments.

In subsequent research, the following factors were found to modify the effects of conformity observed in Asch's research:

1. *Ambiguity of the stimulus.* In Asch's experiments, the lines differed enough so that it was almost impossible to make an error of judgment about which line matched the standard line. However, Asch discovered that as the actual differences in the length of the lines decreased, the amount of conformity within the group increased. Also, Deutsch and Gerard (1955) found that when subjects had to rely on memory in making their judgments, more conformity occurred. The more ambiguous situations are actually closer to real-life situations, where attitude changes are influenced by groups, because most attitudes, unlike lines, cannot be measured objectively.

2. *Unanimity of the majority.* Asch had found that when the unanimity of the false majority was broken, conformity to the group decreased. This phenomenon was confirmed by Allen and Levine (1971), who found that if at least one other person also disagreed with the majority, his presence provided both moral support and an external source of information that served to validate the subject's opinion.

3. *Commitment to a decision.* In Asch's experiment, the subject reported his judgment after the other group members had spoken. But if the subject must commit himself *before* hearing the group's opinions he displays less conformity. For example, Deutsch and Gerard found a rate of conformity of twenty-five percent among subjects who had not made a previous commitment, sixteen percent among subjects who wrote down their own judgment privately first, and only six percent among subjects who made a public commitment before hearing the group's judgments.

In summary, the greatest amount of conformity to group attitudes should occur in a situation where an individual does not have a definite initial attitude, the attitude itself is fairly hard to define objectively, and there is unanimous agreement about the attitude in the group. Possible differences in personality characteristics between conforming and independent individuals are presented in box 22.2.

Persuasive Communications and Attitude Change

Thus far, we have examined the influence of groups on changes in attitudes. However, not all attitude change can be attributed to group factors. We are constantly bombarded by more impersonal appeals by way of television, radio, magazines, books, speeches, and the like. These appeals are directly aimed at changing our attitudes and opinions about the importance of things, such as cleaning our teeth or bathrooms, buying bigger or smaller cars, voting for a particular candidate, changing our opinions about cigarette smoking or energy consumption. Studies on the effects of persuasive appeals on attitude change generally focus on one of the following areas: (1) the attributes of the *communicator* or message-sender, (2) the characteristics of the *persuasive message,* and (3) the personality factors that cause *recipients* to either accept or resist the persuasive communication.

Box 22.2

Conformity and Personality

The experimental studies using the Asch conformity model have investigated various group aspects of conforming behavior. But do some individuals have characteristics that predispose them to conforming behavior? Crutchfield (1955) provided us with clues about the kinds of people who resist or yield under social pressure. Some of the most common differences he found between yielders (conformists) and resisters (independents) are listed below:

Yielders to social pressure (conformists)

1. Were submissive, compliant, and overly accepting of authority figures,
2. Operated within narrow and prescribed limits on their behavior,
3. Showed a strong need to control their impulses, that is, were inhibited,
4. Vacillated, were unable to make decisive choices, and
5. Were highly suggestible, oriented toward the evaluations of others.

Resisters of social pressure (independents)

1. Took leadership roles, were dominant in social relationships,
2. Were self-reliant, able to rely on own judgments,
3. Were active and energetic,
4. Sought and enjoyed aesthetic and sensuous experiences, and
5. Were persuasive in arguments, able to win others over to their own point of view.

Characteristics of the Communicator

Prestige

Associating a product with a well-known personality is one of the oldest and most frequently used methods of persuading people to buy a product (see fig. 22.3): "Here comes George Hunely in his Johnny Carson suit and Joe Namath boots to play tennis with his Rod Laver racquet. He runs into Stephanie Long, getting out of her car that has been endorsed by Wilt Chamberlain and serviced at a transmission shop recommended by Zsa Zsa Gabor. She is wearing a lipstick that has been worn by Bianca Jagger." Although these attempts at persuasion are rather obvious, there are more subtle ones in which the prestige of the *source* of a message can strongly affect attitudes and opinions. For example, in one of the first controlled experimental studies of the effects of prestige, Hovland and Weiss (1951) presented taped communications on a number of topics, such as the advisability of selling nonprescription antihistamines and the practicality of building nuclear-powered submarines. Although all subjects heard the same messages, half of them were told that the message came from a prestigious source and half were told it came from a nonprestigious source. For example, the antihistamine message came from either a physician or a work-

If Colgate is just a kid's cavity fighter, how come Walt Frazier won't brush with anything else?
One-on-one, nobody gets past New York Knick star Walt Frazier. Not the biggest guy in the league, not even tomorrow's superstar. But basically Walt is a team player . . . a man who has the knack of getting people to work together smoothly. On the court and off. Maybe that's why Walt Frazier is a Colgate man.
Colgate is a toothpaste for people who get together with people. It freshens breath as long as a leading mouthwash, as clinical test results show. And the taste is brisk and clean.
Only your dentist can give teeth a better fluoride treatment than Colgate with MFP. But a great cavity fighter can be a powerful breath freshener, too.
If you like people, be sure you brush with Colgate. Walt Frazier wouldn't think of brushing with anything else.
Colgate MFP
Colgate with MFP...the breath-freshening cavity fighter.
©1973, Colgate-Palmolive Company

Figure 22.3 The use of prestigious individuals to sell products is common in advertising. With Walt Frazier, the specific basis for prestige may include expertise, attraction, trustworthiness, and, for some people, perceived similarity. (Courtesy Colgate-Palmolive Company.)

ing man, while the nuclear submarine message came from either a prominent American physicist or an editorial in *Pravda,* the newspaper of the Soviet communist party. Under all these conditions, the subjects who had been told that the message came from a prestigious source were much more likely to agree with and change their attitudes toward the communication.

At about the same time, Asch (1952) performed a similar study. A message that contained the following statement was read to the subjects: "I hold it that a little rebellion, now and then, is a good thing, and as necessary in the political world as storms are in the physical." Half the subjects were informed that the statement had been made by Thomas Jefferson, while the other half were told that Nikolai Lenin had made it. Opinions about the statement were remarkably different in the two groups: the subjects who believed that Jefferson had made the statement were favorably disposed toward the message; the other group rejected the message. In some cases, the basis of the communicator's status is *expertise;* for example, the physician on antihistamines, the physicist on nuclear submarines, and Rod Laver on a tennis racquet. In other cases, the communicator's status is based on personal attractiveness rather than expertise; for example, Zsa Zsa Gabor on transmissions. In still others, the prestige may derive from the *trustworthiness* of the communicator; for example, Jefferson versus Lenin. Yet again, the persuasive appeal may be based on *fear* (see box 22.3). Although most research studies have not separated these elements to observe their relative effects, some studies on the factor of trustworthiness deserve our consideration.

Trustworthiness and Intentions

One of the quickest ways for a communicator to lose an audience is to give the impression that he does not actually believe what he is saying. People are usually suspicious about the intentions of salespeople. If it is clear that a salesperson is only after a sale and has no real interest in the customer, his attempts to persuade are likely to fail. An experiment by Walster, Aronson, and Abrahams (1966) demonstrated this effect. In what these investigators called a *self-serving* condition, subjects heard a convicted criminal arguing in favor of more individual freedom and less police power. In the non-self-serving condition, the prisoner argued in favor of stronger police powers. Attitude change occurred only in the non-self-serving condition because the listeners believed that the convict had to be more sincere to argue on behalf of a belief that would preclude his gaining early freedom. Another way to increase the credibility or trustworthiness of a communicator is to have him "overheard," when he apparently is unaware that he is being listened to. For example, Walster and Festinger (1962) had subjects listen in on a segment of a "therapy session" that contained a standard persuasive argument. Half the subjects thought the therapist was *aware* of their presence, while the other half were led to believe he was *unaware* of them. The subjects' subsequent change in attitude about the persuasive argument was significantly greater if they believed the therapist was *unaware* of their presence. Although the results of this study have been difficult to replicate, this principle of persuasive communication may have inspired all the supposedly candid endorsements of toothpastes and laundry soaps we see on television. The advertisers may be attempting to create a situation where the audience "looks in" on a typical everyday scene in Mrs. Jones's laundry room. However, these messages often fail because the typical audience is unable to identify with Mrs. Jones's neat hairdo and

Box 22.3
Fear and Persuasion

It is not uncommon for the source of a persuasive communication to use fear or threats to back up their message. Parents are forever telling their children that they will get run over if they rush into the street without looking. The advertisements of the American Cancer Society tell us we will die if we keep smoking "coffin nails." Nations back up their communications with other nations by threatening embargos or even war. Short of carrying out the threatened action, does fear work in changing attitudes?

More than a dozen major research studies have investigated the relationship between the amount of fear produced by a persuasive communication and the amount of subsequent attitudinal and behavioral change. The results show that an extremely threatening message is most likely to change behaviors that follow *immediately* after a simple and direct message. For long-term attitude change, however, a *moderate* amount of fear is better. This seems to be related to the fact that people, especially if they are initially highly anxious, tend to cope with extreme threats by simply blocking them out of awareness (e.g., Janis, 1968).

clothing and the immaculate room in which she washes her clothes. Thus, in addition to expertise, trustworthiness, and personal attraction, *perceived similarity* to the communicator is sometimes important.

Similarity. The more similarities a recipient can see between a communicator and himself, the greater the chances that the persuasive message will be accepted. This is why many politicians resort to kissing babies and eating fried chicken at election time. Although they may dislike doing both, they want to appear similar to the "common people."

On a more mundane scale, Brock (1965) effectively demonstrated the importance of similarity in a study done in a paint store. One group of salesmen were instructed to tell customers that they had just painted their own houses with the same *amount* of paint the customer was requesting. They then recommended either a higher or lower priced paint. Another group told customers they had used *twenty times* the amount of paint on their own house as that requested by a customer and they too recommended either a lower or higher priced brand. The salesmen who claimed to have used a similar amount of paint sold more paint than those who represented themselves as dissimilar (see table 22.2).

Table 22.2 Percentage of paint purchasers who changed decision in direction of influence attempts by salesmen who used a similar or dissimilar amount of paint on their own houses. Note that the similarity effect was found whether the attempt was made to change to a higher or lower priced paint.

Direction of influence attempt	Similar	Dissimilar
To a lower price level	73%(16)	45%(10)
To a higher price level	55%(12)	32%(7)
Total	64%(28)	39%(17)*

*Chi-square, p. 05

Source: Adapted from Brock, T.C., "Communicator-recipient similarity and decision change." *Journal of Personality and Social Psychology*, 1965, 1, pp. 650–654. Copyright 1965 by the American Psychological Association. Reprinted by permission.

One word of caution for anyone who plans to use the characteristic of similarity to put something over on an unsuspecting audience. If he fails, and the audience perceives his lack of expertise, untrustworthiness, unpleasant personality, or dissimilarity, the consequent attitude change may be in the opposite direction. This is known as the *boomerang effect* and has been demonstrated in a study of attitudes about civil rights (Abelson and Miller, 1967). In this study, the experimenter interviewed people in the park, while an accomplice deliberately tried to be as personally obnoxious as possible and expressed views that completely opposed those of the experimenter. The result was that the attitudes of the interviewees changed toward those of the experimenter and away from those of the accomplice. The same effect can result if the trustworthiness or expertise of a communicator is undermined—as in cases of public fraud and deception on the part of political, business, or even scientific figures of note. People may dissociate themselves from attitudes formerly endorsed by communicators who have lost their image as persons who are worthy of trust.

Characteristics of the Persuasive Message

While it is fairly obvious that the communicator's characteristics may affect the persuasiveness of his communications, subtle features of the communication itself influence the way it is received. Two aspects of message presentation that have been researched by psychologists are *one- versus two-sided* arguments and the effects of *primacy* and *recency*.

One- Versus Two-Sided Communications

If you wanted to persuade an audience to vote for a certain candidate for political office, what would be the most effective procedure; to emphasize your candidate's good points and ignore the opposition, or present the viewpoints of both candidates and discuss why your candidate's position is better? The answer provided by research is that it depends on your audience.

If the audience supports your candidate, is relatively uneducated, and is unaware of the opposing side's position, it is better to use a one-sided presentation (Hovland et al., 1949). A two-sided presentation may simply confuse these people and perhaps suggest arguments against your candidate that they had not thought of before.

However, if you are addressing an audience that is relatively well educated and aware of the positions of both your candidate and the opposition, it is better to use a two-sided presentation. According to Hovland and his colleagues, there are several reasons for this. First, discussing both sides of an issue may make your presentation seem more *objective* and less of an attempt to force your candidate on the audience. Second, you may seem more broad-minded and *credible* if you appear willing to consider both sides of an issue. Third, by acknowledging that the audience is aware of the other side of an issue you are also acknowledging that they are intelligent enough to have given some thought to the matter. In this way, you support their sense of *self-esteem*. In some cases, it may be enough to acknowledge the fact that opposing arguments exist, without elaborating on them. With a well-educated audience, Jones and Brehm (1970) found greater attitude change when the presentation simply mentioned the existence of opposing positions, compared with a straight one-sided presentation. Fourth, Lumsdaine and Janis (1953) found that two-sided arguments were more effective in producing resistance to subsequent attempts by the opposition to change opinions. McGuire et al. (1961) have termed this phenomenon the *innoculation* effect. Just as a small dose of typhoid will stimulate the body to produce antibodies to ward off a severe infection, a small dose of an opposing argument may stimulate enough counterarguments to defend against a stronger persuasive attempt at a later time.

All of the persuasion methods considered so far, assume a somewhat passive audience. The most effective persuasion technique is *role playing* (box 22.4).

Effects of Primacy Versus Recency

Suppose that there is also a speaker for the opposition candidate, and you must decide who will appear first. Which order would be more effective: you present your speech first and have the other speaker follow you, or the opposition presents his speech first? If you choose the first alternative, you are assuming

Box 22.4
"Don't Just Stand There—
Do Something!"

All the studies on persuasive communication reviewed in the text assume that the audience or target group is passive—either listening to a speaker or watching television. However, more than one researcher has found that an effective way to get a message across is to involve the recipient in acting out the content of the message. This has become known as the *role-playing* technique.

Role-playing was used by Mann and Janis (1965) with great effect to reduce smoking habits and to increase negative attitudes toward smoking. They recruited young women volunteers, all of whom were heavy smokers, to participate in a role-playing sequence depicting a cancer patient. The women had to act the role of the patient as the doctor told her she had cancer and then continue the role-playing by telling her friends and family, being admitted to hospital, and facing an early death. This procedure had the immediate effect of reducing daily cigarette consumption by almost fifty percent for the experimental group as a whole. Moreover, the reduction was still apparent during a follow-up study eighteen months later.

that because the audience is fresh, it will remember more of your speech (the *primacy* effect). If you choose to go last, you are assuming that the audience will remember more of the most recent speech they have heard (the *recency* effect). Miller and Campbell (1959) did an extensive study on this issue and found that if two speakers make their presentations on the same night, one after the other, and the audience is asked to recall the content immediately after the meeting, there will be no differences in recall (see table 22.3). However, if both speeches are made in one week and the audience is not tested until the following week, the first speech will be recalled better than the second—a *primacy* effect. On the other hand, if you give your speech one week, the opposition gives his the second week, and the audience is tested for recall the second week, the opposition's speech will be remembered better—a *recency* effect (see table 22.3). So the critical aspect of primacy and recency in persuasive communications is not the order itself but the interval between the first and second presentation and also between the presentations and the recall test.

Table 22.3 Results from the Miller and Campbell study on primacy and recency effects. A positive number indicates that the first communication had the greatest effect (i.e., primacy). A negative number indicates the second communication was more influential (i.e., recency).

Primacy and Recency in Attitude Formation

Condition	Change	Direction
Communication 1, communication 2, test	− .06	None
Communication 1, communication 2, one week, test	2.11	Primacy
Communication 1, one week, communication 2, test	−1.67	Recency
Communication 1, one week, communication 2, one week, test	.11	None

Source: Adapted from Miller, N. & Campbell, D.T. "Recency and primacy in persuasion as a function of the timing of speeches and measurements." *Journal of Abnormal and Social Psychology*, 1959, *59*, pp. 1–9. Copyright 1959 by the American Psychological Association. Reprinted by permission.

Characteristics of Recipients

We have considered some characteristics of the message sender and several aspects of the actual presentation of the message. Now we will describe a few factors related to the recipient of a persuasive communication: (1) how much *discrepancy* does the recipient perceive between his own position on an issue and the position of the communicator and (2) which individual *personality* characteristics will determine whether a recipient will accept or reject a persuasive communication.

Effects of Discrepancy

The degree to which a member of an audience is willing to change an opinion or attitude depends on the amount of discrepancy he perceives between his own and the communicator's position. In general, there seems to be a *curvilinear* relationship between the size of the discrepancy and the amount of attitude change. That is, if the discrepancy is small to moderate, the recipient tends to move toward the communicator's position. But if the communicator's position is extremely discrepant, the recipient may completely reject his opinion. For example, an educational "expert" might be able to persuade a group of middle-class parents at a parent-teachers' meeting that exposing their children to a small, or even moderate amount of sex-education materials in the school is beneficial for the children's development and learning. However, if the expert goes too far, and begins advocating nude encounter groups or exposure to pornographic movies in the classroom, he would probably not achieve much attitude change.

Hovland, Harvey, and Sherif (1957) devised the terms "latitude of acceptance" and "latitude of rejection" to describe this effect. An increase in discrepancy between the speaker and audience, within the listeners' latitude of acceptance, is likely to lead to increasing attitude change. However, once the speaker enters the audience's *latitude of rejection,* attitude change will decrease (see fig. 22.4).

Several experimental studies have supported the hypothesis of this curvilinear relationship between size of the discrepancy in attitudes and the amount of attitude change. For example, Rhine and Severance (1970) presented messages to students, arguing for small, moderate, or large increases in tuition. Students were influenced much less by the message about a large increase in tuition than by the messages about small or moderate increases. Another way of viewing this effect is to consider it in three stages (Aronson et al., 1963). (1) When a message is close to one's own position, there is not much room for attitude change; that is, you already agree. (2) If a message is moderately different from your own position, a certain amount of arousal, or *dissonance* occurs, and you may try to resolve the discrepancy, which in most cases will involve some attitude change. (3) However, if the discrepancy is too large, it may be easier

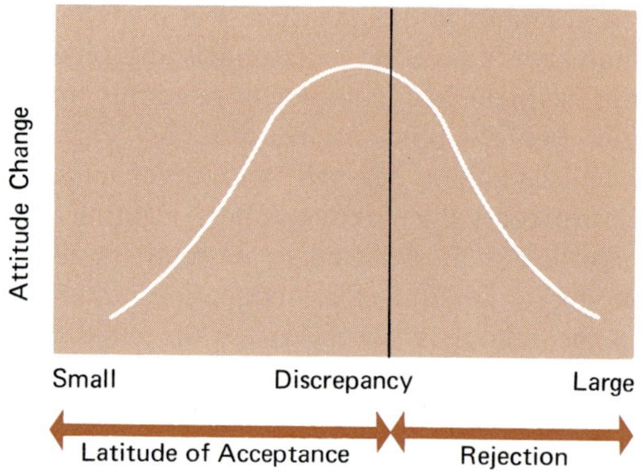

Figure 22.4 Idealized relationship found between size of discrepancy between message sender's and receiver's attitudinal positions. Note that the small and moderate discrepancies fall within the recipient's "latitude of acceptance." Large discrepancies fall in region of rejection.

to reject the communicator (he is less credible) than to try to reconcile the differences in attitudes.

Personality Characteristics

Even if someone used all the information that we have discussed to devise a persuasive message which is guaranteed to have an effect, chances are that not everyone in the audience would accept it. Some individuals refuse to change their opinions under any circumstances. Others, on the other hand, are so easily persuaded that they are willing to sign on the dotted line after the opening sentence. In other words, *individual differences* among people will play a part in determining the success or failure of any communication.

One characteristic that predisposes people to accept or resist persuasion is *authoritarianism.* This includes the tendency of some individuals to rely on external and high-status sources for their view of the world. Thus the latitude of acceptance of any message for highly authoritarian people is restricted to opinions presented by sources that they consider to have high status. Wright and Harvey (1965) tested this phenomenon by presenting subjects who had been rated high or low in terms of authoritarianism with the same message. But, in one case, the message was attributed to a prestigious source; in the other, it was credited to a nonprestigious source. Persons who were highly authoritarian changed their attitudes only under the high-status condition. Those with a low degree of authoritarianism responded similarly to both conditions; that is, they paid more attention to the content of the message than to the status of the source. So if a group of students (low status) attempts to persuade a group of faculty members (high status), which also happens to be strongly authoritarian, the students would do well to sprinkle their presentation liberally with quotations from famous scholars or scientists. However, faculty who are not especially authoritarian may not be so easily impressed, and may be more inclined to argue the content of your proposal.

Another personality factor that affects the persuadability of a recipient is *self-esteem.* A person's degree of self-esteem is related to whether he evaluates himself positively or negatively. A number of studies have shown a *negative relationship* between self-esteem and amount of attitude change. That is, the higher an individual's self-esteem, the less likely he will be persuaded to change his attitudes (Cohen, 1959). Several explanations are possible. One is the now-familiar *prestige-suggestion* effect; that is, persons with low self-esteem will perceive almost everyone else as having higher status than themselves. And we already know that this characteristic will produce a greater degree of attitude change. Another possible reason is that people who lack self-esteem are less able to cope with discrepancies; that is, they cannot argue against or even deny the message, as individuals with high self-esteem are capable of doing. Some psychologists have reasoned that women are generally more susceptible to persuasion than men because women have lower levels of self-esteem. But the issue is not a simple one (see box 22.5).

One way to test the hypothesis that persons with low self-esteem simply lack the resources to deal with persuasive communications, especially threatening ones, would be to present two kinds of messages—one that is nonthreatening and one that contains a personal threat. Gollob and Dittes (1965) did this in an experiment using subjects with high and low self-esteem. The nonthreatening communication dealt with the best method for conducting cancer research and was primarily impersonal and technical. The threatening message implied that a cure for cancer would never be discovered and that the listeners themselves were likely to get cancer during their lifetimes. What would the *"low self-esteem equals low resources"* theory predict? In the nonthreatening condition, the resource needed to counteract persuasion is the ability to evaluate arguments and to marshal counterarguments. Persons with high self-esteem presumably have more of these resources and

Box 22.5
Sex Differences and Persuadability

Although most studies on persuasion have involved male subjects, some research indicates that females are more easily influenced by persuasive communications than males (e.g., McGuire, 1968). What are some possible explanations for this difference?

One possibility advanced by McGuire is that females may be genetically or constitutionally more susceptible to social influences than males. This idea is likely to be rejected out-of-hand by advocates of women's liberation (McGuire is a man), but there is also no objective evidence as yet to support McGuire's hypothesis.

Other, more social causes of the sex difference have greater empirical support. For example, there is ample evidence that parents differentially reward conforming and independent behaviors in young boys and girls (e.g., Block et al., 1969). Moreover, because of differences in educational and occupational opportunities males tend to be placed in dominant and independent positions, while females tend to be placed in subordinate, more submissive positions. Yet another reason for the sex difference in persuadability is that most research situations have been so masculinized (male status figures, choice of automobiles, and so forth) that female subjects have "gone along for the ride," without any real interest in resisting the persuasive communications.

More importantly, the heavy use of male-oriented research situations gives males the advantages of being more familiar with and skilled in them than are females. As we have already learned, the more expertise one has, the more willing one is to resist persuasive attempts. In other words, if female situations were used in research, perhaps the sex differences in persuadability would be less apparent.

should show less attitude change. However, under the threatening condition, the individual's personal resources must be strong enough to absorb the personal implications of the argument and still consider the content of the message. Persons with high self-esteem are presumably better able to do this and should still show *some* (but not too much) attitude change. The person whose self-esteem is low, on the other hand, should be unable to cope with the personal threat and should either deny the message completely or even change his attitude in the opposite direction (the boomerang effect). This is indeed what happened. Gollob and Dittes found that under both conditions, there was a small amount of positive attitude change among subjects with high self-esteem. In the nonthreatening situation, persons with low self-esteem showed a large positive change in the direction of the message, but when threatened, they showed either no change or a small change away from the position argued in the communication.

Thus the differences in the persuadability of persons who are rated high or low in self-esteem seem to be related to differences in cognitive and emotional resources. In most situations, persons with low self-esteem are relatively vulnerable to persuasive attempts. However, if the communication is too threatening to them, they may choose to ignore it or deny it, so that their meagre resources will not be overwhelmed.

Individual Factors in Attitude Change

Most of the research considered so far has focused on social factors that influence attitudes and attitude change. We will now turn to the *intrapsychic* aspects of attitude change. A large body of research over the past two decades has focused on the importance that individuals place on maintaining some consistency among their attitudes, beliefs, and behaviors. (See fig. 22.5.) For example, suppose you like and respect someone very much, but you hear that he has done something that is repugnant to you. This knowledge tends to produce a state of *inconsistency* and tension, which you will probably try to resolve. How can you reduce the inconsistency in liking a person who does things you consider to be obnoxious? You might believe the information about his objectionable be-

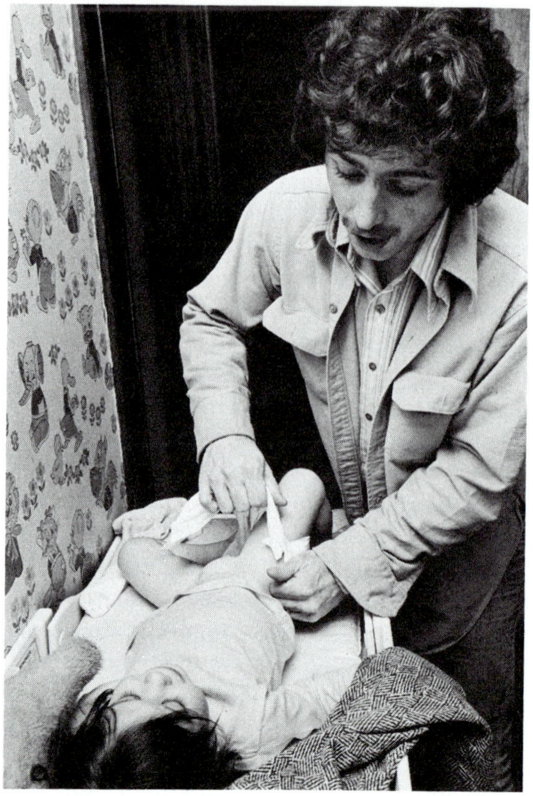

Figure 22.5 An illustration of a dissonance approach to attitude change. Get him to do a few things around the house and after a time, attitudes may change to be consonant with the new sex-role behaviors. Note that the initial attitude-discrepant activities should be ones he enjoys doing. Scrubbing floors should come later, after the attitude change is underway. (Photo courtesy © Alex Webb, Magnum.)

havior and like him less. Or you might deny the information ("Someone is spreading spiteful rumors") and continue to like the person. Theories of *cognitive consistency* attempt to deal with this kind of problem. The theories reviewed here make the following assumptions: *First,* people prefer to have attitudes, emotions, and cognitions about the world that are consistent with one another—that is, they try to keep contradictions and conflicts to a minimum, and, *second,* if inconsistencies or conflicts do occur, people will strive to reduce them in a variety of ways.

The two main approaches involving consistency theory are *balance theory* and the *theory of cognitive dissonance.* We will examine each of these theories in turn and then consider how learning theorists have attempted to explain some of the results obtained in consistency theory experiments by applying the principles of learning and conditioning.

Balance Theory and Attitude Change

One early formulation of consistency theory was put forward by Heider (1946, 1958). He referred to a notion from biology, *homeostasis,* to describe a "normal" state of affairs, both biologically and cognitively. Homeostasis refers to a state in which a system is in *equilibrium,* with all elements balancing each other to form a stable whole—hence the term *balance* theory. If change in any of the elements occurs (in this case, changes in feelings, perceptions, or beliefs), other elements in the system must change to restore equilibrium or balance.

In the case of attitudes, Heider defined two relationships that can be treated as elements in the cognitive system. The first relationship is *sentiment* or "liking," and is represented as either positive (+) or negative (−). The second is a *unit relationship,* which refers to the perception that certain things "belong together" in the world. Things that are considered to be positively related (e.g., Tom owns a car) may be represented by (+), and things that are unassociated (e.g., Tom does *not* have a crewcut) may be represented by a (−).

Heider was particularly interested in the case where an individual's cognitive system contained three elements: a person's (P) attraction toward another (O), a person's (P) attitude toward an object (*x*), and a person's (P) perception of another person's (*O*) attitude toward the same object (*x*). In figure 22.6, you will see that there is a number of possible configurations of these relationships. Let's imagine that (*P*) is yourself, O is an acquaintance, and x is an attitude toward abstract art. In figure 22.6a, you like your acquaintance [P(+)O], you approve of abstract art [P(+)x], and your friend also approves [O(+)x]. In figure 22.6b, you continue to like your acquaintance and abstract art, but your friend does *not* like abstract art [O(−)x]. Which state, *a* or *b,* seems most comfortable to you? If you choose *a,* you have chosen the balanced state rather than the unbalanced one.

One easy way of determining whether a set of relations among any number of elements is balanced is to multiply all the signs in the system. If the *product* is *positive,* the system is *balanced;* if the product is *negative,* the system is *unbalanced.* Try the following exercise: Go through all the examples in figure 22.6 and decide which ones seem comfortable to you and which do not. Then, multiply the signs on each and determine which sets are balanced and which are not. (Sets a, c, d, and e are balanced in fig. 22.6.) Do the balanced ones seem more comfortable than the unbalanced ones? Price, Harburg, and Newcomb (1966) did a systematic study, using similar examples, and found a significant preference for balanced states. However, there was one exception: The balance predic-

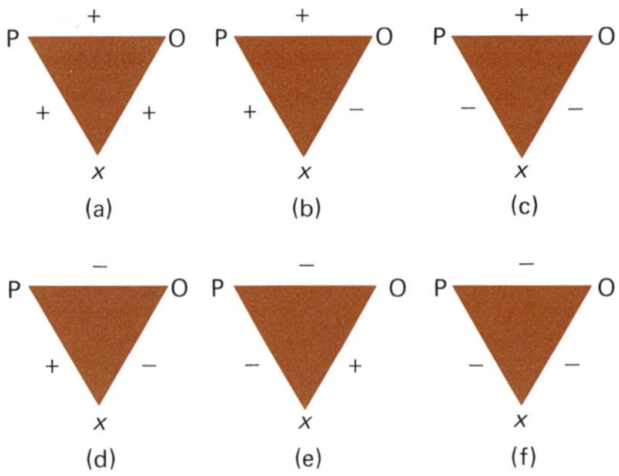

Figure 22.6 Balanced and unbalanced triadic relationships: P = self, O = other, and x = attitude object.

tion held only when the relationship between *P* and *O* was positive [*P*(+)*O*]. When this relationship was negative [*P*(−)*O*], subjects did not seem to care whether their attitudes agreed. Thus the basic postulate presented earlier—that people prefer states of cognitive consistency—seems to hold only when they perceive a positive relationship between themselves and another person.

What about the second postulate that when inconsistency occurs, there will be a tendency to restore consistency? Look again at figure 22.6b, in which you and your friend disagree about modern art. Would you experience a tendency toward change here? If so, you could change either your opinion of modern art (fig. 22.6c), or your liking for your friend (fig. 22.6d). Both states would be balanced. Or you could simply say that opinions about art are not important, and therefore, no inconsistent system exists in the first place (i.e., there is no *line* between P and x). Some research evidence indicates that subjects make more changes in unbalanced than in balanced triads. Rodrigues (1967), for example, found that subjects chose to change relationships in unbalanced triads to make them balanced. Morrissette (1958) showed that if subjects were presented with triadic systems with some relationships missing, they were completed in a way that would balance the system. However, when highly emotional elements are involved, bringing the system into balance can be difficult, as shown in box 22.6.

So the balance theory does seem to provide some evidence for the two basic postulates of cognitive consistency theory. However, subsequent research has also demonstrated that the theory has some limitations. For example, in the triadic case, balance theory holds only if sentiment or *liking relationships* are *positive* (Price et al., 1966). In addition, balance theory holds only for atti-

Box 22.6

The Eternal Triangle

The examples of balance theory in the text have dealt with situations where a relationship exists between two people, and they both have attitudes toward the same object. It is also possible to think about relationships between three people. One that is especially intriguing is the "eternal triangle." Let's consider the case in which a woman likes two men:

Roberta is dating George, but she also has a lover, Antonio. As long as George and Antonio do not know about one another (i.e., no line connects them), everything is fine. But if they do find out about each other, their relationship is certain to be negative. This fact, together with the two positive relationships they have with Roberta, will produce an unbalanced system (+ + −). What will happen? There are a number of ways to regain a balanced relationship. Both men could reject Roberta for deceiving them, and the system would dissolve (− − −). Or, after rejecting Roberta, the men might find they have many things in common and become good friends (− − +). Or Roberta, under pressure from the men, may be forced to decide between them (+ − − or − + −). Finally, they may resolve the problem by deciding that the three of them will live together in an atypical *menage à trois* (+ + +).

tudinal issues that are perceived to be *relevant* or central to a relationship (Zajonc and Burnstein, 1965a). And other sources of consistency, such as the desire to like and be liked—that is, *positivity,* or the tendency to *reciprocate* feelings and attitudes—may sometimes override the balance principle (Zajonc and Burnstein, 1965b).

Cognitive Dissonance Theory and Attitude Change

Like balance theory, the theory of cognitive dissonance is based on the two major postulates of consistency we mentioned earlier. Simply stated, the theory holds that when two contradictory cognitions are held simultaneously, changes will be made to restore consistency (Festinger, 1957). Actually, the two theories are similar: You can substitute *consonance* for balanced states and *dissonance* for unbalanced states. The main differences between the two approaches are in the amount and type of research conducted. The cognitive dissonance approach to attitudes has produced a large amount of what is often ingenious and exciting research. Unfortunately, we can examine only a small part of it here, including studies in the areas of postdecision dissonance, justification of effort, and attitude-discrepant behavior.

Postdecision dissonance

Suppose you have just enough money to buy a small used car, and you have a choice between a small foreign car and a small American-made car. Suppose too that you have made an exhaustive study of all the pros and cons of each car in terms of engineering, mileage, availability of parts, and the two cars come out about even. Thus you decide to buy the foreign car on an impulse. After making this decision, would you have a lower opinion of the American car? Or would you have a higher opinion of the foreign car you bought? Research has shown that these kinds of attitude changes are common following a difficult choice. That is, people tend to increase the value of a chosen alternative and decrease the value of the nonchosen alternative.

In one early study of the reduction of postdecision dissonance, Brehm (1956) showed college women eight products, such as a stopwatch, a radio, or a toaster. First, the subjects rated each product in terms of how much they would like to own it. The experimenter then offered each subject two products and asked her which one she would like to keep. Some subjects were shown two products that had been rated as equally desirable, the *high-dissonance* situation. Subjects in the *low-dissonance* situation were given the choice between one desirable and one undesirable product; that is, no conflict was involved in the choice. After the choices had been made, the subjects were asked to rate all the products again. As predicted, the women in the high-dissonance situation increased their ratings of the chosen object significantly and devalued the nonchosen object. Before-and-after ratings in the low-dissonance situation were about the same. A more recent field study by Knox and Inkster (1968) tested the same effect at a racetrack. They asked bettors, both before and after they had placed their bets, about the chances of each horse winning the next race. Results showed a significant increase in the chances they gave their chosen horse after placing their bets.

In both studies, the dissonance or inconsistency was created when the subjects were forced to choose one of several attractive alternatives and, therefore, had to reject the others. The main method of reducing this kind of inconsistency is simply to change one's attitude toward the alternatives—to increase the value of the chosen one and decrease the evaluation of the nonchosen ones. An example of a dissonance study that stresses the effects of observing one's own choice is given in box 22.7.

Justification of Effort

In a way, the changes in attitude that occur following a decision or choice serve to *justify* or rationalize that choice for the individual. The same effect might occur when someone has put a large amount of work or effort into some activity that does not lead to much. How would you react to the dissonance aroused by "going through hell" for something and then discovering that it was not worth the trouble? Paradoxically, one way to reduce the dissonance would be to increase your liking for the activity or object, which would make the effort seem more justifiable.

> **Box 22.7**
>
> *Feedback Makes the Heart Grow Fonder*
>
> The dissonance theory principle—that to reduce dissonance, people tend to bring their attitudes into line with their perceived behavior—was demonstrated in an ingenious study by Valins (1966). Valins attached male subjects to an apparatus that recorded and amplified their heart rate. In other words, they could hear how fast their heart was beating. He then presented a series of slides of seminude women, presumably to measure the effects of sexual arousal on heart rate. However, there was a catch. Instead of playing back the subject's actual heart rate, Valins amplified a prerecorded tape of changes in heart rate that was coordinated with certain slides. Postexperimental attractiveness ratings of all the women showed that degree of attractiveness was determined by changes in the feedback of false heart rate rather than by the subject's actual heart rate. It was as though the subject, when he heard what was apparently his own heart beating faster, said to himself, "I must really like that woman!" This simply demonstrated principle, of changing one's attitudes to bring them into line with perceived behavior, underlies most of the dissonance studies discussed in the text.

In an early study by Aronson and Mills (1959), female students were recruited to join groups that would discuss the psychology of sex. Half the students were subjected to a severe initiation and half went through a mild initiation before actually joining the discussion group. In the *severe initiation,* the male experimenter interviewed each applicant, presumably to screen out persons who were not "open enough" to participate. As part of this screening procedure, the girls were required to read aloud twelve obscene words and to recite two vivid descriptions of sexual activity. In the *mild initiation,* nonobscene words and materials were used.

All subjects then listened in on groups in which the preplanned discussions of sex were extremely dull, tedious, and boring. In fact, most of the talking was done by accomplices of the experimenter, who described the sex life of invertebrates. After listening to these groups, the subjects were asked to give their impressions of the groups and to rate them in terms of interest and enjoyment. As predicted, subjects who had been subjected to the severe initiation rated the discussions as more enjoyable and interesting than did the other subjects (see table 22.4). Apparently, the subjects who went through the difficult and embarrassing initiation to join the group needed to view the activities as more favorable to justify that effort. The same results were obtained when different degrees of electric shock were used as an initiation to a group (Gerard and Mathewson, 1966).

Given these results on arousal of dissonance and change in attitudes, perhaps the army has known what it was doing all along. Because basic training and initiation into the army are so obnoxious and difficult, they may serve, strangely enough, as an efficient means of increasing the army's attractiveness for new recruits. One fact should be kept in mind, however: Almost all the effects of dissonance on attitude changes occur

Table 22.4 Mean attractiveness ratings for both discussion and participants in the control, mild and severe initiation conditions. Note the increased favorability ratings of women in the severe initiation condition.

	Initiation Condition		
Rating Scales	Control (n=21)	Mild (n=21)	Severe (n=21)
Liked Discussion (9 scales)	80.2	81.8	97.6
Liked Participants (8 scales)	89.9	89.3	97.7
Total	170.1	171.1	195.3

Source: Adapted from Aronson, E. & Mills, L. "The effects of severity of initiation on liking a group." *Journal of Abnormal and Social Psychology,* 1959, *59,* pp. 177–181. Copyright 1959 by the American Psychological Association. Reprinted by permission.

mainly for *volunteers,* that is, people who *choose* to participate, not for persons who are forced to participate, either in the experiments or in military service (Davis and Jones, 1960).

Attitude-Discrepant Behaviors

Sometimes a person engages in behaviors that are inconsistent with his attitudes or values. For example, you may find yourself telling a lie to someone, although there is no good reason for doing so. Or you may be at a speech or a lecture and, out of politeness, applaud the speaker, even though you do not like him. In these cases of attitude-discrepant behavior, dissonance is likely. As in the situations we described earlier, the reduction of dissonance will often involve an increase in the favorableness of the attitude to bring it into line with the behavior.

A study by Festinger and Carlsmith (1959) not only demonstrated this effect but aroused much controversy among dissonance theorists and learning theorists. These experimenters recruited subjects to perform a series of manual tasks, which turned out to be extremely boring. After an hour or so, the subjects were told that the purpose of the experiment was to study the effects of different expectations on the performance of the tasks and that they could help by waiting for the next subject and telling him that the experiment was exciting and highly enjoyable. Subjects were told that if they did this, they would be paid either one dollar or twenty dollars for their assistance. A control group was asked to tell the next subject what they really thought about the experiment. At the end of the experiment, all subjects completed a questionnaire that included a rating of how enjoyable they had actually found the experimental task to be.

Put yourself in the place of the experimental subjects who had been asked to lie about an obviously dull study. Would you feel some dissonance between the positive attitude you communicated to the next subject and your actual feelings? Probably so. How would you reduce this dissonance? If you are like most people, you might be inclined to increase your liking of the task to bring it more in line with what you told the next subject. However, there is an added catch to this study—the money paid for telling the lie. The results showed that the favorable change in attitude toward the task occurred *only* when subjects were given one dollar to tell the lie; no change was observed in subjects who were paid twenty dollars. Why? Presumably, dissonance was aroused in both situations, but the subjects who received twenty dollars could justify their attitude-discrepant behavior by saying "I was paid to do it." In other words, the money justified the behavior. But this way out was not possible for those who received one dollar (nobody tells lies for one dollar), so they reduced the dissonance by changing their attitudes toward the task in a more favorable direction. Although this study has been replicated in various settings and with different tasks, there are some problems with the underlying assumptions (see box 22.8).

Learning Versus Dissonance Theory

We have just described a study of attitude change in which a small reward produced greater attitude change than did a large reward; that is, one dollar produced more favorable change than did twenty dollars. This result directly contradicts the learning theorists' principle of reinforcement and attitude change—the *larger* the reward, the greater the attitude change. In fact, several studies have shown that when subjects are asked to write an essay about a topic from a point of view that is the opposite of their own beliefs, attitude change is greatest among those who are paid the larger sums of money (Janis and Gilmore, 1965).

What sense can we make out of these opposing predictions and results? One possible solution was offered by Carlsmith et al. (1966), who noted that the dissonance effect for the smallest reward was usually obtained under conditions in which the attitude-discrepant behavior was open to *public* scrutiny—performed in front of other people. The results of learning experiments involving large incentives have typically been obtained when the attitude-discrepant behavior was *private* in nature, writing an essay or making a private decision. Carlsmith and his colleagues reasoned further that if this is the case, one

Box 22.8
Dissonance Over Dissonance Theory

Although dissonance theory is currently the most popular of the theories of attitude change at an individual level, it is not without its problems.

The first problem is how to specify more precisely the conditions under which dissonance is likely to be aroused. For example, Festinger and Carlsmith simply assumed that the task they used would be perceived as dull by the subjects and that to tell the next subject it was enjoyable would be attitude-discrepant; telling a lie, in this case. But for some people, an hour or so spent on a routine task that involves little thinking may be a relief, even somewhat therapeutic. These people would not experience dissonance. Or what about the subject who does not believe that telling lies is particularly undesirable or immoral under these circumstances; after all, they lied in the cause of "the scientific study of behavior." So the theory requires a more exact definition of what dissonance is and greater specification of the conditions under which it will or will not be aroused.

A second problem concerns the strategies for reducing dissonance, once it has been aroused. Attitude change is not the only way of reducing dissonance, but the theory has tended to ignore the alternatives. For example, in the postdecision dissonance situation, one way to reduce dissonance is to simply not think about the nonchosen alternatives any more, rather than devalue them relative to the chosen one. Or you might tell yourself that dissonance is an integral part of any choice that involves equally attractive alternatives and that you should learn to live with this fact, rather than try to rearrange your attitudes after each choice.

This last alternative, tolerating rather than attempting to reduce dissonance, is perhaps the greatest challenge to the theory. All consistency theories assume that inconsistency is a noxious state for human beings, and thus individuals will strive to reduce it at almost any cost. The problem with this assumption is that, if carried to its logical conclusion, we would all become compulsive neurotics or paranoid schizophrenics. If contradictions and dissonance are an integral part of our existence, we would have to deny and distort much of that reality, while struggling to maintain cognitive consistency. Therefore, as a limited theory, dissonance theory has much to offer, but it cannot, almost by definition, be a general theory of individual attitude change.

would expect dissonance to occur *only* under the public, not the private conditions; in other words, smaller rewards would lead to greater changes in attitude in publicly discrepant behaviors, while larger rewards would lead to more attitude change when the discrepant behavior was more private in nature.

To test this possibility, they conducted an experiment that was similar to Festinger's and Carlsmith's study on lying to the next experimental subject about how enjoyable a dull task had been. However, they included two conditions. In one, the lie was told directly and publicly to the next subject (the *role-play*) condition. In the second *(essay)* condition, subjects were required to write in private about how enjoyable the dull task had been. As you can see in figure 22.7, the results supported these predictions. Positive change in attitude occurred for small rewards only in the public, role-playing condition (the dissonance prediction). In the private, essay condition, larger rewards led to more positive attitude change (the learning theory prediction).

Overall, dissonance theory has provided some research support for the two basic postulates of the consistency theory of attitude change that we presented at the beginning of this section. All forms of dissonance reduction we have examined seem to contain a common theme: When individuals are faced with an inconsistency between their actions and attitudes and there are no ready-made excuses available, they tend to restore consistency by changing their attitudes in the direction of justifying or rationalizing the behavior they are engaging in.

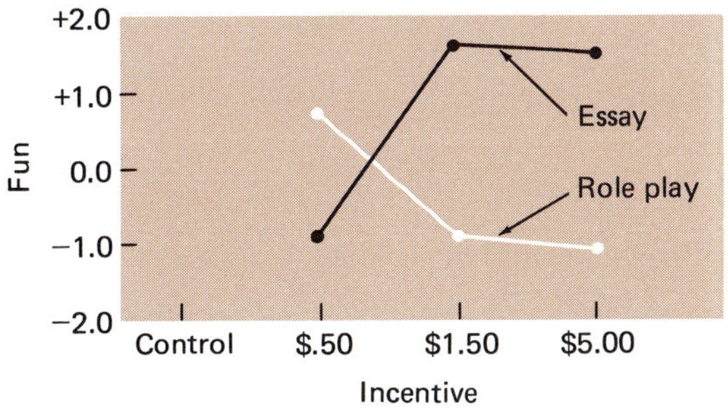

Figure 22.7 Attitude change as a function of increased incentive under conditions of private (essay) and public commitment (role-play). Note that the dissonance prediction of less attitude change with increased incentives holds under the public, role-playing condition. The learning theory prediction of more attitude change with increased incentives holds under the private, essay condition. (From Carlsmith, J.M., Collins, B.E. and Helmreich, R.L. Studies in forced compliance: I. The effect of pressure for compliance on attitude change produced by face-to-face role-playing and anonymous essay writing. *Journal of Personality and Social Psychology,* 1966, *4,* pp. 1–13. Copyright 1966 by the American Psychological Association. Reprinted by permission.)

Summary

The chapter has covered a number of sources for the formation and change of attitudes. In particular, we examined the influence of group factors, persuasive communication, and individual striving for cognitive consistency.

Group sources of attitude change include the influence of reference groups and pressures towards group conformity found in most membership groups. Field experiments have demonstrated that reference groups of which an individual is not a member can still influence attitudes. More limited laboratory experiments have shown that the degree of conformity to group norms is influenced by the ambiguity of the stimulus situation, unanimity of the group consensus, and degree of prior individual commitment to the norm.

In the area of research on persuasive communication, the relative prestige, expertise attractiveness, trustworthiness, and perceived similarity of a communicator have been found to influence the acceptance of a persuasive message. The failure of a communicator to meet minimal requirements on any or all of these factors may lead to a boomerang effect—movement away from acceptance of the message. Aspects of the persuasive communication itself that have been investigated are the use of one- versus two-sided messages and whether arguments are presented first (primacy effect) or last (recency effect). Research on recipient characteristics has demonstrated a curvilinear relationship between amount of attitude change and the degree of discrepancy between the initial positions of the recipient and the persuasive message. The personality characteristics of authoritarianism and self-esteem have been shown to affect the degree of receptivity of recipients to persuasive communications.

Finally, two major consistency theories of attitude change have been presented. The theory of cognitive balance and the theory of cognitive dissonance have been used to explain why and when individuals are susceptible to attitudinal changes. The main assumptions of these theories are that people prefer that their cognitive beliefs and attitudes be consistent, and that they will strive to regain this consistency when it is threatened by dissonance or imbalance. Three major areas of research by cognitive dissonance theorists are postdecision dissonance, justification of effort, and attitude-discrepant behavior.

23

Psychology and Social Issues

In Chapter 21 we discussed the implications of social psychology for conflict and war. What does this branch of psychology have to offer with respect to solving other social problems such as racial conflict, aggression, and crime and delinquency? Although this question is often asked, psychologists are understandably reluctant to give general or simplistic answers. Instead, they have chosen to break the problem down into more limited questions about behavior, questions that are amenable to scientific investigation. In this chapter, the emphasis will be on such research in social psychology and its applications to current social problems such as race relations, television and violence, and crime and delinquency.

Race Relations

Over the past few decades, there has been considerable conflict and debate about the best path to take toward improved race relations in the United States. Many public policies have favored the strategy of *integration,* which has resulted in desegregation laws and school busing programs. However, some members of minority groups view this strategy as a disguised form of assimilation, which would lead to the disappearance of distinct racial and ethnic cultural groups. As an alternative, many blacks, Mexican-Americans, and American Indians have organized pluralistic movements to establish the uniqueness and independence of their cultures, sometimes through violent methods of confrontation.

Is there any research in social psychology that addresses itself to the issue of race relations in the United States? The answer is yes. First, we will examine studies that are relevant to the issue of integration and then consider research on aspects of the independence movements.

Integration and Attitude Change

One of the strongest arguments in favor of desegregation, or legally imposed contact between races, is that daily contact between people of different races will eventually lead to a modification of racial attitudes. In other words, if people of different races must deal directly with each other, they will get to know one another as people rather than as stereotypes. Also, if an individual is constrained by convention to act politely to a member of a minority group, then in time his attitudes will tend to fall in line with his behavior. The result of this attitude change will be lessening of hostility between races.

The notion that attitudes can be changed by placing people in situations where they must act in ways that are contrary to their usual patterns of behavior has been thoroughly explored in a number of laboratory and field experiments. In fact, in dissonance theory (see Chapter 22), this principle of attitude change is called, appropriately enough, *forced compliance*. As a principle of change in racial attitudes and as a basic concept in the integrationist movement, the notion of forced compliance seems to contradict the idea expressed by some political and religious leaders that it is impossible to legislate morality, including racial morality. Let's look at what empirical research in psychology has to say about this issue. (See fig. 23.1.)

At first glance, the research evidence for the positive effects of desegregation on racial attitudes appears to be strong (Pettigrew, 1969). Studies in natural settings such as public housing projects, desegregated department stores, government offices, police departments, and naval vessels have repeatedly shown that the attitudes of blacks and whites toward each other have improved as a result of increased contact. A good example of this kind of research is a study by Deutsch and Collins (1951) of two public housing projects in New York City that had been ordered to desegregate under new state laws. Two segregated housing projects in nearby New Jersey were selected as controls. One strong feature of the research setting was that people were assigned to the desegregated projects without regard to their race or personal preferences. Thus the results can be attributed

Figure 23.1 Psychologists sometimes discuss or analyze racism in an abstract and impersonal way. But to victims of racism, the consequences are painfully real and inescapable. (Courtesy Peter L. Gauld, Freelance Photo Guild, Inc., New York.)

primarily to the effects of desegregation rather than selection bias, or preference.

Comparisons between randomly selected samples of housewives in the housing projects revealed some striking differences (see table 23.1). Seventy-five percent of the black and white women in the desegregated projects were in favor of interracial housing, as compared with only twenty-five percent of the women in the segregated projects. Furthermore, white women in the desegregated projects showed much more respect and liking for black women than did white women in the segregated projects, and they were also more willing to discuss personal matters with black women than were segregated white women. As one white housewife explained: ". . . my ideas changed altogether. They're just people . . . they're not any different." Another commented, "I've really come to like it. I see they're just as human as we are." Notice how these expressions of changed attitudes reveal the nature of the old stereotypes. Prior to having daily contact with black women, these women had not viewed blacks as humans!

Negative Effects of Interracial Contact

Although this study, and many others like it, have provided strong support for the notion that desegregation may lead to successful integration, other studies have painted a less optimistic picture. In a study of an interracial boys' camp, Mussen (1950) found that after four weeks, of the boys that changed attitudes, twenty-eight white boys displayed significantly less prejudice toward black campers while twenty-seven white boys showed greater prejudice and hostility. In a study of a desegregated southern college, researchers found little attitude change among white students, who continued to make remarks such as "Negroes smell" and "Niggers are inferior" (Cole, Steinberg, and Burkheimer, 1968). Not only does increased contact strengthen the prejudice of some whites, but it may also have detrimental effects on the blacks involved. Katz and Benjamin (1960),

Table 23.1 Percentages of white housewives in integrated versus desegregated projects who reported positive attitudes toward black people.

Degree of Esteem	Integrated Interracial Projects		Segregated Bi-Racial Projects	
	Koaltown (103)	Sacktown (90)	Bakerville (100)	Frankville (101)
Respect Negroes living in the project; view them as equal to white people in the project	72%	79%	43%	39%
Feel Negroes are inferior; characterize them as low-class, childish, primitive, etc.	11	13	37	35
Neutral or ambivalent	17	8	20	26

Source: From *Interracial housing: A psychological evaluation of a social experiment*, by M. Deutsch and M. Collins. University of Minnesota Press, 1951. Used by permission using a realistic interracial laboratory setting, reported an increase in feelings of inferiority and self-doubt among some black students following face-to-face contact with authoritarian white students.

How can we account for these differences in the effects of interracial contact? What can we make of the arguments of the integrationists?

One possible explanation is based on the idea that behavioral change must follow genuine changes in attitude; that is, attitude change cannot be forced. After reviewing studies of racial contact, Amir (1969) concluded that interracial contact only strengthens or reinforces already-existing attitudes. In other words, whites who are extremely prejudiced against blacks to begin with will become even more negative when their contacts with blacks increase, whereas whites whose initial attitudes toward blacks are positive or fairly neutral tend to feel more positive as a result of increased interracial contacts. Another possible explanation was offered by Allport (1954), who believed that increased interracial contact leads to favorable attitude change only when both races (1) have equal status in the contact situation, (2) seek or work for common goals, (3) are dependent on each other, and (4) have positive support from authorities, law, and custom. A systematic research program developed by Dr. Stuart Cook has investigated each of these factors (see box 23.1).

Allport's conditions may help explain the conflicting results obtained in the studies already discussed. For example, the public housing study may have met most of these conditions, but it is doubtful whether any of them were met in the study conducted at the

Box 23.1

Making Interracial Contacts Work

To test the effects of interracial contacts on attitude change, Cook (1970) devised an unusual simulation experiment. Forty highly prejudiced white subjects from a large southern city were recruited to work part-time for a month on a special group project. The project involved a series of complex decisions in which all members had to cooperate for the task to succeed. Unknown to the white prejudiced subjects, however, the other members of the group were accomplices of the experimenter who had been carefully trained to play certain roles and elicit certain responses from the subjects. One of the accomplices was black.

The situation was arranged to maximize the total impact of the situation on the subjects' attitudes toward black people. First, everyone had jobs of equal status, and the experimental assistants always included their black colleagues in discussion and decisions. Second, the task was set up so that it could only be achieved cooperatively; that is, no individual could be successful without the help of the team. Third, the black and white confederates of the experimenter showed a willingness to share personal matters during lunch-time conversations. And fourth, the social norms of the group favored racial contact rather than disapproving of it.

In a controlled experimental setting where deliberate attempts are made to create a favorable atmosphere for interracial contact, what happens to the prejudiced attitudes of white subjects? Approximately forty percent of the subjects showed a substantial positive change in independently measured racial attitudes over the period of a month. An additional forty percent showed no significant change in attitudes, and twenty percent became even more prejudiced toward blacks. Therefore, we can conclude that only *some* prejudiced whites will change their attitudes substantially in a positive direction when the conditions for interracial contact are favorable. Investigations of the personality characteristics that differentiate those who do not are now being carried out.

desegregated southern college. It is also interesting to note that, according to Allport's conditions, lasting changes in racial attitudes will depend on whether extensive changes are made in our political, economic, and social institutions. In other words, integration is only possible in a truly egalitarian society. If this is true, it will be pointless to concentrate exclusively on changing attitudes until conditions of inequality have been changed.

Effects of School Desegregation

Although we have just mentioned one study on the effects of school desegregation, the topic deserves special mention because of its current importance and the research it has generated. In a massive study on school desegregation, Coleman et al. (1966) found that the effects of desegregation on academic achievement among blacks were largely positive. In particular, the study showed that black students who attend desegregated schools not only perform better but have a stronger sense of control over their own lives than do their counterparts in segregated schools. As you will see later, this sense of control is a significantly new development among young black people, and its implications go far beyond simply doing well in school. Further analysis of Coleman's data has shown that his findings with respect to the positive effects of desegregation hold only for schools in which classrooms are desegregated. McPartland (1969) discovered that black students who were effectively segregated within supposedly desegregated schools showed no academic gains, when compared with black students who attended segregated schools. This result reminds us again of Allport's four conditions for successful integration. Desegregated schools that maintain segregated classrooms probably continue to regard black students as inferior ("They will lower the standards"). And, of course, keeping the races separate prevents the emergence of common goals and interracial friendships. A note of caution must be added to Coleman's findings. Since he failed to assess the basic effects of social class and economic conditions on school performance *across* social class, his findings could be attributed to these factors rather than to the personality and interpersonal factors suggested in his report.

Pluralistic Movements: A Question of Power and Identity

Although some individuals tend to associate arguments for separating the races with white racist segregationists, there has been a fairly continuous history of separatist movements among American blacks as well (Cruse, 1968). In recent years, several radical black groups and some black leaders have again called for the establishment of a separate black nation, with complete political and economic independence. However, most black people do not support this form of separation. In a survey of fifteen American cities, Campbell and Schuman (1968) found that only eight percent of blacks supported the concept of a separate black nation, whereas more than seventy percent believed in some form of political and economic integration that would provide blacks with a fair share of economic benefits and control over the institutions that most directly affected them.

Another form of separation that has received much stronger support among blacks as well as Mexican-Americans and American Indians might be called cultural and psychological pluralism. For example, more than ninety percent of the black people Campbell and Schuman interviewed said that blacks should take more pride in the history of their race, and forty-two percent expressed their conviction that black children should be taught at least one African language in school. Thus, it seems that in the minds of most

Figure 23.2 The emergence of militancy and the sometimes violent assertion of racial pride and power in recent years are dramatic evidence that fundamental changes in race relations have been taking place in the United States. (Courtesy Charles Harleutt © Magnum Photos, Inc.)

blacks, the issue of separation is related less to political and economic separation than to what has been loosely called "black power," which includes both the desire for a reasonable share of power within the system and the desire to rebuild a sense of personal and racial identity distinctly black. (See fig. 23.2.)

Before we consider how the movement to build both political power and black pride has helped to shape urban change and militant protest, it will be useful to examine some of the effects that centuries of white domination have had on the development of self-identity among racial minorities in the United States.

White-Imposed Black Identity

The most persistent message that white society has conveyed to young black children is that they are different from white people because of their supposedly inherent inferiority. Because white norms have defined blacks as deviants rather than as a unique race and people in their own right, black children have grown up under the influence of negative stereotypes (Fanon, 1967). Therefore, it is not surprising that many blacks have tended to accept these stereotypes as being the truth about themselves. Although research cannot convey the tragic experience of black socialization, it can document some of its effects.

In 1947 Clark and Clark demonstrated in a clear and effective way what was happening to many American black children. These investigators used the simple procedure of presenting black and white children, ages three to eight, with two dolls—one white and one brown. The children were then asked which doll they preferred and why. The results showed that beginning at age three, both black and white children showed a marked preference for the white doll, and rejected the brown one. For example, sixty-eight percent of the black children chose the white doll as the "nicest one," and at least seventy-one percent said that the brown doll "looks bad." Although this well-known study has been criticized on methodological grounds, and more recent research has produced additional evidence of positive rather than negative identity among young black children, the early findings stand as an indictment of white racism. A more personal example of learned negative identity is given in box 23.2.

Fortunately, some blacks have managed to avoid these negative self-definitions, as illustrated by the long history of black affirmation, protest, and rebellion. Today it appears that this sense of black pride has become more developed and widespread than at any time in the history of American race relations, as illustrated by the activities of militant groups such as The Panthers, The Brown Berets and the American Indian Movement. However, the most unforgettable expressions were the massive riots in black ghettos during the late 1960s.

Black Protest and Rioting

Caplan and Paige (1968) found that the median age of participants in the Detroit riot of 1967 was only eighteen and that more than sixty percent of the rioters, compared with thirty percent of nonrioters, were born and raised in Detroit. Therefore, it is inappropriate to blame the riots on newcomers or "outsiders." More significantly, those who participated in the riots revealed a greater sense of black consciousness and black pride than did nonparticipants: Rioters rated black people as more dependable, smarter, and more courageous than white people, whereas blacks who opposed the rioting rated whites as superior in terms of these characteristics.

In another study of young blacks living in the riot area of Detroit, Forward and Williams (1970) found additional evidence for Caplan's and Paige's analysis. Young blacks who were opposed to the rioting felt powerless to shape their own lives and tended to blame both their own ghetto condition and the riots on black people: "They're just a lot of hoodlums and looters"; "If they worked harder to improve themselves instead of rioting, we'd be better off." On the other hand, those who supported the riots not only were more confident of their ability to shape events, if given the chance, but emphatically blamed the rioting on the white system that excluded and oppressed them.

Although some of the rioting can be attributed to greed or a desire to inflict harm or simply have some fun, the primary implication of these studies is that riots are a clear sign that changes are taking place in the self-definition and racial identity of a new generation of black people in America. The notions of compromise and assimilation—inherent in the popular white conception of integration, are being discarded by a growing minority of young blacks as well as Mexican-Americans and American Indians. Instead, these young

Box 23.2

Racism and Negative Identity

An additional illustration of the learned rejection of blackness was provided by Coles (1967), who analyzed drawings and paintings done by black children. For example, Coles described the paintings of a six-year-old black girl (see box fig. 23.2) in a southern school as follows:

> *For a long time—four months in fact—Ruby never used a black or brown except to indicate soil or ground; even then she always made sure they were covered by a solid covering of green grass. She did, however, distinguish between white and Negro people. She drew white people larger and more life-like. Negroes were smaller, their bodies were less intact. A white girl, we both knew to be her own size, appeared several times taller. While Ruby's own face lacked an eye in one drawing, an ear in another, the white girl never lacked any features. Moreover, Ruby drew the white girl's hands and legs carefully, always making sure they had the proper number of fingers and toes. Not so with her own limbs, or those of any other Negro children she chose (or was asked) to picture. A thumb or fore-finger might be missing, or a whole set of toes. The arms were shorter, even absent or truncated. (Coles, 1967.)*

These pictures and hundreds of others are fairly direct expressions of the black child's conception of himself as deviant, inferior, and even deformed in comparison with white people. It would be difficult to find a more graphic indictment of white racism.

Box Figure 23.2 Drawings by Ruby, a six-year-old black girl. On the left is Ruby's drawing of a black girl; on the right, her drawing of a white girl. (From *Children in Crisis,* R. Coles, by permission of Little, Brown & Co., in association with the Atlantic Monthly Press. Copyright © 1966 by Robert Coles.)

Figure 1. Negro girl by Ruby at age 6.

Figure 2. A white girl by Ruby at age 6.

people are seeking ways of confronting white society, in an effort to rebuild a sense of racial identity and to express this identity in a push for justice and equality. How whites are reacting and will react to these changes is not only a topic for further research, but a question on which the future of race relations rests in this country. Of course, the militant strategy is only one of many paths being developed by minority groups in an effort to build a truly equalitarian and pluralistic society.

Television and Violence

The second social issue we will consider is whether watching violence on television has any effect on subsequent aggressive behavior. This issue has aroused so much public concern that a special advisory committee on television and social behavior was set up to study the matter and report its findings to the surgeon general of the U.S. Public Health Service (1972). After reviewing dozens of research studies, the committee concluded that a modest relationship did exist between exposure to televised violence and aggressive behavior. However, it also noted that the research in this area was not entirely consistent or conclusive.

Results of studies on the effects of televised violence are inconsistent and occasionally contradictory. Over the years, psychologists have developed theories that lead to contradictory predictions. For instance, *catharsis theories* predict that aggressive fantasies, including those seen on television, can serve to drain off violent impulses and, therefore, *reduce* actual aggressive behavior. *Social learning theories,* however, predict that televised violence will *increase* violent behavior because it provides learning cues and vicarious reinforcements for aggression. We will examine these two approaches in turn, paying special attention to the research evidence for and against them.

Catharsis Approach

Most catharsis theories derive from Freud's notion that man possesses an *aggressive instinct*—a biologically based supply of aggressive energy that constantly requires some form of release. Freud believed that the aggressive instinct could be expressed directly through overt action or indirectly through aggressive fantasies and dreams. To the extent that an individual can release this energy by participating vicariously in televised violence, he would have less energy available for actual aggressive behavior. Thus in a literal sense, televised violence serves as a release, or catharsis of pent-up aggressive feelings.

The small amount of evidence in favor of this approach comes mainly from the research of Feshbach and his colleagues. In early laboratory studies, these researchers subjected students to a frustrating situation in which they failed at a virtually impossible task and then allowed half of them to write aggressive stories. The students who had the opportunity to express fantasy aggression showed less overt aggression toward the source of their frustration than did the other students (Feshbach, 1955). Unfortunately, these results have not been supported consistently by other studies (Kenney, 1953; DeCharms and Wilkins, 1963). And even if there were solid experimental support for Feshbach's finding, would it generalize to situations outside the laboratory?

In 1971 Feshbach and Singer conducted a field experiment to test the hypothesis. After obtaining the cooperation of authorities, they set up two different schedules of television viewing for two randomly selected groups in a boys' home. For six weeks, one group of boys watched programs that rated high in terms of violence, "Gunsmoke," "Combat," and the like. The second group was exposed to programs containing a minimal amount of aggression; for example, "Gilligan's Island"

and "Lost in Space." When the investigators analyzed the amount of aggressive behavior the two groups displayed during the six-week experimental period, they found that the boys who watched violent programs became significantly less aggressive, while boys who watched the nonaggressive programs became more aggressive. No generalizations could be made, however, because when Feshbach and Singer tried the same experiment in private boys' schools, they found no differences in the effects of television viewing on actual aggression.

Overall, the research evidence for the *catharsis theory*—that viewing televised violence should reduce actual aggression—is both scarce and inconsistent. It seems that aggression is reduced only under specific conditions and among particular types of people. But as yet, we know very little about either the people or the conditions that might be involved.

Social Learning Theory

Social learning theory makes exactly the opposite prediction for the effects of televised violence on behavior; in other words, violent television programs will cause an *increase* in actual aggression rather than a decrease because they provide behavior patterns that children may *imitate* in subsequent aggressive behaviors. Extreme cases of this effect have been reported, in which actual homicides have been patterned after specific television episodes. But television also provides many examples of how to be aggressive successfully or to be successful *because* you are aggressive. This last point highlights the role of vicarious *reinforcement* in teaching children to increase their aggressive behavior. If television heroes are consistently rewarded with fame, fortune, or sex for being aggressive, then viewers are likely to want to try it too (e.g., Bandura, 1971).

Earlier chapters described an experiment in which an inflatable Bobo doll was used to support the commonplace observation that children imitate adults' aggressive behavior toward others. (Bandura, Ross, and Ross, 1961). In an unstructured, "free-play" situation in a nursery school, an adult model played with the Bobo doll for ten minutes, and performed a specific series of movements—pushed the doll, sat on it, hit it with a hammer, and so forth. The adult then left the room and observers, behind one-way mirrors, recorded the children's behavior. The results showed that these children were far more aggressive in terms of specific imitative behavior than were another group of children who watched an adult play with tinker toys for ten minutes. What is even more important for our discussion is the fact that the children displayed the same amount of imitative behavior after watching a filmed version of a model hitting the doll as they did when the model was in the room (Bandura and Mischel, 1965).

An interesting side effect of Bandura's studies discussed in Chapter 10 was that boys tended to imitate the model's "masculine" behavior (hitting with a hammer), while girls tended to imitate only "feminine" behaviors (sitting on the doll, pushing). So, although a high level of aggressive imitation or *modeling* was observed, the exact nature of what was imitated was modified by factors such as sex and, presumably, age, class, and race. Because many investigators have been able to replicate these results, the findings are accepted as valid in controlled laboratory studies. But do they generalize to television viewing? Again, we must look to a field experiment that tests the effects of television in a real-life setting.

Stein and Friedrich (1971) showed three different kinds of television programs to nursery school children in class; extremely violent programs, neutral programs, and programs that emphasized nonaggressive and helpful behavior. The amount of aggression that each group of children displayed was measured over a four-week period and measurements were made again two weeks later. The results showed no overall differences in actual aggression among the three groups. However, the violent programs increased the amount of aggressive behavior in a small number of children who were above average in terms of aggressive behavior before the experiment began, whereas the neutral and nonaggressive programs did not. Thus the research support for the social learning hypothesis that televised violence will *increase* subsequent aggression seems reasonably well established, although the results are not entirely consistent.

Factors that Inhibit or Facilitate Aggression

Thus far, we have considered the general question of whether violent television programs affect the behavior of viewers. The

Box 23.3

How American Men View Violence

Disregarding the findings of the experts for the moment, how does the American public feel about violence? What kinds of violence do they believe are justified, and presumably not unwelcome, on their television sets? A national survey of 1,400 American men showed marked differences in the definition of what constitutes violent behavior (Kahn, 1972). For example, eighty-two percent of black men who were interviewed said that police beating students was violent behavior, but only fifty-two percent of white men considered this behavior to be violent (see box fig. 23.3). Similarly, fifty-nine percent of the blacks and thirty-two percent of the whites believed that police shooting looters was violent behavior. On the other hand, thirty-nine percent of the white and only twenty-three percent of the black men defined student protest as violent, while twenty-three percent of the whites and fifteen percent of the blacks thought sit-ins could be defined as a form of violence.

In general, blacks approved of violence in the service of social change more than they favored violence for social control. Whites, especially older men, approved of violence more often in the context of social control and less often in the context of social change. What kind of violence do you usually see on your television screen?

What is violence?	white	black
Police beating students:	52%	82%
Police shooting looters:	32%	59%
Police stopping people to frisk them:	13%	34%
Denying people's civil rights:	46%	70%
Looting:	87%	74%
Burglary:	64%	70%
Student protest:	39%	23%
Sit-in:	23%	15%
Draft-card burnings:	59%	51%

Box Table 23.3 Shown are differences between black men and white men in the actions that they define as violent. Blacks are more likely than whites to think of police use of force as violent (beating students, shooting looters); whites are more likely than blacks to think all forms of protest are violent (sit-ins, draft-card burnings, looting).

Source: R.L. Kahn, "Violent man: who buys bloodshed and why" *Psychology Today,* 1972, *6,* p. 83. Copyright 1972 by Ziff-Davis Publishing Company. Reprinted by permission of *Psychology Today* Magazine.

available evidence supports the conclusion of the surgeon general's special advisory commission (1972) that there is indeed a "modest relationship" between televised and actual aggression and that the influence is stronger for young people who are predisposed to be highly aggressive. Within this context, we will consider several additional factors that appear to inhibit or facilitate the expression of aggression. (See box 23.3.)

Frustration

Everyone knows how frustration can make one feel extremely angry and ready to take out anger in some form of hostility. The *frustration-aggression* theory (Dollard and Miller, 1939) discussed in Chapter 16, one of the first modern psychological theories of aggression, was based on this principle. However, subsequent research showed that aggression is not the only response to frustration. Instead of attacking, a person may withdraw, do nothing, or simply persist in performing the ongoing activity. (Miller, 1941; Buss, 1961). Nevertheless, when frustration does elicit an aggressive response, the degree of aggression is greater when the frustration is related to personal insults rather than to environmental obstacles (Buss, 1966) and when it is perceived to be imposed arbitrarily (Fishman, 1965). Furthermore, the amount of overt aggression a person will display is related to whether the frustration is anticipated (Berkowitz, 1962) or whether there are supportive cues in the environment (Berkowitz and LePage, 1967).

Depersonalization

Another factor that seems to facilitate aggressive behavior is the extent to which an aggressor is able to *depersonalize* his intended victim. The person who views other people as objects or as nonhumans finds it easier to insult or inflict harm on them.

A simple laboratory demonstration of this effect was set up by Zimbardo (1969). In a "learning" experiment half the subjects were dressed as shown in figure 23.3 and were not introduced to each other (*depersonalized* condition); the other half could see each other and knew one another's names. The experiment required that subjects read lists of words to each other and administer shocks for any errors made. The average duration of shocks was twice as long in the depersonalized group as it was in the control group.

In a more striking demonstration of the

Figure 23.3 *Depersonalized* (anonymous) subjects in Zimbardo's experiment. The similarity between the uniforms shown here and those worn by the Ku Klux Klan during their rituals may be more than coincidental. (Reprinted from Zimbardo, P., "The human choice: individuation, reason and order versus deindividuation, impulse and chaos." In *Nebraska Symposium on Motivation,* Vol. 17, W.J. Arnold and D. Levine (Eds.). Copyright 1969 by the University of Nebraska Press. Photo Courtesy of Dr. Philip Zimbardo.)

same effect, Milgram (1965a) set up a situation now considered ethically questionable by many in which the experimenter required the "teacher" (subject) to *increase* the level of shock for each error the "pupil" made. Because the pupil was a paid accomplice (i.e., he only acted as if he were being shocked), errors began to pile up quickly, and the subjects found that they had to deliver stronger and stronger shocks (from 15 up to 450 volts). In the higher ranges (over 100 volts), the pupil began to moan; at 180 volts, he cried out and begged the teacher to stop. At 315 volts, he let out a prolonged agonized scream and was not heard from again! Despite these realistic effects, sixty-seven percent of subjects continued to increase the shock for each error (or no response) until they reached the maximum of 450 volts. Here the voltage regulator was clearly marked "Extreme Danger," and they had heard nothing from the pupil for several minutes.

One factor that had the effect of reducing the level of shocks (i.e., the subjects refused to continue) was the degree of proximity between subject and victim. Only thirty-four percent of the subjects defied the experimenter and refused to continue when the victim was in another room and the only contact with him was by way of the response lights. When the victim was in the next room and could be heard through an open door, thirty-eight percent defied the experimenter. But when the victim was in the same room and could be seen and heard, sixty-six percent refused to increase the level of shock.

The effect of distance on aggression is similar to the difference between sticking a bayonet in an enemy in face-to-face combat and dropping bombs on victims that will never be seen or heard. However, physical proximity is not the most crucial aspect of depersonalization (see box 23.4) as evidenced by the apparent willingness of some

Box 23.4

"I Was Just Obeying Orders"

The degree to which a person adopts the ethic of *individual conscience* (decide for yourself) or the ultimate *legitimacy of authority* (obey orders) is another important factor in facilitating or inhibiting aggression. This factor was prominent in Milgram's research, which was described in the text. Another example was provided by Kelman and Lawrence (1972) in a survey of 989 American citizens at the time Lt. William Calley was tried for the massacre of unarmed civilians at My Lai. Note the subjects' responses to item B in box figure 23.4: "What would you do if ordered to shoot all the inhabitants in a Vietnamese village?" Fifty-one percent of the subjects said they would follow orders and shoot. Among those who accepted the ethic of individual conscience or personal responsibility (PR), only nineteen percent said they would follow orders, while sixty-eight percent of those who accepted the ethic of *governmental responsibility* (GR) reported they would follow orders and shoot. Thus Kelman's and Lawrence's survey corroborates Milgram's findings; that is, the individual who believes that his superiors are ultimately responsible for what he does is more likely to commit violent acts against other people.

Box Table 23.4 Attitudes toward Lt. Calley's actions in the My Lai massacre by 989 U.S. citizens at the time of Calley's trial. The total sample is broken down into two groups: those who hold an ethic of personal responsibility (PR) for their actions and those who believe it is important to follow orders given by legitimate authorities, that is, *government responsibility* (GR). Note the large differences in responses between these two groups.

	Attitudes toward Calley's actions	total sample	PR approvers	GR disapprovers
A	What would most people do if ordered to shoot all inhabitants of a Vietnamese village?			
	Follow orders and shoot:	67%	37%	82%
	Refuse to shoot:	19%	42%	9%
B	What would you do in this situation?			
	Follow orders and shoot:	51%	19%	68%
	Refuse to shoot:	33%	65%	17%
C	Overall opinion of Calley's action:			
	Right—what any good soldier would do under the circumstances:	29%	3%	49%
	Wrong—but hard for him to know right or wrong in this situation:	39%	33%	34%
	Wrong—clear violation of military code:	6%	15%	3%
	Wrong—violation of morality regardless of military code:	17%	43%	5%
D	Calley's actions justified if people he shot were Communists:			
	Agree:	37%	11%	53%
	Disagree:	51%	85%	34%
E	Calley's actions justified because better to kill some S. Vietnamese civilians than risk lives of American soldiers:			
	Agree:	47%	17%	67%
	Disagree:	39%	70%	21%
F	In World War II it would have been better to kill some German civilians than risk the lives of American soldiers:			
	Agree:	53%	29%	68%
	Disagree:	29%	57%	15%
G	In terms of rights and wrongs, how do Calley's actions compare with bombing raids that also kill Vietnamese civilians?			
	Similar:	56%	38%	63%
	Different:	32%	51%	24%

Source: H.C. Kelman & L.H. Lawrence, "Violent man: American response to the trial of Lt. William Calley," *Psychology Today*, 1972, ***6***, p. 79.

American soldiers in Vietnam to kill women and children at close range. As you can see in box 23.4, the degree to which an individual relies on authority is also important. A third factor is the ability to define people as nonhuman. Interviews with soldiers involved in the My Lai massacre showed that these men considered the Vietnamese people to be subhuman—as "gooks," "kinks," and even animals. Indeed, many of the remarks that were made during the massacre sounded as though a pig hunt was in progress, rather than a massacre of human beings (Hersch, 1970).

In a similar manner, television writers can build up a character's "bad guy" image to such an extent that the viewer is almost relieved when he is killed ("He was nothing but vermin anyway"). This is even more serious when the bad guys are consistently portrayed as Indians, Mexicans, or outcasts of our society.

Norms and Legitimacy

In one sense, the soldiers at My Lai, the television writers, and the subjects in the experiments we have described all acted in a similar manner. They were responding to what they perceived to be legitimate *norms* governing aggression in their respective situations. Norm means a standard of behavior that is accepted by a particular society or group. The soldiers at My Lai were extremely suspicious and mistrustful of the Vietnamese (even children can set booby traps), and the general norm was to "get them before they get us." The television writers can hardly be blamed for portraying "bad guys" who "deserve" to be exterminated because the norms of the larger society have already created the "bad guys."

A much clearer demonstration of how group norms can affect aggressive behavior was demonstrated in another study of Milgram's (1965b). In a replication of his learning-shock study, he introduced a situation where the subject had to join two other "teachers" to decide on the strength of the shocks the "pupil" would receive. When the other two confederates indicated that the experimenter was wrong to ask them to administer severe shocks (i.e., they invoked the norm of nonaggression), the amount of aggression dropped sharply.

However, other people do not have to be present to invoke pro- or antiaggressive norms. Berkowitz and Green (1966) used clips from a boxing film as cues for aggression. One sequence showed a particularly unfair and dirty fight in which the winner gouged, hit below the belt, and in general violated the rules with impunity. The other portrayed a clean version of the fight. Surprisingly, the subjects who saw the first clip displayed *less* aggression than did those who saw the clean version! Thus catharsis was obviously not the major factor. The critical difference was whether the subject perceived the aggression to be *legitimate*. The viewing of unjustified violence seemed to inhibit aggression, probably because norms about fair play and justice were invoked. If the literal depiction of violence is not as important as the norms that are evoked to justify it, then television and other communications media have a tremendous responsibility to the public. However, in the last analysis, it is narrow-minded to put the entire blame on television because it represents only one segment of a larger society that has developed norms to justify aggression and violence in a wide range of situations and toward a number of different groups. (See fig. 23.4.)

Crime and Delinquency

In the mind of the general public, one of the most important social issues is the incidence of crime and delinquency. In some cities, people live in constant fear of becoming the victim of an assault, mugging, rape, or burglary.

Figure 23.4 Violence on television is difficult to overlook because it is a constant feature of many programs. (Copyright © 1968. Ziff Davis Publishing Company. Reprinted by permission of *Psychology Today* Magazine.)

Crimes committed by young people are of special concern because they seem to indicate that something is wrong with society itself. There is also more hope that so-called delinquents may be easier to rehabilitate than are older, "hard-core" criminals.

Delinquency research is one of the oldest fields in social psychology and psychologists have developed many different theories about the causes of delinquent behavior. These theories fall into two broad classes: Those that locate the sources of delinquency within the individual; and those that put the blame on the social and economic system. We will look first at a sample of the evidence for each type of theory and then examine recent evidence that conflicts with these approaches.

Individual Sources of Delinquency

Genetic Abnormalities

Much excitement was generated several years ago when it was discovered that males with an extra Y chromosome (XYY) are found in institutions for the criminally insane much more frequently than would be expected on the basis of their numbers in the general population (Court-Brown et al., 1968). The XYY syndrome is often associated with large physical size, low IQ, and strong aggressive tendencies. However, further studies have not been able to replicate this result consistently (Clark et al., 1970). One problem is that the XYY syndrome occurs so rarely in the general population that an adequate baseline survey estimate is extremely difficult to obtain. Moreover, because the proportion of persons who commit crimes (detected or not) will also contain a small proportion of XYY individuals, this genetic explanation would account for only a very small proportion of the problem, even if the hypothesis were strongly supported.

Physical Types

The idea that certain personality or behavioral characteristics may be related to body types was introduced in Chapter 17. W. H. Sheldon, one of the founders of this approach, was the first to extend this line of thinking to delinquency (Sheldon et al., 1949). Extensive research has given some support to the notion that there is a relationship between the *mesomorph* (or athletic) type of physique and delinquency (Glueck and Glueck, 1959). This relationship would make sense for crimes that involve strength and agility (e.g., unarmed robbery or assault). However, because only official records (arrested and convicted) were used in the Glueck's research, it is possible that the police may have unintentionally been looking for athletic-looking suspects rather than obese or thin ones ("How could that fat kid roll that big guy?").

Learning Disabilities

Another approach that has become popular in recent years is to relate delinquency to a variety of learning problems such as dyslexia and hyperactivity. These basic perceptual and motor problems may cause a child to fail in school and thus create feelings of frustration and inadequacy, which in turn may be expressed in delinquent behavior (Grim, 1968). Once again, although this hypothesis is certainly plausible and worthy of further investigation, it probably cannot explain more than a small proportion of delinquent or criminal activity.

Low Self-Esteem

There is substantial evidence for the existence of a relationship between low self-esteem and delinquency among institutionalized youths (Deitz, 1969). Moreover, this low self-esteem seems to be tied to continued failure of these youths in important life-roles such as student, employee, and the like. (Gold, 1970). Whether failure in school, arrests, and decline in self-esteem occur in any particular order is at present unclear, but the reliability of the findings warrants further study.

When we begin talking about life-*roles,* we are moving away from characteristics that are predominantly individualistic and toward properties that link people to social systems. (See box 23.5.) For example, the association between failure at school and delinquency (or failure at an occupation and crime) may reflect more of a problem with the educational system or occupational structure than with the characteristics of individuals. Because social and economic systems usually exist prior to and survive after any single individual, it is reasonable to believe that low self-esteem and delinquent behavior are a consequence rather than a cause of failure at school or at work. With this argument in mind, we will now examine several theories that focus on socioeconomic sources of delinquency.

Socioeconomic Sources of Delinquency

Poverty

Perhaps the bulk of contemporary social theories of delinquency and crime place the blame on low income and low social status. One well-known example of *status deprivation theory* was developed by Cohen (1955), who contended that although many working-class individuals value the same things which middle- and upper-class people do (e.g., money, house, prestige), their depressed economic and social situation cuts them off from any hope of achieving these goals. Therefore, rather than strive for the impossible, lower-class youths, particularly males, develop their own systems of rewards and prestige. These attainable goals and rewards are often achieved by membership in a gang (Whyte, 1943), and unfortunately, many of their activities (e.g., running numbers, stealing, or fighting) are defined as illegal by the dominant society. As a result, a greater number of lower-class or poor people become involved in serious crime. Notice that Cohen's theory attributes the problem to the socioeconomic and status systems—that is, the lack of access to valued goals by a section of society—rather than to individual traits. This idea had been developed more fully by Merton (1957) and was elaborated as the theory of *blocked-opportunity* by Cloward and Ohlin (1960).

Gang Membership

The gang as a social source of criminal behavior has been investigated intensively, and

Box 23.5

Social Conditions and Personal Reactions

The importance of taking into account both social conditions and personality factors when considering delinquency (or any behavior) is demonstrated in the following interview with a 15-year-old from Detroit:

> *You get kicked out of one place and you move a couple of blocks to the next pig pen. One of my "uncles" gets a truck, and we load up all we got and go somewhere else. After we dump the junk in the new joint, I cruise out cool on the street and look for whose ass I know I can whip. I'm "bad," man. I'm mean. After I drag the street once, I know what's shakin'. I know whose big and who ain't and what's goin' on. I don't mess with the guys that can beat me till I find out who's chicken, and then I try a couple of them. I move in slow, but hard, and the next day, everybody knows. Then they know "mess with me and you die." Nobody pushes with me and nobody says nothin' about my mother. Man, you got to push or suck hind titty where I live. I don't suck no hind titty. That's all. They fool with me and they in a whole world of trouble. You a whitey. You don't know nothin' about it. You can go downtown any time and nobody says nothin' to you. I got the color and I can't go nowhere except with my own kind. You try it and see how you like it. (McNeil, 1967, pp. 101–102.)*

Are you certain you could stay out of trouble if you had to move every other week because you were unable to pay your rent or had to live in a neighborhood where you not only had to protect yourself from your neighbors, but had to avoid the police? These are some of the socio-economic factors involved in delinquency. On the other hand, individual factors also play a part. While one individual will cope by going out on the street and establishing his identity and position, another will do so by simply staying indoors all day.

most of the studies have focused on gangs formed by lower-class males. However, we should point out that there has always been a certain amount of gang activity among middle-class males, and female gangs have emerged in New York City in recent years. Furthermore, you should not overlook the fact that gangs also exist in high places: It was a gang called the "Plumbers" that burglarized the national headquarters of the Democratic Party in 1972 and touched off the Watergate scandal.

Sutherland (1947) was one of the first theorists to pinpoint the small-group processes that make it extremely difficult for a member of a delinquent gang to be deviant; in other words, nondelinquent. Gang leadership tends to be highly authoritarian, and severe sanctions are imposed on members who deviate from group norms. Sometimes the external threat of other gangs or the police strengthens rather than weakens these internal processes for conformity (Whyte, 1943). As we have already indicated, most of these research findings concern lower-class street gangs, but it is recognized by most sociologists that these group forces are present, to some extent, even in more loosely-knit criminal associations (Short and Strodtbeck, 1965).

Broken Families

Perhaps the social factor that most people think of as the major cause of delinquency is family background. In the case of male juveniles, the absence of a father in the home is considered critical for later delinquent behavior (Nye, 1958). However, more extensive investigations have shown that the absence of the father may be less important than how disturbed the family relationships are. A child whose father is consistently brutal, drunk, or rejecting may be affected more profoundly than is a fatherless child (Siegman, 1966; Ainsworth, 1962). In any case, family research, like research on poverty and gangs has concentrated on the problems of lower-class and nonwhite families, rather than those of the middle-class.

The "Typical" Delinquent

All the theories and supporting research data we have discussed thus far seem to define the delinquent in a way that conforms to the general public's conception of what he is like. In other words, the typical delinquent is a lower-class nonwhite male who belongs to a gang, comes from a broken home, and may have chromosomal abnormalities or learning disabilities.

There is one critical problem with this popular image of the typical delinquent: the research support is based on *official* police and court statistics and on comparisons between youths who are caught (and sometimes institutionalized) and youths who are not caught for unlawful behavior. For example, the crime reports issued by the Federal Bureau of Investigation consistently show that the percentage of nonwhite males who are arrested and convicted is much larger than is warranted by the number of nonwhite males in the general population. However, studies of *undetected* delinquent behavior, based on self-reports obtained from large samples of youths and adults, show that *social class* and *racial differences* are actually much *smaller* than *official statistics* would indicate; in some cases, there is *no difference* at all. Before we illustrate these startling results in detail, we should point out that only three to five percent of the self-confessed crimes and delinquent acts reported in surveys of both adults and youths were ever detected by the authorities. If official statistics are based on such a small percentage of actual criminal and delinquent behavior, we must question the validity of theories and conclusions that are based on them.

In one of the more comprehensive and systematic studies in undetected delinquency, Gold (1970) surveyed a randomly drawn sample of 522 youths in Flint, Michigan. Using interviewing techniques that guaranteed the respondent's anonymity, he asked the youths about an extensive list of delinquent acts they might have committed within the previous three years. Details of a few of the confessed offenses were probed at length to ascertain the accuracy of the information. Also, a study on the validity, or truthfulness of responses was carried out (see box 23.6).

Gold's results were consistent with official FBI statistics on only one count: Males admitted to significantly more offenses than did females. Furthermore, his results did not support the popular notion that female delinquency consists largely of sexual promiscuity, running away from home, and/or problems with parents: These acts accounted for only eleven percent of the offenses committed by females. The most important finding was that *no racial* differences existed in the number of undetected delinquent acts and that the differences between *social classes* were much smaller than were indicated by official statistics. For example, the ratio of working-class to middle-class youths who were arrested and convicted was eight to one. But in Gold's study of self-reported crimes committed by these groups, the ratio was three working-class youths for every two middle-class youths! Also, official statistics show that blacks and Mexican-Americans are arrested and convicted in far greater proportions than is warranted by their numbers in the general population. But in Gold's data, there were *no differences* in the number of offenses committed by blacks and whites (see table 23.2).

These results, which are supported by similar studies in other cities (Akers, 1970; Hirschi, 1969; Clark and Wenninger, 1962), have two important implications. One, most social theories of delinquency will have to be

Box 23.6

How Valid Are Self-Reports?

The apparent differences between official crime statistics and *self-reported* criminal activity are critically important for both theory and practice. But how do we know whether people are telling the truth when they say they have committed undetected crimes? Gold (1970) attempted to answer this question by including a *validation* study in his research on self-reported delinquency in Flint, Michigan. Without the respondents' knowledge, he contacted their friends and acquaintances and questioned them in detail about any offenses they knew the subject had committed. Gold was able to do this for 125 of the 522 respondents in his sample, with the following results: In seventy-two percent of the cases, the reports of friends and acquaintances corroborated the subjects' reports; in seventeen percent of the cases, the subject had lied to the investigator. Eleven percent of the cases were questionable. As shown in box figure 23.6, there are some slight, but not significant overall differences across groups in terms of sex, social class, and race. When the data were broken down by kinds of offenses, he found that boys lied most often about drinking, carrying concealed weapons, and shoplifting, while girls tended to lie about stealing and sexual activities.

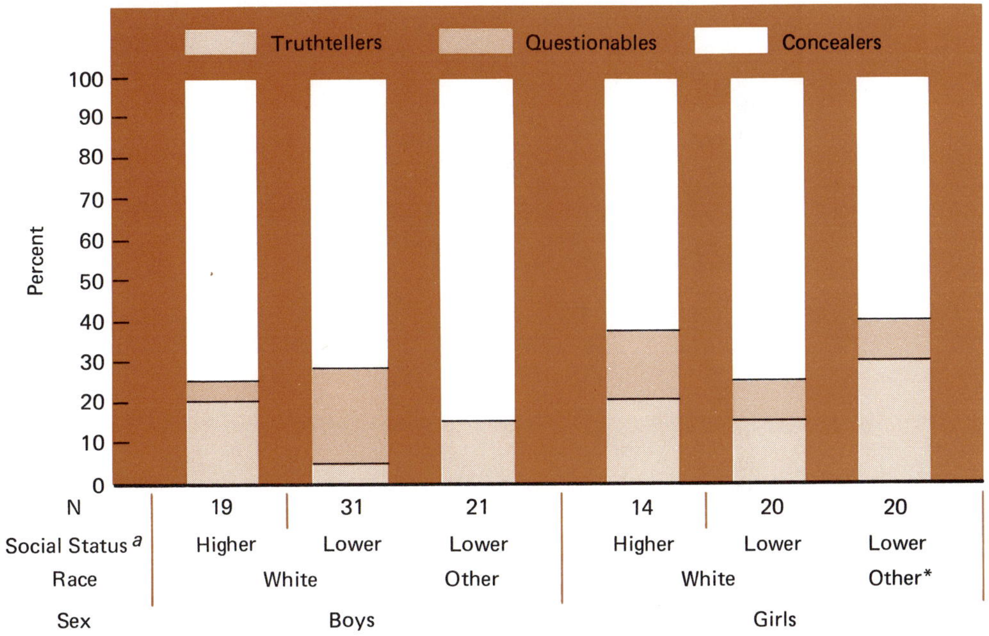

* No difference between groups is statistically reliable at the .20 level by Chi Square or Fisher Exact Test.

[a] "Higher" and "lower" status is largely a distinction between white-blue-collar workers.

Box Figure 23.6 The proportion of youths in the self-reported delinquency study in Flint, Michigan, who told the truth, concealed known offenses, or were questionable. (From *Delinquent Behavior in an American City* by Martin Gold. Copyright 1970 by Wadsworth Publishing Company. Reprinted by permission of the publisher. Brooks/Cole Publishing Company, Monterey, California.)

Table 23.2 Percentage frequencies of delinquent acts reported by black and white youths broken down by sex. Overall, there is significantly more delinquent behavior by boys than girls, but *no differences* in overall frequency between the two racial groups.

Proportions of lower-status white and Negro boys and girls who committed each offense					
Percent	Race: Sex:	White boys	Negro boys	White girls	Negro girls
	N:	67	52	83	36
60		Shoplifting Trespass Theft Drinking	Shoplifting		
50			Theft Trespass Fornication		
40		Truancy	Entering Truancy Concealed weapon Drinking Gang fighting	Truancy Drinking	Drinking
30		Threatened assault Property destruction Gang fighting Stealing car part or gas	Threatened assault Property destruction	Shoplifting Entering Trespass	Shoplifting
20		Concealed weapon UDAA* Fornication False ID or age Assault	Assault Extortion	Theft	Trespass Theft Threatened assault
10		Extortion Running away	Armed robbery False ID or age Running away		Truancy
		Striking parents Armed robbery Arson Fraud	Fraud UDAA* Stealing car part or gas Striking parents	Gang fighting Running away Striking parents Threatened assault Fornication Assault Property destruction	Fornication Gang fighting False ID or age Assault—running away Property destruction Entering Extortion

Source: From *Delinquent behavior in an American city,* by Martin Gold. Copyright © 1970 by Wadsworth Publishing Company. Reprinted by permission of the publisher, Brooks/Cole Publishing Company, Monterey, California.

revised because it is patently wrong to say that crime and delinquency are mainly working-class problems. To be adequate, future theories will have to encompass middle-class and upper-class crime as well. Two, the fact that there are large discrepancies between the amount of actual crime and delinquency and the number of arrests and convictions across race and class have focused attention on the judicial system itself. Why are disproportionate numbers of the working-class (white as well as nonwhite) arrested and convicted? Obviously, the answer will be complex and will involve much rethinking and new research. Part of the problem may be caused by the class and racial prejudices of police officers and court officials. Another factor may be the less intentional prejudice that results in a phenomenon called *self-fulfilling* prophecy. That is, because police officers accept the stereotype of the typical delinquent that is supported by FBI statistics and sociological theories, they are on the lookout for this kind of offender. Those who are arrested then become another statistic among statistics that defined them as potential delinquents in the first place, and thus the cycle (or prophecy) is complete. The youths who are arrested may even come to apply this stereotype to themselves and begin to act accordingly (see box 23.7).

But where do these stereotypes and biases originate? One contemporary approach to this question has been based on Karl Marx's insights into social classes and their relationships to economic and political power. The main hypothesis of this approach is that the racial and class biases that exist in the criminal justice system are part of a larger system of conflict between classes and interest groups (Quinney, 1970). In other words, the idea that the "delinquent" or "criminal" is found primarily in one racial group or class is a convenient justification for creating and maintaining economic, political, and social inequality (Sarbin, 1969).

Box 23.7
Getting Caught

We know from studies of undetected delinquency that only a small percentage of delinquent behavior ever comes to the attention of the police or courts. But what happens if you do get caught? Does it deter you from repeating your delinquent activity? Although there is no confirmed evidence as yet, we have reason to believe that the answer may be no.

In one study of "hard-core" criminals, Robins (1966) found that the two best predictors of continued delinquency and crime were early delinquent behavior and commitment to a correctional institution. In his study on undetected delinquency in Flint, Michigan, Gold (1970) was able to match twenty youngsters who had been caught with twenty that had not been caught, according to age and type of offense. Surprisingly, eleven of the twenty that had been caught subsequently committed *more* offenses than those *who had not* been caught. Five committed the same number of offenses, and only four subsequently committed fewer offenses than those who had not been apprehended. If these results are replicated in a larger study, what would be some possible reasons for the fact that arrest and conviction appear to lead to more rather than less crime? One possibility is that youths who are caught are somehow different (more reckless or impulsive?) from those who are not. On the other hand, the police may be on the lookout for "known" delinquents. However, neither factor accounts for the increases in *undetected* crimes. Maybe the act of being caught labels the youth as a "bad kid," and he subsequently increases his delinquent activity because he has accepted this image of himself. Also, if he is sent to a correctional institution or prison it may simply be a matter of learning how to survive both behind bars and when he is released with a criminal record. These issues are beginning to attract the attention of researchers as well as officials in the criminal justice system.

Whether alternatives to the current theories will be developed and research will be done to test them remains to be seen. But in any case, serious theoreticians of criminology and conscientious administrators of justice can no longer ignore the fact that there are far more similarities than differences among social classes and races in terms of actual crime.

Summary

In this chapter, we have investigated three different areas of *applied research* in psychology; race relations, television and violence, and crime and delinquency.

With respect to race relations, we saw that desegregation is the strategy most often used to achieve the ideal of integration among racial groups. The cognitive dissonance theory predicts that this type of "forced compliance" will eventually lead to improved racial attitudes among participants. However, research on the effects of racial contact on attitude change indicated that several conditions must be met before interracial contact will be beneficial: The participants must have equal status, share common goals and activities, be mutually dependent, and have the support of local authorities and customs.

Those who advocate an independent strategy toward race relations are concerned that integration may simply perpetuate current discrepancies of power among racial groups. The results of national surveys indicate that although black people as a whole do not support the idea of political and economic separation, they overwhelmingly support the reestablishment of a sense of black cultural pride and identity. Research has also demonstrated that white-imposed identities can lead to feelings of self-hate and self-rejection among black and brown children.

Research on the issue of whether exposure to violence on television has any effect on actual aggressive behavior has produced contradictory results. There was some empirical support for the prediction of social learning theorists that televised aggression facilitates actual aggression through learning. There was less support for the catharsis theory, which predicts that television can serve as a safety valve for violent impulses and thus reduce aggression. We saw that the following factors serve to heighten or decrease the behavioral expression of aggression: the degree of frustration, the number of aggressive cues in the environment, the extent to which the intended victim is depersonalized, and the degree to which social norms that sanction either aggressive or nonaggressive behavior are elicited.

In the section on crime and delinquency, we said that some researchers have investigated the following individual factors that might contribute to criminal and delinquent behavior: chromosomal abnormalities, physical characteristics, learning disabilities, and negative self-concepts. Although these approaches showed promise of making important contributions to our understanding of delinquent behavior, chromosomal abnormalities and learning disabilities occur so rarely in the general population, that they cannot be used to explain the behavior of most delinquents.

Other researchers have looked to the socioeconomic system to uncover the sources of crime and delinquency. The study of poverty, gang membership, and broken families as the causes of delinquency has tended to define delinquency as a predominantly lower-class phenomenon. The main source of data for these approaches, official police and court records, certainly supports this view. However, more recent studies of undetected delinquency, which rely on self-report measures, show that there are no racial differences in the overall distribution of delinquent activity and that the differences between social classes are much smaller than official records indicate. Thus social theories about crime and delinquency and the administration of law enforcement and justice are in need of revision.

Throughout this book, we have demonstrated that the purpose of basic research in psychology is to establish empirically based principles of behavior through the use of the scientific method. We have also shown how the knowledge gained in basic psychological research can be applied to issues and problems in real life. In this final chapter, you have seen some of the difficulties involved in applying psychological knowledge and methods to social problems. Obviously, psychology alone cannot provide all the insights and answers, but the attempt will be beneficial for both psychology and society. The confrontation of real-life problems tends to expose the gaps and weaknesses in current psychological theory and research very quickly. Also, as we have seen, it exerts pressure on researchers to supplement traditional laboratory techniques with field-oriented research methods. For society, psychological research may stimulate public concern about certain issues and, hopefully, provide some objective data on which to base the policy decisions that affect us all.

Appendix 1: Concepts in Statistics

This appendix will help explain the statistical terms and techniques used throughout this book. It is meant only as an immediately accessible tool; it is no substitute for the courses in statistics and research design that those who are seriously interested in psychology should take.

To begin a scientific study, an investigator must choose a domain or fairly specific focus. A psychologist, for example, may choose to study attitude change, classical conditioning, neurotransmission, or any of a wide variety of topics perhaps best exemplified by scanning the contents of this textbook. Often he may be unaware of making a deliberate choice because his curiosity about a particular topic has led directly to the research.

The investigator's next step is likely to be quite explicit. He must count or measure something within his domain of interest; for example, test items that are answered in a certain way, the number of conditioned responses, or the latency of a polysynaptic reflex. This something that he measures or scores might be called a *variable,* and the variable he chooses will reflect his skill as a scientist because it must meet several criteria: (1) it is expected to yield information about the domain, (2) it must be capable of being counted or measured, and (3) it should show variation that can be associated with other variables. Cost, effort, and accuracy of measurement should be considered. If his study includes several variables, each must be considered in turn. And, of course, measurements must be made on a *sample of subjects,* which also involves careful choices.

Sampling Procedures

Let's examine the term *sample of subjects,* taking subjects (or *S*s) first. The subjects of a psychological study will usually be a number *(N)* of human beings or animals, although a number of neurons or other cells could be used, especially in biopsychology. If human subjects are used, the scientist must often make decisions concerning sex, age, health, intelligence, economic status, ethnic group, availability, or any other characteristics of potential importance to the study. Many studies will require the use of a nonhuman species, and careful consideration must be given to the species' characteristics that are relevant to the study, as well as to their availability, cost, and maintenance.

It is extremely unlikely that a measurement can be made on all subjects of interest. No matter how much we would like to measure all mankind (or all Americans, all college sophomores, or all left-handed persons), this usually is not possible. Therefore, we define the large group (e.g., all mankind, all women, all voters) as the *population,* and we draw a subset or *sample* from this population. Often the sample is drawn randomly from the population, which means that any subject in the population has an equal chance of being included in the sample. There are sophisticated and efficient techniques for choosing a sample, such as *stratified, random sampling.* Political pollsters are particularly adept at sophisticated sampling procedures. If the sampling is correctly and carefully done, the characteristics of the sample will (within limits) reflect the characteristics of the population.

In practice, fully satisfactory sampling is hard to achieve. Consider, for instance, whether an Australian aborigine really has an equal chance of being included in a study conducted at an American university from which the findings are generalized to "mankind." Nevertheless, techniques can be instituted that help avoid choosing a *biased,* or unrepresentative sample. One of the most useful techniques is to assign numbers to all potential subjects and then, by using a list or table of random numbers, force the choice of sufficient subjects for the sample. This helps the investigator avoid the common biases that might occur if, for instance, he went into an animal colony room (without his random-number table) and attempted to choose a "random" sample of animals for a particular study. Under these conditions, he would be likely to pick larger, sleeker, and tamer animals than would be found in a randomly selected group. A similar but more subtle bias might enter into the selection of a human sample if the investigator used the telephone book to represent the population at large. It is easy to forget that many people do not have a telephone. Thus a representative number of persons would be entirely missing from such a sample, with possibly disastrous results if their characteristics were different enough to invalidate a study that excluded them.

One of the most common experimental designs includes the selection of two or more samples from a population. Often, one of them is used as a base comparison or *control* group, while the others are manipulated in some way prior to measurement. Any changes related to the manipulation can then be assessed by referring to the control group.

Now let us examine some typical methods of presenting data.

Presentation of Data

Distribution of Scores

Assume that we have the following array of scores representing the number of times animal subjects entered the wrong alley, or a *cul de sac,* while being trained to traverse a maze: 11, 7, 7, 9, 12, 10, 9, 11, 8, 8, 8, 9, 10, 10, 9. These scores can be shown as a frequency distribution by putting the occurrences, or frequency, opposite the score.

Score (or X)	*Frequency (or f)*
7	2
8	3
9	4
10	3
11	2
12	1

They can also form a frequency histogram (see fig. A.1). Or a frequency polygon can be formed (see fig. A.2).

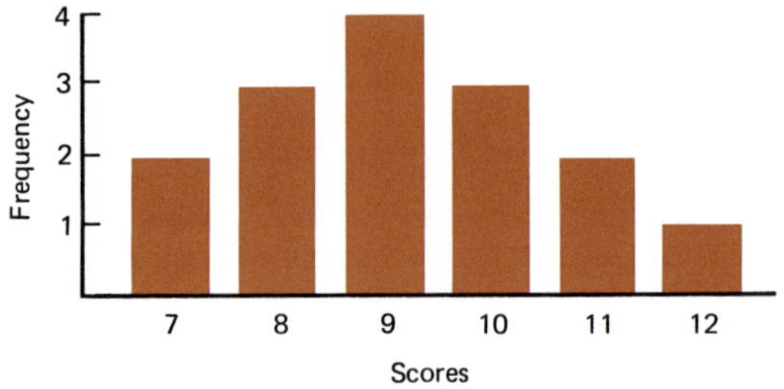

Figure A.1 A frequency histogram.

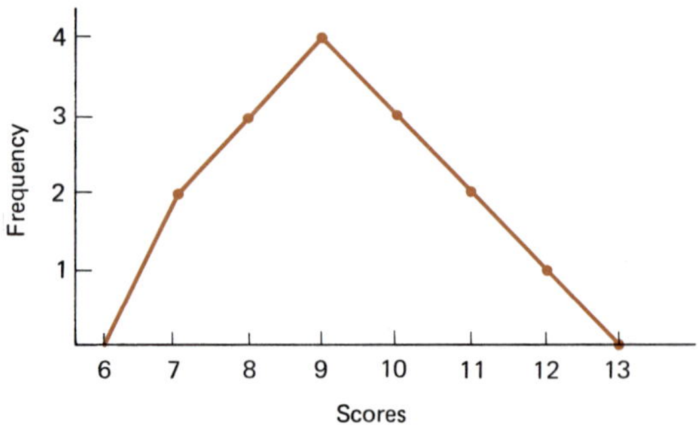

Figure A.2 A frequency polygon.

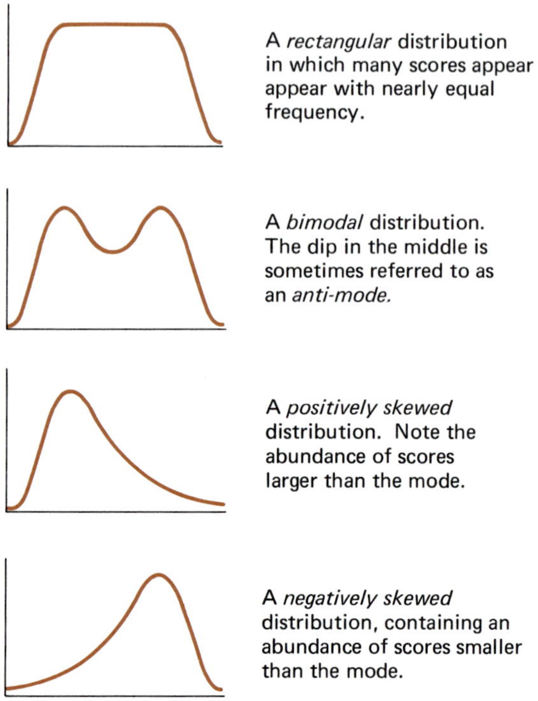

A *rectangular* distribution in which many scores appear appear with nearly equal frequency.
A *bimodal* distribution. The dip in the middle is sometimes referred to as an *anti-mode.*
A *positively skewed* distribution. Note the abundance of scores larger than the mode.
A *negatively skewed* distribution, containing an abundance of scores smaller than the mode.

Figure A.3 A few kinds of distributions.

Measures of Distribution

Mode

Both the histogram and the polygon are convenient for visually inspecting the shape or form of the data distribution. In our example, the data are distributed more or less symmetrically about the *mode* of nine, that is, the most frequently appearing value. However, other kinds of distributions are often seen (see fig. A.3). The shape of the distribution also has important implications for statistical computations and interpretations. We shall return to this point later.

Mean

For most computations, the scores themselves are used. For example, we can compute the mean, or arithmetic mean of our scores by adding, or summing all the scores and dividing the result by the number (N) of scores in the array. Thus

$$11 + 7 + 7 + 9 + 12 + 10 + 9 + 11 + 8 + 8 + 8 + 9 + 10 + 10 + 9 = 138.$$

And because there are fifteen scores, the mean is

$$138 \div 15, \text{ or } 9.2.$$

The Greek letter Σ is used to indicate the summing operation, and a bar placed over the letter or symbol that represents the array

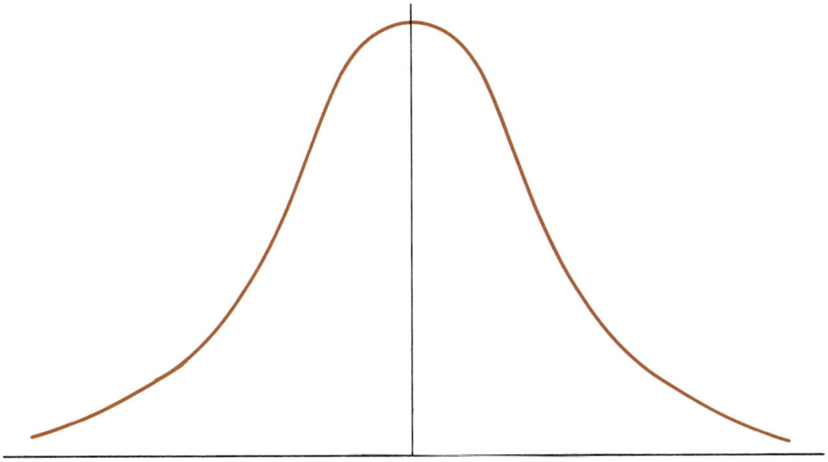

Figure A.4 A unimodal, symmetric distribution.

often indicates the mean of the array. Using these symbols, the above operation is shown as follows:

$$\overline{X} = \frac{\Sigma X}{N} = \frac{138}{15} = 9.2.$$

When the need arises, subscripts or superscripts can be placed on these symbols to indicate precisely which value or operation is meant. Both the *mode* and the *mean* are measures of *central tendency* of a distribution.

Median

Another useful measure of central tendency is the median. In a simple array of scores, the median is the midmost score (if there is an odd number of scores) or halfway between the two middle scores (if the number of scores is even). In our example of fifteen scores, the median is the eighth largest score, or nine. Note that the scores were arranged in order of magnitude to obtain the median. If the scores are too numerous to rearrange into order of magnitude, the median can easily be computed using a frequency distribution.

When a distribution is completely symmetrical, the mean, median, and mode are all equal to the same value (see fig. A.4). When a distribution is skewed, however, the mean is affected by the extreme values and is often a less satisfactory measure of central tendency than the median. Note in figure A.5

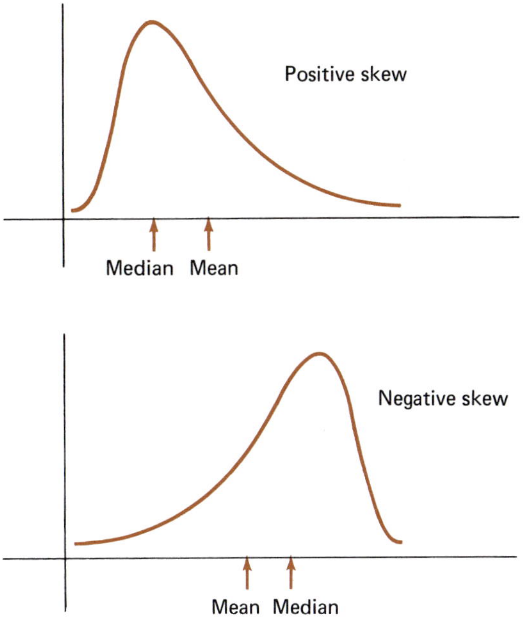

Figure A.5 Effects of skew.

that the mean is always located toward the elongated "tail" of the skewed distribution.

The mean, median, and mode are all *statistics,* computed from a sample. The equivalent concepts that refer to the total population are called *parameters.* For the reasons outlined previously, these parameters usually cannot be computed directly; therefore, we *estimate* their values by computing statistics on a sample from the population. The mean of a sample is an unbiased estimate of the mean of the population, often shown as M or the Greek letter μ (Mu). In our example, $\overline{X} = 9.2$ estimates the parameter, μ_X, of the unknown population. There are procedures for computing the accuracy of the estimate as well. These depend on the sample *variance,* which will be discussed below.

Dispersion of Scores

Another salient characteristic of a distribution is the spread, or dispersion of scores. The two distributions in figure A.6 have the same mean, but one is much more dispersed than the other. One simple measure of dispersion is obtained by subtracting the lowest score from the highest; this is called the range. Another, called the *variance,* is somewhat harder to compute but is an excellent measure of score dispersion and has many useful properties.

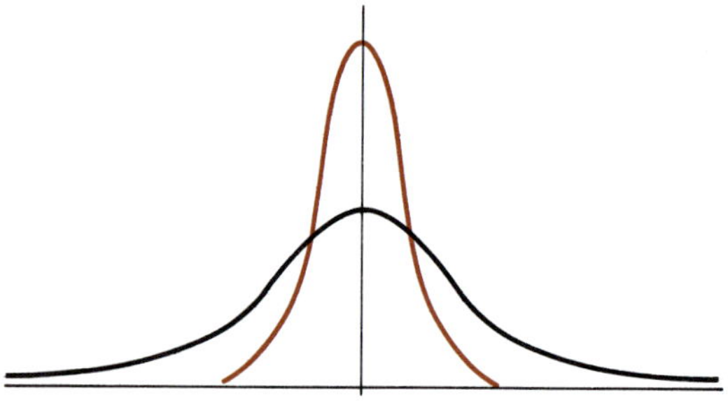

Figure A.6 Two distributions with equal means but different dispersion.

Variance. The sample variance, s^2, can be computed as follows:

1. Compute the mean of the sample.
2. Subtract the mean from every score and square the result.
3. Sum these squared *deviation scores.*
4. Divide the sum by $N - 1$. This gives the variance.

The algebraic formula is

$$s^2 = \frac{\Sigma(X - \overline{X})^2}{N - 1}.$$

The following example illustrates the computation of variance:

Score (or X_i)	$X_i - \overline{X}$	$(X_i - \overline{X})^2$
2	−2	4
3	−1	1
3	−1	1
4	0	0
5	1	1
5	1	1
6	2	4
$\Sigma X_i = 28$	$\Sigma(X_i - \overline{X}) = 0$	$\Sigma(X_i - \overline{X})^2 = 12$

$$\overline{X} = \frac{\Sigma X_i}{N} = \frac{28}{7} = 4.$$

$$s_x^2 = \frac{\Sigma(X_i - \overline{X})^2}{N - 1} = \frac{12}{6} = 2.$$

In this simple example, the "scores" were chosen so that the mean would be an integer, or whole number. Naturally, this is not often the case with real data. To avoid the difficulty of working with a mean that includes a fractional component (e.g., $\overline{X} = 3.714$) the following algebraically equivalent formula for computing the sample variance usually is used.

$$s^2 = \frac{\Sigma X^2 - \frac{(\Sigma X)^2}{N}}{N - 1}.$$

This formula may look more complex than the *defining* formula first given, but it is much easier to use in most cases. Consider its use with the following "data":

X_i	X_i^2
2	4
4	16
4	16
7	49
7	49
8	64
9	81

$\Sigma X_i = 41 \qquad \Sigma X_i^2 = 279 \qquad (\Sigma X_i)^2 = 1681$

$$s_x^2 = \frac{\Sigma X_i^2 - \frac{(\Sigma X_i)^2}{N}}{N-1} = \frac{279 - \frac{1681}{7}}{6} = 6.65.$$

Note that the mean, $\overline{X}$, was never computed. However,

$$\overline{X} = \frac{\Sigma X_i}{N} = \frac{41}{7} = 5.857.$$

Using this value in the defining formula for the sample variance would have resulted in much more labor. With the aid of a good desk calculator, one can obtain ΣX_i, ΣX_i^2, and N in just one "pass" through the data, and s^2 can be calculated with minimal effort. Indeed, some modern machines yield a value for s^2 in a "single stroke"—that is, by pushing only one key—after entering the data.

The sample variance, s_x^2, estimates the population variance, σ_x^2 or V_x. Usually σ_x^2 is unknown, and we must work with available estimates. In those cases where the complete population is available, we can compute the population variance directly by using

$$\sigma_x^2 = \frac{\Sigma(X_i - \mu_x)^2}{N} = \frac{\Sigma X_i^2 - \frac{(\Sigma X_i)^2}{N}}{N}.$$

Actually, the above formulas were used for many years to calculate sample variance, until it was realized that the estimate of population variance obtained in this way was consistently too small, or *biased*. This bias is corrected by using N − 1 in the denominator of the formulas for sample variance. This is necessary because the calculations for sample variance involve the use of the sum or the mean of the same scores, thus using up one *degree of freedom (df)* from the array. For instance, given the scores 1, 3, 5, and 7, we have four degrees of freedom. There are no constraints on any of the scores: any could have some other value. However, as soon as we begin a calculation that involves their sum $(1 + 3 + 5 + 7 = 16)$ or their mean, one of the scores is no longer free to assume another value; if one number is erased, we can easily see what it had to be. In other words, we have lost one degree of freedom, and this loss is reflected by the use of N − 1 in the formula for sample variance.

Standard Deviation

The square root of the variance $(\sqrt{s_x^2})$ is called the standard deviation, s_x, and is another measure of dispersion. When scores from a sample or population are rather divergent or dispersed, s_x^2 and s_x will be relatively large. When the scores are more tightly clustered, s_x^2 and s_x will be relatively small.

When plotted as a histogram or polygon, many arrays of data will reveal a tendency for many scores to be near a central value, while extremely low or high scores are rare. This results in a unimodal distribution, which can be characterized fairly well by just two parameters: where the center of the distribution is located and how widely dispersed the scores are. Usually these functions are served by the mean and the standard deviation, respectively. If the scores happen to form a so-called normal (or Gaussian) curve, these two parameters specify their distribution exactly. Because of this convenient property, the familiar bell-shaped, normal probability curve is widely used—perhaps overused—for data analyses, and tables relating areas under the curve are included in almost every statistics textbook. Many analyses involve distributions made up of *means of samples* drawn from the same population. In this situation, the use of normal-curve-statistics is justified because a distribution of means tends to be normal, regardless of the forms of the sampling distributions from which they were taken. This is known as the *Central Limit Theorem.*

Deviation Scores

It often is convenient to express scores as *deviation scores,* obtained by subtracting the mean from each raw score. This does not change the shape of the distribution; it merely centers the distribution over zero on the X-axis and expresses about half the scores as negative numbers. Deviation scores are often indicated by the use of lowercase letters—for example, $x_i = X_i - \overline{X}$, or $y_i = Y_i - \overline{Y}$. Of course, the sum of the array of deviation scores is zero, as is the mean.

Next, the deviation scores can be *standardized* by dividing them by s_x. By standardizing the deviation scores, any normally distributed variable can be fit onto a single standard-normal, or *unit-normal* curve; this operation also allows the use of a single table for looking up areas and other features that may be needed. Standardized scores usually are indicated by the use of the letter z, and are often called z-scores. The mean of a z-score distribution is zero, its variance equals 1.0, and its standard deviation equals 1.0.

Normal Curve

Some of the features of the standard-normal curve are shown in figure A.7. The distribution is centered over zero, and the tails of the distribution are *asymptotic* to the X-axis—that is, they approach the axis but do not meet it. Since the height of the curve is a function of the expected frequency of each score, we would expect extremely large or extremely small (large negative) scores to appear only rarely.

The total area under the curve is set equal to 1.0. Subportions can be defined and their areas can be computed by using the integral calculus. These areas represent probabilities. For example, we may ask: What is the probability of randomly obtaining a score which, after standardization, falls between zero and -1.0 z? The answer, as shown in figure A.7, is .34. This means that, on the average, a score falling within these limits will occur 34 times out of 100; alternatively, it means that a score will fall outside these limits an average of 66 times out of 100.

There are several conventional ways of dividing up the area under curves: one method involves division into 100 equal parts; another involves division into 4 equal parts. Let's consider the former method first.

Centiles and Quartiles

If we draw 99 vertical lines under the curve in such a way that we obtain 100 equal areas, we have divided it into centiles (sometimes called percentiles). Near either tail, the lines will have to be farther apart to include sufficient area in this shallow part of the curve; near the center the lines will be quite close together. The first line in from the left tail defines the first centile, or C_1: i.e., we would expect 1 percent of the scores to be smaller than this and 99% to be larger. A similar statement could be made for all the other centiles. The 25th, 50th, and 75th centiles

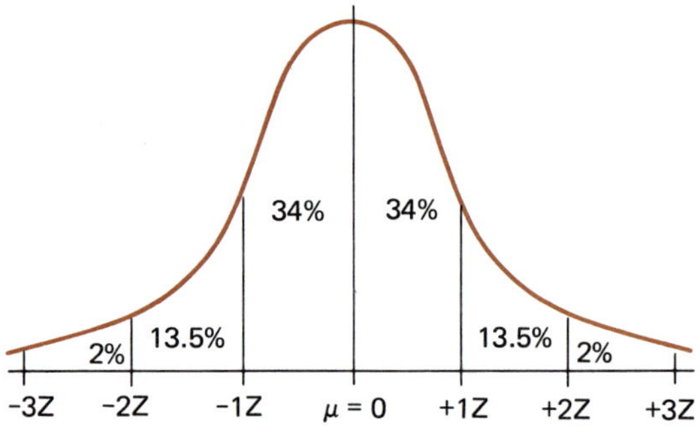

Figure A.7 Some percentages of areas under portions of a unit-normal curve.

warrant further attention. C_{50}, of course, divides the area into two equal parts and is another useful definition for the median. The 25th centile is also called the first *quartile,* or Q_1, because it divides the area into proportions of one-fourth and three-fourths. The 75th centile is the third quartile, or Q_3. Half the distance along the X-axis between Q_1 and Q_3 yields another measure of dispersion, called the *semi-interquartile range,* or *Q*. The formula is simply

$$Q = \frac{Q_3 - Q_1}{2}.$$

Z-Score Transformations

Many transformations that depend on z-scores will be familiar to you. For example, IQ scores are no longer obtained by dividing mental age by chronological age. Instead, an intelligence test is given to a large sample, and the mean and standard deviation are computed. Let's assume that these are 67 and 8.3, respectively. An individual score, say 78, is then standardized as follows to yield a z-score:

$$z_x = \frac{X - \overline{X}}{s_x} = \frac{78 - 67}{8.3} = \frac{9}{8.3} = 1.08.$$

Although this z-score would be a perfectly useful index of intelligence, it is usually transformed to the more familiar IQ form by multiplying by a constant and adding a constant.

$$IQ = 100 + 15\,z_x = 100 + 16.2 = 116.$$

This last process adds no information, but it does eliminate negative numbers and decimal fractions. Although most IQ transformation equations use the additive constant 100, some use a multiplicative constant of 14, 16, or some other number. The Army General Classification Test uses a multiplicative constant of 20.

To interpret a particular "IQ," one must know what constant was used. T-scores (often used in ROTC) use an additive constant of 50 and a multiplier of 10. College Board (SAT) scores use an additive constant of 500 and a multiplier of 100; thus a SAT score of 450 means that the individual placed one-half standard deviation below the mean. The SAT scores, however, refer to a special population of students, not to the general populations, and therefore are not equivalent to IQs. These different methods of representing scores are actually just slightly different ways of reporting relative standing, using a normal curve. Examples of this equivalence are illustrated in figure A.8.

Areas under the standard-normal curve are given in table A.1. The values in the column labeled *z* are in standard deviation units (and fractions) measured *from the middle,* or $\mu = 0$. Because the curve is symmetrical, only positive values are necessary. Any of the area relationships in figure A.8 may be checked by using the table.

Confidence Limits of the Mean

As we mentioned previously, it would be possible to draw many samples of the same size (say $N = 25$) from a population and compute the mean for each. Each separate sample mean would be an estimate of, but not usually exactly equal to the population mean. We could make a histogram or polygon using these means and then compute the mean of the means and the standard deviation of the means. Unless further information is available, the mean of the distribution of sample means is our best estimate of the population parameter, μ, and can be used as such. The standard deviation of sample means has been given a distinctive name, the *standard error of the estimate,* or $s_{\bar{x}}$. The logic of this term may be clearer if you recall that each mean yields an *estimate* of the population mean, and $s_{\bar{x}}$ is a simple way of indicating the amount of dis-

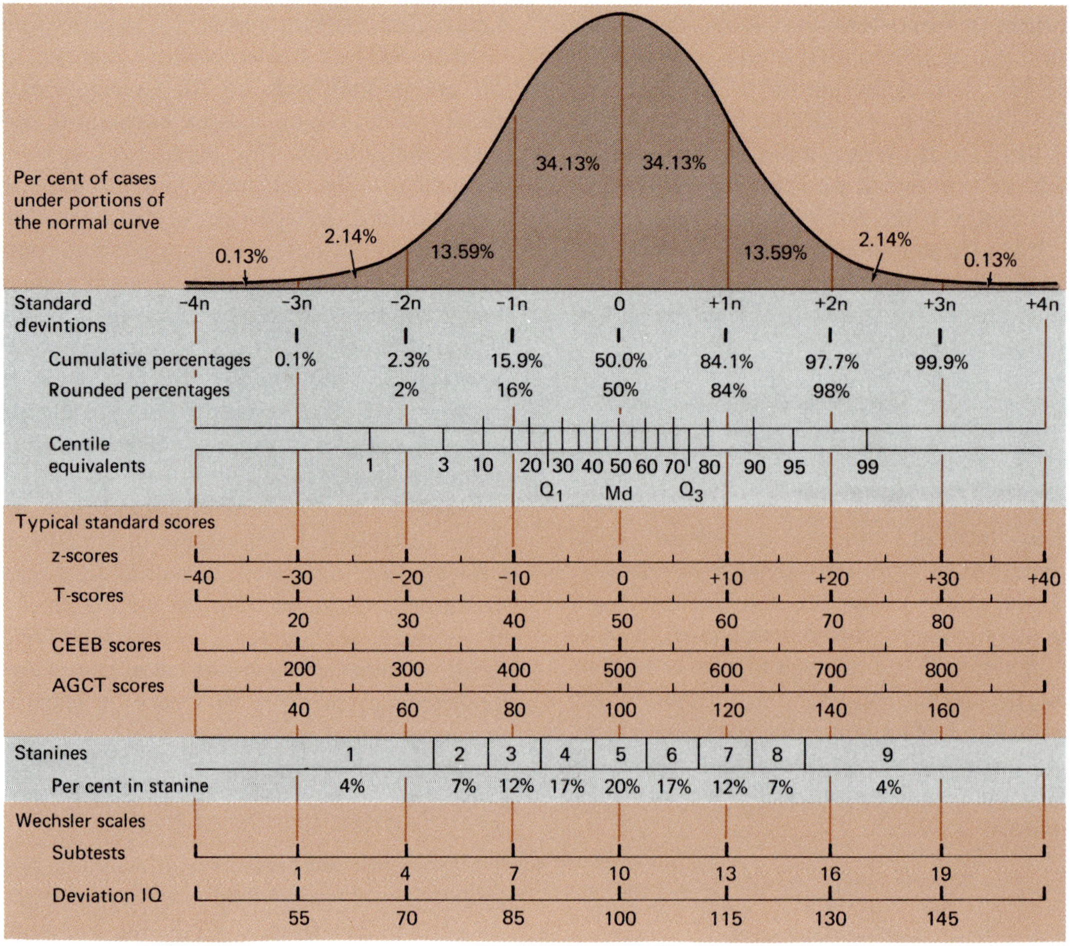

Figure A.8 Centiles and standard scores in a normal distribution.

persion, or scatter in the distribution of means. In practice it is unnecessary to draw many samples and actually calculate $s_{\bar{x}}$, because it has been shown that

$$s_{\bar{x}} = \frac{s_x}{\sqrt{N}}.$$

Thus we would only have to draw one sample of N = 25, calculate its standard deviation (say 10), and use the above formula. Thus:

$$s_{\bar{x}} = \frac{s_x}{\sqrt{25}} = \frac{10}{\sqrt{25}} = \frac{10}{5} = 2.$$

We could take the mean of the same sample (say 23) and use table A.1 to compute the 95 percent confidence limits for the mean. The confidence limits will define a range of values that we would expect to include the mean of 95 out of 100 samples drawn in the same way from the same population. To do this, we find the z-value that includes 47.5 percent of the area measured from the mean toward one tail of the distribution. This is the shaded area in figure A.9; $z = 1.96$ includes such an area. If we take the area between $z = -1.96$ and $z = +1.96$, then 95 percent of

Table A.1 Areas in one tail of and under the normal curve.

TABLE 1

AREAS UNDER THE NORMAL CURVE

From the Arithmetic Mean to Distances $\frac{x}{s}$ of $\frac{x}{\sigma}$ from the Arithmetic Mean z

Expressed as Decimal Fractions of the Total Area 1.0000

This table shows:

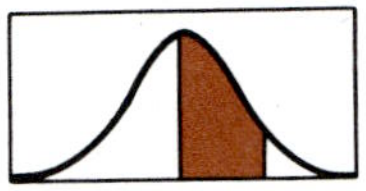

z	.00	.01	.02	.03	.04	.05	.06	.07	.08	.09
0.0	.0000	.0040	.0080	.0120	.0160	.0199	.0239	.0279	.0319	.0359
0.1	.0398	.0438	.0478	.0517	.0557	.0596	.0636	.0675	.0714	.0753
0.2	.0793	.0832	.0871	.0910	.0948	.0987	.1026	.1064	.1103	.1141
0.3	.1179	.1217	.1255	.1293	.1331	.1368	.1406	.1443	.1480	.1517
0.4	.1554	.1591	.1628	.1664	.1700	.1736	.1772	.1808	.1844	.1879
0.5	.1915	.1950	.1985	.2019	.2054	.2088	.2123	.2157	.2190	.2224
0.6	.2257	.2291	.2324	.2357	.2389	.2422	.2454	.2486	.2518	.2549
0.7	.2580	.2612	.2642	.2673	.2704	.2734	.2764	.2794	.2823	.2852
0.8	.2881	.2910	.2939	.2967	.2995	.3023	.3051	.3078	.3106	.3133
0.9	.3159	.3186	.3212	.3238	.3264	.3289	.3315	.3340	.3365	.3389
1.0	.3413	.3438	.3461	.3485	.3508	.3531	.3554	.3577	.3599	.3621
1.1	.3643	.3665	.3686	.3708	.3729	.3749	.3770	.3790	.3810	.3830
1.2	.3849	.3869	.3888	.3907	.3925	.3944	.3962	.3980	.3997	.4015
1.3	.4032	.4049	.4066	.4082	.4099	.4115	.4131	.4147	.4162	.4177
1.4	.4192	.4207	.4222	.4236	.4251	.4265	.4279	.4292	.4306	.4319
1.5	.4332	.4345	.4357	.4370	.4382	.4394	.4406	.4418	.4429	.4441
1.6	.4452	.4463	.4474	.4484	.4495	.4505	.4515	.4525	.4535	.4545
1.7	.4554	.4564	.4573	.4582	.4591	.4599	.4608	.4616	.4625	.4633
1.8	.4641	.4649	.4656	.4664	.4671	.4678	.4686	.4693	.4699	.4706
1.9	.4713	.4719	.4726	.4732	.4738	.4744	.4750	.4756	.4761	.4767
2.0	.4772	.4778	.4783	.4788	.4793	.4798	.4803	.4808	.4812	.4817
2.1	.4821	.4826	.4830	.4834	.4838	.4842	.4846	.4850	.4854	.4857
2.2	.4861	.4864	.4868	.4871	.4875	.4878	.4881	.4884	.4887	.4890
2.3	.4893	.4896	.4898	.4901	.4904	.4906	.4909	.4911	.4913	.4916
2.4	.4918	.4920	.4922	.4925	.4927	.4929	.4931	.4932	.4934	.4936
2.5	.4938	.4940	.4941	.4943	.4945	.4946	.4948	.4949	.4951	.4952
2.6	.4953	.4955	.4956	.4957	.4959	.4960	.4961	.4962	.4963	.4964
2.7	.4965	.4966	.4967	.4968	.4969	.4970	.4971	.4972	.4973	.4974
2.8	.4974	.4975	.4976	.4977	.4977	.4978	.4979	.4979	.4980	.4981
2.9	.4981	.4982	.4982	.4983	.4984	.4984	.4985	.4985	.4986	.4986
3.0	.49865	.4987	.4987	.4988	.4988	.4989	.4989	.4989	.4990	.4990
3.1	.49903	.4991	.4991	.4991	.4992	.4992	.4992	.4992	.4993	.4993
3.2	.4993129									
3.3	.4995166									
3.4	.4996631									
3.5	.4997674									
3.6	.4998409									
3.7	.4998922									
3.8	.4999277									
3.9	.4999519									
4.0	.4999683									
4.5	.4999966									
5.0	.4999997133									

From *Rugg's Statistical Methods Applied to Education* (with corrections), reprinted by arrangement with the publishers, Houghton Mifflin Company. A more detailed table of normal curve areas, but in two directions from the arithmetic mean, is given in Federal Works Agency, Work Projects Administration for the City of New York, *Tables of Probability Functions*, National Bureau of Standards, New York, 1942, Vol. II, pp. 2-388.

TABLE 2

AREAS IN ONE TAIL OF THE NORMAL CURVE AT SELECTED VALUES OF $\frac{x}{s}$ OR $\frac{x}{\sigma}$ FROM THE ARITHMETIC MEAN

This table shows:

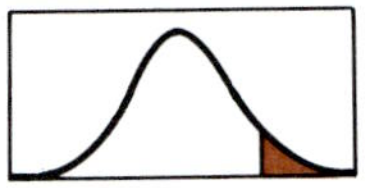

or

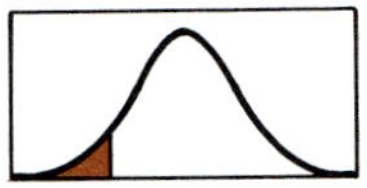

$\frac{x}{S}$ or $\frac{x}{\sigma}$	.00	.01	.02	.03	.04	.05	.06	.07	.08	.09
0.0	.5000	.4960	.4920	.4880	.4840	.4801	.4761	.4721	.4681	.4641
0.1	.4602	.4562	.4522	.4483	.4443	.4404	.4364	.4325	.4286	.4247
0.2	.4207	.4168	.4129	.4090	.4052	.4013	.3974	.3936	.3897	.3859
0.3	.3821	.3783	.3745	.3707	.3669	.3632	.3594	.3557	.3520	.3483
0.4	.3446	.3409	.3372	.3336	.3300	.3264	.3228	.3192	.3156	.3121
0.5	.3085	.3050	.3015	.2981	.2946	.2912	.2877	.2843	.2810	.2776
0.6	.2743	.2709	.2676	.2643	.2611	.2578	.2546	.2514	.2483	.2451
0.7	.2420	.2389	.2358	.2327	.2296	.2266	.2236	.2206	.2177	.2148
0.8	.2119	.2090	.2061	.2033	.2005	.1977	.1949	.1922	.1894	.1867
0.9	.1841	.1814	.1788	.1762	.1736	.1711	.1685	.1660	.1635	.1611
1.0	.1587	.1562	.1539	.1515	.1492	.1469	.1446	.1423	.1401	.1379
1.1	.1357	.1335	.1314	.1292	.1271	.1251	.1230	.1210	.1190	.1170
1.2	.1151	.1131	.1112	.1093	.1075	.1056	.1038	.1020	.1003	.0985
1.3	.0968	.0951	.0934	.0918	.0901	.0885	.0869	.0853	.0838	.0823
1.4	.0808	.0793	.0778	.0764	.0749	.0735	.0721	.0708	.0694	.0681
1.5	.0668	.0655	.0643	.0630	.0618	.0606	.0594	.0582	.0571	.0559
1.6	.0548	.0537	.0526	.0516	.0505	.0495	.0485	.0475	.0465	.0455
1.7	.0446	.0436	.0427	.0418	.0409	.0401	.0392	.0384	.0375	.0367
1.8	.0359	.0351	.0344	.0336	.0329	.0322	.0314	.0307	.0301	.0294
1.9	.0287	.0281	.0274	.0268	.0262	.0256	.0250	.0244	.0239	.0233
2.0	.0228	.0222	.0217	.0212	.0207	.0202	.0197	.0192	.188	.0183
2.1	.0179	.0174	.0170	.0166	.0162	.0158	.0154	.0150	.0146	.0143
2.2	.0139	.0136	.0132	.0129	.0125	.0122	.0119	.0116	.0113	.0110
2.3	.0107	.0104	.0102	.00990	.00964	.00939	.00914	.00889	.00866	.00842
2.4	.00820	.00798	.00776	.00755	.00734	.00714	.00695	.00676	.00657	.00639
2.5	.00621	.00604	.00587	.00570	.00554	.00539	.00523	.00508	.00494	.00480
2.6	.00466	.00453	.00440	.00427	.00415	.00402	.00391	.00379	.00368	.00357
2.7	.00347	.00336	.00326	.00317	.00307	.00298	.00289	.00280	.00272	.00264
2.8	.00256	.00248	.00240	.00233	.00226	.00219	.00212	.00205	.00199	.00193
2.9	.00187	.00181	.00175	.00169	.00164	.00159	.00154	.00149	.00144	.00139

$\frac{x}{S}$ or $\frac{x}{\sigma}$	.0	.1	.2	.3	.4	.5	.6	7.	.8	.9
3	.00135	$.0^{3}968$	$.0^{3}687$	$.0^{9}483$	$.0^{3}337$	$.0^{3}233$	$.0^{3}159$	$.0^{3}108$	$.0^{4}723$	$.0^{4}481$
4	$.0^{4}317$	$.0^{4}207$	$.0^{4}133$	$.0^{6}854$	$.0^{6}541$	$.0^{6}340$	$.0^{6}211$	$.0^{5}130$	$.0^{6}793$	$.0^{6}479$
5	$.0^{6}287$	$.0^{6}170$	$.0^{7}996$	$.0^{7}579$	$.0^{7}333$	$.0^{7}190$	$.0^{7}107$	$.0^{9}599$	$.0^{8}332$	$.0^{8}182$
6	$.0^{9}987$	$.0^{9}530$	$.0^{9}282$	$.0^{9}149$	$.0^{10}777$	$.0^{10}402$	$.0^{10}206$	$.0^{10}104$	$.0^{11}523$	$.0^{11}260$

From *Tables of Areas in Two Tails and in One Tail of the Normal Curve*, by Frederick E. Croxton.

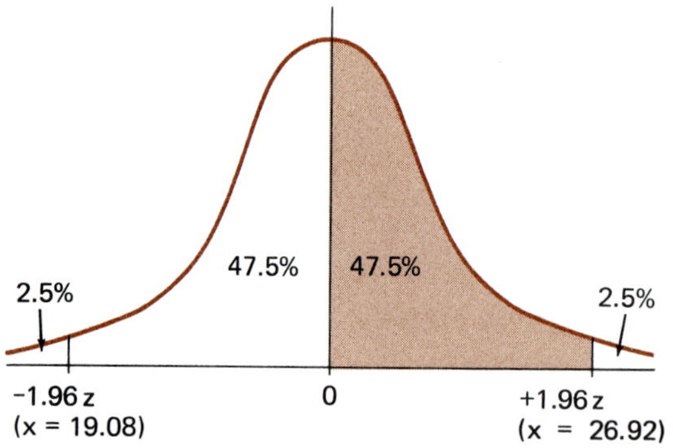

Figure A.9 Confidence limits which include ninety-five percent of the area.

the total area is included. All we have to do is transform these values into the terms of our sample mean and standard error. Because

$$z = \frac{X - \overline{X}}{s_{\overline{x}}},$$

it is also true that

$$z = \frac{\overline{X} - \mu}{s_{\overline{x}}}.$$

Therefore, to find the lower limit of the confidence interval, we substitute z = −1.96 in the second equation:

$$-1.96 = \frac{\overline{X}_L - 23}{2}$$
$$23 - 2(-1.96) = \overline{X}_L$$
$$23 - 3.92 = \overline{X}_L = 19.08.$$

To find the upper limit, let z = +1.96: in other words,

$$+1.96 = \frac{\overline{X}_U - 23}{2}$$
$$23 + 3.92 = \overline{X}_U = 26.92.$$

From these calculations we may be "95 percent confident" that the real, or population mean lies between 19.08 and 26.92. Drawing larger samples would decrease this range because the size of the standard error of the mean would be decreased. Confidence limits for 95 percent or 99 percent of the area are commonly used.

Tests of Statistical Significance

To help assess the outcome of many experiments, the above principles are used in a somewhat different form. For instance, we can draw two samples from a population—a control group and an experimental group. These designations should be assigned randomly. The experimental group will be subjected to some manipulation, such as a special training regimen or drug treatment while the control group will not. The groups will be treated similarly in *every other way*. We can compute the $\overline{X}_C$ and $s_{\overline{x}_C}$ for the control group and calculate the 95 percent (or 99 or 99.9 percent) confidence limits for this mean. Then we can compute the $\overline{X}_E$ for the experimental group and see whether it falls within or outside these confidence limits. If it falls *outside* we are justified in claiming that the experimental manipulation had some effect. Such a result is called a statistically significant outcome. What, if any, theoretical or practical significance there may be remains to be seen, but a finding of statistical significance is a necessary first step. Lacking this outcome, we simply explain any fluctuation of the experimental group mean *within* the confidence limits as unknown or random fluctuation that lacks significance.

Null Hypothesis

In testing a formal hypothesis such as the one just described, we assume, for the purpose of the test, that the means for the experimental group ($\overline{X}_E$) and the control group ($\overline{X}_C$) are equal. This is known as the *null hypothesis* and is illustrated as follows:

$$H_O : \overline{X}_E = \overline{X}_C.$$

The alternative hypothesis can be shown as

$$H_A : \overline{X}_E \neq \overline{X}_C.$$

The H is tested by choosing confidence limits for $\overline{X}_C$ and ascertaining whether $\overline{X}_E$ falls inside or outside these limits. If it falls inside, we "accept" the null hypothesis of no difference and make no further interpretation. If it falls outside, we "reject" H_0 and "accept" H_A. This is called a statistically significant result, and the difference in means is assumed to be related to something (usually the experimental treatment) other than random fluctuation.

It is conventional to describe the confidence limits in a slightly different way when testing a hypothesis. Rather than speak of 95 percent confidence limits, we speak of a 5 percent *level of significance* for the test. This is referred to as alpha-level = .05 ($\alpha = .05$) (or 1.0 minus the level of confidence). The α-level (usually .05 or .01) should be chosen before the experiment is conducted. The choice of $\alpha = .05$ implies that $\overline{X}_E$ will exceed the predetermined confidence limits 5 percent of the time for no reason other than random fluctuation. When this happens, we will make an error in rejecting H_0. This is called a Type I error, and it means that we claim or believe that there is a statistically meaningful difference between the means when in fact no such difference exists. We can lower the chance of making a Type I error by choosing a very small alpha-level (say $\alpha = .001$). However, this increases our chances of erroneously accepting H_0 when in fact H_A is true. This is known as a Type II error. Because of this reciprocal relationship between the two types of error, it is customary to take a 1 percent or 5 percent chance of Type I error ($\alpha = .01$ or .05) and attempt to lower the chances of Type II error by increasing the size of the sample to whatever extent is economically or practically feasible.

t-Tests

Statisticians have known for some time that the use of the normal curve as a reference for calculations on significance levels is not really warranted unless the population variance (σ) is known or the sample size is over 30. W. S. Gosset showed that for smaller samples and for tests using the sample standard deviation or standard error, a closely related curve (more accurately, a family of curves) should be used. Although these curves are similar to the normal curve, they have more area in the tail portions. The t-distribution, as these are called, is widely available in statistics textbooks and is perhaps the most frequently used reference for examining the possible statistical significance of a difference. For example, the summary notation, "$t = 2.41$, $df = 18$, $p \leq .05$" would inform us that the t-value we calculated is high enough to reject H_0 at the 5 percent level of significance. If we saw "$t = 1.61$, $df = 24$, $p > .05$," we would know that H_0 must be accepted rather than rejected because the mean difference fell within the 95 percent confidence limits.

In t-tests the standard error usually is computed (for more accuracy) from both samples, and it is called the standard error of the difference:

$$t = \frac{\overline{X}_1 - \overline{X}_2}{s_{\bar{x}_1 - \bar{x}_2}}.$$

A t-test can be used for randomly drawn samples or for matched or correlated samples. Using the same subjects twice—testing them once before the experimental treatment and once afterward—is an example of a matched or correlated sample.

Analysis of Variance

An important extension of the t-test, developed by Sir Ronald Fisher, is called the analysis of variance. It permits the simultaneous testing of two, three, four, or more means. The reference distribution for this test has been named the F-distribution, in honor of

Fisher, and it is widely available. For this test, the null hypothesis takes the form

$$H_O : \overline{X}_1 = \overline{X}_2 = \overline{X}_3 = \ldots = \overline{X}_n,$$

while the alternative hypothesis is that one or more of the means is *not* equal to the others. If H_O is rejected, then H_A is accepted, and additional tests must be conducted to determine which mean (or means) is different. Most simply conceived, the F-ratio test consists of a numerator, which represents the variance of the sample means around the common or grand mean, and a denominator, which is a variance estimate derived from a pooled estimate of variance within each sample. The denominator is essentially equivalent to the square of the standard error and is called, appropriately, the *error term*. The numerator contains chance or random variation as well, but, even more important, it reflects any differences among the means attributable to experimental manipulations. If these manipulations have caused the sample means to be quite different, the result will be a large variance estimate in the numerator of the F-ratio, and the results probably will be interpreted as statistically significant in reference to the F-distribution.

To use the F-distribution, two different ν's (degrees of freedom) must be known: one value for the numerator (ν_1, usually one less than the number of means being compared) and one for the denominator (ν_2, which is essentially a residual and must be calculated). For example, a simple F-value might be reported as "$F(2,40) = 5.94$; $p < .01$." This would mean that H_O must be rejected and that a search for which mean (or means) is different is in order.

One of the important advantages of using the analysis of variance (ANOVA) arises from the possibility of comparing the same scores in two or more ways in the same experiment. For example, we could test speed of learning by using 10 subjects assigned to each cell in a matrix such as the following:

	Shock Level		
Drug Level	5	10	15
.01			
.02			
.03			

ANOVA would allow us to determine whether the intensity of the shock changed learning speed, whether drug level changed learning speed, and whether there was a joint effect of drug and shock. We can also use larger designs (and more dimensions). Because of the number of hypotheses being tested, the F-values and p-values usually are presented in a summary table.

Chi-Square Test

Another statistic that is commonly used to test the statistical significance of differences in counts or frequencies is known as the chi-square (χ^2) test. Usually H_O takes the form that group frequencies are equal or that they are distributed according to some known or predetermined proportions, and H_A states that they are unequal or not distributed according to the predetermined proportions. After calculation of the value for χ^2, and the degrees of freedom available, we refer to a table of the chi-square distribution to discover whether the result is statistically significant.

Regression and Correlation

If two or more scores are collected from each subject in a sample, it becomes possible to determine whether there is a relationship between the arrays of scores. For example, if we measure both height and weight in a sample of people, we would expect a *positive* association between these variables, although not a perfect one. In other words, although exceptions will occur, shorter people on the average weigh less than taller people. These data can be used for a bivariate plot, as shown in figure A.10.

With practice, visual examination of such bivariate plots can yield a good estimate of the magnitude of the relationship, even before numerical methods are applied. Examine the examples shown in figure A.11, for instance.

When a graphical estimate is not precise enough, we can compute a numerical value for one or more statistics that are measures of association. These include the *covariance,* any of a number of *correlation coefficients* and the *regression coefficient*.

Covariance

To compute the *covariance,* we must cross-multiply the deviation score on one variable $(X - \overline{X})$ with the deviation score on the other variable $(Y - \overline{Y})$ for each subject, add all these products, and then divide the sum by $N - 1$. The defining form of the formula is

$$\text{covariance} = s_{xy} = \frac{\Sigma(X - \overline{X})(Y - \overline{Y})}{N - 1}.$$

To avoid having to work with fractional quantities, the following algebraically equivalent formula is usually used.

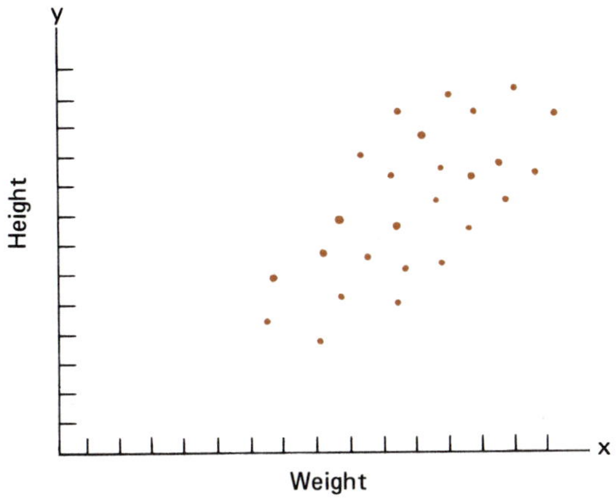

Figure A.10 An example bivariate plot.

$$\text{cov} = s_{xy} = \frac{\Sigma XY - \dfrac{(\Sigma X)(\Sigma Y)}{N}}{N - 1}.$$

Note how closely this formula resembles the formula for variance.

As we would expect, *analysis of covariance* can be conducted on arrays of potentially related variables. Although the covariance is a measure of association, it is difficult to interpret any particular value because the metric used for each variable has an important effect on the magnitude of the statistic. The value for the covariance between height and weight would be very different if height were mea-

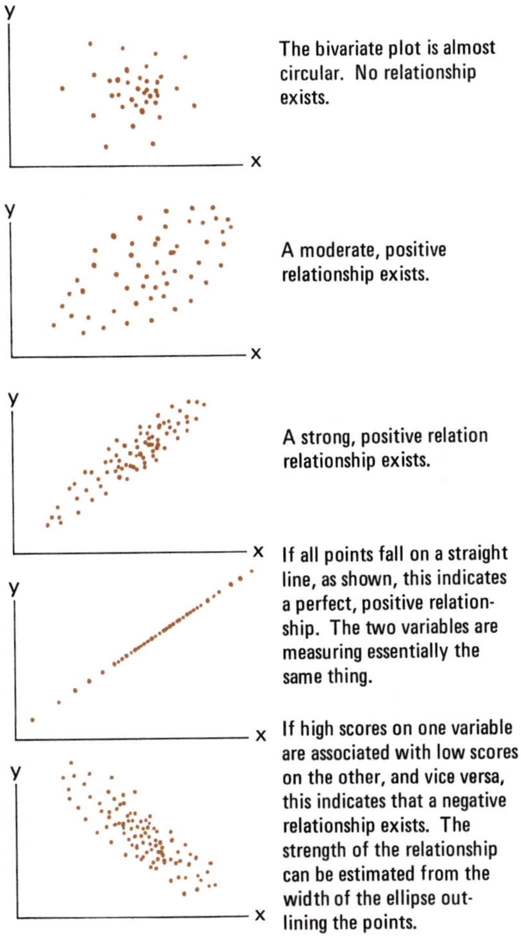

Y
X
The bivariate plot is almost circular. No relationship exists.
A moderate, positive relationship exists.
A strong, positive relation relationship exists.
If all points fall on a straight line, as shown, this indicates a perfect, positive relationship. The two variables are measuring essentially the same thing.
If high scores on one variable are associated with low scores on the other, and vice versa, this indicates that a negative relationship exists. The strength of the relationship can be estimated from the width of the ellipse outlining the points.

Figure A.11 Bivariate plots showing different amounts of positive or negative association.

sured in miles rather than inches. To avoid this problem, *standard scores* can be used because such scores include a correction for metric: that is, each deviation score ($X - \overline{X}$, $Y - \overline{Y}$) has been divided by the relevant standard deviation,

$$z_x = \frac{X - \overline{X}}{s_x} \quad \text{and} \quad z_y = \frac{Y - \overline{Y}}{s_y}$$

and thus a dimensionless quantity has been obtained.

$$z_x = \frac{X - \overline{X}}{s_x} = \frac{\text{height in inches minus mean height in inches}}{\text{standard deviation in inches}}.$$

As you can see, the "inches" metric appears in both numerator and denominator; therefore, they cancel out. Of course, the same would occur with any other metric, so z-scores and statistics derived from them are metric-free.

Correlation Coefficient

The quantity obtained by cross-multiplying the standardized scores, adding their products, and dividing the sum by N − 1 yields a statistic known as the correlation coefficient (r_{xy}), or the *Pearsonian product-moment correlation coefficient* (named after Karl Pearson, who developed it). The z-score formula for r_{xy} is seldom used for actual computations. Instead, one of several algebraically equivalent forms is used:

$$r_{xy} = \frac{\Sigma z_x z_y}{N - 1} = \frac{\dfrac{\Sigma(X - \overline{X})(Y - \overline{Y})}{(s_x)\ (s_y)}}{N - 1} = \frac{\dfrac{\Sigma(X - \overline{X})(Y - \overline{Y})}{N - 1}}{\sqrt{(s_x^2)(s_y^2)}}$$

$$= \frac{s_{xy}}{\sqrt{(s_x^2)(s_y^2)}} = \frac{\Sigma(X - \overline{X})(Y - \overline{Y})}{\sqrt{[\Sigma(X - \overline{X})^2][\Sigma(Y - \overline{Y})^2]}} = \frac{\Sigma XY - \dfrac{(\Sigma X)(\Sigma Y)}{N}}{\sqrt{\left[\Sigma X^2 - \dfrac{(\Sigma X)^2}{N}\right]\left[\Sigma Y^2 - \dfrac{(\Sigma Y)^2}{N}\right]}}$$

Although the final form may appear to be the most difficult one, it is actually much easier to use than the others. Note the use of this formula in the following example:

	X—Scores		*Y—Scores*		
S	*(high school grades)*	*X*²	*(college grades)*	*Y*²	*XY*
1	2.9	8.41	3.2	10.24	9.28
2	2.5	6.25	2.0	4.00	5.00
3	3.5	12.25	3.2	10.24	11.20
4	2.8	7.84	3.0	9.00	8.40
5	2.7	7.29	2.5	6.25	6.75
6	3.0	9.00	2.5	6.25	7.50
Σ	17.4	51.04	16.4	45.98	48.13

$(\Sigma X)^2 = 302.76 \qquad (\Sigma Y)^2 = 268.96$

$$r_{xy} = \frac{\Sigma XY - \dfrac{(\Sigma X)\ (\Sigma Y)}{N}}{\sqrt{\left[\Sigma X^2 - \dfrac{(\Sigma X)^2}{N}\right]\left[\Sigma Y^2 - \dfrac{(\Sigma Y)^2}{N}\right]}} = \frac{48.13 - \dfrac{(17.4)\ (16.4)}{6}}{\sqrt{\left[51.04 - \dfrac{302.76}{6}\right]\left[45.98 - \dfrac{268.96}{6}\right]}} = \frac{.57}{\sqrt{.667}} = .70.$$

The correlation obtained, $r_{xy} = .70$, is a *description* of the association between grades in high school and grades in college. Of course, in an actual study, a much larger N would be used. The statistic, r_{xy}, is an estimate of the population parameter sometimes shown as $\mathbf{R}_{xy}$ or ρ_{xy} (rho). Procedures exist for testing whether the obtained r_{xy} is significantly different from zero; that is, whether there is any association between the variables. One of these procedures involves the t-distribution introduced earlier. It is also possible to test the obtained r_{xy} against any known or hypothesized value of ρ_{xy} by using Fisher's z-transformation.

A bivariate plot of the "data" on grades is shown in figure A.12. Even from these few points, we can see that there has been some *restriction of range:* there are no data points plotted at values below 2.0. It is easy to see why this might occur in this case: students with lower high school grades are less likely to go to college and we need *both* grades for each person to plot one point. In other examples, however, a restriction of range may be less easy to spot. Therefore, all data should be carefully examined for such a possibility since a restriction will tend to *lower* the value obtained for r_{xy}.

Regression Coefficient

If, as is often the case, we want to *predict* the value of one variable before it is measured

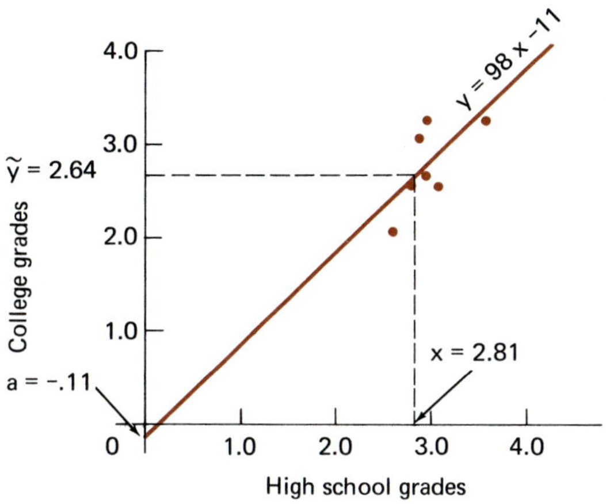

Figure A.12 A bivariate plot between high school and college grades. A geometric solution for predicting a y-score, $\tilde{y}$.

(say college grades) from the known value of a related variable (say high school grades), we can compute a regression coefficient, $b_{y \cdot x}$. This is read as "the regression of Y on X" and is used to estimate an unknown value, $\tilde{Y}$, from a known value, X_K. The formula is similar to that for the correlation coefficient.

$$b_{y \cdot x} = \frac{\Sigma XY - \frac{(\Sigma X)(\Sigma Y)}{N}}{\Sigma X^2 - \frac{(\Sigma X)^2}{N}}.$$

Using the sample data concerning high school and college grades, we compute the value of $b_{y \cdot x}$ as follows:

$$b_{y \cdot x} = \frac{.57}{(51.04 - \frac{302.76}{6})}$$
$$= \frac{.57}{.58}$$
$$= .98.$$

Although the value for the regression coefficient did not exceed 1.0 in this case, it can do so. The value of a correlation coefficient *cannot;* it can range only from −1.0 (perfect negative relationship) through 0.0 (no relationship) to +1.0 (perfect positive relationship).

To predict an unknown Y-score, $\tilde{Y}$ (e.g., average college grades for a high school student who has grade point average of X = 2.81), we would use the following formulas (using the computed $b_{y \cdot x} = .98$):

$$a = \overline{Y} - b\overline{X}$$
$$= \frac{16.4}{6} - (.98)\left(\frac{17.4}{6}\right)$$
$$= 2.73 - (.98)(2.9)$$
$$= 2.73 - 2.84$$
$$= -.11.$$

$$\tilde{Y} = a + bX$$
$$= -.11 + (.98)(2.81)$$
$$= -.11 + 2.75$$
$$= 2.64.$$

The predicted college grade average is 2.64. This value also can be obtained graphically. On a bivariate plot, $b_{y \cdot x}$ is the *slope* of a straight line placed through the points in such a way that the sum of the *squared deviations* of the points from the line is minimized (least-squares criterion). The Y intercept of the line is *a*. When the slope, *b*, and the intercept, *a*, are known, the regression line is completely determined. A bivariate plot showing the regression line, $b_{y \cdot x}$, was shown in figure A.12.

In situations such as the example above, X is called the predictor variable and Y is called the *criterion* variable. Predicted Y-scores ($\tilde{Y}$s) are only estimates and, lacking a perfect relationship ($r = +1.0$ or $r = -1.0$), an error may be contained in any estimate. Such errors could be seen, for instance, by predicting college grades for an entire high school class and then waiting to see what average grades they actually achieved. The difference between any pair $(Y - \tilde{Y})$ would be an *error of estimate*. These errors could be placed in a frequency distribution, and the standard deviation could be calculated. This quantity, known as the *standard error of the estimate* ($s_{y \cdot x}$), can be obtained more easily by using the formula

$$s_{y \cdot x} = \sqrt{\left(\frac{n-1}{n-2}\right) s_y^2 (1 - r^2)}.$$

Using our data, we would first compute

$$s_y^2 = \frac{\Sigma Y^2 - \frac{(\Sigma X)^2}{N}}{n-1}$$

$$= \frac{45.98 - \frac{268.96}{6}}{5}$$

$$= \frac{1.15}{5}$$

$$= .23,$$

and then

$$s_{y \cdot x} = \sqrt{\left[\frac{5}{4}\right][.23][1 - (.70)^2]}$$

$$= \sqrt{\left(\frac{5}{4}\right)(.23)(.51)}$$

$$= .38.$$

Because $s_y = \sqrt{s_y^2} = \sqrt{.23} = .48$, the value for $s_{y \cdot x}$ shows that we have decreased the variation somewhat by considering the relationship between the X and Y variables.

From the value of $s_{y \cdot x} = .38$, we would be able to derive confidence limits for any prediction in the usual way. Note that the value for $s_{y \cdot x}$ is essentially the value of s_y^2 *corrected* for the magnitude of the relationship r_{xy}. As r_{xy} approaches 1, $s_{y \cdot x}$ approaches zero, which informs us that there is no error in estimates when there is a perfect relationship. Usually, a perfect relationship does not exist, so there is some error of estimate. If we conceive of these errors as random and uncorrelated, we can obtain several more formulas that are useful in psychological testing.

Reliability and Validity

Any test we use should be an accurate measuring tool, as a first step. This accuracy, or lack of it, is called the reliability of a test. Reliability can be estimated in a variety of ways. For example, we can split a test into two halves (say odd- and even-numbered items) and calculate a correlation coefficient between the two parts. The result is known as a *split-half reliability coefficient,* and from it we can estimate the accuracy, or reliability of the test as a whole. On the other hand, we can painstakingly construct two comparable or parallel forms of the same test and give both forms to a large group of subjects. Although we should obtain similar means and variances from the two forms, the arrays of scores will not be identical because errors of measurement have been involved. If we compute the error variance, s_e^2, and the total (or observed) variance, s_x^2, then the *reliability coefficient* ($r_{x_1x_2}$) between the two forms will be given by

$$r_{x_1x_2} = 1 - \frac{s_e^2}{s_x^2}.$$

If $s_e^2 = s_x^2$, then reliability equals zero. As s_e^2 becomes smaller, the reliability coefficient approaches its upper limit of 1.0.

After the reliability or accuracy of a test has been established (usually $r_{x_1x_2} = .9$ or more is acceptable, although a coefficient this high has not been achieved as yet for some tests—for example, some tests of neurosis or psychosis), then we are free to determine the validity of the test by correlating test scores with a *criterion* of some kind. The *validity coefficient* we obtain will indicate how accurately the test can predict later performance. Choosing a suitable variable as a criterion may be quite difficult. Prediction of grades may be straightforward and relatively simple, but quantifying such things as happiness or presence or absence of a neurosis or psychosis may present the researcher with a formidable task. For this reason, a new test is often validated against an accepted test. A new intelligence test, for example, may be validated against the Stanford Binet or the Wechsler Adult Intelligence Scale (WAIS), because a vast literature about these tests exists and they are very well known. The validity coefficient serves as a tie between the new test and the older, well-known tests.

Many other measures of association are used, including the rank-order coefficient (R or ρ) and the contingency coefficient (C). The rank-order coefficient is essentially a Pearsonian product-moment correlation coefficient, computed on *ranks* of scores rather than on the actual scores. For example, the scores 1, 3, 17, and 100 could rank 1, 2, 3, and 4. If our measuring technique is good enough to rank subjects (this is called *ordinal* measurement), but is not good enough to measure accurately the interval between scores (called *interval*, or *ratio* measurement), then we use a rank-order coefficient of correlation. Because of its similarity to r_{xy}, the ρ (rho) statistic has essentially the same uses and limits as those outlined for r_{xy}. The contingency coefficient, on the other hand, is useful for indicating the degree of association between categorical variables (e.g., male or female versus left- or right-handed). It ranges in value from zero to less than +1.0. This can be seen from its formula, as only the + (or positive) root is used.

$$C = \sqrt{\frac{\chi^2}{N + \chi^2}}$$

Nonparametric Statistics

In conclusion, we should mention that the techniques used to estimate parameters in classical statistics are not the only ones available. A whole family of nonparametric (or distribution-free) statistics can also be used. We can turn to one of these if the assumptions underlying the derivation of a parametric test cannot be met, because using the parametric test under these circumstances may yield meaningless results. However, if the parametric assumptions *can* be met, then use of a nonparametric statistic usually will result in loss of power; that is, although a real difference between means may exist, it may not be found. However, because of the ease and speed with which many nonparametric tests can be applied to small samples, it is sometimes convenient to use them anyway, keeping in mind the possibility that some power may be lost. If you are interested in the subject of nonparametric statistics, we refer you to Siegel (1956) or Bradley (1968).

Appendix 2: The Authors

Kurt Schlesinger

Is professor of psychology and a fellow of The Institute for Behavioral Genetics at the University of Colorado, Boulder, Colorado. He received his B.A. and M.A. degrees at San Francisco State College and his Ph.D. degree in psychology at the University of California, Berkeley. He has held teaching appointments at the University of North Carolina, Chapel Hill, and research positions at The Jackson Laboratory, Bar Harbor, Maine, and at Yale University. At the undergraduate level he has taught courses in general introductory psychology, biological psychology, and behavioral genetics. Graduate teaching has been in the area of biological psychology and behavioral genetics. Dr. Schlesinger's research interests include genetic and neurochemical correlates of alcohol preference, audiogenic seizures, and learning and memory storage processes. Authored chapters 1, 2, 5, 15 and 16.

Philip M. Groves

Is professor of psychology in the biopsychology area of the Department of Psychology, University of Colorado, Boulder. He received B.A. degree in psychology from U.C.L.A., M.A. in psychology from San Diego State College, and Ph.D. in psychobiology from the University of California at Irvine. He has taught physiological psychology at the undergraduate and graduate levels, as well as a variety of other specialized courses in the neurosciences. Dr. Groves' research interests concern the biological correlates of behavior, especially changes in the activity of single neurons in the brain during simple forms of learning such as habituation and sensitization. More recently, he has worked on the modes of action of amphetamine, the antipsychotics, and other psychotropic drugs on neuronal activity in the central nervous system, and the relation of such effects to the known biochemical and behavioral correlates of acute and long-term drug administration. Authored chapters 3, 13, and 14. Coauthored chapters 6 and 7 with Stephen Young.

Desmond S. Cartwright

Is professor of psychology at the University of Colorado, where he teaches courses in personality adjustment, personality assessment, and multivariate analysis. He obtained his B.A. at the University of London in 1951 and his Ph.D. at the University of Chicago in 1954. He has done research on psychotherapy, delinquency, and gangs, all in relation to personality. His publications include *Psychological Adjustment* (with Carol I. Cartwright), Rand McNally, 1971; *Introduction to Personality* (co-edited with B. Tomson and H. Schwarz), Brooks-Cole, 1975. He has published more than fifty articles in scientific journals and served as editor of the journal *Multivariate Behavioral Research*. From 1966 to 1971 he was a fellow of the American Psychological Association, Division 5, evaluation and measurement, and a member of the Psychometric Society. He is a past president of the Society of Multivariate Experimental Psychologists. Authored chapter 17.

John R. Forward

Is presently an associate professor of psychology at the University of Colorado where he teaches courses in introductory psychology, social psychology, social problems, and small group and organizational behavior. Born in Latrobe, Tasmania in 1939, he completed B.A. studies at Melbourne University (Australia) and obtained a Ph.D. in Social Psychology at the University of Michigan in 1967. Research has included published studies of achievement in group settings, control factors in educational settings, riot behavior, the use of volunteers in juvenile court settings, and methodological studies in social psychology. His study of the 1968 Detroit riot won the Gordon Allport Award for Best Research in Intergroup Relations in 1970. Authored chapters 21, 22, and 23.

William F. Hodges

Is associate professor of psychology at the University of Colorado. Received both his undergraduate and graduate training at Vanderbilt University in clinical psychology, receiving his Ph.D. in 1967. He did his internship in clinical psychology at the Duke University Medical Center. For the past ten years, he has been intensely involved in community mental health and has served as a mental health consultant for high schools, junior high schools, elementary schools, and is now involved in primary prevention programs involved in primary prevention programs at the pre-school level. He is involved in a training program in community mental health at the University of Colorado and supervises graduate students in field placement settings in the community. His research interests have been in the area of anxiety research, coping processes, and biofeedback. Authored chapter 20.

Steven F. Maier

Is associate professor of psychology in the Department of Psychology, University of Colorado at Boulder. He received a B.A. in biology from New York University and M.A. and Ph.D. degrees in psychology from the University of Pennsylvania. He has taught introductory psychology and courses in learning and motivation at both the undergraduate and graduate level. Dr. Maier's research interests are in the area of learning and motivation and center on the effects of exposure to events which the organism cannot control. Authored chapters 11 and 12.

Richard K. Olson

Is assistant professor of psychology at the University of Colorado. He received his B.A. from Macalester College in 1963, and his Ph.D. from the University of Oregon in 1970, where his research was in the areas of human information processing and perception. He became interested in the development of perceptual skills and joined the developmental psychology area at the University of Colorado in 1970. He currently conducts research in perception and perceptual development and teaches courses in child development and perception. Other activities include research on the development of sensorimotor skills at favorite Colorado ski slopes. Authored chapters 8 and 9.

Victor Ryan

Is assistant professor of psychology at the University of Colorado. He received his bachelor's degree from Northwestern University in 1965, and his Ph.D. in Clinical Psychology from the University of Michigan in 1970. He currently teaches clinical psychology and psychotherapy, directs the University Psychology Clinic, and has a small therapy private practice. His research interests involve outcome and process studies of psychotherapy, particularly behavior modification and innovative treatment techniques. Authored chapter 19.

Barbara Sanders

Received her bachelor's degree from the University of Wisconsin and her Ph.D. from Yale University. She was a member of the faculty at the University of Colorado for five years, and taught courses in developmental psychology, cognitive development, and early experience. Her research at that time was concerned with learning and cognitive development. Her interest in the development of sex differences originated in a graduate seminar on the effects of early experience, a seminar which she taught for several years. She is currently a postdoctoral fellow at the Institute for Behavioral Genetics in Boulder, where she is conducting research on alcohol sensitivity and on hormones and behavior. Authored chapter 10.

Carol J. Schneider

Received her bachelor's degree in psychology from the University of Wisconsin in 1960, and the Master of Arts and Ph.D. degrees in psychology from the University of Colorado in Boulder in 1963 and 1965 respectively. She is currently assistant clinical professor, Department of Psychiatry, University of Colorado Medical School; staff psychologist, Student Health Service; and lecturer, Department of Psychology, University of Colorado at Boulder. She has taught undergraduate and graduate courses in clinical psychology. Dr. Schneider has done research studies on sex differences in social behavior in Rhesus monkeys, the etiology and classification of psychiatric problems among college students, and various aspects of the battered child syndrome. Authored Chapter 18.

James R. Wilson

Is associate director of the Institute for Behavioral Genetics at the University of Colorado, Boulder, and is associate professor of psychology and of environmental, population and organismic biology at the same institution. Before completing an undergraduate degree in mathematics at the University of Arizona, he joined the army and spent five years as a construction engineer and helicopter pilot; he assisted in the survey of the Distant Early Warning line on the arctic coast of Alaska. He completed an A.B. in psychology at the University of California,

Berkeley, in 1959 and received a Ph.D. from the same institution in 1968, under the direction of Professor Frank A. Beach. His current research emphasizes the genetic and endocrinological bases of behavior. Authored chapter 4 and Appendix 1.

Stephen J. Young

Obtained the B.A. degree at Los Angeles State College and Ph.D. from the University of California at Los Angeles in the field of perception. Currently faculty research associate in the Department of Psychology at the University of Colorado, Dr. Young has taught courses in perception, experimental psychology, and statistics. His research interests include visual perception and information processing, neuronal correlates of behavior, and quantitative models of perceptual processes. Coauthored chapters 6 and 7 with Philip Groves.

Glossary

ablation technique the process of disconnecting one structure from others in the nervous system without destroying it.

absolute refractory period the period of time occurring immediately after the action potential during which a nerve cell cannot produce another action potential.

absolute threshold the minimal stimulus energy required for detection.

accessory sexual structures sexual structures other than the genitals and germ-producing cells (gonads). In the male, the accessory sexual structures include the epididymis and vas deferens; in the female, the uterus and Fallopian tubes or oviducts.

accommodation occurs when the child changes his mental structures to incorporate some new experiences into his mental space.

acetylcholine a molecule released by the presynaptic membrane which has an effect on the postsynaptic neuron. Hence, acetylcholine is a neurotransmitter.

acetylcholinesterase the enzyme which degrades the neurotransmitter, acetylcholine.

achromatic a "colorless" or white light.

acquired motives previously neutral stimuli which acquire motivational properties by association.

action potential the electrical discharge of a single nerve cell; the all-or-nothing electrical activity propagated down the axon of a nerve cell.

activation the state of arousal or excitement of an organism.

adaptive value refers to a trait which contributes to the fitness of an organism where fitness is the number of offspring an individual contributes to the next generation.

addiction refers to a compulsive use and search for a particular drug.

adenine one of the bases in both DNA and RNA.

adenohypophysis the anterior division of the pituitary gland; includes the *pars distalis* and the *pars intermedia;* releases seven different hormones; derives embryologically from mouth tissue.

adipsia lack of drinking.

adrenal cortex *see* adrenal glands.

adrenal glands compound endocrine glands located on the kidney; medullary portion is under direct neural control, and is source of adrenalin; cortical portion is controlled partly by ACTH, and partly by other mechanisms, and is the source of several steroid hormones.

adrenergic refers to synapses at which norepinephrine is the neurotransmitter.

adrenergic blocking agents drugs which inhibit the normal activity of the sympathetic nervous system. An example of such a drug is dichloroisoproterenol.

adrenocorticotrophic hormone from the *pars distalis* of the pituitary; major effect is on cortex of the adrenal glands where it effects release of about ten different adrenocortical hormones; does not control the adrenal medulla or mineralcorticoid production from the adrenal cortex.

adrenocorticotrophic hormone (ACTH) hormone from the *pars distalis* of the pituitary: stimulates formation and release of several different steroid hormones of the adrenal cortex (e.g., cortisone).

affect technical term for emotional feelings. In depression, "affect is sadness;" in schizophrenia "affect is flattened."

affective disorders psychopathology in which the primary disturbance is to the individual's emotions, feelings, or moods.

afferent nerves nerves which carry information toward the central nervous system.

affiliative behavior the desire to be with other people; to join a group; to associate with others.

affinity the propensity with which a drug attaches itself to a receptor on the cellular membrane.

aggressive children children who respond to nonnurturing environments by aggressive behavior.

agonist a compound which has an effect on a structure. For example, nicotine mimics the effects of acetylcholine at certain synapses. Hence, nicotine is an agonist (so is acetylcholine).

agonistic behavior activity which includes fighting or threat of fighting, but does not include predation.

alpha blocking desynchronization of the alpha waves in the electroencephalogram following some novel sensory stimulus. Characteristic of a sudden shift of attention.

alpha waves highly synchronized changes in voltage occurring in the human electroencephalogram with frequencies between 8 and 13 hertz (i.e., cycles per second).

amino-acid-transfer (RNA) a type of RNA which functions to activate amino acids to allow them to become incorporated into growing protein chains.

amnesia partial or total lack of recall for the past.

anal character a group of personality traits associated with fixation at the anal stage of psychosexual development. They include being obstinate, miserly, and orderly to an extreme degree.

analeptic drugs which at some doses cause seizures or convulsions.

anal stage the second stage in Freud's theory of psychosexual development, focused upon the processes of elimination. Typically this stage is dominant in the second year of life.

analysis-by-synthesis model a model of perception in which information received immediately before and after incoming information, as well as prior knowledge and expectations can influence our perception of incoming information.

analysis of variance a statistical technique with which several sources of variation (for example, sex, age, education) can be examined using one set of data.

androgenized female a genetic female whose sexual structures are masculinized by the presence of certain hormones during prenatal development. In humans this situation has resulted from the overproduction of androgens by the adrenal cortex, and has been caused accidentally by the administration of certain hormones to the mother during pregnancy.

androgens male hormones; major source is the testes, but also produced by the adrenal cortex, the placenta, and the ovary; largely responsible for male body conformation, and some male behaviors; may be important in aggressive behavior.

androstenedione a specific type of male hormone, or androgen.

anoxia refers to a drop in the normal supply of oxygen to the fetus. It is the most serious problem during abnormal childbirth.

antagonist a compound which inhibits the response of a structure. For example, curare inhibits the action of acetylcholine at the neuromuscular junction. Hence, curare is an antagonist.

antibiotics drugs which have been used to inhibit the manufacture of proteins in the nervous system.

anticholinesterases those drugs which inhibit the activity of acetylcholinesterase.

anticipatory guidance reducing the stress associated with normal transitional phases of life by helping people anticipate the problems associated with such changes and helping them cope more effectively.

anticonvulsants a class of drugs which prevents the occurrence of seizures or convulsions. Dilanten is an example of a drug commonly given to prevent epileptic seizures.

antidiuretic hormone hormone secreted by the posterior pituitary which acts on the renal collecting tubules to increase their permeability to water.

antimuscarinic agents drugs which inhibit the activity of postganglionic parasympathetic nerves.

appetitive stimuli pleasurable stimuli. Stimuli that the organism will approach.

applied research research directed toward the undertaking and solution of behavioral and social problems.

approach-approach conflicts conflict produced when an organism makes a choice between two attractive incentives.

approach-avoidance conflicts conflict produced when an organism must choose an incentive which has both positive properties (approach) and negative properties (avoidance).

aqueous humor a liquid in the chamber between the cornea and lens of the eye.

archetypes in Jung's theory, archetypes are inherited dispositions for particular kinds of experience. Examples include the shadow, which refers to tendencies that must be repressed in order to survive in society (tendencies such as bestiality); and the wise old man, which refers to tendencies to seek and revere wisdom.

arithmetic mean a specific type of mean; computed by adding together all the scores in a distribution and dividing this sum by the number of scores.

assimilation the incorporation and representation of external events into presently available mental structures, without significantly changing those structures.

association the connecting agent between mental events proposed by the British Empiricists.

association cortex the bulk of cerebral cortex which does not receive direct sensory information nor carry out direct control of the muscles; (i.e., cerebral cortex which is not strictly sensory nor motor).

association nuclei functional groups of cell bodies in the thalamus which send connections to association cortex.

attachment the social bond formed in infancy between infant and mother or caretaker.

attention a mechanism which admits some information or sensations and excludes others.

attitude a basic disposition toward behavior that includes both beliefs and positive or negative feelings about persons, objects, or events.

attitude-discrepant behavior public behavior that is contrary to previously held attitudes.

attitudes of mind: introversion and extroversion Jung's famous theory of introversion-extroversion held that people differ in whether they are mainly attentive to things outside themselves (extrovert) or to matters inside themselves (introvert).

auditory cortex the portion of cerebral cortex responsible for receiving information from the ears.

authoritarian attitudes a set of attitudes and personality characteristics found in highly prejudiced people. Includes a high degree of deference to authority.

autism psychopathology of childhood characterized by extreme withdrawal from the external world. Autistic children are often mute and self-destructive from earliest infancy.

autonomic division that portion of the peripheral nervous system responsible for glandular activity and emotional responses such as sweating, crying, etc.

autoshaping a phenomenon in which pigeons exposed to a light paired with food come to peck at the light.

autosomes the chromosomes of cells are divided into two classes: the so-called sex chromosomes which are responsible for sex determination, and all other chromosomes collectively referred to as autosomes. In the case of human cells the chromosome complement consists of 23 pairs of chromosomes; one pair, the X and Y chromosomes are referred to as sex chromosomes, the other 22 pairs are termed autosomes.

aversive conditioning form of behavior modification in which an individual is systematically punished for undesirable behaviors, thereby decreasing the likelihood of their occurrence. Often used in conjunction with operant conditioning.

aversive stimuli unpleasant stimuli, stimuli that the organism will avoid.

avoidance-avoidance conflicts conflict produced when an organism must choose between two incentives, both of which have negative attributes.

avoidance response a response that prevents the occurrence of an aversive event.

axon an extension from the nerve cell which conducts information away from the cell body.

axon collaterals branches off of the axon of a nerve cell which allow information to be conducted to more than one place.

axon hillock the point on a nerve cell where the axon joins the cell body.

axon terminals the endpoints of an axon which form small swellings and contain synaptic transmitter substance.

Babinsky reflex a fanning of the toes when the sole of the infant's foot is stimulated. This reflex usually disappears by the sixth month.

bacteriophages a type of virus which attacks bacteria. Often abbreviated as "phage."

balance theory a form of cognitive consistency theory where if the product of all signed relationships in an attitude system is positive, there is no tendency toward change. If the product is negative, there is a tendency to change attitudes to restore balance.

basal ganglia collective term referring to accumulations of nerve cell nuclei located deep within the cerebral cortex. Refers to structures such as the caudate nucleus, the putamen, globus pallidus and the amygdala.

basic research research directed toward establishing fundamental and general principles of behavior. Need not be directly related to social or behavioral problems.

basilar membrane the structure of the organ of corti upon which the hair cells are located.

behavioral pharmacology *see* psychopharmacology.

behaviorism an approach to psychology founded by John B. Watson, which stresses the objective measurement of behavior.

behavior modification also known as "behavior therapy." Forms of psychotherapy based on principles from learning theory.

binocular disparity the difference in the location of images on the retina of the two eyes resulting from their differing angles of view.

binocular vision vision using both eyes.

biofeedback a techniquc in which biological signals, such as heart rate, electroencephalographic activity or blood pressure are converted to visual or auditory signals so that individuals become aware of them (i.e. biological signals are "fed back" to the subject).

biogenic amines a group of chemical synaptic transmitter substances in the peripheral and central nervous systems including norepinephrine, serotonin, and dopamine, among others.

biological half-life the amount of time required for a tissue to metabolize half the administered dose of a drug.

biotransformation the process by which drugs are chemically altered to the form in which they can be excreted.

boomerang effect an attempt to change attitudes may have an effect opposite to that intended.

brain stem the lower part of the brain; usually includes structures such as the medulla, the pons and the mesencephalon.

brightness the perceptual character of a light which varies with the light's physical intensity.

brightness contrast the influence on the brightness of a light by the brightness of surrounding lights.

canalization the return of growth to the original trajectory after an environmental insult has caused the individual's growth pattern to deviate from the normal path.

Cannon-Bard theory (thalamic theory); theory which suggests that emotional stimuli simultaneously act on the cortex resulting in the emotional experience *and* initiate certain bodily changes.

catchment areas geographic areas or populations served by an agency or institution.

catecholamines a class of neurotransmitters which includes norepinephrine and epinephrine.

categorical perception perception of graded physical stimuli as belonging to discrete categories.

catharsis the release of emotional tensions, as in "crying it out" or furiously confronting someone and "getting it off your chest." At one time Freud thought that catharsis was the main thing needed to effect a cure of hysteria. In recent research it has been proposed that watching violence on T.V. allows for a catharsis of hostile emotions.

catharsis theories the assumption that providing socially acceptable outlets for the expression of sex or aggression will reduce socially inappropriate expression of these drives.

caudate nucleus a group of cell bodies forming part of the basal ganglia.

cell theory the theory which states that all living organisms are made up of cells, which are the structural and functional units of life.

cellular membrane a subcellular structure which surrounds and encloses cells. Its functions are varied and include transport of materials in and out of cells, and in the case of nerve cells is responsible for the propagation of the nerve impulse along the axon.

centiles 100 parts of a frequency distribution, all equal in area; cf. quartiles.

central nervous system all nervous tissue contained within the skull and spinal column.

central theory in motivation refers to theories which postulate that the mechanisms which mediate the behavior are located in the central nervous system (as opposed to peripheral structures).

cerebellum the large, convoluted structure lying in back of the cerebral hemispheres and on top of the pons.

cerebral hemisphere the large, convoluted covering of the brain.

character disorders psychopathology which is often similar to neurotic disorders but in which the character style is more fixed and difficult to treat. Often external motivation (parents or law) compels them to seek treatment, rather than internal discomfort being involved in treatment motivation.

chemotherapy treatment of psychological disorders by means of drugs. Typical kinds of drugs include tranquilizers, antipsychotics, and antidepressants.

child abuse any willful or impulsive injury inflicted on a child by his parents or caretakers, using anything but an open hand on any part of the body other than the buttocks.

childhood schizophrenia psychopathology of childhood similar to autism, but with seemingly normal development before withdrawal.

cholinergic synapses at which acetylcholine is the neurotransmitter.

chromosomes subcellular structure, located in the nucleus of cells, on which are located the genes, or the genetic material.

chunking the grouping together of items into larger organized units.

circadian rhythm a 24-hour cycle or variation in behavioral or physiological processes.

classical conditioning learning procedure in which the learned behavioral change is induced by the temporal sequencing of two stimuli.

client-centered therapy Carl Rogers' form of psychotherapy, which emphasizes the therapist's acceptance and empathic understanding of the client, as well as the personality of the therapist himself.

clinical psychology branch of psychology which deals with research and practice in the areas of diagnosis, treatment, and consultation.

coaction persons working on the same task but not talking or interacting with one another. Parallel performances.

cochlea a bony, snail-like structure containing the receptor organ for hearing.

coefficient of genetic determination a statistical expression which is the amount of variance due to heredity divided by the total population (or phenotypic) variability.

cognitive demon the hypothetical mechanism which combines stimulus features in the pandemonium model of perception.

collateral ganglia accumulation of nerves of the parasympathetic nervous system. Many preganglionic parasympathetic fibers synapse on postganglionic nerves in collateral ganglia.

community mental health a branch of community psychology that focuses on community-oriented strategies to reduce or eliminate mental health problems.

community psychology a field of psychology that focuses on the individual in relation to his social environment. The concern is for the effect of broad social forces on the life of the individual and includes issues such as social injustice, the distribution of power and resources, and ways in which communities can support self-determination, self-competence and a sense of belongingness.

complementary any two colored lights which can be mixed in appropriate amounts to produce white light are complementary lights.

complex cortical cells cells of the visual cortex which respond but optimally to light bars like those for simple cortical cells except that the response can be obtained over a region of the retina rather than only in a specific location.

complex sound a sound consisting of more than one sine-wave component.

comprehensive community mental health center a federally funded mental health center that provides five essential services in order to receive building and staffing funds from the federal government. The essential services are: inpatient, outpatient, emergency, partial hospitalization and consultation and education.

compulsions actions which are repeated over and over in an attempt to rid oneself of the anxiety; often associated with obsessive thoughts.

concrete operations mental operations which are demonstrated by the child's ability to perform certain conceptual tasks. The concrete operational stage is the third major stage in Piaget's theory of development.

conditioned emotional response a technique to measure the classical conditioning of fear, A CS is paired with shock, and degree of conditioning is assessed by presenting the CS while the subject is responding to obtain food. The measure of conditioning is the amount of suppression of food motivated responding produced by the CS.

conditioned response a learned response to a CS that occurs by virtue of the temporal sequencing of a CS and a UCS.

conditioned stimulus initially neutral stimulus that precedes the US in classical conditioning.

cones visual receptors responsible for color vision and vision under higher illumination levels.

confidence limits the upper and lower limits of an interval which can be predicted to contain the value of a (unknown) parameter; e.g., the sample mean $\pm$ 2 standard deviations defines confidence limits within which the population mean should fall 95% of the time.

conformity to group norms adherence to group standards for the sake of social acceptance.

conservation the ability to recognize the identity of a substance, quantity, volume or number when they have undergone certain transformations such as a change in shape. The child develops this ability during the concrete operational stage.

consolidation theory a theory of memory which suggests that memory takes some time to become stored after a learning experience.

consultation advice, recommendation, and support provided by mental health professionals to caregivers within a community, such as ministers, police, courts, public health nurses, welfare workers, politicians, and teachers in order to help them respond more effectively to people they serve who have emotional problems.

consummatory behavior the response of an organism in the presence of an incentive which reduces a drive. In the case of a hungry animal, for example, chewing food is a consummatory response.

content analysis coding literature, newspaper articles or magazine content according to research-based categories.

contiguity the presentation of two events overlapping in time.

contingency a relationship between two events in which the presentation of one is dependent on the occurrence of the other.

contingency coefficient a type of correlation coefficient; used when scores can be categorized, but not measured more accurately (nominal scale); CC has smaller range than Pearsonian correlation coefficient.

convergence in depth perception, the rotation of the eyes toward the nose in order to fixate points closer to the observer.

cornea the transparent front area of the eye through which light enters and is first refracted.

corpus callosum the largest single fiber bundle in the nervous system which interconnects the two cerebral hemispheres.

corpus luteum a temporary endocrine gland formed within the cavity left in the ovary after ovulation; chief product is progesterone.

correlation coefficient a standardized measure of the degree of association between 2 (or more) variables; does not imply causation; there are several different kinds of correlation coefficients; can range in value from −1.0, through 0 to +1.0.

cortex *see* adrenal glands.

cotwin control method method used to assess the effects of environmental stimuli—in this method twins are treated as nearly alike as possible except on one variable. After some time the performance of both twins is measured and any difference between them can be attributed to the effects of the single variable on which the twins were treated differently.

counseling much the same as psychotherapy, although the emphasis may be more in the direction of providing information, direction, or support. A common example would be vocational or career counseling.

covariance a measure of the degree to which two (or more) variables are related; not a standardized statistic, but the *correlating coefficient* is.

crisis intervention a form of time limited, brief psychotherapy given to people experiencing a crisis and who are having difficulty coping with it. It is assumed that during this time, people are particularly receptive to treatment.

critical period a stage of development during which an organism is optimally ready to learn certain types of responses.

crossing over the process by which chromosomes exchange physical material during cell division.

cross-tolerance the phenomenon by which use of a particular drug, say ethyl alcohol, renders an individual more tolerant to another type of drug, say the barbiturates.

curare a drug which affects certain types of neural activity. It is an antagonist of acetylcholine, particularly at the neuromuscular junction.

curvilinear a relationship between two variables where high and low levels on one variable predict better to levels on the other variable than do moderate levels on the first variable.

cytology also known as cell biology. That biological discipline which studies the structure and function of cells.

cytoplasm all the intracellular material which is not contained within the nucleus.

cytosine one of the bases in both DNA and RNA.

dark adaptation the increase in sensitivity to light which occurs when illumination is lowered.

dark adaptation curve a graph showing how rods and cones vary in sensitivity over time following a change in illumination from light to dark.

Darwinian (grasping) reflex if a rod contacts the newborn's hand, he will curl his fingers tightly around it and may support most of his weight if the rod is raised.

decibel a logarithmic unit employed in the measurement of sound intensity.

decision demon the hypothetical mechanism in the pandemonium model that "decides" which of several alternative cognitive demons is responding most strongly and, therefore, which pattern is being presented.

degree of freedom a number equal to the number of quantities which were free to vary; in simple statistics, often equal to one less than the number of observations in a category.

dehydroepiandrosterone a specific type of male hormone, or androgen.

delta waves changes in voltage occurring in the electroencephalogram characterized by frequencies between 1 and 3 hertz.

dendrites extensions from the cell body of a nerve cell which conduct information toward the cell body; the receiving end of a nerve cell.

deoxyribonucleic acid (DNA) the genetic material. A large molecule (macromolecule) found in the nucleus of cells which is responsible for genetic inheritance. DNA has two functions: it serves as a template for the synthesis of more DNA; and it serves as a template for the synthesis of another macromolecule, ribonucleic acid (RNA).

depersonalization the process of viewing other people as objects or nonhuman entities. Often used as a justification for the use of destructive violence against them.

depressants those drugs which suppress the activity of the nervous system. Many depressant drugs, however, have certain stimulant properties.

depth perception the ability to perceive three-dimensional objects or objects at different distances from the observer.

derepression in molecular genetics, refers to a molecule which allows a gene which is not normally functioning to express itself.

determinism the idea that behavior is guided by internal and external stimuli. In this sense the opposite of a rational position.

diastolic phase the action of the heart; when the heart expands blood enters it from the venous system. This is referred to as the diastolic phase and it determines the amount of blood which will be pumped into the body during the next contraction of the heart.

dihydrotestosterone a specific type of male hormone, or androgen.

dimensions: extroversion and neuroticism these dimensions are found in the empirical studies carried out by Eysenck. They form a fundamental part of Eysenck's theory of personality. According to this theory, every single person can be tested and given a unique pair of numbers indicating their degree of extroversion (vs. introversion) and of neuroticism (vs. stability).

discrimination training the reinforced presentation of one stimulus and the nonreinforced presentation of a different stimulus.

dispersion of scores the degree to which scores differ from each other, with some being high, some average, and some low.

displacement originally part of Freud's theory, displacement means the shifting of emotional energy from its original connection with an unacceptable idea into connection with an acceptable idea. Thus in the dream some irrelevant thing like a hat becomes the center of concern, the energy from a wish to expose oneself having been displaced onto the hat. In more recent work on aggression the term displacement refers to a redirection of hostile emotion onto some new, mainly unprovocative object. A person furious with his boss may go home and kick the cat. That would be displacement of hostility.

dissociative reaction states which include amnesia, fugue states, and multiple personalities. Person tries to psychically escape all knowledge of and responsibility for undesirable behavior.

dizygotic fraternal twins, that is, twins which develop from two fertilized eggs.

doctrine of innate ideas the belief that some contents of the mind are innate.

dominant if two parental types are crossed to produce offspring (F_1 hybrids), and if the two parents differ on a trait, the parental trait which is expressed in the offspring is referred to as the dominant trait.

dose the amount of a drug necessary to produce an effect.

dose-response relation the quantitative relation between the amount of a drug administered to an organism and the size of the response exhibited by the organism or the tissue.

Down's syndrome *see* trisomy 21.

drug dependence the habitual use of any drug without the ability to stop that use without suffering emotional or physical withdrawal symptoms.

drugs of abuse those drugs which have a high potential of being abused and against which a given society has legislated.

drug therapy *see* chemotherapy.

dualism Descartes' division of behavior into two classes, voluntary and involuntary.

duplication the process by which DNA codes for the synthesis of more—or daughter—DNA.

duplicity theory of vision the theory of a dual (rod-cone) visual system.

ED50 that amount of a drug which produces an effect in 50 percent of the organisms.

efferent nerves nerves which carry information away from the central nervous system.

ego one of three agencies in Freud's second theory. The ego guides behavior so as to maximize instinctual gratification within the limits set by reality and by conscience. The other two agencies are the Id and the superego.

egocentrism a term employed by Piaget in both perceptual and social contexts. It refers to the fact that young children find it difficult to take or understand a point of view other than their own. They tend to think that others see or feel things the same way they do.

electroconvulsive shock electrical current usually delivered by means of electrodes attached to the scalp which induces motor convulsions.

electroconvulsive therapy (ECT) the most widely-employed form of shock therapy, in which convulsions are induced by means of electrical current. The procedure is sometimes accompanied by reduced psychotic or depressive symptoms.

electroshock therapy (EST) *see* electro-convulsive therapy.

embryonic stage the stage of prenatal development beginning with attachment of the zygote to the uterine wall and ending two months later. All major organ systems begin to develop during this stage.

encounter groups groups which meet either over an extended period of time, or for lengthier sessions ("marathons") over a briefer time-span. In such groups the leader endeavors to promote honest self-disclosure and dealing with others.

endocrine function refers to glandular secretion *into* the bloodstream.

engrams a term used to describe the "memory trace" or the physical entity which is presumed to underlie a memory.

enzymes organic catalysts. Protein molecules which catalyze nearly all chemical reactions which occur in cells.

EPSP abbreviation for "excitatory post-synaptic potential."

equiloudness contour a graph indicating the sound intensities required to make different frequencies equally loud.

ergs in Cattell's theory an erg is a primary source trait of motivation. An erg corresponds to a functional unity discovered through empirical analysis of correlation data. The erg for sex underlies correlations among wishes like wanting to be with your sweetheart, wanting to make love, and so on.

escape an instrumental learning paradigm in which an aversive event is removed by the occurrence of a response.

escape response a response that terminates an aversive stimulus.

estradiol benzoate a form of estrogen or female hormone; often used for therapeutic or experimental purposes.

estrogens female hormones; major source is the ovary, but also produced by the placenta, the adrenal cortex, and the testes; largely responsible for female body conformation and some female behaviors, such as estrous (heat) behavior.

ethology that branch of zoology which studies the behavior of animals.

excitatory postsynaptic potential a brief depolarization of a nerve cell membrane potential produced by excitatory synaptic transmission.

excitatory synapses a functional contact between two nerve cells in which one cell causes the other to depolarize; i.e., one cell excites another with which it makes synaptic contact.

existential therapies collective term for forms of psychotherapy based on existential theories. Such therapies typically emphasize acceptance of one's aloneness and vulnerability, and the importance of personally meaningful choices and decisions.

exocrine function refers to glandular secretion elsewhere (e.g., into gut, onto surface of body) than into the bloodstream.

exteroceptive stimuli stimuli that impinge on the exterior of the organism.

extinction the gradual disappearance of a learned behavior produced by presenting the CS alone in classical conditioning and by removing the reinforcer in instrumental learning.

F_1 hybrid that population or generation of animals produced by mating together two parental types.

F_2 *see* second filial generation.

factor analysis a statistical procedure for finding out what few main underlying variables are responsible for various trait measures being correlated. For example, it has been found that the variable of emotional stability underlies the positive correlations between measures of calmness, steadiness, and ability to make decisions.

family therapy group method in which the clients are two or more members of the same family. The therapist works with the family unit (or sub-unit) in straightening out distorted communication, resolving familial problems, etc.

fear-effort hypothesis a hypothesis developed to explain the critical period during which animals imprint. If exposed to the object too early the animals cannot follow the object well (they cannot expand much effort), and if exposed too late they are fearful of the object.

feature analysis model the view that perception depends upon the recognition of elementary features of a stimulus pattern.

feature demon the hypothetical mechanism in the pandemonium model which responds to a particular stimulus feature.

features the basic units of analysis of a stimulus pattern.

fetal stage the stage of prenatal development beginning with the third month of pregnancy and continuing until birth. Organ systems become more differentiated during this stage.

field dependence-independence a dimension of cognitive ability reflected in performance on visual tasks which require a subject to deal with information despite the presence of distracting cues in the background or field. The field independent person is less distracted by the background cues than the field dependent person.

field experiment a research study done in a real-life setting that attempts to utilize all the controls and procedures of a laboratory experiment.

fitness value the number of offspring an organism contributes to the next generation who themselves reach reproductive age.

fixation an intensification of a particular stage in psychosexual development due to excessive gratification or deprivation. As a result that kind of psychosexual organization always remains strong in the personality. The person may become an oral, anal, or phallic character as a result.

fixed interval schedule of reinforcement in which reinforcement is delivered for the first response which occurs beyond a fixed designated period of time following the preceding reinforcement.

fixed ratio schedule of reinforcement in which reinforcement is delivered after a fixed number of responses.

follicle stimulating hormone (FSH) hormone from the *pars distalis* of the pituitary; stimulates growth of Graafian follicle (containing ovum) in the ovary; stimulates spermatogenesis in the testes; stimulates production and release of ovarian estrogen.

forced compliance the condition of being induced to act in a manner contrary to one's beliefs or attitudes. A research situation used by cognitive dissonance researchers.

formal operations is the fourth and final in Piaget's sequence of cognitive development, emerging around twelve years of age. It is characterized by the ability to perform complete mental operations and abstractly consider the consequences of various mental hypotheses.

formants the four limited frequency regions in which the energy of speech sounds is concentrated.

formant transition a shift in the frequency of a formant.

fovea the slightly indented, central region of the retina. In this region, cones are most numerous and rods are extremely sparse.

free association Freud's psychoanalytic technique, in which the patient is instructed to say spontaneously whatever comes into his mind. One of the major means by which the analyst comes to understand the patient's unconscious conflicts.

frequency distribution a table showing how often each response, or each class of responses, occurred.

frequency histogram a type of bar graph where the length or height of each bar represents the number of responses which occurred for each category or class.

frequency polygon similar to a frequency histogram; only the end-points of the bars are shown, and these points are connected by straight lines between adjacent points.

frequency theory the theory of pitch and loudness in which pitch depends on the frequency of vibration of the basilar membrane.

frustration blocking of on-going goal-directed behavior.

frustration-aggression hypothesis the hypothesis which states that frustration (defined as blocking goal-directed behavior) results in aggression.

fugue state individual flees from scene where he was uncomfortable and is amnesic for the past.

functional autonomy hypothesis which states that motives may become independent of their origins. For example, money may acquire a value in and of itself, rather than because it is useful in purchasing goods such as food, dress, etc.

functional disorders disease in which psychological causes are involved in producing the psychopathology.

functions in Jung's theory, the four functions are the four basic ways in which the mind relates to the environment: thinking, feeling, sensing, and intuiting.

fundamental the lowest frequency in a sound.

galvanic skin response skin resistance changes during arousal and emotions. This change in skin resistance during arousal has been called the galvanic skin response (GSR).

gametes germ cells. Male and female gametes join to form the zygote.

"genetic factors in psychosis" current research shows that there is some inherited predisposition in an individual who becomes manic-depressive or schizophrenic.

gender identity one's perception of oneself or sense of identity as male or female.

genes the basic unit of hereditary transmission. An amount of DNA located on the chromosomes.

genital stage the final stage in Freud's theory of psychosexual development. In this stage all of the previously developed part-instincts are integrated under the dominance of genital and procreative drives. This stage is normally achieved in late adolescence.

genotype the genetic constitution of an organism.

Gestalt psychologists a school of psychologists who emphasized the relationships between elements of a stimulus in perception.

Gestalt therapy a form of psychotherapy, pioneered by Fritz Perls, which emphasizes ongoing awareness of one's feelings.

globus pallidus a group of cell bodies forming a part of the basal ganglia.

glucocorticoids steroid hormones from the *Zona fasciculata* of the adrenal cortex; cause breakdown of lymph tissue to form sugar and glycogen; examples include cortisone and cortisol; *see* adrenal glands.

gonadotropins hormones from the *pars distalis* of the pituitary which have major effects on the gonads (ovaries or testes).

gonads the germ-producing organs; in the male, the testes, which produce sperm; in the female, the ovaries, which produce eggs or ova.

graafian the follicle within the ovary where the ovum or egg matures prior to ovulation.

Graduated Reciprocation in Tension-reduction plan (GRIT) an international peace plan that relies on a series of small unilateral moves that build the basis for further tension-reduction if the other side reciprocates.

grey matter nervous tissue consisting primarily of cell bodies and fine, unmyelinated nerve fibers, such as small axons and dendrites.

group conformity agreement with a group opinion for the sake of social approval when the individual opinion may be different from the group's.

group therapy psychotherapy conducted in a group setting. Unlike individual therapy, group therapy emphasizes the need for group members to be therapeutic for one another. Understanding the dynamics of the group may be as, or more, important than understanding individual dynamics.

growth hormone (STH) hormone from the *pars distalis* of the pituitary; stimulates growth of bone, connective tissue and muscle.

guanine one of the bases in both DNA and RNA.

habituation a decrease in an unlearned response to a repetitive stimulus.

hair cells the receptor for audition.

harmonics the frequency components of a complex sound.

hedonism in psychology refers to that motivational concept which states that organisms behave in such a way as to maximize pleasure and minimize pain. Closely related to the philosophical meaning of the word which refers to the fact that pleasure is the highest good.

hertz the number of cycles per second. The unit of frequency in sound measurement.

heterozygosity the condition in which two genes at one locus are different alleles. An *AA* genotype is referred to as a homozygote; an *Aa* individual is referred to as a heterozygote.

hippocampus a large structure in the forebrain which, in humans, may be involved in the transfer of short-term to long-term memory.

Holzinger's H' a statistic used to estimate the contribution of genetic variables to total phenotype variability in human behavioral genetic research.

homeostasis an optimal level of functioning maintained by regulatory "homeostatic mechanisms"; for example, mechanisms which regulate sodium concentrations in the body fluids, or mechanisms which regulate internal body temperature.

homologous two like chromosomes are said to be identical. For example, one X chromosome is the homolog of the other X chromosomes.

Homo sapiens scientific name for man—the human species.

homozygosity the condition in which two genes at one locus are identical alleles. An *Aa* genotype is referred to as a heterozygote; an *AA* genotype is referred to as a homozygote.

hormone a chemical messenger produced by a specific gland, released into the blood, and effective at some distance from its source.

hue the basic color of a light.

humanistic psychologists psychologists that deemphasize the causes of human behavior and focus on the growth potential of man and his ability to make free choices about the goals of life.

Huntington's Chorea heritable, degenerative disease of the central nervous system. Particularly the basal ganglia are involved. The disease is transmitted as a single dominant gene. Typically, the disease develops in individuals between 30 and 40 years of age.

hydrogen bonds a type of chemical bonding in which an atom acts as both a hydrogen ion donor and exceptor. Type of bonding which binds the two strands of DNA, which together form the double helix, together.

hyperactivity psychopathological behavior in which the child is constantly active, has almost nonexistent attention span and cannot be calmed by normal means. Stimulant drugs often have the reverse effect and act to calm these children.

hypercomplex cortical cells cells of the visual cortex which require more complex stimulus patterns for optimal response than those required by simple and complex cells.

hyperopia farsightedness. An optical defect in which the lens is too close to the retina for near accommodation.

hyperpolarized a voltage difference which is larger than the resting membrane potential; i.e., the inside of the cell is more negative than normal.

hypersomnias sleep disorders characterized by an apparent need for too much sleep.

hypnosis the process by which hypnotism or a trance-like state is induced.

hypnotics drugs which induce drowsiness and sleep. Such drugs are also referred to as sedatives. One class of drugs which are referred to as hypnotics or sedatives are the barbiturates.

hypnotism the procedure of inducing in someone an often sleeplike condition of heightened suggestibility.

hypothalamus the group of nuclei just above the pituitary gland which controls its functions and is involved in eating, drinking, sleeping, and a variety of other "motivated" behaviors.

hypothalamic hyperphagia overeating and obesity resulting from destruction of the ventromedial nuclei of the hypothalamus.

hypothalamic hyperphagia (dynamic) that phase of hypothalamic hyperphagia during which the animal eats ravenously and gains weight.

hypothalamic hyperphagia (static) that phase of hypothalamic hyperphagia which follows the dynamic phase and during which the animals no longer eat ravenously and do not continue to gain weight.

iconic memory the sensory memory for visual information.

id one of three agencies in Freud's second theory. The Id represents the instinctual forces in personality. The other two agencies are the ego and the superego.

implosive therapy form of behavior modification based on extinction principles. In implosive therapy, the client is exposed to vivid, anxiety-arousing scenes in imagination. When the anxiety is not accompanied by the imagined disastrous consequences, it hopefully extinguishes.

imprinting a special form of learning in which a young animal of certain species (e.g. greylag geese), if exposed to a particular stimulus very early in life, seems to form a special form of bond; e.g., a young bird imprinted on a man may, when grown, orient its sexual display to a man rather than another bird.

inbred a system of mating in which individuals who are related to each other more closely than by chance are mated.

indigenous paraprofessional a paraprofessional recruited from the community that he or she serves. The term "indigenous" is generally used when the community is a poverty area and the paraprofessional is a member of a minority group.

inducible in molecular genetics, refers to a gene which can become functional in the presence of certain molecules (the inducer).

in-group perception of the superiority of one's own group relative to other groups.

inhibition a force which exerts an influence in the opposite direction from excitation.

inhibitory postsynaptic potential a brief hyperpolarization of a nerve cell membrane potential produced by inhibitory synaptic transmission.

inhibitory synapses a functional contact between two nerve cells in which one cell causes the other to hyperpolarize; that is, one cell prevents another from firing.

inhibitory synaptic transmission synaptic transmission between two nerve cells in which one cell prevents another from firing.

innate categories are those qualities of the mind which may be inborn, such as some of the perceptual functions present in early infancy which do not seem to be very dependent on environmental experience. The term was originally used by the philosopher Immanuel Kant, and stands in contrast to John Locke's "tabula rasa."

innoculation a technique of attitude change where persons are exposed to a small amount of a counter-argument to enable them to defend against later propaganda attempts.

insomnia the class of disorders characterized primarily by an inability to sleep.

instrumental learning learning procedure in which the learned behavioral change is produced by the presence of a contingency between a response and reinforcer.

interoceptive stimuli stimuli that impinge on the interior of the organism.

interposition in perception, when one object blocks part of another from view.

interval schedules schedule of reinforcement in which reinforcement is delivered for the first response which occurs beyond a designated period of time following the preceding reinforcement.

intrinsic activity once a drug has attached itself to a receptor it can initiate its biological activity; the degree to which the drug is biologically active is called the intrinsic activity of the drug.

intrinsic nuclei functional groups of cell bodies within the thalamus which are responsible for making connections solely within the thalamus.

introspection the examination of one's own inner feelings, thoughts, sensations, etc.

ions charged molecules which exist in the body fluids, both inside and outside of cells.

IPSP abbreviation for "inhibitory post-synaptic potential."

iris a ring of muscles in front of the lens which forms the pupil and controls its size.

isogenicity pertains to the state in which all the individuals in a given population are genetically identical.

James-Lange theory theory which attempts to explain emotional experiences. The theory states that emotional stimuli first result in certain bodily changes and that these changes, in turn, result in the subjective experience of the emotion.

karyotyping a technique which prepares chromosomes for microscopic examination.

kinesthetic sense the sense which provides information about the position and state of body movement via muscle and joint receptors.

LD50 that amount of a drug which is lethal to fifty percent of the animals.

latency stage the fourth stage in Freud's theory of psychosexual development. It lasts from about age six to the time of puberty. It is characterized by an absence of interest in sexual matters.

latent learning the type of learning which occurs in situations where the organism is not given a reinforcement, but for which learning can be said to have occurred due to performance increments in the same situation once reinforcement is introduced into the situation.

lateral hypothalamus those areas of the hypothalamus located away from the midline.

lateral inhibition the form of opposition found between center and surround responses in ganglion cell receptive fields.

latitude of acceptance a range on an attitude scale that meets with a person's approval.

latitude of rejection a range on an attitude scale that meets with a person's disapproval.

law of effect Thorndike's principle that responses followed by satisfying states of affairs are strengthened and responses followed by discomforting states are weakened.

law of independent assortment law of genetics which states that genes on different chromosomes separate independently of each other during cell division.

law of segregation law of genetics which states that two allelic genes separate during cell division with any residual effects. Also known as Mendel's first law.

learned helplessness the failure to learn to escape and avoid aversive events which results from prior exposure to inescapable aversive events.

learning set learning how to learn a particular task.

lens a transparent organ between cornea and retina. Its shape is varied to affect accommodation.

lesion technique to remove or destroy a structure or group of structures in the nervous system.

libido in psychoanalytic theory, refers to the energy of the sexual instinct.

lie detection a technique used to detect lies. The assumption is that telling a lie is arousing and that this arousal, in turn, is reflected in a variety of physiological measures, including the galvanic skin response, rates of respiration, etc.

limbic system a large, interconnected group of structures in the central nervous system believed to be important in emotional behavior, learning, and memory; this system includes such structures as the hippocampus, septal nuclei, amygdala, hypothalamus, and others.

linear perspective in perception, the fact that parallel lines converge in the retinal image as they recede from the observer, such as the convergence of railroad tracks as they recede into the distance.

linked genes located on the same chromosome. Linked genes tend to be transmitted together and thus do not obey Mendel's law of independent assortment.

locus a place, or location, on a chromosome occupied by a gene.

long-term memory storage system in which information is kept for long periods of time.

luteinizing hormone (LH) hormone from the *pars distalis* of the pituitary; stimulates ovulation in the female; stimulates androgen production and release from testes; sometimes called Interstitial Cell Stimulating Hormone (ICSH).

luteotrophic hormone (LTH) hormone from the *pars distalis* of the pituitary; enhances secretion of progesterone by the corpus luteum in many species; also called prolactin, in some species.

manic-depressive psychosis depressive affect alternates with manic or euphoric affect. Lithium-carbonate is currently the treatment of choice and this often results in complete control of this disorder.

maturation organ and behavioral systems develop through an interaction of biological growth and environmental influences. Maturation refers to growth processes which are primarily governed by biological forces.

maturational level the particular level achieved by the maturation process. (*See* motivation.)

mean a measure of central tendency; a mean may be an arithmetic mean, a geometric mean, or a harmonic mean; roughly equivalent to *average*.

medial hypothalamus those areas of the hypothalamus located near the midline of the brain.

median a measure of central tendency; equivalent to a score which divides a distribution into two equal parts, with one-half of the scores being larger than the median and one-half being smaller; equivalent to the 50th centile.

meditation a technique used to achieve a state of consciousness that practitioners describe as a fully alert, but relaxed state.

medulla *see* adrenal glands.

medulla oblongata that division of the brain nearest the top of the spinal cord.

meiosis type of cell division which occurs in germ cells.

memory span the number of items that can be remembered shortly after one presentation of a series of items.

Mendel's first law *see* law of segregation.

Mendel's second law *see* law of independent assortment.

mental health worker a trained, and often experienced, psychotherapist, but typically one without an advanced degree in a mental health specialty.

mesmerism the term used to describe the hypnotic trance in the nineteenth century, so-called after one of the early hypnotists, Mesmer.

mesomorph medium, well-proportioned, or athletic body type.

messenger RNA (mRNA) a class of RNA which is DNA-like; that is, the base composition of mRNA is similar to that of the DNA on which it was synthesized. This class of RNA codes for the synthesis of specific proteins.

miasma theory an early theory of public health that assumed that all diseases were caused by a poisonous gas given off by waste materials. Applied to community mental health, the theory proposes that mental health problems can be eliminated by modifying the environment to remove psychological miasmas such as poverty and social injustice.

midbrain that portion of the brain stem above the pons and below the thalamus and hypothalamus.

"milieu therapy" similar to the "therapeutic community." Treatment, usually in a hospital setting, in which the ward environment is deliberately structured to provide maximum therapeutic benefit. The total program may include such things as group meetings, work assignments, and recreational therapy.

mirror-image phenomenon the research finding that groups that are antagonistic hold the same negative attitudes toward each other.

mitosis type of cell division which occurs in somatic cells.

mixed-motive a game that allows for both cooperative (both players win) and competitive (one wins/other loses) strategies.

mode the most frequently occurring response, or class of responses, in a frequency distribution.

modeling is a term used by social learning theorists to refer to the child's behavioral development associated with copying the actions, attitudes and feelings of other people in his environment.

monomers part of the structure of DNA—refers to the nucleotides which are the repeating units in DNA, composed of a phosphate group, a sugar and a base.

monozygotic a kind of twin in which both individuals are genetically identical. Occurs when a single fertilized egg splits to produce two organisms.

moratorium a waiting period, specifically a time of waiting during adolescence, in this period, according to Erikson, the adolescent needs time out from premature demands to develop a firm adult identity. Earlier identity elements need time to be integrated.

moro reflex when the infant is suddenly moved or dropped, he throws his arms out and then draws them in toward his chest.

motion parallax the phenomenon in which objects moving past an observer tend to move faster across the retina when they are nearer, and slower when they are far away.

motor cortex the portion of cerebral cortex involved in bodily movement.

Müllerian duct the embryological tissue from which the female accessory sexual structures (i.e., the uterus and Fallopian tubes) are derived.

Müllerian inhibiting substance (MIS) a substance released during fetal development of males; causes regression of the Müllerian ducts; probably made by the seminiferous tubules.

multiple personality reactions an internal dissociative reaction, where several different personalities exist within the same person, often without knowledge of each other.

Muscarinic agents term which collectively refers to drugs which stimulate the activity of postganglionic parasympathetic nerves.

myelin sheath the fatty substance surrounding the axons of certain nerve cells.

myopia nearsightedness. An optical defect in which the lens is too far from the retina for accommodation of far distances.

narcolepsy a sleep disorder characterized by uncontrollable and irresistible attacks of sleepiness.

National Institute of Mental Health a division of the Department of Health, Education and Welfare of the federal government, founded in 1946 to promote mental health services in the states and to support research and training in fields related to mental health.

natural childbirth generally refers to childbirth without the mother's use of anesthetics. Mothers are usually prepared for natural childbirth by a series of exercises to promote mental relaxation and physical conditioning.

natural selection the process by which certain individuals in a population are more fit (survive and reproduce) in a given environment.

negative reinforcement an instrumental learning paradigm in which an aversive event is removed by the occurrence of a response.

neurasthenic insomnia a syndrome which is characterized by subjective reports of an inability to sleep, frequent awakenings during the night, an inability to fall asleep, and other symptoms.

neurohypophysis the part of the pituitary which derives embryologically from brain tissue; includes the *pars nervosa* (2 hormones) and the *median eminence* (up to 9 releasing factors or hormones).

neuromuscular junction the fuctional connection between a nerve and a muscle. Similar to a synapse which is the functional connection between two nerves.

neuron the nerve cell, the basic cellular component of the nervous system.

neurosis psychopathology in which reality testing is intact.

neurotic depression psychopathological reaction to loss characterized by feelings of sadness and low self-worth.

neurotic reactions psychopathology in which the person's reaction to stress is more severe and lasts longer than the transient disorders, but the personality disorganization of the psychotic reaction is not present.

neurotransmitter a class of compounds which are released from presynaptic neurons and have an effect on postsynaptic nerves. For example, acetylcholine, norepinephrine, etc.

Nodes of Ranvier small gaps along the length of the myelin sheath surrounding nerve cell axons.

nonopponent neurons lateral geniculate neurons which respond similarly (e.g., increase their firing rate) to all wavelengths of light. The amount of response varies according to wavelength.

non-zero sum game a game in which it is possible for both players to win something for each play.

noradrenalin *see* norepinephrine.

norepinephrine hormone secreted by the adrenal medulla; especially effective in raising blood pressure by constricting blood vessels; may be associated with anger; same as noradrenalin.

normal curve a graph of a normally distributed variable; mean, median, and mode are equal; curve is symmetrical; described by a specific mathematical function.

nuclear membrane a subcellular structure which surrounds the nucleus and which regulates transport of material into and out of the nucleus.

nucleotides the repeating unit in the DNA molecule—refers to a phosphate group, a sugar and a base.

nucleus a subcellular structure which contains the genetic material, that is the chromosomes.

objective test according to Cattell, an objective test is a portable, miniature situation, in which the subject cannot readily guess the meaning of his responses. For example, a subject may be asked to press a key as soon as a flickering light fuses into a steady beam (known as critical flicker fusion). In Cattell's studies it has been found that the higher fusion frequencies indicate greater general alertness of the person's brain.

obsessions neurotic psychopathology in which the person cannot get his mind off certain topics which bother him. Thoughts, words, or impulses keep him mentally occupied.

omission training an instrumental learning paradigm in which the occurrence of an appetitive event is prevented by the occurrence of a response.

operant conditioning form of behavior modification in which desirable behaviors are reinforced by the therapist, thereby increasing the likelihood of their occurrence, while undesirable behaviors are generally ignored. The reinforcers for appropriate behavior may be tangible goods, like food or cigarettes, or social praise. Often used in conjunction with aversive conditioning.

opponent neurons lateral geniculate neurons which excite maximally to one wavelength of light (e.g., red) and maximally depress their firing rate to another wavelength (e.g., green).

opponent process theory of color vision a theory proposing four color process in opposing pairs, that is, red vs. green and blue vs. yellow.

optic nerve the nerve formed by the axons of ganglion cells as they exit from the retina out the back of the eye.

oral fantasies complex imaginations of events which are satisfying in ways that involve the mouth, such as eating, drinking, kissing, sucking, and so on.

oral stage in Freud's theory of psychosexual development, the oral stage is the very first in life. It is dominant during the first year after birth. In this stage the mouth is the focus of excitement.

organ of corti the receptor organ for hearing.

organic disorders disease with physical causes for the psychopathology, for example, brain tumor.

organismic valuing process in Rogers' theory, the organismic valuing process is the reaction of "good" or "bad," "pleasant" or "unpleasant" that the organism spontaneously has to any environmental object, event, or quality. It is contrasted with valuing based upon what other people think we should like or prefer.

orienting reflex a complex series of behavioral and physiological responses that occur to a novel stimulus including desynchronization of the EEG, pupillary dilation, the galvanic skin response, etc.

ossicles the bones of the middle ear which connect the tympanic membrane to the oval window.

out-group the perception of the inferiority of other group(s) when compared with a group of which one is a member.

outreach a strategy in community mental health in which people who are in need of mental health or community psychology services are contacted in the community rather than waiting until such people request such services.

oval window the membrane which introduces sound energy to the cochlea.

ovary female reproductive organ; major source of the female hormones (estrogens and progesterone); source of eggs (ova), the female gametes.

overanxious and withdrawn children children who are so shy and fearful often either become overanxious and cling to others or withdraw and become daydreamers.

oxytocin hormone released by the posterior pituitary; increases motility of smooth muscle of oviduct and uterus; effects let-down of milk in female mammals, after sucking stimulus.

paired associate learning the learning of a series of items presented in two member pairs.

pandemonium model a model of perception characteristic of those involving feature analysis.

paradoxical sleep also termed rapid eye movement sleep, the stage of sleep characterized by an electroencephalogram, that is, low voltage and desynchronized. The stage of sleep during which most dreaming occurs.

parameters theoretical attributes of a population; usually not known; estimated by statistics derived from a sample from the population. For example, the mean height of a random sample of all women in Idaho would be an estimate of the parameter which is the actual mean height of *all* the women in Idaho.

paraprofessional a person with minimal training who provides mental health and community services to the community.

parasomnias disorders of sleep in which behavior characteristic of waking occurs during sleep, for example, sleepwalking.

parasympathetic division one division of the autonomic nervous system which is responsible for conservation of energy.

parathyroid an endocrine gland embedded (usually) in the thyroid gland; important for regulation of calcium level in blood; necessary for life.

parenteral all routes of administration of a drug which do not involve the alimentary canal. This latter route of administration is referred to as the oral route.

parity strategy a game strategy that aims to equalize the resources of players on both sides.

pars distalis the largest, most anterior part of the pituitary; source of six major hormones; specific hormone release (or inhibition) from this division is controlled by releasing (or inhibitory) factors from the *median eminence.*

partial hospitalization hospitalization given to mental patients for only part of the day or during the night. The purpose of the program is to increase involvement of mental patients with the community and reduce dependence on hospitalization.

partial report experiment an experiment in which the subject is requested to report a portion of the items in a brief visual display by a cue which appears shortly after the display.

parturition the process of giving birth to a live young; the act of birth.

payoff matrix the rewards and/or costs for each and every mutual choice in a two-person game.

perceptual defense a defense which protects the person from arousal of unacceptable ideas and wishes by distorting perception. Threatening materials are simply not seen or heard.

peripheral nervous system all nervous tissue contained outside the skull and spinal column.

peripheral theories in motivation, refers to theories which postulate that the mechanisms which mediate the behavior are located in peripheral (as opposed to central nervous system) structures.

perservation-consolidation hypothesis a hypothesis which attempts to explain the time-dependent aspects of memory storage by postulating that ongoing neural activity in some circuits must continue for some time after learning for memory to become permanent, that is, consolidated.

phages *see* bacteriophage.

phallic stage the third stage in Freud's theory of psychosexual development. The focus of interest is upon the male genitals or upon the lack of them in girls. This stage is dominant during the period three to five years of age.

phenotype any measurable trait.

phenylketonuria (PKU) a heritable disease. Individuals suffering from this disease lack the liver enzyme phenylalanine hydroxylase which converts phenylalanine to tyrosine. The disease is transmitted as an autosomal recessive gene.

phenylpyruvic acid an abnormal phenylalanine metabolite. Individuals suffering from phenylketonuria produce this metabolite because they lack the enzyme phenylalanine hydroxylase which converts phenylalanine to tyrosine.

phonemes speech sounds we combine to make up words.

photopic threshold curve a graph showing absolute threshold for conversion as a function of wavelength.

photopic vision vision under high levels of illumination involving the cones.

pineal gland a small, unpaired endocrine gland located in the head, above the mid-brain; has been implicated in the timing of puberty, in circadian cyclicity, and in skin color changes (in amphibians).

pitch the characteristic of sound which depends most on its frequency.

pituitary gland the master gland of the body responsible for the functions of all other endocrine glands.

placenta temporary endocrine and nutritive organ formed in the uterus during pregnancy; transfers nutrients from circulation of mother to the fetus; manufactures several of the hormones necessary for maintenance of pregnancy and normal function.

place theory the theory of pitch and loudness in which pitch depends on the place of maximal stimulation along the basilar membrane.

polarization a difference in voltage between two points; usually refers to the difference in voltage across the nerve cell membrane.

polydipsia excessive drinking.

polygenically means many genes; specifically, refers to traits which are determined by many (polygenic) genes.

polypeptides a molecule composed of several peptides each of which, in turn, is made of many amino acids joined together by peptide bonds.

polyribosome the unit of protein synthesis. Refers to that structure made of messenger RNA and ribosomes on which cells manufacture proteins.

polyurea excessive urination.

pons that division of the brain just above the medulla oblongata and including the cerebellum, superior and inferior colliculi, portions of the reticular formation, certain cranial nerve nuclei, etc.

populations at risk a group of people with identifiable characteristics that research has indicated have a higher than average probability of developing a particular problem.

positive reinforcement instrumental learning paradigm in which the presentation of an appetitive event is made contingent on the occurrence of a response.

postdecision dissonance a state of discomfort that results from having to choose only one of two or more highly attractive alternatives.

postganglionic neurons in the autonomic nervous system refers to those nerves which run from either chain ganglia, collateral ganglia or terminal ganglia to the organs which are being innervated.

postsynaptic cell the cell receiving information from another by means of synaptic transmission.

preganglionic neurons in the autonomic nervous system, refers to those fibers which originate in the central nervous system and synapse on postganglionic nerves.

pregnant mare serum gonadotropin (PMSG) a hormone recovered from the blood of pregnant horses which has FSH-like properties when administered to females of many species; useful to stimulate ovarian follicle growth experimentally.

preoperational stage the stage in Piaget's sequence which follows the sensorimotor stage at about age two and ends around age five or six. The child uses abstract verbal and imagery representation during this stage but he is not yet able to perform concrete operations.

preparedness a dimension of ease of conditionability determined by the biological nature of the organism.

presynaptic cell the cell transmitting information to another cell by means of synaptic transmission.

prevalence rate the rate of all known individuals belonging to a certain category (in treatment or belonging to a particular diagnostic category) on a certain date. Usually expressed in terms of number per 100,000 population.

primacy where attitude change is influenced more by the first of a series of arguments.

primal therapy Arthur Janov's historically-oriented form of psychotherapy, in which the client is led to a vivid re-experiencing of painful childhood incidents and memories, hopefully with a reduction in tension and distorted ways of having old needs met.

primary lights three lights differing in wavelength composition which when mixed in varying amounts will produce most of the colors we see.

primary prevention intervention strategies that are designed to eliminate the cause of emotional problems and thus eventually reduce the incidence of these problems.

primary reinforcers a reinforcer that does not depend on prior learning for its reinforcing power.

primary source traits in Cattell's work on personality he has sought to find through statistical procedures those dozen or so traits which are absolutely basic to all variations in personality. These are the primary source traits.

principle of equipotentiality the principle established by Karl Lashley that suggests regions of the cerebral cortex, within limits, are equivalent in their ability to store memories.

principle of mass action a principle established by Karl Lashley which suggests that within limits the amount of cerebral cortex destroyed is more critical for determining how much memory is disturbed rather than the particular area that is destroyed.

proactive interference the interfering effect of old learning on the retention of new material.

probabilities the relative frequencies of events observed in a large sample, or over the long run.

progesterone a steroid hormone produced by the ovary (also by adrenal cortex and by placenta); a major effect is to prepare the wall of the uterus so that implantation of the fertilized egg(s) is possible; estrogens and androgens are biosynthesized from it.

projection a mechanism of defense in which undesirable wishes or characteristics are seen in other people, but not in the self. For example a hostile person in whom hostility is unacceptable may project the hostility onto others and believe that they are persecuting him.

projective technique a method of estimating a person's characteristic needs, conflicts, defenses, emotional reactions, and other features of strength and weakness in the personality. Commonly the method requires the subject to respond freely to some ambiguous stimuli such as inkblots, pictures of social situations, or incomplete sentences. The theory holds that the person projects inner needs, etc., into these responses.

proteins large molecules which consist of long series of amino acids held together by peptide bonds. Two important classes of proteins can be distinguished; these are structural proteins and enzymes. The synthesis of proteins is coded for by mRNA which, in turn, is synthesized on DNA.

prototype reactions infant reactions to early experiences in the Freudian oral and anal stages of development. They are presumed to set the pattern for later personality development.

proximodistal development development of infant motor control proceeds from more central (proximal) to more peripheral (distal) regions of the body.

pseudohermaphrodite an individual who has both male and female sexual structures. The term is derived from the names Hermes and Aphrodite, a god and goddess in Greek mythology. The simpler term, hermaphrodite, is usually restricted to individuals who possess gonadal tissue of both sexes, that is, both ovarian and testicular tissue.

psychiatric hospitalization confinement in a mental hospital or psychiatric ward of a general hospital, usually because the person is dangerous to himself or to others, or is unable to cope effectively with daily demands. Such hospitalization may be either voluntary or involuntary (through the legal system).

psychiatric nursing nursing specialty which deals with the care and treatment of people with psychological disturbances.

psychiatric social work branch of social work which emphasizes the care and treatment of psychologically disturbed people.

psychiatry branch of medicine which deals with diagnosis and treatment of psychological disorders.

psychoanalysis Freud's term for his theory of personality, as well as the technique he devised for the investigation and treatment of neurotic disorders.

psychodrama therapeutic technique in which an individual—the "Protagonist"—is chosen by the larger group to work on a current or past problem in his life. The therapist assigns to other participants various roles (spouse, father, etc.) in the Protagonist's life. The psychodrama is a spontaneous enactment of the situations and feelings which are troublesome to the Protagonist.

psychological tests devices and methods whereby numbers are assigned to people, indicating their relative standing on some personality trait such as intelligence or adventurousness or strength of motive for achievement.

psychopathology abnormality of personality development and/or behavior.

psychopharmacology an area of research which studies the effects of drugs on behavior for the purpose of understanding the mechanism which mediates the behavior.

psychosocial development development of the person in terms of relationships with other people. In Erikson's theory there are stages of psychosocial development, beginning with trust in the first year of life, autonomy in the second year and so on.

psychosocial identity a term in Erikson's theory of psychosocial development. It refers to a synthesis of previously developed characteristics and capabilities. When achieved it is represented in the statements "I am what I believe in, what services I choose to give, what hopes and aspirations I have, and what work I can uniquely do."

psychosomatic psychopathology in which the individual has a true organic disease which is present or made worse at times of emotional stress.

psychosomatic symptoms physical symptoms, for example, headache, or skin rash which become present or are made worse at times of emotional stress.

psychosurgery brain surgery performed to alleviate psychological difficulties, particularly psychotic or depressive symptoms.

psychotherapist one who does psychotherapy —usually a trained clinical psychologist, psychiatrist, counselor or social worker.

psychotherapy treatment of emotional or behavioral problems by psychological means.

psychotherapy research research on psychotherapy, typically classified as either outcome (e.g., assessing the effectiveness of a form of psychotherapy) or process (assessing the components, such as client or therapist personality characteristics, that relate to the quality of outcome).

psychotic depression psychopathology characterized by sad affect and personality disorganization.

punishment an instrumental learning paradigm in which the occurrence of an aversive event is contingent on the occurrence of a response.

pupil the hole formed by the iris of the eye. It varies in size to control the amount of light entering the lens.

putamen a group of cell bodies forming part of the basal ganglia.

Q-sort a Q-sort is a set of cards each bearing a descriptive statement like "I am an intelligent person" or "I keep my cool in most situations." These 100 or so cards are then arranged in piles, going from "those most like me" to "those least like me."

questionnaire a questionnaire is a collection of questions or other verbal items to which a subject responds in a simple fashion such as "true" or "false," or "never," "sometimes," or "always." Questionnaires are among the most widely used psychological tests for assessing personality traits.

radioactively labelled a molecule in which one of the atoms has been made radioactive. Many types of radioactively labelled molecules are used in biological research for a variety of purposes.

range a statistic computed by subtracting the lowest score in a distribution from the highest score.

rank-order coefficient a type of correlation coefficient, computed from score *ranks*, rather than from actual scores. Used when accuracy of actual scores is in doubt, but relative rankings are clear.

raphé nuclei functional groups of cell bodies in the brain stem that contain the neurotransmitter, serotonin, and are involved in the maintenance of sleep.

ratings estimates of another person's characteristics of personality, based on some acquaintance. Often they are expressed in numerical terms. For example: "0 = makes no everyday decisions . . . 3 = makes everyday decisions with moderate speed and efficiency . . . 6 = makes everyday decisions with exceptional speed and good judgment."

rational-emotive therapy Albert Ellis' form of psychotherapy, which emphasizes the understanding and correction of the client's misconceptions about himself and his world.

rationalism a philosophy which states that the behavior of organisms is guided in terms of the expected outcome of such behavior. Closely related to the philosophy of free-will.

rationalizations a set of beliefs adopted by an individual that supports and defends their behavior even though the true sources of that behavior may lie elsewhere.

ratio schedule schedule of reinforcement in which reinforcement is delivered on the completion of a designated number of responses.

reaction formation a drastic method of defending against an unacceptable wish. The personality as a whole is changed so as to express exactly the opposite of that wish. Thus prudishness is a reaction formation against sexual interest.

reaction time the time it takes from the presentation of some event to the subject's designated response.

recency where attitude change is influenced more by the last of a series of arguments.

receptive field that region or area of the retina, which when stimulated, affects the response of a particular cell in that cell's receptive field.

receptors in the context of pharmacology, this term refers to a molecule on the cell surface with which the drug interacts.

receptor layer the layer of the retina consisting of the rods and cones.

recessive if two parental types are crossed to produce offspring (F_1 hybrids), and if the two parents differ on a trait, the parental trait which is not expressed in the offspring is referred to as the recessive trait.

reciprocity strategy a game strategy in which one player matches the strategy of the other player.

recognition test test for memory in which the subject is presented with the items to be remembered along with other items. The subject's task is to indicate which of the items are the ones to be remembered.

recording techniques methods used to study the nervous system in which various types of electrical activity are monitored by electronic recording equipment.

reference groups a group whose standards of behavior are accepted by an individual as their own.

refraction the bending of light rays produced by lenses.

regression coefficient a statistic (or parameter) used to predict a score or value (usually unknown) in one array by using a score or value in another array from the same subject; closely related to the correlation coefficient.

reinforcement in Thorndikian (instrumental or operant) conditioning, the procedure of following the occurrence of the correct response by the reinforcing stimulus. In Pavlovian (classical) conditioning, following the conditioned stimulus with the unconditioned stimulus.

reinforcer a stimulus that promotes the learning of an instrumental response when its presentation is made contingent on the response.

relative refractory period the period of time shortly after an action potential during which the nerve cell must be stimulated with a higher than normal stimulus in order to produce another action potential.

reliability a statistic (or parameter) used to indicate accuracy of measurement; usually expressed as a correlation coefficient, for example, the correlation between scores achieved on a test on one occasion and scores on the same test on a later occasion.

repressed in molecular genetics, a gene which is not functioning due to the presence of a molecule (the repressor) which prevents its expression.

repression withdrawal of energy from an idea of instinctual gratification. As a result the idea cannot become conscious and remains part of the contents of the unconscious system.

residential rehabilitation a form of tertiary prevention that focuses on helping people whose social effectiveness has been reduced (perhaps because of emotional problems) to function appropriately in the context of his or her family.

resistance Freud's term for patient behavior which interferes with the flow of free associations.

resting membrane potential the voltage difference between the outside and inside of a nerve cell at rest (i.e., when it is not carrying action potentials).

retention interval the interval of time between learning some material and the test of memory for that material.

reticular formation the central core of the brain stem on both sides which runs from the upper portions of the spinal cord to the thalamus.

retina the receptive organ of the eye.

retrieval cues stimuli that aid in finding an item in memory.

retroactive interference the interfering effect of new learning on the retention of old material.

retrograde amnesia a kind of memory loss in which recently acquired information is lost after some neural trauma, whereas information acquired a long time ago, that is, long before the trauma, is retained.

retrograde amnesia gradient a relationship between the amnestic effects of electroconvulsive shock or other memory impairing treatment, and the severity of the impairment. Generally, such "gradients" illustrate that treatments which impair memory become less and less effective as the time between original learning and the treatment increases.

reversibility is a mental operation wherein the child can reverse a sequence of events. It allows the child to conserve and recognize the identity of transformations.

rhodopsin the rod photopigment. The chemical in rods which reacts to light.

ribonucleic acid (RNA) a large molecule synthesized on DNA. Three different types of RNA exist; they are messenger RNA, ribosomal RNA and transfer RNA. RNA codes for the synthesis of proteins.

ribosomal RNA a class of RNA. That class of RNA which together with certain proteins constitutes a ribosome.

ribosomes a subcellular structure composed of ribosomal RNA and proteins.

rods visual receptors responsible for vision under dim illumination.

rooting reflex when the newborn is touched on his cheek, he automatically turns his head to contact the object with his mouth.

round window the membrane of the cochlea which relieves pressure changes in the organ induced by sound.

runaways children attempt to cope with a stressful environment by fleeing from it, thus giving a cry for help for themselves and their families.

rules the ways in which features are combined in the feature analysis view of perception.

saturation the purity of a hue. The degree to which a hue is not washed out by mixture with white light. Pink is desaturated red.

schemes sequences of sensorimotor behavior which form an integrated structure for the achievement of some goal or the representation of an event.

schizophrenia one of the forms of psychopathology classified as psychosis. There are four major types—simple, hebephrenic, catatonic, and paranoid. Gross disturbances of thinking, feeling, and action are present.

school psychology branch of psychology in which psychological principles and findings are applied to educational settings. Common activities include testing, counseling, and consultation to teachers and staff.

sclera a tough membrane forming the outer surface of the eye except in the region of the cornea.

scotopic threshold curve the curve describing the absolute threshold for vision as a function of wavelength under low levels of illumination, that is, under rod vision.

scotopic vision vision under dim illumination where rods are employed.

secondary prevention strategies that are designed to treat the symptoms of emotional problems. Traditional psychotherapy, crisis intervention, and suicide prevention are all examples of secondary prevention programs. In each case, the problems already exist before the intervention is used.

secondary reinforcers a reinforcer that depends on prior learning for its reinforcing power.

second filial generation that population or generation produced by mating together two organisms of the first filial, or F_1 hybrid generation.

secular trend the trend for each successive generation to be slightly taller than the preceding generation.

sedatives *see* hypnotics.

selective attention the ability to select for perception and analysis one of many stimuli impinging on the sensory receptors.

selective biological activity a term used to define the activity of a drug. The term biological activity implies that the drug effects a cellular process, and selective implies that at a low concentration one effect of the drug predominates.

selective breeding a technique used in genetic research in which animals are selected for reproduction on the basis of some measurable trait. If the trait selected for is determined in part by genetic factors selective breeding will be successful.

self-actualization the idea, important in the humanistic psychology of, for example, Maslow, that all individuals strive to maximize their potentials.

self-concept in Rogers' theory the self-concept is a fluid pattern of ideas about who one is, what one's capabilities are, whether these are good or bad, and so on.

self-fulfilling prophecy when an expectation for one's self or another elicits the expected behavior which would not have occurred in the absence of the expectation.

self-stimulation behaviors which animals engage in and for which they are rewarded with electrical currents administered to certain parts of the brain.

semi-interquartile range a measure of dispersion; computed by subtracting the score at the first quartile (25th centile) from the score at the third quartile (75th centile) and dividing the result by 2.

semipermeable membrane a membrane or barrier between the inside and outside of cells which allows certain substances to pass through it but restricts the passage of other substances.

sensitivity training group interaction method in which participants learn to communicate honestly and effectively with one another. Typically considered a means for personal growth, rather than psychotherapy per se.

sensorimotor stage the first stage in Piaget's sequence during which the infant represents his world in terms of direct sensory and motor action patterns. This stage ends around age two with the emergence of language and abstract imagery.

sensory memory the first stage of memory in which input information is held very briefly.

sensory relay nuclei functional groups of cell bodies in the thalamus responsible for relaying sensory information to the sensory areas of the cerebral cortex.

separation anxiety often occurs in young children when they are spatially separated from their mother or father. If the child feels he has control over the separation and can regain contact by his own actions, he may not show any anxiety symptoms such as crying.

serial learning the learning of a series of items presented one at a time.

serial position curve a function which plots accuracy of retention against the position of the item in the learned list.

serial position effect the improved retention for items of the beginning and end of a serial list.

serotonin a neurotransmitter; precursor to the pineal hormone melatonin.

sex chromosomes those chromosomes in the total genome (all the chromosomes) which determine an organism's genetic sex. In humans, the X and Y chromosomes are the sex chromosomes.

sex-linked traits the expression of which are controlled by genes on the sex-chromosomes.

sexual problems any physical or emotional impediments to the full enjoyment of human sexuality.

shading patterns of brightness or darkness that provide information about depth.

shadowing technique a procedure in which a subject is asked to report the information received by one ear while both ears are receiving different techniques.

shape constancy the fact that the shape of an object is perceived accurately despite different orientations and, therefore, retinal images.

shaping the technique of reinforcing successive approximations to the desired response.

sheltered workshop a vocational rehabilitation center for people with limited skills to teach them, in a nondemanding atmosphere, skills and appropriate behaviors that would permit them to survive in a regular work setting.

short-term memory storage system in which information is kept for only short periods of time.

signal detection theory a theory accounting for the factors which affect light, false alarms, noises, and correct rejection in the detection of a stimulus.

simple cortical cells cells of the visual cortex which respond optimally to a bar of light of a certain width and orientation illuminating a particular place on the retina.

simulation game a research technique that attempts to set up a small-scale replica of a real-life situation.

sine wave the simplest pattern of air pressure variation over time producing sound.

situational insomnia a sleep disorder created by some precipitating circumstance which interferes with an individual's ability to sleep.

size constancy the fact that the size of an object is perceived accurately despite being seen from different orientations or distances, and therefore, casting different retinal images.

skewed a distribution (or frequency histogram or polygon) which is *not* symmetrical, but which has relatively more high scores than low scores, or vice versa.

skin conductance the reciprocal of skin resistance. Skin resistance, in turn, refers to the resistance of the skin to the flow of an electric current.

sleep paralysis an inability to move upon awakening from sleep.

sleep spindles periodic waves in the electroencephalogram characterized by frequencies between ten and fourteen hertz that occur primarily during stage 2 sleep.

slow-wave sleep the relatively deep stage of sleep characterized by large, slow variations in voltage in the electroencephalogram at frequencies of from 1 to 3 hertz.

social comparison theory the theory that people need to evaluate their opinions and abilities by comparing them to others who are similar to themselves.

social drift hypothesis the hypothesis that serves as an alternative explanation to the assumption that social disorganization is a cause of psychosis. According to this hypothesis people with minimal social skills migrate to that part of the city with the greatest social disorganization, since fewer demands for social interactions are placed on them there.

social epidemiology the study of social forces that play a causative role in the development of emotional problems.

social learning theories based on principles of operant learning, but including also the assumption that vicarious learning (imitation) is an important basis of social learning.

social norms accepted and expected patterns of belief and behavior established by a group or society.

sociopathic personalities individuals who often commit criminal acts without remorse or concern with the amoral behavior affects on others.

somatic cells all cells which do not form part of the organism's germ plasm.

somatic division that portion of the peripheral nervous system responsible for bodily movement and sensation.

somatosensory cortex the portion of cerebral cortex responsible for receiving sensory information from the body surface and muscles.

somatotrophic growth hormone from the *pars distalis* of the pituitary; has major effect on bone and muscle growth.

sound spectograph a plot of the frequency of a sound, or sounds, as a function of time.

species-specific behaviors behavior which occurs in all, or nearly all members of a species providing only that they be of the appropriate age and sex.

spectral absorption curve a graph indicating the amount of light energy absorbed by an object at different wavelengths.

split-brain technique the technique for studying the functions of the cerebral hemispheres in which the corpus callosum and other large fibers that interconnect the two cerebral hemispheres are severed.

spreading depression a phenomenon in which neural tissue is depressed by the application of salt solutions.

S-R theory a theory which holds that learning consists of the establishment of connections between stimuli and responses.

stabilized images a light pattern which is set up to illuminate the same part of the retina regardless of eye movements.

standard deviation a measure of dispersion; equivalent to the square root of the *variance*.

standard error of the difference the standard deviation of an array of difference scores, for example, post-test score minus pre-test score; can be computed without actually forming an array of difference scores.

standard error of the estimate the standard deviation of a distribution of scores formed by subtracting a predicted score from a true score, for all scores; a measure of the accuracy of prediction.

standard-normal a *normal curve* which has a mean (and median and mode) of 0 and a variance of 1.0.

state-dependent learning the phenomenon in which memory for some task may not occur when the organism is put into a different "state," for example, a drug state different from the one in which original learning took place.

statistically significant outcome a result or outcome which is not likely to be due to chance; one which is probably due to some aspect of the experimental manipulation.

status deprivation theory based on the assumption that crime is the result of attempts to achieve culturally valued goals (wealth, power) which are inaccessible by legitimate means because of poverty or discrimination.

stereotypes a rigid, often inaccurate and overgeneralized view of a group, race, or ethnic culture.

Steven's law a law relating perceived magnitude to the physical magnitude of a stimulus.

stimulants those drugs which facilitate the activity of the nervous system. However, many stimulant drugs have depressant properties.

stimulation method to artificially stimulate by chemical or electrical means a particular structure or group of structures in the nervous system.

stimulus generalization the tendency for learned responses to occur to stimuli other than those used during original learning.

stop consonants consonants in which air is momentarily held (stopped) then abruptly let out in order to produce them, such as "ba," "pa."

storefront mental health center a psychological service center designed to help people within low income areas. By using storefronts in the community being served, the impersonal, distant institutional image is eliminated and the center is more accessible to the people it serves.

strain a line of animals maintained through inbreeding. In order for a line to be referred to as an inbred strain it must have been mated brother by sister for at least 20 consecutive generations.

stranger anxiety occurs in some infants around six to eight months of age when they become frightened of strangers.

strata in Cattell's theory the personality is organized in layers or *strata*. Lower layers refer to more circumscribed activities or characteristics, such as suspiciousness. Higher layers refer to broader traits such as anxiety, in which suspiciousness plays only one part among many other characteristics, such as emotional instability.

subliminal stimulus a stimulus is one which is strong enough to have some measurable influence on a person, but not strong enough to be consciously detected.

suicide prevention a form of crisis intervention designed to help people having difficulty coping with stress to help them choose another alternative solution other than death.

superego one of three agencies in Freud's second theory. The superego functions like a censorship or judge, often harshly criticizing the ego. It derives from taking over parental criticisms, prohibitions, and imperative moral commands. The other two agencies are the ego and the id.

supernormal period a period after an action potential during which some nerve cells are more easily stimulated than normal.

sympathetic division one division of the autonomic nervous system which is responsible for mobilization of energy for emergencies.

sympathetic ganglionic chain sympathetic nervous system accumulations of nerve cell bodies running parallel to the spinal cord. Place where the preganglionic fibers of the sympathetic nervous systems synapse with the postganglionic fibers of this system.

sympathomimetic agents drugs which mimic the action of the sympathetic division of the autonomic nervous system are collectively referred to as sympathomimetic drugs. An example of such a drug is amphetamine.

synapse the functional contact between two nerve cells.

synapses the functional contacts between one nerve cell and another.

synaptic transmission the process of the transmission of information between two nerve cells; that is, functional transfer of information between two nerve cells at the synapse.

systematic desensitization a form of behavior modification pioneered by Joseph Wolpe. In systematic desensitization, the therapist strives to establish relaxation responses, rather than anxiety responses, to previously threatening situations.

systolic phase the contraction of the heart. That phase of the heart's action during which blood is pumped into circulation because of the contraction of the heart.

tabula rasa is the Latin phrase used by the philosopher John Locke to characterize the nature of the newborn infant's mind as a blank tablet, awaiting the imprint of experience.

t-distribution a distribution (actually a family of distributions) which is symmetrical and similar to the normal distribution, but with more area in the tails; useful for assessing statistical significance when parameters are unknown, but statistics are available.

tectorial membrane a stiff membrane. One of the two major structures of the organ of corti.

template hypothetical internal representations of patterns which respond when external patterns match their characteristics.

terminal ganglia accumulations of largely preganglionic parasympathetic nerve fibers which synapse onto postganglionic nerves in these ganglia which are located near or in the organs being innervated.

tertiary prevention intervention strategies designed to eliminate problems that result from having emotional problems. Often referred to as rehabilitation, the purpose of such programs is to help people with emotional problems function appropriately in the family, community and on jobs.

testicular feminization a situation which arises in genetic males whose body cells are insensitive to the androgens produced by the testes. These individuals develop female genitalia and, at puberty, the body is further feminized by the small amounts of estrogen which are normally produced by the testes.

testis male reproductive organ; often located extra-abdominally; in scrotum; major source of male hormones, the androgens; source of spermatazoa; the male gametes.

testosterone a specific type of male hormone, or androgen.

T-groups groups which provide sensitivity training.

thalamus the large group of nuclei at the top of the brain stem which relays sensory information to the cerebral cortex; also connects to motor and association cortex.

thematic apperception test (TAT) one of a class of psychological tests which are collectively referred to as projective tests. Individuals are shown somewhat ambiguous stimuli and asked to make up stories about what they see. The assumption is that they project into their stories something of their own personality, desires, needs, etc.

theme interference a term presented by Gerald Caplan to describe a bias or prejudice on the part of a community caregiver toward a client that prevents the caregiver from being effective in serving the client's needs.

theories of cognitive consistency theories that assume that attitude change will occur whenever an individual is aware of contradictions among their attitudes and behaviors.

theory of blocked-opportunity the theory that crime is the result of the reaction to barriers placed in the way of reaching culturally desirable goals.

theory of cognitive dissonance a form of cognitive consistency theory: The assumption that people experience discomfort with discrepancies between attitudes and behaviors and seek to reduce such discrepancies by changing their attitudes.

therapeutic community a therapeutic treatment approach first developed by Maxwell Jones in a London hospital in which the entire hospital setting provides a supportive social environment. Patients participate with staff in decisions involving treatment and discharge and assume responsibility for the overall treatment program of the hospital.

therapeutics a branch of pharmacology which deals with the medical uses of drugs.

thresholds the minimal physical difference or amounts required for the perception of a difference between stimuli or the presence of a stimulus.

thymidine one of the four bases in DNA. This base is one of the differences between the composition of DNA and RNA. The corresponding base in RNA is uracil.

thyroid gland a bi-lobed endocrine gland located in the neck; controlled by pituitary thyroid stimulating hormone (TSH); synthesizes and releases thyroid hormones which have a major effect on metabolic rate of cells of the body.

thyrotrophic hormone from the *pars distalis* of the pituitary; major effect is on thyroid gland where it causes increased production and release of thyroid hormones.

timbre the characteristic of sound which differs between different instruments playing the same note. Timbre depends mainly on the harmonic composition of the sound.

toxic psychoses psychotic disorganization of the personality due to organic (physical) causes.

traits a relatively enduring quality or capacity or tendency of personality. Usually a trait is a disposition that differs in strength in different people. Examples include impulsiveness, cautiousness, or agility.

tranquilizers drugs which are used in psychiatric practice. Tranquilizers are commonly classified into minor tranquilizers, which have antineurotic properties, and major tranquilizers, which have antipsychotic properties.

transactional analysis form of psychotherapy, pioneered by Eric Berne, which emphasizes understanding the interactions ("transactions") between people and modifying them in the direction of greater maturity.

transcription the process by which DNA codes for the synthesis of RNA.

transference the patient's projection of early feelings, wishes or conflicts onto the therapist or other individuals.

transient situational reactions psychopathology which often represents the normal person's response to overwhelming stress. The response usually subsides quickly with or without supportive help.

translation the process by which RNA codes for the synthesis of proteins.

trichromatic theory of color vision the theory that the different colors we perceive derive from the responses of three types of cones, each containing different photopigments.

trisomy a chromosomal abnormality in which the affected individual has 3 chromosomes 21. Also known as Down's syndrome.

true breeding the fact that all the offspring produced are identical to the parental type and that all their offspring, in turn, will also be like the parental types.

tuning curve a curve indicating the range of frequencies to which a particular auditory cell responds and the amount of response.

Turner's syndrome an abnormal condition in which females are born with only one X chromosome, instead of the normal complement of two X chromosomes.

twin comparison studies research method used in human behavioral genetics in which the similarities on a behavioral trait within pairs of twins are compared to those found in other types of relatives, or in random samples selected from the general population.

twins-reared-apart method a method employed in human behavioral genetic research. Similarities and differences in behavioral traits are compared in twins reared in the same environment (twins-reared together) and those reared in different environments, for example, twins given up for adoption and placed into different homes.

two-process theory a theory which holds that classical conditioning and instrumental learnings interact, with classical conditioning providing the motivation for instrumental responding.

tympanic membrane the eardrum.

types commonly occurring patterns of qualities, such as: extrovert, meaning: a) focused upon people and objects outside of oneself, b) interested in actions rather than thoughts, c) outgoing, lively, fun-loving.

umbilical cord the passage by which oxygen and food are carried from the placenta to the fetus.

unconditional cooperation a game strategy in which a player will cooperate regardless of whether the other player is cooperative or exploitive.

unconditional positive regard in Rogers' theory, one person may like and respect another regardless of particular behaviors or characteristics, that is, one may have unconditional positive regard for another person. It is contrasted with conditional positive regard: liking depends on the person's living up to our expectations.

unconditioned response unlearned response to an unconditioned stimulus.

unconditioned stimulus a stimulus that elicits a response without prior learning.

unconscious one of three parts of the mind in Freud's first theory. The others are the conscious and preconscious. The unconscious contains ideas which have been repressed.

undetected delinquent behavior delinquency statistics based on self-report rather than on official police or court records. Specifically, those delinquent acts reported by persons who have not been arrested for the acts.

unilateral strategy making a cooperative or conciliatory move without having any guarantee that it will be reciprocated.

uracil one of the four bases in RNA. This base is one of the differences between the composition of DNA and RNA. The corresponding base in DNA is thymidine.

variable interval schedule of reinforcement in which reinforcement is delivered for the first response which occurs beyond a designated period of time following the preceding reinforcement, one where the time period varies from trial to trial.

variable ratio schedule of reinforcement in which reinforcement is delivered after a number of responses that varies from trial to trial.

variance a measure of dispersion; can be computed by subtracting the mean from each score, squaring the result, adding these squares, and dividing by the number of scores (for a population) or by one less than the number of scores (for a sample).

vestibular sense the sense of balance.

visual cliff a device developed to present a visual depth or drop off. A piece of glass protects the subject from actually falling off the edge.

visual cortex the portion of cerebral cortex responsible for receiving information from the two eyes.

visual spatial acuity the ability to discern variations in light over space.

vitreous humor a jelly-like material in the eye chamber bounded by lens and retina.

vocational rehabilitation a form of tertiary prevention designed to help people whose effectiveness has been reduced because of emotional problems or other problems such as illness or injury (particularly former mental patients) to function appropriately in a work setting.

voice onset time the time between the expulsion of air and the beginning of vibration by the vocal cords.

volley effect the ability of several nerve fibers as a group to convey higher frequency pulsations than the individual fibers. While one fiber recovers, another is ready to respond.

Weber's law a law relating the threshold difference between a comparison and standard stimulus to the physical magnitude of the standard stimulus.

white matter nervous tissue consisting primarily of myelinated nerve fibers.

Wolffian duct the embryological tissue from which the male accessory sexual structures (e.g., the epididymus and vas deferens) are derived.

xanthines a class of drugs which have stimulating properties on the central nervous system. One example is caffeine.

XYY syndrome a genetic abnormality thought to be associated with excessive tendencies toward aggression.

zero-sum game a game in which one player's gain (or reward) is the other player's loss. There is no possibility of mutual rewards.

z-scores scores which have been transformed by subtracting the mean from each and dividing the result by the standard deviation; used in tables of the standard normal curve.

zygote fertilized cell formed by the union of male and female gametes.

References

Abelson, R., & Miller, J. Negative persuasion via personal insult. *Journal of Experimental Social Psychology,* 1967, *3,* 321–333.

Adametz, J.H. Rate of recovery of functioning in cats with rostral reticular lesions. *J. Neurosurg.* 1959, *16,* 85–98.

Aguilera, D.C., Messick, J.M., & Farrell, M.S. *Crisis intervention: Theory and methodology.* St. Louis: C.V. Mosby Co., 1970.

Ainsworth, M. The effects of maternal deprivation: A review of findings and controversy in the context of research strategy. In *Deprivation of maternal care: A reassessment of its effects.* Geneva, Switzerland: World Health Organization, 1962.

Akers, R. L. Socio-economic status and delinquent behaviors: A retest. *Journal of Research on Crime and Delinquency,* 1964, *1,* 38–46.

Alexander, F., & French, T.M. *Psychoanalytic therapy.* New York: Ronald Press, 1946.

Allen, V., & Levine, J. Social support and conformity: The role of independent assessment of reality. *Journal of Experimental Social Psychology,* 1971, *7,* 48–58.

Allison, J. Respiratory changes during transcendental meditation. *Lancet,* 1970, *1,* no. 7651.

Allport, F.H. *Social psychology.* Cambridge, Mass.: Riverside Press, 1924.

Allport, G.W. *The nature of prejudice.* Cambridge, Mass.: Addison-Wesley, 1954.

———. *Personality: A psychological interpretation.* New York: Holt, Rinehart and Winston, 1937.

Alpern, H.P., & Marriott, J.G. Short-term memory: Facilitation and disruption with cholinergic agents. *Physiology and behavior,* 1973, *11,* 571–575.

Altrocchi, H. Mental health consultation. In S.E. Golann and C. Eisdorfer (eds.), *Handbook of community mental health.* New York.: Appleton-Century-Crofts, 1972.

American Psychological Association. *A career in psychology.* Washington, D.C.: American Psychological Association, 1970.

Amir, Y. Contact hypothesis in ethnic relations. *Psychological Bulletin,* 1960, *71,* 319–342.

Anastasi, A. *Differential psychology.* New York: Macmillan, 1958.

Anderson, J.R., & Bower, G.H. *Human associative memory.* Washington, D.C.: V.H. Winston and Sons, 1973.

Ansbacher, J.L., & Ansbacher, R.R. *The individual psychology of Alfred Adler.* New York: Basic Books, 1956.

Aronson, E., & Mills, J. The effects of severity of initiation on liking for a group. *Journal of Abnormal and Social Psychology,* 1959, *59,* 177–181.

Aronson, E., Turner, J., & Carlsmith, M. Communicators' credibility and communicator discrepancy as determinants of opinion change.

Journal of Abnormal and Social Psychology, 1963, *67,* 31–36.
Asch, S.E. Effects of group pressure upon the modification and distortion of judgments. In H. Guetzkow (ed.), *Groups, leadership and men.* Pittsburgh: Carnegie Press.
———. *Social psychology.* Englewood Cliffs, N.J.: Prentice-Hall, 1952.
Aserinsky, E., & Kleitman, N. Regularly occurring periods of eye motility, and concomitant phenomena during sleep. *Science,* 1953, *118,* 273.
Atkinson, J.W. The achievement motive and recall of interrupted and completed tasks. *Journal of Experimental Psychology,* 1953, *46,* 381–390.
———. Towards experimental analysis of motives, expectations and incentives. In J.W. Atkinson (ed.), *Motive in fantasy, action, and society.* New York: D. Van Nostrand, 1958.
Atkinson, J.W., & McClelland, D.C. The projective expression of needs. II The effect of different intensities of the hunger drive on thematic apperception. *Journal of Experimental Psychology,* 1948, *38,* 643–658.
Atkinson, R.C., & Shiffrin, R.M. Human memory: A proposed system and its control processes. In J.T. Spence & K.W. Spence (eds.), *The psychology of learning and motivation: Advances in research and theory, Vol. 2.* New York: Academic Press, 1968.
Austin, C.R., & Short, R.V. *Reproduction in mammals: 3-hormones in reproduction.* London: Cambridge University Press, 1972.
Azrin, N.H., & Holz, W.C. Punishment. In W.K. Honig (ed.), *Operant behavior.* New York: Appleton-Century-Crofts, 1966.
Baez, L.A. Role of catecholamines in the anorectic effects of amphetamines in rats. *Psychopharmacologia,* 1974, *35,* 91–98.
Baldwin, J. Predisposing and situationally instigating aggressive expressions: A person-situation analysis. Unpublished doctoral thesis. University of Colorado, Boulder, Colorado, 1975.
Bakan, D. *The duality of human existence.* Chicago: Rand-McNally and Co., 1966.
Bandura, A. *Aggression: A social learning analysis.* Englewood Cliffs, N.J.: Prentice-Hall, 1973.
———. *Social learning theory.* New York: McCaleb-Seiler, 1971.
Bandura, A. & Mischel, W. Modification of self-imposed delay of reward through exposure to live and symbolic models. *Journal of Personality and Social Psychology,* 1965, *2,* 698–705.
Bandura, A., Ross, D., & Ross, S.A. Imitation of film-mediated aggressive models. *Journal of Abnormal and Social Psychology,* 1963, *66,* 3–11.
———. Transmission of aggression through imitation of aggressive models. *Journal of Abnormal and Social Psychology,* 1961, *63,* 575–582.
Bard, M. Training police as specialists in family crisis intervention. U.S. Department of Justice, Law Enforcement Assistance Administration, National Institute of Law Enforcement and Criminal Justice, U.S. Government Printing Office, 1970.
Barnes, J.M., & Underwood, B.J. 'Fate' of first-list associations in transfer theory. *Journal of Experimental Psychology,* 1959, *58,* 97–105.
Barondes, S.H., & Cohen, H.D. Puromycin effect on successive phases of memory storage. *Science,* 1966, *151,* 5594–5595.
Barry, H., III, Bacon, M.K., & Child, I.I. A cross-cultural survey of some sex differences in socialization. *Journal of Abnormal and Social Psychology,* 1957, *55,* 327–332.
Bartlett, F.C. *Remembering.* Cambridge: Cambridge University Press, 1932.
Baruch, G.K. Maternal influences upon college women's attitudes toward women and work. *Developmental Psychology,* 1972, *6,* 32–37.
Bateson, G. Minimal requirements for a theory of schizophrenia. *Archives of General Psychiatry,* 1960, *2,* 477–491.
Baumrind, D. Socialization and instrumental competence in young children. *Young Children,* 1970, *26,* 104–119.
Bayley, N. Individual patterns of development. *Child Development,* 1956, *27,* 45–74.
Beach, F.A. The descent of instinct. *Psychological Review,* 1955, *62,* 401–410.
———. Effects of injury to the cerebral cortex upon the display of masculine and feminine mating behavior by female rats. *Journal of Comparative Psychology,* 1943, *36,* 169–198.
———. *Hormones and behavior.* New York: Hoeber, 1948.
———. Instinctive behaviors: Reproductive activities. In S.S. Stevens, *Handbook of experimental psychology.* New York: John Wiley & Sons, 1951.
———. The snark was a boojum. *American Psychologist,* 1950, *5,* 115–124.
Beck, E.C., & Doty, R.W. Conditioned flexion reflexes acquired during combined catalepsy and de-efferentiation. *Journal of Comparative and Physiological Psychology,* 1957, *50,* 211–216.
Bedford, J.A. & Anger, D. Flight as an avoidance response in pigeons. Paper read at the meeting of the Midwestern Psychological Association, Chicago, 1968.
Berger, R.J. Experimental modification of dream content by meaningful verbal stimuli. *Brit. J. Psychiat.,* 1963, *109,* 722–740.
Berkowitz, L. *Aggression.* New York: McGraw-Hill, 1962.

Berkowitz, L., & Geen, R. Film violence and the cue properties of available targets. *Journal of Personality and Social Psychology,* 1966, *3,* 525–530.

Berkowitz, L., & LePage, A. Weapons as aggression-eliciting stimuli. *Journal of Personality and Social Psychology,* 1967, *7,* 202–207.

Berlyne, D.E. *Conflict, arousal and curiosity.* New York: McGraw-Hill, 1960.

Berne, E. *Games people play.* New York: Grove Press, 1964.

Bettelheim, B. *The children of the dream.* New York: Avon Books, 1969.

———. *The empty fortress.* New York: Free Press, 1967.

———. *Love is not enough.* New York: Free Press, 1950.

Binswanger, L. Existential analysis and psychotherapy. In F. Fromm-Reichmann & J.L. Moreno (eds.), *Progress in psychotherapy,* 1956.

Black, K. A survey of student suicide in higher education within the Southwestern Rocky Mountain states. Unpublished dissertation, University of Denver, 1971.

Blakemore, C. The representation of three dimensional space in the cat's striate cortex. *Journal of Physiology.* (London), 1970, *209,* 155–178.

Blakemore, C., & Nachmias, J. The orientation specificity of two visual aftereffects. *Journal of Physiology.* (London), 1971, *213,* 157–174.

Blau, P. Cooperation and competition in a bureaucracy. *American Journal of Sociology,* 1954, *59,* 530–535.

Block, J.H., Haan, N., & Smith, M.B. Socialization correlates of student activism. *Journal of Social Issues,* 1969, *25,* 143–177.

Bloom, B.L. *Changing patterns of psychiatric care.* New York: Behavioral Publications, 1974.

———. *Community mental health: A historical and critical analysis.* Morristown, N.J.: General Learning Press, 1973.

———. The 'medical model,' miasma theory, and community mental health. *Community Mental Health Journal,* 1965, *1,* 333–338.

Blurton-Jones, N.G., & Konner M.J. Sex differences in behavior of London and Bushman children. In R.P. Michael & J.H. Crook (eds.), *Comparative ecology and behavior of primates.* New York: Academic Press, 1973.

Bolles, R.C. Species specific defense reactions and avoidance learning. *Psychological Review,* 1970, *77,* 32–48.

Bonime, W. *The clinical use of dreams.* New York: Basic Books, Inc., 1962.

Bower, G.H., & Clark, M.C. Narrative stories as mediators for serial learning. *Psychonomic Science,* 1969, *14,* 181–182.

Bower, T.G.R. *Development in infancy.* San Francisco: Freeman, 1974.

———. The object in the world of the infant. *Scientific American,* 1971, *225,* 30.

———. The visual world of infants. *Scientific American,* 1966, 80–92.

Bradley, J.V. *Distribution-free statistical tests.* Englewood Cliffs, N.J.: Prentice-Hall, 1968.

Bransford, J.D., & Franks, J.J. The abstraction of linguistic ideas. *Cognitive Psychology,* 1971, *2,* 331–350.

Breen, R.A., & McGaugh, J.L. Facilitation of maze learning with post-trial injections of picrotoxin. *Journal of Comparative Physiology and Psychology,* 1961, *54,* 498–501.

Brehm, J.W. Post-decision changes in desirability of alternatives. *Journal of Abnormal and Social Psychology,* 1956, *52,* 384–389.

Breland, K., & Breland, M. The misbehavior of organisms. *American Psychologist,* 1961, *16,* 681–684.

Broadbent, D.E. Attention and the perception of speech. *Scientific American,* 1962, *206,* 143–151.

———. *Perception and communication.* New York: Pergamon Press, 1958.

Brobeck, J.R., Larsson, S., & Reyes, E. A study of the electrical activity of the hypothalamic feeding mechanism. *Journal of Physiology.* (London), 1956, *132,* 358–364.

Brobeck, J.R., Teppermand, J., & Long, C.N. Experimental hypothalamic hyperphagia in the albino rat. *Yale Journal of Biology and Medicine,* 1943, *15,* 831–853.

Brock, T.C. Communicator-recipient similarity and decision change. *Journal of Personality and Social Psychology,* 1965, *1,* 650–654.

Bronfenbrenner, U. Children in mainland China: A view from another planet. Talk presented at the University of Colorado, April 12, 1974a.

———. The origins of alienation. *Scientific Ameri-*tions—a social psychologist's report. *Journal of Social Issues,* 1961, *17,* 45–56.

———. The origins of alienation. *Scientific American,* 1974b, *231,* 53.

———. *Two worlds of childhood: U.S. and U.S.S.R.* New York: Russell Sage Foundation, 1970.

Bronson, F.H., & Desjardins, C. Aggression in adult mice: Modification by neonatal injections of gonadal hormones. *Science,* 1968, *161,* 705–706.

Broun, P.L., & Jenkins, H.M. Auto-shaping of the pigeons key peck. *Journal of the Experimental Analysis of Behavior,* 1968, *17,* 1–8.

Broverman, I.K., Vogel, S.R., Broverman, D.M., Clarkson, F.E., & Rosenkrantz, P.S. Sex-role stereotypes: A current appraisal. *Journal of Social Issues,* 1972, *28,* 59–78.

Brown, B.R. Saving face. *Psychology Today,* 1971, *4,* (12), 55–59.

Brown, D.G. Sex role development in a changing culture. *Psychological Bulletin,* 1958, *55,* 232–242.

Brown, J.S. *The motivation of behavior.* New York: McGraw-Hill, 1961.

Brown, R. *Social psychology.* New York: The Free Press, 1965.

Bruce, D.J., Evans, C.R., Fenwick, C.R., & Spencer, V. Effect of presenting novel verbal material during slow wave sleep. *Nature,* 1970, *225,* 873–874.

Buchwald, J., Halas, E.S., & Schramm, S. Changes in cortical and subcortical unit activity during behavioral conditioning. *Physiology and Behavior,* 1966, *1,* 11–22.

Buchwald, J., & Humphrey, G. An analysis of habituation in the specific sensory systems. In E. Stellar and J. Sprague (eds.), *Progress in Physiological Psychology, Vol. 5.* New York: Academic Press, 1974.

Budzynski, T.H., Stoyva, J.M., Adler, C.S., & Mullaney, D.J. EMG biofeedback and tension headache: A controlled outcome study. *Psychosomatic Medicine,* 1973, *35,* 484–496.

Burt, C. The genetic determination of differences in intelligence: A study of monozygotic twins reared together and apart. *British Journal of Psychology,* 1966, *57,* 137–153.

Buss, A. Instrumentality of aggression, feedback and frustration as determinants of physical aggression. *Journal of Personality and Social Psychology,* 1966, *3,* 153–162.

———. *The psychology of aggression.* New York: John Wiley & Sons, 1961.

Butler, J.M. Self-concept change in psychotherapy. In S.R. Brown and D.J. Brenner (eds.), *Science, psychology, and communication: Essays honoring William Stephenson.* New York: Teachers College Press, 1972.

Butler, R.A. Discrimination learning by rhesus monkeys to visual-exploration motivation. *Journal of Comparative and Physiological Psychology,* 1953, *46,* 95–98.

———. Incentive conditions which influence visual exploration. *Journal of Experimental Psychology,* 1954, *48,* 19–23.

Bykov, K.M. *The cerebral cortex and the internal organs.* New York: Academic Press, 1957.

Cabak, V., & Najdanovic, R. Effects of undernutrition in early life on physical and mental development. *Arch. Dis. in Child.,* 1965, *40,* 532–534.

Cameron, N. *Personality development and psychopathology.* Boston: Houghton Mifflin Company, 1963.

Campbell, A., & Schuman, H. *Racial attitudes in fifteen American cities.* Institute for Social Research, University of Michigan, Ann Arbor, Michigan, 1968.

Campos, T.J., Langer, A., & Krowitz, A. Cardiac responses on the visual cliff in prelocomotor human infants. *Science,* 1970, *170,* 196.

Cannon, W.B. *The wisdom of the body.* New York: W.W. Norton & Co., 1932.

Caplan, G. *Principles of preventive psychiatry.* New York: Basic Books, 1964.

Caplan, N.S., & Paige, J.M. A study of ghetto rioters. *Scientific American,* 1968, *219,* 15–21.

Carlsmith, J.M., Collins, B.E., & Helmreich, R.L. Studies in forced compliance: I. The effect of pressure for compliance on attitude change produced by face-to-face role-playing and anonymous essay writing. *Journal of Personality and Social Psychology,* 1966, *4,* 1–13.

Carmichael, L., Hogan, H.P., & Walter, A.A. An experimental study of the effect of language on the reproduction of visually perceived forms. *Journal of Experimental Psychology,* 1932, *15,* 73–86.

Cartwright, D.S. *Introduction to personality.* Chicago, Illinois: Rand McNally, 1974.

Cattell, R.B. *Personality and mood by questionnaire.* San Francisco: Jossey-Bass, 1973.

Cattell, R.B., Eber, H., & Tatsouka, M. *Handbook for the 16PF.* Champaign, Illinois: Institute for Personality and Ability Testing, 1970.

Cattell, R.B., Horn, J.L., Sweney, A.B., & Radcliffe, J.A. *Handbook for the motivation analysis test.* Champaign, Illinois: Institute for Personality and Ability Testing, 1964.

Cattell, R.B., Schmidt, L.R., & Bjerstedt, A. Clinical diagnosis by the objective-analytic personality batteries. *Journal of Clinical Psychology* Monograph Supplement, July 1972.

Ciaccio, N.V. A test of Erikson's theory of ego epigenesis. *Developmental Psychology,* 1971, *4,* 306–311.

Clark, G. R., Telfer, M.A., Baker, D., & Rosen, M. Sex chromosomes, crime and psychosis. *American Journal of Psychiatry,* 1970, *126,* 1659–1663.

Clark, J.R., & Wenninger, E.P. Socio-economic class and area as correlates of illegal behavior among juveniles. *American Sociological Review,* 1962, *27,* 826–834.

Clark, K., & Clark, M. Racial identification and preference in Negro children. In T. Newcomb and E. Hartley (eds.), *Readings in social psychology.* New York: Holt, Rinehart and Winston, 1947.

Clark-Stewart, K.A. Interactions between mothers and their young children: Characteristics and consequences. *Monographs of the society for research in child development,* 1973, *38.*

Cloward, R.A., & Ohlin, L.E. *Delinquency and opportunity.* New York: Free Press, 1960.

Cofer, C.M. *Motivation and emotion.* Glenview, Illinois: Scott Foresman and Co., 1972.

Cohen, A.K. *Delinquent boys*. New York: Free Press, 1955.
Cohen, A.R. Some implications of self-esteem for social influence. In C.I. Hovlund and I.L. Janis (eds.), *Personality and persuasibility*. New Haven, Conn.: Yale University Press, 1959.
Cohen, B.H. Some-or-none characteristics of coding behavior. *Journal of Verbal Learning and Verbal Behavior*, 1966, *5*, 182–187.
Cole, S., Steinberg, J., & Burkheimer, G.J. Prejudice and conservatism in a recently integrated southern college. *Psychological Reports*, 1968, *23*, 149–150.
Coleman, J. *Abnormal psychology and modern life*. Chicago: Scott Foresman and Company, 1956.
———. *Abnormal psychology and modern life*. Chicago: Scott Foresman and Company, 1972.
Coleman, J.S. et al. Equality of educational opportunity. Washington, D.C., H.E.W. Government Printing Office, 1966.
Coles, R. *Children in crisis: A study of courage and fear*. Boston: Little, Brown & Co., 1967.
Collard, E.D. Achievement motive in the four-year-old child and its relationship to achievement expectancies of the mother. Unpublished doctoral dissertation, University of Michigan, 1964.
Collins, A., & Quillian, M.R. Retrieval time from semantic memory. *Journal of Verbal Learning and Verbal Behavior*, 1969, *8*, 240–247.
Conrad, R. Acoustic confusion in immediate memory. *British Journal of Psychology*, 1964, *55*, 75–84.
Conrad, R., & Hull, A.J. Information, acoustic confusion and memory span. *British Journal of Psychology*, 1964, *55*, 429–432.
Constantinople, A. An Eriksonian measure of personality development in college students. *Developmental Psychology*, 1969, *1*, 357–372.
———. Masculinity-Femininity: An exception to a famous dictim? *Psychological Bulletin*, 1973, *80*, 389–407.
Cook, S.W. Motives in a conceptual analysis of attitude-related behavior. *Nebraska Symposium of Motivation*, 1969, *17*, 179–231.
Cottrell, N., Wack, D., Sekerak, G., & Rittle, R. Social facilitation of dominant responses by the presence of an audience and the mere presence of others. *Journal of Personality and Social Psychology*, 1968, *9*, 245–250.
Court-Brown, W.M., Jacobs, P.A., & Price, W.H. Sex chromosome aueuploidy and criminal behavior. In J.M. Thoday and A.S. Parkes (eds.), *Genetic and environmental influences on behavior*. Edinburgh: Oliver & Boyd, 1968.
Cruse, H. *Rebellion and revolution*. New York: Morrow, 1968.
Crutchfield, R.S. Conformity and character. *American Psychologist*, 1955, *10*, 191–198.
Cumming, J., & Cumming, E. *Ego and milieu*. New York: Atherton, 1962.
D'Andrade, R.G. Sex differences and cultural institutions. In E.E. Maccoby (ed.), *The development of sex differences*. Stanford: Stanford University Press, 1966.
Davis, C.M. Self-selection of diets by newly weaned infants. *American Journal of Diseases of Children*, 1928, *36*, 651–679.
Davis, K.E., & Jones, E.E. Changes in interpersonal perception as a means of reducing cognitive dissonance. *Journal of Abnormal and Social Psychology*, 1960, *61*, 402–410.
Davitz, J.R. *The language of emotion*. New York: Academic Press, 1969.
Dawes, H.C. An analysis of two-hundred quarrels of preschool children. *Child Development*, 1934, *5*, 139–157.
DeCharms, R., & Wilkins, E. Some effects of verbal expression of hostility. *Journal of Abnormal and Social Psychology*, 1963, *66*, 462–470.
DeFries, J.C., & Hegmann, J.P. Genetic analysis of open-field behavior. In G. Lindzey & D.D. Thiessen (eds.), *Contributions to behavior-genetic analysis: The mouse as a prototype*. New York: Appleton-Century-Crofts, 1970.
DeFries, J.C., & McClearn, G.E. Social dominance and Darwinian fitness in the laboratory mouse. *The American Naturalist*, 1970, *104*, 408–411.
Deitz, G.E. A comparison of delinquents with non-delinquents on self-concept, self-acceptance and parental identification. *Journal of Genetic Psychology*, 1969, *115*, 285–295.
Dement, W., & Kleitman, N. The relation of eye movements during sleep to dream activity: An objective method for the study of dreaming. *Journal of Experimental Psychology*, 1957, *53*, 339–346.
Dement, W.C., & Wolpert, E.A. The relation of eye movements, body motility, and external stimuli to dream content. *J. Exp. Psychology*, 1958, *55*, 543–553.
Dennis, W. Causes of retardation among institutional children: Iran. *Journal of Genetic Psychology*, 1960, *96*, 47–59.
Dennis, W. & Dennis, M.G. The effect of cradling practices upon the onset of walking in Hopi children. *Journal of Genetic Psychology*, 1940, *56*, 77–86.
Deutsch, J.A. The cholinergic synapse and the site of memory. *Science*, 1971, *174*, 788–794.
———. An experimental study of the effects of cooperation and competition upon group process. *Human Relations*, 1949, *2*, 196–231.
———. The effect of motivational orientation upon threat and suspicion. *Human Relations*, 1960, *13*, 123–139.
Deutsch, M., & Collins, M. *Interracial housing: A*

psychological evaluation of a social experiment. Minneapolis: University of Minnesota Press, 1951.

Deutsch, M., & Gerard, H.B. A study of normative and informational social influences on individual judgment. *Journal of Abnormal and Social Psychology,* 1955, *51,* 629–636.

De Valois, R.L., & Jacobs, G.H. Primate color vision. *Science,* 1968, *162,* 533–540.

DeVore, I. Male dominance and mating behavior in male baboons. In F.A. Beach, *Sex and behavior.* New York, London, and Sydney: John Wiley & Sons, 1965.

Diamond, B.L. Sirhan B. Sirhan: A conversation with T. George Harris. *Psychology Today,* 1969, *3,* 48–56.

Diamond, M. A critical review of the ontogeny of human sexual behavior. *Quarterly Review of Biology,* 1965, *40,* 147–175.

Dixon, N.F. Apparent changes in the visual threshold as a function of subliminal stimulation. *Quarterly Journal of Experimental Psychology,* 1958, *10,* 211–215.

Dollard, J., Doob, L.W., Miller, N.E., Mowrer, O.H., & Sears, R.R. *Frustration and aggression.* New Haven: Yale University Press, 1939.

Dollard, J., & Miller, N. *Personality and psychotherapy: An analysis in terms of learning, thinking, and culture.* New York: McGraw-Hill, 1950.

Dreger, R.M. Behavioral classification project. *Journal of Consulting Psychology,* 1964, *28,* 1–13.

Duffy, E. Activation. In N.S. Greenfield and R.A. Sternbach (eds.), *Handbook of psychophysiology.* New York: Holt, Rinehart and Winston, Inc., 1972.

———. *Activation and behavior.* New York: John Wiley & Sons, 1962.

Duncan, C.P. The retroactive effect of electroshock on learning. *Journal of Comparative Physiological Psychology,* 1949, *42,* 32–44.

Dunlap, K. Are there any instincts? *Journal of Abnormal Psychology,* 1919, *14,* 35–50.

Dweck, C.S., & Reppucci, N.D. Learned helplessness and reinforcement responsibility in children. *Journal of Personality and Social Psychology,* 1973, *25,* 109–116.

Eayrs, J.T., & Levine, S. Influence of thyroidectomy, and subsequent replacement therapy upon conditioned avoidance learning in the rat. *Journal of Endocrinology,* 1963, *25,* 505–513.

Eccles, J. The synapse. *Scientific American,* January, 1954.

Edwards, A.L. *Statistical analysis.* (3rd ed.) New York: Holt, Rinehart and Winston, 1969.

Edwards, D.A. Early androgen stimulation and aggressive behavior in male and female mice. *Physiology and Behavior,* 1969, *4,* 333–338.

Egan, G. *Encounter: Group processes for interpersonal growth.* Belmont, Calif.: Brooks/Cole, 1970.

Eimas, P.D. Speech perception in infants. *Science,* 1971, *171,* 303–306.

Eimas, P., & Corbit, J. Selective adaptation of linguistic feature detectors. *Cognitive Psychology,* 1973, *4,* 99–109.

Ellis, A. *Reason and emotion in psychotherapy.* New York: Lyle Stuart, 1962.

Engberg, L.A., Hansen, G., Welker, R.L., & Thomas, D.R. Acquisition of key pecking via auto shaping as a function of prior experience: Learned laziness? *Science,* 1972, *178,* 1222–1224.

Epstein, A.N., & Teitelbaum, P. Regulation of food intake in the absence of taste, smell, and other oropharyngeal sensations. *Journal of Comparative Physiology and Psychology,* 1962, *55,* 753–759.

Erikson, E. *Childhood and society.* New York: W.W. Norton & Co., Inc., 1963.

Erikson, E.H. *Young man Luther.* New York: W.W. Norton & Co., 1958.

———. *Identity: Youth and crisis.* New York: W.W. Norton & Co., 1968.

Erlenmeyer-Kimling, L., & Jarvik, L.F. Genetics and intelligence: A review. *Science,* 1963, *142,* 1477–1479.

Etzioni, A. Nonconventional uses of sociology as illustrated by peace research. In P.R. Hazarfeld, W.H. Sewall, and H.L. Wilensky (eds.), *The uses of sociology.* New York: Basic Books, 1967.

Eysenck, H.J. *The biological basis of personality.* Springfield, Illinois: Charles C Thomas, 1967.

———. The effects of psychotherapy: An evaluation. *Journal of Consulting Psychology,* 1952, *16,* 319–324.

———. *The scientific study of personality.* London: Routledge and Kegan Paul, 1952.

Fanon, F. *Black skins, white masks.* New York: Grove Press, 1967.

Faris, R.E.L., & Dunham, H.W. *Mental disorders in urban areas.* Chicago: University of Chicago Press, 1939.

Fay, A.S. The effects of cooperation and competition on learning and recall. Unpublished master's thesis, George Peabody College, 1970.

Fenigstein, A., & Buss, A.H. Association and affect as determinants of displaced aggression. *Journal of Research in Personality,* 1974, *7,* 306–313.

Fenz, W.D., & Velner, J. Physiological concomitants of behavior indexes in schizophrenia. *Journal of Abnormal Psychology,* 1970, *76,* 27–35.

Feshbach, S. The drive-reducing function of fantasy behavior. *Journal of Abnormal and Social Psychology,* 1955, *59,* 3–11.

Feshbach, S., & Feshbach, N. The young aggressors. *Psychology Today,* April, 1973, 90–95.
Feshbach, S., & Singer, R.D. *Television and aggression.* San Francisco: Jossey-Bass, 1971.
Festinger, L. A theory of social comparison processes. *Human Relations,* 1954, *7,* 107–140.
Festinger, L., & Carlsmith, J. Cognitive consequences of forced compliance. *Journal of Abnormal and Social Psychology,* 1959, *58,* 203–210.
Festinger, L., Riecken, H., & Schachter, S. *When prophecy fails.* Minneapolis, Minn.: University of Minnesota Press, 1956.
Fetz, E.E. Operant conditioning of cortical unit activity. *Science,* 1969, *163,* 955–958.
Finichel, O. *The psychoanalytic theory of neurosis.* New York: W.W. Norton, 1945.
Fiske, D.W., & Maddi, S.R. *Functions of varied experience.* Homewood, Illinois: Dorsey Press, 1961.
Fisher, S. *Body experience in fantasy and behavior.* New York: Appleton-Century-Crofts, 1970.
Fishman, C. Need for approval and the expression of aggression under varying conditions of frustration. *Journal of Personality and Social Psychology,* 1965, *2,* 809–816.
Forssberg, A., & Larsson, S. On the hypothalamic organization of the nervous mechanism regulating food intake. Part II. Studies of isotope distribution and chemical compositions in the hypothalamic region of hungry and fed rats. *Acta Physiologica Scandinavia,* 1954, *32,* Supplement 115, 41–63.
Forward, J.R., & Williams, J.R. Internal-external control and black military. *Journal of Social Issues,* 1970, *26,* 75–91.
Frankl, V.E. *Man's search for meaning: An introduction to logotherapy.* New York: Washington Square Press, 1963.
Freemon, F.R. *Sleep research: A critical review.* Springfield, Ill.: Charles C Thomas, 1972.
Freud, A. *The ego and the mechanisms of defense* (Rev. ed.) New York: International Universities Press, 1966.
Freud, S. (1923). *The ego and the id.* New York: Norton, 1962.
———. (1926). *The problem of anxiety.* New York: Norton, 1963.
———. Recommendations for physicians on the psychoanalytic method of treatment. In *Collected Papers, Volume 3.* New York: P.F. Collier, Inc., 1963.
———. (1915). Repression. In *Collected Papers, Volume 4.* New York: Basic Books, 1959.
———. (1905). Three contributions to the theory of sex. In A.A. Brill (ed.), *The basic writings of Sigmund Freud.* New York: Modern Library, 1938.
Fried, R. *Introduction to statistics.* Oxford University Press, 1969.
Friedman, S.M. An empirical study of the castration and Oedipal complexes. *Genetic Psychology Monographs,* 1952, *46,* 61–130.
Fromm, E. *The anatomy of human destruction.* New York: Holt, Rinehart and Winston, 1973.
Fromm, E., & Shor, R.E. *Hypnosis: Research developments and perspectives.* Chicago: Aldine Atherton, 1972.
Fuller, J.L., & Thompson, W.R. *Behavior genetics.* New York: John Wiley & Sons, 1960.
Fuster, J.M., & Alexander, G.E. Neuron activity related to short-term memory. *Science,* 1971, *173,* 652–654.
Gallo, P.S. The effects of increased incentives on the use of threat in bargaining. *Journal of Personality and Social Psychology,* 1966, *4,* 14–20.
Gamson, W.A., & Modigliani, A. *Untangling the cold war: A strategy for testing rival theories.* Boston: Little, Brown & Co., 1971.
Garai, J.E., & Scheinfeld. Sex differences in mental and behavioral traits. *Genetic Psychology Monograph,* 1968, *77,* 169–299.
Garcia, J., & Koelling, R. Relation of cue to consequence in avoidance learning. *Psychonomic Science,* 1966, *4,* 123–124.
Gardner, E. *Fundamentals of neurology.* Philadelphia: W.B. Saunders Company, 1968.
Gardner, G.G. The psychotherapeutic relationship. *Psychological Bulletin,* 1964, *61,* 426–439.
Gazzaniga, M. The split-brain in man. *Scientific American,* August, 1967.
Gellhorn, E. *Principles of autonomic-somatic integrations: Physiological basis and psychological and clinical implications.* Minneapolis: University of Minnesota Press, 1967.
Gerard, H.B., & Mathewson, G.C. The effects of severity of initiation on liking for a group: A replication. *Journal of Experimental and Social Psychology,* 1966, *2,* 278–287.
Gergen, K. *The psychology of behavior exchange.* Reading, Mass.: Addison-Wesley, 1969.
Gewirtz, J.L. The course of infant smiling in four child-rearing environments in Israel. In B.M. Foss (ed.), *Determinants of infant behavior.* New York: John Wiley & Sons, 1965.
Gibson, E.J. Learning to read. *Science,* 1965, *148,* 1066–1072.
———. *Principles of perceptual learning and development.* New York: Appleton-Century-Crofts, 1969.
Gibson, E.J., Gibson, J.J., Pick, A.D., & Ossor, H. A developmental study of the discrimination of letter-like forms. *Journal of Comparative and Physiological Psychology,* 1962, *55,* 898.
Gibson, E.J., & Walk, R.D. The 'visual cliff.' *Scientific American,* 1960, *202,* 64–71.
Glanzer, M., & Cunitz, A.R. Two storage mechanisms in free recall. *Journal of Verbal Learning and Verbal Behavior,* 1966, *5,* 351–360.

Gleitman, D.H. Place learning without prior reinforcement. *Journal of Comparative and Physiological Psychology,* 1955, *48,* 77–79.

Glucksberg, S., & King, J. Motivated forgetting mediated by implicit verbal chaining: A laboratory analog of repression. *Science,* 1967, *158,* 517–519.

Glueck, S., & Glueck, E.T. *Predicting delinquency and crime.* Cambridge: Harvard University Press, 1959.

Gold, M. *Delinquent behavior in an American city.* Belmont, Calif.: Brooks/Cole, 1970.

Gold, P.E., Macre, J., & McGaugh, J.L. Retrograde amnesia gradients: Effects of direct cortical stimulation. *Science,* 1973, *179,* 1343–1345.

Goldberg, P. Are women prejudiced against women? *Transaction,* 1968, *5,* 28–30.

Goldman, R., Jaffa, M., & Schachter, S. Yom Kippur, Air France, dormitory food and the eating behavior of obese and normal people. *Journal of Personality and Social Psychology,* 1968, *10,* 117–123.

Gollob, H.F., & Dittes, J.E. Effects of manipulated self-esteem on persuasibility depending on threat and complexity of communication. *Journal of Personality and Social Psychology,* 1965, *2,* 195–201.

Goodall, J.V. *In the shadow of man.* Boston: Houghton-Mifflin, 1971.

Goodenough, D.R., Shapiro, A., Holden, M., & Steinschriber, L. A comparison of "dreamers" and "nondreamers"; Eye movements, electroencephalograms and the recall of dreams. *Journal of Abnormal and Social Psychology,* 1959, *59,* 295–302.

Goodman, L.S., & Gilman, A. *The pharmacological basis of therapeutics.* New York: Macmillan Company, 1970.

Goodwin, D.W., Powell, B., Bremer, D., Hoine, H., & Stern, J. Alcohol and recall: State-dependent effects in man. *Science,* 1969, *163,* 1358–1360.

Gorbman, A., & Bern, H.A. *A textbook of comparative endocrinology.* New York: John Wiley & Sons, 1962.

Gordon, B. Influence and social comparison as motives for affiliation. *Journal of Experimental and Social Psychology,* 1966, *1,* 55–65.

Goy, R.W., & Resko, J.A. Gonadal hormones and behavior of normal and pseudohermaphroditic nonhuman female primates. *Rec. Prog. Horm. Res.,* 1972, *28,* 707–732.

Green, H. *I never promised you a rose garden.* New York: Signet, 1964.

Greenson, R.R. *The technique and practice of psychoanalysis.* New York: International Universities Press, 1967.

Gregory, R.L. *Eye and brain: The psychology of seeing.* New York: McGraw-Hill, 1966.

Griffith, R.M., Miyagi, O., & Tago, A. The universality of typical dreams: Japanese vs. Americans. *American Anthropologist,* 1958, *60,* 1173–1179.

Grim, P., Kohlberg, L., & White, S.H. Some relationships between conscience and attentional processes. *Journal of Personality and Social Psychology,* 1968, *8,* 239–252.

Grossman, S.P. Eating and drinking elicited by direct adrenergic or cholinergic stimulation of hypothalamus. *Science,* 1960, *132,* 301–302.

Group for the Advancement of Psychiatry. Psychopathological disorders in childhood: Theoretical considerations and a proposed classification. 6, No. 62. New York: Mental Health Materials Center, 1966.

Gulick, L.W. *Hearing: Physiology and psychophysics.* New York: Oxford University Press, 1971.

Gurin, G., Veroff, J., & Feld, S. *Americans view their mental health: A nationwide interview survey.* New York: Basic Books, 1960.

Haines, D.B., & McKeachie, W.J. Cooperative versus competitive discussion methods in teaching introductory psychology. *Journal of Educational Psychology,* 1967, *58,* 386–390.

Hallowitz, E., & Riessman, F. The role of the indigenous nonprofessional in a community mental health neighborhood service center program. *American Journal of Orthopsychiatry,* 1967, *37,* 766–778.

Hammond, K.R. New directions in research on conflict resolution. *Journal of Social Issues,* 1965, *21,* 44–46.

Hammond, K.R., & Householder, J.E. *Introduction to the statistical method.* New York: Alfred A. Knopf, 1967.

Hammond, K.R., Todd, F.J., Wilkins, M., & Mitchell, T.O. Cognitive conflict between two persons: Application of the lens model paradigm. *Journal of Experimental and Social Psychology,* 1966, *2,* 243–260.

Hampson, J.L., & Hampson, J.G. The ontogenesis of sexual behavior in man. In W.C. Young (ed.), *Sex and internal secretions.* (3rd ed.) Baltimore: Williams and Wilkins, 1961.

Harlow, H.F. The formation of learning sets. *Psychological Review,* 1949, *56,* 51–65.

———. The nature of love. *American Psychologist,* 1958, *13,* 673–685.

Harlow, H.F., & McClearn, G.E. Object discrimination learned by monkeys on the basis of manipulation motives. *Journal of Comparative and Physiological Psychology,* 1954, *47,* 73–76.

Harlow, H.F., & Suomi, S.J. Nature of love—simplified. *American Psychologist,* 1970, *25,* 161–168.

Harlow, H.F., & Zimmerman, R.R. Affectional responses in the infant monkey. *Science,* 1954, *130,* 421–432.

Harman, W.W., McKim, R.H., Mogar, R.E., Fadiman, J., & Stolaroff, M.J. Psychedelic agents in creative problem solving: A pilot study. *Psychological Report,* 1966, *19,* 211–227.

Harris, T.A. *I'm OK—you're OK.* New York: Harper and Row, 1967.

Hart, Benjamin L. *Experimental neuropsychology.* San Francisco: W.H. Freeman & Company, 1969.

Hartley, R. Children's concepts of male and female roles. *Merrill-Palmer Quarterly,* 1959, *6,* 84–91.

Hartmann, D.P. Influence of symbolically modelled instrumental aggression and pain cues on aggressive behavior. *Journal of Personality and Social Psychology,* 1969, *11,* 280–288.

Hasler, A.D. Guideposts of migrating fish. *Science,* 1960, *131,* 785–792.

Hebb, D.O. Drives and the CNS (conceptual nervous system). *Psychological Review,* 1955, *62,* 234–254.

———. *The organization of behavior.* New York: John Wiley & Sons, 1949.

Heider, F. Attitudes and cognitive organizations. *Journal of Psychology,* 1946, *21,* 107–112.

———. *The psychology of interpersonal relations.* New York: John Wiley & Sons, 1958.

Helfer, R., & Kempe, C.H. *The battered child.* (2nd ed.) Chicago: University of Chicago Press, 1974.

Helson, H. Adaptation level theory. In S. Koch (ed.), *Psychology: A study of a science.* New York: McGraw-Hill, 1959.

Henchy, T., & Glass, D. Evaluation apprehension and the social facilitation of dominant and subordinate responses. *Journal of Personality and Social Psychology,* 1968, *10,* 446–454.

Hendin, H. Black suicide. *Columbia Forum,* 1969, *12,* 13–17.

Heron, W. The pathology of boredom. *Scientific American,* 1957, January.

Heron, W., Doane, B.K., & Scott, T.H. Visual disturbances after prolonged perceptual isolation. *Canadian Journal of Psychology,* 1956, *10,* 13–18.

Herrnstein, R.J. Method and theory in the study of avoidance. *Psychological Review,* 1969, *76,* 49–69.

Hersh, S. *My Lai 4: A report on the massacre and its aftermath.* New York: Vintage Books, 1970.

Hershey, A.D., & Chase, M. Independent functions of viral protein and nucleic acid growth of bacteriophage. *Journal of Genetic Physiology,* 1952, *36,* 39–56.

Hess, E.H. Natural history of imprinting. *Anals of New York Academic Science,* 1972, *193,* 124–136.

———. The relationship between imprinting and motivation. In M.R. Jones (ed.), *Nebraska Symposium on Motivation,* 1959.

Heston, L.L. The genetics of schizophrenia and schizoid disease. *Science,* 1970, *167,* 249–256.

Hilgard, E. *Hypnotic susceptibility.* New York: Harcourt, Brace, Jovanovich, 1965.

Hirschi, T. *Causes of delinquency.* Los Angeles: University of California Press, 1969.

Hodgkin, A., & Huxley, A. Action potentials recorded from inside nerve fiber. *Nature,* 1939, *144,* 710–711.

Hodgkin, A., & Keynes, R. Experiments on the injection of substances into squid giant axons by means of a microsyringe. *Journal of Physiology,* 1956, *131,* 592–616.

Hoffman, H.S., & Fleshler, M. Aversive control with the pigeon. *Journal of the Experimental Analysis of Behavior,* 1959, *2,* 213–218.

Hoffman, L.W. Early childhood experiences and women's achievement motives. *Journal of Social Issues,* 1972, *28,* 129–155.

Hollander, X. *The happy hooker.* New York: Warner, 1971.

Hollingshead, A.B., & Redlich, F.C. *Social class and mental illness: A community study.* New York: John Wiley & Sons, 1958.

Holmes, T.H., & Rahe, R.H. Social readjustment rating scale. *Journal of Psychosomatic Research,* 1967, *11,* 213–218.

Honzik, M.P. Developmental studies of parent-child resemblance in intelligence. *Child Development,* 1957, *28,* 215–228.

Hopkins, J. Unpublished mimeographed report, National Center for Prevention of Child Abuse, University of Colorado Medical School, Denver, Colo., 1970.

Horney, K. *New ways in psychoanalysis.* New York: Norton, 1939.

Hovland, C.I., Harvey, O.J., & Sherif, M. Assimilation and contrast effects in reactions to communication and attitude change. *Journal of Abnormal and Social Psychology,* 1957, *55,* 224–252.

Hovland, C., Lumsdaine, A., & Sheffield, F. *Experiments on mass communication.* Princeton: Princeton University Press, 1959.

Hovland, C., & Weiss, W. The influence of source credibility on communication effectiveness. *The Public Opinion Quarterly,* 1951, *15,* 635–650.

Howard, J. *Please touch.* New York: McGraw-Hill, 1970.

Howarth, E., & Eysenck, H.J. Extraversion, arousal, and paired-associate recall. *Journal of Experimental Research in Personality,* 1968, *3,* 114–116.

Hubel, D.H., & Wiesal, T.N. Receptive fields and functional architecture in two non-striate visual areas (18 and 19) of the cat. *Journal of Neurophysiology,* 1965, *28,* 229–289.

———. Receptive fields, binocular interaction, and functional architecture in the cat's visual cortex. *Journal of Physiology*, (London), 1962, *160*, 106–154.

———. Receptive fields and functional architecture of monkey striate cortex. *Journal of Physiology*, (London), 1968, *195*, 215–243.

Hughes, C.C., Trembly, M., Rappoport, R.N., & Leighton, A.H. *People of cove and woodlot*. New York: Basic Books, 1960.

Hundelby, J.D. The measurement of personality by objective tests. In P. Kline (ed.), *New approaches in psychological measurement*. New York: John Wiley & Sons, 1973.

Hundelby, J.D., Pawlik, K., & Cattell, R.B. *Personality factors in objective test devices*. San Diego: Robert R. Knapp, 1965.

Jacobsen, C.F. Functions of the frontal association area in primates. *Archives of Neurological Psychiatry*, 1935, *33*, 558–569.

Jacobson, E. *Progressive relaxation*. Chicago: University of Chicago Press, 1938.

Jaffe, J.H. Drug addiction and drugs of abuse. In L.S. Goodman & A. Gilman (eds.), *The pharmacological basis of therapeutics*. (4th ed.) London: The Macmillan Co., 1970.

Jaffe, J.H., & Sharpless, S.K. Pharmacological denervation supersensitivity in the central nervous system: A theory of physical dependence. *Proceedings of the Association for Research on Nervous and Mental Disorders*, 1968, *46*, 226–246.

James, W. *Principles of psychology*. New York: Holt, Rinehart and Winston, 1890.

———. Subjective effects of nitrous oxide. *Mind*, 1882, *7*, 185–208.

Janis, I. When fear is healthy. *Psychology Today*, 1968, *1*, 46–49, 60–61.

Janis, I., & Gilmore, B. The influence of incentive conditions on the success of role-playing in modifying attitudes. *Journal of Personality and Social Psychology*, 1965, *1*, 17–27.

Janis, I.L., & Mann, L. Effectiveness of role-playing in modifying smoking habits and attitudes. *Journal of Experimental Research on Personality*, 1965, *1*, 84–90.

Janov, A. *The primal scream*. New York: G.P. Putnam, 1970.

Jasper, H.H. *Epilepsy and cerebral localization*. W. Penfield and T.C. Erickson (eds.), Springfield: Charles C Thomas, 1941, 401.

Jasper, H., & Shagass, C. Conditioning the occipital alpha rhythm in man. *Journal of Experimental Psychology*, 1941, *28*, 373–388.

Jessor, R., Graves, T.D., Hanson, R.C., & Jessor, S.L. *Society, personality and deviant behavior*. New York: Holt, Rinehart and Winston, Inc., 1968.

John, E.R. *Mechanisms of memory*. New York: Academic Press, 1967.

John, E.R., Bartless, F., Shimokochi, M., & Kleinman, D. Neural readout from memory. *Journal of Neurophysiology*, 1973, *36*, 893–924.

Joint Commission on Mental Illness and Health. *Action for mental health*. New York: Basic Books, 1961.

Jones, E. *The life and work of Sigmund Freud*. New York: Basic Books, Inc., 1953.

Jones, M. *Beyond the therapeutic community*. New Haven: Yale University Press, 1968.

———. *The therapeutic community*. New York: Basic Books, 1953.

Jones, R., & Brehm, J. Persuasiveness of one and two-sided communications as a function of awareness there are two sides. *Journal of Experimental and Social Psychology*, 1970, *6*, 47–56.

Jost, A. Recherches sur la différenciation sexuelle de l'embryon de Lapin. I. Introduction et embryologie génitale normale. *Archives d'Anatomie Microscopique et de Morphologie Experimentale*, 1947, *36*, 151–200.

Jouvet, M. Telencephalic and rhombencephalic sleep in the cat. In G. Wolstenholme, and M. O'Connor (eds.), *CIBA Foundation Symposium, The nature of sleep*. London: Churchill, 1961.

Jouvet, M., Mouret, J., Chouvet, G., & Siffre, M. Toward a 48-hour day: Experimental bicircadian rhythm in man. In F.O. Schmitt and F.G. Worden (eds.), *The neurosciences. Third study program*. Cambridge: MIT Press, 1974.

Juel-Nielson, N. *Individual and environment*. Copenhagen: Munksgaard, 1965.

Julesz, B. Texture and visual perception. *Scientific American*, February, 1965.

Jung, C. *Man and his symbols*. New York: Doubleday, 1964.

Jung, C.G. *Psychological types*. New York: Harcourt, Brace, 1923.

———. *Psychology and religion*. New Haven, Conn.: Yale University Press, 1938.

Kagan, J. *Personality development*. New York: Harcourt Brace Jovanovich, Inc., 1971.

Kagan, J., & Moss, H.A. *Birth to maturity: A study in psychological development*. New York: John Wiley & Sons, 1962.

Kagan, S., & Madsen, M.C. Cooperation and competition of Mexican, Mexican-American and Anglo-American children of two ages under low instructional sets. *Developmental Psychology*, 1971, *5*, 32–39.

———. Rivalry in Anglo-American and Mexican-American children of two ages. *Journal of Personality and Social Psychology*, 1972, *24*, 214–220.

Kahn, R. Who buys bloodshed and why. *Psychology Today*, 1972, *6*, 47–48, 82–84.

Kallman, F.J. The genetic theory of schizophrenia: An analysis of 691 schizophrenic twin index families. *American Journal of Psychiatry,* 1946, *103,* 309–322.

———. The genetics of psychoses: An analysis of 1,232 twin index families. In *Congress International de Psychiatrie,* Paris, VI, Psychiatrie Sociale Rapports, Paris: Herman and Cie, 1950.

Kamin, L.J. Predictability, surprise, attention, and conditioning. In B.A. Campbell and R.M. Church (eds.), *Punishment and aversive behavior.* New York: Appleton-Century-Crofts, 1969.

Katz, I., & Benjamin, L. Effects of white authoritarianism in biracial work groups. *Journal of Abnormal and Social Psychology,* 1960, *61,* 448–456.

Kaye, H. Infant sucking behavior and its modification. In L.P. Lipsitt and C.S. Spiker (eds.), *Advances in child development and behavior, Vol. 3.* New York: Academic Press, 1967.

Kelman, H., & Lawrence, L. Violent man: American response to the trial of Lt. William L. Calley. *Psychology Today,* 1972, *6,* 41–45, 78–82.

Kenny, D. An experimental test of the catharsis hypothesis of aggression. Ann Arbor, Michigan: University Microfilms, 1953.

Kesner, R.P., & Connor, H.S. Independence of short- and long-term memory: A neural system analysis. *Science,* 1972, *176,* 432–434.

Keynes, R. The nerve impulse and the squid. *Scientific American,* December, 1958.

Kinsey, A.C., Martin, C.E., & Pomeroy, W.B. *Sexual behavior in the human male.* Philadelphia and London: W.B. Saunders, 1948.

Kinsey, A.C., Pomeroy, W.B., Martin, C.E., & Gebhard, P.H. *Sexual behavior in the human female.* Philadelphia and London: W.B. Saunders, 1953.

Kleitman, N. Patterns of dreaming. *Scientific American,* November, 1960.

———. *Sleep and wakefulness.* (2nd ed.) Chicago: University of Chicago Press, 1963.

Kline, P. *Fact and fantasy in Freudian theory.* London: Methuen, 1972.

Kline, P., & Grindley, J. A 28-day case study with the M.A.T. *Journal of Multivariate Experimental Personality and Clinical Psychology,* 1973, *1,* 13–22.

Klopfer, P.H., McGeorge, L., & Barnett, R.J. Maternal care in mammals. *Module in biology, no. 4.* Reading, Mass.: Addison-Wesley, 1973.

Knox, R.E., & Douglas, R.L. Low payoffs and marginal comprehension. Paper presented at meeting of the Western Psychological Association, San Diego, March, 1968.

Knox, R.E., & Inkster, J.A. Post decision dissonance at post time. *Journal of Personality and Social Psychology,* 1968, *4,* 319–323.

Kohlberg, L.A. A cognitive-developmental analysis of children's sex-role concepts and attitudes. In E.E. Maccoby (ed.), *The development of sex differences.* Stanford University Press, 1966.

Kohlberg, L. Development of moral character and moral ideology. In M.I. Hoffman and L.W. Hoffman (eds.), *Review of child development, Vol. I.* New York: Russell Sage Foundation, 1964.

Köhler, W. *The place of value in a world of facts.* New York: Liverright, 1938.

Kramer, M. Epidemiology, biostatistics and mental health planning. In R.R. Morrow, G.D. Klee, and E.G. Brody (eds.), *Psychiatric epidemiology and mental health planning.* Washington, D.C.: American Psychiatric Association, 1967.

Krech, D., Rosenzweig, M.R., & Bennett, E.L. Relations between brain chemistry and problem-solving among rats raised in enriched and impoverished environments. *Journal of Comparative Physiological Psychology,* 1962, *55,* 801–807.

Kringlen, E. *Heredity and environment in the functional psychoses.* An Epidemiological clinical twin study, Oslo: Universitetsforlaget, 1967.

Kuo, Z.Y. A psychology without heredity. *Psychology Review,* 1924, *31,* 427–451.

Lang, P.J., & Lazovik, A.D. Experimental desensitization of a phobia. *Journal of Abnormal and Social Psychology,* 1963, *66,* 519–525.

Langer, T.S., & Michael, S.T. *Life stress and mental health.* New York: Macmillan, 1963.

Lashley, K.S. An experimental analysis of instinctive behavior. *Psychological Review,* 1938, *45,* 445–472.

———. In search of the engram. *Symposium of Social Experimental Biology, No. 4.* Cambridge, Eng.: Cambridge University Press, 1950.

———. Studies of cerebral function in learning. V. The retention of motor habits after destruction of the so-called motor areas in primates. *Archives of Neurological Psychiatry,* 1924, *12,* 249–276.

Lazarus, A. *Clinical behavior therapy.* New York: Brunner/Mazel, 1972.

Lazarus, R.S., Yousem, H., & Arenberg, D. Hunger and perception. *Journal of Personality,* 1953, *21,* 312–328.

Lehrman, D.S. The reproductive behavior of ring doves. *Scientific American,* November, 1964.

Leighton, A. *My name is legion.* New York: Basic Books, 1959.

Lejeune, J., Grautier, M., & Turpin, R. Etude des chromosomes somatiques de neuf enfants mogoliens. *Comptes Rendus de l'Academie des Sciences,* Paris, 1959, *248,* 1721–1722.

Lenneberg, E.H. On explaining language. *Science,* 1969, *164,* 635–643.
Levanthal, H., Jones, S., & Trembly, G. Sex differences in attitude and behavior change under conditions of fear and specific instructions. *Journal of Experimental and Social Psychology,* 1966, *2,* 387–399.
Lewis, D.J., Misanin, J.R., & Miller, R.R. Recovery of memory following amnesia. *Nature,* 1968, *220,* 704–705.
Liberman, A.M. The grammar of speech and language. *Cognitive Psychology,* 1970, *1* (4), 301–321.
Lieberman, M.A., Yalom, I.D., & Miles, M.B. *Encounter groups: First facts.* New York: Basic Books, 1973.
Lindemann, E. Symptomatology and management of acute grief. *American Journal of Psychiatry,* 1944, 101. In H.J. Parad (ed.), *Crisis intervention: Selected readings.* New York: Family Service Association of America, 1965.
Lindsay, P.H., & Norman, D.A. *Human information processing: An introduction to psychology.* New York: Academic Press, 1972.
Lindsley, D.B. Emotion. In S.S. Stevens (ed.), *Handbook of experimental psychology.* New York: John Wiley & Sons, 1951.
———. Emotions and the EEG. In M.L. Reymart (ed.), *The second international symposium on feelings and emotions.* New York: McGraw-Hill, 1950.
Lipsitt, L. Learning capacities of the human infant. In R.J. Robinson (ed.), *Brain and early behavior.* London: Academic Press, 1969.
Lorenz, D. The companion in the bird's world. *Auk,* 1937, *54,* 245–273.
Lovaas, O.I. Some studies on the treatment of childhood schizophrenia. In J. Schlein (ed.), *Research in psychotherapy,* Vol. III. Washington, D.C.: American Psychological Association, 1968.
Lowell, E.L. The effect of need for achievement on learning and speed of performance. *Journal of Psychology,* 1952, *33,* 31–40.
Lubin, A. Performance under sleep loss and fatigue. In S.S. Kety, E.V. Evarts, and H.L. Williams (eds.), *Sleep and altered states of consciousness.* Baltimore: Williams and Wilkins Co., 1967.
Luce, R.D., & Raiffa, H. *Games and decisions.* New York: John Wiley & Sons, 1957.
Luborsky, L., Chandler, M., Auerback, A.H., Cohen, J., & Bachrach, H.M. Factors influencing the outcome of psychotherapy. *Psychological Bulletin,* 1971, *75,* 145–185.
Lumsdaine, A.A., & Janis, I.L. Resistance to counterpropaganda produced by one-sided and two-sided propaganda presentations. *The Public Opinion Quarterly,* 1953, *17,* 311–318.
Maccoby, E.E. Sex differences in intellectual functioning. In E.E. Maccoby (ed.), *The Development of Sex Differences.* Stanford: Stanford University Press, 1966.
MacDonald, J. *Rape: Offenders and their victims.* Springfield, Ill.: Charles C Thomas, 1971.
Maier, S.F., Seligman, M.E.P., & Solomon, R.L. Pavlovian fear conditioning and learned helplessness: Effects on escape and avoidance behavior of (a) CS-US contingency, and (b) the independence of the US and voluntary responding. In B.A. Campbell and R.M. Church (eds.), *Punishment and aversive behavior.* New York: Appleton-Century-Crofts, 1969.
Mandler, G. Organization and memory. In K.W. Spence & J.R. Spence (eds.), *The psychology of learning and motivation: Advances in theory and research, Vol. I.* New York: Academic Press, 1967.
Marcia, J.E. Development and validation of ego identity status. *Journal of Personality and Social Psychology,* 1966, *3,* 551–558.
Martin, E. Verbal learning theory and independent retrieval phenomena. *Psychological Review,* 1971, *78,* 314–333.
Maslow, A.H. A dynamic theory of human motivation. *Psychological Review,* 1943, *50,* 370–396.
———. *Motivation and personality.* (2nd ed.) New York: Harper & Row, 1970.
Masserman, J.H. Drugs, brain and behavior. An experimental approach to experimental psychoses. *Journal of Neuropsychiatry,* 1962, *3,* 104–113.
Masters, W.H., & Johnson, V.E. *Human sexual response.* Boston: Little, Brown, and Co., 1966.
May, R. *Existential psychology.* New York: Random House, 1961.
McClearn, G., & DeFries, J. *Introduction to behavioral genetics.* San Francisco: W.H. Freeman and Company, 1973.
McClelland, D.C. Toward a theory of motive acquisition. *American Psychologist,* 1965, *20,* 321–333.
McClelland, D., Atkinson, J.W., Clark, R.A., & Lowell, E.L. *The achievement motive.* New York: Appleton-Century-Crofts, 1953.
McClintock, C.G., Harrison, A., Strand, J., & Gallo, P. International-isolationism strategy of the other player and two-person game behavior. *Journal of Abnormal and Social Psychology,* 1963, *67,* 631–635.
McGaugh, J.L. In D.P. Kimble (ed.), *Anatomy of memory.* Palo Alto, California: Science and Behavior Books, 1965.
———. Time-dependent processes in memory storage. *Science,* 1966, *153,* 1351–1358.
McGaugh, J.L., & Petrinovich, L.F. Effects of drugs on learning and memory. *International Review of Neurobiology,* 1965, *8,* 139–196.
McGaugh, J.L., & Thompson, C.W. Facilitation of simultaneous discrimination learning with

strychnine sulphate. *Psychopharmacologia,* 1962, *3,* 166–172.
McGeoch, J.A. *The psychology of human learning.* New York: Langmans, 1942.
McGinnies, E. Emotionality and perceptual defense. *Psychological Review,* 1949, *56,* 244–251.
McGuire, W.J. The effectiveness of supportive and refutational defenses in immunizing and restoring beliefs against persuasion. *Sociometry,* 1961, *24,* 184–197.
———. Personality and susceptibility to social influence. In E.F. Borgatta and W.W. Lambert (eds.), *Handbook of personality theory and research.* Chicago: Rand-McNally, 1968.
McNamara, H.J., Long, J.B., & Wike, E.L. Learning without response under two conditions of external cues. *Journal of Comparative and Physiological Psychology,* 1958, *49,* 477–480.
McNeil, E.B. *The quiet furies.* Englewood Cliffs, N.J.: Prentice-Hall, 1967.
McPartland, J. The relative influence of school and classroom desegregation on the academic achievement of ninth grade Negro students. *Journal of Social Issues,* 1969, *25,* 93–102.
Mead, M. *Male and female.* New York: William Morrow, 1949.
———. *Sex and temperament.* New York: William Morrow and Mentor, 1935.
Mehesh, Maharishi Yogi. *On the bagavad-gita: A new translation and commentary.* Baltimore: Penguin Books, 1969.
Melten, A.W., & Irwin, J.M. The influence of degree of interpolated learning on retroactive inhibition and the transfer of specific responses. *American Journal of Psychology,* 1940, *53,* 173–203.
Melzoff, J., & Kornreich, M. *Research in psychotherapy.* New York: Atherton Press, 1970.
Menninger, W.C. *Psychiatry in a troubled world.* New York: Macmillan, 1948.
Merton, R. *Social theory and social structure.* New York: Free Press, 1957.
Mewhort, D. Familiarity of letter sequences, response uncertainty, and the tachistoscopic recognition experiment. *Canadian Journal of Psychology,* 1967, *21,* 309–321.
Mewhort, D., Merlikle, P., & Bryden, M. Transfer from iconic to short-term memory. *Journal of Experimental Psychology,* 1969, *81,* 89–94.
Michael, R.P. (ed.). *Endocrinology and human behavior.* London: Oxford University Press, 1968.
Milgram, S. Liberating effects of group pressure. *Journal of Personality and Social Psychology,* 1965 (b), *1,* 127–134.
———. Some conditions of obedience and disobedience to authority. *Human Relations,* 1965 (a), *18,* 57–75.
Miller, G.A. The magical number seven, plus or minus two: Some limits on our capacity for processing information. *Psychological Review,* 1956, *63,* 81–97.
———. Psychology as a means of promoting human welfare. *American Psychologist,* 1969, *24,* 1063–1075.
Miller, L.K., & Hamblin, R.L. Interdependence, differential reward and productivity. *American Sociological Review,* 1963, *28,* 768–778.
Miller, N.E. The frustration-aggression hypothesis. *Psychological Review,* 1941, *38,* 337–342.
———. Learnable drives and rewards. In S.S. Stevens (ed.), *Handbook of experimental psychology.* New York: John Wiley & Sons, 1951.
———. Studies of fear as an acquired drive: I. Fear as motivation and fear-reduction as reinforcement in the learning of new responses. *Journal of Experimental Psychology,* 1948, *38,* 89–101.
Miller, N., & Campbell, D.T. Recency and primacy in persuasion as a function of the timing of speeches and measurements. *Journal of Abnormal and Social Psychology,* 1959, *59,* 1–9.
Miller, N., & Zimbardo, P. Motives for fear-induced affiliation: Emotional comparison or interpersonal similarity? *Journal of Personality,* 1966, *34,* 481–503.
Miller, R.J. Cross-cultural research in the perception of pictorial materials. *Psychological Bulletin,* 1973, *80,* 135–150.
Millon, T. *Modern psychopathology.* Philadelphia: W.B. Saunders, 1969.
Mills, K., Sobell, M., & Schaefer, H. Training social drinking as an alternative to abstinence for alcoholics. *Behavior Therapy,* 2.
Milner, B. Amnesia following operation on temporal lobes. In C.W.M. Whitty and Zangwill (eds.), *Amnesia.* London: Butterworth and Co., 1966.
———. The memory defect in bilateral hippocampal lesions. *Psychiatric Research Reports,* 1959, *11,* 43–52.
Mischel, W. Delay of gratification in choice situations. *NIMH Progress Report,* Stanford University, 1962.
———. *Personality and assessment.* New York: John Wiley & Sons, 1968.
———. Sex-typing and socialization. In P.H. Mussen (ed.), *Carmichael's manual of child psychology.* (3rd ed.) New York: John Wiley & Sons, 1970.
Money, J. Components of eroticism in man: I. The hormones in relation to sexual morphology and sexual drive. *Journal of Nervous and Mental Disease,* 1961, *132,* 239–248.
Money, J., & Ehrhardt, A.A. *Man and woman, boy and girl.* Baltimore: Johns Hopkins University Press, 1972.
Moore, B.R. The role of directed Pavlovian reactions in simple instrumental learning in the pigeon. In R.A. Hinde and J.S. Hinde (eds.),

Constraints on learning. New York: Academic Press, 1973.
Moreno, J.L. *Psychodrama.* (2nd ed.) New York: Beacon House, 1946.
Morrisette, J. An experimental study of the theory of structural balance. *Human Relations,* 1958, *11,* 239–254.
Moruzzi, G., & Magoun, H.W. Brain stem reticular formation and activation of the EEG. *Electroencephalography and Clinical Neurophysiology,* 1949, *1,* 455–473.
Moss, H.A. Sex, age, and state as determinants of mother-infant interactions. *Merrill-Palmer Quarterly,* 1967, *13,* 19–36.
Mower, O.H. "Sin," the lesser of two evils. *American Psychologist,* 1960, *15,* 301–304.
Mpitsos, G.J., & Davis, W.J. Learning: Classical and avoidance conditioning in the mollusk Pleurobranchaea. *Science,* 1973, *180,* 317–320.
Mucha, T.F., & Reinhardt, R.F. Conversion reactions in student aviators. *American Journal of Psychology,* 1970, *127,* 493–497.
Müller, G.E., & Pilzecker, A. Experimentelle Beiträge zur Lehre vom Gedachtniss. *Psychologishe Zeitschrift,* 1900, *1,* 1–288.
Müller, G.E., & Schumann, F. Experimentelle Beiträge zur untersuchung des Gedachtnisses. *Zeitschrift für Psychologie,* 1894, *6,* 81–90.
Murray, H.A. *Thematic apperception test manual.* Cambridge, Mass.: Harvard University Press, 1943.
Mussen, P. Some personality and social factors related to changes in children's attitudes toward Negroes. *Journal of Abnormal and Social Psychology,* 1950, *45,* 423–441.
Mussen, P., & Rosenzweig, M. *Psychology: An introduction.* Boston: D.C. Heath, 1973.
Myens, R.E. Function of corpus callosum in interocular transfer. *Brain,* 1956, *79,* 358.
Myers, A.K., & Miller, N.E. Failure to find a learned drive based on hunger; Evidence for learning motivated by "exploration." *Journal of Comparative and Physiological Psychology,* 1954, *47,* 428–436.
Myers, I.B. *Manual for the Myers-Briggs type indicator.* Princeton, N.J.: Educational Testing Service, 1962.
Naranjo, C. Present-centeredness: Technique, prescriptions, ideal. In H. Fagan and I.L. Shepard (eds.), *Gestalt therapy now.* New York: Science and Behavior Books, 1970.
National Institute of Mental Health, United States Department of Health, Education and Welfare, Mental Health Publication No. 5027, Washington, D.C.: Government Printing Office, 1970.
Neisser, U. *Cognitive psychology.* New York: Meredith Publishing Company, 1967.
Newcomb, T.M. *The acquaintance process.* New York: Holt, Rinehart and Winston, 1961.
———. *Personality and social change: Attitude formation in a student community.* New York: Dryden Press, 1943.
Newcomb, T.M., Koenig, K.E., Flacks, R., & Warwick, D.P. *Persistence and change: Bennington College and its students after 25 years.* New York: John Wiley & Sons, 1967.
Newman, H.H., Freeman, N., & Holzinger, K.J. *Twins: A study of heredity and environment.* Chicago: University of Chicago Press, 1937.
Nidich, S., Seeman, W., & Seibert, M. Influence of transcendental meditation on state anxiety. *Journal of Consulting and Clinical Psychology,* forthcoming.
Noblin, C.D. Experimental analysis of psychoanalytic character types through the operant conditioning of verbal responses. Unpublished doctoral dissertation, Louisiana State University, 1962.
Noyes, A.C., & Kolb, L.C. *Modern clinical psychiatry.* Philadelphia: W.B. Saunders, 1968.
Nye, F.I. *Family relationships and delinquent behavior.* New York: John Wiley & Sons, 1958.
Olds, J. Pleasure centers in the brain. *Scientific American,* October, 1956.
Olds, J., Disterhoft, J., Segal, M., Kornblith, C., & Hirsh, R. Learning centers of the rat brain mapped by measuring the latencies of conditioned unit responses. *Journal of Neurophysiology,* 1972, *35,* 202–219.
Olds, J., & Milner, P. Positive reinforcement produced by electrical stimulation of septal area and other regions of rat brain. *Journal of Comparative Physiology and Psychology,* 1954, *47,* 419–437.
Olds, J., & Olds, M.E. Interference and learning in paleocortical systems. In J.F. Delafresnaye, A. Fessard, R.W. Gerard, and J. Konorski (eds.), *Brain mechanisms and learning.* Oxford: Blackwell Scientific, 1961.
Olshansky, S. The vocational rehabilitation of ex-psychiatric patients. *Mental Hygiene,* 1963, *52,* 556–561.
Olson, R.K. Children's sensitivity to pictorial depth information. *Perception and Psychophysics,* 1975, *17,* 59–64.
Oppenheimer, E. (ed.) *The CIBA collection of medical illustrations, vol. 2: Reproductive system.* Summit, N.J.: CIBA, 1954.
Orme-Johnson, D.W. Autonomic stability and transcendental meditation. *Psychosomatic Medicine,* 1973, *4,* (July, August).
Orme, M.T. The nature of hypnosis: Artifact and essence. *Journal of Abnormal and Social Psychology,* 1959, *58,* 277–299.
Osgood, C.E. *An alternative to war or surrender.* Urbana, Ill.: University of Illinois Press, 1962.
Oskamp, S. Effects of programmed strategies on cooperation in the prisoner's dilemma and other mixed-motive games. In L.S. Wrights-

man, J. O'Connor, and N. Baker (eds.), *Cooperation and competition: Readings in mixed-motive games.* Monterey, Calif.: Brooks/Cole, 1972.

Oswald, I., Taylor, A.M., & Treisman, M. Discriminative responses to stimulation during human sleep. *Brain,* 1960, *83,* 440–453.

Overmier, J.B., & Seligman, M.E.P. Effects of inescapable shock upon subsequent escape and avoidance responding. *Journal of Comparative and Physiological Psychology,* 1967, *63,* 28–33.

Overton, D.A. State-dependent or 'dissociated' learning produced with pentobarbital. *Journal of Comparative and Physiological Psychology,* 1964, *57,* 3–12.

Papousek, H. Individual variability in learned responses in human infants. In R.J. Robinson (ed.), *Brain and early behavior.* London Academic Press, 1969.

Parten, M.B. Social participation among preschool children. *Journal of Abnormal and Social Psychology,* 1933, *27,* 243–269.

Patterson. G. A social engineering technology for retraining aggressive boys. In H. Adams & L. Unihel (eds.), *Georgia symposium in experimental clinical psychology, Vol. 2.* Elmsford, N.Y.: Pergamon Press, 1970.

Penfield, W., & Jasper, H. *Epilepsy and the functional anatomy of the human brain.* Boston: Little, Brown and Company, 1954.

Perkins, C.C. An analysis of the concept of reinforcement. *Psychological Review,* 1968, *75,* 155–172.

Peris, F., Hefferline, R.F., & Goodman, P. *Gestalt therapy.* New York: Dell, 1965.

Pessin, J. The comparative effects of social and mechanical stimulation on memorizing. *American Journal of Psychology,* 1933, *45,* 263–270.

Petersen, L.R., & Petersen, M.J. Short term retention of individual items. *Journal of Experimental Psychology,* 1959, *58,* 193–198.

Pettigrew, J.D. The neurophysiology of binocular vision. *Scientific American,* 1972, *227,* 84–96.

Pettigrew, T.F. Racially separate or together. *Journal of Social Issues,* 1969, *25,* 43–69.

Piaget, J. *The language and thought of the child.* Trans. by M. Gabain. London: Routledge & Kegan Paul Ltd., 1926.

———. *The origins of intelligence in the child.* Trans. by M. Cook. New York: International Universities, 1952.

Piaget, J., & Inhelder, B. *The child's conception of space.* New York: Norton, 1967.

Pilisuk, M., & Skolnick, P. Inducing trust: A test of the Osgood proposal. *Journal of Personality and Social Psychology,* 1968, *8,* 121–133.

Poser, E.G. The effect of therapist training on group therapeutic outcome. *Journal of Consulting Psychology,* 1966, *30,* 283–289.

Posner, M.I., & Rossman, E. Effect of size and location of informational transforms on short-term retention. *Journal of Experimental Psychology,* 1965, *70,* 496–505.

Postman, L., & Stark, K. The role of response availability in transfer and retention. *Journal of Experimental Psychology,* 1969, *79,* 168–177.

Prechtl, H., & Beintema, D. The neurological examination of the fullterm newborn infant. *Little club clinics in developmental medicine,* No. 12, 41. London: Spastics Society Medical Information Unit and William Heinemann Medical Books, Ltd., 1964.

Premack, D. Reinforcement theory. In D. Levine (ed.), *Nebraska symposium on motivation, Vol. 13.* Lincoln: University of Nebraska Press, 1965.

Price, K.O., Harburg, E., & McCleod, J.M. Positive and negative affect as a function of perceived discrepancy in ABX situations. *Journal of Personality and Social Psychology,* 1966, *3,* 265–270.

Pritchard, R.M. Stabilized images on the retina. *Scientific American,* 1961, *204,* 72–78.

Pruitt, D.G. Reward structure and cooperation: The decomposed prisoner's dilemma game. *Journal of Personality and Social Psychology,* 1967, *7,* 21–27.

Quinney, R. *The social reality of crime.* Boston: Little, Brown, and Co., 1970.

Rank, O. *Will therapy and truth and reality.* New York: Alfred A. Knopf, 1945.

Ratliff, R. *Mach bands: Quantitative studies on neural networks.* San Francisco: Holden-Day, 1965.

Reimanis, G. Psychosocial development, anomie, and mood. *Journal of Personality and Social Psychology,* 1974, *29,* 355–357.

Reitman, J. Mechanisms of forgetting in short-term memory. *Cognitive Psychology,* 1971, *2,* 185–195.

Resorla, R.A. Pavlovian conditioning and its proper control procedures. *Psychological Review,* 1967, *74,* 71–80.

Resorla, R.A., & LoLordo, V.M. Inhibition of avoidance behavior. *Journal of Comparative and Physiological Psychology,* 1965, *59,* 406–412.

Resorla, R.A., & Solomon, R.L. Two-process learning theory: Relationships between Pavlovian conditioning and instrumental learning. *Psychological Review,* 1967, *74,* 151–182.

Rheingold, H. (ed.) *Maternal behavior in mammals.* New York: John Wiley & Sons, 1963.

Rheingold, H.L. The modification of social responsiveness in institutional babies. *Monographs of the Society for Research in Child Development,* 1956, *21,* (2, Whole No. 63).

Rhine, R., & Severence, L. Ego-involvement, discrepancy, source credibility and attitude change. *Journal of Personality and Social Psychology,* 1970, *16,* 175–190.

Richter, C.P. Sleep and activity: Their relation to the 24-hour clock. In S.S. Kety, E.V. Evarts, and H.L. Williams (eds.), *Sleep and altered states of consciousness,* 1967, 8–29.

Rieff, B. From swampcott to swamp. *American Psychological Association Division of Community Psychology Newsletter,* 1971, *4,* 1–3.

Riesman, D. The young are captives of each other. *Psychology Today,* 1969, *3,* 28–31.

Riessman, F. A neighborhood-based mental health approach. In E.L. Cowen, E.A. Gardner, and M. Zax (eds.), *Emergent approaches to mental health problems.* New York: Appleton-Century-Crofts, 1967, 162–184.

Ring, K., Lipinski, C.E., & Braginsky, D. The relationship of birth order to self-evaluation, anxiety reduction and susceptibility to emotional contagion. *Psychological Monographs,* 1965, *79,* (Whole No. 603).

Rioch, M.J. Pilot projects in training mental health counselors. In E.L. Cowen, E.A. Gardner, and M. Zax (eds.), *Emergent approaches to mental health problems.* New York: Appleton-Century-Crofts, 1967.

Rioch, M.J., Elkes, G., Flint, A.A., Usdansky, B.S., Newman, R.G., & Silber, E. National Institute of Mental Health pilot study in training of mental health counselors. *American Journal of Orthopsychiatry,* 1963, *33,* 678–689.

Rodrigues, A. Effects of balance, positivity and agreement in triadic social relations. *Journal of Personality and Social Psychology,* 1967, *5,* 472–476.

Rogers, C. *Client-centered therapy.* Boston: Houghton-Mifflin, 1951.

———. *Counseling and psychotherapy.* Boston: Houghton-Mifflin, 1942.

Rogers, C.R. A theory of therapy, personality, and interpersonal relationships, as developed in the client-centered framework. In S. Koch (ed.), *Psychology: A study of a science, Vol. III.* New York: McGraw-Hill, 1959.

Rogers, C.R., & Stevens, B. *Person to person: The problem of being human.* New York: Simon and Schuster Pocket Books, 1971.

Rokeach, M. *Beliefs, attitudes and values.* San Francisco: Jossey-Bass, 1968.

Rokeach, M., & Mezei, L. Race and shared belief as factors in social choice. *Science,* 1966, *151,* 167–172.

Rosen, B., Barn, A., & Cramer, M. Demographic and diagnostic characteristics of psychiatric out-patient clinics in the U.S.A., 1961. *American Journal of Orthopsychiatry,* 1964, *34,* 455–468.

Rosenberg, and Sutton-Smith, B. A revised conception of masculine-feminine differences in play activity. *Journal of Genetic Psychology,* 1961, *34.*

Rosenhan, D.L. On being sane in insane places. *Science,* 1973, *179,* 250–258.

Rosenkrantz, P., Vogel, S., Bee, H., Broverman, I., & Broverman, D. Sex-role stereotypes and self-concepts in college students. *Journal of Consulting and Clinical Psychology,* 1968, *32,* 287–295.

Rosenzweig, S.A. A transvaluation of psychotherapy—A reply to Hans Eysenck. *Journal of Abnormal and Social Psychology,* 1954, *49,* 298–304.

Ruch, T., & Patton, H. *Physiology and biophysics.* Philadelphia: W.B. Saunders Company, 1965.

Roberts, R., & Shettles. *From conception to birth: The drama of life beginnings.* Harper & Row, 1971.

Rundus, D. Analysis of rehearsal processes in free recall. *Journal of Experimental Psychology,* 1971, *89,* 63.

Rundus, D., Loftus, G., & Atkinson, R.C. Immediate free recall and delayed three-week recognition. *Journal of Verbal Learning and Verbal Behavior,* 1970, *9,* 684.

Russell, W.R. *Brain, memory, learning: A neurologist's view.* London: Oxford University Press, 1959.

Russell, W.R., & Nathan, P.W. Traumatic amnesia. *Brain,* 1946, *69,* 280–300.

Sadler, W. *Modern psychiatry.* St. Louis: Mosly, 1945.

Sakel, M. *The pharmacological shock treatment of schizophrenia.* New York: Nervous and Mental Disease Publishing Co., 1938.

Sarbin, T.R. *The myth of the criminal type.* Wesleyan University Press, 1969.

Satir, V. *Conjoint family therapy.* Palo Alto, Calif.: Science and Behavior Books, 1967.

Scarr, S. Genetic factors in activity motivation. *Child Development,* 1966, *37,* 663–673.

———. Social introversion-extroversion as a heritable response. *Child Development,* 1969, *40,* 823–832.

Schachter, S. The interaction of cognitive and physiological determinants of emotional states. In L. Berkowitz (ed.), *Advances in experimental social psychology.* New York: Academic Press, 1964.

———. *The psychology of affiliation.* Stanford, Calif.: Stanford University Press, 1959.

———. Some extraordinary facts about obese humans and rats. *American Psychologist,* 1971, *26,* 129–144.

Schachter, S., Goldman, R., & Gorden, A. Effects of fear, food deprivation and obesity and eating. *Journal of Personality and Social Psychology,* 1968 (a), *10,* 91–97.

Schachter, S., & Gross, L.P. Manipulated time

and eating behavior. *Journal of Personality and Social Psychology,* 1968, *10,* 98–106.
Schachter, S., & Singer, J. Cognitive, social and physiological determinants of emotional state. *Psychological Review,* 1962, *69,* 379–399.
Schaller, G.B. The behavior of the mountain gorilla. In I. DeVore (ed.), *Primate behavior.* New York: Holt, Rinehart and Winston, 1965.
Schallz, A.B., Animura, A., & Kastin, A.J. Hypothalamic regulatory hormones. *Science,* 1973, *179,* 341–350.
Schiller, B. Verbal, numerical and spatial abilities of young children. *Archives of Psychology,* 1934, No. 161.
Schlosberg, H. Three dimensions of emotion. *Psychological Review,* 1954, *61,* 81–88.
Schofield, W. *Psychotherapy: The purchase of friendship.* Englewood Cliffs, N.J.: Prentice-Hall, 1964.
Schreiber, F. *Sybil.* New York: Warner Publications, 1974.
Schuster, C.R. Psychological approaches to opiate dependence and self-administration by laboratory animals. *Federation Proceedings,* 1970, *29,* 2–5.
Schuster, C.R., & Thompson, R. Self administration of and behavioral dependence on drugs. *Annual Review of Pharmacology,* 1969, *9,* 483–502.
Schutz, W.C. *Joy.* New York: Grove Press, 1967.
Schwartz, B., & Coulter, G. A failure to transfer control of key pecking from food to escape from and avoidance of shock. *Bulletin of the Psychonomic Society,* 1973, *1,* 307–309.
Searles, H. *Collected papers on schizophrenia and related subjects.* New York: International Universities Press, 1965.
Sears, R.R. Development of gender role. In F.A. Beach (ed.), *Sex and behavior.* New York: John Wiley & Sons, 1965.
Sears, R.R., Maccoby, E.E., & Levin, H. *Patterns of child rearing.* New York: Harper & Row, 1957.
Segal, D.S. The role of norepinephrine in behavioral arousal. Unpublished Ph.D. Dissertation, University of California at Irvine, 1970.
Segal, D., & Mandell, A. Behavioral activation of rats during intraventricular infusion of norepinephrine. *Proceedings of the National Academy of Sciences,* 1970, *66,* 289–293.
Seiden, R.H. Campus tragedy: A study of student suicide. *Journal of Abnormal and Social Psychology,* 1966, *71,* 389–399.
Selfridge, O.G., & Neisser, U. Pattern recognition by machine. *Scientific American,* 1960, *203,* 60–68.
Seligman, M.E.P. Can we immunize the weak? *Psychology Today,* 1969, June, 42–44.
———. On the generality of laws of learning. *Psychological Review,* 1970, *77,* 406–419.
Seyle, H. *The physiology and pathology of exposure to stress.* Montreal: ACTA, 1950.
Sharpless, S., & Jasper, J. Habituation of the arousal reaction. *Brain,* 1956, *79,* 655–680.
Sheldon, W.H., Hartl, E.M., & McDermott, E. *Varieties of delinquent youth: An introduction to constitutional psychiatry.* New York: Harper, 1949.
Sherif, M., Harvey, O.J., Whie, B.J., Hood, W.E., & Sherif, C.W. *Intergroup conflict and cooperation: The robber's cave experiment.* Norman, Okla.: University of Oklahoma Book Exchange, 1961.
Sherif, M., & Sherif, C. *Social psychology.* New York: Harper & Row, 1969.
Sherman, J.A. Problem of sex differences in space perception and aspects of intellectual functioning. *Psychological Review,* 1967, *74,* 290–299.
Shields, J. *Monozygotic twins.* London: Oxford University Press, 1962.
Shields, J., Gottesman, I.I., & Slater, E. Kallmann's 1946 schizophrenic twin study in the light of new information. *Acta Psychiatrica Scandinavica,* 1967, *43,* 385–396.
Shirley, M.M. The first two years. Institute of Child Welfare Monograph, No. 7. Minneapolis: University of Minnesota Press. Copyright 1933, renewed 1961 by the University of Minnesota.
Short, J.F., & Strudtbeck, F.L. *Group process and gang delinquency.* Chicago: University of Chicago Press, 1965.
Sidowsky, J.B., Wycoff, L.B., & Tabory, L. The influence of reinforcement and punishment in a minimal social situation. *Journal of Abnormal and Social Psychology,* 1956, *52,* 115–119.
Siegel, A.E., & Siegel, S. Reference groups, membership groups, and attitude change. *Journal of Abnormal and Social Psychology,* 1957, *55,* 360–364.
Siegel, S. *Non-parametric statistics for the behavioral sciences.* New York: McGraw-Hill, 1956.
Siegman, A.W. Father absence during early childhood and anti-social behavior. *Journal of Abnormal and Social Psychology,* 1966, *71,* 71–94.
Silverman, P.R. Services to the widowed: First steps in a program of preventive intervention. *Community Mental Health Journal,* 1967, *3,* 37–44.
———. Widowhood and preventive intervention. *The Family Coordinator,* 1972, *21,* 95–102.
Skeels, H.M. Adult status of children with contrasting early life experiences: A follow-up study. *Monographs of the society for research in child development,* 1966, *31,* (Whole No. 105).
Skodak, M., & Skeels, H.M. A final follow-up of one hundred adopted children. *Journal of Genetic Psychology,* 1949, *75,* 85–125.

Slobin, D.I. (ed.) *The ontogenesis of grammar: A theoretical symposium.* New York: Academic Press, 1971.

Snyder, R. In quest of dreaming. In H.A. Witkin & H.B. Lewis (eds.), *Experimental studies of dreaming.* New York: Random House, 1967.

Solomon, L. The influence of some types of power relationships and game strategies upon the development of interpersonal trust. *Journal of Abnormal and Social Psychology,* 1960, *61,* 223–230.

Solomon, R.L., & Corbit, J.D. An opponent-process theory of motivation: II. Cigarette addiction. *Journal of Abnormal Psychology,* 1973, *81,* 158–171.

Somjen, G. *Sensory coding in the mammalian nervous system.* New York: Appleton-Century-Crofts, 1972.

Spence, D.P., & Gordon, C.M. Activation and measurement of an early oral fantasy: An exploratory study. *Journal of the American Psychoanalytic Association,* 1967, *15,* 99–129.

Sperling, G. The information available in brief visual presentations. *Psychological Monographs,* 1960, *74,* No. 11.

Sperry, R. Cerebral organization and behavior. *Science,* 1961, *133,* 1749–1757.

Sperry, R.W. The great cerebral commisure. *Scientific American,* January, 1964.

Sperry, R.W., Stamm, & Miner, N. Relearning tests for interocular transfer following division of optic chiasma and corpus callosum in cats. *Journal of Comparative Physiology and Psychology,* 1956, *49,* 529.

Spiro, M.E. *Kibbutz: Venture in utopia.* Cambridge: Harvard University Press, 1956.

Spock, B. *Baby and childcare.* New York: Pocket Books, 1957.

Stampfl, T.G., & Levis, D.J. Essentials of implosive therapy: A learning theory based on psychodynamic behavioral therapy. *Journal of Abnormal and Social Psychology,* 1967, *72,* 496–503.

Steele, B. Personal Communication, 1973.

Stein, A., & Friedrich, L. Television content and young children's behavior. In J. Murray, E. Rubenstein, and G. Comstock (eds.), *Television and social learning.* Government Printing Office, 1971.

Stein, L. Psychopharmacological substrates of mental depression. In S. Garattini and M.N.G. Dukes (eds.), *Antidepressant drugs.* Amsterdam: Excerpta Medica Foundation, 1967, International Congress Series, No. 122.

Stellar, E. The physiology of motivation. *Psychological Review,* 1954, *61,* 5–22.

Stephens, W.N. *The family in cross-cultural perspective.* New York: Holt, Rinehart, and Winston, 1963.

Sterman, M.B., Lucas, E.A., & MacDonald, L.R. Periodicity within sleep and operant performance in the cat. *Brain Research,* 1972, *38,* 327–341.

Sternberg, S. High-speed scanning in human memory. *Science,* 1966, *153,* 652–654.

Stevens, S.S. The psychophysics of sensory function. In W.A. Rosenblith (ed.), *Sensory communication.* Cambridge, Mass.: M.I.T. Press, 1961.

·Stoller, R.J. *Sex and gender.* New York: Science House, 1968.

Strole, L., Langner, T.S., Michael, S.T., Opler, M.K., & Rennie, A.C. *Mental health in the metropolis.* New York: McGraw-Hill, 1962.

Strumwasser, F. The demonstration and manipulation of a circadian rhythm in a single neuron. In J. Aschoff (ed.), *Circadian clocks.* Amsterdam: North-Holland Publishing Co., 1965.

Strupp, H.H., Fox, R.E., & Lessler, K. *Patients view their psychotherapy.* Baltimore: Johns Hopkins University Press, 1969.

Strupp, H.H., Wallach, M.S., & Wogan, M. Psychotherapy experience in retrospect: Questionnaire survey of former patients and their therapists. *Psychological Monographs,* 1964, *78,* 11 (Whole No. 588).

Strupp, R.H., & Bergin, A.E. Some empirical and conceptual bases for coordinated research in psychotherapy. *International Journal of Psychiatry,* 1969, *7,* 18–90.

Sullivan, H.S. *The interpersonal theory of psychiatry.* New York: Norton, 1953.

Surgeon General's Scientific Advisory Committee on Television and Social Behavior. *Television and growing up: The impact of televised violence.* Washington: H.E.W., 1972.

Sutherland, E. *Principles of criminology.* New York: J.P. Lippincott & Co., 1947.

Sutton-Smith, B. Cross-cultural study of children's games. *American Philosophical Society Yearbook,* 1961, 426–429.

———. Play, games, and controls. In J.P. Scott and S.F. Scott (eds.), *Social control and social change.* Chicago: University of Chicago Press, 1971.

Szasz, T. The myth of mental illness. *American Psychologist,* 1960, *15,* 113–118.

Tanner, J.M. Physical growth. In P.H. Mussen (ed.), *Carmichael's manual of child psychology, Vol. I.* (3rd ed.) New York: John Wiley & Sons, 1970.

Tart, C.T. *Altered state of consciousness.* New York: John Wiley & Sons, 1969.

Teitelbaum, P. Appetite. *Proceedings of the American Philosophical Society,* 1964, *108,* 464–472.

Teitelbaum, P., & Cutawa, J. Spreading depression and recovery from lateral hypothalamic damage. *Science, 147,* 61–63.

Teitelbaum, P., & Epstein, A.N. The lateral hypothalamic syndrome: Recovery of feeding and drinking after lateral hypothalamic lesions. *Psychology Review,* 1962, *69,* 74–90.

Terman, L.M., & Tyler, L.E. Psychological sex differences. In L. Carmichael (ed.), *Carmichael's manual of child psychology.* New York: John Wiley & Sons, 1954.

Thiessen, D.D. *Genetic organization and behavior.* New York: Random House, 1972.

Thomas, D.R. Stimulus selection, attention, and related matters. In J.H. Reynierse (ed.), *Current issues in animal learning.* Lincoln: University of Nebraska Press, 1970.

Thomas, E. Role of postural adjustments in conditioning of dogs with electrical stimulation of the motor cortex on the unconditioned stimulus. *Journal of Comparative and Physiological Psychology,* 1971, *76,* 187–199.

Thompson, R.F. *Foundations of physiological psychology.* New York: Harper & Row, 1964.

Thompson, T., & Schuster, C.R. *Behavioral pharmacology.* Englewood Cliffs, N.J.: Prentice-Hall, Inc., 1968.

Thorndike, E.L. Animal intelligence: An experimental study of associative processes in animals. *Psychological Review, Monograph Supplement,* 1898, *2,* 8.

Thorpe, W.H. *Learning and instinct in animals.* London: Methuen, 1956.

Tinbergen, N. Ethology's warning. *Psychology Today,* 1974, *7,* no. 10, 65–80.

———. *The study of instinct.* Oxford: Clarendon Press, 1951.

Toder, N.L., & Marcia, J.E. Ego identity status and response to conformity pressure in college women. *Journal of Personality and Social Psychology,* 1973, *26,* 287–294.

Tolman, E.C., & Honzik, C.M. Introduction and removal of reward and maze performance in rats. *University of California Publications in Psychology,* 1930, *4,* 257–275.

Tolman, E.C., Tryon, R.C., & Jeffress, L.A. A self-recording maze with an automatic delivery table. *University of California Publications in Psychology,* 1929, *4,* 99–112.

Triplett, N. The dynamogenic factors in pacemaking and competition. *American Journal of Psychology,* 1897, *9,* 507–533.

Truax, C.B., & Carkhuff, R.R. Experimental manipulation of therapeutic conditions. *Journal of Consulting Psychology,* 1965, *29,* 119–124.

———. *Toward effective counseling and psychotherapy.* Chicago: Aldine, 1967.

Tryon, R.C. Genetic differences in maze-learning ability in rats. *Yearbook of the National Society for the Study of Education,* 1940, *39(L),* 111–119.

Tuddenham, R.D. Studies in reputation: I. Sex and grade differences in school children's evaluations of their peers. *Psychology Monograph,* no. 333, 1952, 1–39.

Tulving, E. Subjective organization and effects of repetition in multitrial free recall. *Journal of Verbal Learning and Verbal Behavior,* 1966, *5,* 193–197.

Tulving, E., & Osler, S. Effectiveness of retrieval cues in memory for words. *Journal of Experimental Psychology,* 1968, *77,* 593–601.

Tulving, E., & Pearlstone, Z. Availability versus accessibility of information in memory for words. *Journal of Verbal Learning and Verbal Behavior,* 1966, *5,* 381–391.

Underwood, B.J. *Experimental psychology.* New York: Appleton-Century-Crofts, 1949.

———. "Spontaneous recovery" of verbal associations. *Journal of Experimental Psychology,* 1948, *38,* 429–439.

Valins, S. Cognitive effects of false heart-rate feedback. *Journal of Personality and Social Psychology,* 1966, *4,* 400–408.

Vandenberg, S.G. The heredity abilities study: Heredity components in a psychological test battery. *American Journal of Human Genetics,* 1962, *14,* 220–237.

———. Primary mental abilities or general intelligence: Evidence from twin studies. In J.M. Thoday & A.S. Parks (eds.), *Genetic and environmental influences on behavior.* New York: Plenum Press, 1968.

Vandenberg, S.G., & Johnson, R.C. Further evidence on the relation between age of separation and similarity in I.Q. among pairs of separated identical twins. In S.G. Vandenberg (ed.), *Progress in human behavior genetics.* Baltimore: Johns Hopkins Press, 1968.

VanLawick-Goodall, J. *In the shadow of man.* Boston: Houghton-Mifflin, 1971.

———. Tool using in primates and other vertebrates. In D.S. Lehrman, R.A. Hinde, & E. Shaw (eds.), *Advances in the study of behavior.* New York: Academic Press, 1970.

Van Wimersma Greidanus, T.B., Wijnen, H., Deurloo, J., & De Wied, D. Analysis of the effect of progesterone on avoidance behavior. *Hormones and Behavior,* 1973, *4,* 19–30.

Vetter, H. *Principles of abnormal psychology,* 1972.

Wagner, A.R. Stimulus selection and a modified continuity theory. In G.H. Bower & T.J. Spence (eds.), *The Psychology of Learning and Motivation, Vol. 3.* New York: Academic Press, 1969.

Wagner, A.R., Rudy, J.W., & Whitlow, J.W. Rehearsal in animal conditioning. *Journal of Experimental Psychology Monograph,* 1973, *97,* 407–426.

Wallace, R.K. Physiological effects of transcendental meditation. *Science,* 1970, *16,* 1751–1754.

Wallace, R.K., & Benson, H. The physiology of meditation. *Scientific American,* 1972, *226,* 34–90.

Wallace, R.K., Benson, H., Wilson, A.F., & Garrett, M.D. Decreased blood lactate during transcendental meditation. *Federation of American Societies for Experimental Biology,* Federation Proceedings, 1971, *30,* (March, April), 376.

Wallace, R.K., Benson, H., & Wilson, A.F. A wakeful hypometabolic physiologic state. *American Journal of Physiology,* 1971, *221,* (Sept.), 795–799.

Waller, A.D. Concerning emotive phenomena: II. Periodic variations of conductance of the palm of the human hand. *Proceedings of the Royal Society* (London) B, 1919–1920, *91,* 17–32.

Walls, G.L. The vertebrate eye and its adaptive radiation. *Cranbrook Institute Science Bulletin,* 1942, no. 19, xiv & 785.

Walk, R.D., & Gibson, E.J. A comparative and analytical study of visual depth perception. *Psychology Monograph,* 1961, *75.*

Walster, E., Aronson, E., & Abrahams, D. On increasing the persuasiveness of a low prestige communicator. *Journal of Experimental and Social Psychology,* 1966, *2,* 325–342.

Walster, E., & Festinger, L. The effectiveness of "overheard" persuasive communications. *Journal of Abnormal and Social Psychology,* 1962, *65,* 395–402.

Waterman, A.S., Geary, P.S., & Waterman, C.K. Longitudinal study of changes in ego identity status from the freshman to the senior year at college. *Developmental Psychology,* 1974, *10,* 387–392.

Watson, J.B. *Behaviorism.* (Rev. ed.) New York: W.W. Norton & Company, 1924, 1930.

———. *Psychological care of infant and child.* New York: W.W. Norton & Company, Inc., 1928.

Watson, J.D., & Crick, F.H.C. Molecular structure of nucleic acids. A structure for deoxyribose nucleic acids. *Nature,* 1953, *171,* 737–738.

Waugh, N.C., & Norman, D.A. The measurement of interference in primary memory. *Journal of Verbal Learning and Verbal Behavior,* 1968, *7,* 617–626.

Webb, W.B. *Sleep: An active process.* Glenview, Illinois: Scott Foresman and Co., 1973.

Weitzman, B. Behavior therapy and psychotherapy. *Psychological Review,* 1967, *74,* 300–317.

Werner, H. *Comparative psychology of mental development.* Chicago: Follett Publishing Co., 1948.

Westbrook, W.H., & McGaugh, J.L. Drug facilitation of latent learning. *Psychopharmacologia,* 1964, *5,* 440–446.

Whalen, R.E. (ed.). *Hormone and behavior.* New York: Van Nostrand, 1967.

Wheeler, L. Motivation as a determinant of upward comparison. *Journal of Experimental and Social Psychology,* Supplement, 1966, *1,* 27–31.

Whiting, J.W.M., & Child, L.L. *Child training and personality.* New Haven: Yale University Press, 1953.

Whyte, W.F. *Street corner society.* Chicago: University of Chicago Press, 1943.

Wickelgren, W.A. Acoustic similarity and retroactive interference in short-term memory. *Journal of Verbal Learning and Verbal Behavior,* 1965, *4,* 53–61.

Williams, H.L. The problem of defining depth of sleep. In S.S. Kety, E.V. Evarts, & H.L. Williams (eds.), *Sleep and altered states of consciousness.* Baltimore: Williams and Wilkins Co., 1967, 277–287.

Williams, H.L., Holloway, F.A., & Griffiths, W.J. Physiological psychology: Sleep. In P.H. Mussen & M. R. Rosenzweig (eds.), *Annual Review of Psychology,* 1973, *24,* 279–316.

Williams, H.L., Morlock, H.C., & Morlock, J.V. Instrumental behavior during sleep. *Psychophysiology,* 1966, *2,* 208–215.

Williams, R.L., & Karacan, I. Clinical disorders of sleep. In G. Usdin (ed.), *Sleep research and clinical practice.* New York: Brunner/Mazel, Publishers, 1973, 23–57.

Wilson, W.P., & Zung, W.W.K. Attention, discrimination and arousal during sleep. *Archives of General Psychiatry,* 1966, 15, 523–528.

Witkin, H.A., Lewis, H.B., Hertzman, M., Machover, K., Meissner, P.B., & Wapner, S. *Personality through perception,* G. Murphy (ed.). New York: Harper & Brothers, 1954.

Wolfe, J.B. Effectiveness of token-reward for chimpanzees. *Comparative Psychology Monographs,* 1936, *12.*

Wolman, B.B. Schizophrenia and related disorders. In B.B. Wolman (ed.), *Handbook of clinical psychology.* New York: McGraw-Hill, 1965, 976–1029.

Wolpe, J. *Psychotherapy by reciprocal inhibition.* Stanford, Calif.: Stanford University Press, 1958.

Woodworth, R.S., & Schlosberg, H. *Experimental psychology.* New York: Holt, Rinehart, and Winston, 1959.

Wortis, J. *Fragments of an analysis with Freud.* Indianapolis: Bobbs-Merrill, 1963.

Wright, J.M., & Harvey, O.J. Attitude change as a function of authorization and punitiveness. *Journal of Personality and Social Psychology,* 1965, *1,* 177–180.

Wrightsman, L.S., Davis, D.W., Lucker, W.G., Bruininks, R., Evans, J., Wilde, R., Paulson, P., & Clark, G. Effects of other person's race and strategy upon cooperative behavior in a prisoner's dilemma game. Paper presented at the meeting of the Midwestern Psychological Association, Chicago, May, 1967.

Wrightsman, L.S. Effects of waiting with others on changes in felt level of anxiety. *Journal of Abnormal and Social Psychology,* 1960, *61,* 216–222.

Wurtman, R., & Axelrod, J. The pineal gland. *Scientific American,* 1965, *213,* 50.

Wyden, P., & Wyden, B. *Inside the sex clinic.* New York: Signet, 1971.

Wynne, L., & Solomon, R.L. Traumatic avoidance learning: Acquisition and extinction in dogs deprived of normal peripheral autonomic function. *Genetic Psychology Monographs,* 1955, *52,* 241–284.

Yaffe, S.J., Krasner, J., & Catz, C.S. Variations in detoxication enzymes during mammalian development. *Annals of the New York Academy of Sciences,* 1968, *151,* 887–899.

Yalom, I.D. *The theory and practice of group psychotherapy.* New York: Basic Books, 1970.

Yaroush, R., Ekstrand, B.R., & Sullivan, M.J. Effect of sleep on memory. II. Differential effect of the first and second half of the night. *Journal of Experimental Psychology,* 1971, *88,* 361–366.

Yolles, S.F. The tragedy of suicide in the U.S. Public Service Publication No. 1558. Washington, D.C.: U.S. Government Printing Office, 1955.

Young, W.C. (ed.). *Sex and internal secretions, vols. I and II.* Baltimore: Williams and Wilkins, 1961.

Young, W.C., Coy, R.W., & Phoenix, C.H. Hormones and sexual behavior. In J. Money (ed.), *Sex research: New developments.* New York: Holt, Rinehart and Winston, 1965.

Zajonc, R.B. *Social psychology: An experimental approach.* Belmont, Calif.: Brooks/Cole, 1966.

Zajonc, R.B. & Burnstein, E. The learning of balanced and unbalanced social structures. *Journal of Personality,* 1965(a), *33,* 153–163.

———. Structural balance, reciprocity and positivity as sources of cognitive bias. *Journal of Personality,* 1965(b), *33,* 570–583.

Zajonc, R.B., & Sales, S. Social facilitation of dominant and subordinate responses. *Journal of Experimental and Social Psychology,* 1966, *2,* 160–168.

Zamble, E. Classical conditioning of excitement anticipatory of food reward. *Journal of Comparative and Physiological Psychology,* 1967, *63,* 526–529.

Zax, M., & Cowen, E.L. Early identification and prevention of emotional disturbance in a public school. In E.L. Cowen, E.A. Gardner, and M. Zax (Eds.), *Emergent approaches to mental health problems.* New York: Appleton-Century-Crofts, 1967.

Zax, M., & Specter, G.A. *An introduction to community psychology.* New York: John Wiley & Sons, 1974.

Zeigler, H.P. Trigeminal deafferentation and feeding in the pigeon: Sensorimotor and motivational effects. *Science,* 1973, *182,* 1155–1158.

Zemp, J.W., Wilson, J.E., Schlesinger, K., Boggan, W., & Glassman E. Brain function and macromolecules. I. Incorporation of uridine into RNA of mouse brain during short-term training experience. *Proceedings of the National Academy of Science,* 1966, *55,* 1422–1431.

Zigmond, M.J., & Stricker, E.M. Recovery of feeding and drinking by rats after intraventricular 6-hydroxydopamine or lateral hypothalamic lesions. *Science,* 1973, *182,* 717–720.

Zimbardo, P. The human choice: Individuation, reason and order versus deindividuation, impulse and chaos. In W. Arnold and D. Levine (Eds.), *Nebraska Symposium on Motivation,* 1969, *17,* 237–307.

Zinchenko, V.P., van Chzhi-Tsin, & Tarakanov, V.V. The formation and development of perceptual activity. *Soviet Psychology and Psychiatry,* 1963, *2,* 3–12.

Zubeck, J.P. (Ed.) *Sensory deprivation: Fifteen years of research.* New York: Appleton-Century-Crofts, 1969.

Zubin, J., & Barrera, S.E. Effect of convulsive therapy on memory. *Proceedings of Social Experimental and Biological Medicine,* 1941, *48,* 596–597.

Zuger, B. Gender role determination: A critical review of the evidence of hermaphroditism. *Psychosomatic Medicine,* 1970, *32,* 449–467.

Zwislocki, J. Analysis of some auditory characteristics. In R.D. Luce, R.R. Bosh, & E. Galante (eds.), *Handbook of mathematical psychology, Vol. III.* New York: John Wiley & Sons, 1965.

Index

A

B

C

E

N

O

P

Q

R

S

T